SECRETS OF HEAVEN

The New Century Edition
of the Works of Emanuel Swedenborg

Jonathan S. Rose
Series Editor

Stuart Shotwell
Managing Editor

EDITORIAL COMMITTEE

Wendy E. Closterman

Lisa Hyatt Cooper

George F. Dole

Sylvia Shaw

Alice B. Skinner

A Disclosure of
SECRETS OF HEAVEN
Contained in
SACRED SCRIPTURE
or
THE WORD OF THE LORD
Here First Those in
Genesis
*Together with Amazing Things Seen
in the World of Spirits & in the Heaven of Angels*

EMANUEL SWEDENBORG

Volume 1

Translated from the Latin by Lisa Hyatt Cooper
With a Reader's Guide by William Ross Woofenden and Jonathan S. Rose
An Introduction by Wouter J. Hanegraaff
And Notes by Reuben P. Bell, Lisa Hyatt Cooper, George F. Dole, Robert H. Kirven,
James F. Lawrence, Grant H. Odhner, John L. Odhner, Jonathan S. Rose,
Stuart Shotwell, Richard Smoley, and Lee S. Woofenden

SWEDENBORG FOUNDATION
West Chester, Pennsylvania

© Copyright 2008 by the Swedenborg Foundation, Inc. All rights reserved. No part of this publication may be reproduced or transmitted in any form or by any means, electronic or mechanical, including photocopying, recording, or any information storage or retrieval system, without prior permission from the publisher. Printed in the United States of America. This book is printed on acid-free paper that meets the ANSI Z39.48-1992 standard.

Originally published in Latin as *Arcana Coelestia,* London, 1749–1756. The present volume is indicated in red type in the list below:

Volume number in this edition	Text treated	Volume number in the Latin first edition	Section numbers	ISBN (of hardcover except where noted)
1	Genesis 1–8	1	§§1–946	978-0-87785-486-9
				978-0-87785-504-0 (pb)
2	Genesis 9–15	1	§§947–1885	978-0-87785-487-6
3	Genesis 16–21	2 (in 6 fascicles)	§§1886–2759	978-0-87785-488-3
4	Genesis 22–26	3	§§2760–3485	978-0-87785-489-0
5	Genesis 27–30	3	§§3486–4055	978-0-87785-490-6
6	Genesis 31–35	4	§§4056–4634	978-0-87785-491-3
7	Genesis 36–40	4	§§4635–5190	978-0-87785-492-0
8	Genesis 41–44	5	§§5191–5866	978-0-87785-493-7
9	Genesis 45–50	5	§§5867–6626	978-0-87785-494-4
10	Exodus 1–8	6	§§6627–7487	978-0-87785-495-1
11	Exodus 9–15	6	§§7488–8386	978-0-87785-496-8
12	Exodus 16–21	7	§§8387–9111	978-0-87785-497-5
13	Exodus 22–24	7	§§9112–9442	978-0-87785-498-2
14	Exodus 25–29	8	§§9443–10166	978-0-87785-499-9
15	Exodus 30–40	8	§§10167–10837	978-0-87785-500-2

Library of Congress Cataloging-in-Publication Data

Swedenborg, Emanuel, 1688–1772.
  [Arcana coelestia. English]
  A disclosure of secrets of heaven contained in Sacred Scripture, or, The Word of the Lord : here first those in Genesis, together with amazing things seen in the world of spirits and in the heaven of angels / Emanuel Swedenborg ; translated from the Latin by Lisa Hyatt Cooper ; with introductions by Wouter J. Hanegraaff and William Ross Woofenden ; annotated by Lisa Hyatt Cooper and Richard Smoley.
      p. cm. -- (The new century edition of the works of Emanuel Swedenborg)
  Includes bibliographical references (v. 1, p.   ).
      ISBN 978-0-87785-486-9 (hard cover) — ISBN 978-0-87785-504-0 (pbk.)
  1. New Jerusalem Church—Doctrines. 2. Bible. O.T. Genesis—Commentaries.
3. Bible. O.T. Exodus—Commentaries. I. Cooper, Lisa Hyatt. II. Smoley, Richard, 1956– III. Title. IV. Series: Swedenborg, Emanuel, 1688–1772.
  Works. English. 2000.

BX8712.A8 2006
230'.94--dc22

2006011298

Senior copy editor, Alicia L. Dole. Cover design by Caroline Kline and Karen Connor. Text designed by Joanna V. Hill. Typesetting and diagrams by Alicia L. Dole. Index to prefaces, reader's guide, introduction, and notes by Chara Cooper Daum, Alicia L. Dole, Kate Mertes, and Chara M. Odhner. Ornaments from the first Latin edition, 1749.

Paperback cover image: NASA, C. R. O'Dell and S. K. Wong (Rice University)

Certain Scripture quotations so identified in the annotations are from the New Revised Standard Version Bible, copyright © 1989 National Council of the Churches of Christ in the United States of America. Used by permission. All rights reserved.

For information about the New Century Edition of the Works of Emanuel Swedenborg, contact the Swedenborg Foundation, 320 North Church Street, West Chester, PA 19380 U.S.A.

Contents

Series Editor's Preface, by Jonathan S. Rose	1
Translator's Preface, by Lisa Hyatt Cooper	3
Works Cited in the Translator's Preface	13
Selected List of Editions of *Secrets of Heaven*	14
A Reader's Guide to *Secrets of Heaven,* by William Ross Woofenden and Jonathan S. Rose	17
Works Cited in the Reader's Guide	60
Swedenborg's *Magnum Opus,* by Wouter J. Hanegraaff	63
Works Cited in the Introduction	125
Short Titles and Other Conventions Used in This Work	131

Secrets of Heaven

[Author's Table of Contents]	143

Genesis Chapter 1

§§1–5 / [The Essential Nature of the Word]	145
Text of Genesis Chapter 1	147
§§6–13 / Summary of Genesis 1	148
§§14–63 / Inner Meaning of Genesis 1	150
§§64–66 / [Content and Mode in the Word]	179

Genesis Chapter 2

§§67–72 / [Secrets of the Other Life]	182
Text of Genesis Chapter 2:1–17	183
§§73–80 / Summary of Genesis 2:1–17	184
§§81–130 / Inner Meaning of Genesis 2:1–17	185
Text of Genesis Chapter 2:18–25	205
§§131–136 / Summary of Genesis 2:18–25	206

§§137–165 / Inner Meaning of Genesis 2:18–25	206
§§166–167 / [Representations of Inner Meaning]	218
§§168–181 / Our Resurrection from Death and Entry into Eternal Life	218

Genesis Chapter 3

§§182–189 / Our Entry, Once Revived, into Eternal Life (Continued)	221
Text of Genesis Chapter 3:1–13	222
§§190–193 / Summary of Genesis 3:1–13	223
§§194–233 / Inner Meaning of Genesis 3:1–13	223
Text of Genesis Chapter 3:14–19	240
§§234–240 / Summary of Genesis 3:14–19	241
§§241–279 / Inner Meaning of Genesis 3:14–19	241
Text of Genesis Chapter 3:20–24	258
§§280–285 / Summary of Genesis 3:20–24	259
§§286–313 / Inner Meaning of Genesis 3:20–24	260
§§314–319 / Our Entry into Eternal Life (Continued)	272

Genesis Chapter 4

§§320–323 / What the Life of the Soul or Spirit Is Like	275
Text of Genesis Chapter 4	276
§§324–336 / Summary of Genesis 4	278
§§337–442 / Inner Meaning of Genesis 4	279
§§443–448 / Several Examples from Spirits of Opinions They Adopted during Their Physical Lives Concerning the Soul or Spirit	327

Genesis Chapter 5

§§449–459 / Heaven and Heavenly Joy	331
Text of Genesis Chapter 5	334

§§460–467 / Summary of Genesis 5	336
§§468–536 / Inner Meaning of Genesis 5	336
§§537–546 / Heaven and Heavenly Joy (Continued)	361

Genesis Chapter 6

§§547–553 / Heaven and Heavenly Joy [Continued]	365
Text of Genesis Chapter 6:1–8	368
§§554–559 / Summary of Genesis 6:1–8	368
§§560–598 / Inner Meaning of Genesis 6:1–8	369
Text of Genesis Chapter 6:9–22	395
§§599–604 / Summary of Genesis 6:9–22	396
§§605–683 / Inner Meaning of Genesis 6:9–22	396
§§684–691 / The Communities That Make Up Heaven	438

Genesis Chapter 7

§§692–700 / Hell	442
Text of Genesis Chapter 7	445
§§701–704 / Summary of Genesis 7	446
§§705–813 / Inner Meaning of Genesis 7	447
§§814–823 / The Hells (Continued): The Hells of Those Who Spent Their Lives in Hatred, Revenge, and Cruelty	504

Genesis Chapter 8

§§824–831 / The Hells (Continued): The Hells of Those Who Spent Their Lives in Adultery and Lechery; in Addition, the Hells of Deceivers and Witches	511
Text of Genesis Chapter 8	517
§§832–837 / Summary of Genesis 8	518

§§838–937 / Inner Meaning of Genesis 8   519

§§938–946 / The Hells (Continued): Misers' Hells, the Foul Jerusalem and Outlaws in the Wilderness, and the Feces-Laden Hells of Those Who Have Pursued Sensual Pleasure Alone   588

Notes and Indexes

Notes   595
Works Cited in the Notes   653
Index to Prefaces, Reader's Guide, Introduction, and Notes   659
Index to *Secrets of Heaven,* volume 1   673
Biographical Note   759

Series Editor's Preface

JONATHAN S. ROSE

THIS first of the fifteen volumes of Emanuel Swedenborg's *Secrets of Heaven* begins with a translator's preface, a reader's guide, and an introduction to the work. At the risk of increasing that superabundance of introductory matter, it seems advisable to add this brief survey of the three pieces to help the reader choose a starting point among them. Each of these introductory essays applies to the full fifteen volumes, insofar as comment on the whole can be anticipated in this first volume of the set.

The lead essay is offered by the translator, Lisa Hyatt Cooper. It is the ideal opening for readers who have an interest in her philosophy of translation. However, the translator's preface also includes material that gives it wider applicability: a discussion of several challenging terms in Swedenborg's text. Particularly recommended are Cooper's comments on the word "bodily," since that term has additional meanings in this translation beyond those it usually carries in English.

The reader's guide, composed by William Ross Woofenden and Jonathan S. Rose, has as its main function the explanation of the expositional structure of *Secrets of Heaven*. It is recommended for anyone unfamiliar with *Secrets of Heaven* and anyone who intends to study the biblical exposition of the work. To meet the needs of those with a historical or biographical interest in Swedenborg, this essay also briefly reviews where *Secrets of Heaven* fits into the author's life and corpus as a whole. Furthermore, it elucidates some unique concepts and some problematic content in greater detail than can be attempted in the explanatory notes that appear at the conclusion of the translation text.

Wouter J. Hanegraaff's introduction describes different approaches, from the religious to the secular, that have been taken to *Secrets of Heaven* over time. It presents the notion of correspondences, which is key to a full understanding of Swedenborg's exegesis. It also gives a detailed summary of the work's contents. For those seeking to set the work in its historical context, Hanegraaff's essay shows how those contents relate—and how they do not relate—to the history of thought in general and of

Western esotericism in particular. It includes some reflections on the history of allegorical interpretations of Scripture and argues that *Secrets of Heaven* is unique in its interpretive approach. It closes with some reflections on the early reception of the work.[1]

The brief account of Swedenborg's life should not go unmentioned in this list, though in fact it appears at the end of the volume, on page 759.

The main feature of the volume is of course the translation itself, which begins on page 143, and that too is a possible starting point. Indeed, the first chapter can be recommended as a kind of course in brief on Swedenborg's method, and some readers may want to begin there and return to the introductory matter afterward. Swedenborg himself seems to have encouraged readers to take from his rich and voluminous text what they could and what they most needed. It is our hope that the same principle will be followed with respect to the ancillary material that accompanies his work in these volumes.

---

1. Those who wish to know more about the historical reception of *Secrets of Heaven* are invited to consult chapters 6–9 of Hanegraaff's monograph *Swedenborg, Oetinger, Kant: Three Perspectives on the Secrets of Heaven* (West Chester, Pa.: Swedenborg Foundation, 2007), 57–114.

Translator's Preface

THE work before you, *A Disclosure of Secrets of Heaven Contained in Sacred Scripture, or the Word of the Lord, . . . Together with Amazing Things Seen in the World of Spirits and in the Heaven of Angels,* is a translation of Emanuel Swedenborg's *Arcana Coelestia Quae in Scriptura Sacra, seu Verbo Domini Sunt, Detecta: Una cum Mirabilibus Quae Visa Sunt in Mundo Spirituum, et in Coelo Angelorum,* published in London between 1749 and 1756.[1] Though traditionally this work has been identified by its Latin short title, *Arcana Coelestia,* throughout the present edition it will be referred to by the English short title *Secrets of Heaven.*

The Latin Sources of the Translation

As my source for the first volume of the eight-volume Latin original, I used the facsimile edition issued by the Swedenborg Institut (Swedenborg [1749] 1962?). For subsequent volumes, my source was the electronic facsimile prepared by Junchol Lee under the sponsorship of Je Hyung Bae, and published on compact disk by Philip Kyung Bae, all of the Bayside Korean Church (Swedenborg [1749–1756] 1999).

Though my translation is thus based on the first edition, I have also incorporated many of the emendations in the excellent third Latin edition, prepared by P. H. Johnson and others (Swedenborg [1749–1756] 1949–1973), as modified by John Elliott's errata.[2] For volumes 3 through 15

---

1. For the original publication, see Swedenborg 1749–1756. Bibliographic data for versions of *Secrets of Heaven* mentioned here may be found in the selected list of editions that appears after the list of works cited in this preface. For bibliographic information about Swedenborg's other published theological works in their original printings, see pages 133–136 below. Translations in this preface are those of the author.

2. See Elliott 1999. I should add that I have been able to incorporate the emendations offered by the third Latin edition *only where I am aware of them.* Some are not marked in any way in that edition. See, for instance, §2342:1 in the third edition, where a reading of the rough draft manuscript, *absque impuris et profanis* ("without impure and profane things"), is silently substituted for the reading of the first printed edition, *absque impuris* ("without impure things"). A copy of Elliott's errata may be found in the Swedenborg Library at Bryn Athyn College, Bryn Athyn, Pennsylvania. (For the numbers that designate passages of Swedenborg's works, see note 3 below.)

of this edition I have also been able to consult Swedenborg's draft manuscript of the work in the phototype edition (Swedenborg 1916). The number of errors in the text is not high, and the most frequent type of error is misnumbering, either of internal cross-references or in scriptural citations. It is fairly rare to encounter problems that significantly affect meaning.

This translation presents the original eight Latin volumes in fifteen English volumes. Each of the original Latin volumes has been split in two, except for the slender second volume, which was left whole and constitutes the third English volume. For a table aligning the Latin with the English volumes, see the copyright information on page iv.

Typographic and Numbering Conventions

The bulk of *Secrets of Heaven* is a verse-by-verse exposition of the inner meaning of Genesis and Exodus, but at the beginning of the early chapters and the end of all chapters Swedenborg also adds reports of his spiritual experiences. In the first Latin edition, mentioned above, this and some other similar material is in italics. For ease of reading, the current translation removes the italics from these passages and marks them instead with vertical red rules in the margins.

On the other hand, I have added italics in many instances, to draw attention to phrases and individual words from the verses of Genesis and Exodus—phrases and words whose inner meaning Swedenborg sometimes discusses at length. (In the course of these discussions, he often quotes Scripture to demonstrate or illustrate the meaning, and the italics in such "proof passages" are his.)

Swedenborg numbered his theological works in sections extending anywhere from a few lines to several pages in length.[3] John Faulkner Potts, in preparing a concordance to the material, added subsection numbers, which I have taken from handwritten marks in the margins of Potts's own copy of the second Latin edition.[4] These differ slightly from

---

3. Swedenborgian scholars typically use these section numbers, rather than page numbers, in citing Swedenborg's texts. They are uniform in most editions. In the volumes of *Secrets of Heaven*, section numbers where no work is specified should be understood to refer to *Secrets of Heaven*. For example, a bare reference to "§90" would mean "*Secrets of Heaven* §90."

4. Potts's copy is held in the Swedenborg Library, Bryn Athyn, Pennsylvania. For Potts's concordance itself, see Potts 1888–1902.

the subsection numbers in currently available translations and editions. I have also added a very small number of my own subsection numbers (such as §§1474:2, 1486:2).[5]

Verse numbering and (in a few instances) chapter breaks vary in different language editions of the Bible, and Swedenborg's citations sometimes differ from those used in English Bibles. The present translation for the most part silently and consistently adopts the versification of the King James and other standard Protestant Bibles.[6]

Problematic Vocabulary in *Secrets of Heaven*

Seven terms used by Swedenborg deserve special attention: *Lord, Jehovah, church, heavenly, spiritual, earthly,* and *bodily.*

Swedenborg consistently refers to the Deity as "the Lord" *(Dominus),* and by this term, as he explains in §§14 and 15, he means the one God of the created universe and at the same time the incarnation of this one God in Jesus Christ. As a name for the Divine, it is equivalent to the Hebrew term אֲדֹנָי *(ădōnāi),* and also to the Greek term ὁ κύριος *(ho kúrios)* frequently used by Jesus' disciples. Although the Deity may incorporate both masculine and feminine or transcend gender altogether, the present edition refers to the Lord by masculine pronouns.

One of the names for the Deity in the Hebrew Bible is represented by the "tetragrammaton"—the four Hebrew consonants יהוה *(yhvh).* Modern scholars generally agree that the name was pronounced "Yahweh," but Swedenborg followed the practice of his day in rendering it as Jehovah, and I have carried this spelling over into the translation.

Swedenborg divides the world's religious history into five phases and uses the term *ecclesia,* or "church," to refer to each. According to this system, the earliest church lasted up to an era represented by the Flood and was replaced by what Swedenborg calls simply "the ancient church," which in turn survived until Abraham's time. With Abraham began the Jewish

---

5. In the text, subsections are indicated in square brackets starting with the second subsection, [2]. In references, the subsection is indicated after the colon; thus §1474:2 indicates the second subsection of section 1474.

6. The discrepancies in Bible versification are particularly noteworthy where they coincide with chapter breaks in *Secrets of Heaven,* as occurs twice: in the transition from Exodus 7 to 8 in volume 10, and in the transition from Exodus 21 in volume 12 to Exodus 22 in volume 13.

church, with the Lord's first advent the Christian church, and with the publication of Swedenborg's theological works a new church. This fourth turning point, according to Swedenborg's later account, coincided with the Last Judgment, begun in 1757, and with the Lord's Second Coming, which he explains more as spiritual than as physical events.[7]

The spiritual world, in Swedenborg's description, is divided into three realms: heaven, hell, and the world of spirits, the last being a place of entry for the spirits of those who have recently died. Heaven is divided into two kingdoms, a heavenly one and a spiritual one. The heavenly kingdom is so called because it is the truest embodiment of heavenly qualities. The motivation of angels who live in it is love, especially love for the Lord. The spiritual kingdom is oriented more toward the spirit and the neighbor than the Lord, and the angels there are motivated more by truth than by love.

The terms "heavenly," "spiritual," and "earthly" *(coelestis, spiritualis, naturalis)* are each used by Swedenborg in more than one way. When he speaks of something as heavenly or as spiritual, he can mean that it is not hellish. Alternatively, he can mean that it does not belong to the physical world; and when he speaks of something as earthly, he can mean that it *does* belong to the physical world. But there is a third, more technical sense in which he uses these three terms. In this case "heavenly" refers to something emotive or volitional, "spiritual" to something intellectual, and "earthly" to a lower, more pragmatic level of the human psyche on which the two higher levels express themselves, in our everyday concerns, desires, knowledge, and actions. This third sense is illustrated in the accompanying chart (see figure 1).

"Bodily" *(corporeus)* is perhaps the most troublesome term I have struggled with in my translation, since it depends on a view of the psyche that is not current in Western culture. Swedenborg sees certain drives or passions or urges and even thought patterns as having their seat in or chief effect on the human body, and he refers to them as bodily. These are mainly connected with a self-centered attitude, and sometimes even with

---

7. While Swedenborg believed, on the basis of his encounters with the spiritual world, that an epochal "final judgment" was imminent (see §2121), he did not experience it until after the publication of the final volume of *Secrets of Heaven*. For more on the Last Judgment, see his 1758 work *Last Judgment* and his *True Christianity*, published in 1771, §§753–791. For the meaning of the Last Judgment and the Second Coming in *Secrets of Heaven*, see §§2117–2133, 3900:9, 4060:5, 4229–4231, 4332–4335.

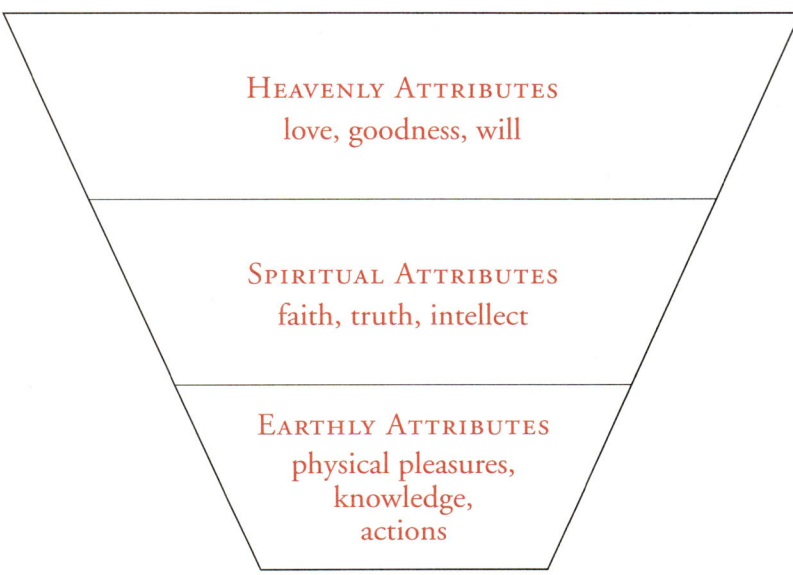

Figure 1. Attributes classified by Swedenborg as heavenly, spiritual, and earthly

a desire for power, status, and control (self-love) as opposed to a desire for worldly advantages (materialism). He therefore describes ambition (see §49 of his 1768 work *Marriage Love*) and despotism (see §507:2 of his 1771 work *True Christianity*) as varieties of bodily love. The problem is not simply that the translation "bodily" might be incomprehensible to the reader but that in many instances where it seems comprehensible it will mislead by suggesting too narrow a range of possibilities. *Secrets of Heaven* 8, for instance, contains the statement that "trouble, misfortune, and grief . . . enable bodily and worldly concerns . . . to fade away and in effect die out." What is the reader likely to picture as "bodily concerns"? Perhaps the basic human need for food, clothing, and shelter, or maybe a desire for sensual pleasures, but probably not abusiveness or emotional manipulation or a host of other coercive behaviors. Because people today do not commonly draw this particular connection between body and mind, English has no appropriate word for it, and I have had to content myself with "bodily," despite its disadvantages.

Swedenborg's Renderings of Scripture

Swedenborg's Scripture quotations constitute a distinct problem for the translator. The Latin into which they are rendered from the original Hebrew and Greek is very literal, by Swedenborg's deliberate choice. In an unpublished work called *The Old Testament Explained* (= Swedenborg 1927–1951), written shortly before *Secrets of Heaven,* Swedenborg explains why he preferred the Latin translation of the Bible by the German scholar Sebastian Schmidt (1617–1696), which became his main source for scriptural quotations in *Secrets of Heaven*:[8]

> The fact that many people have not absorbed any other meaning from the Word[9] than the literal one is a truth so obvious that anyone can recognize it. . . . It is an obvious truth, I say, because no one cares about anything else these days. The reason is that we concentrate on the most superficial realities and on the earthly realm—so much so that people have no idea at all what spiritual realities are.
>
> As a result, even translators themselves, holding similar convictions, have paid little attention to translating the actual words of the text from their source (as Schmidt has) but have concentrated solely on elegant speech (as most have). So they have changed the words themselves [to ones] that simply tell the story. In this way they remove all the light that dwells exclusively in the meaning to be developed out of the actual words of God Messiah.
>
> When they do this, the letter kills, because then the reader believes that it holds nothing inside it but what other history books do. So the reader despises the Word itself of God Messiah and rejects it.[10]

Swedenborg here distinguishes between "the words themselves," which he considers it the translator's duty to represent, and "the literal meaning," or

---

8. For Schmidt's translation, see Schmidt 1696 or Schmidt and Swedenborg 2005, the latter being a facsimile with Swedenborg's annotations.

9. As can be seen from the full title of *Secrets of Heaven* given above, "the Word" is the term commonly used in Swedenborg's tradition to refer to the Bible. It has a slightly limited application in Swedenborg's use; see *Secrets of Heaven* 10325.

10. *The Old Testament Explained* (= Swedenborg 1927–1951) §2073. This passage was brought to my attention by John Elliott in a presentation he made on Swedenborg and Schmidt to a conference on the translation of the Neo-Latin of Emanuel Swedenborg held August 23–26, 1992, at the Academy of the New Church Swedenborg Library in Bryn Athyn, Pennsylvania; see ANCC and SF 1992, 122. The reference to "the letter that kills" is 2 Corinthians 3:6: "The letter kills, but the spirit gives life."

the bare storyline, which he believes to be leading the readers of his time astray. "Elegant speech," or in other words, idiomatic translation, makes it too easy for the reader to become immersed in the "simple telling of the story" and to view that story (the "letter" that "kills") as the whole message. A translation of the "words themselves," on the other hand, because it is inherently difficult to read, enables the reader to see that the true message must lie deeper. It is the "actual words of God Messiah," and sometimes even the phonemes that go to make up the words, that hold "all the light" of the inner meaning. Admittedly there are passages elsewhere in which Swedenborg points to the emotion behind the words and to the overarching idea presented by the words as the true inner meaning (§§1492, 1756:1, 2077:1, 2157, 2275, 2343:2). His actual translations, however, tend to hew closely to the philosophy he expresses in the *Old Testament Explained* passage, and in rendering them into English I have tried for a literalism that does not sacrifice comprehensibility.

For example, Swedenborg is scrupulous in representing a gender-neutral Hebrew word for a human being, such as אָדָם *('ādām)*, by a gender-neutral Latin equivalent (usually *homo*), even in Genesis 2:25, which speaks of "the human and his wife," and I have preserved this wording, despite the apparent oddity of it. I have striven to maintain concrete imagery, such as the mention of kidneys, which were viewed as the seat of emotion ("I, Jehovah, am examining the heart, testing the kidneys," Jeremiah 17:10, §348), or the slightly unusual reference to the top of a mountain as a head ("Let those who live on the crag sing; from the head of the mountains let them shout," Isaiah 42:11, §795:4). Less easy to defend is my attempt to adhere to Swedenborg's word order, which closely tracks the Hebrew word order. I describe the practice as harder to defend because the inversion of expected patterns is much more noticeable in English, in which the order of words is a more significant indicator of grammatical function than in Latin. (Latin generally prefers to use word endings for this purpose.) Still, word order mattered to Swedenborg (see, for instance, §§47, 915), and I have kept the inversions I could, such as the one in the second half of Isaiah 42:11, quoted just above.

On the other hand, I have tried to reflect Swedenborg's departures from word-for-word equivalency as well. His renderings of a given verse are capable of varying from place to place, and I have attempted to follow him. An example may be found in the quotation of Isaiah 30:17 in §§390, 649. Swedenborg changes a preposition slightly from one section to the next, so in §390 the verse reads "One thousand will flee at the reproach of one, and at the reproach of five you will flee," and in §649 it reads "One thousand will flee before the reproach of one, before the reproach of five you will flee." Another example appears in Swedenborg's three quotations of Hosea 6:2:

§93: "He will bring us to life after two days; on the third day he will revive us, and we will live before him."

§720: "He will bring us to life after two days; on the third day he will raise us up and we will live before him."

§901:5: "Jehovah will bring us to life after two days; on the third day he will revive us, so that we may live before him."

The change from "he" to "Jehovah," from "revive" to "raise up" and back, from "and we will live" to "so that we may live"—all these represent variations in the Latin; and there were other variations in the renderings of this verse that I was unable to bring across.

Paradoxically, though, despite his scrupulous attention to all elements of form, Swedenborg does not seem greatly concerned with precision of quotation. The words he puts between quotation marks are occasionally paraphrases, adapted to suit the context in which they appear. Even when there is no obvious reason for a change, he will make substitutions. In §402:2, for instance, he quotes Zechariah 8:3 as speaking of "the mountain of Zion" (that is, Mount Zion) when the phrase in the original is "the mountain of Jehovah Sabaoth." In his quotation of Isaiah 55:4 in §666:2, instead of repeating "peoples," as the Hebrew does, he makes the second word "nations." The quotation of Isaiah 7:22 in §680:5 changes "he will eat butter," as it appears in the Hebrew, to "they will eat butter." Frequently Swedenborg will change a "your" to a "his" or vice versa. I prefer not to treat these departures as errors, because their prevalence in the work of an author so attuned to certain kinds of detail suggests that the modern preoccupation with letter-perfect quotation is alien here. To hold Swedenborg to those standards would result in an explosion of annotations and risk misleading readers about his intentions. I leave most instances unmarked.

In addition, the citation that Swedenborg supplies after a quotation will often include verses not actually quoted. See §424, where in a discussion of the word *artisan* Swedenborg quotes from Jeremiah 10:8–9 but includes verse 3 in his citation because it speaks of a craftsperson. In §934:2, Ezekiel 8:2 is listed because of its great similarity to 1:27.

Instead of translating a Hebrew or Greek word, Swedenborg will occasionally transliterate it. One example is the *qippod* of Zephaniah 2:14

quoted in §655:2. For the most part I have carried such transliterations over into the English and provided information about them in the endnotes.

Acknowledgments

In the course of my work on *Secrets of Heaven,* I have occasionally consulted the translation of John Elliott (Swedenborg [1749–1756] 1983–1999) and even more rarely the version by John Clowes, as revised by Potts.[11] Elliott had a large influence on my development as a translator, and specifically as a translator of this work, since I served under him as American reader for the last six of his twelve volumes and as Latin consultant for the last five of the twelve. He was an unfailingly kind and generous teacher and colleague, and I hope I have managed to pay tribute to his independence of thought by taking my own quite different approach.

I have also had the help of a large number of scholars and assistants. Lee S. Woofenden was my main Latin consultant on this first volume, and I benefited from his knowledge of Hebrew as well. John L. Odhner was also a Latin consultant for several of the early chapters. Both of them provided references and other information used in the annotations. Kristin King, Shirley G. Gladish, and Rob Lawson acted as my literary editors, correcting my trajectory at its start in important ways; as I translate the remaining fourteen volumes of this title, their influence will make an increasing difference. I cannot say enough about the genius, care, attention to detail, patience, and kindness of my editors, Jonathan S. Rose and Stuart Shotwell. George F. Dole has specifically helped me understand the Hebrew underlying some of the Scripture quotations, but even more importantly, his steady sense of gratitude and joy in the work we are doing has warmed my spirit. These last three—Jonathan, Stuart, and George, my fellow translators—have awed and enlightened me with their penetrating analysis of and insights into translation in general and Swedenborgian translation in particular. All the members of the New Century Edition committee, past and present, have provided significant direct and indirect help; in addition to Jonathan, Stuart, and

---

11. The original rendering by Clowes can be found in Swedenborg [1749–1756] 1783–1806; although slightly different from the electronic form I used, the revision by Potts can now most easily be found in Swedenborg [1749–1756] 1995–1998.

George, they are Wendy E. Closterman, David B. Eller, Robert H. Kirven, Sylvia Shaw, and Alice B. Skinner. Reuben P. Bell has shared his expertise in science (especially human anatomy), in the history of science, and in Swedenborg's science, and has infected me with his tremendous enthusiasm for all matters scientific and theological. Mats Eskhult answered many questions about Hebrew. Alicia L. Dole, the senior copy editor of the series, has caught an amazing array of errors.

The Swedenborg Foundation was supportive of this project even before its inception and has shown unwavering commitment since. Several other foundations and many individuals have also contributed generously to it.

To all these I am indebted, and to countless other people as well. Everyone who has praised or criticized, encouraged or questioned, prayed for, talked about, or hoped in my work and the work of the New Century Edition has made a positive difference, and I thank them with a full heart.

LISA HYATT COOPER
Bryn Athyn, Pennsylvania
April 2008

Works Cited in the Translator's Preface

The Academy of the New Church College (ANCC) and the Swedenborg Foundation (SF). 1992. Transactions of the conference on the translation of the Neo-Latin of Emanuel Swedenborg held August 23–26, 1992, at the Academy of the New Church Swedenborg Library. Bryn Athyn, Pa.: Bryn Athyn College of the New Church Swedenborg Library. Photocopied.

Elliott, John. 1999. *Errata in the Third Latin Edition of* Arcana Caelestia. Photocopied.

Potts, John F. 1888–1902. *The Swedenborg Concordance. A Complete Work of Reference to the Theological Writings of Emanuel Swedenborg; Based on the Original Latin Writings of the Author.* 6 vols. London: Swedenborg Society.

Schmidt, Sebastian, trans. 1696. *Biblia Sacra sive Testamentum Vetus et Novum ex Linguis Originalibus in Linguam Latinam Translatum.* Strasbourg: J. F. Spoor.

Schmidt, Sebastian, trans., and Emanuel Swedenborg, annotator. 2005. *Biblia Sacra sive Testamentum Vetus et Novum ex Linguis Originalibus in Linguam Latinam Translatum, ad Fidem Exemplaris Annotationibus Emanuelis Svedenborgii Manu Scriptis Locupletati.* . . . Edited by R. L. Tafel. Bryn Athyn, Pa.: Academy of the New Church. First edition: 1872, Stockholm: Photolithographic Society.

Swedenborg, Emanuel. [1749–1756] 1783–1806. *Arcana Coelestia: or Heavenly Mysteries Contained in the Sacred Scriptures, or Word of the Lord, Manifested and Laid Open; Beginning with the Book of Genesis. Interspersed with Relations of Wonderful Things Seen in the World of Spirits and the Heaven of Angels.* 12 vols. [Translated by John Clowes]. Vols. 1–8, London: R. Hindmarsh. Vols. 9–10, London: J. Hodson. Vols. 11–12, London: J. Hodson and E. Hodson.

———. 1927–1951. *The Word of the Old Testament Explained.* 10 vols. Translated and edited by Alfred Acton. Bryn Athyn, Pa.: Academy of the New Church.

———. [1749–1756] 1995–1998. *Arcana Coelestia.* 12 vols. Translated by John Clowes, and edited and revised by John Faulkner Potts. West Chester, Pa.: Swedenborg Foundation. A revision of the translation by Clowes listed above as Swedenborg [1749–1756] 1783–1806.

Selected List of Editions of *Secrets of Heaven*

1. Edition of the Draft Latin Work

Swedenborg, Emanuel. 1916. *Emanuelis Swedenborgii Autographa Editio Phototypica.* Vols. 10–14. Stockholm: Lagrelius & Westphal. A phototyped edition of the rough copy mss. collected in Swedenborg's papers in the Royal Academy of Sciences, Stockholm, codices 8, 10, 80, 9, 15, 16, 17, 18, 19, 20, 21, 22, 23, 24, 25, 26 (in approximate sequential order).

2. Editions of the Published Latin Work

Swedenborg, Emanuel. 1749–1756. *Arcana Coelestia, Quae in Scriptura Sacra, seu Verbo Domini Sunt, Detecta: . . . Una cum Mirabilibus Quae Visa Sunt in Mundo Spirituum, et in Coelo Angelorum.* 8 vols. [London: John Lewis].
———. [1749–1756] 1833–1842. *Arcana Coelestia Quae in Scriptura Sacra seu Verbo Domini Sunt, Detecta: . . . Una cum Mirabilibus Quae Visa Sunt in Mundo Spirituum et in Coelo Angelorum.* 13 vols. Edited by J.F.I. Tafel. Tübingen: Zu-Guttenberg.
———. [1749–1756] 1949–1973. *Arcana Caelestia Quae in Scriptura Sacra seu Verbo Domini Sunt Detecta: Nempe Quae in Genesi et Exodo Una cum Mirabilibus Quae Visa Sunt in Mundo Spirituum et in Caelo Angelorum.* 8 vols. Edited by P. H. Johnson, E. C. Mongredien, and John E. Elliott. London: Swedenborg Society.

3. Facsimiles of the First Latin Edition

Swedenborg, Emanuel. [1749] 1962? *Arcana Coelestia, Quae in Scriptura Sacra, seu Verbo Domini Sunt, Detecta: Hic Primum Quae in Genesi. Una cum Mirabilibus Quae Visa Sunt in Mundo Spirituum, et in Coelo Angelorum.* Vol. 1. Basel: Swedenborg Institut.
———. [1749–1756] 1999. *Arcana Coelestia, Quae in Scriptura Sacra, seu Verbo Domini Sunt, Detecta: . . . Una cum Mirabilibus Quae Visa Sunt in Mundo Spirituum, et in Coelo Angelorum.* 8 vols. Bayside, New York: Bayside Korean Church. In digital image format on compact disk.

4. English Translations of the Published Work

Swedenborg, Emanuel. [1750] 1750. *Arcana Caelestia: or, Heavenly Secrets, Which Are in the Sacred Scripture, or, Word of the Lord, Laid Open: . . . Together with the Wonderful Things That Have Been Seen in the World of Spirits, and in the Heaven of Angels.* [Translated by John Marchant]. [London: John Lewis]. Published as six separate chapters, this concurrent translation of volume 2 of the first Latin edition was commissioned by Swedenborg himself.

———. [1749–1756] 1783–1806. *Arcana Coelestia: or Heavenly Mysteries Contained in the Sacred Scriptures, or Word of the Lord, Manifested and Laid Open; Beginning with the Book of Genesis. Interspersed with Relations of Wonderful Things Seen in the World of Spirits and the Heaven of Angels.* 12 vols. [Translated by John Clowes]. Vols. 1–8, London: R. Hindmarsh. Vols. 9–10, London: J. Hodson. Vols. 11–12, London: J. Hodson and E. Hodson.

———. [1749–1756] 1857–1860. *The Heavenly Secrets Which Are in the Holy Scripture, or Word of the Lord, Uncovered . . . Together with the Wonders Which Have Been Seen in the World of Spirits, and in the Heaven of Angels.* 12 vols. [Translated by George Harrison]. London: William White.

———. [1749–1756] 1983–1999. *Arcana Caelestia, Principally a Revelation of the Inner or Spiritual Meaning of Genesis and Exodus.* 12 vols. Translated by John Elliott. London: Swedenborg Society.

———. [1749–1756] 1995–1998. *Arcana Coelestia.* 12 vols. Translated by John Clowes, and edited and revised by John Faulkner Potts. West Chester, Pa.: Swedenborg Foundation. A revision of the translation by Clowes listed above as Swedenborg [1749–1756] 1783–1806.

5. Translations of the Published Work in Other Languages

Versions of the work in its entirety have been or are being produced in Danish, Dutch, French, German, Japanese, Korean, Portuguese, and Swedish. Extracts of it have been published in Danish, French, German, Latvian, Norwegian, Russian, Spanish, and Swedish.

A Reader's Guide to *Secrets of Heaven*

WILLIAM ROSS WOOFENDEN
and
JONATHAN S. ROSE

Outline

I. The Place of *Secrets of Heaven* in Swedenborg's Life and Work
    a. Transitional Works and Preparatory Manuscripts
    b. The Writing and Publishing of *Secrets of Heaven*
    c. Later Works and How They Relate to *Secrets of Heaven*

II. Finding One's Way through *Secrets of Heaven*
    a. Structure as a Guide
    b. How Swedenborg Marked the Structure of the Work
    c. Geometrical Reasoning and Repetition within the Middle Field
    d. The Advantage of the Structure for Readers

III. Unique Content
    a. The Spiritual World
    b. The Nature of God
    c. Rebirth
    d. Correspondences
    e. The Sequential Churches
    f. A Perspective beyond Time and Space

IV. Content That May Be Problematic for Today's Readers
    a. Attitudes toward Race and Gender
    b. Troublesome Vocabulary I: "Affection"
    c. Troublesome Vocabulary II: "Bodily"

V. Valediction

Works Cited in the Reader's Guide

ON the title pages of the eight volumes of his Latin work *Arcana Coelestia* (Secrets of Heaven), Emanuel Swedenborg (1688–1772) makes clear that the work contains two types of material: exegesis of Genesis and Exodus, and presentations of his own spiritual experiences.[1] In the author's table of contents at the beginning of the first volume, he clarifies the relationship between these two: that there is unsuspected deeper meaning throughout the Old Testament, which he intends to expound, and that in order to understand that deeper meaning, one has to understand the nature of spiritual reality.[2] The work then goes on to present the elements contained in the inner meaning, proceeding chapter by chapter and verse by verse. In addition, each chapter of biblical interpretation is both preceded and followed by brief presentations of a different sort, ranging from accounts of his paranormal experiences to reasoned expositions of theological principles.

The resulting work was his *magnum opus.* In size, its eight volumes (fifteen in this English edition) far exceeded both the earlier masterwork that had brought him fame in Europe—his *Philosophical and Metallurgical Works*[3]—and all seventeen of the theological titles he was yet to publish. Furthermore, none of his later books was more than a single volume

---

1. The repeated element in the volume titles is *Arcana Coelestia Quae in Scriptura Sacra, seu Verbo Domini Sunt, Detecta: Una cum Mirabilibus Quae Visa Sunt in Mundo Spirituum, et in Coelo Angelorum* (A Disclosure of Secrets of Heaven Contained in Sacred Scripture, or the Word of the Lord, . . . Together with Amazing Things Seen in the World of Spirits and in the Heaven of Angels). Swedenborg does not actually use any word parallel to the English *exegesis,* referring to an explanation or critical exposition of the meaning of a text. He says simply that the "secrets of heaven" (Latin *arcana coelestia*) of the biblical text will be "disclosed" (*detecta,* literally, "uncovered"). This specification of his purpose seems to be intended to distinguish the work from the multitude of other biblical exegeses that preceded it, as well as to play on such titles as *Arcana Naturae Detecta* (Secrets of Nature Disclosed; 1722), a work by the Dutch microscopist Antoni van Leeuwenhoek (1632–1723) that Swedenborg himself owned and admired (see note 23 below). The first clause of the title was thus a learned reference to (and appeal to) the Enlightenment fascination with scientific and experiential knowledge. The theme of actual experience was reinforced by the later reference to "amazing things *seen.*"

2. See also *Secrets of Heaven* 66 on symbolism, representation, and inner meaning in the Bible. On the numbered references to Swedenborg's text, see page 22 and note 9.

3. Swedenborg's *Philosophical and Metallurgical Works,* published in 1734, appeared in three large volumes totaling 1,418 pages. The first of these three volumes is traditionally known as Swedenborg's *Principia.* The first edition of *Secrets of Heaven* appeared in eight volumes and totaled 4,559 pages. For bibliographic information about Swedenborg's works in their original printings, see pages 133–138 below.

in length in the original Latin. In the aspirations of its content as well, the work stands out from the rest. Tackling as it does an exposition of just two of the many books in the Bible, its mass as well as its content communicates that there is a tremendous wealth hidden within the humble words of Scripture.

For all its size, though, *Secrets of Heaven* is a thoroughly disciplined and focused work. In creating it, Swedenborg seems to have set himself the daunting task of sifting an unfathomably vast quantity of spiritual meaning and writing a comparatively small, highly concentrated, and consistently structured book. He states as much at the conclusion of the first chapter:

> This, then, is the Word's inner meaning, the true and genuine life in it, which does not reveal itself at all in the literal meaning. But the number of secrets hidden within is so large that volumes would fail to unfold all of them. I have offered just a few, of a type confirming that regeneration is the theme and that it progresses from outer to inner self.[4]

Thus the text presents itself as but a minimal and concentrated selection of all that could have been offered.

I. The Place of *Secrets of Heaven* in Swedenborg's Life and Work

The work was written at a critical juncture in its author's life. *Secrets of Heaven* was the first major work Swedenborg published after his life took a dramatic turn in middle age. He had already had a distinguished career as a scientist, philosopher, engineer, and government supervisor of the mining industry in his native Sweden. Along the way he had intensely studied first the mineral kingdom and then the field of human anatomy and physiology. He published a number of works in both areas: his best-known work on mineralogy was the *Philosophical and Metallurgical Works* of 1734, already mentioned; his most notable publications on human anatomy and physiology were *Dynamics of the Soul's Domain*

---

4. *Secrets of Heaven* 64. This and all other quotations from *Secrets of Heaven* in this reader's guide are by Lisa Hyatt Cooper.

(1740–1741) and *The Soul's Domain* (1744–1745). As he was writing and publishing this last work, however, he underwent a profound spiritual reorientation. One harbinger of this change was the vividness of his dreams of this period (July 1743 to December 1744), which are recorded in his unpublished work *Journal of Dreams*. He assigned tremendous significance to them, analyzing them carefully in his journal. About two-thirds of the way through this period, at Easter 1744, he had a powerful vision of Jesus Christ (*Journal of Dreams* [= Swedenborg 2001] §§51–54) that seems to have been a particularly significant turning point.

a. Transitional Works and Preparatory Manuscripts

Along with the intensity of his dreams, Swedenborg's Christ vision was a precursor to a new state that he subsequently described as a condition of being simultaneously aware of both the physical world and the spiritual world that interpenetrates it.[5] He reported that it was through this experience of the spiritual world that he came to see Scripture as containing an inner sense; and although the concept of an inner sense in Scripture was by no means new, the particular meaning claimed for Scripture by Swedenborg is unique.

During the transitional period journaled in his dream diary, Swedenborg was moved to write a small work, *Worship and Love of God*. Two parts of the work were published in early 1745, but Swedenborg abandoned the effort after writing some initial fragments of a third. A mélange of nearly all Swedenborg's many interests, both past and to come, *Worship and Love of God* included material on cosmology, anatomy, theology, philosophy, and psychology, conveyed in lush, poetical prose; it is a kind of *Paradise Lost* imbued with an Enlightenment passion for scientific pursuits as well as with the fresh excitement of spiritual awakening. As such, it deals with the material in the first two chapters of Genesis (the creation of the world and the first humans), but without quoting or directly interpreting the biblical account.

Exactly why Swedenborg abandoned *Worship and Love of God* is not certain; a clue is given in a second-hand account in which he is reported to have had another Christ vision in April 1745. He is quoted as saying of that event: "From that day I gave up all practice of worldly letters and

---

5. Early descriptions of this simultaneous presence in both worlds can be found in *Spiritual Experiences* (= Swedenborg 1998–2002) §§[3a], [8a], and they continue throughout his theological works.

devoted my labor to things spiritual."⁶ Apparently he came to see *Worship and Love of God* as inspired by worldly ambition or vanity; in giving it up, he commenced a search for some purer form of expression of his religious insights.

As Swedenborg sought for this more spiritual mode, he began creating his own indexes and concordances to the Bible. By the end of 1745, he had begun to write a verse-by-verse exposition of Genesis and other Bible books in a lengthy series of manuscripts now given the general title *The Old Testament Explained*.⁷ By February 1747, this work filled 1,951 large manuscript pages. It constitutes the first tentative approach to the exegetical format Swedenborg would take up in *Secrets of Heaven*.

Swedenborg included within *The Old Testament Explained* accounts of his spiritual experiences, and the interaction between the exegetical and experiential material throughout the text is of great interest. Eventually, however, he began a separate diary of these accounts of notable occurrences in the spiritual world, which he apparently referred to as *Spiritual Experiences*.⁸ This became another manuscript work of thousands of pages, which was launched with frequent entries in mid-summer of 1746 and continued for nearly twenty years, albeit only sporadically at the end of that period.

b. The Writing and Publishing of *Secrets of Heaven*

The Old Testament Explained, too, despite the massive effort invested in it, was soon left unfinished and unpublished. In late November or the beginning of December 1748, Swedenborg began writing *Secrets of Heaven* (Acton 1927, 131–134). Although the new work differed quite markedly in content from *The Old Testament Explained* and *Spiritual Experiences*, it is clearly descended from them. The similarities include the mixture of abundant expositional material and first-hand spiritual

---

6. Quoted in Acton 1927, 114. Compare the slightly different translation in Tafel 1875, 36. For the original, see Hallengren 1989. This explanation of Swedenborg's abandonment of *Worship and Love of God* is essentially the same as that assumed by Acton 1927, 106–118, with the first sentence of 119.

7. See Swedenborg 1927–1951. The traditional English titles of the works in this series are *The History of Creation, The Coming Messiah,* and *The Historical Word Explained,* or, for the latter, simply *The Word Explained*.

8. On the title *Spiritual Experiences,* see Odhner 1998, ii–iv.

experiences. In *Secrets of Heaven* Swedenborg also continued a practice—initially adopted in his scientific works—of numbering paragraphs sequentially from the beginning to the end of the work.[9] By extending such numbering continuously across the volumes of the work, Swedenborg was able to index and cross-reference them even before the volumes themselves appeared in print. (The more usual practice of indexing by page numbers cannot be begun until the pages are typeset.)

The differences between Swedenborg's former attempts at exegesis and *Secrets of Heaven* are less objectively definable than the similarities; but it can be said that in *The Old Testament Explained,* Swedenborg's exegesis relies heavily on the philosophical principles he had developed earlier in his life. Furthermore, in the works that immediately preceded *Secrets of Heaven,* "we meet with occasional expressions of uncertainty as to what the internal sense of a given passage is, or what the meaning of a given representation seen in the other world. . . . But no such thing can be said of the works that were written after [this] period" (Acton 1927, 144). With *Secrets of Heaven,* Swedenborg leaves the uncertainties of his former attempts at exegesis and steps forward in absolute confidence to detail the inner meaning of Scripture.

Having retired from his position as assessor of the board of mines in July 1747, Swedenborg was free to devote himself to his writing. He took up rented lodgings in London and finished composing the first volume of *Secrets of Heaven* by June 1749, whereupon he personally saw it through the press. By the following year he had returned to Stockholm, where he wrote at his own home, shipping a fair copy[10] of the work to London to be printed. This arrangement meant that he was left with the rough copy; and though he usually destroyed such drafts, in the case of *Secrets of Heaven* volumes 2–8 (volumes 3–15 in the current edition) he

---

9. Other authors of the Enlightenment era also favored this device, which is still utilized in scientific, mathematical, and reference works. In the current edition, the actual paragraphing has been changed to suit modern standards, but Swedenborg's numbering of these "sections" has been retained. It is customary to use these section numbers rather than page numbers to refer to passages in his works. (In Swedenborgian scholarship these sections themselves are sometimes referred to simply as "numbers.") As some sections are extremely lengthy, later scholars supplied further subsection divisions. In references, the subsection is indicated after the colon, as in §995:2, indicating the second subsection of section 995. In the translation text itself, subsections are indicated in square brackets starting with the second subsection, [2].

10. The term "fair copy" has largely gone out of use, and in this age of the ubiquitous printed word probably requires an explanation. It refers to the neatly rewritten copy made from the rough draft of a handwritten document.

did not do so, perhaps in order to preserve a backup in case the manuscript was lost in transit. This rough draft was found among his papers after his death and survives to this day in the archives of the Swedish Royal Academy of Sciences.[11]

By 1756 he had published all eight volumes of the first edition, at the rate of approximately one per year (two volumes were issued in 1753 and none in 1755). All volumes were published anonymously and without printer information on the title pages.[12]

The second volume is a special case. The first volume had not sold well (*Spiritual Experiences* [= Swedenborg 1998–2002] §4422), and Swedenborg was apparently eager to try new formats to spark interest among readers. He commissioned an English translation of volume 2 that was published in the same year as the original Latin volume, and he arranged to have the six chapters of the Latin version printed and sold separately.[13] These experiments were not attempted again in any subsequent volume, but the idea that readers might prefer smaller books seems to have stayed with Swedenborg. He went on to publish several much smaller works, and never again anything remotely as large as the full *Secrets of Heaven* series.

c. Later Works and How They Relate to *Secrets of Heaven*

In a sense, *Secrets of Heaven,* like *The Old Testament Explained* and *Worship and Love of God* before it, was left unfinished—assuming, that is, that Swedenborg's intention in the work was to complete a survey of all or most of Scripture, as occasional comments in it would lead one to

---

11. A phototype facsimile of the rough draft is available in Swedenborg 1916.

12. The man who originally played the role we might now identify as that of publisher or marketer was John Lewis, and the actual printer of the books was John Hart. The biographical data on these two figures is scanty. Lewis seems to have been in the trade from 1739 to at least 1758. Hart died in 1762 (*Court Magazine* 1762, 730). For the correspondence between Swedenborg and Lewis and Hart, see Acton 1948–1955, 510–511, 514–516. See also the final page (328) of the first Latin edition of Swedenborg's *Marriage Love,* which gives a list of theological books Swedenborg had issued to that date (1768) and advises readers that *Secrets of Heaven* is "still being sold" by "Mistr. Hart. Printer, in Poppings Court Fleetstreet," and "Mistr. Lewis, in Pater noster row near Cheapside." For more on Lewis, see Tafel 1877, 492–497. *Secrets of Heaven* was at one time also available from John Nourse (died 1780), a prominent dealer in foreign and scholarly books on the Strand, and Richard Ware (died 1756), who sold religious works on Amen Corner near St. Paul's Cathedral (Tafel 1877, 499; Raven 2007, 143, 160, 198). It should be noted that *Secrets of Heaven* was printed at Swedenborg's expense, and in that sense he himself was the publisher.

13. One scholar (Acton 1948–1955, 510–511) suggests that these innovations were proposed to Swedenborg by his bookseller, John Lewis (see note 12 above).

suspect.[14] But in another sense, it could be said that Swedenborg never stopped writing *Secrets of Heaven*. Alfred North Whitehead famously remarked that "the safest general characterization of the European philosophical tradition is that it consists of a series of footnotes to Plato," alluding not just to the systematic scheme of thought of Plato's works but "to the wealth of general ideas scattered through them" (Whitehead 1969, 53). Similarly, many ideas that first appear in *Secrets of Heaven* are developed more fully and systematically in his later publications. There are only a few significant theological concepts in the whole of his religious writings that are not dealt with to some degree in this first of his published theological works.

In 1758 Swedenborg published five smaller titles, most of which explicitly build on the larger work. *Heaven and Hell* and *New Jerusalem* contain copious footnotes and summaries directing readers back to fuller treatment of topics in *Secrets of Heaven,* and *White Horse* more or less requotes Bible passages on the nature of Scripture that have already been treated there. *Other Planets* is an almost verbatim extract of some of *Secrets of Heaven*'s experiential material. The one exception is *Last Judgment;* in overall subject it strikes out on its own, describing the great event anticipated for centuries in Christian belief as in fact having already taken place in 1757 C.E.—and not as the mythic apocalypse, but as a vast reordering of the spiritual world invisible to mortal eyes. Most of Swedenborg's later works, as well, including the last, *True Christianity,* contain references back to *Secrets of Heaven.* Thus it forms a central and significant part of his theological corpus.

II. Finding One's Way through *Secrets of Heaven*

As has been noted, Swedenborg implies that *Secrets of Heaven* is nowhere near as sizeable as he could have made it. He perceived an infinity of

---

14. The passages in which Swedenborg anticipates discussing Bible books beyond the end of Exodus are collected in Dole 2005, 101–102 note 10, with reference to the eight original Latin volumes:

> At *Secrets of Heaven* 66, Swedenborg anticipates dealing with material in Joshua, Judges, Samuel, and Kings. He states thereafter that he will, "with the Lord's divine mercy," deal with later Bible books as follows: in the first volume of *Secrets of Heaven* (published in 1749) he anticipates treating Numbers (see *Secrets of Heaven* 296), Leviticus (§643:4), Deuteronomy (§730:4), Jonah (§1188:2), Deuteronomy, Joshua, and Judges (§1444:4), Joshua and Judges (§1616:1), and 1 Samuel (§1672); in the second volume (published in 1750) he anticipates treating Numbers (§2280:7); in the third volume (published in 1751) Elijah and Elisha (§2762:2); in the fourth volume (published in 1752) material in

meaning within Scripture (§1936:2). Thus in his eyes, his task in *Secrets of Heaven* was not to bulk out the biblical text into a multivolume commentary, but to extract certain elements from that scriptural infinity for detailed presentation—the result being still necessarily vast. In communicating these details drawn from infinitude, he built a work that has challenged commentators to supply a theory or principle of its organization in order to guide readers.

The traditional organizational pattern is based on the fact that Swedenborg describes three major themes in the inner meaning of Scripture.[15] They are: (1) what is referred to (in the traditional translation of the term) as the *internal historical sense,* which focuses on the history of the "churches," or what we might refer to as the dominant religious cultures in Western history; (2) the *spiritual sense,* which deals with the human process of preparation for heaven known as "rebirth"; and (3) the *heavenly sense,* which concerns the divine process of transformation, elsewhere translated "glorification," that is, the process whereby God became a human being and a human being became God.[16]

Numbers and Leviticus (§4434:10). Of particular interest is a mention in the eighth and last volume (published in 1756) of his expectation to deal with material in Revelation (§10400:2), which was realized in *Revelation Unveiled*. . . . These references may not be taken as unequivocal promises of seriatim treatment of the books mentioned, but they are fully compatible with such an expectation. Also intriguing is a note at §9362 in volume seven (published in 1754) that he would be including interchapter material on the inhabitants of other planets "right up to the end of the Book of Exodus" *(usque ad finem Libri Exodi).* There is no hint at this point that this will mark the end of this particular exegetical project.

15. Although Swedenborg views the literal meaning of Scripture as a sacred and crucial foundation for its inner content (*Secrets of Heaven* 9433:3; *True Christianity* 210, 212–214), he generally has but few words to say about the literal storyline. Instead he focuses on the deeper layers of meaning. See also the translator's preface, pages 8–9.

16. A key reference in this regard is *Secrets of Heaven* 4279:2–3, which indicates that each of the three heavens (see below on pages 38–39) has its own layer of meaning within Scripture, and introduces the term "inner narrative meaning" (equivalent to the "internal historical sense" in the older translations) for the lowest of the three. Swedenborg's nomenclature varies, however, from one passage to another. At another point, for example, he defines the three types of meaning as the outer meaning (the literal), the inner meaning (the spiritual), and the deepest meaning (the heavenly); see his discussion at *Secrets of Heaven* 10614:2. Elsewhere he makes a slightly different numerical division, saying that "the Word's inner meaning . . . at each and every point focuses exclusively on the Lord and his kingdom" (§49:4). It does seem that he is being flexible in his terminology. Still other characterizations of these various senses are possible: Odhner 1930, 51 refers to the three inner senses as "the proximate sense," "the celestial-spiritual sense," and "the supreme sense"; Lamm [1915] 2000, 225, generalizes by referring to the increasing universalization of the three senses as they move from outer to inner.

Though these themes will be briefly discussed below, as an organizational pattern they require extensive discussion that puts them beyond the scope of this introductory essay.[17] Here the focus will be on the structural rather than the thematic aspects of organization.

a. Structure as a Guide

Structure is an organizing principle that Swedenborg himself provided for his work. He established the structure in his first chapter and maintained it with great consistency, though the publication of *Secrets of Heaven* took place over an eight-year span.

The principle of this structure is that (with some exceptions) each chapter is divided into three distinct parts. The main part is the middle of the three, the exegesis itself; before and after each passage of exegesis there are smaller, separate, nonexegetical treatises.

For the purposes of this discussion, the small, nonexegetical treatise at the beginning of each chapter can be called the "front field"; the extended exegesis, the "middle field"; and the small, nonexegetical treatise at the end, the "end field." It is most convenient to describe these three parts in reverse order.

The end field contains brief discussions deriving from Swedenborg's reported visits to the other world. That is, it is not necessarily an "account" of his visits, but a description of what the other world is like, based on those visits; it consists of topics illustrated by narratives. Examples are heaven, hell, the speech of angels, and so forth. In the original Latin edition, the end fields were set in italics; in the current edition, the device of a red marginal rule has been substituted, because such extensive runs of italic text do not agree with modern eyes.

The middle field, too, is very simple to describe: it always contains Swedenborg's exegesis of the Bible. Printed in roman type, both in the Latin original and in this edition, it constitutes about 90 percent of the text of *Secrets of Heaven*.[18]

The front field has been saved for last because it is a little more complicated. It serves a variety of purposes. In the first fifteen chapters,

---

17. For further discussion of the thematic organization of *Secrets of Heaven,* see Wunsch 1929; its charts are edited and explained in Woofenden 1992–1993.

18. There are two small exceptions to the exclusive use of roman type in the middle field: §§14–15 (at the beginning of the middle field of chapter 1) and 166–167 (at the end of the middle field of chapter 2) are set in italics in the first edition.

Swedenborg uses it either to discuss his method of interpreting the Bible or again to treat topics illustrated by his spiritual experiences. These "experiential" passages, too, are in italics in the original Latin edition, like those in the end field, and are marked off by a red rule in this edition. In the first fifteen chapters of Genesis, the front field generally shares the topics of the end field, providing beginnings or continuations of those topics. Commencing with the sixteenth chapter, however, Swedenborg switches to roman type and starts using the front field for short disquisitions on various independent topics in the Bible: the nature of its inner meaning; the Last Judgment; and similar themes. In the chapters that cover Genesis 41–50, the front field disappears; but when it returns, in the chapters that treat Exodus 1–40, it remains a major element in roman type, discussing charity and faith serially through volume after volume.

b. How Swedenborg Marked the Structure of the Work

Swedenborg clearly marked the points at which one field yields to another, offering typographic and formatting devices as navigational helps to the reader.[19] These various devices are shown in figure 1 on pages 28–29; an overview will be provided here.

The front field opens with the chapter heading. Swedenborg's chapters correspond to those of the Book of Genesis and the Book of Exodus; in fact, Swedenborg simply gave his own chapters the names of the Bible books—"Genesis 5," in the case of the example shown in figure 1 on page 28. The chapter designation is followed by a descriptive heading of the contents of the front field (in the example, "Heaven and Heavenly Joy").

At the conclusion of the front field, Swedenborg inserted an ornament that extends from margin to margin. This is the signal for the middle field—which contains the exegetical material—to begin. The Bible book title is given again ("Genesis 5") and the text of the Bible chapter is quoted, or at least as much as Swedenborg plans to discuss in one burst. (As has been mentioned, the front field is nonexistent in the chapters corresponding to Genesis 41–50, and those chapters begin immediately

---

19. The ornaments carefully specified by Swedenborg to mark out different repeating components of his book are omitted in other editions of *Secrets of Heaven*. This is to be regretted, as these devices are in their way as much a part of the work as the words he wrote, and the reader can be spared some confusion about Swedenborg's intentions if they are represented in some manner or other.

1

The "front field." Under a chapter title corresponding to the Bible chapter being explained, and then under a secondary descriptive heading, most chapters open with a passage of material that either **relates information about the spiritual world** deriving from Swedenborg's experiences (as do the openings of the chapters treating Genesis 1–15, set off by italics in the first edition and by a vertical red line in this edition), or **discusses theological matters** (as do the openings of chapters treating Genesis 16–40, Exodus 1–40). Often these passages run in a connected series from one opening or closing portion of a chapter to the next.

Genesis 5

Heaven and Heavenly Joy

449 NO one yet realizes what heaven and heavenly joy are. Those who have considered either subject have formed such a crude, generalized picture that it is hardly any picture at all.

Spirits who have only recently come into the next life from the world have allowed me to see with perfect clarity what idea of heaven and heavenly joy they had formed. When left to their own devices as if they were still in the world, you see, they think the same way they did there. Let me offer just a few examples.

Genesis 5

1. This is the book of the births of the human, on the day on which God created the human; in God's likeness he made the human.
2. Male and female he created them. And he blessed them. And he called their name Human Being on the day on which they were created.
3. And the human lived one hundred thirty years. And he fathered [a child] in his likeness, after his image. And he called his name Seth.
4. And after the human fathered Seth, his days were eight hundred years. And he fathered sons and daughters.
5. And all the days that the human lived were nine hundred thirty years. And he died.
6. And Seth lived one hundred five years and fathered Enosh.

2

The "middle field," part 1: the biblical text. Under the restated chapter title (in the example here, "Genesis 5") the text then **quotes the complete biblical text** to be considered in this portion of the exegesis.

Summary

460 THIS chapter deals specifically with the propagation of the earliest church in later generations, almost up to the time of the Flood.

461 The earliest church in its original form, which was a heavenly church, is what is called the human and God's likeness (verse 1).

462 The second church, which was not as heavenly as the earliest, is called Seth (verses 2, 3).

463 The third church is called Enosh (verse 6), the fourth Kenan (verse 9), the fifth Mahalalel (verse 12), the sixth Jared (verse 15), the seventh Enoch (verse 18), and the eighth Methuselah (verse 21).

464 The church called Enoch is described as developing doctrine out of the things revealed to and perceived by the earliest church. Although this doctrine was not of any use at that point, it was preserved for use by later generations. This is expressed in the words *Enoch was no more, because God took him* (verses 22, 23, 24).

465 The ninth church was called Lamech (verse 25).

466 The tenth, and the progenitor of three churches that followed the Flood, is Noah. This church must be called the *ancient church* (verses 28, 29).

3

The "middle field," part 2: the summary. Next, under the heading "Summary," the text **gives a brief overview** of the inner meaning of the entire chapter.

Figure 1 (including facing page). Schematic of the five basic elements that recur within the "three-field" chapter structure of *Secrets of Heaven*.

Inner Meaning

468 WHAT was stated and demonstrated in the last chapter shows that names symbolize heresies and doctrines, and this in turn suggests that the names in the present chapter stand not for individuals but for some larger entity. Here they symbolize the doctrines—the churches—that were preserved (despite undergoing changes) from the time of the earliest church up to Noah.

A church tends to dwindle over time, however, until at last it remains with only a few. The few among whom it remained at the time of the Flood were called Noah.

469 Genesis 5:1. *This is the book of the births of the human, on the day on which God created the human; in God's likeness he made the human.*

The *book of births* is the enumeration of those who were part of the earliest church. *On the day on which God created the human* means that the human became spiritual. *In God's likeness he made the human* means that the human became heavenly. So it is a depiction of the earliest church.

470 What follows establishes clearly enough that the *book of births* is the enumeration of those who were part of the earliest church. From here up to chapter 11, or to Eber, names never refer to individuals but to some development.

Heaven and Heavenly Joy (Continued)

537 A spirit once latched onto me at my left, asking whether I knew how he could get into heaven. I was permitted to answer that being allowed into heaven was up to the Lord alone, since only he knows what we are like.

A large number of people coming from the world seek nothing more than to enter heaven, not having the least idea what heaven or heavenly joy is. They do not realize that heaven is the sharing of love, or that heavenly joy is the joy this love imparts. Those who do not know are first taught what heaven and its joy are, and one of the ways they learn is through personal experience.

For example, one spirit who himself had recently arrived from the world shared the same desire for heaven [as the first spirit]. To give him a sense of heaven's nature, his inner recesses were opened up so that he could feel something of heavenly joy, but when he felt it, he started to wail and writhe, begging to be released. He was so distressed that survival was impossible, he said. As a result, his inner reaches were closed off to heaven and he then revived.

This demonstrates how anxiety and the gnawing of conscience torture people who are let in to heaven for just a short time, if they are not right for it.

538 Another group with no idea what heaven is like was also making an effort to get in. They were told that unless they possessed a faith inspired by love, entering heaven was as dangerous as walking through fire; but they still insisted. On reaching the "front entryway"—the lower realm of angelic spirits—they received such a blow that they went tearing off in the opposite direction as fast as they could go. From this they learned how much danger there was in merely approaching heaven before the Lord had prepared them to feel the emotions that come with faith.

4

The "middle field," part 3: the exegesis itself. Under the heading "Inner Meaning," the specific portion of the Bible chapter under discussion is treated in detail, using the following pattern:

First, a **preview section** starts with the **requoting of a complete verse or more,** in italics.

Second, the preview section continues with a **series of propositions,** each of which consists of a component part of the verse, in italics, followed by a brief statement of its inner meaning.

Finally, **each proposition is given a detailed explanation,** usually with supporting reasoning or evidence.

After the entire verse has been explained, the next verse is treated according to the same pattern, in which each proposition is repeated and individually discussed. For more detail, see figure 2 on pages 32–33.

5

The "end field." Under a descriptive heading, chapters end with **material based on Swedenborg's experiences in the spiritual world,** again often running in a connected series from one opening or concluding portion of a chapter to the next. In this case, note the continuation of material from the beginning of the chapter (shown on the facing page). These passages, too, are set off by italics in the first edition and by a vertical red line in this edition.

with quoted Bible text.) After quoting the Bible passage, he gives a brief overview of the inner meaning (the "Summary") and delimits it with another margin-to-margin ornament. Then the exegesis proper begins, under the heading "Inner Meaning."

In some chapters, the interpretation is handled in bursts of a dozen verses or so. In such cases, Swedenborg inserts large asterisks to show that one burst has ended and that the pattern of Bible quotation, summary, and discussion of inner meaning is going to begin again.

The conclusion of the middle field exegesis is marked by another margin-to-margin ornament. The end field then commences with a large-type heading; after it concludes—sometimes with an ornament and sometimes without, depending on how much space is available on the page—the cycle begins again with a new chapter and a new front field.

c. Geometrical Reasoning and Repetition within the Middle Field

The two smaller portions of the chapters, the front field and the end field, are straightforward, easy to navigate, and contain relatively little repeated material.[20] The middle fields of the chapters, however, which contain the serial exposition of the biblical text, have a complex, repetitious structure, which has proved confusing for some readers. This structure is nevertheless highly orderly—it shows clear signs of Swedenborg's devotion to empiricism, to responsible scientific discipline. It does so in three particular ways: in a meticulous attention to detail, in a pervasive concern for consistency, and in a strict adherence to "geometrical reasoning."

Its attention to detail is reflected in its methodical and systematic exposition of Genesis and Exodus.[21] Its concern for consistency is shown by its copious cross-references, which Swedenborg developed with the help of his own extensive manuscript index to the work.

Its geometrical reasoning warrants a closer examination, as it forms a template for much of the work. It to some degree emulates a mathematical proof of the type presented in the geometry of Euclid (flourished around

---

20. So dominant is the exegetical material in the middle field that the front field and the end field have traditionally been labeled the "interchapter" material, even though they are within the chapters, not between them, as the term would suggest.

21. There are exceptions. In places where the Bible story itself is repetitious, most notably in the building of the tabernacle in the last six chapters of Exodus, Swedenborg spares the reader from a full exegesis of material already thoroughly explained. He also truncates his exegesis of some genealogical passages.

300 B.C.E.), in which propositions are first stated and then argued and proven, and subsequent propositions refer back to points already established. This systematic approach involves and even depends on a fairly high degree of repetition.

Swedenborg introduces these propositions in a section that acts as a preview, or a small table of contents, of the sections immediately following. (An example of a preview in §893, along with the ensuing pattern of exegesis, appears in figure 2 on pages 32–33.) These previews appear regularly throughout the text. In them, he first restates a portion of the biblical text, usually at least a complete verse and sometimes as many as a dozen verses or more. Then he presents a series of propositions. Each proposition consists of a phrase of that biblical text followed by a brief assertion of its inner meaning.[22] Previews may at first be hard to identify, since unlike other elements in the work they are not distinguished in an obvious way from the rest of the text. The clearest indicators are *(a)* a relatively large block of text from Genesis or Exodus in italics at the beginning of the section and *(b)* the lack of commentary, cross-references, or quotes from other parts of the Bible in the rest of the section.

Each preview is then followed by a series of sections that takes up its propositions one by one. A given proposition, including both the biblical phrase to be expounded and the brief assertion of its inner meaning, is restated at the beginning of the full exegesis. (In this edition, the propositions and restatements have been italicized by the translator to clarify their connection to the verse under discussion.) The evidence then brought forward to argue the proposition is of three kinds: scriptural proofs from elsewhere in the Bible; logical argumentation; and the testimony of Swedenborg's own spiritual experiences. These explanations often lead to miniature essays on a wide array of topics. They are far from being mere set pieces, however; they are always engaging, even in some cases delightful. Now and then, when he comes to a word in the Bible narrative that frequently occurs elsewhere in Scripture, he pauses

---

22. The size of the individual propositions remains remarkably consistent throughout *Secrets of Heaven,* but the scope of the preview sections that contain them increases and the frequency of those previews decreases as *Secrets of Heaven* unfolds. In other words, in the early volumes Swedenborg tends to preview only one verse or a few verses at a time, so the preview sections are as a result quite small. In later volumes, he tends to preview many more verses at once, so the list of propositions expands to cover several pages. (It should be noted that Swedenborg does not himself use the term *proposition* for these statements; this is a term derived from the geometrical/mathematical model he is following.)

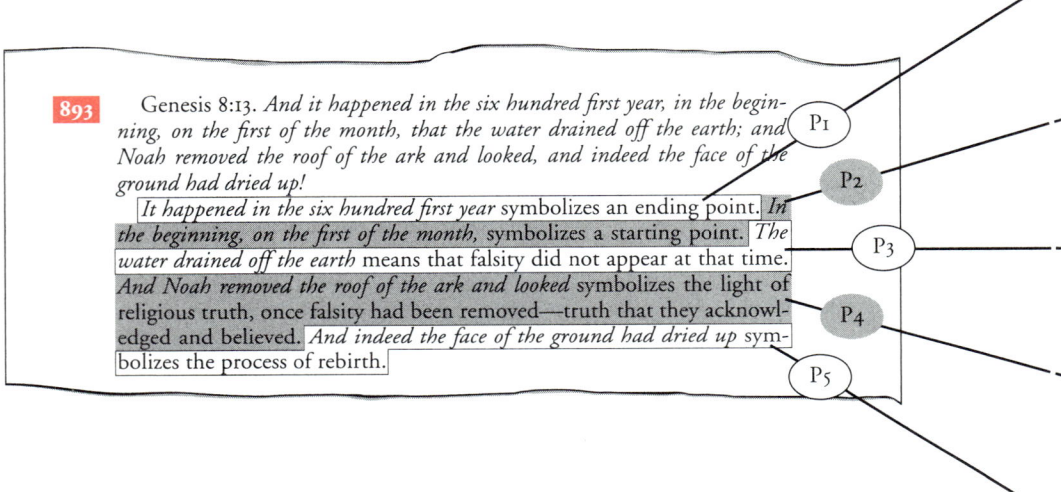

Figure 2. A preview section and its propositions (shown on this page), with arrows indicating the full explanations in later sections (shown on the facing page). In this example, Genesis 8:13 is first quoted in italics in §893. Then, in the same section, the preview proper begins, with the presentation of various propositions (here labeled P1, P2, P3, P4, and P5 and boxed or shaded for emphasis). Each proposition consists of a portion of the biblical text followed by a brief assertion of its inner meaning. The propositions are then restated in the second subsection of §893 (P1) and in §§894, 895, 896, and 898 (P2 through P5, respectively) and are given a more extended explanation, including cross-references to other passages in the Bible and other sections in *Secrets of Heaven*. The number of propositions in a preview may vary, because a given Bible verse may be broken into a different number of component parts than that shown in this example and multiple verses may be presented. (The usual pattern of exposition in *Secrets of Heaven* is to assign separate section numbers to the preview and the exegesis; this example is unusual in that the explanation of P1 does not appear under a separate section number.)

[2] The symbolism of *it happened in the six hundred first year* as an ending point is established by the symbolism of *six hundred,* given at Genesis 7:6, §737. Six hundred symbolizes a beginning and specifically, in that verse, the beginning of a time of trial. Its end is designated by the same number after a whole year has passed (so that *it happened* at the end of a year). That is the reason for adding *in the beginning, on the first of the month,* which symbolizes a starting point.

The Word designates any whole period by a day, week, month, or

894. The symbolism of *in the beginning, on the first of the month,* as a starting point is now evident.

Additional implications of these words are too deep to describe. The important thing is that the time it takes to regenerate is not fixed, in such a way that we can say, "Now I have finished." The states of evil and falsity that each of us has inside are beyond counting. They exist not only as individual states but also as multilayered composites and need to be dispelled to the point where they no longer appear, as already noted [§719]. In some of our states we can be described as more perfect, but in countless

895. The meaning of *the water drained off the earth* as the fact that falsity did not appear at that time can be seen from earlier statements [§§857, 868, 887]. Specifically it means that in the people of this church, falsity was siphoned away from the contents of their will. The *earth* here symbolizes human will, which is nothing but corrupt desire, and that is why it says that the water drained off the earth. The *ground* in us, as I have said [§875:3], is in our intellectual part, where truth is sown. By no means does "ground" exist in our volitional part, which in spiritual people is separate from the intellectual part. That is why the statement that the face of the ground had dried up comes later in the verse.

896. *Noah removed the roof of the ark and looked* symbolizes the light of religious truth, once falsity had been removed—truth that they acknowledged and believed. This can be seen from the symbolism of removing the roof as taking away whatever blocks the light. Since the *ark* symbolizes the people of the ancient church who were regenerating, the *roof* cannot symbolize anything but what blocked them from seeing heaven [or the sky], that is, the light. What got in the way was falsity. This is why it says that they *looked,* or saw. In the Word, seeing symbolizes understanding and believing. Here it means that they acknowledged the truth and put their faith in it.

898. The symbolism of *and indeed the face of the ground had dried up* as the process of rebirth is established by the meaning of the *ground* as people in the church, dealt with frequently in earlier sections [§§386, 566, 872]. The face of the ground is said to have *dried up* when falsity no longer appears.

to provide an extensive analysis of biblical passages that include that word: see, for example, §3300 on the word "red," §8261 on the word "song," and §8581 on the word "rock." The work abounds in cross-references to these biblical demonstrations and topical amplifications.

After all the propositions of a given preview section have been taken up, another preview section introduces the next subset of the chapter to be discussed.

This method provides for thoroughness, but at some cost in repetition. By the time a given scriptural phrase has received its full exegesis, it has been quoted at least four times and the same brief assertion of its inner meaning has been given twice. The purpose of the repeated quotation of the Bible verses can perhaps be illustrated by the analogy of the modern hyperlink: one iteration of a Bible verse in context "links" forward to the next, where it is requoted at the start of a preview; and that in turn links to a proposition further on in the preview that contains the phrase yet again, along with a brief assertion of its inner meaning; and this proposition is restated word for word at the beginning of the full exegesis to act as the final link in the chain. Where a modern writer might strive for variation, Swedenborg avoids it, because the "hyperlink" effect would be lost if the wording did not repeat.

One effect of this continual requotation of Bible verses in the middle field of the chapter is that some readers have the sense that the exposition is continually recommencing. To take one verse of the text shown in figure 1 as an example, Swedenborg states verse 1 of Genesis 5 for the first time after the margin-to-margin ornament at the end of §459. He then gives a general impression of its inner meaning in §461. In §469 he presents the preview for this verse, which repeats the verse again, followed by three brief propositions as to the inner meaning of its component parts; but it is not until §§470–474 (not fully shown in the figure), which include a further repetition of these propositions one by one, that the full exposition is stated. Thus the "outer meaning" is only after some postponement assigned a comprehensible inner meaning in Swedenborg's exegesis.

Swedenborg no doubt appreciated the fact that this method provided several different "optical powers" with which to view the biblical text. That is, first the reader sees the text whole, without any commentary whatever; then in smaller pieces with a little of its inner meaning; and finally in even smaller pieces with much more explanation. (Though the metaphor of the microscope is not his, as a scientist fascinated by such devices, he probably would have liked it.)[23] His method of explanation serves at once to preserve the view of the outer, literal context and to reveal the inner and deeper. Although to readers unfamiliar with his approach the initial iterations may create the appearance of false starts, in time they become consistent and familiar increments of vision that magnify the inner sense.

d. The Advantage of the Structure for Readers

The type devices Swedenborg carefully employed, and his division of the book into front, middle, and end fields, combine to give readers remarkable flexibility in approaching *Secrets of Heaven.* A reader who understands the structure of the book can easily read only the front-field discussions of doctrine, or only the middle-field biblical interpretation, or only the interwoven front-and-end-field topical discussions of the other world, without feeling the need of the other components to provide supporting material. In fact, as previously mentioned, Swedenborg himself later published a section of the end-field components as an independent volume *(Other Planets)*.

Swedenborg clearly designed his structure to allow for this independent treatment of themes. He notes in §71 that one of the topics he presents in the front and end fields would wind up "scattered and disconnected if it were mixed in with explanations of scriptural texts." His solution: "By the Lord's divine mercy I will add it in a more orderly fashion at the beginning and end of each chapter in addition to making remarks along the way." Likewise in §6627 he says that the function of the discussion of doctrine in the front field is to present in orderly and connected fashion the theology that is scattered piecemeal through the exegetical part of the book.[24]

There are other indications as well that Swedenborg deliberately planned the form of the text so that readers could dip into it to find precisely what they need. For those who open the text to look up a given verse in Genesis or Exodus, he provides an abundance of cross-references to

---

23. Swedenborg built his own microscope in 1713 and read the works of the great microscopists of his day (Dole and Kirven 1992, 16–17, 86).

24. He does not, however, indicate his rationale for breaking up the discussion serially over many chapters.

related material earlier in *Secrets of Heaven* (sometimes to points made just one or two sections before). For readers who wish to pursue only the material in the front field or the end field, he provides explicit signposts pointing to the resumption of each topic farther on in the text. For example, after discussing "heaven and heavenly joy" in the front field of chapter 5, in §459 he notes, "More on this subject follows at the end of the chapter." (He may also have intended such promises as an incentive to spur readers through the more difficult exegesis of the middle field.) Apparently to encourage this selective use of his work, he included a table of contents for the topics derived from his experiences in the spiritual world.[25]

III. Unique Content

Whichever path one chooses to take through *Secrets of Heaven,* or whatever fields one traverses on the way, there are some aspects of Swedenborg's theology that it will benefit the reader to know in advance, particularly his views on the realm of the afterlife, the nature of God, the process of spiritual rebirth, correspondence, and what could be called the spiritual or religious history of the human race.

a. The Spiritual World

Swedenborg knew that one of the greatest drawing points of his new theology lay in its depiction of the spiritual world that exists within and alongside the material world. That spiritual world is exclusively populated by human beings whose bodies have died; there are no separately created angels or devils in Swedenborg's theology. Human beings differ

---

25. A decade after finishing *Secrets of Heaven,* Swedenborg published another exegetical work, *Revelation Unveiled.* This too includes spiritual experiences (traditionally referred to as "memorabilia") at the end of each chapter of exegesis. In this case we know for a fact that he intended readers to begin by reading the spiritual experiences, because he said so in cover letters that he sent out with the volume. In a letter to his friend Gabriel Beyer (1720–1779), he writes: "At the end of every chapter are Memorabilia separated from the text by asterisks. The Herr Doctor [Beyer] will be so good as to read these first" (Acton 1948–1955, 610). He made a similar recommendation in less direct terms to the Swedish ambassador to France: "As [the accounts of spiritual experiences] contain several remarkable particulars, they may probably excite the reader to their first perusal" (Acton 1948–1955, 612).

from any other creatures on this planet in that they have both a spiritual and a physical component from birth. While we are alive in this world, our spirit senses physical reality through the agency of our physical body. After that body passes away we come into *direct* sensation through the spiritual senses we have always had.[26] Therefore sensual experience in the spiritual world is more real and vivid, and one feels more awake and aware than in this world. It is true that our surroundings in the spiritual world are not fixed and immutable as we like to think the physical world is, but curiously enough that lack of fixity does not make the spiritual world less "real." In §§320–323, 443–448, Swedenborg takes great pains to describe the shift from our dim, dreamlike physical existence to the unimaginable clarity and intensity of purely spiritual life, in statements such as the following:

> Spirits' powers of sensation are much more highly developed than when they lived in the body, as is their gift for thinking and speaking. These abilities are so much greater that they can hardly even be compared [§321]. . . . When the body has been laid aside, sensation lives on with much greater acuity and perfection [§322:2]. . . . Far from living a dim kind of life, . . . [spirits] live a clear and intensely vivid life [§443]. . . . The truth is that life continues, and continues in such a way that it passes from darkness into broad daylight. [§448]

The grand divisions that Swedenborg found in the spiritual world and his terms for them are worth cataloging briefly here, though his description is subject to complexities and uncertainties that make a full account impossible. The spiritual world does not consist simply of heaven; and though there is a place called heaven there, there are multiple levels within it. The boundaries between these and the arrangements of communities within them are not accidentally arrived at, says Swedenborg, but are the result of the groupings of various types of love and wisdom. (For a rough "map" of the other world, see figure 3 on page 38.)

---

26. Swedenborg asserts that what made it possible for him to experience the afterlife while he was still living was the possession of spiritual senses. In *Secrets of Heaven* 994:4, he reports: "By means of inner sight, I was allowed to see the objects of the next life more clearly than I can see the objects of the world." For his remark that all human beings have the same ability, at least in latent form, see *Secrets of Heaven* 69.

In a pleonasm typical of the divisions of Swedenborg's constantly self-mirroring terminology, the highest or third level of heaven is called the "heavenly" level—the heavenly heaven. It is primarily associated with love and goodness (as will be shown in more detail below). It correlates with the physical world's earliest "church," or religious culture (again, the term "church" in Swedenborg's theology will be explored below).

The middle or second level is called the "spiritual" level. It is primarily associated with wisdom and truth—that is, with the intellectual rather than the affective components of human life. It correlates with what is called the "ancient" church, which came after the "earliest," or "heavenly," church.

Below that is the area variously called the lowest, first, outer, or earthly heaven. It is difficult to extract a clear picture of it from the varying

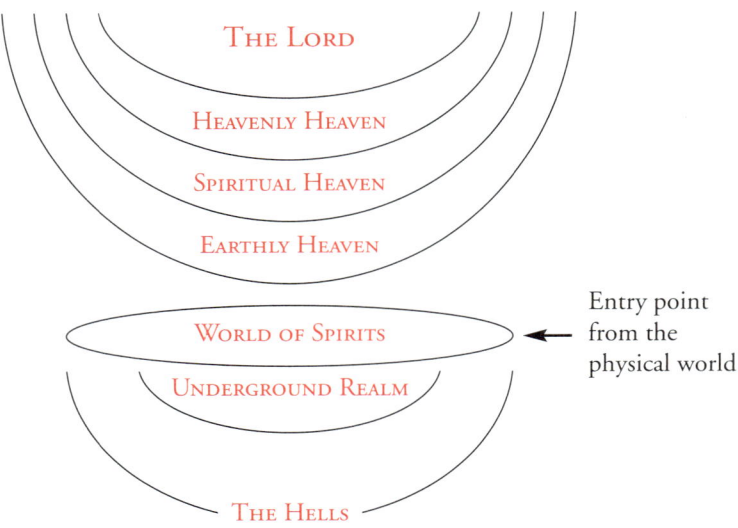

Figure 3. The spiritual world in Swedenborgian theology

descriptions set down by Swedenborg in the course of his theological writings, but briefly put, it seems to act as an outer court, so to speak, for each of the heavens above, like the two courts surrounding the Temple in Jerusalem in biblical times (*Secrets of Heaven* 9741:3).

Below the earthly heaven is the "world of spirits" (to be distinguished from "the spiritual world," a broader term that applies to the entire spiritual universe including the heavens, the hells, and the world of spirits that lies between them). To the world of spirits go all human spirits immediately or shortly after the death of the body. This too is a vast world with many communities within it. After a limited stay there, people in the world of spirits are either raised to heaven, sent to hell, or relegated temporarily to an area call the "underground realm" or "lower earth" (Latin *terra inferior*).[27]

This last place, the somewhat mysterious "underground realm," is surrounded below and on all sides by the lowermost area of the spiritual world, hell itself—or more properly the hells, plural, as there are many different varieties to match the people who live there. The underground realm must be distinguished from the hells, whose residents never relocate; by contrast the underground realm is a sort of "reeducation area" for good people who are stubbornly attached to false ideas. No punishment for punishment's sake is involved, as in the somewhat similar concept of Purgatory—as soon as those who dwell there have learned new ways of thinking, they are taken up into heaven:

> People in the church who have filled their minds with thoughts mired in the world and the earth, and who have tied religious truth to such thinking . . . are sent down to the underground realm. There they face struggles that last till the worldly and earthly elements are detached

---

27. For a brief overview of this process, see *Secrets of Heaven* 5852. In Swedenborg's account, the period spent in the world of spirits varies greatly. Some spirits go almost immediately to heaven or hell upon dying (*Heaven and Hell* 426), but the vast majority do linger in the world of spirits for at least some time; the minimum stay there would be a few weeks (*Heaven and Hell* 426). Before the Last Judgment that occurred in 1757, some people had been allowed to remain there for centuries (*Revelation Unveiled* 866:2); but all such people were removed in 1757 and maximum times became much shorter. In three passages written after that, Swedenborg gives progressively diminishing maximum lengths of stay. In 1757 he mentions a maximum of fifty years (*Spiritual Experiences* [= Swedenborg 1978] §5529); in 1758, thirty years (*Heaven and Hell* 426); and in 1766, twenty years (*Revelation Unveiled* 866:2).

from the religious truth, and new ideas are introduced that prevent the two from ever joining back together. It is when they reach the end of this process that they are lifted into heaven. . . . The only way these worldly and earthly elements can be detached and removed is by battles against falsity, and the battles go like this: The inhabitants of the underground realm find themselves beset with illusions and with falsities based on the illusions, circulated by the hellish spirits all around them. The Lord, however, working through heaven, refutes the false thinking while also instilling truth. (§7090:3)

The hells below and surrounding the underground realm are inhabited by humans who during their own lives on earth made a clear and lasting choice for evil instead of good. Although there is still some use for them in the grand scheme, their love for harming others necessitates that they be kept apart from the rest of the spiritual world.

As varied and remarkable as the spiritual world is in this vision of it, considered from the divine perspective the part of it that constitutes the three heavens takes a single form, that of a human being. Swedenborg calls this effigy the "greatest human," *maximus homo* in Latin, or as it is also translated, "the universal human." Thus individual human souls can be described in terms of the region of the overall effigy to which they correspond: in addition to being referred to as heavenly, spiritual, or earthly, they may be said to live near some anatomical location in the universal human. (Souls in hell are said to live "under the feet" of the universal human; see §3637.)

People in the other world have another distinctive nomenclature as well that overlaps with terms used in other faiths in a possibly confusing way. In *Secrets of Heaven* the inhabitants of heaven may be called good spirits, angelic spirits, or angels; and the good spirits or angels of the lowest heaven are distinguished again into heavenly and spiritual.[28]

---

28. *Secrets of Heaven* 459, 1525. Swedenborg does state in §1752:2 that "angel" is a term applicable to inhabitants of all three levels of heaven, although he adds that it is best suited to the inhabitants of the highest heaven. In *Secrets of Heaven* he alternates between referring to the inhabitants of lower heavens as "good spirits" and "angelic spirits" and calling them "angels"; for examples of the latter usage, see *Secrets of Heaven* 1802:1–2, 5658:3. In later works his terminology shifts decisively. He refers to all the inhabitants of heaven as "angels," and applies the terms "good spirits" and "angelic spirits" to people in the world of spirits who have not yet entered heaven (see *Heaven and Hell* 479:5, 517:2; *Divine Love and Wisdom* 140; *Revelation Unveiled* 875:4).

In *Secrets of Heaven,* Swedenborg depicts the world of spirits as full for the most part of evil spirits and demons (§2121); in a later work, *Last Judgment,* he describes the change mentioned above (page 24) that took place in this region in 1757 C.E., by which the world of spirits was cleansed of these evil souls (see also *True Christianity* 753–791; *The Lord* 61). The inhabitants of hell he refers to as satans, devils, demons, and evil spirits. Some specific types among the latter group are referred to as satyrs and sirens.

At the same time that the other world can be envisioned as distinct from this one, it can also be understood to fully overlap the world in which physical humans dwell. Thus Swedenborg describes each of us as constantly accessible to influences from spirits in the other world, both bad and good. When the essence of our intentions and actions is good, good spirits draw closer and support us; when it is evil, evil spirits draw closer and good spirits move away to a distance. We are in the welter of an ongoing combat, though by God's mercy we do not directly perceive it.[29]

b. The Nature of God

Swedenborg must have expected that his depiction of the afterlife would be in some respects implicitly familiar to his readers: he occasionally observes that people have an almost instinctive understanding of the spiritual world and life after death.[30] The Christian of his day probably found another aspect of Swedenborg's theology more surprising—namely, his Christology. The briefest summary of this system is that Jesus Christ was to God what our body is to our soul; that is, Jesus was the embodiment in flesh of the infinite Creator. He was different from any other person in that he had no mortal father (or, as we might now say, no genetic material from a human father). God was his father and Mary was his mother; God supplied Jesus with a divine soul, and Mary supplied him with a human body and a human mind, along with all the accompanying frailties,

---

29. Sometimes, according to Swedenborg, we experience this spiritual combat indirectly as feelings of unease, anxiety, anger, grief, or despair (see *Secrets of Heaven* 1917, 5036:2, 6202).

30. For this intuitive belief in the afterlife, see, for example, *Heaven and Hell* 602; *Marriage Love* 28; and especially *Divine Providence* 274.

including the evil that had accumulated through generations of human sin committed by Mary's forebears.[31]

What is particularly Swedenborgian in this picture is that Jesus' inborn, inherited evil gave evil spirits access to his mind. Thus even while Jesus was walking the earth and performing miracles and teaching, inwardly his own mind was the arena for a grand struggle between the forces of good and evil. Because of the strength of his divine soul, Jesus was able to allow goodness to completely triumph in a way no other human does. But in other respects, his story is our story, with the exception that if goodness triumphs in us we will become angels, rather than God, as Jesus did. This process of "transformation"—the process whereby Jesus' humanity was made divine through a prolonged struggle with "the hells"—is a major theme of the Bible, as Swedenborg reads its inner meaning.

One consequence of this radical Christology is that it makes the Creator and the Redeemer one and the same person. Swedenborg rejects the Trinity of persons in the Godhead; there is instead a Trinity of aspects. There is a Trinity in the Lord, but a Trinity like that of the spirit, the body, and the actions of an individual (*Secrets of Heaven* 9303:4–5; *The Lord* 46:3). One divine person (and Swedenborg argues that there could not possibly be more than one infinite being [*Divine Love and Wisdom* 27]) includes the three aspects traditionally known as the Father, the Son, and the Holy Spirit. Swedenborg has many names for the one God—for example, God, Jehovah,[32] or the Deity—but the one he prefers, offering a clear explanation of his usage almost at the very outset of *Secrets of Heaven* (§14), is the Lord (Latin *Dominus*).

In Swedenborg's revelation, this Divine Being is all powerful in heaven and on earth. There is no Devil (with a capital *D*) of equal negative power. Rather, the forces of evil that are commonly called "the

---

31. It is important to distinguish this "inherited evil" from the concept of "original sin" that appears in other Christian theologies. Inherited evil stems from the human propensity to do evil, which according to Swedenborg accumulates and is passed on from generation to generation, only to be effaced through the process of individual regeneration. Original sin, by contrast, stems from the disobedience of Adam and Eve in Eden. For examples of Swedenborg's discussion of inherited evil, see *Secrets of Heaven* 313, 966, 2308, 8550.

32. For the term Jehovah, see the discussion on pages 600–601 note 28.

Devil" are all the individual spirits in hell acting in concert.[33] They do not amount to a power equal in any way to the Divine, any more than darkness has any active ability to resist and oppose light.

This omnipotent power, in Swedenborg's description, sustains all things. God's love and wisdom, or, to put it another way, his goodness and truth, constantly flow into everything in the universe. Without such inflow, all things would cease to exist. Goodness and truth flow first into the higher and lower heavens, then into angelic spirits of the world of spirits, and through them into the higher levels of the minds of those humans still in their bodies on earth. It flows as well even into the evil spirits in the hells; but those spirits pervert it into evil and falsity, and redirect it upward from below. Ultimately that evil and falsity flow into the lower parts of our minds—and thus our struggle begins.

c. Rebirth

Our own personal success in the struggle against evil is made possible, in Swedenborg's account, by the success achieved by Jesus Christ, specifically in the transformation process by which humanity and divinity were united in him. The humanity that he acquired from his ordinary human mother had all the same potential infirmities that afflict the rest of the human race. By drawing on the divine potential dwelling within, Jesus gradually, methodically, and completely faced and overcame the power of the hells, restoring a balance between heavenly and hellish forces impinging on persons on the earthly plane. Swedenborg asserts that this process undertaken by the Lord throughout his life on earth is what is meant by redemption. Although that redemption did not amount to automatic salvation for all, it did restore a spiritual balance and make an individual's redemption and salvation possible. Our personal redemption is, in Swedenborg's exegesis, another great theme of the inner meaning of the Bible. At a deep level, the Bible is the universally applicable roadmap that will lead to heaven each person who wills and acts in such a way as to be spiritually regenerated.

---

33. In a few passages (*Secrets of Heaven* 6605; *True Christianity* 68), Swedenborg goes so far as to assign these hellish spirits a collective representation as an infernal monster opposed to the collective representation of angelic societies, but this symbolic figure never constitutes a challenge to the omnipotence of God in Swedenborgian theology. God remains firmly in charge of the entire universe, including hell (see *Heaven and Hell* 536–544).

In Swedenborgian terminology, the term "rebirth" refers to an overall process of spiritual regeneration. It occurs in seven stages, which Swedenborg correlates with the seven days of creation in Genesis 1.[34]

The first day, with its dark and formless void, corresponds to the initial state of darkness and emptiness when the unregenerate individual is utterly unaware of spiritual life. The light that pierces this darkness parallels the first opening of the individual's awareness of God: "As we advance further into the light, it dawns on us that the Lord exists and that he is goodness and truth itself" (§20).

The second day, on which God distinguishes between the waters, corresponds to the separation between the individual's inner and outer being. "Before we are reborn, we do not know even that an inner being exists" (§24:2). "At present," notes Swedenborg, "the second stage rarely comes into play without trouble, misfortune, and grief" (§8).

On the third day, God divides the dry land from the water; in Swedenborg's reading, this represents the individual's knowledge of truth and goodness being stored in the memory. The sprouting of the first plants symbolizes our initial, crude belief that "the good we do and the truth we speak come from ourselves, when the reality is that all good and truth come from the Lord" (§29:1). This is the point at which we repent of the wrongs we have done and intended.

On the fourth day, God creates the sun and moon. Swedenborg identifies these respectively with love and the faith that arises from love, as they come to life in the individual.

The fifth day, with the first appearance of animated creatures, represents the beginning of the individual's understanding that "we cannot so much as think a good thought or will a good result or consequently do a good deed except through the Lord's power" (§39:1). "In the fifth stage,"

---

34. The process of regeneration is described differently in Swedenborg's last published theological work, *True Christianity* 509–625. There the term refers to one of the stages in a tripartite process of repentance, reformation, and regeneration. The beginning of repentance, obviously, is the recognition that one is acting wrongly (*True Christianity* 525–527); it also includes examining oneself, acknowledging the wrong one has done, praying, and beginning a new life (*True Christianity* 528–531). Reformation is a restructuring of one's thoughts, which leads to a new understanding (*True Christianity* 571). Regeneration is a rebirth into a new intention to do good, a stage at which doing good ultimately becomes second nature, replacing even the need for the old intention and discernment (*True Christianity* 601–606). Despite the differences in description and division between the accounts in *Secrets of Heaven* and *True Christianity,* the overall process is essentially the same. For a chart correlating the two schemas, see Kirven 2003, 40–41.

says Swedenborg, "we . . . strengthen ourselves in truth and goodness" (§48). He observes elsewhere that "the things we then produce have life in them and are called the fish of the sea and the birds in the heavens" (§11).

The sixth day, in which human life is brought forth in the image of God, represents the sixth stage, "the point at which we . . . become spiritual people, who are called [God's] image" (§48).

Rebirth is complete on the seventh day, for "the heavenly person is the seventh day, on which the Lord rests" (§74). At this point love becomes the dominant force in the individual's life.

The mechanism of this rebirth process is twofold. The first component is will, referred to as intentionality or volition in some translations; the second is intellect, also referred to as discernment or understanding. Each of these components has its own constellation of related terms. The will is the faculty that feels love; the intellect is the faculty that has thoughts and reflections. The will or volition enables human beings to experience purposefulness, values, intent, and emotion, while the intellect or discernment enables the experience of wisdom, intelligence, reflection, and thought. These constellations line up as shown in figure 4.[35]

AFFECTIVE ELEMENTS	COGNITIVE ELEMENTS
will	intellect
(volition)	(understanding)
love	faith
love for the Lord	love for the neighbor
goodness	truth
the heavenly	the spiritual
warmth	light

Figure 4. Correspondences of will and intellect in Swedenborg

---

35. The content and design of figure 4 were suggested by Lisa Hyatt Cooper.

These alignments constantly recur in *Secrets of Heaven,* leading to numerous passages such as the following:

> The inner self has two elements: a heavenly one and a spiritual one. These two elements form a single whole when the spiritual element comes from the heavenly one. To put the same thing another way, the inner self has two elements: goodness and truth. These two elements form a single whole when truth comes from goodness. Or to put it yet another way, the inner self has two elements: love and faith. These two elements form a single whole when faith comes from love. Or to put it yet again another way, the inner self has two elements: will and intellect. These two elements form a single whole when the intellect comes from the will [§1577:2]. . . . Spiritual people acknowledge spiritual and heavenly types of truth and goodness, but their acknowledgment stems from faith—as do their actions—and not as much from love. Heavenly people believe and perceive truth and goodness of spiritual and heavenly kinds, but they acknowledge no other faith than one that springs from love; and love is also what moves them to action [§81:1]. . . . The last verse dealt with heavenly things, which belong to love. The current verse deals with spiritual things, which have to do with faith [§418:1]. . . . Just as holy love and the good actions that it gives rise to are heavenly things, the true ideas of faith and the good actions that faith gives rise to are spiritual things. [§419][36]

What constantly works against our intention to do good and our ability to discern truth is the overriding delusion that we have our own life apart from God. This sense of autonomy or selfhood (the term for which is traditionally rendered by merely transcribing the Latin word for it, *proprium*) is both a stumbling block to us and a blessing given by God that makes free will possible. If we can live *as if* we were beings independent of God, while realizing intellectually that all things both good and evil are flowing into us from without, we can perform the acts of discernment and will that will lead to our rebirth.

This rebirth is ultimately built on the semiconscious memories of the encounters we had with good and truth when the thoughts and feelings of angels entered our minds and hearts in childhood (see *Secrets of*

---

36. These and several other illustrative passages in this essay were brought to the attention of the authors by Lisa Hyatt Cooper.

Heaven 8, 561). At that time our discernment was not sufficiently deluded and evasive to discount this influence. These angelic influences, which Swedenborg calls a "remnant," assist us when trouble strikes us and we begin the work of rebirth.

d. Correspondences

Figure 4 also illustrates another important mechanism of the functioning of the universe, which Swedenborg terms *correspondence.* The figure shows warmth correlated with will/love/goodness, and light with intellect/faith/truth. Warmth, however, is not just an analog of love; it is actually *caused by* divine love, just as light is caused by divine wisdom. Events on earth are actually caused by events in the spiritual world through correspondence, and thus the earthly world, in response to the spiritual world, offers images of that spiritual world.[37] Each of the elements of inner meaning in the Bible reflects realities in the spiritual world. That meaning appears differently to us, depending on the depth of our understanding, and also differently to different dwellers in the spiritual world, depending on their particular spiritual location and orientation.

Unfortunately, any straightforward definition of correspondence fails to capture the incredible richness of the Swedenborgian concept. For example, the elements in figure 4 correspond to one another not only along vertical lines, but along horizontal lines as well: "Goodness and truth need to correspond to each other. The better they correspond, the more they unite" (*Secrets of Heaven* 2269:3). *Secrets of Heaven* does, however, include a concentrated treatment of correspondence (see the end fields to Genesis chapters 23 through 43). It can also be glimpsed in action throughout Swedenborg's exegesis.

e. The Sequential Churches

The Swedenborgian concept of "churches" rests on the concept of correspondence. Swedenborg holds that only one of the many religions existing at any given time carries the primary responsibility for maintaining the spiritual connection between heaven and earth. This is not to say that the other religions are unnecessary; in fact, Swedenborg's theology is

---

37. Even earthly wars are correspondences of spiritual events. See *Divine Providence* 251:3: "All wars, regardless of the civil issues involved, portray states of the church in heaven and are corresponding images" (translation by George F. Dole).

unusual in its insistence that a diversity of religions is requisite to lead the varied peoples of humanity to salvation (*Divine Providence* 326:10). Yet in any given epoch, as Swedenborg describes human history, a single monotheistic religion has formed humanity's corresponsive bond with heaven. Each of these key religions is in its turn termed "the church." Thus "church" in Swedenborg generally does not refer to a particular Christian denomination (such as the Catholic church or the Protestant church) or to a physical church building. Instead it means a specific historical entity—a broad human community that has particular religious viewpoints in common. During a church's time of preeminence, its spiritual manifestation occupies the central territory in the world of spirits, and all other religions are grouped around it (see *Last Judgment* 48; *Sacred Scripture* 105:3). In the spiritual-religious history sketched out by Swedenborg in *Secrets of Heaven,* as of the time he wrote that work there had been four "churches" in this world: (1) the earliest, or most ancient, church; (2) the ancient church; (3) the Jewish church; and (4) the Christian church.

The concept of sequential churches is significant for the reader of *Secrets of Heaven* because in Swedenborg's reading the first two books of the Bible have an inner meaning that relates to the earliest church on earth, to the spiritual developments that surrounded its fall, and to its replacement by what is here referred to as the "ancient church." Thus much of *Secrets of Heaven* is taken up with the nature of this first "heavenly" church and its immediate successor, the "spiritual" church. The biblical story of the Flood marks the transition point at which the earliest church lost its centrality in the spiritual world. According to Swedenborg, such transitions are periods of devastating upheaval on the spiritual plane.

A significant difference between the heavenly church and the spiritual church can be seen in the difference in the way the will and the intellect were interrelated in each church. During the period of the first church, the will and the intellect were united, but when that church lost its spiritual preeminence and was superseded by the ancient church, which had a corrupted will, the will and the intellect became separable: "The Lord ... provided that the will should be split off from the intellect."[38] This separation

---

38. *Secrets of Heaven* 640. On the interrelationship of the will and the intellect in these churches and in people then and now, see also *Secrets of Heaven* 310:1, 398, 641, 757, 875:3–5, 895, 927:2, 933:4.

was something of a compromise, inasmuch as the "integrated" state is far preferable spiritually, as long as the will is good; but it was also fortunate inasmuch as it enabled the intellect to rise above the flood of evil desires coming out of the now corrupted will and lead the individual to a higher state; without it, salvation and even life itself would not have been possible for these corrupted people. And as people today generally fall into this category—"The intellect and [the] will are as clearly distinguished in us as they could possibly be" (§641)—it is thus possible for our intellect to advocate a better course of action for us than our will would naturally prefer. Swedenborg hints at what our fate would be if it were not for this divine providence:

> The final inheritors of the earliest church could not be reborn since . . . intellectual capacities and volitional capacities formed one mind in them. So they could not detach the ideas in their intellect from the urges of their will and therefore could not cycle back and forth between heavenly and spiritual pursuits on the one hand and bodily and worldly pursuits on the other. Instead they felt perpetual coldness toward the things of heaven and perpetual warmth for the objects of their desire, so that for them no alternation was possible. (§933:4)

f. A Perspective beyond Time and Space

The different, apparently separate aspects of content discussed above are unusual enough in themselves, but they present the added difficulty of mapping directly onto one other. Swedenborg observed the afterlife as a world apart from time and space (*Secrets of Heaven* 1274; *Heaven and Hell* 162). It has features that are *analogous* to time and space, but it is beyond those constraints. Therefore things that seem utterly separate to those of us living in this world of time and space, such as *(a)* the earliest religious history of aggregate groups within the human race, *(b)* the psychological suffering experienced by Jesus Christ, and *(c)* an attitude within a single individual living in the twenty-first century, are from the point of view of the spiritual world linked and related. Similarly in *Secrets of Heaven* it is not always clear what is, or rather what is not, part of the topic at hand.

For example, although at one point the reader may be certain that the topic is *(a)* people who lived many thousands of years ago on the planet, the immediately succeeding sentence or paragraph may manifestly refer to *(b)* the inner world of Jesus Christ while on earth, and then mention how this might apply to *(c)* the reader's life or to *(d)* the human experience in general. At times, there is no apparent frame of reference at all. Swedenborg might simply mention "the rational mind," and not tell us whose mind he means. Though the reader may at first feel the absence of this frame of reference, in fact there is such a frame, albeit spiritual in nature; and that frame of reference is absolutely everything across all time. It is the universal human experience, and also smaller increments thereof; and the divine human experience, along with its infinite resonance.

According to Swedenborg, then, the entire universe, which includes both the spiritual and the material worlds, has a parallel in Scripture, in all its inner and outer layers, and this universe within Scripture again parallels the complexities of a single human being; because the archetypal human being was Christ, who both *was* the Word and came to fulfill it. Furthermore, these layers and levels have complex relationships with time and space. As mentioned above, the earliest church was "heavenly," which means that it occupied the highest territory of the mind or spirit. Later churches descended from that height. And similarly, each individual starts out among heavenly angels in infancy, and then moves down to lower associations as he or she grows up. And because all who have ever lived are still alive in the spiritual world, there is a sense in which the past is not the past but is still present, in which time becomes analogous to space: by moving upward through the spiritual world, Swedenborg is able to visit people from an earlier time in earthly history.

This holographic aspect of reality in Swedenborg's worldview has been discussed by recent scholars.[39] Swedenborg himself describes it in *The Old Testament Explained:*

> In each least word of the Divine Word there lie concealed in the present, infinite things which are yet to be and which are effigied in the things that exist at the time. Moreover, just as things future lie concealed in things present, so also things universal in things singular. For the universal is, in the most distinct way, the complex of all singulars. If we may use a comparison, their relation is not unlike that of a beam of light; each beam, even the least, contains in itself the complete effigy of that object—whether it be a human form or a grove of trees or an entire countryside—which a great number of beams simultaneously

---

39. See Dole 1988, 374–381, and Talbot 1988, 443–448.

carry forward and present to the sight of the human eye. So every single word delivered by the mouth of Jehovah God is a like beam, as it were, containing a universal series of things, only the least part whereof comes to the sight of our eye, that is to say, to the understanding of the human mind.[40]

IV. Content That May Be Problematic for Today's Readers

Secrets of Heaven, having been written in the eighteenth century, naturally presents readers with certain challenges that arise from that implicit context. It is worth briefly examining several of these potential difficulties: first, the attitudes toward race and gender in the work, and then some vocabulary common in Swedenborg's day that has since fallen out of use.

a. Attitudes toward Race and Gender

Treatment of race and gender in Swedenborg's work often forms a strong contrast with the overall message of *Secrets of Heaven.* At times words that speak of the highest love and wisdom share the page with language that today seems harsh and judgmental. Modern readers may be unaware that these negative assertions were commonplace or even rather mild by the combative norms of eighteenth-century theological discourse.

Swedenborg originally wrote for the largest and most influential audience available through mid–eighteenth-century channels of publication: wealthy, educated, Christian, western European males. That audience was nonetheless relatively small and far more uniform than the global readership made available by today's methods of publication and greatly increased rates of literacy. Today's readership includes, of course,

---

40. *Old Testament Explained* (= Swedenborg 1927–1951) §250 (translation adapted). In the comparison with the beam of light, Swedenborg seems to be thinking of the effect seen in a pinhole camera, where an entire scene is conveyed through a very small aperture. See *Secrets of Heaven* 2343:2 for another passage suggestive of holography: "All parts of the Word contain an orderly sequence of thoughts like this one, but the actual sequence cannot disclose its true nature when each word is explained by itself. Such an explanation makes the words seem disconnected and breaks up the continuity of meaning. The sequence becomes clear only when we embrace all the words in a single view or perceive them all in a single glance of the mind, as people do who focus on the inner meaning and view everything by the Lord's heavenly light."

both genders, and has much greater diversity in ethnic, religious, and educational background. Some statements made to the original readership about others then outside the group—in particular Jews, and to a lesser extent women and black Africans—are likely to strike today's readers as misguided, harsh, and prejudiced. Yet they are interwoven with the theology.

Some statements about black Africans in *Secrets of Heaven* may seem offensive. The dark skin of Ethiopians, for example, is occasionally used as an analogy for evil (*Secrets of Heaven* 876, 3540:1; see also *Revelation Explained* [= Swedenborg 1994–1997] §780:5). Yet Swedenborg refers to Ethiopians collectively as "a good nation" (*Spiritual Experiences* [= Swedenborg 1978] §5946:6). In fact, in the present work (§2604) and others (see the references on page 647 note 478) he generally gives black Africans high praise.

The most acute of these problematic areas, and yet the most inextricable, is the work's expressed attitude toward Jews. Swedenborg bluntly states more than once that Jews were and are "the worst of all nations" (*Secrets of Heaven* 3858:8, 3881:10; see also the list of references in §10566). He presents them as avaricious and contemptuous, and given to violence, cruelty, and vengeance even against each other. (For some of the harsher such statements see §§4865:2–3, 6963:2, 8301:5, 9320:3–4, 10033:6.) Particularly surprising, especially given his apparent knowledge of the long history of Jewish mysticism, is his assertion that Jews have no love for what is spiritual or internal (§§908:3, 1861:12, 3147:10, 9942:14). Perhaps the closest he comes to positive characterizations is to say that Jews have an extraordinary capacity for outward holiness (§§8588:5, 9962) and that a few live in mutual love and not in contempt for others (§3479:4), but in context these statements are still essentially negative. Harsh statements like these are not ubiquitous, but they do occur here and there from one end of the work (§276:2) to the other (§10566).[41] They cannot be simply extricated or

---

41. Similar attitudes can be found here and there in Swedenborg's later theological works as well: for instance, his last major theological work includes a section toward the end on Jews that is similarly critical (*True Christianity* 841–845). It is curious to note that in his published work on Genesis and Exodus, Swedenborg is strongly critical of Jews but makes hardly a mention of Catholics or Protestants. (For a few subtle criticisms of Roman Catholicism in the work, see §§4738:2–4, 7272:3, 10412:2; and in §10040 Jews are criticized, and then some Catholics are said to be much the same.) Yet in his later published work on the book of Revelation, *Revelation Unveiled,* the pattern is reversed. That work is strongly critical of Catholics and even more so of Protestants, and scarcely mentions Jews.

excised from the text, because from Swedenborg's theological point of view the corrupt nature of the Jewish religion before Jesus' birth is integral to the spiritual history of the churches: it serves to explain both the need for that birth as a new dawn and the intensity of Jesus' ensuing inner struggle.

In buttressing this negative view, Swedenborg cites Scripture and his own spiritual experiences. Scripturally he turns particularly to the dark picture of the Jews attributed to Moses in Deuteronomy 9:4–6; 32:28, 32–33; and to Jesus in John 8:44 (§§4751:3, 9320:3–4). And when he sees Jews in the afterlife, he reports their spiritual condition as generally miserable (see §§940–941).

Yet at the same time, in *Secrets of Heaven* and other works, Swedenborg shows a fondness for the Hebrew Scriptures, including the language itself in which they were written: he says that of all earthly languages, the lettering and sounds of Hebrew come closest to those of angelic language (*Heaven and Hell* 260). He sees deep meaning behind the tabernacle, the Temple, and ancient Jewish rituals and practices. Very early in the current work he chides Christians for their ignorance of and lack of interest in the treasures that lie within the Old Testament (*Secrets of Heaven* 2).

Biographical details support this more rounded view of his attitude. Early in life he lived for years with a brother-in-law, Erik Benzelius (1675–1743), who was a major proponent of Judaic studies at the University of Uppsala. Both Benzelius and Swedenborg may have studied with Johan Kemper (died 1714 or 1716), the author of a Christian Kabbalah (Dole 1990, 5–6; Hanegraaff 2005, 138). A friend of Swedenborg's in Amsterdam points out that Swedenborg made no distinction between himself and Jews, with whom he sometimes socialized (Cuno 1947, 166). As a result of these evidences, both positive and negative, scholars have been sharply divided on whether to characterize him and his works as philo-Semitic or anti-Semitic.[42]

Perhaps some of this dichotomy can be explained by looking at the norms of seventeenth- and eighteenth-century debate. Swedenborg is in some ways a creature of his times in his own chosen style of theological argumentation. As a scholar of post-Reformation theology succinctly puts it, "Polemics was the order of the day" (Preus 1970, 33). Not only

---

42. Among those who see Swedenborg's life and works as philo-Semitic are Toksvig 1983, 209, and Schuchard 1988; see also Dole 1990. Duker 1956 and Hanegraaff 2005 see and argue for an anti-Semitism there instead; their case is not weak. See also Bell 1995; Rose 2005, 81–82.

were theological positions then "almost always defined and argued over and against the errors of others" (Erwin 2006, 55), but Swedenborg and his contemporaries had a habit of taking their opponents' points to absurd conclusions that their opponents themselves would never draw (Preus 1970, 33).

Swedenborg often writes in sweeping generalizations. He is not hesitant to paint whole nationalities, races, or religions with a single, broad brushstroke, whether positive or negative. In various places he makes approving or disapproving statements about the Dutch, the British, the French, the Germans, and the Chinese; about Africans as a whole; about Roman Catholics, Muslims, and Protestant clergy; and even about all people on this planet. Such statements imply that the same things can be said of each member of the above categories. Nevertheless, in other passages he will state that every individual is different; all people are their own unique love and their own unique understanding; no two people or voices or even hand gestures are ever identical at any given point in time or even throughout all time (*True Christianity* 32:1–2).

It is difficult to reconcile his criticisms of various religions and groups of people with other statements he makes in this and later works that are universally loving, inclusive, and ecumenical. For example, in a later work that is marked by much polemical language against both Protestants and Catholics, he nevertheless strongly asserts that every human being is the neighbor who is to be loved and no one is to be despised (*True Christianity* 406–411). In another work he writes that all people are predestined for heaven and none for hell (*Divine Providence* 329–330). In the present work he declares that if love instead of doctrine were to become the primary focus of Christianity, in a moment all hatred between Christians would evaporate and Catholics, Calvinists, Lutherans, and Evangelicals would become one church (§1799:4). In broader terms, as has been mentioned, he asserts that all the world's religions are needed (*Divine Providence* 326:10). Furthermore, they all include rules for life that when followed have the power to bring salvation to their adherents (*Divine Providence* 253–254). This is a particularly striking departure from the views of his time. And in making these statements, he never singles out Jews or any other religious group or nationality as an exception to the rule; he presents these as universal truths. The two sets of statements, the positive and the negative, coexist in this and Swedenborg's other works seemingly independently, without acknowledging or interacting with each other.

Ultimately, Swedenborg says that the same corrupting forces, which he identifies with the snake in the Garden of Eden, have assaulted all of humanity over time. The snake can do no more than bite the heel, but human susceptibility to that bite has allowed its venom to bring down one great religion after another:

> The pages to come, . . . by the Lord's divine mercy, will reveal how the snake destroyed those lowest things [on the earthly plane] in pre-Flood people through a focus on the senses and through self-love. They will show how the snake destroyed them among Jews through a concern with sensory experiences, tradition, and trivialities, and through self-love and materialism. Then they will show how the snake has destroyed and is destroying people at the present day through sensory, scientific, and philosophical matters, and once more through self-love and materialism. (*Secrets of Heaven* 259:2)

By contrast, any negativity one can find in Swedenborg's statements about women is somewhat milder, although still jarring. For the most part, the statements regarding gender in *Secrets of Heaven* are surprisingly balanced, given the extreme lack of balance between the sexes in the eighteenth century. Two early statements in the work, however, may be taken as lending support to domination of men over women, especially in the context of marriage. The first occurs in §266, in reference to these phrases from the curse God places on Eve: "your obedience will be to your husband; and he will rule over you" (Genesis 3:16). In his commentary on this verse, Swedenborg states:

> Every law and commandment has something heavenly and spiritual as its source and true origin. So this law for marriage stating that a wife should be under the influence of her husband's good sense also has a heavenly, spiritual origin, since she acts on desire, which is self-centered, and not so much from reason as a man does.

Here Swedenborg apparently identifies wives with emotion, desire, and self-centeredness, and husbands with reason and good sense; he also implies that this biblical injunction is to be taken literally, and that the husband is intended to be the dominant partner in a marriage. The other such statement, in §568:2, presents a similar view:

> The female sex is such by nature and formation that the will or desire rules over the intellect. Every fiber in the female body is attuned

> to this, and it is the feminine nature. The male sex, on the other hand, is formed in such a way that intellect or reason reigns supreme. Every fiber in the male body is attuned to this, and it is the masculine nature. Marriage between the sexes results from these circumstances, as does a union between will and intellect in every individual.
>
> Today no will for good exists but desire instead—and yet a modicum of intellect or rationality is possible. This is why so many laws about men's privileges and wives' submission were laid down in the Jewish church.

This statement does add a striking nuance, that in an individual of either gender, will and intellect have a kind of marriage. But again, the statement as it applies literally to husbands and wives may be read as supporting and encouraging male domination.

Counterbalancing statements found in this and other works, however, make it seem unlikely that this was Swedenborg's true intent. A theme that runs throughout his works is that the desire to dominate over and control others for selfish reasons is the most hellish desire of all (*Secrets of Heaven* 10038:2; *Supplements* 61; *Divine Love and Wisdom* 142, 144, 273). One statement speaks specifically of the destructive nature of a desire for control within marriage:

> Any love of control of one over the other utterly destroys marriage love and its heavenly pleasure. . . . There is freedom for neither one when there is control. One is the servant; and so is the one in control, because he or she is being driven like a servant by a need to be in control.[43]

A paragraph toward the end of *Secrets of Heaven* implies an invitation to the reader to reflect more deeply on the relationship between the sexes. In it Swedenborg first makes a strong statement to the effect that by divine design, men, but not women, are to be engaged in the acquisition of knowledge; women are instead to play an emotional rather than a cognitive role (§8994:4). Yet in the sentences immediately following, he qualifies this by saying that although such is the case in the Lord's spiritual kingdom, in the heavenly kingdom the reverse is true: wives there play a more intellectual, and husbands a more emotional, role (§8994:4; see also §915).

---

43. *Heaven and Hell* 380:1–2; see also *Marriage Love* 248. This translation is by George F. Dole.

b. Troublesome Vocabulary I: "Affection"

Beyond the difficulties raised by eighteenth-century presentations of race and gender, two terms of that era also need a short introduction. For people in Swedenborg's day, these terms evoked an entire complex of meaning, but in our time they denote something considerably narrower. One is the Latin word *affectio*. (As it happens, study of this word further illumes Swedenborg's attitude toward women, insofar as that term comes into play in his definitions of the difference between women and men.) In older translations of Swedenborg, this very important and very difficult term was translated with the deceptively familiar word *affection*. The deception arises from the fact that the Latin word only rarely means what the English word *affection* means, despite the similarity of its appearance. The Latin term is a meaning-complex including every form of *being emotionally affected:* love (and here alone "affection" is a true rendering), hate, envy, desire, greed, joy, grief, and so forth, in every intensity, escalating from a subconscious reaction through a mere frisson of emotion, a vague mood, an intense but temporary response, on into habitual response, inclination, and long-standing disposition. It stands in Swedenborg's psychology as counterbalancing that other great mechanism by which the Divine works on the human, namely, thought: a glance back at figure 4 on page 45 will show affective elements (on the left) balanced by cognitive elements (on the right).

In this new translation it has been possible to render this important concept with more variety. However, the reader is encouraged, in considering passages that describe the affective life of humankind, to look for the presence of a much more powerful and overarching concept than mere "emotionality." What Swedenborg is referring to is the entirety of our affective response to stimuli, whether external (from the physical world) or internal (the inflowing of the Divine). This response is of vital importance because it gives rise to thought and understanding. The cognitive element, as derivative of the emotional, stands somewhat pale in comparison.

c. Troublesome Vocabulary II: "Bodily"

In Swedenborg's time, psychological theory divided the psyche differently than we do today. For reasons too technical to consider here, drives such as ambition and the desire for honors and dignities were grouped with the pleasures taken by the physical senses.44 Consider this list of some of the "bodily" and sensual pleasures from *Secrets of Heaven* 995:2 (with emphasis added for those items that we would not consider "bodily" today):

> *Pleasure in owning property and having other wealth;*45 *the pleasure of rank and high office in government;* pleasure connected with love in marriage and with *love for babies and children; pleasure in friendship and social contact;* auditory pleasure, or pleasure in the sweetness of song and music; visual pleasure, or pleasure in the many kinds of beauty that exist, such as elegant clothes, fine mansions with all their furnishings, beautiful gardens, and similar objects whose symmetry makes them delightful; olfactory pleasure, or pleasure in sweet scents; gustatory pleasure, or pleasure in the wonderful flavor and useful qualities of food and drink; and tactile pleasures.

There is no current English term that captures this particular range of meanings. All a translator of Swedenborg can do is to plug in "bodily" or "focused on the body" or some even more vague term such as "personal," and hope that the reader, having been alerted by introduction or annotation, will bear in mind the larger category that the concept of "bodily" things included for Swedenborg and others of his time.

This by no means exhausts the unusual terms, or unusual uses of familiar terms, that the reader will encounter in *Secrets of Heaven;* but few are as global as those that have been touched on here.

V. Valediction

If Swedenborg's work is a mountain or even a range of mountains, accessible by various paths and fields, possessing a vast wealth to be mined, a

---

44. Sometimes, however, Swedenborg splits off the pleasures of the senses as a kind of subcategory of the bodily; for an example, see *Secrets of Heaven* 242–243. There are many other similar passages as well. The key passage in which Swedenborg explicitly groups "all the pleasing affections" of the bodily senses with the pleasure of gaining dignity and honor is *Draft of a Rational Psychology* (= Swedenborg 2001) §228.

45. Sometimes the love for riches is explicitly defined as a "worldly" drive in distinction to a "bodily" one; see *Secrets of Heaven* 8993:3 and *Marriage Love* 49, as well as the definition of "worldly things" in the passage mentioned in the note above, *Draft of a Rational Psychology* (= Swedenborg 2001) §228.

perusal of it is a journey of exploration.[46] Like a mountain journey, reading *Secrets of Heaven* offers great rewards of personal insight. It provides vistas of the human soul both dark and luminous, as well as a great system of thought for comprehending the Bible and even the universe. There *are* steep trails ahead, as well as easy ascents; but however difficult the climb may look, Swedenborg makes it as simple as he can.

So let the reader not be daunted; it is a journey worth taking.

---

46. Besides the works by Wunsch and Woofenden mentioned in note 17 above, other useful material for the student of *Secrets of Heaven* can be found in the introduction by Wouter J. Hanegraaff, who provides varying opinions on and additional details of many of the foregoing topics. It has been published in a longer form, augmented with further historical discussion, in Hanegraaff 2007.

Works Cited in the Reader's Guide

Acton, Alfred. 1927. *An Introduction to the Word Explained.* Bryn Athyn, Pa.: Academy of the New Church.

———. 1948–1955. *The Letters and Memorials of Emanuel Swedenborg.* 2 vols. Bryn Athyn, Pa.: Swedenborg Scientific Association.

Bell, Reuben P. 1995. "Swedenborg and the Kabbalah." *Arcana* 1(4):23–32.

The Court Magazine; or, Royal Chronicle of News, Politics, and Literature, for Town and Country. November 1762 (vol. 1). London: I. Pottinger.

Cuno, J. C. 1947. *J. C. Cuno's Memoirs on Swedenborg.* Translated by Claire E. Berninger. Bryn Athyn, Pa.: Academy Book Room.

Dole, George F. 1988. "An Image of God in a Mirror." In *Emanuel Swedenborg: A Continuing Vision,* edited by Robin Larsen and others. New York: Swedenborg Foundation.

———. 1990. "Philosemitism in the Seventeenth Century." *Studia Swedenborgiana* 7(1):5–17.

———. 2005. "Swedenborg's Modes of Presentation, 1745–1771." In *Emanuel Swedenborg: Essays for the New Century Edition on His Life, Work, and Impact,* edited by Jonathan S. Rose and others. West Chester, Pa.: Swedenborg Foundation.

Dole, George F., and Robert H. Kirven. 1992. *A Scientist Explores Spirit.* New York City and West Chester, Pa.: Swedenborg Foundation.

Duker, Abraham G. 1956. "Swedenborg's Attitude toward the Jews." *Judaism* 5(3):272–276.

Erwin, R. Guy. 2006. "On *True Christianity:* An Introduction to Swedenborg's Most Comprehensive and Systematic Theological Writing from the Standpoint of the Religion of His Contemporaries." In *True Christianity,* by Emanuel Swedenborg, translated by Jonathan S. Rose. Vol. 1. West Chester, Pa.: Swedenborg Foundation.

Hallengren, Anders. 1989. *Carl Robsahm: Anteckningar om Swedenborg, med en inledande självbiografisk text av Emanuel Swedenborg, Svar på brev från en vän.* Stockholm: ABA Cad/Copy & Tryck.

Hanegraaff, Wouter J. 2005. "Emanuel Swedenborg, the Jews, and Jewish Traditions." In *Reuchlin und seine Erben: Forscher, Denker, Ideologen und Spinner,* edited by Peter Schäfer and Irina Wandrey. Ostfildern: Jan Thorbecke.

———. 2007. *Swedenborg, Oetinger, Kant: Three Perspectives on the Secrets of Heaven.* West Chester, Pa.: Swedenborg Foundation.

Kirven, Robert H. 2003. *A Concise Overview of Swedenborg's Theology.* Newtonville, Mass.: J. Appleseed & Co.

Lamm, Martin. [1915] 2000. *Emanuel Swedenborg: The Development of His Thought.* Translated by Tomas Spiers and Anders Hallengren. West Chester, Pa.: Swedenborg Foundation.

Leeuwenhoek, Antoni van. 1722. *Arcana Naturae Detecta.* Leiden.

Odhner, Hugo Lj. 1930. "Notes on the Calendar Readings." *New Church Life* 50:41–52.

Odhner, J. Durban. 1998. Translator's preface to *Emanuel Swedenborg's Diary, Recounting Spiritual Experiences during the Years 1745 to 1765.* Vol. 1. Bryn Athyn, Pa.: General Church of the New Jerusalem.

Preus, Robert D. 1970. *The Theology of Post-Reformation Lutheranism.* Vol. 1. Saint Louis, Mo.: Concordia Publishing House.

Raven, James. 2007. *The Business of Books: Booksellers and the English Book Trade 1450–1850.* New Haven: Yale University Press.

Rose, Jonathan S. 2005. "Swedenborg's Garden of Theology: An Introduction to Swedenborg's Published Theological Works." In *Emanuel Swedenborg: Essays for the New Century Edition on His Life, Work, and Impact,* edited by Jonathan S. Rose and others. West Chester, Pa.: Swedenborg Foundation.

Schuchard, Marsha Keith. 1988. "Swedenborg, Jacobitism, and Freemasonry." In *Swedenborg and His Influence,* edited by Erland J. Brock and others. Bryn Athyn, Pa.: Academy of the New Church.

Swedenborg, Emanuel. 1916. *Emanuelis Swedenborgii Autographa Editio Phototypica.* Vols. 10–14. Stockholm: Lagrelius & Westphal. A phototyped edition of the rough copy mss. collected in Swedenborg's papers in the Royal Academy of Sciences, Stockholm, codices 8, 10, 80, 9, 15, 16, 17, 18, 19, 20, 21, 22, 23, 24, 25, 26 (in approximate sequential order).

———. 1927–1951. *The Word of the Old Testament Explained.* 10 vols. Translated and edited by Alfred Acton. Bryn Athyn, Pa.: Academy of the New Church.

———. 1978. *The Spiritual Diary.* 5 vols. Translated by George Bush, John H. Smithson, and James F. Buss. New York: Swedenborg Foundation. First edition of this translation: 1889–1902, London: J. Speirs.

———. 1994–1997. *Apocalypse Explained.* 6 vols. Translated by John C. Ager, revised by John Whitehead, and edited by William Ross Woofenden. West Chester, Pa.: Swedenborg Foundation.

———. 1998–2002. *Emanuel Swedenborg's Diary, Recounting Spiritual Experiences during the Years 1745 to 1765.* 3 vols. Translated by J. Durban Odhner. Bryn Athyn, Pa.: General Church of the New Jerusalem. The first three volumes, in English, of the six volumes of Swedenborg's Latin work *Experientiae Spirituales,* edited by J. Durban Odhner (Bryn Athyn, Pa.: Academy of the New Church, 1983–1997). Further volumes forthcoming.

———. 2001. *Swedenborg's Dream Diary.* Edited by Lars Bergquist and translated by Anders Hallengren West Chester, Pa.: Swedenborg Foundation.

Tafel, R. L. 1875. *Documents Concerning the Life and Character of Emanuel Swedenborg.* Vol. 1. London: Swedenborg Society.

———. 1877. *Documents Concerning the Life and Character of Emanuel Swedenborg.* Vol. 2, parts 1 and 2. London: Swedenborg Society.

Talbot, Michael. 1988. "The Holographic Paradigm." In *Emanuel Swedenborg: A Continuing Vision,* edited by Robin Larsen and others. New York: Swedenborg Foundation.

Toksvig, Signe. 1983. *Emanuel Swedenborg: Scientist and Mystic.* New York: Swedenborg Foundation. First edition: 1948, New Haven: Yale University Press.

Whitehead, Alfred North. 1969. *Process and Reality.* New York: Free Press. First edition: 1929, New York: Macmillan.

Woofenden, William Ross. 1992–1993. "Doctrinal Patterns in *Arcana Coelestia.*" *Studia Swedenborgiana* 7(4):31–47; 8(1):49–77; 8(2):29–53; 8(3):43–63.

Wunsch, William F. 1929. *The World within the Bible: A Handbook to Swedenborg's "Arcana Coelestia."*

Swedenborg's *Magnum Opus*

WOUTER J. HANEGRAAFF

Outline

    I. Approaches to Swedenborg

   II. A Key to the Secrets: Swedenborg's Doctrine of Correspondences

  III. The Structure of *Secrets of Heaven*

  IV. The First Strand: Method, History, and Doctrine
      a. The Method of Biblical Exegesis
      b. History and the Styles of the Word
      c. Teachings about Charity and Faith

   V. The Second Strand: Biblical Exegesis
      a. Genesis on the Development of Churches
      b. Genesis on the Lord's Inner Development
      c. Exodus on the Spiritual Church

  VI. The Third Strand: Accounts of Memorable Occurrences
      a. Heaven, Hell, and Their Inhabitants
      b. The Universal Human Constituted of Angelic Communities
      c. Hells and the Process of Devastation

 VII. Concluding Remarks

Appendix

Works Cited in the Introduction

EMANUEL Swedenborg (1688–1772) began publishing his multivolume biblical exegesis *Secrets of Heaven* in 1749 and ceased publishing it in 1756. The full title given in the first of the eight volumes (other volume titles vary slightly) is *Arcana Coelestia, Quae in Scriptura Sacra, seu Verbo Domini Sunt, Detecta: Hic Primum Quae in Genesi: Una cum Mirabilibus Quae Visa Sunt in Mundo Spirituum, et in Coelo Angelorum* (A Disclosure of Secrets of Heaven Contained in Sacred Scripture, or the Word of the Lord, Here First Those in Genesis: Together with Amazing Things Seen in the World of Spirits and in the Heaven of Angels). For two hundred years it has been known as *Arcana Coelestia* (Secrets of Heaven), or simply (among Swedenborg's followers) as the *Arcana*. In this edition an English title has been adopted. Ostensibly the work interprets the meaning of Genesis and Exodus; but it is more than just an exegesis, as it includes accounts of Swedenborg's spiritual experiences and some extended doctrinal tracts. Before taking a closer look at these different strands of *Secrets of Heaven,* it will be necessary to briefly discuss the three basic modes in which Swedenborg's work has been approached.

I. Approaches to Swedenborg

It is not possible to interpret and contextualize Swedenborg's work without clearly positioning oneself with respect to a central but traditionally sensitive issue in Swedenborg scholarship: the problem of his sources. Broadly speaking, three opinions can be distinguished here. First, according to what might be called an "orthodox" Swedenborgian perspective, Swedenborg's insights have their source directly in heaven. Since it was the Lord[1] himself who disclosed to him the secrets of heaven as well as the true meaning of the biblical Scriptures, Swedenborg was obviously not dependent on any mundane traditions or sources, whether religious, philosophical, or scientific. From this perspective, any attempt at understanding Swedenborg by means of historical contextualization and the critical study of sources is not only futile, but fundamentally misguided.

Second, according to a more moderate, "providentialist" variant of the orthodox perspective, the Lord's guidance was already discreetly at work during Swedenborg's scientific career. His passionate search for rational understanding, concerned with problems such as the interaction between soul and body, can be seen with hindsight as a necessary preparation for his visionary career: Swedenborg first needed to push strict scientific inquiry as far as he could, and discover for himself the inherent limitations of reason, before he was ready for the Lord to provide him with the direct visionary insight that science could never give. From this perspective, the study of mundane sources may not be decisive, but is legitimate and interesting: at the very least, it provides us with edifying illustrations of the Lord's providential designs.

---

1. Since "the Lord" is the standard way of referring to God in Swedenborg's system, I will adopt this term here.

INTRODUCTION

From a third perspective, that of the historian, it is simply impossible to either verify or disprove the believer's claim that Swedenborg's insights were inspired by heaven. The historian of religions and religious ideas is bound to a stance of "methodological agnosticism" regarding the existence or nonexistence of heaven.[2] From this perspective it becomes critically important to investigate what sources and traditions may have influenced Swedenborg's thinking, and ask whether such influences might help us understand—and even "explain," at least partially—the nature and foundations of his mature worldview. It is important to understand that even in instances where such research happens to suggest a very strong dependence of Swedenborg on previous sources and traditions, it can never amount to a conclusive demonstration, in any strict scientific sense, that he was *not* inspired by heaven: "providential" interpretations may be superfluous and hence irrelevant to the historian, but in principle they always remain possible.

Since the author of the present introduction is not a Swedenborgian, and therefore cannot approach Swedenborg's *Secrets of Heaven* from either the first or the second perspective, it should be obvious that the following analysis will be informed by a historical-contextual approach, based upon a stance of "agnostic" neutrality regarding the ultimate source of Swedenborg's insights. Among previous scholars who have taken a similar approach, we can distinguish between two main lines of interpretation regarding Swedenborg's sources. Major biographers such as Martin Lamm (Lamm [1915] 2000) and Inge Jonsson (Jonsson 1970; Jonsson 1979; Jonsson [1971] 1999) have strongly emphasized the continuity between Swedenborg's scientific and visionary phase: as formulated by Jonsson, "In order to explain rationally his continuous experiences with spirits and angels during and after the great spiritual crisis around the middle of the 1740s, Swedenborg needed to make only small changes in his psycho-physical theorizing, mainly simplifications."[3] Thus Swedenborg's scientific and philosophical worldview—based upon broadly Cartesian foundations, and strongly influenced by rationalist

---

2. That is to say, in his or her role of historian. Privately he or she may or may not be convinced of the existence of heaven; the point is that such personal beliefs cannot be verified or falsified by those who do not already share them. For a detailed discussion of "empirico-historical" research and the necessity in that context of "methodological agnosticism," see Hanegraaff 1995.

3. Jonsson 1979, 251. Here and in the rest of the introduction, translations of secondary sources from other languages are by the author unless stated otherwise. Quotations from *Secrets of Heaven* are those of Lisa Hyatt Cooper; passages from later volumes than the present one are the draft versions current as of this writing.

thinkers such as Gottfried Wilhelm Leibniz (1646–1716), Christian Wolff (1679–1754), and Nicolas de Malebranche (1638–1715)—is of decisive importance for understanding his mature theosophy: although the latter may at first sight look like a sharp break with the scientific theorizing of the past, it is actually a spiritual reformulation of it.

Other Swedenborg specialists, such as, for example, Ernst Benz (Benz [1969] 2002) and Marsha Keith Schuchard (Schuchard 1995; Schuchard 1998; Schuchard 1999; Schuchard 2001), while not denying the relevance of Swedenborg's scientific background, suggest that the essential sources of his spiritual worldview lie elsewhere. Swedenborg is presented by them as a modern representative of Western esotericism,[4] whose worldview is ultimately based upon such currents as Neoplatonism, the Hermetic philosophy of the Renaissance, Jewish and Christian Kabbala, and the Christian theosophy of Jacob Boehme (1575–1624) and his followers.

One obvious problem with this second interpretation is the paucity of explicit references on Swedenborg's part to Western-esoteric authors and traditions;[5] but authors in favor of an "esoteric Swedenborg" tend to explain this fact by suggesting that he must have intentionally suppressed them because he feared that quotations from Kabbalists and mystics might discredit his work in the eyes of his rationalist readers. In the absence of many explicit source references, the alleged dependence of Swedenborg's worldview on traditional esoteric cosmologies is defended by invoking the structural similarity that is claimed to exist between them. Unfortunately, however, if one studies these comparisons, one finds that they tend to be quite superficial, certainly if compared with the detailed critical discussions by authors such as Jonsson, who argue in favor of Swedenborg's dependence on rationalist and scientific models and concepts. Although the present author began his research in the expectation of finding significant debts on Swedenborg's part to Western-esoteric traditions, close study of *Secrets of Heaven* and other works, as well as of the relevant secondary literature, has ended up convincing him that the "exoteric" Swedenborg defended by Lamm and Jonsson is much closer to the truth than the "esoteric" one.[6]

---

4. On Western esotericism see the foundational studies of Antoine Faivre (Faivre 1994; Faivre 2000). See also Hanegraaff 1996–1998; Hanegraaff 2004c.

5. It is well known to Swedenborg scholarship that in two separate letters to his friend Gabriel Beyer (1720–1779), Swedenborg denied ever having read Boehme (Tafel 1877, 251, 260), and in the second letter described his deliberate avoidance of the work of other theologians.

6. With respect to Swedenborg's alleged debt to the Jewish and Christian Kabbala, see Hanegraaff 2004a.

This is not to deny, however, that Swedenborg was aware of a range of philosophers of nature influenced by hermetic, alchemical, and Kabbalistic traditions. His library catalog shows that he owned books of this kind; he must have had some familiarity with the outlines of Jacob Boehme's system (although mostly indirectly, by mediation of Johann Konrad Dippel [1678–1734]);[7] he sometimes uses terminology derived from the Paracelsian tradition; he was certainly familiar with the Cambridge Platonists Henry More (1614–1687) and Ralph Cudworth (1617–1688) as well as with the Christian Kabbalist Franciscus Mercurius van Helmont (1614–1698); and he was seriously influenced by the "divine physics" of his contemporary Andreas Rüdiger (1673–1731). However, we should realize that it was quite normal for an erudite scientist and natural philosopher in the first half of the eighteenth century to be acquainted with such authors and their ideas: they were still very much a normal part of acceptable philosophical and scientific discourse, and in fact it would have been strange if Swedenborg had *not* been aware of them. Generally, however, he seems to have been interested in their more strictly philosophical insights concerning the workings of Nature and its relation to the soul. The influence of the authors just mentioned does not add up to an "esoteric philosophy" in the sense of an integrated religious worldview based upon hermetic, alchemical or Kabbalistic foundations and referring to supra-rational sources of revelation *(gnosis);* nor is there evidence for belief on Swedenborg's part in a "perennial philosophy" passed on and kept alive by divinely inspired teachers through the ages.[8]

Indeed, Swedenborg seems to belong to the select group of true innovators in the history of Western religion: rather than as a link in the chain of esoteric authors from antiquity to modern times, he must be seen as the founder of a new type of Christianity that eventually became

---

7. A possible line of influence that should be further investigated, not least in light of Swedenborg's lengthy sojourns in London, is the English Behmenist tradition, including authors such as John Pordage (1607 or 1608–1581) and Jane Leade (1623–1704). In reading the descriptions of visionary experiences by these and other Christian theosophers (for a useful selection, see Versluis 2000; and see also Versluis 1999), one cannot but be vividly reminded of Swedenborg's visions; but while quite some attention has been given to alleged Kabbalistic influences, references to the English Behmenists are strangely absent in the secondary literature. In exploring the possibility of such influences, however, one should not lose sight of the great differences between Behmenist theosophy and Swedenborg: for example, the former is based entirely on a specific doctrine of the Fall (or rather, several successive Falls) which has no parallel in the latter.

8. On Swedenborg's relation to this current, see Hanegraaff 2005.

of fundamental importance not only for the small church groups that developed directly from it, but for various new kinds of Western esotericism as well. That Swedenborg's work has become of extremely great importance to Western-esoteric currents since the eighteenth century is not in any doubt; but since later esotericists often combined authentic Swedenborgian concepts with ideas that are alien to his worldview, one might say that this is the case in spite of Swedenborg's intentions rather than because of them.[9]

II. A Key to the Secrets: Swedenborg's Doctrine of Correspondences

If we wish to understand Swedenborg's *Secrets of Heaven,* we first need to understand the nature of his famous "doctrine of correspondences." And it is highly significant, as will be seen, that this doctrine is first presented not in a revelatory work but in one of the last products of his "scientific period." In 1741 or 1742, shortly before the religious crisis that would transform him from a scientist into a visionary, Swedenborg wrote a short and technical philosophical work entitled *A Hieroglyphic Key to Natural and Spiritual Arcana by Way of Representations and Correspondences.*[10] Seven years later appeared the first volume of what was to be his first and

---

9. Whether Swedenborg's worldview should be categorized as "Western esoteric" depends on how one defines the latter domain. For an analysis with reference to Faivre's authoritative definition, see Williams-Hogan 1998, who concludes that one of Faivre's four "intrinsic characteristics" of Western esotericism—that is to say, "living nature"—does not figure in Swedenborg. With respect to the influence of Swedenborg on later esoteric traditions—as distinct from the development of the organized Swedenborgian New Church—see, for example, Brock and others 1988, Larsen and others 1988, Wilkinson 1996. It is clear that Swedenborgian ideas very quickly became syncretized with various ideas of different provenance, many of which were actually at variance with Swedenborg's own views.

10. Swedenborg's unpublished manuscript *Clavis Hieroglyphica Arcanorum Naturalium et Spiritualium, per Viam Representationum et Correspondentiarum* (referred to as *Draft of a Hieroglyphic Key* throughout this edition, or simply *Hieroglyphic Key*) was translated into English by Robert Hindmarsh (1759–1835) in 1792 (= Swedenborg 1792), by James John Garth Wilkinson (1812–1899) in 1847 (= Swedenborg 1847), and by Alfred Acton (1867–1956) in the Swedenborgian journal *The New Philosophy* 1916–1917 (Swedenborg 1916–1917; reprinted in Swedenborg 1984, 157–194). The quotations in the text refer to this most recent translation, which is the only one with added section numbers. Swedenborg's use of the term "hieroglyphics" obviously reflects an understanding of that term that pre-dates the correct understanding of Egyptian hieroglyphs that emerged in the wake of the deciphering of the Rosetta Stone by Jean-François Champollion (1790–1832); since the Renaissance at least, there existed a widespread discourse about hieroglyphs as mysterious language possibly reflecting the original language of humankind (see, for example, Dieckmann 1970).

largest visionary work: the *Arcana Coelestia,* translated in the present edition as "Secrets of Heaven." As the very titles indicate, both publications are explicitly devoted to "arcana," or secrets; but whereas the earlier work discusses the correspondences between natural and spiritual secrets, the later one purportedly concentrates on "heavenly" secrets only. Nevertheless, at closer examination the earlier work turns out to be precisely what the title would seem to promise: we will see that it is in fact a major "key" to understanding Swedenborg's *Secrets of Heaven,* and illustrates the remarkable continuity between one of his last scientific/philosophical works and his first visionary one.

In the *Hieroglyphic Key,* we are not dealing with a "mystical" doctrine based upon supra-rational revelatory insights, but with a product of straightforward rationalist argumentation, ultimately based upon mathematics.[11] Highly trained in contemporary philosophy and mechanical science, and acutely aware of their implications, Swedenborg saw himself faced with the specter of materialist reductionism: did intellectual honesty and respect for inescapable facts require him to dismiss traditional concepts of the soul and of a supreme divine reality as mere pious illusions, since everything that had once been attributed to God and the soul could now be reduced to the workings of blind mechanical forces and material realities? As a Christian, Swedenborg found this unacceptable. Should we, then, simply close our eyes to the evidence of science, and refuse to listen to the arguments of reason, in a blind and irrational "leap of faith"? Should we perhaps seek to sideline science altogether by adopting a Platonist or Neoplatonist idealist perspective, insisting that the material realities studied by science are ultimately just illusory shadows of the divine ideas, which alone are "real"? For the scientist Swedenborg, these were no solutions at all: by beating a retreat along such escape routes, one in fact admits intellectual defeat. In short, reducing the "higher" realities of God and the soul to the "lower" reality of matter was no less unacceptable to Swedenborg than the alternative of reducing the "lower" realities (studied by science) to the status of mere shadows of the "higher" ones. How to escape from this dilemma?

Any reader who, allured by the esoteric-sounding title, opens Swedenborg's *Hieroglyphic Key* in the expectation of being introduced to

---

11. See Jonsson 1970, 308–309, about Swedenborg's dream of a "universal mathesis" (see also *Hieroglyphic Key* 25; as is common in Swedenborgian studies, text citations refer not to page numbers but to section numbers—in this case, those added by Acton in the translation of 1916–1917).

realms of mystery and the occult, is bound to be sobered up by the dry formalism of the first sentences: "As long as motion endures so long does *conatus* endure; for *conatus* is the motive force of nature. But *conatus* alone is a dead force" (*Hieroglyphic Key* 1). This is a general statement about physical nature: nature has a motive force, technically referred to as *conatus,* which causes motion. Swedenborg continues with a second sentence of identical structure, which states that what is true on the level of physical nature has its exact correspondence on the level of psychology: the human mind, too, has a driving force, referred to as the will, and this force causes action. He concludes with a third sentence, which states that on the theological level, as well, there is something that corresponds precisely with the levels of nature and the mind: this is divine providence, which is at the root of God's divine operation. Thus we end up with a simple picture based upon the idea of three corresponding "levels of meaning":

God	Providence	→	Divine operation
Humanity	Will	→	Action
Nature	*Conatus*	→	Motion

Essentially, what Swedenborg does in the rest of his *Hieroglyphic Key* is systematically develop this idea by giving twenty further examples of how constellations of concepts pertaining to the material world correspond with constellations of concepts pertaining to humankind and to the divine. Almost every example consists of a similar set of three corresponding short propositions, followed by a longer explanation of what the propositions mean, a set of arguments to confirm the truth of the propositions, and finally a set of general "rules" that can be inferred from them. For instance, example III states that on the physical level there is no motion without *conatus* but conversely there can be *conatus* without motion; this is because if each and every *conatus* were to "break out into open motion, the world would perish, since there would be no equilibrium" (*Hieroglyphic Key* 10). Likewise on the psychological level there is no action without will, but conversely there is will without action: humanity would not be able to survive if there were not many "checks and resistencies" (*Hieroglyphic Key* 11) that keep us from acting out every single impulse of the will, thus causing us to moderate our actions. And likewise, on the level of the divine there is no divine operation without providence, but conversely some providence is "not operative or effective": although God "provided and willed that all men should be saved," if his providence were invariably to take effect, it would mean that humanity's free will would be overruled. Since free will is essential to morality, we find that there are indeed "those who resist the Divine grace; and upon such men this providence cannot be effective and operative" (*Hieroglyphic Key* 12).

Anybody familiar with Swedenborg's mature religious vision will recognize here one of his fundamental ideas; and in several other places, the *Hieroglyphic Key* contains clear prefigurations of his mature spiritual worldview.[12] The significant fact is that such ideas are here presented as logical inferences within a pre-revelatory work of technical rationalist philosophy. To understand how the latter laid the foundations for *Secrets of Heaven*, we need to take a closer look at the basic theory.

The all-important thing to note is that none of the three levels can or should be "reduced" to any other. It would not be correct to understand Swedenborg as saying that what is known as providence on the divine level somehow manifests as will on the human level (that is to say, that providence is the hidden essence of the will), or that the natural force of *conatus* manifests as providence on the divine level (that is to say, that what looks like providence is really a form of *conatus*), and so on. To explain Swedenborg's actual meaning, it may be useful to invoke an example taken from the domain of music. A physicist from another planet who taps into an earthly music hall might make a recording of a symphony by Johannes Brahms (1833–1897) and, in order to report back to his or her people, produce a complete and accurate description of its physical qualities: every single sound, up to the tiniest nuance, can be reduced to exact patterns of physical frequencies and graphically represented on frequency charts. As far as strictly physical realities are concerned, nothing about the symphony needs to be missing in such a

---

12. See, for example, *Hieroglyphic Key* 28 about the doctrine of the two suns: "In man or the microcosm there is no other sun than his soul or spiritual mind whence comes intelligence. But God is the sun of wisdom, or wisdom itself, just as the sun of the world is the sun of light." See also §§30–31 about heaven and hell as states of being created by an individual's "loves": "Love of the highest good brings forth happiness, and this, heaven. . . . But love of evil brings forth unhappiness, and this, hell. . . . Heaven signifies the most perfect joy . . . this joy is inexpressible . . . it is called heaven which also signifies the heavenly society itself." In *Secrets of Heaven* the loves are defined more specifically as "love for God and one's neighbor" *versus* "self-love and love for the world"; for this definition of "loves" there is a precedent in *Hieroglyphic Key* 38 [proposition 4] and 39. Compare this with §46 there about the doctrine of "ends" or "loves"; and with §31 about the absence of doctrine in the "beginning of creation" (referred to in *Secrets of Heaven* as the "earliest church").

representation: it can give a complete description of it. But of course, from the perspective of human listeners, it is anything but complete—in fact, it is wholly irrelevant to them. Listeners do not hear ordered frequency patterns, and such patterns are of no interest to them; they are listening to music. To them, the music contains a message that the interplanetary scientist cannot possibly deduce from his charts; and that message carries an emotional content that his equipment cannot pick up. Some members of the earthly audience may be musicologists: in addition to enjoying the music, they are trained to also analyze it. Their training makes them aware of multiple patterns and connections that are not consciously recognized by the other listeners and can be only indirectly inferred by the interplanetary scientist.[13] And finally, we happen to know that Brahms himself believed that he was directly inspired by God, who used him as a "channel" for divine revelation: "straightaway the ideas flow in upon me, directly from God."[14] Some listeners may follow Brahms's belief, and perceive his music as a divine revelation, a message to humanity in a form perceptible to humankind; others may be more skeptical and hold that Brahms was mistaken in thinking that his music flowed into his mind from a divine source. While the former have no means of proving the divinity of Brahms's message to the skeptics, the latter have no means of disproving it either. But what can be said is that according to some listeners at least, the symphony has a religious or *divine* level of meaning in addition to the *human* and the *physical* ones:

I	God's message	Divine
II	Brahms' symphony	Human
III	Frequency charts	Physical

Now the question is: to what extent can we learn something about one level by studying another?

To begin at the lowest level: studying the scientist's frequency charts evidently does not get us even one step closer to understanding the higher levels of either the symphony or its divine original. It is true that without the frequencies there would be no music—just as without physical bodies

---

13. The interplanetary scientist's frequency charts might be compared, in this regard, to a black-and-white photograph of a colored scene: one can observe in it subtle differences in tones of gray, but has no way of translating them into the colors they reflect.

14. Quotation according to an interview with Brahms in the fall of 1896, as recorded in Abell 1964, 21.

there is no humanity—but the fact that humanity has a physical substratum does not mean that knowledge of the physical level teaches us anything that is relevant to the human one: our knowledge of the frequencies is relevant to physicists but wholly irrelevant to listeners or musicologists.

Second, at the intermediate level of listening to the symphony (or of studying it as musicologists), we again fail to approach even one step closer to the lowest level—that of the frequencies (but neither is there any reason why we should, since we have just seen that such knowledge is irrelevant to the listener).

But might listening to the middle level of the music get us closer to understanding the highest level, that is to say, the divine message? Here—for the first and, as will be seen, the only time—the answer must be positive. But while it is true that the (musical) medium is meant to convey a (divine) message, obviously it is not true that the medium is the message.

Before returning to that crucial point below, we must complete our inquiry into the possibilities of inter-level translation by asking ourselves whether studying the highest, divine level might teach us something about the lower ones. Again the answer must be negative: just as listening to music does not teach us anything about the lower level of frequencies, likewise we cannot assume that direct access to God's mind would teach us something about the intermediate level of music (let alone about the even lower one of frequencies). Divine revelation teaches us about the divine; it does not consist of information about "outward" humanity or material realities.

Our example of a symphony allows us to draw three conclusions, all of which are highly relevant to understanding Swedenborg's doctrine of correspondences.

First, while studying "human" realities may teach us something about the divine, studying physical realities does not contribute anything to our understanding of either human realities or divine ones. What we learn from studying physics is relevant to physics only; by studying nature we learn about nature—and nothing more. I suggest that this insight helps explain why Swedenborg entirely dropped the study of physical science once he had developed his doctrine of correspondences.[15]

---

15. Supporting evidence in this regard can be found in Swedenborg's later works as well; see, for example, *True Christianity* 12:8.

His worldview contained *three* fundamental levels—natural (that is, physical, material), human, divine—but while he still discussed all three of them in his *Hieroglyphic Key*, he chose to ignore the physical level once he had convinced himself that science in and of itself cannot teach us anything about the soul or God (that is, humanity and the divine). As a result, scientific discussions no longer play a leading role in *Secrets of Heaven* and the rest of his revelatory works. Swedenborg henceforth concentrates on only two of the three levels, now referred to as external and internal, or this world and the other one. Henceforth when Swedenborg speaks of the external world, what he actually means is the human life-world.

Second, the musical example illustrates how we can have one phenomenon (a symphony) with three levels of meaning (physical, human, divine), which *correspond to one another but cannot be reduced to one another*. A specific melody clearly corresponds directly with a specific pattern of frequencies (and, one imagines, with a certain strand of thought in God's message); but suggesting that we discover the real meaning of the melody by printing out the frequency graph is no less absurd than suggesting that we discover the real meaning of the frequency graph by playing the melody. Each of the three levels is discrete and has its own autonomous reality, none of the three can replace any other, and none can be reduced to any other. Hence Swedenborg can write in his *Hieroglyphic Key* that

> the principal matter must be expressed not by identical terms, but by different terms proper to each class . . . and, in fact, by terms which at first sight do not seem to signify or represent the same thing. For it is not at once comprehended that will corresponds to *conatus,* and providence to will; or that the rational mind corresponds to nature, and God to the rational mind. (*Hieroglyphic Key* 4 [rules 2–3])

Terms like will and *conatus* "signify or represent the same thing"— that is to say, providence—*not* in the sense that they actually mean the same thing as providence (for that is precisely the point: providence is providence only on its own proper level, the divine), but that will on the human level and *conatus* on the physical level *correspond to* what is providence on the divine level. In other words: none of the three can be reduced to any other.

Third, the musical example shows that there is something unique about the intermediate or human level: it is the only one that can be studied in order to discover something about *another* level. Studying frequency charts does not teach us anything about either music or the divine message it intends to convey; and direct access to God's mind does not teach us anything about his musical message or about physical frequencies. By studying physics we learn about physics; by studying the divine we learn about the divine. By studying the intermediate human level, however, we can by means of analogy learn something about the highest level, that of the divine, as well. And this, I suggest, provides us with another key to understanding *Secrets of Heaven.* As will be explained in more detail below, this work is based upon Swedenborg's direct visionary experiences, on the one hand, and on his biblical exegesis, on the other. In other words, he claims that we may learn about the divine in two ways. Firstly, by direct contact with it: a privileged way of knowledge that, at least at present, is hardly ever available to others than Swedenborg himself (through "things heard and seen," as Swedenborg called it; see most famously *Heaven and Hell* 1 and the full title of that work). And secondly, by interpreting God's message to humanity, the Bible. Again, the doctrine of correspondences as explained in the *Hieroglyphic Key* provided him with a theoretical basis and justification for his project, since it states that the meaning of a term on the human level may be very different from its meaning on the higher level of the divine. On that basis, it can be assumed that the "outer meaning" of biblical terms and expressions corresponds with an "inner meaning" that may not be immediately apparent, or not apparent at all. If so, it becomes critically important to decode the Bible, and unveil the "arcana" hidden in it. The key that breaks the code, however, cannot be found in the Bible itself but has to be revealed by direct contact with the highest level (just as it requires divine grace to hear the divine message present in the symphony).

It was emphasized above that Swedenborg was searching for an alternative to both material reductionism and "(Neo)platonic" idealism (the first of which would reduce the higher to the lower, whereas the second would reduce the lower to the higher). The doctrine of correspondences developed in his *Hieroglyphic Key* went a long way towards formulating such an alternative, but it could not entirely solve the dilemma. Even though the human and material levels are discrete and autonomous, the relation in terms of ontological status between the divine, the human, and the physical realms still needed to be explained. That Swedenborg finally came to assume—somewhat ambiguously and half-heartedly—a clear-cut ontological hierarchy among the three levels of reality, along broadly (Neo)platonic lines, is evident from the final paragraph of the

Hieroglyphic Key: "Exemplars are in the spiritual world; images and types are in the soul's kingdom;[16] but simulacra in nature" (*Hieroglyphic Key* 67 [rule 1]). The status of physical nature as a domain that contains merely simulacra further helps explain why—reluctantly and after much inner struggle, for his heart was with science—he chose largely to ignore it in his subsequent writings. We are left, then, with a broadly Platonic distinction between the spiritual world that contains "exemplars," and a human world of autonomous but secondary status, which contains images and types reflecting the exemplars.

In an earlier analysis, I argued that Swedenborg's doctrine of correspondences was attractive to him

> *not* because it unites mind and nature, but for precisely the *contrary* reason: because it solved (for him) the Cartesian dilemma. It enabled him to retain a fundamental distinction between spirit and nature (modeled upon the distinction between *res cogitans* and *res extensa*); to continue seeing spirit as the active cause and nature as the passive substance "acted upon" by spirit; but to explain that relationship *without* having to assume the existence of mechanisms of instrumental causality. (Hanegraaff 1996–1998, 428)

I still maintain that this analysis is correct as far as Swedenborg's original scientific project is concerned, that is to say, the project of clarifying the relation between soul and body. The *Hieroglyphic Key* essentially contains his solution to this problem. At the same time, however, by distinguishing three rather than two levels, it goes beyond the framework of Cartesian dualism and opens up an entirely new set of problems, concerning the relation between what is properly human and what is properly divine. Swedenborg's solution of the Cartesian dilemma—by suggesting that there is a relation of correspondence rather than of causal influence[17] between soul and body—remains important for understanding the genesis

---

16. Contrary to the frequent mistranslation "animal kingdom" (suggesting the kingdom of the animals), *anima* refers to the human soul; that is to say, Swedenborg is speaking of the world of the (human) soul. On the Neoplatonic features in Swedenborg, see also Lang 2000, 28–33.

17. This is not to deny that Swedenborg sometimes refers to "causality" in the sense that spiritual realities are ultimately the origin of everything (see, for instance, *Secrets of Heaven* 2993, 5711, 6048:2, 8211:2, 8812:5). My point here is that we are not dealing either with "instrumental" causality (as in natural mechanics) or with "occult causality" (where the cause somehow "beams down" or "transmits" invisible influences through space). The philosophical problem with notions of occult causality between soul and body is that one must assume the existence of some kind of "intermediate" substance or reality through which influences are transmitted.

of his worldview, and a broadly Cartesian framework remains visible, for example, in Swedenborg's insistence that "nature is dead."[18] But *Secrets of Heaven* is no longer much concerned with investigating that physical world: the attention now shifts to the human and divine levels, and Swedenborg's mature worldview is carried by the conviction that these, too, are not causally related but stand in a relation of correspondence. Having established these intellectual foundations, we have now to take a closer look at Swedenborg's *magnum opus*.

III. The Structure of *Secrets of Heaven*

Swedenborg's *Secrets of Heaven* was written in the period 1748–1756. It was published anonymously in eight volumes over eight years from 1749 on. The complete work consists of 10,837 numbered sections of varying length, plus four short prefaces without number.

In order to find one's way through this massive work, it is necessary first of all to see that it consists of three interwoven but autonomous strands: the shortest one consists of "introductory parts" about matters of method, history, and doctrine; the longest one consists of a systematic and extremely detailed exegesis of Genesis and Exodus (including complete translations of both):[19] and a strand of intermediate but very substantial length is referred to as *Memorabilia*, or memorable occurrences: accounts of Swedenborg's experiences in the spiritual world. For an analytical overview of the three strands, see the appendix, pages 119–124.

The first strand, that of the "introductory parts," is divided into two sections. It is logical that Swedenborg sets this strand apart from the two others, for it is here that he discusses and seeks to legitimize the basic assumptions on which the entire work is founded. The first part of this

---

18. This conclusion is found in *Hieroglyphic Key* 15 [correspondence 1], and would remain a constant in Swedenborg's visionary phase (see Williams-Hogan 1998, especially 220–222).

19. See Cole 1977 about Swedenborg's Hebrew Bible. In fact he seems to have used the bilingual Hebrew/Latin Bible published by Everard van der Hoogt (1642–1716) in 1740 *(Biblia Hebraica secundum Editionem Belgicam Everardi van der Hoogt . . . Una cum Versione Latina Sebastiani Schmidii)* which contained the Latin translation of Sebastian Schmidt (1617–1696) printed in parallel columns next to the Hebrew; apart from that, he also used Schmidt's translation separately: his copy survives, and is full of marginalia and underlinings (see Schmidt and Swedenborg 1872). As demonstrated by Cole, there is no conclusive evidence for the claim of August Nordensköld (1754–1792) that Swedenborg "translated Genesis, Exodus and the Apocalypse directly from the originals" (Nordensköld 1790, 87, as quoted in Cole 1977, 30).

strand is theoretical and methodological, containing explanations and justifications of his general approach to biblical exegesis; and this part can be further analyzed, as will be seen, into discussions of method and discussions of history. The second part is doctrinal, and focuses on the theological concepts of charity and faith.

The second and the third of the three strands focus on the two levels of reality that, as explained in the previous section, are basic to *Secrets of Heaven:*

Divine	Strand 3: Accounts of Memorable Occurrences
Human	Strand 2: Biblical Exegesis
Physical	—

The second strand, that of biblical exegesis, is quantitatively the longest. It consists of an extremely detailed interpretation of how the Lord manifests himself on the intermediate, human level, that is to say, through the Bible. Referring to my musical analogy, Genesis and Exodus can be compared to two great symphonies, the divine meaning of which is decoded by Swedenborg note by note, and melody by melody: the role assumed by him might be compared to that of a divinely inspired musicologist, who analyzes the symphonies not just according to worldly canons but discloses their "real meaning" as revealed to him from up above.

The third strand, the memorable occurrences, is shorter but still of very substantial length and is based upon Swedenborg's direct experiences of the higher, heavenly, or "inner" level of reality: here we are not dealing with interpretations but with direct accounts of "things heard and seen." The physical level to which Swedenborg had devoted most of his early career is not systematically treated in *Secrets of Heaven,* although some discussions pertaining to physics can be found scattered through the work.

IV. The First Strand: Method, History, and Doctrine

In this section we will first be looking at how Swedenborg describes the method of biblical exegesis used by him in the second strand of *Secrets of Heaven.* Next we will discuss his beliefs about the historical development of religious consciousness. And finally, we will analyze his doctrine of "charity and faith."

a. The Method of Biblical Exegesis

The first sentence of *Secrets of Heaven* contains in a nutshell the thesis fundamental to the whole work:

> The Word in the Old Testament contains the secrets of heaven, and every single aspect of it has to do with the Lord, his heaven, the church, faith, and all the tenets of faith; but not a single person sees this in the letter. (*Secrets of Heaven* 1)

Here we are introduced right away to Swedenborg's basic assumption about biblical exegesis: Scripture, or the Word, has an "inner meaning" that cannot possibly be grasped from the outer, or literal, meaning,[20] and therefore a correct interpretation of the Bible requires divine revelation. Only "very few" people (§13) have been granted such revelation, and Swedenborg is one of them:

> The Lord in his divine mercy has granted me the opportunity for several years now, without break or interruption, to keep company with spirits and angels, to hear them talking, and to speak with them in turn. Consequently I have been able to see and hear the most amazing things in the other life, which have never before come into people's awareness or thought. (*Secrets of Heaven* 5)

Swedenborg is not content with merely making a categorical statement about his unique status and authority as interpreter of the Bible. While the inner meaning of Scripture cannot be inferred from the literal meaning and therefore has to be revealed, the fact *that* an inner meaning exists can be rationally deduced by anybody who believes that the Bible is God's word. For how else could one explain that it contains so many passages that are simply unintelligible if taken literally, and others that describe things so "abominable" as to be clearly far below God's dignity? This point is repeated many times, and must be seen as a major impetus behind his gigantic exegetic labors: to Swedenborg's critical, rational, and scientifically-trained mind, conventional ideas of the Bible as God's word

---

20. The theoretical basis for this fundamental assumption is, of course, provided by the doctrine of correspondences as developed in the *Hieroglyphic Key,* as we have seen: "The principal matter must be expressed not by identical terms, but by different terms proper to each class . . . and, in fact, by terms which at first sight do not seem to signify or represent the same thing" (*Hieroglyphic Key* 4 [rules 2–3]).

just did not make any sense. What, for example, to make of an evidently nonsensical sentence as found in Genesis 49:17: "Dan is a snake on the path, an asp on the track, biting the horse's heels, and its rider will fall off the back"?[21] And what about passages that may be intelligible in themselves, but are mediocre, useless, or even offensive?

> Would anyone expect God's Word to mention the revolting affair of Lot's daughters? . . . How about the story in which Jacob peeled some rods, laying them bare down to the white and placing them in the water troughs to make the flock bear mottled, speckled, and spotted lambs? . . . They would lack any importance; it would be all the same whether we knew them or not, if they did not enfold a divine secret deep inside them. Otherwise they would not differ in any way from other histories . . .[22]

The new rationalist Bible criticism that emerged during Swedenborg's lifetime would, of course, come to that precise conclusion. Swedenborg, however, reasoned differently. If one assumes that the Bible is divinely inspired from the first word to the last, and acknowledges at the same time that this is not borne out by the text's literal meaning, the only solution is to assume that it simply does not mean what it seems to mean. The Bible *has* to contain "secrets" (*arcana*) that contain its actual hidden life; without that life, it cannot be the Word of the Lord (*Secrets of Heaven* 2). In choosing this formulation, Swedenborg explicitly draws an analogy with biological organisms. A mere material body is dead; it can be called a living being only if it has a soul in it (§3). Likewise the outer letter of the Bible is dead; it can only be the Word of the Lord—who is Life himself—if it contains a hidden dimension of life.

This hidden dimension cannot be inferred from the literal text at all. As will be seen, Swedenborg treats Genesis and Exodus as gigantic coded texts, the actual meaning of which must be disclosed by a process of decoding. Every single word means something else than what it means on the surface. Technically this procedure is a clear example, albeit in an

---

21. This is one of several examples given by Swedenborg in *Secrets of Heaven* 1984:2. Later he would devote several sections to the sentence's inner meaning: §§6398–6401.

22. *Secrets of Heaven* 2310:3. Swedenborg goes as far as saying that the Ten Commandments, as well, are unremarkable as far as the literal meaning is concerned: "the rules they lay down . . . are rules that non-Jews also acknowledge and have codified in their laws" (*Secrets of Heaven* 2609:1).

extreme form, of what is known as allegorical exegesis.²³ Traditional biblical hermeneutics distinguished generally between the *sensus literalis* or *historicus* (literal or historical sense) of the Bible, on the one hand, and the *sensus spiritualis* or *mysticus* (spiritual or mystical sense) that largely relied on various types of allegorical exegesis, on the other.²⁴ Allegorical exegesis came to be applied to the Old Testament as early as several centuries B.C.E.; it was promoted as the central method of biblical exegesis by the Jewish philosopher Philo of Alexandria in the first century C.E. and by the Christian theologian Origen in the third, and became the standard approach throughout the Middle Ages (Longenecker 1975, 45–48). This dominance came under sharp attack during the Reformation: the doctrine of *sola scriptura* (Scripture alone) implied that only the *sensus literalis/historicus* was to be accepted. Martin Luther (1483–1546) sharply attacked Origen's approach, and John Calvin (1509–1564) did the same in an even more uncompromising manner. As explained by

---

23. In his useful handbook to *Secrets of Heaven*, written from a Swedenborgian perspective, William F. Wunsch (1882–1969) made a point of denying that Swedenborg's method is allegorical (Wunsch 1929, especially chapter 5), claiming that his method does not entail a rejection of the literal meaning. There are problems with this assertion. First, as evidence of Swedenborg's view that "the sense of the letter (or Scripture as it stands and reads) is the sense from which any teaching for the guidance of Christian life is to be formulated, and on which it should be capable of being rested back" (Wunsch 1929, 20), Wunsch refers to a text written much later, around 1762: Swedenborg's unpublished manuscript *De Scriptura Sacra seu Verbo Domini ab Experientia*, variously referred to as *De Verbo, The Word from Experience,* or *Sacred Scripture*, as in Wunsch's case; and currently known as *Draft of "Sacred Scripture"* (see Swedenborg 1997). Wunsch admits that this explicit acceptance of the literal meaning is not found in *Secrets of Heaven* (Wunsch 1929, 20 note 11); therefore it is most plausibly seen as evidence of a later change of opinion or emphasis on Swedenborg's part, which should not be projected backwards to the time when he wrote *Secrets of Heaven*. There is abundant evidence against Wunsch's view: see §§1874–1875 about the literal meaning "dying away completely," which is presented as "purification"; and compare this with the preface that precedes §2760 ("what thick darkness people plunge into—dragging others with them—by interpreting everything literally" [*Secrets of Heaven* preface to Genesis 22]). Second, it is not by any means as clear as suggested by Wunsch that the classic exponents of allegorical exegesis rejected the literal meaning. On this point, see Longenecker (1975, 29, 45–48) about the case of Philo of Alexandria (around 15 B.C.E.–50 C.E.).

24. But more complex subdivisions are common as well. Origen (around 185 to around 254 C.E.) had distinguished between the literal, the moral, and the mystical sense. But the mystical sense could be divided further into allegorical and anagogical, leading to the four classic senses of Scripture. A frequently quoted example was the word *Jerusalem*: literally it means a city, morally it is a virtue, allegorically it is the church, and anagogically it is heaven. The division could be further complicated by dividing the literal sense into strictly historical and figurative (see Williams 1948, 20; the classic study of the four senses of Scripture is Lubac 1959).

Hans-Joachim Kraus in his standard history of the historical-critical study of the Old Testament, according to the Lutherans and Calvinists,

> with any allegorical interpretation, the human voice imperceptibly mixes itself through God's speech. Within the wide space of allegorical possibilities of interpretation, Man with his ideas settles down and claims his rights—in a place where he should keep silent, and merely listen and ask. Whoever seeks for allegories in the Bible, leaves the solid ground of the letter and of history. . . . In allegory, the Word of God is turned into a fictitious word of Man. Therefore the warning call is: "Cavete ab allegoriis!" (Beware of allegories). For example when 1 Corinthians 10:4 says "and that rock was Christ," Luther explicitly points out that here, too, there should be no room for "allegoria or spiritual interpretation." He continues: "It was not a case of figurative speech, but a matter of great seriousness, God's word, that gives life, and the right faith was there. Therefore this did not just seem to happen to them [the apostles], but it really happened." From this passage . . . one can see how Luther smells in any allegory the acute danger that the historical reality of God's Word will be dissolved into general meaning-contents, and thus into unsubstantial illusions. (Kraus 1982, 14)

One might perceive an irony in the fact that Swedenborg, whose religious worldview was developed entirely from Lutheran foundations (although, of course, he eventually went far beyond them) and for whom Roman Catholicism was self-evidently a perversion of the original Christian message, came to reject these fundamental Lutheran principles in favor of an exegetical method that in fact returns straight to Philo, Origen, and mainstream medieval biblical hermeneutics.[25] Philo, for example,

> was prepared to interpret allegorically anything that might derogate the dignity of the inspired words of God: anything that is nonsensical in the creation accounts, that is reprehensible in the legal portions, or that is trivial in the historical narratives of the Pentateuch. . . . The *prima facie* meaning must normally be pushed aside—even counted as offensive—to make room for the intended spiritual meaning underlying the obvious; though . . . at times he seems willing to consider literal and allegorical exegesis as having "parallel legitimacy." In the main, however,

---

25. See also the discussion in Lamm [1915] 2000, 224–237, especially 227.

exegesis of Holy Writ was for him an esoteric enterprise which, while not without its governing principles, was to be dissociated from literal interpretation. (Longenecker 1975, 46)

But for very minor details, these lines could as well have been written about Swedenborg. In his standard biography, Martin Lamm in fact concluded not only that Swedenborg's exegetical method is "exactly the one Philo of Alexandria and Origen followed," but also that the concrete exegetical results are often identical: a comparison between Philo's and Swedenborg's interpretations of certain specific passages in Genesis showed striking affinities (Lamm [1915] 2000, 227–231). Having pointed out that this does not need to imply a direct dependence of Swedenborg on Philo, Lamm concluded that Swedenborg must be seen as the "late inheritor" of an uninterrupted exegetical tradition:

> The only difference between [Swedenborg's] results and those of his predecessors is, all in all, that his results have been adapted to his philosophical system, whereas the latter have allowed their explications to illustrate their respective systems. Like his forerunners, Swedenborg so freely used allegorical interpretation to reshape the meaning of Scripture that it became possible for him to incorporate his whole philosophical system in his exegesis and to form a logically consistent theological doctrine out of this hermeneutical operation. When he repeatedly stresses in his theological works that he has learned all the teachings of his church from reading the Word, he is certainly sincere. All the same, it is quite the opposite. He has independently formed a philosophical-theological view that he then point for point finds corroborated in his biblical studies. (Lamm [1915] 2000, 231–232)

Lamm slightly overstates his case here, and creates some confusion by assuming a contradiction that is actually only apparent. Claiming that anything one knows comes only from reading the Bible is a commonplace of Protestant pious discourse; but Swedenborg never meant to imply that he had learned his teachings by reading the Word unaided. On the contrary, he claims that its true meaning was revealed to him by the Lord: in other words, it was only thanks to direct divine inspiration that he was able, as formulated by Lamm in the above quotation, to "learn all the teachings of his church from reading the Word." It is true that Swedenborg's approach can technically be categorized as "allegorical," but it differs from the allegorical tradition more strongly than

Lamm suggests. The key to Swedenborg's specificity is, precisely, his Protestantism. While Roman Catholicism had always assigned to the *pietas fidelium* ("the piety of the faithful," that is to say, the tradition of pious consensus) an authority equal to that of the Bible, Swedenborg's attitude is strongly marked by the characteristic Protestant emphasis on the Bible as the sole and exclusive source of divine revelation. Not unlike Luther himself, Swedenborg had emerged from his religious crisis with a profound feeling of the absolute sovereignty of the Lord and his Word: instead of listening to our own merely human opinions, clinging to our own pet ideas (scientific and rationalist ones in his case) and thereby "mixing our own voice through God's speech,"[26] we must wholly submit to the Lord and allow him to guide us in every respect. This quintessentially Protestant ethos permeates Swedenborg's dream diary (see Swedenborg 2001) and is essential for understanding his *Secrets of Heaven*. From such a perspective, the task of trying to understand the Lord's Word must receive a new urgency, and lead to an approach that is qualitatively different from the somewhat more relaxed attitude of the traditional allegorists in the Roman Catholic tradition. In reading the Bible they could allow themselves to be guided by the *pietas fidelium,* in which the Holy Spirit was believed to be invisibly at work. But for Swedenborg, as for Luther, traditional opinion was the product of mere human thinking and had no divine authority whatsoever: the individual creature finds himself face to face with the Lord Himself, who communicates with him through his Word. This Word is clear and unequivocal. It does not have many layers of meaning, as in traditional allegorical exegesis, but only two: the outer and the inner.[27] The inner meaning is no longer understood by human beings, and therefore the Lord himself now reveals it again to humankind through his chosen instrument Emanuel Swedenborg.

Paradoxically, then, Swedenborg's allegorical exegesis of the Bible is a radical but entirely logical outcome of Protestant biblicism. It reflects a profoundly felt wish to listen to the Lord's pure and unadulterated Word. Human opinions and traditions are suspect in principle, and are not

---

26. I am referring to the formulation by Hans-Joachim Kraus (1982, 14) quoted earlier.

27. This, at least, is the general perspective that dominates *Secrets of Heaven*. It is, however, possible to find some passages (see, for example, §4294, 4605–4609) that suggest a subdivision of further levels of meaning within the inner meaning.

allowed to interfere. The great Bible Code can be broken only by the Lord himself.

b. History and the Styles of the Word

A historical-critical approach to the Bible always remained alien to Swedenborg:

> Some people during bodily life had devoted themselves exclusively to biblical criticism when reading the Word, without much concern for the meaning, and their thoughts were represented as lines that were shut off rather than open-ended, and woven into a network.
>
> Some of these people were once with me, and everything I thought and wrote became tangled in confusion. My thinking was virtually imprisoned, because they narrowed it down to the words themselves, turning my attention away from the meaning so forcefully that they completely wore me out. Yet they considered themselves wiser than others![28]

Swedenborg did, however, attempt to differentiate among various "styles" in the Bible (called "modes" in the current translation), and connect them with different historical stages in the development of human and religious consciousness. Most sublime is the style of the "earliest church," about which more will be said below. The first chapters of the Bible—the stories concerning the creation, the Garden of Eden, and everything else up to the time of Abraham—are written in this style. On the face of it they may seem to be about earthly and worldly things, but in fact everything in them should be understood only in a spiritual and heavenly manner: by means of a narrative or quasi-historical sequence the members of the earliest church presented inner truths, and this gave them "the fullest pleasure possible" (*Secrets of Heaven* 66:1). Because the parts of the Bible written in this style should not be taken literally at all, they are different from those written in the "narrative" or "historical" style. The stories from Abraham onwards and the books of Joshua,

---

28. *Secrets of Heaven* 6621. (When Swedenborg writes that these people were "with" him, he refers to their being present with him in spiritual form.) It is also worth noting that Swedenborg finds no value in research into biblical history: "Viewed in themselves, however, the narratives do little to improve us. They have no effect at all on our eternal life, because in the other world historical detail is obliterated from memory" (§1886).

Judges, Samuel, and Kings are historically accurate *and* have an inner meaning: "The historical events in these books are exactly what they appear to be in the literal sense, but as a whole and in detail they still contain an entirely different meaning on the inner plane." A third, "prophetical," style is described by Swedenborg as an offspring of the style of the earliest church, but as differing from it because it is not continuous and does not take a quasi-historical form. Parts written in this style only make sense from the internal perspective, for if taken literally they are "choppy, and almost completely unintelligible." And finally there is the style of the Psalms of David, which "is midway between the prophetic style and people's usual way of speaking" (§66:2).

These statements should be seen in connection with *Secrets of Heaven* 10325, where Swedenborg says explicitly that only those books that have the inner meaning belong to the Word, and lists all of them. According to Swedenborg, the Old Testament Word consists of only the five Books of Moses, Joshua, Judges, 1 and 2 Samuel, 1 and 2 Kings, the Psalms, Isaiah, Jeremiah, Lamentations, Ezekiel, Daniel, Hosea, Joel, Amos, Obadiah, Jonah, Micah, Nahum, Habakkuk, Zephaniah, Haggai, Zechariah, and Malachi. And within the New Testament he accepts only the four Gospels and the Book of Revelation. This means, of course, that such traditionally important parts of the Bible as, for example, the Old Testament Book of Job or the Song of Solomon, and most of the New Testament (including the Acts of the Apostles and all the Epistles) were considered by Swedenborg as not directly inspired by heaven. This fact has worried some of Swedenborg's admirers. For example, on March 18, 1766, Gabriel Beyer asked Swedenborg for clarification about the letters of the apostles and Paul, and Swedenborg responded on April 15:

> In respect to the writings of the apostles and Paul, I have not quoted them in the *Arcana Coelestia,* because they are doctrinal writings, and consequently are not written in the style of the Word, like those of the prophets, of David, of the Evangelists, and the Book of Revelation. The style of the Word consists altogether of correspondences, wherefore it is effective of immediate communication with heaven; but in doctrinal writings there is a different style, which has indeed communication with heaven, but mediately. . . . The writings of the apostles are, nevertheless, good books of the church, insisting upon the doctrine of charity and its faith as strongly as the Lord Himself has done in the Gospels

and the Book of Revelation; as may be seen and found evident by every one who in reading them directs his attention to these points.[29]

Apart from the four biblical "styles," Swedenborg also distinguishes between a sequence of four historical "churches" (that is, prior to the fifth, new church) each one of which had its own "Word":

> To speak more specifically, the Word has existed at every period, though not the Word we have today. The earliest church, which came before the Flood, had one form. The ancient church, which followed the Flood, had another. The Jewish religion had the Word written by Moses and the prophets. And lastly the [Christian] church had the Word written by the Gospel writers. (*Secrets of Heaven* 2895)

The members of the earliest church, before the Flood, were "heavenly people" who lived in daily company with the angels. They had no priests or external cult, nor did they need a written Word: their "Adamic intellect"[30] allowed them to communicate directly with the angels and have an intuitive grasp of the divine truth. Thus they knew by direct perception what was good and true, and had the Word "written on their hearts." They perceived worldly things by the senses and simultaneously understood them spiritually: "everything they saw (or sensed in any other way) represented and symbolized the heavenly and spiritual qualities of the Lord's kingdom to them" (§2896).

The members of the "ancient church," after the Flood, were spiritual but no longer heavenly,[31] and as a result they "learned rather than perceived what the representations and symbolisms involved" (§2897:1). The perfect love and knowledge that had characterized the members of the earliest church had begun to degenerate; and since they could no longer grasp the truth intuitively, the members of this second church had to rely on faith. In order to read the signs of God in nature, they developed an elaborate system of signs, images, emblems, and hieroglyphs. The ancient church fell into decay when the leaders began to misuse their knowledge

---

29. Third letter of Swedenborg to Beyer (Tafel 1877, 240–241). Swedenborg finishes the letter by pointing out that Paul's statements in 2 Romans 28, concerning justification by faith, have been misunderstood.

30. For this term (which is not used by Swedenborg himself), see Benz [1969] 2002, 452.

31. For the distinction between heavenly and spiritual, see pages 90–92 below.

of the hieroglyphs to promote their own power, as a result of which their priestly office declined to magical superstition, idolatrous cults, and polytheism. Thus the sacred science of hieroglyphs, which had originally been based on the true correspondence of heaven and earth, was perverted into a tool for demonic sorcery. They did have a written Word, containing narrative and prophetical parts, but this Word has gotten lost. Its narrative parts were called *Jehovah's Wars;* they were "written in a prophetic mode and were for the most part fictional" (2897:1) like those of Genesis 1–11 in our present Bible.[32] The prophetical parts were called *Utterances* and were (like the narrative parts) written in a style similar to the prophetical style in our Old Testament. Swedenborg derives the titles of these two parts of the ancient Word *(Liber Bellorum Jehovae* and *Enuntiata)* from Numbers 21:14 and 27.

With the revelation of the Ten Commandments followed the third, or "Jewish church" (2899), which represents a further stage of decline. The Jewish law and sacrificial cult are merely outward representations, but at least they do hide the authentic divine truth; as Ernst Benz has put it in his important Swedenborg biography, they are "a trick of reason" by which the inner divine truths are preserved for posterity in outward forms and symbols, even though the members of the Jewish church themselves were no longer capable of understanding what these symbols meant. Thus the Jewish church was "a last resort in the era of the general decline of religion" (Benz [1969] 2002, 456). Their Word was, of course, the Old Testament; and the meaning of its "representations and symbols" is the subject of Swedenborg's *Secrets of Heaven.* The Jewish church came to its end with the destruction of Jerusalem and the diaspora (*Secrets of Heaven* 4057).

The Christian church is the fourth one in line. Christ did away with the worship of mere outward show and refocused attention on the inward truths of faith. However, this did not lead to the return of the Golden Age, for the human race was no longer able to understand the truth as it was revealed to them. In fact only the original apostolic congregation was still pure, and with the development of Roman Catholicism the Christian

---

32. This is, of course, somewhat confusing: the "narrative" parts are written in the "prophetical" style, but the contents are actually similar to those written in the style of the earliest church. These three styles are kept separate when Swedenborg speaks of our Bible, but are here mixed together in his description of the lost Word of the ancient church.

church quickly degenerated into what would eventually be a travesty of the true church. The Protestant Reformation, with its emphasis on literal interpretation, has not succeeded in leading the church back to the true understanding of the Word. The Word of the fourth church obviously consists of the New Testament added to the Old Testament. Christ spoke "from divinity itself, so everything he said also represented and symbolized divine concerns and therefore the heavenly concerns of his kingdom and church" (§2900).

Swedenborg's revelations now mark the beginning of the fifth, or "new," church, which will be established among the few who "can now be educated," but whom only the Lord knows. Of these "chosen," who lead a good life based on faith and love, few in fact will be found in the present church; for in the past, too, it has always been among people outside the church that new religions were established.[33]

Having distinguished four "styles" of the Word, as well as four churches prior to the appearance of the new church, Swedenborg furthermore describes how each church goes through four "stages of corruption":[34]

> First people would start to forget what was good and true and would quarrel over it; then they would despise it; in the third place they would refuse to acknowledge it; and in the fourth they would profane it. (*Secrets of Heaven* 3899)

After the fourth and final state of perversion of a church, a new one is instituted. From *Secrets of Heaven* it is clearly evident that Swedenborg saw his own writings as heralding the new church. Only towards the end of his life, however, would he make the radical claim that they were in fact the new Word, and that their publication represented what was meant by the Second Coming.[35]

c. Teachings about Charity and Faith

Having discussed the stages of perversion of a church by means of a detailed exegesis of Matthew 24, Swedenborg moves on to Matthew 25

---

33. *Secrets of Heaven* 3898:3. See also, for example, §2986.

34. This phrase is used in §3754. Interestingly, Swedenborg discusses the development of the churches by means of a detailed exegesis of Matthew 24 (beginning with §3353, and ending with 4424).

35. *True Christianity* 779, with point 8 preceding it. See also Tafel 1877, 757.

in order to discuss the meaning of the Second Coming and the fate of the soul after death. The Coming of the Son of Man should not be taken literally: it refers not to a judgment at the end of history, but to what happens to every individual person after death. Swedenborg takes the occasion to polemicize against the Protestant doctrine of salvation by faith alone: "The fruits of faith are simply a life in keeping with the precepts of faith. Living according to them is what saves us, then. Believing without living does not" (*Secrets of Heaven* 4663). This leads him to a preliminary discussion of the "essential ingredients of charity" as listed in Matthew 25:34–36: "I was hungry and you gave me something to eat. I was thirsty and you gave me a drink. I was a foreigner and you gathered me in; naked and you put a robe around me. I was sick and you visited me. I was in jail and you came to me" (§4954).

This turns out to be the upbeat for the extensive discussions of "charity and faith" that take up the remainder of what we have referred to as the "first strand" of *Secrets of Heaven*. Implicit in these discussions is a general framework of correspondences and associations that may be presented in a systematic form (see figure 1), and that guides discussions throughout *Secrets of Heaven*. What we have here is the basic Swedenborgian concept of love and faith as ultimately inseparable, but analytically

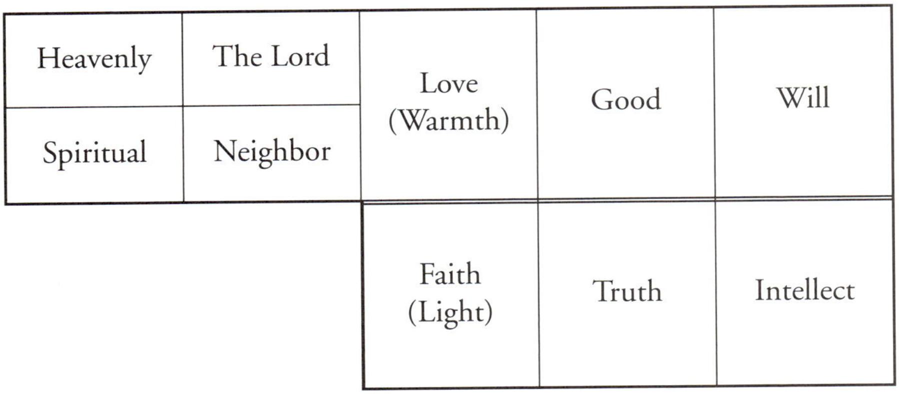

Heavenly	The Lord	Love (Warmth)	Good	Will
Spiritual	Neighbor			
		Faith (Light)	Truth	Intellect

Figure 1. General correspondences in *Secrets of Heaven*

distinguishable as the "higher" and the "lower" dimension respectively of one and the same divine reality:[36]

> The material world has two components to its life force: warmth and light. The spiritual world has two components to its: love and faith. Warmth in the material world corresponds to love in the spiritual world, and light in the material world corresponds to faith existing in the spiritual world. That is why love is meant when spiritual warmth or fire is mentioned, and faith is meant when spiritual light is mentioned. . . . The world's sun generates the warmth and light of the material world, but heaven's sun generates spiritual warmth and light, or love and faith. Heaven's sun is the Lord. The warmth radiating from him as the sun is love, and the light radiating from him as the sun is faith. (*Secrets of Heaven* 7082–7083)

If we follow Swedenborg in his biblical exegesis as well as in his memorable occurrences we see how all other dimensions of the spiritual world and of morality are structured around this basic distinction. Swedenborg begins right away by pointing out that among the people of the ancient church there were differences of opinion regarding matters of faith, but that these were considered of secondary importance: "People acknowledged all who led a good, charitable life as members of the church and called them sister or brother, no matter how strongly they disagreed on the truth that is now called religious truth" (§6628). In other words, charity took precedence over faith.

The commandment to "love one's neighbor" is discussed in detail. The people of the ancient church distinguished various categories of "neighbor" and had precise guidelines about how charity should be exercised towards each of these categories.[37] The Lord himself is the neighbor in the highest degree; everybody else is the neighbor in the measure that

---

36. Again, Swedenborg's discussions are sometimes confusing, and the framework given here is complicated by various factors; for example, the fact that he sometimes uses the term "spiritual" in a broader sense (as in the next quotation in the text, from *Secrets of Heaven* 7082–7083), sometimes in a more restricted sense (as when he uses "spiritual" as a term referring to a subdivision of love). My concern here is not to attempt to create a theological synthesis that harmonizes all variations in Swedenborg's terminology, but to present the general framework that structures his "teachings about charity and faith" in *Secrets of Heaven*.

37. *Secrets of Heaven* 6705. See also §§7259–7260 for further information about these categories.

the Lord resides in him or her; and everybody is also his or her own neighbor. This last dimension of the command, however, ranks lowest: of course one must provide oneself with the necessities of life in order to be in a condition to exercise charity towards others, but the basic commandment—repeated many times by Swedenborg—is that "self-love and love for the world," which are the root of all evil, must be overcome in favor of "love for one's neighbor and for the Lord." These two loves are of a different kind: the first and lower one, love for one's neighbor, is called "spiritual" while the second and higher one, love for the Lord, is called "heavenly." This same basic distinction between spiritual and heavenly recurs in Swedenborg's description of the structure of heaven, as will be seen.

Crucial to Swedenborg's moral teaching is his doctrine of dominant or ruling loves. Neither our beliefs nor our outward behavior are essential to our salvation (that is to say, the Protestant doctrine of justification by faith alone is rejected along with the Roman Catholic emphasis on good works); what matters is the inner motivational drive, or ruling love, that guides our actions and behavior. We are each ultimately motivated by "love for that which we hold as our goal" (§7081), and it is only this ruling or dominant love that molds our character and determines our fate after death. For example, it does not matter if we have done many good deeds during our life, if we did them out of self-love or love for the world (for example, because we wanted to be praised as benefactors of humanity). We must do it out of genuine love for our neighbor and for the Lord. Even worse is the Protestant idea of justification by faith, regardless of love:

> Faith devoid of love resembles light devoid of warmth, which is what winter light is like. Faith combined with love resembles light combined with warmth, which is what the light of spring is like. It is known that everything grows and flourishes in spring's light, and that everything droops and dies in winter's light. The same holds true for faith and love. (*Secrets of Heaven* 7084)

There are two mental powers in a person: intellect and will. The will has been given to humans for the sake of the good of love, the intellect for the sake of the truth of faith. It is not possible to separate the two, that is to say, to "understand and speak truth while willing and doing evil." If a person were to do this, one mental power would be looking upward towards heaven and another downward towards hell, and the person would be suspended between them. Such a thing cannot and does not happen, simply because the will (linked to love and the good) has precedence over the intellect (linked to faith and truth): "the will carries a person along, with the intellect in support" (7180).[38]

Swedenborg's discussions become slightly more complicated because he sometimes speaks of "love" *(amor)*, sometimes of "charity" *(charitas)*, while using both terms in combination with only one theoretical counterpart: "faith" *(fides)*. Charity and faith, and the relation between them, are described by him with characteristic scholastic precision:

> Charity is an inner passion consisting in a heartfelt desire to do good to one's neighbor as the greatest pleasure in one's life and to do so without reward. . . . Faith, on the other hand, is an inner passion consisting in a heartfelt desire to know what is true and good, not for the sake of doctrine as the ultimate goal but for the sake of life. What ties this passion to that of charity is the desire to behave according to the truth and therefore to actually *do* the truth. (*Secrets of Heaven* 8033–8034)

One might wonder how this definition of charity, as an "inner passion" and a "desire" that springs from the heart, can be combined with Swedenborg's insistence on the will. Exerting one's will so as to act charitably is not sufficient for salvation, because it concerns only the external. Is it really possible, however, to change one's heart and one's inward passions or desires by a sheer act of will? Answering that questions brings us to Swedenborg's doctrine of regeneration.

Swedenborg states that in order to enter heaven, one must be "born anew from the Lord" by "accept[ing] spiritual life" (§8548). However, nobody is born with such spiritual life, for from one's parents one receives only physical life. We are all born in what would traditionally be called a "state of sin":

> We are each born into the evils of self-love and materialism passed on by our parents. Every fault that we take on as second nature through habit we pass on to our offspring, as part of a long sequence reaching back to our parents, grandparents, and great-grandparents. Our resulting

---

38. It would be beyond the scope of this discussion to go into the relation of this perspective with some statements elsewhere in *Secrets of Heaven*, according to which will and intellect might nevertheless be seen as having been separated after the Flood (*Secrets of Heaven* 310:1, 398, 640–641, 875:3–5, 895, 927:2, 933:4).

inheritance of evil eventually grows so large that our own, independent spark of life is nothing but evil through and through. This unending chain is not broken or altered except by a life of faith and neighborly love received from the Lord. (*Secrets of Heaven* 8550)

Like John Locke (1632–1704), one of the major influences on his thought, Swedenborg adamantly rejected the philosophical doctrine of "innate ideas,"[39] believing instead that at birth a person is a *tabula rasa,* and for gaining knowledge is dependent on the senses. Since the senses do not give us access to the inner or heavenly realities, we are dependent in this regard on revelation. As explained by Martin Lamm in his excellent discussion of Swedenborg's doctrine of regeneration, we find ourselves in a state of "permanent equilibrium" between our hereditary tendencies towards evil on the one hand, and God's continuous efforts to show us the way to heaven on the other (see Lamm [1915] 2000, 271–274). When we are in the process of being regenerated we experience acute temptations, caused by evil spirits who are fighting with good spirits for dominion over our soul. It is we ourselves who have to exert our free will to allow the "new birth" to take place within us by choosing the side of heaven, in a constant battle with our evil tendencies and the temptation by evil spirits. It is initially by means of faith, aided by reason, that we accept the new truth shown to us; and as part of this process, "charity is planted [deeper and deeper] . . . until it takes over" (§8856). Once this happens, charity has become our "true will," and this remains unchangeable after death (8853–8858, 8958–8969). Swedenborg was convinced that he had undergone this very process of regeneration during the time of his spiritual crisis; it was only thanks to the Lord having fought for him that he was able to finally gain the victory.[40] In sum: human beings cannot be reborn without help from the Lord, but it is up to us to make the decisive step of choosing the good.

The remaining parts of the "first strand" of *Secrets of Heaven* are devoted to a series of specific subjects, some of which have already been touched upon before and some of which would be developed at much

---

39. About this point, and on the entire doctrine of regeneration, see the discussion in Lamm [1915] 2000, chapter 10, especially 266–274.

40. On the Lord fighting for one during regeneration, see §8969.

greater length in Swedenborg's later works. These subjects include the meaning of the forgiveness of sins, freedom and free will, marriage love, baptism, the Holy Supper, the body and outer appearance of spirits after death, providence, secular authorities (laws, rewards and punishments, priests, officers, monarchs, and so on), and finally the nature of God, the correct understanding of the Trinity, and the Lord's passion and glorification. If read against the theoretical background outlined above, these parts speak for themselves and therefore need not be summarized here.

V. The Second Strand: Biblical Exegesis

To understand the motivation behind Swedenborg's gigantic exegetical labors on Genesis and Exodus, we must keep in mind that the Word was for him quite literally "the means for uniting heaven and earth." It "comes from the Lord and was sent down to us through heaven" and was "not written only for people on earth but also for the angels present with us, . . . which is why the Word has the nature it does and why it is unlike any other piece of literature" (*Secrets of Heaven* 2310:2).

There is in fact a dramatic difference between how angels perceive the Word and how human beings perceive it. Angels perceive the inner meaning, and nothing else:

> They know nothing whatever of the literal contents, or the most obvious meaning of even one word, still less the names of different lands, cities, rivers, and people that come up so frequently in the narrative and prophetic parts. All they picture are the things those words and names symbolize. Adam in Paradise, for instance, brings the earliest church to their minds—and not even the church itself but its belief in the Lord. Noah brings up the picture of that church's remnant among its successors, lasting up to Abram's time. Abraham never makes them think of a man who lived long ago but of a saving faith, which he represented. And so on. . . .
>
> Several people found themselves carried up into heaven's outermost entry hall while I was reading the Word, and they spoke to me from there. They said that they had no inkling of a single word or letter there but saw only the things symbolized on the next deeper level of meaning. These things, according to their description, were so beautiful, followed

in such a perfect sequence, and affected them so deeply that they called it glory.[41]

The complete and utter ignorance of the angels concerning the literal meaning finds its exact counterpart in the no less radical ignorance of human beings concerning the inner meaning. As pointed out earlier, and as repeated many times by Swedenborg himself, it is indeed impossible to infer the inner meaning from the literal meaning. Each single word functions as a code for an abstract or spiritual concept. To bring this point home, it suffices to give a small sample of some biblical words and their decoded meaning:

David = the Lord
Asshur = skewed reasoning
Egypt = factual information
Cloud = the Word according to its literal meaning
Tyre = (religious) knowledge
Power and glory = the inner meaning
Peter = faith
James = charity
John = good works
Jewels = the tenets of faith
Road/path = truth
Horse = the intellect
Rider = one who has intelligence
Heel = lowest part of the earthly level
Sea = (religious) knowledge
Heart = desire for good
Eyes = intellect
Ears = obedience
Hand = power
Earth = the church
Earthquake = alteration in the state of the church
Eagles = a person's rational dimension

These examples can be multiplied at will. The undeniable genius of Swedenborg's biblical exegesis—bearing in mind that from a Swedenborgian perspective it should be considered, rather, as evidence of the

---

41. *Secrets of Heaven* 64–65. See also §1876.

divine origin of that exegesis—consists in the fact that his decodings are used consistently throughout *Secrets of Heaven,* and that he manages to come up with a coherent narrative of the inner meaning.

The subject of the Word as a whole, once decoded in this manner, is regeneration (§64); and this process is described as exemplified in the life and inner development of the Lord, on the one hand, and in the historical development of religious consciousness, on the other.[42] As for the book of Genesis, these two themes are distributed as shown in figure 2 on page 98.

For Exodus the situation is easier: the entire book is devoted to the spiritual church founded by the Lord.

a. Genesis on the Development of Churches

The account of the six days of creation in Genesis 1 is interpreted as referring to the six consecutive stages in human regeneration: from the initial stage of being "dead" to the stage of a fully developed spiritual person. The seventh day refers to the individual who has progressed from there to the highest stage, that of a "heavenly person," and the description of the garden of Eden is actually a description of that person's nature and constitution. Swedenborg then reveals that this "person" actually stands for the earliest church, and proceeds to describe how this church slowly declined from its original heavenly state. This happened because the members "ardently sought autonomy" (*Secrets of Heaven* 137), that is to say, began to let themselves be guided by self-love and love for the world. From this they began to believe only what their physical senses told them (their sensory part being represented by the serpent in paradise), and to "examine closely the tenets of faith in the Lord, to see whether they were true" (§192). This attitude of criticism and skepticism is represented by eating from the tree of knowledge. They were now under the influence of evil, although an earthly goodness remained with them. No longer willing to believe anything but what they apprehended by the senses,

---

42. Wunsch 1929, chapter 7, distinguishes three levels, by adding the dimension of "individual regeneration." Although the description of the Lord's development is certainly intended by Swedenborg as an ideal model to be emulated in the life of the individual, and at places can be read as referring to individual regeneration, it is clear already from Wunsch's own overviews (see especially chart 1 on page 129 there) that this third dimension is not an autonomous and independent one (it appears in Genesis 1, but this chapter is at the same time devoted to the "historical" dimension; and elsewhere it appears only occasionally within chapters devoted to the two other dimensions, and as "illustration" [Wunsch 1929, 46] of the Lord's life). Generally on the problems of Wunsch's charts, see Woofenden 1992–1993.

Spiritual Development of the Lord	Chapter	Historical Development of Religious Culture
	1	✓
	2	✓
	3	✓
	4	✓
	5	✓
	6	✓
	7	✓
	8	✓
	9	✓
	10	✓
	11	✓
✓	12	
✓	13	
✓	14	
✓	15	✓
✓	16	
✓	17	
✓	18	
	19	✓
✓	20	
✓	21	
✓	22	
	23	✓
✓	24	
✓	25	✓
✓	26	
✓	27	
✓	28	
✓	29	✓
	30	✓
✓	31	
✓	32	✓
✓	33	
	34	✓
✓	35	
✓	36	
✓	37	
	38	✓
✓	39	
✓	40	
✓	41	
✓	42	
✓	43	
✓	44	✓
✓	45	
✓	46	
✓	47	
	48	✓
	49	✓
	50	✓

Figure 2. Distribution of twin themes concerning regeneration in the chapters of Genesis in *Secrets of Heaven*

they were well on their way to hell; but to prevent them from having to end up there, the Lord promised that he would come into the world. Swedenborg describes the further degradation of the church, through several generations down to the Flood; the members eventually could no longer apprehend any truth at all, developed an "animalistic nature" (239), and turned away from everything belonging to faith and love. Cain means "the teaching that faith was separate from love" (325), while Abel means charity; the murder of the latter by the former means the victory of heretical doctrines over charity. A new faith was however provided by the Lord, by means of which charity was implanted anew; Seth means this new faith, and Enosh the charity implanted by means of it. Swedenborg continues by describing a number of further churches, represented in the Bible as persons (apart from Seth and Enosh, he mentions Kenan, Mahalalel, Jared, Enoch, Methuselah, Lamech, and Noah). All of these churches derive from the first one called Humankind, and are considered branches of the earliest church. From the church called Noah arose three classes of doctrine, referred to as Shem, Ham, and Japheth; they eventually perished in the Flood, that is to say, in a deluge of evil and falsity (603); but the ark, meaning "a member of this church" (*homo hujus Ecclesiae,* that is, Noah), was saved, thus ensuring the survival of the truth and good residing with him (639).

Thus ended the earliest church. After the Flood, a new church had to come into existence. This ancient church is referred to as "Noah and his sons." Swedenborg now becomes somewhat less easy to follow in his narrative of this church's development. Its members originally had one doctrine; but they wished "to explore religious truth in a self-directed way," and did so by means of rational argumentation; as a result they sank into "error and perversions" (975). In the commentaries to Genesis 10 (§§1131–1137) we find an excellent example of Swedenborg's extreme tendency toward systematic categorization:

- Sons of Japheth: those who engaged in outward worship corresponding to inner worship
- Sons of Gomer and Javan: those who engaged in a form of it that was further removed from inner worship
- "The islands of the nations": those whose worship was even further removed
- Sons of Ham: those who revered knowledge, facts, and ritual and separated them from any deeper properties
- Sons of Cush: those who revered the knowledge of spiritual things

- Sons of Raamah: those who revered the knowledge of heavenly things
- Nimrod: those who engage in outward worship that holds evil and falsity within it
- Descendants of Mizraim: those who take facts, apply logic to them, and in this way invent new forms of worship for themselves; and those who turn religious knowledge into a mere system of fact
- Canaan: Outward without inward worship
- Shem: Inward worship
- The church established by Eber had outward worship (Joktan) and inward (Peleg)

With Genesis 12 we reach the parts of the Bible written as "true history" (§1401). As we have seen, these parts are to be regarded as historically accurate *and* as carrying an inner meaning. According to the literal meaning, the stories about Abraham, Isaac, and Jacob and what follows describe the third, the "Hebrew church" (§1850:2); but according to the inner meaning they are about the life of the Lord. We will return to them below.

From this point on, references to the historical "churches" in *Secrets of Heaven* no longer add up to a more or less continuous narrative, but consist of various specific observations about churches. A general line of further development can, however, be distilled from them. After the final decline of the ancient church, a new one was created:

> The new sky and earth were the Hebrew church, which again had its final period, or last judgment, when it became idolatrous. So a new church was raised up, this time among Jacob's descendants. It was called the Jewish religion and was nothing more than a religion that *represented* charity and faith. In that religion, among Jacob's descendants, there was no charity or faith, so there was also no religion, but only a representation of a religion. The reason was that direct communication of the Lord's kingdom in the heavens with any true religion on earth was impossible, so indirect communication was set up through representations. The final period or last judgment of this so-called church occurred when the Lord came into the world, because representative acts—specifically sacrifices and other rituals like them—came to an end at that point. The demise of these rituals was achieved by the extermination of Jacob's descendants from the land of Canaan.
>
> Afterward, a new sky and earth were created. That is, a new church was created, which has to be called the nascent [Christian] church. It was started by the Lord and afterward grew gradually stronger, and in

its early days it possessed charity and faith. The Lord predicts the death of this church in the Gospels, as does John in the Book of Revelation, and its death is what people call the Last Judgment. Not that heaven and earth will now be obliterated, but that a new church will be raised up in some region of the globe, leaving the current church to remain in its superficial worship, as the Jews remain in theirs.[43] The worship of these people is devoid of charity and faith, or in other words, of religion, as is fairly well known. (*Secrets of Heaven* 1850:2–4)

What we read here is that the true "Hebrew" church degenerated to a pseudo-church referred to as the "Jewish" one. Likewise the "Primitive" Christian church based upon the Lord's teachings degenerated to a pseudo-church, referred to as the Christian one. The general pattern is that charity and true faith get lost, and mere outward worship and a focus on doctrine divorced from charity take their place. The general process of the degeneration of churches is again taken up, in great detail, in §§2312–2468, referring to Genesis 19, and in §§2901–2986, referring to Genesis 23. From here on, Swedenborg continues discussing in general terms the nature and development of a true "spiritual" and "heavenly" church, sometimes also using the occasion to add further detail to his earlier description of specific churches (thus for example in the commentaries in §§4811–4930 on Genesis 38, which interprets Judah as meaning the "Jewish church," and Tamar as meaning the "genuine church"). These long exegetical chapters become increasingly technical, with much space devoted to detailed descriptions of questions such as, for example, "the union of earthly truth with spiritual goodness by various means" (§3902). We notice that throughout all these discussions, the general framework remains the one described above, which links love to good and faith to truth, and subdivides love into spiritual and heavenly. One excellent further example of this approach (but many more could be given) is the commentary on Genesis 48 (§§6216–6306), which deals with "the church's intellect (consisting of truth) and its will (consisting of goodness). Ephraim means the church's intellect; Manasseh, its will" (6216).

b. Genesis on the Lord's Inner Development

Swedenborg leaves it in no doubt that the members of the Jewish church had become focused on outward things so completely that they had

---

43. On anti-Semitism in Swedenborg, see Hanegraaff 2004a.

entirely lost touch with internal verities and had in fact become incapable of spiritual understanding (see also Hanegraaff 2004a). By the time this church had reached its final stages of decay, human consciousness had sunk to the lowest point in history; and it was at that point of deepest darkness that the Lord appeared on earth.

The chapters from Genesis 12 on are considered historically accurate, as we have seen, but their inner meaning is not about Abraham and his descendants but about the inner development of the Lord in his years of infancy, childhood, and boyhood. His inner development was one that led from a state of darkness to one of light, thus providing the ideal model of the development that each human individual should undergo. The ensuing interpretations do not, however, add up to a coherent account in temporal sequence: Swedenborg does not give us a coherent, sequential spiritual biography of the Lord's inner life. While the descriptions do convey a sense of how the Lord only gradually became aware of his true identity and his mission,[44] Swedenborg hardly presents this in a narrative form but mostly speaks in abstract terms about the various aspects of his spiritual maturation. For example, he points out that the phrase "Go from your land" means that he was to withdraw from bodily and worldly concerns (*Secrets of Heaven* 1407); that "there was famine in the land" means the scarcity of knowledge that still affected the Lord when he was young (§§1459–1460); that "Abram went down into Egypt to reside as an immigrant" means that he was taught concepts from the Word (1461); that the wars described in Genesis 14 mean the spiritual battles the Lord fought;[45] and so on. These discussions again tend to become quite technical; for example, when they deal with the precise processes by which the Lord's human quality came to be joined to his divine quality (represented by Lot and Abraham respectively);[46] by which his rational side came to fruition through "the influence of his inner self on his outer self's desire for information" (1890); by which truth was connected with good within this rational side (1898–1902); by which "spiritual heavenliness influenced facts on the earthly plane and united with them" (5396b); and so on (3012–3212). Throughout, the discussions bear the imprint of

---

44. Wunsch 1929, 57–69, links the stories of Abraham, Isaac, Jacob, and Joseph quite directly to stages in the Lord's biography. While the broad outlines of this interpretation may be correct, I find the connection less clear-cut.

45. *Secrets of Heaven* 1651–1756. See also §§2764–2869.

46. *Secrets of Heaven* 1535–1618. See also §§1985–2116.

Swedenborg's systematic scientific mind: the awakening to divine consciousness is described by means of a dry and precise technical language, reminiscent of physics or chemistry. It would be beyond the scope of this introduction to analyze these discussions in detail: any value they may have for the reader lies not in the broad outlines of the message, as already sketched above, but in the specific details of Swedenborg's commentary on each and every verse.

c. Exodus on the Spiritual Church

The same is very much true for Swedenborg's interpretation of Exodus. If large parts of Genesis dealt with the inner processes by means of which the Lord came to full spiritual consciousness, the whole of Exodus deals with the church that he founded. Again the presentation is not in temporal sequence and takes the form of often highly abstract generalized statements. To get a sense of what this means, it is sufficient to take the example of Exodus 1:1–6. The biblical text is given as follows. To clarify the relation with Swedenborg's interpretation, the passage is subdivided by the present author into six numbered segments; these are different than the verse divisions.

> [1] And these are the names of the sons of Israel coming to Egypt with Jacob (a man and his household they came): [2] Reuben, Simeon, Levi, and Judah; Issachar, Zebulun, and Benjamin; Dan and Naphtali, Gad and Asher. [3] And every soul issuing from Jacob's thigh was seventy souls. [4] And Joseph was in Egypt.
> [5] And Joseph died, and all his brothers, and all that generation. [6] And the children of Israel reproduced and burgeoned, and multiplied and proliferated greatly, greatly, and the earth was filled with them. (*Secrets of Heaven* 6633)

In Swedenborg's reading this means:

> [1] The nature of the church after truth has been introduced into secular facts in regard to truth and goodness.
> [2] This whole process of the establishment of the church, from start to finish (the names of the twelve sons of Jacob and the tribes named after them meaning all aspects of goodness and truth, that is, of love and faith).
> [3] Everything produced by general truth, which was complete.
> [4] There was a heavenly quality within the earthly level.
> [5] The situation with the inner plane of the church had now changed, and likewise the situation with the outer plane in particular and general.

[6] The church's truth grew in goodness; it grew tremendously in the truth that comes from goodness, until the church was full.[47]

The development of the "spiritual church" having been described in these highly abstract terms, its deliverance by the Lord begins to be described from Exodus 3 on: the members of the church are taught that the Lord will deliver them, and "that he will take them to heaven after they have been given many different kinds of truth and goodness" (*Secrets of Heaven* 6825). Swedenborg continues to systematically apply this truth-good duality; for example, by asserting that Moses represents the goodness of divine law, and Aaron, its truth.[48]

Those who belonged to the true spiritual church were delivered; but those in the church who were governed by faith separated from charity, and who therefore remained "steeped in falsity and evil," underwent damnation. This process of damnation is the true meaning of the eleven[49] plagues of Egypt, each one of which is interpreted in great detail as representing a "stage of devastation." Swedenborg continues by interpreting the wanderings through the desert as the further preparation of those belonging to the spiritual church before the Lord's coming. In order for them to be led to heaven, they first had to be "conducted safely through the midst of damnation and then underwent spiritual challenges, the Lord always at their side" (§8039). This process, too, including all the struggles, is described in the greatest detail. In Exodus 19 we are told about "the Lord's revelation of divine truth from heaven" (8748). The Ten Commandments given in Exodus 20 are interpreted in detail as "the divine truth that needs to be grafted onto goodness in people belonging to the Lord's spiritual church" (8859). The laws, regulations, and punishments given from Exodus 21 on are obviously given a spiritual sense, as referring to offenses against the truth espoused by faith and the good embraced by charity, as well as "falsity . . . in doctrine, and evil . . . in life" (9246). Having interpreted Exodus 24 as describing the essential

---

47. *Secrets of Heaven* 6636 and 6644. The interpretation of part [1] is explained further and at length in §§6637–6639; of [2] in 6640; of [3] in 6641–6642; of [4] in 6643; of [5] in 6645–6646; and of [6] in 6647–6649.

48. *Secrets of Heaven* 6940. See also §7184: Reuben and Simeon and their clans represent elements of faith; Levi and his clans, elements of charity; Aaron and his clans, elements of theology; Moses, elements of divine law.

49. On these eleven rather than ten plagues, see Cole 1977, 31: in his van der Hooght/Schmidius Bible (see footnote 19 above), Swedenborg counted eleven rather than ten plagues, by including the turning of Aaron's rod into a water-serpent.

nature of the Word (9370), Swedenborg interprets the sanctuary and the ark of the covenant, as well as the various other technical descriptions beginning with Exodus 25, in a spiritual sense:

> The dwelling place would represent heaven itself; the ark in it, the deepest heaven; and the testimony or law in the ark, the Lord. The bread of presence on the table, and the lamp stand, would represent heavenly qualities received from the Lord in the heavens, and Aaron's garments would represent the spiritual qualities received from him there.[50]

The consecration of Aaron and his sons to the priesthood refers to the glorification of the Lord in his human incarnation, and Swedenborg then moves on to the establishment by the Lord of a "representative church" among "people who do good out of love for and faith in the Lord," and the bond between the Lord and that church (10326). The church could not be established among the Israelite people, because they were wholly externally oriented and would only have profaned the holy things of heaven if these had been disclosed to them (see Hanegraaff 2004a). Exodus 35 is said to "summarize all the varieties of goodness and truth in the church and in heaven on which worship of the Lord is based" (10725).

And then, quite surprisingly, Swedenborg suddenly gives up. The inner meaning of Exodus 36–40 is not explained because, as stated by him for each of these five chapters separately, everything in it can easily be deduced from what has been said previously.[51] In this manner Swedenborg's extraordinarily detailed decoding of Genesis and Exodus comes to an incredibly abrupt end. After thousands of pages, the reader is preparing himself for some kind of grand finale; instead, the entire work ends without even a conclusion, as if interrupted in mid-thought. Referring to my earlier analogy, *Secrets of Heaven* ends like an "unfinished symphony."

VI. The Third Strand: Accounts of Memorable Occurrences

In this section we will first give a general overview of how Swedenborg looks at the nature and structure of heaven and hell, and how he

---

50. *Secrets of Heaven* 9455. See also §9592.

51. Swedenborg makes that statement in each of the five "summary" parts of the last five chapters of Exodus: §§10750, 10767, 10782, 10807, 10832,

describes their inhabitants. Next we will discuss his celebrated concept of the "universal human." And finally we will take a look at what he writes about hells and the process of spiritual devastation.

a. Heaven, Hell, and Their Inhabitants

While Swedenborg himself attached very great importance to his sentence-by-sentence exegesis of the Word, there can be no doubt that his eventual success as a religious author must be attributed, rather, to his visionary accounts of "things heard and seen" in heaven and hell. *Secrets of Heaven* originally does not seem to have attracted many readers,[52] and those that were interested tended to quickly zoom in on the spectacular accounts of memorable occurrences (even a biblicist theologian like Friedrich Christoph Oetinger [1702–1782], with his great interest in questions of biblical exegesis, was no exception in this regard).[53] Swedenborg himself appears to have realized at one point that, from what we would nowadays call a public relations perspective, the memorable occurrences were by far his strongest "selling point," and decided to adapt his publishing strategy. In 1758, that is, two years after the final volume of *Secrets of Heaven* was published, no fewer than five much smaller works appeared, four of which draw heavily on the nonexegetical parts of his *magnum opus*.[54] Two of them have their basis in what we have called the "first strand" of *Secrets of Heaven*: *De Nova Hierosolyma et Ejus Doctrina Coelesti* (The New Jerusalem and Its Heavenly Teaching)[55] is dependent on the "Teachings about Charity" and "Teachings about Charity and Faith" (see the appendix for the relevant sections), and the contents of *De Equo Albo* (The

---

52. See Dole 2000, especially note 4. See also Wilkinson 1996, 62: "It sold miserably." These assessments have their source in a passage in Swedenborg, *Spiritual Experiences* (= Swedenborg 1998–2002) §4422: "I received a letter saying that not more than four copies had been sold within 2 months, and when this was made known to the angels, they were indeed surprised, but they said that it must be left to the Providence of the Lord, and that it is such that it compels no one. . . ."

53. On Oetinger's reception of Swedenborg, see Hanegraaff 2007.

54. See Dole 2000, 1. The exception is *De Ultimo Judicio* (Last Judgment). Woofenden 2002, 88, points out that it "broke new ground theologically by its claim that the long-expected last judgment predicted in the Bible has already taken place in the spiritual world by the time this work was published." In this context it is interesting to compare the passages in *Secrets of Heaven* about the Last Judgment (especially §§2117–2134, 4661–4664, 4807–4809), where it is interpreted as referring, rather, to the individual "judging him- or herself" after death.

55. Throughout the present edition, the short title *New Jerusalem* is used.

White Horse) are largely drawn from *Secrets of Heaven* 2760–2763. Most influential, however, became the two books that have their basis in the memorable occurrences: *De Telluribus in Mundo Nostro Solari* (known as *Other Planets*) is an only slightly edited republication of the final parts of the "third strand" (see the appendix for the relevant sections); and Swedenborg's most popular work, *De Coelo et Ejus Mirabilibus, et de Inferno* (Heaven and Its Wonders and Hell), is a much amplified and rearranged presentation of material found throughout the rest of the memorable occurrences.[56]

As pointed out by George F. Dole, Swedenborg was "clearly concerned to convey the connection between *Heaven and Hell* and *Secrets of Heaven*" (Dole 2000, 3). Not only were the contents of the smaller book referred to as "secrets of heaven" in §1, but *Heaven and Hell* is heavily annotated with cross-references to *Secrets of Heaven* (see, for example, Swedenborg 2000, 451–454). Dole draws the logical conclusion that

> Swedenborg intended *Heaven and Hell* at least in part as a vehicle for information already published in *Secrets of Heaven*. As well as demonstrating a striking concern for consistency, the cross-references clearly indicate a hope that it would attract the reader to that larger work. (Dole 2000, 4)

Indeed, with the exception of the final parts on the inhabitants of other planets, the memorable occurrences strand consists entirely of information about heaven and hell, and their inhabitants.[57] Swedenborg first speaks of what happens to people when they awake from death and enter into eternal life (§§168–189, 314–319, 320–323, 443–448), and continues with a general sketch of heaven and hell, as well as what may be seen—surprising in an author with a Lutheran background—as an equivalent of purgatory (449–459, 537–553, 684–700, 814–831, 938–970, 1106–1113). We will come back to this below. A short part is devoted to the present condition of the members of the earliest church (they are now very high up in heaven and live in a state of supreme happiness), as well

---

56. Throughout the present edition, the short title *Heaven and Hell* is used. Of the 603 sections of *Heaven and Hell*, 45 are direct quotations from *Secrets of Heaven* (see the table of parallel passages in Swedenborg 2000, 503).

57. Note that §§4523–4534 and 4622–4634 can be read as a summary version of the whole, and amount to an ideal short introduction to Swedenborg's view of heaven and hell.

as of their later descendants up to those who perished in the Flood and are now in one of the lowest hells (1114–1129, 1265–1272). The heavenly world of spirits and angels is described in rich detail at intervals throughout §§1273–1885, which include long discussions of subjects such as the angels' and spirits' manner of perception (1383–1400, 1504–1520), their speech (1634–1650, 1757–1764), and how they understand the inner meaning of the Word (1767–1777, 1869–1879). From here, Swedenborg moves on to a series of specific subjects: the differences between, and heavenly origins of, visions, dreams, and prophecy (1966–1983); the Last Judgment, as actually referring not to an event on earth but to the after-death fate of the individual (2117–2134); the state of children in the other life (2289–2309); the difference between outer memory, which belongs to the body, and inner memory, which belongs to the spirit (the latter constituting the individual's "Book of Life" in which everything he or she has ever thought, said, or done is written down up to the tiniest detail, and on the basis of which he or she is judged after death; §§2469–2494); the after-death fate of peoples and nations that were born outside the church (generally they are described much more mildly than the Jews and especially the Christians, most of whom are seen as much worse than the non-Christians; §§2589–2605); how marriage and adultery are regarded in heaven (2727–2759);[58] and true human freedom as opposed to the pseudo-freedom that comes from hell (2870–2893). Having discussed these specific aspects, Swedenborg again returns to the general picture. He first provides a long theoretical discussion of what is meant by representations and correspondences (2987–3003, 3213–3227, 3337–3352, 3472–3485); and from that perspective he proceeds to a very detailed description of the structure of the heavenly "universal human," on which more below.[59] Finally, there are paragraphs about the nature of sicknesses (all of them have their origin in hell; §§5711–5727); the two angels, one spiritual and one heavenly, and the two infernal spirits—more precisely, an evil spirit and a genius, or demon—that are always present with, and fight

---

58. These passages can be seen as the seed of a complete book, *Delitiae Sapientiae de Amore Conjugiali* (Wisdom's Delight in Marriage Love; current English title: *Marriage Love*), published by Swedenborg in 1768.

59. On the universal human, see §§3624–3649, 3741–3750, 3883–3896, 4039–4055, 4218–4228, 4318–4331, 4403–4421, 4523–4534, 4622–4634, 4652–4660, 4791–4806, 4931–4953, 5050–5062, 5171–5190, 5377–5396, 5552–5573.

over the soul of, each individual (see especially §§5977–5980); and the nature of the soul and the "inflow" of the divine into it.[60]

b. The Universal Human Constituted of Angelic Communities

If we take the accounts of memorable occurrences as a whole, and try to combine their discussions about various aspects of heaven and hell into a coherent picture, we can draw some conclusions that are never made explicit by Swedenborg himself but are nevertheless implicit in his work. To begin with, Swedenborg states that "the whole of heaven has been formed to correspond with the Lord and his divine humanity. Human beings have been formed to correspond in absolutely every particular with heaven, and through heaven with the Lord" (*Secrets of Heaven* 3624). In other words, there are three levels: the Lord himself, his heavenly manifestation as a "universal human" of enormous proportions, and the human being as a small version of the universal human. About the Lord himself, as he exists in and of himself, Swedenborg in fact says practically nothing; but the fact that the universal human "represents"[61] him means that the two cannot be conflated, and the same is implied by statements such as that the Lord appears as the sun to the inhabitants of heaven,[62] and that inhabitants of the third heaven "see the Lord himself" (§3475).

Much attention, in contrast, goes to the heavenly universal human. Universal it certainly is: "the Lord's heaven is immense—so immense as to surpass all belief. The inhabitants of our planet are very few, by comparison—almost like a pond in relation to the ocean" (3631). Essential to Swedenborg's concept is that this entire heavenly universal human *consists of* spirits and angels, who are ordered in spiritual and angelic communities. In long descriptions between §§3624 and 5573, he discusses the anatomy of this universal human's body in meticulous detail, describing how every one of its organs is constituted of specific communities and sub-communities, the spiritual orientation of which corresponds to the inner sense of the components of human anatomy. One cannot but be reminded here of the detailed anatomical studies

---

60. On spiritual influence and divine inflow, see §§6053–6058, 6189–6215, 6307–6327, 6466–6496, 6598–6626.

61. See §2996.

62. See §§1521, 3636, 3638; but in §1529 we read that the Lord appears to heavenly angels in the third heaven as the sun, but to spiritual angels as the moon.

that had occupied Swedenborg in his scientific work during the years immediately preceding his spiritual crisis and the results of which were published in his *Oeconomia Regni Animalis* (Dynamics of the Soul's Domain; 1740–1741). In addition, several scholars have seen in Swedenborg's universal human a clear example of Kabbalistic influence as well. Usually in this regard they have referred to the figure of *Adam Kadmon*,[63] while seldom mentioning the equally obvious parallels in the *Schi'ur Koma* tradition about the measures of God's mystical body.[64] But given the absence in Swedenborg of any explicit references to Jewish sources in that regard, how convincing is it to explain his universal human as an instance of "borrowing"? Elsewhere it has been argued by the present author that we are dealing here with a case of phenomenological similarity that is insufficient as proof of actual dependence (Hanegraaff 2004a). Anybody acquainted with the ancient idea that the human being is a microcosmos corresponding with the macrocosmos can draw the logical conclusion—without any need for Kabbala—that if a human being is a small world, the large world must be a human being;[65] and Swedenborg himself quite explicitly refers to the concept of the microcosmos in discussing the universal human. In doing so, however, with characteristic attention to logical consistency and completeness he distinguishes between the inner and the outer self, corresponding to the inner heaven and the outer cosmos:

> The inner self is made in the image of heaven, and the outer self, in the image of the world. In fact the inner self is heaven in its smallest form, while the outer self is the world in *its* smallest form, so that the person is a microcosm. (*Secrets of Heaven* 6057)

Thus we see that the doctrine of the two worlds and the doctrine of macrocosmos and microcosmos are combined, so as to yield a *double* picture: heaven relates to its individual inhabitant as a universal human to a

---

63. See Lamm [1915] 2000, 255 and following; Williams-Hogan 2000 (the latter author does not, however, conclude that Swedenborg's universal human is an example of Kabbalistic influence; rather, she emphasizes the importance of Neoplatonism).

64. The exception is Idel 1997, who briefly discusses Swedenborg in this context. On the tradition as such, see also Scholem 1977; Schäfer 1988.

65. Some examples of authors who in fact did draw that conclusion are Giovanni Pico della Mirandola ([1463–1494]; see Pico della Mirandola 1942, 380); Cornelius Agrippa ([1486–1535]; *De Occulta Philosophia* [The Occult Philosophy] vol. 3, chapter 13; see Agrippa 1992, 437–439); and Paracelsus ([1493–1541]; *Opus Paramirum* 1:2; see Paracelsus 1925, 94–95).

small, and likewise the external physical universe relates to the individual living person as macrocosmos to microcosmos. The grand and the small mirror one another on a visible as well as an invisible, or outward and inward, level. Now, this fundamental Swedenborgian concept appears to be inseparable from another basic assumption: his denial of any essential distinction between humans, spirits, angelic spirits, and angels, or put differently, his *radical humanization* of heaven (those of us who have lived the right kind of life become spirits, angelic spirits, and angels in the next life).[66] Swedenborg's doctrines of the universal human and of the continuity from human beings to angels follow with strict logical necessity from only two axioms: (1) his firm belief in the difference between a higher and a lower world, and (2) his acceptance of the traditional notion of the human being as microcosmos. For an extremely systematic thinker like him, the combination of the two inevitably brought up the question: If a human being is the universe in miniature, what then is a human being's parallel in heaven? Obviously there were two candidates: angels, and the spirits of the deceased. But since earth is modeled on heaven in all details, the existence of two kinds of microcosm in heaven would require two kinds in the material world as well, whereas actually we know that here on earth we have only human beings. Therefore, conceptual symmetry demanded that in heaven too, there would be only *one* kind of entity; and since the existence of angels as well as the survival of death are attested by the Bible, logically the only remaining possibility is that angels are in fact none other than the spirits of the deceased.[67]

---

66. Swedenborg speaks of three heavens, inhabited by spirits, angelic spirits, and angels, further subdividing each of the three into heavenly and spiritual ones (see, for example, §459; but notice that elsewhere he seems to divide heaven into two parts: see §4931). At times he treats these categories as somewhat fluent, sometimes using "angels" as shorthand for all three categories. The distinctions are important, and used consistently, but the essential point for him is that all inhabitants of heaven have originally lived as human beings on earth (see, for example, §1114: "Angels and spirits, or in other words, human beings after death..."; §1880: "to speak generally of spirits and angels, who are all human souls living on after the death of their body"). The concept is at odds with traditional Jewish as well as Christian notions, mystical or otherwise, of the relation between angels and human beings; see the longer discussion in Hanegraaff 2004a, note 55.

67. Swedenborg's distinction of three categories in heaven, each again subdivided into spiritual and heavenly, in no way contradicts this, for the distinction between spirits, angelic spirits, and angels is not ontological but has to do merely with successive levels of spiritual attainment. As such, each of the three, or six, categories finds its counterpart among living human beings. A human being's spiritual orientation during life on earth is decisive for the category to which he or she gravitates after death.

We begin to see how complex Swedenborg's concept of heaven really is, when we realize next that—in spite of the enormous proportions involved—the universal human in fact exists outside space and time:

> The form of heaven is astounding and completely mind-boggling, because it far surpasses any concept of forms we can possibly develop by looking at worldly objects, even when we analyze them. All heavenly communities are organized into that form, and amazing to say, they exhibit a circular motion that accords with it, though angels and spirits do not feel the motion. The situation resembles the earth's daily rotation on its axis and its annual revolution around the sun, which the inhabitants do not sense. . . .
>
> The forms that are still deeper—and more universal—are incomprehensible, . . . because the word *forms* carries with it the notion of space and of time. At the depths where heaven exists, nothing is perceived in terms of space and time (because they are proper to nature) but in terms of state, and of variations and changes in state.[68]

It follows that although spirits and angels experience concrete spatial environments—landscapes with woods, rivers, houses, and so forth—in which all kinds of things seem to happen to them in temporal sequence, all this is ultimately no more than a dreamlike illusion.[69] Spirits and angels in fact never go anywhere at all:

> All communities in the other world . . . maintain their own constant position in relation to the Lord, who appears to the whole of heaven as the sun. What is surprising—and hardly any will believe it, since they cannot understand it—is that the communities there maintain this same position in relation to *everyone* there. No matter where you are, which way you turn, or how you move around, communities that appear on your right are always on your right, and those on your left are always on your left, even when you turn your face or move your body from quarter to quarter. . . .
>
> Everyone . . . appears upright, head above and feet below. . . . Those in heaven have their heads toward the Lord. . . . The hellish, on

---

68. *Secrets of Heaven* 4041, 4043. See also §3356: "in the other world there is no concept of space or time but of state instead."

69. For further confirmation of that point, see §3633.

the other hand, appear in angels' eyes with their head down and their feet up.[70]

It is not too difficult for the reader to imagine that souls might subjectively experience a life in heavenly time and space even though they are actually "fixed" in a certain position in the body of the universal human; for, after all, we all know how we can travel in our dreams while actually remaining in bed. But how a soul can possibly be "fixed" in any location at all, if there is no space to begin with, remains truly impossible to understand. One is not surprised, therefore, to find that Swedenborg—who is elsewhere always concerned with rationality and logical consistency—emphasizes in the strongest possible terms that *these* marvels are simply beyond human intelligence.

c. Hells and the Process of Devastation

These distinctions between the Lord himself, the universal human as his heavenly representation, and heaven as perceived from the perspective of its inhabitants having been discussed, it remains to briefly discuss the two other environments in which human beings may find themselves after death: hell, and the place of spiritual devastations. About hell we can be short. Just like heaven it consists of innumerable communities (referred to as specific "hells," some of which are described in detail). They all exist outside the universal human "on different levels in all directions under the sole of the foot" (*Secrets of Heaven* 3640), and apparently in upside-down position. This is enough, of course, to suggest that all the hells together must surely form some grand being in human form, just as the heavenly communities do. Swedenborg draws that conclusion explicitly in one isolated passage in *Secrets of Heaven,* and restates it in *Heaven and Hell,*[71] but

---

70. *Secrets of Heaven* 3638, 3641. See also §1274.

71. *Secrets of Heaven* 694: "By the Lord's arrangement and through mutual love, heaven forms a single human being with a single animating soul, so it looks toward a single goal: the preservation and salvation of all to eternity. In contrast, hell, out of its sense of autonomy and through self-love and materialism—through hatred, in other words—forms a single devil with a single animus, so it looks toward a single goal: the destruction and damnation of all to eternity." *Heaven and Hell* 553: "I have not been allowed to see what form hell itself is in overall. I have only been told that in the same way that all heaven as a single entity resembles a single human being . . . so all hell as a single entity resembles a single devil and can be manifested as a likeness of a single devil" (translated by George F. Dole).

elsewhere in *Secrets of Heaven* he seems to contradict it: "It is wrong to believe that any devil has existed from the beginning of creation other than those who once were people."[72] There is reason to assume that this reflects a certain amount of hesitation on Swedenborg's part concerning a subject on which he held somewhat conflicting ideas. If the heavenly universal human represents the Lord, it is logical to conclude that such an infernal grand being must represent his counterpart, the Devil; but this would seem to give the Devil a status precisely equal to that of the Lord, which has far-reaching and troubling theological implications.

Swedenborg is equally evasive about a final aspect of the afterlife that sits somewhat uneasily with the sharp ethical dualism of his system. Again and again, he makes clear that there is no such thing as a gray area between heaven and hell: those whose life is ruled by love for one's neighbor and for the Lord go to heaven, those whose life is ruled by self-love and love for the world go to hell.[73] There is nothing in between. And yet, he does speak of an after-death state that allows human beings to be purged of their "falsity" so as to be eventually admitted to heaven.[74] People who absorbed such falsity "in their naiveté and ignorance" spend a considerable length of time "in an underground realm" (located "under the left foot [of the universal human], out in front a little"), where they undergo the process of devastation before finally being carried into heaven.[75] Clearly this aspect of Swedenborg's teaching is reminiscent of what is known in Roman Catholicism as purgatory: a concept that was rejected by the Reformation, and appears in a Lutheran context only very rarely, and in a later period.[76]

---

72. *Secrets of Heaven* 968; and on this point see also *Heaven and Hell* 544.

73. For good examples of this sharp dualism, see §§7178–7182, 7366–7377, 8033–8037.

74. This state is not to be confused with that in the "world of spirits," on which see, for example, 5427:1, 5852.

75. *Secrets of Heaven* 698, 1106–1113; see also §§4944, 4947.

76. See the concept of "hades" introduced by Johann Heinrich Jung-Stilling (1740–1817) in his *Theorie der Geister-Kunde* (1808), and taken up by Johann Friedrich von Meyer (1719–1798) in his *Hades* (von Meyer 1810; for an exhaustive study, see Fabry 1989).

VII. Concluding Remarks

A general reception history of Swedenborg's thought falls beyond the scope of this introduction. Much has been written about his influence on later generations, including great names like William Blake (1757–1827), Friedrich Wilhelm Joseph von Schelling (1775–1854), Johann Wolfgang von Goethe (1749–1832), Johann Caspar Lavater (1741–1801), Honoré de Balzac (1799–1850), Feodor Dostoevsky (1821–1881), Charles Baudelaire (1821–1867), August Strindberg (1849–1912), Ralph Waldo Emerson (1803–1882), Helen Keller (1880–1968), Arnold Schönberg (1874–1951), and Jorge Luis Borges (1899–1986).[77] While the importance of Swedenborgian concepts for these and many other writers, poets, artists, musicians, and philosophers is not in any doubt, it is much more difficult to assess the importance of *Secrets of Heaven* specifically. After all, many of the ideas that we find in it can be found in other and later works by Swedenborg as well, and unless authors are explicit about their sources or give precise quotations, one often cannot know exactly what they have read. This problem is greatly aggravated by the fact that, as we have seen, several of Swedenborg's most popular later writings are in fact re-edited versions of materials from *Secrets of Heaven:* when authors appear to be influenced by his ideas about heaven and hell or the inhabitants of other planets, they may well have found them in those later publications rather than in *Secrets of Heaven* itself. To make matters worse, the further we move forward in history, away from Swedenborg's own time, the more we have to reckon with indirect transmission of his ideas: very frequently people seem to have picked up some of his ideas from second-hand and not necessarily accurate accounts, and relatively few nonmembers of the New Church may have taken the trouble to actually read Swedenborg's works (see Wilkinson 1996, 19). Among those who did, many dipped into them rather than reading them from cover to cover, and for many such readers the shorter books were no doubt more convenient than the massive and forbidding *Secrets of Heaven*. And finally, among those who did read the latter, one may well wonder how many took the trouble to read the theoretical and exegetical parts: here, too, the memorable occurrences were no doubt most attractive to most readers.

---

77. Among the more important overviews, in whom most of these figures and many others are discussed, see Bergmann and Zwink 1988, Larsen and others 1988, Brock and others 1988.

These patterns become evident already during the earliest stage of the reception history of *Secrets of Heaven,* which is essentially restricted to the German domain: it was here that Swedenborg found his most important commentators and critics during his own lifetime, in the persons of Johann August Ernesti (1701–1781), Friedrich Christoph Oetinger, and Immanuel Kant (1724–1804).[78] The considerable early interest in Swedenborg among German intellectuals[79] had much to do with Oetinger's translation of excerpts from *Secrets of Heaven,* published as early as 1765 in his *Swedenborgs und anderer irrdische und himmlische Philosophie* (Swedenborg's and Others' Earthly and Heavenly Philosophy; Oetinger 1977): it is this translation of selected fragments taken from the memorable occurrences, rather than Swedenborg's original, on which many of them appear to have depended.[80] In France *Secrets of Heaven*'s reception history begins considerably later, mainly due to the fact that French translations do not seem to have become available before 1841.[81] An English translation of *Secrets of Heaven* volume 2, by John

---

78. These authors' reception of Swedenborg is discussed in detail in Hanegraaff 2007.

79. See Benz 1947, 264: the theologian Philipp Matthäus Hahn (1739–1790) devoted large parts of his diary of 1766 to comments on Swedenborg, who was likewise studied by scholars and theologians like Jeremias Friedrich Reuss (1700–1777), Johannes Kies (1713–1781), Heinrich Wilhelm Clemm (1725–1775), Johann Ludwig Fricker (1729–1766), and various people from the nobility. Benz claims that "in the correspondence of Württembergian scholars and pietists in these years, Swedenborg's person and doctrine are one of the most frequently treated subjects" (Benz 1947, 264).

80. The first complete German translation, by J.F.I. Tafel (1796–1863), appeared only as late as 1845–1869. See Benz 1947, 274–280, about a failed attempt during the 1780s to realize a German translation of *Secrets of Heaven* made by the publisher Johann Friedrich Hartknoch ([1740–1789], the same person who had published Kant's *Dreams of a Spirit-Seer* [Kant 1766]).

81. The first Swedenborg translations in French were made in Berlin, by French authors associated with the esoteric group that would later become known as the Illuminés d'Avignon: Antoine-Joseph Pernety (1716–1796) published *Les merveilles du ciel et de l'enfer et des terres planétaires et astrales* (The Wonders of Heaven and Hell and of the Planetary and Astral Earths) in 1782, Louis Joseph Bernard Philibert Guyton de Morveau ([1738–1786]; known as de Brumore) brought out his *Traité curieux des charmes de l'amour conjugal dans ce monde, et dans l'autre* [Curious Treatise on the Charms of Marriage Love in This World and the Other] in 1784, and it was followed by Pernety's *La sagesse angélique sur l'amour divin et sur la sagesse divine* [Angelic Wisdom on Divine Love and Divine Wisdom] in 1786. All these translations were severely criticized by Swedenborgians for the liberties that they took with the originals (see Sjödén 1985, chapter 2). In 1788 followed a compilation taken from various works, by Jean François D'Aillant de la Touche (1744?–1827?), who may either have made the translations himself or have acted as coordinator and editor of translations made by others; it was published anonymously as *L'abrégé des ouvrages d'Em. Swedenborg* (Abridged

Marchant,[82] was published simultaneously with the first Latin edition, in 1750; but this translation is extremely rare, and it seems that only two copies of it survive (Tafel 1877, 974; Hyde 1906, page 139). The complete *Secrets of Heaven,* translated by John Clowes (1743–1831), first appeared in English in twelve volumes from 1783 to 1806; but when the first volume came out, *Heaven and Hell* had already been available for five years, in a 1778 translation by William Cookworthy (1705–1780) and Thomas Hartley (1708–1784), and various other works by Swedenborg had become available by 1806.[83] As for Sweden, Swedenborg's home country, a "Philanthropic and Exegetic Society" devoted to publication and translation of his works existed for a few years (1786–1789), but managed only to get a few small parts into print; publication of Swedenborg's works long remained impossible due to suppression by the ecclesiastical and secular authorities.[84] *Secrets of Heaven* only began to be published in Swedish translations from 1821 on (see Hyde 1906, pages 190–194).

When all is said and done, the history of Swedenborg's *Secrets of Heaven* and its reception is not devoid of a tragic dimension. While Swedenborg spent countless hours on his extraordinarily detailed exegesis of (almost) each and every verse of Genesis and Exodus, very few readers outside the New Church ever seem to have been interested in

---

Presentation of Emanuel Swedenborg's Works; = Swedenborg 1788). The *Abridged Presentation* of 1788 has been described as "one of the most important events in the history of Swedenborgianism" (Sjödén 1985, 52), not in the last place because both the refutation of the New Church by Augustin de Barruel (1741–1820) and Balzac's references to Swedenborg are entirely dependent on this compilation. The first integral French translations after those by Pernety and de Brumore appeared from 1819 to 1824; they were made by a Freemason and Librarian of the Royal Library at Versailles, Jean Pierre Moët (1721–1806 or 1807). Moët also translated *Secrets of Heaven* in its entirety, but this translation remained unpublished (see Hyde 1906, page 688). The manuscript was consulted by Jean-François-Étienne Le Boys des Guays (1794–1864)—who severely criticized it—while he was working on his own translation that would finally be published between 1841 and 1854 (on the early history of Swedenborgian influence in Europe, see Sjödén 1985, 23–35, 51–52, 65–71, 95–124; see also Wilkinson 1996, 112–116).

82. Some sources give this name as Merchant. Though some biographical details are known about him, his dates of birth and death are not. (Hyde 1906, page 731, lists them incorrectly.)

83. See Dole 2003a, 8–9, for editions of Swedenborg's *Divine Love and Wisdom* (1763) and Dole 2003b, 6–7, for editions of his *Divine Providence* (1764).

84. See also Jonsson [1971] 1999, 196–197; interestingly, Hyde 1906, page 200, describes one Swedish translation of excerpts from *Secrets of Heaven,* by Johann Gustav Halldin (1737–1825), dated as early as 1784. In addition to English, French, German, and Swedish, Hyde 1906, pages 189–190, lists manuscripts of translations into Russian dated between 1851 and 1863.

this aspect of his work. Even such a biblicist theologian as Oetinger—not to mention Kant—quickly passed over the exegetical parts, to focus almost all his attention on the memorable occurrences; and this attitude has remained dominant ever since. Swedenborg's lasting fame and influence are undoubtedly based upon his spectacular visions, not upon his tireless efforts as an interpreter of the Bible.

What remains is the unquestionable importance of *Secrets of Heaven* as a huge reservoir of religious ideas and concepts, from which emerged a comprehensive worldview of startling originality and internal consistency. It is not difficult to understand that Swedenborg's extraordinarily graphic and detailed visionary descriptions of heaven and hell were bound to appeal to the imagination of many readers; but it would be a mistake to see this "romantic" appeal as the only reason for his wide-ranging influence up to the present day. A major key to understanding that influence lies in Swedenborg's *rationality*. His scientifically trained mind, used to the dry discipline of logic and always alert to the rational consistency of concepts, is dominantly visible throughout *Secrets of Heaven;* and many of the religious and moral questions that he sought to answer are those of a man of the Enlightenment. The result was a worldview based upon supra-rational revelation but presented in rational terms and congenial to modern mentalities. It is therefore not surprising that basic Swedenborgian concepts came to be adopted by spiritualists and other occultists during the nineteenth century, and that they can be encountered even in contemporary "New Age" contexts that have no room for biblical exegesis.[85] Although Swedenborg himself would have seen such hybrid spiritualities as unfortunate mixtures of truth and falsity, from a historical perspective they testify to the continued vitality of Swedenborg's thought.

---

85. As demonstrated in Hanegraaff 2004b.

Appendix

The Structure of Secrets of Heaven

IN order to find one's way through Swedenborg's *Secrets of Heaven* it is necessary to see that it consists of three interwoven but autonomous strands: the shortest one consists of "introductory parts" about matters of method, history, and doctrine, the longest one consists of a systematic and extremely detailed exegesis of Genesis and Exodus (including complete translations of both),[86] and a strand of intermediate but very substantial length is referred to as memorable occurrences: accounts of Swedenborg's experiences in the spiritual world. The contents of the three strands can be analyzed as follows.[87]

The First Strand: Method, History, and Doctrine (Introductory Passages and Unnumbered Prefaces)

[Unnumbered introductory note]. The essential nature of the Word: §§1–5. The inner life of the Word: 64–66. Secrets of the other life: 67–72. Representations of inner meaning: 166–167. Author's preface [to Genesis 16]. The Word's inner meaning: 1886–1889, 1984. Author's preface [to Genesis 18]. More on the Word's inner meaning: 2135, 2310–2311, 2495, 2606–2609. Author's preface [to Genesis 22]. The white horse: 2760–2763. History of the Word: 2894–2900. The name Jesus Christ: 3004–3011. Narrative detail in the Word: 3228–3229. Matthew 24: 3353–3356, 3486–3489, 3650–3655, 3751–3757, 3897–3901, 4056–4060, 4229–4231, 4332–4335, 4422–4424. The close of the age: 4535. Matthew 25: 4635–4638, 4661–4664, 4807–4810, 4954–4959, 5063–5071. Teachings on charity: 6627–6633

---

86. On the translation included in *Secrets of Heaven*, see note 19 in the preceding essay.

87. To clarify the structure, I have subdivided the three strands. Titles have been added where necessary.

Teachings about Charity 6703–6712, 6818–6824, 6933–6938, 7080–7086, 7178–7182, 7255–7263, 7366–7377, 7488–7494, 7623–7627, 7752–7762, 7814–7821, 8033–8037, 8120–8124, 8252–8257, 8387–8394, 8548–8553, 8635–8640, 8742–8747, 8853–8858, 8958–8969, 9112–9122

Teachings about Charity and Faith 9239–9245, 9363–9369, 9443–9454, 9585–9591, 9701–9709, 9796–9803, 9974–9984, 10167–10175, 10318–10325, 10386–10392, 10519–10522, 10591–10597, 10714–10724, 10740–10749, 10760–10766, 10773–10781, 10789–10806, 10815–10831

The Second Strand: Biblical Exegesis

Genesis:	Summary:	Inner Meaning:
1	6–13	14–63
2:1–17	73–80	81–130
2:18–25	131–136	137–167
3:1–13	190–193	194–233
3:14–19	234–240	241–279
3:20–24	280–285	286–313
4	324–336	337–442
5	460–467	468–536
6:1–8	554–559	560–598
6:9–22	599–604	605–683
7	701–704	705–813
8	832–837	838–937
9	971–976	977–1105
10	1130–1138	1139–1264
11	1279–1282	1283–1375
12	1401–1402	1403–1502[88]
13	1535–1539	1540–1618
14	1651–1658	1659–1756
15	1778–1782	1783–1868
16	1890–1891	1892–1965
17	1985–1986	1987–2116
18	2136–2141	2142–2288
19	2312–2316	2317–2468
20	2496–2497	2498–2588

---

88. Section 1503 is missing.

21	2610–2614	2615–2726
22	2764–2765	2766–2869
23	2901–2902	2903–2986
24	3012–3014	3015–3212
25	3230–3233	3234–3336
26	3357–3361	3362–3471
27	3490	3491–3623
28	3656–3657	3658–3740
29	3758–3759	3760–3882
30	3902–3903	3904–4038
31	4061	4062–4217
32	4232	4233–4317
33	4336	4337–4402
34	4425	4426–4522
35	4536	4537–4621
36	4639	4640–4651
37	4665	4666–4790
38	4811–4812	4813–4930
39	4960–4961	4962–5049
40	5072	5073–5170
41	5191–5192	5193–5376
42	5396b[89]–5397	5398–5551
43	5574	5575–5710
44	5728–5730	5731–5845
45	5867	5868–5975
46	5994	5995–6052
47	6059–6061	6062–6188
48	6216–6217	6218–6306
49	6328–6332	6333–6465
50	6497	6498–6597
Exodus:	**Summary:**	**Inner Meaning:**
1	6634–6635	6636–6694
2	6713–6714	6715–6806
3	6825	6826–6920
4	6939–6941	6942–7068

---

89. Section 5396 was inadvertently repeated. The two paragraphs designated by that number are distinguished by the addition of *a* and *b* in this edition.

5	7087	7088–7169
6	7183–7184	7185–7245b[90]
7	7264–7265	7266–7357
8	7378	7379–7474
9	7495	7496–7619
10	7628	7629–7741
11	7763	7764–7798
12	7822–7823	7824–8020
13	8038–8039	8040–8110
14	8125	8126–8241
15	8258–8259	8260–8370
16	8395	8396–8540
17	8554–8555	8556–8626
18	8641	8642–8732
19	8748	8749–8845
20	8859	8860–8946
21	8970	8971–9103
22	9123	9124–9231
23	9246	9247–9349
24	9370	9371–9437
25	9455	9456–9577
26	9592	9593–9692
27	9710–9712	9713–9789
28	9804	9805–9966
29	9985	9986–10158
30	10175a[91]	10176–10310
31	10326	10327–10376
32	10393–10394	10395–10512
33	10523	10524–10584
34	10589–10600	10601–10707
35	10725	10726–10733
36	10750	——

---

90. Section 7245 was inadvertently repeated. The two paragraphs designated by that number are distinguished by the addition of *a* and *b* in this edition.

91. Section 10175 was inadvertently repeated. The two paragraphs designated by that number are distinguished by the addition of *a* and *b* in this edition.

37	10767	——
38	10782	——
39	10807	——
40	10832	——

The Third Strand: Accounts of Memorable Experiences

Death Our resurrection from death and entry into eternal life: 168–189, 314–319. What the life of the soul or spirit is then like: 320–323. Several examples from spirits of opinions they adopted during their physical lives concerning the soul or spirit: 443–448

Heaven Heaven and heavenly joy: 449–459, 537–553. The communities that make up heaven: 684–691

Hell 692–700. The hells of those who spent their lives in hatred, revenge, and cruelty: 814–823. The hells of those who spent their lives in adultery and lechery; in addition, the hells of deceivers and witches: 824–831. Misers' hells; the foul Jerusalem and robbers in the wilderness; the feces-laden hells of those who have pursued sensual pleasure alone: 938–946. Other hells: 947–970

Spiritual devastation 1106–1113

Antediluvian history The earliest church: 1114–1129. The pre-Flood people who died out: 1265–1272

The world of spirits and angels Location in the "universal human"; place, distance, and time in the other life: 1273–1278, 1376–1382. The ability of spirits and angels to perceive things; auras in the other life: 1383–1400, 1504–1520. The light angels live in; their magnificent gardens and their dwellings: 1521–1534, 1619–1633. The way spirits and angels talk: 1634–1650, 1757–1764. Sacred Scripture, or the Word, which conceals a divine message that lies open to the view of good spirits and angels: 1767–1777, 1869–1879. General information about spirits and angels: 1880–1885

Visions, dreams, prophecy 1966–1983

The Last Judgment 2117–2134

The state of children in the other world 2289–2309

The power of recall that we keep after death 2469–2494

The lot and condition in the other world of nations and peoples born outside the church 2589–2605

The way marriage and adultery are viewed in heaven 2727–2759

Human freedom 2870–2893

Representation and correspondence 2987–3003, 3213–3227, 3337–3352, 3472–3485

The universal human 3624–3649, 3741–3750, 3883–3896, 4039–4055, 4218–4228, 4318–4331, 4403–4421, 4523–4534, 4622–4634, 4652–4660, 4791–4806, 4931–4953, 5050–5062, 5171–5190, 5377–5396, 5552–5573

Disease 5711–5727

The angels and spirits with us 5846–5866, 5976–5993

Spiritual influence, and soul-body interaction 6053–6058, 6189–6215, 6307–6327, 6466–6496, 6598–6626

The inhabitants of other planets 6695–6702. Mercury: 6807–6817, 6921–6932, 7069–7079, 7170–7177. Venus: 7246–7254. Mars: 7358–7365, 7475–7487, 7620–7622, 7742–7751. Jupiter: 7799–7813, 8021–8032, 8111–8119, 8242–8251, 8371–8386, 8541–8547, 8627–8634, 8733–8741, 8846–852. Saturn: 8947–8957, 9104–9111. The moon: 9232–9238. Why the Lord wanted to be born on our planet and not another: 9350–9362. Planets in outer space; their inhabitants, spirits, and angels: 9438–9442. First planet: 9578–9584, 9693–9700, 9790–9795. Second planet: 9967–9973, 10159–10166. Third planet: 10311–10317, 10377–10385, 10513–10518. Fourth planet: 10585–10590, 10708–10713. Fifth planet: 10734–10739, 10751–10759, 10768–10772. Sixth planet: 10783–10788, 10808–10814a, 10833–10837

Works Cited in the Introduction

Abell, Arthur M. 1964. *Talks with Great Composers.* Garmisch-Partenkirchen: G. E. Schroeder.

Agrippa, Cornelius. 1992. *De Occulta Philosophia Libri Tres.* Edited by V. Perrone Compagni. Leiden, New York, Köln: E. J. Brill.

Benz, Ernst. 1947. *Swedenborg in Deutschland: F. C. Oetingers und Immanuel Kants Auseinandersetzung mit der Person und Lehre Emanuel Swedenborgs, nach neuen Quellen bearbeite.* Frankfurt am Main: Vittorio Klostermann.

———. [1969] 2002. *Emanuel Swedenborg: Visionary Savant in the Age of Reason.* Translated by Nicholas Goodrick-Clarke. West Chester, Pa.: Swedenborg Foundation.

Bergmann, Horst, and Eberhard Zwink, eds. 1988. *Emanuel Swedenborg 1688–1772: Naturforscher und Kundiger der Überwelt. Zum Werk des gelehrten Naturforschers. Zu Werk und Einfluss des Visionärs und Theologen. Zur Wirkungsgeschichte eines Naturphilosophen.* Stuttgart: Württembergische Landesbibliothek.

Brock, Erland J., and others, eds. 1988. *Swedenborg and His Influence.* Bryn Athyn, Pa.: Academy of the New Church.

Cole, Stephen. 1977. "Swedenborg's Hebrew Bible." *The New Philosophy* 80:28–33.

Dieckmann, Liselotte. 1970. *Hieroglyphics: The History of a Literary Symbol.* St. Louis, Mo.: Washington University Press.

Dole, George F. 2000. Translator's preface to *Heaven and Hell,* by Emanuel Swedenborg, translated by George F. Dole. West Chester, Pa.: Swedenborg Foundation. 1–6.

———. 2003a. Translator's preface to *Divine Love and Wisdom,* by Emanuel Swedenborg, translated by George F. Dole. West Chester, Pa.: Swedenborg Foundation. 1–10.

———. 2003b. Translator's preface to *Divine Providence,* by Emanuel Swedenborg, translated by George F. Dole. West Chester, Pa.: Swedenborg Foundation. 1–9.

Fabry, Jacques. 1989. *Le théosophe de Francfort Johann Friedrich von Meyer (1772–1849) et l'ésotérisme en Allemagne au XIXe siècle.* 2 vols. Berne, etc.: Peter Lang.

Faivre, Antoine. 1994. *Access to Western Esotericism.* Albany: State University of New York Press.

———. 2000. *Theosophy, Imagination, Tradition: Studies in Western Esotericism.* Translated by Christine Rhone. Albany: State University of New York Press.

Hanegraaff, Wouter J. 1995. "Empirical Method in the Study of Esotericism." *Method and Theory in the Study of Religion* 7:99–129.

———. 1996–1998. *New Age Religion and Western Culture: Esotericism in the Mirror of Secular Thought.* Leiden, New York, Köln: E. J. Brill, and Albany: State University of New York Press.

———. 2004a. "Emanuel Swedenborg, the Jews, and Jewish Traditions." In *Reuchlin und seine Erben: Forscher, Denker, Ideologen und Spinner,* edited by Peter Schäfer and Irina Wandrey. Ostfildern: Jan Thorbecke. 135–154.

———. 2004b. "Spectral Evidence of New Age Religion: On the Substance of Ghosts and the Use of Concepts." *Journal of Alternative Spiritualities and New Age Studies* 1:35–58.

———. 2004c. "The Study of Western Esotericism: New Approaches to Christian and Secular Culture." In *New Approaches to the Study of Religion,* edited by Peter Antes, Armin W. Geertz, and Randi Warne. Berlin and New York: De Gruyter. Vol. I, 489–519.

———. 2005. Entry for "Tradition." In *Dictionary of Gnosis and Western Esotericism,* edited by Wouter J. Hanegraaff and others. Leiden, etc.: E. J. Brill. 1125–1135.

———. 2007. *Swedenborg, Oetinger, Kant: Three Perspectives on the Secrets of Heaven.* West Chester, Pa.: Swedenborg Foundation.

Hooght, Everardus van der. 1740. *Biblia Hebraica secundum Editionem Belgicam Everardi van der Hoogt, Collatis Aliis Bonae Notae Codicibus, Una cum Versione Latina Sebastiani Schmidii.* Leipzig: Wolfgang Deer.

Hyde, James. 1906. *A Bibliography of the Works of Emanuel Swedenborg, Original and Translated.* London: Swedenborg Society.

Idel, Moshe. 1997. "Il mondo degli angeli in forma umana." *Rassegna mensile d'Israel* 63:1–76. Hebrew original in *Jerusalem Studies in Jewish Thought,* edited by J. Dan and J. Hacker, Jerusalem, 1986, 1–66.

Jonsson, Inge. 1970. "Swedenborg's Doctrine of Correspondence." *The New Philosophy* 73:299–327.

———. 1979. "Emanuel Swedenborgs Naturphilosophie und ihr Fortwirken in seiner Theosophie." In *Epochen der Naturmystik: Hermetische Tradition im wissenschaftlichen Fortschritt,* edited by Antoine Faivre and Rolf Christian Zimmermann. Berlin: Erich Schmidt.

———. [1971] 1999. *Visionary Scientist: The Effects of Science and Philosophy on Swedenborg's Cosmology.* West Chester, Pa.: Swedenborg Foundation.

Jung, genannt Stilling, Heinrich. 1808. *Theorie der Geister-Kunde, in einer Natur-, Vernunft- und Bibelmässigen Beantwortung der Frage: Was von Ahnungen, Gesichten und Geistererscheinungen geglaubt und nicht geglaubt werden müsste.* Nürnberg: Raw'schen Buchhandlung.

Kant, Immanuel. 1766. *Träume eines Geistersehers, erläutert durch Träume der Metaphysik.* Riga: Johann Friedrich Hartknoch.

Kraus, Hans-Joachim. 1982. *Geschichte der historisch-kritischen Erforschung des Alten Testaments.* 3rd expanded ed. Neukirchen-Vluyn: Neukirchener Verlag.

Lamm, Martin. [1915] 2000. *Emanuel Swedenborg: The Development of His Thought.* Translated by Tomas Spiers and Anders Hallengren. West Chester, Pa.: Swedenborg Foundation.

Lang, Bernhard. 2000. "On Heaven and Hell: A Historical Introduction to Swedenborg's Most Popular Book." In *Heaven and Its Wonders and Hell,* by Emanuel Swedenborg, translated by George F. Dole. West Chester, Pa.: Swedenborg Foundation. 9–64.

Larsen, Robin, and others, eds. 1988. *Emanuel Swedenborg: A Continuing Vision. A Pictorial Biography and Anthology of Essays and Poetry.* New York: Swedenborg Foundation.

Longenecker, Richard. 1975. *Biblical Exegesis in the Apostolic Period.* Grand Rapids, Mich.: William B. Eerdmans.

Lubac, Henri de. 1959. *Exégèse médiévale: Les quatre sens de l'Écriture.* Paris: Aubier.

Meyer, Johann Friedrich von. 1810. *Hades: Ein Beytrag zur Theorie der Geisterkunde. Nebst Anhängen: öffentliche Verhandlungen über Swedenborg und Stilling, ein Beyspiel des Ahnungsvermögens und einen Brief des jüngeren Plinius enthaltend.* Frankfurt am Main: J. C. Hermann.

Nordensköld, August. 1790. "Remarks by Mr. A. N. on the Different Editions of the Bible Made Use of by Emanuel Swedenborg." *New-Jerusalem Magazine* no. 1:87–88.

Oetinger, Friedrich Christoph. 1765. *Swedenborgs und anderer irrdische und himmlische Philosophie zur Prüfung des Besten ans Licht gestellt.* 2 parts. Ed. K.C.E. Ehmann 1858; facsimile reprint as *Swedenborgs irdische und himmlische Philosophie* (ed. E. Beyreuther) in Oetinger, *Sämtliche Schriften* 2. Abt., 2 Bd., J. F. Steinkopf: Stuttgart 1977.

Paracelsus. 1925. *Medizinische, naturwissenschaftliche und philosophische Schriften.* Edited by Karl Sudhoff. Vol. 9, *"Paramirisches" und anderes Schriftwerk der Jahre 1531–1535 aus der Schweiz und Tirol.* München and Planegg: Barth.

Pico della Mirandola, Giovanni. 1942. *De Homine Dignitate, Heptaplus, De Ente et Uno.* Edited by Eugenio Garin. Florence: Vallecchi.

Schäfer, Peter. 1988. "*Shi'ur Qoma*: Rezensionen und Urtext." In *Hekhaloth-Studien.* Tübingen: J.C.B. Mohr (Paul Siebeck).

Schmidt, Sebastian, trans., and Emanuel Swedenborg, annotator. 1872. *Biblia Sacra sive Testamentum Vetus et Novum ex Linguis Originalibus in Linguam Latinam Translatum ad Fidem Exemplaris Annotationibus Emanuelis Svedenborgii Manu Scriptis Locupletati. . . .* Edited by R. L. Tafel. Stockholm: Photolithographic Society.

Scholem, Gershom. 1977. "*Schi'ur Koma*: Die mystische Gestalt der Gottheit." In *Von der mystischen Gestalt der Gottheit: Studien zu Grundbegriffen der Kabbala.* Frankfurt am Main: Suhrkamp. 7–47.

Schuchard, Marsha Keith. 1995. "Yeats and the 'Unknown Superiors': Swedenborg, Falk, and Cagliostro." In *Secret Texts: The Literature of Secret Societies,* edited by Marie Mulvey Roberts and Hugh Ormsby-Lennon. New York: AMS Press. 114–168.

———. 1998. "Leibniz, Benzelius, and the Kabbalistic Roots of Swedish Illuminism." In *Leibniz, Mysticism and Religion,* edited by Allison P. Coudert, Richard H. Popkin, and Gordon M. Weiner. Dordrecht, Boston, London: Kluwer Academic Publishers. 84–106.

———. 1999. "Emanuel Swedenborg: Deciphering the Codes of a Celestial and Terrestrial Intelligencer." In *Rending the Veil: Concealment and Secrecy in the History of Religions,* edited by Elliott R. Wolfson. New York, London: Seven Bridges Press. 177–207.

———. 2001. "Dr. Samuel Jacob Falk: A Sabbatian Adventurer in the Masonic Underground." In *Millenarianism and Messianism in Early Modern European Culture: Jewish Messianism in the Early Modern World,* edited by M. D. Goldish and R. H. Popkin. Dordrecht, Boston, London: Kluwer Academic Publishers. 203–226.

Sjödén, Karl-Erik. 1985. *Swedenborg en France.* Edsbruk: Almqvist & Wiksell.

Swedenborg, Emanuel. 1740–1741. *Oeconomia Regni Animalis in Transactiones Divisa.* 2 vols. Amsterdam: François Changuion. English version: *The Economy of the Animal Kingdom Considered Anatomically, Physically, and Philosophically,* 2 vols., translated by Augustus Clissold, Bryn Athyn, Pa: Swedenborg Scientific Association, 1955. First edition of the English translation: 1845, London: W. Newbery, H. Bailliere.

———. 1749–1756. *Arcana Coelestia, Quae in Scriptura Sacra, seu Verbo Domini Sunt, Detecta.* 8 vols. [London: John Lewis].

———. [1750] 1750. *Arcana Caelestia.* Vol. 2. [Translated by John Marchant]. [London: John Lewis].

———. 1758a. *De Equo Albo, de Quo in Apocalypsi, Cap. XIX: Et Dein de Verbo et Ejus Sensu Spirituali seu Interno, ex Arcanis Coelestibus.* London: [John Lewis].

———. 1758b. *De Telluribus in Mundo Nostro Solari, Quae Vocantur Planetae, et de Telluribus in Coelo Astrifero, deque Illarum Incolis, Tum de Spiritibus et Angelis Ibi: Ex Auditis et Visis.* London: [John Lewis].

———. 1758c. *De Ultimo Judicio, et de Babylonia Destructa: Ita Quod Omnia, Quae in Apocalypsi Praedicta Sunt, Hodie Impleta Sunt: Ex Auditis et Visis.* London: [John Lewis].

———. 1768. *Delitiae Sapientiae de Amore Conjugiali.* Amsterdam.

———. [1758] 1778. *A Treatise Concerning Heaven and Hell.* Translated by William Cookworthy and Thomas Hartley. London: James Phillips.

———. [1758] 1782. *Les merveilles du ciel et de l'enfer et des terres planétaires et astrales.* Translated by Antoine-Joseph Pernety. Berlin: G. J. Decker.

———. [1749–1756] 1783–1806. *Arcana Coelestia: or Heavenly Mysteries.* 12 vols. [Translated by John Clowes]. London: R. Hindmarsh (vols. 1–8), J. Hodson (vols. 9–10), J. and E. Hodson (vols. 11–12).

———. 1784a. *Clavis Hieroglyphica Arcanorum Naturalium et Spiritualium, per Viam Repraesentationum et Correspondentiarum.* London: Robert Hindmarsh.

———. 1784b. *Traité curieux des charmes de l'amour conjugal dans ce monde, et dans l'autre.* Translated by [de] Brumore (Louis Joseph Bernard Philibert de Morveau). Berlin and Basel: George-Jacques and J. Henri Decker.

———. 1786. *La sagesse angélique sur l'amour divin et sur la sagesse divine.* 2 vols. Translated by Antoine-Joseph Pernety. Lyons.

———. 1788. *Abrégé des ouvrages d'Ém. Swédenborg.* Prepared by Jean François D'Aillant de la Touche. Stockholm [Strasbourg]: Exegetical and Philanthropical Society.

———. 1792. *An Hieroglyphic Key to Natural and Spiritual Mysteries, by Way of Representations and Correspondences.* Translated by Robert Hindmarsh. London: R. Hindmarsh.

———. 1821. *Himmelska lönnligheter.* 3 vols. Translated by J. Tybeck and J. A. Sevén. Stockholm: Pro Fide et Charitate. This Swedish translation of *Secrets of Heaven* extended only as far as §3649.

———. 1841–1854. *Arcanes célestes.* 16 vols. Translated by Jean-François-Étienne Le Boys des Guays. Saint-Amand (Cher): Librairie de *La Nouvelle Jérusalem.*

———. 1845–1869. *Himmlische Geheimnisse.* Translated by J.F.I. Tafel. 16 vols. Tübingen: Verlags-Expedition.

———. 1847. *A Hieroglyphic Key to Natural and Spiritual Mysteries, by Way of Representations and Correspondences.* Translated by James John Garth Wilkinson. London: William Newbery, and Boston: Otis Clapp.

———. 1916–1917. "A Hieroglyphic Key to Natural and Spiritual Arcana by Way of Representations and Correspondences." [Translated by Alfred Acton]. *The New Philosophy* 19:305–319; 20:32–52.

———. 1984. "Hieroglyphic Key to Spiritual and Natural Arcana." In *Psychological Transactions and Other Posthumous Tracts 1734–1744.* Translated by Alfred Acton. 2nd ed. Bryn Athyn, Pa.: Swedenborg Scientific Association.

———. 1997. *The Sacred Scripture or Word of the Lord from Experience.* In *Three Short Works,* translated by N. Bruce Rogers. Bryn Athyn, Pa.: General Church of the New Jerusalem.

———. 1998–2002. *Emanuel Swedenborg's Diary, Recounting Spiritual Experiences during the Years 1745 to 1765.* 3 vols. Translated by J. Durban Odhner. Bryn Athyn, Pa.: General Church of the New Jerusalem. The first three volumes, in English, of the six volumes of Swedenborg's Latin work *Experientiae Spirituales,* edited by J. Durban Odhner (Bryn Athyn, Pa.: Academy of the New Church, 1983–1997). Further volumes forthcoming.

———. 2000. *Heaven and Its Wonders and Hell, Drawn from Things Heard and Seen.* Translated by George F. Dole, with an introduction by Bernhard Lang. West Chester, Pa.: Swedenborg Foundation.

———. 2001. *Swedenborg's Dream Diary.* Edited by Lars Bergquist and translated by Anders Hallengren. West Chester, Pa.: Swedenborg Foundation.

Tafel, R. L. 1877. *Documents Concerning the Life and Character of Emanuel Swedenborg.* Vol. 2, parts 1 and 2. London: Swedenborg Society.

Versluis, Arthur. 1999. *Wisdom's Children: A Christian Esoteric Tradition.* Albany: State University of New York Press.

———. 2000. *Wisdom's Book: The Sophia Anthology.* St. Paul, Minn.: Paragon House.

Wilkinson, Lynn R. 1996. *The Dream of an Absolute Language: Emanuel Swedenborg and French Literary Culture.* Albany: State University of New York Press.

Williams, Arnold. 1948. *The Common Expositor: An Account of the Commentaries on Genesis, 1527–1633.* Chapel Hill, N.C.: University of North Carolina Press.

Williams-Hogan, Jane. 1998. "The Place of Emanuel Swedenborg in Modern Western Esotericism." In *Western Esotericism and the Science of Religion: Selected Papers Presented at the 17th Congress of the International Association for the History of Religion, Mexico City 1995,* edited by Antoine Faivre and Wouter J. Hanegraaff. Louvain: Peeters. 201–252.

———. 2000. "Emanuel Swedenborg and the Jewish Kabbalah: Organic or Syncretic Relationship?" Paper presented at the symposium "Western Esotericism and Jewish Mysticism," 18th Quinquennial Congress of the International Association for the History of Religions, Durban, South Africa, August 5–12, 2000.

Woofenden, William Ross. 1992–1993. "Doctrinal Patterns in *Arcana Coelestia.*" *Studia Swedenborgiana* 7(4):31–47; 8(1):49–77; 8(2):29–53; 8(3):43–63.

———. 2002. *Swedenborg Explorer's Guidebook: A Research Manual for Inquiring New Readers, Seekers of Spiritual Ideas, and Writers of Swedenborgian Treatises.* 2nd ed. West Chester, Pa.: Swedenborg Foundation.

Wunsch, William F. 1929. *The World within the Bible: A Handbook to Swedenborg's "Arcana Coelestia."* New York: The New-Church Press., repr. Kessinger publ. n.d.

Short Titles and Other Conventions Used in This Work

MORE detailed information on several of the following points can be found in the translator's preface.

Volume designation *Secrets of Heaven* was originally published in eight volumes; in this edition all but the second original volume have been divided into two. Thus Swedenborg's eight volumes now fill fifteen volumes, of which this is the first. It corresponds to approximately the first half of Swedenborg's volume 1.

Section numbers Following a practice common in his time, Swedenborg divided his published theological works into sections numbered in sequence from beginning to end. His original section numbers have been preserved in this edition; they appear in red boxes in the outside margins. Traditionally, these sections have been referred to as "numbers" and designated by the abbreviation "n." In this edition, however, the more common section symbol (§) is used to designate the section numbers, and the sections are referred to as such.

Subsection numbers Because many sections throughout Swedenborg's works are too long for precise cross-referencing, Swedenborgian scholar John F. Potts (1838–1923) further divided them into subsections; these have since become standard. They are indicated by bracketed numbers that appear in the text itself: [2], [3], and so on. Since the beginning of the first subsection coincides with the beginning of the section, it is not labeled in the text.

Citations of Swedenborg's text As is common in Swedenborgian studies, text citations of Swedenborg's works refer not to page numbers but to section numbers, which are uniform in most editions. In citations the section symbol (§) is generally omitted after the title of a work by Swedenborg. Thus "*Secrets of Heaven* 29" refers to section 29 (§29) of Swedenborg's *Secrets of Heaven*. Subsection numbers are given after a colon; a reference such as "29:2" indicates subsection 2 of section 29. The reference "29:1" would indicate the first subsection of section 29, though that subsection is not in fact labeled in the text.

Citations of the Bible Biblical citations in this edition follow the accepted standard: a semicolon is used between book references and between chapter references, and a comma between verse references. Therefore "Matthew 5:11, 12; 6:1; 10:41, 42; Luke 6:23, 35" refers to Matthew chapter 5, verses 11 and 12; Matthew chapter 6, verse 1; Matthew chapter 10, verses 41 and 42; and Luke chapter 6, verses 23 and 35. Swedenborg often incorporated the numbers of verses not actually represented in his text when listing verse numbers for a passage he quoted; these apparently constitute a kind of "see also" reference to other material he felt was relevant, and are generally retained in this edition without annotation. This edition also follows Swedenborg where he cites contiguous verses individually (for example, John 14:8, 9, 10, 11), rather than as a range (John 14:8–11).

Quotations in Swedenborg The manner in which Swedenborg used the various conventions of quotation in the first edition suggests that he did not feel it necessary to belabor the distinction between direct quotation and paraphrase of the Bible; neither did he mark his omissions from or minor changes to material he quoted, a practice in which this edition generally follows him. One exception consists of those instances in which Swedenborg did not include a complete sentence at the beginning or end of a Bible quotation. The omission in such cases has been marked in this edition with added points of ellipsis.

Italicized terms Any words in indented scriptural extracts that are here set in italics reflect a similar emphasis in the first edition.

Special use of vertical red rule The opening passages of the chapters treating Genesis 1–15, as well as the ends of all chapters, contain material that derives in some way from Swedenborg's experiences in the spiritual world. Swedenborg specified that the text of these passages be set in continuous italics to distinguish it from exegetical and other material. For this edition, the heavy use of italic text was felt to be antithetical to modern tastes, as well as difficult to read, and so such passages are instead marked by a vertical red rule in the margin.

Changes to and insertions in the text This translation is based on the first Latin edition, published by Swedenborg himself. It incorporates the silent emendation of minor errors, not only in the text proper but in Bible verse references. The text has also been changed without notice where the verse numbering of the Latin Bible cited by Swedenborg differs from that of modern English Bibles. Throughout the translation, references or cross-references that are implied but not stated have been inserted in brackets. Unless an endnote indicates otherwise, all square brackets [ ] represent an insertion of material that was not present in the first edition.

Endnotes Comments on the text are printed as endnotes, which are referenced by superscript numbers appearing in the main text. A reverse reference is given in the endnote itself. To find the location of the text treated in endnote 49, for example, the reader would turn back to the indicated section, §30, and the indicated subsection, [2]. The initials of the writer or writers (listed on the title page) are given in square brackets at the end of each note. Translations of material quoted in the endnotes are those of the indicated writer, except where otherwise specified or in cases in which the cited source is a translated text.

Titles of Swedenborg's works References to Swedenborg's writings in this work accord with the short titles listed below, except where other translations are cited by the annotators. In this list, the short title is followed by the traditional translation of the title; by the original Latin title, with its full translation; and finally by the place and date of original publication if Swedenborg published it himself, or the approximate date of writing if he did not. The list is chronological within each of the two groups shown—the published theological works, and the nontheological and posthumously published works. The titles given below as theological works published by Swedenborg are generally not further referenced in lists of works cited in the preface, introduction, and endnotes.

Theological Works Published by Swedenborg

Secrets of Heaven
Traditional title: *Arcana Coelestia*
Original title: *Arcana Coelestia, Quae in Scriptura Sacra, seu Verbo Domini Sunt, Detecta: . . . Una cum Mirabilibus Quae Visa Sunt in Mundo Spirituum, et in Coelo Angelorum* [A Disclosure of Secrets of Heaven Contained in Sacred Scripture, or the Word of the Lord, . . . Together with Amazing Things Seen in the World of Spirits and in the Heaven of Angels]. London: 1749–1756.

Heaven and Hell
Traditional title: *Heaven and Hell*
Original title: *De Coelo et Ejus Mirabilibus, et de Inferno, ex Auditis et Visis* [Heaven and Its Wonders and Hell: Drawn from Things Heard and Seen]. London: 1758.

New Jerusalem
Traditional title: *New Jerusalem and Its Heavenly Doctrine*
Original title: *De Nova Hierosolyma et Ejus Doctrina Coelesti: Ex Auditis e Coelo: Quibus Praemittitur Aliquid de Novo Coelo et Nova Terra* [The New Jerusalem and Its Heavenly Teaching: Drawn from Things Heard from Heaven: Preceded by a Discussion of the New Heaven and the New Earth]. London: 1758.

Last Judgment
Traditional title: *The Last Judgment*
Original title: *De Ultimo Judicio, et de Babylonia Destructa: Ita Quod Omnia, Quae in Apocalypsi Praedicta Sunt, Hodie Impleta Sunt: Ex Auditis et Visis* [The Last Judgment and Babylon Destroyed, Showing That at This Day All the Predictions of the Book of Revelation Have Been Fulfilled: Drawn from Things Heard and Seen]. London: 1758.

White Horse
Traditional title: *The White Horse*
Original title: *De Equo Albo, de Quo in Apocalypsi, Cap. XIX: Et Dein de Verbo et Ejus Sensu Spirituali seu Interno, ex Arcanis Coelestibus* [The White Horse in Revelation Chapter 19, and the Word and Its Spiritual or Inner Sense (from *Secrets of Heaven*)]. London: 1758.

Other Planets
Traditional title: *Earths in the Universe*
Original title: *De Telluribus in Mundo Nostro Solari, Quae Vocantur Planetae, et de Telluribus in Coelo Astrifero, deque Illarum Incolis, Tum de Spiritibus et Angelis Ibi: Ex Auditis et Visis* [Planets or Worlds in Our Solar System, and Worlds in the Starry Heavens, and Their Inhabitants, As Well as the Spirits and Angels There: Drawn from Things Heard and Seen]. London: 1758.

The Lord
Traditional title: *Doctrine of the Lord*
Original title: *Doctrina Novae Hierosolymae de Domino* [Teachings for the New Jerusalem on the Lord]. Amsterdam: 1763.

Sacred Scripture
Traditional title: *Doctrine of the Sacred Scripture*
Original title: *Doctrina Novae Hierosolymae de Scriptura Sacra* [Teachings for the New Jerusalem on Sacred Scripture]. Amsterdam: 1763.

Life
Traditional title: *Doctrine of Life*
Original title: *Doctrina Vitae pro Nova Hierosolyma ex Praeceptis Decalogi* [Teachings about Life for the New Jerusalem: Drawn from the Ten Commandments]. Amsterdam: 1763.

Faith
Traditional title: *Doctrine of Faith*
Original title: *Doctrina Novae Hierosolymae de Fide* [Teachings for the New Jerusalem on Faith]. Amsterdam: 1763.

Supplements
Traditional title: *Continuation Concerning the Last Judgment*
Original title: *Continuatio de Ultimo Judicio: Et de Mundo Spirituali* [Supplements on the Last Judgment and the Spiritual World]. Amsterdam: 1763.

Divine Love and Wisdom
Traditional title: *Divine Love and Wisdom*
Original title: *Sapientia Angelica de Divino Amore et de Divina Sapientia* [Angelic Wisdom about Divine Love and Wisdom]. Amsterdam: 1763.

Divine Providence
Traditional title: *Divine Providence*
Original title: *Sapientia Angelica de Divina Providentia* [Angelic Wisdom about Divine Providence]. Amsterdam: 1764.

Revelation Unveiled
Traditional title: *Apocalypse Revealed*
Original title: *Apocalypsis Revelata, in Qua Deteguntur Arcana Quae Ibi Praedicta Sunt, et Hactenus Recondita Latuerunt* [The Book of Revelation Unveiled, Uncovering the Secrets That Were Foretold There and Have Lain Hidden until Now]. Amsterdam: 1766.

Marriage Love
Traditional title: *Conjugial Love*
Original title: *Delitiae Sapientiae de Amore Conjugiali: Post Quas Sequuntur Voluptates Insaniae de Amore Scortatorio* [Wisdom's Delight in Marriage Love: Followed by Insanity's Pleasure in Promiscuous Love]. Amsterdam: 1768.

Survey
Traditional title: *Brief Exposition*
Original title: *Summaria Expositio Doctrinae Novae Ecclesiae, Quae per Novam Hierosolymam in Apocalypsi Intelligitur* [Survey of Teachings for the New Church Meant by the New Jerusalem in the Book of Revelation]. Amsterdam: 1769.

Soul-Body Interaction
Traditional title: *Intercourse between the Soul and Body*
Original title: *De Commercio Animae et Corporis, Quod Creditur Fieri vel per Influxum Physicum, vel per Influxum Spiritualem, vel per Harmoniam Praestabilitam* [Soul-Body Interaction, Believed to Occur either by a Physical Inflow, or by a Spiritual Inflow, or by a Preestablished Harmony]. London: 1769.

True Christianity
Traditional title: *True Christian Religion*
Original title: *Vera Christiana Religio, Continens Universam Theologiam Novae Ecclesiae a Domino apud Danielem Cap. VII:13–14, et in Apocalypsi Cap. XXI:1, 2 Praedictae* [True Christianity: Containing a Comprehensive Theology of the New Church That Was Predicted by the Lord in Daniel 7:13–14 and Revelation 21:1, 2]. Amsterdam: 1771.

Nontheological and Posthumously Published Works by Swedenborg Cited in This Volume

Philosophical and Metallurgical Works
Traditional title: *Principia*
Original title: *Principia Rerum Naturalium sive Novorum Tentaminum Phaenomena Mundi Elementaris Philosophice Explicandi* [Basic Principles of Nature or of New Attempts to Explain Philosophically the Phenomena of the Natural World]. 3 vols. Dresden and Leipzig: 1734.

Dynamics of the Soul's Domain
Traditional title: *Economy of the Animal Kingdom*
Original title: *Oeconomia Regni Animalis in Transactiones Divisa* [Dynamics of the Soul's Domain, Divided into Treatises]. 2 vols. Amsterdam: 1740–1741.

Quotations on Various Philosophical and Theological Topics
Traditional title: *A Philosopher's Note Book*
Original title: [Untitled]. Written around 1741.

Draft on Sensation
Traditional title: *Sensation*
Original title: *De Sensatione, seu de Corporis Passione* [On Sensation, or the Passive Organs of the Body]. Written before or during 1742

Draft of a Rational Psychology
Traditional title: *Rational Psychology*
Original title: [Untitled]. Written before or during 1742.

Draft on the Fiber
Traditional title: *The Fiber*
Original title: [Untitled]. Written around 1742.

Draft of a Hieroglyphic Key
Traditional title: *Hieroglyphic Key*
Original title: *Clavis Hieroglyphica Arcanorum Naturalium et Spiritualium per Viam Representationum et Correspondentiarum* [A Hieroglyphic Key to the Secrets of Material and Spiritual Things by Way of Representations and Correspondences]. Written around 1742.

Journal of Dreams
Traditional title: *Journal of Dreams*
Original title: [Untitled]. Written between July 1743 and December 1744.

Draft on the Five Senses
Traditional title: *The Five Senses*
Original title: [Untitled]. Written before or during July 1744.

The Soul's Domain
Traditional title: *The Animal Kingdom*
Original title: *Regnum Animale, Anatomice, Physice, et Philosophice Perlustratum* [The Soul's Domain Thoroughly Examined by Means of Anatomy, Physics, and Philosophy]. 3 vols. The Hague, London: 1744–1745.

Worship and Love of God
Traditional title: *Worship and Love of God*
Original title: *Pars Prima de Cultu et Amore Dei; Ubi Agitur de Telluris Ortu, Paradiso, et Vivario, Tum de Primogeniti seu Adami Nativitate, Infantia, et Amore. Pars Secunda de Cultu et Amore Dei; Ubi Agitur de Conjugio Primogeniti seu Adami, et Inibi de Anima, Mente Intellectuali, Statu Integritatis, et Imagine Dei. Pars Tertia, de Vita Conjugii Paris Primogeniti.* [Part 1: Concerning the Worship and Love of God; In Which Is Discussed the Earth's Origin, Paradise, and the Garden, and Then the Birth

of the Firstborn, or Adam, His Infancy, and Love. Part 2: Concerning the Worship and Love of God; In Which Is Discussed the Marriage of the Firstborn, or Adam, and Therein the Soul, the Understanding Mind, the State of Wholeness, and the Image of God. Part 3: Concerning the Life of the Firstborn Married Couple]. London: 1745.

Notes on the Creation Story
Traditional title: *History of Creation*
Original title: *In Nomine Domini. Historia Creationis a Mose Tradita. Ex Smidio et ex Castellione* [In the Name of the Lord. The Creation Story Passed Down by Moses. Based on Schmidt and Castellio]. Written during summer 1745.

Passages on the Coming Messiah
Traditional title: *The Messiah About to Come*
Original title: *De Messia Venturo in Mundum* [On the Messiah Who Is Going to Come into the World]. Written before or during November 1745.

The Old Testament Explained
Traditional title: *The Word Explained*
Original title: *Explicatio in Verbum Historicum Veteris Testamenti* [The Historical Word of the Old Testament Explained]. Written from November 1745 to February 1747.

Spiritual Experiences
Traditional title: *The Spiritual Diary*
Original title: *Experientiae Spirituales* [Spiritual Experiences]. Written from 1745 to 1765.

Revelation Explained
Traditional title: *Apocalypse Explained*
Original title: *Apocalypsis Explicata secundum Sensum Spiritualem, Ubi Revelantur Arcana, Quae Ibi Praedicta, et Hactenus Recondita Fuerunt* [The Book of Revelation Explained as to Its Spiritual Meaning, Which Reveals Secret Wonders That Were Predicted There and Have Been Hidden until Now]. Written from 1758 to 1759.

Draft of "Sacred Scripture"
Traditional title: *De Verbo*
Original title: *De Scriptura Sacra seu Verbo Domini ab Experientia* [On Sacred Scripture, or the Word of the Lord, from Experience]. Written around 1762.

Biblical Titles

Swedenborg refers to the Hebrew Scriptures as the Old Testament and to the Greek Scriptures as the New Testament; his terminology has been adopted in this edition. As was the custom in his day, he refers to the Pentateuch (Genesis, Exodus, Leviticus, Numbers, and Deuteronomy) as the books of Moses, or simply as "Moses"; for example, in §218 he writes "in Moses we read the following" and then quotes a passage from Exodus. Similarly, in sentences or phrases introducing quotations he sometimes refers to the Psalms as "David," to Lamentations as "Jeremiah," and to the Gospel of John, the Epistles of John, and the Book of Revelation as simply "John." References given in parentheses after the quotations specify their sources.

Secrets
of
Heaven

First seek God's kingdom and its justice
and you will gain all.

—Matthew 6:33

[Author's Table of Contents]

THE "secrets[1] of heaven" that have been disclosed to us in Sacred Scripture, or the Lord's Word,[2] can be found in the exposition of the Word's inner meaning. To learn about the nature of this meaning, see what my experience has shown in §§1767–1777 and 1869–1879; and see too what appears in the body of the text in §§1–5, 64, 65, 66, 167, 605, 920, 937, 1143, 1224, 1404, 1405, 1408, 1409, 1502 at the end, 1540, 1659, 1756, 1783, 1807.

Accounts of the wonders I have seen in the world of spirits and in the heaven of angels[3] are appended at the beginning and end of each chapter. In this first volume they are as follows:[4]

1.	Our resurrection from death and entry into eternal life	§§168–181
2.	Our entry, once revived, into eternal life (continued)	182–189
3.	Our entry into eternal life (continued)	314–319
4.	What the life of the soul or spirit is then like	320–323
5.	Several examples from spirits of opinions they adopted during their physical lives concerning the soul or spirit	443–448
6.	Heaven and heavenly joy	449–459
7.	Heaven and heavenly joy (continued)	537–546
8.	Heaven and heavenly joy (continued)	547–553
9.	The communities that make up heaven	684–691
10.	Hell	692–700
11.	The hells of those who spent their lives in hatred, revenge, and cruelty	814–823
12.	The hells of those who spent their lives in adultery and lechery; in addition, the hells of deceivers and witches	824–831
13.	Misers' hells; the foul Jerusalem and outlaws in the wilderness; and the feces-laden hells of those who have pursued sensual pleasure alone	938–946
14.	A different set of hells than those already mentioned	947–970
15.	Spiritual devastation	1106–1113
16.	The earliest church, called "humankind," or Adam	1114–1129
17.	The pre-Flood people who died out	1265–1272

18. Location in the "universal human";[5] in addition, place
    and distance in the other life 1273–1278
19. Location and place in the other life; distance and time
    there as well (continued) 1376–1382
20. The ability of spirits and angels to perceive things; auras
    in the other life 1383–1400
21. Perception and auras in the other life (continued) 1504–1520
22. The light in which angels live 1521–1534
23. The light in which angels live (continued); their
    magnificent gardens and their dwellings 1619–1633
24. The way spirits and angels talk 1634–1650
25. The way spirits talk (continued) and how it varies 1757–1764
26. Sacred Scripture, or the Word, which conceals a divine
    message that lies open to the view of good spirits and
    angels 1767–1777
27. Sacred Scripture or the Word (continued) 1869–1879
    General information about spirits and angels 1880–1885

Genesis

1

THE Word in the Old Testament[6] contains secrets of heaven, and every single aspect of it has to do with the Lord,[7] his heaven, the church, faith, and all the tenets of faith; but not a single person sees this in the letter. In the letter, or literal meaning, people see only that it deals for the most part with the external facts of the Jewish religion.

The truth is, however, that every part of the Old Testament holds an inner message.[8] Except at a very few points, those inner depths never show on the surface. The exceptions are concepts that the Lord revealed and explained to the apostles, such as the fact that the sacrifices symbolize the Lord,[9] and that the land of Canaan and Jerusalem symbolize heaven (which is why it is called the heavenly Canaan or Jerusalem [Galatians 4:26; Hebrews 11:16; 12:22; Revelation 21:2, 10]), as does Paradise.[10]

2

The Christian world, though, remains deeply ignorant of the fact that each and every detail down to the smallest—even down to the tiniest jot[11]—enfolds and symbolizes spiritual and heavenly matters; and because it lacks such knowledge, it also lacks much interest in the Old Testament.

Still, Christians can come to a proper understanding if they reflect on a single notion: that since the Word is the Lord's and comes from him, it could not possibly exist unless it held within it the kinds of things that have to do with heaven, the church, and faith. Otherwise it could not be called the Lord's Word, nor could it be said to contain any life.[12] Where, after all, does life come from if not from what is living? That is, if not from the fact that every single thing in the Word relates to the Lord, who is truly life itself? Whatever does not look to him at some deeper level, then, is without life; in fact, if a single expression in the Word does not embody or reflect him in its own way, it is not divine.

[3] Without this interior life, the Word in its letter is dead. It resembles a human being, in that a human has an outward self and an inward one, as the Christian world knows.[13] The outer being, separated from the inner, is just a body and so is dead, but the inward being is what lives and allows the outward being to live.[14] The inner being is a person's soul.

In the same way, the letter of the Word by itself is a body without a soul.

[4] The Word's literal meaning alone, when it monopolizes our thinking, can never provide a view of the inner contents. Take for example this first chapter of Genesis. The literal meaning by itself offers no clue that it is speaking of anything but the world's creation, the Garden of Eden (Paradise), and Adam, the first human ever created.[15] Who supposes anything else?

The wisdom hidden in these details (and never before revealed) will be clear enough from what follows. The inner sense of the first chapter of Genesis deals in general with the process that creates us anew—that is to say, with regeneration—and in particular with the very earliest church;[16] and it does so in such a way that not even the smallest syllable fails to represent, symbolize, and incorporate this meaning.[17]

[5] But without the Lord's aid not a soul can possibly see that this is the case. As a result, it is proper to reveal in these preliminaries that the Lord in his divine mercy has granted me the opportunity for several years now, without break or interruption, to keep company with spirits and angels, to hear them talking, and to speak with them in turn.[18] Consequently I have been able to see and hear the most amazing things in the other life, which have never before come into people's awareness or thought.

In that world I have been taught about the different kinds of spirits, the situation of souls after death, hell (or the regrettable state of the faithless), and heaven (or the blissful state of the faithful). In particular I have learned what is taught in the faith acknowledged by the whole of heaven. All of these topics will, with the Lord's divine mercy, be explored further in what follows.

Genesis 1

1. In the beginning, God created heaven and earth.[19]
2. And the earth was void and emptiness; and there was darkness on the face[20] of the abyss. And the Spirit of God was constantly moving on the face of the water.
3. And God said, "Let there be light," and there was light.
4. And God saw the light, that it was good; and God made a distinction between light and darkness.
5. And God called the light day, and the darkness he called night. And there was evening and there was morning, the first day.
6. And God said, "Let there be an expanse in the middle of the waters, and let it exist to make a distinction among the waters, in the waters."
7. And God made the expanse, and he made a distinction between the waters that were under the expanse and the waters that were over the expanse; and so it was done.
8. And God called the expanse heaven. And there was evening and there was morning, the second day.
9. And God said, "Let the waters under heaven be gathered into one place, and let dry land appear," and so it was done.
10. And God called the dry land earth, and the gathering of waters he called seas. And God saw that it was good.
11. And God said, "Let the earth cause the sprouting on the earth of the tender plant, of the plant bearing its seed, of the fruit tree making the fruit that holds its seed, each in the way of its kind," and so it was done.
12. And the earth produced the tender plant, the plant bearing its seed in the way of its kind, and the tree making the fruit that held its seed in the way of its kind, and God saw that it was good.
13. And there was evening and there was morning, the third day.
14. And God said, "Let there be lights in the expanse of the heavens to make a distinction between day and night; and they will act as signals and will be used for seasons for both the days and the years.
15. And they will act as lights in the expanse of the heavens to shed light on the earth"; and so it was done.
16. And God made the two great lights: the greater light to rule by day and the smaller light to rule by night; and the stars.
17. And God placed them in the expanse of the heavens, to shed light on the earth,
18. and to rule during the day and during the night, and to make a distinction between light and darkness; and God saw that it was good.

19. And there was evening and there was morning, the fourth day.

20. And God said, "Let the waters cause the creeping animal—a living soul—to creep out. And let the bird flit over the land, over the face of the expanse of the heavens."

21. And God created the big sea creatures, and every living, creeping soul that the waters caused to creep out, in all their kinds, and every bird on the wing, of every kind. And God saw that it was good.

22. And God blessed them, saying, "Reproduce and multiply and fill the water in the seas, and the birds will multiply on the land."

23. And there was evening and there was morning, the fifth day.

24. And God said, "Let the earth produce each living soul according to its kind: the beast, and that which moves, and the wild animal of the earth, each according to its kind"; and so it was done.

25. And God made each wild animal of the earth according to its kind, and each beast according to its kind, and every animal creeping on the ground according to its kind; and God saw that it was good.

26. And God said, "Let us make a human in our image, after our likeness; and these[21] will rule over the fish of the sea and over the bird in the heavens, and over the beast, and over all the earth, and over every creeping animal that creeps on the earth."

27. And God created the human in his image; in God's image he created them; male and female he created them.

28. And God blessed them, and God said to them, "Reproduce and multiply, and fill the earth and harness it, and rule over the fish of the sea and over the bird in the heavens and over every living animal creeping on the earth."

29. And God said, "Here, now, I am giving you every seed-bearing plant on the face of all the earth and every tree that has fruit; the tree that produces seed will serve you for food.

30. And every wild animal of the earth and every bird in the heavens and every animal creeping on the earth, in which there is a living soul—every green plant will serve them for nourishment." And so it was done.

31. And God saw all that he had done and, yes, it was very good. And there was evening and there was morning, the sixth day.

Summary

6 THE six days or time periods, meaning so many consecutive stages in a person's regeneration, are these, in outline:

The first stage is preliminary, extending from infancy to just before regeneration, and is called void, emptiness, and darkness. The first stirring, which is the Lord's mercy, is the Spirit of God in constant motion on the face of the water.

In the second stage, a distinction is drawn between the things that are the Lord's and those that are our own. The things that are the Lord's are called a "remnant" in the Word.[22] In this instance the "remnant" refers principally to religious knowledge acquired from early childhood on. This remnant is stored away, not to reappear until we arrive at such a stage.

At present the second stage rarely comes into play without trouble, misfortune, and grief, which enable bodily and worldly concerns—things that are our own—to fade away and in effect die out.[23] The things that belong to the outer self, then, are separated from those that belong to the inner self, the inner self containing the remnant that the Lord has put aside to await this time and this purpose.

The third stage is one of repentance. During this time, at the prompting of the inner self, we speak devoutly and reverently and yield a good harvest (acts of neighborly kindness, for instance). These effects are lifeless nonetheless, since we suppose that they come of our own doing. They are called the tender plant, then the seed-bearing plant, and lastly the fruit tree.

In the fourth stage, love stirs and faith enlightens us. Before this time we may have spoken devoutly and yielded a good harvest, but we did so in a state of trial and anguish, not at the call of faith and kindness. In consequence they are now kindled in our inner self and are called the two lights.

In the fifth stage, we *speak* with conviction and, in the process, strengthen ourselves in truth and goodness. The things we then produce have life in them and are called the fish of the sea and the birds in the heavens.

In the sixth stage, we *act* with conviction and therefore with love in speaking truth and doing good. What we then produce is called a living soul and a beast. Because we begin to act as much from love as from conviction, we become spiritual people, who are called [God's] image.

In regard to our *spiritual* lives, we now find pleasure and nourishment in religious knowledge and acts of kindness; and these are called our food. In regard to our *earthly* lives, we still find pleasure and sustenance in things relating to our body and our senses, which cause strife until love takes charge and we develop a heavenly character.

Not everyone who undergoes regeneration reaches this stage. Some (the great majority, these days) arrive only at the first stage, some only at the second, some at the third, fourth, or fifth, very few at the sixth, and almost no one at the seventh.²⁴

Inner Meaning

14 FROM this point on, the term *Lord* is used in only one way: to refer to the Savior of the world, Jesus Christ; and the name "Lord" is used without any additions.

He is acknowledged and revered as Lord throughout heaven because he possesses all power in heaven and on earth.

He also commanded this when he said, "You address me as 'Lord.' You speak correctly, because so I am" (John 13:13). And his disciples called him Lord after the resurrection.²⁵

15 In the whole of heaven no one knows of any other Father than the Lord, since the Father and the Lord are one. As he himself said:

"I am the way and the truth and life." Philip says, "Show us your Father." Jesus says to him, "After all the time I've spent with you, don't you know me, Philip? Whoever has seen me has seen my Father. How then can you say, 'Show us your Father'? Don't you believe that I am in my Father and my Father is in me? Believe me, that I am in my Father and my Father is in me." (John 14:6, 8, 9, 10, 11)

16 Genesis 1:1. *In the beginning, God created heaven and earth.*

The word *beginning* is being used for the very earliest times. The prophets frequently call them "the days of old."²⁶

"The beginning" includes the first period of regeneration too, as that is when people are being born anew and receiving life. Because of this, regeneration itself is called our new creation [2 Corinthians 5:17; Galatians 6:15]. Almost everywhere in the prophetic books, the words *creating, forming,* and *making* stand for regenerating, though with differences.²⁷ In Isaiah, for example:

All have been called by my name, and I have created them for my glory; I have formed them; yes, I have made them. (Isaiah 43:7)

This is why the Lord is called Redeemer, One-Who-Forms-from-the-Womb, Maker, and Creator, as in the same prophet:

I am Jehovah,[28] your Holy One, the Creator of Israel, your Monarch. (Isaiah 43:15)

In David:[29]

The people created will praise Jah.[30] (Psalms 102:18)

In the same author:

You send out your spirit—they will continue to be created—and you renew the face of the ground.[31] (Psalms 104:30)

Heaven, or the sky, symbolizes the inner self, and the *earth,* before regeneration occurs, symbolizes the outer self, as may be seen below [§§17, 24:3, 27].

Genesis 1:2. *And the earth was void and emptiness, and there was darkness on the face of the abyss, and the Spirit of God was constantly moving on the face of the water.*

Before regeneration a person is called the *void, empty earth,* and also soil in which no seed of goodness or truth has been planted.[32] *Void* refers to an absence of goodness and *empty* to an absence of truth. The result is *darkness,* in which a person is oblivious to or ignorant of anything having to do with faith in the Lord and consequently with a spiritual or heavenly life. The Lord portrays such a person this way in Jeremiah:

My people are dense; they do not know me. They are stupid children, without understanding. They are wise in doing evil but do not know how to do good. I looked at the *earth,* and there—void and emptiness; and to the *heavens,* and these had no light. (Jeremiah 4:22, 23, 25)

The *face of the abyss* means our cravings and the falsities these give rise to; we are wholly made up of cravings and falsities and wholly surrounded by them. Because no ray of light is in us, we are like an abyss, or something disorganized and dim.

Many passages in the Word also call such people abysses and sea depths, which are drained (that is, devastated) before a person is regenerated. In Isaiah, for instance:

Wake up, as in the days of old, the generations of eternity! Are you not draining the sea, the waters of the great abyss, and making the depths of the sea a path for the redeemed to cross? May those ransomed by Jehovah return! (Isaiah 51:9, 10, 11)

An individual of this type, observed from heaven, looks like a dark mass with no life at all to it.[33]

The same words involve an individual's overall spiritual devastation—a preliminary step to regeneration.[34] (The prophets have much more to say about it.)[35] Before we can learn what is true and be affected by what is good, the things that stand in the way and resist have to be put aside. The old self must die before the new self can be conceived.[36]

19 The *Spirit of God* stands for the Lord's mercy, which is portrayed as *moving constantly*, like a hen brooding over her eggs. What is being brooded over in this instance is what the Lord stores away in us, which throughout the Word is called "a remnant" [or "survivors"].[37] It is a knowledge of truth and goodness, which can never emerge into the light of day until our outer nature has been devastated. Such knowledge is here called the *face of the water*.

20 Genesis 1:3. *And God said, "Let there be light," and there was light.*

The first step is taken when we begin to realize that goodness and truth are something transcendent.

People who focus exclusively on externals do not even know what is good or what is true; everything connected with self-love and love of worldly advantages[38] they consider good, and anything that promotes those two loves they consider true. They are unaware that such "goodness" is evil and such "truth" false.

When we are conceived anew, however, we first begin to be aware that our "good" is not good. And as we advance further into the light, it dawns on us that the Lord exists and that he is goodness and truth itself.

The Lord says in John that we need to know of his existence:

Unless you believe that I am, you will die in your sins. (John 8:24)

We need to know too that the Lord is goodness itself, or life, and truth itself, or light, and consequently that nothing good or true exists that does not come from him. This is also found in John:

In the beginning there was the Word, and the Word was present with God, and the Word was God. Everything was made by him, and nothing that was made was made without him. In him was life, and the life was the light of humankind; but the light appears in the darkness. He was the true light that shines on every person coming into the world. (John 1:1, 3, 4, [5,] 9)

21 Genesis 1:4, 5. *And God saw the light, that it was good, and God made a distinction between light and darkness. And God called the light day, and the darkness he called night.*

The *light* is said to be *good* because it is from the Lord, who is goodness itself.

The *darkness* is whatever looked like light to us before our new conception and birth, because we saw evil as good and falsity as truth; but it is actually darkness—our lingering sense of self-sufficiency.

Absolutely everything that is the Lord's is compared to the day, because it belongs to the light, and everything that is our own is compared to the night, because it belongs to the darkness. The Word draws this comparison in quite a few places.[39]

22 Genesis 1:5. *And there was evening and there was morning, the first day.*

From this we now see what evening and morning mean. *Evening* is every preliminary stage, because such stages are marked by shadow, or by falsity and an absence of faith. *Morning* is all later stages, because these are marked by light, or by truth and religious knowledge.

Evening stands in general for everything that is our own, while morning stands for everything of the Lord's. As David says, for example:

> The Spirit of Jehovah has spoken in me and his words are on my tongue. The God of Israel has said, the rock of Israel has spoken to me. He is like the morning light when the sun rises, like a morning when there are no clouds, when because of the brightness, because of the rain, the tender grass springs from the earth. (2 Samuel 23:2, 3, 4)

Since evening is when there is no faith and morning is when there *is* faith, the Lord's coming into the world is called morning. The period in which he came, being a time of no faith, is called evening. In Daniel:

> The Holy One said to me, "Up till [the day's second] evening, when it becomes morning,[40] two thousand and three hundred times." (Daniel 8:14, 26)

Morning in the Word is similarly taken to mean every coming of the Lord, so that it is a word for being created anew.

23 Nothing is more common in the Word than for a *day* to be understood as meaning the times, as in Isaiah:

> The day of Jehovah is near. Look—the day of Jehovah is coming! I will shake heaven, and the earth will tremble right out of its place, on the

day when my anger blazes up. The time of his coming is near, and its days[41] will not be postponed. (Isaiah 13:6, 9, 13, 22)

In the same prophet:

In the days of old she was old. It will happen on that day that Tyre will be forgotten for seventy years, corresponding to the days of one king. (Isaiah 23:7, 15)

Because a day stands for a time period, it is also taken to mean the state we are in during that period, as in Jeremiah:

Doom to us! For the day has faded, for the shadows of evening have lengthened. (Jeremiah 6:4)

In the same prophet:

If you nullify my compact with the day and my compact with the night, so that there is no daytime or night at their times . . . (Jeremiah 33:20, 25)

And again:

Renew our days as in ancient times. (Lamentations 5:21)[42]

24. Genesis 1:6. *And God said, "Let there be an expanse in the middle of the waters, and let it exist to make a distinction among the waters, in the waters."*

The next step occurs after the Spirit of God—the Lord's mercy—brings out into daylight the knowledge of truth and goodness and provides the first glimmering that the Lord exists, that he is goodness and truth itself, and that nothing is good or true except what comes from him. The Spirit of God then *makes a distinction* between the inner and the outer being, and between the religious knowledge we possess in our inner selves and the secular knowledge belonging to our outer selves.

The inner self is called the *expanse,* the knowledge in the inner self is called the *waters over the expanse,* and the facts belonging to the outer self are called *the waters under the expanse.*

[2] Before we are reborn, we do not know even that an inner being exists, let alone what it is, imagining there is no difference between the two selves. This is because we are absorbed by bodily and worldly interests and merge the concerns of the inner being with those interests. Out of distinct and separate planes we make one dim, confused whole.

Therefore this verse first says that there should be an expanse in the middle of the waters, then that it should exist to make a distinction "among the waters, in the waters," but not that it should make a distinction between one set of waters and another. The next verse says that.

[3] Genesis 1:7, 8. *And God made the expanse, and he made a distinction between the waters that were under the expanse and the waters that were over the expanse, and so it was done; and God called the expanse heaven.*

The second thing we begin to notice while being reborn, then, is that the inner self exists. We become aware that the attributes of the inner self are good feelings and true ideas, which are the Lord's alone.

While we are being reborn, our outer self is such that it still believes we are acting on our own when we do what is good and speaking on our own when we speak what is true. The Lord uses those things—allowing them to seem like our own, since such is our mind-set—to lead us to doing what is good and speaking what is true. Consequently we first learn to distinguish what is *under the expanse;* only then do we learn to distinguish what is *over the expanse.*

Another secret from heaven is that the Lord leads us by means of things that really are our own—both the illusions of our senses and our cravings—but diverts us toward things that are true and good. So every single moment of regeneration carries us forward from evening to morning, just as it takes us from the outer self to the inner, or from earth to heaven. This is why the expanse (the inner self) is now called *heaven.*

Spreading out the earth[43] *and stretching out the heavens* is a customary formula used by the prophets when they speak of our regeneration. In Isaiah, for example:

> This is what Jehovah has said, your Redeemer and the one who formed you from the womb: "I am Jehovah, making all things, stretching *the heavens* out on my own and spreading *the earth* out by myself." (Isaiah 44:24)

Again, where the Lord's Coming is spoken of openly:

> A crushed reed he does not break, and smoldering flax he does not quench; he propels judgment toward truth. [In other words, he does not break our illusions or extinguish our cravings but bends them toward truth and goodness. It continues:][44] God Jehovah creates *the heavens* and stretches them out. He spreads out *the earth* and the things it produces. He gives a soul to the people on it and spirit to everyone walking on it. (Isaiah 42:3, 4, 5)[45]

Several other places could be cited as well.[46]

26 Genesis 1:8. *And there was evening and there was morning, the second day.*

The meanings of *evening, morning,* and *day* are explained above at verse 5 [§§22–23].

27 Genesis 1:9. *And God said, "Let the waters under heaven be gathered into one place, and let dry land appear"; and so it was done.*

When we learn that we have an inner self and an outer, and that truth and goodness come from the inner self—or rather from the Lord by way of the inner self into the outer, even though this is contrary to appearances—this information, this knowledge of truth and goodness, is stored away in our memory. The knowledge takes its place among the secular facts we have learned, because anything instilled in our outward memory, whether earthly, spiritual, or heavenly, lodges there as a fact, and from there the Lord draws on it.

This knowledge is the *waters gathered into one place* and named seas. The outer being itself, on the other hand, is called *dry land*. Immediately afterward it is called earth, as the next verse shows.

28 Genesis 1:10. *And God called the dry land earth, and the gathering of waters he called seas; and God saw that it was good.*

To find *waters* symbolizing religious and secular knowledge, and *seas* symbolizing a body of such knowledge, is quite common in the Word. In Isaiah:

> The earth will be full with the awareness of Jehovah, like the waters covering the sea. (Isaiah 11:9)

In the same prophet, where both kinds of knowledge are portrayed as lacking:

> The water will disappear from the sea, the river will drain away and dry up, and the streams will recede. (Isaiah 19:5, 6)

In Haggai, where a new church is the subject:

> I am shaking *the heavens* and *the earth,* and the sea and the dry land; and I will shake all the nations, and those who are the desire of every nation will come, and I will fill this House[47] with glory. (Haggai 2:6, 7)

And in Zechariah, on the regenerating individual:

> That will be a single day; it is known to Jehovah; it is not *day* or night. And it will happen that at the time of *evening* there will be light. And it will happen on that day that living water will go out from Jerusalem,

part of it to the eastern sea and part of it to the western sea.[48] (Zechariah 14:7, 8)

In a passage in David depicting a devastated person who is being reborn and will come to revere the Lord:

Jehovah does not despise his prisoners; *the heavens* and *the earth,* the seas and every creeping thing in them will praise him. (Psalms 69:33, 34)

In the following passage in Zechariah, the *earth* symbolizes that which receives something put into it:

Jehovah is stretching out *the heavens* and founding *the earth* and forming the human spirit in the middle of it. (Zechariah 12:1)

Genesis 1:11, 12. *And God said, "Let the earth cause the sprouting on the earth of the tender plant, of the plant bearing its seed, of the fruit tree making the fruit that holds its seed, each in the way of its kind"; and so it was done. And the earth produced the tender plant, the plant bearing its seed in the way of its kind, and the tree making the fruit that held its seed in the way of its kind. And God saw that it was good.*

When the *earth* (a person) is so well prepared as to be able to accept heavenly seed from the Lord and to produce good and truth in some degree, that is the time when the Lord first *causes the sprouting* of something tender, called the *tender plant* or grass. Next he stimulates something more useful that reseeds itself—the *plant bearing its seed.* Finally he germinates something good, which reproduces fruitfully—the *tree making the fruit that holds its seed,* each of these *in the way of its kind.*

During regeneration we naturally suppose at first that the good we do and the truth we speak come from ourselves, when the reality is that all good and truth come from the Lord. If we imagine they come from ourselves, then, we are not yet in possession of the life force belonging to true faith (although we can receive it later). We cannot believe yet that they come from the Lord, because we are being prepared to receive the living power of faith. This stage is represented in the story by things that have no living soul; animate creatures represent the stage of living faith to come.

[2] The Lord is the sower of seeds, the *seed* is his Word, and the *earth* is the human being, as he saw fit to say in Matthew 13:19–23, 37, 38, 39; Mark 4:14–20; and Luke 8:11–15. A similar description:

So God's kingdom is like one who tosses seed into the earth and sleeps and rises night and day, and the seed sprouts and grows; how it happens,

> the person does not know. For the earth bears fruit readily—first a shoot, then an ear, then the full grain in the ear. (Mark 4:26, 27, 28)

"God's kingdom" in its broadest sense means the whole of heaven. Less broadly it means the Lord's true church. In its narrow sense it refers to everyone with true faith, which is to say, all who become reborn by living out their faith. Each of these people is also called a heaven (since they have heaven in them) and God's kingdom (since they have God's kingdom in them). The Lord himself teaches this in Luke:

> Jesus was asked by the Pharisees, "When is God's kingdom coming?" He answered them and said, "God's kingdom does not come in an observable way, nor will they say, 'Look here!' or 'Look there!' because—look!—God's kingdom is within you." (Luke 17:20, 21)

This is the third step in our regeneration and the stage at which we repent. The process continues to advance from shadow to light, from evening to morning, and so it says:

[3] Genesis 1:13. *And there was evening and there was morning, the third day.*

30 Genesis 1:14, 15, 16, 17. *And God said, "Let there be lights in the expanse of the heavens to make a distinction between day and night; and they will act as signals and will be used for seasons for both the days and the years. And they will be lights in the expanse of the heavens, to shed light on the earth," and so it was done. And God made two great lights: the greater light to rule by day and the smaller light to rule by night; and the stars. And God placed them in the expanse of the heavens, to shed light on the earth.*

We cannot understand the identity of these great lights very well unless we first know what the essence of faith is and how it develops in those who are being created anew.

The actual essence and life of faith is the Lord alone. No one who lacks faith in the Lord can have life, as he himself said in John:

> Those who believe in the Son have eternal life, but those who do not believe in the Son will not see life; instead, God's anger will rest on them. (John 3:36)

[2] The progress of faith in those who are being created anew is as follows. Initially such people are without any life, as no life exists in evil or falsity, only in goodness and truth. Afterward they receive life from the Lord through faith. The first form of faith to bring life is a memorized

thing—a matter of fact. The next is faith in the intellect—faith truly understood. The last is faith in the heart, which is faith born of love, or saving faith.

In verses 3–13 the things that had no living soul represent factual faith and faith truly understood. Faith brought alive by love, however, is represented by the animate creatures in verses 20–25. Consequently this is the point at which love and the faith that rises out of it are first dealt with, and they are called *lights*. Love is the *greater light* that *rules by day;* faith springing from love is the *smaller light* that *rules by night*.[49] And because they must unite as one, the verb used with "lights" is singular, "let it be" rather than "let them be."[50]

[3] Love and faith work the same way in our inner being as warmth and light work in our outer flesh and are therefore represented by warmth and light. This is why the lights are said to be *placed in the expanse of the heavens,* or our inner being, the greater light in our will and the smaller in our intellect.[51] But they only seem to be present there, just as the light of the sun only appears to be in physical objects. It is the Lord's mercy alone that stirs our will with love and our intellect with truth or faith.

The fact that the *great lights* symbolize love and faith and that they are named sun, moon, and stars can be seen in many places in the prophets. In Ezekiel, for instance:

> When I blot you out I will cover *the heavens* and black out their stars; the sun I will cover with a cloud, and the moon will not make its light shine. All the lamps of light in the heavens I will black out above you, and I will bring shadow over your *land*.[52] (Ezekiel 32:7, 8)

This passage is directed at Pharaoh and the Egyptians. In the Word, these people stand for sensory evidence and factual information, and the idea here is that they used both things to blot out love and faith. In Isaiah:

> The day of Jehovah [comes] to make *the earth* a desolation, since neither the stars of the heavens nor their Orions[53] will shine their light. The sun has been shadowed over in its emergence, and the moon will not radiate its light. (Isaiah 13:9, 10)

In Joel:

> The day of Jehovah has come, a day of shadow and darkness. Before him the earth trembles, the heavens shake, the sun and moon turn black, and the stars hold back their rays. (Joel 2:1, 2, 10)

[2] The following passage in Isaiah discusses the Lord's Coming and the light brought to the nations—in other words, a new church, and specifically the individuals who are in shadow but welcome the light and are being reborn.

> Rise, shine, because your light has come! Look—shadows cover the earth, and darkness, the peoples. And Jehovah will dawn above you; and the nations will walk toward your light, and monarchs, toward the brightness of your rising. Jehovah will become an eternal light to you. No longer will your sun set, and your moon will not withdraw, because Jehovah will become an eternal light to you. (Isaiah 60:1, 2, 3, 19, 20)

In David:

> Jehovah makes *the heavens* with understanding; he spreads *the earth* out on *the waters;* he makes the great lights—the sun to rule during the day and the moon and stars to rule during the night. (Psalms 136:5, 6, 7, 8, 9)

In the same author:

> Give glory to Jehovah, sun and moon! Give glory to him, all you shining stars! Give glory to him, heavens of heavens and waters above the heavens! (Psalms 148:3, 4)

In all these places the sources of light symbolize love and faith.

[3] Because lights represented and symbolized love for and faith in the Lord, the Jewish church[54] was commanded to keep a light burning perpetually, from evening to morning, since every activity that was required of that church represented the Lord. The command for the perpetual light was as follows:

> Command the children of Israel to take oil for the light, to make [the fire of] the lamp go up continually. In the meeting tent, outside the veil that is by [the ark of] the testimony, Aaron and his sons shall arrange it before Jehovah, from evening till morning. (Exodus 27:20, 21)

This symbolizes love and faith, which the Lord kindles and causes to shine in our inner self, and through our inner into our outer self, as will be shown in its proper place [§9783], with the Lord's divine mercy.

Love and faith are first called the great lights, then love is called the *greater light* and faith the *smaller light*. It says that love will *rule during the day* and that faith will *rule during the night*. Because this information is unknown and less accessible than ever at this time—the end of an era—the Lord in his divine mercy has allowed me to lay open the true situation.

It is especially well hidden in these final days because the close of the age has arrived and almost no love exists, consequently almost no faith.[55] The Lord himself predicted this event in words recorded in the Gospels:

> The sun will go dark, and the moon will not shed light, and the stars will fall down from the sky, and the powers of the heavens will be shaken. (Matthew 24:29)

The sun here means love, which has gone dark. The moon means faith, which is not shedding light. The stars mean religious concepts (the powers and forces of the heavens), which are falling down from heaven.

[2] The earliest church acknowledged no faith besides love itself. Heavenly angels[56] too have no idea what faith is if it is not a matter of love. The entirety of heaven gives itself over to love, because no other kind of life than that of love exists in the heavens. Love is the source of all their happiness, which is so immense that not a bit of it can be put into words or grasped in any way by the human mind.

People who dwell in love do love the Lord with all their heart, but they know, say, and perceive that all love comes from the Lord and from nowhere else, as does all life (which is the product of love alone) and so all happiness. Not the smallest measure of love, life, or happiness do they claim to possess on their own.

In the Lord's transfiguration, the great light—the sun—represented the fact that he is the source of all love, since

> His face shone like the sun, while his clothes became like the light. (Matthew 17:2)

The face symbolizes the deepest levels of being, while clothes symbolize the things that issue from those levels. So the sun (love) means the Lord's divinity, and light (the wisdom that rises out of love), his humanity.

Anyone can see perfectly well that no hint of life ever exists without some kind of love and that no trace of joy ever exists unless it results from love. The nature of the love determines the nature of the life and of the joy.

If you were to take the things you love—the things you long for (since longings are bound up with love)—and set them aside, your thought processes would come to an immediate halt and you would be like a corpse. I have learned this through experience.

Self-love and materialism produce an imitation of life and an imitation of joy, but since they are diametrically opposed to genuine love—that is, loving the Lord above all and loving our neighbor as ourselves—it stands to reason that they are not forms of love but of hatred. Notice that the more we love ourselves and worldly goods, the more we hate our neighbor and therefore the Lord.

Genuine love, then, is love for the Lord, and genuine life is a life of love received from him. True joy is the joy of that life.

Only one genuine love can exist, so only one genuine life can exist, and it gives rise to true joy and happiness, like that felt by angels in heaven.

34 Love and faith can never be separated, because they make a single unit. This is why the sources of light when first mentioned are treated as grammatically singular in the statement, "Let there be lights in the expanse of the heavens."[57] Let me report some surprising facts in this connection.

Because the Lord gives heavenly angels this kind of love, love reveals all religious knowledge to them. Love also gives them such a living and shining intelligence that it can hardly be described.

For spirits who learn the doctrinal tenets of faith but lack love, on the other hand, life is so chill and the light so dim that they cannot even approach the near side of the threshold to heaven's entrance hall without fleeing in retreat.

Some say that they had believed in the Lord; but in actuality they had not lived as he taught. The Lord speaks of them this way in Matthew:

> Not everyone saying "Lord! Lord!" to me will enter the kingdom of the heavens, but the one doing my will. Many will say to me on that day, "Lord! Lord! Haven't we prophesied in your name?" (Matthew 7:21, 22)

See also what follows there, up to the end of Matthew 7.

[2] All this makes it clear that people who have love also have faith and consequently heavenly life. The same cannot be said of those who claim to have faith but do not lead a loving life.

A life of faith without love is like sunlight without warmth—the type of light that occurs in winter, when nothing grows and everything droops and dies. Faith rising out of love, on the contrary, is like light from the sun in spring, when everything grows and flourishes. Warmth from the sun is the fertile agent. The same is true in spiritual and heavenly affairs, which are typically represented in the Word by objects found in nature and human culture.

Nonbelief and belief without love are in fact compared to winter by the Lord in Mark where he made predictions concerning the close of the age:

> Pray that your flight not occur in winter, as those will be days of distress. (Mark 13:18, 19)

The "flight" refers to the final days and to an individual's final days before death as well. "Winter" is a life devoid of love. The "days of distress" are the person's wretched condition in the other life.

Humans have two basic faculties: will and intellect. When the will regulates the intellect, the two together make one mind and as a result one life; under those circumstances, what we will and do is also what we think and intend. When the intellect is at odds with the will, though, as when we act in a way that contradicts what we claim to believe, our single mind is torn in two. One part wants to rise up to heaven while the other leans toward hell. And since the will drives everything, we would rush into hell heart and soul if the Lord did not take pity on us.

People who have separated faith from love do not even know what faith is. When they try to picture it, some see it merely as thought. Some view it only as thoughts about the Lord. A few equate it with the teachings of faith.

But faith is more than the knowledge and acknowledgment of all that is encompassed in the teachings of faith. First and foremost it is obedience to everything that faith teaches; and the primary thing faith teaches and requires our obedience to is love for the Lord and love for our neighbor. No one who lacks this possesses faith. The Lord teaches this so clearly in Mark that no one can doubt it:

> The first of all the commandments is "Listen, Israel: The Lord our God is one Lord. Therefore you shall love the Lord your God with all your heart and with all your soul and with all your mind and with all your powers." This is the first commandment. A second, similar one, of course, is this: "You shall love your neighbor as yourself." There is no other commandment greater than these. (Mark 12:28–34)

In Matthew he calls the former the first and great commandment and says that the Law and the Prophets depend on these commandments (Matthew 22:35–40). "The Law and the Prophets" are the teachings of faith, all-inclusively, and the whole Word.[58]

The words *the lights will act as signals and will be used for seasons both for the days and for the years* contain more hidden information than can be spelled out in the present work, even though none of it appears in the literal meaning. The only thing to be said at this time is that spiritual and heavenly things—as a group and individually—go through cycles, for which the daily and yearly cycles are metaphors. The daily cycle begins in the morning, extends to midday, then to evening, and through night to morning. The corresponding annual cycle begins with spring, extends to summer, then to fall, and through winter to spring.

These changes create changes in temperature and light and in the earth's fertility, which are used as metaphors for changes in spiritual and heavenly conditions. Without change and variation, life would be monotonous and consequently lifeless. There would be no recognition or differentiation of goodness and truth, let alone any awareness of them.

The celestial cycles are called "statutes" in the prophets, as in Jeremiah:

> The word spoken by Jehovah, who gives the sun as light for the day, the statutes of moon and stars as light for the night: "These statutes will not depart from before me." (Jeremiah 31:35, 36)

And in the same prophet:

> This is what Jehovah has said: "If my compact with day and night should cease, if I should cease to set the statutes of heaven and earth . . ." (Jeremiah 33:25)

But the subject will be explored further at Genesis 8:22 [§§933–936], the Lord's divine mercy permitting.

38 Genesis 1:18. . . . [59] *and to rule during the day and during the night, and to make a distinction between light and darkness; and God saw that it was good.*

Day means goodness and *night* evil, so in common parlance the good things people do are associated with the day, while the bad things they do are called deeds of the night.

Light means truth and *darkness* falsity, as the Lord says:

> People loved darkness more than light. One who does the truth comes to the light. (John 3:19–21)

Genesis 1:19. *And there was evening and there was morning, the fourth day.*

39 Genesis 1:20. *And God said, "Let the waters cause the creeping animal—a living soul—to creep out. And let the bird flit over the land, over the face of the expanse of the heavens."*

After the great lights are kindled and placed in the inner self, and the outer self is receiving light from them, the time arrives when we first start to live. Earlier, we can hardly be said to have been alive, thinking as we did that the good we perform and the truth we speak originate in ourselves. On our own we are dead and have nothing but evil and falsity inside, with the result that nothing we produce from ourselves has life. So true is this that by our own power we cannot do anything good—at least not anything inherently good.

From the doctrine taught by faith, anyone can see that we cannot so much as think a good thought or will a good result or consequently do a good deed except through the Lord's power. After all, in Matthew the Lord says:

> The one who sows good seed is the Son of Humankind.[60] (Matthew 13:37)

Good cannot come from anywhere but this same unique source, as he also says:

> Nobody is good except the one God. (Luke 18:19)

[2] Still, when the Lord brings us back to life, or regenerates us, he at first allows us to harbor these mistaken ideas. At that stage we cannot view the situation in any other way. Neither can we be led in any other way to believe and then perceive that everything good and true comes from the Lord alone.

As long as our thinking ran along these lines, the truth and goodness we possessed were equated with a tender plant or grass, next with a plant bearing seed, then with a fruit tree, none of which has a living soul. Now, when love and faith have brought us to life and we believe that the Lord brings about all the good we do and the truth we speak, we are compared initially to *creeping animals of the water* and *birds flitting over the land* and later to beasts. All these are animate and are called *living souls*.

The *creeping animals* that the *waters* breed symbolize facts that the outer self knows. *Birds* in general symbolize logical reasoning; they also symbolize matters that we truly understand, which belong to the inner self.

The following verses in Isaiah demonstrate the symbolism of the *creeping animals of the waters*—fish—as facts:

> I came and there was no man.[61] In my censure I will dry up the sea; I will make the rivers a desert; their fish will stink from lack of water and die of thirst; I will dress the heavens in black. (Isaiah 50:2, 3)

[2] Evidence still clearer appears in Ezekiel, where the Lord describes a new temple,[62] the general meaning of which is a new church and an

adherent of the church or person reborn (since everyone who is reborn is a temple to the Lord).

> The Lord Jehovah said to me, "That water, which will go out to the boundary toward the east and go toward the sea, will be channeled down into the sea, and the water [of the sea] will be cured. And it will come about that every living soul that creeps out in any place where the water of the rivers goes will survive; and the fish will be very numerous, because that water goes there and will be cured, and everything will live, wherever the river goes. And it will happen that the fishers will stand over it from En-gedi to En-eglaim; they will be there spreading their nets. Their fish will be of all kinds, like the fish of the great sea, very numerous." (Ezekiel 47:8, 9, 10)

"Fishers from En-gedi to En-eglaim spreading their nets" symbolize people who are to teach the earthly plane of the human mind about the truths that make up faith.[63]

[3] Passages in the prophets establish the fact that birds symbolize logical reasoning and concepts truly understood. In Isaiah, for example:

> I am calling the winged creature from the sunrise, the man I planned on, from a faraway land. (Isaiah 46:11)

In Jeremiah:

> I looked and there, not a human! And every bird of the heavens had fled. (Jeremiah 4:25)

In Ezekiel:

> I will plant a cutting of the tall cedar, and it will lift its branch and make fruit and become a majestic cedar. And every bird of every wing will live under it; in the shade of its branches they will live. (Ezekiel 17:[22,] 23)

And in Hosea, where the subject is a new church, or the regenerate person:

> And I will strike a pact with them on that day—with the wild animal of the field, and with the bird in the heavens and the creature that moves on the ground. (Hosea 2:18)

The wild animal obviously does not mean a wild animal or the bird a bird, because the Lord is sealing a new pact with them.

41 Nothing that is a person's very own has any life in it. When presented to view, it looks hard as bone, and black. Everything that comes from the

Lord, on the other hand, has life. It has a spiritual and heavenly quality and looks like something living and human.[64]

Incredibly, perhaps (although it is absolutely true), each word, each mental image, and each scintilla of thought in an angelic spirit is alive. Passion received from the Lord, who is life itself, permeates every single thing about such a spirit.

Things that come from the Lord, then, contain life because they contain faith in him, and they are symbolized here by *a living soul*. Additionally, they have the equivalent of a physical body, symbolized by *that which moves* or *creeps*. This information remains obscure to the human mind, but since the verse talks about a living soul that moves, I need at least to mention it.

Genesis 1:21. *And God created the big sea creatures, and every living, creeping soul that the waters caused to creep out, in all their kinds, and every bird on the wing, of every kind; and God saw that it was good.*

Fish symbolize facts, as already stated [§40]. In this instance they symbolize facts animated by faith that is received from the Lord, which therefore possess vitality. *Big sea creatures* symbolize general categories of facts, from which come subcategories. (Not one thing exists anywhere in the world that does not belong to some general category. The category allows the particular item to come into being and continue in existence.)[65]

The prophets mention sea monsters or whales a number of times, and when they do, these symbolize general categories of facts. Pharaoh, king of Egypt, representing human wisdom or understanding (that is, factual information in general), is called a large sea creature, as in Ezekiel:

> Here, now, I am against you, Pharaoh, king of Egypt, you great sea creature, lying in the middle of your rivers, who has said, "The river is mine, and I have made myself." (Ezekiel 29:3)

[2] Another:

> Raise a lamentation over Pharaoh, king of Egypt; and you are to tell him, "But you are like a monster in the seas; and you have emerged among your rivers and churned the waters with your feet." (Ezekiel 32:2)

This image symbolizes those who want to use facts (meaning they want to use their own powers) to initiate themselves into religious mysteries. In Isaiah:

> On that day Jehovah, with his steely and great and mighty sword, will exact punishment on Leviathan the stretched-out serpent and on

> Leviathan the coiled serpent; and he will kill the monsters that are in the sea. (Isaiah 27:1)

Killing the monsters that are in the sea means leaving such people without awareness even of general facts. In Jeremiah:

> Nebuchadnezzar, king of Babylon, has devoured me, has churned me up; he has rendered me an empty container, like a sea monster he has swallowed me down, filled his belly with the savors of me, hurled me out. (Jeremiah 51:34)

In other words, "Nebuchadnezzar" has swallowed up all religious knowledge (the "savors") as the sea monster did to Jonah. In Jonah's case the monster stood for people who possess the broad outlines of this knowledge in the form of facts and who wolf them down.

43. Genesis 1:22. *And God blessed them, saying, "Reproduce and multiply and fill the water in the seas, and the birds will multiply on the land."*

Everything with life from the Lord in it reproduces and multiplies beyond measure—not so much during our physical lives, but to an astounding degree in the next life.

In the Word, *reproducing* or being fruitful applies to the elements of love, and *multiplying,* to the elements of faith. Fruit born of love holds the seed by which it multiplies so prolifically.

The Lord's *blessing* in the Word also symbolizes fruitfulness and multiplication, because these are its result.

Genesis 1:23. *And there was evening and there was morning, the fifth day.*

44. Genesis 1:24, 25. *And God said, "Let the earth produce each living soul according to its kind: the beast, and that which moves, and the wild animal of the earth, each according to its kind"; and so it was done. And God made each wild animal of the earth according to its kind, and each beast according to its kind, and every animal creeping on the ground according to its kind. And God saw that it was good.*

Like the earth, we are unable to produce any good unless we have first been sown with religious insights, which enable us to see what to believe and do.

The role of the intellect is to hear the Word, while the role of the will is to do it. To hear the Word and not act is to claim we believe it although we do not live by it. People who act like this separate the two and split their minds. The Lord says they are stupid:

> Everyone who hears my words and does them I compare to a prudent man who built his house on rock. But everyone who hears my words

and does not do them I compare to a stupid man who built his house on sand. (Matthew 7:24, 26)

What the intellect grasps is symbolized, as shown [§40], by creeping animals that the waters cause to creep out and birds flying over the land and over the face of the expanse. What the will is intent on is symbolized by the *living soul* that *the earth* is to *produce,* by the *beast* and *that which creeps,* and by the *wild animal of the earth.*

People who lived in the earliest times used the same kinds of symbols for the contents of the intellect and the will. In consequence, the different types of creature have a similar representation in the prophets and throughout the Old Testament Word.

Beasts are of two kinds: bad (because they are dangerous) and good (because they are tame). Bad animals—bears, wolves, and [feral] dogs, for instance—symbolize evil things in us. Good animals—young cattle, sheep, lambs—symbolize the good, gentle things in us. Because the present theme concerns people who are being reborn, the beasts in this verse are the good, tame ones, symbolizing feelings of affection.

The traits in us that belong to a lower order and rise more out of our body are called the wild animals of the earth; they are cravings and appetites.[66]

Many examples from the Word can clarify the fact that *beasts* or animals symbolize the feelings we have—negative feelings if we are evil, positive feelings if we are good. Take these verses in Ezekiel:

> Here, now, I am yours, [mountains of Israel,] and I will turn to face you so that you may be tilled and sown; and I will multiply human and animal upon you, and they will multiply and reproduce; and I will cause you to live as in your ancient times. (Ezekiel 36:9, 10, 11)

This speaks of regeneration. In Joel:

> Do not be afraid, animals of my field; because the living-places of the desert have become grassy. (Joel 2:22)

In David:

> I was dull-witted; I was like the animals, in God's sight. (Psalms 73:22)

In Jeremiah:

> Look! The days are coming when I will sow the house of Israel and the house of Judah with the seed of human and the seed of animal; and I will watch over them to build and to plant. (Jeremiah 31:27, 28)

This speaks of regeneration.

[2] *Wild animals* have the same symbolism. In Hosea, for example:

> I will strike a pact with them on that day—with the wild animal of the field, and with the bird in the heavens and the creeping animal of the earth. (Hosea 2:18)

In Job:

> Of the wild animal of the earth you are not to be afraid, as you will have a compact with the stones of the field, and the wild animal of the field will be peaceful toward you. (Job 5:22, 23)

In Ezekiel:

> I will strike a pact of peace with you and bring an end on the earth to the evil wild animal, so that people may live securely in the wilderness. (Ezekiel 34:25)

In Isaiah:

> The wild animal of the field will honor me because I have put water in the desert. (Isaiah 43:20)

In Ezekiel:

> In its branches nested every bird of the heavens, and under its branches bred every wild animal of the field, and in its shade lived all the great nations. (Ezekiel 31:6)

This describes Assyrians, who symbolize a person with a spiritual focus and who are being compared to the Garden of Eden. In David:

> Give glory to Jehovah, all you angels of his; give glory from the earth, you sea creatures, fruit tree, wild animal, and every beast, creeping animal, and bird on the wing. (Psalms 148:2, 3, 4, 7, 9, 10)

This lists exactly the same things [as the present chapter]: sea creatures, fruit tree, wild animal, beast, creeping animal, and bird. Unless they symbolized living things in us, they could never be said to give glory to Jehovah.

[3] The prophets draw a careful distinction between the animals *of the earth* and the animals of the field.

It is good things that have been called animals up to this point, just as the people closest to the Lord in heaven are termed living creatures both in Ezekiel [1; 10] and in John:[67]

All the angels stood around the throne and the elders and the four living creatures, and they fell down before the throne on their faces and worshiped the Lamb. (Revelation 7:11; 19:4)

People to whom the gospel is to be preached are also called created beings, since they are to be created anew:[68]

Go throughout the world and preach the gospel to every created being. (Mark 16:15)

More evidence that these words enfold the mysteries of regeneration can be seen in differences between the present verse and the last. The last says that the earth produced the living soul, the beast, and the wild animal of the earth. The present one employs a different order, saying that God made the wild animal of the earth and then the beast. At first we produce results as if on our own, as we do later, too, before developing a heavenly nature. Regeneration, then, starts with the outer self and moves to the inner, which is why a change in the order occurs, and outermost things come first.[69]

All this verifies the premise: In the fifth stage we speak with conviction (an attribute of the intellect) and in the process strengthen ourselves in truth and goodness. The things we then produce have life in them and are called the fish of the sea and the birds in the heavens. And in the sixth stage we act with conviction (an attribute of the intellect) and therefore with love (an attribute of the will) in speaking truth and doing good. What we then produce is called a living soul, an animal. Because this is the point at which we begin to act as much with love as with conviction, we become spiritual people, who are called [God's] image—the very next subject.

Genesis 1:26. *And God said, "Let us make a human in our image, after our likeness; and these will rule over the fish of the sea and over the bird in the heavens, and over the beast, and over all the earth, and over every creeping animal that creeps on the earth."*

To members of the earliest church, whom the Lord addressed face to face, he appeared as a human being. (Many things could be told about these people, but this is not the right time.)[70] As a consequence, they used the term *human* for none but him, or for his qualities. They did not even call themselves human, excepting whatever they could tell he gave them, such as all the good embraced by love and all the truth espoused by faith. These traits they described as human, because they were the Lord's.

[2] As a consequence, the terms *human being* and *son of humankind*[71] in the prophets have the Lord as their highest meaning. At a lower but still internal level, the meaning is wisdom and understanding and accordingly everyone who has been reborn. An example from Jeremiah:

> I looked at the earth, and there—void and emptiness; and to the heavens, and there—no light in them! I looked, and there—not a human! And all the birds of the heavens had fled. (Jeremiah 4:23, 25)

At the inner level, the following passage in Isaiah uses a human being to mean one reborn, and on the highest level the Lord himself, as an exemplar:

> This is what Jehovah, the Holy One of Israel and its fashioner, has said: "I made the earth, and the human being on it I created. My hands stretched out the heavens, and to their whole army[72] I gave commands." (Isaiah 45:11, 12, 13)

[3] For this reason, the prophets saw the Lord as a human being. Ezekiel was one who did:

> Above the expanse was a seeming appearance of sapphire stone, like a throne, and on the likeness of a throne was what looked like the appearance of a person on it, high above. (Ezekiel 1:26)

When Daniel saw the Lord, he called him "Son of Humankind," or human being, which is the same thing:

> I looked, and there! In the clouds of the sky, it was as if the Son of Humankind was coming. And he came to the Ancient One, and they brought him before [the Ancient One]. And he was given power to rule, and glory, and kingship; and all peoples, nations, and tongues will serve him. His ruling power is eternal, a power that will not pass away, and his kingship one that will not perish. (Daniel 7:13, 14)

[4] In fact, the Lord often calls himself Son of Humankind,[73] or human; echoing the prophecy in Daniel that he will come in glory, he says:

> They will see the Son of Humankind coming in the clouds of the sky with strength and glory. (Matthew 24:27, 30)

"The clouds of the heavens" (or sky) is what the literal meaning of the Word is called. "Strength and glory" are terms for the Word's inner meaning, which at each and every point focuses exclusively on the Lord and his kingdom. This focus is what gives the inner meaning strength and glory.

What the people of the earliest church meant when they spoke of the Lord's *image* involves more than can be put into words.

People have no idea whatever that the Lord governs them through angels and spirits, or that at least two spirits and two angels accompany each of them. The spirits create a link with the world of spirits,74 and the angels create one with heaven. We cannot possibly live without a channel of communication open to the world of spirits through spirits and to heaven through angels (and in this way to the Lord through heaven). Our life depends totally on such a connection. If the spirits and angels withdrew from us, we would be destroyed in a second.

[2] As long as we are unregenerate, we are governed in a completely different way than the regenerate. Before regeneration we have with us evil spirits whose grip on us is so strong that the angels, though present, can achieve hardly any results. All they can do is head us off from rushing into the worst kind of evil and divert us toward some form of good. They even use our own appetites to lead us toward good, and the illusions of our senses to lead us toward truth. Under these circumstances we communicate with the world of spirits by means of the spirits around us but not so much with heaven, since the evil spirits are in charge and the angels only deflect their influence.

[3] When we are regenerate, on the other hand, the angels are in charge, inspiring us with all kinds of goodness and truth and instilling a horror and fear of evil and falsity.

Angels do give us guidance, but they are mere helpers; the Lord alone governs us, *through* angels and spirits. Since angels have their assisting role, the words of this verse appear in the plural—"Let us make a human in our image." But since only the Lord rules and manages us, the next verse uses the singular—"God created the human in his image." The Lord states his role clearly in Isaiah:

> This is what Jehovah has said, your Redeemer and the one who formed you from the womb: "I, Jehovah, make all things, stretching *the heavens* out on my own, spreading *the earth* out by myself." (Isaiah 44:24)

The angels themselves confess that they have no power but act only at the Lord's behest.

As far as an *image* is concerned, it is not the likeness of another thing but is *after a likeness* of it, which explains the wording "Let us make a human in our image, after our likeness." A person with a spiritual character is an image, but a person with a heavenly character is a likeness or exact copy.[75] Genesis 1 deals with the spiritual person, Genesis 2 with the heavenly person.

The Lord calls the person of spiritual character (or an "image") a child of light, as he does in John:

> Those who walk in the dark do not know where they are heading. As long as you have the light, believe in the light, in order to be children of light. (John 12:35, 36)

He also calls such a person a friend:

> You are my friends if you do whatever I command you. (John 15:14, 15)

But the person of heavenly character (or a "likeness") he calls God's child in John:

> As many as did accept him, to them he gave the power to be God's children, to those believing in his name, who had their birth not from blood[76] or from the flesh's will or from a man's will but from God. (John 1:12, 13)

52 As long as we are spiritual, we rule the outer self first and from this the inner, as illustrated here in Genesis 1:26: *and they will rule over the fish of the sea and over the bird in the heavens, and over the beast, and over all the earth, and over every creeping animal that creeps on the earth.* When we become heavenly, though, and do good because we love to, we rule the inner self first and from it the outer. The Lord describes this as being true of himself; and as it is true of him, it is also true of the heavenly type of person, who is a likeness of him. The words appear in David:

> You have made him rule over the works of your hands; all things you have put under his feet: the flock and all the herds, and also the animals of the fields, the bird in the heavens, and the fish of the sea—that which travels the paths of the seas. (Psalms 8:6–8)

In this passage, animals receive the first mention, next the bird, then the fish of the sea, because the heavenly person proceeds from love, which belongs to the will. Things are different with the spiritual person, for whom the fish and birds come first and the animals follow; fish and birds are associated with the intellect, which concerns itself with faith.

53 Genesis 1:27. *And God created the human in his image; in God's image he created them.*

Image comes up twice in this verse because faith, which belongs to the intellect, is called *his* image, but love, which belongs to the will, is called *God's* image. Love comes second in the spiritual person but first in the heavenly person.

Male and female he created them.

The inner meaning of male and female was very familiar to the earliest church, although their successors lost touch with this secret when they lost sight of any deeper import to the Word.

These earliest people found their greatest happiness and pleasure in marriage.[77] Whenever they could possibly draw a comparison between something else and marriage, they did so, in order to perceive the happiness of marriage in that other entity.[78] Being people of depth, they enjoyed only the deeper aspects of things. External objects were just for looking at; their thoughts were occupied instead with the things those objects represented. External objects, then, were nothing to them, serving only as a springboard for reflection on inner realities, and these for contemplation of heavenly realities and so of the Lord, who was everything to them. The same process caused them to reflect on the heavenly marriage,[79] which they could tell was the source of the happiness in their own marriages.

As a result, they called the intellect in the spiritual being *male* and the will there *female;* and when the two worked together, they called it a marriage.

That religion initiated the practice, which became quite common, of calling the church Daughter or Virgin[80] (as in "the Virgin Zion," "the Virgin Jerusalem") and also Wife, on account of its desire for good. For more on this, see the treatment of Genesis 2:24 and 3:15.[81]

Genesis 1:28. *And God blessed them, and God said to them, "Reproduce and multiply, and fill the earth and harness it, and rule over the fish of the sea and over the bird in the heavens and over every living animal creeping on the earth."*

The earliest people called the interconnection of intellect and will or of faith and love a marriage, so the generation of any good from that marriage they termed *reproduction,* and the generation of any truth they termed *multiplication.* Because they did so, the prophets did so too; in Ezekiel, for instance:

> I will multiply human and animal upon you, [mountains of Israel,] and they will multiply and reproduce; and I will cause you to live as in your ancient times. And I will do good to you beyond that at your beginnings,

and you will know that I am Jehovah. And I will cause *humankind*—my people Israel—to walk upon you. (Ezekiel 36:8, 9, 10, 11, 12)

Humankind here means the spiritual being, which is also called Israel; the ancient times mean the very earliest church; and the beginnings mean the ancient church, which followed the Flood. The multiplying (of truth) comes before the reproducing (of good) because these verses describe the person who is being reborn, not the one who has been reborn already.

[2] When the intellect couples with the will in us, or faith with love, the Lord through Isaiah calls us a married land:

> No longer will your land be named Devastated; but you will be called I Am Well Pleased with Her, and your land, Married, since Jehovah will take pleasure in you. And your land will be married. (Isaiah 62:4)

The fruits of truth produced by this marriage are called sons, while the fruits of goodness are called daughters, as occurs quite often in the Word.

[3] The *earth is filled* when truth and goodness proliferate, because when the Lord *blesses* and *says things* (that is, operates), goodness and truth grow beyond measure. As he states:

> The kingdom of the heavens is like a mustard seed that you have taken and sown in your field, which to be sure is the smallest of all the seeds; but when it has grown, it is bigger than all the plants and becomes a tree, so that the birds of the sky come and nest in its branches. (Matthew 13:31, 32)

The mustard seed is the good we have before developing a spiritual orientation; it is the smallest of all the seeds, because we suppose that we do good on our own. Anything we do on our own is evil through and through, but since we are engaged in the process of being reborn, we have a trace—the smallest possible trace—of goodness. [4] Later, as faith becomes more closely connected with love, it grows larger—a plant. When the connection is completed, it turns into a tree, and then the birds of the heavens (which here as before [§§11; 40:1, 3; 48] are true ideas, or the contents of the intellect) nest in its branches (the facts we know).

When we are spiritual people or are becoming spiritual, we are subject to conflict; and this is why it says *harness the earth, and rule*.

56   Genesis 1:29. *And God said, "Here, now, I am giving you every seed-bearing plant on the face of all the earth and every tree that has fruit; the tree that produces seed will serve you for food."*

A person whose nature is heavenly enjoys only heavenly things, which are called heavenly food because they harmonize with the life such a person lives. A person whose nature is spiritual enjoys spiritual things, which are called spiritual food because they harmonize with the life this person lives. A person focused on the physical world similarly enjoys earthly things, which are called food because they are vital to such a person; these are mainly facts.

As spiritual people are the subject at present, their spiritual food is depicted by the representative items here. *The seed-bearing plant* represents a spiritual type of this food, as does *the tree that has fruit;* the more general term for both is *the tree that produces seed*. These people's earthly food is described in the next verse.

The seed-bearing plant is every true idea that looks toward a useful goal. *The tree that has fruit* is religious good; the fruit is what the Lord gives the heavenly person, but the seed leading to new fruit is what he gives the spiritual person, which is why it says *the tree that produces seed will serve you for food*.

The next chapter, treating of the heavenly type of person, will demonstrate that heavenly food is called the fruit from a tree.[82] Here the Lord's words through Ezekiel will suffice:

> Beside the river, on its bank, on this side and that, grows every food tree. Its leaf will not fall, and its fruit will not be used up. Month by month it is reborn, because its waters are going out from the sanctuary. And its fruit will serve as food, and its leaf, as medicine. (Ezekiel 47:12)

"Water from the sanctuary" symbolizes the living energy and mercy of the Lord, who is the "sanctuary." The fruit symbolizes wisdom, which is food to people of heavenly character. The leaf is intelligence, which is given to them for a purpose referred to as "medicine."

The idea that spiritual food is called a plant (or grass), though, is expressed in David:

> My shepherd, I will lack nothing. In grassy pastures you make me lie down. (Psalms 23:1, 2)

Genesis 1:30. *"And every wild animal of the earth and every bird in the heavens and every animal creeping on the earth, in which there is a living soul—every green plant will serve them for nourishment"; and so it was done.*

This verse depicts the spiritual person's earthly food. The *wild animal of the earth* symbolizes such a person's earthly plane of existence, as does the *bird in the heavens,* both of which received *for nourishment* the *green plant* or grass. Concerning this person's two kinds of food—both earthly and spiritual—David has the following to say:

> Jehovah causes grain to sprout for the beast and plants for the service of humankind, to bring bread from the earth. (Psalms 104:14)

"The beast" stands for the wild animal of the earth and at the same time for the bird in the heavens, both of which David mentions in verses 11 and 12 of the same Psalm.

59. In this verse the nourishment of the earthly self is restricted to *green plants* for the following reason.

While we are being reborn and learning to concern ourselves with the spirit, we are in constant battle (which is why the Lord's church is described as militant).[83] Up to this point our cravings have controlled us, because our whole being is cobbled together out of nothing but those cravings and the distorted ideas they spawn. We cannot rid ourselves of those longings and distortions instantaneously during regeneration; to do so would destroy us completely, since we have not yet acquired another way of life. Consequently, evil spirits are left with us for a long time to trigger our appetites, which then break down in countless different ways, and break down so thoroughly that the Lord can turn them into something good. This is the way we reform.

In the time of battle, evil spirits leave us no other nourishment than the equivalent of green plants. (Those spirits hold an absolute hatred for everything good and true—for anything having to do with love for the Lord and faith in him, these being the only good and true things that exist—because such things hold eternal life within them.) But from time to time the Lord gives us additional food that can be compared to seed-bearing plants and fruit trees: calm and peace, with their accompanying joy and happiness.

[2] If the Lord were not protecting us every moment, every split second, we would be wiped out instantly. Hatred against any aspect of love for the Lord or faith in him dominates the world of spirits, and the hatred is so deadly that it defies description.

I can testify to the truth of this absolutely. For several years now I have visited the next world and the spirits there, though remaining in my body, and the evil ones (the worst, in fact) have crowded around me, sometimes numbering in the thousands. They have been allowed to spew out their venom and harass me in every possible way, but still they were unable to hurt a single hair on my head, so closely did the Lord guard me.[84]

All these years of experience have taught me a great deal about the nature of the world of spirits and about the conflict that those who are being reborn inevitably suffer if they are to win the happiness of eternal life.

No one, however, can learn enough from a general description to develop an unshakable belief in this information, so the details, with the Lord's divine mercy, must come in what follows.[85]

60 Genesis 1:31. *And God saw all that he had done and, yes, it was very good. And there was evening and there was morning, the sixth day.*

This time it says *very good* but previously it said simply *good*, because now the components of faith combine with those of love to make one entity. A marriage between spiritual and heavenly things has taken place.

61 "Spiritual" is the adjective for anything having to do with religious knowledge. "Heavenly" applies to everything having to do with love for the Lord and for our neighbor. Spiritual things fall in the province of our intellect; heavenly things, in that of our will.

62 The periods and stages of our regeneration—both the whole process and individual cycles within it—divide into *six,* and these six are called our days of creation. Step by step we advance from being nonhuman to being somewhat human, though only a little, then more and more so up to the sixth day, when we become [God's] image.

63 All the while the Lord is constantly fighting on our behalf against evil and falsity and through these battles strengthens us in truth and goodness. The time of conflict is when the Lord is at work (for which reason the prophets call a regenerate person the work of God's fingers [Psalms 8:3, 6; Isaiah 19:25; 29:23; 45:11; 60:21; 64:8; Lamentations 4:2]), and he does not rest until love takes the lead. Then the conflict ends.

When the work progresses so far that faith is united with love, it is called *very good,* since the Lord now makes us likenesses of himself.

At the end of the sixth day, evil spirits retreat and good ones take their place. We are led into heaven, or the Paradise of heaven, described in the next chapter.

64 THIS, then, is the Word's inner meaning, the true and genuine life in it, which does not reveal itself at all in the literal meaning. But the number of secrets hidden within is so large that volumes would fail to unfold all of them. I have offered just a few, of a type confirming that regeneration is the theme and that it progresses from outer to inner self.

That is what angels see in the Word. They know nothing whatever of the literal contents, or the most obvious meaning of even one word, still less the names of different lands, cities, rivers, and people that come up so frequently in the narrative and prophetic parts.[86] All they picture are the things those words and names symbolize. Adam in Paradise, for instance, brings the earliest church to their minds—and not even the church itself but its belief in the Lord. Noah brings up the picture of that church's remnant among its successors, lasting up to Abram's time. Abraham[87] never makes them think of a man who lived long ago but of a saving faith, which he represented. And so on. In sum, they see spiritual and heavenly realities in the Word, completely separate from the words and names.

65. Several people found themselves carried up into heaven's outermost entry hall while I was reading the Word, and they spoke to me from there. They said that they had no inkling of a single word or letter there but saw only the things symbolized on the next deeper level of meaning. These things, according to their description, were so beautiful, followed in such a perfect sequence, and affected them so deeply that they called it glory.

66. The Word has four major modes of writing:

1. The mode of [the people in] the earliest church. Their method of expressing themselves involved thought of the spiritual and heavenly things represented by the earthly, mundane objects they mentioned. Not only did they express themselves in words representing higher things, they also spun those words into a kind of narrative thread to lend them greater life. This practice gave the earliest people the fullest pleasure possible.

This early manner of writing is meant in Hannah's prophecy: "Speak deeply, deeply; let what is ancient come out of your mouth" (1 Samuel 2:3).[88] David calls those representative signs "enigmas from ancient times" (Psalms 78:2, 3, 4). Moses received the present accounts of creation and the Garden of Eden, extending up to the time of Abram, from the descendants of the earliest church.

[2] 2. The narrative mode. This mode is used in the books of Moses[89] from Abram's story on, and in Joshua, Judges, Samuel, and Kings. The historical events in these books are exactly what they appear to be in the literal sense, but as a whole and in detail they still contain an entirely different meaning on the inner plane. What follows will, with the Lord's divine mercy, explain that meaning in order.[90]

3. The prophetic mode. The inspiration for this was the mode used by the earliest church, a manner of writing [the authors] revered. But the prophetic mode lacks the cohesiveness and semi-historical quality of the

earliest church's mode. It is choppy, and almost completely unintelligible except on the inner level, which holds profound secrets forming a well-connected chain of ideas. They deal with our outer and inner beings, the many stages of the church, heaven itself, and—at the very core—the Lord.

4. David's Psalms. This mode is midway between the prophetic mode and people's usual way of speaking. The inner meaning speaks of the Lord under the character of David when he was king.

Genesis 2

67 THE Lord in his divine mercy has given me the opportunity to learn the inner meaning of the Word, which contains deeply hidden secrets that no one has ever been aware of before. No one *can* become aware of them without learning how things stand in the other life, since almost all of the Word's inner meaning looks, speaks, and points to that life. For these reasons, I have been granted the privilege of disclosing what I have heard and seen over the past several years of interaction with spirits and angels.

68 I realize many will claim that no one can talk to spirits and angels as long as bodily life continues, or that I am hallucinating, or that I have circulated such stories in order to play on people's credulity, and so on. But none of this worries me; I have seen, I have heard, I have felt.[91]

69 The Lord created us to be capable of communicating with spirits and angels while still living in our bodies, as people actually did in the earliest times. After all, we are one with spirits and angels. In fact we ourselves are spirits clothed in flesh.

Over time, though, people have immersed themselves so deeply in bodily and worldly concerns that almost nothing else interests them, and so the path has closed; but as soon as the body-driven concerns that absorb us drop away, it opens and we find ourselves among spirits, living life together with them.

70 Now that I may reveal what I have experienced for the past several years, I must begin with the circumstances of our resurrection, or the way in which we leave bodily life to enter eternal life.

To convince me that people live on after death, I was allowed to talk and spend time with many people known to me during their physical life, which I did, not just for a day or a week, but for months and almost as much as a year. Our interactions were the same as they had been in the world.

These acquaintances were positively astounded that while living the life of the body they had been (and many others still are) so skeptical—skeptical to the point that they did not believe they would continue to live after death. The truth, they found, is that little more than a day passes after the demise of the body before we enter the next life, since that life is a continuation of this.

However, the account of our resurrection would end up scattered and disconnected if it were mixed in with explanations of scriptural texts. So by the Lord's divine mercy I will add it in a more orderly fashion at the beginning and end of each chapter in addition to making remarks along the way.

Allow me, then, to offer at the end of this chapter an account of our revival from the dead and entry into eternal life [§§168–181].

Genesis 2

1. And the heavens and the earth were completed, and their whole army.[92]

2. And on the seventh day God completed the work that he had done; and he rested on the seventh day from all the work that he had done.

3. And God blessed the seventh day and consecrated it, because on it he rested from all the work that he had done as God in creating it.

4. These are the births of the heavens and the earth when he created them, on the day on which he, Jehovah God, made the earth and the heavens.

5. And no shrub of the field was yet on the earth, and no plant of the field was yet sprouting, because Jehovah God had not made it rain on the earth. And there was no human to cultivate the ground.

6. And he made a mist rise up from the earth and watered the whole face of the ground.

7. And Jehovah God formed a human, dirt from the ground, and he breathed into the human's nostrils the breath of lives,[93] and the human was made into a living soul.

8. And Jehovah God planted a garden in Eden, on the east, and put in it the human whom he had formed.

9. And Jehovah God caused to sprout from the ground every tree desirable in appearance and good for food, and the tree of lives in the middle of the garden, and the tree of the knowledge of good and evil.

10. And a river was going out from Eden to water the garden, and from there it parted and became four headwaters.

11. The name of the first is Pishon; it is circling the whole land of Havilah, where there is gold.

12. And the gold of that land is good; there is bdellium there, and shoham[94] stone.

13. And the name of the second river is Gihon; it is circling the whole land of Cush.[95]

14. And the name of the third river is Hiddekel;[96] it goes east toward Assyria. And the fourth river is the Phrath.[97]

15. And Jehovah God took the human and put the human in the Garden of Eden to cultivate it and to guard it.

16. And Jehovah God commanded the human concerning it, saying, "From every tree of the garden you definitely may eat.

17. But from the tree of the knowledge of good and evil you may not eat, because on the day on which you eat from it you will surely die."

Summary

73. HAVING been changed from lifeless people to people focused on spirit, we are now changed from spiritual to heavenly; and heavenly people are the subject here (verse 1).

74. The heavenly person is the seventh day, on which the Lord rests (verses 2, 3).

75. The shrub and the plant sprouting from the ground and watered by the mist provide a picture of the factual knowledge and reason in such people (verses 5, 6).

76. The breath of lives breathed into the human provides a picture of the life force in them (verse 7).

77. The garden on the east in Eden depicts their intelligence. The trees in the garden that were desirable in appearance are times when they perceive a thing to be true; the trees good to eat are times when they perceive a thing to be good. The tree of lives portrays their love; the tree of knowledge, their faith (verses 8, 9).

78. The river in the garden depicts wisdom. It branches into four rivers, of which the first is goodness and truth themselves. The second is a knowledge of everything involved in goodness and truth, or in love and faith; these things belong to the inner self. The third is the faculty of reason, and the fourth is secular knowledge, both of which belong to the outer self. All of these flow from wisdom, and wisdom flows from love for the Lord and faith in him (verses 10, 11, 12, 13, 14).

79. People of heavenly character are this kind of garden. They are free to enjoy everything in the garden, but because it is the Lord's, they are not given personal possession of any of it (verse 15).

In addition, they are always allowed to depend on the perception they receive from the Lord to tell them what is good or true. They are not to depend on themselves or the world around them, though; in other words, when they inquire into the mysteries of faith, they are not to rely on sensory evidence or secular knowledge. To do so would be the death of their heavenly quality (verses 16, 17).

Inner Meaning

THIS chapter deals with the heavenly person; the last dealt with the spiritual person, who previously had been lifeless. In modern times, though, people know nothing about the character of a heavenly person and very little about that of a spiritual person or of a lifeless one. Let me clarify the differences through a brief discussion of each type.

1. The only truth and goodness that lifeless people acknowledge are bodily and worldly kinds, and these they revere.

Spiritual people acknowledge spiritual and heavenly types of truth and goodness, but their acknowledgment stems from faith—as do their actions—and not as much from love.

Heavenly people believe and perceive truth and goodness of spiritual and heavenly kinds, but they acknowledge no other faith than one that springs from love; and love is also what moves them to action.

[2] 2. Those who are lifeless fixate purely on bodily and worldly life as their goals. They do not know what eternal life is or what the Lord is. If they have heard about these, they have no belief in them.

Those who are spiritual focus first on eternal life as their goal, and then on the Lord.

Those who are heavenly concentrate first on the Lord as their goal, and then on his kingdom and eternal life.

[3] 3. When the lifeless undergo conflict, they almost always give in. When they are free of conflict, evil and falsity master them, and they are slaves to it. Their restraints are external and include fear of the law and fear of losing their life, wealth, profits, and consequent reputation.

The spiritual are subject to conflict, but they always win. The restraints that curb them are internal ones termed the bonds of conscience.[98]

Heavenly people experience no conflict. If evil and falsity attack them, they spurn them, which is why they are called victors. They have no apparent restraints to curb them, being free, but they do have invisible restraints, which are the goodness and truth they perceive.

82 Genesis 2:1. *And the heavens and the earth were completed, and their whole army.*

This means that we are now spiritual—so much so that we have become "the sixth day." *Heaven* is our inner and *the earth* our outer being. *Their army* is love and faith, and knowledge about love and faith. These things were symbolized earlier by the great lights and the stars.

Scriptural passages quoted in the preceding chapter demonstrate that the inner being is called *heaven* and the outer being is called *earth*.[99] Let me add another from Isaiah:

> I will render a man more rare than solid gold, and a human being [more rare] than the precious gold of Ophir.[100] Therefore I will strike the heavens with terror, and the earth will quake out of its place. (Isaiah 13:12, 13)

And another:

> You will forget Jehovah your maker, who stretches out the heavens and founds the earth. But I will put my words in your mouth, and in the shadow of my hand I will hide you, to stretch out heaven and found the earth. (Isaiah 51:13, 16)

All of this makes it clear that both *heaven* and *earth* refer to humankind.

Although the earliest church forms the subject here, the Word in its inner depths is such that whatever it says about the church applies also to every individual in the church. If we were not each a church, we could not be part of the church. Likewise, anyone who is not a temple to the Lord cannot be what the Temple symbolizes: a church and a heaven.

This is why the earliest church is referred to as a human being in the singular.

83 The verse says that the heavens, the earth, and their whole army are *completed* when we become "the sixth day." At this point faith and love join forces, and when they do, love rather than faith begins to play the leading role—that is, heavenly rather than spiritual qualities take the lead. To put heavenly qualities first is to be a heavenly person.

84 Genesis 2:2, 3. *And on the seventh day God completed the work that he had done; and he rested on the seventh day from all the work that he had* *done. And God blessed the seventh day and consecrated it, because on it he rested from all the work that he had done as God in creating it.*

A heavenly person is *the seventh day*. And since the Lord worked through six days, that individual is called *his work*. Conflict then comes to an end, as a result of which the Lord is said to *rest from all his work*. This is why the seventh day was *consecrated* and named "Sabbath," from [a Hebrew word for] rest. In the process the human being has been made, formed, and created, as the words themselves clearly indicate.

Lack of information is another reason why these secrets—that a person of heavenly character is the *seventh day,* that this explains the *consecration* of the seventh day, and that it was named "Sabbath" for the idea of rest—have continued to lie hidden. No one knows what a heavenly person is, and few what a spiritual person is. Inevitably, in their ignorance, people have considered a spiritual person the same as a heavenly one, when a rather large difference separates the two (see §81).

In regard to the seventh day, evidence that a heavenly person is the seventh day or Sabbath can be found in the identity of the Lord himself as the Sabbath. As he says, "The Son of Humankind is lord even of the Sabbath" (Mark 2:28), meaning that the Lord is the true human being and the Sabbath itself.

He calls his kingdom in the heavens and on earth the Sabbath, or eternal peace and rest.[101]

[2] The earliest church (the subject here) more than all later ones was the Lord's Sabbath.

In every subsequent church, the inmost part, closest to the Lord, has also been the Sabbath.

The same holds true for all regenerate people when they develop a heavenly nature, as they are then likenesses of the Lord. They are past the six days of conflict, or labor.

In the Jewish church, all these considerations were represented by the work days and by the seventh day, the Sabbath. That church had no customs that did not represent something about the Lord and his kingdom.

The ark represented the same kind of thing in its travels and its repose. Its travels in the wilderness represented conflict and trial; its repose, a time of peace. So when it set out on a journey, Moses said, "Rise, Jehovah, and let your enemies scatter, and let those who hate you run from your face"; and when it came to rest, he said, "Come back, Jehovah, to the countless thousands of Israel." This is from Numbers

10:35, 36. Verse 33 of the same chapter portrays the ark as setting out from the mountain of Jehovah "to find rest for them."

[3] Isaiah uses the Sabbath to paint a picture of the heavenly person's quiet rest:

> If you turn your foot back from the Sabbath by not doing your own desire on my holy day; if you refer to those things that belong to the Sabbath as pleasures honoring the holiness of Jehovah, and you honor [the Sabbath] by not going your own ways and not gaining your own desire or speaking a word [of your own]; then you will be a pleasure to Jehovah, and I will make you ride on the heights of the earth and will feed you with the inheritance of Jacob. (Isaiah 58:13, 14)

Heavenly people act not on their own desire but on the Lord's pleasure, which is his desire. So they are blessed with inner peace and happiness (their being "lifted up on the heights of the earth") and at the same time with outer calm and enjoyment (their being "fed with Jacob's inheritance").

86 When spiritual people (who are now the "sixth day") begin to turn heavenly (a process first alluded to here), they have reached the eve of the Sabbath. In the Jewish religion, this was represented by the commencement of the Sabbath observance in the evening. Heavenly people are the morning, soon to be described.

87 A further reason a heavenly person is identified as Sabbath rest is the fact that struggle ends when a person becomes heavenly. Evil spirits retreat and good ones move closer. Heavenly angels approach too, and when they are nearby, evil spirits, unable to be anywhere near, escape far away.

Because we have done none of the fighting ourselves—the Lord does all the fighting for us—he is the one said to *rest*.

88 Spiritual people are called God's work after they have developed a heavenly nature, because the Lord has fought for them all on his own. He is the one who has made, formed, and created them. That is why this verse says that *God completed his work* on the seventh day and, twice, that he rested from all *his work*. The prophets frequently call such people the work of Jehovah's hands or fingers. An example describing the regenerate person occurs in Isaiah:

> This is what Jehovah, the Holy One of Israel and its fashioner, has said: "Do you seek signs from me concerning my children, and command me concerning the work of my hands? I made the earth, and the human being on it I myself created! My hands stretched out the heavens, and

to their whole army I gave commands!" Because this is what Jehovah has said in creating the heavens (he is God, forming the earth and making it; he is firming it; he has not created it a void; he has formed it to be inhabited): "I am Jehovah, and no one is God except me." (Isaiah 45:11, 12, 18, 21)

This passage shows how creating people anew—regenerating them—is the Lord's work alone.

The words *create, form* (or *fashion*), and *make* (or *do*) are used in fairly different ways, as in the preceding quotation from Isaiah, which says "creating the heavens, forming the earth, and making it."[102] Likewise in another passage:

All have been called by my name, and I have created them for my glory; I have formed them; yes, I have made them. (Isaiah 43:7)

The same is true in Genesis 1 and 2, as for instance here, where it says, "He rested from all the work that he had done as God in creating it." The inner meaning maintains a distinct idea for each of these words. Similarly in places where the Lord is called Creator, or Fashioner, or Maker.[103]

Genesis 2:4. *These are the births of the heavens and the earth when he created them, on the day on which he, Jehovah God, made the earth and the heavens.*

The births of the heavens and the earth are the ways in which the heavenly person is formed.

Clearly this verse concerns the formation of a heavenly person. Subsequent details provide additional evidence. The text says, for instance, that no plant had yet sprouted, that there was no human to cultivate the ground, and that Jehovah God formed the human, then every beast and every bird in the heavens. But since the last chapter already told of the formation of these things, the present chapter must be talking about another kind of person.

As further evidence, this verse is the first to use the name *Jehovah God,* where before, in discussing the spiritual person, the text used only *God.* The current chapter speaks of the *ground* and the *field,* the former only of the *earth* or *land.* Finally, this verse initially places *heaven* before *earth* and then *earth* before *heaven.* The reason for this last point is that the *earth* symbolizes the outer self and *heaven* the inner self of a spiritual person, and such a person's reformation begins in the earth, or outer self.

However, because the subject is now a heavenly person, reformation begins in the inner self, or heaven.

90. Genesis 2:5, 6. *And no shrub of the field was yet on the earth, and no plant of the field was yet sprouting, because Jehovah God had not made it rain on the earth; and there was no human to cultivate the ground. And he made a mist rise up from the earth and watered the whole face of the ground.*

The *shrub of the field* and the *plant of the field* in general mean everything that the person's outer self produces. The *earth* is the outer self that the person had when spiritual. The *ground*—and the *field*—is the outer self when the person becomes heavenly. The *rain,* soon afterward called *mist,* is the peaceful calm that follows the end of battle.

91. For one who knows nothing of the conditions a person experiences when changing from spiritual to heavenly, however, the ramifications of all this are impossible to understand, since they are fairly deep mysteries.

When we are spiritual, our outer self is not yet willing to obey and serve the inner self, which causes strife. When we become heavenly, then our outer self starts to obey and serve the inner, which brings an end to strife and the beginning of calm (see §87). The *rain* and *mist* symbolize this calm, because it acts like a mist, coming from our inner self to water and drench the outer self. Such calm, which comes of peace, causes the growth of the "shrub of the field" and the "plant of the field"—specifically, rational ideas and factual knowledge having an origin that is heavenly and spiritual at the same time.

92. None but those who have experienced a state of peace can appreciate the nature of the peaceful tranquility that the outer self enjoys when there is an end to struggle, or to the disquiet of burning desires and misconceptions. That state is so joyful that it surpasses all our notions of joy. It is not simply an end to our struggles but a vibrancy welling up from deep-seated peace, affecting our outer being beyond the capacity of words to describe it.

That state gives birth to religious truth and a loving goodness, which draw their life from the joy of peace.

93. Here is how the Lord, through Ezekiel, depicts the circumstances of a heavenly person who has been gifted with peace and calm, created anew by the rain, and delivered from enslavement to evil and falsity:

> I will strike a pact of peace with them and bring an end on the earth to the evil wild animal; and they will live securely in the wilderness and sleep in forests. And I will make them—and the environs of my hill—a

> blessing and cause the rain to fall in its season; showers of blessing there will be. And the tree of the field will yield its fruit, and the earth will yield its produce, and they will be secure on their own ground; and they will know that I am Jehovah, in that I have broken the straps of their yoke and freed them from the hand of those forcing them to serve them. You are my flock, the flock of my pasture, you are *humankind;* I am your God. (Ezekiel 34:25, 26, 27, 31)

Through Hosea he describes this as happening on the third day (which means the same thing as the seventh, in the Word):

> He will bring us to life after two days; on the third day he will revive us, and we will live before him, and we will know and press on toward knowing Jehovah. His emergence has been prepared like the dawn, and he will come like rain to us, like the late rain watering the earth. (Hosea 6:2, 3)

In a passage from Ezekiel that speaks of the ancient church, he compares it to a young shoot in the field:

> I have made you a young shoot in the field, and you have grown and matured and come into [the time of] the most beautiful of ornaments.[104] (Ezekiel 16:7)

He also compares it to a seedling of Jehovah God's planting and to the work of his hands, in Isaiah 60:21.

94. Genesis 2:7. *And Jehovah God formed a human, dirt from the ground, and he breathed into the human's nostrils the breath of lives; and the human was made into a living soul.*

To *form a human, dirt from the ground* is to form our outer self, which was not previously human; verse 5, after all, says that there was no person to cultivate the ground. To *breathe into the human's nostrils the breath of lives* is to put life into our faith and love. *The human was made into a living soul* means that our outer self has also been brought to life.

95. The subject here is life in the outer self. While the two preceding verses deal with the life in our faith or intellect, the present one deals with the life in the love we feel, or in our will.

So far our outer being has not wanted to obey or serve the inner but has instead kept up a battle with it, so during this time the outer being has not been human. Now, though, when we have taken on a heavenly nature, our outer self is beginning to offer some obedience and service to the inner self and is becoming human, through a living faith and vibrant love. A living faith prepares us to be human; a vibrant love makes us so.

96 It says that Jehovah God *blew in through the person's nostrils.* In ancient times and in the Word, *nostrils* meant anything that was pleasing, from the idea of fragrance, which symbolizes perception. In many places, therefore, we read that Jehovah smelled a restful smell from the burnt offerings and from other offerings representing himself and his kingdom.[105] Since he finds the various aspects of love and faith most pleasing, the text says that he blew the breath of lives in through the nostrils.

For this reason Jehovah's anointed—the Lord—is called the breath [or spirit] of the nostrils (Lamentations 4:20).[106]

The Lord conveyed the same idea by breathing on the disciples, as John reports:

> He breathed on them and said, "Receive the holy spirit." (John 20:22)

97 The nature of the earliest church provides yet another reason for the use of *breathing* and breath as depictions of a life force. The people of that church could perceive the quality of love and faith in others from the quality of their breathing—a quality that gradually changed over the generations. Nothing can be said about this kind of respiration any longer, since time has buried any knowledge of it.[107] The earliest people knew all about it, and people in the next life do too, but no one left on the globe today does.

In consequence, people of the earliest church used wind as a metaphor for spirit or life. So does the Lord when he speaks of our regeneration in John:

> The spirit (wind)[108] blows where it wishes, and you hear its voice but do not know where it may be coming from or where it may be going off to; this is the way with everyone who is born from the spirit. (John 3:8)

David has something similar:

> By Jehovah's word were the heavens made, and by the spirit (wind) of his mouth, the whole army of them. (Psalms 33:6)

And again:

> You gather their spirit, they pass away and return to their dust; you send your spirit out, they continue to be created, and you renew the face of the ground. (Psalms 104:29, 30)

It can be seen in Job that *breath* stands for the vital quality of faith and love:

> There is a spirit in humankind, and the breath of Shaddai[109] makes them understand. (Job 32:8)

Again:

> The spirit of God made me, and the breath of Shaddai gave me life. (Job 33:4)

Genesis 2:8. *And Jehovah God planted a garden in Eden, on the east; and he put in it the human whom he had formed.*

The *garden* symbolizes intelligence, *Eden* love, and the *east* the Lord. So the garden on the east in Eden symbolizes the intelligence of heavenly people, which comes to them from the Lord, love being the conduit.

The inner life in people whose nature is spiritual is structured as follows: The faith they have does allow the Lord to enter into the things they understand, the things they grasp rationally, and the things they know. But since the more superficial levels of their mind are in conflict with the deeper levels, it does not seem as though their intelligence comes from the Lord. It appears to come from themselves and to be a product of their factual information and rational processes.

For people whose character is heavenly, on the other hand, the inner life is patterned in such a way that the Lord enters into their understanding, reason, and knowledge by way of love and the convictions of love. And since they are free of conflict, they can see that this is so.

The structure that so far has stood upside down in the spiritual person, then, returns to its proper position in the heavenly person. The heavenly structure, or the heavenly person, is called the garden on the east in Eden.

The garden *planted by Jehovah God* on the east in Eden is, in the highest sense, the Lord himself.

In the [next] deepest sense (which is also the universal sense), the garden is the Lord's kingdom or heaven, where we are *put* when we become heavenly. At that stage we keep company with angels in heaven and almost come to be one of them. (We were, in fact, created to be in heaven while at the same time living on earth.) All our thoughts then lie open, as do all the individual ideas that make up our thoughts, and all our words and deeds too, if these have anything heavenly or spiritual in them; and this openness extends clear to the Lord. His life, you see, is present in everyone, giving each the ability to perceive.

100 We can see in Isaiah too that a *garden* symbolizes intelligence and *Eden* love:

> Jehovah will comfort Zion, he will comfort all its wastelands, and he will make its wilderness like Eden and its desert like a garden of Jehovah. Joy and gladness will be found in it; acclamation and the voice of song. (Isaiah 51:3)

The prophet uses *wilderness, joy,* and *acclamation* to express the heavenly (or loving) aspects of faith; *desert, gladness,* and *the voice of song* express further spiritual (or intellectual) aspects. The first set of words relates to *Eden,* the second to *the garden.* This particular prophet fairly consistently uses two words for a single idea, one word symbolizing heavenly things, and the other, spiritual things.[110]

For more on the meaning of the Garden of Eden, see the explanation of verse 10, below [§108].

101 The identification of the Lord as the *east* is also evident throughout the Word. In Ezekiel, for example:

> He led me to the gate, a gate that looks out on the path to the east, and look! The glory of Israel's God came by way of the east, and his voice was like the voice of many waters, and the earth shone with his glory. (Ezekiel 43:1, 2, 4)

The practices of the Jewish church represented inner things; and as the Lord is the east, their sacred custom before the Temple was built was to turn their faces to the east when praying.[111]

102 Genesis 2:9. *And Jehovah God caused to sprout from the ground every tree desirable in appearance and good for food, and the tree of lives in the middle of the garden, and the tree of the knowledge of good and evil.*

A *tree* symbolizes perception; a *tree desirable in appearance,* perception of truth, and a *tree good for food,* perception of goodness. The *tree of lives* symbolizes love and the faith it leads to; the *tree of the knowledge of good and evil* symbolizes faith based on evidence from the senses, that is, on secular knowledge.

103 The reason *trees* symbolize different kinds of perception here is that the chapter has to do with heavenly people. The situation is otherwise when spiritual people are the topic.[112] The nature of the subject determines the nature of the things said about it.

104 People today have no idea what perception is. It is an inner feeling for whether a thing is true and good—a feeling that can come only from the Lord—which was very familiar to the people of the earliest church.

The sensation is so clear for angels that it gives them awareness and recognition of truth and goodness, of what comes from the Lord and what from themselves. In addition, it enables them to detect the character of anyone they meet simply from that person's manner of approach or from a single one of his or her ideas.

Spiritual people have no perception, although they have conscience. People who are lifeless do not even have conscience, and many do not know what conscience is, much less perception.

105. The *tree of lives* is love and the faith it leads to; *in the middle of the garden* means in the will that belongs to the inner self.

The main thing the Lord possesses in a person or angel is the will, which the Word refers to as the heart. Since none of us can do good on our own, our will or heart is not ours, even though it is described as ours. What is truly our own is self-interest, which we call our will.

Because the will is the *middle of the garden,* in which stands the tree of lives, and we have no will aside from self-interest, this tree is the Lord's mercy, the source of all love and faith and so of all life.

106. For further explanation of the trees in the garden, or perception; the tree of lives, or love and consequent faith; and the tree of knowledge, or faith based on the senses and secular knowledge, see below [§§125–130, 198–209].

107. Genesis 2:10. *And a river was issuing from Eden to water the garden; and from there it parted and became four headwaters.*

The *river from Eden* symbolizes wisdom born of love (*Eden* being love). To *water the garden* is to give the gift of intelligence or understanding. *From there it parted into four headwaters* portrays intelligence under the image of the four rivers, as discussed below.

108. Since the earliest people compared the human being to a garden, they compared all aspects of wisdom to *rivers;* or rather than compare them they actually *called* them those things, because that was their manner of speaking. The prophets later used the same device, sometimes making the comparison, sometimes using the direct name. An example from Isaiah:

> In the shadows your light will rise, and your darkness will be like daylight; and you will be like a watered garden and like an outlet of water, whose waters will not prove false. (Isaiah 58:10, 11)

This passage is talking about people who accept the gift of faith and love. Another example:

> They are planted as valleys are, as gardens beside the river. Like tents[113] has Jehovah planted them, like cedars beside the water. (Numbers 24:6)

The subject of this verse is regenerate people. In Jeremiah:

> Blessed is the man who trusts in Jehovah. He will be like a tree planted by the water, and above the brook he will send out his roots. (Jeremiah 17:7, 8)

Here is a passage in Ezekiel in which people are not compared to but called a garden, and trees beside the rivers:

> The water made [the cedar] grow; the depths of the water raised it up. A river was winding all around its planting-place and sent out its channels of water to all the trees of the field. Beautiful it became in its size, in the length of its branches, because its root was [going out] to many waters. The cedars cast no shadow on it in the garden of God; the firs were not equal to its branches, and the sycamores did not rival its limbs. No tree in God's garden was equal to it in its beauty. Beautiful he made it in the profusion of its branches, and all the trees of Eden in God's garden strove to match it. (Ezekiel 31:4, 7, 8, 9)

These quotations indicate that in comparing humans (or what humans have inside them) to a garden, the earliest people included the idea of the water or rivers that watered the garden. It is also apparent that they took the water and rivers to mean the things that would stimulate growth.

109 Although wisdom and understanding seem to reside in us, they belong to the Lord alone, as noted [§99], and this is clearly expressed in Ezekiel under representative images of the same kind:

> There! *Water* going out under the doorsill of the House toward the east, because the House faces east. And he said, "That *water* is going out to the boundary toward the east, and it runs down onto the plain and goes to the *sea,* having been channeled out into the *sea,* and the *water* [of the sea] will be cured. And it will come about that every living soul that creeps in any place where the *water of the rivers* goes will survive. And beside the *river,* on its bank, on this side and that, will grow every food tree. Its branch will not wither, and its fruit will not be devoured. Month by month it is reborn, because its *water* comes out from the sanctuary. And its fruit therefore will serve as food, and its leaf as medicine." (Ezekiel 47:1, 8, 9, 12)

In this instance the east symbolizes the Lord, as does the sanctuary from which spring the water and rivers. Likewise in John:

He showed me a pure *river of the water of life,* brilliant as crystal, going out from the throne of God and the Lamb. In the middle of its street and of the *river,* on this side and that, was the tree of life, making twelve fruits, offering up its fruit each month; and the leaf of the tree served as medicine for the nations. (Revelation 22:1, 2)

110. Genesis 2:11, 12. *The name of the first is Pishon; it is circling the whole land of Havilah, where there is gold. And the gold of that land is good; there is bdellium and shoham stone there.*

The *first river, Pishon,* symbolizes the intelligence that goes with a faith based on love. The *land of Havilah* symbolizes the mind; *gold,* goodness; and *bdellium and shoham,* truth. *Gold* comes up twice because it symbolizes the goodness that goes with love and the goodness that goes with a faith based on love. Both *bdellium* and *shoham* are mentioned because one symbolizes truth that belongs to love and the other symbolizes truth that belongs to a faith based on love.

All these qualities belong to a person whose nature is heavenly.

111. Telling more about the inner meaning of these things, however, would be difficult, as people today know nothing about them. They have no concept, for instance, of a faith based on love, of wisdom, or of the intelligence that comes from these. Shallow people know hardly anything but secular facts, which they call understanding and wisdom, and also faith. They do not even know what love is, and many are unacquainted with the will and intellect and the fact that these two combine to form the mind. In reality, each of the above attributes has a distinct and in fact a unique identity; and the Lord attends to the finest possible distinctions in organizing all of heaven according to differences in love and faith, which are endless.

112. People should be aware, though, that the only wisdom comes from love and so from the Lord, and the only intelligence comes from faith and so, again, from the Lord. What is more, all good comes from love and so from the Lord, and all truth comes from faith and so from the Lord. When these things do not come from love and faith and so from the Lord, they are counterfeit, even though they bear the same names as the real entities.

113. Nothing is more common in the Word than for *gold* to symbolize and represent the goodness that belongs to wisdom or to love. All the gold used for the ark, the Temple, the golden table, the lampstands, the utensils, and Aaron's garments had this symbolism and representation.[114]

The prophets use *gold* in a similar way. In Ezekiel, for instance:

> In your wisdom and in your understanding you made yourself riches, and you made *gold* and silver for your treasuries. (Ezekiel 28:4)

This explicitly states that gold and silver (goodness and truth) come from wisdom and understanding. Silver here symbolizes truth, as does the silver in the tabernacle and the Temple.[115] In Isaiah:

> A horde of camels will blanket you, the dromedaries of Midian and Ephah; they will all come from Sheba. *Gold* and frankincense they will carry, and Jehovah's praises they will proclaim. (Isaiah 60:6)

The sages from the East did the same when they came to Jesus at his birth and fell on their faces and worshiped him:

> And they opened their treasure chests and offered him gifts: *gold,* frankincense, and myrrh. (Matthew 2:1, 11)

Here too gold symbolizes goodness. Frankincense and myrrh symbolize things that are pleasing [to the Lord], because they spring from love and faith. This is why they are called "Jehovah's praises." So in David it says:

> And [the poor] will live, and [God] will give them some of Sheba's *gold* and pray for them continually; every day he will bless them. (Psalms 72:15)

114. *Precious stones* in the Word, such as those on the breastplate of judgment and the shoulders of Aaron's ephod, symbolized and represented religious truth. The gold, the fibers of blue-violet, red-violet, and double-dyed scarlet, and the fine linen of the breastplate represented different aspects of love; the precious stones represented aspects of a faith based on love. So did the two memorial stones on the shoulders of the ephod, which were shoham stones in gold settings. (See Exodus 28:9–22.) The Book of Ezekiel openly draws the same connection where it talks about a person who owns heavenly riches—wisdom and understanding:

> You were full of wisdom and perfect in beauty in *Eden, the garden* of God.[116] Every precious stone was your covering: ruby, topaz, diamond; tarshish,[117] *shoham,* and jasper; sapphire, chrysoprase, emerald; and *gold* is what the tambourines and pipes in you were crafted from. On the day when you were *created,* they were prepared; you were perfect in your ways on the day when you were *created.* (Ezekiel 28:12, 13, 15)

The stones here do not mean stones but the heavenly and spiritual qualities of faith, as anyone can see. In fact every stone represented some essential ingredient of faith.

The earliest people, when mentioning the names of various lands, had the symbolism of those places in mind. The same is true of people today who adopt the idea that the land of Canaan and Mount Zion symbolize heaven. When such people hear these names, they do not even think of the land or the mountain but only about the things they stand for. Likewise in the present verse in regard to the *land of Havilah,* which comes up again in Genesis 25:18; in that verse the subject is Ishmael's offspring, who "lived from *Havilah* all the way to *Shur,* which is before Egypt as you come into Assyria."

For people who look at things the way heaven does, what the words of this verse suggest is simply intelligence and what stems from intelligence. They take *circling,* for instance (as in "the river Pishon *circles* the whole land of Havilah"), to mean "flowing in." So the fact that gold settings *circled* the shoham stones on the shoulders of Aaron's ephod (Exodus 28:11) suggests to them that the good we love flows into the truth we believe. There are many other examples.

Genesis 2:13. *And the name of the second river is Gihon; it is circling the whole land of Cush.*

The *second river,* called *Gihon,* symbolizes knowledge about everything involved in goodness and truth, or in love and faith. The *land of Cush* symbolizes our mental abilities.

Will and intellect constitute the mind. The attributes portrayed by the first river belong to the will, while those portrayed by this second river belong to the intellect, which houses our knowledge of goodness and truth.

The *land of Cush,* or Ethiopia, was also rich in gold, precious stones, and perfumes, and these, as stated, symbolize goodness, truth, and offshoots of goodness and truth pleasing [to the Lord], such as a knowledge of love and faith. The symbolism becomes clear above in §113, in the quotations from Isaiah 60:6; Matthew 2:1, 11; and the Psalms of David 72:15.

From the prophets we can see that Cush, or Ethiopia, has the same meaning in the Word as Sheba.[118] Here is an example from Zephaniah that also mentions the rivers of Cush:

> In the morning, he will offer his judgment as a light, because "At that time I will turn toward peoples of transparent speech, so that they may

all call on the name of Jehovah, so that they may serve him with a single shoulder. From the ford of *Cush's* rivers my worshipers will bring me my offering." (Zephaniah 3:5, 9, 10)

And in Daniel, where it speaks of the northern and southern monarchs:

> He will rule over the hidden treasures of gold and silver and over all the desirable things of Egypt. And the *Libyans* and *Ethiopians* will be under his tread. (Daniel 11:43)

Egypt stands for secular knowledge and Ethiopians for religious knowledge. [2] In Ezekiel:

> The dealers of *Sheba* and Raamah were your dealers, in the finest of every perfume, and in every precious stone, and gold. (Ezekiel 27:22)

These commodities again symbolize religious knowledge. In David, where the subject is the Lord and therefore the heavenly individual:

> In his days the upright individual will flourish, as will great peace, until the moon is no more. The monarchs of Tarshish[119] and of the islands will bring their tribute; the monarchs of *Sheba* and Seba will deliver their gift. (Psalms 72:7, 10)

All this symbolizes the heavenly qualities of faith, as is plain from the verses before and after these in the same chapter.[120]

Similar things are symbolized by the queen of Sheba, who came to Solomon and posed riddles, and who carried perfumes, gold, and precious stones to him (1 Kings 10:1, 2, 3). As in the prophets, everything in the narrative portions of the Word symbolizes, represents, and incorporates hidden wisdom.[121]

118   Genesis 2:14. *And the name of the third river is Hiddekel; it goes toward the east, to Assyria. And the fourth river, it is the Phrath.*

The *river Hiddekel* is the ability to reason—that is, the clear-sightedness of reason. *Assyria* is the mind that does the reasoning. The fact that the river *goes east* to Assyria means that this ability comes from the Lord through the inner self to the part of the mind that reasons, which is located in the outer self.

The *Phrath,* or Euphrates, is factual knowledge, which is the final boundary of the mind.

119   The prophets provide clear evidence that *Assyria* symbolizes the reasoning mind, or a person's ability to think rationally. In Ezekiel, for instance:

> Here, *Assyria* was a cedar in Lebanon, beautiful in its branch, and [forming] a shady grove, and tall in its height; and its bough was surrounded by dense growth. The water made it grow; the depth of the *water* raised it up. A *river* was winding all around its planting-place. (Ezekiel 31:3, 4)

The ability to reason is here called a cedar in Lebanon. The bough surrounded by dense growth symbolizes factual information in the memory, which resembles such a bough. Still more plainly in Isaiah:

> On that day there will be a path from Egypt to *Assyria,* and *Assyria* will come into Egypt and Egypt into *Assyria,* and the Egyptians will serve *Assyria.* On that day Israel will be third to Egypt and *Assyria,* a blessing in the middle of the earth, whom Jehovah Sabaoth[122] will bless, saying, "A blessing on my people Egypt and on the work of my hands, *Assyria,* and on my inheritance, Israel!" (Isaiah 19:23, 24, 25)

Here and in many other places, Egypt symbolizes factual information, Assyria the ability to reason, and Israel the ability to understand.

Like Egypt, the *Euphrates* symbolizes secular knowledge—facts—and the sensory impressions on which facts are based. The prophetic parts of the Word make this clear, as in Micah:

> My enemy has said, "Where is Jehovah your God?" A day will come on which he will build your bulwarks. That is the day the set limit will be far off; that is the day when he will come all the way to you from *Assyria,* and to the cities of Egypt and to the *River* [Euphrates].[123] (Micah 7:10, 11, 12)

This is how the prophets spoke about the Coming of the Lord, who was to regenerate us, so that we would come to be like heaven's inhabitants. In Jeremiah:

> What does it matter whether you go to Egypt to drink the waters of the Sihor? And what does it matter whether you go to *Assyria* to drink the waters of the *River* [Euphrates]? (Jeremiah 2:18)

Egypt and the Euphrates alike stand for facts, Assyria for rationalizations constructed out of them. In David:

> You have caused a grapevine to travel from Egypt; you have driven away the nations; you have planted it. You have sent its offshoots all the way out to the sea, and its tendrils to the *River* [Euphrates]. (Psalms 80:8, 11)

In this passage the river Euphrates again stands for sensory and factual information. The Euphrates, after all, formed the boundary of Israel's dominions on the Assyrian side.[124] Similarly for spiritual and heavenly people, facts in the memory are the outer limit of understanding and wisdom.

These words spoken to Abraham have the identical symbolism:

> To your seed I will give this land, from the river of Egypt all the way to the great river, the river *Euphrates*. (Genesis 15:18)

These two boundaries symbolize the same things.

121 How the inner life of heavenly people is organized, or the order in which its constituent parts develop, may be illustrated by these rivers. To be specific, the pattern starts with the Lord, who is the east. From him comes wisdom, through wisdom comes understanding, through understanding comes reason; and reason, in turn, makes the facts we have memorized come alive. This is the proper way for the inner life to be organized, and that is how it is organized in heavenly people.

This is why the elders of Israel, in representing heavenly people, were described as wise, understanding, and knowledgeable (Deuteronomy 1:13, 15). Likewise Bezalel, the maker of the ark, is described as being "filled with the spirit of God, in *wisdom,* in *understanding,* and in *knowledge,* and in every kind of work" (Exodus 31:3; 35:31; 36:1, 2).

122 Genesis 2:15. *And Jehovah God took the human and put the human in the Garden of Eden to cultivate it and to guard it.*

The *Garden of Eden* symbolizes everything in a heavenly person, which is the subject here. *Cultivating the garden* and *guarding it* means that such a person is free to enjoy all of those things but not to claim personal possession of them, because they are the Lord's.

123 Heavenly people acknowledge, because they perceive, that absolutely everything is the Lord's. Spiritual people too acknowledge it, but only in speech, because they have learned it from the Word. Worldly and body-centered people do not accept or agree with the idea; they claim as their own any ability they discover inside themselves, and if they lose it, they consider it completely destroyed.

124 Various things the Lord taught make it clear that wisdom, understanding, reason, and knowledge are not ours but the Lord's. In Matthew, for example, the Lord equated himself with a householder who planted a vineyard, set a hedge around it, and rented it to some growers (Matthew 21:33). In John:

> The spirit of truth will lead you into all truth, since he[125] will not speak on his own authority but will speak whatever he hears. He will give me

glory, because he will take from what is mine and proclaim it to you. (John 16:13, 14)

Again in John:

None of us can acquire anything unless it is given to us from heaven. (John 3:27)

Anyone privileged to learn even just a few of heaven's secrets knows that this is true.

Genesis 2:16. *And Jehovah God commanded the human concerning it, saying, "From every tree of the garden you are definitely to eat."*

To eat from every tree is to depend on perception in order to know and recognize what is good and true; a *tree* is perception, as stated [§102].

The people of the earliest church knew about true faith through revelations, since they spoke with the Lord and angels. They were also taught through visions and dreams, which filled them with the exquisite pleasures of Paradise.

They received from the Lord an uninterrupted state of perception, which enabled them to tell immediately whether or not a thought based on memorized information was true and good. This ability was so unerring that if something false surfaced, it inspired not merely distaste but even horror in them. It is the same with angels.

Later on, the earliest church's perceptive abilities were replaced by a knowledge of truth and goodness based [at first] on the prior revelations and afterward on revelations recorded in the Word.

Genesis 2:17. *"But from the tree of the knowledge of good and evil you may not eat, because on the day on which you eat from it you will surely die."*

The meaning of verses 16 and 17 is that people are allowed to depend on any perception they receive from the Lord to tell them what is true or good but not on themselves or the world around them (in other words, when inquiring into religious mysteries, they are not to rely on sense impressions or facts); and that to do so would be the death of their heavenly quality.

People's desire to rely on sensory evidence or secular knowledge when investigating religious mysteries caused the fall of the earliest church, and specifically of the generation that inherited it, as described in the next chapter. But more than that, it causes the fall of every church, because it breeds not only falsities but also wickedness in life.

When we are under the sway of the world and our bodies, we say in our hearts, "As for faith and its ramifications, if my senses do not teach me to see, or if facts do not teach me to understand, I refuse to believe." In confirmation, we remind ourselves that what holds true on the earthly plane cannot conflict with spiritual realities. So we want our senses to teach us about heavenly and divine affairs. This is as impossible as it is for a camel to go through the eye of a needle.[126] The more we rely on sensory evidence in order to gain wisdom, the more we blind ourselves, to the point that we stop believing in anything, even the existence of a spiritual dimension or of eternal life. That is the consequence of our original assumption.

This is what *eating from the tree of the knowledge of good and evil* means; and the more we eat from it, the more deadened we become.

If we do not rely on the world for our wisdom, on the other hand, but on the Lord, we tell ourselves at heart to believe in the Lord, that is, in all that the Lord has said in the Word, because those are reliable truths. This is the principle on which we base our thinking. We use rational argument, factual knowledge, sensory evidence, and physical phenomena in confirmation, but whatever fails to confirm the Word we put aside.

129. Clearly our assumptions control us, even when they are utterly false. All our knowledge and our sophistry bolster these assumptions, drawing together endless supporting arguments that harden us in our false ideas. If we seize, then, on the premise that we will believe nothing until we see and understand it, we will never be able to believe anything. Spiritual and heavenly concepts remain beyond the range of our eyesight, beyond the grasp of our imagination.

The proper method is to learn wisdom from the Lord, that is, from his Word. Then all goes well, and in addition light is shed on our rational thinking and factual knowledge.

By no means, you see, is the acquisition of knowledge forbidden. Knowledge is useful for our lives, and pleasurable. For a believer no prohibition exists on thinking and speaking the way the well-educated of the world do. But we are to do so on the principle of belief in the Lord's Word and of using earthly truth to confirm spiritual and heavenly truth so far as we can, using language familiar to the academic world. The Lord, not ourselves, must be the source of our principles. This is life; the other way is death.

130. For those wanting to learn wisdom from the *world,* the "garden" is sensory evidence and factual information; their "Eden" is self-love and materialism. Their east is west; that is, they are their own east. Their

Euphrates is all the factual knowledge they have learned—damnable knowledge. Their second river, in the area of Assyria, is insane reasoning and the falsity it spawns. Their third river, in the area of Cush, is principles that advocate evil and falsity, developed out of such reasoning; these are the catechism of their faith. Their fourth is the wisdom that results.[127] The Word describes this wisdom as magic,[128] and that is why Egypt, which symbolizes scholarly learning, also symbolizes occult knowledge, having adopted the magical arts. The reason is given in various places in the Word: they wanted to teach themselves wisdom. Ezekiel speaks of them this way:

> This is what the Lord Jehovih[129] has said: "Here, now, I am against you, *Pharaoh,* king of *Egypt,* you great sea creature, lying in the middle of his rivers, who has said, 'My river is mine, and I have made myself.' And the land of Egypt will become a desolation and wasteland—and they will know that I am Jehovah—because he said, 'The *river* is mine, and I myself have made it.'" (Ezekiel 29:3, 9)

In another passage treating of Pharaoh the Egyptian, the same prophet refers to people of this type as trees of Eden in hell:

> ... when I make him go down into hell, accompanying those going down into the pit. Whom have you come to resemble this way, in glory and in greatness, among the *trees of Eden,* when you were made to go down with the *trees of Eden* into the underground realm,[130] in the midst of the uncircumcised, with those stabbed by the sword? This is Pharaoh and all his horde. (Ezekiel 31:16, 18)

The trees of Eden stand for facts and religious knowledge from the Word, which such people accordingly profane by the use of crooked reasoning.

18. And Jehovah God said, "It is not good for the human to be alone. Let me make him an aid that seems to be his."[131]

19. And out of the soil Jehovah God formed every animal of the field and every bird in the heavens and brought it to the human to see what he would call it. And whatever the human called the living soul, that was its name.

20. And the human gave names to every beast and to the bird in the heavens and to every wild animal of the field; but for the human no aid was found that seemed to be his.

21. And Jehovah God made slumber fall on the human, and he went to sleep. And he took one of his ribs and closed up the flesh in its place.

22. And Jehovah God built a woman out of the rib that he took from the human and brought her to the human.

23. And the human said, "This time, bone from my bones and flesh from my flesh. This is why she will be called 'wife': because she was taken from man."[132]

24. Therefore a man will leave his father and his mother and cling to his wife, and they will become one flesh.

25. And they were both naked, the human and his wife, and did not blush.

Summary

[131] THESE verses deal with later generations of the earliest church, who strove for autonomy.

[132] Human nature is such that we are not content with the Lord's leading but also desire to be led by ourselves and the world, or in other words, to act independently. Consequently the present verses treat of the sense of autonomy yielded to humankind (verse 18).

[133] People are first given the ability to recognize the positive feelings and true concepts given them as gifts by the Lord, but still they seek independence (verses 19, 20).

[134] So they are brought into a state of self-governance and are granted a sense of autonomy, as depicted by the rib from which the woman was built (verses 21, 22, 23).

[135] Then heavenly, spiritual life is linked so closely with the sense of independence that they seem to form a unit (verse 24).

[136] The Lord introduces innocence into their self-direction to keep it from becoming objectionable (verse 25).

Inner Meaning

[137] THREE chapters of Genesis deal generally with the earliest church (called the human) from its first period to its last, when it died. The earlier part of this chapter tells of its heyday, when it formed a heavenly

individual. The current section speaks of that church and its descendants when they ardently sought autonomy.

Genesis 2:18. *And Jehovah God said, "It is not good for the human to be alone. Let me make him an aid that seems to be his."*

Being alone symbolizes being discontent with the Lord's leading and desiring to be led by oneself and the world. An *aid that seems to be his* symbolizes a sense of autonomy, later referred to as the rib from which the woman was built [Genesis 2:22].

The ancients described people who were led by the Lord (the way people of heavenly character are) as living *alone* because evil or rather evil spirits no longer bothered them. In the Jewish church, the same circumstances were represented by the promise that when the other nations had been driven out they would live alone. For this reason the Word predicts several times that the Lord's church would be alone. An example from Jeremiah:

> Rise, go up to a nation at rest, *living securely*. No double doors, no bar on the gate do they have; they live *alone*. (Jeremiah 49:31)

In a prophecy of Moses':

> Israel has lived *securely, alone*. (Deuteronomy 33:28)

Still more explicitly in Balaam's prophecy:

> Look, a people that lives *alone* and is not counted among the nations! (Numbers 23:9)

Here the nations stand for different kinds of evil.

The generation that inherited the earliest church did not wish to live alone or, what is the same, to be heavenly or, again, to be led by the Lord as a heavenly individual. They wanted to be in among the nations, as the Jewish church was. Since this was what they wanted, the verse says that it was not good for the human to be alone. Those who yearn for evil are already involved in it, and they are allowed to have it.

A key to the reason why *an aid that seemed to be his* symbolizes a sense of autonomy lies in the nature of autonomy and in the story that follows. Since the people in the church being discussed here had good character, they were granted self-direction, but of a kind that only appeared to be theirs, which is why the verse says the aid *seemed to be his*.

An endless number of things can be said about self-rule[133] in the individual, specifically about its nature in a body-oriented or worldly person, in a spiritual person, and in a heavenly person.

In carnal, materialistic people, their sense of autonomy is the all-in-all. They know nothing else. If it died, they would think *they* had died, as noted earlier [§123].

Autonomy looks the same in spiritual people. Although they know and admit that the Lord is the life in all things, that he is the giver of wisdom and understanding and so of thought and action, they do not really believe it.

Heavenly people, however, acknowledge that the Lord is the life of all and the giver of thought and action because they perceive that it is so, and they have no desire at all for autonomy. Yet even though they do not seek autonomy, the Lord gives it to them. This autonomy or selfhood is directly bound up with their ability to perceive what is good and true and with their happiness.

Such is the autonomy or selfhood present in angels, and its presence brings them the highest peace and tranquility. Their selfhood is composed of qualities that belong to the Lord, who governs their self-governance, or rather governs them through their self-governance. This selfhood is the epitome of heavenliness; the selfhood of a body-centered person, on the other hand, is hellish. More about autonomy or selfhood will follow, however.

142. Genesis 2:19, 20. *And out of the soil Jehovah God formed every animal of the field and every bird in the heavens and brought it to the human to see what he would call it. And whatever the human called the living soul, that was its name. And the human gave names to every beast and to the bird in the heavens and to every wild animal of the field; but for the human no aid was found that seemed to be his.*

Animals symbolize emotions of a heavenly type; *birds in the heavens* symbolize emotions of a spiritual type. To put it another way, animals symbolize the contents of the will, birds the contents of the intellect. *Bringing them to the human to see, so that he could call them by name,* means granting humankind the ability to recognize the nature of those feelings; the fact that he gave them names means that people recognized the nature of the feelings. At the same time, even though they recognized the nature of the virtuous emotions and true concepts given them as gifts by the Lord, they still strove for autonomy, as expressed in the same words used before: *he did not find an aid that seemed to be his.*

143. These days it may seem strange that in ancient times *animals* and beasts symbolized feelings and similar human qualities. But [in the first place] people then viewed things the way heaven does, and [in the second place] animals represent these qualities in the world of spirits as well. (In fact a quality is represented by an animal whose nature reflects that

quality.) In consequence, when the ancients mentioned the animals they meant nothing else than the qualities.

In the Word, too, no other meaning is intended in any passage that mentions animals in general or in particular. The whole of the prophetic portion is full of these references. Not knowing what each species of animal symbolizes makes it impossible to understand what the Word contains in its inner meaning.

As noted above [§45], animals are of two kinds: bad (because they are dangerous) and good (because they are harmless). The good ones, such as sheep, lambs, and doves, symbolize positive emotions. Here, where the heavenly person (or the heavenly kind of spiritual person) is the subject, that is their symbolism.

Sections 45 and 46 quoted several places in the Word that show that animals in general symbolize feelings, eliminating the need for further demonstration here.

144

In regard to the idea that *naming things* means recognizing their nature, it needs to be realized that the ancients took a name to mean simply the essence of a thing, and *seeing something and naming it* to mean recognizing its nature.[134] This was due to the fact that they gave their daughters and sons names with a relevant meaning. Every name had a unique element that indicated where people were from and what they were like. Explanations further on concerning Jacob's twelve sons will, by the Lord's divine mercy, demonstrate this.[135]

Since names, then, told where people were from and what they were like, that is exactly what naming something meant to those ancient people. Such a manner of speaking was familiar to them, and anyone who fails to understand it will be puzzled by the symbolism.

145

In the Word as well, a *name* means the essence of a thing and *seeing something and naming it* means recognizing its nature, as in Isaiah:

> I will give you the treasures of the dark and the hidden riches of secret places, in order that you may know that I am Jehovah; *the one who gives* you your *name;* the God of Israel. For the sake of my servant Jacob and of Israel my chosen, I have also *called* you by your *name;* I have *surnamed* you, but you do not know me. (Isaiah 45:3, 4)

Calling by name and naming symbolize foreseeing a person's nature. In the same author:

> A new *name* will be *given* to you, which the mouth of Jehovah will declare. (Isaiah 62:2)

This time it means that the person will change, as is evident from the verses before and after it. Again:

> Don't be afraid, Israel, because I have redeemed you; I have *called* you by your *name:* You Are Mine. (Isaiah 43:1)

The message here is that he knows what we are like. Once again:

> Raise your eyes up high and see who has created those things, leading their legions out by number. He will *call* them all by *name.* (Isaiah 40:26)

In other words, he knows everyone. In Revelation:

> You have a few *names* in Sardis that have not defiled their clothes. Those who conquer will be dressed in white clothes, and I will not delete their *name* from the book of life; and I will proclaim their *name* before my Father and before his angels. (Revelation 3:4, 5)

In another place:

> . . . those whose *names* are not written in the Lamb's book of life. (Revelation 13:8)

In none of these places does *names* literally mean names but rather what the people are like. No one knows anyone's name in heaven, either, but each knows what the other is like.

146. From all these explanations you can see how the symbolism interconnects. Verse 18 said, "It is not good for the human to be alone. Let me make him an aid that seems to be his." Next come the animals and birds, which also appeared earlier, and then immediately the same words recur, "For the human no aid was found that seemed to be his." That is, when humans received the ability to recognize their own nature—the nature of their good emotions and true concepts—they still sought independence. After all, when people are such that they want to rule themselves, they begin to despise all that the Lord has to offer them, no matter how clearly those things are presented and illustrated for them.

147. Genesis 2:21. *And Jehovah God made slumber fall on the human, and he went to sleep. And he took one of his ribs and closed up the flesh in its place.*

The *rib,* a chest bone, means that part of our identity which is hardly alive and yet is our very own, so that we love it tenderly. The *flesh in place of the rib* means the part of our identity that *is* alive. *Slumber* means a state brought over us to make it seem to us as if we have autonomy. This state is like sleep because in it we have no idea that we do not live, think, speak, and act on our own; but when we begin to realize how wrong this view is, we are roused from our sleep and wake up.

Our identity or independence—which is indeed our own and is therefore tenderly loved by us—was called a *rib* or chest bone because to the earliest people the chest, with its heart and lungs, symbolized our tender love for others. Since bones are only minimally alive, they symbolized attributes of relatively little value. *Flesh,* however, symbolized attributes that have a living quality.

The reason for these symbolisms lies deeply hidden but was known to the earliest people. It will, with the Lord's divine mercy, be discussed later.[136]

The Word also uses bones as a symbol for a person's sense of self and specifically for a sense of self brought to life by the Lord. In Isaiah:

> Jehovah will satisfy your soul in the barrens, and he will make your *bones* ready; and you will be like a well-watered garden. (Isaiah 58:11)

In the same author:

> Then you will see, and your heart will rejoice, and your *bones* will be like sprouting grass. (Isaiah 66:14)

In David:

> All my *bones* will say, "Jehovah, who is like you?" (Psalms 35:10)

This appears still more clearly in Ezekiel, where it talks about bones that will take on flesh and have breath enter them:

> The hand of Jehovah put me in the middle of the valley, and the valley was full of *bones.* And he said to me, "Prophesy over those *bones,* and you are to say to them, 'Dry *bones,* listen to the word of Jehovah. This is what the Lord Jehovih has said to these *bones:* "See? I am bringing breath into you, and you will live. And I will put tendons on you and bring *flesh* up over you and draw skin over you and put breath in you, and you will live. And you will know that I am Jehovah."'" (Ezekiel 37:1, 4, 5, 6)

[2] Human selfhood, viewed from heaven, looks completely bony, lifeless, and hideous—inherently dead. But once the Lord gives it life, it appears to have flesh. Human selfhood is in fact nothing more than a dead trifle, even though it seems to its owner to be significant and indeed all-important. Anything living in us comes from the Lord's life. If his life

withdrew from us, we would fall dead as a stone. We are merely organs designed to receive life, but the nature of the organ that we are determines how we respond to that life.

Only the Lord has autonomy. By his own power he redeems us and by his own power he saves us. This autonomy or selfhood of his is life, and it causes our selfhood, which is inherently dead, to come alive. The Lord's words in Luke symbolize his selfhood:

> A spirit doesn't have flesh and bones as you see I have. (Luke 24:39, 40)

Another sign was the fact that not a bone of the Passover lamb was to be broken (Exodus 12:46).[137]

150 Our condition when we rely on ourselves or when we think we live by our own power can be compared to *slumber* or unconsciousness. The people of old actually called that condition slumber, and the Word speaks of it as "being flooded with a spirit of slumber" [Isaiah 29:10] and "sleeping a sleep" [Jeremiah 51:39, 57].

The truth that human selfhood is inherently dead, that none of us have any life on our own, is demonstrated in the world of spirits by vivid experience—so vivid that evil spirits, who love nothing but selfhood or a sense of autonomy and obstinately insist that they live independently, become convinced and admit that life is not theirs after all.

I more than any other have been given the opportunity in the last several years to see what "human autonomy" amounts to, finding as I have that not a single one of my thoughts originated in me. I have been able to perceive with utmost clarity that every component idea in my thinking has come from outside, and sometimes I have seen where it came from and how it entered.

Therefore those who suppose they live by their own power have it wrong. By believing that they live independently, they adopt all possible evil and falsity as their own, and this they would never do if they believed the situation to be as it really is.

151 Genesis 2:22. *And Jehovah God built a woman out of the rib that he took from the human and brought her to the human.*

Building means reconstructing what has fallen down. A *rib* symbolizes a sense of self devoid of life. A *woman* symbolizes a sense of self brought to life by the Lord. *Bringing her to the human* means giving people a sense of self.

Unlike their parents, the members of the generation that inherited the earliest church preferred not to have a heavenly character but to lead themselves. They sought selfhood or a sense of autonomy, so it was yielded to them. Still, it was a living selfhood, vivified by the Lord, so it is called a woman and later a wife.

If you give it even a little thought, you can see that woman did not come from the rib of man and that these words involve deeper secrets than have ever yet come to light. The fact that the *woman* symbolizes selfhood is indicated by her being the one who was deceived [Genesis 3:1–6], since nothing ever deceives us besides our self-absorption or, what is the same, love for ourselves and for the material world.

The exact wording is that the woman was *built* out of a rib, not that she was made, formed, or created, as before [§88], where regeneration was discussed. *Build* is used because it means reconstructing what has fallen. It is similar to places where the Word uses *build* of evil, *raise up* of falsities, and *renew* of both. In Isaiah, for instance:

> They will *rebuild* the eternal wastelands, the ancient desolate places they will *raise up,* and they will *renew* the wasted cities, the desolate places of generation after generation. (Isaiah 61:4)

Wastelands here and elsewhere stand for evil, while desolate places stand for falsities; *build* is applied to the former and *raise up* to the latter—a distinction carefully observed in other prophetic passages. In Jeremiah:

> I will *build* you again so that you may be *built up,* virgin Israel.[138] (Jeremiah 31:4)

Nothing evil or false can possibly exist that is not our own and the product of our "autonomy." Human selfhood is wickedness itself, and consequently a human being is nothing but evil and falsity.

This fact has stood out whenever I have seen people's intrinsic characteristics presented visually in the world of spirits.[139] The sight is as ugly as any a painter could paint—with variations, according to the nature of the particular personality involved. It is so hideous that the individual whose traits are being displayed shudders at herself or himself and wants to run, as if from the Devil.[140]

When the Lord gives life to our intrinsic characteristics, though, they look lovely and beautiful—with variations, depending on the particular life involved and the heavenly quality the Lord can add to it. Those provided with charity, or enlivened by it, look like boys and girls with strikingly beautiful faces. Those for whom the quality is innocence look like toddlers, naked but decked out in different ways, with flower garlands around their chests or tiaras on their heads, living at play in diamond-bright air, attuned to the happiness that wells up from deep within.

155 The words *a woman was built out of a rib* conceal more than anyone can ever see in the literal meaning, since the Lord's Word is such that deep down it concerns itself with the Lord himself and his kingdom. This is the source of all life in the Word. In the same vein, the inmost concern here is the heavenly marriage.[141]

The heavenly marriage is something that exists in our selfhood. Moreover, it is because of the heavenly marriage that our selfhood, after being brought to life by the Lord, is called the Lord's bride and wife.

When the Lord brings it to life, our sense of self gives us the ability to perceive all the good desired by love and all the truth taught by faith. So it holds within it all wisdom and understanding, joined to an indescribable happiness.

Still, a few words will not be enough to explain the nature of this living autonomy called the Lord's bride and wife. I can offer only this much: that angels perceive that they live from the Lord, although when not reflecting, they are under the full impression that they live on their own. This living selfhood is a sensation affecting all of them, telling them something has changed whenever they depart in the least from a loving goodness and religious truth. They enjoy their customary peace and happiness, which defies description, when they share in a perception that they live from the Lord.

A living sense of self is also what Jeremiah refers to when he says,

> Jehovah has created something new in the earth: a *woman* will encircle a *man*. (Jeremiah 31:22)

This too is talking about the heavenly marriage, the woman symbolizing a sense of autonomy brought to life by the Lord. She is said to encircle the man because our self-life encircles us as the fleshed-out rib encircles the heart.

156 Genesis 2:23. *And the human said, "This time, bone from my bones and flesh from my flesh. This is why she will be called 'wife': because she was taken from man."*[142]

Bone from one's bones and *flesh from one's flesh* symbolizes the sense of autonomy of our outer being; *bone* symbolizes that autonomy without much life, and *flesh* symbolizes that autonomy with life. The *man*, though, symbolizes our inner being, and because the inner being is intimately coupled with the outer being, as the next verse says, this desire to rule ourselves is here called a *wife*—the term used in the next verse—instead of a woman as before.¹⁴³ *This time* means that it has now been accomplished, because our state has changed.¹⁴⁴

Since *bone of one's bones and flesh of one's flesh* symbolized what is our own in the outer being (which holds the inner being), in ancient times they used *bone of my bones and flesh of my flesh* to refer to anyone who could be called theirs. This was so whether they belonged to the same household or the same clan or had some other relationship. Laban so described Jacob:

> You are certainly my bone and my flesh. (Genesis 29:14)

Abimelech said the same of his mother's brothers and of the clan of his maternal grandfather's household:

> Remember that I am *your bone* and *your flesh*. (Judges 9:1, 2, 3)

The tribe of Israel also described themselves that way to David:

> Here now, we are *your bone* and we are *your flesh*. (2 Samuel 5:1)

The following passage from Isaiah shows that a *man* symbolizes the inner being or, what is the same, someone understanding and wise:

> I am looking, and there is not a *man,* and [seeking] among them, and there is not a counselor. (Isaiah 41:28)

In other words, there is no one wise or understanding. In Jeremiah:

> Dash about through the streets of Jerusalem and see whether you find a *man,* whether he is exercising judgment, seeking truth. (Jeremiah 5:1)

Exercising judgment stands for being wise; and seeking truth, for having understanding.

It is not easy to perceive how the situation stands with all this unless one knows what heavenly people's state is like—that their inner being is distinguished from their outer being. The distinction is clear enough that they can tell what belongs to their inner and what to their outer being. They can also tell how the Lord uses the inner being to regulate the outer.

But the condition of this later generation changed because of their desire for autonomy, which belongs to the outer being. They no longer perceived the distinction between their inner and outer beings; for them it was as if the inner and outer were one. This perception is a result of the desire for autonomy.

160   Genesis 2:24. *Therefore a man will leave his father and his mother and cling to his wife, and they will become one flesh.*

Leaving father and mother is leaving the inner being behind, as it is the inner being that conceives and gives birth to the outer being. *To cling to one's wife* is to have an inner being within our outer being. That they are to be *one flesh* means that the two coexist there. Prior to this time the inner being was spirit, as was the outer being through its connection with the inner. Now, however, they *become* flesh.

By this means, heavenly, spiritual life was linked so closely with the sense of independence that they seemed to form a unit.

161   This later generation of the earliest church was not evil; they were still good. And because they were eager to live in their outer being or selfhood, the Lord granted them their wish. In his mercy, though, he wove a heavenly-spiritual quality into their self-sufficiency.

In order to understand how the inner and outer being act in concert, or appear as one, it is necessary to know how the one exerts an influence on the other. To form at least some idea of this, take action as an example. An action that does not have charity (or love and faith) behind it and the Lord behind that is not an action that can be called either a charitable deed or the fruit of faith.

162   All laws ordaining what is true and right flow from heavenly origins, or from the structure of the inner life in a person who belongs to heaven. Heaven, taken as a whole, *is* a heavenly person because the Lord alone is a heavenly person. He is the totality of each and every thing in heaven and in the heavenly individual. This is how the inhabitants there come to be called heavenly.

Since heavenly origins or the structure of a heavenly person's life is the source from which arises every law ordaining what is true and right—most of all the law for marriage—the heavenly marriage is the source and pattern for all marriages on earth. The heavenly marriage allows for one Lord and one heaven, or one church with the Lord as head. The resulting law for marriage is that there must be one man and one wife. When there are, they represent the heavenly marriage and provide a model of the heavenly person.

Not only was this law revealed to the men of the earliest church, it was also written on their inner being. Consequently a man in those times had just one wife and set up one household. But when the descendants of those earliest people stopped being deep people and became shallow instead, they began to marry many wives.

[2] For the men of the earliest church, the love that belongs to marriage was like heaven itself and its happiness, because their marriages represented the heavenly marriage. When that church started to go downhill, they no longer found happiness in marriage love but in the enjoyment of many partners instead—a pleasure that resides in the outer self. The Lord calls this phenomenon hard-heartedness, the grounds on which Moses allowed them to marry multiple wives. As the Lord himself teaches:

> Because of your hardness of heart Moses wrote you this commandment. From the beginning of creation, though, God made them male and female. Therefore a person shall leave his father and mother and cling to his wife, and the two will become one flesh; so they are no longer two but one flesh. What God has joined together, then, no human shall separate. (Mark 10:5, 6, 7, 8, 9)

Genesis 2:25. *And they were both naked, the human and his wife, and did not blush.*

They were naked and did not blush means that they were innocent; the Lord introduced innocence into their selfhood to keep it from being objectionable.

Human selfhood, as noted [§§39, 59, 154], is nothing but evil; presented in visual form it is extremely ugly. But when infused by the Lord with charitable love and innocence, it appears virtuous and lovely, as stated in §154.

Love for our fellow humans and innocence are what excuse self-centeredness, or a person's evil and falsity. Not only do they excuse it, they almost eliminate it, as anyone can see in young children. When toddlers show love to each other and to their parents while glowing with childish innocence, what is actually evil and false in them does not seem so and even gives pleasure.

This shows that no one can be let into heaven without some innocence, as the Lord said:

> "Allow the little children to come to me and do not stop them. These are the kind who make up God's kingdom. Truly, I say to you: anyone who does not receive the kingdom of God like a little child will not enter it." So taking them up into the curve of his arms, he put his hands on them and blessed them. (Mark 10:14, 15, 16)

The symbolism of their unembarrassed *nakedness* as innocence is highlighted by what followed, when their integrity and innocence deserted them. Then they *blushed* at their nakedness, which seemed like a disgrace to them, and that is why they hid.

Certain representative acts in the world of spirits also demonstrate that unembarrassed nudity symbolizes innocence. When spirits want to exonerate themselves and display their blamelessness, they show themselves naked, to testify to their innocence.

The strongest confirmation of this meaning is supplied by the innocent in heaven, who look like naked toddlers, wearing garlands that reflect their particular kind of innocence. Inhabitants with less innocence appear in beautiful, shimmery clothes—diamondlike silk, you might say—of a kind the prophets sometimes saw angels wearing.[145]

166 This is what the Word contains in this chapter, but the contents I have laid bare are few. Since they have to do with the person of heavenly character, and hardly anything is known about such a person these days, the little I have disclosed must seem murky to some.

167 If people realized how much was hidden in each verse, they would be dumbfounded. So much is hidden that it could never be told. This fact is scarcely visible in the letter.

To give some idea in a few words: In the world of spirits (since it is a representative world) the literal words, just as they are, are represented in a living way, arranged in beautiful display. Any live representation in that world is then perceived in all its finer detail by the angelic spirits in the second heaven. What the angelic spirits see is then perceived by the angels in the third heaven in great richness.[146] These angels see the represented text filled with angelic ideas for which there are no words, and by the Lord's good pleasure, they see it in all its boundless variety. Such is the nature of the Lord's Word.

Our Resurrection from Death and Entry into Eternal Life

168 IN accordance with my promise [§72], I will now relate the steps by which we move from bodily life into eternal life, in order to show how a person is revived. The explanation is based not on hearsay but on my own personal experience.

[169] I was brought into a state in which I was unaware of physical sensation—almost into the condition of someone who is dying. My inner life and thinking remained unimpaired, however, so that I would perceive and remember what was happening. I underwent the same experiences as those who have died and are being revived, when their breathing is at first consistent with continued life and then falls silent.

[170] Heavenly angels were present, occupying the area of my heart, so that I seemed to be at one with them in my heart. We were so close that at last hardly anything of my own remained to me besides thought and the perception that comes with thought. This lasted several hours.

[171] In this way I was removed from communication with spirits in the world of spirits. They assumed I had departed bodily life.

[172] In addition to the heavenly angels occupying the region of my heart, there were two angels sitting at my head. I perceived that this is so for everyone.

[173] The angels sitting at my head were completely silent, communicating their thoughts only by the face, so that I felt something like a new face come over me—two new faces, in fact, since there were two angels.

When the angels perceive that their faces are being mirrored, they know the person is dead.

[174] After recognizing their faces on me, they caused certain changes in the area around my mouth and in this way shared their thoughts with me. (To speak through the area around someone else's mouth is common for heavenly angels.) I was able to perceive their thought-speech.

[175] I smelled a sweet fragrance, like that from an embalmed corpse. Whenever heavenly angels are present, the scent of a dead body comes across as sweet. If evil spirits smell it, they cannot come near.

[176] All the while I remained at one with the heavenly angels, held in a fairly close embrace in the area around my heart, as I perceived and also felt in my pulse.

[177] The idea was instilled in me that angels hold us in any thoughts we have at the moment of death that are devout and holy. I also gathered that when people are dying most of them are thinking about eternal life—few are thinking about their salvation or happiness—so the angels keep them in that thought about eternal life.

[178] The heavenly angels hold us in this thought quite a while before withdrawing and leaving us to the spiritual angels who then become our companions. Meanwhile we fully, if dimly, believe that we are still alive in our bodies.

179 As soon as the internal organs of the body grow cold, our living substances, wherever they are located, are separated out. This would happen even if they were lost in the thousand interlinking passages of a labyrinth.[147] The Lord's mercy, which I had already experienced as a living and powerful pull, is so strong that it could not leave any living element behind.

180 The heavenly angels sitting at my head remained with me a while after I was "revived" without speaking except in their silent way. From their thought-speech I learned that they completely discounted all my misconceptions and falsities. It was not that they ridiculed them; they appeared not to care about them at all.

They speak by thoughts, without sound. This is the way they start to talk with the souls whom they accompany in the beginning.

181 People revived in this way by the heavenly angels are still experiencing a dim sort of life. When it is time to pass the people on to the spiritual angels, the heavenly angels wait a little and then withdraw once the spiritual angels have arrived. I was also shown how the latter enable the reviving soul to receive the use of light. See the beginning of the next chapter for more on this.

Genesis 3

Our Entry, Once Revived, into Eternal Life (Continued)

WHEN heavenly angels are present with the revived, they do not leave them; they love each one. But if our soul is such that we can no longer enjoy the company of heavenly angels, we long to get away from them, at which point spiritual angels arrive and give us the gift of light. Until then, we do not have the use of our sight, only of our thoughts. [182]

I was shown how these angels do their work. They seemed to roll a kind of membrane off my left eye toward the nasal septum to open my eye and give it the use of the light. To the person being revived this seems to be exactly what is happening, but it is only an appearance. [183]

When this small membrane seems to have been rolled off, a dim kind of glow can be seen, like the light seen through the eyelids on waking. We are in a peaceful state, still protected by the heavenly angels. [184]

Next there appears a shadowy something the color of the sky, with a tiny star in it; but I sensed that different people experience this differently.

Afterward something seems to be rolled gently off the face, and we return to consciousness. The angels take the greatest care at this point to prevent any idea from rising out of us unless it is a fairly gentle, loving one. Now we learn that we are a spirit. [185]

This is when we start to live, and at first things are happy and cheerful, since we feel we have entered on eternal life. This stage is represented by a brilliant light with a beautiful golden tinge, symbolizing the fact that our first stage of life is heavenly, with a touch of the spiritual. [186]

Then we are welcomed into a community of good spirits. This is represented by a young adult astride a horse, directing it toward hell, although the horse is unable to move a step. We are represented by a young adult because as soon as we come into eternal life we find ourselves among angels and so seem to ourselves to be in the prime of our youth. [187]

188 The kind of life that comes next is represented by a scene in which the youth dismounts and goes on foot because of the horse's inability to move from the spot. The thought is planted in our minds that we will be taught about truth and goodness.

189 Then some gently rising paths become visible, symbolizing the fact that we will be led gradually toward heaven by a knowledge of truth and goodness and an acknowledgment of our own nature. Unless we acknowledge who we are and learn what is true and good, we can never be led there.

See the continuation at the end of this chapter [§§314–319].

Genesis 3

1. And the snake was crafty above every wild animal of the field that Jehovah God had made, and it said to the woman, "Did God really say, 'You must not eat from any tree of the garden'?"

2. And the woman said to the snake, "We are to eat from the fruit of the tree of the garden.

3. But from the fruit of the tree that is in the middle of the garden, God said, 'You may not eat from it, nor are you to touch it, or you will die from it.'"

4. And the snake said to the woman, "You are not going to 'surely die,'

5. because God knows that on the day when you eat from it, your eyes will be opened and you will be like God, knowing good and evil."

6. And the woman saw that the tree was good for eating, and that it was appealing to the eyes, and a tree desirable for lending insight. And she took some of its fruit and ate, and she gave to her husband too, who was with her, and he ate.

7. And the eyes of both were opened and they realized that they were naked. And they sewed together the leaf of the fig tree and made loincloths for themselves.

8. And they heard the voice of Jehovah God, going alone in the garden at the breeze of the day. And the human hid himself, as did his wife, from Jehovah God's face, in the middle of the tree of the garden.[148]

9. And Jehovah God called to the human and said to him, "Where are you?"

10. And he said, "I heard your voice in the garden, and I was afraid because I was naked, and I hid myself."

11. And he said, "Who pointed out to you that you were naked? You ate from the tree from which I commanded you not to eat, didn't you?"

12. And the human said, "The woman whom you gave to be with me, she gave me from the tree and I ate."

13. And Jehovah God said to the woman, "Why have you done this?" And the woman said, "The snake deceived me and I ate."

Summary

THESE verses deal with the third stage of the earliest church, in which people's eagerness for autonomy amounted to a passion. [190]

Driven by self-love they began at this point to believe nothing that they could not grasp with the physical senses. The snake represents sensory abilities; the woman represents self-love; and the man represents the ability to reason. [191]

The snake (the senses) therefore persuaded the woman to examine closely the tenets of faith in the Lord, to see whether they were true. This is symbolized by the eating from the tree of knowledge. The fact that the man ate symbolizes consent on the part of the human being's rational mind (verses 1–6). [192]

But they perceived that they were behaving wrongly, as symbolized by the fact that their eyes were opened and that they heard Jehovah's voice (verses 7, 8). This remaining trace of perception, together with the leaf of the fig tree that they used in making loincloths for themselves (verse 7), the shame they displayed in hiding in the middle of the tree of the garden (verses 8, 9), and their acknowledgment and confession (verses 10, 11, 12, 13), makes it clear that they retained an earthly kind of goodness. [193]

Inner Meaning

GENESIS 3:1. *And the snake was crafty above every wild animal of the field that Jehovah God had made; and it said to the woman, "Did God really say, 'You must not eat from any tree of the garden'?"* [194]

The *snake* is used here to mean our senses, which we trust.[149] The *wild animal of the field*, here as before [§46], means every emotion in our outer self. The *woman* means selfhood. The snake's words—*"Did God really say, 'You must not eat from any tree'?"*—mean that for the first time they had doubts.

The subject is the third generation of the earliest church, who began to disbelieve what had been revealed unless they could see and feel that it was so. This verse and another just below depict the first phase they went through as a skeptical one.

195 The earliest people did not *compare* various human traits to animals and birds but *called* them such. That was their manner of speaking. This practice persisted in the ancient church, which came after the Flood, and the [Old Testament] prophets perpetuated it.

Snakes was their word for a person's sensory abilities. This was because sense impressions rise directly out of the body, just as snakes lie directly on the ground. Those people referred to false logic concerning the mysteries of faith, when it sprang from sense impressions, as snake venom, and they called the logicians themselves snakes. People who employ this kind of logic spend much time constructing arguments based on things they can sense and specifically on things they can see—things of the earth, their body, the world, and nature—and that is why the snake was described as being *crafty above every wild animal of the field*.

[2] David uses similar words:

> They sharpen their tongue like a snake. The venom of an asp is on their lips. (Psalms 140:3, 4, 5)

This speaks of people who beguile others with their false reasoning. In the same author:

> They go astray from the womb, speaking a lie; they have venom like the venom of a *snake*. Like a deaf poison *asp*, they stop up their ear so as not to hear the voice of those who murmur, of a sage who associates in societies.[150] (Psalms 58:3, 4, 5)

The snake venom refers to specious arguments, which tend to prevent people from even listening to anything wise—the "voice of a sage." That is the source of a customary saying among the ancients that a snake would stop up its ear.[151] In Amos:

> . . . as if you come into the house and lean your hand on the wall and a *snake* bites you. Isn't the day of Jehovah shadow and not light? And isn't there darkness and not radiance on that day? (Amos 5:19, 20)

The hand on the wall stands for our independent powers and for confidence in the evidence of our senses. These cause blindness, as described.
[3] In Jeremiah:

> The sound of Egypt will travel like a *snake*, because they will travel in strength and come with axes against her, as if they were woodcutters. "Let them cut down her forest," says Jehovah, "because it will not be explored. For they have become more numerous than locusts and there is no counting them. The daughter of Egypt has been shamed; she will be delivered into the hand of the people of the north." (Jeremiah 46:20, 22, 23, 24)

Egypt stands for sophistry about divine subjects based on physical sensation and factual knowledge. Sophistic arguments are called the sound of a snake, and the blindness that results is symbolized by the people of the north. In Job:

> They will suck the venom of *asps;* the tongue of a *viper* will kill them. They will not see torrents, streaming rivers of honey and butter. (Job 20:16, 17)

Rivers of honey and butter are spiritual and heavenly qualities, which reasoners "will not see." Their arguments are called the venom of asps and the tongue of a viper. For more on the meaning of a snake, see below at verses 14 and 15 [§§242–251, 254, 257–259].

In ancient times, people who put more trust in what they learned through their senses than in what had been revealed were called snakes. The situation now is even worse, since some people not only believe nothing except what they can see and touch but also use facts unknown to the ancients to confirm their point of view. The result is that they blind themselves far more profoundly.

People who judge heavenly matters on the basis of the senses, book learning, or philosophical reasoning blind themselves so badly that they no longer see or hear anything at all. They become not just deaf snakes but the much more deadly flying snakes the Word also mentions [Isaiah 14:29; 30:6]. To see how they do this to themselves, take their beliefs about spirit as an illustration.

[2] Sense-oriented people, or those who believe only what their senses tell them, deny that spirit exists because they cannot see it. "It isn't anything," they say, "because I can't sense it. If I can see or touch something, then I know it exists."

Scholars, or people who depend on written knowledge for their conclusions, say, "What is spirit but a puff of air, maybe, or body heat?"—or something else within the scope of their learning. "And when it's snuffed out, the spirit vanishes. Don't animals also have a body, physical senses, and something like reason? Yet people say animals are destined to die, while the human spirit is destined to live on."[152] So they deny that spirit exists.

[3] Philosophers, who claim to be keener of intellect than anyone else, speak of spirit in technical terms. These terms they do not even understand themselves, since they debate them, claiming that not a single word that derives from [notions of] matter, organic substance, or extension in space can be applied [to the human spirit]. So they bury the idea in speculation until it disappears from their sight and turns into nothing.

The saner ones admit that thought exists; but when they argue about thought, they eventually come to the conclusion that it will dissolve when the body dies, because they separate it from any kind of substance.[153]

Everyone, then, who analyzes the question on the basis of the senses, written knowledge, or philosophy denies that spirit exists. And when they deny its existence, they believe absolutely nothing that is said about spirit or spiritual things. If you ask the simple at heart, on the other hand, they say that they know it exists because the Lord said they would live on after death. They do not snuff out their rational capacity; instead they make it a living thing by means of the Lord's Word.

197 When the earliest people (whose nature was heavenly) spoke of a snake, they meant watchfulness. They also meant the sensory level of the mind, which enabled them to watch out for any evil that might otherwise hurt them. This is illustrated by the Lord's words to the disciples:

> Here, I'm sending you out as sheep in the midst of wolves. So be *shrewd* as *snakes* and simple as doves. (Matthew 10:16)

Something similar was meant by the bronze snake lifted up in the wilderness [Numbers 21:9]. It symbolized the sensory level in the Lord—the only heavenly person and the only being who watches over and provides for everything. That is why the people who looked on the bronze snake were saved.

198 Genesis 3:2, 3. *And the woman said to the snake, "We are to eat from the fruit of the tree of the garden; but from the fruit of the tree that is in the middle of the garden, God said, 'You shall not eat from it, nor are you to touch it, or you will die from it.'"*

The *fruit of the tree of the garden* means the goodness and truth revealed to [this third generation] by the people of the earliest church. The *fruit of the tree that was in the middle of the garden,* from which they were not to *eat,* means religious goodness and truth, which they were not to learn about from themselves. The ban on *touching* it means that they were also not to think about religious goodness and truth from themselves, or from their senses and the facts they knew. That they would *die from it* means that this is how faith—that is, all wisdom and understanding—would perish.

As stated, the *fruit of the tree* from which they were to eat[154] symbolizes religious goodness and truth, as it had been revealed to this generation by the earliest church; in other words, it symbolizes religious knowledge. This can be seen in the fact that they are told to eat from the *fruit* of the tree of the garden, not from the tree of the garden as before, in chapter 2, verse 16, where the heavenly person or the earliest church is the subject. The *tree of the garden,* as noted there [§125], symbolizes perception of what is good and true. This sort of goodness and truth, because it is a product of perception, is here called fruit. Fruit has the same symbolism in many other places in the Word.

The present verse says that the tree of knowledge was in the middle of the garden, but Genesis 2:9 above says that the tree of lives was in the middle, implying that the tree of knowledge was not. The reason is that the middle of the garden symbolizes the inmost core. The core of the heavenly individual, or the earliest church, was the tree of lives, which is love and the faith that develops out of love. With the people of this ensuing generation (who could be called heavenly-spiritual people), the middle of the garden, or the core, was faith.

Further description is impossible because no one today has any idea at all what the people who lived in that earliest era were like. Their character was completely unlike any found in our own age.

Their character was such (to give just a small idea) that good taught them about truth; that is to say, love taught them what belonged to faith. But when that generation passed away, another with a completely different nature took its place. The new descendants did not learn from good about truth; they did not learn from love about faith's tenets. Instead, from truth they acquired facts about goodness. To put it another way, from religious knowledge they acquired facts about love. And many of them gained little more than facts.

This change was made after the Flood, to prevent the world's destruction.

201 Since the character of the earliest people in the times before the Flood is not to be seen or found these days, it is not easy to explain the real meaning of these words. The real meaning is common knowledge in heaven, though, because those angels and angelic spirits who are called heavenly have the same nature as regenerate people of the earliest days, before the Flood. But the angels and angelic spirits who are called spiritual share the characteristics of regenerate people living after the Flood. Both natures come in unlimited variety.[155]

202 The earliest church, which was a heavenly person, was such that it did not *eat* from the tree of knowledge; it was not from sense impressions and facts that people learned what belongs to faith. In fact they were not allowed even to touch that tree; they were not allowed even to think about any matter of faith on the basis of sense impressions or facts. Had they done so, they would have slipped from a heavenly life into a spiritual life and lower.

Heavenly angels live this same way. Those who are more profoundly heavenly do not even allow faith to be mentioned, nor anything that has a spiritual [rather than heavenly] quality. (If others do mention faith, in its place they perceive love, in an altered form known to themselves alone; whatever has to do with faith they see as stemming from love and goodwill.) They have a still harder time listening to a logical treatment of faith, and least of all can they stand to hear a coldly factual treatment. This is because the Lord gives them a perception through love of what is good and true. From perception they recognize immediately whether a thing is so or not. Consequently when they hear any discussion of faith, they have no other response than "That's true" or "That's not true," because they perceive so from the Lord. Here lies the meaning of the Lord's words in Matthew:

> Your conversation shall be "Yes, yes," "No, no." Anything beyond these comes from evil. (Matthew 5:37)

Such is the meaning of the prohibition on even touching the fruit of the tree of knowledge, since these humans would have fallen prey to evil if they had—which is to say they would have *died from it.*

Heavenly angels, by the way, discuss all kinds of things, just as others do, but their speech, being formed and derived from love, is heavenly. It is harder to describe than the speech of spiritual angels.

203 Spiritual angels, on the other hand, do talk about faith, and they use intellectual, rational, and scientific concepts to confirm their religious beliefs; but they never rely on those concepts for their conclusions about faith. Anyone who does so is in the grip of evil. Spiritual angels too receive from the Lord a perception of everything having to do with faith, but theirs is not the same kind of perception that heavenly angels have. The perception experienced by spiritual angels is an ability supplied by conscience and brought to life by the Lord. It looks like heavenly perception, but it is only spiritual, not heavenly.

Genesis 3:4, 5. *And the snake said to the woman, "You are not going to 'surely die,' because God knows that on the day when you eat from it, your eyes will be opened and you will be like God, knowing good and evil."*

If they ate from the fruit of the tree their eyes would be opened means that if they scrutinized the tenets of faith from a sensory or factual standpoint—that is, from their own minds—they would see clearly that those tenets were not true.[156] Their *being like God, knowing good and evil* means that if they judged good and evil for themselves they would be like God and would be able to lead themselves.

Every verse holds inside it some particular state or change of state within the church. The first few verses spoke of a perception remaining among them that [this self-direction] was unacceptable even though they yearned for it. The present verses speak of a creeping uncertainty about whether it might actually be permissible, because it would allow them to see whether the things they had heard from their elders were true, and their eyes would be opened.

In the end, because self-love began to predominate in them, the text speaks of a state in which they could lead themselves and so resemble the Lord. Self-love carries with it the desire not to be led by the Lord but by oneself and, being led by oneself, to turn to sensory evidence and secular knowledge as the criteria for belief.

What group of people believes more firmly that their eyes are open and that like God they can identify good and evil than those who admire themselves and at the same time boast a good secular education? But what group is more blind? Just ask them and you will find that they have no idea of the existence of spirit, let alone a belief in it. Spiritual life and heavenly life they know nothing about. Eternal life they do not acknowledge, since they believe they will die like brute animals. They positively refuse to recognize the Lord, worshiping themselves and the material world instead.[157] Those who want to speak cautiously say that some Supreme Entity rules all things, although they do not know what it is.

[2] These are their principles, and privately they use many arguments from the senses and from the academic disciplines to prove them. They would do so publicly as well, if they dared.

Such people want to be recognized as gods or as fonts of wisdom, but if you ask them whether they know what it is to lack selfhood, they will answer that it is nonexistence; once deprived of it, they would be nothing. If you ask whether they know what it is to live from the Lord, they consider the concept a fantasy. If you inquired whether they knew what conscience was, they would describe it as nothing more than an imaginary something-or-other good for keeping the common people under control. If you inquired whether they knew what perception was they would do nothing but sneer and call it a sign of religious mania.

This is their wisdom. These are the people who have their eyes open; these are the people who are gods. Principles like these, which they consider clearer than daylight, are their starting points. From there they go on to reason about the mysteries of faith. What is the result but a chasm of the deepest darkness? Such people more than any are snakes that lead the world astray [Revelation 12:9].

But the descendants of the earliest church were not yet like this. What verses 14 to 19 of the current chapter say about them shows what they were later to become.

207 Genesis 3:6. *And the woman saw that the tree was good for eating, and that it was appealing to the eyes, and a tree desirable for lending insight. And she took some of its fruit, and she ate and gave to her husband too, who was with her, and he ate.*

Good for eating means intense desire. *Appealing to the eyes* means delusion. *Desirable for lending insight* means sensual pleasure. These three are properties of our selfhood (or the woman). *Her husband's eating* symbolizes the rational mind's consent (§265).

208 This was the fourth generation of the earliest church. They allowed themselves to be seduced by self-love and were unwilling to believe what had been revealed unless they saw it confirmed by evidence from the senses and by facts.

209 The words employed here—the tree was *good for eating, appealing to the eyes, desirable for lending insight*—are expressions that applied to the nature of the people living in that earliest era. They have to do with the will in particular, because the evils of those people gushed out of their will. Where the Word describes those who came after the Flood, it uses words that refer not so much to the will as to the intellect. Among the earliest people, you see, goodness led to truth, while for the people who followed the Flood, truth led to goodness.

210 To explain what selfhood is: Human selfhood is everything evil and false that wells up out of self-love and materialism. It is the tendency not to believe in the Lord or his Word but in ourselves and to think that what we do not grasp on a sensory or factual basis is nothing. The result of these tendencies is nothing but evil and falsity, which cause us to see everything backward—evil things as good, good things as evil, false things as true, and true things as false. That which exists we consider to be nothing, while that which is nothing we consider to be everything. We call hatred love, darkness light, death life, and the other way around. The Word calls people who succumb to this way of thinking lame and blind.

This, then, is human selfhood, which in itself is hellish and damnable.

Genesis 3:7. *And the eyes of both were opened and they realized that they were naked.*

211

Their eyes were opened means that an inner voice caused them to *realize* and admit *that they were naked,* in other words, that they now lived in evil and no longer in the innocence they had had before.

The fact that the *opening of one's eyes* means an inner voice is indicated by similar instances in the Word. Take Balaam's words describing himself: because he had visions, he calls himself a man whose eyes were open (Numbers 24:3, 4). And when Jonathan tasted some honeycomb and his inner voice told him he had done wrong, it says that his *eyes saw,* so that they were *enlightened* to see what he had not known (1 Samuel 14:27, 29). In many other passages from the Word, *eyes* are taken to mean the intellect and so an inner dictate issuing from it. In David, for example:

212

> Give light to my *eyes* to prevent me from sleeping the sleep of death. (Psalms 13:3)

This stands for a request that light shine on the intellect. In Ezekiel:

> . . . who have *eyes* to see and do not see. (Ezekiel 12:2)

This means those who refuse to understand. In Isaiah:

> Their *eyes* you must smear over, to prevent them from seeing with their eyes. (Isaiah 6:10)

This stands for their being so blind that they could not understand. Moses told the people:

> Jehovah has not given you a heart for knowing or *eyes* for seeing or ears for hearing. (Deuteronomy 29:4)

A heart stands for the will and eyes for the intellect. Isaiah says that the Lord will "open blind *eyes*" (Isaiah 42:7). In the same author:

Out of the darkness and out of the shadows, the *eyes* of the blind will see. (Isaiah 29:18)

213 *They realized that they were naked* means that they recognized and admitted that they were living in evil and not in the innocence they had had before. This can be deduced from the last verse of the previous chapter, where it says, "And they were both naked, the human and his wife, and did not blush." Their lack of embarrassment over their nakedness symbolizes their innocence, as may be seen there [§§163–165].

The symbolism is just the opposite when they do show embarrassment, as is the case here, where they sewed fig leaves together and hid themselves. When innocence is lacking in us, nakedness is a matter of shame and scandal because we are conscious of wrong thoughts.[158] For this reason, nudity in the Word is seen as a bad and shameful thing and is used to portray a perverted church. Ezekiel, for instance, says that the church was naked, bare, and trampled in its blood (Ezekiel 16:7, 22). In the same author:

> Let them leave her *naked* and *bare*, and let her *nakedness* be unveiled. (Ezekiel 23:29)

In John:

> I advise you to buy white clothes, so that you will be dressed and the shame of your *nakedness* will not be exposed. (Revelation 3:18)

And concerning the last days:

> Fortunate are those who are watchful and keep their clothes, to avoid walking *naked* and letting others see their shame. (Revelation 16:15)

In Deuteronomy:

> If a man finds any *nakedness* whatever in his wife, let him write her a document of divorce. (Deuteronomy 24:1)

Likewise Aaron and his sons were required to have linen shorts to cover the flesh of their *nakedness* when they approached the altar to minister; otherwise they would bear their sin and die (Exodus 28:42, 43).

214 They are said to be naked because they have been left to their own devices. Those who are left to their own devices or left on their own no longer retain any understanding or wisdom (that is, faith) and so are stripped of truth and goodness. As a result they live in evil.

215

The fact that our selfhood is nothing but evil and falsity has become clear to me from experience with spirits. Everything they have said to me on their own authority has been so consistently evil and false that I have only had to know they were speaking on their own in order to realize immediately that what they were saying was false. Yet the spirits themselves were so sure of the truth of their assertions that they never doubted them. People on earth who resemble them do the same.

Similarly there have been people who take to debating what constitutes spiritual and heavenly life, or faith, and they always succumb to doubt and even denial, as I have been allowed to see. To cavil about faith is to doubt and deny. Because such people reason from themselves or from a self-centered point of view, they stumble into undiluted falsity and so into an abyss of darkness—that is, of falsity. While they are in this abyss, the slightest objection overpowers a thousand truths, like a speck of dirt sitting on the pupil of the eye that prevents a viewer from seeing the universe and everything in it.

Of these people the Lord says in Isaiah:

> Doom to those who are wise in their own eyes and discerning in their own sight! (Isaiah 5:21)

In the same author:

> Your wisdom and your knowledge turned you away, and you said in your heart, "I am, and there is no one else besides me." But evil whose origin you do not know will come upon you; and a catastrophe that you will not be able to atone for will fall upon you; and a devastation that you do not know will come upon you speedily. (Isaiah 47:10, 11)

In Jeremiah:

> All people have been made stupid by their knowledge, all metalsmiths have been put to shame by their sculpture, because their carvings are a lie and have no breath in them. (Jeremiah 51:17)

A sculpture stands for the falsity we adopt as our own, and carvings for the evil we adopt as our own.

216

And they sewed together the leaf of the fig tree and made loincloths for themselves.

To *sew leaves together* is to make excuses. The *fig tree* is earthly good. To *make loincloths for themselves* is to feel shame. That is how the people of the earliest church spoke in describing this generation of the church.[159]

They were saying that members of this generation had earthly good in place of the earlier innocence, that it hid their evil, and that since they had a merely earthly goodness they felt shame.

217 The symbolism in the Word of a grapevine as spiritual-level good and of a *fig tree* as earthly-level good is completely unknown today because the inner meaning of the Word has been lost. Wherever these words come up, however, that is what they symbolize or refer to. What the Lord said in various parables about vineyards and fig trees had the same meaning.[160] So did his words in Matthew:

> Jesus, seeing a *fig tree* along the way, came to it but found nothing on it except leaves alone. So he said to it, "May fruit not come from you from now to eternity!" Accordingly the fig tree instantly withered. (Matthew 21:19)

These words meant that no good was to be found on the earth, not even good on the earthly plane. The grapevine and fig tree have a similar meaning in Jeremiah:

> "Were they ashamed that they did an abominable thing? They felt no shame at all, and they did not know how to blush. So I will utterly destroy them," says Jehovah. "There are no grapes on the grapevine, no *figs* on the fig tree, and the leaf has fallen off." (Jeremiah 8:12, 13)

This means that all good—both spiritual and earthly—had died out, because people were such that they could not even feel shame. They were like those today who have evil in them but are so far from feeling shame that they brag about it. In Hosea:

> Israel was like grapes in the wilderness when I discovered him. Your ancestors were like first fruit on a young *fig tree* when I saw them. (Hosea 9:10)

And in Joel:

> Do not be afraid, animals of my field; because the tree will bear its fruit, the *fig tree* and the grapevine will yield their strength. (Joel 2:22)

A grapevine stands for spiritual good, a fig tree for earthly good.

218 Genesis 3:8. *And they heard the voice of Jehovah God, going alone in the garden at the breeze of the day. And the human hid himself, as did his wife, from Jehovah God's face, in the middle of the tree of the garden.*

The *voice of Jehovah God, going alone in the garden,* means an inner dictate, which [the people of this generation] dreaded. The inner call was the trace of perception they kept. The *breeze of the day* symbolizes the era when the church still retained a trace of perception. *Hiding themselves from Jehovah God's face* means fearing the inner dictate, as those who are conscious of their evil do. The *middle of the tree of the garden,* in which they hid themselves, symbolizes earthly good. The word *middle* refers to the deepest core. A *tree* is perception, as noted before [§102]; but since they had little perception, the word is used in the singular, as if only one tree were left.

The meaning of *the voice of Jehovah God, going alone in the garden,* as an inner dictate that [the people of this generation] dreaded can be established from the symbolism of *voice* in the Word. *The voice of Jehovah* there is taken to mean the Word itself, teachings about faith, conscience (or an alertness to what is inside us), and every reproof of conscience. As a result, thunderbolts are called *the voices of Jehovah.* An instance appears in John:

> The angel then shouted with a loud voice, like a lion roaring, and when he shouted, the seven thunders uttered their *voices.* (Revelation 10:3, 4)

This stands for the fact that an outer and an inner voice were heard at that time. In the same author:

> In the days of the seventh angel's *voice,* the mystery of God is to come to an end. (Revelation 10:7)

The meaning here is similar. In David:

> Sing to God, make music to the Lord, who is riding on the ancient heavens of heavens. Watch: he will lift his *voice,* a voice of strength. (Psalms 68:32, 33)

The ancient heavens of heavens stand for the wisdom of the earliest church; the voice, for revelation and for an inner call as well. In the same author:

> Jehovah's *voice* is upon the waters; Jehovah's *voice* has power; Jehovah's *voice* is in its glory. Jehovah's *voice* is shattering cedars; Jehovah's *voice* is cutting down fiery flames. Jehovah's *voice* makes the wilderness tremble; Jehovah's *voice* sends the does into labor and strips the forests bare. (Psalms 29:3, 4, 5, 7, 8, 9)

In Isaiah:

> Jehovah will make the perfection of his *voice* heard, since at Jehovah's voice Assyria will panic. (Isaiah 30:30, 31)

The *voice going alone* means that little perception was left, as if it were all by itself and unheard, so to speak. This is evident from the next verse as well, where it says that Jehovah called or shouted to the person. Similarly in Isaiah:

> *The voice of one shouting* in the wilderness; the voice said, "Shout!" (Isaiah 40:3, 6)

The wilderness stands for a church that has no faith. The voice of one shouting stands for a proclamation of the Lord's Coming; and in general for every time his coming is proclaimed, as for instance in the case of regenerate people, who hear an inner call.

221 The symbolism of the *breeze of the day*[161] as an era when the church still retained a trace of perception can be seen from the symbolism of day and night. The earliest people compared the phases of the church to the times of day and night, the day times being a comparison for phases in which the church still enjoyed light. So the breeze of the day is being used as the comparison for a stage at which the church kept some residual perception, allowing them to recognize that they had slipped.

The Lord also uses *day* as the term for a state of faith and *night* as the term for a state lacking in faith. An example in John:

> I have to do the work of him who sent me while it is still *day*. The *night,* in which no one can work, is coming. (John 9:4)

The stages of a person's regeneration are therefore called days in the first chapter.

222 *Hiding themselves from Jehovah's face* means fearing the inner dictate, as those who are conscious of their evil do. This meaning can be ascertained from their answer in verse 10: "I heard your voice in the garden, and I was afraid because I was naked."

The face of Jehovah, or the Lord, is mercy, peace, and everything good, as is clear from the benediction

> Jehovah make his *face* shine on you and *have mercy* on you. Jehovah lift his *face* on you and give you *peace.* (Numbers 6:25, 26)

And in David:

> May God *have mercy* on us and bless us; may he make his *face* shine on us. (Psalms 67:1)

And in another place:

> Many people are saying, "Who will cause us to see good? Lift the light of your *face* on us, Jehovah." (Psalms 4:6, 7)

This is why the Lord's mercy is called "the angel of his *face*" in Isaiah:

> I will mention Jehovah's *mercies.* He repaid [the house of Israel] according to his *mercies* and according to the abundance of his *mercies,* and he became a savior to them. In all their anguish he was not an anguish, and the angel of his *face* saved them. On account of his *love* and on account of his compassion he redeemed them. (Isaiah 63:7, 8, 9)

Since the Lord's face is mercy, peace, and everything good, it is clear that he never looks at anyone except with mercy and never turns his face from anyone. It is we, when we are wrapped up in evil, who turn our faces away. As the Lord said through Isaiah: 223

> Your offenses are what cause a separation between you and your God; and your sins hide his face from you. (Isaiah 59:2)

Likewise it says here that they hid themselves from Jehovah's face because they were naked.

Mercy, peace, and all that is good—Jehovah's face—are what give rise to the inner call in the case of those who have perception (and those who have conscience, too, but in a different way). These qualities always operate in a compassionate manner, but the way we receive them depends on our state. 224

The state of the human in this chapter, or of this generation of the earliest church, was one of earthly good. Those who live in earthly good are such that they hide themselves in fear and shame over their nakedness. Those who lack earthly good, however, do not even hide, because they are shameless. They are spoken of in Jeremiah 8:12 and 13 (see §217 above).

The *middle of the tree of the garden* symbolizes earthly good that brings with it a certain amount of perception, the latter being called the *tree* here. This symbolism can also be seen from [the meaning of] the garden that the heavenly person inhabited, because anything that is good or true is called a *garden.* The connotations vary, depending on the person who cultivates it. 225

Good is not good unless it has at its core something heavenly that supplies perception, or that allows the Lord to supply it. This core is called the *middle* and the Word uses the term the same way.

Genesis 3:9, 10. *And Jehovah God called to the human and said to him, "Where are you?" And he said, "I heard your voice in the garden, and I was afraid because I was naked, and I hid myself."* 226

The meaning of *calling* and of the *voice in the garden* and the reason they *were afraid at being naked* and *hid themselves* has already been explained [§§219–220, 222–224].

It is a common occurrence in the Word for people first to be asked where they are or what is happening,[162] although the Lord already knows everything. The purpose of the inquiry is to give the person an opportunity for acknowledgment and confession.

227

The source of perception, inner dictates, and conscience needs to be understood. Because no one these days knows anything about it, let me say a little.

It is entirely true that the Lord governs us through spirits and angels. When evil spirits start to take control, angels put their effort into deflecting evils and falsities, and conflict results. This conflict is what we sense by means of perception, an inner dictate, or conscience.

From these three sensations, and from the trials we are going through, we would see clearly that spirits and angels are present with us if our focus were not thoroughly physical. Such a focus prevents us from believing anything we hear about spirits and angels. Body-centered people could experience those conflicts a hundred times over and still claim that an overactive imagination or some kind of mental illness lay at the root of them.

I myself have had the opportunity to experience conflict and its vivid sensation thousands upon thousands of times—almost continually now for several years. I have been able to learn what spirits were involved, what they were like, just where they were, at what moment they approached, and what time they left, and I have been allowed to speak to them.

228

It is impossible to describe how keenly angels perceive whether or not the thoughts that enter our minds violate religious truth or a loving goodness. Angels are a thousand times more sensitive to the nature of our thoughts and the timing of their introduction than we are, since we know almost nothing about it.

The smallest piece of our thoughts is more apparent to the angels than the largest is [to us]—which is unbelievable, but absolutely true.

229

Genesis 3:11, 12, 13. *And he said, "Who pointed out to you that you were naked? You ate from the tree from which I commanded you not to eat, didn't you?" And the human said, "The woman whom you gave to be with me, she gave me from the tree and I ate." And Jehovah God said to the woman, "Why have you done this?" And the woman said, "The snake deceived me and I ate."*

The symbolism in all of this is established by previous explanations [§§99, 128–129, 196]: our rational capacity allows itself to be deceived by our sense of autonomy—which we love tenderly—or in other words, by self-love, so that we give no credit to anything we cannot see or feel.

Anyone can see that Jehovah God did not talk to a snake[163] and that in fact there was no snake. Nor did he talk to the sensory part of the mind, symbolized by the snake. Rather, other things are involved. Specifically, people perceived that they had been deceived by their senses, and because they loved themselves, they were eager to know whether the things they heard about the Lord and about faith in him were true. Only then would they be willing to believe.

230 The reigning evil of this generation was self-love. Love of the material world did not form as large a part of the reigning evil as it does now. This was because people lived among their households and clans and did not strive after riches.

231 A single evil afflicted not only the earliest church, before the Flood, but also the ancient church, after the Flood, and the Jewish church, and then the new church or the church among non-Jews that came after the Lord's arrival into the world,[164] just as it afflicts the modern church. It is the evil of not believing the Lord or the Word but trusting oneself and one's senses. The result is an absence of faith, and when faith is absent, so is love for others—a situation that leads to all falsity and evil.

232 Conditions are much worse today than they once were. People can now employ knowledge unavailable to our ancestors in justifying the skepticism bred by their senses. In doing so, they produce so great a darkness that it could never be described. If people knew how great a darkness results, they would be astounded.

233 Examining religious mysteries by the use of factual knowledge is as impossible as it would be for a camel to go through the eye of a needle [Matthew 19:24; Mark 10:25; Luke 18:25]. It is as impossible as it would be for a rib to regulate the purest filaments of the chest and of the heart within it. So coarse—and much coarser—is the dimension of the senses and of technical knowledge in relation to spiritual and heavenly qualities.

Those who limit their investigations to the secrets of nature have difficulty enough laying bare even a single one among *that* uncountable quantity. Think how much greater their failure would be if they tried to find out the secrets of spiritual and heavenly life, of which there are myriads for each and every hidden facet of nature. And this is to say nothing of the fact that their researches plunge them into error, as everyone knows.

[2] Let just this one example serve for illustration.

On our own, we cannot help doing evil and turning away from the Lord. Yet it is not we who act this way but the evil spirits present with us. And it is not the evil spirits but the wickedness itself adopted by them as their own. In spite of this, we do evil and turn away from the Lord, and we are to blame. Still, we cannot live except from the Lord.

On the other hand, we have no ability at all to do good or turn toward the Lord on our own; it is the angels who give us the power. Yet the angels themselves cannot do so. Only the Lord can. Still, we can do good and turn toward the Lord as if we were acting under our own power.

This reality could never be grasped by our senses, by the academic disciplines, or by philosophy. Consult these and they absolutely refute it, even though it is all true in and of itself. The same holds for all other heavenly secrets.

[3] From this we can conclude that people who make sensory evidence and factual knowledge the standard for belief tumble headlong not simply into doubt but even into denial—in other words, into darkness. And since they thrust themselves into darkness, they also subject themselves to every kind of craving. When we believe in something false, we also act on falsity; and when we believe anything spiritual or heavenly to be impossible, we believe that only what belongs to the flesh and the world exists. So we love whatever promotes our self-interest or worldly advantage, and our false premise leads to evil cravings and outright wickedness.

✳ ✳ ✳ ✳

14. And Jehovah God said to the snake, "Because you have done this, a curse on you, above every beast and above every wild animal of the field! You will travel on your belly and eat dirt all the days of your life.

15. And I will put hostility between you and the woman and between your seed and her seed. He will trample you on the head and you will wound him on the heel."

16. And to the woman he said, "I will vastly multiply your pain in conception. In pain you will bear children, and your obedience will be to your husband; and he will rule over you."

17. And to the human he said, "Because you listened to the voice of your wife and ate from the tree concerning which I commanded you, saying, 'You will not eat from it,' a curse on the ground because of you! In great pain you will eat from it all the days of your life.

18. And it will produce thorn and thistle for you, and you will eat the grass of the field.

19. You will eat bread in the sweat of your face until you return to the ground, because from it you were taken. For you are dirt, and to dirt you will return."

Summary

THIS passage portrays the subsequent state of religion, up to the time of the Flood. Because the church completely destroyed itself at that time, these verses also predict that the Lord would come into the world and save the human race.

People no longer wanted to believe anything they could not grasp through their senses, and that is why their sensory capacity, which is the snake, brought a curse on itself and became hellish (verse 14).

Therefore, to prevent humanity from plunging into hell with the whole of its being, the Lord promised he would come into the world (verse 15).

The woman provides a further picture of the church, whose people loved themselves, or their autonomy, so much that they were no longer able to comprehend anything true. This was so even though they had been given the ability to reason—the mental capacity that was to rule in them (verse 16).

The nature of this rational capacity is described too. It is said to have consented and in this way to have brought a curse on itself as well and become hellish, so that no rationality remained but only a skewed logic (verse 17).

The curse and ruination are depicted, as is the animalistic nature of these people (verse 18).

Their aversion for everything having to do with faith and love is described next, and how this changed them from being human to being nonhuman (verse 19).

Inner Meaning

THE earliest people, who were heavenly, did actually see everything they looked at on earth and in the world around them, but their thoughts were devoted to the heavenly or divine attribute it symbolized or represented.[165] Vision was just a means. So their manner of speaking reflected the same trait.

We can all see what that trait was like from our own experience. When we pay close attention to the meaning of a speaker's words, we hear the words, but it is as if we do not. We seem to catch only the meaning.

One who thinks more profoundly does not even notice the meaning of the words but something more universal within.

Ensuing generations of the earliest church, however—the ones discussed in the present verses—were not like their forebears. They loved the worldly and earthly realm, so when they looked at it, their minds clung to it. Their thoughts about this realm were the starting point for their thoughts about the things of heaven and of God. In this way the sensory experience came to be the primary force, not the mere tool it was for their predecessors. And when the worldly and earthly realm becomes the primary force, people base their reasoning about heavenly matters on it and blind themselves.

Our own experience can again show us what this method was like. When we fail to pay attention to the meaning of a speaker's words but concentrate on the words themselves, we gather little of the meaning and still less of any universal significance within the meaning. Sometimes from a single word, or even from a single point of grammar, we leap to judgment about the whole of a speaker's message.

242. Genesis 3:14. *And Jehovah God said to the snake, "Because you have done this, a curse on you, above every beast and above every wild animal of the field! You will travel on your belly and eat dirt all the days of your life."*

Jehovah God said to the snake means that they perceived their reliance on their senses to be at fault. The *curse on the snake above every beast and above every wild animal of the field* symbolizes the fact that the sensory level of their mind turned away from what was heavenly toward what was bodily, bringing a curse on itself. Here as before the *beast* and the *wild animal of the field* symbolize feelings [§46]. The serpent's *traveling on its belly* means that the sensory level could no longer look up toward heavenly values but had to look down toward bodily and earthly ones. *Eating dirt all the days of its life* means that the sensory plane became incapable of living on anything but what was bodily and earthly, so that it turned hellish.

243. In the earliest, heavenly sort of people, the sensory capacities of the body served the inner self obediently, and beyond that they had no interest in those capacities. After they began to love themselves, though, they put sense experience ahead of the inner self. As a result their senses were separated [from anything higher], turned to serving the body, and so were condemned to hell.

244. It has already been shown [§229] that *Jehovah God said to the snake* means that they perceived their reliance on their senses to be at fault, so I will not dwell on the matter.

245. The inner sense of the Word establishes fairly clearly the symbolism of *he said to the snake, "A curse on you, above every beast and above every*

wild animal of the field!" The meaning is that the sensory level of their mind turned away from what was heavenly toward what was bodily, damning itself, or bringing a curse on itself. Jehovah God—the Lord— never curses anyone, is never angry at anyone, never leads anyone into crisis. He does not even punish us, let alone curse us. It is the Devil's crew that does such things. Nothing of the sort could ever come from the fountain of mercy, peace, and goodness.[166]

This passage and many others in the Word describe Jehovah God as not only turning his face away, being angry, punishing, and testing, but even killing—and, yes, cursing.[167] This was in order to foster the belief that the Lord controls and arranges every last detail in the universe, including evil itself, punishments, and times of trial. After accepting this very general idea, people would learn just how he controls and arranges things. They would see that he transforms the evil involved in punishment and in our ordeals into good.

All scriptural teaching and learning begins with the most general things; for this reason the literal meaning abounds in broad ideas.

246 The meaning of the *beast* and the *wild animal of the field* as feelings is established by the things said about beasts and wild animals above at §§45, 46. Let me add to those statements these verses in David:

> Rain you stir up with a will, God. You are the one who strengthens your struggling inheritance. Your *wild animal* will live in it. (Psalms 68:9, 10)

Here even a wild animal stands for a positive feeling, since this is what will live in God's inheritance.

The reason Genesis 3:14, like Genesis 2:19, 20, speaks of the beasts and wild animals *of the field* while Genesis 1:24, 25 speaks of those *of the earth* is that this verse describes the church, or in other words, a person who has been reborn. The first chapter, on the other hand, dealt with the absence of religion, or in other words, a person in need of regeneration. The word *field* applies to the church or the regenerate individual.

247 The serpent's *traveling on its belly* means that the sensory level could no longer look up toward heavenly values as it had before, but only down toward bodily and earthly ones. This can be seen from the fact that in ancient times people used *belly* to symbolize the things that are closest to the earth, *chest* to mean things higher than the earth, and *head* to mean the highest things of all. So here it says that the sensory plane, which by its nature is the lowest plane of the human mind, would travel on its belly because it turned toward earthly things. In the Jewish religion too a tendency toward lower things was symbolized by pressing one's belly down to the ground and by sprinkling dirt on one's head.[168] David puts it this way:

> Why do you hide your face, why forget our misery and our oppression? For our soul has bowed down to the *dirt* and our *belly* clings to the *earth*. Rise up as a helper to us and ransom us for the sake of your mercy. (Psalms 44:24, 25, 26)

Here again we can see that when we turn away from Jehovah's face, our stomach begins to cling to the dirt and the earth.

The belly of the big fish that Jonah was cast into symbolizes the underground realm,[169] as a prophecy in the Book of Jonah shows:

> From the *belly* of hell I shouted; you heard my voice. (Jonah 2:2)

In this verse, *hell* stands for the underground realm.

248. When people fixed their sight on heavenly aims, then, they were said to go upright and to look up or, what is the same, forward. But when they looked toward bodily and earthly goals, they were said to bow to the ground and to look down or backward. Leviticus has an example:

> I, Jehovah, am your God, who brought you out of the land of Egypt to keep you from being slaves to them, and who broke the restraints of your yoke and made you go *upright*. (Leviticus 26:13)

In Micah:

> You will not remove your necks from [the evil planned for you], nor will you go *upright*. (Micah 2:3)

In Jeremiah:

> Jerusalem sinned a sin. For that reason they despised her, because they saw her nakedness. Yes, she groaned and turned *backward*. "From up high he shot fire into my bones and made me go *back*. He rendered me desolate." (Lamentations 1:8, 13)

In Isaiah:

> Jehovah your redeemer is turning the wise around *backward,* and he changes their knowledge into foolishness. (Isaiah 44:24, 25)

249. *Eating dirt all the days of its life* means that the sensory plane became incapable of living on anything but what was bodily and earthly, so that

it turned hellish. This can likewise be seen from the symbolism of dirt or dust in the Word. In Micah, for instance:

> Pasture your people as in the days of old. The nations will see and will be ashamed of all their power. They will lick *dust* like the *snake,* and like the *slitherers* of the earth they will be rattled out of their enclosures. (Micah 7:14, 16, 17)

The days of old stand for the earliest church. The nations stand for those who trust in their own abilities, of whom it says that they lick dust like snakes. In David:

> Before God the barbarians will bow down, and his enemies will lick *dust.* (Psalms 72:9)

Barbarians and enemies stand for those who focus only on earthly and worldly considerations. In Isaiah:

> *Snakes—dirt* will be their bread. (Isaiah 65:25)

Since dirt symbolized those who did not have their eye turned in a spiritual and heavenly direction but in a bodily and earthly one, the Lord ordered his disciples to shake off the dust of their feet if a town or a household was unworthy (Matthew 10:14).

For dirt as a symbol of what is damned and hellish, see more at verse 19 [§278].

Genesis 3:15. *"And I will put hostility between you and the woman and between your seed and her seed. He will trample you on the head and you will wound him on the heel."*

It escapes no one today that this is the first prophecy of the Lord's coming into the world. The words themselves make it clear. From this prediction and from the prophets, even the Jews know that a messiah will come.[170] No one yet, however, knows the specific meaning of each part—the snake, the woman, the snake's seed, the woman's seed, the snake's head that he will trample, and the heel that the snake will wound. An explanation, then, is due.

The *snake* refers in general to all evil and particularly to self-love. The *woman* refers to the church. The *snake's seed* refers to all unbelief. The *woman's seed* refers to faith in the Lord. *He* refers to the Lord himself. The snake's *head* refers to the tyranny of evil in general and of self-love in particular. *Trampling* refers to pushing it down until it travels on its belly and eats dirt. The *heel* refers to what is bottommost on the earthly level, such as an orientation toward the body; this is what the snake is going to wound.

251 The meaning of the *snake* as all evil in general and self-love in particular is due to evil's point of origin. All evil rises out of a fixation on the senses and on facts, which is what the snake first symbolizes. As a consequence, the snake now symbolizes evil itself in any form, and specifically self-love, or hatred directed at others and at the Lord, which is the same as self-love.

Because the evil of hatred is multifaceted, and divides into many general categories and an even larger number of specific forms, the Word distinguishes its forms by speaking of different kinds of snakes. There are generic snakes, cockatrices, asps, bloodletting snakes, and "presters," or fire snakes; there are flying snakes and creeping ones; and there are vipers.[171] The determining factor is differences in their venom, and the venom is hatred. [2] In Isaiah, for instance:

> Do not rejoice through and through, Philistia, that the rod striking you has been broken, because from the root of a *snake* a *cockatrice* will come out, and its fruit will be a flying *fire snake*. (Isaiah 14:29)

The root of a snake is a reliance on the senses and on factual knowledge. A cockatrice is evil from the resulting falsity. A flying fire snake is the kind of desire felt by self-love. The same prophet deals with the same animals in another way using these words:

> They will hatch the eggs of a *cockatrice* and weave the webs of a spider. Whoever eats of their eggs dies, and when one is crushed, a *viper* is hatched. (Isaiah 59:5)

In Revelation 12:3, 9 and 20:2, this snake is called a big red *dragon* and the *ancient snake;* it is also called a devil and satan and the one who leads the whole inhabited world astray. (In this place and others, "devil" never means an individual devil who is the ruler of the others but the total horde of evil spirits—and evil itself.)

252 The meaning of the *woman* as the church can be seen from the heavenly marriage described above in §155. The heavenly marriage is a relationship in which heaven (and so the church) is united to the Lord through its sense of self. In fact heaven and the church are to be found in the feeling of independent existence, because without it there could never be union. When the Lord in his mercy infuses our selfhood with innocence, peace, and goodness, it still seems to be our own, but it becomes heavenly and full of the greatest blessings, as you may see above at §164.

I cannot yet say, though, what a heavenly, angelic identity received from the Lord is like, nor a hellish, diabolical identity generated by ourselves.[172] The difference between them is like the difference between heaven and hell.

Because of the heavenly, angelic sense of self, the Word calls the church a woman, a wife, and a bride, young woman, and daughter.[173] It is called a *woman* in the Book of Revelation:

> ... a *woman* enveloped in the sun, and the moon under her feet, and on her head a crown of twelve stars; and the *dragon* persecuted the *woman* who had given birth to the male. (Revelation 12:1, 4, 5, 13)

Here the woman means the church, the sun means love, the moon means faith, and the stars mean religious truth, as stated before [§§30, 32]. These things the evil spirits hate and persecute with all possible energy. The church is called both a woman and a wife in Isaiah:

> ... because your husband, your maker—Jehovah Sabaoth is his name; and your redeemer, the Holy One of Israel, is called God of the whole earth. For Jehovah has called you as a *woman* abandoned and afflicted in spirit and as the *wife* of his youthful days. (Isaiah 54:5, 6)

Here plural forms are used [in the original] for the husband/maker, because human selfhood is involved too.[174] A woman abandoned and the wife of his youthful days stand specifically for the ancient church and the earliest church. Likewise in Malachi:

> Jehovah has stood as witness between you and the *wife* of your youthful days. (Malachi 2:14)

The church is called a wife and bride in the Book of Revelation:

> I saw the holy city Jerusalem coming down from God out of the sky, prepared as a *bride* dressed up for her husband. "Come, I'll show you the *bride*, the Lamb's wife." (Revelation 21:2, 9)

As for identifying the church as a *young woman* and a *daughter*, the prophets do this often.[175]

The meaning of the *snake's seed* as all unbelief is established by the symbolism of the *snake* as all evil. Seed is what yields a harvest and is also the harvest yielded; in other words, seed is what breeds and is bred. Since the subject here is the church, what is bred is unbelief. Isaiah uses the terms *seed of the evil, seed of an adulterer,* and *seed of a lie* in talking about the Jewish church after it was corrupted:

> Doom to a sinful nation, to a people weighed down with wickedness, to the *seed* of the evil, to ruinous children! They leave Jehovah behind, they have provoked the Holy One of Israel, they have *backed* away, far away. (Isaiah 1:4)

In another place:

> Come up here, you witch's children, *seed* of an adulterer. Are you not the offspring of transgression, the *seed* of a lie? (Isaiah 57:3, 4)

In addition:

> You were thrown out of your grave like a despicable offshoot, because you ruined your land, you killed your people. The name of the *seed* of the evil will go unmentioned forever. (Isaiah 14:19, 20)

These verses are speaking of the snake, or dragon, called Lucifer here.[176]

255. The meaning of the *woman's seed* as faith in the Lord is established by the symbolism of a *woman* as the church. Her *seed* is nothing else but faith. Its faith in the Lord is what causes the church to be a church and to be called one.

Faith is called God's seed in Malachi:

> Jehovah has stood as witness between you and the *wife* of your youthful days. And did he not make [them] one? And is there no spirit in what remains? And why does the one seek God's *seed?* But keep watch in your spirit, to keep [anyone] from betraying the *wife* of your youthful days. (Malachi 2:14, 15)

The wife of one's youthful days is the ancient church and the earliest church. Its seed, or faith, is what is being discussed. In Isaiah:

> I will pour water out on thirsty land, and streams on dry ground; I will pour my spirit out on your *seed* and my blessing on *those descended* from you. (Isaiah 44:3)

This is also about the church. In Revelation:

> The dragon was enraged against the woman and went off to make war with the rest of her *seed*—those who were keeping God's commands and who possess Jesus Christ's testimony. (Revelation 12:17)

And in David:

> I struck a pact with my chosen one; I swore to David my servant, "I will establish your *seed* forever, and I will make his *seed* everlasting and his throne like the days of the heavens. His *seed* will exist forever, and his throne like the sun before me." (Psalms 89:3, 4, 29, 36)

Here David means the Lord; the throne, his kingdom; the sun, love; and the seed, faith.

Not only faith is called "the seed of a woman"; the Lord himself is so called as well. This is partly because he alone gives us faith, so that he alone *is* faith. It is also because he chose to be born and in fact to be born into a religion that had sunk all the way down into a hellish, diabolical kind of selfhood, through self-love and materialism. He was born in order to unite his divinely heavenlike selfhood to a human one, in the context of his human nature, by the use of his divine power, so that they could become one inside him. Had he not united them, the world would have ended in total destruction.

Because the woman's seed is the Lord, then, the text refers to it as "he," not "it."

The fact that the snake's *head* means the tyranny of evil in general and of self-love in particular can be seen in the nature of self-love. Its character is such that it seeks power, and not just power but power over everything on earth. Not stopping there, it strives for control over everything in heaven. Even then it does not rest but aims for power over the Lord. And in fact it still would not rest at that point. This tendency lies hidden in every single glimmer of self-love. Just indulge that love and ease the restraints on it and you will find that it instantly rushes out and swells to those dimensions.

You can therefore see how the snake—the evil of self-love—wishes to dominate, and how it hates anyone it cannot dominate. That is the snake's head, which lifts itself up, and which the Lord tramples down to the ground, so that the snake travels on its belly and eats dirt, as the previous verse says.

This is how Isaiah describes the snake or dragon called Lucifer:[177]

> Lucifer, you said in your heart, "I will scale the heavens; I will raise my throne above the stars of God, and I will sit on the mountain of assembly, on the flanks of the north.[178] I will climb onto the loftiest parts of the cloud; I will become equal to the Highest One." Nevertheless, you will be thrown down to hell, to the sides of the pit. (Isaiah 14:13, 14, 15)

The snake or dragon is also described in the Book of Revelation:

> There was a big red dragon having seven *heads* and ten horns, and on its *heads* were many crowns; but it was thrown onto the earth. (Revelation 12:3, 9)

These verses describe how high it lifts its head. In David:

> Jehovah said to my Lord, "Sit at my right, till I have placed your enemies as a stool for your feet. Jehovah will send the scepter of your strength out from Zion." He will judge the nations. He has filled them with corpses; he has crushed [one who was] *head* over much land. From the river along the way he will drink; therefore he will lift up his *head*. (Psalms 110:1, 2, 6, 7)

258 *Trampling* or crushing [the snake] means pushing it down until it travels on its belly and eats dirt, as has now been demonstrated in this verse and the last. Isaiah has something similar:

> Jehovah has thrown down those who live up high. The exalted city he will humble; he will humble it all the way to the *earth;* he will *level* it all the way to the dust; his *foot* will *tread* on it. (Isaiah 26:5, 6)

Another:

> He will throw them down to the earth with his hand. With his feet the crown of haughtiness will be trampled. (Isaiah 28:2, 3)

259 The meaning of the *heel* as what is bottommost on the earthly level, or the bodily dimension, cannot be known without information on the way the earliest people viewed the various levels inside us. They connected heavenly and spiritual qualities in us with the head and face. They connected the effects of those qualities—charity and mercy, for instance—with the chest. Things on the earthly level they connected with the lower leg. Those that rank fairly low they associated with the foot, and the very lowest earthly and bodily concerns, with the heel. In addition, not only did they connect such attributes with those body parts, they even called them by those names.

The heel also means the bottommost things in the rational mind, which are the facts we know. They are involved in Jacob's prophecy concerning Dan:

> Dan will be a snake on the path, an asp on the track, biting the horse's *heels,* and its rider falls off the back. (Genesis 49:17)

They are also meant in David:

> The wickedness at my *heels* has surrounded me. (Psalms 49:5)

Genesis 25:26 says that when Jacob came out of the womb, he was grasping Esau's *heel* (which is why he was called Jacob) and the meaning here is the same. The name Jacob comes from [the Hebrew word for] "heel" because the Jewish church, symbolized by Jacob, was to wound the heel.[179]

[2] Snakes are able to hurt only the lowest things on the earthly plane. Unless they are a species of viper, they cannot harm the more interior things we have on the earthly plane, still less those on the spiritual plane, least of all those on the heavenly plane. All these things the Lord protects, and he stores them away without our awareness. (What the Lord stores away is called "a remnant" [or "survivors"] in the Word.)[180]

The pages to come, though, by the Lord's divine mercy, will reveal how the snake destroyed those lowest things in pre-Flood people through a focus on the senses and through self-love.[181] They will show how the snake destroyed them among Jews through a concern with sensory experiences, tradition, and trivialities, and through self-love and materialism.[182] Then they will show how the snake has destroyed and is destroying people at the present day through sensory, scientific, and philosophical matters, and once more through self-love and materialism.[183]

260 The foregoing discussion shows that the church of those days learned through revelation that the Lord would come into the world to save them.

261 Genesis 3:16. *And to the woman he said, "I will vastly multiply your pain in conception. In pain you will bear children, and your obedience will be to your husband; and he will rule over you."*

The *woman* now symbolizes the church, on account of the self-dependence the church loved. To *multiply pain vastly* symbolizes conflict, and anxiety stemming from conflict. *Conception* symbolizes all thinking. The *children* she would *bear in pain* symbolize the truth the church would produce in this state. The *husband,* or man, here as before symbolizes the rational capacity [§§207, 229, 238], which the church is to *obey* and which will *rule.*

262 The symbolism of the *woman* as the church has already been mentioned [§§252–253]. Here she symbolizes the church corrupted by the self-dependence that she symbolized earlier—the subject under discussion being the generation that inherited the earliest church, which had become corrupt.

263 When the sensory level of the mind turns away and brings a curse on itself, the consequence is that evil spirits start to fight hard and the angels present with us start to work hard. So *vastly multiplying pain in conception and in the bearing of children* depicts this conflict in our thinking and in the development of true ideas.

264 *Conception* and the *bearing of children* in the Word are taken only in the spiritual sense—conception as the thought and imagination of the heart, and the children born as true ideas. This may be seen in the following words from Hosea:

> Ephraim—like a bird will their glory fly away, abandoning *birth* and the *womb* and *conception.* Even if they bring up their children, I will still bereave them, so that not one *person* is left. Indeed, doom to them, since I will have departed from them. (Hosea 9:11, 12)

Here Ephraim symbolizes the intelligent, or an intelligent understanding of truth, and the children symbolize the true ideas themselves. Hosea has more of the same to say about Ephraim, or the intelligent person who has lost all sense:

> The pains of a woman in labor came on him. He is an unwise child, because at the time when children *break open the womb,* he will not present himself. (Hosea 13:13)

In Isaiah:

> Blush, Sidon, because the sea, the stronghold of the sea spoke, saying, "I was not *in labor,* did not *give birth,* and did not *bring up* young men or raise young women." As when Egypt receives the news, they will *go into labor* over the news from Tyre. (Isaiah 23:4, 5)

Here Sidon stands for people who had religious knowledge but destroyed it by turning it into mere facts so that it became sterile. [2] In the same prophet:

> "Before she *goes into labor* she *gives birth,* and before pain came on her she *delivered* a male. Who has heard a thing like this? Who has seen things like those? Does the earth labor for one day and I cause it to *give birth?*" Jehovah has said. "Am I, the bringer of *birth,* going to close up [the womb]?" your God has said. (Isaiah 66:7, 8, 9)

This deals with regeneration, and the children again symbolize the true ideas belonging to faith. Things that are good and true, because they are the things conceived and born of the heavenly marriage, are also called children by the Lord in Matthew:

> The one who sows good seed is the Son of Humankind; the field is the world; but the seeds are the *children* of the kingdom. (Matthew 13:37, 38)

In John 8:39 the Lord calls the goodness and truth that belong to a saving faith the "children of Abraham." *Seed,* after all (as stated in §255), is faith, and therefore *children,* who come from seed, are the good deeds and true ideas of faith. As a consequence, because the Lord is himself the seed, he called himself the Son of Humankind, meaning the church's faith.

The symbolism of the *husband* or man as the rational capacity can be seen from verse 6 of this chapter, which says that the woman gave to her husband, who was with her, and he ate, which symbolized his consent. The symbolism can also be seen from what was shown about a man in §158, where it means a wise and understanding person. Here, though, because the eating from the tree of knowledge had destroyed wisdom and understanding, the man means the ability to reason, since nothing else was left. The rational capacity imitates, or seems to resemble, an intelligent understanding.

Every law and commandment has something heavenly and spiritual as its source and true origin. So this law for marriage stating that a wife should be under the influence of her husband's good sense also has a heavenly, spiritual origin, since she acts on desire, which is self-centered, and not so much from reason as a man does.[184]

Genesis 3:17. *And to the human he said, "Because you listened to the voice of your wife and ate from the tree concerning which I commanded you, saying, 'You will not eat from it,' a curse on the ground because of you! In great pain you will eat from it all the days of your life."*

The *human,* in *listening to the voice of his wife,* symbolizes a man, that is, the rational faculty, and the fact that it consented. Because the rational mind consented, it also turned away or brought a curse on itself. On this account, the whole outer self did the same, which is what is symbolized by *a curse on the ground because of you.* His *eating from it in great pain,* which means the unhappy condition of life to come, was to last right to the end of that church—*all the days of his life.*

The symbolism of the *ground* as our outer self can be seen in what was said earlier [§90] about the land, the ground, and the field.

People who have been regenerated are no longer called *land* but *ground,* because they have been planted with heavenly seed. The Word in many places also compares them to ground or calls them such. It is our outer self, or the feelings and memory of our outer self, that the seeds of goodness and truth are planted in. They are not sown in our inner self because the inner self lacks anything of our own; things of our own exist in the outer self.

Our inner being holds good qualities and true thoughts. When they seem to have departed, we are then shallow, body-oriented people. Still, the Lord stores those things up in our inner self without our knowing. They do not come out of hiding until our outer self dies, so to speak, as frequently happens in times of trial, misfortune, grave illness, or imminent death.

The ability to reason also belongs to the outer self (§118). In its true character, that capacity is a kind of bridge between the inner self and the outer, because the inner self directs the outer, body-centered self by means of it. But when the rational mind consents [to self-dependence], it separates the outer self from the inner, so that we no longer know the inner self exists. As a result, we also fail to see what understanding and wisdom are, belonging as they do to the inner realm.

269 The things demonstrated above in §245 make it clear that Jehovah God—the Lord—did not *curse the ground,* which is the outer self. The outer self, rather, turned away or separated from the inner self and brought a curse on itself by doing so.

270 The symbolism of *eating from the ground in great pain* as life in an unhappy condition stands out clearly from the verses that come before and after. In addition, the deeper sense of *eating* is living. Furthermore, an unhappy life is the kind that follows when evil spirits start to attack and the angels with us begin to struggle. Life becomes even more unhappy later when the evil spirits start to take command. Those spirits then control our outer self and angels control our inner self, of which so little is left that the angels can hardly cull anything from it to defend us with. The consequence is misery and distress.

People who are spiritually dead rarely feel that kind of misery and distress because they are no longer human, even though they consider themselves more human than others. They have no greater ability to recognize what spiritual and heavenly qualities are or what eternal life is than a brute animal. Like an animal they face down toward the things of earth, or they turn their attention outward to worldly affairs. They foster their own interests exclusively and indulge their tastes and their senses.

To all this their rational mind wholly consents. As they are dead, they would be unable to hold up under any onslaught or trial. If trouble came on them, it would weigh them down too much to allow continued life. In this way they would bring still greater curses on themselves and rush headlong into a damnation even more profoundly hellish. For this reason they are spared until they cross over into the other life, where trials and unhappiness retain no power to kill them. Then they undergo severe troubles. This likewise is what is symbolized by the words *a curse on the ground* and *in great pain will you eat from it*.

271. The symbolism of the *days of his life* as the end of the church's days can be recognized when one considers that this is not talking about an individual but about religion and its stage of development. The end of this church's days came at the time of the Flood.

272. Genesis 3:18. *"And it will produce thorn and thistle for you, and you will eat the grass of the field."*

Thorn and thistle mean the curse and ruination. The fact that he would *eat the grass of the field* means that they would live like animals.

We live like animals when our inner being is so radically separated from our outer being that the inner being cannot direct it except in the most general way. Our identity as human beings we receive from the Lord through our inner selves, but our identity as animals we receive from our outer selves. The outer self separated from the inner is in itself merely an animal; its nature, its desires, its appetites, its delusions, and its sensations are like an animal's, and its physiology is similar as well.[185] Despite the similarities, our outer self has the ability to engage in reasoning—with keen penetration, as it seems to us—and this ability is ours by virtue of the spiritual substance through which the Lord's life can flow into us.[186] But when that self is disconnected from our inner self, the Lord's life is perverted in us and becomes an evil life, which is death, and this is why we are then called dead.

273. The symbolism of *thorn and thistle* as the curse and ruination is established by the fact that field crops and fruit trees symbolize just the opposite—blessings and fertility.

This symbolism of thorn, thistle, brier, bramble, and nettle can be seen in the Word, as in Hosea:

> Look! They have left on account of the ruination. Egypt will gather them; Moph[187] will bury them, [will bury] what is desirable of their

> silver. The *nettle* will inherit them, the *bramble* will be in their tents. (Hosea 9:6)

Here Egypt and Moph stand for those who wish to gain wisdom about divine things from their own minds and the facts that they know. In the same prophet:

> The high places of Aven, the sin of Israel, will be destroyed. *Thorn* and *thistle* will climb over their altars. (Hosea 10:8)

The high places of Aven stand for self-love; thorn and thistle on the altars, for profanation. In Isaiah:

> They are beating their breasts because of the desirable fields, because of the fruitful grapevine. On my people's soil the *brier's thorn* will come up. (Isaiah 32:12, 13)

And in Ezekiel:

> No longer will there be for the house of Israel a *stinging brier* or a *painful thorn* from all their surroundings. (Ezekiel 28:24)

274 The fact that *eating the grass of the field,* or fodder found in the wild, is living like an animal can be seen from Nebuchadnezzar's story in Daniel:

> They will drive you away from humanity, and your dwelling place will be with the *beast of the field.* They will make you eat *grass* like cattle, and seven seasons will pass over you. (Daniel 4:32)

In Isaiah:

> Have you not heard? From far away I did this, from the days of old, and I formed it. Now I have caused it to come, and it will be for tearing down bulwarks, fortified cities, into heaps. And their residents, their hand shortened, have felt panic and shame. They have become *field grass,* and *green grass,* the *grain plant* on the roofs,[188] and a *plowed field* burnt out in front of the standing crop. (Isaiah 37:26, 27)

This explains what field grass and what green grass, the grain plant on the roofs, and a plowed field burnt out mean. It is referring to the time before the Flood, as implied by the words *far off* and *days of old.*

275 Genesis 3:19. *"In the sweat of your face will you eat bread, until you return to the ground, because from it you were taken. For you are dirt, and to dirt you will return."*

Eating bread in the sweat of his face means rejecting what is heavenly. *Returning to the ground from which he was taken* means returning to the external person as it was before regeneration. *Being dirt* and *returning to dirt* means being damned and resembling hell.

276

The symbolism of *eating bread in the sweat of his face* as rejecting what is heavenly can be established by the symbolism of *bread*. *Bread* means everything of a spiritual or heavenly character, which is food for the angels. If they were deprived of it, they could not live, any more than a person deprived of bread or food can. The heavenly and spiritual things existing in heaven also correspond to the bread on earth.[189] Moreover they are represented by bread, as can be seen in many passages.

The Lord is bread because everything heavenly or spiritual comes from him, as he teaches in John:

> This is the bread that came down from heaven. Whoever eats this bread will live forever. (John 6:58)

In consequence, bread and wine are symbols in the Holy Supper.[190] This heavenly aspect was represented by the manna as well [Exodus 16:4–31]. The fact that heavenly and spiritual things are angels' food is also clear from the Lord's words:

> Humankind shall not live on bread alone but on every word coming out of God's mouth. (Matthew 4:4)

That is, humankind is to live on the Lord's life, the source of every heavenly and spiritual quality.

[2] The final generation of the earliest church—which directly preceded the Flood and is the subject of these verses—was so degenerate and so immersed in what belonged to their senses and their body that they refused to hear about religious truth or about the Lord's nature. Nor did they want to know that he was going to come and save them. At the simple mention of those things they turned their backs. Such rejection is depicted by the eating of bread in the sweat of one's face.

It was similar with the Jews, whose nature was such that they would not acknowledge heavenly things and did not want any other Messiah than a worldly one.[191] For that reason, they could not help rejecting the manna (which represented the Lord) and calling it worthless bread. This is why snakes were sent among them (Numbers 21:5, 6).

What is more, the heavenly things that they benefited from in their distress, in their misery, and in their tears they called the bread of distress, the bread of misery, and the bread of tears [Isaiah 30:20; Deuteronomy 16:3; 1 Kings 22:27; Psalms 80:5]. The things they benefited from even while rejecting them are here called the bread of their face's sweat.

277 This is the inner meaning. No one who stresses the literal sense gains any more from it than the fact that humanity would wrest their food from the ground by hard work, or the sweat of their brow. The human being here, though, means not an individual but the earliest church. The ground does not mean ground, the bread bread, or the garden a garden, but things that are heavenly or spiritual, as has been sufficiently illustrated already.

278 *Returning to the ground from which he was taken* symbolizes the church's return to the external person as it was before regeneration, and this is established by the symbolism of the *ground* as the outer self, which was stated earlier [§268].

The symbolism of the *dirt* as that which is damned and resembles hell can be seen from the things said about the snake [§249], where the prediction occurs that it would eat dirt because of its accursedness. In addition to the passages there showing the symbolism of dirt or dust, let me add the following from David:

> All those descending to the *dust* will bow down before Jehovah, and anyone whose soul he did not revive. (Psalms 22:29)

In another place:

> You hide your face; people are troubled. You gather their spirit; they pass away and return to their *dust*. (Psalms 104:29)

In other words, when they turn away from the Lord's face, they pass away or die and so return to the dust, that is, come to be damned and to resemble hell.

279 The idea involved, then, when all these verses are taken in sequence, is this: The sensory capacity turned away from the heavenly side (verse 14). The Lord was to come into the world to reunite the sensory and the heavenly (verse 15). Because the outer self turned away, conflict arose (verse 16), resulting in misery (verse 17), damnation (verse 18), and, in the end, hell (verse 19). These consequences followed one another in that church from the time of the fourth generation through to the Flood.

❋ ❋ ❋ ❋ ❋ ❋

20. And the human called the name of his wife Eve, because "She will be the mother of every living thing."[192]

21. And Jehovah God made leather tunics for the human and his wife and clothed them.

22. And Jehovah God said, "Here, the human has been like one of us, knowing good and evil; and now perhaps people will put out their hand and take from the tree of lives as well, and eat, and live forever."

23. And Jehovah God sent them away from the Garden of Eden to cultivate the ground from which they were taken.

24. And he threw the humans out. And he caused guardian beings[193] to live on the east of the Garden of Eden, and the flame of a sword turning itself, to guard the way to the tree of lives.

Summary

THIS passage as a whole deals with the very earliest church and those in it who fell away. As a result it also deals with that church's descendants through to the time of the Flood, when it passed away. [They were as follows:]

The true church of earliest times, which had a heavenly nature. Because they lived a life of faith in the Lord, this church was called Eve and "the mother of every living thing" (verse 20).

The first generation of descendants, who had a spiritual kind of heavenly good; and *the second and third generations,* who had good on the earthly level, symbolized by the leather tunic that Jehovah God made for the human and his wife (verse 21).

The fourth generation, among whom earthly good began to disappear. Had they been created anew or been taught the heavenly ideas involved in faith, they would have perished. This is the force of the words, "Perhaps people will put out their hand and take from the tree of lives as well, and live forever" (verse 22).

The fifth generation. They were completely deprived of goodness and truth and regressed to the condition they had been in before regeneration. This is being sent away from the Garden of Eden to cultivate the ground from which they were taken (verse 23).

The sixth and seventh generations. They were withheld from the knowledge of anything good or true and were left to their own filthy loves and delusions. This provision kept them from profaning the sacred beliefs of faith. These things are symbolized by the fact that they were thrown out and that guardian beings were caused to live there, together with the flame of a sword, to guard the way to the tree of lives (verse 24).

Inner Meaning

286 UP to this point the text has been dealing with the very earliest people and their regeneration. First it spoke of those who lived like animals and finally became spiritual people. Next it spoke of those who became heavenly people—the ones who made up that earliest church. Then it turned to those who fell away, and their heirs, tracing them in order: the first generation to inherit, the second, the third, and lastly those that followed, right up to the Flood.

These verses at the end of the chapter contain a review extending from the people of the earliest church up to the time of the Flood, which brings closure to all that came before.

287 Genesis 3:20. *And the human called the name of his wife Eve, because "She will be the mother of every living thing."*

The *human* here means the individual of the earliest church, or the heavenly person. His *wife* and the *mother of every living thing* mean the church. The word *mother* is used because this was the first church, while the word *living* is used because this church believed in the Lord, who is life itself.

288 The meaning of the *human* as the individual of the earliest church, or the heavenly person, has already been demonstrated [§277]. In fact, it was shown that the Lord alone is human [§49] and that heavenly people acquire their humanity from him, because they are his likeness [§§50–51]. This is how all who belonged to the church came to be called human, no matter who they were or what they were like. In the end, all that was required was that they appear physically human, so that they could be distinguished from animals.

289 The meaning of a *wife* as the church and in a comprehensive sense as the Lord's kingdom in heaven and on earth has also been demonstrated before.[194] It follows, then, that a *mother* has the same meaning.

The Word frequently uses *mother* for the church. Take Isaiah:

> Where is your *mother's* document of divorce? (Isaiah 50:1)

In Jeremiah:

> Your *mother* has been acutely shamed; *she who gave birth* to you has blushed with embarrassment. (Jeremiah 50:12)

In Ezekiel:

> [You are] your *mother's* daughter, showing disgust for her husband and her children. Your *mother* is a Hittite and your father an Amorite. (Ezekiel 16:45)

The husband stands for the Lord and every heavenly quality, the children for religious truth. A Hittite stands for falsity and an Amorite for evil. In the same author:

> Your *mother* was like a grapevine that resembled you, planted next to the water; fruitful, leafy was she, because of the many waters. (Ezekiel 19:10)

The mother stands for the ancient church.

The earliest church is the main one to be called a mother, because it was the first and was also the only heavenly one, so that the Lord loved it above all others.

The fact that the church was called the mother of *every living thing* by reason of its faith in the Lord, who is life itself, can also be seen from earlier evidence: In no way is it possible for more than a single life force to exist from which all other beings receive life [§2]. Any life that is truly to be life must come by way of faith in the Lord, who is life [§30:2]. And any faith that is to have life within it must come from him and therefore must have him within it [§41].

For this reason, the Word describes the Lord as the only living being. It uses the names *Jehovah who lives* (Jeremiah 5:2; 12:16; 16:14, 15; 23:7; Ezekiel 5:11); *the one who lives forever* (Daniel 4:34; Revelation 4:10; 5:14; 10:6); *the wellspring of life* in David (Psalms 36:9); and *the fountain of living water* in Jeremiah (17:13). It calls heaven, which lives from him, *the land of the living* (Isaiah 38:11; 53:8; Ezekiel 26:20; 32:23, 24, 25, 26, 27, 32; Psalms 27:13; 52:5; 142:5). People who believe in the Lord are called *the living,* as in David: "... who places our soul among the *living*" (Psalms 66:9). Of those who believe, it also says that they are in *the book of life* (Psalms 69:28; Revelation 13:8; 17:8; 20:15). By the same token, those who accept a faith in the Lord are said to be *brought back to life* (Hosea 6:2; Psalms 85:6). Those who do not believe, on the other hand, are by extension called dead, as in Isaiah:

> The *dead* will not live; the Rephaim[195] will not rise again, because you inflicted punishment on them and obliterated them. (Isaiah 26:14)

The dead here stand for people inflated with self-love, and rising again symbolizes entering into life. They are also referred to as victims of

291 This verse [Genesis 3:20] describes the first era, when the church was in the flower of its youth and represented the heavenly marriage. As a result the passage depicts that church as a marriage and gives it the name *Eve* from [the Hebrew word for] life.

292 Genesis 3:21. *And Jehovah God made leather tunics for the human and his wife and clothed them.*

These words symbolize the fact that the Lord taught them about spiritual and earthly goodness. The verbs *make* and *clothe* express the idea of his instruction and a *leather tunic* embodies the idea of spiritual and earthly goodness.

293 None of this symbolism could ever be detected in the literal meaning, although the fact that the words involve something deeper is readily apparent; anyone can see that Jehovah God did not make leather tunics for them.

294 The symbolism of the *leather tunic* as spiritual and earthly goodness likewise escapes people unless it is revealed to them by an unveiling of the inner meaning and then by other places in the Word that use similar terms.

The verse uses the general word *leather*, which implies goat, sheep, and ram skins. In the Word, these symbolize good emotions, charity, and the effects of charity. The sheep used in sacrifices had a similar meaning.

Anyone with a supply of charitable goodness—that is, of spiritual and earthly goodness—is called a sheep. So the Lord is called the shepherd, and people who possess charity are termed sheep, as everyone knows.

295 The reason it says they were dressed in a leather tunic is this: The earliest people were described as naked on account of their innocence. Later, when innocence died, they observed that they were caught up in evil, and that too is described as nudity. But now, in order for all the details to come together as a story, as required by the ancients' manner of speech, they are said to be clothed, so as not to be naked, or involved in evil.[196]

They did possess spiritual and earthly goodness, as is clear from statements and evidence regarding them offered at verses 1 to 13 of the present chapter [§§193, 216–217, 224–225] and from the assertion here that Jehovah God made clothes for them. This verse, you see, concerns not only the first generation in the church but more particularly the second and third generations, who were granted that kind of good.

296 Kid, sheep, goat, badger, and ram skins symbolize spiritual and earthly kinds of good. This can be seen in the inner meaning of the Word where it deals with Jacob and with the ark.

In respect to Jacob: He was dressed in Esau's clothes and (where his hands and neck lay bare) in the skins of goats' kids [Genesis 27:15–16]. When Isaac smelled them, he said, "My son's smell is like the smell of the field" (Genesis 27:22, 27). The symbolism of these skins as spiritual and earthly forms of good will be seen at that location [§3540], with the Lord's divine mercy.

In respect to the ark: The tabernacle covering was made of rams' skins and badgers' skins (Exodus 26:14; 36:19). Whenever Aaron and his sons set out on a journey, they would cover the ark with a blanket of badgers' skin. They did the same with the table [for the bread] and its utensils, the lampstand and its utensils, the golden altar [of incense], and the utensils for ministry and for the altar [of burnt offerings] (Numbers 4:6, 8, 10, 11, 12, [14]). The symbolism of these skins as spiritual and earthly good will be seen at that location as well, with the Lord's divine mercy.[197] Whatever went into the making of the ark, dwelling place, or tent, and even what Aaron wore when dressed in the holy garments, symbolized something heavenly and at the same time spiritual. Not the smallest item existed that did not have its own representation.

Heavenly goodness is unclothed goodness, because it is the deepest good and is innocent. Heavenly good that is spiritual is the first level of good to be clothed, and earthly good is the next, because these two kinds are more external. They are also compared to clothes and are even *called* clothes. An example occurs in Ezekiel, where the subject is the ancient church:

> I *clothed* you with embroidery, gave you shoes of *badger*, *swathed* you in fine linen, and *covered* you in silk. (Ezekiel 16:10)

In Isaiah:

> Put on your finest *clothes,* Jerusalem, you holy city. (Isaiah 52:1)

In the Book of Revelation:

> . . . who have not defiled their *clothing* and will walk with me in *white* because they are worthy. (Revelation 3:4, 5)

The same book also mentions the twenty-four elders wearing white garments (Revelation 4:4).

So the more external kinds of goodness, which are heavenly-spiritual and earthly good, are clothing, and this is why people endowed with the goodness that accompanies charity appear wearing dazzling clothes in heaven. In the current verse, however, because they are still in the body, they wear a leather tunic.

298 Genesis 3:22. *And Jehovah God said, "Here, the human has been like one of us, knowing good and evil, and now perhaps people will put out their hand and take from the tree of lives as well, and eat, and live forever."*

The reason Jehovah God speaks at first in the singular and then in the plural is that *Jehovah God* means the Lord and at the same time heaven with its angels. The fact that *the human knew good and evil* means that people became heavenly and so became wise and understanding. The implied desire that they not *put out their hand and take from the tree of lives* is a refusal to let them be taught the mysteries of faith. If they were taught, they would never be saved to all eternity, which is *living forever*.[198]

299 Here lie two hidden pieces of wisdom. One is that Jehovah God symbolizes the Lord and at the same time heaven. The other is that if those people had learned the mysteries of faith, they would have been destroyed forever.

300 To take up the first: *Jehovah God* means the Lord and at the same time heaven. It needs to be observed that the Word uses different names for the Lord, always for a hidden reason. At one time he is called simply Jehovah, at another Jehovah God, at another first Jehovah and then God, at another the Lord Jehovih, at another the God of Israel, and at another simply God. In Genesis 1, for instance, the only name used is God, and he speaks in the plural there as well—"let us make a human in our image." Not until the next chapter, which treats of heavenly people, is he called Jehovah God.

He is called Jehovah because he alone *is,* he alone lives; the name comes from his *beingness.* He is called God because he is *able* to do anything; the name comes from his powerful *ability.*[199] Evidence for this appears in the Word, in places where the two names are distinguished: Isaiah 49:4, 5; 55:7; Psalms 18:2, 28, 30, 31; 38:15.

For this reason, each angel or spirit who spoke to people on earth they called a god, if they considered that angel or spirit to be capable of accomplishing something. This can be seen in David:

> God stood in the assembly of *God;* in the midst of *the gods* he will pass judgment. (Psalms 82:1)

In another place:

> Who in the heights of the sky will compare with Jehovah, will be like Jehovah, among the children of *gods?* (Psalms 89:6)

Again:

> Acclaim the God of *the gods,* acclaim the Lord of *the lords!* (Psalms 136:2, 3)

Human beings are also called gods by virtue of their power, as in Psalms 82:6; John 10:34, 35. Moses was called a "God to Pharaoh" (Exodus 7:1). For the same reason, the [Hebrew] word for God, *Elohim,* is plural.

Angels have no power at all on their own, however (as they themselves confess), but only receive it from the Lord. Because of this, and since there is only one God, Jehovah God in the Word means the Lord alone. But when anything occurs through the ministry of angels, as in Genesis 1[:26], then the plural is used. Here it also says, "The human has been like one of us, knowing good and evil," that is, has been wise and intelligent. This is because people of heavenly character, being human, could not be compared to the Lord but only to angels.

The other secret is that if they had learned the mysteries of faith, they would have been destroyed forever. Such is the meaning of the words *now perhaps people will put out their hand and take from the tree of lives as well, and eat, and live forever.* The situation is this:

People can reach a point where the structure of their life is turned upside down; they have no interest in receiving life or wisdom from any other source than themselves and their own powers. Under these circumstances, when they hear anything about faith, no matter what it is, they debate in their minds whether it is true or not. Because they make themselves—their sense impressions and the facts they have learned—their authority, they cannot help denying; and when they deny, they blaspheme and profane. They end up with no concern about whether they are intermingling profane and holy things.

If this is what we become, we are so utterly damned when we enter the other life that no hope of salvation remains; and this is because things that are mingled together through profanation cling to each other in their mixed condition. As soon as an image of something holy comes to our minds, the attached image of something profane appears, preventing us from keeping company with any but the damned. (People in the next life—even the spirits in the world of spirits, and more so the angelic spirits—keenly perceive what is present in, and linked with, the ideas that make up our thinking. Their perception is so keen that from a single thought they can tell what we are like.)

Profane things attached in this way to holy things cannot be wrenched apart from them without the tortures of hell—tortures so intense that if we knew about them, we would stay as far away from profanation as we would from hell itself.

That is why the mysteries of faith were never revealed to the Jews, who were like this. So little was revealed to them that they were not even told plainly that they would live on after death[200] or that the Lord was going to come into the world to save them. They were (as they continue to be) kept so deeply ignorant and oblivious that they had no idea (nor do they yet) that we have an inner being or that an inner plane even exists. If they had known it (and if they knew it now), to the point of acknowledging its truth, they are such that they would have profaned it, removing forever any hope of salvation in the next life.[201]

These are the things the Lord meant when he said in John:

> He has blinded their eyes and closed off their heart to prevent them from seeing with their eyes and understanding at heart and turning and being healed by me. (John 12:40)

The Lord also spoke to them in parables without explaining a single one to them "so that seeing, they would not see, and hearing, they would not hear and understand," as he himself says in Matthew 13:13.

For the same reason, all religious mysteries were hidden away from them and veiled in the representative acts and objects of their religion. For the same reason again, that is what the Word's prophetic mode is like, too.

But it is one thing to know and another to acknowledge. When we know but do not acknowledge, it is as if we do not know. If we do acknowledge and then we blaspheme and profane, we are the people the Lord refers to.

303. We build a life through all the things whose truth we persuade ourselves of, that is, the things we acknowledge and believe. What we are not persuaded of—what we do not acknowledge and believe—has no effect on our mind. As a result, we cannot profane holy things unless we are persuaded to the point of acknowledgment and yet deny them.

Those who do not acknowledge are capable of knowing, but it is as if they do not know. They are like people who know things but whose knowledge amounts to nothing. This describes the Jews at the time of the Lord's Coming. Since that is their nature, the Word depicts them as spiritually devastated, or no longer possessing faith.[202] At that point, there is no harm in opening the inner depths of the Word to them because they then resemble sighted people who do not see, hearing people who do not hear, whose hearts are coarsened. The Lord spoke of them through Isaiah:

> Go, and you are to tell this people, "Listen—listen!—but you are not to understand, and see—see!—but you are not to know." Make the

heart of this people fat and make their ears heavy and smear over their eyes, to prevent them from seeing with their eyes and hearing with their ears and understanding in their heart and turning to be healed. (Isaiah 6:9, 10)

[2] Religious mysteries are not opened up to them before they fall into this condition, in which they are devastated or stripped of any continuing ability to believe. The delay until then, as I said, is to make it impossible for them to commit profanation. This too the Lord clearly states in the very next verses in Isaiah:

I said, "How long, Lord?" and he said, "Until the cities are ruined (so that there is not a resident) and the houses (so that there is not a [single] person) and the ground is desolated with ruination; and Jehovah will take humankind away." (Isaiah 6:11, 12)

A person or *humankind* refers to those who are wise, or who acknowledge and believe.

These scenes describe the Jews at the time of the Lord's Coming, as I said; and for the same reasons as then, their cravings (especially their greed) continue to chain them to a condition of desolation.[203] The emptiness is so complete that even if they hear a thousand times about the Lord, about the objects and practices among them that represent the church, and how these symbolize the Lord in every detail, they still acknowledge and believe none of it.

This, then, is the reason that the people who brought on the Flood were thrown out of the Garden of Eden and suffered devastation, to the point where they were unable to acknowledge anything true.

All this evidence indicates that such is the meaning of these words— *to keep people from putting out their hand and taking from the tree of lives as well, and eating, and living forever. Taking from the tree of lives and eating* is learning all about love and faith, to the point of acknowledging it. The plural *lives* is love and faith; *eating* here as before [§125] symbolizes knowing; and *living forever* is not living in the body forever but living on after death in eternal damnation. People who are dead are so called not because they will die after the life of the body but because they will live a life of death, since death is damnation and hell. *Living* has a similar meaning in Ezekiel:

You hunt the souls that belong to my people, and the souls that are yours you keep alive. And you profaned me among my people, to kill souls that must not *die* and to keep souls *alive* that must not *live*. (Ezekiel 13:18, 19)

305 Genesis 3:23. *And Jehovah God sent them away from the Garden of Eden to cultivate the ground from which they were taken.*

Being thrown out of the Garden of Eden means being deprived of all understanding and wisdom. *Cultivating the ground from which they were taken* means becoming body-centered, as they were before regeneration.

The fact that *being thrown out of the Garden of Eden* means being deprived of all understanding and wisdom is established by the symbolism of a garden and of Eden, dealt with above [§§98–100, 107–109]. A *garden* symbolizes understanding or the comprehension of truth. *Eden*, because it symbolizes love, symbolizes wisdom, or the will to do good.

The fact that *cultivating the ground from which they were taken* means becoming body-centered, as they were before regeneration, was shown earlier at verse 19 [§278], where similar words occur.

306 Genesis 3:24. *And he threw the humans out. And he caused guardian beings to live on the east of the Garden of Eden, and the flame of a sword turning itself, to guard the way to the tree of lives.*

Throwing the humans out is completely depriving us of all the will to do good and all comprehension of truth—so completely that those faculties are withheld from us and we cease to be human. *Causing guardian beings to live on the east* is making sure that we cannot enter into any of the hidden wisdom of faith; the *east of the Garden of Eden* is a heavenly quality from which an intelligent understanding comes. The *guardian beings* symbolize the Lord's providence making sure that if we are like this we do not pry into the ideas that compose faith. The *flame of a sword turning itself* symbolizes self-love with its mad desires and the delusions that grow out of them. These desires and delusions are such that although we want to enter there, we are carried in the opposite direction, toward bodily and earthly preoccupations. This is done *to guard the way to the tree of lives,* or in other words, to prevent us from profaning holy things.

307 This deals with the sixth and seventh generations, which met their end in the Flood. They were thrown completely out of the Garden of Eden—that is, separated from any comprehension of truth—and became almost nonhuman; and they were left to their insane desires and delusions.

308 The symbolism of the east and the Garden of Eden has already been demonstrated [§§98–101, 107–109], so there is no need to dwell on them. Several passages in the Word mentioning the *guardian beings,* though, show that they symbolize the Lord's providence making sure we do not incur death by profaning the mysteries of faith, through an insane exploration of them that relies on our own powers, empiricism, or mere facts.

The Jews were such that had they clearly recognized certain realities, they would have profaned the knowledge and been destroyed forever. Those realities were that the Lord would come, that the representative or prefigurative forms in the church symbolized the Lord, that life continues after death, that we have an inner self, and that the Word has an inner meaning. The danger of their profanation was represented by the guardian beings on the appeasement cover[204] atop the ark, on the curtains for the dwelling place, and on the veil, and by the same figures in the Temple (Exodus 25:18, 19, 20, 21; 26:1, 31; 1 Kings 6:23–29, 32, 35). They symbolized the fact that the Lord was on guard.

The ark holding the testimony[205] symbolized the same thing as the tree of lives here—the Lord and the things that belong to heaven, which are exclusively the Lord's. This is why the Lord many times is called the God of Israel seated upon the guardian beings[206] and why he talked with Aaron and Moses from between them (Exodus 25:22; Numbers 7:89).

[2] A clear picture of this appears in Ezekiel in the following words:

> The glory of Israel's God lifted up off the *guardian being* on which it had been and moved to the threshold of the House. He called to the man wearing linen clothes and said to him, "Cross through the middle of the city, through the middle of Jerusalem, and make a mark on the foreheads of the men who are groaning and sighing over all the abominations done in the middle of it." And to the men themselves he said, "Cross through the city behind him and strike! Do not let your eye spare any and do not exercise compassion. Old person, young man, and young woman, and toddler, and women—kill them to annihilation. Defile the House and fill the courtyards with those who have been stabbed." (Ezekiel 9:3, 4, 5, 6, 7)

Further on:

> He told the man wearing linen clothes, "Go in, between the wheels, under the *guardian being,* and fill your palms with embers of *fire* from between the *guardian beings* and scatter them over the city." The *being* stretched its hand out from among the [other] *beings* to the *fire* that was

among the *beings,* picked it up, and put it into the palms of the man wearing linen clothes. And he took it and went out. (Ezekiel 10:1–7)

These verses show that the guardian beings symbolize the Lord's providence working to prevent people from prying into religious mysteries. They also show that for this reason people were left to their mad desires, symbolized here by the fire that was to be sprinkled over the city and by the fact that no one was to be spared.

309 The *flame of a sword turning itself* symbolizes self-love with its mad desires and delusions, which are such that although we want to enter there, we are carried in the opposite direction, toward bodily and earthly preoccupations. So many quotations from the Word are available to prove this symbolism that they would fill pages. Let me offer only these words from Ezekiel:

> Prophesy, and you are to say, "This is what Jehovah has said: 'Say, "A *sword!* A *sword* sharpened and even polished for committing slaughter, sharpened to have a flash of lightning to it!" Let the *sword* be used again a third time, the *sword* of its victims, the *sword* of much stabbing, penetrating to them in their private rooms, so that their heart will dissolve; and it will multiply the stumbling blocks in all their gates. I have put a terror of a *sword* there; oh, it has turned into lightning!'" (Ezekiel 21:9, 10, 14, 15)

The sword stands for our desolation—desolation to the point where we see not a bit of goodness or truth but only the false things that stand in the way; this is the multiplying of stumbling blocks. Let me add these words in Nahum:

> A horse rider rushing up, and the *flame of a sword,* and the *lightning flash* of a spear, and a throng of those stabbed. (Nahum 3:3)

This describes people who wish to pry into the secrets of faith.

310 Each word of this verse [Genesis 3:24] holds such deep secrets that they could never be uncovered. They relate to the inborn character of the people who were destroyed in the Flood, a character completely different from that of the people living after the Flood.

Let me say just a little about it. The most distant ancestors of this generation, who formed the earliest church, had a heavenly character and so were sown with heavenly seed. Their descendants consequently had in them seed from a heavenly source. Because of its heavenly source, the nature of this seed is to cause love to reign throughout the whole mind and unify it.

The human mind has two parts: will and intellect. The will holds love or goodness, the intellect holds faith or truth. From love (goodness) the people of that time perceived what belonged to faith (to truth), so that their minds were unified. The offspring of such people keep the same seed inside them, which is perilous if they turn away from truth and goodness, because they then corrupt their whole mind to such an extent that it can hardly be restored in the other life.

[2] The situation is different for people who do not have heavenly but instead spiritual seed inside them—those living after the Flood, for example, and those who live in modern times. Such people have no love and therefore no will to do good. Faith is still possible, though; in other words, they are able to comprehend truth. Faith or an understanding of truth can lead them to a kind of charity, although they arrive at it by another way. Their way lies through conscience, which is instilled in them by the Lord and is formed out of a knowledge of truth and of the good that results from it. So their circumstances are radically different from those of the people who predated the Flood. Those circumstances will be described later [§398], the Lord in his divine mercy willing.

These are secrets wholly unknown to people today. No one today has any idea what a heavenly person is or even what a spiritual one is, let alone what the implications are for the nature of the human mind and mortal life or for the resulting conditions after death.

311. The otherworld condition of those who died in the Flood is such that they can never live in the world of spirits or coexist with other spirits. They live in a hell separated from other spirits' hells and seemingly placed at the foot of a certain mountain, which appears to be a barrier formed out of their dreadful fantasies and self-deceptions. These dreams and notions of theirs are of a kind that puts other spirits in such a stupor that they cannot tell whether they are alive or dead, since it robs them of all their ability to discern what is true and leaves them without perception.

The people who died in the Flood had held fast to the same delusions when they were alive, and they were destined in the next life to be incapable of ever living among other spirits without bringing a sort of death to them. In consequence, all people of this type became extinct, and the Lord in his divine mercy created new states for the people coming after the Flood.

312. The current verse thoroughly describes the condition of these pre-Flood people in saying, for instance, that they were thrown out—separated from heavenly goodness—and that guardian beings were made to live on *the east of the Garden of Eden*. It is owing to their character that the verse

[literally] says they lived "from" the east "to" the Garden of Eden, in words that can apply only to them. These words cannot be said of the people who lived later; they have to be described as stretching *from the Garden of Eden to the east*. The verse also mentions "the flame of a sword turning itself"; for modern people it would have spoken of "a sword of flame." Nor would it have mentioned a "tree of lives" but a "tree of life." There is still more in the series that can never be explained but can only be understood by angels, to whom the Lord reveals the meaning. Each state holds in it an unlimited number of secrets, and not one of them is known to the human race.

313

From the statements now made about the first human it can be seen that this person did not pass an evil heredity on to everyone alive today and that popular belief is wrong in saying we have no inherited evil except what sprang from that source.[207] It is the primeval church that is the subject here and that is being called "the human." When the name *Adam* is used, it symbolizes the idea that humankind was taken from the ground, or that from being nonhuman, people were made human, in being regenerated by the Lord.[208] This is the origin and this is the meaning of the name.

The truth about inherited evil is that any of us who have actually committed a sin have imposed on ourselves a nature rising out of that sin. The evil is then implanted in our children and becomes hereditary. So it comes from every parent, from every grandparent, great-grandparent, great-great-grandparent, and so on back in order. In this way it multiplies and grows in each succeeding generation and remains with every one of us—and our own sinful deeds add to it. It does not weaken to the point of harmlessness except in those whom the Lord regenerates.

Anyone who pays attention can see this by considering that the bad tendencies of parents remain visible in their children, so that one family can be distinguished from another, and in fact one generation from another.

Our Entry into Eternal Life (Continued)

314

AFTER our revived selves—our souls—have been restored to the light, so that we can look around us, the spiritual angels mentioned before [§182] perform every service for us that we can possibly desire in our new state. They teach us about the things that exist in the other life, but only so far as we can comprehend. To anyone who had been a believer and has an interest they also show the grand and amazing sights of heaven.

[315] But if the revived person or soul is not the kind who wants to learn, he or she then wants to leave the angels' company. The angels are quick to perceive this because in the next life all the ideas involved in our thinking are shared generally. When we are eager to part with the angels, they do not leave us but we disconnect from them. Angels love everyone and want nothing more than to be helpful to us, teach us, and take us up into heaven. That is their highest pleasure.

[316] When we as souls break off with them in this way, we are next welcomed by good spirits, and in their company every possible service is again performed for us. However, if our life in the world was such that we cannot stay among the good, once more we want to get away from them. The process repeats continuously until we come into contact with the type of people whose life in the world was in total agreement with ours. Among them we seem to find our own life. Then, surprising to say, we live the same kind of life with them as we had lived in the body.

As we sink back into that life, we experience a new beginning. Some of us move on from there toward hell after a fairly long time and some after a fairly short time. Those of us who had believed in the Lord, however, from the time of that new beginning are gradually led to heaven.

[317] Some reach heaven more slowly and some more quickly. I have even seen some taken up into heaven immediately after death. Allow me to mention just two examples.

[318] A man came and spoke to me who, as certain signs indicated, had recently departed from life. At first he did not realize where he was, supposing himself to be in the world.

I then informed him that he was in the next life and that he no longer had any possessions—house, money, and so on—but was in another realm, where he lacked everything he had owned in the world. Filled with anxiety over this, he did not know what direction to go or where he would live; but I told him that the Lord alone looks out for him and for everyone. Afterward I left him alone to think as he had thought in the world. He started to wonder (everyone's thoughts can be perceived clearly in the other life) what he should do now, being destitute of everything that had allowed him to stay alive.

Still laboring under this anxiety, he was transferred to the company of spirits with a heavenly nature. They were in the vicinity of the heart[209] and everything he wanted, whatever it was, they helped him with. This done, he was again left alone and, under the inspiration of charity, began to consider how he could repay such great kindness. All this showed that in the life of the body he had possessed the charity that belongs to faith. As a result he was lifted up into heaven instantly.

319 I also watched another person transferred right into heaven by the angels and saw him received by the Lord and shown heaven's glory.

Besides all this, I know from much other experience that it takes time for some people to reach heaven.

Genesis 4

What the Life of the Soul or Spirit Is Like

320 WHAT is life generally like for souls or recently departed spirits after death? Wide experience has shown me that when people come into the next life they do not realize they are there. They think they are still in the world and in fact in their bodies. They are so convinced of this that if you tell them they are spirits, they are amazed and dumbfounded, for two reasons. One is that they seem completely human in respect to their senses, desires, and thoughts. The other is their previous disbelief, when they lived in the world, that they were spirits or (in some cases) that spirits could even be like this.

321 A second thing is that spirits' powers of sensation are much more highly developed than when they lived in the body, as is their gift for thinking and speaking. These abilities are so much greater that they can hardly even be compared. Still, spirits are unaware of the change until the Lord leads them to reflect on it.

322 Avoid succumbing to the false opinion that spirits lack the power of sensation, and sensation much keener than they had while living in the body. I know the opposite to be true from thousands and thousands of experiences. If you do not want to believe, because of assumptions you make about the spirit, keep it to yourself when you enter the other life.[210] There actual experience will make a believer out of you.

Spirits have eyesight, since they live in light, and good spirits, angelic spirits, and angels live in such bright light that the world's noonday light can hardly be compared to it. (More will be said later on [§§1521–1534], with the Lord's divine mercy, about the light that they live in and see by.)

Not only that, they also have hearing, and such sensitive hearing that their [former,] physical hearing cannot be measured against it. They have talked with me almost continually for several years now[211] (but more about their speech will also be told later on [§§1634–1650, 1757–1764], with the Lord's divine mercy).

They have a sense of smell (also dealt with later [§1516], with the Lord's divine mercy).

They have an extremely sensitive sense of touch, from which come the excruciating pangs of hell. All the senses relate to touch, since they are simply different varieties of it.[212]

[2] They have desires and feelings to which, again, the ones they had during physical existence cannot be compared. (These too will be expanded on below [§994:3], with the Lord's divine mercy.)

They think much more clearly and precisely than they did during the life of the body, packing more into a single mental image than they did into a thousand when they engaged in thought during bodily life.

They talk to each other with such great acumen, subtlety, wisdom, and clarity that if we perceived only part of what they said we would be astounded.

In short, they have lost absolutely nothing they need in order to be human—and more perfectly human at that—except flesh and bones, and the accompanying imperfections.

They acknowledge and perceive that during bodily life the spirit was what actually sensed things. Although sensation seemed to take place in their bodies it was not, in fact, physical. Consequently when the body has been laid aside, sensation lives on with much greater acuity and perfection. Life consists in sensation because without it there is no life, and the quality of sensation determines the quality of life, as anyone can recognize.

323 Below, at the end of the chapter, are some examples of people who thought otherwise in the life of the body [§§443–448].

Genesis 4

1. And the human knew[213] Eve, his wife, and she conceived and delivered Cain. And she said, "I have acquired a man: Jehovah."[214]

2. And she went on to deliver his brother Abel; and Abel was a shepherd of the flock, and Cain was one who cultivated the ground.

3. And it happened at the end of some days that Cain brought forward some of the fruit of the ground as an offering to Jehovah.

4. And Abel, too, brought forward some of the firstborn of his flock and of their fat. And Jehovah looked on Abel and on his offering.

5. But Cain and his offering he ignored. And anger kindled strongly in Cain, and his face fell.

6. And Jehovah said to Cain, "Why has anger kindled in you? And why has your face fallen?

7. If you do well, will it not raise you up? And if you do not do well, sin lies at your door. And [Abel] longs for you, but you rule him."

8. And Cain said to Abel his brother . . .[215] And it happened when they were in the field that Cain rose up against Abel his brother and killed him.

9. And Jehovah said to Cain, "Where is Abel, your brother?" And he said, "I do not know. Am I my brother's guardian?"

10. And he said, "What have you done? The voice of your brother's blood is crying out to me from the ground.

11. And now, a curse on you from the ground, which opened its mouth, receiving your brother's blood from your hand!

12. When you cultivate the ground, it will no longer yield its strength to you. A wanderer and fugitive you will be on the earth."

13. And Cain said to Jehovah, "My wickedness is too great to be taken away.

14. Look, you have thrown me out today, off the face of the ground. And I will be hidden from your face and will be a wanderer and fugitive on the earth. And it will come about that anyone who finds me will kill me."

15. And Jehovah said to him, "Therefore anyone who kills Cain will suffer sevenfold vengeance." And Jehovah put a mark on Cain, that no one who found him should strike him.

16. And Cain went out from before Jehovah; and he lived in the land of Nod, to the east of Eden.

17. And Cain knew his wife, and she conceived and delivered Enoch. And [Cain] was building a city, and he named the city after his son, Enoch.

18. And Irad was born to Enoch. And Irad fathered Mehujael, and Mehujael fathered Methushael, and Methushael fathered Lamech.

19. And Lamech took two wives to himself, the name of one being Adah and the name of the other Zillah.

20. And Adah delivered Jabal; he was the father of the tent dweller, and of livestock.[216]

21. And the name of his brother was Jubal; he was the father of everyone playing the harp and the organ.[217]

22. And Zillah in turn delivered Tubal-cain, who trained every artisan in bronze and iron. And Tubal-cain's sister was Naamah.

23. And Lamech said to his wives, Adah and Zillah, "Listen to my voice, wives of Lamech, and with your ears perceive what I say, because I killed a man for my wound and a little child for my bruise."[218]

24. For Cain will be avenged seven times, and Lamech seventy-seven times."

25. And the human knew his wife again, and she delivered a son and called his name Seth, "Because God has restored other seed for me in place of Abel, since Cain killed him."[219]

26. And to Seth in turn a son was born, and he called his name Enosh. Then people began to call on the name of Jehovah.

Summary

324 THE subject here is religious positions developed independently of the church, or in other words, heresies. A new church raised up later, called Enosh, is also treated of.

325 Because the earliest church loved the Lord, it believed in Him, but some people came along who divided faith from love. The teaching that faith was separate from love was named Cain. Charity, which is love for others, was called Abel (verses 1, 2).

326 The way each group worshiped is described. Cain's offering depicts worship motivated by a detached faith while Abel's offering depicts worship motivated by charity (verses 3, 4). Worship based on charity was pleasing, while worship based on a detached faith was not (verses 4, 5).

327 Cain's burning anger and fallen face portrayed a change for the worse in the condition of those who latched on to a separated faith (verses 5, 6).

328 Charity allows us to recognize the quality of faith. In addition, charity wants to exist alongside faith, if faith does not become the chief thing and is not lifted up above charity (verse 7).

329 Charity was blotted out among those who detached faith from it and made faith more important, as illustrated by Cain in his murder of his brother Abel (verses 8, 9).

330 Charity that has been extinguished is called the voice of blood (verse 10), corrupt theology is called a curse from the ground (verse 11), and falsity and evil from that theology are the wanderer and fugitive on the earth (verse 12). Since those people turned away from the Lord, they were in danger of eternal death (verses 13, 14), but faith was the means by which charity

would be implanted from then on, so a sacred ban was placed on the violation of it. This is the mark put on Cain (verse 15). The removal of faith from the seat it used to occupy is Cain's residence to the east of Eden (verse 16).

331. The heresy in a later, expanded form is called Enoch (verse 17).

332. Other heresies rising out of it are also given names, in the last of which—called Lamech—no more faith remained (verse 18).

333. Adah and Zillah mean a new church that now came into being and was portrayed in these women's sons—Jabal, Jubal, and Tubal-cain. The heavenly aspects of the church were represented by Jabal, the spiritual aspects by Jubal, and the earthly aspects by Tubal-cain (verses 19, 20, 21, 22).

334. That church arose when every shred of faith and of charity had been destroyed and the most sacred ban had been violated (verses 23, 24).

335. At the end of the story, after the obliteration of charity by a detached faith (Cain), the Lord granted a new kind of faith—one through which charity would be introduced. That faith is Seth (verse 25).

336. Charity introduced by means of faith is called Enosh, or "another person,"[220] which is the name of that church (verse 26).

Inner Meaning

337. THE subject here is the deterioration of the earliest church, or the falsification of religious teachings. Heresies and sects are described under the names of Cain and his descendants. In connection with this, we need to understand that we can have no idea how the religion was falsified or what that church's heresies and sects were like unless we are thoroughly acquainted with the nature of the true church. With such acquaintance we can recognize how things stood.

The earliest church has already been discussed quite amply. I showed that it was in the form of a heavenly person [§§162:1, 200] and that its adherents did not acknowledge any other faith than one of love for the Lord and for other people [§§32:2, 202, 281]. Through that love they received faith from the Lord, or in other words, a perception of all that belongs to faith [§§104, 125]. They did not even want to use the word *faith* for fear it would be separated from love, as shown earlier (§§200–203).

[2] That is what a person of heavenly character is like, and David, in speaking of the Lord as monarch and of a heavenly person as royal offspring, uses the following images to represent that nature:

> Give your judgments to the monarch, and your justice to the royal offspring. The mountains will bring peace to the people, as will the hills, in justice. Generation after generation will fear you in the lasting of the sun and before the face of the moon. In their days the upright individual will flourish, as will great peace, until there is no moon. (Psalms 72:1, 3, 5, 7)

The sun symbolizes love and the moon faith. The mountains and hills symbolize the earliest church. Generation after generation symbolizes the religions that came after the Flood. It says *until there is no moon* because faith will be love. See also what is said in Isaiah 30:26.

[3] This shows the nature of the earliest church and of its religious thought. Modern times, in which faith comes first, are completely different; but through faith the Lord endows us with charity, and then charity takes highest importance. It follows that religious teachings were falsified in earliest times when people declared their faith and in the process separated faith from love. Those who falsified the religion in this way, dividing faith from love (that is, championing faith alone), were at that time called Cain. To do as they did was scandalous to the earliest people.

338 Genesis 4:1. *And the human knew Eve, his wife, and she conceived and delivered Cain; and she said, "I have acquired a man: Jehovah."*

The *human* and *his wife, Eve,* symbolize the earliest church, as is known. His firstborn or first offspring is faith, which is called *Cain* here. *She said, "I have acquired the man Jehovah,"* means that faith among those called Cain was recognized and acknowledged as a thing in itself.

339 In the three previous chapters I have offered proof enough that the *human* and *his wife* symbolize the earliest church, so that there can be no doubt of it [§§252–253, 277, 288–289]. Since the human and his wife are the earliest church, it makes sense that what was *conceived* and *given birth to* by them could not be anything else [than what was conceived and born in the church].

The earliest people were very familiar with assigning names that had symbolic meaning and in this way creating a genealogy. After all, the church's attributes bear the same relationship to each other: one thing is conceived and born from another and relates to it like a new generation. Consequently it is common for the Word to refer to the church's attributes as times of conception and birth, as offspring, babies, children, daughters, sons, youths, and so on. The prophetic parts are full of such references.[221]

[340] The opening summary of this chapter [§337] establishes the meaning of *she said, "I have acquired the man Jehovah,"* as the fact that faith among those called Cain was recognized and acknowledged as a thing in itself.

Before this it was as if people were unaware of what faith was, because they had a perception of everything involved in faith. When they started to create a distinct doctrine concerning faith, however, they drew out principles they had learned through perception, reduced them into a systematic theology, and named them "I have acquired the man Jehovah," as if they had stumbled onto some new thing. In this way they turned what had been written on their hearts into a set of facts.

In ancient times people gave a name to every new phenomenon and explained the significance of the names in just this way. They explained, for example, that *Ishmael* meant that Jehovah had heard Hagar's unhappiness (Genesis 16:11); that *Reuben* meant "Jehovah has seen my unhappiness" (Genesis 29:32); that *Simeon* meant that Jehovah had heard Leah was not as well loved (Genesis 29:33); and that *Judah* meant "This time I will acclaim Jehovah" (Genesis 29:35). The altar built by Moses was called "Jehovah my banner" (Exodus 17:15). Here the actual doctrine concerning faith was called "I have acquired the man Jehovah," that is to say, Cain.

[341] Genesis 4:2. *And she went on to deliver his brother Abel. And Abel was a shepherd of the flock; and Cain was one who cultivated the ground.*

The church's second-born is charity, symbolized by *Abel* and *brother*. *A shepherd of the flock* is people who do the good that charity inspires. *One who cultivated the ground* is people who lack charity, however attached they may be to a faith separated from love, which is no kind of faith.

[342] The fact that the church's second-born is charity can be seen from the things that the church conceives and gives birth to: nothing but faith and charity. The first children Leah bore to Jacob have the same symbolism: Reuben symbolizes faith; Simeon, faith in action; and Levi, charity (Genesis 29:32, 33, 34). This is also why the tribe of Levi became the priests and represented a shepherd of the flock.

As charity is the church's second-born, it is called a brother and is named Abel.

[343] Everyone can see that *a shepherd of a flock* is one who does the good that charity inspires, because the image is common in the Old and New

Testaments of the Word. One who leads and teaches is called a shepherd, or pastor, while those who are led and taught are termed the flock. No one who fails to lead people to do the good involved in charity or who fails to teach about that good is a true shepherd; no one who fails to follow the path to goodness or to learn about it is part of the flock.

Of course, it is unnecessary to demonstrate this symbolism of shepherd (or pastor) and flock by passages from the Word, but let me mention these anyway. In Isaiah:

> The Lord will give rain for the seed with which you sow the ground, and bread from the produce of the ground. He will *pasture* your *livestock* on that day, in a broad meadow. (Isaiah 30:23)

Bread from the produce of the ground is charity. In the same author:

> The Lord Jehovih will *pasture* his *flock* like a *shepherd*. He will gather the lambs into his arm and carry them on his chest. He will *lead* their new mothers gently. (Isaiah 40:11)

In David:

> *Shepherd* of Israel, listen intently, as you *lead* Joseph like a *flock*. As you sit upon the guardian beings, shine out! (Psalms 80:1)

In Jeremiah:

> I have compared the daughter of Zion to an attractive and delicate woman. *Shepherds* will come to her, and their *flocks* will pitch their *tents* near her all around. They will each *graze* their space. (Jeremiah 6:2, 3)

In Ezekiel:

> The Lord Jehovih said, "I will multiply them like a *flock of people*, like a holy *flock*, like the *flock* of Jerusalem at its set [feast] times; in this way the deserted cities will be filled with a *flock of people.*" (Ezekiel 36:37, 38)

In Isaiah:

> Every *flock* of Arabia will be gathered to you; the *rams* of Nebaioth will wait on you. (Isaiah 60:7)

Those who lead the flock toward neighborly kindness are those who gather the flock; those who do not lead toward neighborly kindness are those who scatter the flock. All togetherness and unity are the result of charity, while all dispersal and disjunction come from a lack of charity.

344 What purpose is there to faith, or to the facts, insights, and teachings of faith, except that we may become what faith teaches us to be? And the primary thing it teaches is charity, as stated in Mark 12:28–34 and Matthew 22:35–40. That is the goal toward which faith looks in all it does. If we do not gain charity, what is knowledge, or doctrine, but a nothing?[222]

345 *One who cultivated the ground* is people who lack charity, however attached they may be to a faith separated from love, which is no kind of faith. This can be seen from what follows—that Jehovah ignored Cain's offering and that Cain killed his brother or, in other words, destroyed the charity that Abel symbolized.

People whose sights were set on bodily and earthly interests were said to cultivate the ground. This can be seen from remarks made at Genesis 3:19, 23 [§§276, 305], where it says that the humans were sent away from the Garden of Eden to cultivate the ground.

346 Genesis 4:3. *And it happened at the end of some days that Cain brought forward some of the fruit of the ground as an offering to Jehovah.*

The end of some days means the passage of time. *Fruit of the ground* means doing what faith requires without loving others. An *offering to Jehovah* means the worship rising out of those deeds.

347 Anyone can see that *the end of some days* means the passage of time. The doctrine called Cain, in its beginning, when it still had a simple quality, did not appear to have been as displeasing as later, which can be seen from the fact that they called the child acquired "the man Jehovah." Neither was faith as completely divided from love in the beginning as it was "at the end of some days" or with the passage of time. This is what happens with all genuine religious teachings.

348 The fact that the *fruit of the ground* means doing what faith requires without loving others is also evident from what follows. Deeds of faith that lack charity are deeds devoid of faith. In themselves they are dead, since they belong exclusively to the outer self. Jeremiah speaks of them this way:

> Why is the path of the godless successful? You planted them; they also took root. They grew; they also produce *fruit*. You are nearby in their mouth but far from their kidneys.[223] How long will the land mourn and the grass of all the fields wither? (Jeremiah 12:1, 2, 4)

"Nearby in their mouth but far from their kidneys" refers to those who advocate a faith detached from charity. It says of them that the land mourns. The same book calls [acts of faith devoid of charity] "the fruit of their deeds":

> The heart is more a usurper than anything else is and is beyond hope. Who really knows the heart? I, Jehovah, am examining the heart, testing the kidneys, and [my purpose is] to give them each as their *ways* deserve, as the *fruit* of their *deeds* deserves. (Jeremiah 17:9, 10)

In Micah:

> The land will become a desolate place because of its residents, in return for the *fruit of their deeds*. (Micah 7:13)

But Amos says this kind of fruit is nonfruit—that is, it is the work of dead people—and both the fruit and the root are destroyed:

> Before their faces I have destroyed the Amorites, whose height was like the height of cedars. And they were strong, like an oak, yet I destroyed their *fruit* upward and their *roots* downward. (Amos 2:9)

And in David:

> Their *fruit* you will destroy from the earth and their *seed* from among the children of humankind. (Psalms 21:10)

But deeds inspired by charity are alive. They are said to send roots below and yield fruit above, as in Isaiah:

> The remaining refugees of Judah's house will put new *root* downward and produce *fruit* upward. (Isaiah 37:31)

To produce fruit upward is to act with charity as motivation. The fruit is called excellent in the same author:

> On that day Jehovah's offshoot will become the beauty and glory—and the earth's *fruit* will become the *excellence* and adornment—of Israel's rescuees. (Isaiah 4:2)

It is also the fruit of salvation, as the same author terms it:

> Drizzle, you heavens, from above, and let the heights of the sky flow with justice. Let the earth open, and let them bear the *fruit of salvation,* and let justice sprout together with it. I, Jehovah, will *create* this. (Isaiah 45:8)

349 The meaning of an *offering* as worship can be established by the representative practices of the Jewish religion. All its sacrifices, the presentation of the first fruits of the land and of all its produce, and the giving over of the firstborn—these are called offerings and constituted that religion's worship. Since all these offerings represented heavenly things and had to do with the Lord, they symbolized true worship. Anyone can recognize this. What is a representative act without the thing it represents? What is the outer shell without inner contents but some dead, idolatrous thing? It is the inner contents, or the Lord working through the inner contents, that give the outer shell life. Clearly, then, all such offerings in a representative religion symbolize worship of the Lord. The symbolism of the individual types will, with the Lord's divine mercy, be given later.[224]

[2] The general meaning of offerings as worship can be seen in many places in the prophets. In Malachi, for instance:

> Who can endure the day of his coming? He will sit smelting and purging silver and will purify the children of Levi and refine them like gold and like silver; and they will be bringing an *offering* to Jehovah in justice. Then the *offering* of Judah and Jerusalem will be sweet to Jehovah, as in the days of old and as in the ancient years. (Malachi 3:2, 3, 4)

An offering made in justice is the inner content that the children of Levi (meaning devout worshipers) will bring. The days of old are the very earliest church, and the ancient years are the ancient church. In Ezekiel:

> On my holy mountain, on the mountain of Israel's high ground, all the house of Israel—that whole land—will worship me. There I will be appeased by them, and there I will seek your *oblations* and the *first fruits* of your *offerings* in all your consecrations. (Ezekiel 20:40)

The oblations and the first fruits of their offerings in their consecrations are again good deeds that charity from the Lord has consecrated. In Zephaniah:

> From the ford of the rivers of Ethiopia, those who adore me will bring my *offering*. (Zephaniah 3:10)

Ethiopia stands for those who possess heavenly attributes: love, charity, and deeds inspired by charity.

Genesis 4:4. *And Abel, too, brought forward some of the firstborn of his flock and of their fat. And Jehovah looked on Abel and on his offering.*

Abel here symbolizes charity, as he did earlier [§§325–326, 341–342]. The *firstborn of the flock* symbolize holiness, which is exclusively the Lord's. The *fat* symbolizes the actual quality of heaven, which is also the Lord's. *Jehovah looked on Abel and on his offering* means that everything connected with charity was pleasing to the Lord, as was all worship springing from charity.

351 *Abel* has already been shown to symbolize charity [§§342–343]. Charity means love for our neighbor. It means mercy too, since if we love our neighbors as we do ourselves we have mercy on them when they are suffering, as we would on ourselves.

352 The symbolism of the *firstborn of the flock* as holiness, which is exclusively the Lord's, can be seen from the place of firstborns in the representative church. They were all holy because they prefigured the Lord, who is the only firstborn.

Love and love-based faith is the firstborn. All love is the Lord's and no particle of love is ours, which is why the Lord is the only firstborn. In the early churches, this fact was represented by the consecration of firstborns and of firstborn animals to Jehovah (Exodus 13:2, 12, 15). It was also represented by the fact that the tribe of Levi was taken in place of all the firstborn and became the priestly order (Numbers 3:40–46; 8:14–20), even though Levi, who on an inner level symbolizes love, was born after Reuben and Simeon, who on an inner level symbolize faith.

The following words in David say that the Lord in respect to his human nature was the firstborn of all:

> The name he will give me is: "You are my father, my God, and the rock of my salvation." Indeed, I will make him the *firstborn,* high above the monarchs of the earth. (Psalms 89:26, 27)

And in John:

> Jesus Christ, the *firstborn* of the dead and chief of the earth's monarchs. (Revelation 1:5)

Take note that the firstborn animals used in worship symbolize the Lord while the firstborn things of the church symbolize faith.[225]

353 Let me address the symbolism of the *fat* as the actual quality of heaven, which also belongs to the Lord. Heaven's quality is made up of everything that belongs to love. Faith too is heavenly when it comes from love. Charity is a heavenly thing. All the good inspired by charity is heavenly. These things are all represented by the fat of the sacrifices, each separate aspect being represented by the fat over the liver (called the omentum), the fat over the kidneys, the fat sheathing the intestines, and the fat over the intestines.[226] These fat deposits were holy and were burned on the altar (Exodus 29:13, 22; Leviticus 3:3, 4, 14;[227] 4:8, 9, 19, 26, 31, 35; 8:16, 25). So they are called the bread of the fire offering for Jehovah's repose (Leviticus 3:5, 16), and this is why the Jewish people were forbidden to eat any of the fat from the animals; these rules were called an "eternal statute throughout their generations" (Leviticus 3:17; 7:23, 25). The statute was given because that church was such that it would not acknowledge anything internal, much less anything heavenly.

[2] The symbolism of fat as the heavenly aspects of charity and the goodness that it inspires can be seen in the prophets, as in Isaiah:

> Why do you weigh out silver for what is not bread and your labor for what does not satisfy? Pay wholehearted attention to me and eat what is good, so that your soul may revel in the *fat*. (Isaiah 55:2)

In Jeremiah:

> I will fill the soul of the priests with *fat*, and my people will receive fully of my goodness. (Jeremiah 31:14)

It is obvious that this does not mean fat but a heavenly-spiritual kind of goodness. In David:

> They are filled with the *fat* of your house, and you slake their thirst with a river of your pleasures, because yours is the wellspring of life. In your light we see light. (Psalms 36:8, 9)

The fat and the wellspring of life stand for the heavenly quality that belongs to love. The river of pleasures and the light stand for the spiritual quality that belongs to a faith rising out of love. In the same author:

> My soul will be filled with *grease* and *fat*, and my mouth will give praise with lips of song. (Psalms 63:5)

Here the fat again stands for a heavenly quality, lips of song for a spiritual one. Clearly something heavenly is meant, since the soul will be filled with it. First fruits themselves—the firstborn produce of the earth—are therefore called fat (Numbers 18:12).

[3] Because heavenly things come in an uncountable number of major categories and an even more uncountable number of specific types, the song Moses recited before the people depicts them generally:

> ... *butter* from the cow and the *milk* of the flock, together with the *fat* of lambs and of rams—the sons of Bashan—and of goats, together

with the *fat* of the kidneys of wheat;[228] and the *blood* of the grape you will drink as unmixed wine. (Deuteronomy 32:14)

No one could ever see what these things mean except in light of their inner meaning. Without the inner meaning, no one could see what butter from the cow is, or the milk of the flock, the fat of lambs, the fat of rams and of goats, the sons of Bashan, the fat of the kidneys of wheat, or the blood of the grape. Without an inner meaning, they would be words and nothing more, when in reality as a whole and individually they symbolize general and specific kinds of heavenly qualities.

354. The meaning of *Jehovah looked on Abel and on his offering* as the fact that everything connected with charity and all worship springing from charity were pleasing to the Lord has been explained previously [§350]. Both what Abel and what an offering symbolize were covered [§§342–343, 349].

355. Genesis 4:5. *But Cain and his offering he ignored. And anger kindled strongly in Cain, and his face fell.*

Cain, as I said [§§325–327, 337:3, 338, 340–341], symbolizes faith detached from love, or at least the kind of doctrinal view that allows faith to be detached. *His offering* and the fact that Jehovah *ignored it* has the same symbolism as before [§345]: that his worship was not acceptable. The *anger kindled in Cain* and the *falling of his face* symbolize a change on the deeper levels; the *anger* means that charity took its leave, and his *face* symbolizes the deeper levels, which, when they change, are said to *fall*.

356. I have already shown that *Cain* symbolizes faith detached from love, or at least the kind of doctrinal view that allows faith to be detached [§340], and that the *offering* which Jehovah *ignored* means that Cain's worship was not acceptable.

357. The symbolism of the *anger kindled in Cain* as the departure of charity is evident from the sequel—that he killed his brother Abel, who symbolizes charity.

Anger is a generalized emotion—our reaction to everything that stands in the way of self-love and the desires that go along with it. This can be clearly perceived in the realm of evil spirits, where anger directed at the Lord is pervasive, because the inhabitants have no charity but only hatred. Whatever does not favor self-love and materialism arouses opposition, which displays itself in anger.

The Word many times attributes anger, wrath, and even fury to Jehovah. But these emotions are ours and are blamed on Jehovah merely because they seem to be his, for the reason just mentioned. So David says:

> He sent against them the *anger of his nostril,* and *wrath,* and *fury,* and anguish, and a delegation of wicked angels. He leveled out a path for *anger;* he did not withhold their soul from death. (Psalms 78:49, 50)

It is not that Jehovah ever sends anger against anyone but that people bring it into themselves. Neither is it he that sends wicked angels, as it says, but we that invite them to come. Consequently it adds that he levels out the path of anger and does not withhold their soul from death. Isaiah accordingly says:

> They will come to Jehovah, and all who *blazed up* against him will be shamed. (Isaiah 45:24)

This shows that anger symbolizes evil or, what is the same thing, a departure from charity.

The meaning of *his face fell* as a change at the deeper levels can be established by the symbolism of the face and of falling. Among the ancients the *face* symbolized the inner depths, because those depths shine out through the face. People's nature in earliest times was such that the face was in complete harmony with what was inside, so that everyone could see in another's face what that other's temperament or mind was like. They considered it heinous to show one thing on the face while thinking another. In those days pretense and fraud were abhorrent. As a result, the face symbolized inner things. When charity shone out from the face, the face was said to be lifted, but when the opposite was true, the face was said to fall. This is also why the Lord is said to lift his face on us (as in the blessing from Numbers 6:26 and Psalms 4:6), meaning that the Lord gives us the capacity to love others.[229]

What the *falling* of the face is can be seen in Jeremiah:

> "I will not make my *face fall* toward you, because I am merciful," says Jehovah. (Jeremiah 3:12)

Jehovah's face is mercy. When he lifts his face on anyone, the meaning is that in his mercy he gives that person the gift of charity. The opposite occurs when he makes his face fall—that is, when a person's own face falls.

Genesis 4:6. *And Jehovah said to Cain, "Why has anger kindled in you and why has your face fallen?"*

Jehovah said to Cain means that conscience spoke. The *kindled anger* and the *fallen face* mean, as they did just above, that charity withdrew and the inner depths changed.

360. There is no need to prove that *Jehovah said to Cain* means that conscience spoke. A similar phrase has already been explained [§219].

361. Genesis 4:7. *"If you do well, will it not raise you up? And if you do not do well, sin lies at your door. And [Abel] longs for you, but you rule him."*

If you do well, will it not raise you up? means if you wish well, charity resides in you. *If you do not do well, sin lies at your door,* means if you do not wish well, there is no charity but only evil. *He longs for you, but you rule him,* means that charity wants to reside in you but cannot because you want to rule over it.

362. This verse presents a picture of the teachings concerning faith that are called Cain, which, because they divided faith from love, also divided faith from charity, the offspring of love.

Wherever a church exists, heresies crop up, because when we think about a single article of faith, we make it the chief one.[230] It is a characteristic of human thought that when we turn our attention to one consideration, we make it more important than another, especially if our fantasies claim it as our own personal discovery. When love for ourselves and for worldly advantages inflates our pride, no circumstance fails to add its consent and support, until we are almost ready to swear that it is true, even if it is false.[231] So those referred to as Cain made faith more essential than love; and since they lived without love, they were helped along in their cause by both self-love and the fantasies that accompany it.

363. The nature of the doctrine of faith that was called Cain can be found in this verse's description of him. The later parts of the verse indicate that charity could have been joined onto faith but only in such a way that charity would rule, not faith. So it says first, *if you do well, it will raise you up,* meaning if you wish well, charity can be present. In the inner sense, doing well means willing well, because good deeds flow from goodwill. Action and will formed a single entity in ancient times. The action allowed people to see the will, because pretense was wholly absent.

What was said earlier [§358] about the face shows that a *raising* [or lifting] symbolizes the presence of charity, since to *lift one's face* is to display charity and the falling of one's face is the opposite.

364. The second phrase was *if you do not do well, sin lies at your door,* meaning if you do not wish well, there is no charity, but only evil. Anyone can see that when *sin lies at the door* it is an evil near at hand and

eager to get in. When charity is missing, after all, ruthlessness and hatred and therefore every kind of evil are present.

The general term *sin* is taken to mean the Devil, and the Devil—or rather the Devil's crew—is nearby when we lack charity. The only thing that chases them from the door is love for the Lord and for our neighbor.

The third thing it says is *he longs for you, but you rule him,* meaning that charity wants to coexist with faith but cannot because faith wants to rule over it, which goes against proper order. As long as faith wants to be in charge, it is not faith. But when charity is in charge, faith is faith. This is because the main concern of faith is charity, as shown before [§344].

Charity can be compared to a flame, which is essential for heat and light, since they come from it. Faith when separated can be compared to light, which without the warmth of the flame is still light, but a wintry light—and there is nothing that does not languish and die in winter's light.

Genesis 4:8. *And Cain said to Abel his brother . . . And it happened when they were in the field that Cain rose up against Abel his brother and killed him.*

Cain said to Abel means a length of time. *Cain,* as I said [§337:3], symbolizes faith separated from love. *Abel* symbolizes charity, the brother of faith, which is why he is called *brother* twice here. The *field* symbolizes every point of doctrine. *Cain rose up against Abel his brother and killed him* means that a detached faith extinguished charity.

These things do not need to be proved by similar passages from the Word beyond the identification of charity as the brother of faith and the symbolism of a field as every point of doctrine.

From the nature or essential character of faith, anyone can see that charity is the *brother* of faith. The brotherhood of these was also represented by Esau and Jacob—another relationship that gave rise to controversy over the birthright and the dominance it entailed. The same brotherhood was represented by Perez and Zerah, Tamar's sons by Judah (Genesis 38:28, 29, 30), a story that also dealt with birthrights. And it was represented by Ephraim and Manasseh (Genesis 48:13, 14), likewise a tale about birthrights and the implied dominance. The same thing was represented by others, too.

Both faith and charity, after all, are the church's offspring. Faith is called a man, as Cain was in the first verse of this chapter, and charity a brother, as in Isaiah 19:2; Jeremiah 13:14;[232] and elsewhere. The union of faith and charity is called a brothers' pact in Amos 1:9.

[2] Something like the relationship symbolized by Cain and Abel was represented by Jacob and Esau, as I said, in that Jacob wanted to supplant Esau. This can be seen in Hosea too:

> . . . to bring on Jacob the consequences of his ways; according to his deeds will [Jehovah] repay him. In the womb he supplanted his brother. (Hosea 12:2, 3)

But Esau, or the charity that Esau represented, was still dominant, as can be seen in the enigmatic prediction of his father Isaac:

> By your sword you will live, and your brother you will serve. And it will happen when you *gain the dominance* that you will force his yoke off your neck. (Genesis 27:40)

In other words, Esau represented a church among non-Jews,[233] or a new church, while Jacob represented the Jewish church. This is why it says so many times that they should acknowledge non-Jewish nations as their brothers and sisters.[234]

In the church of the non-Jews, or the early [Christian] church, they all called each other "sister" or "brother," because of the charity among them. "Sisters and brothers" was also used by the Lord of those who hear the Word and act on it (Luke 8:21); the "hearers" are those who have faith, the "doers" those who have charity. However, those who hear (or say they have faith) and do not act on it (have no charity) are not "sisters and brothers," and the Lord compares them to fools (Matthew 7:24, 26).

368 The symbolism of a *field* as doctrine and therefore as every point of doctrine that deals with faith or charity is clear from the Word. In Jeremiah:

> Mountain of mine in the *field,* your resources, all your treasures I will turn into plunder. (Jeremiah 17:3)

The field stands for doctrine, while resources and treasures stand for the spiritual riches of faith, that is, for teachings of faith's doctrine. In the same author:

> Will the snow of Lebanon desert the rock of my *field?* (Jeremiah 18:14)

Jeremiah 26:18 and Micah 3:12 predict that Zion will be plowed like a *field* when the doctrine concerning faith disappears. In Ezekiel:

> He took some of the seed of the land and put it in a *field* suitable for sowing. (Ezekiel 17:5)

This speaks of the church and its faith. Doctrine is being called a field on account of the seed in it. In the same author:

> And let all the trees of the *field* know that I, Jehovah, will bring down the tall tree. (Ezekiel 17:24)

In Joel:

> The *field* was devastated, the *ground* mourned, because the grain was devastated, the new wine dried up, the oil weakened. The *farmers*[235] were put to shame; the *harvest of the field* was destroyed. All the *trees of the field* withered. (Joel 1:10, 11, 12)

A field here stands for doctrine, trees for knowledge, and farmers for worshipers. In David:

> The *field* and all that is in it will rejoice. Then all the trees of the forest will sing. (Psalms 96:12)

A field cannot rejoice and trees in the forest cannot sing; only something in us can do so, and that something is religious knowledge. In Jeremiah:

> How long will the land mourn and the *grass* of all the *fields* wither? (Jeremiah 12:4)

Again, neither the earth nor the grass of the fields can mourn but only some quality in us that has been ravaged. Likewise in Isaiah:

> The mountains and hills will ring before you with song, and all the *trees of the field* will clap the palms of their hands. (Isaiah 55:12)

The Lord too, in making predictions about the end of the era, refers to the doctrine concerning faith as a field:

> Two will be in the *field*; one will be taken, the other left. (Matthew 24:40; Luke 17:36)

Here the field means both false and true teachings concerning faith, as in the current verse. As the field is doctrine, whoever receives any seed of faith is also called a field, whether it is an individual, the church, or the whole world.

From all this we can now deduce what it means that when they were in the field, *Cain rose up against Abel his brother and killed him*. The meaning is that while both faith and charity grew out of the doctrine concerning faith, faith detached from love could not help completely devaluing charity and in this way extinguishing it. People do the same thing today when they claim that faith alone will save them even if they never perform a single act of neighborly love. So their theory itself annihilates charity, even though they recognize and pay lip service to the idea that faith does not save unless there is love.

370. Genesis 4:9. *And Jehovah said to Cain, "Where is Abel, your brother?" And he said, "I do not know. Am I my brother's guardian?"*

Jehovah said to Cain means a certain perception from deep down that spoke of charity, which is *Abel, your brother. He said, "I do not know. Am I my brother's guardian?"* means that he considered charity worthless, not wanting to act as its servant. So it means that he totally rejected anything having to do with charity. This is what their doctrine had become.

371. When the earliest people described *Jehovah* as *speaking,* they meant perception, because they realized that the Lord made it possible for them to perceive. This capacity for perception lasted only as long as love had primary importance. When love for the Lord came to an end, and love for others consequently did the same, perception died out. To the extent that love remained, perception remained.

This perceptiveness was distinctive to the earliest church. After faith had been separated from love, as it was in those who lived after the Flood, and charity was being acquired by way of faith, conscience took over. Conscience, too, speaks from within, but not in the same way. More on this will, by the Lord's divine mercy, appear later.[236] When conscience dictates, the Word describes it the same way—that is, as speech by Jehovah. Our conscience is formed from the revelations and knowledge of Scripture, and when the Word speaks or supplies an inner dictate, it is the Lord who is speaking. No expression is more common, even today, than "the Lord says" when we refer to a matter of conscience or of faith.

372. Being a *guardian* means serving, like the doorkeepers and gatekeepers in the Jewish religion [2 Kings 7:10–11; 22:4; 23:4; 25:18; Jeremiah 52:24]. Faith is called the guardian of charity here because it must serve charity. But the principles of that doctrine required instead that faith be dominant, as noted at verse 7 [§§362, 365].

373. Genesis 4:10. *And he said, "What have you done? The voice of your brother's blood is crying out to me from the ground!"*

The *voice of his brother's blood* symbolizes violence inflicted on charity. The fact that the blood *cries out* symbolizes guilt. The *ground* symbolizes a schism or heresy.

The symbolism of the *voice of blood* as violence inflicted on charity can be seen from many places in the Word, where a *voice* is taken to mean everything that accuses and *blood* to mean every kind of sin, especially hatred. Those who hate their sister or brother kill her or him in their hearts, as the Lord teaches:

> You have heard that among the people of old it was said, "You shall not *kill;* but whoever *kills* will be subject to judgment." I say to you, though, that any who *are angry* at their sister or brother without cause will be subject to judgment. Once again, any who say "Raca!"[237] to their sister or brother will be subject to the Sanhedrin.[238] But any who say, "Stupid!" will be subject to fiery Gehenna.[239] (Matthew 5:21, 22)

These words refer to different degrees of hatred. Hatred opposes charity, and if it does not kill with its hand, it still does so in its mind or heart, in every way it can. External deterrents alone prevent it from killing with its hand. So every form of hatred is *blood,* as in Jeremiah:

> Why do you amend your ways so as to seek love? Yes, on your hems[240] is found the *blood* of innocent paupers' souls. (Jeremiah 2:33, 34)

[2] Since hatred is *blood,* so is all wickedness, because the source of all wickedness is hatred, as in Hosea:

> False swearing and lying and killing and stealing and the committing of adultery; they rob, and *blood* has followed on *blood.* Therefore the earth will mourn and everyone living in it will waste away. (Hosea 4:2, 3)

In Ezekiel:

> Will you judge the *blood-soaked* city and let it know all its abominations? The city is shedding *blood* in its midst. By your *blood* that you shed you have become guilty. (Ezekiel 22:2, 3, 4, 6, 9)

This is about lack of mercy. In the same author:

> The earth is full of judgment on [crimes of] *blood,* and the city is full of *violence.* (Ezekiel 7:23)

In Jeremiah:

> On account of the sins of Jerusalem's prophets, the transgressions of its priests, who shed the *blood* of the just in its midst, [those same prophets

and priests] wander blind in the streets; they are defiled with *blood*. (Lamentations 4:13, 14)

In Isaiah:

... when the Lord washes away the dirt of Zion's daughters, and has cleansed the *blood* of Jerusalem from its midst, with a spirit of judgment and a spirit of burning. (Isaiah 4:4)

In the same author:

Your palms have been defiled with *blood,* and your fingers with *wickedness.* (Isaiah 59:3)

In Ezekiel:

I passed right by you and saw you trampled in your *blood,* and I told you, "Live in your *blood!*" And I told you, "Live in your *blood!*" (Ezekiel 16:6, 22)

This is about Jerusalem's abominations, which are referred to as blood. [3] The ruthlessness and hatred of the final days are also pictured as blood in Revelation 16:3, 4.

Blood is used in the plural here [in the original language] because everything wicked and abhorrent wells up out of hatred, just as everything good and holy wells up out of love. Those who hate their neighbor would kill him or her if possible, in every way they are capable of, which is to inflict violence on their neighbor; and violence is what *the voice of bloods* properly symbolizes here.

375 *A voice crying out* and *the voice of outcry* are common phrases in the Word. They are used for every situation in which there is any noise, crowd, or hostility, and also where there is elation, as in Exodus 32:17, 18; Zephaniah 1:9, 10; Isaiah 65:19; Jeremiah 48:3. Here the voice makes an accusation.

376 The symbolism of *his blood cries out* as guilt follows in turn, because those who use violence have guilt, as in David:

Evil will kill the ungodly person, and those who *hate* the just individual will incur *guilt.* (Psalms 34:21)

In Ezekiel:

City, by the *blood* that you shed you have become *guilty.* (Ezekiel 22:4)

377 The symbolism of the *ground* here as a schism or heresy can be established by the symbolism of a field. Since a field symbolizes doctrine, the ground containing the field is a schism.

We ourselves are also the ground, and a field too, because doctrine and heresy have been sown in us. Our character comes from the seeds we are sown with. Good, true seed makes us good and true, and evil, false seed makes us evil and false. Those who attach themselves to a particular doctrine are named for that doctrine; those who participate in a schism or heresy are named for that. So the ground here stands for the schism or heresy that is in a person.

378 Genesis 4:11. *"And now, a curse on you from the ground, which opened its mouth, receiving your brother's blood from your hand!"*

A curse on you from the ground means that the schism made [Cain] turn away. *Which opened its mouth* symbolizes what the schism taught. *Receiving your brother's blood from your hand* is the fact that it inflicted violence on charity and extinguished it.

379 These symbolisms can be seen from the preceding sections [§§373–377]. The symbolism of *a curse* as something turned away was also shown before, in §245. Wicked and loathsome acts—that is, acts of hatred—are what turn us away and make us look downward only, toward bodily and earthly concerns, or in other words toward the things of hell. This happens when we send charity into exile and extinguish it, which shatters the bond between the Lord and us. Only charity, which is love and mercy, maintains the bond. Faith without charity is incapable of doing so, since it is no faith but mere knowledge, of a kind that even the Devil's horde can acquire; they are further able to use it for deliberately deceiving the upright and impersonating angels of light. The worst preachers sometimes do the same, with a zeal that seems to spring from piety, although nothing is farther from their minds than what they utter with their lips.

Can there be a person with judgment so unsound as to believe that a memorized faith can have any effect by itself? Or that mere thought based on that faith can have any effect? On the contrary, we all know from our own experience that no one can tell the real value of another's statements and assertions if they do not arise from the will or from genuine intent. It is the will and intention that please us and connect us to one another. Our real identity is whatever we will, not what we think or say without willing it. Our will is what determines our nature and character, because it is the will that has an effect.

If on the other hand our thoughts are good, then the essence of faith, which is charity, lies inside the thought, because goodwill is present. But if we say our thoughts are good, while we live an evil life, we can never desire anything but evil, in which case faith is out of the question.

380 Genesis 4:12. *"When you cultivate the ground, it will no longer yield its strength to you. A wanderer and fugitive you will be on the earth."*

Cultivating the ground symbolizes developing this schism or heresy. *No longer yielding its strength to you* means that it is sterile. *Being a wanderer and fugitive on the earth* means not knowing what is true or good.

381 The meaning of *cultivating the ground* as developing this schism or heresy is established by the symbolism of the *ground,* dealt with just above [§377]. It is evident from this, and from the words themselves, that *no longer yielding its strength* means being sterile. The same thing is also evident from the fact that those who profess faith without charity are professing no faith, as noted [§379].

382 The symbolism of *being a wanderer and fugitive on the earth* as not knowing what is true or good can be seen from the symbolism of *wandering* and *fleeing* in the Word, as in Jeremiah:

> The prophets and priests *wander* blind in the streets; they are defiled with blood. Things that they themselves cannot touch, they touch with their clothes. (Lamentations 4:13, 14)

The prophets stand for those who teach, the priests for those who live according to what is taught. Wandering blind in the streets is not knowing what is good or true. [2] In Amos:

> One plot has received rain and a plot on which it has not rained is drying up. As a result, two or three cities will *wander* to one city to drink water and will not get enough. (Amos 4:7, 8)

The plot that was rained on is teachings about faith that come from charity. The plot or piece of turf on which it did not rain is teachings about faith that are devoid of charity. Likewise, wandering somewhere to drink water is trying to find out what is true. [3] In Hosea:

> Ephraim has been struck; their root has dried up; they will not produce fruit. My God will reject them because they did not heed him, and they will be *wanderers* among the nations. (Hosea 9:16, 17)

Ephraim stands for an intelligent understanding of truth, or faith, because he was Joseph's firstborn.[241] The root that dried up stands for a charity that cannot produce fruit. *Wanderers among the nations* means that they do not know what is true or good. [4] In Jeremiah:

> Go up against Arabia and lay waste to the children of the east. *Flee, wander* far and wide. Hazor's inhabitants have gone down below to live. (Jeremiah 49:28, 30)

Arabia and the children of the east stand for the possession of heavenly riches, or of anything touched by love. When these things have been laid waste and can produce nothing good, they too are said to flee and wander, or to be fugitives and wanderers. Hazor's inhabitants—those who possess the spiritual riches that come with faith—are said to go down below, that is, to perish. [5] In Isaiah:

> All your leaders *wander about* together; on account of the bow they were put in chains. From far away they *fled*. (Isaiah 22:3)

This is about the Valley of Vision,[242] or the delusion that faith is possible without charity. So verse 14 below says that anyone who professes a faith that does not rise out of charity is a wanderer and fugitive, that is, knows nothing about truth or goodness.

383 Genesis 4:13. *And Cain said to Jehovah, "My wickedness is too great to be taken away."*

Cain said to Jehovah symbolizes a limited confession that he was in evil's grip, the confession resulting from a kind of internal pain. *Wickedness too great to be taken away* symbolizes his consequent despair.

384 This shows that a modicum of good still remained in Cain. All the good linked to charity later died out, however, as seen in Lamech, the subject of verses 19, 23, and 24.

385 Genesis 4:14. *"Look, you have thrown me out today, off the face of the ground. And I will be hidden from your face, and I will be a wanderer and fugitive on the earth. And it will come about that anyone who finds me will kill me."*

Being thrown off the face of the ground symbolizes being cut off from all the church's truth. *Being hidden from your face* symbolizes being cut off from all the good inherent in a loving faith. *Being a wanderer and fugitive on the earth* is not knowing what is true or good. *Anyone who finds me will kill me* means that all evil and falsity would destroy him.

386 The symbolism of *being thrown out, off the face of the ground* as being cut off from all the church's truth is established by the symbolism of the *ground*. In its genuine sense it is the church, or those people who make up the church, and so whatever belief the church proclaims, as noted earlier [§§90, 268, 278, 313, 377]. The nuance comes from the subject under discussion. So if a person wrongly adopts a belief (that is, a schism or heresy), that person too is called the ground. *Being thrown off the face of the ground* here, then, means no longer knowing the church's truth.

387. The symbolism of *being hidden from your face* as being cut off from all the good inherent in a loving faith is established by the symbolism of *Jehovah's face*. Jehovah's face, as previously stated [§§222–223, 358], is mercy, the source of all the good taught by a loving faith. So the good that faith teaches is symbolized here by *face*.

388. *Being a wanderer and fugitive on the earth* is not knowing what is true or good, as above [§382].

389. In consequence, *anyone who finds me will kill me* means that all evil and falsity would destroy him.

The situation is this: When we deprive ourselves of charity, we cut ourselves off from the Lord. Charity—love for others and mercy—is the only thing that binds us to the Lord. Without charity, there is disconnection. When there is disconnection, we are left to ourselves, or to our own devices. Under those circumstances, every thought we think is false and every purpose we intend is evil. These are the things that kill a person, or cause a person to be lifeless.

390. Moses shows how those who succumb to falsity and evil fall prey to an unremitting fear of murder:

> And your land will be a ruin and your cities a wasteland. Those of you who are left—I will make their heart *soft* in the lands of their enemies. And *the sound of a driven leaf will pursue them, and they will flee as if fleeing a sword,* and fall when no one pursues them. And they will each collide with their brother as if before a sword, though no one pursues them. (Leviticus 26:33, 36, 37)

In Isaiah:

> Traitors betray and traitorously commit the treachery of traitors.[243] And it will happen that one *fleeing from a terrifying sound* will fall into the pit, and one climbing out of the middle of the pit will be caught in the snare. Their transgression will weigh on them; therefore they will fall and not rise again. (Isaiah 24:16–20)

In Jeremiah:

> Here, I am bringing a *horror* on you; from all your surroundings you will each be driven out before it, and there will be no one to gather the *wanderers*. (Jeremiah 49:5)

In Isaiah:

> "On a horse we will flee," and so you will flee. "And on a swift mount we will ride," so your pursuers will grow swift. One thousand will flee at the reproach of one, and at the reproach of five you will flee. (Isaiah 30:16, 17)

This place and others in the Word depict those who are subject to falsity and evil—how they flee, and how they fear they will be killed. Everything causes them fear because no one is protecting them.

All who have evil and falsity inside hate their neighbor; therefore each of them is eager to kill the others.

The best evidence that those under the sway of falsity and evil are afraid of everyone is provided by evil spirits in the other life. The ones who have deprived themselves of all charity wander and flee. Everywhere they go, whatever communities they may happen upon perceive immediately, on their first approach, what kind of person each of them is. (That kind of perception is possible in the other life.) These communities not only drive such spirits off but also punish them severely and in fact would like to kill them, if they could.

The evil take enormous delight in punishing and torturing each other; in this their greatest joy consists. And to reveal a secret, falsity and evil themselves lie at the root, since what one person desires to do to another returns on that person's own head. Falsity and evil carry with them their own punishment and so also the fear of punishment.

Genesis 4:15. *And Jehovah said to him, "Therefore anyone who kills Cain will suffer sevenfold vengeance." And Jehovah put a mark on Cain, that no one who found him should strike him.*

Anyone who kills Cain will suffer sevenfold vengeance means that there was a sacred ban on violating the faith that was detached in this way. *Jehovah put a mark on Cain, that no one should strike him,* is the fact that the Lord singled out that faith in a special way in order to preserve it.

Before I explain the symbolism of these things on the inner plane, the nature of faith needs to be understood.

The people of the earliest church were such that they acknowledged no other faith than faith from love, so much so that they did not even want to say the word *faith*. Everything involved in faith they subsumed under the idea of love from the Lord. Heavenly angels (described above [§202]) are the same way.

It was foreseen, though, that the human race would not maintain this character but would split faith off from love for the Lord and make it into a doctrine of its own. So it was also provided that faith would indeed be split off but in such a way that through it, or through a knowledge of it, the Lord would give us a heart for charity. In this way, knowledge, or "hearing the message," would come first.[244] Then through that knowledge or hearing the Lord would give us the gift of charity—that is, love for our neighbor, and mercy. The charity acquired by this means not only would be inseparable from faith but also would constitute faith's principal concern.

Afterward conscience took the place of the perception that the earliest church had enjoyed. Conscience, built up through the faith that is attached to charity, would speak from within, not *explaining* what was true but affirming *that* a particular thing was true, and this because the Lord had said so in the Word. For the most part, the churches that came after the Flood—including the early [Christian] church (the first church following the Lord's Coming)—adopted this character.

The same criterion distinguishes spiritual angels from heavenly angels.

394 Now, as these things were foreseen and provided in order to prevent the human race from dying an eternal death, the present verse says that no one was to do violence to Cain, who symbolizes a detached faith. It also says that a mark was placed on him, that is, that the Lord singled faith out in a special way in order to preserve it.

This is hidden knowledge that has never before come to light. The Lord had the same thing in mind when he spoke of marriage and of eunuchs in Matthew:

> There are eunuchs who were born so from their mother's womb. And there are eunuchs who were made so by others. And there are eunuchs who made themselves eunuchs for the sake of God's kingdom. Those who can understand, let them understand. (Matthew 19:12)

"Eunuch" applies to those who enter into the heavenly marriage.[245] The ones who are like heavenly angels are called "those born so from their mother's womb." The ones who are like spiritual angels are called "those made so by others." The ones who are like angelic spirits, who participate in that marriage not so much from charity as from obedience, are called "those who made themselves so."

Anyone who kills Cain will suffer sevenfold vengeance means there was a sacred ban on violating the faith detached in this way. This is established by the symbolism of *Cain* as a detached faith and of *seven* as a sacred ban.

The number seven was held sacred, as is known,[246] because of the six days of creation and because of the seventh day—which is the heavenly kind of person—on which there is peace, repose, a Sabbath. This is why the rituals of the Jewish religion so often involve the number seven, and each time it is seen to stand for something sacred.[247]

For this reason, different stretches of time, long and short, were divided in seven and called weeks. One instance is the long periods before the coming of the Messiah in Daniel 9:24, 25. Laban and Jacob call a period of seven years a week in Genesis 29:27, 28. So wherever the number seven occurs, it is considered as standing for something sacred, or else for a sacred ban, as in David:

Seven times in a day do I praise you. (Psalms 119:164)

In Isaiah:

The light of the moon will be like the light of the sun, and the light of the sun will be *seven times as strong,* like the light of *seven* days. (Isaiah 30:26)

Here the sun is love and the moon is faith from love, which will be like love.

[2] Just as the stages of a person's regeneration are divided into six, which precede the seventh, or the stage of being heavenly, so too are the stages of devastation, which continues until nothing heavenly remains. This was represented by the Jews' many captivities, including the last, in Babylon—a captivity of seven "ages" or seventy years;[248] and several times it is said that the land was to rest during its Sabbaths.[249] Devastation was also represented by Nebuchadnezzar in Daniel:

His heart will change from [that of] a human, and the heart of an animal will be given to him, until *seven* seasons change upon him. (Daniel 4:16, 25, 32)

Concerning the devastation of the final days as described by John:

I saw another sign in the sky, great and awesome: *seven* angels having the *seven* final plagues. (Revelation 15:1, 6, 7)

Revelation 11:2 says that the holy city will be trampled for forty-two months, which is six times seven. In the same author:

> I saw a book written inside and on the back,[250] sealed with *seven* seals. (Revelation 5:1)

Accordingly, different severities and levels of punishment were expressed in sevens, as in Moses:

> If after all this you do not obey me, I will castigate you *seven times* harder for your sins. (Leviticus 26:18, 21, 24, 28)

In David:

> Return *seven times as much* into our neighbors' lap. (Psalms 79:12)

Since a sanction was placed on the violation of faith, then, because faith could be of service (as has already been said [§372]), the present verse states that the person who kills Cain will suffer sevenfold vengeance.

396 The meaning of *Jehovah put a mark on Cain, that no one should strike him,* as the fact that the Lord singled faith out in a special way in order to preserve it is established by the symbolism of a *mark* and of *putting* a mark *on anyone* as singling something out. In Ezekiel, for example:

> Jehovah said, "Pass through the middle of the city, through the middle of Jerusalem, and you are to make a *mark* [that is, make a designation][251] on the foreheads of the men who are groaning and sighing over all the abominations." (Ezekiel 9:4)

Marking their foreheads does not mean setting a mark or line on their foreheads but distinguishing them from others. Likewise in John:

> . . . that they should harm the people who did not have *God's mark* on their foreheads. (Revelation 9:4)

Having a mark also stands for being singled out. [2] The same author uses [a different word][252] for a mark when he speaks of "putting a *mark* on their hand and on their foreheads" [Revelation 14:9]. The people of the Jewish religion represented the fact of this symbolism by the binding of the first and most important commandment onto their hand and forehead, as described in Moses:

> Listen, Israel: Jehovah our God is one Jehovah. You shall love Jehovah your God with all your heart and all your soul and all your powers.

And you shall bind these [words] as a *sign* on your hand; and let them be as brow pieces between your eyes. (Deuteronomy 6:4, 5, 8; 11:13, 18)

This represented the fact that they singled out the commandment concerning love above all the other commandments, which shows what the placement of marks on their hand and forehead symbolizes. [3] In Isaiah:

[The time] to gather all nations and tongues is coming, and they will come and see my glory; and I will *put* a *mark* on them. (Isaiah 66:18, 19)

And in David:

Turn to face me and have mercy on me; give your strength to your servant, and save the child of your serving maid. Make with me a *mark* of goodness, and let those who hate me see and be ashamed. (Psalms 86:16, 17)

All this now establishes what a mark is. No one should suppose that any mark was actually placed on an individual named Cain, because the inner meaning of the Word involves themes completely different from those on the literal plane.

Genesis 4:16. *And Cain went out from before Jehovah; and he lived in the land of Nod, to the east of Eden.*

Cain went out from before Jehovah means that he was cut off from the good inherent in a loving faith. His *living in the land of Nod* is living outside truth and goodness. Living *to the east of Eden* is living by the dictates of the intellectual part of the mind, where love had been before.

To see that *going out from before Jehovah* [or *from Jehovah's face*] means being cut off from the good inherent in a loving faith, review the comments above at verse 14 [§387]. The meaning of his *living in the land of Nod* as living outside truth and goodness is established by the meaning of the [Hebrew] word *nod:* to be a wanderer and fugitive.[253] And being a wanderer and fugitive means being deprived of truth and goodness, as you can also see above [§382].

Living *to the east of Eden* means living by the dictates of the intellectual part of the mind, where before love had reigned supreme; it is also living by the dictates of the rational mind, where before charity had reigned supreme. This is established by earlier statements [§§98, 101] concerning the symbolism of Eden's east, in which the east is identified with the Lord, and Eden, with love.

Among the people of the earliest church, the mind, composed of will and intellect, was unified. The will part of the mind was everything, with the result that the intellect belonged to the will. This was because they made no distinction between love (in the will) and faith (in the intellect), since love was everything and faith belonged to love. After faith was detached from love, however, as it was by those referred to as "Cain," the will no longer ruled in any form. But because in that kind of mind the intellect ruled in place of the will—that is, faith ruled in place of love—it says that Cain lived to the east of Eden. This was due to the singling out of faith (as just described) by the mark put on it to preserve it for the use of the human race.

399 Genesis 4:17. *And Cain knew his wife, and she conceived and delivered Enoch. And [Cain] was building a city, and he named the city after his son, Enoch.*

Cain knew his wife, and she conceived and delivered Enoch, means that this schism or heresy spontaneously produced another called "Enoch." The *city that was built* symbolizes every doctrinal or heretical teaching spawned by it. As the schism or heresy was called "Enoch," it says that *the city was named after his son, Enoch.*

400 *Cain knew his wife, and she conceived and delivered Enoch,* means that this schism or heresy spontaneously produced another. This is the obvious conclusion from all that precedes. It also makes sense in light of verse 1, which says that the human and his wife, Eve, gave birth to Cain; later developments are similar conceptions and births, whether it is the church or heresies that reproduce themselves. For these offshoots the people [of the earliest church] established a genealogy,[254] because they resemble family trees: from a single heresy, once seized upon, many others are born.

401 The reason why the heresy, and each of its doctrinal or heretical teachings, is named *Enoch* can be found to some extent in the name itself, which means the instruction that was initiated or first undertaken at that time.[255]

402 The symbolism of the *city that was built* as every doctrinal or heretical teaching spawned by the original schism can be established from places in the Word where the names of cities occur. None of them refers to an actual city but to some doctrinal or else heretical teaching.

The angels are completely unaware of what a city is and what the name of any city is; they never do and never can have any mental picture of a city, because all their ideas are spiritual or heavenly, as previously shown [§64]. They perceive only what the symbolic meanings are. The

Holy City, for instance (for which another name is Jerusalem the Holy), brings nothing else to their minds than the Lord's kingdom in general or, more particularly, in every individual in whom it exists. The same is true of the city or mountain of Zion; they take the mountain to be the heavenly aspect of faith, the city, to be the spiritual aspect.

[2] The quality itself of being heavenly or spiritual is also depicted by cities, palaces, houses, walls, foundations, fortifications, gates, and the bars on gates, and by the temple at the heart of these. Examples occur in Ezekiel 48; Revelation 21:15–end; 21:2, 10, where the name *Jerusalem the Holy* is used; and Jeremiah 31:38. David uses the name *the city of God, the sanctuary of the dwelling places of the Highest One* in Psalms 46:4. That city is called *Jehovah is there* in Ezekiel 48:35. Isaiah speaks of it this way:

> The children of a foreigner will rebuild your *walls*. All those spurning you will bow down at the soles of your feet, and they will call you Jehovah's *city*, Zion of the Holy One of Israel. (Isaiah 60:10, 14)

In Zechariah:

> Jerusalem will be called the *city* of truth, and Mount Zion, the holy mountain. (Zechariah 8:3)

The city of truth, or Jerusalem, symbolizes the spiritual aspects of faith, and the holy mountain, Zion, symbolizes the heavenly aspects of faith.

[3] Just as a city represents the heavenly and spiritual qualities of faith, so the cities of Judah and Israel symbolize all doctrinal teachings as a whole. When the cities are named, each symbolizes some particular teaching. Which teaching a city symbolizes no one can know without the inner meaning.

Just as cities symbolize doctrinal views, they also symbolize heretical views, and when they are named, each again symbolizes some particular view. At present the following places will show only that *city* in general symbolizes a point of doctrine or of heresy. [4] In Isaiah:

> On that day there will be five *cities* in the land of Egypt speaking the tongue of Canaan and swearing to Jehovah Sabaoth. One will be called the *city* of Heres.[256] (Isaiah 19:18)

The subject here is the systematic study of spiritual and heavenly matters that existed at the time of the Lord's Coming. In the same author:

> Full of riots is the turbulent *city*, the jubilant *city*. (Isaiah 22:1, 2)

This is about the Valley of Vision, or about delusion. In Jeremiah:

> The *cities* of the south have been closed, and there is no one to open them. (Jeremiah 13:19)

This is about people who are in the south,[257] that is, who have access to the light of truth and yet extinguish it. In the same author:

> Jehovah has thought to destroy the *wall* of Zion's daughter. He makes the *bulwark* and the *wall* mourn; together they have been weakened. Her *gates* have sunk into the earth; he has destroyed and smashed the *bars* locking them. (Lamentations 2:8, 9)

Anyone can see here that the wall, bulwark, gates, and bars mean nothing but doctrinal tenets. [5] Likewise in Isaiah:

> This song will be sung in the land of Judah: A *city* strong for us. Salvation will place the *walls* and *bulwark*. Open the *gates,* so that an upright nation keeping faith may walk in. (Isaiah 26:1, 2)

In the same author:

> I will exalt you, I will acclaim your name! You have made a *city* into a heap, a fortified *city* into a ruin. A palace for foreigners will never be built from the *city* to eternity. Therefore a strong people will honor you, a *city* of fearsome nations will be afraid of you. (Isaiah 25:1, 2, 3)

Neither is this passage talking about a city. In Balaam's prophecy:

> Edom will be an inheritance and will rule from Jacob and cause the destruction of the remainder from the *city*. (Numbers 24:18, 19)

Anyone can see that in this passage the city does not literally mean a city. In Isaiah:

> The empty *city* has been broken; every *house* has been closed so that no one will be able to enter. A shouting over the wine in the *streets!* (Isaiah 24:10, 11)

The empty city stands for the empty claims of doctrine. Streets here and elsewhere mean things that are part of the city, whether false or true. In John:

> When the seventh angel poured out his bowl, the big *city* was split into three parts and the *cities* of the nations fell. (Revelation 16:19)

The big city is a heretical point of view, and so are the cities of the nations, as anyone can see. Revelation 17:18 explains that the big city is the woman John saw, and I have already shown [§§252–253] that a woman is a church of the kind being described.

This establishes the symbolism of a city. But because all the details have been linked into a story, people who concentrate on the literal meaning view it as saying simply that Cain built a city and called it Enoch. They can see nothing more in it even though the literal meaning also requires them to believe that the land was well populated, despite the fact that Cain was Adam's firstborn. This is the story line's necessary implication. As noted earlier [§66], though, the custom of the earliest people was to express everything through representative images and weave them into a narrative. This custom gave them the greatest pleasure; it seemed to make everything come alive.

Genesis 4:18. *And Irad was born to Enoch. And Irad fathered Mehujael, and Mehujael fathered Methushael, and Methushael fathered Lamech.*

All these names symbolize heresies stemming from the first one, called Cain. Since we know nothing about them but their names, there is no need to say anything.

The derivation of their names, however, yields a measure of information. Irad's name, for instance, signifies that he descends from a city[258] and so from the heresy called Enoch; and so on.

Genesis 4:19. *And Lamech took two wives to himself, the name of one being Adah and the name of the other Zillah.*

Lamech, the sixth descendant in order, beginning with Cain, symbolizes devastation—a condition in which there is no more faith. The *two wives* symbolize the origin of a new church; *Adah* stands as the mother of that church's heavenly and spiritual attributes, *Zillah* as the mother of its earthly attributes.

The symbolism of *Lamech* as devastation, or the absence of faith, can be seen in verses 23 and 24 below: he killed a man for his wound and a little child for his bruise. *A man* there means faith and *a little child* charity.

The state of a church in general is such that over time it tends to ebb away from true faith and finally terminate without any faith. When faith is gone, the church is described as devastated or ruined. That is what happened in the earliest church among those called followers of Cain. It occurred also in the ancient church, which followed the Flood. It occurred also in the Jewish church, which was so utterly devastated at the time of the Lord's Coming that they did not know anything about him or the fact that he was coming to save them; still less did they know anything about faith in him. It occurred also in the early [Christian] church—the first church following the Lord's Coming—which today is in such complete ruins that no faith remains.

Even so, a nucleus of the church always remains in existence, unrecognized by those whose faith has been destroyed. A remnant of the earliest church, for example, survived until the Flood and continued on after it. That church remnant is called Noah.

408. When a church has been so thoroughly devastated that no more faith remains, it makes a new start; a new light shines out. In the Word, this is called "morning." The reason why the new light or morning does not dawn before devastation is complete is that any manifestation of faith or charity is mingled with something profane, and as long as they are mingled, no light or charity can be introduced. Tares destroy all the good seed.[259] When there is no faith, faith can no longer be profaned, because no one believes what is said anyway.

Those who do not acknowledge and believe something but only know it cannot profane it, as pointed out earlier [§§302–303].

Jews these days, for instance, because they live among Christians, necessarily realize that Christians acknowledge the Lord as the Messiah that they (the Jews) waited and are still waiting for. But they cannot profane the idea because they do not acknowledge or believe it. The same is true of Muslims and the people of unbaptized nations who have heard of the Lord. This was why the Lord came into the world at a time when the Jewish church no longer acknowledged or believed anything.

409. The situation was similar for the heresy named Cain, which over time suffered devastation. It is true that this heresy acknowledged love, but it put faith in first place, ahead of love. The further heresies that it bred gradually deviated from this, and Lamech, the sixth in line, absolutely denied faith. When this era arrived, a new light or dawn emerged and grew into a new church, here called *Adah* and *Zillah,* who are described as Lamech's wives.

They are called the wives of Lamech (who was devoid of faith) just as the inner church and outer church of the Jews (who were also devoid of faith) are called wives in the Word. This was represented in Leah and Rachel, the two wives of Jacob; Leah stood for the outer church and Rachel for the inner. Although this pair of churches appears to be two churches, they are one church, because the external, representative church without the internal church is simply something idolatrous or dead. The internal together with the external, on the other hand, formed one and the same church, as Adah and Zillah do here.

Since "Jacob" or in other words his descendants were, like Lamech, lacking in faith, the church could not remain among them but was transferred to non-Jewish nations, who lived in ignorance rather than faithlessness. Rarely if ever does the church survive among possessors of the truth while they are undergoing devastation. Instead it is transferred to those who know absolutely nothing of the truth, because they embrace faith much more easily.

There are two kinds of devastation. The first takes place with people who know but do not want to know, or who see but do not want to see. This is what Jews were like and what Christians are like today. The second kind takes place with people who neither know nor see anything because they are untaught. This is what the nations outside the Judeo-Christian tradition were like and are like today as well.

When devastation reaches its final stage with those who know but do not want to know, or see but do not want to see, the church springs up anew. It does so not among that group of people but among people whom they call gentiles.[260] This is what happened in the earliest church, which predated the Flood; it is what happened in the ancient church, which followed the Flood; it is what happened in the Jewish church.

The reason new light then shines for the first time is, as I said [§408], that people can no longer profane what is being revealed because they do not acknowledge or believe in its truth.

Many times in the prophets the Lord says that the final stage of devastation has to arrive before a new church can arise. In those places it is called either devastation, which relates to the heavenly aspects of faith, or desolation, which relates to its spiritual aspects. It is also referred to as a culmination and a cutting off. Examples are found in Isaiah 6:9, 11, 12; 24:1–end; 33:8 and following verses; 42:15–18; Jeremiah 25:1–end; Daniel 8:1–end; 9:24–end; Zephaniah 1:1–end; Deuteronomy 32:1–end; Revelation 15, 16, and following chapters.

Genesis 4:20. *And Adah delivered Jabal; he was the father of the tent dweller, and of livestock.*

Adah as before [§405] means the mother of the heavenly and spiritual aspects of faith. *Jabal, the father of the tent dweller and of livestock,* symbolizes teachings about holy love and the good actions that result from it, which are heavenly things.

The symbolism of *Adah* as the mother of faith's heavenly aspects can be seen in her firstborn, *Jabal.* He is called *the father of the tent dweller, and of livestock.* These things are heavenly because they symbolize holy love and the good actions in which it results.

414 The fact that *dwelling in a tent* means holy love is established by the symbolism of *tents* in the Word, as, for instance, in David:

> Jehovah, who will *stay* in your *tent?* Who will *live* on your *holy mountain?* Those walking unblemished and doing justice and speaking truth in their heart. (Psalms 15:1, 2)

This passage tells what it means to live in a tent or on a holy mountain, which it equates with the holy ways of love, that is, with walking unblemished and doing justice. In the same author:

> Their line has gone out into all the earth and their discourse to the end of the world. *He placed a tent for the sun* among them. (Psalms 19:4)

The sun here stands for love. In the same author:

> I will *stay* in your *tent* forever; I will feel safe in the hiding place of your wings. (Psalms 61:4)

The tent stands for something heavenly, the hiding place of the wings for something spiritual that grows out of it. In Isaiah:

> The throne has been strengthened by mercy, and he *sits* on it in truth in David's *tent,* judging and seeking judgment and hastening justice. (Isaiah 16:5)

Again the tent stands for holy love, exercised through the rendering of judgment and the hastening of justice. In the same author:

> Look at Zion, the city of our appointed feast; may your eyes see Jerusalem, a tranquil *dwelling,* a *tent* that does not move. (Isaiah 33:20)

This speaks of the heavenly Jerusalem. [2] In Jeremiah:

> This is what Jehovah has said: "Watch! I am bringing back Jacob's captured *tents,* and I will have mercy on his *dwellings.* And the city will be built on its own [ruin] mound." (Jeremiah 30:18)

The capture of the tents stands for being stripped of heavenly qualities, or holy love. In Amos:

> On that day I will raise up David's fallen *pavilion,* and wall up its breaches, and its ruins I will raise up, and I will rebuild it as in the days of old. (Amos 9:11)

The pavilion (or tabernacle) here likewise stands for heavenly attributes and their holiness. In Jeremiah:

> The whole earth was devastated. Quickly were my *tents* devastated; in an instant, my tent curtains. (Jeremiah 4:20)

And in another place:

> My *tent* was devastated and all my ropes were torn out; my children left me and were no more. I am no longer stretching out my *tent* or setting up my *tent curtains*. (Jeremiah 10:20)

The tent stands for heavenly qualities, the tent curtains and ropes for the spiritual qualities that come from them. In the same author:

> [Others] will seize their *tents* and *flocks;* [others] will carry off for themselves their *tent curtains* and all their vessels and the camels. (Jeremiah 49:29)

This is about Arabia and the "children of the east,"[261] representing people who possess holy, heavenly qualities. In the same author:

> The Lord poured his wrath out into the *tent* of Zion's daughter like fire. (Lamentations 2:4)

This stands for being stripped of everything sacred and heavenly about faith.

[3] The reason why a tent in the Word is taken to mean sacred, heavenly love is that the ancients carried out sacred worship in their tents. When they started to profane the tents with profane types of worship, the tabernacle and later the Temple were built. So tents have the same symbolism as the tabernacle and the subsequent Temple. A godly person is therefore called a tent, a tabernacle, and a temple to the Lord.

It is clear in David that a tent, a tabernacle, and a temple mean the same thing:

> One thing have I asked of Jehovah; this I will seek: that I may remain in Jehovah's *house* all the days of my life to watch Jehovah in sweet pleasure and to make early morning visits in his *Temple*. For he will hide me in his *tabernacle* on the day of evil. He will conceal me in the concealment of his *tent;* on a rock he will lift me up, and now my head will be lifted up against my enemies all around me and I will offer in his *tent* the sacrifices of shouting. (Psalms 27:4, 5, 6)

[4] In the highest sense, the Lord's human quality is a tent, a tabernacle, and a temple. That is why these terms are applied to every heavenly person and to every sacred, heavenly quality too.

The Lord loved the earliest church more than the ones following it, and its people lived alone with each other—divided into their families, that is—holding sacred worship in their tents. For these two reasons their tents were considered more sacred than the Temple, which was eventually profaned. In remembrance of this, the Feast of Booths (or huts) was established. It took place while the people were gathering the land's produce, and during it they lived in huts as the earliest people had (Leviticus 23:39–44; Deuteronomy 16:13; Hosea 12:9).[262]

415 The symbolism of the *father of livestock* as the good actions resulting from holy love can be seen from what was shown above at verse 2 of this chapter [§§343–344]: that the shepherd of the flock symbolizes the good actions that charity inspires. The present verse, though, mentions a father rather than a shepherd, and livestock rather than a flock; and the expression *of livestock* (dependent on *father*) directly follows the word *tent*. This shows that the phrase means good actions coming from holy love.[263] A home or fold for the livestock is the idea; in other words, it is referring to the father of those that lived in tents and livestock pens.

Their symbolism as the goodness produced by heavenly love can also be seen throughout the Word, as in Jeremiah, for instance:

> I will gather the *remnant* of my *flock* from all the lands to which I dispersed them, and I will bring them back to their *folds,* so that they may breed and multiply. (Jeremiah 23:3)

In Ezekiel:

> In a good pasture I will pasture them, and on the mountains of Israel's height will be their *fold.* There will they lie in a good *fold,* and on rich pasture they will graze in Israel's mountains. (Ezekiel 34:14)

The folds and pastures stand for the goodness that love brings about, described as "rich." [2] In Isaiah:

> He will give rain for the seed with which you will sow the ground; and the bread, the produce of the ground, will be rich with fat and oil. He will pasture your *livestock* on that day in a broad meadow. (Isaiah 30:23)

The bread symbolizes what is heavenly, and the fat on which the livestock will graze symbolizes the good actions that result from it. In Jeremiah:

Jehovah has ransomed Jacob; and they will come and sing on Zion's height and stream together toward the goodness Jehovah has bestowed on wheat and on new wine and on oil and on the offspring of *flock* and *herd,* and their soul will be like a watered garden. (Jeremiah 31:11, 12)

This depicts Jehovah's holiness as wheat and oil, the good actions coming from it as new wine and as offspring of flock and herd—livestock. In the same author:

Shepherds and the *flocks* of their livestock will come to the daughter of Zion. They will fix their tents near her all around. They will each graze their space. (Jeremiah 6:3)

The daughter of Zion stands for a heavenly type of church, which is associated with both tents and flocks of livestock.

More evidence that the intended meaning is holy love and the good actions that come out of it can be seen in the fact that Jabal actually was not the first of those that lived in tents and livestock pens. Abel—the human's and Eve's second son—is also called a shepherd of the flock, and Jabal is seventh in line from Cain.

Genesis 4:21. *And the name of his brother was Jubal; he was the father of everyone playing the harp and the organ.*

The name of his brother was Jubal symbolizes teachings about spiritual things in the same church. *The father of everyone playing the harp and the organ* symbolizes the true ideas and good deeds of faith.

The last verse dealt with heavenly things, which belong to love. The current verse deals with spiritual things, which have to do with faith. These are expressed by the *harp and organ.*

The symbolism of stringed instruments—harps and the like—as the spiritual qualities of faith is evident from many things.

It is exactly what the same kind of instruments represented in the worship of the representative church, and what vocal music represented as well, which is why there were so many singers and musicians.[264] The underlying reason is that all heavenly joy makes the heart cheerful, and the cheer was attested to in song that had string instruments added to echo and enhance it. All the heart's emotions carry with them the tendency to spill out in song and so in the accompaniment to a song. The feeling in the heart is heavenly in nature; the song it inspires is spiritual.

[2] The symbolism of songs and other kinds of music as something spiritual is clear to me from angel choirs, of which there are two kinds:

heavenly and spiritual. The singing of the spiritual choirs has a sound reminiscent of [beating] wings that can be compared to the sound of stringed instruments, which makes it easy to distinguish them from heavenly choirs. (They will be described later, with the Lord's divine mercy.)[265]

The earliest people, moreover, assigned anything of a heavenly nature to the heart's province and anything spiritual to the lungs' province. In this way they associated spirituality with any use of the lungs, such as for vocal music and so on; as a result they associated it with the "voices" or sounds of wind instruments. The reason was not only that the heart and lungs represent a kind of marriage, as love and faith do, but also that heavenly angels belong to the province of the heart and spiritual angels belong to that of the lungs.

The presence of these meanings in the current verse can also be seen from the consideration that the Word is the Lord's, but would be devoid of life if it were merely telling that Jubal was the father of those who play the harp and the organ. Nor would it be useful to anyone to know this.

419 Just as holy love and the good actions that it gives rise to are heavenly things, the true ideas of faith and the good actions that faith gives rise to are spiritual things. The function of faith, after all, is to understand not only what is true but also what is good; religious knowledge involves both. But to *be* the kind of person that faith teaches us to be is a *heavenly* thing.

As faith involves both truth and goodness, they are symbolized by the two instruments—harp and organ. A harp is a stringed instrument, as everyone knows, so it symbolizes spiritual truth. An organ, though, is midway between a stringed and a wind instrument, so it symbolizes spiritual good.

420 The Word mentions various instruments, each of which has its own symbolism. These will, by the Lord's divine mercy, be explained in the appropriate places.[266] For the moment let me restrict myself to the following in David:

> I will offer in Jehovah's *tent* the sacrifices of *shouting;* I will *sing* and *make music* to Jehovah. (Psalms 27:6)

The tent expresses the idea of something heavenly, and the shouting, singing, and music-making something spiritual that grows out of it. In the same author:

> *Sing* [for joy] in Jehovah, you who show justice. For the upright, praise of him is beautiful. Give thanks to Jehovah on a *harp;* on a ten-string *lute* make music to him. *Sing* him a new song, make your *strumming*

excel in its *clamor*, because Jehovah's word is upright, and every work of his is done in truth. (Psalms 33:1, 2, 3, 4)

These stand for religious truth; everything said applies to that truth. [2] Spiritual things, which are the truth and goodness involved in faith, were celebrated by harp and lute, by song, and by similar music. The holy or heavenly aspects of faith were celebrated by wind instruments—horns and so on. This is why so many instruments were connected with the Temple and why it says so many times that certain instruments were used in celebrating this thing or that. So the instruments are taken to mean the very qualities themselves that the instruments were honoring, as those just discussed are. [3] In the same author:

> I will give thanks to you on the *lute;* your truth, my God, I will *play as music* to you on the *harp,* Holy One of Israel. My lips will *sing* when I *make music* to you, as will my soul, which you redeemed. (Psalms 71:22, 23)

This too is about religious truth. In the same author:

> Answer Jehovah with thanksgiving; make music to our God on a *harp*. (Psalms 147:7)

The giving of thanks here is about the heavenly aspects of faith, which is why the name Jehovah is used, and making music with a harp is about the spiritual aspects, which is why the name God is used. In the same author:

> Let them praise Jehovah's name in dance; on *tambourine* and *harp* let them make music to him. (Psalms 149:3)

The tambourine stands for good, and the harp, for truth, which the people are praising. [4] In the same author:

> Praise God with the blare of a horn. Praise him on lute and *harp*. Praise him on tambourine and in dance. Praise him on *strings* and *organ*. Praise him with loud cymbals. Praise him with *shouting* cymbals. (Psalms 150:3, 4, 5)

These stand for religious goodness and truth, for which the people are offering praise. Do not imagine that so many instruments would be named if they did not each symbolize something. In the same author:

> Send your light and your truth. Let them lead me; let them bring me to your holy mountain and to your dwelling places. And I will go in to

God's altar, to the God of my happiness and joy, and I will give thanks to you with a *harp,* God, my God. (Psalms 43:3, 4)

These things stand for knowledge of goodness and truth. [5] In Isaiah:

Take a *harp,* circle the city, *strum* well, multiply your *singing,* in order to be remembered. (Isaiah 23:16)

These types of music stand for the attributes of faith and of religious knowledge. Still more clearly in John:

The four living creatures and the twenty-four elders fell down before the Lamb, each of them having *harps* and golden bowls full of pieces of incense, which are the prayers of the godly. (Revelation 5:8)

Anyone can see that they did not have harps but rather that the harps symbolize religious truth, and the golden bowls full of incense symbolize religious good. In David, in Psalms 42:4 and 69:30, the music made by instruments is called praise and thanksgiving. Elsewhere in John:

I heard a sound from the sky like that of many waters. I heard the sound of harpists *strumming on their harps;* they were *singing* a new song. (Revelation 14:2, 3)

And in another place:

Men were standing next to the glassy sea, having *God's harps.* (Revelation 15:2)

It is noteworthy that angels and spirits distinguish sounds on the basis of differences in goodness and truth. They do this with the sounds not only of singing and instruments but also of words, and they refuse to listen to any but those that harmonize. The result is concord between the sounds (and so the instruments) on one hand and the nature and essence of good and truth on the other.

421 *Genesis 4:22. And Zillah in turn delivered Tubal-cain, who trained every artisan in bronze and iron. And Tubal-cain's sister was Naamah.*

Zillah, as noted [§§405, 409], means the mother of the earthly aspects of the new church. *Tubal-cain, who trained every artisan in bronze and iron,* symbolizes teachings about good and truth on the earthly level, *bronze* symbolizing earthly good and *iron* earthly truth. *Tubal-cain's sister Naamah* symbolizes another similar church—or teachings about good and truth on the earthly level—outside the bounds of that church.

422 The way things stood in this new church can be seen from the Jewish church. It was composed of an inner church and an outer church. Heavenly and spiritual qualities made up the inner church, and earthly qualities, the outer. The inner church was represented by Rachel and the outer by Leah. Jacob, however, or rather his descendants (who are meant by the name Jacob in the Word), were such that they had no interest in anything but outward acts, that is, external worship. Jacob received Leah before Rachel, and Leah with her weak eyes represented the Jewish church, while Rachel represented a new church among non-Jewish nations. So the mention of Jacob in the prophets can be taken in both ways—one when the corrupt Jewish church is symbolized and the other when the true external church among other nations is symbolized. When the inner church is meant, it is called Israel.[267] These things, with the Lord's divine mercy, will be dealt with later.[268]

423 *Tubal-cain* is described as one *who trained every artisan* rather than as a father, the way Jabal and Jubal were earlier. The heavenly and spiritual attributes, or deeper qualities, [of that new church] had not existed before, and since these first came into being at that time, Jabal and Jubal are called fathers. But the earthly attributes, or superficial ones, [of that church] had previously existed (although at this point they are connected with [those new] inner things), so he is called not the father but the trainer of an artisan.

424 An *artisan* in the Word symbolizes one who is wise, understanding, or knowledgeable; here, where it is an artisan in bronze or iron, it symbolizes those who know about earthly goodness and truth. In John, for example:

> In an onslaught, Babylon, the big city, will be overthrown, and it will not be found any longer. And the sound of *harpists* and musicians and flutists and trumpeters will not be heard in it any longer. And no *artisan* of any *art* will be found in it any longer. (Revelation 18:21, 22)

Harpists stand for religious truth, as they did above, and trumpeters, for religious good. *An artisan of any art* stands for one who knows about truth and goodness or for the knowledge itself. In Isaiah:

> The *artisan* casts a sculpture, and the metalsmith overlays it with gold and molds chains of silver. [An idolater] seeks out a *wise artisan* to prepare a sculpture, in hopes that it will not be toppled. (Isaiah 40:19, 20)

The artisan stands for those who concoct falsity—the sculpture—for themselves out of their illusions and teach it in a way that makes it seem true. In Jeremiah:

> While they are becoming foolish, they grow stupid. Their education in worthless things is a piece of wood. Silver beaten thin is brought from Tarshish, gold from Uphaz, the work of the *artisan* and of the *metalsmith's* hands, blue-violet fabric and clothing—all of them the work of the *wise*. (Jeremiah 10:3, 8, 9)

These things symbolize a person who teaches falsity and who collects scriptural passages to use in molding a fiction. This is why it is called an education in worthless things and the work of the wise. Such people were once represented by artisans who cast idols (falsities) that they embellish with gold (an imitation of good), silver (an imitation of truth), and blue-violet fabric and clothing (things on the earthly plane that seem to harmonize).

425 The world is still unaware that *bronze* symbolizes earthly good, and that every metal named in the Word is a symbol for something in the inner meaning. Gold, for instance, symbolizes heavenly good, silver symbolizes spiritual truth, bronze earthly good, iron earthly truth, and so on with all the rest. The same is true for stone and wood. The gold, silver, bronze, and wood used in the ark and in the tabernacle symbolize these things, as do those used in the Temple, all of which will be taken up later, with the Lord's divine mercy.[269]

These symbolic meanings shine out in the prophets. In Isaiah, for example:

> You will suck the milk of the nations, and you will suck the nipple of monarchs. For *bronze* I will bring in gold; and for *iron* I will bring in silver; and for wood, *bronze;* and for stones, *iron;* and I will make peace your property, and justice your taskmaster. (Isaiah 60:16, 17)

This is about the Lord's Coming, his kingdom, and the church whose character is heavenly. "For bronze, gold" means heavenly goodness in place of earthly goodness. "For iron, silver" means spiritual truth in place of earthly truth. "For wood, bronze" means goodness on the earthly level in place of goodness on the bodily level. "For stones, iron" means truth on the earthly level in place of truth gained through the senses.[270] In Ezekiel:

> Javan, Tubal, and Meshech were your dealers in human souls; and *vessels of bronze* they sold as your trade goods. (Ezekiel 27:13)

The subject here is Tyre, which symbolizes those who have spiritual and heavenly riches; the vessels of bronze stand for earthly goodness. In Moses:

> . . . a land whose stones are *iron*, and from its mountains you will mine *bronze*. (Deuteronomy 8:9)

Here too the stones stand for truth gained through the senses, iron stands for truth on the earthly plane, or truth in the rational mind, and bronze stands for good on the earthly plane. Ezekiel saw four living creatures (guardian beings) with feet gleaming "like the appearance of burnished *bronze*" (Ezekiel 1:7), where again bronze symbolizes good on the earthly level, because a person's foot represents the earthly level. Daniel likewise saw:

> A man clothed in linen, and his hips were circled with the gold of Uphaz, and his body was like tarshish,[271] his arms and his feet were like the appearance of burnished *bronze*. (Daniel 10:5, 6)

The *bronze* snake mentioned in Numbers 21:9 represented goodness present in the Lord on the level of the senses and on the earthly plane. See the earlier discussion [§197].

The symbolism of *iron* as earthly truth is established not only by the places just cited but also by Ezekiel's words concerning Tyre:

> Tarshish[272] was your dealer, on account of the vastness of all your affluence; for silver, *iron*, tin, and lead they sold your merchandise. Dan and Javan and Meuzal for your trade goods gave *polished iron*; cassia and calamus were in your market. (Ezekiel 27:12, 19)

From these verses and those before and after them in the same chapter it can be seen clearly that heavenly and spiritual riches are being symbolized and that each item named means some specific entity. So do the personal names. The Lord's Word, after all, is spiritual, not mere words.

[2] In Jeremiah:

> Will anyone crush *iron*, *iron* from the north, and *bronze*? Your resources and treasures I will turn into plunder, [in exchange] not for a price but for all your sins. (Jeremiah 15:12, 13)

Iron and bronze stand for earthly truth and goodness. What comes from the north symbolizes the level of the senses and the earthly level, because the earthly level in respect to the spiritual and heavenly level is like northern darkness in relation to southern sunlight. Or it is like a shadow, which Zillah (Tubal-cain's mother) also symbolizes here.[273] Plainly the resources and treasures mean heavenly, spiritual riches. [3] In Ezekiel:

> Take yourself an *iron* griddle and put it as an *iron* partition between yourself and the city; and set your face toward it, and let it be for a siege, and tighten the siege against it. (Ezekiel 4:3)

Clearly iron symbolizes truth here. Truth is considered strong because nothing can resist it. So iron, which symbolizes truth, or the verities of faith, is said to crush and bruise, as in Daniel 2:33, 40. And in John it says:

> To those who conquer I will give authority over the nations, to shepherd them with an *iron rod,* as if clay pots were being crushed. (Revelation 2:26, 27)

In the same author:

> The woman delivered a male child, who is to shepherd all the nations with an *iron rod.* (Revelation 12:5)

[4] An iron rod is the truth in the Lord's Word, as John himself explains:

> I saw the sky opened, when look! A white horse. And the one sitting on it was called faithful and true, and he judges and fights in justice. He was dressed in a garment dyed with blood, and his name is called God's Word. From his mouth issues a sharp saber, and with it he will strike the nations, and he will shepherd them with an *iron rod.* (Revelation 19:11, 13, 15)

427 Genesis 4:23. *And Lamech said to his wives, Adah and Zillah, "Listen to my voice, wives of Lamech, and with your ears perceive what I say, because I killed a man for my wound and a little child for my bruise."*

Lamech as before [§§405, 406] symbolizes devastation. *He said to his wives, Adah and Zillah, that they should perceive with their ears what he said,* is an admission of guilt, which is made only where the church exists, the church being symbolized by *his wives,* as mentioned [§409]. *He killed a man for his wound* means that he destroyed faith, a *man* symbolizing faith, as before [§§340, 367:1]. Killing *a little child for his bruise* is destroying charity. The *wound* and the *bruise* mean that nothing was sound any longer, the *wound* meaning that faith had been abandoned and the *bruise* meaning that charity had been wiped out.

428 The contents of this verse and the next show clearly that *Lamech* symbolizes devastation, since it says that he killed a man and a little child, and that Cain will be avenged seven times, and Lamech seventy-seven times.

429 The symbolism of a *man* as faith can be seen from the first verse of this chapter, in which Eve delivered Cain and said, "I have acquired the man Jehovah." This meant the doctrine concerning faith, which was called "the man Jehovah" [§340]. It can also be seen from earlier remarks [§§158, 265] showing that a man symbolizes the intellect, since the intellect is connected with faith.

From this it is apparent that Lamech also destroyed charity, which is called a little child, because anyone who denies or murders faith also denies and murders the charity that is being born through faith.

430 In the Word a *little child* symbolizes innocence, and charity too, since true innocence is not possible without charity, nor true charity without innocence. There are three levels of innocence, and in the Word they are identified as babies, toddlers, and children. Because true innocence is impossible without true love and charity, three levels of love are symbolized by the same three age groups. Those levels are: a tender love like the kind babies have for their mother or wet nurse; a love like the kind toddlers have for their parents; and charity like the kind children have for their teachers. Isaiah contains an example:

> The wolf will stay with the lamb, and the leopard will lie down with the kid, and the calf and the young lion and the fattened animal [will live] together, and a *little child* will lead them. (Isaiah 11:6)

The lamb, kid, and calf stand for innocence and love in their three degrees. The wolf, leopard, and young lion stand for the opposite. A little child stands for charity. [2] In Jeremiah:

> You do great evil against your own souls, cutting off from yourselves *man* and wife, *toddler* and *baby* in the middle of Judah, so as to prevent a remnant from remaining to you. (Jeremiah 44:7)

"Man and wife" stand for the intellectual properties of truth and the will-oriented properties of good. "Baby and infant" stand for the first levels of love. The identification of babies and children with innocence and charity stands out clearly in the Lord's words in Luke:

> They brought *babies* to Jesus to touch them; he said, "Allow the *little ones* to come to me and do not stop them, because these are the kind who make up God's kingdom. Truly, I say to you: whoever does not accept God's kingdom as a *child* does, will not enter it." (Luke 18:15, 16, 17)

The Lord himself is called a little child in Isaiah 9:6 because he is innocence itself and love itself, and he is there said to be "miraculous, a Counselor, God, Hero, Eternal Father, Prince of Peace."

431 The *wound* and the *bruise* mean the fact that nothing was sound any longer, the *wound* specifically meaning that faith had been abandoned and the *bruise* meaning that charity had been wiped out. This can be seen from the fact that the man is associated with the wound and the child with the bruise. Isaiah uses the same words to depict the abandonment of faith and destruction of charity:

> From the sole of the foot right to the head, there is no soundness in it; wound, bruise, and fresh blow, not pressed out and not bound up and not softened with oil. (Isaiah 1:6)

The wound is used for faith abandoned, the bruise for charity wiped out, and the blow for both.

432 Genesis 4:24. *"For Cain will be avenged seven times, and Lamech seventy-seven times."*

These words mean that they obliterated the faith meant by Cain, although there was a sacred ban on the violation of it, and at the same time they obliterated the charity that was to be born through faith. Charity being far more sacrosanct, the result was damnation, which is what *being avenged seventy-seven times* is.

433 For the meaning of *Cain will be avenged seven times* as the placement of a sacred ban on violating the detached faith meant by Cain, see what was shown at verse 15 [§§392–396]. The symbolism of *seventy-seven times* as being far more sacrosanct and resulting in damnation can be seen from the symbolism of seventy-seven times.

Seven is a holy number because the seventh day symbolizes the heavenly person, the heavenly church, the heavenly kingdom, and in the highest sense the Lord himself. Therefore the number seven means something holy or sacrosanct wherever it occurs in the Word. The holiness or heinousness belongs to the qualities under discussion and is determined by them. Seventy is also holy because it covers seven "ages," an "age" in the Word being ten years.

When anything extremely holy or positively sacrosanct was expressed, the words *seventy times seven times* were used. The Lord, for instance, said that we should not forgive our brother or sister up to *seven times* but up to *seventy times seven* (Matthew 18:21, 22). This means that we should forgive as often as our brother or sister sins, without limit, or to eternity, which is holy. And the fact here that vengeance would be taken seventy-seven times means damnation, because violation was absolutely forbidden.

Genesis 4:25. *And the human knew his wife again, and she delivered a son and called his name Seth, "Because God has restored other seed for me in place of Abel, since Cain killed him."*

The *human* and *his wife* mean the new church previously symbolized by Adah and Zillah. Their *son, whose name she called Seth,* symbolizes a new faith that will allow charity to take hold. *God has restored other seed in place of Abel, since Cain killed him* means that charity, which Cain separated and extinguished, has now been given to this church as a gift by the Lord.

The meaning of the *human* and *his wife* as the new church previously symbolized by Adah and Zillah is not something anyone can know or figure out from the literal sense, because before now, the person and his wife symbolized the earliest church and their descendants. But it can be seen from the inner sense.

It can also be seen from verses 3 and 4 of the next chapter [§485], which say again that the human and his wife gave birth to Seth (though in completely different words), where he symbolizes the first generation to inherit the earliest church. If the symbolism were no different in this verse, there would be no need to repeat it. In the same way, the first chapter told of the creation of the human, the earth's vegetation, and the animals, and the second chapter did likewise. This was for the reason already given [§89], that the first chapter spoke about the creation of the spiritual person and the second about the creation of the heavenly person. Wherever this kind of repetition concerning the very same person or thing is encountered, one occurrence has a different meaning from the other. What the meaning is can never be known except from the inner sense, although the actual thread of the story confirms it.

Besides, *human* and *wife,* wherever they appear, are words symbolizing the church under discussion there, in its role as a progenitor.

The symbolism of their *son, whose name she called Seth,* as a new faith that will allow charity to take hold can be seen from statements made earlier[274] and from the verse saying that Cain had a mark placed on him to prevent his murder [§392].

The chain of events is this: Faith that had detached from love was symbolized by Cain, charity by Abel. This detached faith put an end to charity, as symbolized by Cain's murder of Abel. Faith was preserved to enable the Lord to instill charity by means of it, as symbolized by Jehovah's putting a mark on Cain to keep anyone from killing him. Afterward, it was by means of faith that the Lord endowed people with holy love and the goodness that comes from it, symbolized by Jabal, who was born to Adah. He also granted them the spiritual gift of faith, symbolized by Jabal's brother Jubal. And through these he imparted earthly goodness and truth, symbolized by Tubal-cain, who was born to Zillah. These two verses bring the story to a close and so sum up the state of affairs, which is that the human and his wife symbolize the new church previously referred to as Adah and Zillah; Seth symbolizes faith, through which charity is implanted; and, in the next verse, Enosh symbolizes the charity implanted through faith.

437

The symbolism here of Seth as a new faith that will allow charity to take hold is explained by his name, in that he was so called *because God restored other seed in place of Abel, since Cain killed him. God restored other seed* means that the Lord gave people another kind of faith. *Other seed* is a faith that allows for the growth of charity. For the symbolism of seed as faith, see above at §255.

438

Genesis 4:26. *And to Seth in turn a son was born, and he called his name Enosh. Then people began to call on the name of Jehovah.*

Seth symbolizes a faith that allows for the growth of charity, as noted. *His son, whose name was Enosh,* symbolizes a church that considered charity to be faith's principal concern. *Then people began to call on the name of Jehovah* symbolizes worship from charity in that church.

439

The symbolism of *Seth* as a faith that allows for the growth of charity was shown at the previous verse. The symbolism of *his son, whose name was Enosh,* as a church that considered charity to be faith's principal concern can also be seen from earlier statements.[275] In addition this can be seen from the fact that the child is called Enosh, another name meaning *person*—not a heavenly person but an individual with a spiritual nature, who is *Enosh* here.

It can be seen from the very next words as well: *then people began to call on the name of Jehovah.*

440

The symbolism of *then people began to call on the name of Jehovah* as worship from charity in that church can be seen from the fact that invoking Jehovah's name is a ritual common to all worship of the Lord. The fact that the worship is based on charity is established by the use here of the name Jehovah (the last verse spoke of God) and by the fact that the Lord cannot be worshiped except from charity. Faith that does not come from charity does not lead to worship, because it lives only on the lips, not in the heart.

The Word makes it clear that calling on Jehovah's name is a common practice in all worship of the Lord. Take these words about Abram:

> He built an altar to Jehovah and *called on the name of Jehovah.* (Genesis 12:8; 13:4)

> He planted a grove in Beer-sheba and *there called on the name of Jehovah, the God of eternity.* (Genesis 21:33)

That it is an element of all worship is indicated in Isaiah:

> Jehovah, the Holy One of Israel, has said, "You have not *called on me,* Jacob, and you have wearied of me, Israel. You have not brought me the animal of your burnt offerings, and with sacrifices you have not honored me. I have not made you serve me with your minha[276] nor wearied you with frankincense." (Isaiah 43:22, 23)

This provides a summary of all representative worship.

441. This was not actually when people first started calling on Jehovah's name, as is fairly clear from the information above concerning the earliest church, which more than other churches revered and worshiped the Lord.[277] The fact that Abel brought an offering from the firstborn of his flock is further evidence. So calling on the name of Jehovah here means nothing else than the worship of the new church after the previous one had been destroyed by those called Cain and, later, Lamech.

442. From evidence given in this chapter it is clear that in the earliest era there were many theologies developed outside the church, and many heresies, each of which had its own name. The thinking behind these independent theologies and heresies was much more profound than in modern times because the people of the time were by nature deep thinkers.

Several Examples from Spirits of Opinions They Adopted during Their Physical Lives Concerning the Soul or Spirit

443. IN the other life it is easy to tell what opinions others held during bodily life concerning the soul, the spirit, and life after death. When people are kept in a state like the one they had in the body, they think the

same way they did then, and their thinking is communicated as clearly as if they were talking out loud.

In the case of one spirit[278] who had departed this world not long before, I perceived—and he admitted—that although he believed he would live on as a spirit, he expected to live a vague kind of life. His thinking, since he located life in the body, was that if physical life were withdrawn, only a vague something-or-other would remain. So his picture of the spirit was like that of a ghost. The observation that brute animals too had life, almost as people do, had confirmed him in his opinion. But now he was amazed to see that spirits and angels live in the greatest possible light and in the greatest possible intelligence, wisdom, and happiness, with such keen perception that it can hardly be described. Far from living a dim kind of life, he discovered, they live a clear and intensely vivid life.

444 I talked with another individual who during life in the world had not believed the spirit had any extension in space. On this principle, he had refused to accept any word that involved dimension [to describe the spirit]. I asked him, "What do you think now, as a soul or spirit, about the fact that you possess sight, hearing, smell, sensitive touch, desires, and thoughts, so much so that you feel exactly as if you were still in your body?"

Restricted to the picture he had formed when thinking about the subject in the world, he said, "The spirit consists in thought."

"You once were alive in the world," I was allowed to reply. "Don't you know that physical sight cannot occur without the visual organ—the eye? How can thought, which is inner sight, do so? Doesn't it require an organic substance in order to operate?" He then acknowledged that during the life of the body he had labored under the delusion that spirit is simply thought, without any organic matter or dimension.

"If the soul or spirit was only thought," I added, "we would have no need for a brain the size we have, since the brain is nothing but an organ for our interior senses. If that were not its function, the skull could be hollow and still provide a place for our thoughts to do the work of the spirit. This alone should have convinced you that the spirit is organic, or made of organic substance. And had you considered what impressive activities result when the soul operates on the muscles, it might also have convinced you." He confessed his error and wondered how he could have been so foolish.[279]

445 I said further that the erudite fully believe the soul that lives on after death—the spirit—is abstract thought. Obviously, then, they refuse to accept any term that involves dimension or anything implied by dimension. Thought has no extension apart from the person thinking, but the

person thinking and the objects of thought do have extension. Moreover, if the objects of thought are not dimensional, people objectify them and make them three-dimensional in order to understand them. From this it is abundantly clear that intellectuals take the soul or spirit to be nothing but pure thought. The consequence is an unalterable belief that the soul will vanish when they die.

I spoke with some spirits about the attitude of people alive on earth today who reject belief in the spirit because they cannot see it with their eyes or grasp it scientifically. They deny not only that a spirit has dimension but also that it has substance, because they argue about what substance even is. And since they deny its dimensionality and argue about its substantiality, they also deny that it exists in a place or, consequently, in a human body. The most simple-thinking people, however, can understand that their soul or spirit has its own body.

When I said these things to the spirits, who happened to be among the more simple-thinking, they expressed their amazement that people today could be so stupid. When they heard the terminology that was being argued over (*parts outside of parts*,[280] and so on), they called it jarring, absurd, and pretentious. They said that such things should never take up mental space because they block the path to true understanding.

One new spirit who was talking with me heard that I was speaking about the spirit, and he asked, "What is a spirit?" He thought that he was still living on earth.

"Everyone has a spirit inside," I said. "The living part of us *is* a spirit, and the body only makes it possible for us to spend time on earth. The body—the flesh and bones—has never possessed life or engaged in thought."

He looked doubtful, so I asked, "Have you ever heard of the soul?"

"What is the soul?" he said. "I don't know what the soul is."

"You yourself are now a soul or spirit," I was allowed to say. "You can tell, because you're above my head, not standing on the ground. Don't you realize that?"

He fled in terror shouting, "I'm a spirit! I'm a spirit!"

A certain Jew was also under the firm impression that he was alive in the body.[281] So solid was his belief that he could hardly be persuaded otherwise. When shown that he was a spirit, he continued to insist that he was a person on earth because he could see and hear. That is what people who were body-oriented in the world are like.

I could cite many other instances, but these should suffice to show that it is the spirit within us, not the body, that senses.

448 I have talked to many people I knew in their bodily life, and our conversations have continued a long time, over months and through a year. Our voices were as clear to each other as voices are among friends in this world, but they were heard internally. Sometimes we also engaged in discussions about the human condition after death. They were astounded that no one who is alive in the body knows or believes that she or he will live on after physical life ends, when the truth is that life continues, and continues in such a way that it passes from darkness into broad daylight. For those who believe in the Lord, life grows clearer and clearer.

These people wanted me to tell their friends [on earth] that they were alive and to send letters describing their current status. They themselves had heard much from me about how those friends were doing. [2] "But," I said, "if I were to say or write the things you ask, your friends would not believe me. They would accuse me of hallucinating, laugh at me, and demand signs or miracles before believing. So I would be exposed to their ridicule. Few, perhaps, would believe that those things were true, because they deny at heart that spirits exist. Even those who do not deny are completely unwilling to hear that anyone could talk with spirits."

Such beliefs about spirits never existed in ancient times, only in modern times, when people desire to investigate what the spirit is in a highly intellectual way that relies on skewed logic. With their definitions and theories they deprive spirits of all sensation, and the more erudite they claim to be, the more they do so.

Genesis 5

Heaven and Heavenly Joy

449 NO one yet realizes what heaven and heavenly joy are. Those who have considered either subject have formed such a crude, generalized picture that it is hardly any picture at all.

Spirits who have only recently come into the next life from the world have allowed me to see with perfect clarity what idea of heaven and heavenly joy they had formed. When left to their own devices as if they were still in the world, you see, they think the same way they did there. Let me offer just a few examples.

450 Some, who in the world had seemed more enlightened concerning the Word than others, had latched onto such a false conception of heaven that they thought they could go to heaven just by going up. They imagined that from their height they would be able to govern everything below, so they thought they would be allowed to bask in self-glorification and in their superiority over others.[282]

In order for them to see the error of their thinking, they were raised up on high—such being their fantasy—and were permitted some governance over things below. But they found to their shame that this heaven was an illusion. They discovered that heaven does not consist in altitude but exists wherever people have love and charity (or the Lord's kingdom) inside them, and that it does not involve the desire to be superior to others. The wish to be greater than others is not heaven but hell.

451 One man who had been more influential than others during bodily life retained his desire for power in the other life. I told him that he was in another realm—an eternal one—and that the power he had exercised on earth was dead. "Here," I said, "the only standard by which people are evaluated is the amount of goodness and truth and of the Lord's mercy they possess.

"The situation in this realm," I added, "is just like that on earth, where people acquire status only through wealth or through favor with the head of state. Wealth in this kingdom is goodness and truth, and the

452 I spoke with some spirits who thought heaven and heavenly joy consisted in being greatest. But I told them that the greatest in heaven is the one who is least.[283] Whoever wants to be least has the greatest happiness. Since the person with the greatest happiness is the person who is least, it follows that such a person is the greatest. What is being greatest if not being happiest? Happiness is what the powerful seek in power and what the rich seek in riches.

I added that heaven does not consist in the desire to be least for the purpose of being greatest, because then the hope and longing is to be greatest. Heaven is wishing better for others than for ourselves with all our heart and serving others for the sake of their own happiness, not for any selfish goal but for love.

453 Some have such a simplistic idea of heaven that they think it is just a matter of being let in. They even picture it as a room with a door. The door will open and the doorkeepers there will announce their arrival.

454 The opinion of some is that a life of leisure and being waited on by others constitutes heaven. To these I said that happiness never consists in seeking satisfaction directly from doing nothing. If it did, we would inevitably want to take others' happiness for our own, and if everyone did, no one would be happy. Such a life would not be active but idle, resulting in sluggishness—when as anyone can see life holds no joy unless it is active.

Angelic life consists in usefulness and acts of neighborly kindness. Nothing makes angels happier than giving information to spirits newly arrived from the world and teaching them; serving people on earth, making sure that the evil spirits present with them do not go too far, and inspiring them with good; and reviving the dead as they enter eternal life, eventually taking them to heaven, if the condition of their souls allows it. Angels find more happiness in these activities than could ever be described. In performing them they become images of the Lord. In performing them they love their neighbor more than themselves. This makes heaven.

Usefulness (that is, the good that comes of love and charity) is accordingly the substance, the source, and the measure of the angels' happiness.

When I had finished saying these things, the spirits who thought heavenly joy consisted in relaxing and idly breathing the air of eternal ecstasy were given the opportunity to perceive what such a life would be like. The idea was to embarrass them out of it. They saw that such a life was utterly depressing and that in short order, when inactivity had destroyed all their joy, they would grow sick and tired of it.

455 One of the people reputed most knowledgeable about the Word when he lived in the world had developed an idea of heavenly joy as consisting in a glorious ring of light like the circle of golden rays beaming from the sun. As in the previous example, this dream life of his involved inactivity. To awaken him to his misconception, he was granted this kind of light, and as he stood at its center he felt so much pleasure that, as he himself declared, it was like being in heaven. He could not linger there long, however, because little by little it grew tiresome for him and turned into no joy at all.

456 Some very well informed people claimed that heavenly joy lay in a life spent not in carrying out the good deeds prompted by charity but only in praising and celebrating the Lord. This life they called an active one. But I said that praising and celebrating the Lord is not an active life of the kind meant but a mere side effect of that life. The Lord has no need of praise but wants us to do the good things that charity calls on us to do. That is the activity that determines how happy the Lord can make us.

Those people, smart as they were, still could not find any promise of joy in the good deeds of charity, only the prospect of servitude. But to do such deeds is actually freeing and brings with it indescribable happiness, as the angels testified.

457 Almost all who come into the next life from the world think that hell is the same for everyone and heaven is the same for everyone, when in reality there are unlimited differences and variations in either case. Hell is never exactly the same for one person as for another, nor is heaven—just as there is never one person, spirit, or angel who is exactly the same as another.

When I merely entertained the thought that there could be two people precisely the same or identical, it aroused horror among those in the world of spirits and among the angels of heaven. "All unity is formed out of harmony among many," they said. "The way that the many harmonize determines what kind of unity they have. No monolithic unity lasts, only the unity created by harmony. So every community in the heavens forms a single unit, as do all the communities—or the whole of heaven—taken together. The Lord alone makes this happen, and he does so through love."

One angel calculated only the most general kinds of joy experienced by spirits (in other words, inhabitants of the first heaven) to be around 478.

This indicated how countless the less general kinds must be, and how innumerable the specific kinds that make up each general kind. And considering how many kinds there are in that heaven, you can see how unlimited must be the kinds of happiness in the heaven of angelic spirits and how many more yet in the heaven of angels.[284]

458   At times evil spirits have conjectured that some heaven other than the Lord's could exist. They have received permission to look for it wherever they could. To their own chagrin, they have never been able to locate one.

Evil spirits rush headlong into all kinds of craziness, both because they hate the Lord and because hell is so painful, and these are the kinds of fantasies they seize on.

459   There are three heavens. The first is where good spirits are, the second where angelic spirits are, and the third where actual angels are.

Spirits, angelic spirits, and angels are each as a group divided up into heavenly and spiritual types. The heavenly ones are those whom love has led to receive faith from the Lord, as those who were part of the earliest church did; they have already been described [§§32:2, 34, 202]. The spiritual ones are those whom religious knowledge has led to receive a feeling of charity from the Lord and then to act on it.

More on this subject follows at the end of the chapter [§§537–546].

Genesis 5

1. This is the book of the births of the human, on the day on which God created the human; in God's likeness he made the human.

2. Male and female he created them. And he blessed them. And he called their name Human Being on the day on which they were created.

3. And the human lived one hundred thirty years. And he fathered [a child] in his likeness, after his image. And he called his name Seth.

4. And after the human fathered Seth, his days were eight hundred years. And he fathered sons and daughters.

5. And all the days that the human lived were nine hundred thirty years. And he died.

6. And Seth lived one hundred five years and fathered Enosh.

7. And after Seth fathered Enosh he lived eight hundred seven years. And he fathered sons and daughters.

8. And all Seth's days were nine hundred twelve years. And he died.

9. And Enosh lived ninety years and fathered Kenan.

10. And after Enosh fathered Kenan he lived eight hundred fifteen years. And he fathered sons and daughters.

11. And all Enosh's days were nine hundred five years. And he died.

12. And Kenan lived seventy years and fathered Mahalalel.

13. And after Kenan fathered Mahalalel he lived eight hundred forty years. And he fathered sons and daughters.

14. And all Kenan's days were nine hundred ten years. And he died.

15. And Mahalalel lived sixty-five years and fathered Jared.

16. And after Mahalalel fathered Jared he lived eight hundred thirty years. And he fathered sons and daughters.

17. And all Mahalalel's days were eight hundred ninety-five years. And he died.

18. And Jared lived one hundred sixty-two years and fathered Enoch.

19. And after Jared fathered Enoch he lived eight hundred years. And he fathered sons and daughters.

20. And all Jared's days were nine hundred sixty-two years. And he died.

21. And Enoch lived sixty-five years and fathered Methuselah.

22. And after Enoch fathered Methuselah he walked with God three hundred years. And he fathered sons and daughters.

23. And all Enoch's days were three hundred sixty-five years.

24. And Enoch walked with God and was no more, because God took him.

25. And Methuselah lived one hundred eighty-seven years and fathered Lamech.

26. And after Methuselah fathered Lamech he lived seven hundred eighty-two years. And he fathered sons and daughters.

27. And all Methuselah's days were nine hundred sixty-nine years. And he died.

28. And Lamech lived one hundred eighty-two years. And he fathered a son.

29. And he called his name Noah, saying, "He will console us[285] for our work and for the distress of our hands from the ground, which Jehovah cursed."

30. And after Lamech fathered Noah he lived five hundred ninety-five years. And he fathered sons and daughters.

31. And all Lamech's days were seven hundred seventy-seven years. And he died.

32. And Noah was a son of five hundred years.[286] And Noah fathered Shem, Ham, and Japheth.

Summary

460 THIS chapter deals specifically with the propagation of the earliest church in later generations, almost up to the time of the Flood.

461 The earliest church in its original form, which was a heavenly church, is what is called the human and God's likeness (verse 1).

462 The second church, which was not as heavenly as the earliest, is called Seth (verses 2, 3).

463 The third church is called Enosh (verse 6), the fourth Kenan (verse 9), the fifth Mahalalel (verse 12), the sixth Jared (verse 15), the seventh Enoch (verse 18), and the eighth Methuselah (verse 21).

464 The church called Enoch is described as developing doctrine out of the things revealed to and perceived by the earliest church. Although this doctrine was not of any use at that point, it was preserved for use by later generations. This is expressed in the words *Enoch was no more, because God took him* (verses 22, 23, 24).

465 The ninth church was called Lamech (verse 25).

466 The tenth, and the progenitor of three churches that followed the Flood, is Noah. This church must be called the *ancient church* (verses 28, 29).

467 Lamech is portrayed as not retaining the slightest trace of the earliest church's perception, and Noah is portrayed as a new church (verse 29).

Inner Meaning

468 WHAT was stated and demonstrated in the last chapter shows that names symbolize heresies and doctrines,[287] and this in turn suggests that the names in the present chapter stand not for individuals but for some larger entity. Here they symbolize the doctrines—the churches—that

were preserved (despite undergoing changes) from the time of the earliest church up to Noah.

A church tends to dwindle over time, however, until at last it remains with only a few. The few among whom it remained at the time of the Flood were called Noah.

[2] The waning of the true church until it remains with a few can be seen from other churches that likewise shrank. The remaining few are called "survivors" or "a remnant" in the Word, where they are described as being in the middle or heart of the land.[288]

The situation is the same in general as it is in particular; in other words, what holds true for the church holds true for individual people. Unless the Lord preserved a remnant in each of us, we could only succumb to eternal death, because the remnant holds spiritual and heavenly life within it.[289] Likewise at the general or universal level, unless there were always some with whom the church or true faith survived, the human race would come to an end. For the sake of a handful, we know, the city and in fact the whole nation is preserved.[290]

This is mirrored in the human heart. As long as the heart is healthy, the surrounding organs thrive. When it ails, all the organs deteriorate and the person dies.

The last survivors, [or remnants,] are what Noah symbolizes, since aside from him the whole earth was corrupt, as Genesis 6:12 makes clear.

[3] Remaining traces in each individual and in the church are discussed by the prophets in many places, as in Isaiah:

> The one *left* in Zion and the one *remaining* in Jerusalem will be called holy to *him*—everyone in Jerusalem assigned to life—when the Lord has cleansed the filth of Zion's daughters and washed away the blood of Jerusalem from its midst. (Isaiah 4:3, 4)

What is left—symbolizing the survivors of the church and the remnant in the people of the church—is here described as being holy. After all, those left in Zion and Jerusalem could not have been holy just because they were left there. Likewise in the same author:

> It will be in that day that the *survivors* of Israel and the *refugees* of Jacob's house will no longer continue to lean on the one that strikes them; and it will lean on Jehovah, the Holy One of Israel, in truthfulness. The *survivors* will return, the *survivors* of Jacob, to the mighty God. (Isaiah 10:20, 21, 22)

In Jeremiah:

> In those days and at that time there will be a search for Israel's wickedness, but it will not be there, and for Judah's sins, and they will not be found, because I will pardon the one whom I make a *remainder*. (Jeremiah 50:20)

In Micah:

> The *survivors* of Jacob in the midst of many peoples will be like dew from Jehovah, like showers on the grass. (Micah 5:7)

[4] The remainder or remnant in a person or in the church was also represented by tithes, or portions equaling one tenth, which were holy. As a result, the number ten was also holy, and this is why ten is associated with remnants, as it is in Isaiah:

> Jehovah will take humankind away, and much [territory] will be abandoned in the *middle of the land*. And a *tenth* of it will remain and rebound but is destined for extermination, like an oak or a holm oak when its stump is cast out. *Its stump is holy seed.* (Isaiah 6:12, 13)

Here the remainder is called a holy stump. In Amos:

> This is what the Lord Jehovih has said: "The city going out as a thousand will leave one *hundred remaining*, and the one going out as a hundred will leave *ten remaining* to the house of Israel." (Amos 5:3)

These places and many others in their inner meaning symbolize and describe a remnant. The fact that a city is preserved for the sake of the church's survivors can be seen from what Abraham said of Sodom:

> Abraham said, "Perhaps *ten* may be found there." And [Jehovah] said, "I will not destroy it for the sake of *ten.*" (Genesis 18:32)

469 Genesis 5:1. *This is the book of the births of the human, on the day on which God created the human; in God's likeness he made the human.*

The *book of births* is the enumeration of those who were part of the earliest church. *On the day on which God created the human* means that the human became spiritual. *In God's likeness he made the human* means that the human became heavenly. So it is a depiction of the earliest church.

470 What follows establishes clearly enough that the *book of births* is the enumeration of those who were part of the earliest church. From here up to chapter 11, or to Eber, names never refer to individuals but to some development.

In the earliest era, the human race was divided up into households, clans, and nations. A household comprised a husband and wife and their children along with others of the same clan who served them. A clan comprised several households (the number could be small or large) living not far from each other but not in exactly the same place either. A nation comprised a small or large number of clans.

They lived this way, independently, divided only into households, clans, and nations, in order to preserve the church entire. The purpose was for all households and clans to evolve from one progenitor and so to persist in their love and their true worship.

In addition, each household had its own identity that distinguished it from the next. As everyone knows, children acquire their personality from their parents, as do future generations, and they also inherit characteristic traits of face, and so on, by which they can be recognized. Consequently it pleased the Lord to have them live this way in order to avoid the mingling of different natures and instead to maintain careful distinctions among them.

In this the church represented the Lord's kingdom with great fidelity, because the Lord's kingdom holds countless groups of people, each differing from the next in its love and faith.

This, as noted before [§139], is to live alone and, as also noted [§414], to live in tents. And this is what the Lord was pleased to have the Jewish church do too—live divided into households, clans, and tribes, marrying within the clan—and for the same reason. The subject will, by the Lord's divine mercy, be explored further in what follows.[291]

The meaning of *on the day on which God created the human* as a time when the human became spiritual can be seen from statements made and demonstrated above [§§49–52]. So can the meaning of *in God's likeness he made the human* as a time when the human became heavenly [§§51–52]. *Create* applies to people specifically when they are being created anew or regenerated and *make* when they are being perfected. So the distinctions among creating, forming, and making (or doing) are carefully observed in the Word. Chapter 2 above contains an example, where in talking about the transformation of a spiritual person into a heavenly one it says, "God rested from all the work that he had *done* as God in *creating* it" [Genesis 2:3]. There are many other examples elsewhere. In these places *create* has to do with a person who is spiritual in nature and *make* (that is, *perfect*) with a person who is heavenly in nature. See §§16 and 88.

The fact that God's likeness is a heavenly person, and God's image, a spiritual one, has also been shown above [§§50–51]. An image is *in the* likeness of another thing but a likeness is an exact copy, because a heavenly person is completely under the Lord's guidance, as a likeness of him.

474 Because the current topic, then, is the "births" or propagation of the earliest church, its transformation from spiritual to heavenly is the first thing described here. The other stages of propagation follow from it.

475 Genesis 5:2. *Male and female he created them, and he blessed them and called their name Human Being*[292] *on the day on which they were created.*

Male and female symbolizes the marriage between faith and love. *Calling their name Human Being* means they were a church, which especially deserves the name of Human.

476 The symbolism of *male and female* as the marriage between faith and love has been stated and demonstrated before [§§54–55]. The *male* or a man symbolizes the intellect and everything connected with it, so it symbolizes the qualities of faith. The *female* symbolizes the will or the properties of the will, so it symbolizes the qualities of love. This is also why the woman was named Eve from [the Hebrew word for] life, which belongs exclusively to love.

As a further result, a female also symbolizes the church, again as shown earlier, and a male symbolizes the individual of the church [§§253, 288].

The subject here is the state of the church when it was spiritual, although it soon became heavenly. This is why *male* comes first, just as it did in Genesis 1:26, 27. The word *create* also has to do with a spiritual person. Immediately afterward, however, when the marriage was complete or, in other words, the church had developed a heavenly character, they are called not male and female but Human Being, meaning both, because of the marriage. This is why the next words are *and he called their name Human Being,* which symbolizes the church.

477 The identification of the *human being* with the earliest church has been stated and demonstrated many times before [§§277, 288]. In the highest sense, the Lord himself is the only human being [§49]. The heavenly type of church acquires its name as human from this, because it is a likeness of the Lord [§§50–51]. The spiritual type of church does too, because it is an image of him. But in common usage, a human being is defined as anyone who has a human intellect, [on the supposition that] the intellect makes us human, and [that] having more of it makes one person more human than another; although distinctions among us would [better] be based on the degree of our loving belief in the Lord.

[2] What is mainly called the human is the earliest church and every true religion, and consequently the people in such a religion, or people

characterized by love for and faith in the Lord. The Word makes this clear, as in Ezekiel:

> I will multiply *humankind*—the whole, entire house of Israel—upon you, [mountains of Israel]. I will multiply *human* and animal upon you so that they may multiply and reproduce. And I will cause you to live as in your *ancient times,* and I will do good to you beyond that at your *beginnings.* And I will cause *humankind*—my people Israel—to walk upon you. (Ezekiel 36:10, 11, 12)

The ancient times here symbolize the earliest church, the beginnings symbolize the ancient church, and the house of Israel and the people Israel symbolize the early [Christian] church, or the church among non-Jews. All these churches are being referred to as human beings. [3] In Moses:

> Remember the *days of old,* understand the years of *generation* after *generation,* when the Highest One gave an inheritance to the nations; when he divided the *children of humankind,* he set the boundaries of the peoples according to the number of the children of Israel. (Deuteronomy 32:7, 8)

The days of old mean the earliest church, while "generation after generation" means the ancient churches. The ones being called children of humankind are those who believed in the Lord; their belief is "the number of the children of Israel." A regenerate individual is called a human being in Jeremiah:

> I looked at the earth and there—void and emptiness; and to the heavens, and these had no light! I looked, and there—not a *human!* And every bird of the heavens had flown away. (Jeremiah 4:23, 25)

The earth stands for the outer self and heaven for the inner, the human stands for love of goodness, and the bird of the heavens stands for comprehension of truth. [4] In the same author:

> Look! The days are coming when I will sow the house of Israel and the house of Judah with the seed of *human* and the seed of animal. (Jeremiah 31:27)

The human stands for the inner self and the animal for the outer. In Isaiah:

> Keep your distance from *humans,* whose breath is in their nose, for how much are they worth? (Isaiah 2:22)

The person stands for someone in the church. In the same author:

> Jehovah will send *humankind* far away, and much [territory] will be abandoned in the middle of the land. (Isaiah 6:12)

This is about the devastation of a person to the point where no good or truth remains. In the same author:

> The residents of the land will be destroyed by fire, and the *humanity* left behind will be a pittance. (Isaiah 24:6)

Humanity here stands for those who possess faith. In the same author:

> The paths have been abandoned; the traveler on the path has ceased. They have nullified the compact; they have despised the cities; they have thought nothing of *humankind*. The land mourns and droops. (Isaiah 33:8, 9)

This time "humankind" actually refers to humankind, or a human being, which in the Hebrew [here] is *enosh*.[293] In the same author:

> I will make *humankind* more precious than pure gold, and *humanity* [more precious] than Ophir's gold. Therefore I will shake heaven, and the earth will quake out of its place. (Isaiah 13:12, 13)

Here humankind [in the Hebrew] is called *enosh* the first time, *adam* the second time.[294]

478 The reason the term *adam* is used is that the Hebrew word means *a human*. The person is never called by the proper name Adam but is called *the human*. Clear evidence for this is the fact that here [in verse 2] and earlier the human is spoken of not in the singular but in the plural. What is more, the term refers to both the man and the woman; both together are called *the human*. Anyone can see that this is so from the words themselves, which are, "He called their name Human Being on the day on which they were created" [Genesis 5:2]. Likewise in chapter 1 it says, "Let us make a human in our image, and these will rule over the fish of the sea" (Genesis 1:26, 27, 28). The same words also show that the subject is not some first-created individual of the race but the whole of the earliest church.

479 In the Word, to *call someone's name* such-and-such or call someone by a name symbolizes a knowledge of the person's nature, as shown above [§§144–145]. Here it was the earliest church whose nature was recognized—and recognized as being that of a human taken from the ground, or in other words, regenerated by the Lord. (The word *adam* means "ground.") Later, when the church came to have a heavenly nature, it was recognized as being more human than others because it loved, and so believed in, the Lord.

Genesis 1:26, 27 makes it clear that they were indeed called Human Being *on the day on which they were created,* that is, at the end of the sixth day. This corresponds to the eve of the Sabbath, or the moment when the Sabbath or seventh day started; and the seventh day or Sabbath is the person of heavenly character, as shown before [§§85–87].

Genesis 5:3. *And the human lived one hundred thirty years, and he fathered [a child] in his likeness, after his image, and called his name Seth.*

One hundred thirty years symbolizes the interval before the new church came into being. Because this church was not very different from the earliest one, it says that it was born *in his likeness* and *after his image;* but a *likeness* now has regard to faith and an *image* to love. This church was referred to as *Seth.*

The inner meaning of the *years* and numbers of years that come up in this chapter is not as yet recognized by anyone. Those who concentrate on the literal meaning consider the years to be time-related, but none of the chapters from here to the twelfth contains any history that is literally accurate. Each and every detail instead has a different kind of content. As with the names [§470], so also with the numbers.

The number three occurs frequently throughout the Word, as does the number seven, and each time they occur they symbolize something whose circumstances are holy or sacrosanct. The periods of time and other features involved entail or represent those circumstances. The meaning is the same for short periods as it is for long periods; just as the parts make up the whole, so the smallest fractions make up the largest aggregates. There has to be uniformity across the different magnitudes for a whole to develop out of the parts or for an aggregate to emerge from the pieces in a compatible way. [2] In Isaiah, for example:

> Now has Jehovah spoken, saying, "In *three years* (corresponding to a hired servant's *years*) the glory of Moab will be abased." (Isaiah 16:14)

In the same author:

> The Lord said to me, "In one more *year* (corresponding to a hired servant's *years*) all the glory of Kedar will be consumed." (Isaiah 21:16)

This means both the shortest and the longest periods. In Habakkuk:

> Jehovah, I have heard of your fame; I have been awed, Jehovah, by your work. In the middle of the *years,* bring it to life. In the middle of the *years,* please make it known. (Habakkuk 3:2)

The middle of the years stands for the Lord's Coming. In regard to shorter periods, it stands for every instance in which the Lord comes—when we are being reborn, for example. In regard to somewhat longer periods, it stands for a time when the Lord's church rises up anew. Isaiah also calls this the year of the redeemed:

> The day of vengeance is in my heart, and the *year* of my redeemed has come. (Isaiah 63:4)

The thousand years in which Satan was to be fettered (Revelation 20:2, 3, 7) and the thousand years of the first resurrection (Revelation 20:4, 5, 6) likewise mean not a thousand years but the state of those people. Just as a day is taken to refer to a state, as shown before [§23], so are years; and the number of years describes the states in some way. This clarifies the fact that the intervals mentioned in this chapter also involve the prevailing states, since the state of perception in each church was different from that in another. The differences in their ability to perceive was a result of differences in character—both inherited character and character developed through living.

483 The names that follow—Seth, Enosh, Kenan, Mahalalel, Jared, Enoch, Methuselah, Lamech, Noah—symbolize so many churches, of which the first and most important was the one called *the human.*

For these churches, the most important attribute was perception, so the main distinctions among them in that era were differences in perception.

Concerning perception, let me mention that throughout heaven the perception of goodness and truth alone holds sway. Its nature is such that it can never be described, and it comes in so many different varieties that not one community has the same kind as another. There are general categories and specific kinds of perception in heaven, and the number of general categories cannot be counted; likewise the specific kinds within each category. Both will be discussed later [§§1383–1400, 1504–1520], with the Lord's divine mercy.

In the face of countless general categories, countless specific kinds within each category, and still more uncountable varieties within each kind, it is evident how little the world today knows about heavenly and spiritual matters. Its knowledge is so scant as to amount to almost nothing, since it does not even know what perception is and, if told, does not believe that such a thing exists. It is equally ignorant in other areas.

[2] The earliest church represented the Lord's heavenly kingdom in respect to the various genera and species of perception. But in view of today's thorough ignorance of what perception is, even in its broadest outlines, to recount the categories and types of perception in those churches would be to purvey nothing but the strange and unheard-of.

The people of those churches were divided into households, clans, and nations and contracted marriage within the household or clan for a reason. The reason was to preserve the different categories and types of perception and to transmit them exclusively by reproducing the character of the parents in their children. As a result, those who were part of the earliest church also live together in heaven.

§484 The fact that the church called Seth shared a close similarity with the earliest church can be seen from the fact that it says the human *fathered [a child] in his likeness, after his image, and called his name Seth*. The *likeness* has to do with faith and the *image* with love. This church, you see, was not like the earliest church in loving, and therefore believing in, the Lord, as can be seen from the statement just above, "Male and female he created them, and he blessed them and called their name Human" [Genesis 5:2]. These words, as noted above [§476], symbolize the spiritual person of the sixth day, so that Seth's likeness was to the spiritual person of the sixth day. In other words, love was not so much the primary concern in this church, yet faith was still bound up with love.

§485 *Seth* means another church here than the one previously depicted by Seth, in Genesis 4:25 (see §435 there). Churches whose theologies are different can be called by the same name, as verses 17 and 18 of the last chapter show. Two churches mentioned there were called Enoch and Lamech, while two others in verses 21 and 30 of the present chapter are likewise named Enoch and Lamech.

§486 Genesis 5:4. *And after the human fathered Seth, his days were eight hundred years. And he fathered sons and daughters.*

Days symbolize those times and states in general. *Years* symbolize those times and states in specific. *Sons and daughters* symbolize the truth and goodness they perceived.

§487 The symbolism of *days* as those times and states in general was shown in the first chapter [§23], where the days of creation symbolize nothing else.

It is very common for the Word to call all units of time "days."[295] In this verse the practice is quite obvious, as it also is in verses 5, 8, 11, 14, 17,

20, 23, 27, and 31 below. The general states at those times accordingly are symbolized by days as well. When *years* are mentioned in conjunction with days, the time spans represented by those years symbolize the nature of the states then; in other words, they symbolize the specific states.

[2] The earliest people had particular numbers they used for symbolizing various aspects of the church: three, seven, ten, twelve, and additional ones that they compounded out of these and others. This allowed them to sum up the states of the church. As a result, these numbers contain hidden wisdom that would require a long explanation. It was a way of evaluating different states in the church.

The same phenomenon occurs at many other places in the Word, especially in the prophets. In the rites of the Jewish religion there are also numbers for both timing and measurement in connection with sacrifices, minhas,[296] oblations, and other acts of worship; and everywhere those numbers occur they symbolize holiness in the thing they are applied to.

What these numbers specifically involve, then—the eight hundred in this verse, the nine hundred thirty in the next, and so on for the numbers of years in the following verses—is more than I can ever convey. They all come down to changes in the state of religion among those people, seen in relation to their general state.

Later on, by the Lord's divine mercy, I will need to tell what the simple numbers up to twelve symbolize.[297] Unless this is known first, the symbolism of their products cannot be grasped.

488 The symbolism of days as general states and of years as specific states can also be seen in the Word, as I said [§§482, 487]. Take these words in Ezekiel:

> You have made [the end of] your *days* approach and have come all the way to [the end of] your *years*. (Ezekiel 22:4)

This is about people who do loathsome things and fill their quota of sin, so in regard to the state of such people, *days* describes its general outlines and *years* its specific nature. In David:

> You will add *days* to the monarch's *days;* the monarch's *years* will be like those of generation after generation. (Psalms 61:6)

This is about the Lord and his kingdom. The days and years stand for the state of his kingdom. In the same author:

> I thought about the ancient *days,* the *years* of old. (Psalms 77:5)

The ancient days are the states of the earliest church, and the years of old are the states of the ancient church. In Isaiah:

> The *day* of vengeance is in my heart, and the *year* of my redeemed has come. (Isaiah 63:4)

This stands for the final times; the day of vengeance stands for a state of damnation, and the year of the redeemed, for a state of blessing. In similar words from the same author:

> . . . to proclaim a *year* of good pleasure for Jehovah and a *day* of vengeance for our God, to comfort all who mourn. (Isaiah 61:2)

Here again, both the word *day* and the word *year* are used, and they symbolize states. In Jeremiah:

> Renew our *days* as in ancient times. (Lamentations 5:21)

Here the days obviously stand for the state of those people. [2] In Joel:

> The *day* of Jehovah has come, because it is near: a *day* of shadow and darkness, a *day* of cloud and haze. One like it has not occurred for ages, and after it one will not occur again for the *years* of generation after generation. (Joel 2:1, 2, 11)

Here a day stands for a state of shadow, darkness, cloud, and haze for each person in particular and everyone in general. In Zechariah:

> I will carry off the wickedness of that land in one *day*. On that *day* you will shout, a man to his companion, to [come] under the grapevine and under the fig tree. (Zechariah 3:9, 10)

And in another place:

> There will be a single *day;* it is known to Jehovah; it is not *day* or night. And it will happen that at the time of evening there will be light. (Zechariah 14:7)

Plainly this is about some state [of mind], because it says that there will be a day that is not day or night, and that there will be light at the time of evening.[298] Statements in the Ten Commandments provide further evidence:

> Honor your father and your mother, so that your *days* may be lengthened and so that it may be well with you upon the ground. (Deuteronomy 5:16; 25:15)

The lengthening of days does not symbolize long life but a happy state.

[3] On a literal level, no other meaning for a day can be seen than that of time, but in an inner sense it means a state. Angels, who focus on the inner meaning of the Word, do not know what time is. They have no sun or moon to divide time into units, so they do not know what a day or a year is, only what a state and changes in state are.[299] For this reason, whatever partakes of matter, space, or time dissolves under the gaze of angels alive to the Word's inner meaning. The literal sense of these words from Ezekiel does so, for instance:

> The *day* is near; yes, the *day* of Jehovah is near. The time of the nations will be a *day* of cloud. (Ezekiel 30:3)

And from Joel:

> Oh my, the *day!* For the *day* of Jehovah is near, and [it comes] as devastation. (Joel 1:15)

The day of cloud stands for a cloud, or in other words, falsity. The day of the nations stands for the nations, or in other words, wickedness.[300] The day of Jehovah stands for devastation. When the notion of time is laid aside, there remains the notion of the state that things were in at that time. The situation is the same for the days and years mentioned so frequently in this chapter.

489 The symbolism of *sons and daughters* as the truth and goodness that this church perceived—sons being the truth and daughters the goodness—can be seen from many places in the prophets. The things conceived and born in the church are called daughters and sons in the Word, just as they were in ancient times. An example from Isaiah:

> The nations will walk toward your light, and monarchs, toward the radiance of your dawn. Raise your eyes all around and see: they all gather and come to you. Your *sons* will come from far away and your *daughters* will be nourished at your side. Then you will see and flow toward them, and your heart will be struck with awe and expand. (Isaiah 60:3, 4, 5)

The sons stand for truth, and the daughters, for good. In David:

> Free me and rescue me from the hand of a foreigner's *sons,* whose mouth speaks hollow words. Our *sons* are like plantings grown large in their youthful days; our *daughters* are like corner pieces cut in the shape of the Temple. (Psalms 144:11, 12)

A foreigner's sons stand for pseudo-truths, that is, falsities. "Our" sons stand for doctrinal concepts concerning truth; daughters, for doctrinal concepts concerning good. In Isaiah:

> I will say to the north, "Hand them over!" and to the south, "Do not hinder them! Bring my *sons* from far away and my *daughters* from the end of the earth, leading forth a blind people (and they will have eyes) and the deaf (and they will have ears)." (Isaiah 43:6, 8)

The sons stand for truth, and the daughters, for good; the blind, for those who will see truth, and the deaf, for those who submit to it. In Jeremiah:

> Shame has devoured our fathers' toil from our youth—their smaller livestock, their herd, their *sons,* and their *daughters.* (Jeremiah 3:24)

The sons and daughters stand for truth and good.

[2] To see that *sons* stand for truth, look in Isaiah:

> No longer will Jacob be ashamed and no longer will his face pale. Because when he sees his *sons*—the work of my hands—in his midst, they will revere my name and revere the Holy One of Jacob, and the God of Israel they will dread. Those wandering in spirit will know intelligence. (Isaiah 29:22, 23, 24)

The Holy One of Jacob, the God of Israel, stands for the Lord. The sons stand for regenerate people, who will gain an intelligent understanding of goodness and truth, as these words also explain. In the same author:

> Sing, infertile woman (she had not given birth), because the *sons* of the desolate one are more numerous than the *sons* of the married one. (Isaiah 54:1)

The sons of the desolate one stand for the truth known to the early church (the church among non-Jews) and the sons of the married one for the truth known to the Jewish church. In Jeremiah:

> My tent was devastated and all my ropes were torn out; my *sons* went away from me and were no more. (Jeremiah 10:20)

The sons stand for truth. In the same author:

> His *sons* will be as they once were, and their assembly will be established before me. (Jeremiah 30:20)

Here they stand for the truth known to the ancient church. In Zechariah:

> I will stir up your *sons,* Zion, along with your *sons,* Javan, and I will make you like the sword of a mighty man. (Zechariah 9:13)

Here they stand for truth from a loving faith.

490

The Word frequently uses a *daughter* to stand for good, as in David:

> *Daughters* of kings are among your valued [friends]; the queen stands at your right hand in Ophir's best gold. The *daughter* of Tyre is among your tribute. All glorious is the king's *daughter* within the palace; her clothing is made of gold eyelet. In place of your forebears will be your *sons.* (Psalms 45:9–16)

The goodness and beauty of love and faith are being portrayed by a daughter here. That is why churches are called daughters—because of the good in them. The terms *daughter of Zion* and *daughter of Jerusalem,* for instance, are used in Isaiah 37:22 and in many other places. Churches are also referred to as "the daughter of [my] people" (Isaiah 22:4), "the daughter of Tarshish" (Isaiah 23:10), "the daughter of Sidon" (Isaiah 23:12), and "daughters in the field" (Ezekiel 26:6, 8).

491

Daughters and sons symbolize the same thing in verses 4, 7, 10, 13, 16, 19, 26, and 30 of this chapter. The nature of the particular church determines the nature of the "sons and daughters," or goodness and truth. Here they are the distinct truths and forms of goodness that those people perceived, because these sons and daughters are mentioned in reference to the earliest church, the first ancestor of all the others that followed.

492

Genesis 5:5. *And all the days that the human lived were nine hundred thirty years, and he died.*

Days and *years* here as before [§§482, 487, 488] symbolize those times and states. *He died* means that such perception ceased to exist.

493

There is no need for me to linger any further over the symbolism of *days* and *years* as those times and states. I must only say here that in the world, the necessity for periods of time and units of measure, expressed in numbers, is unavoidable, since they are among the most concrete features of the natural world. But every time such terms are used, the number of days and years (and the numbers used in measurement) symbolize something abstracted from time (and measure). Just what is being symbolized depends on what the number is. This is true of the six days' labor and the holy seventh day, discussed above [§395]. It is true of the jubilee that was proclaimed in the forty-ninth year of every cycle and celebrated in the fiftieth [Leviticus 25, 27]. It is true of the twelve tribes of Israel, matching the number of the Lord's apostles; of the seventy elders [Numbers 11:16, 24–25] and the equal number of the Lord's disciples [Luke 10:1]; and of many other phenomena. The numbers in these places symbolize some special quality, as distinguished from the objects to which they apply. Once the qualities are isolated, their various states are what the numbers symbolize.

The meaning of *he died* as the fact that such perception ceased to exist is clear from the symbolism of the word *die* as applying to everything that ceases to be what it was. In John, for example:

> To the angel of the church in Sardis write, "These words says he who has the *seven* spirits and the *seven* stars: 'I know your works, that you are said to live but are *dead*. Be watchful and strengthen what is left, which is close to *death*, because I have not found your works perfect before God.'" (Revelation 3:1, 2)

In Jeremiah:

> I will expel your mother, who bore you, to another land where you were not born, and there you will *die*. (Jeremiah 22:26)

The mother stands for the church.

[2] The nature of a church, as explained already [§§407, 468], is that it tends to dwindle and deteriorate and its initial integrity dissolves. The main reason is that hereditary evil increases, since all parents add new evil to what they inherited. Every bad thing that parents actually do appears to be second nature, and when they do it repeatedly, second nature it does in fact become. It adds itself to their heredity and is transplanted into their children and ensuing generations. In this way, hereditary evil grows enormous in later generations, as anyone can recognize from seeing children with a bad character that is just like that of their parents and grandparents.

Some very wrongly believe there is no inherited evil aside from that which they say Adam passed on (see §313). The truth is that we all create an evil inheritance by actually committing sin, and this we add to what we have acquired from our parents. So we amass a legacy that endures through all the generations and is never softened, except in those whom the Lord regenerates.

This is the main reason every church degenerates. The same was true for the earliest church.

495 No one can see in what way the earliest church waned without knowing what perception is, since that church was perceptive in a way that none today is. A church's perception consists in a gift from the Lord for perceiving good and truth as the angels do. The good and truth perceived are not so much those of public life as those having to do with love for the Lord and faith in him. What we profess to believe, as confirmed by the way we live, indicates what kind of perception we have, and whether we have any at all.

496 Genesis 5:6. *And Seth lived one hundred five years and fathered Enosh.*

Seth, as noted [§481], is a second church—a less heavenly church than the earliest that gave it birth but still one of the primeval churches. *He lived one hundred five years* symbolizes those times and states, as already explained [§§482, 487, 488]. *He fathered Enosh* means that another church, called Enosh, descended from the previous ones.

497 *Seth*'s identity as a second church—a less heavenly church than the earliest that gave it birth but still one of the primeval churches—is established by the things said about him above at verse 3 [§§484–485]. The situation with churches, as has also been mentioned [§§407, 468, 494:2], is that little by little, as time passes, their essential qualities diminish. The chief reason for this also appears above [§494:2].

498 The meaning of *he fathered Enosh* as the fact that another church, called Enosh, descended from the previous ones can be seen from the fact that the names in the current chapter just symbolize churches.

499 Genesis 5:7, 8. *And after Seth fathered Enosh he lived eight hundred seven years. And he fathered sons and daughters. And all Seth's days were nine hundred twelve years, and he died.*

The *days* and numbers of *years* symbolize those times and states, here as before [§§482, 487, 488]. *Sons and daughters* have the same symbolism as before [§489], and so does *he died* [§494].

500 Genesis 5:9. *And Enosh lived ninety years and fathered Kenan.*

Enosh, as noted [§496], symbolizes a third church—one still less heavenly than the church Seth but still one of the primeval churches. *Kenan* symbolizes a fourth church that came after the others.

501 The churches succeeding one another over time, each described as giving birth to the next, operated much as fruits do, or as their seeds do. The fruit within the fruit or seed within the seed, so to speak, is at the center, deep inside, and each layer of fruit or seed receives life from the layer before it in order. The farther out you go toward the surface, the less there is of the fruit's or the seed's essence, until finally there is only a skin or covering where the fruit or seed ends.

The brain follows the same pattern. Inside it is a fine organic network called the cortical substances. These substances provide a starting point and medium for the soul's operations. Following in order from them come fine coverings, then denser ones, and at last the ones that overlie all of the brain, called meninges. These are bounded by even more inclusive layers and in the end by the one that envelops the whole, which is the skull.[301]

502. These three churches—the human, Seth, and Enosh—constitute the earliest church, although there were differences in how perfectly each of the three perceived things. The first church's perceptivity lessened in all the ensuing churches and became more general, as just described in regard to the fruit or seed, or the brain. Perfection consists in the ability to perceive minute distinctions, and this perfection decreases when the ability is not so refined but more general. A dimmer kind of perception then takes the place of the clearer kind, and in this way perception begins to disappear.

503. The earliest church's perceptive ability was not restricted to an awareness of what was good and true but included happiness and joy in doing good. Without happiness and joy in doing good, perception is not alive; from that happiness and joy it lives. The living quality of love and of the faith that comes from love, such as it was in the earliest church, is a quality we have when we are being useful, or when we adopt the goodness and truth that come from useful activity. Usefulness is the source from which, the means by which, and the measure according to which the Lord gives us life. Nothing useless can have any life in it, because anything that is useless is rejected.

In this, the earliest people were likenesses of the Lord; consequently in their perceptive abilities they became images of him. To be perceptive is to recognize what is good and true and so what is appropriate to faith. One who is under the influence of love is not satisfied with just knowing what is good and true but wants to do it—that is, to be useful.

504. Genesis 5:10, 11. *And after Enosh fathered Kenan he lived eight hundred fifteen years, and he fathered sons and daughters. And all Enosh's days were nine hundred five years, and he died.*

Again the days and numbers of years, the sons and daughters, and the death symbolize what they did before [§§482, 487–489, 494].

505. Enosh, as noted, is the third church, one of the primeval ones but less heavenly and as a result less perceptive than the church Seth, which in turn was not as heavenly and perceptive as the church that gave it birth, called "the human."

These three are the churches that constitute the earliest church. They are like the pit of a fruit or the germ of a seed in relation to the churches that followed. These later churches resemble the outer layers of a fruit or seed by comparison.

506

Genesis 5:12. *And Kenan lived seventy years and fathered Mahalalel.*

Kenan symbolizes the fourth church and *Mahalalel* the fifth.

507

The church called *Kenan* must not be counted as belonging with the three more perfect ones because in its time the more distinct perception of the earlier churches began to become more general. It was like the first, somewhat soft layers of a fruit or seed next to the pit or germ. Conditions in this church are not described, admittedly, but can be seen from later verses—from the description of the churches named Enoch and Noah, for example [§§519, 521–522, 530–531].

508

Genesis 5:13, 14. *And after Kenan fathered Mahalalel he lived eight hundred forty years. And he fathered sons and daughters. And all Kenan's days were nine hundred ten years, and he died.*

The days and the number of years function as previously described [§§482, 487, 488]. Sons and daughters here as before symbolize the truth and goodness they perceived [§§55:2, 486, 489–491], although they perceived it in a more general way. Kenan's death likewise means that [perception] ceased to be what it had been.

509

I need to observe only that all this is in relation to the church's state.

510

Genesis 5:15. *And Mahalalel lived sixty-five years and fathered Jared.*

Mahalalel, as noted, symbolizes the fifth church; *Jared* symbolizes the sixth.

511

Since perception faded, and from being rather acute and distinct became more general and obscure, the vitality of love and of useful activity waned too; the strength of the living force in love and usefulness determines the strength of perception. To recognize truth on the basis of goodness is a heavenly trait.

In addition, the vital force in those who made up the church called Mahalalel was such that they preferred the pleasure gained from truth to the deep satisfaction gained from being useful. This I learned through experience with their kind in the next life.

512

Genesis 5:16, 17. *And after Mahalalel fathered Jared he lived eight hundred thirty years, and he fathered sons and daughters. And all Mahalalel's days were eight hundred ninety-five years. And he died.*

The meanings here are the same as for parallel verses above [§§482, 487–489, 494].

Genesis 5:18. *And Jared lived one hundred sixty-two years and fathered Enoch.*

Jared, as noted, symbolizes the sixth church; *Enoch* symbolizes the seventh.

Nothing is said about the church called *Jared* either, but its nature can be seen from the church Mahalalel before it and the church Enoch after; it is halfway between them.

Genesis 5:19, 20. *And after Jared fathered Enoch he lived eight hundred years, and he fathered sons and daughters. And all Jared's days were nine hundred sixty-two years, and he died.*

The meanings again are the same as those mentioned above [§§482, 487–489, 494]. Anyone can see that their ages did not really extend as far as 962 years in Jared's case and 969 in Methuselah's. The same thing can also be seen from the points that will be made at verse 3 of the next chapter [§575], by the Lord's divine mercy, where the text says, "Their days will be one hundred twenty years." The number of years, then, does not mean the lifetime of any individual but the times and states of the church.

Genesis 5:21. *And Enoch lived sixty-five years and fathered Methuselah.*

Enoch, as mentioned, symbolizes the seventh church, and *Methuselah* symbolizes the eighth church.

What the church Enoch was like will be described immediately below.

Genesis 5:22. *And after Enoch fathered Methuselah he walked with God three hundred years, and he fathered sons and daughters.*

Walking with God symbolizes the doctrine concerning faith. *He fathered sons and daughters* symbolizes doctrinal teachings about truth and goodness.

There were at that time people who developed a theology out of the things perceived by the earliest church and the churches that followed. They designed it to serve as a standard by which everyone could judge what was good and true. The people who did this were called *Enoch,* and what they did was symbolized by the words *and Enoch walked with God.* They also used the name for the theology or set of teachings itself, which is what the name Enoch—"teach"—means.[302]

Additional evidence for this signification is the symbolism of the word *walk* and the fact that he is said to have walked *with God,* not with Jehovah. Walking with God is teaching the doctrine concerning faith and living by it, while walking with Jehovah is living a life of love.

Walk is a figure of speech for living, in such phrases as *walk in the law, walk in the statutes,* and *walk in truth.*[303] At its most basic level, walking has to do with a path, and a path relates to truth and consequently to faith, or to the doctrine concerning faith.

[2] What walking symbolizes in the Word can be established to some extent from the following passages. In Micah:

> He has *pointed out* to you, friend, what is good; and what is Jehovah requiring of you but to carry out judgment and the love of mercy and to be humble *walking with* your *God?* (Micah 6:8)

Walking with God here too symbolizes living—living by the things "pointed out." The expression *with God* appears, but the same phrase in regard to Enoch employs a different [Hebrew] word, one that can also mean *from beside (God);* so it is ambiguous.[304] In David:

> You rescued my feet from tripping, to *walk before God* in the light of the living. (Psalms 56:13)

Walking before God means walking in religious truth—the "light of the living." Likewise in Isaiah:

> The people *walking* in darkness now see great light. (Isaiah 9:2)

The Lord says in Moses:

> I will *walk* in your midst and become your *God,* and you will become my people. (Leviticus 26:12)

This stands for the idea that they would live according to the teachings of the law. [3] In Jeremiah:

> They will spread them out to the sun and to the moon and to the armies of the heavens—those that they *loved,* and that they *served,* and that they *walked* after, and that they *sought.* (Jeremiah 8:2)

A clear distinction is being made here between the activity of love and the activity of faith. That of love is loving and serving; that of faith is walking and seeking. The prophets pay close attention to words and never replace one word with another.

Walking with or before Jehovah, on the other hand, when it comes up in the Word, means living a life of love.

520 Genesis 5:23, 24. *And all Enoch's days were three hundred sixty-five years. And Enoch walked with God and was no more, because God took him.*

All Enoch's days were 365 years means that they were few. *He walked with God* means the doctrine concerning faith, as before [§518]. *He was no more, because God took him,* means that this doctrine was preserved for use by future generations.

He was no more, because God took him, means that this doctrine was preserved for use by future generations. The case with Enoch was that, as stated [§519:1], he took what the earliest church perceived and reduced it to a doctrinal system—a forbidden thing at that time.[305] Recognizing from perception, after all, is completely different than learning from doctrine.

People who have the gift of perception have no need to learn by way of doctrinal formulas what they already know. To illustrate: when we already know how to think effectively, we do not need an artificial system to teach us how. Using such a system would destroy our ability to think effectively, as it does for those who wallow in scholarly dust.[306]

People who recognize what is good and true on the basis of perception receive that intuition from the Lord by an internal route. Those who recognize it on the basis of doctrine receive their knowledge by an external route—the physical senses. The difference is like that between light and darkness.

Furthermore, the perceptions of a heavenly type of person can never be described, because they involve the tiniest, most specific details and take into account all the variety of different conditions and circumstances.

It was foreseen, however, that the perceptiveness of the earliest church would come to an end, and that people thereafter would learn from doctrine how to identify truth and goodness; in other words, they would travel through the dark to arrive at light. In consequence, it says here that "God took him," which is to say that God preserved perception for the use of future generations.

I was given the opportunity in fact to learn firsthand what perception became among the people called Enoch. I experienced it as something generalized and dim, and lacking a certain distinctness, since under these circumstances the mind turns its gaze outward to focus on doctrinal issues.

Genesis 5:25. *And Methuselah lived one hundred eighty-seven years and fathered Lamech.*

Methuselah symbolizes the eighth church and *Lamech* the ninth.

Nothing specific is mentioned about the nature of the church [meant by Methuselah] but its perception did grow general and dim, as can be seen from the description of the church called Noah. So it grew less sound, and as it did, its wisdom and understanding faded.

525 Genesis 5:26, 27. *And after Methuselah fathered Lamech he lived seven hundred eighty-two years. And he fathered sons and daughters. And all Methuselah's days were nine hundred sixty-nine years, and he died.*

The meanings here are the same as for the rest.

526 Genesis 5:28. *And Lamech lived one hundred eighty-two years, and he fathered a son.*

Lamech here symbolizes the ninth church, whose perception of truth and goodness was so general and vague as to be almost nonexistent. So it was a church devastated. The *son* symbolizes the beginnings of a new church.

527 The symbolism of *Lamech* as a church whose perception of truth and goodness was so general and vague as to be almost nonexistent, so that it was a church devastated, is established by the preceding verses. What follows—since the next verse describes this church—establishes the same meaning again.

In the last chapter Lamech symbolized almost the same thing as here, namely, devastation. (For more on this subject, see the previous chapter at verses 18, 19, 23, 24 [§§404–411, 427–432].) The man who fathered him there had almost the same name—Methushael—so that the symbolism is almost the same as well. Methushael and Methuselah symbolize something that is dying, and Lamech something destroyed.[307]

528 Genesis 5:29. *And he called his name Noah, saying, "He will console us for our work and for the distress of our hands from the ground, which Jehovah cursed."*

Noah symbolizes the ancient church. *Consoling us for our work and for the distress of our hands from the ground, which Jehovah cursed,* symbolizes the doctrine that was to restore what had been corrupted.

529 The symbolism of *Noah* as the ancient church, the progenitor of the three churches that followed the Flood, will become clear in what follows, where Noah is treated of at length.

530 The names in this chapter, as noted [§§468:1, 483], symbolize different churches or doctrinal systems (which are the same thing, since a church develops out of doctrine and is called a church because of its doctrine). So Noah symbolizes the ancient church, or the doctrine left from the earliest church.

The way matters stand with churches and their theologies has been mentioned before [§§468, 494:2]: they tend to dwindle until none of the goodness or truth associated with faith remains any longer, and then the Word describes the church as devastated.

Still, a remnant—certain people, no matter how few, in whom religious goodness and truth endure—is always preserved. If that goodness and truth were not preserved in them, there would be no bond joining heaven and the human race together.

[2] About the remnant that exists in an individual person: The fewer the traces [of goodness and truth] remaining with us, the weaker the light that shines on our rational concepts and the facts we know. The light of good and truth flows in from those traces, or rather through them from the Lord. If we had no remnant, we would not be human but much worse than an animal. The smaller a remnant we have, the less human we are; the larger a remnant, the more human. A remnant is like a star in the sky; the smaller it is the less light it gives, and the larger it is the more light it gives.

The few traces that remained from the earliest church were present with those composing the church called Noah. What they retained, though, was not vestiges of perception but of integrity and of the theology derived from the perceptions of the earliest churches. Consequently a new church was now raised up by the Lord for the first time. Because its character was completely different from that of the earliest churches, it must be called the ancient church. It is called ancient because it existed at the end of the centuries preceding the Flood and in the first era following it.

The Lord in his divine mercy willing, this church will be discussed further in what follows.[308]

The symbolism of *consoling us for our work and for the distress of our hands from the ground, which Jehovah cursed,* as the doctrine that was to restore what had been perverted will also, by the Lord's divine mercy, be seen in what follows.[309]

Work means that such people could not perceive what was true without a great deal of effort and anguish. *The distress of our hands from the ground, which Jehovah cursed,* means that they were unable to do anything good. This is how Lamech, or the church that lay in ruins, is described. The *work and labor of our hands* is when people have to rely on themselves or their own powers to find out what is true or do what is good. Anything that then results is the *ground that Jehovah cursed,* that is, something entirely false and evil. For what it means to say that Jehovah curses, see §245.

Consoling, however, relates to the son, Noah, who symbolizes a new rebirth and so a new church, which is the ancient church. This church, or Noah, also symbolizes a time of rest[310] and the consolation that comes with rest, just as it was said of the earliest church that it was the seventh day—the day of the Lord's rest (see §§84–88).

532 Genesis 5:30, 31. *And after Lamech fathered Noah he lived five hundred ninety-five years, and he fathered sons and daughters. And all Lamech's days were seven hundred seventy-seven years, and he died.*

Lamech, as noted [§527], symbolizes a church devastated or in ruins. His *sons and daughters* symbolize what is conceived and born in such a church.

533 As nothing more is said of Lamech, either, than that he fathered sons and daughters, which are the things conceived and born in such a church, there is no need to linger further. Just what the offspring—the daughters and sons—are can be seen from the church itself, since the offspring have the same character as the church.

Both the church called Methuselah and the one called Lamech passed away right before the Flood.[311]

534 Genesis 5:32. *And Noah was a son of five hundred years. And Noah fathered Shem, Ham, and Japheth.*

Noah, as mentioned [§528], symbolizes the ancient church. *Shem, Ham, and Japheth* symbolize the three ancient churches whose progenitor was the ancient church, named Noah.

535 The church called Noah should not be counted among the churches preceding the Flood, as verse 29 makes clear; that church was to "console them from their work and from the labor of their hands from the ground, which Jehovah had cursed." The consolation was that it would survive and endure.

But more will be said about Noah and his sons below,[312] with the Lord's divine mercy.

536 The perceptive ability of the churches that came before the Flood is discussed many times above,[313] but in modern days perception is a wholly unknown thing. The ignorance about it is so great that people are capable of believing it to be a kind of ongoing revelation, or else something instinctive. Some suppose that it is no more than make-believe, while others have other ideas. Yet perception is the epitome of the heavenly character that the Lord gives to those who have a loving belief in him. Perception exists throughout heaven in untold variety, so with the Lord's divine mercy, let me describe below [§§1383–1400] the general kinds as they exist in the heavens.

Heaven and Heavenly Joy (Continued)

A spirit once latched onto me at my left, asking whether I knew how he could get into heaven. I was permitted to answer that being allowed into heaven was up to the Lord alone, since only he knows what we are like.

A large number of people coming from the world seek nothing more than to enter heaven, not having the least idea what heaven or heavenly joy is. They do not realize that heaven is the sharing of love, or that heavenly joy is the joy this love imparts. Those who do not know are first taught what heaven and its joy are, and one of the ways they learn is through personal experience.

For example, one spirit who himself had recently arrived from the world shared the same desire for heaven [as the first spirit]. To give him a sense of heaven's nature, his inner recesses were opened up so that he could feel something of heavenly joy, but when he felt it, he started to wail and writhe, begging to be released. He was so distressed that survival was impossible, he said. As a result, his inner reaches were closed off to heaven and he then revived.

This demonstrates how anxiety and the gnawing of conscience torture people who are let in to heaven for just a short time, if they are not right for it.

Another group with no idea what heaven is like was also making an effort to get in. They were told that unless they possessed a faith inspired by love, entering heaven was as dangerous as walking through fire; but they still insisted. On reaching the "front entryway"—the lower realm of angelic spirits—they received such a blow that they went tearing off in the opposite direction as fast as they could go. From this they learned how much danger there was in merely approaching heaven before the Lord had prepared them to feel the emotions that come with faith.

A certain spirit who in bodily life had considered adultery perfectly harmless was also allowed to cross heaven's first threshold, since that was what he wanted. On arriving there, he began to suffer and to smell his own corpselike stench. These sensations grew until he could no longer stand them. If he had gone any farther, it seemed to him, he would have been destroyed.

Consequently he was banished from there to the underground realm. He felt angry that crossing heaven's first threshold meant undergoing such tortures, since he was entering an environment opposed to adultery. He is one of the unfortunate ones.

540 Almost no one coming into the other life understands what the blessings and happiness of heaven are, since they do not know what deep-seated joy is or what it feels like. They can grasp it only in relation to bodily and worldly kinds of happiness and joy, and whatever they do not know about they consider worthless. Nevertheless, bodily and worldly thrills are relatively worthless and filthy.

In order for those who are honest but ignorant to learn what heavenly joy is and to come to recognize it, they are introduced first into scenes of Paradise that surpass anything they could ever have imagined. (With the Lord's divine mercy, these scenes will be described further on [§1622]). They suppose they have now entered the heavenly Paradise, but they are taught that this is not the true happiness of heaven. Next they experience profound states of joy in their deepest core. Afterward they are carried into a state of peace reaching to the same deep level. They confess that nothing about that peace could ever be captured in word or thought. Finally they are brought into a state of innocence that again reaches right to their deepest level of sensation. This allows them to recognize what true good is like on the spiritual and heavenly planes.

541 Some who had no idea what heavenly joy was were abruptly carried up into heaven. They had been reduced to a condition in which they could be lifted up, their bodily desires and their delusions having been put to sleep. I heard one of them saying to me from there that now for the first time he could feel how much joy there was in heaven. He admitted that he had been grossly deceived, that he had held a very different view, and that he could now perceive the deepest degree of his own joy, which was immeasurably more than he had ever felt at the peak of any sensual experience during his physical existence. He called the pleasures that [he and his companions] usually enjoy foul.

542 In those who are taken to heaven for the purpose of discovering what it is like, bodily desires and delusions are put to sleep, since no one can enter heaven bringing such things along from the world. Either that or they are surrounded with the aura of spirits who moderate the unclean and discordant things in them in a miraculous way. Some people may have their inner recesses opened. These are some of the methods [of preparation], and there are others, depending on the way people have lived and the character they have acquired along the way.

543 Once some spirits eager to explore what heavenly joy was like were granted the opportunity to perceive the deepest level of their own joy, up to the point where they could no longer stand it. It was not angelic joy and barely resembled even the least of such joys, as I could tell when their joy was communicated to me. It was so paltry as to seem rather cold. Still, they pronounced it most heavenly, since it was the deepest of their own joys.

This experience showed not only that there are different levels but also that the deepest level of one kind barely extends to the shallowest or middle level of another. It demonstrated further that when we gain our most profound joy, we are in our own heavenly joy; we cannot bear any deeper variety, which would only end up turning painful for us.

544. A group admitted into the innocent state of the first heaven[314] spoke to me from there and confessed that the condition of that heaven was so glad and joyful that it could never be imagined in the least. This was in merely the first heaven. There are three heavens, and each enjoys a state of innocence, with all its countless variations.

545. In order to teach me about the existence and nature of heaven and heavenly joy, the Lord has given me the opportunity to perceive the pleasures of heavenly joy frequently and for extended periods. Because I have learned these things by actually experiencing them, I possess the knowledge but cannot possibly put it into words.

To offer just an idea of it: The countless pleasures and joys there, which come together to create a single experience shared by all, carry with them a certain emotion. Within that common experience, or that common emotion, are points of harmony among a boundless number of feelings. These individual points of harmony do not come clearly but only vaguely to our awareness, because our perception is extremely generalized. Even so, I was allowed to perceive that there were countless parts, organized in a way that can never be described. Those countless parts flow from the order that exists in heaven, which determines their nature.

[2] The smallest individual elements of an emotion are organized in such a way that they are presented and sensed only as a collective whole, according to the capacities of the person who feels the emotion. In a word, every whole has an unlimited number of parts, organized in the most perfect way; every one of the parts is alive; and every one of them affects us, all the way to our inmost recesses. For the inmost recesses are where heavenly joy comes from.

I also perceived that joy and pleasure seemed to come from my heart, gently permeating all the inmost fibers of my body and thus all the bundles of fibers.[315] The sensation of this joy at the deepest levels made it seem as though each fiber was composed of nothing but joy and pleasure and all the perceptiveness and sensitivity that come with joy and pleasure. The fibers seemed alive with happiness.

The joy we feel in physical indulgence, compared to these joys, is like a coarse, stinging dust compared to the gentlest breath of pure air.

546. The following experience was to teach me what happens with people who are eager to enter heaven but are not of a type that can stay there.

Once while I was in a community in heaven, an angel appeared to me as a little child wearing a wreath of dazzling sky-blue flowers on its head and garlands of other colors circling its chest. From this sign I was able to recognize that I was in a particular community where charity existed. Then into the same community came some upstanding spirits who on entering suddenly became much more intelligent and started talking like angelic spirits.

Next to be admitted was a group of people who claimed to be innocent on their own merits. Their condition was represented to me by a baby spitting up milk. That is what such people are like.

Afterward came people who supposed that their own good thinking made them intelligent. Their condition was represented in their faces, which were angular but reasonably attractive. They appeared wearing pointed hats with a protruding spike. Still, their faces did not seem to be made of human flesh but looked like lifeless sculptures. This is the condition of those who believe that they can make themselves spiritual or acquire faith on their own.

Other spirits were allowed in who were unable to stay there. Overwhelmed with dismay and anxiety, they fled the place.

Genesis 6

Heaven and Heavenly Joy [Continued]

NONE of the souls who come into the other life know what heaven or heavenly joy is. Most think it is a joy they can enter into regardless of how they have lived. Even those who hated their neighbor and indulged in a life of adultery believe this, entirely unaware that heaven is love—a love both mutual and chaste—and that heavenly joy is the happiness welling up from love. 547

Several times I have talked to spirits newly arrived from the world about the conditions of eternal life. "It's important for you to know who the Lord of the realm is, what his style of government is like, and what the form of government is," I pointed out. "On earth, the first thing you have to do on entering another country is to learn the identity and character of the monarch, the nature of the government, and other information about the country. How much more so in this realm, where you'll live forever? 548

"The Lord alone rules not just heaven but the whole universe," I said. "Whoever rules the one rules the other.

"The kingdom in which you now find yourself is the Lord's. The laws of this kingdom are eternal truths, all founded on this solitary law: you are to love the Lord above all and your neighbor as yourself. Not only this, in fact, but if you want to be like angels, you'll have to love your neighbor *more* than yourselves."

[2] To all this they had no answer, because during bodily life they had heard something similar but had not believed it. They were astounded to hear that in heaven people can and do love their neighbor more than themselves (although they *had* heard that they should love their neighbor as themselves).

"Everything good in the next life expands without limit," I told them. "Life bounded by the body is such that we can't progress any farther than loving our neighbor as ourselves, because we're wrapped up in bodily concerns. But when these concerns have been laid aside, love grows purer and purer until at last it is angelic. Angelic love is to love one's neighbor more than oneself.

[3] "That this kind of love is possible you could have known from the love between certain married partners who would prefer death to seeing their spouse injured. You could have known it from the love parents have for their children: a mother would rather starve than see her baby go hungry. And this is true even among birds and animals.

"You could have known it from true friendship in people who risk danger for the sake of their friends. You could even have known it from polite friendship—the pretense that tries to pass for real friendship—in which we offer the better portions to those in our good graces and bear selflessness on our lips (though not in our hearts).

"Last, you could have known it from the nature of love, which is such that its joy is to serve others, not for one's own sake but for the other person's."316

But these things were incomprehensible to those who loved themselves more than others and to those who had been money-grubbing during physical life. Least understanding of all were the misers.

549

The angelic state is such that everyone conveys his or her own blessings and happiness to others. In the next life there is a communication and keen perception of all feelings and thoughts, so that in the sharing of joy each communicates to all and all to each, which essentially makes every individual the center of all the rest. This is how heaven is set up.

As a result, the more people there are to make up the Lord's kingdom, the greater the happiness is; it increases as the numbers increase. This is why heavenly happiness is inexpressible.

Such a sharing of all with one and one with all exists whenever we love another person more than ourselves. But when we wish better to ourselves than to another, self-love takes control. Self-love shares nothing of its own with others except its self-conception, which is actually something extremely filthy. When this conception is perceived by others, we are immediately cut off and rejected.

550

Each and every part of the human body cooperates with the others in both the overall functioning of the whole and the specific functioning of each part. It is the same in the Lord's kingdom, which is like a single human being and is also named the "universal human"; everyone there works together, whether at close quarters or more at a distance, and by many different means. This takes place in accord with the plan established and constantly reinforced by the Lord alone for the sake of everyone's happiness.

551

The whole of heaven and its individual inhabitants without exception trace their origin to the Lord alone, in general and in the smallest particulars. This is the source of order, of unity, of mutual love, and of happiness, because this is what causes individuals to look to the health and happiness of all, and all to that of every individual.

Many experiences have shown me that all joy and happiness in heaven come from the Lord alone. At this point, let me recount just one such experience.

I saw that certain angelic spirits, using the greatest possible care, were making an ornate lampstand, with its lamps and flowers, in the Lord's honor. For an hour or two I was allowed to observe how hard they worked to make absolutely everything beautiful and full of significance. They felt that the labor was their own, but I was able to sense clearly that they could invent nothing by their own power.

Finally, several hours later, they said they had succeeded in making a gorgeous lampstand, with all its representative art, in honor of the Lord, and at this they rejoiced from the depths of their being. I told them, however, that at no time had they designed or created anything on their own but that it was the Lord alone who had done this for them. At first they were scarcely willing to believe it, but being angelic spirits, they received enlightenment and confessed that it was so.

The same is true for all their other representative objects, for all their feelings and thoughts without exception, and so for heavenly joy and happiness; the least of them all come from the Lord alone.

Those who know how to share love are constantly advancing into the springtime of their youth in heaven, and the more millennia they live, the more joyful and happy that springtime is. Their progress continues forever, its never-ending increase determined by their development and growth in the capacity for sharing love, in charity, and in faith.

A woman who dies old, worn out by age, and who lived a life marked by faith in the Lord, charity toward her neighbors, and a happy, loving marriage with her husband—such a woman develops more and more of the bloom of mid- and early womanhood with the passage of years. She takes on a loveliness that eclipses any conception of beauty ever seen by the eye. Virtue and kindness are what shape her and make her a likeness of themselves. They cause the joy and beauty of neighborly love to shine out from the smallest details of her face, so that she becomes a form of charity itself. Some observers have been struck speechless on seeing these women.

[2] The inner workings of charity are such that charity itself is what provides the visible form and is the thing expressed in that form too. This is clear from actual experience in the other life. The whole angel, especially the face, *is* charity, which is both clearly presented to view and

clearly perceived. To see the form is to see inexpressible beauty that touches the deepest, living reaches of the mind, filling them with charity. The beauty of the form provides an image in which religious truth is displayed—truth that is also perceived from that form.

Those who have lived a life marked by faith in the Lord, that is, by the faith that comes of charity, become these visible forms—these beauties—in the next life. All angels are such forms, in unlimited variety. Of them heaven is made.

Genesis 6

1. And so it was that humankind began to multiply on the face of the ground, and daughters were born to them.

2. And the sons of God saw the daughters of humankind, that they were good, and they took wives for themselves from among all whom they chose.

3. And Jehovah said, "My spirit will not denounce humankind forever, because they are flesh. And their days will be one hundred twenty years."

4. The Nephilim[317] were in the land in those days and for a very long time after[318] the sons of God went in to the daughters of humankind, who bore children to them. These were mighty men, who for ages had been men with a name.

5. And Jehovah saw that the evil of the people in the land multiplied; and what the thoughts of their heart fabricated was nothing but evil every day.

6. And Jehovah was sorry that he had made humankind on the earth, and he grieved to himself at heart.

7. And Jehovah said, "I will obliterate the human whom I created from the face of the ground, from human to beast to creeping animal to the bird in the heavens, because I regret that I made these things."

8. But Noah found favor in Jehovah's eyes.

Summary

554 THIS is talking about the condition of the pre-Flood people.

555 It says that where the church existed, appetites (which are the daughters) started to control people. It also says that people forged ties between the teachings of faith and their cravings, hardening themselves in evil and falsity; this is the fact that the sons of God took wives for themselves from among the daughters of humankind (verses 1, 2).

Because doing so deprived people of any remnant of goodness or truth, a new way is predicted of forming people so they could acquire those remnants. The hundred twenty years are the remnants (verse 3).

The Nephilim are those who merged the teachings of faith with their desires and in this way, under the influence of self-love, dreamed up appalling delusions about their own importance compared to that of other people (verse 4).

The result was that no will for what was good or true and no perception of goodness or truth remained (verse 5).

The Lord's mercy is described as regret and heartfelt grief (verse 6). People became such that their desires and delusions could only annihilate them (verse 7). So in order for the human race to be saved, a new church came into being, and this is Noah (verse 8).

Inner Meaning

BEFORE going any further, let me mention the situation of the church that came before the Flood. Its situation was much like that of later churches, such as the Jewish church before the Lord's Coming and the Christian church afterward: all of them perverted and adulterated true religious knowledge.

In specific regard to the people of the church before the Flood, they conceived appalling delusions as time passed. The goodness and truth that belong to faith they merged so thoroughly with their foul desires that almost no trace of either was left to them. When they reached this point, they virtually suffocated themselves. A person lacking any remnant [of goodness or truth], after all, cannot survive. Such a remnant, as noted earlier [§530], is what lifts human life above animal life. A remnant, or rather the Lord working by means of a remnant, is what allows a person to seem human, to learn what is good and true, to reflect on particular instances of it, and so to think and reason. This remnant alone has spiritual and heavenly life in it.

To explain what a remnant is: It is not just the good and true things that we learn out of the Lord's Word from the time we are small and that become stamped on our memory. It is also all the states that rise out of those things, such as a state of innocence from babyhood, a state of love for our parents, siblings, teachers, and friends, a state of charity toward our neighbor and compassion toward the poverty-stricken and needy. In short, it is all states of goodness or truth.

These states, along with the good and true things imprinted on our memory, are called a remnant. The Lord preserves them in us, hiding them away in our inner being without our slightest awareness and carefully separating them from the things that are our own—in other words, from evil and falsity.

The Lord preserves all these states in us in such a way that not even the least significant of them is lost. This I learned from the fact that every one of our states from infancy to extreme old age not only remains in the other life but even returns. When we relive them, they are identical to the experience we first lived through in the world. This happens not only with the good and true things etched on our memory but also with any state of innocence or charity we have experienced. In addition, each and every one of our states of evil and falsity (or malice and delusion) remains and returns as well, in all its minutest detail. And when the latter states come back to us, the Lord tempers them by means of the former. All of which shows that if we had no remnant, we could not help being damned for eternity (see above at §468).

562. The pre-Flood people were such that in the end they had almost no remnant. The cause was their mental character, which inclined them to adopt dreadful, odious persuasions about absolutely everything that happened or that sprang into their thoughts. They did not want to retreat a single step from those delusions or, above all, from self-love, considering themselves godlike and their thoughts divine.[319] A bent for self-deception on this scale has never emerged among any race of people before or since. Such a nature kills by suffocating, and so those people can never be in the vicinity of other spirits in the next life. When present, they rob other spirits of any ability to think, by the pressure of their own immovably determined opinions—not to mention other effects they produce, which are, by the Lord's divine mercy, to be described below [§§1265–1272].

563. Should this kind of self-deception take over, it acts like a glue, and the good feelings and true thoughts that should be our remnant adhere to it. Then remnants can no longer be stored away, and what has already been stored away becomes unavailable. As a result, when people arrived at the height of this kind of delusion, they annihilated themselves and

drowned in an inundation not unlike the Flood. Their extinction is compared to a flood for this reason and, in keeping with the custom of the earliest people, is also depicted as a flood.

564. Genesis 6:1. *And so it was that humankind began to multiply on the face of the ground, and daughters were born to them.*

Humankind symbolizes the human race of that time. The *face of the ground* symbolizes that whole area where the church existed. The *daughters* symbolize what resides in the will of such a person and so symbolize appetites.

565. The symbolism of *humankind* as the human race of that time—an evil and corrupt race—is established by subsequent verses:

> My spirit will not denounce *humankind* forever, because they are flesh. (Genesis 6:3)

> The evil of the *people* in the land multiplied; and everything that the thoughts of their heart fabricated was nothing but evil. (Genesis 6:5)

> I will obliterate the *human* whom I created. (Genesis 6:7)

And from the next chapter:

> All flesh creeping on the earth passed away, and every *human,* in whose nostrils was the breath of living spirit. (Genesis 7:21, 22)

In regard to humanity, it has already been said that the Lord alone is human [§§49, 162] and that from him every heavenly person (or heavenly church) acquires the name of human [§477]. Everyone who is not heavenly acquires the name of human from him too, as do people of all religions whatever. It is what distinguishes us from animals. Still, we are not human, are not different from the animals, except through having a remnant (as noted [§§530, 560]), which is the Lord's. The remnant too enables us to be called human, and since the remnant enables this, and the remnant is the Lord's, again it is from the Lord that we acquire the name of human, no matter how bad we are. We would not be human but the lowest of the animals if we had no remnant.

566. The symbolism of the *face of the ground* as that whole area where the church existed can be seen from the symbolism of the *ground,* since the Word carefully distinguishes *ground* from *the earth* or *the land.* Wherever it appears, *ground* symbolizes the church, or some aspect of the church. This is the origin of the human's name—Adam, which means *ground.*[320]

Often when *the earth* or *the land* is mentioned in the Word, it means the absence of the church or of anything having to do with the church. The first chapter is an example. In it, only the earth or land is mentioned,[321] since the church—the regenerate person—did not yet exist. The ground is first mentioned in the second chapter, because by then the church did exist. Something similar occurs here and in the next chapter:

> All substance would be destroyed from the face of the *ground.* (Genesis 7:4, 23)

This means in the territory where the church was. In the same chapter:

> . . . to keep their seed alive on the face of the *earth.* (Genesis 7:3)

This is about a church yet to be created. The same holds true everywhere in the Word, as in Isaiah:

> Jehovah will have mercy on Jacob and will yet choose Israel and will put them on their *ground;* and the peoples will take them and lead them to their place, and the house of Israel will inherit them upon the *ground* of Jehovah. (Isaiah 14:1, 2)

This is about a church that has been formed; but a place where there was no church is called the *earth* in verses 9, 12, 16, 20, 21, 25, and 26 of the same chapter. [2] In the same author:

> And the *ground* of Judah will make Egypt quake. On that day there will be five cities in the *land* of Egypt speaking the tongue of Canaan. (Isaiah 19:17, 18)

The ground is where the church is and the land is where the church is not. In the same author:

> The *earth* will wander, wander, like a drunkard. Jehovah will punish the army of the heights on high, and the monarchs of the *ground* down on the *ground.* (Isaiah 24:20, 21)

The meaning is similar. In Jeremiah:

> Because of the chastened *ground,* since there was no rain on the *land,* the farmers were put to shame, they covered their head; for even the doe in the *field* gave birth. (Jeremiah 14:4, 5)

The land means the area surrounding the ground, and the ground means the area surrounding the field. [3] In the same author:

§566

> He brought the seed of the house of Israel out from the north *land* and from all the *lands* to which I drove them, and they will live on their *ground*. (Jeremiah 23:8)

The land and lands are where there are no churches; the ground is where the church or true worship is. In the same author:

> I will make the *survivors* of Jerusalem—those left in this *land* and those living in the *land* of Egypt—I will make them a disturbance, an evil to all the kingdoms of the *earth*. And I will send against them sword, famine, and contagion to the point of devouring them off the *ground* that I gave to them and their ancestors. (Jeremiah 24:8, 9, 10)

The ground stands for theology and for the worship it gives rise to. The same holds true for Jeremiah 25:5.[322] [4] In Ezekiel:

> I will gather you from the *lands* to which you have been scattered, and you will acknowledge that I am Jehovah, when I have returned you onto Israel's *ground*, onto the *land* in which I lifted my hand to give it to your ancestors. (Ezekiel 20:41, 42)

The ground stands for inner worship; it is called land when there is no inner worship. In Malachi:

> I will harangue against the devouring pest for you, and it will not spoil the fruit of the *ground* for you; and the grapevine in the field will not be bereft for you. And all nations will call you fortunate, because *you will be a land* of pleasure. (Malachi 3:11, 12)

The land stands for the whole surrounding area and so, quite obviously, for a person, who is called "a land." The ground surrounded by that land stands for the church, or theology. [5] In Moses:

> Sing, you nations, his people. He will atone for his *ground*, his people. (Deuteronomy 32:43)

Clearly this stands for the church among non-Jewish nations, which is called the "ground."[323] In Isaiah:

> Before the child knew to spurn evil and choose good, the *ground* that you despise in the presence of its two monarchs would be deserted. (Isaiah 7:16)

This speaks of the Lord's Coming, saying that the ground prepared for the church—the true doctrine concerning faith—would be deserted. It is clear that the words *ground* and *field* are used in connection with planting, as in Isaiah:

> He will give rain for the seed with which you would sow the *ground*. Cattle and young donkeys working the *ground* . . . (Isaiah 30:23, 24)

And in Joel:

> The *field* was devastated and the *ground* mourned, because the grain was devastated. (Joel 1:10)

From this it can now be seen that the human—called *adam* in Hebrew, from the word for ground—symbolizes the church.

567. The whole region encompassing those who have learned what is taught about true faith is called the church's territory. The land of Canaan was one such place during the time the Jewish church was there. Europe, where the Christian church now exists, is another. The lands and regions outside this are not the church's territory, meaning they are not the *face of the ground.*

Just where that territory was before the Flood can be seen from the lands circled by the rivers that came from the Garden of Eden—rivers that the Word frequently describes as marking the boundaries of the land of Canaan [Genesis 15:18; Deuteronomy 1:7; 11:24; Joshua 1:4; 1 Chronicles 5:9]. Its location can also be determined from what follows, such as the fact that the Nephilim were in the land; and the land they were in was Canaan, as established by the presence of the children of Anak, who were some of the Nephilim (Numbers 13:33).

568. The symbolism of *daughters* as what resides in the will of such a person, and so as cravings, is clear from statements made about sons and daughters, and evidence offered, at verse 4 of the last chapter [§§489–491]. Sons were there shown to symbolize truth, and daughters goodness. *Daughters,* or goodness, belong to the will. But our character determines what our intellect and will are like and so what our "sons and daughters" are like. The current chapter is describing corrupted people, who have no will but raw desire instead, which they consider to be will, and which they also call will. Any feature attributed to a thing has its quality from that thing, and the people said to have these daughters were corrupt, as already shown [§§560, 562–563, 565].

[2] Daughters symbolize what is in the will, and when there is no will for good, they symbolize appetites; sons symbolize what is in the intellect, and when there is no comprehension of truth, they symbolize

delusions. The reason for this lies in the nature of the sexes. The female sex is such by character and formation that the will or desire rules over the intellect. Every fiber in the female body is attuned to this, and it is the feminine nature. The male sex, on the other hand, is formed in such a way that intellect or reason reigns supreme. Every fiber in the male body is attuned to this, and it is the masculine nature. Marriage between the sexes results from these circumstances, as does a union between will and intellect in every individual.324

Today no will for good exists but desire instead—and yet a modicum of intellect or rationality is possible. This is why so many laws about men's privileges and wives' submission were laid down in the Jewish church.325

Genesis 6:2. *And the sons of God saw the daughters of humankind, that they were good, and they took wives for themselves from among all whom they chose.*

The *sons of God* symbolize the teachings of faith. *Daughters* here as before symbolize cravings. *The sons of God saw the daughters of humankind, that they were good, and they took wives for themselves from among all whom they chose,* means that they forged ties between the teachings of faith and their own appetites—appetites of any kind whatever.

The symbolism of the *sons of God* as the teachings of faith is established by the symbolism of *sons*, dealt with just above and in verse 4 of the last chapter [§489], where sons symbolized the church's truth.

The church has truth in the form of doctrinal teachings. Because the people described in the present chapter received them by word of mouth from the earliest people, these teachings were true in the abstract. It is for this reason that they are called the sons of God, and also because of their relation to the desires called the daughters of humankind.

This verse is describing those people's character, showing that they immersed the church's truth—which is holy—in their cravings and in this way defiled it. In doing so they reinforced their own firmly held assumptions.

The way these matters stand is something we can all evaluate by looking at ourselves and the people around us. When we convince ourselves of some idea, we prove its truth to ourselves by the use of every seemingly valid argument—even by arguments that come from the Lord's Word. As long as we cling to our adopted principles and persuasions, we force everything into agreement and harmony with them. The more we dote on ourselves, the more rigidly we stick by those ideas.

Such a description fits the race of people under discussion here. More will be said about them below [§§573, 580–586a, 607:3, 619–637, 659–662, 792–813], by the Lord's divine mercy, in a further description of their hideous delusions. Surprising to say, these delusions are such that those people are never allowed to influence others with their rationalizations; if they did, they would kill all rational power in the spirits around them. They are allowed to influence others only with their desires.

Now it is clear what is meant by *the sons of God saw the daughters of humankind, that they were good, and they took wives for themselves from among all whom they chose.* The meaning is that they forged ties between the teachings of faith and their cravings—cravings of any kind whatever.

571. When we are such that we smother religious truth with our insane longings, we profane the truth and deprive ourselves of any remaining traces [of goodness or truth]. Although these traces stay with us, we cannot bring them to consciousness, since the moment we do so, we desecrate them once again with thoughts that are already defiled. Profanation of the Word creates a kind of callus that dams up all remaining goodness and truth and absorbs it. Be careful, then, not to desecrate the Lord's Word, which—although it is not seen as containing truth by anyone caught up in false assumptions—does contain eternal, living truth.

572. Genesis 6:3. *And Jehovah said, "My spirit will not denounce humankind forever, for this reason: that they are flesh. And their days will be one hundred twenty years."*

Jehovah said, "My spirit will not denounce humankind forever," means that people would no longer be led in the same way. *"For this reason: that they are flesh,"* means because they became body-centered. *"And their days will be one hundred twenty years"* means that they ought to have traces of faith left; and it is a prophecy about the church to come.

573. The meaning of *Jehovah said, "My spirit will not denounce humankind forever,"* as the fact that people would no longer be led in the same way can be seen from context. Prior context shows that people developed the character described there by merging religious teachings or truths with their own desires to the point where they could no longer be shown the error of their ways, or see what was evil. All ability to perceive truth and goodness was snuffed out by their self-deceptions, since the only things they believed true were those that conformed with their theories. Subsequent context will show that people in the church changed after the Flood. What arose in them to take the place of perception was conscience, by which they *could* be rebuked. So the denunciation by Jehovah's spirit symbolizes

an inner voice—either perception or conscience—and Jehovah's spirit itself symbolizes truth and goodness flowing in. Isaiah too says:

> I will not *press my quarrel* forever; I will not rage eternally, since their *spirit* would be overwhelmed before me; and I made their souls. (Isaiah 57:16)

The symbolism of *flesh* as the fact that people became body-centered is established by the symbolism of flesh in the Word, where it is taken to mean both every person in general and a body-centered one in particular.

Flesh is understood as implying all people, in Joel:

> I will pour out my *spirit* on all *flesh,* and your sons and your daughters will prophesy. (Joel 2:28)

The flesh stands for people; the spirit, for truth and goodness flowing in from the Lord. In David:

> Hearer of prayers, to you will all *flesh* come. (Psalms 65:2)

Here flesh stands for all people. In Jeremiah:

> Cursed will the man be who trusts in humankind and uses *flesh* as his arm. (Jeremiah 17:5)

Flesh stands for people, the arm for power. In Ezekiel:

> . . . so that all *flesh* will know . . . (Ezekiel 21:4, 5)

In Zechariah:

> Be silent, all *flesh,* before Jehovah. (Zechariah 2:13)

Here flesh stands for all people.

[2] Flesh is understood as particularly implying a body-centered person, in Isaiah:

> The Egyptian is human and not God, and their horses are *flesh* and not spirit. (Isaiah 31:3)

This stands for the fact that their knowledge was limited to the bodily level. Horses here and elsewhere in the Word stand for the rational level. In the same author:

> They will withdraw to the right and be hungry and will eat on the left and not get enough. They will each eat the *flesh* of their own arm. (Isaiah 9:20)

Flesh stands here for the things that are our own, which are all on the bodily level. In the same author:

> From soul to *flesh* he shall consume [it all]. (Isaiah 10:18)

The flesh stands for bodily preoccupations. In the same author:

> The glory of Jehovah will be revealed and all *flesh* will see it together. A voice says, "Shout!" And he said, "What shall I shout?" "All *flesh* is grass!" (Isaiah 40:5, 6)

Flesh stands for all body-oriented people. [3] In the same author:

> Jehovah will argue his case by fire, and argue it with all *flesh* by his sword; and the number of those stabbed by Jehovah will multiply. (Isaiah 66:16)

Fire stands for punishment inflicted on corrupt desire, the sword for punishment inflicted on falsity, and flesh for bodily preoccupations. In David:

> God remembered that they were *flesh*, a spirit wandering, never to return. (Psalms 78:39)

This is about the people in the wilderness craving flesh, or meat (Numbers 11:32, 33, 34), describing them as body-centered. Their yearning for flesh represented the fact that they desired only bodily rewards.

575 *The days of humankind will be one hundred twenty years* means that they ought to have traces of faith left. In verses 3 and 4 of the last chapter I said that days and years symbolize those times and states [§§482, 487–488], and that the earliest people used different combinations of numbers to symbolize the state of the church and changes in that state [§487:2]. But their method of calculating numbers for the affairs of their church is part of the knowledge that has been lost.

Likewise in the present verse the number of years comes up, and no one can have any idea what the numbers mean without knowing what significance lies hidden in the individual numbers from one to twelve and beyond. It is obvious that they involve some other, hidden meaning, since a life span of 120 years is inconsistent with earlier verses. People in later times did not live a mere 120 years either, as can be seen from those living after the Flood. Chapter 11 says of Shem that he lived 500 years after fathering Arpachshad, that Arpachshad lived 403 years after fathering Shelah, that Shelah also lived 403 years after fathering

Eber, and that Eber lived 430 years after fathering Peleg. Chapter 9, verse 28, says that Noah lived 350 years after the Flood. And so on.

What the number 120 involves can be seen only from its factors, ten and twelve. To be specific, it symbolizes remaining traces of faith. In the Word the number ten—and tenths or tithes as well—symbolizes and represents a remnant preserved by the Lord in the inner self, the remnant being holy because it belongs to the Lord alone. The number twelve symbolizes faith, or all aspects of faith taken as a whole. The number compounded out of these symbolizes a remnant of faith.

The following places establish the fact that *ten*, like *a tenth*, symbolizes a remnant. In Isaiah:

> Many houses will become desolate—large, beautiful ones—without any inhabitant, since *ten* acres of vineyard will yield a single bath, and the sowing of a homer will yield an ephah.[326] (Isaiah 5:9, 10)

This concerns the devastation of spiritual and heavenly qualities. "Ten acres of vineyard will yield a bath" stands for the fact that so few traces of any spiritual quality remain. "The sowing of a homer will yield an ephah" stands for the fact that so few traces of any heavenly quality remain. In the same author:

> And much [territory] will be abandoned in the middle of the land, but a *tenth* of it will remain and rebound; yet it is destined for eradication. (Isaiah 6:12, 13)

The middle of the land stands for the inner self, and the tenth part, for so small a remnant. In Ezekiel:

> You shall have honest scales and an honest ephah and an honest bath. The measure of an ephah and of a bath will be the same, so that a bath may hold a *tenth* of a homer, and an ephah a *tenth* of a homer. Their measure will be according to the homer. And the statute for the oil—the bath for oil—is a *tenth* of a bath out of a kor,[327] *ten* baths being a homer; for *ten* baths are a homer. (Ezekiel 45:10, 11, 14)

This discusses holy attributes of Jehovah in terms of measures, which symbolize different categories of sacred qualities. Ten here symbolizes a remnant of heavenly traits and of the spiritual traits that grow out of them. What would be the point of all these measures and the numbers that specify them if they did not contain some hidden, sacred significance? This applies to chapter 45 of Ezekiel and earlier chapters dealing with the heavenly Jerusalem and the new Temple, to other prophets as well, and to various rituals in the Jewish religion. [2] In Amos:

> The virgin of Israel has fallen; she will not rise again. This is what the Lord Jehovih has said: "The city going out as a *thousand* will leave a *remnant* of one *hundred,* and the one going out as a *hundred* will leave a *remnant* of *ten* for the house of Israel." (Amos 5:2, 3)

Here a remnant is mentioned, of which the smallest part will remain, since it is only a tenth part, or in other words, a remnant of a remnant. In the same author:

> Jacob's pride and his palaces I hate, and I will shut up the city and its abundance. And it will happen that if *ten* men have been *left* in one house they will die. (Amos 6:8, 9)

Ten stands for the remnant, which will hardly last. In Moses:

> Neither an Ammonite nor a Moabite will come into Jehovah's assembly; not even the *tenth* generation of them shall ever come into Jehovah's assembly. (Deuteronomy 23:3)

The Ammonite and Moabite stand for profanation of the heavenly and spiritual attributes of faith, the remnants of which were discussed earlier [§§468, 530, 560–561].

[3] The fact that tithes represent remaining traces can be seen from the discussion above. They are treated of this way in Malachi:

> Bring all *tithes* to the treasure house to be plunder in my House, and let them test me, please, in this: if I do not open to you the floodgates of heaven and pour out on you a blessing. (Malachi 3:10)

"To be plunder in my House" stands for the remnant in our inner self. The remnant is compared to plunder because it is tucked away among all our evils and falsities, so to speak. Through the remnant come all blessings.

All feeling of charity in us, too, comes by way of the remnant in our inner self. This was represented in the religion of the Jews by their giving to the Levite, the immigrant, the orphan, and the widow after they had paid their tithes (Deuteronomy 26:12 and following verses).

[4] Since the remnant is the Lord's alone, tithes are described as "holy to Jehovah," as in Moses:

> All *tithes* of the land—from the seed of the land, from the fruit of the tree—they will be Jehovah's, holy to Jehovah. All *tithes* of herd and

flock, everything that passes under the [shepherd's]³²⁸ crook—a *tithe* will be holy to Jehovah. (Leviticus 27:30, 32)

The *Decalogue* was the Ten Commandments, or the Ten Words,³²⁹ which Jehovah wrote on tablets (Deuteronomy 10:4), and they symbolize a remnant. The fact that they were written by Jehovah's hand symbolizes that the remnant is the Lord's alone. The fact that they reside in the inner self was represented by the tablets.

The symbolism of *twelve* as faith, or as the properties of love and so of faith taken as a whole, can also be demonstrated by many phenomena in the Word: the twelve sons of Jacob and their names, the twelve tribes of Israel, and the Lord's twelve disciples. But these will be covered later [§§3858, 3913:1], by the Lord's divine mercy, especially in chapters 29 and 30 of Genesis.

These numbers alone indicate what the Lord's Word holds at heart, in its inner recesses—what secret treasures lie hidden there, completely invisible to the naked eye but present throughout the whole. Each word hides similar mysteries.

Remarks to be made below [§§660, 661:2] about the pre-Flood people under discussion here will show, with the Lord's divine mercy, that they had few if any remaining traces [of goodness and truth]. Because these traces could not be preserved in them, a prediction appears here concerning a new church called Noah that would have a remnant. This remnant too, with the Lord's divine mercy, will be described below [§§635, 737, 1050].

Genesis 6:4. *The Nephilim were in the land in those days and for a very long time after the sons of God went in to the daughters of humankind, who bore children to them. These were mighty men, who for ages had been men with a name.*

The Nephilim symbolize those who placed no value on anything holy or true because of delusions about their own importance and superiority. *For a very long time after the sons of God went in to the daughters of humankind, who bore children to them,* means that they became so at the point when they merged the teachings about faith with their appetites and convinced themselves of false ideas. They are called *mighty men* from their love for themselves. *For ages they had been men with a name* means that they had been like this before as well.

The symbolism of the *Nephilim* as those who placed no value on anything holy or true because of delusions about their own importance and superiority can be seen from what appears above and just below.

Specifically, it says that they merged doctrinal teachings with their appetites—the symbolic meaning of the two statements that the sons of God went in to the daughters of humankind and that they bore children to them.

People's delusions about themselves and their fantasies grow as they amass more and more contributing arguments, until finally those delusions become permanent. And when they drag religious teachings in, they develop the most rigid point of view, which causes them to completely discount the value of anything holy or true, making themselves into Nephilim.

That tribe of people, who lived before the Flood, is such as described above [§§562–563]; every spirit they meet, no matter who, they choke to death with the most horrendous delusions, which flood out from them like a poisonous, suffocating fog. They strangle those spirits so effectively that the spirits forget how to think, and seem to themselves to be half dead.

Had the Lord by his coming into the world not freed the world of spirits from such a venomous tribe as that, not a single spirit could have survived there. This would have meant the end of the human race, which the Lord governs through spirits. As a result, they now are kept in a hell below a kind of boulder, massive and shrouded in mist, under the heel of the left foot.[330] They make no attempt to rise up out of the place, leaving the world of spirits free of their extremely hostile crowd. This crowd and the toxic effect of their persuasions will be spoken of in another place [§§1265–1272], the Lord in his divine mercy allowing.

These are the ones called Nephilim, who place no value on anything holy or true.

[2] Though the Word does call them Nephilim, it refers to their descendants as Anakim and Rephaim.[331] The following passage in Moses shows that they are called Anakim:

> Those who scouted out the land of Canaan said, "There we saw the *Nephilim,* the children of *Anak* from among the *Nephilim,* and in our eyes we were like locusts, and we were the same in their eyes." (Numbers 13:33)

Moses also shows that they were called Rephaim:

> The Emim previously lived in the land of Moab, a people large and numerous and tall, like the *Anakim.* They themselves were accounted

as *Rephaim,* like the *Anakim,* and the Moabites call them Emim. (Deuteronomy 2:10, 11)

The Nephilim are not mentioned anywhere else, but the Rephaim are, and the prophets describe them in the same way. Isaiah says:

Hell was disquieted below for you, coming to meet you; it stirred up the *Rephaim* for you. (Isaiah 14:9)

This is about hell, where such people are. In the same author:

The dead will not live, the *Rephaim* will not rise, because you inflicted punishment on them and destroyed them and wiped out all memory of them. (Isaiah 26:14)

Here too the subject is their hell, from which they will no longer arise. Again in the same author:

Your dead will live, my corpse; they will rise again. Wake up and sing, you who live in the dirt, because your dew is the dew on the vegetation. But the land of the *Rephaim* you will cast out. (Isaiah 26:19)

The land of the Rephaim is hell, which is what this verse describes. In David:

Will you do a miracle for the dead? Will the *Rephaim* arise, will they acclaim you? (Psalms 88:10)

This likewise deals with their hell and the fact that they cannot rise up to poison the atmosphere in the world of spirits with their dreadful persuasions.

The Lord, however, provided that the human race would no longer steep itself in such appalling fantasies and delusions. The people who lived before the Flood had a nature and psyche that enabled them to absorb such twisted thinking. The reason is not yet known to anyone but will be divulged below [§927], by the Lord's divine mercy.

After the sons of God went in to the daughters of humankind, who bore children to them, means that at the point when they merged the teachings about faith with their corrupt desires they became Nephilim. This meaning can be seen from what was stated and demonstrated just above at verse 2 [§§569–571]: the sons of God symbolize the teachings of faith, and daughters symbolize desire. The child born from this combination is nothing but the practice of viewing the holy attributes of faith as worthless and profaning them.

Our cravings, which spring from self-love and materialism, are diametrically opposed to everything holy and true. They have the upper hand in us, so that when we acknowledge something as holy and true and then submerge it in our desires, our doom is sealed, since those desires cannot be uprooted and dissolved. They cling to every idea we have, and ideas are the means of communication people have with each other in the next life. Consequently, as soon as the suggestion of something holy and true comes up, immediately and directly the profanation and falsity attached to it is perceived. Such people, then, simply must be separated and forced down into hell.

583. The fact that the Nephilim are called *mighty men* from their love for themselves can be seen in many places in the Word where such people are referred to as strong. In Jeremiah, for instance:

> The *mighty* of Babylon stopped fighting; they sit in their strongholds; their *might* fails; they have turned into women. (Jeremiah 51:30)

The mighty of Babylon stand for those who have fallen into the trap of self-love. In the same author:

> A sword against liars—and they will lose their minds; a sword against its *mighty*—and they will feel dismay. (Jeremiah 50:36)

In the same author:

> I saw: they were dismayed and turned back. Their *mighty* were crushed; they fled madly and did not look back. Terror all around! The swift will not flee nor the *mighty* escape. Go up, horses,[332] and run mad, chariots. Let your *mighty ones* leave, Cush, Put,[333] and Lydians. (Jeremiah 46:5, 6, 9)

This is about using rationalization to delude oneself. In the same author:

> How can you say, "We are *mighty ones* and men strong in war"? Moab has been devastated. (Jeremiah 48:14, 15)

In the same author:

> The city was captured, as were its fortifications; it was occupied. And the heart of the *mighty* of Moab on that day became like the heart of a woman in agony. (Jeremiah 48:41)

Jeremiah 49:22 similarly mentions "the heart of the *mighty* of Edom." In the same author:

> Jehovah has ransomed Jacob and won him back from the hand of one *mightier* than he. (Jeremiah 31:11)

This passage uses a different [Hebrew] word for "mighty."³³⁴

It can be seen in Moses that the Anakim (who were offspring of the Nephilim) were described as strong:

> You are crossing the Jordan today, arriving to take possession of nations larger and more numerous than you, of cities large and fortified to the sky, of a people large and tall, the children of the *Anakim,* whom you know. And you have heard, "*Who will stand up to the children of the Anakim?*" (Deuteronomy 9:1, 2)

584. Genesis 6:5. *And Jehovah saw that the evil of the people in the land multiplied; and everything that the thoughts of their heart fabricated was nothing but evil every day.*

Jehovah saw that the evil of the people in the land multiplied means that the will for good began to disappear. *Every fabrication of the thoughts of their heart was nothing but evil every day* means that there was no perception of truth or goodness.

585. *The evil of the people in the land multiplied* means that the will for good began to disappear, as can be seen from what was said above [§568]—that true will no longer existed but only desire. The same meaning can also be seen from the symbolism of the *people in the land*. At the literal level, the land is where the people are. On an inner plane, it is where love is, and since love is a matter of will or else of desire, the land is taken to mean human will itself. It is willing that makes a person human, and not so much knowing and understanding, since knowing and understanding derive from willing. Anything that fails to flow out of our will is something we do not want to know or understand. In fact when we speak and act at variance with our will, it is still a form of will—one far removed from our words and deeds—that controls us.

The land of Canaan (the Holy Land) is taken to stand for love and so for the will of a heavenly type of person, as many passages from the Word can prove. The same is true for the fact that the lands of various nations stand for the love in the hearts of those peoples—generally love for oneself and for worldly gain. But the term occurs so many times that there is not room to spend time on it here.³³⁵

All of this leads to the conclusion that the evil of the people in the land symbolizes evil on the earthly level, present in the will. It is said to have multiplied because it was not completely sinister in everyone; there were some who still wished good to others, although for selfish reasons. Its thorough corruption is *what the thoughts of their heart fabricated.*

586a 336 *What the thoughts of their heart fabricated was nothing but evil every day* means that there was no perception of goodness or truth, because people immersed the teachings of faith in their filthy cravings, as has been said and shown [§§560, 570]. When this happened, all perception died out and in its place came monstrous convictions, or the most entrenched and fatal delusions. These were the cause of their extinction through suffocation. Such death-dealing persuasions are symbolized here by what the thoughts of their heart invented.

When *what the heart fabricates* is mentioned without *the thoughts,* it symbolizes the evil connected with self-love or with desire. An instance occurs in chapter 8 below, where after Noah had made burnt offerings Jehovah said, "I will never again curse the ground on the human being's account, because what people's *hearts fabricate* is evil from their youth" (Genesis 8:21). A *fabrication* is what we make up in our own minds and persuade ourselves is true. [2] In Habakkuk, for instance:

> What use is a sculpture? For its *fabricator* sculpted it—a cast image and that which teaches a lie. For the fabricator trusts in his *fabrication* [and] in the making of mute idols. (Habakkuk 2:18)

A sculpture symbolizes false persuasions based on premises we have conceived and hatched from our own minds. Fabricators are those who persuade themselves of the ideas described as fabrications. In Isaiah:

> Oh, your upside-downness! Will the potter be considered clay because the product says to its maker, "That one did not make me" and the *fabrication* said to its *fabricator,* "That one did not understand me"? (Isaiah 29:16)

A fabrication here stands for self-centered thinking and the resulting conviction that falsity is true. In general a fabrication (or design) is what we make up out of our heart or our will, and also out of our thoughts or persuasions. An example in David:

> Jehovah knows our *fabrication;* he remembers that we are dust. (Psalms 103:14)

In Moses:

> I know their *designs* that they are forming today, before I bring them into the land. (Deuteronomy 31:21)

586b Genesis 6:6. *And Jehovah was sorry that he had made humankind on the earth; and he grieved to himself at heart.*

He was sorry symbolizes mercy. *He grieved at heart* has the same symbolism. *Regret* has to do with wisdom, *grieving at heart* with love.

587 The symbolism of *Jehovah was sorry that he had made humankind on the earth* and of *he grieved at heart* as mercy can be concluded from the fact that Jehovah never has regrets. After all, he foresees absolutely everything from eternity. When he made humankind—that is, when he created people anew and perfected them into heavenly people—he also foresaw that the race would gradually become what it did. Since he saw this ahead, he could not have changed his mind, as is plain in Samuel, who said:

> The Undefeated One of Israel does not lie and will not *be sorry*, since he is not a human, that he should *be sorry*. (1 Samuel 15:29)

And in Moses:

> God is not a man and tells lies, or the offspring of humankind and *has regrets*. Has he said a thing and will not do it, or spoken and will not secure it? (Numbers 23:19)

But regretting or feeling sorry symbolizes having mercy.

[2] Jehovah's mercy—the Lord's mercy—involves each and every thing the Lord does for the human race. Humankind's nature is such that the Lord has mercy on us, and on each of us according to our circumstances. So he has mercy on the state of one whom he permits to be punished and on the state of one to whom he grants good fortune. Punishment is an act of mercy because mercy bends all the evil involved in punishment to good ends. To grant good fortune is also an act of mercy because we never earn any kind of good. The whole human race is evil, and left to ourselves we all plunge into hell. To pull us back out of hell, then, is mercy, and pure mercy at that, since the Lord does not need anyone.

Mercy is called *misericordia* [in Latin] because it removes us from the miseries of hell.[337] It is therefore named in relation to the human race, which is miserable, and is the effect of love for all people because they are miserable.

588 But the Lord is said to feel regret and to grieve at heart because these activities seem to lie at the core of all human mercy. The language of this passage, like that of many others in the Word, goes along with the appearance. The true nature of the Lord's mercy no one can know, because it infinitely transcends all human comprehension. But the nature of our own mercy we recognize, and that nature is to feel sorry and to grieve.

If we did not form an idea of mercy from some other feeling whose nature we do recognize, we could not think or learn anything about it at all. This is why human traits are frequently used to describe Jehovah's attributes, or in other words, the Lord's. For instance, Jehovah—the Lord—is said to punish, lead into crisis, destroy, and burn with anger, when the truth is that he never punishes anyone, never inflicts trouble on anyone, never destroys anyone, and never burns with anger. Because such claims are indeed made about the Lord, then, it follows that regret and grief are also attributed to him, since the one claim is a result of the other. This can be clearly seen from the following places in the Word. [2] In Ezekiel:

> My *anger* will be ended, I will put my *wrath* to rest, and I will *relent*. (Ezekiel 5:13)

Since this verse ascribes anger and wrath to him, it also speaks of him as relenting. In Zechariah:

> "Just as I thought to do *evil* when your ancestors aroused *anger* in me," Jehovah Sabaoth has said, "and I did not *relent*, so, in turn, will I think in those days to do good to Jerusalem and to the house of Judah." (Zechariah 8:14, 15)

It says here that Jehovah thought to do evil when in reality he never thinks to do evil to anyone but good to each and every person. In Moses, when Moses entreated Jehovah:

> "Turn back from the *wrath* of your *anger* and *relent* from the evil done to your people." And Jehovah *relented* from the *evil that* he had said *he would do* to his people. (Exodus 32:12, 14)

Here too wrath and anger are attributed to Jehovah and he is therefore said to have relented. In Jonah, the king of Nineveh said:

> Who knows? Perhaps God will turn and *relent*, to turn back from the *heat* of his *anger*, and we will not be destroyed. (Jonah 3:9)

Once again he is said to relent because he is said to have been angry. [3] In Hosea:

> A change of *heart* has come over me; at the same time my *regrets* have burned. I will not carry out the *wrath* of my *anger*. (Hosea 11:8, 9)

This too speaks of his heart and the regrets burning there, just as the verse under discussion says that he grieved at heart. The regrets clearly stand for great mercy. Likewise in Joel:

> Turn back to Jehovah your God, since he is indulgent and *compassionate,* patient and abounding in *mercy,* and *regretful* over evil. (Joel 2:13)

In this place as well regret plainly symbolizes mercy. In Jeremiah:

> If perhaps they listen and turn back, a man from his wicked way, and I *regret* the evil . . . (Jeremiah 26:3)

Having regret stands for having mercy. In the same author:

> If that nation turns back from its evil, I will *relent* from evil. (Jeremiah 18:8)

Again, relenting stands for having mercy—if they turn back. We are the ones who turn away from the Lord's mercy; the Lord never turns away from us.

These and many other passages in the Word show that it speaks according to human appearances. Anyone who wants to use the appearances in which the statements of the Word are couched to support false premises will have an unlimited supply to choose from.

But using the Word to prove false assumptions is very different from taking the Word at face value. Those who confirm false assumptions start by seizing on a principle that they refuse ever to relinquish or even partially to retract. Instead they scrape together and pile up proofs from every available source, including the Word, until they have so thoroughly convinced themselves of their premise that they can no longer see the truth. [2] Those who take the Word at face value, however, or who believe it with a simple heart, do not start by taking hold of a principle but think, "Since the Lord said it, it is true." And if they are taught how to understand it, by the use of other passages from the Word, they yield to it with joy in their hearts.

It does no harm to believe in all simplicity that the Lord is angry, punishes, relents, or grieves and that we should accordingly fear evil and do good, because it leads to the belief that the Lord sees everything large and small. Once committed to this belief, we receive enlightenment in all other areas—during the next life, if not before. The case is very different with those who delude themselves with their cherished assumptions, helped along by vile self-love and greed.

590 The fact that regret has to do with wisdom, and heartfelt grief with love, cannot be explained clearly to people's understanding. It can only be explained in terms of human experience and so in terms of appearances.

Every concept in our thinking contains something of both intellect and will; to put it another way, it contains something of thought and of love for that thought. If an idea does not draw to some extent on the will, or on love in the will, it is not an idea, because without love we cannot think. There is a kind of marriage, perpetual and inviolable, between thought and will. So the contents of the will or the objects of love in the will are present within the ideas that make up our thinking, or are at least attached to them. From this human experience it seems more or less possible to know (or rather to grasp in some measure) what lies at the heart of the Lord's mercy: wisdom and love.

As a result, the prophets (especially Isaiah) almost everywhere use two terms for every concept, one involving a spiritual quality and the other a heavenly one.[338] The spiritual aspect of the Lord's mercy is wisdom and its heavenly aspect is love.

591 Genesis 6:7. *And Jehovah said, "I will obliterate the human whom I created from the face of the ground, from human to beast to creeping animal to the bird in the heavens, because I regret that I made these things."*

Jehovah said, "I will obliterate the human," means that humanity would annihilate itself. *"Whom I created from the face of the ground"* symbolizes those who were descendants of the earliest church. *"From human to beast to creeping animal"* means that whatever was in their will would annihilate them. *"To the bird in the heavens"* means whatever was in their intellect or thoughts. *"Because I regret*[339] *that I made these things"* symbolizes compassion, as above [§§587–588].

592 The meaning of *Jehovah said, "I will obliterate the human"* as the fact that humanity would annihilate itself is established by what was said above [§588]. That is, Jehovah (the Lord) is described as punishing, testing, doing evil, destroying or killing, and cursing. For instance, Jehovah is said to have killed Er, Judah's firstborn, and Onan, his second (Genesis 38:7, 10), and all the firstborn of Egypt (Exodus 12:12, 29). Jeremiah has an example:

> . . . whom I have *struck* in my *anger* and in my *wrath*. (Jeremiah 33:5)

In David:

> He sent against them the *wrath* of his *anger*, his *ire* and *fury* and *distress*, a *delegation of evil angels*. (Psalms 78:49)

In Amos:

> Will there be *evil* in the city and Jehovah did not do it? (Amos 3:6)

In John:

> . . . seven golden bowls *full of the anger of God*, who lives forever and ever. (Revelation 15:1, 7; 16:1)

All of these banes are said to be from Jehovah, even though the truth is the exact opposite.

The reason they are attributed to him was given above [§§588–589]. A further purpose is to allow people to form first the very general idea that the Lord controls and arranges absolutely everything. Later they can learn that nothing bad comes from the Lord, least of all murder, but that we humans are the ones who bring evil on ourselves and destroy and kill ourselves. Still, it is not we who do so but evil spirits who goad us and lead us on; and yet it is we who do so after all, because we fully believe it is.

This is the reason, then, that the present verse says Jehovah would obliterate the human, when truly it is humans who destroyed and annihilated themselves.

[2] The actual situation is especially clear from those in the other life who undergo the tortures of hell. They are constantly weeping and blaming the Lord for all the negative consequences of their punishment. Those evil spirits in the realm of evil spirits who take pleasure—their greatest pleasure—in hurting and punishing others lay the blame in the same place. The ones they wound and discipline think it is the Lord who does so, but I told them and showed them that absolutely nothing bad comes from the Lord. "On the contrary," I said, "you bring the evil on yourselves.

"The way all things in this other life are arranged and balanced, evil rebounds on the evildoer and turns into the miseries of punishment. This evil cannot be helped. It is described as being tolerated—tolerated for the sake of evil's cure. But the Lord still converts all the negative consequences of punishment into good, so that nothing but goodness ever comes from him."

What this kind of toleration is no one yet realizes. People view the thing that is tolerated as having been carried out by the One who allows it, simply because he allows it. The reality, though, is quite different, as will be explained later [§2447], with the Lord's divine mercy.

593. The symbolism of *whom I created from the face of the ground* as those who were descendants of the earliest church can be seen from several things. The first is that the text speaks of the human he *created* (that is, regenerated) and later of the human whom he *made* (that is, perfected, or in other words, regenerated to the point of becoming heavenly). The second is that it says *from the face of the ground,* the ground being the area where the church is, as shown earlier [§§566–567].

Another indication is that the discussion treats of those who merged the teachings of faith with their appetites. People who had no access to the doctrine of the true faith could not commit this offense. Those outside the bounds of the church live in ignorance about what is true and good, and people who live in ignorance can have a certain kind of innocence even when they say or do something that violates the truth and goodness of faith. They may be driven by a zeal for the worship that they grew up with and that they consequently consider true and good.

The case is completely different with those who have the doctrine of the [true] faith among them. These are capable of mingling truth with falsity, and holiness with profanation. Their lot in the other life is accordingly much worse than the lot of those called gentiles, who will be discussed below, the Lord in his divine mercy willing.[340]

594. The meaning of *from human to beast to creeping animal* as the fact that whatever was in their will would annihilate them can be seen from the symbolism of *human, beast,* and *creeping animal.*

A human is human only by virtue of will and intellect. These faculties distinguish humans from animals. All other characteristics are shared between them. Among the people being described here, every impulse for good and every inkling of truth had died out. Insane longings arose to replace the will for good and absurd delusions to replace the comprehension of truth, and these delusions joined forces with those longings. So after these people had essentially blotted out all remaining traces of will and intellect in this way, they themselves necessarily became extinct.

Prior discussions of beasts and creeping animals have established the fact that all aspects of the will are referred to as these creatures [§§44–46, 246]. Here, though, because of the nature of the people described, beasts do not symbolize positive emotions but negative ones, and consequently corrupt desires. And creeping animals symbolize the lower pleasures—bodily and sensual pleasures.

There is no further need for proof from the Word that animals and reptiles have this symbolism, since examples appear above in §§45, 46, 142, and 143; please see there.

For the symbolism of *the bird in the heavens* as whatever was in their intellect or thoughts, again see above, at §40.

Genesis 6:8. *But Noah found favor in Jehovah's eyes.*

Noah symbolizes a new church. *He found favor in Jehovah's eyes* is the fact that the Lord foresaw that this was the way the human race could be saved.

Noah symbolizes a new church, called the ancient church in order to distinguish between the very earliest church, which preceded the Flood, and the church that followed the Flood.

The states of these two churches were entirely different. That of the earliest church was to receive a perception of good, and so of truth, from the Lord. In the ancient church—"Noah"—the state changed to one of conscience concerning goodness and truth. The difference between conditions in the earliest church and in the ancient church was the difference between having perception and having conscience. Perception is not conscience. Heavenly angels have perception; spiritual angels have conscience. The earliest church was heavenly, but the ancient church was spiritual.

[2] The earliest church experienced direct revelation through personal contact with spirits and angels and also through visions and dreams sent by the Lord. These gave them a general ability to recognize what was good and true, and having recognized this, they confirmed the generalities (axioms, more or less) by countless insights gained through perception. These insights constituted particular details filling in the broad categories to which they belonged. In this way, daily experience corroborated general principle. Whenever they came across something that did not agree with general principle, they perceived that it was wrong, and whenever they came across something that agreed, they perceived that it was right. Heavenly angels are in the same state.

[3] The broad principles of the earliest church—its axioms, in effect—were heavenly, eternal truths. They included the idea that the Lord governs the universe, that he is the source of all goodness and truth and of all life, that our selfhood is pure evil and of itself is dead, and other ideas like these. The people of that church received from the Lord a perception of countless thoughts supporting and harmonizing with these principles.

To them, love was the most important element of faith. It was through love that the Lord enabled them to perceive everything belonging to faith, and so faith to them was love, as already stated [§§32:2, 202, 398].

The ancient church, on the other hand, became totally different, as later sections will reveal, by the Lord's divine mercy.[341]

598 *He found favor in Jehovah's eyes* means that the Lord foresaw that this was the way the human race could be saved. The Lord's mercy concerns the salvation of the whole human race and looks toward this. His favor or grace does too, which is why the human race's salvation is symbolized here.

Noah symbolizes not only a new church but also the faith of that church—the faith that came of charity. So the Lord foresaw that the human race could be saved by the faith that comes of charity. This faith will be described below.[342]

[2] The Word maintains a distinction between mercy and favor, however, and that distinction depends on differences between the kinds of people who receive them. Mercy is appropriate to the heavenly, and favor, to the spiritual. The heavenly acknowledge nothing but mercy while the spiritual acknowledge hardly anything but favor, or grace. The heavenly have no idea what favor is; the spiritual scarcely know what mercy is and consider it one and the same with favor.

These differences result from attitudes of humility in each, which are equally different. Those who are humble at heart beg the Lord for mercy, while those who are humble in their thinking seek his favor. If the latter pray for mercy, they do so in times of trouble, or else they do so with their lips rather than in their hearts.

Since the new church called Noah was not heavenly but spiritual, it is said to have found not mercy but favor in Jehovah's eyes.

[3] The distinction that the Word maintains between mercy and favor, or grace, can be seen in many places where Jehovah is called merciful and favorable, such as Psalms 103:8; 111:4; 112:4; and Joel 2:13. The same distinction is preserved in other places too, such as Jeremiah:

> This is what Jehovah said—"The population of those left by the sword has found *favor* in the wilderness"—as he went to give rest to Israel. From far off Jehovah appeared to me, [saying,] "And with eternal love I have loved you; therefore I drew you to me in *mercy*." (Jeremiah 31:2, 3)

Favor describes a spiritual quality and mercy a heavenly one. In Isaiah:

> Therefore Jehovah will wait, in order to show *favor* to you, and therefore he will lift himself up to have *mercy* on you. (Isaiah 30:18)

Favor again looks to a spiritual quality and mercy to a heavenly one. In a later part of Genesis, where Lot is talking to the angels:

> Look, please; your servant has found *favor* in your eyes, and you have enlarged the *mercy* that you have shown me, keeping my soul alive. (Genesis 19:19)

The fact that favor focuses on spiritual aims, which have to do with faith or the intellect, can be seen here too, where it says [as in Genesis 6:8] that someone "found favor in your eyes." Mercy, however, focuses on heavenly aims, which have to do with love or the will, as can be seen from the statement that the angels had shown mercy and given life to his soul.

❋ ❋ ❋ ❋ ❋ ❋

9. These are the births[343] of Noah: Noah was a just, upright man in his generation. Noah walked with God.

10. And Noah fathered three sons: Shem, Ham, and Japheth.

11. And the land was corrupt before God; and the land was full of violence.

12. And God saw the land, and found it was corrupt, because all flesh had made their way corrupt on the earth.

13. And God said to Noah, "The end of all flesh has come before me, since the land is filled with violence because of them, and indeed, I am destroying them together with the earth.

14. Make yourself an ark of gopher wood;[344] you must make compartments in the ark, and you must tar it inside and out with tar.

15. And this is how you must make it: three hundred cubits[345] for the length of the ark, fifty cubits for its width, and thirty cubits for its height.

16. You must make a window for the ark and complete it to a cubit above. And you must place a door for the ark in its side. Lowest, second-level, and third-level [compartments] you must make in it.

17. And I—yes, I—am bringing a flood of water on the earth, to destroy all flesh (all that has the breath of life in it) from under the heavens; all that is on the earth will pass away.

18. And I will set up my pact with you; and you will enter the ark: you and your sons and your wife and your sons' wives with you.

19. And of every living thing, of all flesh, you must bring pairs of each into the ark, to keep them alive with you. A male and a female they must be.

20. Every kind of bird, and every kind of beast, every kind of everything creeping on the ground—pairs of all must go in to you, to stay alive.

21. And you, take for yourself some food of every type that is eaten and gather it to yourself, and it will serve you and them as food."

22. And Noah did everything that God had commanded him; that is what he did.

Summary

599 THIS is about the state of the church called Noah before rebirth.

600 The people of that church are described as ones who could be reborn (verse 9). Still, out of that church would rise three kinds of theology, and they are Shem, Ham, and Japheth (verse 10).

601 No other people from the earliest church would be capable of rebirth, because of their fearsome convictions and unclean desires (verses 11, 12), through which they would utterly destroy themselves (verse 13).

602 Those in the church called Noah, though, were not like this, and they are portrayed by the ark (verse 14). Their remaining traces [of goodness and truth] are described by the measurements (verse 15). Different features of their intellect are depicted in the window, door, and compartments or decks (verse 16).

603 They would be preserved when everyone else perished in the flood of evil and falsity (verse 17).

604 The true thoughts and good impulses that they had would be salvaged (verse 18), that is, the contents of the intellect and those of the will; the means would be regeneration (verses 19, 20). They would undergo preparation for this step (verse 21). And so it happened (verse 22).

Inner Meaning

605 THE present subject is the formation of the new church called Noah. Its formation is depicted by the ark that took in living things of every kind. But before that new church could come into being, it was necessary—as it always is—for the people in the church to suffer further trials, portrayed by the rising, tossing, and long ride of this ark on the flood waters.

Their eventual transformation into truly spiritual people and their deliverance are depicted by the ebbing of the water and other later details.

No one who sticks exclusively to the literal meaning can see this message. The main reason is that all the elements link together to create a story and present the kind of picture that we expect from a narrative. The people of that time, though, had a manner of writing—most pleasing to themselves—that cloaked everything in symbols, and they would assemble these into a history. The more consistent the thread of the story, the better it suited their way of thinking. The people of those long-ago times, you see, did not spend so much time with bare facts as people today do but engaged in deep thought, which led to the fertile kind of results seen here. This was the wisdom of our ancestors.

Modern scholars[346] may be familiar with the notion that the Flood, the ark, and consequently the description of both symbolize rebirth and the struggles that lead up to it. So they speak metaphorically of regeneration and struggle as flood waters.

What follows will lay out that church's nature in detail; for now I will present just a glimpse of it through these brief remarks.

The earliest church was heavenly, as already noted.[347] The church under discussion here, on the other hand, became spiritual. The earliest church had enjoyed a perception of goodness and truth. This church (the ancient) did not have perception but another kind of inner voice instead that can be called conscience.

[2] But what the world does not yet know and may have difficulty believing is that the people of the earliest church breathed internally; any external breathing was silent. As a result, they also spoke less with words than people afterward did and still do. Instead, like the angels, they spoke in ideas or mental images, which they could communicate by endless changes in facial expression, especially around the lips. This part of the face has countless series of muscle fibers that today cannot work separately but in those times were independent of each other. Using these muscles, they were able to display, signal, and represent their ideas in such a way that what we would now need an hour to express in articulated sounds (that is, words) would have taken them a minute. And they conveyed their message to the grasp and real comprehension of those present much more fully and clearly than words or sentences could ever do. This may seem impossible, and yet it is true.

There are also many others, not from this planet, who spoke and still speak in the same way, as will be described below [§§6814, 7359–7360,

7745–7746, 8022–8026, 8247–8248, 10587–10588, 10708–10710], with the Lord's divine mercy.

[3] In fact I have been able to learn about this internal breathing of theirs—what it was like and how it changed over time. Since their respiration was like the respiration of the angels, who breathe in a similar way, they had access to the deeper concepts involved in thought and were capable of a kind of perception that could never be described. If its nature were described, no one would understand it, and therefore no one would believe it.

This internal breathing vanished little by little among their descendants. In those consumed by horrendous delusions and fantasies, such breathing lost the ability to present any thoughts to them that were not hideously ugly. The effect of this change was [so powerful] that the people themselves could no longer survive, and so they were all wiped out.

608 As internal breathing waned, external breathing almost of the kind we have today gradually replaced it. With external breathing came verbal speech—the speech of articulated sounds. This was now the vehicle for the individual ideas that make up thought.

In the process, the human condition changed radically. People could no longer perceive things in the way they had before but, as a substitute for perception, began to hear another kind of inner voice that can be called conscience. It was similar to conscience, although it was more or less a middle ground between perception and the conscience that some people today are familiar with.[348]

When the ideas that make up thought came to be poured into this type of mold—into spoken words, that is—human beings could no longer receive instruction by way of the inner self as the earliest people had but only through the outer self. The revelations of the earliest church gave way to articles of doctrine, which would first be grasped through the physical senses. These physical sensations would be shaped into concrete images in the memory and then reshaped into ideas—the components of thought. The ideas would provide an avenue and a framework for instruction.

So it was that this church, which came after the earliest church, had a completely different kind of psyche. Had the Lord not imposed on the human race this new psyche or new approach, no one could ever have been saved.

609 Again, because humankind's state-of-being in this church called Noah had altered completely from that in the earliest church, the race no longer could be taught or enlightened in the same way as the earliest people had been. The inner pathways were now blocked off, preventing any contact with heaven except that which lay hidden to consciousness. No channel of instruction lay open but the external one through the senses, as just noted.

Accordingly, the Lord in his providence saw to it that the teachings of faith would be safeguarded for the use of this generation, along with certain revelations made to the earliest church. Cain was the first to collect these teachings and preserve them against destruction. That is why a mark was said to have been put on him to prohibit his murder. (For more on these things, see the discussion of Genesis 4:15 [§§392–396].) Later, Enoch reduced those teachings into a systematic theology. The theology was not at all useful to the people of that time but only to a generation yet to come, which is why it is said that God took him. (For more, see the discussion of Genesis 5:24 [§521].) These are the teachings of faith that the Lord saved up for the use of the posterity or the church now being described. The Lord had foreseen that perception would die out and so had provided that the teachings would endure.

610 Genesis 6:9. *These are the births of Noah: Noah was a just and upright man in his generation. Noah walked with God.*

The *births of Noah* mean a description of the way the new church would be refashioned, or reborn. *Noah was a just and upright man in his generation* means that the church was one that could be endowed with feelings of charity; *just* has to do with the good involved in charity, *upright* with the truth involved. The *generation* is a stage of religious development. *Walking with God* symbolizes the doctrine concerning faith here, as it did above where Enoch was discussed.

611 The meaning of the *births of Noah* as a description of the way the new church would be refashioned, or reborn, can be seen from the things said above at Genesis 2:4 and 5:1 [§§89, 469–474].

612 The meaning of *Noah was a just and upright man in his generation* as the fact that the church was one that could be endowed with feelings of charity is established by the symbolism of *just and upright*. Being *just* has to do with the good involved in charity and *upright* with the truth involved in it. The same meaning can also be seen from the distinguishing feature of that church, which was charity, as will be discussed later [§§640, 765], with the Lord's divine mercy.

The fact that being *just* has to do with the good involved in charity and *upright* with the truth involved in it can be seen from the Word, as in Isaiah:

> They will seek me every day and desire a knowledge of my ways, as a nation that performs *justice* and does not abandon the *rightful judgment*

of its God. They will ask me about *judging justly;* they will want God to come close. (Isaiah 58:2)

Judgment stands for the things advocated by truth, and justice for the things urged by good. *Performing judgment and justice* became a kind of standard formula that meant doing what is true and good; examples appear in Isaiah 56:1; Jeremiah 22:3, 13, 15; 23:5; 33:15; and Ezekiel 33:14, 16, 19. The Lord said:

The *just* will glow like the sun in my Father's kingdom. (Matthew 13:43)

The just stand for people endowed with charity. And in a passage concerning the end of the era:

The angels will go out and separate the evil from the midst of the *just*. (Matthew 13:49)

Here too the just stand for those who display the good that comes of charity.

[2] An upright person, however, symbolizes the truth that grows out of charity. Truth can originate in many other places, but truth that grows out of the good embraced by charity and received from the Lord—this truth is called whole or upright and is referred to as the upright individual, or a person of integrity. One example appears in David:

Those who will stay in your tent, who will live on your holy mountain, are those walking in *integrity* and doing *justice* and speaking truth in their hearts. (Psalms 15:1, 2)

This portrays the upright person. In the same author:

With the holy person you bear yourself in a holy manner; with the *upright man* you show yourself to be *upright*. (Psalms 18:25)

The upright man is upright in consequence of the holiness or goodness embodied in charity. In the same author:

Jehovah will not withhold what is good from those who *walk* in *integrity*. (Psalms 84:11)

[3] The upright individual is one whom goodness inspires to be truthful, or in other words, a person who speaks and acts on truth out of love for others; and this is clear from the way the Word speaks of uprightness. Often it uses the words *walk, path* [or *way*], and *right* or *rectitude* in

connection with the upright person or with integrity, and these words relate to truth. In David, for instance:

> I will instruct the *upright person* about *the path*—how long it takes to reach me. I will *walk* in the *integrity* of my heart in the middle of my house. (Psalms 101:2)

And in the same Psalm:

> The one who *walks the path of the upright person,* that is the one who will wait on me. (Psalms 101:6)

Elsewhere in the same author:

> A blessing on those who are *upright in their path, walking* in Jehovah's law! (Psalms 119:1)

In the same author:

> *Integrity* and *rectitude* will guard me. (Psalms 25:21)

Again in the same author:

> Observe what is *upright* and watch what is *right,* because a man's final possession is peace. (Psalms 37:37)

All of this establishes the fact that justice is ascribed to one who does what is good and uprightness to one who acts on the truth that springs from goodness; and this is the same as performing justice and judgment. Holiness and justice are the heavenly aspect of faith, while integrity and judgment are the spiritual aspect that develops out of the heavenly aspect.

The fact that the *generation* is a stage of religious development is not evident from the literal sense, which tells a story. Because the message here is exclusively an inner one, though, what are symbolized are attributes of faith. The thread of the story too shows that the generation must be a stage of religious development. Several other places in the Word also use *generation* this way. In Isaiah, for example:

> May they rebuild from you the age-old wastelands; the foundations of *generation* after *generation* may you raise up. And the name given to you will be "The one who walls up the breach," "The one who brings back the paths to dwell by." (Isaiah 58:12)

All the elements of this verse symbolize aspects of faith. The age-old wastelands symbolize faith's heavenly qualities laid waste; the foundations of generation after generation symbolize the foundations of faith's spiritual qualities. These had gone to ruin since ancient times, as is also symbolized. In the same author:

> They will rebuild the age-old wastelands, the earlier desolate places they will raise up, and they will renew the wasted cities, the desolate places of *generation* after *generation*. (Isaiah 61:4)

The meaning here is similar. In the same author:

> They will not labor for empty purpose and will not *bear children* for turmoil, because they are the seed of those blessed by Jehovah, as are their *descendants* with them. (Isaiah 65:23)

Here too the bearing of children is ascribed to the properties of faith, and labor, to the properties of love. The latter are described as the seed of those blessed by Jehovah, the former as offspring.

614 To see that *walking with God* symbolizes the doctrine concerning faith, look at earlier statements about Enoch at Genesis 5:22, 24 [§519]. He too was said to have walked with God, which there symbolized the doctrine of faith preserved for the use of later generations. Since this is the generation destined to use it, the phrase recurs here.

615 The present verse offers a general picture of the people of this church—not what they were already like but what they could become. (Future chapters deal with the actual formation of this character [§§838, 977–979].) Specifically, through religious knowledge they would be able to receive the gift of charitable feeling. In this way they would be able to act out of charity, and the goodness connected with charity would allow them to recognize what was true. So the goodness of charity (being just) comes first and the truth of charity (being upright) second.

Charity, as noted before [§§325, 351], is love for our fellow human beings and is mercy. It is a lower grade of love than that which marked the earliest church, whose love was directed toward the Lord. As you can see, love is now declining and becoming shallower, so that it has to be termed charity.

616 Genesis 6:10. *And Noah fathered three sons: Shem, Ham, and Japheth.*

Noah fathered three sons means that three kinds of theology—symbolized by *Shem, Ham,* and *Japheth*—would rise out of that church.

617 The meaning of *Noah fathered three sons* as the fact that three kinds of theology would rise out of that church can be seen from all the earlier statements [§§337, 339, 402, 468] that names stand purely as symbols for various churches or, to put it another way, various theologies. The same applies here. But the sole reason the names come up here is the context, or the connection with what preceded—that the Lord foresaw that people whose minds worked this way would be able to receive a gift for loving others, although they would still give birth to three different kinds of theology. These theologies will be discussed below where Shem, Ham, and Japheth are treated of, the Lord in his divine mercy willing.[349]

618

In order to understand why *Noah was just and upright, he walked with God,* and (in the present verse) *he fathered three sons* all take the past tense even though they look to future events, you need to know that the nature of the inner meaning makes tense irrelevant. The original language suits this quality, since sometimes one and the same word in it can be understood in any tense; likewise, the words are not divided up.[350] This exposes the inner content to clearer view. The language acquires its flexibility from the inner meaning, which is more richly layered than anyone could ever believe, and this is why it does not allow tense or partitioning to place restrictions on it.

619

Genesis 6:11. *And the land was corrupt before God, and the land was full of violence.*

The *land* symbolizes the tribe of people mentioned earlier [§§562–563, 581:1]. It is described as *corrupt* because of their dreadful delusions, and as *full of violence* because of their unclean desires. The name *God* is used from here to the end of the chapter because there was now no church.

620

The symbolism of the *land* as the tribe of people mentioned earlier is established by places above that show the symbolism of the land (or earth) and the ground [§§268, 566].

Land is a term that surfaces repeatedly in the Word, where it means an area—such as the land of Canaan—in which the Lord's true church exists. It also means an area—such as the land of Egypt or another non-Jewish nation—in which the church does not exist. Accordingly it stands for the race of people living there; and since it stands for the race, it also stands for every member of the race there.

An expression such as *the land of Canaan* uses the term *land* for a heavenly love. The lands of non-Jewish nations are so called on account of foul loves. But *ground* is used in reference to faith, which is planted as a seed. As I showed [§566:2], the land means the area surrounding the ground and the ground means the area surrounding a field, just as love is what contains faith and faith is what contains the religious knowledge that is planted.

The use of *land* in the current verse implies a race or tribe in which every element of heavenly love and of the church died away. (How a term applies [in a given context] can be determined from the subject under discussion.)

621

The fact that the land is described as *corrupt* or destroyed because of people's dreadful delusions, and *full of violence* because of their unclean desires, can be seen from the symbolism of the two terms *corruption* and *violence*. The Word never confuses the two but consistently applies whatever term expresses the precise idea involved. This is done with a care so great that the word choices themselves instantly reveal the inner message. Such is the case with *corruption* and *violence* here. *Corruption* describes the traits of an intellect stripped bare, while *violence* describes the traits of a will laid waste. So corruption has to do with self-deception and violence with desire.

622

The relationship of *corruption* to delusions can be seen in Isaiah:

> They will not do evil or *practice corruption* anywhere on my holy mountain, because the *earth* will be full of knowledge from Jehovah. (Isaiah 11:9; parallel in 65:25)

The doing of evil is associated with the will, or cravings, while the practicing of corruption is associated with the intellect, or persuasive lies. In the same author:

> Doom to a sinning nation, to a people weighed down with wickedness, to the seed of evildoers, to children who *corrupt!* (Isaiah 1:4)

Here as elsewhere the non-Jewish nations and the seed of evildoers stand for evil, which is a matter of will or desire, while the people and the children who corrupt stand for falsities, which are a matter of intellect or self-deception. In Ezekiel:

> More *corrupt* are you than they, in all your ways. (Ezekiel 16:47)

Corruption in this verse has to do with the things we understand, reason over, or think about, since *way* is a word symbolizing truth. In David:

> They did a *corrupt thing,* and they made a heinous thing of their work. (Psalms 14:1)

The corrupt thing stands for appalling delusions and the heinous thing for unclean longings, which lay within their work, or from which it sprang. In Daniel:

After sixty-two weeks the Messiah will be cut off, and he will have nothing; and the people of a leader yet to come will *corrupt* the city and the sanctuary, and its end will come in a flood. (Daniel 9:26)

Again the practicing of corruption or destruction stands for persuasive lies, which are described as a flood.

The fact that the land is described as *full of violence* because of unclean desires—especially the desires stemming from self-love, or flagrant arrogance—can also be seen from the Word. *Violence* is the name for the damage people inflict on holy things when they profane them. That is what these pre-Flood people did when they submerged doctrinal concepts in cravings of every kind. In Ezekiel, for example:

I will turn my face from them, and they will profane my hiding place. And if burglars enter it, they will profane it. Make a chain, because the *land* is full of judgment on [crimes of] blood, and the city *is full of violence*. (Ezekiel 7:22, 23, 24)

This describes the violent, identifying them as the kind of people depicted. In the same author:

They will eat their bread with anxiety and drink their water in desolation, so that the land of [Jerusalem] may be stripped of its abundance, on account of the *violence* of all those living in it. (Ezekiel 12:19)

The bread they will eat with anxiety is heavenly food, and the water they will drink in desolation is spiritual drink, both of which they treated violently, that is, profaned. [2] In Isaiah:

Their webs will not be for clothing, and they will not be dressed in their works. Their works are works of wickedness, and the perpetration of *violence* is in the palms of their hands. (Isaiah 59:6)

The webs and clothes refer to objects of mental activity, or of thought, the wickedness and violence to products of the will, or of works. In Jonah:

May they each be turned from their evil way and from the *violence* that is in the palms of their hands. (Jonah 3:8)

The evil way refers to falsities in the intellect, and the violence, to evil in the will. In Jeremiah:

Within a year will come rumor and *violence* in the land. (Jeremiah 51:46)

Rumor stands for properties of the intellect, violence for those of the will. In Isaiah:

> No *violence* has he done, and no deceit is in his mouth. (Isaiah 53:9)

Violence has to do with traits of the will, deceit in the mouth with those of the intellect.

624 The current passage is about circumstances in which there is no church, as can be seen from the fact that from here on the present chapter speaks of *God*, whereas in the first part it spoke of *Jehovah*. When no church exists, the text uses the name *God*, but when a church does exist, it uses *Jehovah*. In Genesis 1, for instance, where there was no church, it said *God*, but later, when a church did exist, it said *Jehovah God*.

Jehovah is an extremely sacred name used nowhere else but in the church. This is not true of *God*, however, since every nation had its gods, and so the name *God* is not as sacred. No one was allowed to mention Jehovah without a knowledge of the true faith; but anyone could speak of God.[351]

625 Genesis 6:12. *And God saw the land, and found it was corrupt, because all flesh had made their way corrupt on the earth.*

God saw the land means that God understood humankind. *It was corrupt* means that there was unmitigated falsity. *Because all flesh had made their way corrupt on the earth* means that humankind's preoccupation with the bodily level had destroyed all comprehension of truth.

626 Anyone can see that *God saw the land* means that God understood humankind. God, after all, who knows absolutely everything from eternity, has no need to look to see whether we are [corrupt]. *Seeing* is a human activity, and consequently (as was noted at verse 6 and elsewhere [§§587–590, 592]) the passage is speaking from a human point of view. In fact the Word goes so far as to say that God uses eyes to see.[352]

627 The meaning of *because all flesh had made their way corrupt on the earth* as the fact that humankind's preoccupation with the bodily level destroyed all comprehension of truth is established by the symbolism of *flesh*. At verse 3 above [§574], *flesh* was described as symbolizing every person in general and one with a bodily focus in particular, or in other words, the whole bodily realm. A *way* symbolizes the comprehension of truth, or truth itself.

The use of *way* or path to describe a comprehension of truth, or truth itself, can be gathered from passages quoted in various places above [§§519:1, 612:3, 622, 623:2]. The following passages also illustrate the connection. In Moses:

Jehovah said, "Get up; go down quickly from here, because your people have *corrupted* themselves, they have suddenly turned back from the *way* that I commanded them. They have made themselves a cast image." (Deuteronomy 9:12, 16)

In this passage it is commandments, which are truths, that were abandoned. [2] In Jeremiah:

> ... whose *eyes* are open to all the *ways* of the sons of humankind, to reward a man according to his *ways* and according to the fruit of his deeds. (Jeremiah 32:19)

These "ways" are a life spent obeying what has been commanded, and the fruit of a person's deeds is a life inspired by charity. So a way relates to truth, truth being contained in the things commanded and required of us. A son of humankind and a man carry the same connotation, as shown before [§§158, 264, 489, 568:2]. These symbols have the same meaning in Jeremiah 7:3 and 17:10. In Hosea:

> I will bring on them the consequences of their *ways,* and their deeds will I return on them. (Hosea 4:9)

In Zechariah:

> "Turn back from your evil *ways* and your evil deeds." As Jehovah Sabaoth thought to do to us according to our *ways* and according to our deeds ... (Zechariah 1:4, 6)

The meaning here is similar to that in the earlier passages, though turned around, since the ways and deeds are evil. In Jeremiah:

> I will give them one heart and one *way.* (Jeremiah 32:39)

A heart stands for goodness, and a way, for truth. In David:

> Make me understand the *way* of your requirements. Remove the *way* of falsehood from me, and favor me with your law. I have chosen the *way of truth*. I will run the *way* of your commandments. (Psalms 119:26, 27, 29, 30, 32, 35)

The way of the divine requirements and commandments is being referred to as the way of truth, and the opposite, as the way of falsehood. [3] In the same author:

> Make your *ways* known to me, Jehovah; teach me your *paths. Lead the way for me* in your *truth* and teach me. (Psalms 25:4, 5)

Again the way clearly stands for truth. In Isaiah:

> With whom has Jehovah taken counsel, and [who] has instructed him, and taught him the *path* of judgment, and taught him knowledge, and made the *way of understanding* known to him? (Isaiah 40:14)

Obviously the way stands for a comprehension of truth. In Jeremiah:

> This is what Jehovah has said: "Stand on the *footways* and see, and ask about the ancient *paths*—which *way* is the good one—and go on it." (Jeremiah 6:16)

Once again the way stands for a comprehension of truth. In Isaiah:

> I will lead the blind on a *way* they have not known; in *paths* they have not known I will lead them. (Isaiah 42:16)

Words used to describe truth include way, path, road, street, and lane, because these lead to truth. Jeremiah contains an example:

> They caused them to stumble on their *way,* on the ancient *roads,* to go on the *paths,* on a *way* that was not paved. (Jeremiah 18:15)

Likewise in Judges:

> In the days of Jael, the *roads* disappeared, and those going on the *paths* went by crooked *roads.* The *lanes* in Israel disappeared. (Judges 5:6, 7)

628 The inner meaning here is that all people everywhere in the land—in the church's territory—had made their way corrupt, so that they did not comprehend truth, since all of them had turned their attention to the bodily plane. This included not only those mentioned in the last verse [Genesis 6:11] but also those referred to as "Noah," specifically discussed both here and in the next verse. Before being reborn, they had the same character as the others. These details come first because the story of their rebirth waits till later [Genesis 8:15–22]. And since little of the church remained, the name *God* rather than *Jehovah* is now being used.

The present verse signals the fact that nothing true had survived, and the next, that nothing good had. The only truth and goodness left was the remnant possessed by the people called "Noah," because without a remnant regeneration is impossible. The doctrinal concepts that they knew about also survived.

There was no comprehension of truth, however, because this is out of the question where no will to do good exists. When will is absent, so too is intellect, and the better or worse the will is, the better or worse the intellect. The earliest people had a will to do good because they loved the Lord, and from this they had a comprehension of truth. This ability to comprehend, though, was completely destroyed along with the will.

A glimmering of truth on the rational plane and a trace of goodness on the earthly plane did remain to the people called "Noah," and for this reason they were capable of rebirth.

Genesis 6:13. *And God said to Noah, "The end of all flesh has come before me, since the land is filled with violence because of them; and indeed, I am destroying them together with the earth."*

God said means that is how it was. *The end of all flesh has come before me* means that the human race could not avoid destruction. *Since the land is filled with violence* means that there was no longer any will to do good. *Indeed, I will destroy them together with the earth,* means that the human race would meet its end when the church died.

The meaning of *God said* as the fact that that is how it was can be seen from this: in Jehovah there is only what is.[353]

The meaning of *the end of all flesh has come before me* as the fact that the human race could not avoid destruction can be seen from the words themselves. It is also established by the symbolism of *flesh* as all people in general and body-oriented ones in particular, as detailed earlier [§574].

The meaning of *the land is filled with violence* as the fact that there was no longer any will to do good can be seen from statements and evidence concerning the symbolism of *violence* offered above at verse 11 [§623].

The last verse predicted that the comprehension of truth would be destroyed in the people of the church, and this verse predicts that the will to do good would be destroyed.

The fact of the matter is that no one has any understanding of truth or will to do good. Not even the people of the earliest church had them. When people develop a heavenly nature, they seem to have a will to do good and an understanding of truth, but the capability is all the Lord's, as they themselves see, acknowledge, and perceive. The same holds true for angels. So entirely is this the case that anyone who fails to see, acknowledge, and perceive the truth of it utterly lacks any comprehension of truth or will to do good.

The independent self of every human being and every angel—even the most heavenly—is mere falsity and evil. As people know, the heavens are not pure in the Lord's sight [Job 15:15], and all good and all truth belong to him alone.

If a person or an angel can be perfected, then by the Lord's divine mercy that individual is perfected and receives what seems to be an understanding of truth and a will to do good. But what she or he has is only an apparent possession.

All people can be perfected and so receive this gift of the Lord's mercy. The way they have lived their lives, in view of the evil they have inherited from their parents, determines the shape in which mercy comes to them.

634 It is tremendously difficult to explain comprehensibly what an understanding of truth and a will to do good are, in the strict sense. The reason for the difficulty is that we consider every thought passing through our minds to be part of our intellect (since that is the name we give it) and every desire entering our heart to be part of our will (since that is the name we give it).

What makes a clear explanation even harder is that many people today are also completely unable to tell the difference between activity in the intellect and activity in the will. When they think something, they say they want it, and when they want something, they say they think it. So again the obstacle is the labels people use.

Yet another barrier to comprehension is the fact that only what relates to their body captures people's interest; that is, their lives are exceedingly shallow.

[2] For all these reasons, people are unaware that each of us has a deeper level inside, and another level deeper than that, and another level that is deepest of all. They do not see that our bodily urges and sense impressions form the outermost surface; our passions and memories, a deeper layer; our loves and rational thoughts, a still deeper layer; and a will to do good and a comprehension of truth, the deepest. These levels are differentiated from one another with the greatest possible clarity. Body-centered people, however, jumble them all together into an undifferentiated whole. This is the source of the belief that when our physical part dies, everything else must too, even though it is at death that we first start to live. Indeed the new life comes to us by way of our inner levels, passing through each level in order.

If our inner dimensions were not clearly distinguished in this way, and if they did not lie one within the other, in the next life we could never become spirits, never become angelic spirits, never become angels. These three groups are differentiated in the same way as the inner levels, which create the plainest demarcation possible among the three heavens.

This explanation casts a little light on what a comprehension of truth and a will to do good are, properly speaking, and shows that they can be ascribed only to a person whose character is heavenly, or to angels in the third heaven.

635. The things said in this verse and the last symbolize the impending destruction of all comprehension of truth and all will to do good during the cataclysm of the pre-Flood church. Among the people who had absorbed appalling delusions and foul desires in the times before the Flood, such destruction was so complete that not even a faint impression of those faculties remained visible. But among the people referred to as "Noah," some traces did last. That remnant was not enough to reestablish in them any ability to understand or to will, only to present them with truth on the rational plane and good on the earthly plane. A person's character, you see, determines how fully the remnant can operate. These people had enough remaining traces of intellect and will to enable them to be reborn. Self-deception did not block or swallow up the Lord's operation through the remnant in them.

Delusions—false premises that have taken root—hinder the Lord's operation at every turn. Unless they are eradicated, their possessor can never be reborn. More on this later [§§660–661, 792–806], with the Lord's divine mercy.

636. The meaning of *I will destroy them together with the earth* as the fact that the human race would meet its end when the church died can be seen from the inclusion of *together with the earth* in this verse. The *earth* or land in the broad sense symbolizes love, as already pointed out [§§585, 620], and consequently the church's heavenly qualities. Here, since no love or any heavenly impulse remained, the earth symbolizes self-love and whatever is hostile to the church's heavenly qualities. People were still considered part of the church, though, since they held on to their religious teachings. As I said [§§566:2, 620], the land or earth means the area surrounding the ground, and the ground means the area surrounding a field, just as love is what contains faith and faith is what contains religious knowledge.

637. To expand on the symbolism of the words *I will destroy them together with the earth* as the fact that the human race would meet its end along with the church: If the Lord's church were completely obliterated from the planet, the human race could never survive. Every last person would die.

The church resembles the heart, as noted earlier [§468:2]. As long as the heart thrives, so can the surrounding organs and limbs. But as soon as the heart dies, everything else dies too. The Lord's church on earth is like the heart; from it the human race—including people outside the church—receives life. Since no one has the faintest idea why this is so, I wish to explain.

The situation of the earth's entire population resembles that of the human body with all its parts.[354] In this body, the church plays the role of the heart. If there were no church supplying the heart's place—a church with which the Lord could be united by means of heaven and the world of spirits—a break would occur. And if there were a break between the human race and the Lord, we would be annihilated immediately.

For this reason, a church has always existed, ever since the first moment of humanity's creation. Even when the church has begun to die out, it has always remained alive in a few people.

[2] The Lord came into the world for the same reason. Had divine mercy not prompted him to come, the whole human race on this planet would have been destroyed, because at that time the church had reached its last stages and hardly any goodness or truth was left.

Because we humans, regarded in ourselves, are much lower than animals, we have no chance at survival unless we are intimately connected with the Lord through heaven and the world of spirits. Left on our own we would plunge headlong into destroying ourselves and everyone else, because the ruination of ourselves and everyone else is all we long for.

Our proper code of life is to love one another as we love ourselves, but what we actually do these days is to love ourselves more than others and thus hate everyone else. Now, with unreasoning animals the case is totally different. Their proper code is the one they live by, and so they live in thorough harmony with their destiny. We humans, though, live exactly opposite to the pattern ordained for us, so if the Lord did not take pity on us, if he did not bind us to him through angels, we could not possibly survive a single moment.

Of this fact humanity is unaware.

638 Genesis 6:14. *"Make yourself an ark of gopher wood; you must make compartments in the ark, and you must tar it inside and out with tar."*

The *ark* symbolizes a member of this church. The *gopher wood* symbolizes such a person's ardent cravings. The *compartments* symbolize a person's two sides—that of will and that of intellect. *Tarring it inside and out* symbolizes being preserved from a flood of desires.

639 The symbolism of the *ark* as a member of this church—the church called Noah—can be seen fairly clearly from its description in subsequent verses. It can also be seen from the fact that the Lord's Word concerns itself throughout with spiritual and heavenly subjects. To put it another way, his Word is spiritual and heavenly.

If the ark (with its specifications of tarring, dimension, and construction) and the Flood had no greater significance than the words themselves suggest, spiritual and heavenly implications would be utterly lacking. The story itself would be everything and would perform no more critical service to humankind than similar literature written by secular authors.

But in every corner of its inmost recesses the Lord's Word contains and enfolds spiritual and heavenly matters, and this leads directly to the conclusion that the ark and everything said of it carries a hidden meaning not yet uncovered.

[2] The same holds true elsewhere, as, for instance, in respect to the little ark with Moses hidden inside that was laid among the rushes by the river's edge in Exodus 2:3. It is even more sublimely true of the sacred ark in the wilderness, built according to the model shown to Moses on Mount Sinai. If it had not represented the Lord and his kingdom in each and every one of its details, it would have functioned as nothing more than a kind of idol or a cult object. Again, take Solomon's temple. It had no innate holiness derived from the gold, silver, cedar, and stone of its construction, but gained all its holiness from the attributes individually represented by those materials. Likewise here; if Noah's ark with the itemized plan for building it did not symbolize some hidden characteristic of the church, the Word would be not the Lord's Word but a string of words devoid of life and no different from the work of any secular writer.

The logical conclusion is that the ark symbolizes a person belonging to the church called Noah, or the church itself.

The symbolism of *gopher wood* as such a person's ardent cravings and of the *compartments* as that person's two sides—the volitional side and the intellectual side—has so far escaped human awareness. No one, moreover, will be able to see how those meanings are symbolized without first hearing how matters stood in the church called Noah.

As I have quite often said [§§32:2, 200, 202, 310, 337, 393, 459, 597], love made it possible for the people of the earliest church to recognize whether something they were hearing formed a part of faith. To put it another way, a will to do good gave them a comprehension of truth. But their descendants inherited also a tendency for desire (which belongs to the will) to gain the upper hand in them. They took the lessons they had learned about faith and drowned them in desire, and the result was that they became Nephilim.

Since the Lord foresaw, then, that if the human race continued in this tendency they would succumb to eternal ruin, he provided that the will should be split off from the intellect. We would not be shaped by a will to do good, as we had been previously; instead through an understanding of truth we would receive a gift for charity, which would resemble a will to do good. Such is the character that was taken on by the new church called Noah, and in consequence they possessed a nature wholly different from that of the earliest church.

Other churches besides this one also existed during the same period—one called Enosh, for example, as described above at Genesis 4:25, 26.[355] There were others too that left behind no such reference or description. Only the church Noah is depicted here, because its nature was so unlike the earliest church's and diverged so radically from it.

641 The people of this church had to reform. The side of a person called the intellect had to reform first, before it was possible for the other side, referred to as the will, to do the same. So the present passage tells how the contents of the will were separated from those of the intellect and how they were concealed and stored away, so to speak, in order to block off any stimulus to the will. Had the appetites of the will been stirred up, it would have destroyed people, as will become clear from later explanations [§§660–661, 751, 760, 927], with the Lord's divine mercy.

These two sides, the intellect and will, are as clearly distinguished in us as they could possibly be. I was able to learn this unmistakably from the fact that intellectual information coming from spirits and angels enters the left side of the head or brain but impulses of the will enter the right side.[356] They affect the face in a similar way. When angelic spirits exert an influence, they waft in like the gentlest possible breezes. When evil spirits arrive, they essentially flood the left side of the brain with dreadful hallucinations and delusions and the right side with cravings. Their influence is like a deluge of fantasies and appetites.

642 Such observations clarify what this initial description of the ark involves, in requiring that the ark be built out of gopher wood, be divided into compartments,[357] and be tarred outside and in with tar. The meaning is that this second side—the will side—would be protected from the Flood and only the intellectual side would lie open, as depicted in verse 16 by the window, the door, and the lowest, second, and third levels.

Maybe these ideas seem unbelievable because they have never occurred to anyone before and people have not pictured the Lord's Word this way. Yet they are completely true. However, they represent the simplest and most general type of secret hidden from human knowledge. If I delved into the details, nobody would comprehend even a single one.

To take up the actual symbolism of the terms: it is clear from the Word that gopher wood means intense cravings and the compartments mean our two sides.

Gopher wood is a kind of wood loaded with sulfur, similar to fir and many others of the same kind. Sulfur is what makes this wood symbolic of cravings because sulfur catches fire quite easily.

The earliest people used gold, silver, bronze, iron, stone, and wood as metaphors and similes for human attributes. Gold stood for the most profound heavenly quality in us, bronze for a heavenly quality less profound, and wood for the lowliest, physical kind, rising out of the first two. Silver, on the other hand, was a metaphor or simile for the deepest possible spiritual quality, iron for a spiritual quality less deep, and stone for the lowest kind. When these substances are mentioned in the Word, the same qualities are symbolized by them on an inner plane. In Isaiah, for instance:

> For *bronze* I will bring in *gold;* and for *iron* I will bring in *silver;* and for *wood, bronze;* and for *stones, iron;* and I will make peace your property, and justice your taskmaster. (Isaiah 60:17)

This passage deals with the Lord's kingdom, which contains not metals like these but heavenly and spiritual elements. The presence of symbolism here is also evident from the fact that the verse speaks of peace and justice. The gold, bronze, and wood mentioned in it are interconnected and symbolize heavenly or will-related qualities, as I said. The silver, iron, and stone too are interconnected and symbolize spiritual or intellectual qualities. [2] In Ezekiel:

> They will prey on your resources, they will plunder your wares—your *stones* and your *wood.* (Ezekiel 26:12)

Obviously the resources and wares mean not those of a worldly type but those of a heavenly and spiritual type. Likewise the stones and wood; the stones are the contents of the intellect, and the wood, those of the will. In Habakkuk:

> A *stone* in the wall cries out, and a beam of *wood* answers. (Habakkuk 2:11)

The stone stands for the lowest plane of the intellect, and the wood, for the lowest plane of the will, which responds whenever a fact is produced from a person's store of sense-based information. In the same author:

> Doom to one who says to *wood,* "Wake up!" and says "Rouse yourself!" to silent *stone.* Will it teach [anyone anything]? Look, it is immobilized in gold and silver, and there is no spirit at its core. But Jehovah is in his holy temple. (Habakkuk 2:19, 20)

Here too wood stands for desire, and stone stands for the lowest level of the intellect, which is why the text connects it with silence and teaching. The absence of spirit at its core means that it does not represent anything heavenly or spiritual, as the Temple with its stone and wood does. The stone and wood are locked up in gold and silver with those who spend no time thinking about the things they represent. [3] In Jeremiah:

> Our water we drink at the cost of silver; our *wood* comes at a price. (Lamentations 5:4)

The water and silver symbolize the assets of the intellect, the wood, those of the will. In the same author:

> . . . saying to *wood,* "You are my father," and to *stone,* "You gave us birth." (Jeremiah 2:27)

The wood stands for desire in the will, from which such people trace their conception, and the stone, for facts learned through the senses, from which they have their birth. Many passages in the prophets talk of serving *wood* and *stone,* where these refer to sculptures of wood and stone. The meaning is that people were slaves to their desires and fantasies. Another expression refers to engaging in adultery with *wood* and *stone,* as in Jeremiah 3:9. In Hosea:

> The people ask questions of their *wood,* and their wand shows them the answer, because a spirit of whoredom has led them astray. (Hosea 4:12)

This stands for looking to a wooden idol—or in other words, to their appetites—for answers. In Isaiah:

> From yesterday a tophet[358] has been prepared; its pyre is *fire* and much *wood;* Jehovah's breath is like a river of burning *sulfur.* (Isaiah 30:33)

The fire, sulfur, and wood stand for filthy desires.

[4] Wood in general symbolizes what exists on the lowest plane of the will. Costly woods, such as cedar and so on, symbolize the good things there. The cedar wood in the Temple has such a meaning, as does the cedar wood used to cure leprosy³⁵⁹ (Leviticus 14:4, 6, 7) and the wood thrown into the bitter water at Marah, making it sweet (Exodus 15:25). These passages will be explained in their places, by the Lord's divine mercy.³⁶⁰ Wood that was not valuable, however, and that was made into idols or used for a funeral pyre or some similar purpose symbolizes cravings. The gopher wood in the current verse was of this type, because of the sulfur. In Isaiah, for instance:

> A day of vengeance for Jehovah! [Zion's] rivers will turn into pitch, and its dirt into *sulfur,* and its land will become burning pitch. (Isaiah 34:8, 9)

Pitch stands for horrendous delusions, sulfur for filthy desires.

644. The symbolism of the compartments as a person's two sides, that of will and that of intellect, is established by previous statements: there is a clear distinction between the two sides called will and intellect, and the result, as noted [§641], is the division of the human brain into two parts referred to as hemispheres.³⁶¹ Intellectual affairs belong to the left hemisphere and volitional ones to the right. This is the broadest division.

Both will and intellect are further divided into parts without number. The concerns of our intellect and the concerns of our will have so many categories that even the general ones could never be labeled or listed, still less the specific ones.

A person is like a kind of miniature heaven that corresponds to the world of spirits and heaven, where the Lord draws distinctions among all the genera and species of intellectual and volitional affairs. He divides them up and organizes them so perfectly that even the smallest has its own distinct identity. More on this below [§§657, 675, 684, 775], by the Lord's divine mercy.

The distinct groupings in heaven are called communities. In the Word they are called dwelling places, and in John 14:2 the Lord calls them places to live. Here they are called compartments, since they were a feature of the ark, which symbolizes a person who is part of the church.

645. The symbolism of *tarring it inside and out with tar* as being preserved from a flood of desire can be seen from what was said above [§§641–642]: the people of this church first needed to reform the functioning of their intellect and so were preserved from a flood of desire, which would destroy all the work of reformation.

The original [Hebrew] text does not actually say "tar with tar" but uses a term that refers to protection. The term comes from one for *atone* or *appease* and therefore involves similar ideas.[362] Atonement, or the appeasement of the Lord, is protection from a flood of evil.

646 Genesis 6:15. *"And this is how you must make it: three hundred cubits for the length of the ark, fifty cubits for its width, and thirty cubits for its height."*

The numbers here as before symbolize the remaining traces and their scarcity. The *length* is their holiness, the *width* their truth, and the *height* their goodness.

647 The symbolism assigned here must necessarily seem bizarre and far-fetched to any reader. It must be hard to accept, for instance, that *three hundred, fifty,* and *thirty* symbolize the remaining traces and how few they were. The same for the symbolism of *length, width,* and *height* as holiness, truth, and goodness.

But in the first place, see the statements and proofs concerning numbers above at verse 3 of this chapter [§575], which showed that one hundred twenty there symbolizes remaining traces of faith. In the second place, anyone can achieve clarity on this point who considers that people intent on the inner meaning, as good spirits and angels are, look beyond everything tied to the earth, the body, and the world alone. Accordingly they look beyond everything connected with numbers and measurement, and yet the Lord gives them a full perception of the Word's message, even though they are completely detached from such things. This being true, those details obviously must involve heavenly and spiritual concerns so remote from the literal meaning that we cannot even see they are meant. All heavenly and spiritual matters are like this, without exception.

Now you can see how insane it is to try to inquire into faith through the use of empirical data and factual knowledge and to believe nothing until this method allows you to grasp it.

648 The heavenly and spiritual symbolism of numbers and dimensions in the Word is plainly indicated by the taking of the measurements of the New Jerusalem and the new temple as recorded by John and Ezekiel. Anyone can see that the New Jerusalem and the new temple symbolize the Lord's kingdom in the heavens and on earth. Clearly that kingdom cannot be physically measured, and yet numerical dimensions of length, width, and height are specified.

From this, anyone can reach the conclusion that the numbers and measurements hold a sacred meaning. In John, for example:

> A reed like a staff was given to me, and the angel stood nearby. He told me, "Get up and *measure* God's *temple* and the altar and those worshiping in it." (Revelation 11:1)

And regarding the New Jerusalem:

> The wall of the *heavenly Jerusalem* was big and high, having *twelve* gates and on the gates *twelve* angels and names written, which are those of the twelve tribes of the children of Israel. On the east were *three* gates, on the north *three* gates, on the south *three* gates, on the west *three* gates. The wall of the city had *twelve* foundations and on them the twelve names of the Lamb's apostles. The one who was talking to me had a golden reed for measuring the city and its gates and its wall. The city lies square, and its *length* is as great as its *width*. So he measured the city with the reed at *twelve thousand* stadia. Its *length* and *width* and *height* were equal. He measured its wall at a *hundred forty-four cubits,* which is the measure of a human, that is, of an angel. (Revelation 21:12, 13, 14, 15, 16, 17)

[2] The number twelve turns up repeatedly in this passage. It is a sacred number because it symbolizes the holy things of faith, as was mentioned above at verse 3 of the present chapter [§577]. (The same thing will be demonstrated below at chapters 29 and 30 of Genesis [§§3858, 3862, 3913:1], with the Lord's divine mercy.) This is why it adds that the measure is the measure of a human, that is, of an angel.

The meaning is similar for the new temple and the new Jerusalem spoken of in Ezekiel, where again they are described by their measurements. See Ezekiel 40:3, 5, 7, 9, 11, 13, 14, 22, 25, 30, 36, 42, 47; 41:1–end; 42:5–15; Zechariah 2:1, 2. In these places too, the numbers have no meaning by themselves. The only meaning is the one abstracted from the numbers, which is that of something holy and either heavenly or spiritual. This holds true for all the dimensions of the ark in Exodus 25:10 as well, and those of the appeasement cover, golden table, dwelling place, and altar in Exodus 25:17, 23; 26; 27:1. Likewise for all the figures and dimensions connected with the Temple in 1 Kings 6:2, 3; and for many others.

Here, though, the numbers representing the measurements of the ark simply symbolize the remnant present in the people of this church when they were being reformed, and the remnant's meager size. This is established by the predominance of the number *five* in those figures, five symbolizing "some" or "a little" in the Word. An example from Isaiah:

> Gleanings will be *left* in it, like what is shaken off the olive tree—*two, three* fruits at the crown of the highest branch; four, *five* on the branches of a productive tree. (Isaiah 17:6)

Two, three, and five stand for a few. In the same author:

> One thousand will flee before the reproach of one, before the reproach of *five* you will flee, until you are *left* as a standing pole on the head of the mountain. (Isaiah 30:17)

Here again five stands for a few. The minimum fine added to any restitution people paid was a *fifth part* (Leviticus 5:16; 6:5; 22:14; Numbers 5:7), and the minimum surcharge when people redeemed an animal, a house, a field, or tithes was also a *fifth part* (Leviticus 27:13, 15, 19, 31).

650 The symbolism of the *length* as the holiness of the remnant, of the *width* as its truth, and of the *height* as its goodness, expressed in numbers, is not so easy to prove by the Word, because the meanings of each relate to the object or entity being described. Length, for example, when ascribed to time symbolizes what lasts to eternity, as in the phrase *length of days* (Psalms 23:6; 21:4). But when ascribed to distance, length symbolizes something holy, and this meaning follows from the former. The case with width and height is similar.

All earthly things have three dimensions, but the same dimensions cannot be applied to heavenly and spiritual things. When applied to something heavenly or spiritual—in abstraction from the dimensions—they mean more perfection or less, and also the nature or amount of the thing. So in the present verse the measurements imply the nature (they were traces) and amount (there were only a few).

651 Genesis 6:16. *"You must make a window for the ark and complete it to a cubit above. And you must place a door for the ark in its side. Lowest, second-level, and third-level [compartments] you must make in it."*

The *window* that was to be *completed to a cubit above* symbolizes the ability to understand. The *door on the side* symbolizes hearing the message. The *lowest, second-level, and third-level [compartments]* symbolize matters of fact, reason, and understanding.

652 The symbolism of the *window* as the ability to understand and of the *door* as hearing the message, and the resulting theme of this verse as a person's intellectual side, are indicated by what was said above. To be specific, the intellect was said to be the means of reformation for the people of that church [§§641, 642].

[Nowadays] people have two kinds of life, one belonging to the will and the other to the intellect. These become two kinds of life when will is absent and desire takes its place. The second, intellectual half is the part then capable of reforming. When the intellect has been reformed, we are able to receive a new will through it, allowing the two (that is, charity and faith) to continue as a single force in our lives.

Since at this point people were such that they had no will, but mere desire instead, the volitional side was closed off, as noted at verse 14 [§§640–642], and the other, intellectual side opened up, as described in the current verse.

Here is what happens during reformation, a process accomplished through conflict and trials. Evil spirits attach themselves to us, and they call up the facts we have heard—the ideas that seem rational to us—and nothing else. Their activity wards off any spirit who would arouse our desires.

There are, you see, two kinds of evil spirit: those who act on our rationalizations and those who act on our cravings. Those who stir up our rationalizations call forth all our misconceptions. They try to persuade us that falsity is truth, and more than that, they even turn our true ideas into false ones. These falsities we must combat when we are going through times of trial (although it is the Lord working through the angels connected to us who actually fights against them).

[2] After these battles have sifted out the falsities and apparently rid us of them, we are ready to accept the truth taught by faith. As long as falsity governs us, of course, we are completely unable to accept religious truth, because the false premises we have adopted stand in the way.

Once prepared in this way to accept religious truth, we can for the first time be sown with heavenly seed—the seed of charity. The seed of charity can never be sown in ground controlled by falsities, but only where truth rules.

That is how the reformation or rebirth of a spiritual person takes place. The same process took place among the people of the church described here, the church called Noah. That is why the current verse discusses the ark's window and door and its lowest, second-level, and third-level compartments or decks. All these things relate to our spiritual or intellectual self.

The above process, then, as churches today know, is to gain faith through hearing.[363] But faith is decidedly not a knowledge of faith's tenets, a knowledge of what should be believed; such knowledge is mere book-learning. Faith is acknowledgment. What is more, acknowledgment is impossible to anyone who lacks the most important element of faith, which is charity—that is, love for others and mercy. Where charity exists, acknowledgment exists, which is to say, faith exists. Anyone who imagines otherwise is as far from understanding what faith is as the earth is from heaven. When charity (the goodness belonging to faith) is present, acknowledgment (the truth belonging to faith) is present.

Consequently, the purpose of our rebirth through matters of fact, reason, and understanding is to prepare the soil of our minds to receive charity. Charity—or rather the living out of charity—then forms the basis of thought and action. At that point we are reformed or reborn, and not before.

655 The symbolism of the *window* to be *completed to a cubit above* as the ability to understand is visible to anyone from the statements just made. Further clarity comes from considering that if the subject is the construction of the ark, and if the ark symbolizes a person in the church, the ability to understand cannot be compared to anything but a window above.

In other places too the Word calls human intellect (in other words, our inner sight) a window, whether that intellect engages in reason or merely rationalizes. In Isaiah, for example:

> Afflicted one, tossed by a whirlwind, disconsolate: I will use rubies for your suns *(windows)*,[364] and make your gates of garnets and your whole border of desirable stones. (Isaiah 54:11, 12)

The word used here for windows is *suns* because of the light that windows let in or transmit. The suns or windows are ideas in the intellect—ones that spring from charity, which is why they are described as rubies. The gates are rational concepts from the same source. The border is organized knowledge and sensory evidence. All of these items have to do with the Lord's church.

[2] All the *windows* in the Temple at Jerusalem represented the same thing. The ones at the top represented matters of understanding, those in the middle represented matters of reason, while those on the bottom represented matters of fact and sense impressions (the annex being three-storied; see 1 Kings 6:4, 6, 8). The *windows* of [the temple in] the new Jerusalem described by Ezekiel (40:16, 22, 25, 33, 36) have a similar representation.

In Jeremiah:

> Death climbed through our *windows,* it came into our palaces, to cut off the toddler in the street, the youths in the avenues. (Jeremiah 9:21)

This is referring to windows of the middle story, which are matters of reason, and it says that these are obliterated. The toddler in the street is newborn truth.

As windows symbolize truth gained through the intellect and reason, they also symbolize falsity resulting from the misuse of reason. An example from the same author:

> Doom to those who build their house on what is not justice and their upper rooms on what is not judgment; who say, "I will build myself a house of [large] dimensions, and upper rooms that are spacious," and cut *windows* out for themselves (and it is paneled in cedar), painting it with vermilion. (Jeremiah 22:13, 14)

The windows stand for falsities adopted as premises. In Zephaniah:

> Packs of animals will lie down in its midst, every wild animal of that nation. Both the spoonbill and the qippod[365] will spend the night among its pomegranates. A voice will sing in the *window;* devastation is at the threshold. (Zephaniah 2:14)

This concerns Assyria and Nineveh, Assyria symbolizing the intellect, here one that has been devastated. A voice singing in the windows stands for misguided logic based on illusions.

By now it is apparent that the *door on the side* symbolizes hearing the message, and there is no need to bring in similar passages from the Word by way of confirmation. After all, the relationship between the ear and the internal sense organs is like that between the door on the side and the window above. And to say the same thing another way, it is like the relationship between hearing (which is the ear's function) and intellectual activity (which is a function of the internal senses).

The symbolism of the *lowest, second-level, and third-level [compartments]* as matters of fact, reason, and understanding also follows.

There are three levels to the contents of the human intellect.[366] The lowest has to do with factual knowledge, the middle with reason, and the highest with understanding. These levels are so clearly distinguished from each other that they never blur, but people are unaware of the distinction because they place life exclusively in what they can sense and learn about. Since they fixate on that level, they cannot see even that their ability to reason is different from their knowledge, still less that their ability to understand is different from it. The reality is that the Lord exerts an influence on our rational thinking through the things we truly understand, and on the data in our memory through our rational thinking, giving life to the senses of sight and hearing. This is true influx; this is the true connection between the soul and the body.[367]

Life could never exist in us if it did not flow from the Lord into the things we truly understand, and through these into the contents of our rational mind, and through these into the facts stored in our memory. Or to be more accurate, it first has to flow into the contents of our will and through these into the things we understand, and so on.

Even though we are enmeshed in falsity and evil, the Lord's life still enters in through the things we will and understand; but our rational mind absorbs those influences according to its form. This makes it possible for us to reason about, to reflect on, and to understand what is true and good. But more on these subjects below [§§6053–6058, 6189–6215, 6307–6327, 6466–6496, 6598–6626], with the Lord's divine mercy; and also something on the way life operates in animals [§§1902:1, 3646, 4776:4–5, 5850, 6323].

658 These three levels—understanding, reason, and knowledge, which are described in a general way as a person's intellectual possessions—are also symbolized by the windows of the three-floor annex to the Temple at Jerusalem (1 Kings 6:4, 6, 8), as noted [§655:2]. They were symbolized earlier as well, by the rivers going out from the Garden of Eden, which was in the east. In that passage, the east symbolizes the Lord, Eden symbolizes love in the will, the garden symbolizes the intelligence that grows out of it, and the rivers symbolize wisdom, reason, and knowledge. See what was said about these things earlier, at Genesis 2:10, 11, 12, 13, 14 [§§107–121].

659 Genesis 6:17. *"And I—yes, I—am bringing a flood of water on the earth, to destroy all flesh (all that has the breath of life in it) from under the heavens; all that is on the earth will pass away."*

The *flood* symbolizes a deluge of evil and falsity. *To destroy all flesh (all that has the breath of life in it) from under the heavens* means that all the descendants of the earliest church destroyed themselves. *All that is on the earth will pass away* symbolizes the people who were part of that church and who adopted its nature.

660 The symbolism of the *flood* as a deluge of evil and falsity is established by statements above concerning the descendants of the earliest church. There it was said that sordid cravings took control of them and that they merged the teachings of faith with those cravings [§§560, 568:1, 570, 582, 593, 640]. The consequence was that they adopted falsities as their convictions [§§562, 581], blotting out everything true or good [§§573, 586a, 627–628, 632, 635], and at the same time shutting off access to the remnant within them so that it could not do its work [§§563, 571]. This inevitably resulted in their self-destruction [§§560, 563, 592, 594, 631, 636, 637].

When the path to the remnant within us is shut off, we cease to be human, because angels can no longer protect us. Evil spirits take thorough possession of us instead, and their only interest and desire is to annihilate us. Such was the cause of the extinction of the pre-Flood race, as portrayed in the worldwide deluge of the Flood.

Furthermore, an influx of fantasies and appetites coming from evil spirits is not unlike a flood, and that is why the Word frequently calls it a flood, as the remarks introducing the next chapter [§705] will show, with the Lord's divine mercy.

661 The meaning of *to destroy all flesh (all that has the breath of life in it) under the heavens* as the fact that all the descendants of the earliest church destroyed themselves can be seen from what was just said. It can also be seen from earlier sections [§§560, 562–563] describing how the mentality that the same people inherited cumulatively from their forebears made them more disposed than others to soak up monstrous convictions of this type. The main reason was that they immersed the religious teachings they possessed in the torrent of their desires and so took on this disposition.

Circumstances are different for those who have never learned what the true faith teaches but live in complete ignorance. They cannot do as that church did; they have no way of profaning holy things and so blocking off access to the remnant within themselves. As a result, they do not drive the Lord's angels away.

[2] The remnant within us, as already stated [§561], includes every lesson in innocence, in charity, in mercy, and in religious truth that we have received from the Lord since childhood. Each and every trace of those lessons is stored away. Without them, innocence, charity, and mercy would be wholly absent from our thinking and our actions. In that case, nothing good or true would be present, and we would be worse

than savage beasts. The outcome would be the same if a remnant of these qualities did stay with us but unclean desires and dreadful, misconceived persuasions blocked its outlet, preventing it from operating. That is what happened with the people predating the Flood who exterminated themselves. They are the ones meant by *all flesh (all that has the breath of life in it) under the heavens.*

[3] *Flesh* symbolizes all people in general, and body-centered people in particular, as shown already [§574]. *The breath of life* symbolizes all life in general, but strictly speaking, it is the life in those who have been reborn. Here, then, it symbolizes the final generation of the earliest church. Although no living faith survived in them, they still had acquired from their ancestors a germ of that faith—which they smothered. It is here called the breath of life; in Genesis 7:22, it is referred to in the phrase, "in whose nostrils was the breath of living spirit."

Flesh under the heavens symbolizes what is limited to our bodily plane, whereas the *heavens* are the truth that we understand and the good that we will. Once our bodily concerns are disconnected from truth in the intellect and good in the will, we can no longer remain alive. What sustains us is the bond we have with heaven, that is, with the Lord through heaven.

662 *All that is on the earth will pass away* symbolizes the people who were part of that church and who adopted its nature. As demonstrated earlier [§§566–567, 620], the earth does not mean the whole inhabited world, only the part that constituted the church. So the verse is not referring to any kind of flood, let alone a worldwide one. It is talking about the death, the "drowning," of those in the church who were cut off from the remnant within them and consequently from any comprehension of truth or will to do good; which is to say that they were cut off from the heavens.

Scriptural passages quoted earlier attest to the symbolism of the *earth* or land as the area where the church existed, and so as the inhabitants of that area.[368] The following verses also confirm the symbolism. In Jeremiah:

> This is what Jehovah has said: "The whole *earth* will be stripped bare, yet I will not make a full end. Because of this the *earth* will mourn and the heavens above will be draped in black." (Jeremiah 4:27, 28)

The earth stands for residents in the area where the church, which had been devastated, existed. In Isaiah:

> I will shake heaven, and the *earth* will quake out of its place. (Isaiah 13:13)

The earth here stands for an individual in the church's territory who is to suffer devastating experiences. In Jeremiah:

> The people stabbed by Jehovah will on that day reach from the ends of the *earth* to the ends of the *earth*. (Jeremiah 25:33)

The ends of the earth here do not mean the entire globe but only the tract of land where the church was. So they symbolize the people who belonged to the church. In the same author:

> I am calling for a sword upon all the inhabitants of the *land*. Upheaval has come all the way to the ends of the *earth*, because Jehovah has a quarrel against the nations. (Jeremiah 25:29, 31)

Again it is not the whole globe that is meant but only the territory of the church and so the inhabitant there, that is, a person who belongs to the church. In this passage the nations stand for falsities. In Isaiah:

> Watch: Jehovah is leaving his place to exact punishment for wickedness in the inhabitant of the *land*. (Isaiah 26:21)

The meaning here is similar. In the same author:

> Are you not listening? Has it not been pointed out to you from the beginning? Do you not understand the foundations of the *earth*? (Isaiah 40:21)

In the same author:

> Jehovah is creating the heavens; he is God, forming the *earth* and making it; he is also establishing it. (Isaiah 45:18)

The earth stands for a member of the church. In Zechariah:

> This is the saying of Jehovah as he stretches out the heavens and founds the *earth* and forms the human spirit in the middle of it. (Zechariah 12:1)

Plainly the earth stands for a person in the church.

The earth (or land) is distinguished from the ground, just as a person in the church is distinguished from the church itself, or as love is distinguished from faith.

Genesis 6:18. *"And I will set up my pact with you; and you will enter the ark: you and your sons and your wife and your sons' wives with you."*

Setting up a pact means that [the people referred to as Noah] would be reborn. That *he was to enter the ark, as were his sons [and his wife] and his sons' wives* means that they would be saved. The *sons* are truth and the *wives* goodness.

664   The last verse was about people who destroyed themselves. This one is about people who were being reborn and so would be saved, who are referred to as "Noah."

665   The meaning of *setting up a pact* as the fact that they would be reborn can be seen clearly from this: No pact can mediate between the Lord and humanity except that of being united by love and faith. So a pact symbolizes union. This kind of union is the heavenly marriage, which is the truest compact. The heavenly marriage, or union, can exist only in those who are reborn, and accordingly a pact in the broadest sense symbolizes rebirth itself. The Lord enters into a compact with us when he regenerates us, and for this reason the ancients saw a pact as representing nothing but regeneration.

The literal meaning gives no clue that the covenant made with Abraham, Isaac, and Jacob and so often renewed with their descendants had to do with any others than those actual people. But they were people incapable of rebirth, since they equated worship with outward observances alone. They also saw holiness in external elements without considering any connection to internal values. So the pacts struck with them could do no more than represent regeneration.

None of their rituals did more than this. Neither did Abraham, Isaac, and Jacob themselves, who represented different aspects of love and faith. These men were like the priests and high priests, who were able to represent a heavenly and very holy priesthood no matter what their character was—even those who were criminal. When people serve to represent something, no thought is given to their personality, only to the quality represented. By the same token, all the monarchs of Israel and Judah—even the worst ones—represented the Lord's royal power. In fact the pharaoh who raised Joseph up over the land of Egypt also represented that power.

This consideration and many others (to be mentioned later, by the Lord's divine mercy) show that the numerous covenants with the children of Jacob were nothing more than rituals that held a representative meaning.[369]

666   The fact that a pact means nothing else than rebirth with all it entails can be seen from numerous passages in the Word that call the Lord himself a covenant [or pact]. The term is applied to him because he is the only one to regenerate us and the only one to whom the reborn individual looks. He is also the all-in-all of love and faith.

The fact that the Lord is the pact itself can be seen in Isaiah:

> I, Jehovah, have called you in justice and am holding your hand and guarding you; and I will give you as a *pact* with the people, as a light for the nations. (Isaiah 42:6)

The pact stands for the Lord, while the light for the nations means faith. Isaiah 49:6, 8 has a similar message. In Malachi:

> Watch: I am sending my angel, and suddenly to his temple will come the Lord, whom you are seeking, and the *angel of the covenant,* whom you desire. Watch: He is coming! Who can endure the day of his coming? (Malachi 3:1, 2)

In this passage the Lord is called the angel of the covenant. The Sabbath is referred to as an *eternal pact* in Exodus 31:16 because it symbolizes the Lord. It also symbolizes us when he has regenerated us to the point of being heavenly.

[2] As the Lord is the pact itself, we can conclude that everything binding us to the Lord is part of the contract. Love and faith, then, are part of it, as is everything that comes of love and faith. These things are the Lord's, and the Lord is in them. Consequently the covenant itself is in those things wherever they are received. And they are not received except in one who has been reborn. Everything in a person reborn that belongs to the Regenerator—the Lord—is part of the compact or, in other words, *is* the compact. In Isaiah, for example:

> My mercy will not withdraw from you, and the *compact* of my *peace* will not recede. (Isaiah 54:10)

The mercy and the compact of peace are the Lord and everything that is his. In the same author:

> Bend your ear and come to me; listen and let your soul live, and I will strike with you an *eternal pact*—the reliable mercies [that I showed] to David. Here, now, I have made him a witness to the peoples, a leader and lawgiver for the nations. (Isaiah 55:3, 4)

David stands for the Lord. The eternal pact consists in attributes of the Lord's and is fulfilled by means of them. These are the things meant by going to him and listening so that our souls may live. [3] In Jeremiah:

> I will give them one heart and one way, to fear me every day, with good result to them and to their children after them. And I will strike an *eternal*

pact with them, [pledging] that I will not turn away from doing good to them; and fear of me I will put into their heart. (Jeremiah 32:39, 40)

These words stand for people who are being reborn. They stand also for qualities in the person who has been reborn, those qualities being the one heart and one way. One heart and one way in turn are charity and faith, which are the Lord's and so are part of the compact. In the same author:

"Look! The days are coming," says Jehovah, "when I will strike a *new pact* with the house of Israel and with the house of Judah unlike the *pact* that I struck with their ancestors, because they nullified my *pact*. But this is the *pact* that I will strike with the house of Israel after these days: I will put my law in the midst of them, and upon their heart I will write it, and I will become their God, and they will become my people." (Jeremiah 31:31, 32, 33)

This explains openly what a covenant is: love for the Lord and faith in him as adopted by one who is regenerating. [4] The same author calls love a *compact with the day* and faith a *compact with the night* (Jeremiah 33:20). In Ezekiel:

I, Jehovah, will become their God, and my servant David will be chief in their midst. And I will strike a *pact of peace* with them and bring an end on the earth to the evil wild animal; and they will live securely in the wilderness and sleep in forests. (Ezekiel 34:24, 25)

This is obviously about regeneration. David stands for the Lord. In the same author:

David will be chief over them forever. I will strike a *pact of peace* with them; it will be an *eternal pact* with them. I will put my sanctuary in their midst forever. (Ezekiel 37:25, 26)

Again this is about rebirth. David and the sanctuary stand for the Lord. In the same author:

I entered into a *pact* with you, and you were mine; and I washed you with water and cleaned your blood off you and anointed you with oil. (Ezekiel 16:8, 9, 11)

Plainly this is about rebirth. In Hosea:

I will strike a *pact* with them on that day—with the wild animal of the field, and with the bird in the heavens and the creeping animal of the earth. (Hosea 2:18)

This stands for regeneration. The wild animal of the field stands for what the will holds, the bird in the heavens for what the intellect holds. In David:

> He has sent redemption to his people; he has commanded his *covenant* forever. (Psalms 111:9)

This stands for rebirth. It is called a covenant or contract because it is given and received.

[5] There are some, however, who do not regenerate. To put it another way, there are some who consider the outward show of worship to be worship, and who value and revere themselves, their own wishes, and their own thoughts as gods. Because they alienate themselves from the Lord, they are portrayed as nullifying the compact. In Jeremiah, for instance:

> They abandoned the *compact* of Jehovah their God and bowed down to other gods and served them. (Jeremiah 22:9)

In Moses:

> Whoever goes against the *compact* by serving other gods—the sun, the moon, the whole army of the heavens—will be stoned. (Deuteronomy 17:2 and following verses)

The sun stands for self-love, the moon for assumptions based on falsities, and the army of the heavens for the falsities themselves.

All of this now indicates that the ark of the covenant, containing the testimony (or covenant), was the Lord himself; that the book of the covenant was the Lord himself (Exodus 24:4, 7; 34:4, 5, 6, 7, 27;[370] Deuteronomy 4:13, 23); and that the blood of the covenant was the Lord himself (Exodus 24:6, 8). The Lord alone is the Regenerator, so the covenant is regeneration itself.

667 The meaning of *he was to enter the ark, as were his sons and his wife and his sons' wives* as the fact that they would be saved can be seen from the things said above. It can also be seen from things said below [§711] showing that they would be saved through being reborn.

668 The fact that the *sons* are truth and the *wives* goodness was also shown earlier, at Genesis 5:4 [§§489–491]. That verse spoke of sons and daughters but this one speaks of sons and their wives, because *wives* are the good connected with truth.

No truth would ever come into being if something good or pleasurable did not exist for it to grow out of. Goodness and pleasure have life in them, but truth does not have any life besides that which it gains from goodness and pleasure. It is from these that truth forms and sprouts. The same applies to faith (a matter of truth), which comes from love (a matter of goodness). Truth is like light. No light exists that does not come from the sun, that is, flame; this is the source from which light develops.

Truth is simply the form of goodness, and faith is simply the form of love. Truth develops out of goodness according to the quality of the goodness, and faith develops according to the quality of love or charity.

This, then, is the reason for the mention of a wife and wives, symbolizing the good connected with truth. For the same reason, the next verse says that two of each, a male and a female, were to enter the ark. Unless good is attached, no regeneration occurs.

669 Genesis 6:19. *"And of every living thing, of all flesh, you must bring pairs of each into the ark to keep them alive with you. A male and a female they must be."*

A *living soul* symbolizes what lies in the intellect. *All flesh* symbolizes what lies in the will. *You must bring pairs of each into the ark* symbolizes the regeneration of these entities. A *male* is something true and a *female* something good.

670 The symbolism of a *living soul* as what lies in the intellect and of *all flesh* as what lies in the will is established by statements made above and others to follow.

In the Word, a *living soul* means every animal in general, no matter what kind, as it did at Genesis 1:20, 21, 24, and 2:19. In the current verse, though, since *all flesh* follows on its heels, it symbolizes the intellectual realm. The reason was given before [§§641, 652–654]: the people of this church first had to be reborn as to the ideas in their intellect. For the same reason, the next verse starts with the mention of birds, symbolizing matters of understanding, or of reason, and moves on to animals, symbolizing matters of will.

Flesh specifically symbolizes the body-centered part of the will.

671 The symbolism of *you must bring pairs of each into the ark to keep them alive* as the regeneration of these entities can be seen from remarks on the previous verse. There it was said that truth can be regenerated only by what is good and pleasurable, and the attributes of faith, therefore, only by the qualities of charity. In consequence the present verse says "pairs of each must go in," or to be specific, both something of the truth that inhabits the intellect and something of the goodness that inhabits the will.

People who have not been reborn have neither an understanding of truth nor a will to do good. (They only appear to have them, although they do have faculties that everyone calls by those names.) They are indeed capable of grasping truth on the rational and factual levels, but such truth is not alive. They are also seemingly able to will what is good, but the goodness is not living. It is like the good deeds that non-Christians do, or even like the good actions of unreasoning animals, and these are merely analogous to good. Truth and goodness can never come to life in us before we regenerate and so before the Lord gives them life.

In the other world people can easily tell what is not alive and what is alive. When they come across truth that is not living, they immediately sense it as something material, fibrous, and shut off. When they come across goodness that is not living, they perceive it as something wooden, bonelike, or stony. The truth and goodness that the Lord has brought to life, though, is open, vibrant, and full of spiritual and heavenly essence, offering unhindered access all the way to the Lord. It displays this nature in every idea and action, down to the tiniest aspects. This, then, is the reason the verse says that pairs were to enter the ark *to be kept alive*.

672 I have already said and shown [§§54, 476, 489–491] that a *male* is something true and a *female* something good.

Every part of us, no matter how small, has something equivalent to a marriage in it. Whatever exists in our intellect, therefore, is coupled with something in our will. Without this mating, or marriage, we produce nothing at all.

673 Genesis 6:20. *"Of the bird by its kind, and of the beast by its kind, of everything creeping on the ground by its kind—pairs of all must go in to you, to stay alive."*

A *bird* symbolizes matters of intellect, a *beast* matters of will, and *something creeping on the ground* both at the lowest level. *Two of each must go in, to stay alive,* here as above symbolizes the regeneration of these entities.

674 The symbolism of a *bird* as matters of intellect or of reason was shown earlier, at §40. So was the symbolism of a *beast* or animal as matters of will, or emotions, at §§45, 46, 142, 143, 246. The symbolism of *something creeping on the ground* as both at the lowest level can be seen from the fact that anything creeping on the ground is as low as possible. The symbolism of *pairs of all must go in, to stay alive,* as the regeneration of these entities was explained at the last verse.

675 The present verse speaks of *every kind* of bird, *every kind* of beast, and *every kind* of creeping thing. In this regard it needs to be known that in each of us the contents of the intellect and of the will divide into countless major categories and an even greater number of specific kinds, each perfectly distinct from the others, even though we are unaware of the fact. During our regeneration, the Lord brings every single one of these forward in its sequence, disentangling it and setting it in its proper place so that he can turn it in the direction of truth and goodness and unite it with them. This he does in many different ways, depending on the states we go through, which are also beyond number.

Still, none of these things—the individual genera and species, the individual stages of our life—can ever be perfected to eternity. Each embraces factors whose number is unlimited when taken separately and even higher when compounded. We do not even realize this is true; still less can we see how we are reborn. That is what the Lord says to Nicodemus about a person's regeneration:

> The spirit blows where it wishes, and you hear its voice, yet you do not know where it is coming from or where it is going off to; this is the way with everyone who is born from the spirit.[371] (John 3:8)

676. Genesis 6:21. *"And take for yourself some food of every type that is eaten and gather it to yourself, and it will serve you and them as food."*

He was to take for himself some food of every type that was eaten symbolizes what is pleasurable and good. *He was to gather it to himself* symbolizes what is true. *It was to serve him and them as food* symbolizes both.

677. To describe the food of people who are to be reborn: Before we can be reborn, we have to be equipped with everything instrumental to rebirth. Good, joyful feelings serve the needs of our will, while truth from the Lord's Word, along with support and confirmation from other sources, serves our intellectual needs. Till we receive this preparation, we cannot be regenerated. Those supplies are our food. That is why we cannot be regenerated before we reach adulthood. But we each have foods particularly appropriate to us that seem to be all our own, and the Lord provides us with them prior to our rebirth.

678. The symbolism of *he was to take for himself some food of every type that was eaten* as what is pleasurable and good can be seen from statements to the effect that pleasure and goodness are the constituents of human life but that truth is not so much so [§§32–34, 503, 590, 668]. This is because truth acquires its life from what is pleasing and good.

From the time of childhood right through to old age, no item of knowledge or reason is ever instilled in us unless it enters by way of something pleasant and good. Because the human soul lives on goodness and pleasure and sustains itself by means of them, they are called food.[372] They actually are food, since the soul could never survive without them, as anyone who is willing to pay attention can see.

679 The symbolism of *he was to gather it to himself* as what is true follows as a consequence, since *gather* is used of the items in our memory; they are "gathered" there. In addition, this clause involves the idea that both—goodness and truth—are collected in us before we undergo regeneration. Without a collection of good feelings and true ideas to serve as instruments for the Lord's work, we could never be regenerated, as just noted. This leads to the conclusion that *it was to serve him and them as food* symbolizes both.

680 Everyone can see that goodness and truth are a person's genuine food. Anyone deprived of them is dead, not living. The kinds of food that our souls feed on when we are [spiritually] dead are the pleasures of evil and the gratifications provided by falsity; these are lethal foods. So are the pleasures and satisfactions afforded by bodily, worldly, and earthly things, which have no inherent life.

What is more, people devoid of life have no idea what spiritual and heavenly food is. They are so ignorant on this score that every time the Word mentions food or bread, they suppose it means physical food. Take, for instance, the phrase from the Lord's Prayer, *Give us daily bread;* they think this refers only to the nourishment of the body, or if their thinking stretches any further, they allow that it also includes the body's other needs, such as clothing, riches, and so on. They even argue bitterly against the notion that any other kind of food is meant. Yet they see clearly that the words before and after this phrase have to do only with heavenly and spiritual concerns and that the Lord's kingdom is the subject of the prayer. They are also capable of grasping that the Word of the Lord is spiritual and heavenly. [2] From this circumstance and others like it, the extent to which people today focus on the body is obvious enough. So is their desire (like that of Jews) to interpret everything the Word says as dealing with the crudest of material concerns.[373]

The Lord himself teaches plainly what food and bread mean in his Word. Of food he speaks this way in John:

> Jesus said, "Work, not for the *food* that perishes, but for the *food* that lasts to eternal life, which the Son of Humankind gives you." (John 6:27)

Of bread he says in the same author:

> Your ancestors ate manna in the wilderness and died. This is the *bread* that came down from heaven so that a person could *eat* of it and not die. I am the living *bread* who came down from heaven; if anyone eats of this *bread,* that person will live forever. (John 6:49, 50, 51, 58)

Some today say, as those who heard this did,

> "This saying is hard. Who can listen to it?" And they backed away and no longer walked with him. (John 6:60, 66)

The Lord told them:

> The words that I am speaking to you are spirit and are life. (John 6:63)

[3] In similar fashion, water symbolizes the spiritual aspects of faith. The Lord speaks of it this way in John:

> Jesus said, "Anyone who drinks this water will be thirsty again. But those who drink the water that I give them will never be thirsty to eternity. Instead, the water that I give them will become a spring of water gushing up in them to provide eternal life." (John 4:13, 14)

People do exist today, however, who resemble the woman the Lord talked to by the spring, when she answered,

> Lord, give me this water, to keep me from being thirsty and coming here to draw! (John 4:15)

[4] Many passages in the Word establish that *food* there stands only as a symbol for spiritual and heavenly nourishment, which is faith in the Lord and love. In Jeremiah, for instance:

> The enemy has stretched its hand out over every pleasant thing in Jerusalem. Because she has seen the nations, they have come into her sanctuary, about which you commanded, "They shall not come into your assembly." All the people are groaning, looking for *bread*. They have exchanged what is pleasant to them for *food* to revive their soul. (Lamentations 1:10, 11)

These words mean no other bread or food than a spiritual kind, since they deal with the sanctuary. In the same author:

> I called out to my lovers; they deceived me. My priests and my elders expired in the city, for they had tried to find *food* for themselves and would have brought their soul back [to life]. (Lamentations 1:19)

The meaning is similar. In David:

> All of them wait for you to give them their *food* in its season. You give to them; they *gather*. You open your hand; they *receive abundant good*. (Psalms 104:27, 28)

This too stands for spiritual and heavenly food. [5] In Isaiah:

> Everyone who is thirsty, come to the *water,* and whoever does not have silver, come, buy and *eat!* And come, without silver and without the price buy *wine and milk!* (Isaiah 55:1)

The wine and milk stand for spiritual and heavenly drink. In the same author:

> The young woman will conceive and deliver a child, and you shall call his name Immanuel. *He will eat butter and honey,* in order to know to spurn what is evil and choose what is *good.* It will happen on account of the abundance of *milk-*making that *they will eat butter,* since butter and honey are what everyone who is *left* in the middle of the land will eat. (Isaiah 7:14, 15, 22)

Eating honey and butter is taking nourishment that is heavenly and at the same time spiritual. Those left in the land stand for remnants [of goodness and truth]. Malachi also discusses these:

> Bring all tithes to the treasure house, so that there may be *food* in my House. (Malachi 3:10)

Tithes stand for remnants. For more on the symbolism of food, see §§56–58, 276.

The best place to learn about heavenly and spiritual food is in the other life. Angels and spirits sustain their life not with the kind of food the world offers but with every word that issues from the Lord's mouth, as he himself teaches in Matthew 4:4.

The situation is that the Lord alone is the life of all. From him comes each and every thing that angels and spirits think, say, or do. This is true not only of angels and good spirits but also of evil spirits. They speak and do evil because that is how they receive and pervert all the good and true things that are the Lord's. The form of the recipient determines the way a thing is received and the effect it has. The case is comparable to that of various objects struck by the sun's light that turn the light they receive into hideous, unpleasant colors according to their makeup and the arrangement and structure of their parts, while other objects turn the light into lovely, pleasing colors.

So the entirety of heaven and the entire world of spirits live on everything that comes out of the Lord's mouth, and every individual there receives life from the same source. Indeed, this applies not only to heaven and the world of spirits but to the entire human race as well. I know that people will scoff, but I can still assert from years of constant experience that it is absolutely true.

Evil spirits in the world of spirits are also reluctant to believe that it is so. For this reason they have received many personal demonstrations, which were so effective that they have begrudgingly confessed the situation to be so.

If angels, spirits, or people on earth were to be deprived of this food, they would die instantly.

682. Genesis 6:22. *And Noah did everything that God had commanded him; that is what he did.*

Noah did everything that God had commanded him means it happened in this way. The repetition of *did* means that it involves both [good and truth].

683. Again, the double mention of *did* means that it involves both. In this connection, it needs to be realized that the Word, especially in the prophets, describes a single phenomenon in two ways. In Isaiah, for instance:

> He has passed by in peace; he did not tread the path with his feet. Who has managed and done it? (Isaiah 41:3, 4)

One expression looks to good, the other to truth. In other words, one looks to what exists in the will, the other to what exists in the intellect. So *passing by in peace* involves qualities of the will, *not treading the path with his feet* qualities of the intellect. The same holds for *managing* and *doing*.

This is how the Word ties together the properties of the will and those of the intellect, that is, those of love and those of faith, or in other words, heavenly attributes and spiritual ones. At each point it achieves a kind of marriage and a reflection of the heavenly marriage. The repetition of a single word here achieves the same purpose.

The Communities That Make Up Heaven

684. THERE are three heavens. Good spirits inhabit the first, angelic spirits the second, and angels the third. Each heaven is deeper and purer than the one before it. The result is that the heavens are perfectly distinct from one another.

The first heaven, the second heaven, and the third heaven are each divided into numberless communities. Each community consists of many people who because of the compatibility and unanimity among them form a single personality, so to speak. And all the communities together form a single human being.

The distinctions among the communities are created by differences in mutual love and in faith in the Lord. Those differences are so far beyond counting that I cannot list even the most universal kinds.

Not the smallest difference exists that is not fitted into its exact place in the overall plan. In this way it can unite with all the other pieces in perfect concord to form a common whole, and the common whole can contribute to unity among the individual pieces. Thus everything combines for the happiness of the whole (rising from the individuals' happiness) and for the individuals' happiness (rising from the happiness of the whole).

In consequence, each angel and each community is an image of the whole of heaven and a kind of heaven-in-miniature.[374]

685 The ties that connect people in the next life are remarkable. They are like family ties on earth, in that some acknowledge others as parents, as children, as siblings, as blood relatives, and as more distant connections. Their love for one another reflects these different levels of relationship. The varieties come in unlimited number. The way they are communicated and perceived is so exquisite that it cannot be described.

People there pay no attention at all to who was whose parent, child, blood relative, or connection on earth. They do not care what a person's outer identity was like, whether the individual had importance or wealth, and so on. They look only at differences in mutual love and in faith, and at what kind of capacity for welcoming love and faith a person has received from the Lord while living in the world.

686 The Lord's mercy is love for all of heaven and all of the human race. It is this mercy—and so it is the Lord alone—that organizes all the elements, large and small, into communities. This same mercy gives rise to the love in marriage and consequently the love parents have for their children. These loves are fundamental and primary. From them come all other loves in boundless variety, organized into communities and delineated with utter clarity.

687 Since that is what heaven is like, no angel or spirit could ever have any life without being part of some community, without joining in harmony with many others. Community is simply harmony among many. No one's life is ever isolated from the life of others.

In fact no angel, spirit, or society could ever have any life—could ever be affected by good, form an intention, be affected by truth, form a thought—without a tight link to heaven and the world of spirits through other members of the group.

It is the same for the human race. Whoever we are, whatever we are like, we need the same kind of link to heaven through the angels with us, and to the world of spirits and even hell through the spirits with us. Otherwise we could never engage in life; we could never be affected by good or truth, never form an intention or thought. Everyone living in the body associates with some community of spirits and angels, despite being totally unaware of the fact. If we were not closely connected to heaven and the world of spirits through the spiritual society we associate with, we could not survive for a minute.

The situation resembles that in the human body. When any part of it lacks connection with the rest through nerve fibers and blood vessels and so lacks the means for performing its function, it ceases to be part of the body. Instead the body immediately isolates it and rejects it as being devoid of life.

When we come into the next life, we are shown the actual communities we lived in and associated with during bodily life. On entering that society after bodily life, we come into the selfsame life we lived while in the body, and on that life we build a new one. Depending on the life we carried out in the body, then, we either go down to hell or are raised into heaven.

688 Since there is this kind of bond connecting all with each and each with all, it also extends to the most minute details of feeling and thought.

689 We are all, as a whole and as individuals, in such flawless balance at the heavenly, spiritual, and earthly levels that none of us can think, feel, or act unless inspired by many others. Yet each of us imagines that we act by ourselves in absolute freedom.

In a similar way, nothing ever exists that is not balanced by its opposite, and also by intermediate steps between them. So each of us by ourselves and numbers of us taken together live in the most perfect balance.

For this reason, nothing bad can happen to anyone without being immediately counterbalanced. When a surplus of evil accumulates, the evil or the person committing it is punished by the law of equilibrium—spontaneously, it seems. But this never occurs except in order that good may come out of it.

This pattern (and so this balance) constitutes the design of heaven, which the Lord alone shapes, arranges, and preserves to eternity.

690 Another fact to be aware of is that no community can ever be completely and absolutely the same as another, and within a community, no individual can ever be exactly like another. To everything there is a concordant and harmonious variety. The Lord brings this variety into order in such a way that everything bends toward a common goal. This he accomplishes by means of our love for him and faith in him. The result is unity.

Accordingly, heaven and its joy are never completely and exactly the same for one person as for another. Just as love and faith come in great variety, so do the heaven and heavenly joy that love and faith contain.

691 So much in general for the communities [of heaven], on the basis of my repeated experience over a long period of time. More detail is to come, with the Lord's divine mercy.[375]

Genesis 7

Hell

692 PEOPLE have only the most general concept of hell,[376] just as they do of heaven, and that concept is almost so vague as to be none at all. It is like the picture of the world at large available to those who have never been outside their cabins in the forest. They know nothing about its empires and countries, let alone its forms of government, and least of all about society and the way people live in society. Until they know these things, their concept of the world cannot be more than the sketchiest notion, which is practically no notion whatever. Likewise with regard to heaven and hell. In reality, both heaven and hell contain too many marvels to count—indefinitely more than any planet could hold.

The vast number of wonders there can be seen from this one thought: Just as no two people ever have the same heaven, no two ever have the same hell, and all the souls that have ever existed in the world since the beginning of creation flock together there.

693 Love for the Lord and for one's neighbor constitutes heaven, as do the joy and happiness it brings. By the same token, spiteful opposition to the Lord and one's fellow human constitutes hell, as do the penalties and torture it brings.

Hatred comes in countless different types and even more variations on those types. For every variety of hatred, there is a hell.

694 By the Lord's arrangement and through mutual love, heaven forms a single human being with a single animating soul, so it looks toward a single goal: the preservation and salvation of all to eternity. In contrast, hell, out of its sense of autonomy and through self-love and materialism—through hatred, in other words—forms a single devil with a single animus, so it looks toward a single goal: the destruction and damnation of all to eternity. Thousands and thousands of times have I experienced the whole effort of hell as turning in this direction. If the Lord, then, did not preserve us all, every single solitary moment, we would be snuffed out.

695 However, the Lord forms and organizes hell in such a way that the bonds and restraints of people's own desires and fantasies hold them fast.

Their whole life consists in those desires and fantasies, and because their life is a living death, it turns into tortures so dreadful that they cannot be described.

The most intense pleasure of their life is to punish, torment, and inflict pain on each other. They use methods utterly unknown in the world. By these methods they know how to trigger acute sensations, exactly as though their victims were still in the body. They also know how to produce appalling, terrifying hallucinations, not to mention many other kinds of frights and terrors. The Devil's crew takes such passionate delight in doing this that if they could increase and intensify the pain and anguish infinitely, they still would not rest satisfied; they would burn to add another infinity of grief. But the Lord negates their efforts and softens their abuse.

Everything in the other life, overall and in particular, exists in such perfect balance that evil punishes itself. In this way, evil contains its own penalty. So does falsity, which rebounds on the person who subscribes to it. We each bring on ourselves our own punishment and torture, and at the same time we bring on the diabolical crowd that inflicts it.

The Lord never sends anyone to hell but wants to lead everyone out. Still less does he inflict pain. Instead, since evil spirits actually run to get there, the Lord turns all the punishment and torment to good and puts it to some use. No penalty can ever exist unless the Lord has some purpose in mind for it, because the Lord's kingdom is a realm of purpose and usefulness. But the purposes that hellish spirits can serve are ignominious. When performing those services, they are not in as much pain, but when they cease to be useful, they are returned to hell.

We each have at least two evil spirits and two angels present with us. Through the evil spirits we have contact with hell, and through the angels we have contact with heaven. If we were not in touch with both, we could not possibly survive for a minute. So every one of us, although completely unaware of the fact, associates with some group of hellish spirits; but their torment is not transmitted to us, because we are undergoing preparation for eternal life. In the other world, we are sometimes shown the community we had been part of, since we go back to it and therefore to the life we had lived on earth. From there we either head toward hell or go up to heaven.

People who do not lead good, charitable lives or allow the Lord to guide them are part of the hellish crowd. After death they become devils themselves.

In addition to hell itself, there is also a process of devastation, described at length in the Word.377 We take with us into the next life innumerable evils and falsities acquired from the sins we have actually committed. These we heap up and twine together, even those of us who have lived honorably. Before the honest can be lifted into heaven, their evils and falsities have to be dispelled, and this process is called devastation.

There are many kinds of devastation, and it can last for a longer or shorter time. Some people are taken to heaven after a very brief period, and some go immediately after death.

699. I have been sent down to hell several times in order to see the torture that those in hell go through and the devastation of those in the underground realm. (Being sent to hell is not a matter of moving from one place to another but of gaining entrance to one of hell's communities while staying in the same place.) Let me report on just one experience.

I had the clear sensation of a kind of pillar drawing around me and growing perceptibly larger. The idea came to me that this was the bronze wall mentioned in the Word, formed out of angelic spirits to keep me safe in my mission to the unfortunates below.[378] While there, I heard plaintive wails like these: "Oh God, oh God! Have mercy on us! Have mercy on us!" These laments continued for a long time. I was allowed to talk with those unhappy people as much as I wanted. Their main complaint concerned the evil spirits, whose sole and burning desire was to cause them pain. They had lost hope, saying that they believed the agony would go on to eternity. But I was able to comfort them.

700. Because there are so many hells, as I said, describing them in an organized way means doing so in this order:

1. The hells of those who spent their lives in hatred, revenge, and cruelty [§§814–823].
2. The hells of those who spent their lives in adultery and lechery; in addition, the hells of deceivers and witches [824–831].
3. Misers' hells; the foul Jerusalem there and outlaws in the wilderness; in addition, the feces-laden hells of those who have pursued sensual pleasure alone [938–946].
4. Next, other hells than these [947–970].
5. Last, those who are undergoing spiritual devastation [1106–1113].

These may be found at the beginnings and ends of the ensuing chapters.

Genesis 7

1. And Jehovah said to Noah, "Enter the ark, you and all your household, because I have seen you before me as a just person in this generation.

2. Of every clean animal you are to take yourself seven each, seven each, a man and his wife; and of the animal that is not clean, two each, a man and his wife;[379]

3. and of the bird of the heavens seven each, seven each, a male and a female, to keep their seed alive on the face of the whole earth.

4. Because in seven more days I will be making rain fall on the earth for forty days and forty nights, and I will obliterate all substance[380] that I have made from the face of the ground."

5. And Noah did everything that Jehovah had commanded him.

❋ ❋ ❋ ❋ ❋ ❋

6. And Noah was a son of six hundred years when the flood of water took place on the earth.[381]

7. And Noah entered the ark, as did his sons and his wife and his sons' wives with him, because of the waters of the flood.

8. Of the clean animal and of the animal that is not clean and of the bird and of everything that creeps on the ground,

9. two each, two each entered to Noah in the ark, a male and a female, as God had commanded Noah.

10. And it happened in seven days that the waters of the flood came on the earth.

❋ ❋

11. In the six hundredth year of Noah's life, in the second month, on the seventeenth day of the month, on that day all the springs of the great abyss burst and heaven's floodgates opened.

12. And there was a downpour on the earth for forty days and forty nights.

❋ ❋ ❋ ❋ ❋ ❋

13. On that very day Noah entered the ark, as did Shem and Ham and Japheth, Noah's sons, and Noah's wife and his sons' three wives with them,

14. they, and every kind of wild animal, and every kind of beast, and every kind of creeping thing creeping on the earth, and every kind of bird, every flying thing, every winged creature.

15. And they entered to Noah in the ark, two each, two each of all flesh that had the breath of life in it.

※ ※

16. And those entering—a male and a female of all flesh—entered as God had commanded him. And Jehovah closed it behind him.

17. And the flood was forty days on the earth, and the waters grew and lifted the ark and it rose off the earth.

18. And the water strengthened and increased greatly on the earth, and the ark went on the face of the water.

※ ※ ※ ※ ※ ※

19. And the water strengthened greatly, greatly on the earth, and all the high mountains that were under the whole heaven were covered.

20. Fifteen cubits upward the water towered, and it covered the mountains.

21. And all flesh creeping on the earth passed away—including the bird and the beast and the wild animal and every crawling thing crawling on the earth—and every human.

22. Everything that had the breath of living spirit in its nostrils, of all that was on dry land, died.

23. And all substance that was on the face of the ground was obliterated, from human to animal to creeping thing to the bird of the heavens, and they were obliterated from the earth. And Noah alone was left, and what was with him in the ark.

24. And the water strengthened on the earth for one hundred fifty days.

Summary

701 THE general topic here is the preparation of the new church. As it had to be prepared in respect to intellectual things earlier, so here it has to be prepared in respect to the things of the will (verses 1–5).

702 Then its times of trial are described—those involving ideas in the intellect (verses 6–10) and those involving the intentions of the will (verses 11, 12).

703 Next, attention turns to the protection and preservation of that church (verses 13–15). But the stage it was going through is described as one in which it wavered (verses 16, 17, 18).

Last of all, the subject becomes the final generation of the earliest church and its nature. They were held in the grip of persuasive lies and of desires that rose out of self-love, so much so that they were destroyed (verses 19–24).

Inner Meaning

THIS chapter speaks in detail of the Flood, which does not symbolize simply the trials that people in the church called Noah had to endure before they could be reborn; it also symbolizes the ruination of those who could not be reborn.

The Word compares both trial and ruination to floods of water, and it also calls them floods directly.

Trial. In Isaiah:

> "For a short moment I abandoned you, but with great compassion I will gather you back. In a *flood* of anger I hid my face from you a moment, but with eternal mercy will I have mercy on you," your redeemer, Jehovah, has said. "For to me it is [like] the *waters of Noah,* to whom I swore that the *waters of Noah* would no longer pass over the earth. So have I sworn that I would not rage against you or censure you. Afflicted one, and storm-tossed, and not gaining comfort!" (Isaiah 54:7, 8, 9, 11)

This is about the regenerating church and about times of trial, which are called the waters of Noah. [2] The Lord himself also calls our struggles a flood in Luke:

> Jesus said, "Everyone who comes to me and listens to my words and does them is like a person building a house. The person dug and went down[382] deep and set a foundation on the rock. For this reason, when a *flood* took place, the river struck that house but was not strong enough to dislodge it, since it was founded on rock." (Luke 6:47, 48)

Anyone can see that the flood here means times when we are tested.

Ruination. In Isaiah:

> The Lord is bringing up over them the *waters of a river, strong and abundant:* the king of Assyria and all his glory; and he comes up over

all their brooks and will go over all their banks, and he will go through Judah. He will *flood in* and pass over; he will reach all the way to their neck. (Isaiah 8:7, 8)

The king of Assyria stands for delusions, for falsities adopted as premises, and for faulty reasoning based on them, which ruin us and which ruined the people living before the Flood. [3] In Jeremiah:

This is what Jehovah has said: "Look! *Water* climbing from the north; and it will become a *flooding river* and will *flood* the earth and its abundance, the city and those living in it." (Jeremiah 47:2, 3)

This is about Philistines, representing those who seize on false premises and use them as a basis for reasoning about spiritual matters. False premises and warped reasoning drown a person, as they did the pre-Flood people.

The Word uses floods of water as a simile and a metaphor for times of both trial and ruin because these are similar phenomena. During them, evil spirits stream in with their persuasive lies and false assumptions and arouse the same kind of thinking in us. With a person who is regenerating these agitations are trials; with one who is not regenerating, they bring ruination.

706 Genesis 7:1. *And Jehovah said to Noah, "Enter the ark, you and all your household, because I have seen you before me as a just person in this generation."*

Jehovah said to Noah means it happened in this way. The name *Jehovah* is used because the topic under consideration is charity. *Enter the ark, you and all your household,* symbolizes what exists in the will, which is the *house. Entering the ark* here is being prepared. *Because I have seen you as a just person in this generation* means having a good quality that makes regeneration possible.

707 The text from here to verse 5 almost restates the contents of the last chapter, without much change. The same is true beyond verse 5. One who is unaware of the inner meaning of the Word necessarily believes that this is mere repetition. It happens in other passages in the Word too, especially in the prophets, where the same idea is expressed by two different phrasings and sometimes is even taken up yet again and redescribed. The reason, though, is the one given before [§§590, 683]: that we have two very distinct faculties called intellect and will and that the Word deals with each individually; such is the cause of the repetition.

What follows will make it clear that this is the situation here.

708 The meaning of *Jehovah said to Noah* as it happened this way can be seen from this, that in Jehovah there is only what is.[383] What he says, happens, and always has happened. The meaning is the same as that in verse 13 of the last chapter [§630] and in other places where Jehovah's speaking means what happens and has happened.

709 The name *Jehovah* is used because the topic under consideration is charity.[384]

In the last chapter, from verse 9 to the end, the name used is not *Jehovah* but *God,* because the subject there was the preparation of "Noah"—in other words, the people of the church called Noah—in respect to their intellectual possessions, which have to do with faith.[385] Here, however, the subject is their preparation as to the contents of the will, which are a matter of love. When ideas in the intellect are under consideration, or in other words, the truth that faith discloses, the name God is used. When the intent of the will is under consideration, or in other words, the good effects of love, the name Jehovah is used. It is not the concerns of the intellect or matters of faith that constitute religion, you see, but the concerns of the will or matters of love. Jehovah is present in our love and charity, not in our faith, unless our faith is a result of love or charity. For this reason the Word compares faith to the night but love to the day. Genesis 1 is an example, where in talking about the great lights it says that the greater light—the sun, symbolizing love—rules by day and the smaller one—the moon, symbolizing faith—rules by night (Genesis 1:14, 16).[386] Something similar occurs in the prophets, in Jeremiah 31:35; 33:20; Psalms 136:8, 9; and in the Book of Revelation 8:12.

710 The symbolism of *enter the ark, you and all your household,* as what exists in the will is clear from what I have just said. The previous chapter, where it dealt with affairs of the intellect, used different words: "You will enter the ark: you and your sons and your wife and your sons' wives with you" (Genesis 6:18). The symbolism of a *house* or household as the will and what it holds is established by numerous places in the Word, as in Jeremiah:

> Their *houses* are transferred to others, their fields and wives together. (Jeremiah 6:12)

The houses, fields, and wives refer to facets of the will. In the same author:

> Build *houses* and live in them; and plant gardens and eat their produce. (Jeremiah 29:5, 28)

The houses to build and inhabit belong to the will, while the gardens to plant belong to the intellect. It is similar in other places. The recurrent phrase *the House of Jehovah* stands for the church, in which love is first and foremost. The house of Judah stands for the heavenly church, and the house of Israel for the spiritual church, because a house is the church. As a consequence, the mind of someone in the church is also a house, containing as it does both volitional and intellectual content, or qualities of charity and faith.

711 The fact that *entering the ark* means being prepared was stated above at Genesis 6:18, but the meaning there was preparation in regard to intellectual things, which are the truths that faith espouses.[387] Here the meaning is preparation in regard to affairs of the will, which are the good impulses of charity, leading to salvation.

To be prepared is to be equipped with true thoughts and good impulses, and unless we are prepared, we can never regenerate, still less be tested. The evil spirits [who are] present with us during those processes stir up everything false and evil in us; and if we lack anything true or good to which the Lord can redirect the evil and falsity, and by which he can disperse it, we go under.

The truth and goodness are remaining traces that the Lord has stored away for just such a purpose.

712 *Because I have seen you as a just person in this generation* means having a good quality that makes regeneration possible, as was explained and demonstrated at Genesis 6:9 [§§612–615]. There, the word *just* had to do with the good involved in charity, and *upright*, with the truth involved in it. There, *generations* was plural because the realm of the intellect was the theme, but here the word is singular because the realm of the will is the theme. The will encloses intellectual things in its embrace, whereas the intellect does not enclose volitional ones.

713 Genesis 7:2. "*Of every clean animal you are to take yourself seven each, seven each, a man and his wife; and of the animal that is not clean, two each, a man and his wife.*"

Every clean animal symbolizes positive emotions. *Seven each* means that these things are holy. *Man and wife* [in this instance] symbolize truth united to goodness. An *animal that is not clean* symbolizes negative emotions. *Two each* means that these things are relatively profane. *Man and wife* [in this instance] symbolize falsity united to evil.

714 The symbolism of *every clean animal* as positive emotions is established by things said and shown about animals before, in §§45, 46, 142, 143, 246.

The reason for this way of symbolizing emotions is that, of ourselves, taken on our own merits, we are nothing but animals. Our sensory abilities, appetites, desires, and feelings are identical to theirs. The good kinds of love that we feel—even the best kinds—such as love for others of our own kind, for children, and for a mate, are also exactly the same, with no difference whatever.

What makes us human and raises us above the beasts is our possession of a deeper plane of life than exists or can ever exist with beasts. That life is the life of faith and love received from the Lord. If it did not lie at the heart of each of the qualities we share with animals, we would never be any different than they are.

Take love for our acquaintances, for a single example. If we loved our peers for selfish reasons only, and nothing more heavenly or godly lay behind it, that would not justify our claim to be human, because animals do the same. Likewise for all other kinds of love.

Consequently, unless the vital force of love from the Lord inhabited our will and the vital force of faith from the Lord inhabited our intellect, we would not be the least bit human. It is the life we have from the Lord that extends our life beyond death, because the Lord attaches us to himself. Once he does, we can reside in his heaven with the angels and live forever.

Even when people live like wild animals, loving only themselves and what centers on themselves, the Lord's mercy is still so great (since it is divine and infinite) that he cannot abandon them. Instead he constantly breathes his life into them through the angels. This life force, although they may receive it in no other way, still grants them the capacity to consider, reflect, and understand whether a thing is good or bad on the planes of morality, public life, worldly interest, or bodily preoccupations, and therefore whether it is true or false.

The earliest people were aware that they were nothing more than animals and beasts and that if they were human it was only because the Lord made them so; and when feeling humble about themselves they confessed as much. So any attribute existing in themselves they not only compared to beasts and birds but also called such. Attributes of the will they compared to and referred to as animals. Attributes of the intellect they compared to and referred to as birds.

They made a distinction, though, between good and wicked feelings. The good ones they likened to lambs, ewes, kids, she-goats, bucks of the goats, rams, young cattle, and adult cattle. This was because these are good, gentle beasts, and useful in our lives, whether for eating or for the use of their hides and wool in our clothing. These in the main are the clean animals.

But those that are bad and savage and that are not useful in our lives are the unclean animals.[388]

716 The symbolism of *seven each* as things that are holy can be seen from what was said about the seventh or Sabbath day above at §§84–87. Those sections say that the Lord is the seventh day and that from him comes the entire heavenly church, or the heavenly person, and in fact the heavenly quality itself, which, because it belongs to the Lord alone, is very sacred. In the Word, accordingly, seven symbolizes holiness.[389] Indeed the inner meaning contains absolutely no suggestion of numbers in places like this, since people absorbed by the inner meaning (angels and angelic spirits, for example) do not even know what a number is and so what *seven* is. As a result, the present verse makes no implication whatever that they took seven pairs of every clean animal or in other words, that they possessed goodness in a seven-to-two ratio to evil. The meaning is that the qualities of will with which the member of the church was being supplied were good ones, holy ones, which as noted [§§677, 679–680] make regeneration possible.

[2] The symbolism of seven as holiness or holy elements can be seen from the rituals of the representative church,[390] in which the number seven crops up so many times. One example is the sevenfold spattering of some of the blood and oil [used in a ritual], as, for instance, in Leviticus:

> Moses took the anointing oil and anointed the dwelling place and everything that was in it and *consecrated* them, and he spattered some of it on the altar *seven times* and anointed the altar and all its utensils to *consecrate* them.[391] (Leviticus 8:10, 11)

Seven times would have had no meaning here at all had holiness not been represented by it. The oil symbolizes the holy quality of love. From another place:

> When Aaron enters the holy place, he shall take some of the young ox's blood and spatter it with his finger on the face of the appeasement cover, toward the east, and he shall spatter some of the blood with his finger before the face of the appeasement cover *seven times*. Likewise, at the altar, he shall spatter some of the blood on it with his finger *seven times,* and he shall *cleanse* it and *consecrate* it. (Leviticus 16:14, 19)

Each and every item here symbolizes the Lord himself and consequently the holiness of love—the blood, the appeasement cover, the altar, the east toward which the blood was to be spattered, and so the number seven as well. [3] It was similar with the sacrifices, discussed in another place:³⁹²

> If a soul sins by mistake, or if an anointed priest sins, to the people's guilt, he shall slaughter a young ox before Jehovah, and the priest shall dip his finger in the blood and spatter some of the blood *seven times* before Jehovah toward the veil of the holy place. (Leviticus 4:1, 3, 5, 6)

Here again seven symbolizes holiness, because the verses are describing atonement, which is exclusively the Lord's function, and as a result they are describing the Lord. Similar rituals were also established for the healing of leprosy as described in another place:

> Using the blood of a flying creature, cedar wood, scarlet cloth, and hyssop, *seven times* the priest shall spatter the person to be cleansed of leprosy and *cleanse* the person. Again, *seven times* [he shall spatter] some of the oil that is on his left palm before Jehovah. And again, using the cedar wood and hyssop and scarlet cloth and flying creature's blood, *seven times* he shall spatter a house where there is leprosy. (Leviticus 14:6, 7, 27, 51)

Anyone can see that there is absolutely nothing meaningful in the cedar wood, scarlet cloth, hyssop, oil, or flying creature's blood, or consequently in the number seven, unless it comes from their function in representing what is holy. If you remove all holy import from them, what remains is a lifeless triviality or something profane and idolatrous. When they symbolize something holy, on the other hand, the worship bound up in them is divine worship, which takes place deep within and is merely represented by the outward acts.

Certainly the Jews had no way of knowing what these things symbolized—the cedar wood, the hyssop, the scarlet cloth, the bird—so no one today does either. Still, if they had only cared to, they could have considered that something holy but beyond their ken was involved. So they could have worshiped the Lord, or in other words, the Messiah who was to come and cure them of their leprosy, that is, of profaning what is holy. Then they could have been saved.³⁹³ As soon as those who think this way and believe these things arrive in the other world, they learn (if they so desire) what every single detail represented.

[4] Something similar is said about the red cow:

> The priest would take some of its blood on his finger and spatter some of its blood toward the face of the meeting tent *seven times*. (Numbers 19:4)

As the seventh day or Sabbath symbolized the Lord and (because of him) the heavenly person and heavenliness itself, in the Jewish religion the seventh day was far more sacred than any ritual. That was the reason for the absolute Sabbath every *seventh year* (Leviticus 25:4) and for the jubilee that was to be proclaimed after *seven Sabbaths* of years, that is, after *seven times seven* years (Leviticus 25:8, 9).

The symbolism of seven at the highest level as the Lord and so as the holiness of love can also be seen from the golden lampstand with its *seven lamps,* which are described in Exodus 25:31, 32, 33, 37; 37:17, 18, 19, 23; Numbers 8:2, 3; Zechariah 4:2. This is what John says about them:

> . . . *seven* golden lampstands; in the middle of the *seven* lampstands was one like the Son of Humankind. (Revelation 1:12, 13)

It is obvious that the lampstand with its seven lamps symbolizes the Lord and that lamps stand for holy love—a heavenly thing—which is why there were seven of them. [5] In the same author:

> From the throne came *seven* fiery lanterns burning before the throne, which are God's *seven* spirits. (Revelation 4:5)

The seven lanterns that came from the Lord's throne are seven lamps. The number seven has a similar meaning where it comes up in the prophets, as in Isaiah:

> The light of the moon will be like the light of the sun, and the light of the sun will be *seven times as strong,* like the light of *seven days,* on the day when Jehovah binds up his people's fracture. (Isaiah 30:26)

The light seven times as strong, like the light of seven days, does not mean any sevenfold strength but the holiness of the love that the sun symbolizes. See also the statements made and evidence offered above at Genesis 4:15 [§395].

These things add to the proof that no number in the Word, no matter what it is, ever has a merely numerical meaning. This too was shown above, at Genesis 6:3 [§§575–578].

717. A further conclusion from all this is that the current passage deals with the things in a person's will, or with a person's good, holy traits,

which have to do with the will. The present verse, after all, says that of clean animals Noah was to take seven each, and the next says the same of birds. Verses 19 and 20 of the last chapter, however, said not that he was to take seven each but two each, or pairs, because the subject there was intellectual matters. Things of the intellect are not holy in themselves, although love, which belongs to the will, makes them holy.

The symbolism of *man and wife* as truth united to goodness is established by the following considerations. A *man* symbolizes truth, which belongs to the intellect, while a *wife* symbolizes goodness, which is a matter of will, both of which were treated of earlier.[394] And a person does not have the smallest particle of thought, the slightest stir of feeling or activity, that does not involve a kind of marriage between intellect and will. Without some kind of marriage, nothing at all is ever produced or comes into existence. The actual organic substances of which we are made, whether taken together or separately, even down to their simplest forms, have in them both a passive and an active nature. If the passive and active did not join together in something that resembles the marriage between a husband and wife, they could not possibly exist in those substances, much less produce anything. This is true throughout the world of nature.[395]

These enduring unions trace their origin and source to the heavenly marriage, which stamps every entity in all of creation, animate or inanimate, with a picture of the Lord's kingdom.

The symbolism of an *animal that is not clean* as negative emotions can be seen from statements made and supported above about clean animals [§§45–46, 142, 143, 246, 714–715].

The term *clean* applies to animals that are tame, well behaved, and useful. *Unclean* animals are the opposite: savage, evil, and useless. They come in different genera and species and in the Word are exemplified by wolves, bears, foxes, swine, and many others, symbolizing various types of craving and malice.

Why does this verse say that unclean animals—wicked feelings—were to be brought into the ark? The situation is this: The present passage is characterizing the people in this church in terms of the ark and its contents, that is, what was brought into it—in other words, what existed in those people before they were reborn. They did have the true ideas and good impulses that the Lord supplied and granted to them before they underwent regeneration, since without a fund of truth and goodness no one could ever regenerate. Here mention is made of the evil in them, symbolized by the unclean animals.

When we are being reborn, there are evils that have to be dispelled, or rather pried loose and tempered, by means of good. None of the evil that we have committed or inherited can ever be removed to the point of complete abolition. It lurks within and is merely loosened and mitigated by the good we receive from the Lord, to the point where it becomes harmless and invisible. This secret has not yet come into common knowledge.

It is the evil we have actually committed that relaxes its grip on us and softens, not so much the evil we have inherited. This too is a matter unknown.

720 The symbolism of *two each* as things that are relatively profane can be seen from the symbolism of the number itself.

Two symbolizes marriage (and when it symbolizes the heavenly marriage it is a holy number), but it also symbolizes the same thing as six. Two has the same relation to three as the six days of labor have to the seventh, holy day of rest. So in the Word the third day is interchangeable with the seventh and involves almost the same meaning. This is because of the Lord's resurrection on the third day. For the same reason, just as the seventh day speaks of the Lord's entry into the world and into his glory (and all the other times he comes as well), so also does the third day. In consequence, the two preceding days are not holy but relatively profane, as in Hosea:

> Come, let us return to Jehovah, because he has injured us and will heal us. He has struck us and will bind us up. He will bring us to life after *two days;* on the *third* day he will raise us up and we will live before him. (Hosea 6:1, 2)

In Zechariah:

> "It will come about in all the earth," says Jehovah, "that *two* parts in it will be cut off, will die, and a *third* will be left in it. And I will lead the third part through fire, and smelt them as silver is smelted." (Zechariah 13:8, 9)

And Psalms 12:6 says that the silver would be very pure when purified seven times.

Just as seven each does not mean seven each but what is holy, then, two each plainly does not mean two each but what is relatively profane. In no way does this imply that the ratio of unclean animals (or negative emotions in those people) to clean animals (or good impulses) was as low as two to seven. On the contrary, we harbor immeasurably more evil than good.

721

The symbolism of *man and wife* as falsity united to evil is clear from the things said directly above. Here *man and wife* is used of unclean animals but just above of clean animals. There it symbolized truth united to good, here falsity united to evil. The nature of the object described determines the meaning of the description.

722

Genesis 7:3. *"And of the bird of the heavens seven each, seven each, a male and a female, to keep their seed alive on the face of the whole earth."*

The *bird of the heavens* symbolizes aspects of intellect. *Seven each* symbolizes what is holy. *A male and a female* symbolizes truth and goodness. *To keep their seed alive on the face of the whole earth* symbolizes the truth that faith espouses.

723

The symbolism of the *bird of the heavens* as aspects of intellect has already been demonstrated [§40], so there is no need to dwell on it.

724

The symbolism of *seven each* as what is holy has also been demonstrated [§716]. Here, though, it symbolizes holy truth, which is holy because of its origin in goodness. There is no such thing as holy truth except for the truth that comes from goodness. We can speak all manner of truth from the Word and so from memory, but unless love (love for our fellow humans) is what brings it to our lips, it can by no means be described as holy. If love and charity are indeed the qualities that bring it forward, on the other hand, we then acknowledge and believe what we are saying, and so it comes from the heart.

The case is the same with faith, which so many people claim is the only thing that saves.[396] Unless love or charity is what gives rise to faith, it is not faith at all. Love and charity are what consecrate faith. The Lord is present in love and charity, not in faith separated from them. Detached faith has our own selves at its core, and in us there resides utter filth. When we separate faith from love, what we privately seek in speaking is either to hear ourselves praised or to profit monetarily.[397]

We can all recognize this phenomenon from our own experience. When an individual claims to love another, to prefer that other to anyone else, to acknowledge that other as more noble than anyone else, and so on, and yet thinks otherwise privately, that individual makes such a claim with the lips alone, denying the words at heart and sometimes even mocking them. People do the same with faith. Here is something I have come to know extremely well from frequent experience: Some of those who most hate the Lord and persecute the faithful in the other life are people who preached about the Lord and faith during bodily life with such eloquence and such a devout facade as to astound their listeners, although they were not speaking from the heart.

725 The symbolism of *a male and a female* as truth and goodness is established by statements made and evidence offered earlier to the effect that a man and a male symbolize truth while a wife and a woman symbolize good.[398] *Male and female* are used of what belongs to the intellect, however, whereas *man and wife* are used of what belongs to the will. This is because a husband and wife represent marriage in a way that male and female do not. Truth acting on its own is completely unable to enter into marriage with goodness—it is possible only for goodness to join with truth—because no truth whatever exists that does not grow out of goodness and so is not coupled with goodness. If you extract goodness from truth, nothing remains but mere words.

726 The symbolism of *to keep their seed alive on the face of the whole earth* as the truth that faith espouses can be seen from the fact that it was through this church that life was given to the seed, the *seed* meaning faith. All the other descendants of the earliest church destroyed the heavenly and spiritual seed in themselves by their foul appetites and appalling delusions. So that the heavenly seed would not die out, though, the people referred to as Noah were regenerated, and this was accomplished by means of spiritual seed. These are the things symbolized.

Those who receive the Lord's life are said to be given life, or kept alive, because only attributes of the Lord's have life in them. Anyone can see so from this idea, that no life at all attaches to things that have no connection with eternal life or that do not look to eternal life. Life that is not eternal is not life; in a short time it ends. Neither is Being an attribute of anything that ceases to be, only of things that never cease to be.[399] So life and Being inhabit only those things that are the Lord's, or Jehovah's, because all Being and all eternal life are his.

By eternal life I mean eternal happiness.

See the remarks and illustrations on this topic at §290.

727 Genesis 7:4. *"Because in seven more days I will be making rain fall on the earth for forty days and forty nights, and I will obliterate all substance that I have made from the face of the ground."*

In seven days symbolizes the beginning of their inward trials. *Rainfall* symbolizes the trials themselves. *Forty days and nights* is a symbol for how long their trials last. *Obliterating all substance that I have made from the face of the ground* means that human self-sufficiency is obliterated, so to speak, when a person is reborn. The same words also symbolize the annihilation of those in the earliest church who destroyed themselves.

728

The symbolism of *in seven days* here as the beginning of their inward trials can be seen from the inner meaning of all the words in the current verse, which deal with the trials of the people referred to as Noah. The general subjects are both the inward trials of the "Noah" element and the total devastation that befell some in the earliest church. As a result, *in seven days* symbolizes not only the start of trials but also the end of ruin.

The reason *in seven days* symbolizes these things is that *seven* is a holy number, as has been said and shown at verse 2 of this chapter [§§716–717], at Genesis 4:15 and 24 [§§395, 433], and at §§84–87. It symbolizes the Lord's arrival in the world and his entry into glory, and it specifically symbolizes every time that the Lord comes to us.

Every arrival of the Lord entails a beginning for those who are regenerating and an end for those who are being destroyed. For the people of this church, his coming was the start of adversity, because when tested, an individual begins to turn into a new person and to regenerate. At the same time it was the end for those in the earliest church who had developed in such a way that the only possible outcome was extinction. By way of a parallel, at the time of the Lord's advent into the world the church was in the final stage of its destruction and a new church was formed.

[2] This symbolism of *in seven days* can be seen in Daniel:

> *Seventy weeks* have been decreed upon your people and upon your holy city, to bring an end to transgression, and to seal up their sins, and to atone for wickedness, and to introduce everlasting justice, and to seal up vision and prophet, and to anoint the Holiest One. And you will know and perceive that from the issuing of the Word to restore and rebuild Jerusalem to the time of Messiah the prince, there will be *seven weeks*. (Daniel 9:24, 25)

The seventy weeks and the seven weeks here symbolize the same thing as seven days: the Lord's Coming. But since this is explicitly a prophecy, the numbers involving a seven mark the period as being even more holy and certain. The use of seven to describe this period symbolizes not only the Lord's arrival but the start of a new church at the same time, as indicated by the statement that the Holiest One would be anointed and Jerusalem would be restored and rebuilt. It also symbolizes a final devastation at the same time, as indicated by the statement that those weeks were decreed upon the holy city in order to bring an end to transgression and to seal up its sin. [3] Similar words occur elsewhere in the Word, as in Ezekiel, where the prophet says of himself:

> I came to the captives at Tel-abib, who were sitting by the river Chebar, and I sat there *seven days,* thunderstruck among them, and it happened at the *end of seven days* that the word of Jehovah came to me. (Ezekiel 3:15, 16)

Here too the seven days stand for the start of a divine visitation, seeing that after the seven days during which Ezekiel sat with the captives the word of Jehovah came to him. In the same author:

> They will bury Gog, in order to cleanse the land for *seven months.* At the end of *seven months,* they will make a careful search. (Ezekiel 39:12, 14)

Again the period of seven stands for the final point of devastation and the start of divine visitation. In Daniel:

> Nebuchadnezzar's heart will change from [that of] a human, and the heart of an animal will be given to him, and *seven seasons* will pass over him. (Daniel 4:16, 25, 32)

This likewise stands for the end of devastation and the start of becoming a new person.

[4] Seventy years of captivity in Babylon represented the same thing. Whether it is seventy or seven, it involves the same meaning—seven days or seven years or the seven "ages" or decades that make up seventy years. The process of devastation was represented by the years of captivity; the beginning of a new church was represented by the liberation and rebuilding of the Temple.

Similar things were represented by Jacob's service with Laban, described in these words:

> "I will serve you *seven years* for Rachel," and he served *seven years.* Laban said, "Fill out this *week* and we will give you her as well for the service that you serve with me yet another *seven years.*" And Jacob did so and filled out this *week.* (Genesis 29:18, 20, 27, 28)

The seven years of servitude here involve a similar meaning, as does the fact that marriage and liberty followed the days of the seven years. This span of seven years was called a week, as it also was in Daniel [9:24, 25].

[5] The command that the people circle Jericho seven times to make the wall fall represented the same thing. It says that on the *seventh day* they got up at dawn and circled the city in the customary way, *seven times*, "and it happened on the *seventh time* that the *seven* priests blew their *seven* trumpets and the wall fell" (Joshua 6:1–20). Had such details been devoid of symbolic meaning, it never would have been ordered that they circle seven times or that there be seven priests and seven trumpets.

These and many other passages (such as Job 2:13; Revelation 15:1, 6, 7; 21:9) show that *in seven days* symbolizes the beginning of a new church and the end of the old. Since the present verse deals both with the people of the church called Noah and their trials and with the last descendants of the earliest church, who destroyed themselves, the *seven days more* cannot symbolize anything else than the start of Noah's trials and the end of the earliest church, or its final ruination and death.

729 The symbolism of *rainfall* as the trials themselves can be seen from the remarks and supporting quotations introducing this chapter [§705]. They showed that a flood or a deluge of water—which is what this rain was—symbolizes not only trials but also devastation. The meaning will also be clear from what is said about the Flood in the sections to follow.

730 The fact that *forty days and nights* is a symbol for how long their trials last stands out clearly from the Lord's Word.

The use of forty as a symbol for the length that times of trial last comes from the fact that the Lord submitted to being tested for forty days, as shown in Matthew 4:1, 2; Luke 4:2; and Mark 1:13. Each and every tradition established in the Jewish church, and in all the other representative churches that preceded the Lord's Coming, foreshadowed him.[400] So the forty days and nights did too, representing and symbolizing every time of struggle in general, and the length that any one time of struggle lasts in particular.

When we are being tried, we experience the devastation or stripping away of everything self-centered and bodily. What is self-centered and bodily has to die—and die through combat and struggle—before we can be reborn as a new being, or in other words, as a spiritual and heavenly being. Because of this, forty days and nights also symbolize the length of time that devastation lasts. They do so here, in a verse that deals with both the trials of the people in the new church known as Noah and the devastation of the pre-Flood people.

[2] The symbolism of *forty* as the duration of both trials and devastation, whether long or short, can be seen in Ezekiel:

> You shall lie on your right side and carry the wickedness of the house of Judah *forty days;* a day for each year is the [task] I have set for you. (Ezekiel 4:6)

Forty stands for the length of time the devastation of the Jewish church lasted. It stands also as a representation of the Lord's struggles, since it says that he was to carry the wickedness of the house of Judah. In the same author:

> I will turn the land of Egypt into wastelands, a ruinous wasteland. It will not be traversed by a human foot, nor will an animal's foot traverse it, and it will not be inhabited for *forty years.* And I will make the land of Egypt a ruin in the middle of ruined lands; and its cities in the midst of wasted cities will be a lonely place for *forty years.* (Ezekiel 29:10, 11, 12)

Again forty stands for the time it takes for them to be devastated (or laid waste) and ruined. On a deeper plane it positively does not mean forty years but only the overall process by which faith is brought to ruin, whether this takes a short or long time. In John:

> Throw out the courtyard that is outside the temple and do not measure it, because it has been given to the nations, which will trample the holy city for *forty-two months.* (Revelation 11:2)

[3] And in the same author:

> The beast was given a mouth speaking grand things and blasphemies, and it was given authority to act for *forty-two months.* (Revelation 13:5)

Here the number stands for the course that devastation runs, since it certainly does not mean a period of forty-two months, as anyone can see.

This time the number mentioned is forty-two, which is the same as forty, for the following reason. Seven days symbolize the end of devastation and a new start while six symbolizes hard work, from the six days of labor or combat. Seven multiplied by six, then, produces forty-two, symbolizing the length of time devastation lasts and the length of time struggles or labor and conflict last for those who are being reborn. This period contains something holy. The round number of forty is a substitute for the exact figure of forty-two, as is clear from the above places in the Book of Revelation.

[4] The fact that the Israelite people wandered in the wilderness for forty years before entering the land of Canaan likewise represented and symbolized the duration of hardship and also of devastation. The former was represented and symbolized by the fact that they did eventually enter the holy land. The latter was represented and symbolized by the fact that everyone who had passed the age of twenty by the time of leaving Egypt, except for Joshua and Caleb, died in the wilderness. Hardships are meant by the things against which the people murmured so many times, and devastation is meant by the plagues and deaths that so often struck.

The symbolism of these events as trials and devastation will be shown where the relevant passages are explained, the Lord's divine mercy permitting.[401] Moses speaks of them this way:

> Remember all the path that Jehovah your God led you on these *forty years* in the wilderness to afflict you, to *test you,* to know what was in your heart, whether you would keep his commandments or not. (Deuteronomy 8:2, 3, 16)

Moses' forty days and forty nights on Mount Sinai are again a symbol for the length of time that struggle lasts, or for the testing of the Lord, as is clear in Moses:

> He was on Mount Sinai *forty days* and *forty nights,* not eating bread, not drinking water, pleading for the people that they not be destroyed. (Deuteronomy 9:9, 11, 18, 25–29; 10:10; Numbers 14:33, 34, 35; 32:8–14)

[5] The reason forty days symbolize the duration of struggles, as noted, is that the Lord allowed himself to be tried by the Devil for forty days. Since everything represented the Lord, if the angels were thinking about trial, that idea was represented visually in the world of spirits by the kinds of things that exist in the world. All the thoughts angels have are made visible in representative form when they pass down into the world of spirits. So the number forty served for the idea of adversity, since the Lord would struggle for forty days. (To the Lord, and consequently to the angels in heaven, the future is the same as the present. What is to come is already here, or what will happen is already an accomplished fact.) This is why the number forty in the representative church was able to represent times of trial, and of devastation as well.

But these things cannot yet be grasped in a satisfactory way, since no one knows about the influence the angelic heavens have on the world of spirits or the fact that the influence works this way.

731 *Obliterating all substance that I have made from the face of the ground* means that human self-sufficiency is obliterated, so to speak, when a person comes to life. This can be seen from earlier statements about selfhood [§§154–155, 164]. Our insistence on autonomy is thoroughly evil and false. As long as it maintains its grip, we are dead. However, when we suffer times of trouble, this sense of autonomy is shaken off; that is, it is loosened and mitigated by the truth and goodness we receive from the Lord. In the process, it is brought to life and yet seems to disappear. The fact that it becomes invisible and harmless is symbolized by *being obliterated* even though it is never obliterated but remains.

The situation is almost like that with black and white. When these two are modified in various ways by rays of light, they turn into beautiful colors, such as blues, yellows, and reds. Through these colors, and depending on the objects they appear in (flowers, for instance), they display themselves as lovely and appealing. Still, they remain inherently and fundamentally black and white.

But since the present verse deals at the same time with the final devastation of the people in the earliest church, *obliterating all substance that I have made from the face of the ground* also symbolizes those who perished. So does verse 23 below [§§807–811].

The *substance that I have made* is every trait (or every person) that had a germ of heaven in it (or who was part of the church). As a result, the current verse and verse 23 below use the word *ground,* symbolizing a person in the church in whom the seed of goodness and truth has been sown. Once evil and falsity had been dispelled, as noted, that seed grew and grew in the people referred to as Noah, although among the pre-Flood people who died it was killed off by tares.[402]

732 Genesis 7:5. *And Noah did everything that Jehovah had commanded him* once again means it happened in this way.

See Genesis 6:22, which twice says that "Noah did"; this verse says it only once. And Genesis 6:22 uses the name God where this verse uses Jehovah. The reason is that the passage there dealt with matters of the intellect while this one deals with matters of the will. Matters of intellect regard matters of will as different and separate from themselves, but matters of will view matters of intellect as united to themselves, or as being one with themselves. The ability to understand, you see, rises from the will. This is why the previous chapter uses the word *did* twice where the present one uses it just once, and why the previous chapter uses the name God where the present one uses Jehovah.

733 Genesis 7:6. *And Noah was a son of six hundred years when the flood of water took place on the earth.*

Noah as a *son of six hundred years* symbolizes the first stage of their trials. The *flood of water on the earth* symbolizes the onset of trial.

734 Earlier sections talked about the truth in the intellect with which the Lord supplied members of the Noah church before they could regenerate (Genesis 6:13–22) and about the good in the will that the Lord also gave them (Genesis 7:1–5).[403] Because the text deals with both, it seems to repeat itself.

The theme here, though, is the trials those people underwent, and at this point it is the first stage and so the onset of trial (verses 6–11). As anyone can see, redundancy enters in once again. The current verse says that Noah was a son of six hundred years when the Flood took place on the earth, while verse 11 says it happened in the six hundredth year of his life, in the second month, on the seventeenth day. Again, verse 7 says that Noah entered the ark with his sons and the wives, while verse 13 below says the same; and verses 8 and 9 say that the animals entered to Noah in the ark, while verses 14, 15, and 16 say the same thing as well. So the present chapter clearly engages in the same kind of repetition of earlier material.

No one who sticks to the literal meaning alone can see any other possibility beyond the fact that some narrative element is being repeated in this way. Here as elsewhere, however, there is not a single syllable that is extraneous or frivolous, because it is the Lord's Word; so repetition never occurs unless it symbolizes something additional. At this point, as before, it means that there is a first testing, which is a testing of our intellectual side, and then a testing of our motives [§§641, 652–654, 670].

The two kinds of trial follow each other in the person who is regenerating. It is one thing, after all, to face a challenge to our intellect and quite another to face one to our motives. A challenge to the workings of our intellect is slight; a challenge to the workings of our will is serious.

735 The reason for the weakness of a challenge to the workings of our intellect, or in other words, to the falsities we adopt, is that our senses lie to us, and the lies they tell us are such that we cannot help participating in them. In consequence, they are easy to dispel.

Take those who restrict themselves to the literal meaning of the Word where it speaks in terms they can grasp and so speaks according to their sensory illusions. If such people maintain a simple belief in those passages because it is the Lord's Word, then even if they are immersed in deceptive appearances, they readily allow themselves to learn better. One who believes that the Lord is angry with the ungodly, punishes them, and does evil to them, for example, easily learns how the case really stands, since the fallacy came from the literal meaning.

Then too some people in all simplicity believe that they can do good on their own and that in the next life they will receive a reward from the Lord if they are intrinsically good. These, too, readily learn that the good they do comes from the Lord and that the Lord rewards them freely, out of mercy.

When people like these find the ideas of their intellect—fallacies like these—tested, the trial is inevitably a light one. It is also their first trial and hardly even seems to be a test. That is the kind of trial under discussion here.

The case is different with another group of people. These are individuals who do not believe the Word in simplicity of heart. On the contrary, they confirm themselves in illusions and falsities because these justify their desires. As a result they heap up a large number of compelling rationalizations based on self-interest and on the facts they know; and then they use the Word to bolster their arguments. So they stamp this way of thinking on their minds and convince themselves that falsity is truth.

736. To describe Noah, or in other words, the people of this new church, they were the kind who had an uncomplicated belief in the things they had received from the earliest church. These were the doctrinal tenets that the people called Enoch had collected and organized into a kind of systematic theology [§§519–521].

Their character was entirely different from that of the pre-Flood people who died in the Flood and who were called Nephilim.[404] These were the people who had merged the teachings of faith with their foul desires and so had seized on horrendous delusions that they would not back away from, no matter how hard others tried to teach them and to show them the falsity of their notions.

People with the same two types of mentality or personality exist today too. The former can regenerate easily, the latter only with difficulty.

737. The symbolism of *Noah, a son of six hundred years,* as the first stage of their trials can be seen from this: From here all the way to Eber in chapter 11, the numbers, the ages in years, and the names have a purely symbolic meaning, just as the ages and names of everyone in chapter 5 did.

The symbolism here of *six hundred years* as the first stage of trial can be seen from the number's major factors, ten and six, which are multiplied twice.⁴⁰⁵ If a larger or smaller number is produced by the use of the same factors, the symbolism does not change.

The number *ten* has already been shown at Genesis 6:3 to symbolize remaining traces [§576]. The symbolism here of *six* as hard work and combat can be seen from many places in the Word. The case is this: preceding verses have discussed our preparation for struggle, which involves receiving from the Lord a supply of truth in the intellect and goodness in the will. This truth and good are in the form of remaining traces, which are not brought to our consciousness until we are regenerating. If the trials we go through are a means to regeneration for us, the remnant we possess is for the use of the angels who attend us. From the remnant they draw out those resources that they can employ in defending us against evil spirits, who attack us by stirring up the falsity in us.

The symbolism of the number ten as the remnant and of six as combat is the reason for the reference to six hundred years, in which the numbers ten and six predominate, symbolizing a time of trial.

[2] The particular symbolism of six as combat or conflict is established by the first chapter of Genesis, which specifies six days for rebirth before a person turns heavenly. During those six days, the combat never lets up, but on the seventh day comes rest. This is the source of the six days of labor and the seventh of Sabbath, symbolizing rest.

For the same reason, a Hebrew slave was to serve for *six years* and go free in the seventh (Exodus 21:2; Deuteronomy 15:12; Jeremiah 34:14). For the same reason, they were to sow the land and gather its produce for *six years* but to leave it fallow in the seventh (Exodus 23:10, 11, 12); and the same for a vineyard. And for the same reason, the seventh year was to be an absolute Sabbath for the land, a Sabbath to Jehovah (Leviticus 25:3, 4).

Because six symbolizes labor and conflict, it also symbolizes the dispersing of falsity. In Ezekiel:

> Here, *six* men were coming by way of the upper gate, which faces north, and each had a weapon for *dispersing* [people] in his hand. (Ezekiel 9:2)

And in the same author's prophecy against Gog:

> And I will make you turn back and will *destroy a sixth of you*⁴⁰⁶ and bring you up from the flanks of the north. (Ezekiel 39:2)

In these verses, six and destroying a sixth stands for dispersing something, the north stands for falsity, and Gog stands for those who wring dogma from the most superficial matters and use it to destroy inner worship. From Job:

> In *six* periods of distress he will liberate you, and in the seventh, evil will not touch you. (Job 5:19)

Here six stands for spiritual battles.

[3] In some of the other occurrences of six in the Word, it does not symbolize hard work, battles, or the dispersing of falsity. Instead it symbolizes the holy quality of faith, because it is drawing a connection with twelve (which symbolizes faith and all properties of faith taken together) and with three (which symbolizes holiness). From those numbers comes this additional, positive meaning of six. One example occurs in Ezekiel 40:5, where it says that the reed a man was using to measure Israel's holy city was six cubits. There are other instances as well.

The reason the positive meaning develops out of those numbers is that spiritual struggles have the holy quality of faith in them. Then too, the six days of labor and combat look to the seventh, holy day.

738 Noah is called a son of six hundred years here because a *son* symbolizes truth in the intellect, as already demonstrated [§§489, 570]. But verse 11 below does not call him a son, because that passage deals with that church's struggles in respect to the workings of its will.

739 The symbolism of the *flood of water on the earth* as the onset of trial follows from the fact that the present subject is struggles in respect to intellectual issues—struggles that come first and are relatively slight, as explained. For this reason it is called a flood of water, not simply a flood, as it is in verse 17 below. Water mainly symbolizes our spiritual possessions, the intellectual elements of faith, and the opposites of these, which are falsities. The Word contains many passages that support this meaning.[407]

[2] The symbolism of a flood of water as times of trial can be seen from the evidence offered in the preface to this chapter [§705]. It can also be seen in Ezekiel:

> This is what the Lord Jehovih has said: "I will make a stormy wind break out in my wrath, and in my anger a *flooding downpour* will take place, and hail stones in my rage, until their full end, so that I destroy the wall that you coated with your foolish plaster." (Ezekiel 13:11, 13, 14)

The stormy wind and flooding downpour stand for the ruination that falsity causes. The wall coated with foolish plaster stands for a fiction that seems to be the truth. In Isaiah:

Jehovah God is a shelter from the *flood,* a shade from the heat, for the spirit of the violent is like a *flood* against a wall. (Isaiah 25:4)

The flood stands for a challenge to our way of thinking, and it differs from a challenge to the intentions of our will, which is called heat. [3] In the same author:

Indeed, the Lord has someone who is strong and mighty, like a flood of hail, a storm of obliteration, like a *flood of* strong, *overflowing water.* (Isaiah 28:2)

This describes different levels of distress. In the same author:

When you cross through the *water,* I will be with you, and [when you cross] through the rivers, they will not *flood over* you. When you go through fire, you will not be burned, and flame will not scorch you. (Isaiah 43:2)

The water and rivers stand for falsity and fantasies, the fire and flame for evil and cravings. In David:

All the godly will pray to you over this at the time when they find you, so in a *flood of* many *waters,* [the waters] will not reach them. You are a hiding place for me; you will save me from anguish. (Psalms 32:6, 7)

The flood of waters stands for trials. Another word for flood[408] is also applied to them in the same author:

Jehovah sits by the *flood,* and Jehovah sits as monarch forever. (Psalms 29:10)

These passages and those prefacing the chapter [§705] show clearly that a flood of water simply symbolizes times of trial and of devastation, even though described as if part of a story, according to the custom of the earliest people.[409]

Genesis 7:7. *And Noah entered the ark, as did his sons and his wife and his sons' wives with him, because of the waters of the flood.*

Noah entered the ark because of the waters of the flood means that while being tested he was protected. His *sons* as before symbolize truth, his *wife* goodness, and the *sons' wives* truth united to good.

Anyone can see that *Noah entered the ark because of the waters of the flood* means that he was protected.

The tests that we undergo are nothing else than battles between the evil spirits and angels who are present with us. The evil spirits summon up every wrong that we have ever done or even considered from childhood on. So they stir up both what is evil and what is false in us and condemn us for it. Nothing gratifies them more; it is the central pleasure of their lives. But through the angels the Lord protects us and prevents evil spirits and demons from pushing beyond the furthest limits of our endurance and drowning us.

742

The fact that Noah's *sons* symbolize truth, his *wife* goodness, and the *sons' wives* truth united to good came up before at Genesis 6:18 [§668], where the same words appear.

Although this verse speaks of Noah's sons, of his wife, and of his sons' wives, the truth and goodness they symbolize are protective truth and goodness in the people themselves referred to as Noah. Such was the mode in which the earliest people wrote the Word, weaving heavenly secrets together to form a story.

743

Genesis 7:8, 9. *Of the clean animal and of the animal that is not clean and of the bird and of everything that creeps on the ground, two each, two each entered to Noah in the ark, a male and a female, as God had commanded Noah.*

As earlier, a *clean animal* symbolizes positive emotions, an *animal that is not clean* symbolizes cravings, a *bird* in general symbolizes thoughts, and *everything that creeps on the ground* symbolizes the sensory level and anything that gives sensual pleasure. *Two each, two each,* symbolizes elements that answer to each other. *They entered the ark* means that they were protected. *A male and a female* symbolizes truth and goodness, as they have done before. *As God had commanded Noah* means it happened in this way.

744

The symbolism of a *clean animal* as positive emotions was stated and shown at verse 2 of this chapter [§§714, 719], so there is no need to linger over it. The same holds true for the symbolism of an *animal that is not clean* as cravings or evil wishes.

745

The general symbolism of a *bird* as thoughts is established by frequent statements about birds above [§§40, 142, 595, 674, 723] indicating that they symbolize intellectual or rational matters. The term there, however, was *bird of the heavens;* here it is simply *bird.* Consequently, in a general way it symbolizes thoughts. There are, after all, many kinds of birds, both clean and unclean. Verse 14 below divides them into birds, flying things, and winged creatures, the clean ones being thoughts based on truth, the unclean ones thoughts based on falsity. They will be discussed in what follows [§§776–778], with the Lord's divine mercy.

746 The symbolism of *everything that creeps on the ground* as the sensory level and anything that gives sensual pleasure was also stated and shown above [§§44, 195–197, 251, 594, 674].

The earliest people used creeping, crawling animals as a metaphor and simile for the things that we acquire through our senses and the things that give us sensual pleasure. Therefore they also called such things by the names of those animals. They did so because those things occupy the lowest plane of existence and seem to creep on our surface, barred from lifting themselves any higher.

747 Anyone can see the symbolism of *two each, two each,* as elements that answer to each other, by considering that such things are pairs. They cannot be pairs unless they answer to each other as do truth and goodness, and evil and falsity. All things display something like a marriage or coupling within them, like the match of truth with goodness or of evil with falsity, because the intellect is married to the will. To put it another way, ideas in the intellect are married to the intentions of the will. In fact everything has its partner or mate, without which it could never remain in existence.

748 I already said at verse 7 above [§741], where it concerned Noah and his sons and the wives, that *they entered the ark* means that they were protected.

749 The symbolism of *a male and a female* as truth and goodness can be seen from what appeared previously at Genesis 6:19, where male and female are used of birds, but *man and wife* are used of the animals.[410] The reason also appeared there; the contents of the will marry the contents of the intellect but the contents of the intellect (regarded in themselves) do not really marry those of the will. The former relationship is like that of husband and wife but the latter like that of male and female. And since the present chapter takes up first the challenge to the ideas in their intellect that the people under discussion faced, as noted [§734], the phrase used is *a male and a female.* It implies combat, or a challenge to one's intellectual concerns.

750 The fact that *as God had commanded* means it happened in this way was shown before at Genesis 6:22 [§682] and in this chapter at verse 5 [§732].

751 The subject under discussion here is the trials of the people in the new church called Noah, but few if any know what goes on in times of trial because few today experience them. Those who do are wholly convinced that it is something inherent in themselves that causes them to suffer. In consequence, let me offer a brief explanation of the matter here.

During such times it is evil spirits who stir up our falsities and evil, as mentioned [§§653, 705:3, 711, 741]. From our memory they stir up everything we have ever considered or committed since childhood. Evil spirits are able to do this with such consummate skill and malice that words cannot describe it. The angels who accompany us, though, bring out the goodness and truth that we have and use it to defend us. The conflict between the parties is what we sense and feel, and it causes our conscience to gnaw at us and torment us.

[2] There are two kinds of trial, one testing the intellect, and the other the will. In struggles involving our intellectual processes, evil spirits stir up only the following: the wrong we have done (symbolized here by the unclean animals), for which they accuse and condemn us; our good deeds (symbolized by the clean animals), which they twist in a thousand ways; our thoughts (symbolized by the birds); and the things symbolized by the animals creeping on the ground. A struggle of this kind is mild, and we perceive it only as the memory of such things, along with a kind of resulting anxiety.

[3] A struggle involving the urges of our will, on the other hand, does not stimulate the memory of our thoughts and deeds in this way. Rather, wicked demons (a name for evil spirits of this type) kindle in us the cravings and vile kinds of love that already permeate us, and so they attack us with our own longings. This they manage so malevolently and covertly that no one could ever believe it was their doing. It takes them only a moment to infiltrate the vital energy that lies behind our longings. In almost no time they change and redirect our desire for goodness and truth into a desire for evil and falsity. We end up totally unaware that this event did not happen on its own, that it did not unfold spontaneously. This kind of trial is very severe, and we perceive it as an excruciating, burning pain inside. It will be discussed below [§§755–757, 760, 845].

The truth of all this I was privileged to see and recognize from repeated experience. I also learned when it was that evil spirits and demons poured and flooded in, where they came from, who they were, and what their methods were. These experiences too will later be described individually, by the Lord's divine mercy.[411]

752 Genesis 7:10. *And it happened in seven days that the waters of the flood came on the earth.* As before, these words symbolize the start of their trials.

753 The symbolism of *seven days* as the start of their trials was demonstrated above at verse 4 [§728]. The words also suggest the same ideas discussed above—that this struggle, involving the thoughts in their intellect, was the start of their trials, or the first struggle [§§641, 652–654, 670, 734]. And the expression provides a conclusion to the passage.

Because this first trial involved the contents of the intellect, the words *waters of the flood* are used to describe it, as they were before at verse 7, and as *a flood of water* was in verse 6. In the strict sense, the term symbolizes just such a trial, which was shown there [§739].

Genesis 7:11. *In the six hundredth year of Noah's life, in the second month, on the seventeenth day of the month, on that day all the springs of the great abyss burst and heaven's floodgates opened.*

The *six hundredth year, second month, and seventeenth day,* symbolizes the next stage of their trials. *All the springs of the great abyss burst* symbolizes the climax of their struggles over the intentions of the will. *Heaven's floodgates opened* symbolizes the climax of their struggles over ideas in the intellect.

The symbolism of the *six hundredth year, second month, and seventeenth day* as the next stage of their trials follows from what has been said so far. From verse 6 up to this point, verse 11, the text has dealt with the first stage of trial, which was a challenge to the concerns of the intellect, but the present passage deals with the next stage, a challenge to the concerns of the will. This is the reason for the restatement of Noah's age. It is expressed the first time as the fact that he was a *son of six hundred years* but here as the fact that the Flood took place *in the six hundredth year of his life, in the second month, on the seventeenth day.*

No one can possibly guess that the years of Noah's life, specified down to the year, month, and day, mean a condition of struggle in respect to the promptings of the will, but this was the way the earliest people spoke and wrote, as noted [§66]. They took particular delight in being able to specify periods and names in order to construct an authentic-sounding history. This is what their wisdom consisted in.

[2] I have already shown, at verse 6 above [§737], that *six hundred years* simply symbolize the first stage of trial. The six hundred years here have a similar meaning, but the months and days are added in order to symbolize the second stage. In fact, *two months* (or *in the second month*) is added, symbolizing the actual combat, as can be seen from the symbolism of the number *two,* given above at verse 2 of this chapter. It was shown to have the same symbolism as six: hard work, combat, and dispersing something. (See the demonstration there.)[412]

The number *seventeen,* however, symbolizes both the beginning and the end of trial, because it is composed of seven and ten. When seven symbolizes the beginning of trial, it implies the phrase *in seven days,* or a seven-day week, which was shown above at verse 4 of this chapter [§728] to symbolize the beginning of trial. But when seven symbolizes the end of trial, as it does below in Genesis 8:4, it is a holy number. Ten, symbolizing the things that remain, is added to the seven because without a remnant we cannot be reborn.

[3] The symbolism of seventeen as the beginning of trial can be seen in Jeremiah, where he was commanded to buy a field in Anathoth from Hanamel, his father's brother. Jeremiah weighed out silver for him, *seventeen shekels of silver* (Jeremiah 32:9). This number also symbolized the people's captivity in Babylon, which represented the trials suffered by the faithful and the devastation suffered by the faithless. In fact it represented the start of trial and at the same time the end of trial, or liberation. All this can be seen from later verses in the same chapter of Jeremiah: verse 36 concerns their captivity, and the next, verse 37, their liberation. A number like this would never have shown up in Jeremiah had it not, like all the other details, entailed secrets from heaven.

[4] The symbolism of seventeen as the start of trial can also be seen from Joseph's age—he was a "son of seventeen years"—when he was sent to his brothers and sold into Egypt (Genesis 37:2). The fact that he was sold into Egypt has a similar representation, as will be demonstrated in the appropriate place [§§4670, 4788, 5886], with the Lord's divine mercy.

That passage in Genesis contains historical details with a representative meaning, and events happened according to the description there. The events of the current passage, though, are made-up history with a symbolic meaning and did not happen according to the literal description here. Yet the components of Joseph's story down to the individual words still involve heavenly secrets as much as those of Noah's story do.

This fact necessarily seems strange, because anywhere that an item of true or made-up history occurs, the mind lingers over the literal meaning, unable to extricate itself, and it therefore believes no symbolism or representation exists beyond the letter. [5] But any intelligent person can see that the Word has some kind of inner meaning in which its life resides. (Its life is not in the letter, which apart from the inner meaning is dead.) Without a deeper meaning, how does a historical fact [in the Word] differ from one reported by any secular author? What use would it be to know in what year, month, and day of Noah's life the Flood took place, if this did not involve some heavenly mystery? Can anyone fail to see that *all the springs of the great abyss burst and heaven's floodgates opened* is a prophetic turn of speech? Other similar arguments could be offered.

The symbolism of *all the springs of the great abyss burst* as the climax of their struggles over the intentions of the will can be established by statements just above about two kinds of trial. One kind involves activity in the intellect, the other the activity of the will, the latter being much more severe than the former. It can also be established by the fact that up to this point the discussion has centered on challenges to the workings of the intellect. More evidence for this meaning comes from the symbolism of the *abyss* as corrupt desires and the falsities that spring from them, as before (§18), and from the following passages in the Word. In Ezekiel:

> This is what the Lord Jehovih says: "When I turn you into a ruined city, like cities that are not inhabited; when I bring up over you an *abyss,* and *many waters* cover you . . ." (Ezekiel 26:19)

The abyss and the many waters stand for the climax of struggles. In Jonah:

> The *waters* circled me right to my soul; the *abyss* surrounded me. (Jonah 2:5)

The waters and the abyss here again stand for the extremity of the trials. In David:

> *Abyss* is shouting to *abyss* at the sound of your *watercourses.* All your breakers and all your *waves* go over me. (Psalms 42:7)

Clearly these things stand for a low point in the struggles. In the same author:

> He rebuked the Suph Sea[413] and it dried up, and he took them through the *abysses as if through the desert.* And he saved them from the hand of the one who hated them and redeemed them from the hand of the enemy. And *water covered their foes.* (Psalms 106:9, 10, 11)

The abysses stand for their trials in the wilderness.

[2] The people of ancient times used an abyss to symbolize hell, and they compared delusional thinking and persuasive lies to water, rivers, and smoke pouring out of an abyss. The hells of some spirits look this way too, like an abyss or like the oceans (to be described later [§8099:2–3], by the Lord's divine mercy).

The evil spirits who carry out a person's devastation and also those who put a person through trial come from such hells. Their fantasies, which they pour into us, and the desires that they use to inflame us are like inundations and vapors coming from such places. (As was noted

[§§50, 687], evil spirits connect us with hell, and angels with heaven.) So when all the springs of the abyss are said to burst, these are the things symbolized.

In Ezekiel one can see that hell is called an abyss and that its loathsome discharges are called rivers:

> This is what the Lord Jehovih has said: "On the day that he went down into *hell,* I caused him to mourn; I made the *abyss* cover him and held back its rivers, and *great waters* were shut in." (Ezekiel 31:15)

John too calls hell an abyss in Revelation 9:1, 2, 11; 11:7; 17:8; 20:1, 3.

757

The symbolism of *heaven's floodgates opened* as the climax of their struggles over ideas in the intellect can be established by the same statements just made. Trials involving the urges of the will, or cravings, simply cannot be detached from trials involving concepts in the intellect. If the two were separated, there would be no struggle, only a deluge of the kind that overwhelms people who live amid the raging fire of their appetites, in which they find the core pleasure of their lives, as hellish spirits do.

The term *heaven's floodgates* comes from the flood of falsities or rationalizations that pours in, as portrayed also in Isaiah:

> One fleeing because of a horrifying sound will fall into a pit, and one climbing out of the middle of the pit will be caught in a snare, because the *floodgates in the heights opened* and the foundations of the earth shook. (Isaiah 24:18)

758

Genesis 7:12. *And there was a downpour on the earth for forty days and forty nights* means that this struggle continued. The *downpour* is the struggle, *forty days and nights* is its duration.

759

The fact that the *downpour* means struggle is plain from statements made and evidence offered earlier concerning the Flood [§§733–757]. It is also plain from the meaning of *the springs of the abyss burst and heaven's floodgates opened* as struggles or times of trial.

760

The symbolism of *forty days and nights* as its duration was shown above at verse 4 [§730].

Forty, as noted there, symbolizes every period that trials last, long or short, and in fact it symbolizes severe trial, which involves the impulses of the will.

We construct a life for ourselves through endless sensual pleasures, through love for the material world and for ourselves, and so through our cravings, which are extensions of those loves. The result is that these qualities and nothing more form the material of our lives. Such a life cannot possibly harmonize with heavenly life. No one can love worldly advantages and heavenly ones at the same time; to love what the world offers is to look downward, to love what heaven offers is to face upward. Still less can we love ourselves and our neighbor at the same time, and least of all the Lord. Those who love themselves hate everyone who fails to serve them. So those who love themselves are utterly alienated from heavenly love and charity, which consists in loving our neighbor more than ourselves and loving the Lord above everything.

This demonstrates how large a gap separates mortal life from heavenly life, which is the reason the Lord uses adversity to regenerate us and bend us into harmony.

That is why this kind of struggle is so severe, since it touches, attacks, destroys, and changes our very life. Consequently the situation is depicted in the words *the springs of the abyss burst and heaven's floodgates opened.*

I have already said [§§741, 751] that spiritual struggle is a battle inside us between the evil spirits and angels present with us, and that we sense this conflict indistinctly in our conscience.

Further vital information about this combat is that angels constantly defend us and deflect the evil that the evil spirits intend against us. They even defend the falsity and evil we have in us, because they know very well where we obtained the falsity and evil: from evil spirits and demons. We never produce anything misguided or wicked out of ourselves. It is the evil spirits with us who produce it and at the same time cause us to believe that it comes from us. Such is their malevolence. What is more, at the same instant that they are filling us with these things and making us believe this way, they are also accusing and condemning us. I can back this claim with many different experiences.

Those lacking faith in the Lord cannot receive light dispelling this belief that they are the source of evil, so they adopt the evil as their own and become just like the evil spirits who accompany them. That is the human condition.

As angels are aware of this, during the trials of regeneration they even defend our falsity and evil. Otherwise we would suffer defeat, since we have nothing in us that is not evil and therefore false and are accordingly nothing more than a heap and conglomeration of evils and resulting falsities.

Spiritual struggles are little known today and are not permitted to the extent that they once were, since people are not under the guidance of religious truth and would consequently succumb. Instead there occur other experiences, such as misfortunes, sorrows, and anxieties rising from earthly and bodily causes; and there is physical illness and disease. To some extent these experiences still subdue and shatter our life of pleasure and desire, and they direct and raise our thoughts to profound and godly themes. But they are not spiritual tests. Spiritual tests cannot take place except with those who receive from the Lord a conscience concerning what is true and good. Conscience itself is the field in which those trials do their work.

763

The topic under discussion so far has been times of trial. Now follows the purpose of such times, which was that a new church might come into being.

764

Genesis 7:13. *On that very day Noah entered the ark, as did Shem and Ham and Japheth, Noah's sons, and Noah's wife and his sons' three wives with them.*

They entered the ark here as before means that they were saved. *Noah* symbolizes qualities of the church. *Shem, Ham, and Japheth* symbolize qualities of the churches that developed out of that church. *Noah's sons* symbolize doctrinal teachings. *Noah's wife* symbolizes the actual church. *His sons' three wives* symbolize the actual churches that developed out of that church.

765

Up to this point, the subject has been the trials of the people in the church who were called Noah. First to be discussed were their trials involving the contents of their intellect, which are the true ideas that compose faith (verses 6–10). Next were their trials involving the contents of their will, which have to do with the good impulses of charity (verses 11, 12). The purpose of these struggles was to bring about the rebirth of the individual belonging to the church—in other words, the birth of a new church—when the earliest church ended.

This church, as already explained [§§371, 597, 607], had a different character than the earliest church. It was a spiritual religion, which is one whose members are reborn by means of the doctrinal precepts of faith. When these precepts have taken root, they allow for the introduction of conscience, which prevents a person from acting contrary to the truth and goodness that faith embraces. Such people can then receive the gift of charity, which governs their conscience, and this becomes their guide to behavior. These details illustrate the nature of the spiritual person—not one who considers faith without charity to be saving but one who views charity as the essential quality of faith and takes it as a basis for action.

The emergence of such an individual, or such a church, was the end in view, and so attention now turns to this church.

We can also see that this church is now the subject from the repetition of what seems to be the same idea. The present verse says, "On that very day Noah entered the ark, as did Shem and Ham, and Japheth, Noah's sons, and Noah's wife and his sons' three wives with them." Verse 7 above makes a similar statement, but in these words: "And Noah entered the ark, as did his sons and his wife and his sons' wives with him." Because the church is now the subject, the sons are mentioned by name—Shem, Ham, and Japheth. When they are called by name, they symbolize the people of the church. When on the other hand they are referred to as sons, without names, they symbolize the true concepts of faith.

In addition, what was said at verses 8 and 9 about the entry of the animals and birds into the ark is repeated in verses 14, 15, and 16, with variations here to suit and adapt it to the church.

767 [414]

The meaning of *they entered the ark* as the fact that they were saved is established by what has already been said [§§667, 711, 741] about entering the ark. Those saved are people in the church called "Noah" and the rest of the churches that descended and branched off from that one, all of whom form the focus of attention here.

768

The symbolism of *Noah* as qualities of the church and of *Shem, Ham, and Japheth* as qualities of the churches that developed out of that church can be seen from the fact that they are not called his sons here, as they were above at verse 7. Instead they are called by their names. When their names appear, they symbolize the people of the church. An individual in the church stands not only for the actual church but also for every trait that characterizes the church. The term *person in the church* is a comprehensive one embracing every attribute of religion, as was previously noted in connection with the earliest church, which was called "the human" [§§64, 339, 477–479]. The same is true of all other people whose names are given. So Noah and Shem, Ham, and Japheth symbolize all characteristics of the [new] church and of the churches that grew out of it—all such characteristics taken as a whole. This is the Word's style and manner of speaking.

[2] Where the prophets mention Judah by name, for instance, he usually symbolizes a church that is heavenly, or whatever characterizes such a church. Where Israel is named, he usually symbolizes a church that is spiritual, or whatever characterizes it. Where Jacob is named, he symbolizes the outer church, because in every religious person, the

church has an inner aspect and an outer. The inner aspect is where the true church resides, and the outer aspect is what comes out of it; this latter is Jacob.

The situation is different when these people are not mentioned by name.

[3] The reason why this is the case is that when people are named, they call the Lord's kingdom to mind by representing it. The Lord is the only human, and he is the totality of his kingdom. Since the church is the Lord's kingdom on earth, the Lord alone is also the totality of the church.

The all-in-all of the church is love, or charity, so a human being (or, what is the same, a person mentioned by name) symbolizes love or charity—that is, the totality of the church. The person's wife then symbolizes simply the church composed of those qualities, as the wives here do.[415]

What kind of churches Shem, Ham, and Japheth symbolize will be explained below, with the Lord's divine mercy.[416]

769. The symbolism of *Noah's sons* as doctrinal teachings is established by the meaning of *sons*, dealt with earlier [§§518, 570]. The church could not exist without doctrinal teachings, so the sons are not simply named, but the fact that they were Noah's sons is added.

770. The symbolism of *Noah's wife* as the actual church and of *his sons' three wives with them* as the actual churches that developed out of that church can be seen from what was just said. The statement was that when the person of the church is mentioned by name, it means the all-in-all of the church or, as the expression goes, the head of the church.[417] A *wife* is then the church, as shown earlier (§§252, 253).

Things are otherwise when the Word refers to either *man and wife* or *male and female*. The man or male then symbolizes intellectual concerns, or the truth that faith embraces, and the wife or female symbolizes the concerns of the will, or the good that faith urges.

771. Since every expression in the Word comes from the Lord, so that divinity dwells in each, it is clear that not a single word or even a single jot[418] exists there that does not symbolize or suggest something deeper. This holds true for the fact that it mentions *three* wives here, calls them wives of *his sons,* and says *with them.* But revealing what each detail involves would take too long. It is enough merely to give a general picture of the most comprehensive notions involved.

772. Genesis 7:14, 15. *They, and every kind of wild animal, and every kind of beast, and every kind of creeping thing creeping on the earth, and every kind*

of bird, every flying thing, every winged creature. And they entered to Noah in the ark, two each, two each of all flesh that had the breath of life in it.

They symbolizes the people of the church as a whole. *Every kind of wild animal* symbolizes all spiritual goodness. *Every kind of beast* symbolizes earthly goodness. *Every kind of creeping thing creeping on the earth* symbolizes all goodness at the sensory and bodily levels. *Every kind of bird* symbolizes all spiritual truth; the *flying thing,* earthly truth; and the *winged creature,* truth gained through the senses. *They entered to Noah in the ark* means as before that these things were saved. *Two each and two each* as before [§747] means pairs. *Of all flesh that had the breath of life in it* means a newly created being, or the fact that they received new life from the Lord.

[773] The symbolism of *they* as the people of the church as a whole, or every quality displayed by this church, is evident from the fact that it refers to the people just named: Noah, Shem, Ham, and Japheth. Although there were four of them, together they form a unit.

Noah, who in general stands for the ancient church, held within him the churches that grew out of the ancient one, as a progenitor or a seed holds such things within it, and this is why *they* symbolizes the ancient church. All the churches referred to as Shem, Ham, and Japheth, taken together, form a single church, called the ancient church.

[774] I have already stated and shown that *every kind of wild animal* symbolizes all spiritual goodness, *every kind of beast* all earthly goodness, and the *creeping thing creeping on the earth* all goodness on the sensory and bodily levels (§§45, 46, 142, 143, 246).

It may at first glance seem wrong to say that a wild animal symbolizes spiritual goodness, but look at the series of subjects. First to be mentioned are *they* (the people of the church), then the wild animal, the beast, and finally the creeping thing. The wild animal involves something more important and nobler than a beast, because the Hebrew word also means a living being, something with a living soul. In this verse, then, it does not mean a wild animal but a living creature with a living soul, since the word for both is the same.[419]

The symbolism of living creatures, beasts, and creeping things creeping on the earth as aspects of the will has been mentioned and demonstrated before.[420] More evidence appears directly below, where birds are discussed.

[775] As all things have their divisions into broad and specific categories, including different kinds of goodness on both the spiritual and earthly

planes, and on the resulting sensory and bodily planes, the present verse says *every kind* for each type. There are so many general categories of spiritual goodness and likewise of spiritual truth that they could never be listed. Still less could the particular varieties composing each general category be listed.

In heaven, all heavenly and spiritual goodness and truth are so carefully distinguished into their genera, and the genera into their species, that only what is perfectly distinct exists there. The forms are so far beyond counting that the number of individual species can be called unlimited. This shows the poverty and near insignificance of human wisdom, which hardly even knows that spiritual goodness and truth exist, let alone what they are.

[2] Earthly goodness and truth emerge and descend from heavenly and spiritual kinds of goodness (and from the truth that springs out of the latter kinds of goodness). Nothing good or true exists on the earthly plane that does not rise out of spiritual goodness, which itself rises out of heavenly goodness. Earthly goodness and truth also depend on the higher levels in order to remain in existence. If the spiritual level withdrew, the earthly level would be nothing.

The facts about the origin of all things are these: Absolutely everything comes from the Lord. The heavenly plane is from him. The spiritual plane comes into existence from him by means of the heavenly plane, as does the earthly plane by means of the spiritual, and the bodily and sensory planes by means of the earthly. Because this is how things come into existence from the Lord, it is also how they remain in existence. As is well known, to continue in existence is constantly to come into existence.[421]

Those who view the rise and genesis of things in any other way—people who worship the material world,[422] for instance, and trace the origin of everything to it—are in the grip of such deadly theories that the phantasms of wild animals in the forest can be described as much more sane. This applies to many individuals who seem to themselves to excel others in wisdom.

776. The symbolism of *every kind of bird* as all spiritual truth, the *flying thing* as earthly truth, and the *winged creature* as truth gained through the senses can be seen from what was said and shown earlier about birds, at §40.

The earliest people compared human thoughts to birds, because that is what thought is like, relative to the activity of the will.

The bird, flying thing, and winged creature mentioned here come one after the other in the same way different levels of mental activity do in humans; we can understand things, reason, and use our physical senses. To overcome all doubt that they symbolize these processes, let me bring forward several more passages from the Word in confirmation. (The passages will also show that animals symbolize just what they were said to.) [2] In David:

> You have made him rule over the works of your hands; all things you have put under his feet: the *flock* and all the *herds,* and also the *animals* of the fields, the *flying thing* in the heavens, and the fish in the sea. (Psalms 8:6, 7, 8)

This speaks of the Lord, describing his rule over us and over the things that are in us. What would governance over animals and birds be, if not this? In the same author:

> The fruit tree and all cedars, the *wild animal* and every *beast,* the *creeping thing,* and the *flying creature on the wing* will give glory to Jehovah's name. (Psalms 148:9, 10, 13)

The fruit tree is a heavenly person, the cedar is a spiritual person. The wild animal, beast, and creeping thing are their good qualities (as in the current verses) and the flying thing on the wing is their true ideas. With these they can give glory to Jehovah's name—which a wild animal, beast, creeping thing, or flying creature could never do. Secular writers can use expressions like these as high-flown figures of speech, but the Lord's Word never uses them that way; it uses them only to symbolize or represent something deeper.423 [3] In Ezekiel:

> The fish of the sea and the *bird* of the heavens and the *wild animal* of the field and every *creeping thing creeping* on the ground and every human who is on the face of the ground will tremble before me. (Ezekiel 38:20)

Obviously the animals and birds here are the kinds of symbols I have described, because what glory would there be for Jehovah in the trembling of fish, birds, and beasts? Can anyone imagine that such wording would be holy if it had no sacred content? In Jeremiah:

> I looked and there, not a *human!* Every *bird* of the heavens had fled. (Jeremiah 4:25)

This stands for the fact that everything good and true had fled. The human here also stands for the good that comes of love. In the same author:

> Those places have been laid waste, so that not a man is passing through, and they do not hear the call of any *livestock*. From the *bird* in the heavens to the *beast,* they have wandered away, they have left. (Jeremiah 9:10)

This too stands for the fact that everything true and good has departed. [4] In the same author:

> How long will the land mourn and the *grass* of all the *fields* wither? Because of the wickedness of those living in it, the *animals* and the *bird* have perished, since they said, "He will not see our latter days." (Jeremiah 12:4)

The animals stand for goodness and the bird for truth, both of which have perished. In Zephaniah:

> I will consume *human* and *animal,* I will consume the *bird* in the heavens and the fish in the sea and stumbling blocks in the godless, and I will cut humanity off from the face of the ground. (Zephaniah 1:3)

The human and animal stand for the things that belong to love and to the good that springs from love. The bird in the heavens and the fish in the sea stand for what belongs to the intellect and so for matters of truth. These are called stumbling blocks because goodness and truth—not animals and birds—are obstacles for the godless. It also says clearly that they are things existing in humanity. In David:

> The trees of Jehovah and cedars of Lebanon that he planted, where the *flying things* nest, receive their fill. (Psalms 104:16, 17)

The trees of Jehovah and cedars of Lebanon stand for spiritual people. The flying things stand for their rational and earthly truth. These kinds of truth are like nests.

[5] In other places, *the birds nested in the branches* was a common turn of speech symbolizing truth. In Ezekiel, for example:

> On a high mountain in Israel I will plant it, and it will lift its branch and make fruit and become a majestic cedar. And every *flying creature of every wing* will live under it; in the shade of its branches they will live. (Ezekiel 17:23)

This image stands for the church among non-Jews—a spiritual church, which is what the majestic cedar means.[424] The bird of every wing stands for truth of every kind. In the same author:

> In its branches nested every *bird* of the heavens, and under its branches bred every *wild animal* of the field, and in its shade lived all the great nations. (Ezekiel 31:6)

This concerns Assyria, which is a spiritual church and is called a cedar. The bird of the heavens stands for the truth that church had, and the animals stand for its goodness. [6] In Daniel:

> Its branch was beautiful and its fruit plentiful, and nourishment for all was in it. Under it the *animal* of the field found shade, and in its branches lived the *flying creatures* of heaven. (Daniel 4:12, 21)

The animal stands for goodness, and the flying creature of the heavens for truth, as anyone can see. What would be the point of saying that birds and animals lived there? Similar meaning lies in the Lord's words:

> The kingdom of God is like a mustard seed that a person took and threw into the garden; and it grew and turned into a large tree, so that the *birds* of the sky lived in its branches. (Luke 13:19; Matthew 13:[31,] 32; Mark 4:[31,] 32)

This shows that a bird symbolizes spiritual truth; a flying thing, earthly truth; and a winged creature, truth gained through the senses. These are the categories into which truth divides.

Truth gained through the senses—through sight and hearing—is said to have wings because it is the most external kind. Wings carry the same implication when applied to other objects.[425]

Since the birds of the heavens symbolize truth in the intellect, and so symbolize thoughts, they also symbolize the opposite, including illusions, or false notions. Because these are a matter of human thought, they too are called birds. An example is the fact that the ungodly would be given as food to the birds of the sky and to the wild animals, that is, to illusions and cravings (Isaiah 18:6; Jeremiah 7:33; 16:4; 19:7; 34:20; Ezekiel 29:5; 39:4). The Lord himself compares fantasies and persuasive lies to birds when he says:

> The seed that fell on the hard path was trampled, and the *birds* of the sky ate it. (Matthew 13:4; Luke 8:5; Mark 4:4, 15)

The birds of the sky mean falsity and only that.

779. The meaning of *they entered to Noah in the ark* as the fact that these things were saved has been mentioned before [§§667, 711, 741, 748, 767]. The symbolism of *two each and two each* is pairs; to learn what pairs mean, see Genesis 6:19 above [§672].

780. The fact that *of all flesh that had the breath of life in it* means a newly created being, or the fact that they received new life from the Lord, is established by the symbolism of *flesh* as every person in general and a body-centered one in particular. This meaning with its proof was presented earlier [§§574, 661]. So flesh *that has the breath of life in it* symbolizes an individual reborn, since within such a person's sense of autonomy lies the Lord's life, which is the vital force of charity and faith.

None of us is anything but flesh, but when the Lord stirs in us the living quality of charity and faith, our flesh comes to life and becomes spiritual and heavenly. Then we are called a new creature (Mark 16:15)[426] because we have been created anew.

781. Genesis 7:16. *And those entering—a male and a female of all flesh—entered as God had commanded him. And Jehovah closed it behind him.*

Those entering symbolizes attributes of the people in the church. *A male and a female of all flesh entered* means that they had every kind of truth and goodness in them. *As God had commanded* means that they had been prepared to receive such things. *And Jehovah closed it behind him* means that people were no longer able to communicate with heaven as the people of the heavenly church had.

782. The discussion so far, to verse 15,[427] has centered on the church and its preservation in the people referred to as Noah. It now turns to conditions in the church and a depiction of them. At first the conditions are depicted as being those already explained. Then the nature of those conditions is portrayed. The individual verses and in fact the individual words suggest this church's particular circumstances.

Because conditions in the church are the present topic, the verse repeats what came just above, and repeats it twice. It says, "And those *entering*—a male and a female of *all flesh—entered,*" while the very last verse said, "And they *entered* to Noah in the ark, two each and two each of *all flesh.*" Repetition like this in the Word signals the fact that a different state is being discussed. If it did not, the repetition would be completely pointless, as anyone can see.

783. The symbolism of *those entering* as attributes of the people in the church can be seen from the above.

The meaning of *a male and a female of all flesh entered* as the fact that they had every kind of truth and goodness in them also follows. The symbolism of *male and female* as truth and goodness has been stated and demonstrated several times before.428

As God had commanded means that they had been prepared to receive such things. This meaning and this identification of the things to be received has already been discussed.429 For the Lord, to command is to prepare someone and to act.

As for the fact that *Jehovah closed it behind him* means that people were no longer able to communicate with heaven the way the people of the heavenly church had, the case is this:

Circumstances in the earliest church allowed its people to communicate internally with heaven and through heaven with the Lord. They loved the Lord, and people who love the Lord are like angels, the only difference being that they are clothed in a body. Their deeper levels were open, offering unhindered access all the way to the Lord.

This new church, however, was different. Its people believed in rather than loved the Lord, and faith led them into charity toward their fellow humans. They could engage in external communication, but not in internal communication, as the earliest people had. Describing the two kinds of communication, though, would take too long.

We all communicate with heaven—even the sacrilegious—through the angels present with us. Without this, we would not be human. But the degree of intimacy varies from very close to very distant, with an unlimited number of steps in between. Spiritual people are wholly incapable of the kind of contact heavenly people have, because the Lord dwells in love and not so much in faith.

This, then, is the meaning of *Jehovah closed it behind him*.

[2] Moreover, heaven was never open after that era in the way that it had been for the people of the earliest church. It is true that many people—Moses, Aaron, and others—later talked to spirits and angels, but the method was entirely different. By the Lord's divine mercy, it will be described below [§5121].

The reason heaven was closed off and remains closed today is a deep secret. Heaven is so tightly shut that people are unaware even that spirits exist, let alone that angels are present with them. They suppose they are completely alone when they are away from companions in this world and thinking privately. The truth is that we are constantly in the company of spirits, who notice and perceive what we are thinking, and what we are intending and scheming. They observe these things as thoroughly and openly as if they stood out for all the world to see. We have no knowledge whatever that this is so, since heaven is so utterly closed to us, but it is positively true.

The reason is that were heaven not sealed off this way in humankind, it would be extremely dangerous for people, since they do not possess faith, much less religious truth, least of all charity. This is also the meaning of the words above at Genesis 3:24 [§§306–310], "Jehovah God threw the humans out and caused guardian beings[430] to live on the east of the Garden of Eden, and the flame of a sword turning itself, to guard the way to the tree of life." See also what was said in §§301, 302, 303.

785. Genesis 7:17, 18. *And the flood was forty days on the earth, and the waters grew and lifted the ark and it rose off the earth. And the water strengthened and increased greatly on the earth; and the ark went on the face of the water.*

Forty days symbolizes the length of time the church called Noah lasted. The *flood* symbolizes the false ideas that still swamped them. *The waters grew and lifted the ark and it rose off the earth* means that this is how they wavered. *The water strengthened and increased greatly on the earth, and the ark went on the face of the water* means that this is how their wavering intensified.

786. The symbolism of *forty days* as the length of time the church called Noah lasted was demonstrated above at verse 4 [§730]. This verse says *forty days,* that one said *forty days and nights,* because the symbolism there was the length of time the trials lasted, the nights being times of anxiety.

787. The symbolism of the *flood* as the false ideas that still swamped the people of that church also follows from earlier statements [§660], because a flood or deluge simply means a flood, or deluge, *of falsity.*

Above, in verse 6 [§739], a flood of water symbolized trials, as shown there, and that flood was also an inundation of falsity—the falsity that evil spirits stir up in us during our trials. A similar flood is meant here, but not in the context of our trials. Accordingly the present verse mentions only a flood, not a flood of water.

788. *The waters grew and lifted the ark and it rose off the earth* means that this is how those people wavered. *The water strengthened and increased greatly on the earth, and the ark went on the face of the water* means that this is how their wavering intensified. The symbolism here will not be apparent until I say what conditions were like in this Noah church.

Noah was not the true ancient church but a kind of progenitor or seed from which that church came, as already pointed out [§773]. Noah and Shem, Ham, and Japheth together constituted the ancient church that came right after the earliest church. All those in the church who were referred to as Noah came from the descendants of the earliest church. Consequently their condition in respect to an evil heredity[431] was almost the same as that of the other descendants, who were destroyed. Because their condition was similar, they could not regenerate and become spiritual in the same way as those who do not inherit such a character. The nature of their heredity was described above, at §310.

[2] Let me explain more clearly how the situation stands. Those—such as Jews—who have descended from Jacob's seed cannot regenerate in the same way as other races. They maintain a creed hostile to genuine faith, acquired not only from principles adopted in childhood and later confirmed but also from heredity. The fact that heredity contributes can be seen from the consideration that their mentality, their mores, and even their faces differ from those of others and these three attributes (by which they can be recognized) are inherited. So also for their deeper qualities, since custom and facial appearance are signs of what lies within. Consequently, converted Jews waver between truth and falsity more than others do.[432]

The same is true of the first adherents of this church, referred to as Noah, because they came from the stock and seed of the earliest people.[433]

Such vacillation is what the present verses depict, as do later verses that say Noah was a man of the ground, planted a vineyard, drank some of the wine, and became so drunk that he lay naked in the middle of his tent (Genesis 9:20, 21).

I was able to tell how small their numbers were from seeing the people of that church represented in the world of spirits as a tall, slender man dressed in bright white, standing in a cramped room. Yet these were the people who preserved the doctrinal teachings of faith, which they had among them.

The details here portray the faltering of the people in this church. First the waters—falsities—grew, then they lifted the ark and it rose off the earth. Next the water strengthened and increased greatly on the earth, and finally the ark went on the face of the water. But describing the different stages of vacillation would be both tedious and useless. It is enough to know they are depicted here. All that needs explaining is the meaning of the phrases *it rose off the earth* and *it went on the face of the water*. The symbolism is not evident to anyone who has not learned how we are held back from evil and falsity. Since this is unknown I must explain it briefly.

All people in general, and even those who are regenerate, are such that unless the Lord held them back from evil and falsity they would throw themselves headlong into hell. At any moment that we are not withheld, we rush there precipitately, as I have discovered through various experiences. The horse mentioned in §§187, 188 also represented this.

To be held back in this way is no different than being lifted up or *rising,* so that the evil and falsity are perceived as being below and the person above. More about such elevation will come later, with the Lord's divine mercy.[434]

This lifting up or rising is what the ark symbolized in rising off the earth and going on the face of the water.

790 The symbolism of *water* here and below as falsity is established by the passages dealing with a flood of water that were cited from the Word in the prefatory section of this chapter and at verse 6 [§§705, 739]. The quotations in those two places show that floods of water symbolize times of desolation and trial, which carry the same consequences as false notions, since desolation and trial are nothing but deluges of the falsities stirred up by evil spirits. The symbolism of flood water as falsities comes from the general meaning of water in the Word as something spiritual, that is, as the things we truly understand, grasp rationally, and know about. Because water symbolizes these things, it also symbolizes their opposites, since every falsity, being a matter of thought, is a "fact," so to speak, and seems capable of being grasped rationally and understood.

The symbolism of water as things that are spiritual can be seen from many places in the Word.[435] In support of its symbolism as falsity, though, I offer the following in addition to previous quotations.[436] [2] In Isaiah:

> This people spurned the *waters* of Shiloah, which go gently. Therefore (look, now!) the Lord is bringing up over them the *waters of a river, strong and abundant;* and it will come up over all their brooks and go on all their banks. (Isaiah 8:6, 7)

The waters going gently stand for things that are spiritual, waters strong and abundant for things that are false. In the same author:

> Doom to a land casting shadow with its wings,[437] a land across the rivers of Cush, that sends ambassadors onto the sea and [puts them]

in rattan vessels on the *face of the water*. Go, speedy envoys, to a nation marked out and trampled, whose land the *rivers* plunder. (Isaiah 18:1, 2)

Here they stand for the falsities that belong to a "land casting shadow with its wings." [3] In the same author:

When you cross through the *water*, I will be with you, and [when you cross] through the *rivers*, they will not drown you. (Isaiah 43:2)

The water and rivers stand for difficulties and for falsities. In Jeremiah:

What does it matter whether you go to Egypt to drink the *waters* of the Sihor? And what does it matter whether you go to Assyria to drink the *waters* of the river? (Jeremiah 2:18)

The waters stand for the falsities produced by crooked reasoning. In the same author:

Who is this who rises like a *river*, whose *waters* churn like *rivers*? Egypt rises like a *river*, and like *rivers* its *waters* churn, and it said, "I will go up; *I will cover the land*; I will destroy the city and those living in it." (Jeremiah 46:7, 8)

The waters stand for the falsities produced by crooked reasoning. [4] In Ezekiel:

This is what the Lord Jehovih has said, "When I turn you into a devastated city, like cities that are not inhabited; when I bring up over you an *abyss*, and *many waters cover you*, and I make you go down with those going down into the pit . . ." (Ezekiel 26:19, 20)

The waters stand for evil and the falsity it engenders. In Habakkuk:

You trod the *sea* with your horses, the mud of many *waters*. (Habakkuk 3:15)

The waters stand for falsity. In John:

The dragon hurled *water* like a *river* from its mouth after the woman to cause her to be swallowed up by the *stream*. (Revelation 12:15, 16)

The water here stands for falsities and lies. In David:

Put out your hands from high up, rescue me and free me from the *many waters*, from the hand of a foreigner's children, whose mouth speaks a *lie,* and their right hand is the right hand of *falsity.* (Psalms 144:7, 8)

The many waters clearly stand for falsities. A foreigner's children also symbolize falsities.

791 These verses, then, have dealt with Noah, or in other words, the regenerate people called Noah, who were in the ark and rose above the water. Now comes a description of the earliest church's descendants caught under the water, or submerged in it.

792 Genesis 7:19, 20. *And the water strengthened greatly, greatly on the earth, and all the high mountains that were under the whole heaven were covered. Fifteen cubits upward the water towered, and it covered the mountains.*

The water strengthened greatly, greatly on the earth means that persuasive lies piled up in this way. *And all the high mountains that were under the whole heaven were covered* means that all the good effects of charity were obliterated. *Fifteen cubits upward the water towered, and it covered the mountains* means that nothing was left of charity: *fifteen* symbolizes what is so meager as to be hardly anything.

793 From here to the end of the chapter, the topic being discussed is the pre-Flood people who perished, as can be seen from the individual parts of the description. Anyone alive to the inner meaning can tell instantly what the subject is, even from a single word, and even more easily from the connections among many words. When the topic changes, different words suddenly come into use, or else the previous words are linked together in a new way. The reason for the shift is that spiritual themes have their own special vocabulary and heavenly themes have theirs, or to put it another way, intellectual matters have their own vocabulary and volitional ones theirs. Ruination, for example, is a word that applies to spiritual things, while devastation applies to heavenly things; a city has to do with spiritual things, while a mountain has to do with heavenly things; and so on. The same holds true for the ways that words link together.

No one could help being surprised to learn that in Hebrew it is often sound that distinguishes the two. In words that belong to the spiritual category, the first three vowels [of the Hebrew alphabet] usually predominate. In those that capture heavenly qualities, the last two vowels do.[438]

The changing of topics here can be recognized by such signs, and also by the repetition involved (as discussed previously [§§435, 683, 707, 734,

765, 782]). To be specific, it says again here, "And the water strengthened greatly, greatly on the earth," as the last verse also said. The fact of a switch can also be recognized from everything that follows.

And the water strengthened greatly, greatly on the earth means that persuasive lies piled up in this way, as is established by statements made and evidence offered just above concerning *water*. They showed that flood waters symbolize falsities. Because the falsity (or the false persuasions) intensified, the current verse says that the water strengthened *greatly, greatly,* this being a superlative in the original language.

By falsities I mean false premises and false persuasions. These increased tremendously among the pre-Flood people, as remarks above [§§560, 562, 581, 660–661, 705:3, 736] concerning them make clear.

Self-delusion grows tremendously when it taints truth with perverted desires, that is, when it uses truth to justify self-love and materialism. In doing so, it corrupts truth and forces it to cooperate in a thousand different ways. What person is there who has either absorbed or manufactured false principles, without using a plethora of facts at his or her disposal—even from the Word—to confirm them? Is there a heresy in existence that does not seize on this kind of support? And if heresy comes across arguments that do not harmonize, it compels them to yield anyway, explaining and distorting them in a variety of ways until they no longer disagree.

[2] Take those who embrace the premise that faith alone, without the good deeds of charity, brings salvation. Are they not capable of weaving together a whole system of theology out of the Word? And yet they do not care about, they do not pay attention to, they do not even see the Lord's words that a tree is recognized by its fruit and that a tree not bearing good fruit will be cut down and thrown into the fire (Matthew 7:16, 17, 18, 19, 20; 12:33). What could be more pleasing than to live by the desires of our flesh and still be saved? To merely know what is true without doing a single scrap of good?

Every perverse yearning that we cultivate goes into making up the life of our will, and every falsity that we adopt as a premise or as a conviction goes into making up the life of our intellect. These two kinds of life combine into one when we merge the doctrinal teachings of faith with our cravings. By this means we each form a kind of personal soul, and the quality of its life remains unchanged after death. As a result, nothing is more important for us than to know what is true. When we know what is true—and know it in such a way that it cannot be perverted—it cannot be infused with corrupt desires and do deadly harm. What should we take more to heart than our eternal life? If we destroy our soul during bodily life, do we not destroy it forever?[439]

795 The meaning of *all the high mountains that were under the whole heaven were covered* as the fact that all the good effects of charity were obliterated can be seen from the symbolism of *mountains* among the earliest people.

Among the earliest people, mountains symbolized the Lord, because it was on mountains that they held worship to him. Their reason for doing so was that mountains were the highest points on earth. Consequently mountains symbolized heavenly qualities—love and charity, and so the good effects of love and charity, which are heavenly—and the people also referred to these things as "most high."

Employing an opposite sense, the Word also refers to those who are conceited—and accordingly to self-love itself—as mountains.

Mountains in the Word symbolize the earliest church too, because they rise so high above the earth and in this way are (in a sense) closer to heaven, the origin of everything.

[2] The symbolism of mountains as the Lord and all the heavenly qualities that come from him (in other words, the good effects of love and charity) is established by the following places in the Word. These passages reveal the particular meanings of mountains, since the way things stand with each and every object depends on the subject at hand. In David:

> The *mountains* will bring peace, as will the *hills*, in justice. (Psalms 72:3)

The mountains stand for love for the Lord, the hills for neighborly love, of the type the earliest church possessed. Because it possessed this type of love, mountains and hills in the Word symbolize that church as well. In Ezekiel:

> "On my *holy mountain,* on the *mountain* of Israel's *high ground,*" says the Lord Jehovih, "where all the house of Israel—the whole of that house in the land—will serve me . . ." (Ezekiel 20:40)

The holy mountain stands for love for the Lord; the mountain of Israel's high ground, for charity toward others. In Isaiah:

> It will happen in the end of days that the *mountain of Jehovah's house* will stand firm, will become the head of the *mountains,* and will be loftier than the *hills.* (Isaiah 2:2)

Here they stand for the Lord and so for every heavenly quality. In the same author:

> Jehovah Sabaoth will make for all peoples on this *mountain* a banquet of rich foods. And he will swallow up on this *mountain* the enveloping layers.⁴⁴⁰ (Isaiah 25:6, 7)

The mountain stands for the Lord and so for every heavenly quality. [3] In the same author:

> It will be that on every *high mountain* and on every *lofty hill* there will be brooks, channels of water. (Isaiah 30:25)

The mountains stand for the good effects of love, the hills for the good effects of charity. Out of these come the true ideas that make up faith, which are the brooks and channels of water. In the same author:

> You will have song like the holy observance of a feast at night, and joy of heart like that of one who goes about with a flute to come onto *Jehovah's mountain*, toward *Israel's rock*. (Isaiah 30:29)

Jehovah's mountain stands for the Lord in relation to the good that comes of love. Israel's rock stands for the Lord in relation to the good that comes of charity. In the same author:

> Jehovah Sabaoth will come down to wage war on Zion's *mountain* and on its *hill*. (Isaiah 31:4)

The mountain of Zion here and in many other places stands for the Lord and so for every heavenly quality (love), while hills stand for a lesser heavenly quality (charity). [4] In the same author:

> Take yourself up onto a *high mountain*, you who bring good news to Zion. Lift your voice with strength, you who bring good news to Jerusalem. (Isaiah 40:9)

Going up onto a high mountain and bringing good news is worshiping the Lord in love and charity, which lie at our deepest level and are therefore described as being highest. (What lies deepest is also referred to as highest.) In the same author:

> Let those who live on the *crag* sing; from the *head of the mountains* let them shout. (Isaiah 42:11)

Those who live on a crag stand for those who live in charity. Shouting from the head of the mountains stands for worshiping the Lord with love. In the same author:

> How gratifying on the *mountains* are the feet of the one who brings good news, who lets people hear about peace, who brings good news of something *good,* who lets people hear about salvation. (Isaiah 52:7)

Bringing good news on the mountains stands in a similar way for preaching about the Lord—and worshiping him—from teachings about love and charity. In the same author:

> The *mountains and hills* will ring before you with song, and all the trees of the field will clap the palms of their hands. (Isaiah 55:12)

This stands for worshiping the Lord in love and charity (which are the mountains and hills) and in the faith that grows out of them (which is the trees of the field.) [5] In the same author:

> I will turn all my *mountains* into a road, and my paths will be *lifted high.* (Isaiah 49:11)

The mountains stand for love and charity, a road and paths for the truth belonging to faith that springs from them. These are said to be lifted high when truth does develop out of love and charity, since these are the deepest entities in us. In the same author:

> The one who trusts in me will own the land as an inheritance and will inherit my *holy mountain.* (Isaiah 57:13)

This stands for the Lord's kingdom, where there is nothing but love and charity. In the same author:

> From Jacob I will produce seed, and from Judah, the heir to my *mountains;* and the ones I have chosen will own it. (Isaiah 65:9)

The mountains stand for the Lord's kingdom and for heavenly kinds of goodness. Judah stands for the heavenly church. In the same author:

> This is what the *High* and *Exalted One* dwelling to eternity has said—and The Holy One is his name: "*High* and holy I will dwell." (Isaiah 57:15)

The height mentioned here stands for holiness, which is the reason that mountains, because they stand high above the earth, symbolize the Lord and his holy, heavenly qualities. And this is why the Lord also issued the law from Mount Sinai.

The Lord too was referring to love and charity when he mentioned mountains in speaking about the end of the age, saying that whoever was in Judea should then flee into the *mountains* (Matthew 24:16; Luke 21:21; Mark 13:14). In this passage, Judea stands for the church after it had been devastated.

796. Since the people of the earliest church held their sacred worship on mountains, the ancient church also carried out ritual sacrifices on mountains and built high places. So too, consequently, did all the representative churches of that era, and even the surrounding nations. Abram's adherence to this practice can be seen in Genesis 12:8; 22:2. Its use among the Jews before the building of the Temple can be seen in Deuteronomy 27:4, 5, 6, 7; Joshua 8:30; 1 Samuel 9:12, 13, 14, 19; 10:5; 1 Kings 3:2, 3, 4. Its use among other nations can be seen in Deuteronomy 12:2; 2 Kings 17:9, 10, 11. Its use among Jewish idolaters can be seen in Isaiah 57:7; 1 Kings 11:7; 14:23; 22:43; 2 Kings 12:3; 14:4; 15:3, 4, 34, 35; 16:4; 17:9, 10, 11; 21:3; 23:5, 8, 9, 13, 15.

797. From all this it can now be seen what the water that covered the mountains symbolizes: the fact that persuasive lies wiped out all the good effects of charity.

798. The meaning of *fifteen cubits upward the water towered, and it covered the mountains,* as the fact that nothing was left of charity, and the symbolism of *fifteen* as what is so meager as to be hardly anything, can be seen from the symbolism of *five*. This was dealt with above at Genesis 6:15 [§649], where it was shown that according to the Word's mode of expression, or in its inner meaning, five symbolizes a small amount. And since fifteen is made out of five, symbolizing a little, and *ten,* symbolizing what remains (as shown above at Genesis 6:3 [§576]), it has to do with the remnant these people possessed, which hardly amounted to anything. The falsities of which people had persuaded themselves were so enormous that they eradicated everything good.

How the case stands with the remnant stored inside people was described earlier [§§562–563, 571]: false premises and especially distorted convictions, as they existed among these pre-Flood people, locked up any surviving traces [of truth and goodness] and shut them away so entirely that they could not be brought out again. If they had been, they would have been falsified immediately. The vital force of delusions is such that it not only rejects everything true and soaks up everything false but also perverts any truth that does come near.

799
Genesis 7:21, 22. *And all flesh creeping on the earth passed away—including the bird and the beast and the wild animal and every crawling thing crawling on the earth—and every human. Everything that had the breath of living spirit in its nostrils, of all that was on dry land, died.*

All flesh creeping on the earth passed away means that those who belonged to the final generation of the earliest church died out. *Including the bird and the beast and the wild animal and every crawling thing crawling on the earth* symbolizes their self-deceptions. The *bird* symbolizes an attachment to falsity, the *beast* symbolizes corrupt desires, the *wild animal* symbolizes sensual pleasure, and the *crawling thing* symbolizes bodily and earthly yearnings. These different impulses are contained within the self-deceptions, and taken together they are called *every human*. *Everything that had the breath of living spirit in its nostrils* symbolizes those who were part of the earliest church and had the *breath of living spirit in their nostrils*—that is, who had lived a life of love and of a faith based on love. *Of all that was on dry land* symbolizes people who no longer had any of that life. *They died* means that this life expired.

800
The meaning of *all flesh creeping on the earth passed away* as the fact that those who belonged to the final generation of the earliest church died out can be seen from later sections that describe their delusions and desires [§§803, 806, 808].

Here for the first time they are called *flesh creeping on the earth,* because they became obsessed with sensory and bodily matters. The earliest people compared sense impressions and bodily concerns to creeping animals, as noted earlier [§§195–197], so that when the text mentions flesh creeping on the earth, it symbolizes the kind of people who have become entirely absorbed in what is sensory and bodily.

Previous statements and evidence [§574] have shown that flesh symbolizes everyone, when used in a broad sense, and body-centered people, when used in a narrow sense.

801
The portrayal of these pre-Flood people reveals what the literary mode of the earliest people was like and so what the prophetic mode was like. The chapter from here to the end describes those people, telling of their delusions in the current verse and of their appetites in verse 23 below. In other words, it depicts the condition of the ideas in their intellect and then the condition of the impulses in their will.

Although nothing in them was [truly] a matter of understanding or will, the contrary thoughts and impulses they had must still be called such. These include their distorted convictions, which are anything but matters of understanding, since they are the product of thought and of twisted logic; and their cravings, which are anything but a matter of will.

Those people are described, as I was saying, in respect first to their distorted convictions and next to their cravings, which is why the statements of verse 21 here are repeated in verse 23 below, although in a different order.

[2] The prophets used the same manner of expression. Its basis is the existence of two vital forces in us, one belonging to the ideas of the intellect, and the other to the intentions of the will. The two kinds of life force are perfectly distinct from each other. We consist of both, and although they are separate in people today, the one still has an influence on the other and for the most part unites with it. The fact that they unite can be established and illustrated by much supporting evidence, as can the way they unite.

Since we consist of these two sides, then—of intellect and will—and since the one side affects the other, when the Word draws a picture of a human being it depicts each of the two sides separately. This is the reason for the repetition, which would otherwise be a defect.

The same is true with every facet of reality, because different abstract phenomena exactly mirror conditions in the people who experience them. They are attributes of those people because they arise out of them. An abstract phenomenon separated from the person subject to it, or from a substance underlying it, has no reality at all. This is the reason the Word describes things as having two parts, in the manner detailed above. Doing so makes the portrayal of every phenomenon complete.

An indication that the present verse is talking about delusions and verse 23 about appetites is that the present verse mentions birds first and then beasts. Birds symbolize different aspects of the things we understand or find logical, while beasts symbolize different aspects of the things we intend. When matters of desire are described, however, as they are below in verse 23, beasts are named first and then birds. This device is used because, as noted, each side influences the other, so that to describe them this way is to give a full description.

Including the bird and the beast and the wild animal and every crawling thing crawling on the earth symbolizes their self-deceptions. *Birds* symbolize an attachment to falsity, the *beast* symbolizes corrupt desires, the *wild animal* symbolizes sensual pleasure, the *crawling thing crawling* symbolizes bodily and earthly yearnings, and these different impulses are contained within the self-deceptions. The symbolism here is established by earlier demonstrations of the meaning of birds and beasts. A treatment of birds appeared at §40 and above at verses 14 and 15 of this chapter [§§776–778]. A treatment of beasts also appeared in the latter place [§774] and at §§45, 46, 142, 143, 246 as well.

Because birds symbolize matters of understanding, reason, and fact, they also symbolize the opposites of these—corrupt reasoning, falsity, and attachment to falsity.

These words portray the self-deceptions of a pre-Flood person in their entirety, specifically the feelings of attachment to falsity, corrupt desires, sensual pleasures, and bodily and earthly yearnings that their self-deceptions carried with them. All these impulses are inherent in a person's delusions, although no one realizes it. We tend to consider a false premise or conviction an irreducible unit, or else a single generalized concept, but we are very wrong. The situation is completely otherwise. Each of our feelings derives its manifestation and its nature from resources in our intellect and in our will. Our whole being, then, with all that we understand and all that we will, enters into every emotion that we have and in fact into the most detailed, minute aspects of our emotions.

This has become clear to me from a wealth of experience. [2] To mention a single example, in the other life spirits can be recognized by just one of the individual ideas that go into their thinking. The angels even receive from the Lord an ability merely to look at a person and fathom immediately what the person's character is, without making the slightest mistake.[441] This shows clearly that every one of our ideas, every one of our feelings, and indeed every shred of feeling in us, no matter how small, is an image and portrait of us. To put it another way, each of these contains an element—whether closely or distantly related—of every thought in our intellect and every impetus of our will.

These verses, then, describe the appalling convictions of a pre-Flood person and how they carry with them attachment to falsity, attachment to evil (corrupt desires), sensual pleasure, and bodily and earthly yearnings. All these impulses are inherent in such convictions, in which bodily and earthly yearnings predominate—and not only in those convictions as a whole but in the most detailed, minute aspects of them.

If we realized the extent of the consequences for one false assumption or one false persuasion, we would be horrified. Each is like an effigy of hell. But if we adopt it in all innocence or ignorance, the falsity of it is easily dispelled.

The added phrase *every human* means that these things existed in the people under discussion. It is a general closure that embraces everything before it. Such tags occur in many places.⁴⁴²

Everything that had the breath of living spirit in its nostrils symbolizes those who were part of the earliest church and had the *breath of living spirit in their nostrils*—that is, who had lived a life of love and of a faith based on love. This can be seen from what was said earlier at §§96, 97.

Life was what the earliest people meant when they referred to *breath in the nostrils.* Breath is the vital physical force that corresponds to spiritual things, just as the beating of the heart is the vital physical force that corresponds to heavenly things.

The people spoken of here are the pre-Flood people who had inherited from their ancestors the rudiments of a heavenly quality (although it came to be snuffed out or smothered). That is why it says *everything that had the breath of living spirit in its nostrils.*

[2] These words also conceal an even deeper meaning, one dealt with in §97.⁴⁴³ This deeper secret is that the people of the earliest church breathed internally, so that their breathing was harmonious with and similar to the breathing of the angels. More on this later [§§1118–1120, 3892, 7361], with the Lord's divine mercy. Such respiration varied with all the phases their inner being went through. It changed over time in their descendants, however, up to this final generation, in whom everything angelic died out. When that happened, they forfeited their ability to breathe in unison with the angelic heaven as well. This was the real reason for their extinction, which is why it now says that they passed away and that those with the breath of living spirit in their nostrils died.

[3] From this time, inner breathing ceased—and along with it people's contact with heaven, and therefore the ability to intuit things in a heavenly way—and external breathing took its place. Since contact with heaven ceased in the process, the people of the ancient church (which was the new church) were no longer capable of a heavenly character, as the earliest people had been, but only a spiritual one. This will be dealt with below, though, the Lord in his divine mercy willing.⁴⁴⁴

The conclusions follow logically that *of all that was on dry land* symbolizes people who no longer had any of that life and that *they died* means that this life expired. And since the whole living force of love and faith had been eradicated, the term *dry land* appears.

Dry land is a place without water, that is, where there is no longer anything spiritual, let alone heavenly. The conviction that falsity is true destroys any spiritual or heavenly quality by suffocating it, so to speak, as we can all see from much experience, if we pay attention. Once people have laid hold of an opinion, even if it is utterly false, they stick to it so obstinately that they do not want even to hear anything that contradicts it. They positively refuse to be taught, even if you place the truth before their very eyes. This applies still more strongly to those who treat their misguided opinions with a sort of reverential awe. People who rebuff all truth and pervert what they do allow themselves to hear, suffusing it with their fantasies, are like this.

They are the ones symbolized here by the dry land, which has neither water nor grain on it, as in Ezekiel:

> I will turn the rivers into *dry ground* and sell the land into the hand of the evil and strip the land and its abundance. (Ezekiel 30:12)

Turning the rivers into dry ground stands for a condition in which nothing spiritual remains. And in Jeremiah:

> Your land has become *dry ground*. (Jeremiah 44:22)

Dry ground stands for a ruined and devastated land, where nothing true or good remains.

807 Genesis 7:23. *And all substance that was on the face of the ground was obliterated, from human to animal to creeping thing to the bird of the heavens, and they were obliterated from the earth. And Noah alone was left, and what was with him in the ark.*

All substance was obliterated symbolizes cravings, which are a product of self-love. *That was on the face of the ground* symbolizes the descendants of the earliest church. *From human to animal to creeping thing to the bird of the heavens* symbolizes the nature of their evil. The *human* is the actual nature, the *animal* is cravings, the *creeping thing* sensual pleasure, and the *bird of the heavens* the falsity that grows out of these. *And they were obliterated from the earth* sums it up by saying that the earliest church passed away. *Noah alone was left, and what was with him in the ark,* means that those who made up the new church were kept alive, *what was with him in the ark* being everything that belonged to the new church.

808 The symbolism of *all substance was obliterated* as cravings, which are a product of self-love, is established by the next few phrases, which describe the cravings through the creatures that represent them. *Substance* has to do with matters of the will, because in human beings, everything rises out of the will, that is to say, everything emerges from the will and feeds off it. The will is a person's real substance, a person's real self.

The cravings or corrupt desires of the pre-Flood people grew out of self-love. There are two very broad categories of selfish desire; one has to do with self-love, the other with love of worldly gain. We can crave only what we love, so cravings are a matter of love. The pre-Flood people were dominated by self-love and therefore by the appetites connected with it. They loved themselves so intensely that they considered themselves gods, not acknowledging any god higher than themselves. This was their conviction.

809

The symbolism of *that was on the face of the ground* as the descendants of the earliest church is established by the symbolism of the *ground* as the church and so as everything that belongs to the church. This has already been detailed [§§386, 566–567]. Since the verse describes substance that was on the face of the ground as being obliterated, the meaning is that the people in the earliest church who were like this were wiped out.

The word *ground* is used here, but the word *earth* in verse 21 above, because intellectual traits are never described as being the church; only qualities of the will are. A bare knowledge of faith and reasoning that supports faith does not in the least constitute the church or a member of the church. Charity in the will does. Every essential quality comes from the will. As a result, doctrinal concepts also do not make the church unless they look to charity in their whole and in every part. When they do this, charity becomes the purpose, and the purpose behind a doctrinal concept is what reveals its quality—whether it really embodies the church or not.

The Lord's church, like his kingdom in the heavens, consists solely of love and charity.

810

From human to animal to creeping thing to the bird of the heavens symbolizes the nature of these people's evil. The *human* is the actual nature, the *animal* is cravings, the *creeping thing* sensual pleasure, and the *bird of the heavens* the falsity that grows out of these. This is established by the symbolism of all these things as dealt with above [§§803–804], so there is no need to linger over them.

811

They were obliterated from the earth sums it up by saying that the earliest church passed away. *Noah alone was left, and what was with him in the ark,* means that those who made up the new church were kept alive, *what was with him in the ark* being everything that belonged to the new church. These things also need no further explanation, because they are self-evident.

812

Genesis 7:24. *And the water strengthened on the earth for one hundred fifty days* symbolizes the ending point of the earliest church. *One hundred fifty* is an ending point and a starting point.

813 The symbolism of these words as the ending point of the earliest church and of *one hundred fifty* as an ending point and a starting point is not so susceptible to proof from the Word as the meanings of the simpler numbers, which appear over and over. Still it can be deduced from the fact that the number *fifteen,* dealt with above at verse 20 [§798], symbolizes what is so meager as to be hardly anything. All that much more so the number one hundred fifty, which is a product of fifteen and ten, since the latter symbolizes remaining traces. Multiplying a small amount—a half, quarter, or tenth, for instance—results in an even smaller product, so small finally as to be almost nothing.[445] In consequence, it is a conclusion or ending point. The same number appears again in Genesis 8:3 ("the waters receded at the end of one hundred fifty days"), where the meaning is similar.

We need to view the numbers in the Word quite separately from the literal meaning. They are added simply to spin out the thread of the story found in the letter, as stated and shown before [§§482:1, 755:4, 5]. Where seven occurs, for instance, it means holiness, with no reference whatever to the periods of time and the measurements that it usually quantifies. Angels, who perceive the inner meaning of the Word, know nothing of time and measure, let alone what number is specified. Yet when we read the Word, they fully understand it.[446] Wherever a number comes up, then, they are unable to form any idea of a number but picture instead the phenomenon that the number symbolizes. So by the number here they understand the ending point of the earliest church, and in verse 3 of the next chapter they understand the starting point of the ancient church, which was the new church.

The Hells (Continued): The Hells of Those Who Spent Their Lives in Hatred, Revenge, and Cruelty

814 THERE are people who nurse a murderous hatred and therefore meditate revenge, seeking nothing short of their victim's death and not resting until they have achieved it. Spirits like this are kept in a deep, cadaverous hell—one that reeks with a stench like that given off by corpses. Strange to say, the people there enjoy the stench so much that they prefer it to the most pleasant smells; such is their horrendous nature and the crazy thinking it spawns. The odor described actually wafts from that hell. When the place yawns open—as it rarely does, and then just briefly—so foul a smell pours out that spirits cannot stay in the vicinity.

Some demons, or rather avenging furies, were let out of that hell in order for me to discover what they were like. They infected the air with such poisonous and pestilential fumes that the spirits around me could not remain. At the same time they affected my stomach in such a way that I threw up.

[2] They presented themselves in the form of a young child with a tolerably attractive face and a concealed dagger, whom they sent to me with a flask in hand. From this I learned that they had a taste for murder, either by dagger or poison, under the guise of innocence. The bodies of the spirits themselves were naked and quite black.447

Soon, though, they were sent back into their cadaverous-smelling hell, and then I was able to watch the path of their descent. They headed to the left, keeping level with my left temple and going quite a distance without moving downward. Later they did descend, traveling first into a fire that appeared, then into a cloud of fiery smoke like that from a furnace, and directly afterward to a point below the furnace and in front, where many dark and gloomy caves led farther down. Along the way, they were constantly devising evil plots and schemes. Their intended victims were primarily the innocent, whom they targeted without cause. While passing through the fire, they wailed loud and long.

When released from their hell, they take with them a kind of ring that allows others to identify where they come from and what they are like. The ring is set with spikes which are made of something like bronze and which they grip tightly and twist with their hands—a sign that they are this type of spirit and that they are under restraint.448

Some take so much pleasure in hatred and the revenge it inspires that they are not content simply to kill the body but long to destroy the soul as well, although the Lord redeems the soul. They are lowered though a dark hole toward the bowels of the earth, the depth to which they go being determined by the intensity of their hatred and the vengefulness growing out of it. A dreadful terror and horror then strike them, while they are being held in the grip of their lust for revenge. As that desire grows, they slip even farther down.

Later they are sent to a place beneath Gehenna,[449] where big, terrifying, round-bellied snakes appear, as lifelike as if they actually existed. They torture the vengeful spirits with their bites, which the spirits experience just as vividly as they do the snakes. Spirits feel these sensations—corresponding as they do to the spirits' lives—as keenly as people living in the body feel bodily sensation.

Meanwhile they live out their dreadful fantasies, wallowing in them for ages, until they no longer know that they were once human. By no other method can the way of life that they acquired from such acts of hatred and revenge be extinguished.

816 The different general kinds of hatred and vengefulness are beyond counting, the specific kinds still more so, and the hell for one kind is not the same as the hell for another. So it is impossible to list each in order. For this reason, let me simply report on some examples I have seen.

One spirit who seemed to be a noble came to me. (Spirits have appeared to me as if in clear daylight, and even more clearly than that, but to my inner eye, since the Lord in his divine mercy has let me interact with them.) As soon as he arrived, he pretended, by sly nodding, to show that he had many things he wanted to share with me, asking whether I was a Christian. I answered yes. He said he was, too, and asked to be alone with me so that he could tell me something privately. "In this life," I answered, "no one can be alone, the way people on earth think they can. Many other spirits are close by."

He came nearer anyway, stealing up from behind to the back of my head. I could then tell that he was an assassin. While he was there I felt a stab to the heart and then to the brain—the kind a person could easily die from. But because the Lord was keeping me safe, I was unafraid. What trick he was using I cannot say.

Thinking I was dead, he told some other spirits that he had just come from a murder victim of his, one to whom he had dealt a fatal blow from behind. He claimed a skill at keeping people from knowing what was happening until they fell dead, and from suspecting he was anything but innocent. From this I could tell that he had recently departed life, where he had committed the same kind of crime.

The punishment of such spirits is horrible. After enduring ages of hellish torment, they end up with faces so loathsome, so shockingly deformed, that they are not faces but almost like flax, drained of all color. In other words, these spirits strip themselves of everything human; then everyone who sees them shudders at the sight. Consequently they wander in the shadows like wild animals.

817
A certain spirit from a room in hell that was off to the left side came to me and talked with me. I was allowed to perceive that he was a criminal type.

This is how his misdeeds in the world were exposed: he was sent fairly far down into the underground realm that was in front and a little to the left, and there he began to dig a hole, as people do for burying the dead. This made me suspect that he had committed some fatal deed during bodily life. Next there appeared a bier swathed in black, and soon a man rose off it and approached me. He told me with saintly restraint that he was dead, probably as a result of poisoning by that man. This had been his dying thought, although he did not know whether it was an unfounded suspicion.[450]

When the wicked spirit heard this, he confessed that he had done the deed. Punishment followed his confession. Twice he was rolled into the black grave he had dug and became as black himself in face and body as Egyptian mummies. In this condition, he was lifted up high and carried around in front of spirits and angels, while people shouted, "What a devil!" He also turned cold, so that he belongs among the cold in hell; and he was sent to hell.

818
Under the buttocks is a fearsome hell where the inhabitants seem to attack each other with knives. Like furies they thrust their knives at the chests of others, but the moment they strike, the knife is always taken from them. They are individuals who hated others so much that they burned to murder them viciously. From this they drew their appalling nature.

The hell was opened up (but only slightly, because of their terrible cruelties) for me to see what their savage hatred was like.

819
There is a large, oblong lake to the left, level with the lower parts of the body. Along the front bank, the residents see grotesque snakes of the types that live in standing water, spreading disease on their breath. On the left bank and farther away are seen cannibals eating one another, sinking their teeth into each other's shoulders. Even farther away on the left appear huge fish, monstrous whales that swallow people down and then spit them out. At the farthest end, on the opposite bank, can be seen the most horribly deformed faces, especially those of old hags, so disfigured that they cannot be described, the owners of the faces running every which way as if insane. On the right-hand bank are people who try

to kill each other with instruments of torture, the instruments varying with the different kinds of villainy they have at heart. The middle of the lake is uniformly black, like a stagnant pond.

Several times I saw people being led to this lake, which surprised me. But I learned about the situation from several others who were leaving. They said that the ones arriving were people who cherished against their neighbor a deep-seated hatred that erupted at every opportunity, affording them supreme pleasure. Nothing had delighted them more, I heard, than hauling their fellow creatures up before a judge and having them sentenced to punishment and—if the penalties of law did not prevent it—to execution.

Into such horrors are people's hatreds and cruelties transformed after life in the body. The fantasies that result seem absolutely real to those people.

820 Those who engaged in robbery or piracy during physical life, love stinking, reeking urine above every other kind of fluid. They also seem to themselves to live among sewage of this kind and in bad-smelling ponds.

One outlaw approached me grinding his teeth. To my surprise I could hear the sound of the grinding as clearly as from a person on earth, even though these criminals do not have teeth. He admitted that he would much rather live in malodorous, urinous dampness than among the purest waters and that the stench of urine was what pleased him. He said that he preferred spending time in vats of urinous liquid to any other kind and that he wanted to make his home there.

821 There are some who maintain an outwardly honest face and honest life to avoid arousing suspicion that they are anything but upright. They eagerly pursue every method of so appearing in order to rise to prominent positions and to get rich without risking their reputation. For this reason they do not act openly. Instead they use agents to strip others of their goods by devious stratagems, not caring in the least whether the families they plunder die of starvation. If it could remain out of sight to the world, they would do the job themselves without a pang of conscience. Still, their character is the same as if they had committed the act themselves. They are covert thieves, and their particular type of hatred involves pride, greed, ruthlessness, and deceit.

[2] When people like this arrive in the other world, they claim to be innocent, saying they have done nothing wrong, since they have never been caught. To demonstrate their blamelessness, they take off their

clothes and stand naked, giving witness to their purity. When they are questioned, others perceive exactly what they are like from every word they speak and every thought they think, although they themselves do not realize this is happening.

Every acquaintance they come across in the next life they desire to kill, untroubled by remorse. In their hands they hold an axe and a hammer, while at their feet they seem to have another spirit lying face up, whom they strike. They do not go so far as to spill blood, however, being fearful of death. What is more, they are unable to toss their weapons from their hands, although they try with all their might, in order to keep from being seen for what they are. They do not want the fierceness of their disposition to show in front of spirits and angels.

They occupy a place in the middle distance, under the feet and toward the front.

There is a type of hatred toward others that prompts people to enjoy injuring and abusing everyone. The more damage they can inflict, the greater their pleasure. Many of them are from the lowest social strata. However, there are others not of that class who have the same visceral reactions but better superficial manners, having been brought up to live in polite society, and holding legal penalties in due regard.

After death they appear unclothed from the waist up, their hair unkempt. One will rush at another, grab the other's shoulders in a violent grip, tumble over the person's head, circle briefly, return, and slug away relentlessly.

Those whom I described as better behaved act similarly but first exchange courtesies, then go around behind the other's back to attack with their fists. When they see each other face to face, they greet each other and then circle behind again to strike their blows. In this way they preserve appearances.

These spirits are seen on the left at a middling height, some distance away.

Whatever we have done during bodily life, and even whatever we have thought, gradually comes back in the other life. When the hostile, spiteful, underhanded actions we have taken return, the individuals we hated and secretly plotted against also appear before us, and appear in an instant. That is how things operate in the next life. (Later sections [§§6893, 7498], by the Lord's divine mercy, will deal with this kind of presence.) The negative thoughts we have had about the people are also plain to see, since everyone's thoughts are perceptible. Miserable states result; hidden hatreds erupt openly.

Bad people find that all their misdeeds and thoughts come back with vivid realism in this way, but good people do not. With them, all states of goodness, friendship, and love return, bringing with them the highest pleasure and happiness.

Genesis 8

The Hells (Continued): The Hells of Those Who Spent Their Lives in Adultery and Lechery; in Addition, the Hells of Deceivers and Witches

UNDER the heel of the right foot is the hell of those who enjoyed cruelty and also adultery and felt the greatest pleasure of their lives in those two things. It is remarkable that people who were cruel while living in the body also practiced adultery more than any others. Such people live in this hell.

There they inflict cruelties in unspeakable ways. In their imaginations they create [giant] mortarlike vessels (similar to those used for grinding herbs) and pestles, which they use to crush and torture everyone they can. They also conjure up executioners' broadaxes, or something like them, as well as trephines[451] with which they viciously maul each other—and other grim devices besides.

In that hell are a number of Jews who once treated gentiles in the same cruel ways. Today the hell is still growing, the main additions coming from the so-called Christian world. These "Christians" obtained all the joy of their lives from adultery, and most of them were also abusive.

[2] Sometimes their delight is transformed into the reek of human dung, an odor that pours out copiously when the hell opens. I sensed the smell in the world of spirits and almost passed out. This fecal stench comes and goes in hell. It consists of the inhabitants' pleasure in adultery, converted into a horrible aroma.

As time passes and they finish a certain amount of time living in such scenes, they are left alone, sitting in pain, and seem to turn into misshapen skeletons, although they remain alive.

Level with the soles of the feet, in front and fairly far away, is a hell called Gehenna containing shameless women who centered all their pleasure on committing adultery. They regarded adultery as not just acceptable but honorable and lured the unblemished and innocent into it under various high-minded guises.

A sort of fiery glow appears there, like the one that a large conflagration would cast in the air. There is also a blast of heat, which I was able to feel through the warmth that spread from there to my face. And an odor drifts out that resembles the smell of singed bones and hair.

Sometimes this hell turns into a mass of loathsome snakes that bite the inhabitants. Once bitten they long for death, but they cannot die.

Some women released from the place came to me and said it was hot there. They reported that when they are allowed to approach a certain community of good spirits, the heat turns into intense cold. The temperature, they said, then fluctuates between extremes of blazing heat and freezing cold, which also tormented them miserably.

They have intervals during which they are aroused and aflame with lust; but conditions change for them, as noted.

826. There were some of each sex from the so-called Christian world who during bodily life considered their adulteries not only allowable but even sacred and for this reason contracted group "marriages" (as they so profanely called them) under the appearance of sanctity.[452]

As I watched, they were sent to Gehenna, but when they arrived there, a change occurred. Gehenna's fiery glimmer, which is red-hot, became white-hot at their approach, and their inability to get along together became perceptible. As a result, that iniquitous troupe of theirs was removed and transferred to an area behind the back—to another world, I heard, where they would sink into the water and then move on to a new Gehenna created for them.

An indescribable sort of hiss could be heard in [the first] Gehenna, but the hissing or whispering there was duller than the sound made by these people who polluted what is holy with their adulteries.

827. There are some men who hide behind a love for marriage and a love for children in order to commit treacherous deeds. Their behavior prevents any suspicion on a husband's part that they as his guests are anything but chaste, innocent friends. Under such appearances and many others, they commit adultery in relative safety. These people live in a hell under the buttocks and in the filthiest excrement where, because they are among the deceitful, they undergo such devastation that they finally seem to turn into skeletons.

People like this do not even know what conscience is. I talked to them, and they were surprised that anyone might have a conscience or claim that adultery violates it. I told them that for adulterers of their type, who have no compunction, it is as impossible to come into heaven as it is for a fish to rise into the air or for a bird to fly up into the ether.453 Let them only edge close to heaven and they feel as though they would suffocate. The pleasure they feel turns into a stinking smell. They can only be thrust down into hell. Eventually they come to appear skeletal, with little life left, because this is the kind of life they have obtained for themselves, and when they lose it, only a tiny amount of truly human life remains.

There are men who like nothing better than deflowering virgins—that is, who take the greatest pleasure in virgins and in robbing them of their virginity without any thought of marriage or children. When they have stolen the bloom of their virginity, they abandon them in disgust or prostitute them.

Men who have lived this kind of life have contravened the order of nature, of the spirit, and of heaven. They violate not only marriage love, a love held very sacred in heaven, but also innocence, which they wound and murder when they take innocent girls, who could have had the love of marriage instilled in them, and introduce them instead to the life of a whore. (People know that the first blossoming of love is what introduces young women to the chaste love in marriage and unites the minds of married partners.)454

Because heaven's holiness is founded on marriage love and innocence, and these men are inward murderers (as described), in the other life they suffer punishment of the most severe kind. They seem to themselves to be riding a frenzied horse that bucks them up into the air, throwing them off, apparently in danger of their lives; such is the terror that strikes them. Later they see themselves under the belly of the maddened horse and soon seem to go up through the horse's rump into its stomach. Then suddenly it appears to them as if they are in the belly of a woman, a foul slut, who changes into a huge dragon.455 There they remain hidden and in pain. This punishment recurs many times over hundreds and thousands of years, until the offenders gain a horror for such desires.

I have heard that their children are worse than others, since they inherit this quality from their fathers. Accordingly, when people of this kind engage in sexual intercourse, it rarely produces offspring, and such babies as are born do not live long.456

Some during their bodily life think lewdly and turn whatever others say into something indecent, even if the subject is holy, and they continue to do so even into adulthood and old age, when nothing of earthly lust remains to goad them. Neither do they stop thinking and speaking this way in the other world. Since in that world their thoughts are shared generally, and sometimes present themselves in obscene form to the eyes of other spirits, they cause offense.

Their punishment consists in being laid out flat before the spirits they have hurt and spun quickly from left to right like a scroll. Then they are spun crosswise in another position, and then in yet another, stripped naked in the sight of all, or else half-naked (depending on the nature of their debauchery). All the while they suffer shame. Next they are twirled horizontally by their head and feet as if around an axis. Resistance is triggered in them, together with pain, since two forces are acting, one spinning one direction and the other pushing back. So the procedure tears them apart in an agonizing way.

At the end of all this, the individuals have a chance to remove themselves from the gaze of other spirits, and they are filled with shame. Still there are some spirits who test them to see whether they will persist in such behavior. But as long as they continue to feel humiliation and pain, they shy away from it. So they hide, despite the fact that others know just where they are.

This punishment appeared in front, some distance away.

[2] There are also boys, adolescents, and young men who in their youthful folly and lust have taken it as a principle (a horrendous one) that a wife—especially one who is young and beautiful—should not belong to her husband but to themselves and others like them. The only role they leave to the husband is as head of household and educator of the children. In the other life they are distinguished by the childish sound of their voices. They are at the back and fairly high up.

The ones who have hardened themselves in these principles and in actually living their lives by them undergo wretched punishment in the other life. They suffer dislocation and rearticulation of their joints, or having their limbs wrenched in one direction and then the other. The spirits who administer the punishment know how to create the illusion of a body and along with it the physical sensation of pain. The back-and-forth motion and the resistance to it induced in them at the same time tear at them so violently that they seem to themselves to be ripped into minute shreds, with excruciating pain. The process repeats until, struck with horror for a life based on such principles, they abandon their former way of thinking.

830 Some people fool others with great subtlety and craft, presenting a pleasant face and pleasant speech but inwardly concealing poisonous

deceit. In this way they captivate others for the purpose of destroying them. Their hell is more forbidding than others' hells, more forbidding even than the one murderers are in. They seem to themselves to live among snakes, and the more hurtful their plots had been, the more dreadful, poisonous, and numerous appear the snakes that surround and torture them. They have no idea that these are not snakes, the pain and torment they feel being the same. Few will believe this, perhaps, and yet it is true.

These are people who premeditate the frauds they practice, and find the highest pleasure of their life in them.

Dissemblers are chastised in several different ways, according to the nature of their deceit. In general, the communities banish such people rather than tolerate them. Whatever a spirit thinks, those nearby immediately know and perceive it, so they can tell if any duplicity is at work and what kind of duplicity it is. In consequence, after being driven away from society, they end up sitting alone. They then appear to have a broad face, equal in width to four or five others' faces. They wear a wide, white straw hat[457] and sit like images of death, racked with pain.

There are others who by nature are given to deception, so that they do not act from forethought or under cover of a false appearance. They are recognized instantly, and their thinking is perceived plainly. They even boast about their dishonesty, as if wanting to appear clever. These people do not have the same kind of hell. But more on charlatans later [§§947, 957–960, 1271, 6197], by the Lord's divine mercy.

831

There are women who lived a life of indulgence, focusing their energies on themselves and the world and centering their whole lives and all the pleasure of life on external decorum. As a result polite society valued them more than others. From practice and habit they learned to behave in socially acceptable ways in order to tap into others' desires and sensual pleasures. This they did under a pretense of respectability but with the desire to control. Consequently their lives became a sham and a lie. They attended church just as others did, but for no reason except to appear honorable and devout. Furthermore, they lacked any conscience and were very much drawn to immoral and adulterous conduct, so far as it could be kept hidden.

Their thinking remains the same in the next life. What a conscience is they do not know, and they scoff at people who use the word. They get inside others' feelings, whatever those may be, simulating honesty, piety, mercy, and innocence, and using these as covers for deception. Whenever outward restraints are removed from them, they plunge into the most criminal obscenities.

[2] In the other life, these women become sorceresses or witches, some of whom are called sirens.[458] There they eagerly take up arts unknown in the world. They are like sponges that soak up wicked and cunning methods, for which they have such a talent that they put them directly into practice. The stratagems unknown in this world that they learn there are these:

> They can throw their voices, so that it seems as though the sound were coming from good spirits somewhere else.
> They can seem to be with several people at once, convincing others that they are present almost everywhere.
> They can speak as though they were many people talking simultaneously and in many places at once.
> They can deflect what flows in from good spirits and even from angelic ones and immediately twist it to their own advantage in a variety of ways.
> They can impersonate another by seizing on the person's patterns of thought and mimicking them.
> They can induce affection for themselves in anyone by worming their way into the actual emotions the person is feeling.
> They can suddenly drop out of sight and turn invisible.
> They can create the appearance of a dazzling white flame—the sign of an angel—around their head, and this in front of a large number of spirits.
> They have different ways of pretending innocence, even causing babies to appear and kissing them.
> And they inspire the people they hate to kill them (since they know they cannot die) and then publicly accuse them of being murderers.

[3] In my case, using consummate skill they dredged up out of my memory everything bad that I had ever thought or done. While I was sleeping, they talked to others exactly as if I were speaking, managing to dupe those spirits; and what they said was false and lewd. They have many other devices as well.

Their nature is so persuasive that not a trace of hesitation can be detected in it. For this reason their ideas are not shared generally, as other spirits' ideas are. Their eyes are like snakes' eyes, as people say, turning their unflinching, conscious gaze in every direction.

These witches or sirens are punished severely, some in Gehenna, some surrounded by snakes in a kind of assembly hall. The punishment of some consists in being torn apart and buffeted in various ways, with the greatest pain and anguish. After a while they are ostracized and turn into seeming skeletons from head to toe.

More on this subject follows at the end of the chapter [§§938–946].

Genesis 8

1. And God remembered Noah, and every wild animal and every beast that was with him in the ark. And God made a wind pass over the earth, and the waters subsided.

2. And the springs of the abyss and the floodgates of heaven were stopped up, and the downpour from the sky was held back.

3. And the waters receded off the earth, going and coming back, and the waters disappeared at the end of one hundred fifty days.

4. And the ark came to rest in the seventh month, on the seventeenth day of the month, on the mountains of Ararat.

5. And the waters were going and disappearing till the tenth month; in the tenth [month], on the first of the month, the heads of the mountains appeared.

* *

6. And it happened at the end of forty days that Noah opened the window of the ark that he had made.

7. And he sent out a raven, and it went out, going and coming back till the water dried up off the earth.

8. And he sent a dove out from him, to see whether the water might have lessened off the face of the ground.

9. And the dove did not find a resting place for the sole of its foot, and it returned to him, to the ark, because there was water over the face of the whole earth; and he put his hand out and took it and brought it in to himself, into the ark.

10. And he waited yet another seven days and proceeded to send the dove out from the ark.

11. And the dove returned to him at evening time, and look: the torn-off leaf of an olive tree in its mouth! And Noah realized that the water had lessened off the earth.

12. And he waited yet another seven days and sent a dove out, and it never returned to him again.

13. And it happened in the six hundred first year, in the beginning, on the first of the month, that the water drained off the earth; and Noah removed the roof of the ark and looked, and indeed the face of the ground had dried up!

14. In the second month, on the twenty-seventh day of the month, the earth dried up.

*   *

15. And God spoke to Noah, saying,

16. "Go out of the ark, you and your wife and your sons and your sons' wives with you,

17. every wild animal that is with you, of all flesh, including the bird and the beast and every creeping thing creeping on the earth. Take them out with you, and let them swarm throughout the earth and reproduce and multiply on the earth."

18. And Noah went out, as did his sons and his wife and his sons' wives with him,

19. every wild animal, every creeping thing, and every bird—everything creeping on the earth. By their families they went out of the ark.

*   *

20. And Noah built an altar to Jehovah and took of every clean animal and of every clean bird and offered burnt offerings on the altar.

21. And Jehovah smelled a restful smell, and Jehovah said in his heart, "I will never again curse the ground on the human being's account, because what human hearts fabricate is evil from their youth. And I will never again strike every living thing as I have done.

22. Throughout all the days of the earth to come, sowing and reaping and cold and heat and summer and winter and day and night will not end."

Summary

832 NOW comes the second series about the people of the new church, who are being called Noah, and about the state they are in from the time following their trials until their rebirth and beyond.

833 The first state[459] after their trials; their vacillation between truth and falsity, which continues until truth begins to appear (verses 1–5).

The second state, which has three parts: at first the truth belonging to faith still does not shine clearly, then it does shine out, along with charity, and later the good effects of charity shed a brilliant light (verses 6–14). **834**

The third state, when they start acting and thinking in terms of charity; this is the first state the reborn person goes through (verses 15–19). **835**

The fourth state, when they act and think in terms of charity; this is the second state for the reborn person (verses 20, 21). **836**

Last, this new church, revived as a replacement for the earlier one; a description of it (verses 21, 22). **837**

Inner Meaning

THE last two chapters spoke of the new church called Noah, or of the people in that church. First it dealt with the preparation they underwent for receiving faith and for receiving charity through faith. Then it dealt with the trials they suffered, and later the way they were protected when the earliest church died out. What comes now is the state they were in following their trials, described in the order in which it developed. **838**

This is also the order in which it develops in every person who is regenerating. The Lord's Word is such that where it talks about one person it talks about anyone and everyone, with differences according to each individual's character. This type of meaning is present everywhere in the Word.

Genesis 8:1. *And God remembered Noah, and every wild animal and every beast that was with him in the ark. And God made a wind pass over the earth, and the waters subsided.* **839**

God remembered symbolizes the end of trial and the beginning of renewal. *Noah* symbolizes the people of the ancient church, as he did before. *Every wild animal and every beast that was with him in the ark* symbolizes everything that was in those people. *And God made a wind pass over the earth, and the waters subsided,* symbolizes putting everything in its proper place.

The symbolism of *and God remembered* as the end of trial and the beginning of renewal can be seen from statements made above and below.[460] **840**

Specifically, *God remembers* means that he shows mercy. His remembrance is mercy, which is ascribed mainly to the period following struggles, since new light then radiates. As long as our trials continue, we think the Lord is absent, since evil demons disturb us, sometimes to the point where despair almost prevents us from believing God exists at all. But the Lord is closer then than we can possibly believe. When the trouble ends, we find comfort, and then we first believe the Lord is present. That is why *God remembered* (since it seems as though he remembers) symbolizes the end of struggle and the beginning of renewal.

God and not Jehovah is said to remember because this is still the state before rebirth. When we have been reborn, Jehovah's name is indeed used, as it is in verses 20 and 21 at the end of the chapter. The reason it is not used here is that faith has not yet united with charity. The point at which we can first be described as regenerate is when we act out of charity. It is in charity that Jehovah is found, not so much in faith before it unites with charity. In the other world, charity is our actual existence and life. Existence itself and life itself is Jehovah, and so until we exist and live, it is not Jehovah but God who is said to be present with us.

841 *Noah* symbolizes the people of the ancient church, as he did before, and *every wild animal and every beast that was with him in the ark* symbolizes everything that was in those people. This can be seen from previous remarks about Noah [§466] and about the symbolism of a wild animal and a beast.

A *wild animal* is understood in two senses in the Word: as those things in us that are living and as those things that are dead. The reason it stands for things that are living is that the Hebrew word means "living thing."[461] But since the earliest people in their humility recognized themselves as wild animals, the same word also symbolized the things that are dead inside a person.

Here a wild animal symbolizes both what is living and what is lifeless, combined, as they usually are in an individual after struggle. Things that are alive and dead, or things that are the Lord's and those that are a person's own, seem so jumbled together that the person barely knows what is true or good. At that stage, however, the Lord reduces everything into order and puts it in its place, as can become clear from what follows.

For the symbolism of the wild animal as those things in us that are alive, see the discussion of Genesis 7:14 above and also in this chapter at verses 17 and 19 [§§774, 908, 916:1]. Its symbolism as things inside us, including those that are dead, can be seen from evidence concerning wild animals and beasts offered several times earlier, as in §§45, 46, 142, 143, 246.

The symbolism of *and God made a wind pass over the earth, and the waters subsided,* as putting everything in its proper place is established by the symbolism of the *wind* in the Word. The wind is used as a metaphor, a simile, and even a name for all spirits, both good and evil. The original language uses the same word for both spirits and the winds.[462]

During our struggles—which are the *waters* that subsided, as shown before [§§705, 739, 790]—it is evil spirits that flood in. They crowd in on us with their delusional thinking and stir up the same kind of thinking in us. When something banishes these spirits, or rather the hallucinations they induce, the Word describes the wind (and in fact the east wind) as the agent.

[2] For an individual who is being tested, the circumstances surrounding the end of the struggle's commotions (or waters) are the same as those for a larger collection of people, as I have learned from much experience. Evil spirits in the world of spirits sometimes form gangs and cause disturbances, but they are dispersed by other groups of spirits that generally approach from the right and so from the east. These groups strike such fear and terror into the evil spirits that they cannot think about anything but running away. Though they had ganged together, they scatter in all directions, and this is the way in which such coalitions of spirits mobbing together for evil purposes are dissolved. The groups of spirits who disperse them by this method are called an east wind. Countless other ways of disbanding them exist, and these too are called east winds. With the Lord's divine mercy, they will be described below [§§1398, 2128, 4793:5, 7679:1]. When the evil spirits have scattered, and the mob and its agitation are past, a calm or silence occurs.

The case is similar for an individual during times of trial. In those periods, the person is surrounded by a crowd of the same type of spirits as above, and after they have been driven off or dispelled, there is a kind of calm—the first step in putting everything where it belongs.

[3] Before being reduced to order, it is very common for everything to fall into confusion or seeming chaos. This allows things that cling together poorly to separate, and when they have separated, the Lord arranges them in their place.

Nature offers parallels, since in it too each and every thing first falls into some degree of disorder before being put in order. If the skies did not storm, causing unlike elements to scatter, the air would never clear; destructive forces would amass and wreak havoc.

The human body displays the same characteristic. Unless all the components of the blood, whether compound or pure, were continuously and cyclically combined and pumped into a single heart first and mingled there, the fluid component would coagulate in a fatal way. The individual elements would never be distributed to perform their proper functions.463

It is the same with a person who is regenerating.

[4] The wind—specifically the east wind—simply symbolizes the dispersal of falsity and evil (or, what is the same, of evil spirits and demons) and the organizing of them that follows. This can be seen in the Word, as, for instance, in Isaiah:

> You will disperse them, and the *wind* will carry them off, and a *storm* will scatter them. And you will rejoice in Jehovah; in the Holy One of Israel you will glory. (Isaiah 41:16)

The dispersal (of evil) is compared here to a wind and the scattering to a storm. When this occurs, those who are reborn will rejoice in Jehovah. In David:

> Look! The monarchs assembled; they passed by together; they saw. So they were stupefied; they were bewildered; they rushed away. Terror seized them there—pain like that of one in labor. With an *east wind* you will shatter them.464 (Psalms 48:4, 5, 6, 7)

This describes the terror and confusion that the east wind brings over such spirits. The description stems from things that happen in the world of spirits, because the Word's inner meaning involves such things. [5] In Jeremiah:

> It will make their land something shocking; like an *east wind* I will scatter them before their enemy. I will turn toward them with my neck and not my face on the day of their disaster. (Jeremiah 18:16, 17)

Here again the east wind stands for the dispersal of falsity. Something similar is represented by the east wind that dried up the Suph Sea465 to allow the children of Israel to cross, as mentioned in Exodus:

> Jehovah drew back the Suph Sea by means of a strong *east wind* the whole night, and he made the sea into dry land, and the water was divided. (Exodus 14:21)

The water of the Suph Sea represented something much like what the waters of the Flood do in the present verse. This can be seen from the fact that the Egyptians, who represented the wicked, drowned, while the children of Israel, who represented the regenerate (as Noah does in the present verse), walked across. The Suph Sea, like the Flood, represented damnation and also times of trial. So the east wind represented the dispersal of the water, that is, the abatement of damnation's evils or a person's trials. The parallels can also be seen in the Song of Moses, which he sang after the Israelites had crossed that sea (Exodus 15:1–19), and in Isaiah:

> Jehovah will exterminate the tongue of Egypt's sea and wave his hand over the river in the fierceness of his *wind* and strike it into seven rivers and make way [for them as they walk] in their shoes. And there will be a path for the *survivors* of his people who will remain from Assyria, as there was for Israel when they went up from the land of Egypt. (Isaiah 11:15, 16)

The path for the survivors of the people left from Assyria stands for the process of putting things in their proper place.

843 Genesis 8:2. *And the springs of the abyss and the floodgates of heaven were stopped up, and the downpour from the sky was held back,* means that their trials ended. The *springs of the abyss* symbolize evils, which belong to the will. The *floodgates of heaven* symbolize falsities, which belong to the intellect. The *rain* symbolizes trial itself in general.

844 From here to verse 6 the chapter speaks of the first state the people of this church experienced after their trials. The contents of this verse symbolize the end of those struggles.

Challenges to the intent of their will and to the ideas in their intellect have already been dealt with. The *stopping-up of the springs of the abyss* symbolizes the end of struggles involving their will, while the *stopping-up of the floodgates of heaven* symbolizes the end of struggles involving their intellect. These symbolisms have been mentioned and illustrated before at Genesis 7:11 [§§756–757], and the symbolism of rain as trial itself at Genesis 7:12 [§759], so there is no need to spend any more time corroborating them.

845 The reason the springs of the abyss symbolize a testing of the will's intents and the floodgates of heaven a testing of the intellect's ideas is as follows.

It is our volitional side that hell drives, and not so much our intellectual side, unless this is saturated with corrupt desires, which come from the will. Evil, which is a matter of will, is what condemns us and drags us down toward hell. Falsity does not do so to the same extent unless coupled with evil (since the one then follows after the other).

The large numbers of people who subscribe to falsity and yet are saved provide evidence for this. Many non-Christians, whose lives have been marked by earthly charity and by mercy, fall into this category, as do Christians whose beliefs have been adopted in simplicity of heart. Ignorance and simplicity themselves excuse such people, since innocence can inhabit those qualities.

[2] The situation is otherwise for people who have hardened themselves in falsity and from this contracted such a dishonest way of life that they deny and reject all truth. Their way of life has to be destroyed before any seed of truth or goodness can be planted in them. It is worse, however, for those who have hardened themselves in falsity on the basis of desire, so that falsity and desire have come to form a single life force. They are the ones who plummet into hell.

This is why trials involving attributes of the will are symbolized by the springs of the abyss, which are the hells, while trials involving attributes of the intellect are symbolized by the floodgates of heaven, which are rain clouds.

846 Genesis 8:3. *And the waters receded off the earth, going and coming back, and the waters disappeared at the end of one hundred fifty days.*

The waters receded off the earth, going and coming back, symbolizes vacillation between truth and falsity. *The waters disappeared at the end of one hundred fifty days* means that the trials ended. *One hundred fifty days* here as before symbolizes an ending and starting point.

847 The symbolism of *the waters receded off the earth, going and coming back,* as vacillation between truth and falsity is established by earlier statements. I said that the flood water or deluges connected with Noah symbolized times of trial [§§705, 739, 756, 790], and since the subject here is the first state following trials, the waters that receded, going and coming back, can symbolize nothing else but a wavering between truth and falsity.

The nature of this wavering, though, cannot be known without a knowledge of what trials or "temptations" are. The type of struggle determines the type of vacillation afterward. When the trial involves heavenly qualities, the vacillation is between good and evil. When the trial involves spiritual qualities, the vacillation is between truth and falsity. And when the trial is earthly, the vacillation is between the things we crave and their opposites.

[2] There are many kinds of struggle. The general types are heaven-oriented, spiritual, and earthly, and it is important to avoid confusing

them. Only those who love the Lord are subject to heaven-oriented trials. Spiritual trials come to those who have charity for their fellow human. Earthly tribulation has nothing to do with the other two kinds, and it is not really a trial, or temptation, but merely anxiety rising out of an attack on earthly kinds of love. The anxiety is stirred by misfortune, illness, or morbid constitution of the blood and the body fluids.466

This brief discussion can give some idea of what is involved in our trials: distress and anxiety over things that conflict with what we love. For those who love the Lord, whatever attacks love for the Lord produces deep pain, and this is trial on the heavenly plane. For those who love their neighbor, or in other words, those who feel charity, anything that attacks that love triggers the sting of conscience, and this is spiritual trial. [3] But earthly trials, which many people call temptations (while they refer to the pain they feel as the pangs of conscience), are not temptations, or tests. They are merely an anxiety sparked by an assault on what they love. Examples are times when they worry that they will be, or feel that they have been, deprived of their position, worldly goods, reputation, physical pleasures, bodily life, and so on. Still, these experiences are apt to do some good.

For those who practice earthly charity—and so for all kinds of heretics, non-Christians, and idolaters—temptations or trials are also possible, resulting from attacks on the way they live their faith, which is precious to them. But these are just woes that mimic spiritual crises.

When our trials are over, we experience a kind of wavering, and if our trials have been spiritual, it is a vacillation between truth and falsity, as can be seen clearly enough from the fact that trial is the beginning of regeneration.

The whole process of rebirth exists in order for us to receive new life, or rather to receive life at all. It exists in order that from being nonhuman we may become human, or from being dead may become alive. So when our previous way of life, which was no better than animal life, breaks down in times of trouble, we cannot help faltering between truth and falsity after the trouble has passed. Truth belongs to the new life, falsity to the old. Unless the earlier way of life is destroyed and this uncertainty takes hold, spiritual seed cannot possibly be sown in us, since there is no soil for it.

[2] When disintegration of the prior life is complete, on the other hand, and such hesitation takes its place, we are left with almost no idea what is true or good. We are so unsure that we scarcely know whether

anything is true. For instance, we can wonder whether we are capable of doing the good that charity urges (or good works, as people call them) under our own power, when the exercise of our powers involves a sense of merit. Our minds are so cloudy and dark at this point that if someone says that people cannot do any good or earn any merit on their own or under their own power, that all good comes from the Lord and all the credit is the Lord's, we can only sit there stupefied. It is the same with all other religious questions. Yet slowly, bit by bit, light begins to pierce the murk or darkness we live in.

[3] Regeneration is exactly like human development. When babies are born, they live in great mental darkness, knowing almost nothing, so at that stage general impressions enter their minds first. By degrees, as specifics are introduced into the general ideas, those ideas grow more distinct, and still more distinct when the specifics acquire even greater detail. In this way, the particular sheds light on the general, allowing a person to see not only that such things exist but also of what quality they are. The case is the same with everyone emerging from spiritual trial.

Conditions are similar for those in the other life who, since they had held false notions, go through the process of devastation.

This state is called vacillation and is portrayed here by the waters that receded, going and coming back.

849   Clearly it now follows that *the waters disappeared at the end of one hundred fifty days* means that the trials ended. The symbolism of *one hundred fifty days* as an ending and starting point is established by the things said about this number above at Genesis 7:24 [§813]. Here it is an ending point for vacillation and a starting point for new life.

850   Genesis 8:4. *And the ark came to rest in the seventh month, on the seventeenth day of the month, on the mountains of Ararat.*

The ark came to rest symbolizes rebirth. The *seventh month* symbolizes holiness. The *seventeenth day of the month* symbolizes something new. The *mountains of Ararat* symbolize a bit of light.

851   The symbolism of *the ark came to rest* as rebirth can be seen from this, that the *ark* symbolizes the people of this church, and everything in the ark symbolizes what those people had inside them, as shown frequently above [§§602, 638–658, 667–681, 713–726, 740–751, 764–784, 811]. When the ark is said to have *come to rest,* then, the meaning is that the same people were regenerating.

The literal story line does indeed seem to suggest that the settling of the ark symbolizes an end to the wavering (discussed at the last verse) that followed their trials. The wavering, however, which is doubt and confusion about truth and goodness, does not end here but lasts a long time, as will also become clear below.[467]

This shows that the inner sense always has some other implication; and since that implication is unknown, let me reveal it here. After spiritual people have endured tribulation, they too become the Lord's *rest*, just as the heavenly person does, and they also become a *seventh* thing—not the seventh day, as the heavenly person does, but the seventh month. Concerning the heavenly person as the Lord's Sabbath rest and as the seventh day, see §§84–88. Since there is a difference between heavenly and spiritual people, though, the original language uses a word meaning "Sabbath" for the heavenly person's repose and another, from which the name *Noah* comes and which more strictly means "rest," for the spiritual person's repose.[468]

852. The symbolism of the *seventh month* as holiness is abundantly clear from §§84–87, 395, 716 above, where this is demonstrated. The holiness implied here parallels what Genesis 2:3 said about the person of heavenly character: that the seventh day was consecrated because God rested on it.[469]

853. The symbolism of the *seventeenth day* as something new can be seen from remarks and supporting evidence concerning the number seventeen at Genesis 7:11, §755, where it symbolizes a beginning. Every beginning is something new.

854. The symbolism of the *mountains of Ararat* as a bit of light is established by the symbolism of a *mountain* as the good that comes of love and charity (§795) and of *Ararat* as a bit of light—the light that a regenerate person enjoys.[470]

The new glimmer—the first glimmer—that comes to the regenerate individual never rises out of a knowledge of faith's truth but out of charity. Faith's truths are like rays of light; love, or charity, is like a flame. The enlightenment of one who is regenerating does not radiate from the truth belonging to faith but from charity. The truths themselves are the rays that beam from it. So one can see that the mountains of Ararat symbolize this kind of light.

Such light is the first to shine after a time of struggle, and because it is the first, it is dim and is called a bit of light, not full light.

855. These explanations show what the elements of the current verse mean on an inner plane: the spiritual person embodies a holy restfulness that results from the new glimmer of understanding radiated by charity. The angels perceive these details in all their amazing variety, arranged in a

delightful pattern. If we could possess ourselves of just one idea like theirs, thousands and thousands of other insights along manifold lines would enter into it and touch our hearts. Those thoughts are completely beyond description. Such is the Lord's Word throughout its inner meaning, even though it looks like an unpolished history in its literal meaning—as does the current verse (despite the symbolism given): *The ark came to rest in the seventh month, on the seventeenth day of the month, on the mountains of Ararat.*

856. Genesis 8:5. *And the waters were going and disappearing till the tenth month; in the tenth [month], on the first of the month, the heads of the mountains appeared.*

The waters were going and disappearing means that falsity began to be dispersed. The *tenth month* symbolizes the truth belonging to the remnant. *On the first of the month the heads of the mountains appeared* symbolizes religious truth that then began to be visible.

857. The meaning of *the waters were going and disappearing* as the fact that falsity began to be dispersed can be seen from the words themselves. It can also be seen from the remarks just above explaining verse 3, which says that the waters receded, going and coming back, where the present verse says that the waters were going and disappearing. Both phrases symbolize vacillation between truth and falsity, but the meaning here is that such vacillation lessened.

To waver after a period of trial, as I said [§849], is not to know what is true; but as the wavering gradually ends, the light of truth appears. The reason for the darkness is that as long as we are at this stage, our inner self—that is, the Lord working through our inner self—cannot act on the outer self. The inner self holds the remnant described earlier [§§561, 661:2], which is a desire for goodness and for the truth it leads to. The outer self contains cravings and the falsity they lead to. Until these outer attributes are overcome and eliminated, no channel lies open for goodness and truth coming from the inner self, that is, from the Lord through the inner self.

[2] An additional purpose of our trials, then, is to subdue our external qualities and make them obedient to inner qualities. Anyone can see this by considering that as soon as our interests are attacked and crushed, the way they are by misfortune, sickness, and mental illness, our cravings start to shut down. As they shut down, we start talking devoutly. But the minute we return to our previous condition, the outer self takes over and we barely think about religious subjects. Something similar happens in the last hour of death, when our bodily drives begin to die away.

From this everyone can see what the inner self and outer self are, what the remnant is, and how the cravings and sensual pleasures of the outer self block the Lord from operating through the inner being. By the same token it is easy to see what else is accomplished by our struggles or inward pangs, called the gnawings of conscience: subordination of the outer self to the inner. Obedience in the outer self is simply a state in which cravings and consequent falsities do not obstruct, resist, or smother the desire for goodness and truth. An end to perverse longings and misguided thinking is what the going and disappearing of the waters depicts here.

858 The symbolism of the *tenth month* as the truth belonging to the remnant is established by the symbolism of *ten* as a remnant (§576) and by what was said just above about the remnant in the inner self.

859 The symbolism of *on the first of the month the heads of the mountains appeared* as religious truth that then began to be visible is established by the symbolism of *mountains* as the good effects of love and charity (§795). The *heads* start to show when we are being reborn and given a conscience and, through conscience, charity.

Those who think they see mountaintops, or religious truth, from any other perspective than that of a loving, charitable goodness are completely mistaken. Otherwise, Jews and blasphemous gentiles[471] would also be able to see the truth, even though they lack such goodness.

The mountaintops are the first points of light to appear.

860 From this it is also possible to see that all regeneration advances from evening to morning, as Genesis 1 says six times in discussing a person's rebirth. Verses 2 and 3 here portray the evening, verses 4 and 5 the morning. The emergence of the mountaintops depicts the first light or dawn of this state.

861 Genesis 8:6. *And it happened at the end of forty days that Noah opened the window of the ark that he had made.*

It happened at the end of forty days symbolizes the time that the previous state lasted and the point at which the next commenced. *Noah opened the window of the ark that he had made* symbolizes the second state, when religious truth appeared to them.

862 The symbolism of *it happened at the end of forty days* as the time that the previous state lasted and the point at which the next commenced is established by the symbolism of *forty*. In a passage that, referring to times of trial, mentions forty days and forty nights, forty is a symbol for the length that times of trial last (§730). Here, because the subject is the state that follows struggles, it says forty days but not nights. The reason the text speaks only of days is that charity now begins to appear. The Word compares charity to the day and calls it day, while the early faith that is not yet very tightly bound up with charity it compares to the night, and calls night. An example is Genesis 1:16; and there are other passages.

Another reason that the Word refers to faith as night is that it obtains its light from charity, as the moon does from the sun. So the Word compares faith to the moon and calls it a moon, and it compares love, or charity, to the sun and calls it the sun.

Forty days, and the length of time they symbolize, relate both to what comes before and to what comes after, which is why it says *at the end of* forty days. In this way, they symbolize the duration of the previous state and the commencement of the state presently under discussion.

Now begins a description of the second state following periods of struggle for the people in this church.

863 *Noah opened the window of the ark that he had made* symbolizes the second state, when religious truth appeared to them. This can be seen from the final words of the last verse (saying that the heads of the mountains appeared) and their meaning; from the symbolism of a window; and from the fact that this is the first moment of light. A *window*, dealt with above at §655, symbolizes the intellectual side of things and consequently religious truth, which is the same thing.

As for the intellectual realm or the religious truth that the window symbolizes, I must make the same remark as before [§§854, 859]: No religious truth is at all possible unless it develops out of the goodness that goes with love or with charity, just as nothing truly belongs to the intellect unless it rises out of something in the will. If you take away volition, there is no comprehension, as demonstrated several times already [§§112, 585, 590, 628]. So if you take away charity, there is no faith.

But since the human will is undiluted greed, the Lord made a miraculous provision to prevent us from plunging the contents of the intellect—religious truth—into our selfish desires. He divided what belongs to the intellect from our will by the specific means of conscience, which he infuses with charity. Without this miraculous act of providence, no one could ever have been saved.

864 Genesis 8:7. *And he sent out a raven, and it went out, going and coming back till the water dried up on the earth.*

He sent out a raven, and it went out, going and coming back, means that falsity still troubled them. The *raven* symbolizes falsity. *Going and coming back* symbolizes the stage they were in, which fluctuated in just this way. *Till the water dried up on the earth* symbolizes apparently getting rid of falsity.

The meaning of *he sent out a raven, and it went out, going and coming back,* as the fact that falsity still troubled them can be seen from the symbolism of a raven and of going and coming back, discussed below.

This describes the second state following times of trial for a person who is regenerating. In it, the truths that faith espouses, representing the first points of light, start to appear. Conditions are such that falsity constantly interferes, making the period resemble dawn with its half-light, which overlaps the lingering dark of night. That is why it is symbolized by a raven here.[472]

In spiritual people, especially before they have been reborn, falsity is like dense patches of cloud, because they cannot learn any religious truth except from information that the Word reveals, and the Word states everything in a general way. Generalities are nothing but splotches of cloud, since every general statement embraces thousands upon thousands of individual concepts and every individual concept embraces thousands upon thousands of particulars. The details making up the individual concepts are what shed light on the general ideas. Such details are never revealed to humankind, both because they cannot be described and because we cannot grasp them and so cannot acknowledge or believe them. They run contrary to the illusions of our senses, which we surrender to and do not easily allow to be destroyed.

[2] The case is entirely different with heavenly people, who receive perception from the Lord. It is possible to introduce the individual concepts and the particulars of those concepts to them. For example, it is possible to instill in them the idea that true marriage involves one husband and one wife, that it represents the heavenly marriage, and that such a marriage therefore can hold heavenly happiness within it, which the marriage between one man and many wives never can. Spiritual people who have learned this from the Lord's Word yield to it, so they accept as a matter of conscience that polygamous marriage is a sin. Beyond this their knowledge does not extend. Heavenly people, though, perceive a thousand arguments confirming it and shudder at the idea of contracting marriage with multiple partners.[473]

Since spiritual people possess only general knowledge, and this is what forms their conscience, and since the general teachings of the Word are adapted to sensory illusions, clearly numberless misconceptions attach themselves to such teachings and seep in among them. These misconceptions cannot be done away with. They are symbolized by the raven that went out, going and coming back.

866 The symbolism of the *raven* as falsity is established in general by explanations and illustrations above regarding birds [§§40, 745, 776, 803], showing that they symbolize matters of understanding, reason, and fact, and the opposites of these, which are rationalization and falsity. The Word depicts both the positive and negative types in the different species of bird. Birds that are gentle, pretty, and clean portray true ways of understanding, but birds that are fierce, ugly, and unclean portray false ones, depending on the specific type of truth or falsity. Thick, dense falsity is depicted by owls and ravens—by owls because they inhabit the dark of night, by ravens because they are black. In Isaiah, for instance:

Owl and *raven* will live there. (Isaiah 34:11)

These words occur in a passage that speaks of the Jewish church as containing sheer falsity,[474] which the owl and raven depict.

867 The symbolism of *going and coming back* as the stage they were in, which fluctuated in just this way, can be seen from the falsities that plague people during the first and second stages after their trials. As false ideas then flit through the mind, they depart and return, for the reason given above: the person can and does learn only the most comprehensive generalizations. These generalizations give entry to some very fanciful notions that arise from a bodily, sensory, and worldly source, and that do not harmonize with the truth taught by faith.

868 The symbolism of *till the water dried up on the earth* as apparently getting rid of falsity can be seen from the circumstances a person faces when being reborn.

Everyone today believes that the evil and falsity we have in us is wholly dispelled and abolished when we regenerate, so that when our rebirth is complete, nothing evil or false remains. People suppose we are then pure and righteous, as if we had been washed and rinsed with water. But this belief is absolutely false. Not a single evil or falsity is so thoroughly dispelled as to be abolished. Everything we inherited at infancy and everything we acquired through our actions remains, so that even when we have become regenerate we consist of unrelieved evil and falsity. Souls after death go through experiences that demonstrate this fact to them.

The same thing is also clear enough from the consideration that we have no goodness or truth whatever except from the Lord and that all our vices and distortions come from our selfhood. If people—or spirits, or even angels—were left on their own for even the smallest moment, they would make a spontaneous rush for hell. For this reason the Word says that heaven is not pure [Job 15:15]. The angels acknowledge this, and no one who fails to acknowledge it can be among them. The Lord's mercy alone frees them from hell, indeed removes them from hell and keeps them from voluntarily plunging right back in.

Angels perceive plainly that the Lord keeps them from running headlong into hell. Good spirits do too, up to a point. But evil spirits, like people on earth, do not believe it, although they have been shown many times. A description of my experiences on this subject will appear below, by the Lord's divine mercy.475

[2] The human condition, then, is such that we can never banish anything evil or false so completely as to eliminate it, since evil and falsity make up those aspects of life that are all our own. Because of this, when the Lord uses times of trouble to regenerate us, in his divine mercy he subdues our evil and falsity to the point where they look dead, although they are not; they are merely so well conquered that they cannot stand up to the goodness and truth the Lord gives us.

Through our times of trouble the Lord also gives us a new capacity for receiving goodness and truth. He endows us with conceptions of what is good and true, and feelings of affection for it, and whatever is evil and false can then be bent in that direction. He also introduces into our general ideas (as described above [§848:3]) more specific ones, and into these the most specific, which are hidden to us and of which we are totally unaware, since they lie beyond the reach of our comprehension and perception. This subconscious knowledge serves as a reservoir or container into which the Lord can pour neighborly love, which itself holds the innocence he can instill.

These things, when mixed together in marvelous balance in a person, spirit, or angel, can present an image of a rainbow, which is why a rainbow was used as the sign of the pact mentioned in Genesis 9:12, 13, 14, 15, 16. For more on this, with the Lord's divine mercy, see there [§§1036–1056].

When we have come into this form, we are called regenerate. Everything evil and false in us remains, but then everything good and true is also preserved. Bad people find that all the forms of evil and falsity they had indulged in during bodily life return in exactly the same form in the next life, where they turn into the hallucinations and punishments of hell. Good people in the next life, though, recall all the states marked by goodness and truth that they had experienced—states of friendship, love for others, and innocence—along with the attendant joys and pleasures, now increased and multiplied beyond measure.

This, then, is the apparent eradication of falsity symbolized by the drying up of the water.

869 Genesis 8:8. *And he sent a dove out from him, to see whether the water had lessened off the face of the ground.*

The *dove*[476] symbolizes the truth and goodness of faith in one who is being reborn. *He sent a dove out from him to see* symbolizes the right conditions for taking in faith's truth and goodness. *Whether the water had lessened* symbolizes falsities that get in the way. The *face of the ground* is things that people in the church have in them. The word *ground* is used because this is the first stage a person goes through in becoming a church.

870 The symbolism of a *dove* or pigeon as the truth and goodness of faith in one who is being reborn can be seen from the symbolism of a dove in the Word—especially the one that settled on Jesus when he was baptized, as told in Matthew:

> After he was baptized, Jesus went up immediately out of the water, and here, the heavens opened! And he saw God's spirit coming down like a *dove* and lighting on him. (Matthew 3:16, 17; told also in John 1:32; Luke 3:21, 22; Mark 1:10, 11)

The dove simply symbolizes the holy quality of faith, while baptism itself symbolizes rebirth. So in relation to the new church that was to arise, it symbolizes faith's truth and goodness, which the people of that church receive through the Lord's regeneration of them.

[2] The use of pigeon chicks and turtledoves as sacrifices and burnt offerings in the Jewish religion represented and involved similar things. This can be seen in the individual passages that speak of those offerings: Leviticus 1:14–end; 5:7–10; 12:6; 14:21, 22; 15:14, 15, 29, 30; Numbers 6:10, 11; Luke 2:22, 23, 24. Anyone can grasp that they symbolized such things, for the simple reason that they had to have represented something. If not, the gesture would be hollow rather than divine in any way. The church's outward motions are lifeless; all their life comes from within, and what is within comes from the Lord.

[3] A dove's general symbolism as the use of the intellect for religion can also be seen in the prophets, as in Hosea:

> Ephraim will be like a simpleminded *pigeon:* no heart. They called Egypt; they left for Assyria. (Hosea 7:11)

In the same author:

> Ephraim will quake like *fowl* from Egypt and a *dove* from the land of Assyria. (Hosea 11:11)

In these verses, Ephraim stands for a person endowed with understanding, Egypt for a knowledgeable person, Assyria for a logical one, and the dove or pigeon for everything having to do with the intellectual side of religion. The passages are about the spiritual church's rebirth. In David:

> Jehovah, do not hand the *turtledove's* soul over to the wild animal. (Psalms 74:19)

The wild animal stands for those who have no love for their neighbor; the soul of a turtledove, for a life of faith.

See the remarks and evidence above at §§40, 776, [777, 778] in respect to birds, showing that they symbolize matters of understanding. Tame, pretty, clean, and useful birds symbolize ideas in the intellect that are true and good, while rapacious, ugly, unclean, and useless ones symbolize the opposite—that is, ideas that are false—as does the raven, here set opposite the dove.

The symbolism of *he sent a dove out from him to see* as the right conditions for taking in faith's truth and goodness becomes clear from the series of ideas. It can also be deduced from the ensuing treatment of the three stages of regeneration[477] that follow times of trial for the people being discussed. The three times the dove was sent out symbolize those three stages.

The words here most directly involve an examination of those people, since it says that Noah sent the dove out from him to see specifically (as comes next) *whether the water might have lessened.* The question posed by these words was whether falsity was still so overwhelming that they could not accept the truth and goodness of faith. But the Lord has no use for investigation, since he knows absolutely everything, so at a deeper level, the words symbolize not an examination but prevailing conditions. Here they mean the first stage, when falsity still got in the way, as symbolized by the words *whether the water had lessened.*

872 The *face of the ground* is what people in the church have in them, the word *ground* being used because this is a person's first stage in becoming a church. This can be seen from the symbolism of the ground (dealt with before [§§386, 566]) as people in the church, who are referred to as the ground when the seed of faith's truth and goodness can be sown in them. Prior to that they are referred to as the land, or the earth. The first chapter of Genesis, for instance, speaking of a time before people have developed a heavenly character, uses *land* to describe them, but the second chapter, dealing with a time when they have become heavenly, uses *ground* and *field* to describe them. Something similar occurs in the present chapter.

The words *land* (or *earth*) and *ground* by themselves indicate what the symbolic meaning on the inner plane is, not just here but throughout the Word.

In an overall sense, the ground symbolizes the church; and because it symbolizes the church, it also symbolizes the people who belong to the church, since, as noted before [§82], every individual in the church *is* a church.

873 Genesis 8:9. *And the dove did not find a resting place for the sole of its foot, and it returned to him, to the ark, because there was water over the face of the whole earth; and he put his hand out and took it and brought it in to himself, into the ark.*

The dove did not find a resting place for the sole of its foot means that none of faith's goodness or truth could root itself. *It returned to him, to the ark,* symbolizes goodness and truth that seemed to be religious in those people. *Because there was water over the face of the earth* means that falsity was still overflowing. *He put his hand out* symbolizes their personal power. *And took it and brought it to himself, into the ark,* means that they did good and thought about truth under their own direction.

874 This scene depicts the first stage of regeneration following trial for the people of this church, a stage common to everyone who is being reborn: we imagine that we are doing good deeds and thinking true thoughts under our own power. Because we still cannot see clearly at all, the Lord lets us think this way.

Still, none of the good we do and none of the truth we contemplate while holding this opinion (a mistaken one) is the kind of goodness or truth that makes a part of faith. Nothing that we produce from ourselves can be good, because it *is* from ourselves—an impure and very unclean source. From an impure and unclean source nothing good can spring, because we are always thinking about how deserving and righteous we are. Some people, as the Lord teaches in Luke 18:9–14, go further and despise others in comparison with themselves. Others do other things just as bad. Self-centered desires add themselves to the mixture, making the exterior look good, although the interior is filthy.

As a consequence, the good that we do at this stage is not the good that belongs to faith. It is the same with the truth that we think. Even if the idea we adopt is absolutely true and is in itself a valid religious concept, nonetheless as long as we adopt it for selfish reasons, it has no religious good within it. Any truth, in order to be theologically true, has to have the good of faith from the Lord within it. That is when it first becomes good and true.

The meaning of *the dove did not find a resting place for the sole of its foot* as the fact that none of faith's goodness or truth could root itself can be seen from this: a *dove* symbolizes religious truth, and a *resting place for the sole of the foot* means becoming rooted. The reason it could not root itself comes up later: falsity was still overflowing. But no one can understand how the situation stands without learning how a spiritual person is reborn.

[2] Spiritual people have to have seeds of knowledge planted in their memory—knowledge of what faith is, drawn from the Lord's Word or from doctrinal precepts distilled out of it. (The ancient church acquired this knowledge from what had been revealed to the earliest church.) From the memory, their minds then need to be supplied with material for the intellect; but as long as they are awash in falsity, religious truth cannot take root, no matter how densely it has been sown. Such truth clings only to the surface, or memory, and the soil does not become suitable until falsity has been driven away so that it no longer appears, as noted before [§§842:4–5, 868:2].

[3] For spiritual people, the ground itself is prepared in the intellectual part of the mind. When preparation is complete, the Lord instills the goodness of charity and then a conscience. Conscience becomes the basis for the person's actions, or in other words, the channel through which the Lord puts into effect the goodness and truth connected with faith.

In this way, the Lord divides the workings of the intellect in a spiritual person from those of the will so that they never coalesce. If they did, it would necessarily destroy the person forever. [4] In the people of the earliest church the two did converge, as they also do in heavenly angels; but in the people of this church they did not, nor do they in spiritual people generally.

It does look as though the neighborly good that they do comes from their will, but this is just an appearance and an illusion. All the neighborly good they do is the Lord's alone and comes through conscience rather than will. If the Lord allowed us to act from our own will one tiny bit, we would do evil instead of good, and we would do it out of hatred, vengefulness, and cruelty.

[5] The situation is similar in regard to the truth that spiritual people think and talk about. If they did not think and speak from conscience, and so from some good quality belonging to the Lord, they could never think or speak truth, except the way the Devil's horde does when impersonating angels of light.

These things are quite obvious in the other life.

This explanation shows how regeneration proceeds and what it means for spiritual people: a separation of the intellectual part of the mind from the volitional part by means of conscience. The Lord forms the conscience in their intellectual part, and the deeds that come out of it seem to come from their will, although they really come from the Lord.

876 The symbolism of *it returned to him, to the ark,* as goodness and truth that seemed to be religious can be seen from statements above [§874] and just below.

Liberation is symbolized on an inner level not by the dove's return to the ark but by its being sent from the ark and *not* returning, as indicated by what follows. Verse 12, for instance, says that Noah sent the dove out and it never returned to him again. Verses 15 and 16 say that he himself was ordered to leave the ark, and verse 18, that he did.

The *ark* symbolizes the circumstances of these people before rebirth. Under such circumstances they were captives or prisoners, beset on all sides by evil and falsity, or by the flood waters. So *returning* to Noah, to the ark, signals the relapse of goodness and truth (as meant by the dove) into that condition.

Anything good we intend to do when motivated by self-interest comes back to us, because it focuses on us; we want the world or the angels to see what we are doing, or we desire to earn a place in heaven, or we hope to be the greatest in heaven. Those are the urges inherent in self-interest and in every idea connected with it, however convincing the outer appearance of religious goodness and truth. The goodness and truth that faith embraces is good and true inside, from the very core; that is, the goodness and truth of faith comes entirely from the Lord by way of our deepest levels. When it comes instead from ourselves, or depends on our merits, it is dirty on the inside although apparently clean on the outside, just like a foul-smelling prostitute with a beautiful-looking face or like an Ethiopian person, or rather an Egyptian mummy, dressed in white clothing.⁴⁷⁸

877. The symbolism of *there was water over the face of the earth* as the fact that falsity was still overflowing is established by the symbolism of *flood water* as falsity. This symbolism has been proved satisfactorily before [§§739, 757, 790, 842], so that the meaning is clear from the words themselves.

878. *He put his hand out* symbolizes their personal power, and *he took it and brought it in to himself, into the ark,* means that they did good and thought about truth under their own direction. This can be seen from the symbolism of a *hand* as power and so here as the personal power that they exercised. *Putting out* one's hand, *taking* a dove, and *bringing it in to oneself* is laying claim to the truth meant by the dove and using it for one's own purposes.

The symbolism of a *hand* as power, authority, and the arrogant self-assurance these impart, is established by many scriptural passages, such as this one from Isaiah:

> I will exact punishment on the fruit of the bloated heart of Assyria's king because he said, "In the *power of my hand* have I acted, and in my wisdom, because I have understanding." (Isaiah 10:12, 13)

The hand obviously stands for personal power, to which Assyria's king attributed his success; hence the punishment inflicted on him. In the same author:

> Moab will stretch out its *hands* in its own midst—as a swimmer stretches them out to swim—and [Jehovah] will lay their arrogance low, together with the floodgates⁴⁷⁹ of their *hands*. (Isaiah 25:11)

The hands stand for personal power resulting from a sense of superiority to others and so from arrogance. [2] In the same author:

> Their residents, *their hand shortened,* have felt panic and shame. (Isaiah 37:27)

Having shortened hands stands for lacking any power. In the same author:

> Will the clay say to its potter, "What are you doing?" or will your work say, "[My maker] has no *hands*"? (Isaiah 45:9)

Not having hands stands for not having any power. In Ezekiel:

> The monarch will mourn and the chieftain will be clothed in shock, and the *hands* of the people of the land will be uneasy. (Ezekiel 7:27)

The hands stand for various kinds of power. In Micah:

> Doom to those who contemplate wickedness and practice evil on their beds, because they do it in the morning light, and because their *hand* is as a god.[480] (Micah 2:1)

Their hand stands for their personal power, which they trust in as their god. In Zechariah:

> Doom to shepherds who are good for nothing, abandoning the flock! A sword against their *arm* and against their *right-hand* eye! Their *arm* will utterly shrivel and their *right-hand* eye go utterly dark. (Zechariah 11:17)

[3] Because a hand symbolizes different kinds of power, the Word frequently calls humanity's evil ways and false thinking the *works of their hands*.[481] Evil grows out of selfishness in our will, and falsity out of selfishness in our intellect. This fact becomes clear from the nature of human selfhood [or autonomy], which is unremitting evil and falsity. For a description of human selfhood in these terms, see above at §§39, 41, 141, 150, 154, 210, 215.

Since hands in general mean power, the Word many times attributes hands to Jehovah, or the Lord, and in those places, on an inner level, hands mean omnipotence. In Isaiah, for instance:

> Jehovah, *your hand* is lifted high. (Isaiah 26:11)

Here the hand stands for divine power. In the same author:

> Jehovah stretches out *his hand,* they are all consumed. (Isaiah 31:3)

Again it stands for divine power. In the same author:

> Concerning the work of *my hands* do you command me? *My hands* spread out the heavens, and to their whole army I gave commands! (Isaiah 45:11, 12)

Again it stands for divine power.

The Word frequently refers to regenerate people as the work of Jehovah's hands. In the same author:

> *My hand* founded the earth, and *my right hand* measured the heavens by palm-breadths. (Isaiah 48:13)

The hand and the right hand stand for omnipotence. [4] In the same author:

> Is *my hand* shortened, so that redemption fails; or do I not have in me the *power* to rescue? (Isaiah 50:2)

This stands for divine power. In Jeremiah:

> You brought your people Israel out of the land of Egypt by signs and portents, and by a *strong hand,* and by an *outstretched arm.* (Jeremiah 32:17, 21)

This stands for divine power, and verse 17 uses the word *power* where verse 21 uses *hand*.[482] The saying that the people of Israel were brought out of Egypt by a strong hand and an outstretched arm comes up repeatedly [Deuteronomy 4:34; 5:15; 7:19; 26:8; Psalms 136:11–12]. In Ezekiel:

> This is what the Lord Jehovih has said: "On the day when I chose Israel and *raised my hand*[483] to the seed of the house of Jacob and became known to them in the land of Egypt, I *raised my hand* to them to bring them out of the land of Egypt." (Ezekiel 20:5, 6, 23)

In Moses:

> Israel saw the *massive hand* that Jehovah used against the Egyptians. (Exodus 14:31)

[5] These passages now make it quite clear that a hand symbolizes power. In fact the symbolism was so strong that a hand also came to serve as a representation of power. This is visible in the miracles performed in Egypt, when Moses was commanded to stretch out his staff or his hand in order to accomplish a given result. For example:

> Moses *stretched out his hand* and hail fell on Egypt. (Exodus 9:22)

> Moses *stretched out his hand* and darkness fell. (Exodus 10:21, 22)

> Moses *stretched out his hand* and staff over the Suph Sea[484] and it dried up. And he *stretched out his hand* and it returned to its place. (Exodus 14:21, 27)

No clear-thinking person can believe that there was any power in Moses' hand or staff. Rather, since the act of lifting and stretching out a hand symbolized divine power, it had become representative [of that power] in the Jewish religion. [6] The instance in which Joshua extended a javelin was similar:

> Jehovah said, "*Stretch out the javelin that is in your hand* toward Ai, because I will deliver it into your *hand.*" When Joshua stretched out the *javelin that was in his hand,* they came into the city and seized it, and Joshua did not draw back the *hand* with which he had stretched out the javelin until he had exterminated all the residents of Ai. (Joshua 8:18, 19, 26)

This shows what the case was with the representative acts and objects that formed the external ritual of the Jewish religion. It also shows what the Word is like, in that the particulars of its outward meaning do not seem as if they would be representative of the Lord and his kingdom. This applies to the examples here of times when leaders stretched their hands out, and to all other details as well. Their representative nature will never be clear as long as our minds cling exclusively to the literal narrative.

The same evidence indicates how far the Jews fell away from a true understanding of the Word and the rituals of their religion, since they identified worship with outward forms alone. They went so far as to ascribe power to Moses' staff[485] and Joshua's javelin, when in reality these were no more powerful than a piece of wood. It was because those objects symbolized the Lord's omnipotence, and because heaven viewed them this way, that signs and wonders occurred when those men stretched out a hand or a staff as ordered. The same is true of the fact that when Moses raised his *hands* on top of the hill, Joshua won, and when he dropped them Joshua lost, which led others to support his *hands* (Exodus 17:9–13).[486]

[7] The situation was similar when one person, seeking to transfer power, laid hands on another to consecrate that other, as the people did to the Levites (Numbers 8:9, 10, 12) and as Moses did to Joshua when Joshua was to take his place (Numbers 27:18, 23). This is the source of modern rites of ordination and benediction that involve the laying on of hands.

The extent to which a hand symbolized and represented power can be seen from the stories of Uzzah and Jeroboam, which the Word tells in the following way.

Concerning Uzzah: Uzzah *put* (his hand) *out* onto the ark of God, grasped it, and died for doing so (2 Samuel 6:6, 7). The ark represented the Lord and so represented everything that was sacred and heavenly. Uzzah's "*putting* it *out*" onto the ark represented his own, independent power, or human autonomy. Because human autonomy is profane, the word *hand* does not appear in the text (although it is implied) to prevent the angels from being aware that anything so profane touched something holy. And since he put it out, he died.

[8] Concerning Jeroboam: It happened that when he heard the word that the man of God had shouted in denunciation of the altar, Jeroboam *put his hand out* from the altar, saying, "Seize him!" And his *hand* that he had *put out* in denunciation of the man shriveled up, and he could not draw it back to himself. He said to the man of God, "Please entreat Jehovah your God to restore my *hand* to me." And the man of God entreated Jehovah, and his *hand* was restored to him and became as it had been before (1 Kings 13:4, 5, 6).

Here again *putting out a hand* symbolizes a person's own, independent power or autonomy, which is profane. Jeroboam wanted to violate what was holy by putting his hand out toward the man of God, so his hand shriveled, but since he was an idolater and incapable of profaning anything, as noted earlier [§§303, 408, 661:1], his hand was restored.

The symbolism and representation of a hand as power can be deduced from objects in the world of spirits that have a representative meaning. Sometimes an arm becomes visible there—a bare arm, possessing such tremendous strength that it could crush bone and pound one's deepest marrow more or less into oblivion. The arm strikes so much terror into the inhabitants that their hearts turn to water. And it actually does have the strength that it seems to have.[487]

Genesis 8:10, 11. *And he waited yet another seven days and proceeded to send the dove out from the ark. And the dove returned to him at evening time, and look: the torn-off leaf of an olive tree in its mouth! And Noah realized that the water had lessened off the earth.*

He waited another seven days symbolizes the start of the second stage of regeneration. *Seven days* symbolizes holiness, since the current subject is charity. *And he proceeded to send the dove out from the ark* symbolizes the right conditions for taking in the goodness and truth of faith. *And the dove returned to him at evening time* means that goodness and truth began to show just a little bit. *Evening time* resembles conditions during the half-light that precedes morning. *And look: the torn-off leaf of an olive tree in its mouth,* symbolizes a very small quantity of religious truth. The *leaf* means truth, an *olive tree* means the good that charity inspires, *torn off* means that this is the source of religious truth, and *in its mouth* means that it became visible. *And Noah realized that the water had lessened off the earth* means that these things were now possible because falsity was not so overpowering that it got in the way, as it had previously.

880 The symbolism of *he waited another seven days* as the start of the second stage of regeneration can be seen from this: the clause describes the interval between the first stage (discussed just above in verses 8 and 9) and the second (discussed here in verses 10 and 11). To weave its story, the text uses the words *he waited* to stand for the interval.

The facts with respect to the second stage of rebirth can be seen to some extent from what was stated and shown concerning the first stage, in which religious truth could not yet put down roots because falsity was getting in the way. Religious truth first takes root when we begin to acknowledge and believe it. Until then, it has no roots. The things that we hear from the Word and hold in our memory are no more than seeds sown there.

Roots, however, do not develop until we receive and welcome charitable goodness. The goodness embraced by faith, that is, the good urged by charity, is what gives root to the truth taught by faith. The situation is like that of seed cast on the earth while winter still holds sway and the earth remains frozen. The seed lies there, but it does not grow roots. As soon as the warming sun of early spring thaws the ground, though, the seed begins to develop roots, at first growing them inside and then extending them into the earth. So it is with the planting of spiritual seed; no roots grow until the goodness of charity warms it. Then it first develops roots internally and afterward sends them out.

[2] We have three parallel, unified layers within us: earthly, spiritual, and heavenly. Our earthly level receives no life at all except from the spiritual; our spiritual level receives no life at all except from the heavenly; and our heavenly level receives life from the Lord alone, who is life itself.

To offer a somewhat fuller picture, our earthly level is a reservoir that holds spiritual qualities, or a container into which they are poured; and our spiritual level is a reservoir that holds heavenly qualities, or a container into which they are poured. Through our heavenly level, we receive life from the Lord. This is what influx is.[488] The heavenly aspect is everything good connected with faith or (in a spiritual person) the goodness connected with charity. The spiritual aspect is truth, which definitely does not become a part of our faith unless it has inside it the goodness that belongs to faith, or the goodness of charity, which in turn has within it life itself from the Lord.

To present a still clearer view of what is entailed, our earthly dimension involves carrying out a *work of charity*[489] by means of our physical body, whether in deed or word. But this dimension in itself is dead. It has no life except from the spiritual dimension lying behind the work; and the spiritual dimension has no life except from the heavenly dimension, which comes from the Lord. Because of him a deed is called good; nothing is good unless it comes from the Lord.

[3] This being the case, everyone can see that in any charitable deed, the act itself is just a function of the material body; whatever vitality it possesses comes from the religious truth that underlies it. Furthermore, religious truth is itself just a lifeless entity; anything alive in it comes from religious goodness. Religious goodness, again, has no life except from the Lord alone, who is goodness itself and life itself.

This demonstrates why heavenly angels are unwilling to hear about faith, still less about good deeds (see §202), because they trace the origin of each to love. They act on their faith out of love, and even the good works of faith are something they do out of love, so that for them, both the works and the faith vanish and only love and the good that comes of it remain. Within their love the Lord is present.

Because these angels have such heavenly ideas, they are kept separate from the angels described as spiritual. Their way of thinking and consequent manner of speech is much harder to grasp than the spiritual angels' thought and speech.

Seven symbolizes holiness, since the current subject is charity. This is established by the symbolism of seven as discussed earlier at §§395 and 716. Another reason the text inserts *seven* here is to link everything into the story, because *seven* and *seven days* in the inner meaning adds a kind of sanctity, a quality this second stage has from its heavenly aspect, that is, from charity.

The symbolism of *and he proceeded to send the dove out from the ark* as the right conditions for taking in the goodness and truth of faith can be deduced from statements made at verse 8 [§871], where the words are almost the same. A difference is that verse 8 says he sent the dove out from himself. The reason for the difference is also given there:[490] The people under discussion were at that time putting truth and goodness

883 *The dove returned to him at evening time* means that goodness and truth began to show just a little bit, *evening time* resembling conditions during the half-light that precedes morning. This can be seen from the things said above at verse 9⁴⁹¹ and from the reference here to evening time. Concerning evening, see the statements made at Genesis 1 [§22], which says six times that there was evening and there was morning. *Evening* is a term connected with regeneration, specifically with the phase when we are still living in shadow, or when not much light at all shines inside us as yet. The actual morning is portrayed in verse 13 by "he removed the roof of the ark and looked."

The fact that [in the original language the word for] evening meant the half-light before morning explains the frequent references to evening in the Jewish religion.[492] It also explains why their Sabbaths and feast days began in the evening and why Aaron was commanded to light the sacred lamp at evening (Exodus 27:[20,] 21).[493]

884 *And look: the torn-off leaf of an olive tree in its mouth,* symbolizes a very small quantity of religious truth. The *leaf* means truth, an *olive tree* means the goodness that charity inspires, *torn off* means that this is the source of religious truth, and *in its mouth* means that it became visible. This can be seen from the symbolism of an olive tree, and it shines out from the words themselves. The fact that it was only a leaf indicates the meagerness of the amount.

885 The symbolism of a *leaf* as truth is established by numerous passages in the Word comparing us to, or actually calling us, trees. In those places, fruit symbolizes the good espoused by charity and a leaf the truth to which it leads (and charity and truth also function the same way fruit and leaves do). In Ezekiel, for example:

> Beside the river, on its bank, on this side and that, grows every food tree, whose *leaf* does not fall and whose *fruit* is not used up; month by month it is reborn, because its waters are going out from the sanctuary. And its *fruit* will serve as food, and its *leaf,* as medicine. (Ezekiel 47:12; Revelation 22:2)

The tree stands for the people of a church that embodies the Lord's kingdom. The fruit stands for the good that results from love and charity, and the leaf, for the truth that develops out of it. That truth is used for the instruction and regeneration of the human race, which is why the leaf is said to serve as medicine. In the same author:

> Will he not tear out its roots and cut down its *fruit*, and it will wither? All the *torn-off* [leaves][494] of its new growth will wither. (Ezekiel 17:9)

This is about a devastated grapevine (church), of which the fruit (goodness) and what is torn off the new growth (truth) will wither in this way. [2] In Jeremiah:

> Blessed is the man who trusts in Jehovah. He will be like a tree planted by the water. His *leaf* will be green; in a year of shortage, he will not worry. And he will not leave off making *fruit*. (Jeremiah 17:7, 8)

The green leaf stands for the truth that composes faith and so for the faith itself that springs from charity. David has similar words in Psalms 1:3. In the same prophet:

> There are no grapes on the grapevine and no figs on the fig tree, and the *leaf* has fallen off. (Jeremiah 8:13)

Grapes on the vine stand for spiritual goodness, and figs on the fig tree for earthly goodness. The leaf stands for truth, which falls off in this way. Isaiah 34:4 is parallel. Something similar is meant by the fig tree that Jesus saw and on which he found nothing but *leaves*, so that it withered (Matthew 21:[19,] 20; Mark 11:13, 14). The fig tree in this case specifically refers to the Jewish church, in which there was no longer any earthly goodness. The doctrinal precepts of faith (or truth) preserved among them are the leaves. A church that has been devastated is such that it knows the truth but does not want to understand it. The same applies to people who say they know the truth, or the tenets of religion, yet possess none of charity's goodness. They are only fig leaves, and they wither.

The symbolism of an *olive tree* as the goodness that charity inspires can be seen from the scriptural symbolism not only of an olive tree but of oil as well.

Olive oil was used along with perfumes to anoint priests and kings and also as fuel for lamps. (For the former, see Exodus 30:24, [25]; for the latter, Exodus 27:20.) The reason for using olive oil in anointings and in lamps was that it represented every heavenly quality and consequently all the good effects of love and charity. The oil is the very essence of a tree, virtually its soul, just as the heavenly dimension or goodness of love and charity is the very essence or soul of faith. That is the source of its representation.

Many passages in the Word can confirm that oil symbolizes the heavenly aspect or goodness of love and charity, but since the present verse mentions the olive tree, let me offer a few passages that demonstrate the meaning of the olive tree alone. In Jeremiah:

> "An *olive tree* green and beautiful with shapely fruit" is the name Jehovah had given you. (Jeremiah 11:16)

The name applies to the earliest church, which was heavenly (and which served as a basis or foundation for the Jewish church). As a result, everything in that church that had a representative function looked toward heavenly qualities and, through heavenly qualities, to the Lord. [2] In Hosea:

> Its branches will spread, and its honor will resemble an *olive tree,* and it will have a scent like Lebanon's. (Hosea 14:6)

Here the subject is the planting of a church whose honor is the olive tree, or in other words, the goodness that comes of love and charity. A scent like Lebanon's is a devotion to the religious truth that rises out of that goodness. Lebanon is an allusion to cedars, which symbolize spiritual entities, or in other words, religious truth. In Zechariah:

> There were two *olive trees* next to the lampstand, one to the right of the oil dish and one on the left of it. These are the two offspring of *pristine oil,* standing next to the Lord of the whole earth. (Zechariah 4:3, 11, 14)

The two olive trees stand for what is heavenly and what is spiritual, and so for the love that characterizes the heavenly church and the charity that characterizes the spiritual. These churches stand at the Lord's right and left hands. The lampstand symbolizes the Lord, just as it represented him in the Jewish church. The lamps symbolize heavenly attributes that yield spiritual attributes, just as a flame yields rays of light, or illumination. [3] In David:

> Your wife is like a fruitful grapevine at the sides of your house; your children are like the saplings of *olive trees.* (Psalms 128:3)

The "wife like a grapevine" stands for the spiritual church. The children stand for true concepts that make up faith, which are called olive tree saplings because they grow out of charitable goodness. In Isaiah:

> Gleanings will be left in it, like what is shaken off the *olive tree*—two or three fruits at the crown of the branch. (Isaiah 17:6)

This is about the remnant inside us. Olive trees stand for a heavenly remnant. In Micah:

> You will tread the *olive* (but not anoint yourself with *oil*) and the juice in the grapes (but not drink wine). (Micah 6:15)

And in Moses:

> You will plant and cultivate vineyards but not drink wine; you will have *olive trees* within all your borders but not anoint yourself with *oil*. (Deuteronomy 28:39, 40)

These passages describe an ample supply of doctrinal teachings about the goodness and truth inherent in faith, which these people's character nonetheless caused them to reject.

All of these places show that a leaf symbolizes religious truth and an olive tree symbolizes charitable goodness. They also show the meaning of the olive leaf carried in the dove's mouth to be similar: that the people of the ancient church were now able to see a small amount of religious truth springing out of the goodness that charity inspires.

887 The meaning of *the water had lessened off the earth* is that these things were now possible because falsity was not so overpowering that it got in the way. This is established by the symbolism of the same words above in verse 8 [§871].

Regarding the fact that in the second stage (the stage referred to by this verse) falsity was not so overpowering that it got in the way, as it had previously, the situation is this: All the falsity we latch on to stays with us; as already mentioned [§868], not one false idea is obliterated. But when we are being reborn, true ideas are sown in us, and the Lord bends our false thinking in the direction of those ideas. Then falsity seems to have been dispelled, and it is the goodness he gives us as a gift that accomplishes this.

888 Genesis 8:12. *And he waited yet another seven days and sent the dove out, and it never returned to him again.*

He waited another seven days symbolizes the beginning of the third stage. *Seven days* symbolizes holiness. *And sent the dove out* symbolizes the right conditions for receiving the goodness and truth of faith. *The dove did not return to him again* symbolizes a liberated state.

889 The symbolism of *he waited another seven days* as the beginning of the third stage and of *seven days* as holiness is established by remarks concerning the second stage just above [§§880–881], where similar words occur.

890 The symbolism of *and sent the dove out* as the right conditions for receiving the goodness and truth of faith is likewise established by things said above at verse 10 [§882]. The words are the same and so is the meaning, except that the subject there is the second stage and here it is the third.

The third stage is depicted in the dove's not returning, Noah's removal of the ark's roof, and his eventual departure from the ark because the face of the ground, and the earth, had dried up.

891 The symbolism of *the dove did not return to him again* as a liberated state follows logically. It also follows from the consideration that the dove—religious truth, or the truth of faith—like the other birds, the animals, and Noah, was no longer trapped in the ark by the flood water. As long as it stayed on the ark, buffeted by the flood water (falsity), its state was one of slavery, of captivity or imprisonment. This state, along with the state of trial, is portrayed above in Genesis 7:17, which said that the waters grew and lifted the ark and the ark rose off the earth. It is portrayed in Genesis 7:18 as well, which said that the water strengthened and the ark went on the face of the water. Its state of freedom is depicted in the fact that not only Noah but everything else with him too went out of the ark (which occurs later in the present chapter, verses 16, 17, 18, 19).[495] The first of them all to leave was the *dove,* that is, religious truth that grows out of goodness, because all freedom comes from the goodness connected with faith, that is, from a love for what is good.

892 We first come into a state of freedom after we have regenerated; until then, we are in a state of slavery. Enslavement occurs when cravings and falsity rule over us; freedom results when a fondness for what is good and true takes charge. As long as we are enslaved, we have no perception of the actual state of affairs. The first perception dawns when we come into freedom.

In a state of slavery, when cravings and falsity take control, those of us under their yoke think we are enjoying freedom; but this is grossly untrue. At such a time, we are carried away by the pleasure that our vices and the indulgence of them brings us, or in other words, by the pleasure that selfish kinds of love bring us. Since it is pleasure that engrosses us, we see it as freedom.

Whenever some specific passion leads us, no matter what direction it goes, if we follow it, we consider it a liberating thing. But it is devilish spirits—whose company we keep and whose stampede we join—that sweep us along. This we consider the epitome of freedom. In fact we believe life would become positively miserable and even end if we were deprived of such a condition. It is not merely that we know of no other kind of life; we also receive the impression that no one can make it into heaven except through misfortune, poverty, and renunciation of pleasure. But this is untrue, as I have learned from much experience, which I will describe later, the Lord in his divine mercy willing.[496]

[2] We never come into a free condition until we have regenerated and until the Lord leads us by means of a love for what is good and true. Once we arrive there, we are able to see and perceive for the first time what liberty is, because we then realize what life is and what true pleasure in life and happiness are. Up to that time, we do not even know what goodness is, and occasionally we refer to the height of evil as the greatest good. When people who enjoy a state of freedom given by the Lord observe a life of perverted desire and false thinking, and particularly when they sense it, they are as horrified as if they saw hell gaping open before their very eyes.

As most people today have absolutely no idea what a life of freedom is, let me offer this brief definition: freedom, or a life of freedom, is solely and simply being led by the Lord.

Many things come up, however, that make it impossible for people to believe that this kind of life is a free one. For one thing, we suffer times of trial (whose whole purpose is to deliver us from the tyranny of diabolical spirits). For another, we recognize nothing as pleasing and good but the attainment of our selfish and worldly desires. In addition, we form false opinions about all facets of heavenly life. For these reasons, explanations are less effective as educational tools than reports of actual experience are. Let me relate such experiences at a future point, then, by the Lord's divine mercy [§§2870–2893].

Genesis 8:13. *And it happened in the six hundred first year, in the beginning, on the first of the month, that the water drained off the earth; and Noah removed the roof of the ark and looked, and indeed the face of the ground had dried up!*

It happened in the six hundred first year symbolizes an ending point. *In the beginning, on the first of the month,* symbolizes a starting point. *The water drained off the earth* means that falsity did not appear at that time. *And Noah removed the roof of the ark and looked* symbolizes the light of religious truth, once falsity had been removed—truth that they acknowledged and believed. *And indeed the face of the ground had dried up* symbolizes the process of rebirth.

[2] The symbolism of *it happened in the six hundred first year* as an ending point is established by the symbolism of *six hundred,* given at Genesis 7:6, §737. Six hundred symbolizes a beginning and specifically, in that verse, the beginning of a time of trial. Its end is designated by the same number after a whole year has passed (so that *it happened* at the end of a year). That is the reason for adding *in the beginning, on the first of the month,* which symbolizes a starting point.

The Word designates any whole period by a day, week, month, or year, even if that period is a century or a millennium. An example is the "day" in Genesis 1, meaning the time it took a person in the earliest church to be reborn. On an inner plane, a day and a year just stand as symbols for a span of time, and since they are symbols for a span of time, they symbolize a state, so that a *year* throughout the Word is taken to stand for a time and a state. In Isaiah, for instance:

> . . . to proclaim a *year* of good pleasure for Jehovah and a *day* of vengeance for our God, to comfort all who mourn. (Isaiah 61:2)

This is about the Lord's Coming. In the same author:

> The *day* of vengeance was in my heart, and the *year* of my redeemed had come. (Isaiah 63:4)

Here too the day and year stand for a time and a state. In Habakkuk:

> Jehovah, in the middle of the *years,* bring your work to life; in the middle of the *years,* please make it known. (Habakkuk 3:2)

The years stand for a time and a state. In David:

> God, you are he, and your *years* are not used up. (Psalms 102:27)

The years stand for spans of time and for the fact that God is timeless. Likewise in the present verse the year of the Flood in no way means a year as such but a stretch of time lasting an undetermined number of years, and at the same time, a state. See previous discussions of years in §§482, 487, 488, 493.

894 The symbolism of *in the beginning, on the first of the month,* as a starting point is now evident.

Additional implications of these words are too deep to describe. The important thing is that the time it takes to regenerate is not fixed, in such a way that we can say, "Now I have finished." The states of evil and falsity that each of us has inside are beyond counting. They exist not only as individual states but also as multilayered composites and need to be dispelled to the point where they no longer appear, as already noted [§719]. In some of our states we can be described as more perfect, but in countless others we cannot. In the other life, those who were reborn during bodily life and who lived lives of faith in the Lord and charity toward their neighbor are constantly being perfected.

The meaning of *the water drained off the earth* as the fact that falsity did not appear at that time can be seen from earlier statements [§§857, 868, 887]. Specifically it means that in the people of this church, falsity was siphoned away from the contents of their will. The *earth* here symbolizes human will, which is nothing but corrupt desire, and that is why it says that the water drained off the earth. The *ground* in us, as I have said [§875:3], is in our intellectual part, where truth is sown. By no means does "ground" exist in our volitional part, which in spiritual people is separate from the intellectual part. That is why the statement that the face of the ground had dried up comes later in the verse.

With the people of the earliest church, the "ground" was in their volitional part, and the Lord sowed it with the seed of goodness. As a result, they were able to recognize and perceive truth from the viewpoint of goodness, or in other words, to acquire faith from love. If the same thing happened today, it would necessarily destroy us forever, because our will is completely perverted.

[2] What happens when seed is sown on the will side, and what when it is sown on the intellectual side, can be seen from this: The people of the earliest church received revelations that initiated them into a perception of goodness and truth from the time they were very small. Because the seed was sown on their will side, they perceived innumerable things without further instruction; the Lord gave them the ability to look at one general concept and recognize particular ideas and individual details. These we now have to learn before we can know them, and yet we are hardly able to see even one in a thousand.

People in a spiritual church recognize only what they learn and so what they know about, remember, and believe to be true. In fact if they learn falsity, and it becomes stamped on their minds as truth, they believe it. They cannot help perceiving it as true because they are persuaded it is so. Those who have a conscience hear a kind of inner voice, but the voice does no more than tell them a thing is true because it is what they have heard and learned. This standard forms their conscience, as can be seen from people with misguided consciences.

896 *Noah removed the roof of the ark and looked* symbolizes the light of religious truth, once falsity had been removed—truth that they acknowledged and believed. This can be seen from the symbolism of removing the roof as taking away whatever blocks the light. Since the *ark* symbolizes the people of the ancient church who were regenerating, the *roof* cannot symbolize anything but what blocked them from seeing heaven [or the sky], that is, the light. What got in the way was falsity. This is why it says that they *looked,* or saw. In the Word, seeing symbolizes understanding and believing. Here it means that they acknowledged the truth and put their faith in it.

Knowing the truth, acknowledging it, and believing it are three entirely different things. Knowledge is the first step of rebirth, acknowledgment is the second, and belief is the third. The differences among knowing, acknowledging, and believing can be seen from the fact that the worst people are capable of knowing without acknowledging; take Jews, for instance, and those who try to destroy the teachings of the church with their specious arguments.[497] The faithless, moreover, are capable of acknowledging as well as knowing and, in some moods, of preaching, confirming doctrine, and persuading others of its truth, all with great zeal. But they cannot put faith in it if they are not believers. [2] Those who have faith know, acknowledge, *and* believe. They have charity and they have conscience. So faith can by no means be attributed to anyone—no one can be said to believe—except one who possesses these traits. This, then, is to be regenerate.

Mere knowledge of the elements of faith is a matter of memory and does not involve the rational mind's assent. Acknowledgment of the tenets of faith requires some assent on the part of the rational mind—a state of mind produced by certain considerations, with a view to certain ends. The possession of faith, though, is a function of conscience, that is, of the Lord working through conscience.

This reality can best be seen in the inhabitants of the other world. Many of those who merely know the truth are in hell. The same goes for those who acknowledge it, since their acknowledgment in earthly life came only in certain moods, as stated. In the next life, when they realize that the things they preached, taught, and convinced others of are actually true, they are quite amazed. They acknowledge those things only when reminded that they had preached them. But everyone who truly believed is in heaven.

§897. Since the subject here is regenerate people in the ancient church, *looking* [or seeing] symbolizes acknowledging and believing. This symbolism can be seen in the Word. In Isaiah, for instance:

> You have not *looked* to its maker, and the one who formed it from long ago you have not *seen*. (Isaiah 22:11)

This is about the city of Zion. Not seeing the one who formed it from long ago is failing to acknowledge him, still less to put faith in him. In the same author:

> Make the heart of this people fat and make their ears heavy and smear over their eyes, to prevent them from *seeing with their eyes* and hearing with their ears and understanding in their heart and turning and being healed. (Isaiah 6:9, 10)

Seeing with the eyes stands for acknowledging and believing. In the same author:

> The people walking in darkness *have seen* great light. (Isaiah 9:2)

This is about nations that had received the faith. It is like the current verse where it says "he removed the roof and saw." In the same author:

> On that day, the deaf will hear the words of the Book, and out of the darkness and out of the shadows the *eyes of the blind will see*. (Isaiah 29:18)

This is about the conversion of the nations to the faith. Seeing stands for embracing the faith. In the same author:

> You who are deaf, listen! And you who are blind, *look and see!* (Isaiah 42:18)

The meaning is similar. [2] In Ezekiel:

> ... who have *eyes to see and do not see,* who have ears to hear and do not hear, because they are a rebellious house. (Ezekiel 12:2)

These words mean, "who are able to understand, acknowledge, and believe, but do not wish to."

The representation of the Lord by the bronze serpent in the wilderness provides clear evidence that seeing symbolizes believing, since everyone who looked at it was cured. Moses describes it this way:

> "Put the snake on a pole, and it will happen that all who have been bitten and *see* it will live." It happened that if a snake bit a man and he *looked* at the bronze snake, he lived. (Numbers 21:8, 9)

From this everyone can see that looking or seeing symbolizes faith. What could *seeing* in this passage be if not an act representing faith in the Lord?

Another conclusion from this is that on an inner level, Jacob's firstborn—Reuben, whose name comes from a word for seeing[498]—symbolizes faith. See earlier remarks concerning the church's firstborns at §§352 and 367.

898 The symbolism of *and indeed the face of the ground had dried up* as the process of rebirth is established by the meaning of the *ground* as people in the church, dealt with frequently in earlier sections [§§386, 566, 872]. The face of the ground is said to have *dried up* when falsity no longer appears.

899 Genesis 8:14. *And in the second month, on the twenty-seventh day of the month, the earth dried up.*

The *second month* symbolizes all the stages that precede rebirth. The *twenty-seventh day* symbolizes holiness. *The earth dried up* means that they were reborn. These words are the conclusion to the verses above and the beginning of all that follows.

900 The symbolism of the *second month* as all the stages that precede rebirth can be seen from the symbolism of *two* in the Word. Two symbolizes the same thing as six, which is the fighting and hard work that come before rebirth. So here it means all the stages we go through before becoming regenerate.

The longest and shortest intervals in the Word are generally split in three or in seven and are called days, weeks, months, years, or "ages."[499] Three and seven are holy; two and six, being just one less, are not holy but relatively profane, as shown before (§720).

Three and seven also mean something sacrosanct, each because of its connection with the Last Judgment, predicted as coming on the third or else the seventh day.[500] Every person—both collectively and individually—has a last judgment when the Lord comes. There was a last judgment when the Lord came into the world. There will be a last judgment when he enters into his glory. There is a last judgment when he comes individually to each person. There is also a last judgment for each person who dies. This last judgment is the third day and the seventh day, which is holy for those who have lived good lives but unholy for those who have lived evil lives. Consequently, a third day and a seventh is predicted for those judged worthy of death and for those judged worthy of life, so that the numbers symbolize what is unholy for those with a verdict of death but what is holy for those with a verdict of life.

Two and six, the numbers just before three and seven, bear a relationship to them and symbolize in general every preceding stage. This is the meaning of the numbers two and six, and the meaning adapts to the subject at hand and to whatever the subject applies to, which the numbers describe.

All of this will become clearer from the discussion of the number twenty-seven in the next section.

The symbolism of the *twenty-seventh day* as holiness is established by this: The number is the product of three multiplied by itself twice; three times three is nine, and nine times three is twenty-seven, so that three is dominant in the number. This is how the earliest people calculated their numbers, and they understood them purely as standing for some quality.

The fact that three symbolizes the same thing as seven can be seen from remarks in the previous section. The secret reason is that the Lord rose again on the third day. The Lord's resurrection in itself involves everything that is sacred and entails the resurrection of all people. That is why the Jewish religion came to use this number in a representative way and why it is a holy number in the Word. The situation resembles that in heaven, where there are no numbers; a generalized and reverent idea of the Lord's resurrection and of his arrival in the world replaces the numbers three and seven there.

[2] The symbolism of three and seven as holiness is established by the following passages in the Word. In Moses:

> Those touching a dead body will be unclean *seven days*. They shall atone for themselves in this matter on the *third day,* and on the *seventh day* they will be clean. And if they have not atoned for themselves on the *third day,* then on the *seventh day* they will not be clean. Those who touch one stabbed by a sword, or a dead body, or a human bone, or a grave will be unclean *seven days*. A clean person shall spatter [water] on the unclean person on the *third day* and on the *seventh day,* and the clean one will expiate the unclean on the *seventh day.* The unclean shall wash their clothes and rinse with water and will be clean in the evening. (Numbers 19:11, 12, 16, 19)

It is quite clear that these things are representative, in other words, that the outward circumstances symbolize something internal. This is true, for instance, of the uncleanliness ascribed to one who had touched a dead body, a victim of stabbing, a human bone, or a grave. All these things on an inner level symbolize a person's own propensities, which are dead and profane. The same is also true of the fact that they were to wash with water and would then be clean in the evening. So the third and seventh days were representative too, symbolizing holiness, since on those days the person would achieve atonement and would therefore be clean.

[3] The same applies to those who returned from battle against the Midianites, of whom it says,

> Camp outside the camp *seven days,* every one of you who has killed a soul and every one who has touched a victim of stabbing. You shall atone for yourselves on the *third day* and on the *seventh day.* (Numbers 31:19)

Had this been mere ritual, neither the third day nor the seventh would have represented or symbolized holiness and atonement. They would have been something dead, like a result without means and a means without a purpose, or to put it another way, like a result separated from a means separated from its purpose.[501] So it would not have been the least bit divine.

The coming of the Lord to Mount Sinai clearly indicates that the third day represented and therefore symbolized something holy. These are the commandments concerning that event:

> Jehovah said to Moses, "Go to the people and *consecrate* them today and tomorrow, [telling them] to wash their clothes and be ready for the *third day,* because on the *third day,* Jehovah will come down, in the eyes of all the people, onto Mount Sinai." (Exodus 19:10, 11, 15, 16)

[4] Joshua's passage across the Jordan on the third day suggests the same thing. It is described this way:

> Joshua commanded, "Pass through the middle of the camp and command the people, saying, 'Get provisions ready for yourselves, because in *three days* you are crossing this Jordan, to come in to inherit the land.'" (Joshua 1:11; 3:2)

The crossing of the Jordan represented the entrance of the children of Israel—regenerate people, that is—into the Lord's kingdom. Joshua, who led them in, represented the Lord himself, and it occurred on the third day.

Since the third day like the seventh was holy, the *third* year was set up as a "year of tithes," and the people then behaved in a godly way by doing charitable work (Deuteronomy 26:12 and following verses). Tithes represented the remnant in us, which is holy because it is the Lord's alone.

Jonah's *three days and three nights* in the fish's belly (Jonah 1:17) obviously represented the Lord's burial and resurrection on the third day (Matthew 12:40).

[5] The symbolism of three as this kind of sanctity can also be seen in the prophets, as in Hosea:

> Jehovah will bring us to life after two days; on the *third day* he will revive us, so that we may live before him. (Hosea 6:2)

Here too the third day plainly stands for the Lord's coming and his resurrection. In Zechariah:

> It will come about in all the earth that two parts in it will be cut off, will die, and a *third* will be left in it. And I will lead the *third part* through fire, and smelt them as silver is smelted, and test them as gold is tested. (Zechariah 13:8, [9])

The third part, or the number three, here again stands for holiness. One third involves the same thing as three, as does a third of a third, which comes up in the current verse, since three is a third of a third of twenty-seven.

The meaning of *the earth dried up* as the fact that they were reborn can be seen from the things said earlier at verses 7 and 13 [§§868, 895:1, 898] about the drying up of the water, the earth, and the face of the ground.

Genesis 8:15, 16. *And God spoke to Noah, saying, "Go out of the ark, you and your wife and your sons and your sons' wives with you."*

God spoke to Noah symbolizes the Lord's presence with the people of this church. *Going out of the ark* symbolizes liberty. *You and your wife* symbolizes the church. *Your sons and your sons' wives with you* symbolizes truth and a goodness bound up with truth in those people.

The symbolism of *God spoke to Noah* as the Lord's presence with the people of this church can be seen from the Word's inner meaning.

The Lord talks to every individual, because anything good or true that a person wills or thinks comes from the Lord. We each have at least two evil spirits and two angels with us. The evil spirits stir up our evils, but the angels inspire goodness and truth. Everything good or true that the angels inspire in us is the Lord's, so the Lord is constantly talking to us. He talks very differently, though, to one person than to another. With those who allow themselves to be swept up by evil spirits, the Lord speaks like one absent or far away, so that he can barely be said to speak at all.

But with those whom he leads, the Lord speaks more directly. The fact that no one can ever think anything good or true except by the Lord's power makes this sufficiently clear.

[2] The degree of love we feel for our neighbor and of faith we have determines the extent to which the Lord can be described as present with us. The Lord is present in neighborly love because he is present in everything good, but he is not as present in so-called faith devoid of love. Faith without love and charity is a detached or disconnected thing. Wherever there is union, there must be a uniting medium, and the only uniting medium is love and charity.

Anyone can see this by considering that the Lord shows mercy to everyone, loves everyone, and wants to make everyone happy forever. As a result, those who lack sufficient love to have mercy on others, love them, and want to make them happy cannot unite with the Lord, because they are unlike him and are anything but his image.[502] To gaze at the Lord through the lens of supposed faith and yet hate others is not only to stand far removed from the Lord, it is also to put a deep, hellish gulf between yourself and the Lord, a gulf you will fall into if you try to approach him. Hatred for other people is that intervening, hellish chasm.

[3] The Lord's presence with us first becomes possible when we love our neighbor. Within love is the Lord, and so far as we have love, the Lord is present. Moreover, so far as the Lord is present, he talks to us. We are unaware that it is not our own thinking, but not a single idea, not a single particle of an idea, originates in us. Whatever is evil and false we acquire from hell, through evil spirits, and whatever is good and true we acquire from the Lord, through angels. This is influx. It endows us with life and creates the link between our soul and our body.[503]

These things suggest what it means that God spoke to Noah. Saying something to a person (as he does in Genesis 1:29; 3:13, 14, 17; 4:6, 9, 15; 6:13; 7:1) is different from speaking to someone.[504] Speaking to Noah, here, is being present, because the current subject is the person reborn, who has received the gift of charitable feeling.

905 The symbolism of *going out of the ark* as liberty can be seen from earlier statements [§891] and from the thread of the story itself, with its pattern of connections.

The time that Noah spent in the ark, surrounded by flood water, symbolized being in captivity—that is, being tossed about by evil and falsity or, what amounts to the same thing, by the evil spirits who spark our spiritual battles. From this it follows that leaving the ark symbolizes liberty.

The Lord's presence involves liberty; the one is a consequence of the other. The more present the Lord is, the freer we are. In other words, the more we love goodness and truth, the more freely we act. That is the nature of the Lord's influence, coming by way of angels.

Hell's influence, on the other hand, coming by way of evil spirits, brings with it the forceful effort to dominate. Those spirits connive at nothing else than to put us so completely under their yoke that we become nothing and they become everything. When they are everything, then we are one of them—and hardly even one of them, but like a nobody in their eyes. So when the Lord delivers us from their control and removes their yoke, a battle begins. And when we have been delivered—reborn—the Lord leads us so gently by means of angels that it is anything but a yoke, anything but domination. Through pleasure and happiness we are led and loved and esteemed. This is what the Lord teaches in Matthew:

> My yoke is mild and my burden is light. (Matthew 11:30)

The situation is quite the opposite among evil spirits, who consider us worthless, as I said, and would torture us every second if they could. This I know from a great deal of experience that I will relate further on, with the Lord's divine mercy.[505]

The symbolism of *you and your wife* as the church can again be seen from the series of ideas, as can the symbolism of *your sons and sons' wives with you* as truth, and a goodness bound up with truth, in those people. The symbolism of *you* as people in the church is obvious, and the symbolism of a *wife* as the church, of *sons* as truth, and of *sons' wives* as the goodness bound up with truth has been shown many times before [§§668, 742, 769–770]. So there is no need to tarry over it here.

Genesis 8:17. "...[506] *every wild animal that is with you, of all flesh, including the bird and the beast and every creeping thing creeping on the earth. Take them out with you, and let them swarm throughout the earth and reproduce and multiply on the earth.*"

Every wild animal that is with you, of all flesh, symbolizes everything that was alive in the people of this church. The *bird* here as before symbolizes the ideas in their intellect. The *beast* symbolizes the urges of their will. Both of these belong to the inner self. *Every creeping thing creeping on the earth* symbolizes the corresponding attributes in the outer self. *Take them out with you* symbolizes the level of freedom they had. *And let them swarm throughout the earth* symbolizes the way the inner self acts on the outer. *Let them reproduce* symbolizes increases in goodness. *Let them multiply* symbolizes increases in truth. *On the earth* means in the outer self.

908   The symbolism of *every wild animal that is with you, of all flesh,* as everything that was alive in the people of this church can be seen from this: The wild animal refers to a quality in Noah, or in other words, in the people of this church, now that they had regenerated. And it plainly looks ahead to the bird, beast, and creeping thing, since it says, "every wild animal that is with you, of all flesh, including the bird and the beast and every creeping thing creeping on the earth."

The word for *wild animal* in the original language strictly means life or a living thing, yet in the Word it means not only a living thing but also a relatively nonliving thing: a wild animal.[507] (You can see why those who do not grasp the Word's inner sense will sometimes be at a loss as to its meaning.) The reason the word means both living and nonliving is that the people of the earliest church, in humbling themselves before the Lord, confessed that they were nonliving, were not even good animals but wild beasts. They knew intimately that this is what humans are, viewed in themselves or as independent creatures. So the same word means both a living thing and a wild animal.

[2] The meaning of a wild animal as a living thing is evident in David:

> Your *wild animal* will live in it [God's inheritance].[508] You will strengthen the wretched person with your goodness, God. (Psalms 68:9, 10)

The wild animal, because it will live in God's inheritance, simply means a regenerate person and consequently, as here, a living quality in such a person. In the same author:

> Every *wild animal* of the forest is mine, the beasts on a thousand mountains. I know every bird of the mountains, and the *wild animal of my field* is with me. (Psalms 50:10, 11)

The wild animal of the field "with me," that is, with God, also[509] stands for a regenerate person and so for the living qualities in that person. In Ezekiel:

> In its branches nested every bird of the heavens, and under its branches bred every *wild animal of the field.* (Ezekiel 31:6)

This passage describes the spiritual church as a plant, so the phrase stands for the living qualities in the people of that church. In Hosea:

> I will strike a pact on that day with the *wild animal of the field* and with the bird in the heavens. (Hosea 2:18)

This is about people regenerating, with whom a pact will be struck. So strong is the meaning of a wild animal as a living thing that even the guardian beings or angels seen by Ezekiel are called *four "wild animals"* (Ezekiel 1:5, 13, 14, 15, 19; 10:15).

[3] The fact that a wild animal in the Word is taken in the opposite sense of a nonliving thing, or a savage creature, can be seen in many places. Let these alone serve for proof. In David:

> Do not hand the soul of your turtledove over to the *wild animal*. (Psalms 74:19)

In Zephaniah:

> The city became a wasteland, a lair for the *wild animal*. (Zephaniah 2:15)

In Ezekiel:

> They will no longer be plunder for the nations, and the *wild animal* of the land will not eat them. (Ezekiel 34:28)

In the same author:

> On its wreckage will live every bird of the heavens, and among its branches will stand every *wild animal of the field*. (Ezekiel 31:13)

In Hosea:

> I will devour them there like a lion; the *wild animal of the field* will rip them apart. (Hosea 13:8)

In Ezekiel:

> . . . given to the *wild animal* of the land and to the bird in the heavens as food . . . (Ezekiel 29:5)

This phrase recurs often.[510]

The Jews stuck exclusively to the literal meaning, understanding a wild animal as a wild animal and a bird as a bird, unwilling to see (much less acknowledge) any deeper content in the Word or to learn about it. As a result, they were so cruel, so feral, that they found pleasure in refusing to bury enemies killed in battle, leaving the bodies out to be eaten by the birds and wild animals.[511] This also demonstrates clearly what a wild animal a human being is.

909 The *bird* symbolizes the ideas in their intellect and the *beast* the urges of their will, which belong to the inner self, while *every creeping thing creeping on the earth* symbolizes the corresponding attributes in their outer self. These things are established by the symbolism of a *bird* as discussed previously at §§40 and 776 and of a *beast* as discussed at §§45, 46, 142, 143, 246. The fact that a *creeping thing creeping on the earth* symbolizes the corresponding aspects of the outer self follows naturally, because the *creeping thing creeping* is a reference to both the bird (intellectual traits) and the beast (traits of the will).

The earliest people called sensory information and physical pleasure *creeping things creeping* because they are just like creeping things creeping on the earth. The same people also compared the human body to the earth or to the ground, and even called it earth or ground, as here, where the *earth* just means our outer self.

911 [512] This is how it happens that a creeping thing creeping symbolizes the corresponding attributes in their outer self: In a person reborn, external traits respond to internal values, which is to say that they are obedient to them. Our outward aspects are reduced to obedience when we regenerate, and then we become an image of heaven. But until we have been reborn, external considerations overpower spiritual and heavenly ones, and then we are an image of hell.

The proper order is for heavenly concerns to govern spiritual ones and through these to govern earthly ones and through these, finally, to govern bodily ones. But when bodily and earthly demands control spiritual and heavenly ones, the hierarchy is destroyed, and when it is destroyed, we are an image of hell. For this reason, the Lord restores the proper order through regeneration. Once it has been restored, we become an image of heaven. This is the way the Lord draws us out of hell, and this is the way he lifts us up to heaven.

[2] Let me explain briefly how the correspondence of the outer self with the inner then stands. Everyone who has regenerated is a kind of miniature heaven, or a model or image of the whole of heaven—which is why the Word also calls our inner being a heaven.[513] Things in heaven are structured in such a way that the Lord governs spiritual elements through heavenly ones and earthly elements through spiritual ones. So he governs all of heaven as a single individual, and heaven accordingly is

also called the "universal human." The scheme is the same for every person within heaven. When we reflect this hierarchy, we are each a miniature heaven or, to put it another way, a kingdom of the Lord, since we have the Lord's kingdom inside us. Then external traits correspond to—that is, they obey—internal values in us just as they do in heaven. In the three heavens, which together present the image of a single person, spirits form the outer self, angelic spirits an intermediate self, and angels the inner self (§459).

[3] The case is the opposite for those who locate life exclusively in bodily desires, or in other words, in cravings, physical pleasures, appetites, and indulgence of the senses. These are people who find nothing enjoyable unless it feeds their love for themselves and for worldly advantages, which is the same as feeding their hatred toward anyone who does not cater to and serve them. Because these people's bodily and earthly drives take precedence over spiritual and heavenly ones, not only do their outward attributes fail to correspond or obey, they even put up total opposition. The proper hierarchy is utterly destroyed, and since it is utterly destroyed, those people can only be images of hell.

912. The symbolism of *take them out with you* as the level of freedom they had can be seen from the discussion above at verse 15 [§905] showing that going out of the ark symbolizes liberty.

913. *And let them swarm throughout the earth* symbolizes the way the inner self acts on the outer, *let them reproduce* symbolizes increases in goodness, *let them multiply* symbolizes increases in truth, and *on the earth* means in the outer self. All this can be seen from the general line of reasoning. It can also be seen from earlier remarks and illustrations [§§43, 55] concerning the symbolism of *reproducing* and *multiplying,* showing that the Word uses the former in connection with good and the latter in connection with truth. The symbolism of the *earth* as the outer self was likewise demonstrated earlier [§§16, 82]. Consequently there is no need to spend time proving these things.

The present verse speaks of the way the inner self acts on the outer after we have regenerated, revealing that good first reproduces itself and truth first multiplies when the outer self is reduced into correspondence or obedience. It can never happen before that, because bodily desires rebel against goodness, and sense impressions rebel against truth. The former snuff out love for goodness, and the latter extinguish love for truth.

Good reproduces and truth multiplies in the outer self—good reproducing itself in our feelings, and truth multiplying in our memory. The outer self throughout which good and truth swarm and on which they reproduce and multiply is here called the earth.

914 Genesis 8:18, 19. *And Noah and his sons went out, as did his wife and his sons' wives with him, every wild animal, every creeping thing, and every bird—everything creeping on the earth. By their families they went out of the ark.*

Noah and his sons means the people of the ancient church. *Went out* means came into being. *His wife and his sons' wives with him* means the church itself. *Every wild animal and every creeping thing* symbolize good things in them—the *wild animal,* good things in the inner self, and the *creeping thing,* good things in the outer self. *And every bird, everything creeping on the earth,* symbolizes truth—the *bird,* truth in the inner self, and the thing *creeping on the earth,* truth in the outer self. *By their families* means pairs. *They went out of the ark* means, as above, that they all came into being; and at the same time it symbolizes a condition of freedom.

915 *Noah and his sons* means the people of the ancient church, *went out* means came into being, and *his wife and his sons' wives* means the church itself. This meaning is indicated by the story line, which suggests that the ancient church therefore came into existence, since these words are final ones, summing up all that came before.

When the Word describes the church, it uses either the phrase *man and wife* or the phrase *a human and his wife.*[514] When it uses *man and wife,* the man symbolizes an element of the intellect, or something true, while the wife symbolizes an element of the will, or something good. When it uses *a human and his wife,* the human symbolizes the good that love embraces, or love, while the wife symbolizes the truth that faith espouses, or faith. So the human symbolizes the core quality of the church, while the wife symbolizes the church itself. This comes up over and over in the Word.

Since up to this point the text has been speaking of the formation of a new church upon the death of the earliest church, Noah and his sons here symbolize the people of the ancient church, while his wife and his sons' wives with him symbolize the church itself. For this reason, the order of the phrases here differs from that of verse 16, which says, "Go out, you and your wife, and your sons and your sons' wives with you." This links *you* with *wife,* and *sons* with *sons' wives,* so that *you* and *sons* symbolize truth, while *your wife* and *your sons' wives* symbolize good. In the current verse, though, the order is not the same, for the reason (as stated) that *he and his sons* symbolizes the people of the church while *his wife and his sons' wives* symbolizes the church itself. The clause is a conclusion to all that came before.

It was not Noah who constituted the ancient church but his sons, Shem, Ham, and Japheth, as noted before [§§773, 788]. In a sense, there were three churches that formed this ancient church, about which I will say more below, by the Lord's divine mercy.[515] These churches came forward as if born from a single church—the one called Noah. That is why the present verse says *Noah and his sons* and then *his wife and his sons' wives*.

Every wild animal and every creeping thing symbolize good things in them—the *wild animal,* good things in the inner self, and the *creeping thing,* good things in the outer self. In addition, *every bird, everything creeping on the earth* symbolizes truth—the *bird,* truth in the inner self, and the *thing creeping on the earth,* truth in the outer self. This is established by the statements and explanations at the previous verse [Genesis 8:17] concerning the wild animal, the bird, and the creeping thing creeping. (That verse referred to a *creeping* thing *creeping* because it symbolized both the goodness and the truth in the outer self.)

Because these words sum up the preceding verses, they include this addendum about the church, specifically about its goodness and truth, and the phrase indicates what kind of church it was: a spiritual one. It also shows that it became the kind of church that placed its chief emphasis on charity, or goodness, which is why the verse mentions the wild animal and creeping thing first and the bird and thing creeping afterward.

[2] A church is called spiritual when it acts from charity, or from the good that charity urges, and never when it claims to have faith without charity. Under those circumstances, it is not even a church. After all, what do the church's teachings about faith deal with if not charity? And why would the church teach anything about faith if not to have its teachings carried out? To know and think as faith teaches cannot have any reality; doing what faith teaches—this alone exists. A spiritual church first becomes a church when it acts as bidden by charity, charity being the true teaching of faith. To put it another way, this is when a person in the church first becomes a church.[516] Consider: what is a commandment? It does not order us to know a precept but to live by what it says. This is when we first have the Lord's kingdom inside us, because the Lord's kingdom consists solely in mutual love and the happiness it brings.

[3] There are some who divide faith from charity and believe that the source of salvation is faith—a faith that is devoid of the good deeds urged by charity. They are followers of Cain, who kill their brother Abel, that is, charity. They are also like birds circling over a corpse, because such a faith is a bird and the corpse is a person who lacks charity. They scrape together

a pseudo-conscience that tells them they can behave like devils, hate and persecute their neighbor, spend their whole lives in adultery, and yet be saved, as is extremely familiar in the Christian world. What could be sweeter to us than to hear and persuade ourselves that we can be saved, even if we live like a savage beast? Even non-Christians see that this is false, and many of them shudder at Christian teachings when they observe how Christians live. Another conclusion to be drawn is that nowhere do people live in a more despicable way than in the Christian world.

917 The fact that *by their families* means pairs can be seen from previous statements about the entry of the clean animals seven by seven and of the unclean animals two by two (Genesis 7:2, 3, 15). The current verse, however, says that they went out by families. It says families and not seven at a time or two at a time because at this point the Lord has brought all elements into such good order that they represent families.

In a regenerate person, virtues and truths (or the attributes of charity and so the attributes of faith) relate to each other in such a way that they all regard each other as blood relatives and kin. That is to say, they regard each other as belonging to families that spring from the same stock or the same progenitor. The situation resembles that in heaven (§685). This is how the Lord organizes our positive qualities and true ideas.

The specific meaning here is that each and every form of good looks at its related truth as being united in marriage with itself. The way charity in general views faith is the same way that a single good impulse in particular always views a single truth.

A general rule is not general unless it emerges from specific cases. It is from the specific cases that the general rule has its existence and from them that it is described as general. The situation is the same in each of us; whatever we are like generally, we are like in every smallest detail of our feelings and thoughts. These form our constituent parts; these make us what we are as a whole. So when people have been reborn, they become the same in the most minute respects as they are overall.[517]

918 The fact that *going out of the ark* also involves a condition of freedom can be seen from remarks just above at verse 16 about going out of the ark [§905].

The nature of a spiritual person's freedom is indicated by the fact that the Lord governs such people through conscience. Those whose conscience governs them, or who act in accord with their conscience, act freely. Nothing repels them more than violating their conscience. Acting against conscience is hell to them; obeying conscience is heaven. From this anyone can see that the latter is freeing.

The Lord governs spiritual people through a conscience that shows them what is good and true. This conscience, as noted [§§310:2, 393, 875:3], is formed in the intellectual part of their mind and so is separate from the contents of their will. Since conscience is totally separate from the urges of our will, we obviously can never do anything good on our own. And since all religious truth comes from religious good, we obviously never think anything true on our own, only under the Lord's power. The appearance that we do it on our own is only an appearance. Moreover, as this is how things work, a person who is truly spiritual also acknowledges and believes it.

From this it stands to reason that the spiritual person's conscience is a gift from the Lord, that it is like a new will, and therefore that the person who has been created anew is supplied with a new will and from this a new intellect.

919 Genesis 8:20. *And Noah built an altar to Jehovah and took of every clean animal and of every clean bird and offered burnt offerings on the altar.*

Noah built an altar to Jehovah symbolizes the practice of representing the Lord. *He took of every clean animal and of every clean bird* symbolizes the good effects of charity and [the true ideas] of faith. *And offered burnt offerings on the altar* symbolizes all the worship growing out of these things.

920 This verse depicts the worship of the ancient church in general, using the images of an altar and a burnt offering, which were the main elements in all representative worship. First, however, I need to tell what the worship of the earliest church was like and how people came to worship the Lord in a representative manner.

The people of the earliest church had no other kind of worship than internal worship—the kind of worship in heaven. In that church, heaven communicated with humankind in such a way as to form a single unit with it. The method of communication was perception, which is discussed frequently above.[518] So because the people of that church were angelic and had depth, they did not care about superficial bodily or worldly things, although they were, of course, aware of them. In the individual objects of the senses, rather, they perceived something divine and heavenly.

When they saw a tall mountain, for example, they did not picture a mountain but perceived the idea of height, and the idea of height led them to the idea of heaven and the Lord. This is how it came about that the Lord was said to live on the heights, that he was called the Highest One and Most Exalted, and that worship of him was later held on mountains.

It was the same with all other phenomena. When they thought of morning, for instance, they did not think of the early hours of the day but of the quality of heaven, which is like the morning or dawn in a person's mind. So they called the Lord the morning, the east, and the dawn. Likewise when they perceived a tree with its fruit and leaves, they ignored these details, seeing in them instead the representation of a human being—love and charity being the fruit, and faith, the leaves. As a result they not only compared members of the church to a tree (and to a whole paradise), and character traits to the fruit and leaves, but also called them such.

This is what people who have a heavenly, angelic way of thinking are like.

[2] Everyone is capable of realizing that our general viewpoint governs all our specific perceptions, including, of course, all our sense impressions, whether acquired through our eyes or ears. In fact we lack any interest in the objects of our senses unless they make part of that overall picture. To those whose hearts are glad, for instance, everything they hear or see appears cheerful and smiling. But to the depressed, everything they see or hear seems grim and melancholy. The same is true in all other cases as well, because our general mood pervades everything and causes us to see and hear everything within the context of our overall mood. Nothing outside that context is even visible but is virtually absent or irrelevant.

The situation was the same with the people of the earliest church. Whatever they saw with their eyes had a heavenly character for them. So for them, absolutely everything seemed alive. This indicates what their worship of God was like: internal and not at all external.

[3] When the church deteriorated, as it did in succeeding generations, and that perception, that communication with heaven, began to die out, the situation started to change. People were no longer perceiving anything of heaven in the objects of their senses as earlier generations had, but only things of the world, and the less perception they had left, the more this tendency increased. At last their final inheritors, who lived just before the Flood, saw nothing but what was worldly, physical, and earthly in those objects.

By this means, heaven was separated from humankind and ceased to communicate with it, except in a very remote way. A line of contact with hell then opened for humanity, and this became the source of their general perspective, which in turn is the source of all particular notions, as has been noted. After that, when the suggestion of something heavenly came up, they discounted it, until finally they did not even want to admit that anything spiritual or heavenly existed. So humankind's condition turned upside down.

[4] Since the Lord foresaw that this was what the human condition would become, he arranged for religious teachings to remain preserved and available, so that from them people could learn what was heavenly and what was spiritual. Those teachings, obtained from the people of the earliest church, were gathered by the individuals known as Cain and as Enoch, who have already been discussed. This is why it is said of Cain that a mark was put on him to prevent his murder, and of Enoch that God took him. See the treatment of these details at Genesis 4:15, §§392, 394, and at Genesis 5:24 [§521].

These doctrinal formulations consisted exclusively in symbolic language and so in what seem to be enigmatic sayings, telling what was meant by things found on earth, such as mountains (symbolizing heavenly attributes and the Lord), the morning and the east (again heavenly attributes and the Lord), different kinds of trees and their fruits (people and their heavenly qualities), and so on.

In such things did their articles of doctrine consist, and they were gathered together out of the signs and symbols of the earliest church. In consequence, their writing exhibited the same character. Since what they admired for its antiquity (and felt they could discern) in that literature was the divine and heavenly component, they were allowed to establish for themselves a form of worship based on similar features. That was the inspiration for their worship on mountains, in groves, and among the trees; for their open-air sculpture; and for the altars and burnt offerings that eventually became the main features of all worship.

The people of the ancient church initiated this worship, and from them it spread to their descendants and to all the surrounding nations, as did many other aspects of their worship. This will be discussed later [§§1238, 1241, 2180:4], the Lord in his divine mercy willing.

The symbolism of *Noah built an altar to Jehovah* as the practice of representing the Lord can be seen from the things just now said.

All the ritual of the ancient church represented the Lord, as did the ritual of the Jewish religion. But the chief item representing him came to be the altar, along with the burnt offering. Because it was clean animals and birds that were offered, the representation matched the symbolism involved, clean animals meaning the good effects of charity, and clean birds, the true ideas of faith. When the people of the ancient church offered up such creatures, it meant symbolically that the gifts they offered the Lord consisted of these attributes. Nothing else can be offered to the Lord that is pleasing to him.

Their descendants, however, like the surrounding nations and the Jews too, corrupted the practice, not realizing that it had any symbolic meaning and viewing all worship as an external affair.

[2] The fact that the altar was the main object to represent the Lord can also be seen from this: Before the establishment of any other kind of ritual, before construction of the ark, before the building of the Temple, there were altars, even among non-Jewish nations.

We see that when Abram came to the mountain on the east of Bethel, he constructed an *altar* and called on Jehovah's name (Genesis 12:8). He was ordered to offer Isaac up as a burnt offering on an *altar* (Genesis 22:2, 9). Jacob built an *altar* at Luz, which is Bethel (Genesis 35:6, 7). And Moses built an *altar* at the foot of Mount Sinai and offered a sacrifice (Exodus 24:4, 5, 6). This was before the establishment of the sacrifices and before the construction of the ark, around which they later conducted their worship in the wilderness.

By the same token, we know about the existence of altars among non-Jewish nations from the story of Balaam, who told Balak to build seven *altars* and prepare seven heads of cattle and seven rams (Numbers 23:1–7, 15–18, 29, 30). And it was decreed that those nations' *altars* should be destroyed (for instance, Deuteronomy 7:5; Judges 2:2). So the use of altars and sacrifices in the worship of God was not an innovation on the part of the Jews.

In fact before people knew anything about slaughtering cattle and the smaller livestock on altars, they were building them as memorials.

[3] The symbolism of *altars* as the practice of representing the Lord, and of *burnt offerings* as the resulting worship of him, is clearly evident in the prophets. One example is Moses' prophecy concerning the tribe of Levi, to whom the priesthood was assigned:

> They will teach your judgments to Jacob and your law to Israel. They will put incense in your nostrils and a *whole* [burnt offering][519] on your *altar*. (Deuteronomy 33:10)

This is about the totality of worship. "They will teach your judgments to Jacob and your law to Israel" stands for inner worship. "They will put incense in your nostrils and a 'whole [burnt offering]' on your altar" stands for outward worship that corresponds to inward worship. So the verse stands for the totality of worship. In Isaiah:

> On that day, humanity will look to its maker, and its eyes will regard the Holy One of Israel; and it will not look to *altars,* the work of its hands. (Isaiah 17:7, 8)

Looking to altars plainly stands for representative worship in general, which was to be abolished. In the same author:

> On that day there will be an *altar to Jehovah* in the middle of the land of Egypt and a pillar to Jehovah by its border. (Isaiah 19:19)

Here too the altar stands for external worship. [4] In Jeremiah:

> The Lord has deserted his *altar,* has despised his sanctuary. (Lamentations 2:7)

The altar stands for representative worship, which became idolatrous. In Hosea:

> Ephraim multiplied *altars* for sinning; it had *altars* for sinning. (Hosea 8:11)

The altars stand for every act of representative worship cut off from its inner meaning and so for idolatrous practices. In the same author:

> The lofty places of Aven, the sin of Israel, will be destroyed. Thorn and thistle will climb over their *altars.* (Hosea 10:8)

Again the altars stand for idolatrous worship. In Amos:

> On the day that I exact punishment on Israel for its transgressions, I will also bring punishment on the *altars* of Bethel, and the *horns of the altar*[520] will be chopped off. (Amos 3:14)

Once more the altars stand for representative practices that became idolatrous. [5] In David:

> They will bring me to your holy mountain and to your dwelling places, and I will go in to *God's altar,* to God, my happiness and joy. (Psalms 43:3, 4)

The altar obviously stands for the Lord. So the construction of an altar in the ancient and Jewish churches stood for the practice of representing the Lord.

Since the principal means for carrying out worship of the Lord were burnt offerings and sacrifices and these were consequently the principal symbols for representative worship, it stands to reason that the altar symbolized representative worship itself.

922
The symbolism of *he took of every clean animal and of every clean bird* as the good effects of charity and the true ideas of faith has been demonstrated before. The symbolism of an *animal* as the good effects of charity was shown in §§45, 46, 142, 143, 246 and of a *bird* as the true ideas of faith in §§40, 776.

Cattle, lambs and goats, and turtledoves or pigeon chicks were used in burnt offerings (Leviticus 1:2–17; Numbers 15:2–15; 28:1–end). These animals were clean, and each of them symbolized some particular attribute of heaven. Since they had a symbolic meaning in the ancient church and a representative meaning in the subsequent churches, it can be deduced that burnt offerings and sacrifices were nothing but representations of inner worship. It can also be deduced that when separated from internal worship, they were idolatrous.

Anyone of sound reason can see this. What is an altar but a heap of stone? What is a burnt offering or sacrifice but the slaughter of an animal? If it is divine worship, it must represent something heavenly that the worshipers know about and acknowledge and that inspires them to worship the One whom they are representing. [2] The only person who can fail to realize that these things represented the Lord is one who absolutely refuses to develop any understanding of the Lord.

The lens through which the One represented is to be seen, acknowledged, and believed is that of inner qualities, namely, charity and the faith that springs from it. This is quite evident in the prophets, as in Jeremiah:

> Jehovah Sabaoth, the God of Israel, has said, "Add your burnt offerings to your sacrifices and eat the meat. I did not speak to your ancestors *or command them* (on the day when I brought them out of the land of Egypt) *concerning the matters of burnt offering and sacrifice,* but this word I commanded them, saying '*Obey my voice* and I will become your God.'" (Jeremiah 7:21, 22, 23)

Hearing or obeying a voice is obeying the law, which has to do entirely with the one and only commandment, that they were to love God above all and their neighbor as themselves because the law and the prophets consist in this (Matthew 22:37–40; 7:12). In David:

Jehovah, *sacrifice and gift you have not wished for, burnt offering and sin sacrifice you have not sought.* I have desired to do your will, my God, and *your law* is in the middle of my belly. (Psalms 40:6, 8)

[3] In Samuel, when Samuel said to Saul,

> Does *Jehovah take as much satisfaction in burnt offerings and sacrifices as in obedience to Jehovah's voice?* Look: *obedience is better than sacrifice,* attentiveness than the fat of rams. (1 Samuel 15:22)

Micah tells what obeying his voice is:

> Am I to meet Jehovah with *burnt offerings,* with calves that are offspring of a year?[521] Will Jehovah take satisfaction in *thousands of rams,* in myriads of rivers of oil? He has pointed out to you, friend, what is good; and what is Jehovah requiring of you but to *carry out judgment and the love of mercy* and to be humble walking with your God? (Micah 6:6, 7, 8)

These are the things that burnt offerings and sacrifices of clean animals and birds symbolize. In Amos:

> If you offer me *your burnt offerings and gifts, I will not accept them,* and the peace offering of your fattened animals I will not regard. Let *judgment* flow like the water and *justice* like a mighty river. (Amos 5:22, 24)

Judgment is truth and justice is goodness, both of them flowing from charity, which is the burnt offerings and sacrifices of the inner self. In Hosea:

> *Mercy I wish for and not sacrifice,* and the knowledge of God *rather than burnt offerings.* (Hosea 6:6)

These passages show what quality sacrifices and burnt offerings have where there is no charity or faith. They also show that clean animals and clean birds symbolized and therefore represented the good effects of charity and [the true ideas] of faith.

The symbolism of *and he offered burnt offerings on the altar* as all the worship growing out of these things is evident from what has been said so far. Burnt offerings were the main element in the worship of the representative church, as were sacrifices later on, which will be discussed below [§§2165:3, 2177:1–4, 2180, 3880:8–9], by the Lord's divine mercy.

The fact that burnt offerings symbolize all representative worship as a whole can also be seen in the prophets, as in David:

> Jehovah will send your help from his sanctuary, and from Zion he will sustain you. He will remember all your gifts and make your *burnt offering* fat. (Psalms 20:2, 3)

And in Isaiah:

> All who keep the Sabbath and avoid profaning it—I will bring them to my holy mountain. Their *burnt offerings* and their sacrifices will bring great pleasure on my *altar*. (Isaiah 56:6, 7)

The burnt offerings and sacrifices stand for all worship. Burnt offerings stand for worship from love, sacrifices for worship from the faith that comes of love.

Internal attributes are described here by external actions, as they so often are in the prophets.

924. Genesis 8:21. *And Jehovah smelled a restful smell, and Jehovah said in his heart, "I will never again curse the ground on the human being's account, because what human hearts fabricate is evil from their youth. And I will never again strike every living thing as I have done."*

Jehovah smelled a restful smell means that worship rising out of those things was pleasing to the Lord. *And Jehovah said in his heart* means that it would no longer happen this way. *I will never again curse the ground* means that humanity would no longer turn its back in this way. *On the human being's account* means in the way people among the earliest church's descendants had done. *Because what human hearts fabricate is evil from their youth* means that the volitional side of the human mind is completely evil. *I will never again strike every living thing as I have done* means that people could no longer destroy themselves in this way.

925. *Jehovah smelled a restful smell* means that worship rising out of those things—in other words, worship inspired by charity and by the faith that comes of charity, as symbolized by the burnt offering—was pleasing to the Lord. This meaning was mentioned at the previous verse [§922:2–3].

The Word often says that Jehovah smelled a restful smell, chiefly from burnt offerings, and in each of those places it symbolizes something pleasing or welcome. Passages describing him as smelling a restful smell include the following: From burnt offerings, Exodus 29:18, 25, 41; Leviticus 1:9, 13, 17; 23:12, 13, 18; Numbers 28:6, 8, 13; 29:2, 6, 8, 13, 36. From other kinds of sacrifice, Leviticus 2:2, 9; 6:15, 21; 8:21, 28; Numbers 15:3,

7, 13. Both are referred to as fire offerings that served as a restful smell for Jehovah, meaning that love and charity were the source. In the Word, fire and fire offerings associated with the Lord and with worship of him symbolize love.

Bread has a similar meaning, so that representative worship employing burnt offerings and sacrifices is also called the bread of a fire offering to Jehovah that served as a restful smell (Leviticus 3:11, 16).

[2] A *smell* symbolizes something pleasing and welcome, as a result of which the Jewish religion also used it to represent something pleasing and attributed the smelling of it to Jehovah, or the Lord. This is because the good embraced by charity and the truth espoused by a faith that stems from charity correspond to pleasant, agreeable smells.

Auras in the heaven of spirits and angels can demonstrate that this correspondence does exist and can show what its nature is like. In that world, auras of love and faith exist, and the inhabitants perceive them distinctly. The auras are such that when a good spirit or an angel or a community of good spirits or angels comes on the scene, others immediately discern (if the Lord pleases) what kind of love and faith the spirit, angel, or community has. They can tell this from a distance, and the perception grows stronger at close quarters. It is incredible yet absolutely true: this is how communication and perception in the other life work. When the Lord pleases, then, there is no need to probe extensively to find out what a soul or spirit is like, since it can be recognized at the person's first approach.

These auras have their counterpart in earthly aromas. The correspondence between the two is clear from this, that in the world of spirits, when it pleases the Lord, auras of love and faith are manifestly embodied in clouds of sweet, pleasant fragrances and are manifestly perceived there.

[3] This explains why a *restful smell* symbolizes something pleasing, why the Jewish religion came to use fragrances in a representative way, and why they saw Jehovah, or the Lord, as sensing the restful smell.

A restful smell is a peaceful smell, or in other words, the pleasing quality of peace. Peace enfolds in a single embrace each and every facet of the Lord's kingdom, because the state of the Lord's kingdom is a state of peace. All the happy states that result from love for the Lord and faith in him emerge in a state of peace.

What has just been said shows not only how the case stands with representative worship but also why the Jewish religion used incense, for which an altar was provided in front of the veil and the appeasement cover [of the ark]. The same discussion shows why offerings of frankincense had a place among their sacrifices, and also why they used so many fragrant extracts in their incense, frankincense, and anointing oil. So it demonstrates that in the Word a restful odor, the burning of incense, and perfumes all symbolize the heavenly characteristics of love, and the spiritual characteristics of faith derived from them—in general, anything pleasing that develops out of them. [4] In Ezekiel, for example:

> On my holy mountain, on the mountain of Israel's high ground, there all the house of Israel—the whole of that house in the land—will serve me; there I will *accept* them. And there I will seek your raised offerings and the first fruits of your gifts in all your consecrations; because of the *restful smell* I will *accept* you. (Ezekiel 20:40, 41)

The restful smell applies to the burnt offerings and gifts, that is, to worship inspired by charity and the faith that comes of charity, this worship being what the burnt offerings and gifts symbolize. Such worship is accordingly "accepted," which is what the scent means. In Amos:

> I have hated, I have spurned your feasts, and I will not *smell* [the incense of] your holidays,[522] because if you offer me your burnt offerings and gifts, they will not *be accepted*. (Amos 5:21, 22)

Here the smell explicitly means something pleasing or acceptable. Of Isaac's blessing on Jacob instead of Esau we read:

> When Jacob had stepped close, and Isaac had kissed him and *smelled the smell* of his clothes, he blessed him and said, "See: the *smell* of my son, like the *smell* of a field that Jehovah has blessed." (Genesis 27:26, 27)

The smell of the clothing symbolizes earthly goodness and truth, which is pleasing because it harmonizes with heavenly and spiritual goodness and truth. Its pleasing quality is expressed as the *smell of a field*.

926 The meaning of *Jehovah said in his heart* as the fact that it would no longer happen this way will be seen from what follows.

When Jehovah is spoken of as *saying,* it means only that a thing happens or does not happen in this way (or that it is to happen or not to happen in this way). After all, nothing else can be said about Jehovah than "He is."[523]

Actions or traits that passages in the Word often attribute to Jehovah are mentioned for the sake of those whose minds cannot grasp anything beyond ordinary human experience. That is why the literal sense has the nature that it does. The simple at heart can learn from the appearances with which we all live. They hardly venture beyond what their senses reveal to them, so the Word speaks at their level of understanding. Such is the case here with the statement that Jehovah said something in his heart.

I will never again curse the ground on the human being's account means that humanity would no longer turn its back in the way people among the earliest church's descendants had done. This can be seen from earlier statements about the posterity of the earliest church. For the inner-level symbolism of *cursing* as turning away, see above (§§223, 245).

[2] The situation here and in what follows can also be seen from previous descriptions comparing the earliest church's later generations, which perished, with the new church called Noah. (That situation includes the fact that people no longer turned their backs, as members of the earliest church had done, and that they were no longer able to destroy themselves.) As noted in those places [§§310:1, 398, 640, 875:4], the will and intellect of people in the earliest church constituted a single mind. For them, in other words, love was planted in the volitional side, and at the same time so was faith, which filled the second part of the mind, or the intellectual side. Their descendants consequently inherited a will and an intellect that formed a single unit. So when self-love and the mad desires that it spawns started to take over their volitional side, displacing love for the Lord and charity toward their neighbor, it totally corrupted not only the volitional side, or the will, but at the same time the intellectual part, or the intellect. The corruption intensified when the final generation merged falsity with their cravings and by this means became Nephilim.[524] Having become Nephilim, they could not be salvaged, because their mind on both its sides—that is, their whole mind—was destroyed.

[3] But since the Lord foresaw this, he also provided that humankind should be rehabilitated. The means would be an ability to reform and regenerate the second or intellectual part of their mind and to receive in it the seed of a new will. The new will is conscience, through which the Lord puts into action the good urges of love or charity and the true ideas of faith.

In this way, by the Lord's divine mercy, humankind was restored.

These are the things symbolized in the current verse by *I will never again curse the ground on the human being's account, because what human hearts fabricate is evil from their youth. And I will not strike every living thing again as I have done.*

928. The meaning of *what human hearts fabricate is evil from their youth* as the fact that the volitional side of the human mind is completely evil is established by the statements just above; *what the heart fabricates* has no other meaning.

We think that we have a will to do good, but we are wholly mistaken. When we do good, it is not our will but a new will that is the Lord's—and so the Lord himself—that moves us to do so. By the same token, when we think and speak what is true, the source is a new intellectual capacity coming out of the new will and so the Lord again. People who have been reborn are entirely new people, formed by the Lord, so they are said to be *created anew*.[525]

929. The meaning of *I will not strike every living thing again as I have done* as the fact that people could no longer destroy themselves in this way now stands out clearly.

This is the situation: When we have regenerated, we are held back from the evil and falsity that are in us. Under those circumstances, we are conscious only of doing and thinking what is good and true on our own, but this is an appearance, an illusion. It is the result of being held back from evil and falsity, and held back with great force. What is more, since we are withheld from evil and falsity, we cannot destroy ourselves. If we were given leeway or left on our own to even a slight extent, we would plunge into all possible evil and falsity.

930. Genesis 8:22. *"Throughout all the days of the earth to come, sowing and reaping and cold and heat and summer and winter and day and night will not end."*

Throughout all the days of the earth to come symbolizes all time. *Sowing and reaping* symbolizes the regenerating person and so the church. *Cold and heat* symbolizes the condition of a person who is regenerating, which is cold and hot toward the acceptance of faith and charity; *cold* symbolizes no faith or charity but *heat* symbolizes faith and charity. *Summer and winter* symbolizes the condition of an already-regenerate person in respect to new movements of the will, which alternate the way summer and winter do. *Day and night* symbolizes the condition of this same regenerate person in respect to concepts in the intellect, which alternate the way day and night do. *They will not end* is the fact that this will happen throughout all time.

931. The symbolism of *throughout all the days of the earth to come* as all time, is established by the symbolism of a *day* as the times; see §§23, 487,

488, 493. So a *day of the earth* here is all time, as long as the earth lasts—that is to say, as long as an inhabitant remains on the planet. Inhabitants first come to an end when the church ceases to exist, because when the church is gone, humankind loses contact with heaven, and when that contact ends, every earth-dweller dies out.

The church is like a person's heart and lungs, as already mentioned.[526] As long we have a heart that is sound, and lungs, too, we are alive. The same is true of the church in relation to the universal human, which is the whole of heaven.[527] That is why the present verse says, "Throughout all the days of the earth, sowing and reaping and cold and heat and summer and winter and day and night will not end."

This also indicates that the planet will not last forever but will have its end as well, since it says, "throughout all the days of the earth," that is, as long as the earth exists.

[2] People believe, though, that the end of the earth is the same as the Last Judgment mentioned in the Word, where the culmination of the age, the day of divine visitation, and the Last Judgment are dealt with.[528] They are wrong. A last judgment comes to every church when it goes through the process of devastation, which is the stage at which there is no longer any faith in it.

The earliest church had its last judgment when it perished, as it did among its final descendants, just before the Flood. The Jewish church had its last judgment when the Lord came into the world. A last judgment has yet to come, too, when the Lord comes into his glory. Not that the earth and the world will then be destroyed but that the church will.[529] Afterward, however, the Lord always brings a new church back to life. So at the time of the Flood, he raised up the ancient church, and at the time of his Coming, he raised up the early [Christian] church among non-Jews. It will be the same when the Lord comes into his glory.

This is also what "the new heaven and the new earth" means [Isaiah 65:17; 66:22; Revelation 21:1]. [3] The case resembles that of every regenerate person, who becomes a part of the church—becomes a church, in fact—after being created anew. The inner self of such people is called a new heaven and their outer self a new earth.

In addition, every individual also has a last judgment at death, because at that time, depending on how we behaved in the body, we receive a verdict of either death or life.[530]

An indication that the end of the age, the cataclysm, and the Last Judgment have no other meaning and therefore do not imply the world's obliteration is clear from the Lord's words in Luke:

> On that *night* there will be two in one bed; one will be taken, the other *left*. Two will be grinding together; one will be taken and the other *left*. Two will be in the field; one will be taken and the other *left*. (Luke 17:34, 35, 36)

The last stage is called the night here because there will be no faith, that is, no charity. It says that some people will be left, which clearly indicates that the world will not be annihilated at that time.

932 The symbolism of *sowing and reaping* as the regenerating person, and so the church, needs no confirmation from the Word because it occurs so many times. Not only is a field—and consequently the sowing of it—used as a metaphor and simile for a person, but seed is used in the same way for the Lord's Word, and the produce or harvest, for the effect it has. Everyone understands this meaning because its appearance in the Word has made it common in everyday speech.

The general subject here is humankind as a whole and the fact that the time will never come when there are no seeds being planted in us by the Lord, whether we are inside or outside the church, that is, whether we know the Lord's Word or not. Without seed planted by the Lord, no one can do a whit of good. [2] Even among non-Christians, every charitable kindness is seed from the Lord. The good that non-Christians do is not a result of the true faith, as it can be among people inside the church, but it can become so. Non-Christians usually live a life of charity in the world, and when those who do so are instructed by angels in the other life, they embrace and welcome the teachings of true faith and the faith that comes of charity much more easily than Christians. More about this later [§§1032–1033, 2589–2605, 2861:1, 3263:2], with the Lord's divine mercy.

The specific subject here is the regenerating individual and the fact that the church will never cease to exist in at least one place on earth. That is what "throughout all the days of the earth there will be sowing and reaping" means.

The fact that there will always be sowing and reaping, or that the church will always exist, connects with the message of the last verse: that people could no longer destroy themselves in the way the final generation of the earliest church had done.

Cold and heat symbolizes the condition of a person who is regenerating, which is cold and hot toward the acceptance of faith and charity; *cold* symbolizes no faith or charity, but *heat* symbolizes [faith and] charity. This can be seen from the symbolism of cold and heat in the Word, which uses the terms to describe a person who is regenerating, or one who has regenerated, or the church. It can also be seen from the context above and below, which deals with the church. The last verse said that people could no longer destroy themselves in the same way. The present verse says that the church will always exist, first depicting what happens when it comes into existence—that is, when a person is reborn as a church[531]—and soon after discussing the nature of a person who has already become regenerate. So it deals with every phase that people in the church pass through.

[2] There is only one really good way to see that when we are regenerating we go through these phases of cold and heat, or of faith and charity absent and present. That is through experience and through reflection on our experience. Few people regenerate, though, and few if any of those who regenerate can or do reflect on the state of their regeneration. So let me say a few words about it.

When we are being reborn, we receive life from the Lord, since up till then we cannot be said to have been alive. A life focused on the world and the body is not really life; only a life that is heavenly and spiritual is real. We receive real life from the Lord through regeneration, and since before that time we lack any life, we alternate between no life and true life—that is, between no faith or charity and some faith and charity. Here, cold symbolizes a lack of faith and charity, and heat, the presence of some faith and charity.

[3] This is the situation: Whenever we are caught up in bodily and worldly concerns, we experience a lack of faith and charity, or coldness. At such times our bodily and worldly interests—and so our self-interest—are active. As long as we are wrapped up in them, we are devoid of or distant from belief and neighborly love, so that we do not even think about heavenly and spiritual matters. The reason for the disconnection is that a heavenly focus and a bodily focus can never coexist in us, since the human will is lost beyond recall. When our bodily desires and the urges of our will stop agitating and fall quiet, though, the Lord works through our inner self, and we then come into faith and charity, which are called "heat" here. When we return to a bodily focus, we go back into the cold, and when the body and everything connected with it fade away almost to

the point of vanishing, we regain the warmth, and so on in cycles. Such is the human condition—heavenly and spiritual values cannot coexist with bodily and worldly values in us but must alternate with them.

These are the things that take place in every regenerating person, lasting just as long as the process of regeneration does. There is no other way for us to be reborn, or in other words, from being dead to come alive, for the reason already given: our will is lost beyond recall. This will is entirely separate from the new will that we receive from the Lord and that is the Lord's, not ours.

All this now indicates what cold and heat symbolize here.

[4] Anyone who has been reborn can see from experience that this is how the matter stands. That is to say, when bodily and worldly considerations absorb us, we are absent and distant from internal ones. Not only do we fail to think at all about them but we also sense a kind of chill inside us. When bodily and worldly demands quiet down, on the other hand, we come under the influence of faith and charity.

Such an individual can also see from experience that these two phases alternate. So when bodily and worldly concerns start to overflow and try to dominate, we enter a period of distress and trial. The crisis lasts until we have been reduced to a state in which our outer self obeys our inner self—an obedience that is utterly impossible except when the outer self grows still and almost vanishes.

The final inheritors of the earliest church could not be reborn since, as noted [§§310:1, 398, 640, 875:4, 927:2], intellectual capacities and volitional capacities formed one mind in them. So they could not detach the ideas in their intellect from the urges of their will and therefore could not cycle back and forth between heavenly and spiritual pursuits on the one hand and bodily and worldly pursuits on the other. Instead they felt perpetual coldness toward the things of heaven and perpetual warmth for the objects of their desire, so that for them no alternation was possible.

934 The symbolism of *cold* as no love (that is, no charity) or faith, and of *heat* or fire as love (or charity) and faith, is attested by the following passages in the Word. In John, when he addressed the church of Laodicea:

> I know your deeds, that you are neither *cold* nor *hot*. If only you were *cold* or *hot!* But since you are lukewarm and neither *cold* nor *hot,* I am about to spit you out of my mouth. (Revelation 3:15, 16)

Being cold stands for having no charity, and being hot, for having a wealth of it. In Isaiah:

> This is what Jehovah has said: "I will rest and watch in my established position, like a sheen of *heat* on the light, like a cloud of dew in the *heat of harvest.*" (Isaiah 18:4)

This passage is about planting a new church. The heat on the light and the heat of harvest stand for love and charity. In the same author:

> Jehovah's *fire* is on Zion and his furnace is in Jerusalem. (Isaiah 31:9)

Fire stands for love. In respect to the guardian beings that Ezekiel saw:

> What the living creatures looked like: Their appearance was like *burning embers of fire,* like the appearance of lamps. The *fire* was moving along among the living creatures, and it had brilliance, and from the *fire* went out lightning. (Ezekiel 1:13)

[2] And in the same author, describing the Lord:

> Above the expanse that was over the head of the guardian beings was a seeming appearance of sapphire stone, like a throne. And on the likeness of a throne was what looked like the appearance of a person on it, high above. And I saw the seeming form of a *fiery ember,* like the form of *fire,* within him all around, from the appearance of his hips and up; and from the appearance of his hips and down I saw the seeming appearance of *fire,* which had a brilliance all around. (Ezekiel 1:26, 27; 8:2)

The fire stands for love. In Daniel:

> The Ancient One sat; his throne was *fiery flames,* its wheels a *burning fire.* A river of *fire* was pouring forth and going out from before him. Thousands upon thousands were waiting on him, and myriads upon myriads were standing before him. (Daniel 7:9, 10)

The fire stands for the Lord's love. In Zechariah:

> "I will be to them," says Jehovah, "a wall of *fire* all around." (Zechariah 2:5)

This is about a new Jerusalem. In David:

> Jehovah makes the spirits[532] his angels, the *flaming fire* his attendants. (Psalms 104:4)

The flaming fire stands for something heavenly and at the same time spiritual.

[3] Since fire symbolized love, it also came to be used for representing the Lord, as is evident from the *fire* on the altar of burnt offering, which was never put out (Leviticus 6:9, 12, 13), representing the Lord's mercy. That is why Aaron had to burn incense with *fire* taken from the altar of burnt offering before he could go in to approach the appeasement cover (Leviticus 16:12, 13, 14). Furthermore, in order to symbolize the Lord's acceptance of the worship, fire was sent down from heaven and consumed the burnt offerings (Leviticus 9:24, for instance, and elsewhere).

In the Word, fire also symbolizes self-love and its craving, with which heavenly love cannot harmonize. That is why two of Aaron's sons were devoured by fire for using *foreign fire* in their sacrificial burning (Leviticus 10:1, 2). Foreign fire is the totality of self-love and love of worldly gain, as well as all the cravings that accompany those loves.

Besides, ungodly individuals experience heavenly love in no other way than as a burning, consuming fire. For this reason, the Word describes the Lord as a consuming fire. The fire on Mount Sinai that represented the Lord's love or mercy, for instance, was perceived by the people as a devouring fire, which is why they told Moses not to make them listen to Jehovah God's voice or look at the *huge fire* or they would die (Deuteronomy 18:16). This is what the Lord's love or mercy looks like to people inflamed with self-love and materialism.

935   The things already said about cold and heat establish the symbolism of *and summer and winter* as the condition of an already-regenerate person in respect to new movements of the will, which alternate the way summer and winter do. The two extremes for people undergoing the process of regeneration are like cold and heat, but for people who have regenerated they are like summer and winter.

The clue to the fact that the previous phrase describes a regenerating person and the present phrase a regenerate one is that the previous phrase mentions cold first and heat second, while the present phrase mentions summer first and winter second. People who are regenerating start with cold, that is, with no faith or charity, but when they have been reborn they start with charity.

[2] Regenerate people go back and forth between having no charity at one time and some charity at another. This is clear to see because everyone, even a person reborn, has nothing but evil inside; all goodness is the Lord's alone. Since the regenerate have nothing but evil inside, they cannot help seesawing, living now in a kind of summer (in charity) and now in winter (no charity). These cycles exist to bring them into increasing perfection and so into increasing happiness.

Regenerate people go through these cycles not only while they are living in the body but also when they come into the other life. Without alternations that resemble those of summer and winter in matters of the will, and day and night in matters of the intellect, the regenerate would never be perfected or made happier. Their ups and downs in the other world, though, are like the summertime and wintertime changes that occur in temperate zones, and like the daytime and nighttime changes that occur in the spring.

[3] The prophets too portray these phases in terms of summer and winter, day and night, as in Zechariah:

> And it will happen on that day that living water will go out from Jerusalem, part of it to the eastern sea and part of it to the western sea;[533] in *summer* and in *winter* it will happen. (Zechariah 14:8)

This concerns a new Jerusalem, or the Lord's kingdom in heaven and on earth, and conditions in each, which are described as summer and winter. In David:

> God, yours is the *day*, yours also the *night*. You prepared the light and the sun. You set up all the boundaries of the earth. You formed *summer* and *winter*. (Psalms 74:16, 17)

These things involve similar meanings. Likewise in Jeremiah the fact that neither the *compact with the day* nor the *compact with the night* was to be nullified, so that daytime and night would occur at their times (Jeremiah 33:20).

936. The symbolism of *day and night* as the condition of this same regenerate person in respect to concepts in the intellect, which alternate the way day and night do, is established by statements just above.

Summer and winter have to do with the contents of the will because of the warmth and cold involved, since matters of the will grow warm or cold. But day and night have to do with the contents of the intellect because of the light and dark involved, since matters of the intellect exist in light or darkness.

Because the statements made here are self-evident, they need no confirmation from similar passages in the Word.

937. The above also shows what the Lord's Word is like in its inner meaning. In its literal sense it seems so unsophisticated that we necessarily see it as speaking only of sowing and reaping, cold and heat, summer and winter, day and night, when in reality these details involve secrets that were known to the ancient or spiritual church. The actual, literal words act in just this

way—as extremely ordinary containers, so to speak, whose finer details hold heavenly secrets in such great number and of such great importance that not one millionth of them could ever be fully explored. When angels look with the Lord's eyes at those common, everyday words, drawn from an earthly vocabulary, they can see the whole process of regeneration and also the condition of both a regenerating and a regenerate person, in all their boundless variety. Humankind, on the other hand, sees hardly anything.

The Hells (Continued): Misers' Hells, the Foul Jerusalem and Outlaws in the Wilderness, and the Feces-Laden Hells of Those Who Have Pursued Sensual Pleasure Alone

938 OF all people, misers are the vilest and think the least about life after death, the soul, and the inner being. They do not even know what heaven is. This is because of all people they do the least to elevate their thinking, which they completely saturate and drench with bodily and earthly preoccupations. The result is that when they enter the other world, for a long time they fail to realize that they are spirits, remaining firmly convinced instead that they are still in the body.

Their thoughts, dragged down to the bodily and earthly level by their greed, turn into dreadful hallucinations. Strange to say, but true, in the next life the grossly avaricious seem to themselves to live in cellars where their money is stored and where they are overrun with rats. Despite the rats, they do not leave until they grow unbearably tired of the situation, at which point they finally emerge from these tombs of theirs.

939 Evidence that the ideas composing the thoughts of sordid misers turn into sordid hallucinations can be seen in their hell, which is deep down under the feet. Out of it wafts a cloud of steam, like the steam from pigs being skinned in a trough. That is where misers' houses are. The people who go there are dark-looking at first, but when they have their hair scraped off, as pigs do, they seem to themselves and to each other to grow lighter in color.[534] But the process still leaves a mark indicating that this is their nature, no matter where they go.

A dark-looking spirit who had not yet been shunted into his own hell (because he was to stay longer in the world of spirits) was sent down to that locale. He was not very miserly, but even so, while he lived he had harbored a malicious envy of others' wealth. When he arrived, the misers there ran away, saying that since he was dark, he was a robber and so would kill them. Misers flee such people in tremendous fear for their lives. Finally they discovered that he was not that lawless and told him that, if he wanted to turn lighter, all he had to do was to be stripped of his hair, as was happening to the pigs right there in plain view, and then his color would grow lighter. But he did not want this. He was taken up among the spirits.

This hell is where most of the Jews who had been appallingly greedy go.[535] When they come near other spirits, the stench of rats announces their presence.

Speaking of Jews, let me tell how wretched their condition is after death—at least the condition of those who had been rapacious and despised others in comparison with themselves (from the inborn arrogance of their belief that they alone were the chosen people). Let me also say something about their cities and about some outlaws in the wilderness.

During bodily life they had dreamed up and proved to their own satisfaction the idea that they were destined to arrive in Jerusalem—in the Holy Land there—and possess it, unwilling to see that the New Jerusalem means the Lord's kingdom in the heavens and on the earth. When they reach the next life, their delusion causes them to see a city that is to the left of Gehenna[536] and a little out in front of it, which they enter in a mob. The city is full of putrid-smelling mud, though, and for this reason is called the foul Jerusalem. There they run around through the streets, ankle deep in muck and mud, complaining and howling.

(With their eyes they see cities, and streets too. Such things are represented to them as in clear daylight. I myself have seen cities several times.)

[2] I observed one rather shadowy spirit coming from this foul Jerusalem. A kind of gate opened. There were some wandering stars around him, especially on his left. (Wandering stars around a spirit symbolize falsity in the world of spirits; the case is different with stars that do not wander.) He came up and attached himself from above to my left ear, which he seemed to touch with his mouth in order to speak with me. He did not talk in a clearly audible voice, as others do, but inwardly, to himself, though still in such a way that I could hear and understand it.

He said that he was a Jewish rabbi and that he had lived in that muddy city for a long time. "The streets you have to go on there," he said, "are nothing but muck and mud. And there's nothing to eat but mud."

"Since you're a spirit, why should you want to eat?" I asked.

"I do eat," he said, "and when I want to eat, no one offers me anything but mud. So I complain bitterly.

"What's to be done, then?" he went on to ask. "I can't find Abraham, Isaac, or Jacob."

I told him a few things about the patriarchs. "There's no point in looking for them," I added. "If you do find them, they won't be able to help you at all." And I said some other, rather hard-to-grasp things. "You should not be looking for anyone but the Lord alone," I went on. "He's the Messiah, whom the Jews despised during their lives. He rules the whole of heaven and all the earth without anyone else's help."

"Where is he?" the rabbi anxiously asked me several times.

"You find him everywhere," I said, "and he hears and knows everyone." But then some other Jewish spirits dragged him away.

941 There is another city on the right of Gehenna too, or between Gehenna and the lake,[537] where the better Jews seem to themselves to live. But the city changes for them as their fantasies change. At one point it turns into a collection of small towns, at another into a lake, and at another back into a city. The residents have a fear of robbers, but as long as they are in the city they are safe.

Between the two cities is a kind of triangular space dark with shadows. That is the home of the outlaws, who are Jews but of the worst kind. Anyone they come across they torture cruelly. The Jews are so terrified of these outlaws that they call them "Lord," and they call the wilderness the outlaws live in "the [Holy] Land."

To keep those who enter the city on the right-hand side safe from the bandits, a good spirit stands at one corner of the city limits and welcomes arrivals.[538] When they reach the spirit, they bow down to the ground and enter at the spirit's feet. That is the ritual they go through to get into the city.

One spirit came up to me quite suddenly. "Where did you come from?" I asked.

"I ran in terror from the thieves, because they kill people, and chop, roast, and boil them," was the answer. "Where can I be safe?"

"What place, what land are you from?" I asked.

Out of fear, the spirit did not dare to answer more than, "The land is the Lord's." (As noted, they call the wilderness the [Holy] Land and the thieves Lord).

[2] Then some of these outlaws came up, and they were very dark. They had deep voices, like giants' voices, and wherever they make an appearance they inflict an amazingly palpable fear and horror. I asked who

they were. They said they were looking for goods to loot. "Where do you expect to pile your loot?" I asked. "Don't you know that you're spirits and can't make off with loot or pile it up? Such are the delusions of the evil!"

"We live in the wilderness, looking for plunder," they answered, "and we torture the people we run into." While they were with me they finally admitted that they were spirits, but they still could not be persuaded to believe they were not living in their bodies.

There are Jews who wander around in this way, making talk about indiscriminately murdering, chopping, roasting, and boiling others, even if the victims are Jews or friends of theirs. This has allowed others to recognize their character, despite the fact that they dare not divulge it in the world.[539]

Not far from the foul Jerusalem is yet another city called Gehenna's Judgment.[540] This is the home of people who claim heaven for themselves on the strength of their own righteousness and who condemn others for not living out the same fantasies.

Between this city and Gehenna appears a kind of bridge, pretty enough, of a dingy, grayish color, where there is a dark-looking spirit they fear, who keeps them from crossing. On the other side of the bridge, you see, appears Gehenna.

There are some for whom sensory pleasure was their sole aim during bodily life. The only thing they loved was indulging in luxury and living on delicacies and rich food. They focused entirely on themselves and the material world, considered divine things worthless, and lacked faith and charity. After death they are at first brought into the same kind of life they had in the world. There is a place out in front, to the left, and down a little, which offers unending fun, games, dancing, feasting, and conversation. This is where they go, and while there they are completely unaware that they are not in the world.

But the scene changes. In a little while they descend into a hell below the buttocks, a hell of mere excrement. The kind of pleasure just described, which belongs strictly to the body, turns into excrement in the other life. I have seen people there carting dung and complaining bitterly.

There are some women who have risen from a sordid and lowly condition to become rich. Vain as a result, they have dedicated themselves to pleasure and to a lazy, pampered life, reclining like queens on cushions, sitting at table to feast, and caring for nothing. When they come together in the other life, they go at each other in a shocking fashion, punching, scratching, pulling each other's hair, and turning into furies.[541]

This is not the case, however, with women who have been born into the creature comforts and pleasures of life and have been brought up to these advantages since infancy—queens, for instance, and other nobility, and the rich too. Although they live a life of sensual gratification, luxury, and grandeur, as long as they also live one of faith in the Lord and charity toward their neighbor they are among the happy in the next life.

To forswear life's pleasures, power, and wealth in order to earn heaven through one's suffering is wrong. What is meant in the Word is to think of pleasures, power, and wealth as nothing compared to the Lord, and the life of the world as nothing compared to the life of heaven [Matthew 19:21–24; Mark 10:21–25; Luke 18:22–25].

946   I talked with some spirits about the prospect that few will believe all these things can happen in the other world. People have no conception of life after death, except for a vague, general notion, which is no conception at all, and they harden themselves in this notion by the fact that they cannot see a soul or spirit with their eyes. Furthermore, although scholars affirm that the soul or spirit exists, they get bogged down in inventing technical terms that dim—no, extinguish—any understanding of the subject.[542] Because of this, and because they focus on themselves and worldly advantages and rarely on the common good or heaven, scholars have even less belief than sense-oriented people do.

The spirits I was talking to were amazed that humankind could be this way despite knowing that nature itself, in each of its kingdoms, provides so many varied wonders of which people are unaware. Take just the human inner ear, for example; a whole book could be filled with astounding and unheard-of facts about it, and everyone trusts those facts. But say anything about the spiritual world, which gives rise to each and every detail of nature's kingdoms, and hardly anyone believes it. The reason, as noted, is people's confirmed prejudice that the spiritual world is nothing because they do not see it.

Notes & Indexes

Notes

Notes to the Author's Table of Contents

1. The Latin word here translated "secrets" is *arcana,* which generally refers to sacred secrets or mysteries; the English equivalent, "arcana," has a similar sense, but has come to have a more limited use. Most previous translations of this work retained the Latin title *Arcana Coelestia,* literally, "heavenly arcana." [RS]

2. Although the use of the term "the Word" for the Bible was common in Swedenborg's time, his conception of "the Word" does not include all the books of which the Bible is generally understood to be composed. He generally limits his definition of "the Word" to those parts of Scripture that he believes to have an inner meaning throughout: the Pentateuch (Genesis, Exodus, Leviticus, Numbers, Deuteronomy), the historical books (Joshua, Judges, 1 and 2 Samuel, 1 and 2 Kings), the Psalms, the prophets (Isaiah, Jeremiah, Lamentations, Ezekiel, Daniel, Hosea, Joel, Amos, Obadiah, Jonah, Micah, Nahum, Habakkuk, Zephaniah, Haggai, Zechariah, Malachi), the Gospels (Matthew, Mark, Luke, John), and Revelation. He thus omits certain parts of the Hebrew Scriptures, such as 1 and 2 Chronicles, Ruth, Proverbs, and the Song of Solomon, as well as the writings of the apostles in the Greek Scriptures. For a discussion of his reasons for these omissions, see his letter to his friend Gabriel Beyer (1720–1779) dated April 15, 1766, cited in Acton 1948–1955, 612–613, and quoted in the introduction to this volume, pages 86–87. On the use of the term "the Lord" in Swedenborg's writings, see note 7. [GFD, RS]

3. Swedenborg describes the next world as being divided into three major areas: heaven, hell, and a middle region called the world of spirits (see §5852, for example). A fourth area could be added: the "underground realm" (see note 169). [LHC] In his 1758 work *Heaven and Hell* 421, Swedenborg says, "The world of spirits is neither heaven nor hell but a place or state between the two. It is where we first arrive after death, being in due time either raised into heaven or cast into hell from it depending on our life in this world." (The translations from *Heaven and Hell* quoted in these notes are those of George F. Dole.) Angels form an extremely important part of Swedenborg's metaphysical system. Key aspects of his thought in this regard are that angels are persons in the strict sense, not abstract forces or entities. They have bodies as we do, and even wear clothing and live in houses in heaven (*Heaven and Hell* 73–77, 177–190). Moreover, angels were not originally created as such: every angel was at one point a person alive either on this earth or on some other planet (see his 1758 work *Other Planets* 1). Much of Swedenborg's information about the unseen worlds is reported in the form of conversations with angels. [RS]

4. Swedenborg later came to refer to these "accounts of the wonders . . . seen in the world of spirits and in the heaven of angels" with the Latin term *memorabilia.* Traditionally they have been referred to in English as either "memorabilia" or "memorable relations"; in the annotations to this edition they are called "accounts of memorable occurrences," or some variation of that term. (Strictly speaking, the first separate "memorable occurrences"

distinctly labeled in small caps in the first editions appeared in Swedenborg's 1766 work *Revelation Unveiled,* but the term has since been applied to the shorter accounts embedded in his previous material.) Because of their basis in Swedenborg's spiritual experiences, these accounts are also sometimes referred to as "experiential" material (as opposed to doctrinal or exegetical). Swedenborg apparently saw the experiential material in the *Secrets of Heaven* volumes as the reader's easiest avenue of access to the work; in order to distinguish it, he had it printed in italics, in slightly larger type, and with more space between the lines. In this table of experiential material in the first volume, the first edition (the Latin edition of 1749) cites the passages by page number, an odd exception to Swedenborg's customary use of section numbers to refer to his text. He may have felt that the use of page numbers would make these topics more accessible to the browsing reader. The corresponding section numbers have been substituted in this edition. It should be noted that this first volume of the present edition contains about half the material in the first volume of Swedenborg's edition; so that when he here refers to "accounts of the wonders" (Latin *mirabilia*) appearing "in this first volume," the reader must understand that the passages cited after §946 appear now in volume 2. The same applies to the section numbers cited just above in the text. [SS]

5. Swedenborg describes heaven as having the form of a single human being, which he calls *maximus homo,* here translated "universal human." See §§550, 911:2, and the sections referred to here by Swedenborg. See also note 209 below. [LHC]

Notes to Genesis Chapter 1, §§1–66

6 (in §1). This edition follows Swedenborg's practice of referring to the Hebrew Scriptures as the Old Testament and the Greek Scriptures as the New Testament. On the meaning of the term "the Word," see note 2. [JSR]

7 (in §1). "The Lord" here refers to Jesus Christ. Although Swedenborg's theology is thoroughly monotheistic, to denote God he uses many names and terms from philosophical and biblical backgrounds (God, the Divine Being, the Deity, the Divine Human, the One, the Infinite, the First, the Creator, the Redeemer, the Savior, Jehovah, God Shaddai, and many more). The most frequently occurring term, however, is "the Lord" (Latin *Dominus*). Here and generally throughout, "the Lord" refers to Jesus Christ as the visible manifestation of the one and only God. See §14. For a brief summary of Swedenborg's theology, see *True Christianity* 2–3. [JSR, RS]

8 (in §1). The idea that Scripture possesses an inner meaning is an ancient one. Some of the earliest interpretations of the Bible using such a method come from Philo of Alexandria (also known as Philo Judaeus; about 15 B.C.E–50 C.E.), whose works interpret Scripture in the light of Greek philosophy. The most significant accounts of the Bible's inner meaning in early Christianity come from the church fathers Clement of Alexandria (about 150–between 211 and 215 C.E.) and Origen (about 185–about 254 C.E.). Origen wrote, "Among those narratives which appear to be recorded literally there are inserted and interwoven others which cannot be accepted as history but which contain a spiritual meaning" (Origen, *On First Principles,* book 4, chapter 3, in Origen 1966, 290). For a discussion of the similarities between Swedenborg's perspective on the Bible and those of the church fathers, see Tulk 1994, 19–33. Another influential exposition of the inner meaning of Genesis appears in the compendium of Jewish mystical knowledge known as the *Sefer ha-Zohar,* or "Book of Splendor," attributed to the circle of

Rabbi Moses de Leon (about 1250–1305) in thirteenth-century Spain. The *Zohar* is the principal work of the Kabbala, the mystical doctrine of Judaism. According to Kabbalistic teaching, there are four levels of meaning to Scripture, ranging from the literal to the mystical (see Matt 2004 and Scholem 1974, 174). Swedenborg's familiarity with these earlier sources is a matter of scholarly debate, but it is generally acknowledged that he had at least a broad conception of them, and indeed his interpretations often accord with them (see Lamm [1915] 2000, 55–58, 227–231). On the other hand, although he himself does occasionally show awareness of theories of an inner meaning much like his own (see, for example, §606), he repeatedly insists that his theology is derived from personal spiritual experience. [RS]

9 (in §1). For instances in which the inner meaning of sacrifices is explained, see Matthew 26:26–28, Mark 14:22–24, and Luke 22:19–20, where Jesus refers to the bread and wine of the Passover meal as his body and blood. He also uses the term "blood of the covenant," which recalls a sacrifice offered by Moses just after he received the Ten Commandments, as described in Exodus 24:4–8. See also Ephesians 5:2; Hebrews 7:27; 9:26. [LHC, JLO] The Epistle to the Hebrews draws an elaborate analogy between the sacrifices ordained by the Mosaic Law and Christ's sacrifice, adding that the Law is "a shadow of good things to come," that is, of Christ's coming; see Hebrews 9; 10:1. (The term "the Law," so capitalized, refers loosely to the books of Genesis, Exodus, Leviticus, Numbers, and Deuteronomy, and in particular to the injunctions of divine worship laid on the Jewish people there.) [RS]

10 (in §1). See Luke 23:43, where Jesus on the cross promises a criminal who is also being executed, "Today you will be with me in Paradise." See also Revelation 2:7. [LHC, JLO] The word *Paradise* comes from a Persian word meaning "park" or "enclosure"; it appears in Hebrew as פַּרְדֵּס *(pardēs)* and in Greek as παράδεισος *(parádeisos)*. Early on, however, it came to serve as a metaphor for heaven. [RS]

11 (in §2). The phrase "down to the tiniest jot" means down to the smallest letter, which in the Hebrew alphabet is yod (י). The word "jot" comes from the name of the Greek letter iota, which in turn comes from the same source as yod. [LHC]

12 (in §2). Here Swedenborg appears to be thinking of John 1:4: "In it [the Word] there was life, and that life was the light for humankind." [RS]

13 (in §3). Swedenborg is not necessarily limiting his conception of the "Christian world" to Christianity proper. In §54 of his 1763 work *Sacred Scripture,* he uses the term to include not only the Reformed Church (that is, Calvinists) and Catholics but Jews as well. See also note 14. [RS, GFD]

14 (in §3). Swedenborg here alludes to a dynamic that infuses his work, as it does practically all of Christianity from its earliest origins: the contrast between the "outer"—equated with the purely physical, which, taken on its own, is lifeless—and the "inner," which is what gives life. This contrast between the inner self and the outer self is a common theme in the Christian tradition, going back to Jesus himself, who strongly emphasized the difference between external appearances of piety and the inner motivation. See the parable of the Pharisee and the tax collector, Luke 18:10–14; also Matthew 23:27: "Woe to you, scribes and Pharisees, hypocrites, because you make yourselves like bleached tombs, which do indeed look beautiful from the outside, but inside are full of the bones of the dead and uncleanness of every kind." The dynamic can be seen in

Paul's Epistles as well: see 2 Corinthians 4:16: "Although our outer self is perishing, our inner self is nevertheless being renewed day by day." Similarly, Paul contrasts those who are Jews "outwardly" with those who are Jews "inwardly"; the former have a circumcision that is "outward in the flesh," while the latter have one "of the heart, in the spirit, and not in the letter" (Romans 2:28–29). [RS]

15 (in §4). The creation story is one area in which *Secrets of Heaven* differs radically from most earlier allegorical interpretations of Scripture (see note 346). The latter assume that the opening of Genesis does indeed attempt to explain the creation of the world and humankind (see, for example, Philo 1993, 3–5; Matt 2004, 107 and following). Swedenborg, by contrast, asserts that this passage is not dealing with actual cosmogenesis, but with the spiritual life of an individual human being. [RS]

16 (in §4). Swedenborg uses the term *ecclesia,* or "church," in a number of ways. Here, as often, it does not denote a group of Christians but instead refers to one of five major phases Swedenborg assigns to the world's religious history. In general Swedenborg calls the first phase the earliest church, the second the ancient church, the third the Jewish church (up to the time of Christ), the fourth the Christian church, and the fifth a new church. In the early volumes of the present work, though, he often adds another, called the Hebrew church, between the ancient and Jewish churches. [LHC]

17 (in §4). "Represent" (Latin *repraesentare*) and "symbolize" *(significare)* are heavily used terms in Swedenborg's theology. The two have related but distinguishable meanings. Both indicate the presence of an inner meaning in an object, person, name, or action, but symbolism directs our attention to the meaning itself (especially as communicated by words), whereas representation generally directs our attention to the living enactment of that meaning (especially by persons). One result, as described in §§665 and 1361, is that a person who represents something good does not actually have to be good; an evil monarch, to use Swedenborg's own example, can represent the Lord's power. In §920, in the first volume of the first edition, Swedenborg makes clear that these distinctions parallel certain of the divisions in the world's religious history he calls churches (see note 16). Members of the earliest church, he says, had the ability to perceive the inner meaning without effort; their perceptiveness was replaced in the ancient church by the codified knowledge of symbolism. In §1361:3, also in the first volume, he adds that when the church with an intuitive gift for symbolism came to an end, representation took the place of symbolism. However, by the third volume (that is, starting at §2760), Swedenborg becomes fairly consistent in assigning representative meaning to the individuals who appear in a story and symbolic meaning to everything else. A typical example occurs in §3131, which expounds a phrase in Genesis 24:29, "And Laban ran to the man outside at the spring." Swedenborg describes this as symbolizing the predisposition that goodness has toward truth; running symbolizes predisposition, and a man symbolizes truth, as does a spring, but Laban *represents* a desire for what is good. These distinctions apply only where Swedenborg is using the word *symbolize* in a technical sense. Often he uses it much more broadly. For more on these distinctions in inner meaning in relation to various modes of biblical discursion, see §66. For a very brief overview of the history of biblical interpretation as it relates to Swedenborg's views, see Smoley 2005, 27, and the references given there. [LHC, GHO]

18 (in §5). Swedenborg here, writing in late 1748 or early 1749, mentions that his consciousness of the spiritual world began "several years" ago and has continued in an

unbroken fashion. (He uses the same phrase, "several years," in similar contexts elsewhere in the present volume, in §§59:2, 67, 70, 150, 227, and 322:1, although in the last two of these instances he adds the nuance that his dual consciousness throughout that time has been "almost" continual.) Nevertheless, fixing a particular date to the shift is difficult, because Swedenborg gives somewhat conflicting evidence. In discussing it, he never gives a range of dates; he invariably assigns it either a single date or a fixed number of months or years before the time of writing. Yet the stated or implied date generally recedes the older he gets; that is, in the late 1740s, he places it in 1745; in the 1750s through 1766, he places it in 1744; and after 1766 he places it in 1743. See Tafel's recapitulation (Tafel 1877, 1118–1127). This receding date may have been the effect of simple forgetfulness, or it may have been the result of an evolving understanding of the significance of various turning points and changes in consciousness he experienced between 1743 and 1745. [JSR]

19 (in the text of Genesis 1:1). Swedenborg's translations of the Hebrew and Greek Scriptures into Latin were deliberately literal, and an attempt has been made in this translation to reflect this literal quality. For his translations in the current work, Swedenborg relied heavily on the Latin version of Scripture produced by Sebastian Schmidt (1617–1696), both in the independent Latin version (1696), and in the bilingual (Hebrew and Latin) van der Hooght–Schmidt version of 1740 (on Swedenborg's use of the latter, see Cole 1977, 33). Though he admired the Schmidt version for its faithfulness, he did also make alterations based on his reading of the Hebrew and Greek. Readers who compare his versions with standard English translations may therefore notice variations from those texts. As a general rule they have not been noted in this edition. For further discussion of the translation of biblical passages in this edition, see the translator's preface, pages 8–11. [LHC, SS]

20 (in the text of Genesis 1:2). The Hebrew word for "face" (פָּנִים *[pānîm]*) is plural, and Swedenborg very often renders it literally, with a Latin plural, as here *(faciebus)*. He speaks explicitly of the importance of grammatical number with respect to several other words (see, for example, §§30:2, 50:3, 253, 304, 374:3), but not this one. It has been rendered in the singular to accord with English usage. [LHC]

21 (in the text of Genesis 1:26). On the meaning of the shift here from the singular, "a human," to the plural, "these," see §478. [JSR]

22 (in §8). The "remnant" (also rendered "survivors") to which Swedenborg refers consisted of Israelites and Judeans who survived the conquest of Israel by Assyria in 721 B.C.E. and of Judah by Babylon in 581 B.C.E. He draws a symbolic connection between this biblical remnant and the traces of goodness and truth every individual acquires as a child, which disappear from consciousness during adulthood but remain stored away for use during the process of rebirth. Key passages on the remnant include §§468, 530, 560–563, 576, 1050, 1906, 2284, 5135:2–4, 5342, 5897. Section 468 quotes a number of biblical occurrences: Isaiah 4:3; 10:20–22; Jeremiah 50:20; Amos 5:3; Micah 5:7. [LHC]

23 (in §8). The Latin phrase here translated "bodily and worldly concerns—things that are our own" is *ea quae sunt corporis & mundi, ita quae sunt propria,* literally, "those things that are of the body and the world, thus which belong to the self." In Swedenborg's theology, the phrase the "things of the body," and other forms of reference to the body, evoke an entire meaning-complex that is difficult for modern readers to recover. Aspects of this meaning-complex include the physical, material body; a certain class of

psychological affects; and the physiological responses accompanying the latter. For instance, Swedenborg associates with the body not only a love for oneself, but a passion for dignities and honors, as well as the love of dominating over others. The primary reason for this association is that these drives are seen as having a secondary physical effect on the body according to a physiology stemming from ancient and Renaissance medical science. The modern reader should be aware, then, that "bodily concerns" may include such drives as ambition and pride, and are often, though not exclusively, connected with self-love. Love of oneself is generally cast in a negative light by Swedenborg, though it is approved as a practical necessity to enable one to better love and care for others (see *Secrets of Heaven* 6933–6938; *True Christianity* 405:1, and *True Christianity* 403–405 generally). By way of indicating the difficulties of this topic, it can be observed that though a love of wealth is traditionally considered selfish, in Swedenborg's system it is considered not "bodily" but "worldly." See also the translator's preface, pages 6–7, and the reader's guide, pages 57–58. [SS]

24 (in §13). Swedenborg describes the seventh stage in the next chapter, which tells what happened on the seventh day of creation. See §§74, 84–88. [LHC]

25 (in §14). See John 20:2, 13, 15, 18, 20, 25, 28; 21:7, 12, 15, 16, 17, 20; Mark 16:19, 20, which Swedenborg identifies in §2921:6 as passages in which Jesus' disciples call him "Lord" after his resurrection. See also Luke 24:3, 34; John 21:21; Acts 1:6; 2:36; 7:59–60; 8:16; 1 Corinthians 4:5; 9:1, 5; Hebrews 7:14. [LHC, JLO]

26 (in §16). For references to "the days of old," see Deuteronomy 32:7; Psalms 44:1; 77:5; 143:5; Isaiah 23:7; 37:26; 51:9; 63:9, 11; Jeremiah 46:26; Lamentations 1:7; 2:17; 5:21; Amos 9:11; Micah 5:2; 7:14, 20; Malachi 3:4. [LHC]

27 (in §16). The Hebrew original of Genesis uses three distinct words for creation: בָּרָא *(bārā),* "create"; יָצַר *(yāṣar),* "form"; and עָשָׂה *('āśā),* "make." [RS]

28 (in §16). Following a Christian practice of his times, Swedenborg used "Jehovah" as a rendering of the tetragrammaton, יהוה, "YHVH" (or "YHWH"), the four-letter name of God in the Hebrew Scriptures. In earliest times, Hebrew was written only with consonants; a system for indicating vowels was not perfected until the eighth century of the Common Era, and even in most modern Hebrew texts, vowels are not marked. The current scholarly reconstruction of the original pronunciation of the name is "Yahweh": see *Theological Dictionary of the Old Testament,* under "YHWH." A strict understanding of the Second Commandment, "You are not to take the name of YHVH your God in vain" (Exodus 20:7), led pious Jews to avoid pronouncing the name aloud; instead the name אֲדֹנָי *(ădōnāi,* literally meaning "my lord") was read. To indicate this, vowels similar to those in *Adonai* were added to YHVH, creating the form *Jehovah.* At occurrences of the combination אֲדֹנָי יהוה *(ădōnāi yhvh),* "the Lord YHVH," the vowels for אֱלֹהִים *(ĕlōhîm),* or "God," are added to the four consonants instead, again in adapted form, to make יְהֹוִה *(yĕhôvih).* Swedenborg carefully represents this as "Jehovih." For a traditional Jewish view of this vocalization, see Gikatilla 1994, 148–149. "Yahweh" itself, יַהְוֶה *(yahweh),* may be grammatically an imperfect causative form of the verb הָיָה *(hāyā),* "to be," meaning "he who causes to be" or "he creates" (Cross 1973, 65). This identification is controversial, however. Swedenborg himself connects the name "Jehovah" with being: see *True Christianity* 19:1, where he says the name means "I am" (see Exodus 3:14, 15; 6:3). Some modern English Bibles use the name "Jehovah,"

while others render the term as "Lᴏᴏʀᴅ," so capitalized; "Lord," in capital and lowercase; "Yahweh"; "Aᴅᴏɴᴀɪ"; or even "God." [GFD, RS]

29 (in §16). As was the custom in his day, Swedenborg refers to Psalms as a book of David. [LHC]

30 (in §16). "Jah" is a shortening of the name Jehovah. Jewish esoteric thought ascribed the different names of God to different aspects of the divine. "Jah" or "Yah" (Hebrew יָהּ *[yāh]*) was associated with divine wisdom and mercy (Gikatilla 1994, 4–5, 325). [RS, LHC]

31 (in §16). The Latin word here translated "they will continue to be created" is *creabuntur*, a simple future form. Its subject is the world of living things, which are dependent on God for their existence. The original Hebrew has an imperfect verb form here, indicating an action that is continuous or not yet completed. Many English versions of the Bible render this word "they are created." [RS]

32 (in §17). Swedenborg seems to have in mind Christ's parable of the sower and the seed, in which individuals are likened to ground on which the "seed" of the word is sown (Mark 4:3–20). See §29:2. [RS]

33 (in §18). Here, in a transference of perspective common in his works, Swedenborg describes a spiritual viewpoint in terms of the geography of the spiritual world. "To see from heaven" is in his theology to see people, intellectual movements, or philosophical abstractions in the "higher" light that prevails in heaven, even if those entities themselves are "lower down" in the spiritual, or even in the physical, world. (Aspects of the mind that are more spiritual can be described as both "higher" and "more inward," and less spiritual aspects as "lower" and "more outward." See also Swedenborg [1771] 2006, 739 note 455.) The nature of heaven's light, as Swedenborg explains it, is that it reveals the true underlying nature of the thing or person seen, but shows it as a pictorial or animated graphic (*Secrets of Heaven* 4674:2–3; *Heaven and Hell* 131; his 1768 work *Marriage Love* 269:3; *True Christianity* 281:12, 462:11). This light does not always flow down into spiritual areas below heaven, but when it does, it radically changes the appearance of things there (*Heaven and Hell* 553; *True Christianity* 187:2). Swedenborg reports seeing people's inner natures represented in the light of heaven as people (*Secrets of Heaven* 6626; *Revelation Unveiled* 341:2); animals (see Swedenborg's posthumously published theological work *Revelation Explained* [= Swedenborg 1994–1997] §1005:3); birds (*True Christianity* 42, 334:8); monstrous, mythological, or biblical creatures (see the 1763 work *Divine Love and Wisdom* 254; *Marriage Love* 521:1; *True Christianity* 388:1, 389:7); or lifeless objects (see the 1763 work *Divine Providence* 226; *True Christianity* 31:4, 110:8, 113:4). For similar visions of the inner soul of certain individuals as dark or inanimate masses, see Swedenborg's posthumously published *Spiritual Experiences* (= Swedenborg 1998–2002) §§1271, 3215, 4060. For related phenomena, see notes 64, 139. [JSR, SS]

34 (in §18). The spiritual "devastation" to which Swedenborg alludes here is common in religious literature. A classic account of it is given by the psychologist and philosopher William James (1842–1910), who speaks of the progress from a "sick soul" to a "divided self" and finally to regeneration, or spiritual rebirth—which is often the result of a conversion experience (see James 1910, 136–188). One term frequently applied to this "devastation" is the "dark night of the soul," from the poem of the same name by the sixteenth-century Spanish mystic John of the Cross (1542–1591; see John of the

Cross 1990). Swedenborg endured a similar crisis in the years 1743–1745, which marked his transformation from scientific investigator to spiritual visionary. Swedenborg's *Journal of Dreams,* a record he kept during the months March–October 1744, gives a vivid account of his internal upheavals during this period; see Swedenborg 2001b. [RS]

35 (in §18). For prophetic depictions of spiritual devastation, see the following passages, which are quoted among others on this topic in §5376: Isaiah 6:9–13; 13:6; 16:4; 33:8, 9; 42:14, 15; 49:17–19; 51:17–23; Ezekiel 36:3–12; Zephaniah 1:14–18. [LHC]

36 (in §18). Compare Ephesians 4:22–24; Colossians 3:9–10. [LHC, JLO]

37 (in §19). For Bible passages mentioning "the remnant," which is sometimes also rendered "survivors," see note 22. [LHC]

38 (in §20). On Swedenborg's concepts of self-love and the love of worldly advantages, see note 23. [SS]

39 (in §21). For comparisons between day and night in the Bible (implicit and explicit), see the passages quoted in §22, as well as the following passages, which are quoted in §2353: Micah 3:5, 6; Luke 17:34; John 9:4; 11:9, 10. [LHC]

40 (in §22). "Up till [the day's second] evening" means "when the night becomes morning." In addition to the usual meaning as the time when day turns into night, Swedenborg considered the word "evening" in Old Testament idiom to apply as well to the twilight before dawn. Compare *Secrets of Heaven* 883, "Evening meant the half-light before morning," and a similar statement in §2323:1. Compare also *Secrets of Heaven* 7844, 10135:5, where Swedenborg discusses the Mosaic phrase "between the evenings" (Exodus 12:6; 16:12; 29:39, 41; 30:8; Leviticus 23:5; Numbers 9:3, 5, 11; 28:4, 8) and defines it as meaning "overnight," that is, during the period between twilight at the end of one day and twilight at the beginning of the next. [LHC]

41 (in §23). The phrase "its days" here refers literally to the final days of Babylon. [LHC]

42 (in §23). Swedenborg here introduces two quotes by saying that they came from "the same prophet," namely, Jeremiah, yet one of them is from Jeremiah and the other from Lamentations. This is because Swedenborg, like others in his day, saw Lamentations as a book by Jeremiah. [LHC]

43 (in §25). The Latin word represented here by "spreading out" *(expandere)* and the one represented by "expanse" in the preceding verse *(expansum)* are forms of the same word. In other words, the "expanse" is what is "spread out." [LHC]

44 (in §25). This bracketed interpolation is Swedenborg's. [LHC]

45 (in §25). Though Isaiah 42:4 is cited, it is not in fact represented in the quotation. Swedenborg frequently gives the numbers of such extra verses in the context of the material he actually quotes; they constitute a kind of "see also" reference. In general, such citation anomalies are not noted further in the annotations to this work. See the discussion of Swedenborg's quotation practices in the translator's preface, pages 8–11. [JSR, SS]

46 (in §25). In §9596:4, 6 Swedenborg quotes the following verses, which speak of stretching out the heavens: Psalms 104:2; Isaiah 40:22; 45:12; 51:15; 54:2; Zechariah 12:1. [LHC]

47 (in §28). The "House" means the Temple in Jerusalem, here and in later quotations in §§109, 308:2, 576:3, 680:5; and in Swedenborg's general reference in §710. [JSR]

48 (in §28). The "eastern" sea here, from the perspective of Jerusalem, refers to the Dead Sea, and the "western" sea refers to the Mediterranean. [JSR]

49 (in §30:2). Here Swedenborg begins to set out one of the central themes of his work: the dynamic between goodness and truth. Goodness is associated with love and the will; truth is associated with faith and the intellect. Swedenborg's entire system is based on the relationship between these two forces, which, as he notes here, entails the superiority of goodness (here, as love) over truth (here, as faith). He furthermore associates these two forces, goodness and truth, with the "heavenly" and the "spiritual" respectively, the former being more inward and closer to the Lord than the latter. In *Heaven and Hell* 20–27, Swedenborg describes heaven itself as being divided into separate kingdoms based upon the angels' capacity to resonate with the Lord. Those who resonate with him on the basis of goodness, through love, are in a higher heaven, and are called "heavenly," while those who resonate with him on the basis of truth—that is, through the intellect—are called "spiritual." It would be hard to overstate the importance of this dynamic in Swedenborg's thought. Much of *Secrets of Heaven,* as well as of his other writings, is devoted to expanding on it. For further discussion, a diagram of this dynamic, and illustrative passages, see the reader's guide, pages 45–46. [RS]

50 (in §30:2). In both the original Hebrew and Swedenborg's Latin version, Genesis 1:14 combines a plural subject with a singular verb. (The Hebrew is יְהִי מְאֹרֹת *[yəhî məʾōrōt]*; the Latin is *sit luminaria*.) The disagreement in number cannot easily be represented in English. [LHC]

51 (in §30:3). Swedenborg characterizes the mind as being possessed of two basic faculties: the *will* (Latin *voluntas,* elsewhere in this edition rendered "volition" or "intention") and the *intellect* (Latin *intellectus,* also translated "understanding" and "discernment"); see §35. In Swedenborg's use, *intellect* has a somewhat broader connotation than it has today, one more consonant with its use in the system of the medieval Christian philosophers who were known as the Scholastics. For example, in the philosophy of the major figure of Scholastic thought, Thomas Aquinas (1224 or 1225–1274), which underlies the terminology of much of philosophical language up to and including Swedenborg's time, *intellect* encompasses all of what we associate with the faculties of mind, not only the capacity to reason and understand, but the capacity to perceive ideas in the abstract, as well as the ability to be aware of itself (Shallo 1923, 115–116). The complementarity of will and intellect is also something Swedenborg shares with Scholastic thought. Aquinas, for example, observes, "We can easily understand why these powers include one another in their acts, because the intellect understands that the will wills, and the will wills the intellect to understand. In the same way, the good is contained under the true, inasmuch as it is an understood truth, and the true under the good, inasmuch as it is a desired good" (*Summa Theologiae* 82:4; translation in Pegis 1948, 366–367). Note again the complementarity of the "true" and the "good." [RS]

52 (in §31:1). The Latin word here *(terra)* and the Hebrew word for which it stands (אֶרֶץ *[ʾereṣ]*) mean both "land" and "earth." Swedenborg emphasizes it as he does many other instances of words for earth and sky in §§25, 28, 29, 30. [LHC]

53 (in §31:1). "Orions" seems to mean simply constellations. Swedenborg used the Latin word *oriones* here, which is the hypothetical plural of *Orion,* the mythological hunter for whom one of the constellations is named. The Hebrew word, as the third Latin edition points out, is the plural of כְּסִיל *(kəsîl),* which is the name for the same constellation. [LHC]

54 (in §31:3). On the meaning of "church" here, see note 16. [LHC]

55 (in §32:1). "The close of the age" (*consummatio saeculi,* in the Latin) is a scriptural term referring to a time of final judgment on the world. The concept pervades Daniel, Revelation, and parts of Matthew; see Matthew 13:39, 40 for a specific example of the term. In Swedenborg's system the Last Judgment does not refer to the end of the earth as we know it; rather to a purgation of the spiritual world that makes it possible for a "new church" to be established on earth. It also marks the commencement of an era when spiritual truths that were formerly hidden are to become accessible to human minds. Swedenborg regarded his own works as a crucial component of this new revelation. In his 1758 book *Last Judgment,* he states that this event took place in the spiritual world in 1757, the year after the last volume of *Secrets of Heaven* was published. For more on the Last Judgment, see note 529. [LHC, RS]

56 (in §32:2). These are angels of the heavenly kingdom rather than the spiritual kingdom; see note 49. [LHC]

57 (in §34:1). On this treatment of "lights" as a singular, see §30:2 and note 50. [LHC]

58 (in §36). "The Law and the Prophets" refer to two main sections of the Hebrew Scriptures: the Law or Torah, comprising the five books of Moses: Genesis, Exodus, Leviticus, Numbers, and Deuteronomy; and the Prophets, including Isaiah, Jeremiah, Lamentations, Ezekiel, and the twelve minor prophets. Since Swedenborg here explains the phrase as referring to "the whole Word," he is apparently extending it as well to parts of a third section of the Hebrew Scriptures known as the "Writings," which includes poetic and philosophical works such as the Psalms, Proverbs, and Ecclesiastes; but see also notes 2 and 86. (Swedenborg included Daniel among the Prophets, but in the Hebrew Scriptures it is included in the Writings.) [RS]

59 (in §38). The following clauses depend grammatically on verse 17, quoted above at §30. For a discussion of the treatment of quotations in this text, see the translator's preface, pages 8–11, and also page 132 above. [LHC]

60 (in §39:1). The Latin phrase here translated "the Son of Humankind" is *Filius Hominis,* traditionally rendered "the Son of Man." Elsewhere in this edition it has sometimes been rendered "the Human-born One." The force of the phrase is literally "someone descended from the human race," "someone who was born human," and therefore "someone human" (see §49:3). It is difficult to estimate the original range of meaning of the term, however. In the Old Testament, the phrase almost always applies to a human being (as opposed to the Divine), and seems to encourage humility by emphasizing the person's mere humanness. In the New Testament it in most cases arguably denotes Jesus Christ, as Swedenborg clearly takes it to mean in the passage at hand; but scholars differ widely on whether it carries (1) the same humble force there as it does in the Old Testament, (2) a virtually opposite exalted and apocalyptic meaning, (3) some combination of the two, or (4) something else altogether. See Borsch 1967. [JSR]

61 (in §40:1). Here and elsewhere in this translation, where the word "man" appears it almost always reflects a Latin word *(vir)* that in its most common usages refers specifically to a male person. When Swedenborg uses this word in quotations from the Old Testament, it is usually a translation of one of two Hebrew words that again refer specifically to a male person (אִישׁ *['îš]* and גֶּבֶר *[geber]*). In New Testament quotations it is usually a translation of the Greek word ἀνήρ *(anér),* which is likewise gender-specific. In

addition to these words, the Latin, Hebrew, and Greek languages also have words that connote a human being without specifying his or her gender (in Latin, the word *homo;* in Hebrew, the words אָדָם *[ādām]* and אֱנוֹשׁ *[ĕnôš];* in Greek, the word ἄνθρωπος *[ánthropos]*). In §§476 and 915 Swedenborg ascribes significance to the distinction between these gender-specific and gender-inclusive terms, so the distinction has been preserved in this translation. [LHC]

62 (in §40:2). Swedenborg is referring to Ezekiel's prophecy of the restoration of the Temple in Jerusalem after the destruction of the first Temple by the Babylonians in 586 B.C.E. The vision of the new temple is described at length in Ezekiel 40–41. [RS]

63 (in §40:2). Swedenborg probably has in mind Christ's well-known invitation to the disciples, "Follow me and I will make you fishers of men" (Matthew 4:19; Mark 1:17). Compare his statement from one of the last books of his theological period, the 1769 work *Soul-Body Interaction* 20, where he describes being asked what a spiritual fisher is: "I said that in the Word, a fisherman spiritually understood is someone who inquires into and teaches earthly truths and then does the same with spiritual truths, in a rational manner" (this and all other translations from *Soul-Body Interaction* in these notes are by George F. Dole). In support of this statement he then cites Ezekiel 47:9–20 as well as Matthew 4:19 and Mark 1:17. [SS, RS]

64 (in §41). Abstract qualities, according to Swedenborg, become visible as objects in the next life. See *Heaven and Hell* 173–176, where by way of illustration he mentions the appearance of beautiful tree groves and gardens in the vicinity of angels who are especially intelligent. See also §6200 of the present work, which describes a wavelike manifestation of thought. For related phenomena, see notes 33, 139. [LHC]

65 (in §42:1). Swedenborg is alluding to an issue which was much discussed in Scholastic philosophy, and which persisted down to his own day. The genus, or "general category" (in Swedenborg's Latin, *commune*), forms a kind of backdrop that enables the individual, or a particular item *(particulare),* to take existence. That is to say, a table cannot exist unless there is some category of tables as a whole that enables it to come into being (McCormick 1940, 51). [RS]

66 (in §45). On the meaning of the reference to those traits that arise out of the body, see note 23. The important point is that the cravings and appetites Swedenborg refers to here may include such nonphysical yearnings as a desire for honor, privilege, and power. [SS]

67 (in §46:3). In Swedenborg's day, it was the custom to refer to the Book of John, the Epistles of John, and the Book of Revelation simply as "John." Swedenborg commonly follows this practice. [JSR]

68 (in §46:3). The word translated "created beings" here is *creaturae,* from the verb *creare,* "create." The *-tura* ending referred originally to a process (here, the process of creation) but eventually to the product of the process (here, something created). This ending is a form of the future active participle, and Swedenborg seems to have its forward-looking quality in mind here, since he says "they are to be created anew." [LHC]

69 (in §47). On the concept of outer as opposed to inner in Swedenborg's theology, see notes 14 and 33. [JSR]

70 (in §49:1). One significant later passage discussing the people of the earliest church is §§1114–1129. [LHC]

71 (in §49:2). On the term "son of humankind," see note 60. [JSR]

72 (in §49:2). On the stars and other heavenly bodies as an "army," see note 92. [LHC]

73 (in §49:4). Aside from the passages in Matthew that Swedenborg cites just below in the text, passages in which Christ refers to himself as the Son of Humankind include Matthew 8:20; 9:6; 10:23; 11:19; 12:8, 32, 40; 13:37, 41; 16:13, 27, 28; 17:9, 12, 22; 18:11; 19:28; 20:18, 28; 24:37, 39, 44; 25:13, 31; 26:2, 24, 45, 64; Mark 2:10, 28; 8:38; 9:12, 31; 10:33, 45; 13:26; 14:21, 41, 62; Luke 5:24; 6:5, 22; 7:34; 9:22, 26, 44, 56, 58; 11:30; 12:8, 10, 40; 17:22, 24, 26, 30; 18:8, 31; 19:10; 21:27, 36; 22:22, 48, 69; John 1:51; 3:13, 14; 5:27; 6:27, 53, 62; 8:28; 12:23; 13:31. [SS]

74 (in §50:1). On the world of spirits, see note 3. [LHC]

75 (in §51). Other scholars see the actual meaning of the Hebrew words for "image" and "likeness" as differing slightly from Swedenborg's interpretation here. צֶלֶם (*selem*, "image") "means predominantly an actual plastic word, a duplicate, sometimes an idol (1 Samuel 6:5; Numbers 33:52; 2 Kings 11:18); a painting (Ezekiel 23:14).... [However,] דְמוּת (*dəmût*, 'likeness') is a verbal abstraction and means predominantly something abstract: 'appearance,' 'similarity,' 'analogy' (Ezekiel 1:5, 10, 26, 28), but also 'the copy' (2 Kings 16:10)" (Rad 1972, 57–58). [RS]

76 (in §51). The noun in the phrase here translated "from blood" is actually plural in the Latin, which is *ex sanguinibus*—literally, "from bloods"; these words are in turn a literal translation of the Greek, which is also plural: ἐξ αἱμάτων (*ex haimáton*). It should be noted that Swedenborg assigns significance to the plural form of the word in §374, where he deals with Genesis 4:10, in which Jehovah tells Cain, "The voice of your brother's blood is crying out." The word for blood there is plural in the original Hebrew (דָּמִים [*dāmîm*]). Swedenborg describes blood in general as meaning hatred and the plural form in Genesis 4:10 as symbolizing violence; and indeed Brown, Driver, and Briggs 1996 say that the Hebrew plural is sometimes associated with "rude violence." Swedenborg goes on to imply that the reason the plural means violence is that "everything wicked and abhorrent wells up out of hatred, just as everything good and holy wells up out of love." Furthermore, Swedenborg saw human blood as a compound of three "bloods" (see note 463), so even aside from the symbolic value of the plural, it would have been natural for him to use this plural in his rendering of this biblical passage. [LHC, RS, SS]

77 (in §54). Swedenborg later wrote a work on marriage—his 1768 work *Marriage Love*. In it he defines chastity not as celibacy, but as sexual love within a monogamous marriage, because "it comes from the Lord and answers to the marriage of the Lord and the church" (*Marriage Love* 143; this and all other translations from *Marriage Love* in these notes are by George F. Dole). The work, in fact, begins with a description of a wedding in heaven (*Marriage Love* 19–22; compare *True Christianity* 746:4–749). [RS]

78 (in §54). Perhaps an example of a subject susceptible to comparison to marriage would be music. These earliest people, as Swedenborg describes them, might for instance have seen a marriage between the mechanics of a piece—melody, harmony, rhythm, and so on—and the feeling expressed in it. They might then have been pleased, in listening to it, not only by the form and content of the music itself but also by the way form and content combined in reflection of a marriage. [LHC]

79 (in §54). By "heavenly marriage" Swedenborg here means the "marriage" between goodness and truth or love and wisdom. See §§155, 162, 252. See also note 141. [LHC]

80 (in §54). In a time when a woman was identified primarily in terms of her marital status, the term represented here by "virgin" (*virgo* in Latin; בְּתוּלָה *[bətûlā]* in Hebrew; παρθένος *[parthénos]* in Greek) had as much to do with a woman's dependence on her father and eligibility for marriage as with her lack of sexual experience. Where possible, the word has been translated "young woman." [LHC]

81 (in §54). The relevant treatment of Genesis 2:24 (the first edition erroneously reads 2:23 here) is in §162; the relevant part of the discussion of Genesis 3:15 is in §253. For biblical references to the church as the Daughter and the Virgin, see note 175. [SS]

82 (in §57). For the meaning of crop-producing trees in Genesis 2, see §§102, 125. See also §199. [LHC]

83 (in §59:1). The allusion is to the traditional term "Church Militant" (that is, combating for Christ), referring to those members of the Christian church alive on earth, as contrasted to the "Church Triumphant," referring to the souls in heaven. (See *New Catholic Encyclopedia* 2003, under "church.") [RS]

84 (in §59:2). The vexation of the regenerating soul by evil spirits is a common theme in Christian literature. The most famous instance is that of the third-century ascetic St. Anthony of the Desert (around 250–around 350 C.E.), as recounted in the *Life of St. Anthony* by the church father Athanasius (about 295–373 C.E.). At one point we are told, "Coming one night with a multitude of demons, [the Devil] so cut him with stripes that he lay on the ground speechless from the excessive pain. For he affirmed that the torture had been so excessive that no blows inflicted by man could ever have caused him such torment" (Athanasius 1927, 198). [RS]

85 (in §59:2). Details concerning the struggles involved in regeneration are scattered throughout the work, and in particular throughout the treatments of Genesis 7 and 14–16; see, for example, §§751 and 1820. [LHC]

86 (in §64). By the narrative parts, Swedenborg means the five books of the Pentateuch (Genesis, Exodus, Leviticus, Numbers, Deuteronomy), as well as Joshua, Judges, the two books of Samuel, and the two books of Kings. By the prophetic parts he means Psalms and the major and minor prophets. See §66 and, for an even more detailed listing, §2606. [LHC]

87 (in §64). Abraham and the Abram just mentioned are the same man (see Genesis 17:5). When Swedenborg speaks in the previous sentence about the earliest church's successors, he is talking about various phases of the ancient church, represented by the descendants of Noah listed in Genesis 10 and 11; see §§1130, 1279–1282. Abram is a transitional figure, representing the final, effete stages of the ancient church and the beginning of its own successor, the "representative church," or Jewish religion; see §§1282, 1361, 1375. Because Abram is that figure's name at the point in his life when he represents the transition, Swedenborg so names him. The reason for the shift to the name Abraham immediately afterward, in a more general statement about angelic views on the man, is probably that this is the name by which he is more commonly known. [LHC, SS]

88 (in §66:1). Most biblical translators understand these words from 1 Samuel 2:3 differently. Swedenborg's translation is identical with that of Schmidt 1696. A literal translation of the Hebrew might be, "Do not multiply in speaking high, high, let go out a-forward-thing from your mouth" אַל־תַּרְבּוּ תְדַבְּרוּ גְּבֹהָה גְבֹהָה יֵצֵא עָתָק מִפִּיכֶם *('al-tarbû tədabbərû gəbōhā gəbōhā yēṣē 'ātāq mippîkem)*. Usually the negation is taken to

apply to all the verbs, the word for "high" is taken to mean haughty, and the word for "forward thing" is taken to mean arrogance. The New Revised Standard Version, for instance, reads: "Talk no more very proudly, let not arrogance come from your mouth." Schmidt and Swedenborg apparently understood the concept of forwardness to refer to being "forward" in years—that is, advanced in age. [LHC]

89 (in §66:1). As was the custom in his day, Swedenborg refers to the books of Genesis, Exodus, Leviticus, Numbers, and Deuteronomy simply as "Moses." [JSR]

90 (in §66:2). There is evidence that Swedenborg originally planned for *Secrets of Heaven* to cover more than Genesis and Exodus—perhaps even the whole Bible. In this volume alone, he anticipates offering an exposition of Leviticus (see §643:4) and Numbers (see §§296, 730:4). See the reader's guide, pages 24–25 note 14. [LHC]

Notes to Genesis Chapter 2, §§67–181

91 (in §68). Swedenborg lived in an age that was increasingly enamored of empirical observation and inductive reasoning from it. Thus he often (as here) backs up his claim to have experience of the spiritual world by asserting that it rests on the evidence of the senses—in this case the internal senses, which were opened up in him as a result of divine mercy, as he says in §67 above. Swedenborg often emphasizes that sensory perception is a comparatively low form of cognition compared to the internal senses; see §§102–104, 127. [GFD, SS, RS]

92 (in the text of Genesis 2:1). The word in Latin here translated "army" is *exercitus,* a rendition of the Hebrew צָבָא (*sābā*), whose plural, צְבָאוֹת (*sǝbā'ôt*), is sometimes translated as "hosts." The idea is that the angels and stars constitute the "armies" of the Lord (Brown, Driver, and Briggs 1996, under צָבָא). See also note 122. [RS]

93 (in the text of Genesis 2:7). The unusual plurals in the phrase "breath of lives" here and "tree of lives" below in verse 9 are retained because they represent plurals in Swedenborg's Latin versions of these phrases, which are literal translations of the Hebrew. Swedenborg explains elsewhere that two lives are meant: the life of love and the life of faith (§304; see also §3623). On other unusual plurals in Swedenborg's Latin, see notes 20, 76 above. [LHC, GFD]

94 (in the text of Genesis 2:12). Swedenborg here transliterates the Hebrew word שֹׁהַם (*šōham*). The identification of the stone is uncertain. [LHC]

95 (in the text of Genesis 2:13). Some scholars agree with Swedenborg in identifying this Cush (or Kush) with Ethiopia (see §117), but the more literal-minded point out that Ethiopia is not circled by a river and lies far from the other rivers mentioned in this passage. There are other candidates, but the exact identification will probably remain uncertain. Whatever the quibbles of scholars, this Cush is subsumed into the symbolic complex that Swedenborg identifies with Ethiopia (see, for example, §1163). [SS]

96 (in the text of Genesis 2:14). The Hiddekel is the Tigris. [LHC]

97 (in the text of Genesis 2:14). The Phrath is the Euphrates. [LHC]

98 (in §81:3). The Latin word here translated "conscience" is *conscientia,* a word that encompasses the concepts of both conscience and consciousness (Chadwick and Rose 2008, under *conscientia;* see also §608). [RS]

99 (in §82). There are a great many Scripture passages quoted in the previous chapter (from somewhere other than Genesis 1) that mention "heaven" or "earth": see §§17,

22–25, 28–29, 31, 34, 37, 40, 46, 49–50, 52, 55, 58. In that chapter Swedenborg explicitly draws the connection between "heaven" and the inner being in §24:3, and between "earth" and the outer being in §27. [JSR]

100 (in §82). On the terms "man" and "human being" here, see note 61. [LHC]

101 (in §85:1). For more on the association of the Lord's kingdom with the Sabbath, see §8495 and the passages quoted there, including Isaiah 56:7; Jeremiah 17:24, 25; Ezekiel 20:12. For its association with peace, see §3780 and the passages quoted there, including Isaiah 9:6, 7; 32:17, 18; 52:7; 54:10; Jeremiah 16:5; Haggai 2:9; John 14:27. [LHC, JSR]

102 (in §88). For the three Hebrew words for creation that are referred to here, see note 27. [RS]

103 (in §88). Passages in which the Lord is called Creator, Fashioner, or Maker include Isaiah 17:7; 22:11; 40:28; 42:5; 43:1, 15; 44:2, 24; 49:5; 54:5. [LHC]

104 (in §93). "The most beautiful of ornaments" (עֲדִי עֲדָיִים [*ʿădî ʿădāyîm*]) may refer to menarche, the onset of menstruation; the text is usually emended to read עֵת עִדִּים (*ʿēt ʿiddîm*), "the time of periods." [LHC]

105 (in §96). On Jehovah's smelling a restful smell, see the passages cited in §925:1. [LHC]

106 (in §96). The Latin word here translated "breath [or spirit]" is *spiritus,* a single word that means both breath and spirit, as does the Hebrew word in Lamentations (רוּחַ [*rûaḥ*]). The bracketed material is inserted here because English lacks a word that simultaneously implies both. See also note 108. [LHC]

107 (in §97). Swedenborg himself experienced changes in respiration that he associated with altered states of consciousness. He remarks that even as a child he had been accustomed to exercise what he called "inner respiration" while praying (*Spiritual Experiences* [= Swedenborg 1998–2002] §§3320, 3464). When as a mature man he wrote in a state of inspiration, he found his breath would almost stop (*Spiritual Experiences* [= Swedenborg 1998–2002] §3320). [RS]

108 (in §97). The parenthetical interpolations of the word "wind" here and in the quotation from Psalms 33:6 below are Swedenborg's. [LHC]

109 (in §97). Shaddai (שַׁדַּי [*šaddai*]) is a name for God, already archaic by the time the Hebrew Scriptures were written. The etymology and meaning are unknown, but it is often translated as "Almighty." Recent scholarship suggests that it comes from a Semitic root meaning "mountain"; thus Shaddai may mean "the mountain [god]" (Cross 1973, 52–55). Swedenborg discusses the name at length in §1992. [LHC, RS]

110 (in §100). Here Swedenborg explicitly describes a feature of his biblical exegesis that will frequently recur: the interpretation of the elements of sense pairs in Hebrew poetry (here, for example, wilderness and desert, joy and gladness, acclamation and the voice of song) as relating to the heavenly (or good) and the spiritual (or true), respectively. For the fullest exposition of this method of interpretation, see *Sacred Scripture* 81, 84–88 (repeated with variations in *True Christianity* 248, 250–253); see also *Secrets of Heaven* 793, 5502. The currently accepted analysis of these word pairs as a component of the poetical conventions of Hebrew verse entered Christian scholars' discussion of the Bible during Swedenborg's lifetime. See Hrushovski-Harshav 2007, 598–600, for further discussion. [SS, JSR, LHC]

111 (in §101). Compare Swedenborg's description of orientation in heaven: "They call 'east' where the Lord is seen as the sun." Consequently, the angels in heaven face east no

matter in which direction they turn—a fact that Swedenborg acknowledges to be somewhat difficult for humans to understand (*Heaven and Hell* 141–143). [RS]

112 (in §103). The phrase "when spiritual people are the topic" appears to be a reference back to §§56–57. [LHC]

113 (in §108). The Hebrew word translated as "tents" here (*tentoria* in the Latin) actually means "sandalwoods" (which in Latin would be *santalos,* as Swedenborg renders it elsewhere). The context of the quotation—"How good are your tents, Jacob; your dwellings, Israel! They are planted as valleys are, as gardens beside the river. Like sandalwoods has Jehovah planted them"—suggests that the Latin translation is mistaken and that the tents are actually the item being compared here rather than the item to which something else is compared. The cause of the misreading, as the third Latin edition points out, is probably that the Hebrew words for these two objects are nearly identical: אֲהָלִים (*'ăhālîm*) means "sandalwoods," and אֹהָלִים (*'ōhālîm*) means "tents." [LHC]

114 (in §113). It is possible that "Temple" (*templo*) here is an error for "tabernacle" (*tabernaculo*), because the other items listed, and especially Aaron's garments, are more closely associated with the tabernacle than with Solomon's temple. But see note 115 as well. By the tabernacle here Swedenborg would mean specifically the main tent, or "dwelling place." For the use of gold in the tabernacle, its furniture, and Aaron's garments, see Exodus 25, 26, 28, 30. For its use in Solomon's temple, see 1 Kings 6, 7; 1 Chronicles 28, 29; 2 Chronicles 3, 4. [LHC]

115 (in §113). The translation here is based on reading *Tabernaculo* (tabernacle) for *Arca* (ark), as suggested in the third Latin edition. See Exodus 26, 27 for the use of silver in the tabernacle. See 1 Chronicles 28, 29 for its use in the Temple. It is worth noting, however, that in §296 Swedenborg treats the ark as standing for the structure in which it was housed; the discussion of the ark there starts off with a description of the coverings for the dwelling place and proceeds through all the other furniture and the utensils. This may also explain the difficulty discussed in note 114 just above. A similar problem occurs in §2784. [LHC]

116 (in §114). These verses are addressed to the king of Tyre as the object of Ezekiel's prophecy. Tyre was a Phoenician trading city on the coast of the Mediterranean Sea in what is now southern Lebanon; the king was in Eden only in the metaphorical sense of being in Paradise. [LHC, SS]

117 (in §114). Swedenborg here transliterates the Hebrew word "tarshish" (תַּרְשִׁישׁ [*taršîš*]). Brown, Driver, and Briggs 1996 define it as "a precious stone, perhaps yellow jasper, or other gold-coloured stone." [LHC]

118 (in §117:1). Swedenborg means here that the areas known in biblical times as Cush (by which he apparently means Ethiopia; see note 95) and Sheba have the same *spiritual* meaning, as the passage goes on to demonstrate. Physically, the two areas were separated by the Red Sea. Cush was in eastern Africa, south of Egypt; Sheba was in the southwestern corner of the Arabian peninsula. The people for whom these two areas were named were related to each other: Sheba was the grandson of Cush (Genesis 10:7; 1 Chronicles 1:9). [JSR, LHC]

119 (in §117:2). "Tarshish" (Hebrew תַּרְשִׁישׁ [*taršîš*]) here does not refer to a precious stone (as it does in §114 above; see note 117), but to a distant country whose exact location is unknown (see also Jonah 1:3). Most authorities place it in Spain (Brown, Driver, and Briggs 1996, under II תַּרְשִׁישׁ). [RS]

120 (in §117:2). See Swedenborg's explanations of various verses from Psalm 72 in §§113, 337:2, 795:2, 1171:1, 4735:8, 6435:7, 9209:5, 10438:3. [LHC]

121 (in §117:2). On what is meant by "the narrative portions" and "the prophets" in Scripture, see note 86. [LHC]

122 (in §119). *Sabaoth* is a Hebrew term (צְבָאוֹת *[ṣəḇāʾôṯ]*) meaning "legions." *Jehovah Sabaoth* means "Jehovah of the Legions," the legions being the "heavenly host"—either the angels or, when viewed on a more concrete level, the sun, moon, and stars. See also note 92 on Genesis 2:1. [LHC, RS]

123 (in §120). This bracketed gloss, and the other two in subsequent quotations in this section, are Swedenborg's. [LHC]

124 (in §120). Swedenborg views the land of Canaan as extending farther than is generally thought. He saw it as stretching to the Euphrates River—presumably on the north rather than the east, since he describes the borders of Canaan as being the Mediterranean, the Nile, the Jordan, and the Euphrates (see, for example, §5196). His reason, as he says at the end of §4454, is that these were considered the borders of Canaan in scriptural times, by the evidence of Genesis 15:18. According to 2 Samuel 8:3–6, David did take land in the area of the Euphrates and place garrisons in Syria. [LHC]

125 (in §124). The pronoun "he" here refers to "the spirit of truth." [SS]

126 (in §128). See Matthew 19:24; Mark 10:25; and Luke 18:25. Swedenborg's Latin reproduces the Greek original. Although Swedenborg does explain the inner meaning of the word "camel" here (see *Heaven and Hell* 365:3), this word in the Greek may be a misunderstanding of the Aramaic, the language in which Jesus spoke. In that tongue, *gamla*, "camel," is a homonym of *gamla*, "rope." What Jesus might have originally said was "It is easier for a *rope* to go through the eye of a needle . . ." (Lamsa 1933, xiv). There are other explanations of the phrase as well. [RS, LHC]

127 (in §130). Since Swedenborg is describing a pseudo-wisdom that sees west as east, so to speak, he reverses the order of the rivers mentioned in Genesis 2:11–14. The fourth, the Phrath or Euphrates, becomes the first; the third, in Assyria, becomes the second; the second, in Cush, becomes the third; and the first becomes the last. [LHC, JSR]

128 (in §130). For a reference to such false wisdom as magic, see, for example, Isaiah 47:8–15. [LHC]

129 (in §130). The origin of "Jehovih" as an alternate spelling of "Jehovah" is explained in note 28. [LHC]

130 (in §130). For a discussion of the inner meaning of the Hebrew term used here, אֶרֶץ תַּחְתִּי (*ʾereṣ taḥtî*), "underground realm," see note 169 below. [JSR]

131 (in the text of Genesis 2:18). The Latin phrase here translated "an aid that seems to be his," *tanquam apud illum*, has numerous possible meanings. This English rendering is based on Swedenborg's clarification in §140. [LHC]

132 (in the text of Genesis 2:23). The point of the elliptical expression "This time, bone from my bones and flesh from my flesh" is that in this current act of creation, God has created bone from Adam's bones and flesh from his flesh, as opposed to what Adam was offered as companions before—that is, the animals, who were not from his bone and flesh. The derivation of the word "wife" described in the rest of the verse depends upon the Hebrew, in which the word for man (or husband) is אִישׁ (*ʾîš*), while that for wife (or woman) is אִשָּׁה (*ʾiššā*), so that the word for the latter seems to be "taken from" the former. Many English versions of the Bible express the wordplay by rendering the

verse thus: "She shall be called woman, because she was taken out of man" (Genesis 2:23). [RS, LHC]

133 (in §141). In this passage the words "self-rule," "self-governance," "autonomy," "sense of autonomy," "autonomy or selfhood," and "selfhood" are used to translate the Latin *proprium,* literally meaning that which is proper to oneself. The term has an equivocal meaning in Swedenborg, as this passage suggests. Sometimes it simply means "self" in a neutral sense; sometimes it is equated with the evils arising from desire and selfishness (see, for example, Swedenborg's 1763 work *The Lord* 17); and at other times, as at the end of this passage, it is said to be a source of heavenly peace and happiness. In essence Swedenborg holds that, as all good comes from the Lord, all evil comes from self-will. Consequently, regeneration radically changes one's sense of self. The idea goes back to Christ himself: "Those who find their soul shall lose it, and those who lose their soul for my sake shall find it" (Matthew 10:39). Similarly in Galatians 2:20: "I am crucified with Christ. Nevertheless I do live; yet not I, but Christ lives in me." [RS]

134 (in §144). The identity of a thing with its name was a central feature of ancient Semitic thought. In Hebrew, for instance, the word דָּבָר *(dābār)* can mean both "word" and "thing" (Brown, Driver, and Briggs 1996, under דָּבָר). The Babylonians as well saw the two as interwoven: "For the Babylonians, a thing does not exist unless it has a name; unless it has one, it is not known; it does not exist" (Contenau 1947, 127). [RS]

135 (in §144). Elsewhere in *Secrets of Heaven* Swedenborg discusses both the literal and the inner meanings of the names of Jacob's twelve sons: Reuben (§§3861–3863), Simeon (§§3869–3872), Levi (§§3873–3877), Judah (§§3880–3881), Dan (§§3920–3923), Naphtali (§§3927–3928), Gad (§§3934–3935), Asher (§§3938–3939), Issachar (§§3956–3957), Zebulun (§§3960–3961), Joseph (§3969), and Benjamin (§§4591–4592). [JSR]

136 (in §148). Swedenborg discusses the correspondence of bone in §§5560–5563, and the first part of that passage, §§5560–5561, may have been the kind of treatment he had in mind in promising to talk about the *reason* for the symbolism. But see also §155 just below. [LHC]

137 (in §149:2). Passover is a celebration of Israelite deliverance from Egypt as described in Exodus 12. It included the sacrifice of an unblemished lamb. [LHC]

138 (in §153). On the word *virgin,* see note 80. [LHC]

139 (in §154). Here Swedenborg alludes to a striking feature of the spiritual world: the characteristics, moods, and thoughts of individuals may be represented around them in any of a vast variety of displays (see also notes 33, 64). For example, a hypocrite is said to create a display like a snake shedding its skin (*Spiritual Experiences* [= Swedenborg 1998–2002] §4351), and those who think obscene things actually project obscene displays around them (*Spiritual Experiences* [= Swedenborg 1998–2002] §1695). The displays emanating from good people, however, may be extremely beautiful (*Spiritual Experiences* [= Swedenborg 1998–2002] §2350). Spirits are said to actually use such projections as adjuncts to their speech (*Secrets of Heaven* 1641:2) or as complete substitutes for it (§1764); and as tools to educate children in the next world (§2299). [SS]

140 (in §154). Swedenborg here casually mentions "the Devil," which readers might take to mean one supreme "Satan," or "Lucifer," that is, an angel who was cast down and became the ruler of hell (a concept based on Isaiah 14:12; see also note 176), or else

a single evil force opposite God. Both conceptions were general among Christians in Swedenborg's times; but in fuller discussions elsewhere, Swedenborg asserts that they are false. In his usage, "the Devil" is a collective term for hell (see §251:2 of the present work; *Heaven and Hell* 311, 544; *Last Judgment* 14). His terminology for those who dwell in hell is flexible. He sometimes uses the term "evil spirits" to apply to all those in hell; but at other times he speaks of two classes of people in hell, one called "evil spirits," or "satans," and the other called "devils," or "demons." The distinction is outlined in *Divine Love and Wisdom* 273 and *Divine Providence* 310:3, and mentioned in *Heaven and Hell* 311:2 and *True Christianity* 281:12. Where Swedenborg makes the distinction, "evil spirits" are associated with false thoughts, love for the world, and justification of obsessions with evil, whereas "demons" are associated with demonic loves, love for oneself, and acting out obsessions with evil. In these cases he consistently describes "devils" or "demons" as more profoundly wicked than "evil spirits" or "satans." [JSR]

141 (in §155). The theme of the heavenly marriage occurs frequently in the Christian tradition. The source of this metaphor lies in the Old Testament, which portrayed Israel as the bride of the Lord: Hosea 1–3 depicts Israel as a faithless wife, and the Song of Songs was from an early time regarded as an allegory of love between God and Israel (Schmithals 1997, 166–167). In the New Testament, Revelation describes "the holy city, the new Jerusalem, coming down from God out of the sky, prepared as a bride dressed up for her husband" (Revelation 21:2). The "bride" is "the Lamb's wife" (Revelation 21:9; see §253). The union between Christ and the Church is thus portrayed as a heavenly marriage. In the Western esoteric tradition, this metaphor has a meaning closer to Swedenborg's, where the spiritual element is the Lord, and the physical "self" is the bride. See also note 79. [RS]

142 (in §156). For this derivation of the word "wife" from "man," see note 132. [RS]

143 (in §156). Although in Swedenborg's Latin the word "woman" (Latin *mulier*) is used in Genesis 2:22 and the word "wife" (Latin *uxor*) is used in verses 23 to 25, the same Hebrew word אִשָּׁה (*'iššā*) underlies them both. In making this change here from "woman" to "wife" Swedenborg follows a long-standing tradition in Latin translations of the Bible. [JSR]

144 (in §156). Presumably what was accomplished was the acquisition of autonomy. [LHC]

145 (in §165). This mention of angels in bright clothing seen by Old Testament prophets is probably a reference to the visions of otherworldly human beings wearing linen seen by Ezekiel (Ezekiel 9:2, 3, 11; 10:2, 6, 7) and Daniel (Daniel 10:5; 12:6, 7); compare *Revelation Explained* (= Swedenborg 1994–1997) §951:4. See also *Heaven and Hell* 180, 519. [JSR]

146 (in §167). Swedenborg says a little more about the three heavens in §§459, 684, 1642. Early in *Secrets of Heaven* he refers to them as the heaven of good spirits, the heaven of angelic spirits, and the heaven of angels (as late as §2026 he is referring to a heaven of angelic spirits as a separate thing from the heaven of angels), but later he tends simply to number them first, second, and third, and to describe the inhabitants of all of them, or at least of the second and third heavens, as angels. He devotes a chapter of his *Heaven and Hell* (§§29–40) to discussing this subject. The apostle Paul also speaks of a third heaven, in 2 Corinthians 12:2. [LHC]

147 (in §179). The Latin phrase here translated "interlinking passages of a labyrinth," *labyrintheis nexibus,* may be an allusion to the phrase *labyrintheis . . . flexibus,* "the labyrinthine windings," which occurs in an ancient Latin poem about the original labyrinth in Greco-Roman mythology (Catullus 64:114). Here Swedenborg seems also to be obliquely referring to a criticism raised by Deism, a philosophical outlook that during his lifetime could be defined roughly as a belief in God based on inborn knowledge, reason, and experience, without acceptance of revelation or traditional religion. The Deists mocked as impossible and absurd the idea that at the Last Judgment the physical bodies of the dead were to be reconstituted by God, no matter where their component parts had ended up over the millennia (see a sample of such a critique in Voltaire [1764] 1962, 452 [under "Resurrection," second section]). This common Christian doctrine, based on various passages of the Bible, including Revelation 20:23, was also rejected by Swedenborg (see, for example, *Secrets of Heaven* 5078:3); but in the present passage, he reserves to divine power the ability to reconstitute the nonphysical "living substances" of the dead, no matter what the circumstances of their final disposition at death. For more on the Last Judgment in Swedenborg's theology, see notes 55, 529. [JSR, SS]

Notes to Genesis Chapter 3, §§182–319

148 (in the text of Genesis 3:8). "Tree" here is usually taken as a collective noun for all the trees in the garden, among which the woman and her husband were walking, but Swedenborg sees significance in the singular form of the word, as he explains in §218. [LHC]

149 (in §194). In some Christian traditions, the Fall has been equated with enslavement to sensory perception. The Orthodox theologian Maximus the Confessor (580–662) observes, "If a man exercises only sensory discrimination between pain and pleasure in the body, thus transgressing the divine commandment, he eats from the tree of knowledge of good and evil, that is to say, he succumbs to the mindless impulses that pertain to the senses" (*Philokalia* 1979–1984, 2:149). Swedenborg's emphasis is slightly different from that of theologians like Maximus. He understands the Fall more in cognitive terms (that is, as a belief in the evidence of the senses), rather than in merely physical terms (as a surrender to the distractions of pleasure and pain). [RS]

150 (in §195:2). The Latin phrase here translated "of a sage who associates in societies," *sociantis sodalitia sapientis,* may aim to retain the hypnotic effect of both the alliteration and the obscurity of the Hebrew original: חוֹבֵר חֲבָרִים מְחֻכָּם (*ḥôbēr ḥăbārîm məḥukkām*). On the asp stopping its ear, see note 151. [LHC]

151 (in §195:2). The idea that snakes can be charmed and pacified by certain types of speech, song, or instrumental music dates back to ancient times. Snakes were said to make themselves resistant to being thus charmed by stopping up their ears. See, for example, the statement in a commentary of church father Augustine (354–430) on Psalms 57:5 in the Vulgate Latin Bible (Psalms 58:6 in English Bibles), the same passage Swedenborg addresses here. In Augustine's report of the attempts of one of the Marsi (the ancient magicians and snake-charmers of central Italy) to charm a snake out of its cave, he notes: "It is said that when the snake is unwilling to come out, it presses one ear to the ground and stops the other ear with its tail in order not to hear the words by which it feels itself being compelled" (Augustine *Enarrationes in Psalmos* 57.7; translation by JSR). On the general notion that some serpents are able to resist being charmed, see Jeremiah 8:17. [JSR, SS]

152 (in §196:2). Philosophers and scientists of the Enlightenment period were especially intrigued with the question of the difference between animals and humans. Some thinkers averred that animals did not have souls; others were just as confident that they did. Some saw the distinguishing feature of humanity as the possession of the reasoning soul (compare Swedenborg's view in *Heaven and Hell* 39), and others, like the putative speaker here, argued that if animals did not have souls, humans could not possess them either—since a human being is only a special form of animal. For a fuller discussion and refutation of this argument, see *Secrets of Heaven* 4760:2, 5114:5. For further resources and discussion of the general topic of the animal during the Enlightenment, see Swedenborg [1771] 2006, 688 note 67. [JSR, SS]

153 (in §196:3). Swedenborg is here reflecting on a philosophical debate that generated much controversy in his own day and continues down to the present: Does mind, or consciousness, precede physical existence, or is it an epiphenomenon, that is, a side-effect, of matter? The "sense-oriented people" here are those who give no credence to anything but sensory experience, believing that only the experience of the senses gives rise to consciousness. In his later work *Soul-Body Interaction* (published in 1769), Swedenborg characterizes this as the view of the disciples of Aristotle (384–322 B.C.E.)—that is, the adherents of Scholastic philosophy. The followers of Gottfried Wilhelm Leibniz (1646–1716) adhere to a notion of "preestablished harmony," where the soul and body operate in parallel without any physical interaction. These could be the philosophers Swedenborg has in mind here who "separate [thought] from any kind of substance." (Swedenborg considers spiritual "substance" a necessary medium for thought. See, for instance, §444. Concerning spiritual substance, see note 186.) In the summary in *Soul-Body Interaction* 19, the followers of René Descartes (1596–1650) seem closest to Swedenborg's own view, insofar as they hold to the doctrine of "spiritual influx," granting primacy to the unseen realities rather than to those we can see and touch. In fact, Descartes's view of this issue was considerably more complex than the summary in *Soul-Body Interaction* suggests. Descartes felt the need to assert the essential independence of soul and body—that is, of mind and brain—while acknowledging their interdependence in numerous capacities, and, moreover, insisting that the soul could survive the body after death. In his mature philosophy, he posited the substantial union of mind and body, while granting that certain mental functions were independent of the brain (Gaukroger 1995, 388–394). In the early modern era, as in ours, a tremendous amount of literature was written on the mind-body issue, though no theory then or now has won universal approval. [RS]

154 (in §199). The text here actually reads "which they were not to eat," but the sense suggests that this is an error. Both Potts 1888–1902 (6:308, under "Tree" at this section number) and Elliott in his translation (Swedenborg [1749–1756] 1983–1999) apparently make this emendation. [LHC]

155 (in §201). In §459 Swedenborg explains that there are three heavens and that each contains spiritual inhabitants and heavenly inhabitants. For more on this, see Swedenborg's chapters on the two kingdoms and three heavens of the other world in *Heaven and Hell* (§§20–28, 29–40). See also notes 49, 146. [LHC]

156 (in §204). When Swedenborg says the people described in Genesis 3:4, 5 would see that the tenets of faith were not true, he means they would see that relying on their

own standard of truth would *not* destroy their wisdom and understanding, contrary to the contents of verses 2, 3. [LHC]

157 (in §206:1). In the phrase "worshiping . . . the material world," Swedenborg does not mean that those in question literally build altars to worship anything, but rather that in their thinking they substitute material causes for processes otherwise viewed as requiring divine intervention; for example, the creation of the world. They hold that the material (or "natural") world is everything that exists; there is nothing transcendent or beyond that world. (These people were sometimes called Naturalists, a term that often has a different application today.) To Swedenborg "worshiping the material world" (or "worshiping nature") was shorthand for having no spiritual life whatsoever or, essentially, ascribing to atheism. For just a few of the many other references to people of this type in his works, see *Secrets of Heaven* 775:2, 2343:8, 2993, 3175:1, 4214:2, 4950; *Heaven and Hell* 102, 313, 353, 464, 488:3; *Divine Love and Wisdom* 46, 69, 162, 349:2. [SS]

158 (in §213). See §§1073, 1079, 1088, where Swedenborg discusses the symbolism of Noah's nakedness. [RS]

159 (in §216). The superlative term "earliest church" here might be taken as implying that the earliest people said such things of generations of their church that were *later* than their own. It is more likely, however, that Swedenborg is using "earliest" here as an umbrella term that includes many generations. Indeed, he seems in discussing the first seven chapters of Genesis to use "earliest church" in two ways: in a strict sense to mean the first, pure state represented by "Adam" (see, for example, §66:1; sometimes referred to as "the very earliest church"); and in a wider sense, as here, to mean the pure state and also all the other spiritual "generations," or stages of descent, down to "the Flood" (see, for example, §231). [JSR]

160 (in §217). For parables about vineyards and fig trees, see Matthew 20:1–16; 21:28–32; 24:32; Mark 12:1–11; 13:28; Luke 13:6–9; 20:9–16; 21:29–30. [LHC]

161 (in §221). "The breeze of the day" here is, in Latin, *per auram seu spiritum diei*—literally, "in the breeze, or the spirit, of the day." Swedenborg is trying to reflect two different nuances of the Hebrew רוּחַ *(rûaḥ)*, which means both "wind" and "spirit." See also note 106. [RS]

162 (in §226). For such queries, see Genesis 3:13; see also Genesis 16:8 and 21:17 (and the discussion of these verses at §§1931, 2693); Exodus 4:2; Ezekiel 37:3; Matthew 20:32; 26:50; Mark 10:51; Luke 18:41; John 5:6; 18:4, 7; 20:15; 21:15–17. [LHC]

163 (in §229). This is a reference to Genesis 3:14, in which God curses the snake. [LHC]

164 (in §231). By "the church among non-Jews" (*ecclesia gentium,* in the Latin) Swedenborg seems to mean the early Christian church as expanded by Paul to include non-Jews (see, for example, Acts 9:15; 13:47). Specifically, the Latin word here translated as "non-Jews" is *gentium,* literally, "nations"; the traditional translation is "Gentiles." Swedenborg uses this term differently in different contexts. In §367 below, the term clearly means "non-Jews" as opposed to Jews; in *Heaven and Hell* 516, it means certain unspecified non-Christians who are also not Muslims. In *Heaven and Hell* 308, he uses the term to refer to "people who are outside the church, where the Word is not found," and this seems to be the core meaning of the term as he employs it (see §410 below). In sum it would be safe to say that, although in the current passage the term refers to those

§247

within the church, in most instances when Swedenborg speaks of "Gentiles" he refers to those who are outside the church of a given dispensation. [LHC, GFD, RS]

165 (in §241). On the difference between "symbolism" and "representation" in Swedenborg's theology, see note 17. [LHC]

166 (in §245). Swedenborg here states what will become a recurring if minor theme of his theology: The common biblical description of divine action in the language of human emotion is in fact merely a subjective redescription in terms we understand rather than an objective statement about the nature of the divine. (Among many passages, §§257, 588:1, 1093, 1408:3, 1874, 2553, 3425:4, 3605:4 could be cited; for a fuller list, see Swedenborg's references to *Secrets of Heaven* in the footnote to *Heaven and Hell* 545.) This preliminary instance of the theme is unusual in its ascription of evil events to "the Devil's crew," a phrase that must be taken figuratively, as Swedenborg does not subscribe to the notion of the Devil as an independent being (see note 140). His reiterated denial of the anger of God is a response both to the frequency of such anthropomorphizing in the Bible and to the criticisms of contemporary atheists and Deists (see note 147) that the God of the Bible is implausibly capricious and unforgiving. These critics cited instances of an apparently cruel and wrathful God in the Bible, or the sanctioning of cruel human conduct by God, as evidence that the Scriptures were not divine revelation but the product of human minds. [RS, SS]

167 (in §245). For a sampling of the many passages in the Old Testament that characterize God as turning his face away from people, see Ezekiel 7:22; as being angry toward people, see Exodus 4:14; Numbers 11:1; 32:13; Deuteronomy 29:27; as punishing people, see Exodus 32:34; Leviticus 26:18, 24; Jeremiah 44:13; as testing (or tempting) people, see Genesis 22:1; Deuteronomy 13:3; as killing or slaying people, see Genesis 38:7, 10; Psalms 78:34; Lamentations 2:21; Amos 4:10; and as cursing people, see Deuteronomy 30:7; Proverbs 3:33; Jeremiah 17:5; 48:10; Malachi 2:2; 4:6. [JSR]

168 (in §247). For biblical references to sprinkling dirt (or dust) on one's head, see Joshua 7:6; 2 Samuel 1:2; 15:32; Lamentations 2:10; Ezekiel 27:30. [LHC]

169 (in §247). The Latin phrase here translated "underground realm" is *infera terrae*, literally, "low areas of the earth." When the English phrase "underground realm" appears again at the end of the passage, it stands for a slightly different Latin phrase: *terra infera*, "the low earth." These Latin phrases are two of six similar, more or less interchangeable ways in which Swedenborg denotes "the underground realm," a low-lying area below the world of spirits (see note 3) but above hell. The other four phrases are: (1) that which Swedenborg uses most often, *terra inferior*, literally, "the lower earth," paralleling the Hebrew phrase אֶרֶץ תַּחְתִּי (*'ereṣ taḥtî*), which appears in Ezekiel 31:14, 16, 18; (2) *terra inferiorum*, literally, "the land of low places," paralleling the Hebrew phrase אֶרֶץ תַּחְתִּיּוֹת (*'ereṣ taḥtiyyôt*), which appears in Ezekiel 26:20; 32:18, 24; (3) *inferiora terrae*, literally, "low places of the earth," paralleling the Hebrew phrase תַּחְתִּיּוֹת אֶרֶץ (*taḥtiyyôt 'āreṣ*), which appears in Psalms 63:9; 139:15; Isaiah 44:23; and (4) simply *infera*, "low areas." The underground realm is an area for good people who are nevertheless strongly attached to false ideas. As Swedenborg describes the spiritual geography of the underground realm, it is surrounded below and on all sides by the hells themselves; the people there are unwittingly subject to the negative influence of the hells. Yet from above, it enjoys support from and contact with angels and heaven. In the underground realm,

and particularly in pits within that realm (to which biblical mentions of "the pit" correspond), people undergo a process called "devastation" to disabuse them of their false notions. This involves sometimes lengthy, painful, shattering experiences, but afterward the people who undergo them are lifted up into heaven with a great sense of consolation and relief. See *Secrets of Heaven* 4728, 4940–4950, 7090; *Heaven and Hell* 513 and its note a; *Revelation Unveiled* 845:2. [JSR]

170 (in §250). On Swedenborg's attitude toward Jews, see note 182 and the reader's guide, pages 51–55. Jewish Messianism is based on references in the Hebrew Scriptures to an anointed one (Hebrew מָשִׁיחַ *[māšîaḥ]*, sometimes transliterated in English as Mashiach or Moshiach), such as Psalms 2:2; 18:50; Isaiah 45:1; Lamentations 4:20; and on many prophecies seen as related, such as Isaiah 11. [JSR]

171 (in §251:1). Swedenborg here lists different types of snakes that occur in Scripture, some of which are no longer thought to exist. The meaning of "bloodletting," "flying," and "creeping" snakes seems obvious enough. By "generic snakes" he apparently means nonpoisonous snakes. A "cockatrice" (Latin *regulus*) was thought to be able to kill by breathing on or even looking at its victims. An "asp" (Latin *aspis*) was poisonous. A "prester or fire snake" (Latin *prester* or *serpens ignitus*) had a bite thought to cause a burning sensation or death by swelling. A "viper" (Latin *vipera*) was a poisonous snake that produced live offspring rather than eggs and was thought to be able to cause internal damage to a human being in a way that other snakes could not; see §259:2. [JSR]

172 (in §252). Later on in the work Swedenborg does explore the nature of heavenly and hellish identity; see §§694, 1044, 1049, 1594:5, 3812–3813, 3994:1, 5660:3, 8497. [LHC]

173 (in §253). On the biblical themes of wife and bride, see note 141; on the church as young woman and daughter, see note 175. [RS]

174 (in §253). The Hebrew words in the quotation for "your husband" (בְּעָלַיִךְ *[bōʿălayik]*) and "your maker" (עֹשַׂיִךְ *[ʿōśayik]*) are plural in form but singular in meaning. Gesenius 1949 under בַּעַל associates the plural here with majesty. [LHC]

175 (in §253). For references of this type to a young woman and daughter, see, for example, Isaiah 7:14; 23:12; 37:22; 47:1; Jeremiah 14:17; 31:4; Lamentations 1:15; 2:13; or the passages conveniently quoted in §2362, including Micah 4:8; Zephaniah 3:14; Zechariah 9:9; Revelation 14:4, 5. [LHC, RS]

176 (in §254). The passage from which this quotation is taken, Isaiah 14:3–23, literally concerns the king of Babylon. In verse 12, however, the king is addressed as הֵילֵל *(hêlēl)*, defined in Brown, Driver, and Briggs 1996 as "shining one," and sometimes translated as "Lucifer." From there the identification with the Devil follows readily; the two were equated in Christian lore as early as the third century (Russell 1981, 130–131). As for the connection between the Devil and the snake, or dragon, it is stated explicitly in Revelation 12:9: "And the great dragon was cast out, the old serpent called the Devil and Satan, which deceives the whole world." [RS, LHC]

177 (in §257). On the identification of the snake and the dragon called Lucifer, see note 176. [LHC]

178 (in §257). "The flanks of the north" are the most remote northern areas. [LHC]

179 (in §259:1). The Hebrew root of the name Jacob is עָקֵב *(ʿāqēb)*, or "heel." The verb עָקַב *(ʿāqab)*, which has the same root, means "to follow at the heel," thus, figuratively, to assail in a furtive way, or per Swedenborg's reading at Genesis 27:36, to supplant.

The latter passage is a good example of how Hebrew plays on the literal and figurative meanings in its account of Jacob. [RS] In saying that the Jewish church was to wound the heel, Swedenborg is doubtless referring to the betrayal of Jesus by Judas, who also, like Jacob, was seen by Swedenborg as representing the Jewish church (see *Secrets of Heaven* 4751; *The Lord* 16; *True Christianity* 130). [LHC]

180 (in §259:2). On the concept of the remnant in the Bible, see note 22. [LHC]

181 (in §259:2). Throughout his treatment of Genesis 6 (§§554–683) Swedenborg describes how self-love corrupted the desires and thoughts of people living just before the Flood. [LHC]

182 (in §259:2). Swedenborg's attitude toward the Jews echoes much of the Christian tradition. On the one hand, the Jews are the preservers of the true religion handed down from the most ancient church; on the other hand, the Jewish religion is assailed for its degeneracy, corruption, and literalism. The tensions and ambiguities reflected in this attitude go back to the New Testament. The Gospel of John, for example, states that "salvation is of the Jews" (John 4:22), but the Gospel also stresses the role of "the Jews" as Christ's enemies and persecutors (see, for example, John 7:1; 19:31). Modern scholars tend to see these views as reflections not of Christ's actual teachings, but of tensions between the Jewish synagogue and the nascent Christian community in the late first century C.E. (for one example, see Schmithals 1997, 258–277). See also the reader's guide, pages 51–55, which cites several passages pertinent to Swedenborg's statement here in §259:2. [RS] The "pages to come" to which Swedenborg is referring here may include such passages as §§1094, 1200, 1205. [LHC]

183 (in §259:2). Swedenborg describes the harmful effect of over-reliance on sensory evidence and logic in such passages as §§1072, 2568, 2588, 4658. [LHC]

184 (in §266). For a discussion of Swedenborg's attitudes toward gender, see the reader's guide, pages 55–56. [JSR]

185 (in §272). On the fascination of Swedenborg's age with the difference between animal and human, see note 152. [SS]

186 (in §272). Swedenborg uses the term *substance,* both here and generally, to refer to what he sees as the spiritual equivalent of matter. See *Marriage Love* 31. [LHC]

187 (in §273). "Moph" is a transliteration of the Hebrew name for the Egyptian city of Memphis. [RS]

188 (in §274). "The grain plant on the roofs" is the growth that arose from seeds mixed into the mud of which roofs were commonly made in Middle Eastern countries. Though it grew rapidly with the rains, it either dried up quickly in the ensuing sun or was burned off before it could attain its usual height. See *International Standard Bible Encyclopedia* (Orr 1960), under "grass"; compare Psalms 129:6. [SS]

189 (in §276:1). Swedenborg saw the material world as caused by the spiritual world and as therefore reflecting it; that is, physical phenomena and events *offer images of*— are "responsive to" or "correspond to"—spiritual phenomena and events. As noted by Swedenborg in §4, the primary purpose of this work is to demonstrate that the Bible contains levels of spiritual meaning that can at least in part be discovered by a knowledge of specific correspondential relationships. [GFD, RHK]

190 (in §276:1). The Holy Supper is the term Swedenborg generally uses for the Christian rite of Communion, or the Eucharist, a sacramental consumption of bread

and wine initiated by Jesus Christ on the eve of his Crucifixion (see Matthew 26:26–29; Mark 14:22–25; Luke 22:14–20). [LHC]

191 (in §276:2). This last phrase echoes John 18:36: "Jesus answered, 'My kingdom is not of this world.'" [LHC] Swedenborg here reflects a common Christian polemic against Judaism: that it sought political liberation for the Jewish nation rather than collective salvation for humanity. See also the reader's guide, pages 51–55. [RS]

192 (in the text of Genesis 3:20). This verse is a play on the similarity of the Hebrew name חַוָּה (Ḥavvā), usually translated "Eve," and the Hebrew verb for "live," חָיָה (ḥāyā). [LHC]

193 (in the text of Genesis 3:24). The Hebrew for "guardian beings" is כְּרֻבִים (kərubîm), often translated "cherubim," a plural form. The traditional translation for the singular, "cherub," has—unfortunately for the purposes of translation—come to be associated with the "cupid," or diminutive winged angel figure (for which the correct technical term is the Italian *putto*). Originally the cherub seems to have been regarded as "the living chariot of the theophanic God" (Brown, Driver, and Briggs 1996, under כְּרוּב, quoting 2 Samuel 22:11 and Psalms 18:10: "he rode upon a cherub"). The celebrated vision in Ezekiel 1 describes the cherubim as having the faces of a man, ox, lion, and eagle (later equated with the Four Evangelists in Christian iconography). For Swedenborg, the cherub signifies above all a "guardian being," placed to keep humans who were oriented toward sensory experience from entering realms of sacred experience, which would be harmful for them; see §§306, 308, 2761:4. [RS]

194 (in §289). For the meaning of a wife (or woman) as the church, see §§54, 250, 252–253, 255, 262. In §29:2 Swedenborg defines God's kingdom in the broadest sense as heaven and in a narrower sense as the church. [SS]

195 (in §290). The Hebrew word translated Rephaim (רְפָאִים [rəpā'îm]) is usually taken to represent either of two separate words, of which one refers to giants and the other means "the enervated," or in other words, "ghosts." The latter is the sense that most translators assign in this passage, but Swedenborg seems to understand the word in the former sense, since he says that they stand for people who are "inflated" (see the text immediately after the quotation). In §581:2 and elsewhere he connects the Rephaim of this verse with the Nephilim (see §§581–583), who are taken to be giants; see note 317. [LHC]

196 (in §295). In regard to the ancients' manner of speech, see §66. [LHC]

197 (in §296). See §§9471, 9630–9632, where Swedenborg discusses the mention of badger and ram skins in Exodus. Although this passage again (see note 90) suggests that he expected *Secrets of Heaven* to reach at least as far as Numbers (see similar references in §§730:4, 2280:7, 4434:10; see also the reader's guide, pages 24–25 note 14), as it turned out he did not proceed beyond Exodus. [LHC]

198 (in §298). As Swedenborg makes clear in §304, the phrase "living forever" paradoxically refers not to salvation but to damnation. [LHC]

199 (in §300). Swedenborg, like many scholars then and now, considered the divine name in Hebrew (יהוה [yhvh]) to be derived from the verb "to be" (הָיָה [hāyā]), and the short and long Hebrew words for God (אֵל [ēl] and אֱלֹהִים [ĕlōhîm]) to be connected with a word for power (אֵל [ēl]), which is identical in form with the shorter word for God. See also note 28. [LHC]

200 (in §302). Swedenborg may be thinking of passages such as Ecclesiastes 9:5: "The living know that they will die, but the dead know nothing and have no reward any more, because their memory is forgotten." See also Psalms 146:4: "When they breathe their last, they will return to the ground; on that day their thoughts will perish." See also Genesis 3:19; Ecclesiastes 9:10; Isaiah 26:14; 53:12; Ezekiel 18:4. [RS, LHC, SS]

201 (in §302). On Swedenborg's attitude toward Jews, see note 182 and the reader's guide, pages 51–55. [JSR]

202 (in §303:1). For passages that Swedenborg may be thinking of here, see those quoted in §5376, including the following: Isaiah 24:1–23; 51:17–23; Ezekiel 12:19, 20; 26:19–21; 36:3–12; Matthew 24:15, 16. In the Gospels Christ frequently stresses the lack of faith of his hearers: see Matthew 6:30; 8:10, 26; 14:31; 16:8; Mark 4:40; Luke 7:9; 8:25; 12:28; 17:6; 18:8. [LHC, RS]

203 (in §303:2). Swedenborg here is picking up a longstanding, though regrettable, polemic against the greed of the Jews. This is possibly a reflection of his upbringing in the Protestant church of his day. The Protestant reformer Martin Luther (1483–1546), although at first inclined to be sympathetic to the Jews after his break with the Catholic Church, was disappointed by their response to his evangelizing and ended his career indulging in anti-Semitic vituperations (see, for example, Luther 1543). See also note 182 and the reader's guide, pages 51–55. [RS]

204 (in §308:1). The traditional term for this cover is "mercy seat." Sitting on the ark that contained the two tablets inscribed with the Ten Commandments, it was topped with two gold, winged figures—the guardian beings—and was the site of God's presence with the Israelites (see Exodus 25:17–22). The name for the item in Hebrew, כַּפֹּרֶת *(kappōreṯ)*, comes from כִּפֶּר *(kipper)*, a verb whose basic meaning is to cover, although it is most commonly used in the more abstract sense of "covering" transgression by atonement. The same root can be seen in the familiar Hebrew term *Yom Kippur*, "Day of Atonement," on which the high priest made a sin offering whose blood was spattered on the appeasement cover (see Leviticus 16; the role of the appeasement cover in the sacrifice is described in verses 13–15 there). [LHC, GFD, SS]

205 (in §308:1). "The testimony" here is the Ten Commandments. [LHC]

206 (in §308:1). See 2 Kings 19:15; Isaiah 37:16. Without being called God of Israel, he is said to sit on (or, in some translations, between) the guardian beings in 1 Samuel 4:4; 2 Samuel 6:2; Psalms 80:1; 99:1. [LHC]

207 (in §313). Swedenborg seems to be attacking the notion of original sin, the idea that all humans inherited the primordial sin of Adam, a doctrine first articulated by Augustine. See Kelly 1960, 361–366. As the passage goes on to say, however, he is not denying the heritability of sin, simply the idea that all inherited sin can be traced back to Adam. He asserts instead that each person's hereditary evil comes from her or his biological parents (*Marriage Love* 525:1; *True Christianity* 469). At §494 below, he indicates that hereditary evil is the cause of the decline of every church. See also §788 and the discussion of inherited evil in the reader's guide, page 42 note 31. [RS]

208 (in §313). אָדָם *(ʾāḏām)* is the Hebrew word for humankind; it can be translated as "Adam" or as "a human," "the human race," and so forth. It is related to the word for "ground," אֲדָמָה *(ʾăḏāmā)*. The Latin captures the flavor of the Hebrew, since the word for a human is *homo* and "from the ground" is *ex humo*. [LHC]

209 (in §318). The communities of the next life come together to form a single human being, each community serving the function of a different body part of that being, as described in §§550, 686–687, 1285:2, and in the material following each of Swedenborg's separate discussions of chapters 27–42 in Genesis. [LHC]

Notes to Genesis Chapter 4, §§320–448

210 (in §322:1). Although Swedenborg describes the spiritual world as a place of complete honesty, where any spoken words that diverge from the speaker's true opinions sound noticeably strained and harsh, people nevertheless retain the option of keeping silent; see *Revelation Unveiled* 294:1; *Divine Providence* 224:3. [JSR]

211 (in §322:1). For more details on the dates of Swedenborg's spiritual awakening, see note 18. [JSR]

212 (in §322:1). What Swedenborg means here is that the five senses are simply different modes of detecting the impingement of various particles on the human body. He discusses his theory of the senses extensively in his unpublished manuscript of 1744, *Draft on the Five Senses* (= Swedenborg 1976b). There he uses the term "touch" both in a general sense, as the detection of particles impinging on any organs of sense, and in its narrower meaning of "the sensation perceived by the nerve fibers of the skin." In §444 of that work he states: "The origin of all sensation is from touch [in the broad sense], or external impulse. . . . The sensations of touch [in the narrow sense], taste, and smell arise from a touch [in the broad sense], or impulse of heavy particles, . . . but the sense of hearing and of sight [is] from a touch, or impulse, of particles not heavy, but of active force, that is of particles of the atmosphere." See also his posthumously published manuscript *Draft on Sensation* (= Swedenborg 1984), 150–151. [SS]

213 (in the text of Genesis 4:1). The verb "know" here and in verses 17 and 25 means to have sexual intercourse with. It is a literal translation of the Latin verb here *(cognoscere)*, which in turn is a literal translation of the Hebrew verb (יָדַע *[yāḏaʿ]*). [LHC]

214 (in the text of Genesis 4:1). The Hebrew here is associating the verb קָנָה *(qānā)*, "get," with the name קַיִן *(qayin)*, "Cain." In the Hebrew, there is an ambiguous particle (אֵת *[ʾet]*) before "Jehovah". Most translators take the particle as a preposition meaning "with," but Swedenborg takes it in its other possible function: as indicator of a direct object, which sets "Jehovah" in apposition with "a man." The result is the translation here, "I have acquired a man: Jehovah." Contrast the New Revised Standard Version: "I have produced a man with the help of the Lord." [LHC]

215 (in the text of Genesis 4:8). The clause "And Cain said to Abel his brother" appears incomplete, in both Hebrew and Latin. [LHC]

216 (in the text of Genesis 4:20). Jabal is obviously not the father of livestock, but of those who own livestock. The Hebrew extends the sense of the first clause to the second by a figure of speech called zeugma (or, more specifically, protozeugma), an unequal linking of sentence elements. The passage may also be seen as an example of ellipsis, the purposeful omission of a word or words for rhetorical or poetic effect. However, see the inner meaning of this figure of speech, as explained by Swedenborg in §415 (and see also the discussion in note 263). [SS]

217 (in the text of Genesis 4:21). The instrument referred to as an organ here is probably a set of pipes through which the player blows. In §419 Swedenborg describes an

organ as midway between a stringed and a wind instrument, so perhaps he is thinking of a reed organ, which is blown but has a stringlike reed that vibrates. [LHC, LSW]

218 (in the text of Genesis 4:23). Lamech is saying that he takes something more than the "eye for an eye" vengeance later sanctioned in Exodus 21:23–25, Leviticus 24:19–20, Deuteronomy 19:21, and mentioned by Jesus in Matthew 5:38. That is, Lamech has killed a man for simply wounding him and a child for merely bruising him. The same extreme vindictiveness is also expressed in the next verse: "For Cain will be avenged seven times, and Lamech seventy-seven times." It is possible that the Hebrew original incorporates an old boasting-song, here taken as a reflection of the increased arrogance of the generations of Cain (Rad 1972, 111). [LHC, RS]

219 (in the text of Genesis 4:25). The Hebrew original that underlies this verse associates the verb שִׁית *(šît)*, "put" (here represented by "restored"), with the name שֵׁת *(šēt)*, "Seth." [LHC]

220 (in §336). The Hebrew name represented by "Enosh," אֱנוֹשׁ *(ĕnôš)*, is a word meaning "person." [LHC]

221 (in §339). As Swedenborg indicates, the prophetic parts of the Bible are full of references to these terms. Some passages he may have in mind include Isaiah 7:14; 39:7; Jeremiah 29:6; Ezekiel 14:16, 18; Hosea 9:11; Malachi 3:3. [RS]

222 (in §344). This is an echo of 1 Corinthians 13:2: "Though I have the gift of making prophecies, though I understand all mysteries and all knowledge, and though I have all faith, faith to move mountains, if I do not have charity, I am nothing." [RS]

223 (in §348). The ancient Hebrews regarded the kidneys as a seat of the emotions, much as the heart still is regarded in our culture. See, for example, Job 19:27; Psalms 16:7; 73:21; Proverbs 23:16. [LHC, RS]

224 (in §349:1). On the symbolism of specific types of offerings, see, for example, §§923, 2177, 2830, 3880:8–9, 4581, 8080:1, 8088, 9223, 9990–9994, 10042, 10053:1, 10097, 10137. [LHC]

225 (in §352). For "the firstborn things of the church," see §338. [LHC]

226 (in §353:1). Because of the bad press that fatty foods receive in current culture, the passages quoted in this section may be startling to modern readers. Among the active peoples of ancient times, however, the high caloric content of fat was particularly valued for its sustaining properties. A link between body fat and fertility, supported by modern research (see Frisch 2004), may also have been known to the ancients. Consequently, fat was often regarded as the most desirable part of the sacrifice, not only among the Hebrews but among other Mediterranean cultures. See, for example, the Greek myth in which Prometheus deceives Zeus by using the fat of a sacrificed ox as an enticement (Hesiod *Theogony* 533–553, in Evelyn-White 1914, 118–119). Furthermore, the parts of the sacrificial animal containing fat burned best and were thus seen as most suited for use in worship ceremonies. [RS, SS, LHC]

227 (in §353:1). Leviticus 3:15 is also pertinent. [LHC]

228 (in §353:3). "The fat of the kidneys of wheat" may mean either "the white of the kernels" by a color analogy, or "the best wheat" by an analogy with the most desirable part of an animal sacrifice, the fat (see note 226). Such a figure of speech is called a catachresis, or forced trope. Compare the modern mixed metaphor "the cream of the crop." However, other theories have been advanced to explain the phrase. [LHC, SS]

229 (in §358). Numbers 6:26 says, "May Jehovah lift his face on you and give you peace." Psalms 4:6 says, "Lift the light of your face on us, Jehovah." [LHC]

230 (in §362). Swedenborg seems to be alluding to a possible etymological meaning of "heresy." The word comes from the Greek αἵρεσις *(haíresis),* a noun meaning "sect" that is derived from the Greek verb αἱρεῖν *(haireîn),* "to choose." From this etymological point of view, a "heresy" would result from choosing one aspect of traditional doctrine and overemphasizing it. See Liddell and Scott 1968, under αἵρεσις; *Oxford English Dictionary,* under "heresy." [RS, SS]

231 (in §362). Compare Swedenborg's earlier scientific publication *Dynamics of the Soul's Domain* (= Swedenborg [1740–1741] 1955), part 1, §18, in which he describes his own anatomical researches: "I have observed . . . that as soon as I came across something that had never been discovered before, I would begin (perhaps as a result of self-love) to grow blind to the findings and even the best delineated discussions of others [on the subject]. I would attempt to base an entire series of rational conclusions on my discovery; along the way I would lose the ability to search honestly for, and keep in mind, the universal principles that should have been brought to bear on my individual findings, and to categorize the details under those universal principles. Indeed, when I tried to extrapolate principles from my observations, I would think I was seeing many points of confirmation in other areas, but what I was seeing was not in fact true." (Translation by JSR.) [SS, LSW, JSR]

232 (in §367:1). The Hebrew of Jeremiah 13:14 says, literally, "And I will smash them, a man against his brother" (וְנִפַּצְתִּים אִישׁ אֶל־אָחִיו *[vənippaṣtîm 'îš 'el-'āḥîv]*). Both Isaiah 19:2 and Jeremiah 13:14 appear to use "a man" and "his brother" in a negative sense. [LHC]

233 (in §367:2). For more about the "church among non-Jews," see note 164. [LHC]

234 (in §367:2). It is not entirely clear which passages are referred to here, but the prophets sometimes speak of other nations as being equally under God's protection and mercy. Examples are Amos 9:7; Isaiah 19:23–25. The term translated here as "brothers and sisters" (and in other inclusive ways below) is *fratres,* which can apply collectively to siblings of either gender, and which also applies to people unrelated except by their common humanity. [LHC, LSW]

235 (in §368). Swedenborg's sudden inclusion of farmers in this list of instances of the word *field* may surprise English readers. The verbal connection is more clear in Latin, in which the word for a farmer, *agricola,* is obviously formed (in part, at least) from the Latin word for a field, *ager.* [LHC]

236 (in §371). On the shift from perception to conscience in people who lived after the Flood, see, for example, §§393, 573, 597. [LHC]

237 (in §374:1). *Raca* is a Greek form of an Aramaic word meaning "empty," "worthless," "idle." Here it is used as a term of abuse (Liddell and Scott 1968, under ῥακά). [LHC, RS]

238 (in §374:1). The term "Sanhedrin" refers to any of several councils of the Jews in Palestine under Roman occupation. Although the function of the councils is a matter of scholarly dispute—they seem to have served a mixture of executive, judicial, legislative, and religious functions—clearly this particular Sanhedrin is envisioned as a court of law. [SS]

239 (in §374:1). "Gehenna" is short for the Valley of the Children of Hinnom (גֵיא בֶן־הִנֹּם [gê ben-hinnōm]) south of Jerusalem, where the children of Israel once "passed their children through the fire" (sacrificed them) for Moloch, the god of the Ammonites. Josiah, king of Judah, obeying the commands of the recently rediscovered Torah, defiled this site in his campaign against idolatry (2 Kings 23:10), and in keeping with this historical defilement, it was later used as a refuse dump. The Old Testament refers to this valley in several places (for instance, Jeremiah 7:31–32), and by New Testament times "Gehenna" had become more or less synonymous with hell (and in some versions of the Bible today is so translated). In Mark 9:43–45, Christ, quoting Isaiah 66:24, describes Gehenna as a place for the wicked, "where their worm does not die, and the fire is not quenched." [LHC, RS]

240 (in §374:1). In both the Hebrew and the Latin, the word here translated "hems" (Hebrew כָּנָף [kānāp]; Latin *ala*) can also mean "wings"; see note 425. [LHC, JSR]

241 (in §382:3). Ephraim was actually born after his brother Manasseh (Genesis 41:51), but their grandfather Jacob in blessing them "set Ephraim before Manasseh" (Genesis 48:20), giving Ephraim the rights of the firstborn. A note in the third Latin edition refers the reader to §3325 (see subsection 10), which mentions the displacement of Reuben by Ephraim as Jacob's own firstborn as reported in 1 Chronicles 5:1. [LHC]

242 (in §382:5). The Valley of Vision is mentioned in Isaiah 22:1. [LHC]

243 (in §390). The phrase "traitors betray and traitorously commit the treachery of traitors" here echoes the repetition in the Latin, *perfidi perfide agunt, et perfidia perfidorum perfide faciunt,* which in turn reflects the repetition in the original Hebrew: בֹּגְדִים בָּגָדוּ וּבֶגֶד בּוֹגְדִים בָּגָדוּ (*bōgədîm bāgādû ûbeged bōgədîm bāgādû*). [JSR]

244 (in §393). "Hearing the message" here is an allusion to Romans 10:17: "Therefore faith comes from hearing the message, and the message is heard through God's word." [LHC]

245 (in §394). For Swedenborg, the ideal condition of man and woman is that they should be united as one, a spiritual marriage that occurs in heaven. On this same passage from Matthew 19:12, compare *Marriage Love* 156:2: "'Eunuchs who make themselves eunuchs for the sake of the kingdom of God' means individuals who refrain from the evils of promiscuity in marriage. Clearly, it does not mean Italian eunuchs [that is, castrated men]." For more on the heavenly marriage, see notes 79, 141; for more on this sense of "eunuch," see *Revelation Explained* (= Swedenborg 1994–1997) §710:28–30. [RS, LSW]

246 (in §395:1). The universality of the sacred character of the number seven is sometimes explained by the fact that it is a "virgin" number (the only one between one and ten that is neither the product nor the divisor of any of the others), that it referred to the seven classical planets (the moon, Mercury, Venus, the sun, Mars, Jupiter, and Saturn), or that it reflects the seven notes of the octave. Swedenborg here gives the most common reason cited in the Judeo-Christian tradition. See, for example, Philo *On the Creation* (= Philo 1993) §§30–43; and for more explanation by Swedenborg, §433 below. As Swedenborg goes on to note, however, the number has negative connotations as well, indicating a period of "devastation." What unites these two concepts is perhaps the idea that the number seven represents a complete cycle. [RS]

247 (in §395:1). On the sacred significance of the number seven in general, see note 246; on its sacred significance in Scripture in particular, see, for example, the passages quoted in §716, including Leviticus 8:10, 11; 16:14, 19; Isaiah 30:26; Revelation 1:12, 13;

4:5; the passages quoted in §2252:3: Leviticus 23:15; 25:8, 10; and the passages quoted in §2830:3, including Numbers 28:11, 12, 18–20, 26–28. [LHC]

248 (in §395:2). In §433 Swedenborg explains that a biblical "age" (Latin *saeculum*) is a decade. Elsewhere he also uses the term for centuries and whole eras. [LHC]

249 (in §395:2). See Exodus 23:10, 11 and Leviticus 25:2–5, which indicate that the land of the Israelites was to be left fallow every seventh year. The six years before the fallow are thus, in the exhaustion of the soil, representative of the devastation in which all heavenly properties of the individual are used up. The Sabbath is not, strictly speaking, one of the stages of spiritual devastation, but rather the symbol of the end of such devastation, that is, of regeneration. See §8539:2: "[The state before regeneration] is signified by the six days that precede the seventh, and . . . [the state after regeneration] is signified by the seventh day, or the Sabbath." [SS, LHC, LSW]

250 (in §395:2). The book in question was most likely a scroll, so that "inside and on the back" means on both sides of the rolled up sheet of paper. [LHC]

251 (in §396:1). The bracketed gloss here is Swedenborg's. [LHC]

252 (in §396:2). The text here makes a distinction that is surprisingly difficult to convey in the translation itself. There are two words used for "mark" in the original Greek form of the Book of Revelation, σφραγίς *(sphragís)* and χάραγμα *(cháragma)*. Swedenborg represents *sphragís* with the Latin word *signum*, and *cháragma* with the Latin word *character*. The Latin, then, literally says: "A mark is also called a character in the same author" *(signum vocatur etiam character apud Eundem)*. In all other quotations from the Bible in this section, whether from Old or the New Testament, he uses the word *signum*, here translated with either "mark" or "sign." [LHC]

253 (in §398). The name Nod comes from נוֹד, *nôḏ* (Brown, Driver, and Briggs 1996, under II נוֹד), which comes from נוד, *nûḏ*, "to wander." [RS]

254 (in §400). Swedenborg has more to say about this kind of genealogy at §339. [LHC]

255 (in §401). Swedenborg is basing this statement on the derivation of the Hebrew חֲנוֹךְ *(ḥănôk),* "Enoch," from the verb חָנַךְ *(ḥānak),* "train," "train up" (Brown, Driver, and Briggs 1996, under חָנַךְ). See §519:1. [RS]

256 (in §402:4). *Heres* in Hebrew means "destruction." In Isaiah's original this reference to "the city of Heres" is probably a pun on the Hebrew name for the Egyptian city of Heliopolis, which is עִיר הַחֶרֶס *('îr haḥeres),* "the city of the sun," while "city of destruction" is עִיר הַהֶרֶם *('îr haherem),* a phrase only slightly different in sound (Brown, Driver, and Briggs 1996, under חֶרֶס). [RS]

257 (in §402:4). The Latin phrase here translated "in the south," *in meridie,* may also mean "at noon." [RS]

258 (in §404). In a note at this point in his translation (Swedenborg [1749–1756] 1983–1999, 1:143), Elliott observes that the actual meaning of the name Irad (עִירָד *['îrāḏ])* is unclear and that the definition Swedenborg gives here is apparently based on a combination of the noun עִיר *('îr),* which means "a city," with יָרַד *(yāraḏ),* which means "to go down." [LHC]

259 (in §408). This is an allusion to Matthew 13:24–30, 36–43, a parable in which tares (the growth of some type of weed, probably darnel) are compared to "the children of the wicked one." They arise in the field of the world alongside the good and are not gathered in until the harvest (the end of the world), when they are separated from the good and burned. [SS, LHC]

260 (in §410). In Swedenborg's usage, "gentiles" *(gentes)* seems to refer to anyone who is not involved with the church of a given dispensation; that is, "outsiders." See note 164. [RS, SS]

261 (in §414:2). The "children of the east" are mentioned in Jeremiah 49:28, the verse previous to the one just cited here. The phrase was quoted and explained in §382:4. [SS]

262 (in §414:4). The Feast of Booths, or Sukkot, is still celebrated by modern Jews, who build a temporary shelter outdoors and eat their meals in it (even sleeping in it if weather and health permit). It occurs on the fifth day after Yom Kippur, in September or October by the Gregorian calendar. [RS]

263 (in §415:1). What Swedenborg seems to be saying here (with reference to Genesis 4:20, "he was the father of the tent dweller, and of livestock") is that although the words "father" and "of livestock" are understood together, in the original text the word for "of livestock" actually stands next to the word for "tent," which implies that what the livestock symbolize (goodness) grows out of that which the tent symbolizes (holy love). [LHC]

264 (in §418:1). King David appointed 288 official musicians (1 Chronicles 25:7); see also 1 Chronicles 9:33; 15:16–22; 25:1–31; 2 Chronicles 5:12, 13. [LSW]

265 (in §418:2). For discussion of these choirs, see §§1648–1649, 2595–2596, 3350–3351, 3893, 8115. [LHC]

266 (in §420:1). Swedenborg's statement here that explanations of individual instruments in Scripture will occur at the "appropriate places" may be another indication that at the time of writing, he planned *Secrets of Heaven* as a full exegesis of all Scripture; see note 90 and the reader's guide, pages 24–25 note 14. Ultimately, however, the primary exegesis in *Secrets of Heaven* was limited to Genesis and Exodus. The musical instruments mentioned in these two biblical books are the organ (Latin *organum*), whose meaning is given here; the harp (Latin *cithara*), here and at §4138; the tambourine (Latin *tympanum*), in §§4138, 8337; one type of trumpet (Latin *jobel*), at §8802; and another type of trumpet (Latin *buccina*), at §§8815, 8823, 8915. [LHC, JSR]

267 (in §422). For passages in the prophets about Jacob and Israel, both favorable and unfavorable, see, for example, Isaiah 9:8; 10:20; 27:6; Jeremiah 31:7. See also the many passages quoted and discussed in *Revelation Explained* (= Swedenborg 1994–1997) §433. [JSR]

268 (in §422). For Swedenborg's discussion of the symbolism of Leah and Rachel, see, for example, his treatment of Genesis 29, and in particular §§3817–3821. For a discussion of the inner and outer part of the church represented by Jacob, see, for instance, §4292. [LHC]

269 (in §425). On the sacred and symbolic use of these materials, see the explanations of Exodus 25–30 in volumes 14 and 15. [LHC]

270 (in §425). In Swedenborg's theology, the earthly level is the mind's lowest level and is closely connected with the physical world but remains a step above the body and its senses. See §§259, 4038; see also note 23. [LHC]

271 (in §425). For tarshish as a precious stone, see note 117. [LHC]

272 (in §426:1). For the place called Tarshish, see note 119. [RS]

273 (in §426:2). The name Zillah itself also means "shadow." In identifying the north with darkness and the south with light, Swedenborg presumes a readership in the northern hemisphere. [LHC]

274 (in §436). Though Swedenborg refers to Seth as a new faith in §335, he apparently intended the text of the present section to provide the full explanation. [SS]

275 (in §439). Swedenborg links Enosh with charity at §§336, 436, and 438. [SS]

276 (in §440). *Minha* is a Hebrew word (מִנְחָה *[minḥā]*) whose general meaning is "an offering" and whose specific meaning is "a grain offering." [LHC]

277 (in §441). For passages above in the main text that mention the closeness between the Lord and the earliest church, see §§49:1, 125, 337:1, 393, 414:3, 4. [JSR, LHC]

278 (in §443). This person is identified as a man named Dippel in Swedenborg's *Spiritual Experiences* (= Swedenborg 1998–2002) §3890, where the same story is told. This Dippel is almost certainly Johann Konrad Dippel (1673–1734), a physician and radical Pietist who wrote works critical of the Protestant clergy under the name "Christianus Democritus" (see Tafel 1877, 1138–1139). [LHC, SS]

279 (in §444). The man in question seems to have been an adherent of Cartesian dualism: Descartes affirmed "that the mind or soul of man is entirely different from the body." He also contended that, unlike the body, mind does not possess the quality of extension in space, that is, dimensionality or divisibility (Descartes [1641] 1968, 162–164). Swedenborg indicates in the following section that these ideas would lead one to believe that the soul is extinguished after death. [RS] Compare Swedenborg's *Dynamics of the Soul's Domain* (= Swedenborg [1740–1741] 1955), part 2, §216. [SS]

280 (in §446). The Latin phrase here translated "parts outside of parts" is *partes extra partes,* loosely translatable as "parts external to other parts" or "parts distinct from other parts." The French philosopher Descartes (see note 153) believed that the necessary properties of corporeal as opposed to spiritual objects were (1) being extended in space, (2) having parts that were distinct from other parts *(partes extra partes),* (3) being divisible, and (4) existing in a particular place. Cartesians (as the disputants in question seem to be; see note 279) would claim that the soul does not adhere to the principle of *partes extra partes,* and thus it cannot have dimension or exist in a place. The failure to conform to this principle would also mean that the soul could not have such parts as the human head, torso, limbs, etc. In other words, by this thinking the soul must lack all the components of the human form. By contrast, the more naive spirits mentioned at the end of the section, who are not blinded by philosophical cant, can readily understand that the soul possesses a spiritual human form made out of a spiritual substance. For a discussion of the issue of extension in early Enlightenment philosophy, with a note on the history of the term *partes extra partes,* see Pasnau 2007. [SS]

281 (in §447). Swedenborg is apparently alluding to a common view, held both by Jews and by non-Jews, that Judaism does not teach the existence of an afterlife. "The belief that the soul continues its existence after the dissolution of the body is a matter of philosophical or theological speculation rather than of simple faith, and is accordingly nowhere expressly taught in Holy Scripture" (*The Jewish Encyclopedia* 1910, 6:654; see also Scholem 1974, 333–334). The picture is not quite so simple, however. The Talmud makes many references to "Gehenna" (compare note 239) and "the world to come" (Bialik and Ravnitzky 1992, 568–574), and many Kabbalists teach the *sod ha-gilgulim* ("the mystery of the cycles"—that is, reincarnation; see Scholem 1974, 344–350). [RS]

Notes to Genesis Chapter 5, §§449–546

282 (in §450). There is an echo in this passage of the dispute among the disciples about "which of them should be the greatest" (Mark 9:33–35; Luke 22:24–26; see note 283). See also *Marriage Love* 7. [RS]

283 (in §452). This is an allusion to Luke 22:26: "Let the greater among you be as the younger; and the one who rules be as the one who serves." [RS]

284 (in §457). There is more detail on the three heavens in §459 just below; see also §§684, 1642, and the extended treatment of the subject in Swedenborg's *Heaven and Hell* 29–40. See also note 146. [LHC]

285 (in the text of Genesis 5:29). The Hebrew is drawing a connection between the name Noah and a verb for "console," נִחַם *(niḥḥam)*. The original root has to do with "rest," a meaning elucidated below at §851. [LHC, RS]

286 (in the text of Genesis 5:32). Based on the notion of one's having "become a child" (been born) at a certain point in the past, "a son of (so many) years" is a Hebraism meaning simply "(so many) years old" and is often translated in that way. [LHC]

287 (in §468:1). On names that stand for heresies and doctrines, see, for example, §§324–325, 331–336. [LHC]

288 (in §468:2). Isaiah 7:22 actually mentions survivors in the middle of the land; Isaiah 5:8, 6:12, and 24:13 imply the idea. [LHC]

289 (in §468:2). The subject of the remnant in the individual is introduced in §19. [LHC]

290 (in §468:2). See the quotation of Genesis 18:32 at the end of §468. [LHC]

291 (in §471). For Swedenborg's discussions later in the work on the reasons for the Israelite laws limiting marriage to one's own people (Numbers 36:6–9), and forbidding it with others (Exodus 34:16; Deuteronomy 7:3, 4), see *Secrets of Heaven* 3024:7, 3665:4, 4444:4–6, 8998. For more on the reasons why the earliest church followed this practice, see *Secrets of Heaven* 483:2, 1159:3, 1246. [LHC, JSR]

292 (in §475). The Hebrew word for "human being" is אָדָם *('ādām)*; see note 208. Many translations, including the King James, the Latin Vulgate, and the Greek Septuagint, render it as a proper name, Adam, in this verse. Swedenborg uses the Latin equivalent of the common noun, *Homo,* meaning "a human being." In §478 Swedenborg states that the first human "is never called by the proper name Adam but is called *the human,*" although in §566:1 he acknowledges that the word is also used as a name. [RS, LHC]

293 (in §477:4). On the word *enosh,* see note 220. [LHC]

294 (in §477:4). On the word *adam,* see notes 208 and 292. [LHC]

295 (in §487:1). See, for example, Ezekiel 4:6, which explicitly equates a day with a year. [RS]

296 (in §487:2). For the definition of a minha, see note 276 on Isaiah 43:22, 23. [LHC]

297 (in §487:2). For the meaning of one, see §§1013, 1285, 1316. For that of two, see §§649, 720, 755:2, 900. For that of three, see §§482, 720, 900, 901. For that of four, see §1686. For that of five, see §§649, 798, 1686. The significance of six has already been explained in §§62, 84–85; that of seven, in §§395, 433, 482:1 (see also notes 246 and 247). For the meaning of eight, see §2044. For that of nine, see §§1988, 2075. The meaning of ten has been touched on in §468:4. For the meaning of eleven, see §9616. For that of twelve, see §§575, 577, 648:2. This is only a very small sampling of passages that deal with the meaning of these numbers. For other perspectives on the meaning of sacred numbers, see Schneider 1995 and Lawlor 1982. [LHC, RS]

298 (in §488:2). In other words, since the literal meaning is paradoxical, there must be another meaning. [LHC]

299 (in §488:3). For more on this subject, see *Heaven and Hell* 162–169. Swedenborg's footnotes at §§165 and 167 there give extensive references back to various topics relating to state and time in *Secrets of Heaven*. [RS, SS]

300 (in §488:3). Swedenborg assigns negative connotation to "the nations" in §§139, 249 as well. In later sections, such as 1025:7, he sometimes assigns this expression a positive connotation. [LHC]

301 (in §501). Swedenborg has no difficulty here comparing the tissue layers surrounding a seed in a fruiting body with the brain and its meninges. The underlying rationale for this comparison is the *contiguum* concept appearing early in his scientific period and coming to maturity in his theological works. According to this concept, such layers are derived successively one from another in a causal series, each layer being a little less perfect than the one before. They are related—but not equivalent—structures. This anatomical principle appears in the theological works as the principle of distinct levels (traditionally rendered "discrete degrees"), which is necessary, along with the principle of correspondence, for describing how the divine order devolves from spiritual to physical levels in a step-by-step process. [RPB]

302 (in §519:1). On the name Enoch see note 255. [LHC]

303 (in §519:1). For the phrase "walk in the law," see Exodus 16:4; Psalms 78:10; 119:1. For "walk in the statutes," see Leviticus 26:3; Ezekiel 5:6–7; 18:9, 17; 36:27. For "walk in truth," 1 Kings 2:4; Psalms 26:3. [LHC]

304 (in §519:2). The word in Micah 6:8 to which Swedenborg refers here is עִם *('im)*; the word in Genesis 5:22 is אֶת *('et)*. The words are virtual synonyms. [LHC, GFD]

305 (in §521). Swedenborg here differs from much of Jewish and Christian tradition, which portrays Enoch as a figure of extraordinary sanctity who attained the heights of mystical experience. The pseudoepigraphical *Book of Enoch,* for example, which dates to the first and second centuries B.C.E., describes him as "a righteous man, whose eyes were opened by God, [and who] saw the vision of the Holy One in the heavens" (*Enoch* 1.2, in Charles 1913, 188). [RS]

306 (in §521). The Latin phrase here translated "scholarly dust" is *pulvis scholasticus*. This was a common phrase; among other things, it was the title of at least two books published in Germany as early as the 1590s (Götting 1592 and Waldung 1595), and had a long life in its German form, *Schulstaub*. It referred literally to the acrid dust that collects on the upper edges of books, but functioned as a derogatory reference to the petty subjects of study pursued by fanatical scholars. Swedenborg uses similar phrases in *Dynamics of the Soul's Domain* (= Swedenborg [1740–1741] 1955), part 2, §207; and *The Soul's Domain* (= Swedenborg [1744–1745] 1960) §9 (though the latter instance is obscured in translation). [SS]

307 (in §527). Swedenborg seems to connect the names Methushael and Methuselah with the Hebrew word מוּת *(mût),* "die." It is unclear with what Hebrew word, if any, he might be associating "Lamech." [LHC]

308 (in §530:2). The ancient church is dealt with throughout the next six chapters (§§547–1382). [LHC]

309 (in §531). Although Swedenborg gives no further explanation for this biblical phrase, the role of the people meant by "Noah," who embraced "the doctrine that was to restore what had been perverted," and the spiritual changes taking place during that

time are major focuses of the exegesis of Genesis chapters 6 through 9. See especially §§596–598, 607–609, 640, 736. [JSR]

310 (in §531). Swedenborg is drawing a connection between the name Noah and a Hebrew word for rest, נוּחַ *(nûaḥ)*. See also note 285 on the text of Genesis 5:29. [LHC]

311 (in §533). By the biblical chronology, Lamech dies five years before the Flood, Methuselah in the year of the Flood. Jewish legend says that Methuselah died just before God closed up the ark (Gaer 1966, 70). [RS]

312 (in §535). For passages discussing the meaning of Noah and his sons, see §§597, 617, 736, 764–771, 773, 915, 975, 1060–1105; for the meaning of his further offspring, §§1140–1264. [JSR]

313 (in §536). For passages discussing the perceptive ability of the churches that came before the Flood, see §§104, 125, 126, 202, 225, 371, 483, 495, 502, 503, 521. [JSR]

314 (in §544). The translation here is based on reading *statum innocentiae primi coeli,* "innocent state of the first heaven," for the first Latin edition's *coelum innocentiae primi coeli,* "heaven of innocence of the first heaven." Compare Swedenborg's unpublished manuscript *Spiritual Experiences* (= Swedenborg 1998–2002) §832, where the term "innocent state" is used in what appears to be a preliminary draft of this section. [LHC]

315 (in §545:2). Swedenborg's use of the term *fiber* here is specific for individual nerve fibers. Like other scientists of his day, he was aware of the bundling of these into fascicles, and of fascicles into nerves, and he reserves the use of the term "nerve" to these tertiary bundles of fibers, as would a scientist today. See *Dynamics of the Soul's Domain* (= Swedenborg [1740–1741] 1955), part 1, §157: "A fiber is a unit of the first order, a fascicle of fibers a unit of the second order, and a nerve a unit of the third order." For Swedenborg's descriptive anatomy and derivation of this system, see his posthumously published manuscript *Draft on the Fiber* (= Swedenborg 1976a) §§1–327. [RPB]

Notes to Genesis Chapter 6, §§547–691

316 (in §548:3). In the last three paragraphs, Swedenborg seems to follow the traditional Christian delineation of four different types of love: *eros,* or romantic, sexual love; *storge,* family feeling; *philia,* friendship; and *agape,* "charity" or selfless love. See Liddell and Scott 1968, under ἀγάπη *(agápē),* ἔρως *(éros),* φιλία *(philía),* στοργή *(storgḗ);* and Lewis [1960] 1988, throughout. [RS]

317 (in the text of Genesis 6:4). The meaning of "Nephilim" (נְפִלִים *[nəp̄ilîm]* in the Hebrew) is obscure. In the Bible it occurs in only one other place, Numbers 13:33 (see §567), and even there it has to be explained. The best working translation seems to be "giants." [RS]

318 (in the text of Genesis 6:4). The phrase here translated "and for a very long time after" represents the Latin words *et quam maxime postquam*—literally, "and as long as possible after." The Hebrew is וְגַם אַחֲרֵי־כֵן אֲשֶׁר *(vəḡam 'aḥărê-ḵēn 'ăšer),* which most translators take to mean something like "and even afterward, when." [LHC]

319 (in §562). The pre-Flood people, as Swedenborg describes them here and elsewhere, are reminiscent of arrogant semi-divine beings that occur in other traditions. The most familiar ones in the West are the Titans of Greek mythology, who challenged the authority of the gods. Hesiod's *Theogony* says: "These sons whom he begot himself great Heaven used to call Titans (Strainers) in reproach, for he said that they strained

and did presumptuously a fearful deed" (Hesiod *Theogony* 208–210, in Evelyn-White 1914, 94–95). Hindu and Buddhist cosmology speaks of the *asuras,* or demigods, who are jealous of the gods and perpetually wage war with them (Zimmer 1951, 76). [RS]

320 (in §566:1). On the apparent derivation of the name Adam from the Hebrew word for "ground," see note 208. For more on the name, see note 292. [RS]

321 (in §566:1). On the translation of the single Latin word *terra* with the two English words "earth" and "land," see note 52. Contrary to the observation Swedenborg makes here, the Latin word rendered by the word "ground" *(humus)* does in fact appear once in the first chapter, near the end of verse 25, as does the Hebrew word underlying it (אֲדָמָה *['ădāmā]*). (On this Hebrew word, see also note 208.) Swedenborg elsewhere reiterates the importance of the distinction between "earth" or "land" and "ground" (see §§90, 268, 620, 662, 872, 895), but assigns a wide and varied range of meanings to each term, depending on context. At times the meanings even overlap. For example, "earth" is here said to mean "the absence of the church or of anything having to do with the church" and "ground" is said to mean "the church." In §662 "earth" is said to mean "a person in the church" and "ground" is said to mean "the church itself." In §872 "earth" is said to refer to people before "the seed of faith's truth and goodness can be sown in them" and "ground" is said to mean "people in the church." Nevertheless in each context the distinction between the two terms is emphasized as important. [LHC, SS]

322 (in §566:3). Jeremiah 25:5 reads, "Turn, please, each of you from your evil and from the wickedness of your deeds, and live on the ground that Jehovah gave you and your ancestors from age to age." [LHC]

323 (in §566:5). For more about the "church among non-Jewish nations," see note 164. [LHC]

324 (in §568:2). For a discussion of Swedenborg's attitudes toward gender, see the reader's guide, pages 55–56. [JSR]

325 (in §568:2). The chief instance of the relationship described here, in which the male is privileged and the female submits to his direction, can be found in Genesis 3:16, when Jehovah tells the woman, "Your obedience will be to your husband; and he will rule over you." But Swedenborg is probably also referring to laws in which the lower status of women is merely implicit. See, for example, the tenth commandment (Exodus 20:17), "You shall not covet your neighbor's house. You shall not covet your neighbor's wife or male slave or female slave or ox or donkey or anything that is your neighbor's," where a wife is included among a list of possessions; or Leviticus 15:19–33, where menstruation is described in the same terms of uncleanliness as the discharge of an infection; or Numbers 5:11–31, which repeatedly speaks of a wife as subject to her husband's authority. [SS, RS]

326 (in §576:1). A bath (בַּת *[bat]*) is a Hebrew liquid measure equal to about twenty-four quarts or twenty-three liters. The statement "ten acres of vineyard will yield a single bath" consequently means that ten acres will produce enough grapes to make about twenty-four quarts of wine. The Latin word here translated "acre" *(jugerum)* and the Hebrew word for which it stands (צֶמֶד *[ṣemed]*) mean the amount of land a yoke of oxen could plow in a day, which, according to Lewis and Short (1879; see under *jugerum*) is more like two-thirds of an acre. A homer (חֹמֶר *[ḥōmer]*) is a dry or liquid measure equal to ten ephahs or ten baths, so "the sowing of a homer will yield an

ephah" means that sown seed will produce tenfold. An ephah (אֵיפָה *['êpā]*) is a dry measure equal to about twenty-one quarts or about twenty-three liters. (See Metzger and Coogan 1993, 796.) [LHC]

327 (in §576:1). A kor (כֹּר *[kōr]* in Hebrew) is the same as the liquid measure called a homer (see note 326); that is, about sixty gallons or 225 liters. [LHC]

328 (in §576:4). This bracketed interpolation is Swedenborg's. [LHC]

329 (in §576:4). The term *Decalogue* comes from the Greek for "ten words"; it reflects the underlying Hebrew word דְּבָרִים *(dəbārîm),* which literally means "words." The Hebrew, however, also has the meaning "commandments," and both senses are reflected in Swedenborg's gloss here, "the Ten Commandments, or the Ten Words" (Brown, Driver, and Briggs 1996, under דָּבָר). [RS]

330 (in §581:1). Swedenborg often describes position in the other world in relation to the human body. It is not always clear what body he means, but the foot mentioned here is likely part of the universal human he describes in §550. See also note 209. [LHC]

331 (in §581:2). On the "Nephilim," see note 317. "Anakim" is a plural word for giants taken from the Hebrew עֲנָקִים *('ănāqîm);* see Deuteronomy 1:28; 2:10, 11, 21; 9:2; Joshua 11:21, 22; 14:12, 15. On the "Rephaim," see note 195. [LHC]

332 (in §583). The translation here is based on reading "Go up, horses" *(ascendite equi)* for the first Latin edition's "Mount the horses" *(ascendite equos).* The reading "Go up, horses" occurs when this same biblical passage is quoted in §§1164:1, 1195, 2799:16, 5321:11. [LHC]

333 (in §583). "Cush" here refers to Ethiopia (see note 95) and "Put" to Libya. [LHC]

334 (in §583). The Hebrew word for "mighty" in Genesis 6:4 and in the previous quotes from Jeremiah is גִּבּוֹר *(gibbôr).* The word in Jeremiah 31:11 is חָזָק *(ḥāzāq).* The former word, *gibbôr,* is related to גֶּבֶר *(geber),* "man," and is used exclusively of males—whether human or animal. The second of the two words for "mighty," *ḥāzāq,* seems to have a connotation of hardness and is used of metals, wind, sounds, and swords as well as of people, animals, and God. [LHC, GFD]

335 (in §585). In a great many passages elsewhere, Swedenborg explores the inner meaning, or rather meanings, of the land of Canaan. For one example, see *Secrets of Heaven* 5757, which gives a range of meanings with references. See also Swedenborg's 1758 work *New Jerusalem* 5. [SS]

336 (in §586a:1). This paragraph and the next are both numbered 586 in the first Latin edition. Traditionally, this paragraph has been numbered 586, and the next, 586a; the current edition labels them 586a and 586b, respectively. [LHC]

337 (in §587:2). Swedenborg is drawing a connection between the root *miser-* in the Latin word for "mercy," *misericordia,* and the appearance of the same root in the Latin word for "miseries." The root relates to pity and wretchedness. (The second root in the word *misericordia* is *cor, cord-,* referring to "the heart.") [LHC]

338 (in §590). For examples of the use in the prophets of two terms, one involving a spiritual quality and the other a heavenly, see the passages quoted in §612, which include Psalms 15:1, 2; 25:21; 37:37; Isaiah 58:2; the passages quoted in §983, which include Jeremiah 3:14–16; 23:3; and the passages quoted in §1259, which include Isaiah 9:2, 3; 11:10–12; 14:32; 25:7. See also note 110. (For Swedenborg's inclusion of Psalms among the prophetical books of the Bible, see note 86.) [LHC]

339 (in §591). The reading "regret" *(paenitet)* for the first Latin edition's "regretted" *(paenituit)* is adopted from the immediately preceding full quotation of this verse. [LHC]

340 (in §593). On the spiritual condition of non-Christians, see, for example, §§1032–1033, 1059. [LHC]

341 (in §597:3). The rest of the discussion of Genesis 6 and all the treatment of Genesis 7 and 8 concern this shift. For specific passages on ways in which people in the ancient church differed from people in the earliest church, see, for example, §§605–609, 615, 628, 640, 784, 865. [LHC]

342 (in §598:1). For a description of this faith, see, for example, §§1025:1, 1072:2, 1079. [LHC]

343 (in the text of Genesis 6:9). "Births" is a literal translation of the Latin word here *(nativitates)*, which is a literal translation of the Hebrew word (תּוֹלְדֹת *[tôlǝdōṯ]*). It means a history, often including genealogy. [LHC]

344 (in the text of Genesis 6:14). "Gopher" is a Hebrew word (גֹפֶר *[gōp̄er]*). Although Swedenborg does explain in §643:1 that gopher wood is "a kind of wood loaded with sulfur, similar to fir," the exact identity of the wood remains uncertain. [LHC]

345 (in the text of Genesis 6:15). A cubit is an ancient measure equal to the length from the tip of the middle finger to the elbow, or between seventeen and twenty-two inches (between forty-three and fifty-six centimeters). [SS]

346 (in §606). Swedenborg is perhaps referring to a school of biblical interpretation in historical Christianity usually called either allegorical or spiritual exegesis, in which things and persons as well as storylines are interpreted symbolically for a meaning that may or may not correlate closely with the literal text. The New Testament itself is replete with an early form, called typology, of this method of reading the Jewish Scripture (that is, a figure or event in the Jewish Scripture is interpreted as prefiguring some aspect of the Christ event). For example, 1 Peter 3:20–21 asserts that Noah and his family being saved in the midst of the waters by the ark refers directly to the Christ who would be coming to save through the waters of baptism (the Flood and ark are the types; baptism and Christ are the antitypes, that is, the things foreshadowed). Augustine, whose work Swedenborg read with care, construed the dimensions of Noah's ark as corresponding to the dimensions of Christ's body (*City of God* 15:26; see also 15:27). Metaphoric reading of the Jewish Scriptures expanded greatly in the third and fourth centuries through Alexandrian exegetes Origen and Athanasius and continued to develop for another thousand years primarily in the Latin church through some of the greatest Christian authors (Jerome [around 347–around 420], Gregory the Great [540–604], the Venerable Bede [672 or 673–735], Bernard of Clairvaux [1090–1153], and Richard of St. Victor [died 1173]). This tradition finally waned during the Renaissance, when scholarly focus turned with a new fascination to the study of biblical texts in their historical formation, and emphasizing the "plain sense" of Scripture captured the day, though scholars in Swedenborg's century were still aware of the allegorical tradition. The two-volume *Medieval Exegesis: The Four Senses of Scripture* (Lubac 1998) is the best study of this tradition of interpretation. [JFL]

347 (in §607:1). On the heavenly nature of the earliest church, see, for example, §§85, 201–202. [LHC]

348 (in §608). In this discussion it is important to remember that *conscientia,* the Latin word here translated "conscience," can also mean "consciousness." See note 98. [RS]

349 (in §617). On the approaches to religion symbolized by Shem, Ham, and Japheth, see, for example, §§975, 1062, 1083. [LHC]

350 (in §618). The exact meaning of the Latin clause here translated "the words are not divided up," *nec distinguit inter voces,* is not entirely certain. It may refer to the fact that the Word in its earliest form was not divided up into sentences by punctuation, this being a later innovation; see §§4987, 5578, and 7191. It may also refer to the fact that in early manuscripts no breaks between words were marked, allowing for wide ranges in interpretation that are a common feature of rabbinical exegesis. In regard to tense, Hebrew does not have the kind of tense that modern English does. Instead it has two "aspects," one for continuous or repeated action and the other for single events. In English translation, the former is usually rendered as a present or future and the latter as a past, but that is due more to the requirements of English than to the content of the Hebrew. [LHC, RS]

351 (in §624). On the sanctity of the name Jehovah, see note 28. [RS]

352 (in §626). Psalms 11:4 and Isaiah 33:20, 37:17, for instance, speak of God as seeing with his eyes. [LHC]

353 (in §630). The Latin for this last clause reads *apud Jehovam non sit nisi quam Esse,* literally, "with Jehovah, there is nothing but being." The concept of being, *esse,* is an important part of Swedenborg's philosophical system. In accord with much of the Western philosophic tradition since the Middle Ages, he distinguishes between *esse,* "being" in its pure sense, and *existere,* "being" as it is manifested. See *True Christianity* 21: "The underlying divine reality is intrinsic reality *[esse],* and is also an intrinsic capacity to become manifest *[existere]*" (translation by Jonathan S. Rose). In *Divine Love and Wisdom* 14, he writes, "Wherever there is reality *[esse],* there is manifestation *[existere]*: the one does not occur without the other" (translation by George F. Dole). [RS, RHK]

354 (in §637:1). In Swedenborg's system, the human figure has correspondences at many levels. Here he indicates that humanity on earth resembles a single individual. In *Heaven and Hell* 59–77, he says that all of heaven has this form (see note 5 above), as well as each community in heaven (compare note 209 above). Moreover, each community in heaven has its place in this body (see *Heaven and Hell* 65). Similarly, here on earth the church constitutes the heart of humanity, as this passage indicates. [RS]

355 (in §640). For the description of the church represented by Enosh, see §439. [LHC] The temporal overlap of the church of Enosh with that of Noah is supported by the life spans given in the genealogy of Genesis 5, according to which Enosh, the son of Seth, would have been alive for eighty-four years after Noah was born. [LSW]

356 (in §641). Swedenborg was not the first thinker to localize mental functions in different parts of the brain. Attempts were made in this direction as early as the medieval era, when mental function was frequently said (for example) to be centered in the brain's ventricles (Gaukroger 1995, 278). Swedenborg himself, in *The Soul's Domain,* suggested that the cerebrum is the residence of the will, while the cerebellum is the residence of "nature," that is, involuntary or autonomic processes (Swedenborg [1744–1745] 1960, §394 note m). But Swedenborg does in this and similar passages (for example, *Secrets of Heaven* 3884, 4052) appear to have anticipated modern brain research by assigning different functions to the left and right hemispheres of the brain. See §644. For Swedenborg's manuscripts on the cerebrum, unpublished during his lifetime, see

Swedenborg 1976d; other earlier discussions of brain form and function can be found in *Dynamics of the Soul's Domain* (= Swedenborg [1740–1741] 1955) and *Draft on the Fiber* (= Swedenborg 1976a). [RHK, RS, SS]

357 (in §642). The translation here is based on reading "that [there were to be] compartments" *(quod mansiones)* for the first Latin edition's "what the compartments [were]" *(quid mansiones)*. The original Latin is plausible in itself, but does not accurately represent the verse it summarizes, Genesis 6:14. Elliott's translation (Swedenborg [1749–1756] 1983–1999) also assumes the emendation. [LHC]

358 (in §643:3). The word *tophet* is Hebrew (תָּפְתֶּה *[topteh]*). It is usually considered a proper noun, the name of a location in the Valley of Ben-Hinnom (that is, Gehenna) used for human sacrifice. On Gehenna, see note 239. [LHC, RS]

359 (in §643:4). Although the skin disease mentioned in the Leviticus verses is no longer thought to be leprosy, that is the traditional interpretation of the Hebrew term (צָרַעַת *[ṣāra'at]*). Leviticus (14:34, 44, 55) applies the term to a house or garment, suggesting that it may refer to a type of fungus (Brown, Driver, and Briggs 1996, under צרעת). Swedenborg translates it with the Latin term for leprosy *(lepra)*. [LHC, RS]

360 (in §643:4). See §§8354–8356 for Swedenborg's explanation of the passage in Exodus. *Secrets of Heaven* does not extend as far as Leviticus (see note 90 and the reader's guide, pages 24–25 note 14). [LHC]

361 (in §644). On Swedenborg's recognition of the division of functions between the two hemispheres of the brain, see note 356. [RS]

362 (in §645). Swedenborg is saying (in the previous sentence) that the Hebrew text actually reads "protect it with tar" rather than "tar it with tar." The question, then, is why he chose to translate the verb as "tar" rather than as "protect." The verb at issue, כָּפַרְתָּ *(kāpartā)*, may be etymologically related either to the noun for tar, כֹּפֶר *(kōper)*, or to כִּפֶּר *(kipper)*, a verb whose concrete meaning is "cover" but whose more common, abstract meaning is "atone" or "appease" (see note 204). Though dictionaries disagree on the point, Swedenborg clearly accepts both connections. On the basis of the relationship with *kōper*, "tar," he feels justified in translating it simply with the verb "to tar." However, on the basis of the verb's relationship with *kipper*, "cover" or "atone," he identifies the real meaning as "protect," for two possible reasons. One is that covering the ark with tar is the same as protecting it with tar. The other is that Swedenborg describes atonement as a form of protection (see the following sentence in the section). This meaning, "protect," provides a parallel with the symbolism of preservation that Swedenborg gives for the expression "tarring with tar." No matter whether *kāpartā* is in fact related by etymology to *kōper* or *kipper*, it is associated with both by sound, since all three Hebrew words are based on the same string of consonants. [LHC]

363 (in §654). Swedenborg is probably alluding here to Romans 10:17. In Swedenborg's works, this type of locution ("as churches today know") often, though not invariably, seems to be an indirect reference to the Epistles of Paul. See, for example, *Secrets of Heaven* 1563:1, 4286:1 (references to such passages as 2 Corinthians 4:16; Romans 2:28–29); *Secrets of Heaven* 1659:2 (a reference to Hebrews 5:9–10, among others); *Marriage Love* 426 (a reference to Romans 7:22–23). Contrast, however, *True Christianity* 104 and *Divine Providence* 150:1, which use a similar locution but quote books other than the Epistles in support of their points. [SS, LSW, LHC]

364 (in §655:1). The gloss in parentheses is Swedenborg's; he apparently felt it necessary to add the clarification because the Hebrew word (שְׁמָשׁוֹת *[šəmāšōṯ]*) literally means "suns" but connotes "windows" in this context. [LHC]

365 (in §655:2). Swedenborg here inserts a Latin transliteration of the Hebrew word קִפֹּד *(qippōḏ)*, the meaning of which is uncertain. Elsewhere (§1188:4, for instance), Swedenborg, like Schmidt 1696, translates the word as *anataria,* a water-loving bird of prey capable of eating ducks; the exact species is unknown. [LHC]

366 (in §657). On the intellect, see note 51. [RS]

367 (in §657). The Latin term used here is *influxus*. In Swedenborg's usage, it can mean "influx," "inflow," or "spiritual influence." In the present translation the rendering "influx" is reserved for instances in which Swedenborg uses the word in the narrow, technical sense common in philosophical disputes in the seventeenth and eighteenth centuries, disputes specifically about how the soul acts on the body (see note 153). The point Swedenborg is making here is that the true explanation of what the philosophers call "influx" in their convoluted theorizing is simply the Lord's influence as just described. For further discussion, see §§6053–6058, 6189–6215, 6307–6327, 6466–6496, 6598–6626 below in the present work. For a topical index to later passages on this subject throughout *Secrets of Heaven,* see *Heaven and Hell* 603:5–8. [JSR, SS]

368 (in §662). Sections 620 and 636 do suggest that "earth" (or "land") symbolizes the people who live in a given area, but the most detailed treatment, in §566, uses Scripture to demonstrate that "earth" or "land" often symbolizes areas where the church does *not* exist, and that a third term, "ground," symbolizes the church's territory. See also note 321. [LHC]

369 (in §665). On the inner meaning of covenants, see, for example, §§1023, 1038, 1864. [LHC]

370 (in §666:5). The first Latin edition cites Exodus 24:4, 5, 6, 7, 27, and does not cite Exodus 34 at all here, but there is no verse 27 in Exodus 24. The only verse in the five books of Moses that specifically refers to a "book of the covenant" is Exodus 24:7. The others listed here have to do directly or indirectly with the written law. The third Latin edition emends the reference to 24:4–7, 34:27. [LHC]

371 (in §675). The full force of this biblical quotation is difficult to capture in English. The Greek word for "spirit" in John's original is πνεῦμα *(pneûma)*; Swedenborg's Latin is *spiritus*. Both of these words have broader meanings than "spirit" in English: they refer to "breath" and "wind" as well as what we normally associate with "spirit" (Liddell and Scott 1968, under πνεῦμα; Chadwick and Rose 2008, under *spiritus*). See also note 106. [RS]

372 (in §678). The human tendency to measure what is good by what is pleasurable figured importantly in Greek and Roman theories of human psychology and therefore in ancient philosophy. The challenge of living well, according to many ancient philosophers, lay in determining what was truly good, not just what appeared to be good, because the pleasure deriving from true good would ultimately be superior to any pleasure that tended toward self-destruction (see, for example, Plato *Republic* 2:505–506). Swedenborg likewise judges pleasure by its ultimate goal. In §§994–995 below, he lists the various pleasures of human life, both those connected with the will and those

connected with the understanding, and insists that "no one is ever forbidden to enjoy personal and sensory pleasures" as long as those pleasures originate "in the good impulses of neighborly love and in the true ideas comprising faith in the Lord" and thus conduce to helping the individual lead a useful life. See also his 1745 work *Worship and Love of God* 82:2; and his unpublished 1742 work *Draft of a Rational Psychology* (= Swedenborg 2001a) §§457–459. [SS]

373 (in §680:2). The phrase "the crudest of material concerns" here may be a veiled reference to the search for alchemical information supposedly hidden in the Bible (compare *Sacred Scripture* 23:4). There were numerous alchemical readings of Scripture in Swedenborg's times; see Principe and Newman 2001, 398; Matton 1988. On Swedenborg's attitude toward Jews, see note 182 and the reader's guide, pages 51–55. [JSR]

374 (in §684). For a more detailed elaboration of the schema of the three heavens set out in this section, see *Heaven and Hell* 29–40, a passage that contains many footnote references back to further discussion in *Secrets of Heaven* itself. [RS]

375 (in §691). For more on the communities of heaven, see, in the treatment of Genesis, the material at the ends of chapters 27–42 (§§3624–3649, 3741–3750, 3883–3896, 4039–4055, 4218–4228, 4318–4331, 4403–4421, 4523–4534, 4622–4634, 4652–4660, 4791–4806, 4931–4953, 5050–5062, 5171–5190, 5377–5396, 5552–5573). [LHC]

Notes to Genesis Chapter 7, §§692–823

376 (in §692). For a condensed portrait of the hells, see *Heaven and Hell* 536–588. For discussions of hell in *Secrets of Heaven* see, in the treatment of Genesis, the material here at the beginning of chapter 7; and at the end of chapter 7, the beginning and end of chapter 8, the beginning of chapter 9, and the end of chapter 43 (§§692–700, 814–831, 938–970, 5711–5727). [LHC, RS]

377 (in §698). On devastation in the Bible, see the many passages quoted in §5376, including Psalms 40:2; Isaiah 6:9–13; 24:1–23; 51:3; Ezekiel 12:19, 20; 36:3–12. [LHC]

378 (in §699). Swedenborg is referring here to the bronze wall mentioned in Jeremiah 1:18 and 15:20. [LHC]

379 (in the text of Genesis 7:2). The phrase "a man and his wife," which occurs twice in this verse, refers to the animals; it is a literal rendering of the Latin *virum et uxorem ejus*, which is in turn a literal rendering of the original Hebrew אִישׁ וְאִשְׁתּוֹ *('îš və'ištô)*. The phrase is elsewhere translated "the male and his female" (in the King James Version) or "the male and its mate" (in the New Revised Standard Version). [RS]

380 (in the text of Genesis 7:4). The Hebrew word for "substance," יְקוּם *(yəqûm)*, can mean "living things" or possessions in general, as in Deuteronomy 11:6 (Brown, Driver, and Briggs 1996, under יקום). [RS]

381 (in the text of Genesis 7:6). On the Hebraism "a son of (so many) years," see note 286. [LHC]

382 (in §705:2). The translation here is based on reading "went down" *(penetravit)* for the first Latin edition's "goes down" *(penetrat)*. Elliott (Swedenborg [1749–1756] 1983–1999) also adopts the past tense for this verb in his translation. [LHC]

383 (in §708). On the relationship between "Jehovah" and Being, see note 353. [RS]

384 (in §709). This passage is reminiscent of Kabbalistic teachings that the names of God reflect different aspects of the divine nature. The name יהוה (YHVH), "Yahweh" or "Jehovah," is associated with the merciful aspect of the divine; אֱלֹהִים *(ĕlōhîm),* "God," with the severe aspect (Gikatilla 1994, 248). Here Swedenborg associates Jehovah with charity, Elohim with faith. [RS]

385 (in §709). For a summary of changes preparatory to rebirth in the people called "Noah," see §§600–604, 608–609. [LHC]

386 (in §709). For a discussion of these verses, see §§30–36 above. [RS]

387 (in §711). Swedenborg's cross-reference here seems slightly inaccurate. In explaining Genesis 6:18 at §667, he does not say that to enter the ark means being prepared; he says that it means being saved. Earlier than that, however, in §653, where Genesis 6:16 is explained, he describes the process of sifting out false ideas as a preparation—that is, for regeneration and thus for salvation. See also §§654, 671, 701, 706, 709. [SS]

388 (in §715). On bad and savage animals, see §45 above. [RS]

389 (in §716:1). On the symbolism of the number seven in Scripture, see §395 and note 247. [RS]

390 (in §716:2). By the term "the rituals of the representative church," Swedenborg means the rituals enjoined on the Jews in the Hebrew Scriptures. He indicates what he means by a representative church in §§101, 349:1, 730:4–5, 1437. [LHC]

391 (in §716:2). The Latin words here translated "consecrated" and "consecrate" stem from the verb *sanctificare,* which is related to the Latin word for "holy," *sanctus.* This is no doubt why, for the purposes of this discussion of holiness, Swedenborg emphasized these words. [LHC]

392 (in §716:3). The first edition incorrectly identifies the Book of Numbers as the source of the quotation that follows at this point, and mentions no book name where the citation is given following the quotation; so the reading "in another place" has been accepted instead, to echo the phrase, "from another place," just above in the section. This is Swedenborg's normal reference for a different passage from the same Bible book that has just been cited. In keeping with this practice of Swedenborg's, the reading "in another place" has been supplied for the reading of the first edition, "in Leviticus" *(in Levitico),* before the next quotation. [LHC]

393 (in §716:3). On Swedenborg's attitude toward Jews, see note 182 and the reader's guide, pages 51–55. [JSR]

394 (in §718). On the symbolism of a man or husband, and of a woman or wife, see §§158, 265, 429, 476, 668. Compare also §§54, 489–490, 568, 570, 672. [LHC]

395 (in §718). The complementary qualities of activeness and passivity entered Western thought most forcefully in the philosophy of Aristotle; see in particular *Physics* 3:1–3 (200b–202b), where they are utilized to describe motion and change: the mover or changer is active, the moved or changed passive. Over the course of his works, Swedenborg turns to this contrast numerous times to distinguish complementary qualities or forces. In *Secrets of Heaven* 4653:1, speech is said to be active, and hearing passive; in 6987, spoken thought is said to be active, and unspoken thought passive; in *Divine Love and Wisdom* 178, gases are active and solids are passive; in *Soul-Body Interaction* 11, the spiritual is said to be active and the material to be passive; in *True Christianity* 110:6, the Lord is said to be active in us, and

by flowing into us, to make us active also—an inflow without which we would be completely passive. Compare also *Worship and Love of God* 80, where love is defined as the quintessential emotion belonging to the union of active and passive forces. It is interesting to note that although Swedenborg uses marriage here in *Secrets of Heaven* 718 as an indicator of close union, he does not label either party to it as exclusively active or passive. [SS]

396 (in §724). Swedenborg here refers to the Protestant doctrine of the justification by grace through faith alone. The doctrine holds that God forgives people's sins and saves them from damnation through the grace he bestows because of their faith, not through any merit they have won by doing good works for others; it was particularly, though not exclusively, held by Lutherans. For further discussion of the doctrine by Swedenborg, see *True Christianity* 355–377 (and also his 1763 work *Faith* 44–72); for a recent, brief overview adding significant historical nuance, see Erwin 2006, 90–92. [SS]

397 (in §724). This was written in a time and place in which the outward show of piety was a prerequisite for public office and a career in the church could be quite lucrative. The subversion of religion for private advantage is a prevalent theme in Swedenborg's theological writings (see, for example, *Secrets of Heaven* 2027:3, 2261:2, 2329:1, 2354:2, and *Revelation Unveiled* 784, 799, to mention just a few passages), though it is often stated obliquely, as here. [LHC]

398 (in §725). On the symbolism of a man or male, and of a wife or a woman, see §718 and the sections referred to in note 394. [LHC]

399 (in §726). On Being, see note 353. [RS]

400 (in §730:1). The other representative churches mentioned here are those that existed at the time of the ancient church. See §§796, 9280:2. [LHC]

401 (in §730:4). Several of the matters mentioned here (the story of Joshua and Caleb, the wandering and death in the wilderness, and many of the plagues and slaughters the Israelites suffered) occur in the Book of Numbers, which Swedenborg apparently originally intended to cover in *Secrets of Heaven* (see the reader's guide, pages 24–25 note 14). However, for the symbolism of the people's murmurings against God (and his servants), see the explanations of Exodus 14:10–15; 15:24–25; 16:2–12; 17:1–7 (§§8158–8181, 8344, 8351–8358, 8402–8499, 8556–8591). Additionally, the massacre or plague referred to in Exodus 32:35 is explained in its place as symbolizing devastation (§§10496, 10510–10512). [LHC]

402 (in §731). On the dispelling of evil mentioned here, see §719. On the symbolism of tares, see note 259. [LHC]

403 (in §734). For the passages to which Swedenborg refers here on the truth in the intellect, see §§640–642, 651–658; for the passages on the good in the will, see §§701, 709–710, 713–721, 732. [LHC]

404 (in §736). On the "Nephilim," see §§581–583 and note 317. [LHC]

405 (in §737:1). That is, 6 × 10 × 10. [LHC]

406 (in §737:2). The Latin phrase here translated "destroy a sixth of you" is *Sextabo te*. The Hebrew is שִׁשֵּׂאתִיךָ (*šiššētîḵā*), which most modern translators understand to mean "I will lead you on," but the verb appears to resemble the Hebrew word for "six" (שֵׁשׁ [*šēš*]), and the verb that Swedenborg (like Schmidt 1696) uses (*sextare*) is accordingly based on the Latin word for "six" (*sex*). Hebrew-Latin lexicons of Swedenborg's day such as Alberti 1704 and Buxtorf 1735 use this same Latin verb to define the Hebrew. The closest analogy in English would be *decimate,* derived from the Latin *decem,* or

"ten," whose original meaning was to destroy one out of ten (*Oxford English Dictionary*, under "decimate"). [LHC, RS]

407 (in §739:1). For Bible passages relating to water, see the verses quoted in §§28, 108–109, 680:3, and 790. [LHC]

408 (in §739:3). The Latin word translated "flood" or "overflow" in all the other quotations here and in §705 is *inundatio* (or one of its variants). The one used in the quotation of Psalms 29:10 is *diluvium,* which is the same word that Swedenborg uses in quotations from Genesis. These distinctions reflect differences in the original language; the Hebrew word used in Psalms 29:10 (מַבּוּל *[mabbûl]*) is the same as that used in Genesis and is different from the term used anywhere else in the Old Testament. [LHC]

409 (in §739:3). For more on this symbolic mode of writing among the earliest people, see §66. [LHC]

410 (in §749). This seems to be a slight misstatement. Genesis 6:19 does refer to "every living thing" as being male and female, and the meaning of "male" and "female" is given in §672. But it is in Genesis 7:2, 3 that the expression "man and wife" is applied to animals and "male and female" to birds, and the explanation of this distinction appears in §725. [LHC]

411 (in §751:3). Swedenborg refers, perhaps, to such experiences as related in §§814–831, 938–969. His *Journal of Dreams* (Swedenborg 2001b) and his diary *Spiritual Experiences* (Swedenborg 1998–2002 and Swedenborg 1978) offer examples too numerous to cite. [LHC, RS]

412 (in §755:2). The equivalence of two and six is explained at verse 2 (§720); the actual meaning of six is treated more fully at verse 6 (§737). [LHC]

413 (in §756:1). Suph (סוּף *[sûp]*) is a Hebrew word for "reed," and the name of the sea is usually rendered either "Sea of Reeds" or "Red Sea." Swedenborg, though, consistently uses the transliteration. [LHC]

414 (in §767). There is no §766 in Swedenborg's original text. [LHC]

415 (in §768:3). Swedenborg's reference to a "person's" wife recalls his use of similar phrasing at Genesis 2:18–25 and in his discussion of those verses in §§131–167, where he describes Adam, like Noah here, as standing for people in general, male and female. [LHC]

416 (in §768:3). On the churches symbolized by Shem, Ham, and Japheth, see, for example, §§975, 1062, 1083. [LHC]

417 (in §770). The "head of the church" is an expression used in the Epistles to refer to Christ; see Ephesians 1:22, 23; 5:23; Colossians 1:18. [LHC, LSW]

418 (in §771). On the word "jot," see note 11. [LHC]

419 (in §774). The Hebrew term Swedenborg refers to here is חַיָּה *(ḥayyā)*. The same word is used in Ezekiel for the four guardian beings (see Ezekiel 1:5), and it may be that Swedenborg has those beings or something like them in mind when he mentions "a living creature with a living soul." [RS, JSR, LHC]

420 (in §774). On the symbolism of all kinds of animals, see §§45–46, 142, 143, 246, 714–715, 719. For the symbolism of creeping things specifically, see §§44, 195–197, 251, 594, 674, 746. [LHC]

421 (in §775:2). The Latin phrase here translated "to continue in existence is constantly to come into existence" is *substantia est perpetua existentia*—a common theological maxim (see §§3483, 5084:3; see also *Marriage Love* 380:8; *Soul-Body Interaction* 4).

Swedenborg frequently built on it; see §§3648, 4322, 4523:3, 5116:3, 5377, 6040:1, 6482, 9502, 9847, 10076:5, 10152:3, 10252:3, 10266; *Heaven and Hell* 106, 303; *Divine Love and Wisdom* 151–152; *Divine Providence* 3:2; *Soul-Body Interaction* 9:1; *True Christianity* 46, 224:1. This notion is referred to as commonplace in part 5 of Descartes's *Discourse on Method* (Descartes [1637] 1968, 64): "It is certain, and it is an opinion commonly held among theologians, that the action by which [God] conserves [the world] now is the same as that by which he created it." Elsewhere Descartes offers this explanation: "The present time has no causal dependence on the time immediately preceding it. Hence, in order to secure the continued existence of a thing, no less a cause is required than that needed to produce it at the first" (Descartes [1641] 1952, 131). Thomas Aquinas makes a similar statement about all "creatures," that is, created things: "The being of every creature depends on God, so that not for a moment could it subsist [have independent existence], but would fall into nothingness were it not kept in being by the operation of the Divine power" (*Summa Theologiae* 1:104:1; translation in Aquinas 1952). In support of his position, Aquinas in turn cites another Church Father, Gregory the Great, specifically his *Moralia in Job* (Ethical Disputations on Job) 16:37; he is probably thinking of Gregory's statement there that "all things subsist in him [God]. . . . No created thing avails in itself either to subsist or to move." This Scholastic theory of perpetual creation is also discussed by the Anglo-Irish philosopher George Berkeley (1685–1753) in his work *The Principles of Human Knowledge* (Berkeley [1710] 1952) §46. [JSR, SS, RS]

422 (in §775:2). On the meaning of the phrase "people who worship the material world," see note 157. [SS]

423 (in §776:2). For a similarly emphatic distinction between mere metaphor and the living correspondence of biblical imagery, see §§8989:11, 9272:2, 9828:4. [SS]

424 (in §776:5). For the meaning of the expression "the church among non-Jews," see note 164. [LHC]

425 (in §777). Swedenborg probably has in mind here the fact that the Hebrew word for "wing" (כָּנָף *[kānāp]*) is used for other kinds of extremities, as, for instance, the edge of a garment (1 Samuel 15:27) and the farthest reaches of the earth (Isaiah 24:16). See also note 240. [LHC]

426 (in §780). Mark 16:15 mentions "all creation" or "every creature." 2 Corinthians 5:17 and Galatians 6:15 speak of a "new creation" or "new creature." [LHC]

427 (in §782). The translation here is based on reading "verse 15" instead of the first edition's apparently erroneous reference to verse 11. [LHC]

428 (in §783). On the symbolism of the phrase "male and female," see §§718, 725, and the sections referred to in note 394. [LHC]

429 (in §783). For previous discussion of this preparation to receive, see §§709, 711; on goodness and truth as what is to be received, see the explanations of Genesis 6:21, 22 (§§676–683). [LHC]

430 (in §784:2). On these guardian beings, see note 193. [RS]

431 (in §788:1). On evil heredity, see note 207. [RS]

432 (in §788:2). On Swedenborg's attitude toward Jews, see notes 182 and 203, and the reader's guide, pages 51–55. [JSR]

433 (in §788:2). The "earliest people" referred to here are presumably the fallen of the earliest church. [LHC]

434 (in §789). On this spiritual elevation, see, for example, §§1044:3, 1857:3, 2116:2. [LHC]

435 (in §790:1). On the meaning of water as spiritual things, see the biblical passages quoted and explained in §§28, 680:3. [LHC]

436 (in §790:1). On the meaning of water as falsity, see the biblical passages previously quoted and explained in §§705, 739. See also note 435. [LHC]

437 (in §790:2). The land seems to be pictured as a huge bird throwing a shadow with its wings or, alternatively, perhaps a cloud of locusts. Swedenborg, Schmidt 1696, and some other older Bible translators read the key Hebrew word as meaning "shadowing"; modern translators take it as referring to the sound of bird or insect wings. The Hebrew root in question is צָלַל (*ṣālal*), which represents several homographs, including one that means to be dark and one that means to tingle in the ears. [LHC]

438 (in §793). In the Hebrew alphabet, the first three vowels correspond roughly to English *a*, *e*, and *i*; the last two, to *o* and *u*. In later comments on this subject, Swedenborg gradually moves the *a* vowel into the heavenly category. See *Heaven and Hell* 241; *Sacred Scripture* 90; and *True Christianity* 278. [LHC]

439 (in §794:2). Possibly an echo of Matthew 10:28 ("Do not fear those who kill the body but cannot kill the soul. Instead fear one who is able to destroy both body and soul in hell.") or Mark 8:36 ("What good does it do a person to gain the whole world and lose his or her soul?"). [RS, LHC]

440 (in §795:2). "The enveloping layers" here are the layers of cloth in which people wrapped their faces when mourning. See Brown, Driver, and Briggs 1996, under לוֹט. The literal meaning of the passage quoted is unintelligible without its full context; it says that on Mount Zion, that is, in Israel, Jehovah will "swallow up" or obliterate the veil of mourning that conceals the people; in other words, he will end their sufferings. [LHC, SS]

441 (in §803:2). Swedenborg emphasizes that while it is possible to tell lies on earth, it is not possible to do so in heaven, where "no one can conceal inner character by facial expression and pretend." This is because angels can see the quality of others "instantly, from their faces" (*Heaven and Hell* 48). Moreover, as indicated in §925:2, in heaven it is even possible to discern the nature of a being from his or her aura. See also note 210, and notes 33, 64, and 139. [RS]

442 (in §804). Swedenborg describes Genesis 7:10; 8:14, 18–19; 9:7; 10:30; 20:16; 22:18, 23; 27:17, 45; 29:13; 37:1; and Exodus 15:9 as offering summations by means of a particular phrase, though many different phrases are used, and they do not always appear in final position in translations of the Bible. See §§753, 899, 915, 916, 1018, 1249, 2578, 2854, 2866, 3546, 3617, 3810, 4667:1, 9483. [LHC]

443 (in §805:2). The breathing described in §97 is also discussed in §607. On Swedenborg's experience of internal breathing, see note 107. [LHC, RS]

444 (in §805:3). For later discussion of this second church as a spiritual church, see §§875:4, 916. In §1120, the change in respiration of the earliest people is more directly linked to a decline in their state of love and faith and an increase in their falsity. [SS]

445 (in §813). Swedenborg seems to be viewing fifteen and ten as symbolizing fractional amounts, which vanish into almost nothing when multiplied together. [LHC]

446 (in §813). According to Swedenborg, there are always angels with everyone (*Secrets of Heaven* 697). When people read Scripture, the angels who are with them follow along,

so to speak, and yet the angels understand the contents in a spiritual way, while people tend to remain in an earthly understanding (*Secrets of Heaven* 1767, 3735:2). In this way Scripture provides a link between heaven and earth (*Heaven and Hell* 305). Although Swedenborg states here in a general way that angels "fully understand" Scripture when we read, elsewhere he cites various factors that either improve or inhibit their understanding. For example, angels' understanding is improved when children read Scripture (*Secrets of Heaven* 1776, 1871), or when adults read it because they love to do so (*Secrets of Heaven* 1767), or view it as a sacred text (*Secrets of Heaven* 3735:2), or read it with innocence (*Secrets of Heaven* 3839:1) or as part of a quest for truth and for guidance in life (*Secrets of Heaven* 9188:8). The angels' understanding decreases when people bring predetermined false notions to their reading, or read primarily for worldly or selfish reasons (*Secrets of Heaven* 9039:1, 9188:8, 10551:3). [JSR]

447 (in §814:2). This detail does not seem to have racial implications. Swedenborg seems to have a positive view of black people in general, and in fact specifically states that "of non-Christians, the Africans are especially valued in heaven. They accept the good and true things of heaven more readily than others do" (*Heaven and Hell* 326). See also note 478. [RS]

448 (in §814:2). Swedenborg also describes this ring and its spikes in his *Spiritual Experiences* (= Swedenborg 1998–2002) §1280. There is no indication what part of the body it circles, if any. One possibility is that it may be like a dog collar. [LHC]

449 (in §815). On the hell called Gehenna in the spiritual world, see §§825–826. On Gehenna in the Bible, see note 239. [LHC, RS]

450 (in §817). For a more detailed version of this same story, see *Spiritual Experiences* (= Swedenborg 1998–2002) §1260. [LHC]

Notes to Genesis Chapter 8, §§824–946

451 (in §824:1). A trephine is a version of a trepan, a small surgical saw used to saw skulls open (*Oxford English Dictionary,* under "trepan," "trephine"). [RS]

452 (in §826). The exact sect or sects Swedenborg has in mind are not ascertainable, but there is no small supply of candidates. The broad extent of conjugal experimentation among Christian groups is documented as early as about 200 by Clement of Alexandria; he writes scathingly of the Carpocratians, who "think that wives ought to be common property" and thus "bring scandal down upon the name of Christ" (*Stromata* 3:2). He also describes similar Christians, without labeling them, who practiced "sexual intercourse in common" as a "mystical communion" (*Stromata* 3:4). Another obscure Christian group, the Adamites, which seems to have begun around Clement's era, is said to have tried to emulate the original innocence of Adam and Eve by, among other practices, rejecting the sacrament of marriage. Their views resurfaced among Christian groups from time to time over the centuries. Swedenborg's readers had ample opportunities to become aware of these heretical groups. The Adamites, for instance, were mentioned as a curiosity by both ancient and contemporary writers—for example, perhaps by Clement himself (see the vague reference to the "followers of Prodicus" in *Stromata* 3:4); certainly by Epiphanius (after 310–403), another early Christian writer, in his *Panarion* (heresy 52; see Epiphanius 1990, 189); by Augustine (*On Heresies* 31; see Augustine 1956, 76–77, 150–151); and by the radical French writer of 1694–1778, Voltaire (Voltaire

1924, under "Nakedness"). In his other writings, Swedenborg shows himself to be very familiar with ancient Christian sects in general (see *True Christianity* 378:2) and with contemporary variations such as the Quakers and Moravians (see his 1763 work *Supplements* 83–90). [SS]

453 (in §827). The term "ether" in this sense refers to a subtle and invisible atmosphere believed to surround the earth at a level above the familiar atmosphere; compare *Revelation Unveiled* 907 and *Marriage Love* 188:3. (For a summary of the various meanings of this term in Swedenborg, see Swedenborg [1771] 2006, 696 note 116.) [RS]

454 (in §828). For a discussion of how love unites the minds of marriage partners, see *Marriage Love* 179. [RS]

455 (in §828). This may be an echo of Revelation 17:1–5, which refers to a "whore," "a woman sitting upon a scarlet beast, full of blasphemous names." [RS]

456 (in §828). The assertion that the children of seducers perish early is unusual to Swedenborg, and the specification that he has been told this by others is striking. He elsewhere (for example, §8550) states that the impure habits of a parent are passed on to a child as evil, but the implication of such passages is that the evil has spiritual, not physical, consequences. In addition, in *Marriage Love* 392 he says that the Lord so orders the universe that even evil people love and care for their children. However, the actions of men such as are here described are counter to the ideal of faithful monogamy, a state that Swedenborg saw as divinely ordained for the generation of physical progeny (see *Marriage Love* 481); so it is at least consonant with his theology that the intercourse of those who flouted married love should prove unproductive. Furthermore, the belief that the children of parents who engage in sexual irregularities are defective can be found in at least one other author of the early modern era (see the instance cited in Harvey 1994, 26). In any case, when children failed to thrive, it would have been logical to seek in the actions of the parents for an explanation. [SS]

457 (in §830). The translation here is based on reading "straw hat" *(pileo canneo)*, as in *Spiritual Experiences* (= Swedenborg 1998–2002) §2498 and Elliott's translation (Swedenborg [1749–1756] 1983–1999), for the first Latin edition's "fleshy hat" *(pileo carneo)*. [LHC]

458 (in §831:2). Sirens were mythological creatures who lured sailors to their deaths by sweet singing, or, as in Homer's *Odyssey* (12:39–54, 158–200), by offering knowledge. Swedenborg has more to say about spiritual sirens in §§959, 1983; *Marriage Love* 505:2; and *True Christianity* 80:1. [LHC, RS]

459 (in §833). In §§833–836 Swedenborg lists four states depicted in Genesis 8. This is the first of three interconnected numbering systems he uses for the states portrayed in this chapter. The second numbering system initially comes up in the next section, §834, and the third in §§835–836. The first system, with its four elements, covers states that Swedenborg defines as those coming after times of trial. The second system, containing three elements, appears to cover the states of a person who is in the process of being reborn. The third system, containing two elements, appears to cover the states of a person who has achieved rebirth. For more about the states covered by the second numbering system, see §§869–892, especially §§880:1, 890, and note 477. When Swedenborg reaches the explanation of the verses involved in the third numbering system (Genesis 8:15–21, §§903–929), he ceases to number the states at all. [LHC]

460 (in §840). In his references to "statements made above and below," Swedenborg seems to be referring generally to his treatment of the process of spiritual rebirth, which at this point turns from trial to renewal. That is, it is not the notion of "God remembering" that he has treated before and will treat later, but trial and renewal, respectively. See his summary of the previous two chapters of the book in §838, where he notes that the text has been dealing with the trials the people of the new church called Noah suffered and that "what comes now is the state they were in following their trials." The phrase "and God remembered" symbolically marks this turning point. (For a general discussion of the symbolism of the actions and emotions ascribed to God, see §588.) [SS]

461 (in §841). For the Hebrew word in question, see note 419. [RS]

462 (in §842:1). On the word for "spirit" and "wind" in Hebrew, see note 161. [LHC]

463 (in §842:3). This description is based on Swedenborg's considerable work on the blood as the medium for the soul in his *Dynamics of the Soul's Domain* (= Swedenborg [1740–1741] 1955), part 1, §§36–115. In his premise, there are three "bloods": (1) the *animal spirits* (the spirituous fluid, or "fluid of the soul," delivered via the nerves from the cerebrum to the tissues); (2) the *purest blood* (lymph, or blood plasma without the cellular components); and (3) the *red blood* (a compound of the above, with the addition of the cells). These three fluids are combined in the heart and then distributed to the various parts of the body. Each of these "bloods" has its own specific function as it contributes to the essential function of the whole. Swedenborg's system is based partly on Descartes's system of psychophysiology, which also posited the existence of "animal spirits" that mediated between soul and body (Gaukroger 1995, 272–273). [RPB, RS]

464 (in §842:4). The third Latin edition supplies "the ships of Tarshish" *(naves Tarshishi)* as the object that is shattered. [LHC]

465 (in §842:5). On the name Suph Sea, see note 413. [LHC]

466 (in §847:2). In *Dynamics of the Soul's Domain* (= Swedenborg [1740–1741] 1955) part 1, §62, Swedenborg lists five qualities of the blood that determine the condition of the life it brings to the body, one of which is the blood's constitution, or chemical integrity. When he speaks here of the "morbid constitution of the blood," he brings a progressive understanding of physiology as biochemistry to bear on his comments. It is worth detailing here that despite the apparent reference to the Hippocratic doctrine of the "four humors" of bodily fluids that governed the body's state of health, Swedenborg was in fact operating far beyond it. First, the Hippocratic model had been superseded by the "spagyric" (that is, alchemical, or in modern terminology, biochemical) model for the external origin of disease developed by Paracelsus (1493–1541). Second, from Swedenborg's studies of the disciplines of chemistry and histology, he knew much about blood, lymph, cerebrospinal fluid, and the fluid that percolated within the tissues; and he was aware that the state of those fluids was dependent upon local chemical conditions. Thus he was working from a surprisingly modern biochemical model for the state of the fluids in the body. Third, he added his own findings on the blood and its components. [RPB]

467 (in §851). For this long period of vacillation, see the sections from here up to the explanation of verse 12 (§§888–892), where Swedenborg describes the process of gradual enlightenment as finally coming to completion. [LHC]

468 (in §851). On the meaning of "Noah," see note 285. "Sabbath" comes from the Hebrew שָׁבַת *(šābat)*, a verb that also means "rest," but has a different root than the word

for "Noah." Swedenborg indicates here that the two terms are used for different levels of spiritual development. [RS]

469 (in §852). This discussion of Genesis 2:3 appears in §§84–87, a passage mentioned in the previous sentence. [LHC]

470 (in §854). Although there is no obvious Hebrew root suggesting that אֲרָרַט (ărāraṭ) means "illumination" (Brown, Driver, and Briggs 1996, under אֲרָרַט), it is possible that Swedenborg saw a connection with the word אוֹר ('ôr), "light." [LHC, RS]

471 (in §859). On Swedenborg's attitude toward Jews, see note 182 and the reader's guide, pages 51–55. On the term "gentiles," see note 164. [JSR]

472 (in §865:1). As Swedenborg no doubt knew, the raven has had ambiguous connotations in the Western tradition, some of them derived from its color (see §866), some from its behavior as it was released from the ark, for reasons Swedenborg gives. Occasionally it symbolizes the Devil himself. Augustine interpreted its cry as indicating the onomatopoetic *"Cras! Cras!"* (Latin for "Tomorrow! Tomorrow!"), representing the sinner who puts off repentance till tomorrow (Charbonneau-Lassay 1991, 238–239). [RS]

473 (in §865:2). This brief rejection of polygamy (compare §162) is amplified in later passages such as *Heaven and Hell* 379 and *Marriage Love* 332–356. [SS]

474 (in §866). On Swedenborg's attitude toward Jews, see note 182 and the reader's guide, pages 51–55. [JSR]

475 (in §868:1). Although Swedenborg touches on the topic of the Lord as the sole restraint that keeps us from plunging ourselves into the hells in §§5854:2, the experiential material that he is referring to here is probably to be seen in the extended discussion of human freedom in §§2870–2893. [SS]

476 (in §869). "Because of its mild and peaceful habits, its attachment to its mate, even its color and its song, the dove, from the beginning of ancient humanity's use of symbols, has been taken as the ideogram of peace, purity, simplicity, patience in suffering, and conjugal fidelity" (Charbonneau-Lassay 1991, 229 and following). As a symbol of peace, it is linked to the olive branch that it carries in the story of the Flood. In the New Testament, it is a symbol of the Holy Spirit: see Matthew 3:16; Mark 1:10; Luke 3:22; and John 1:32–34. For Swedenborg's interpretation of the dove in these passages, see §870:1. [RS]

477 (in §871). The three stages that Swedenborg mentions here are a subdivision of the second state following times of trial. See §§834, 880:1, 890, and note 459. [LHC]

478 (in §876). The contrast Swedenborg is apparently trying to make here is one of darker and lighter color as corresponding to moral evil and goodness. Swedenborg first selects an Ethiopian person as an image of blackness to be contrasted with white clothing; he then switches to what he apparently considered an even blacker image: an Egyptian mummy, which would add the further factors of grotesqueness and death. For other passages in which Swedenborg mentions the blackness of Ethiopians, see *Secrets of Heaven* 3540:1; *Revelation Explained* [= Swedenborg 1994–1997] §780:5; for passages where he mentions the blackness of mummies, see *Secrets of Heaven* 817; *Revelation Unveiled* 153:12; *True Christianity* 595:1. This is not to say that Swedenborg had a low opinion of black Africans, however; he elsewhere accords them higher praise than the other races of the earth including his own; see *Marriage Love* 114 in the context of §§103–114. He praises their rationality, intelligence, and receptivity to spiritual goodness and truth; see *Heaven and Hell* 326, 514; *Last Judgment* 51; *True Christianity* 837–839. [JSR]

479 (in §878:1). The Hebrew word here—usually read as אֲרֻבּוֹת (*ărubôt*)—occurs only once in the Bible. Modern translators generally view it as meaning something like "trickery." However, Swedenborg's Latin translation here shows that he read the word as אֲרֻבּוֹת (*ărubbôt*), "floodgates." This reading is plausible because the only difference between the two words is in the vowels, which were added to the written Hebrew long after the original texts were composed. As the third Latin edition points out, Swedenborg's reading of the word is the same as that of Tremellius and Beza 1669. [LHC]

480 (in §878:2). The word translated "god" in this verse is usually translated as "power" or some equivalent. The New Revised Standard Version, for instance, reads, "Alas for those who devise wickedness and evil deeds on their beds! When the morning dawns, they perform it, because it is in their power." The Hebrew word is אֵל (*ēl*), which represents two related homographs; one can mean "a powerful person," "god," or "God," and the other means simply "power." See also note 199. Swedenborg, like Schmidt 1696, renders it *deus,* "god." [LHC]

481 (in §878:3). For examples of biblical passages mentioning the works of people's hands, see Deuteronomy 27:15; 2 Kings 22:17; Psalms 9:16; 28:4; 115:4; 135:15; Isaiah 2:8; 17:8; 37:19; Jeremiah 1:16; 10:3; 25:6, 7, 14; 32:30; 44:8; Revelation 9:20. [LHC]

482 (in §878:4). The indented excerpt just given in the text is solely from Jeremiah 32:21, despite the reference to both verse 17 and verse 21 supplied there by Swedenborg. That citation is in accordance with his usual practice of listing related verses along with the numbers of the verses he is actually quoting. (On Bible quotations in Swedenborg, see note 45 above and the translator's preface, pages 8–11.) Jeremiah 32:17 says, "You made the heavens and the earth by your great power and by your outstretched arm." [LHC]

483 (in §878:4). The phrase "raised my hand" is a figure of speech meaning "made a vow." [LHC]

484 (in §878:5). Concerning the name Suph Sea, see note 413. [LHC]

485 (in §878:6). The Jewish tradition has many legends associated with Moses' staff. It was said to have been created in the week of creation and handed down from Adam to Seth and then down to Jacob and Joseph. Jethro, Moses' father-in-law, was given it as a gift from Pharaoh and stuck it in the ground in his garden. Neither he nor any of the strong men of his country could pull it out. Moses succeeded in removing it, proving that it was he that would free the Children of Israel from slavery (Gaer 1966, 146–147). [RS]

486 (in §878:6). Exodus 17:9–13 describes a battle between the Israelites, led by Joshua, and a band of Amalekites, which Moses watched from atop a nearby hill, holding his staff. When he grew tired, his arms were supported by Aaron and Hur. [LHC]

487 (in §878:8). Other references to this arm appear in §§4934–4935; Swedenborg's *Heaven and Hell* 231 (at the end); *True Christianity* 136:5; and his *Spiritual Experiences* (= Swedenborg 1998–2002) §§881, 1754. [LHC]

488 (in §880:2). For the meaning of "influx" here, see note 367. For the idea of influx in the contemporary debate about the interaction of the soul and the body, see note 153. [RS]

489 (in §880:2). The phrase "a work of charity," which could also be translated as "a labor of love," may be an allusion to 1 Thessalonians 1:3; Hebrews 6:10; and possibly Galatians 5:6. [LSW]

490 (in §882). The explanation that follows actually comes in the discussion of verse 9; see §878. [LHC]

491 (in §883). The translation here is based on reading "9" for the first Latin edition's "8." See §876. [LHC]

492 (in §883). On the literal meaning of the word "evening" in the Old Testament, see note 40. Many references to evening can be found in Leviticus 11 and 15 and Numbers 19. [LHC]

493 (in §883). As another indication of the special significance of evening, and of half-light or twilight in general, it could be noted that in §6110:6 Swedenborg says that there is no night in heaven, but only evening, followed by the twilight that precedes morning. See also §§2323, 10114:2, 10135. [LSW]

494 (in §885:1). This bracketed interpolation is Swedenborg's. [LHC]

495 (in §891). The verse references here are substituted for the first Latin edition's 15, 16, 17, 18. [LHC]

496 (in §892:1). For later passages in which Swedenborg speaks against religious practices of self-punishment and renunciation of wealth and pleasure, see §§945, 3951:2, 5573:2; *Heaven and Hell* 528, 535. [LSW, LHC]

497 (in §896:1). On Swedenborg's attitude toward Jews, see note 182 and the reader's guide, pages 51–55. [JSR]

498 (in §897:2). Swedenborg here is accepting the biblical association of the name רְאוּבֵן (rə'ûbēn), or "Reuben," with the verb רָאָה (rā'ā), "to see." See Genesis 29:32: "And Leah conceived and bore a son and called his name Reuben, because she said, 'Jehovah has seen my affliction, for now my husband will love me.'" [RS]

499 (in §900). Concerning the word "ages," see note 248. [LHC]

500 (in §900). Figurative predictions of a final devastation lasting some period involving the number seven may be found in Isaiah 23:15–17; Jeremiah 25:11, 12; Ezekiel 39:9–12; Daniel 9:24–25. Predictions of a resulting redemption or of resurrection on the third or seventh day may be seen in Isaiah 30:26; Hosea 6:1, 2; Jonah 1:17–2:10; Luke 13:32; John 2:19–21. See Swedenborg's discussion of these and related passages in §§728, 1825, 2788, 6508, 9228. On the Last Judgment as it appears in Swedenborg's later writings, see note 529. [LHC]

501 (in §901:3). In mentioning "purpose" here (Latin *finis*), Swedenborg apparently has in mind the Scholastic idea of the "final cause," the reason for which something is done or made. If something is done to no end, he is suggesting, it is purposeless and therefore dead. See Shallo 1923, 184, 193. [RS]

502 (in §904:2). "They are unlike him and are anything but his image" is an inverted echo of Genesis 1:26, which speaks of a person as God's likeness and image. [LHC]

503 (in §904:3). For the meaning of "influx" here, see note 367. For the idea of influx in the contemporary debate about the interaction of the soul and the body, see note 153. [RS]

504 (in §904:3). Swedenborg is drawing a distinction between two Hebrew verbs—דִּבֶּר (dibber), which appears in the clause "God spoke to Noah" in Genesis 8:15, and אָמַר ('āmar), which appears in all the verses listed here. Swedenborg uses the Latin verb *loqui* ("speak") for the former, and *dicere* ("say") for the latter. [LHC]

505 (in §905). On the general desire that evil spirits have to inflict torment, see, for example, §§954, 959, 5863–5864. [LHC]

506 (in §907). The following phrases continue from verse 16, quoted at §903. [LHC]

507 (in §908:1). For the Hebrew word in question, see note 419. [RS]

508 (in §908:2). The bracketed gloss here is Swedenborg's. [LHC]

509 (in §908:2). Swedenborg says "also" here because the word for "wild animal" in this particular phrase in Psalms 50:11 (זִיז [zîz]) is not the one that he has translated as "wild animal" elsewhere, not even in the phrase "every wild animal of the forest" in the first part of the quote, from verse 10. He is in effect saying, "This second word for 'wild animal' is just as much a symbol for the regenerate person as is the other word for 'wild animal' previously quoted." [LHC, RS]

510 (in §908:3). The unmentioned substance, in the passage just quoted, that is threatened to be given as food to "the wild animal" and "the bird" is human flesh. For other passages that mention corpses becoming food for wild animals and birds, see, for example, Deuteronomy 28:26; Psalms 79:2; Jeremiah 7:33; Ezekiel 34:5, 8. [LHC]

511 (in §908:3). The Bible gives no instances in which Jews themselves deny anyone burial, though such denial is often the subject of warning and prophecy. See note 510. [JSR]

512 (in §911:1). There is no §910. Elliott (Swedenborg [1749–1756] 1983–1999, 1:358) suggests, "Possibly a section which refers to beasts meaning things of the will has been accidentally omitted." [LHC]

513 (in §911:2). This is perhaps a reference to Luke 17:21: "The kingdom of God is within you." [LHC]

514 (in §915). Swedenborg is referring to the Hebrew word אִישׁ ('îš) when he speaks of a "man" here and to the word אָדָם ('ādām) when he speaks of a "human," and Genesis 2 has several examples of each. See the translation of Genesis 2:22–25 in this volume (after §130), where the distinction between the two words is preserved. See also note 379 on the text of Genesis 7:2, and note 61. [LHC]

515 (in §915). For more on these churches, see, for example, §§975, 1062, 1083. [LHC]

516 (in §916:2). On the identification of an individual person as a church, see §§82, 869, 872. [LHC]

517 (in §917). The idea that the human being serves as both a microcosm and a macrocosm is extremely important in Swedenborg's thought. Most commonly he describes a larger collective as resembling an individual: that is, heaven takes the form of the universal human (see notes 5, 209, and 354), and even humanity on earth resembles the human form. Here, by contrast, the individual is taken as a macrocosm: each of her or his smallest parts reflects the whole, in a manner that a modern person might describe as holographic. [RS]

518 (in §920:1). On the topic of perception, see, for example, §§104, 125, 202–203, 371, 483, 502–503, 521, 597. [LHC]

519 (in §921:3). This bracketed interpolation is Swedenborg's, although the same bracketed insertion a few lines later is not. [LHC]

520 (in §921:4). The horns of the altar were projections from the four corners. Their origin is obscure, as is their sacramental function, though in 1 Kings 1:50, 2:28 fugitives seize on the horns when seeking refuge, and in ceremonies described in Exodus 29:12, Leviticus 4:30, and other passages the horns are either anointed or smeared with sacrificial blood. Perhaps originally they served as posts to secure the sacrificial victims, a use mentioned in Psalms 118:27, though biblical scholarship tends to frown on this explanation. The passage cited here (Amos 3:14) makes clear that the horns were considered an integral part of the altar that could not be removed without desecrating the whole. [SS]

521 (in §922:3). "Offspring of a year" is a Hebraism meaning one year old. Compare note 286. [LHC]

522 (in §925:4). The Latin phrase translated "I will not smell . . . your holidays" is *non odorabor cessationes vestras*. Its exact meaning is subject to conjecture, and it is worth noting that the conventional understanding of the passage from Amos is quite different. The Hebrew verb represented by the Latin *odorabor* and the English "smell" is in this Bible passage generally taken by scholars in the metaphorical sense of "delight in." The Hebrew represented by the Latin *cessationes* and the English "holidays" may also mean "assemblies." For these reasons, the phrase as a whole usually appears in English Bibles as something like "I will not delight in your assemblies." [LHC]

523 (in §926). This statement echoes Exodus 3:14, in which Jehovah declares, "I am who I am." See also note 353. [LHC]

524 (in §927:2). For more on the "Nephilim," see §§581–583 and note 317. [LHC]

525 (in §928). The phrase "created anew" here may be an allusion to 2 Corinthians 5:17; Galatians 6:15. [LSW]

526 (in §931:1). Strictly speaking, Swedenborg has not yet mentioned the lungs in these comparisons, which occur in §§468:2 and 637:1. His own index of *Secrets of Heaven* gives the present passage as the first relevant location in the work. However, he goes on to include the lungs with the heart in §§2054, 2853:3, 2913:3, 4217:3, 4423:1. In §§2913:3 and 4217:3 he specifically mentions §637 as the passage that supports his statement, and in §4423:1 he mentions §468 as well, so §§468:2 and 637:1 are clearly the passages he is thinking of here in §931:1. See also §§418, 9276:6, 9400:2; *Heaven and Hell* 328; *Sacred Scripture* 105; *True Christianity* 268. [SS]

527 (in §931:1). This "universal human" is defined at §§550 and 911:2. For other discussion, see also notes 5, 209, 330, 354, 517. [LHC]

528 (in §931:2). For passages that specifically mention "the culmination of the age," see Matthew 24:3; Luke 21:7; see also Daniel 9:27. For "the day of visitation," see Isaiah 10:3; Hosea 9:7. Although the phrase "Last Judgment" does not occur in Scripture, judgment scenes do appear in Daniel 7:9–14; Matthew 24:3–14; 25:31–46; Revelation 20:11–15. [JSR]

529 (in §931:2). This comment foreshadows a crucial aspect of Swedenborg's later thought: the idea that the Last Judgment of the dispensation of the Christian Church took place in the spiritual world in 1757. He went on to describe this event in his 1758 work *Last Judgment*, but here he speaks of it in apparent unawareness of the central place the event would someday have in his own theology. (This passage, published in 1749, contains one of his first allusions to this judgment. Another early reference, written on February 13, 1748, appears in his journal *Spiritual Experiences* [= Swedenborg 1998–2002] §765; there he relates a vision of the number 57, guessing at its connection with the year 1657.) According to Swedenborg, the Last Judgment essentially consists of a purgation of the world of spirits, which, since the time of Christ, had accepted those who were externally but not internally good. These people had managed to construct a kind of counterfeit heaven in their realm, which began to obstruct the communion of heaven and earth. Their expulsion from the world of spirits does not result in an apocalypse of the conventional sort, but enables heaven to communicate with earth in a more direct manner than was previously possible. This in turn lays the groundwork for the creation of a new church. [RS, LSW]

530 (in §931:3). For more on how this individual judgment occurs, and the role of the individual's will in it, see *Secrets of Heaven* 4663:1; *Heaven and Hell* 545–549. [JSR]

531 (in §933:1). See note 516. [LHC]

532 (in §934:2). The Latin word here translated "spirits" is *spiritus,* the word Swedenborg usually uses to refer to spirits living in the spiritual world. However, the underlying Hebrew word, רוּחַ *(rûaḥ),* can mean breath, wind, or spirit, and here interpreters see the word as referring to the four winds; see Brown, Driver, and Briggs 1996, under רוּחַ, definition 2.a. Compare note 161. [LHC]

533 (in §935:3). The "eastern" sea here, from the perspective of Jerusalem, refers to the Dead Sea, and the "western" sea refers to the Mediterranean. [LHC]

534 (in §939). The reference to color is not racial here; see note 447. The usual methods for debristling pigs after slaughter included burning the bristles off in a very hot and quickly spent fire of dry tinder, and brushing away the ashes; or scalding the pig and scraping off the bristles. See Hartley 1979, 226–227. [JSR, SS]

535 (in §940:1). On Swedenborg's attitude toward Jews, see note 182 and the reader's guide, pages 51–55. [JSR]

536 (in §940:1). For more about Gehenna, see §§825–826 and note 239. [LHC]

537 (in §941:1). The "lake" referred to here may be the one described in §819. [LHC]

538 (in §941:1). A parallel passage in *Spiritual Experiences* (= Swedenborg 1998–2002) §728 says that it is the better spirits who enter the city on the right. [LHC]

539 (in §941:2). On Swedenborg's attitude toward Jews, see notes 182 and 203, and the reader's guide, pages 51–55. [JSR]

540 (in §942). The phrase here translated "Gehenna's Judgment" also appears in Matthew 23:33. It is variously translated; in the King James Version, for instance, it is rendered as "the damnation of hell," and in the New Revised Standard Version as "being sentenced to hell." [LHC]

541 (in §944). The three Furies of Greek and Roman myth were female avengers, minor deities who punished criminals for their crimes. [LHC]

542 (in §946). In Swedenborg's time the existence of the soul was in general not doubted, though there was much scholarly debate about its nature and qualities. For an overview of some aspects of this debate that Swedenborg at one time thought worth transcribing, see his *Quotations on Various Philosophical and Theological Topics* (= Swedenborg 1976c), 10–27, 162–184, 187–203, 259–289, 346–377, 400–420. This notebook, left unpublished by him but known to have been written around 1741, contains quotations on the soul (among other topics) both from ancient sources (Plato [427–347 B.C.E.], Aristotle, Augustine, and Scripture) and from various scholars of the seventeenth and eighteenth centuries: René Descartes, Nicolas de Malebranche (1638–1715), Gottfried Wilhelm Leibniz, Giovanni Francesco Gemelli Careri (1651–1725), Andreas Rydelius (1671–1738), Christian Wolff (1679–1754), and George Bernard Bilfinger (1693–1750). As Swedenborg observes here, these scholars' discussions of the topic are indeed highly technical in nature. [JSR]

Works Cited in the Notes

Acton, Alfred. 1948–1955. *The Letters and Memorials of Emanuel Swedenborg.* 2 vols. Bryn Athyn, Pa.: Swedenborg Scientific Association.

Alberti, Paul Martin. 1704. *Lexicon Novum Hebraeo-Latino-Biblicum.* Saxony.

Aquinas, Thomas. 1952. *Summa Theologiae.* Translated by the Fathers of the English Dominican Province, and revised by Daniel J. Sullivan. Vols. 19–20 of *Great Books of the Western World.* Chicago: Encyclopedia Britannica.

Athanasius. 1927. *Select Works and Letters.* In vol. 4 of *Nicene and Post-Nicene Fathers,* series 2, edited by Philip Schaff and Henry Wace. Edinburgh: T. & T. Clark.

Augustine. 1956. *The De Haeresibus of Saint Augustine: A Translation with an Introduction and Commentary.* Translated and annotated by Liguori G. Müller. Washington, D.C.: Catholic University of America Press.

Berkeley, George. [1710] 1952. *The Principles of Human Knowledge.* In vol. 35 of *Great Books of the Western World.* Chicago: Encyclopedia Britannica.

Bialik, Hayim Nahman, and Yehoshua Hana Ravnitzky. 1992. *The Book of Legends: Sefer ha-Aggadah.* Translated by William G. Braude. New York: Schocken.

Borsch, Frederick Houk. 1967. *The Son of Man in Myth and History.* Philadelphia: Westminster Press.

Brown, Francis, S. R. Driver, and Charles A. Briggs. 1996. *The Brown-Driver-Briggs Hebrew and English Lexicon.* Reprint, with Strong's numbering added, Peabody, Mass.: Hendrickson Publishers, Inc.

Buxtorf, John. 1735. *Lexicon Hebraicum et Chaldaicum.* Basil: Episcopiana.

Chadwick, John, and Jonathan S. Rose, eds. 2008. *A Lexicon to the Latin Text of the Theological Writings of Emanuel Swedenborg (1688–1772).* London: Swedenborg Society.

Charbonneau-Lassay, Louis. 1991. *The Bestiary of Christ.* Translated and abridged by D. M. Dooling. Harmondsworth, Middlesex, England: Arkana/Parabola Books.

Charles, R. H., ed. 1913. *The Apocrypha and Pseudepigrapha of the Old Testament.* Vol. 2: *Pseudepigrapha.* Oxford: Oxford at the Clarendon Press.

Cole, Stephen. 1977. "Swedenborg's Hebrew Bible." *The New Philosophy* 80:28–33.

Contenau, G. 1947. *La Magie chez les Assyriens et les Babyloniens.* Paris: Payot.

Cross, Frank Moore. 1973. *Canaanite Myth and Hebrew Epic: Essays in the History of the Religion of Israel.* Cambridge, Mass.: Harvard University Press.

Descartes, René. [1641] 1952. *Objections against the Meditations and Replies.* Translated by Elizabeth S. Haldane and G.R.T. Ross. In vol. 31 of *Great Books of the Western World.* Chicago: Encyclopedia Britannica.

———. [1637] 1968. *Discourse on Method.* In *Discourse on Method and the Meditations,* translated by F. E. Sutcliffe. Harmondsworth, Middlesex, U.K.: Penguin.

———. [1641] 1968. *Meditations.* In *Discourse on Method and the Meditations,* translated by F. E. Sutcliffe. Harmondsworth, Middlesex, U.K.: Penguin.

Epiphanius. 1990. *The Panarion of St. Epiphanius, Bishop of Salamis: Selected Passages.* Translated by Philip R. Amidon. New York: Oxford University Press.

Erwin, R. Guy. 2006. "On *True Christianity:* An Introduction to Swedenborg's Most Comprehensive and Systematic Theological Writing from the Standpoint of the Religion of His Contemporaries." In *True Christianity,* by Emanuel Swedenborg, translated by Jonathan S. Rose. West Chester, Pa.: Swedenborg Foundation.

Evelyn-White, Hugh G. 1914. *Hesiod, The Homeric Hymns, and Homerica.* Cambridge, Mass.: Harvard University Press/Loeb Classical Library.

Frisch, Rose E. 2004. *Female Fertility and the Body Fat Connection.* Chicago: University of Chicago Press.

Gaer, Joseph. 1966. *The Lore of the Old Testament.* New York: Grosset & Dunlap.

Gaukroger, Stephen. 1995. *Descartes: An Intellectual Biography.* Oxford: Oxford University Press.

Gesenius, William. 1949. *Hebrew and Chaldee Lexicon to the Old Testament Scriptures.* Translated by Samuel Prideaux Tregelles. Grand Rapids, Mich.: William B. Eerdmans.

Gikatilla, Joseph. 1994. *Gates of Light: Sha'arey Orah.* Translated by Avi Weinstein. San Francisco: HarperSanFrancisco.

Götting, Heinrich. 1592. *Pulvis scholasticus: Das ist: Schuhlstaub, Von Mühe, Unlust und Widerwertigkeit, so ein uleissiger und getrewer Praeceptor oder Schulmeister in seiner Schulen haben und ausstehen muss: Sampt angehengtem kurtzen Bericht, Wes er sich darinnen widerumb zugetrösten habe.* Erfurt.

Hartley, Dorothy. 1979. *Lost Country Life.* New York: Pantheon Books.

Harvey, A. D. 1994. *Sex in Georgian England: Attitudes and Prejudices from the 1720s to the 1820s.* London: Phoenix Press.

Hooght, Everard van der. 1740. *Biblia Hebraica Collatis Aliis Bonae Notae Codicibus Una cum Versione Latina Sebastiani Schmidii.* 2nd ed. Leipzig: Deer.

Hrushovski-Harshav, Benjamin. 2007. "Prosody, Hebrew." In *Encyclopaedia Judaica,* edited by Fred Skolnik and Michael Berenbaum. 2nd ed. 16:595–623. Detroit: Thomson Gale.

James, William. 1910. *The Varieties of Religious Experience.* New York: Longmans, Green & Co.

The Jewish Encyclopedia: A Descriptive Record of the History, Religion, Literature, and Customs of the Jewish People from the Earliest Times to the Present Day. 1910. 12 vols. Edited by Cyrus Adler and others. New York: Funk & Wagnalls.

John of the Cross, Saint. 1990. *Dark Night of the Soul.* Translated by E. Allison Peers. New York: Doubleday.

Kelly, J.N.D. 1960. *Early Christian Doctrines.* Rev. ed. San Francisco: Harper & Row.

Lamm, Martin. [1915] 2000. *Emanuel Swedenborg: The Development of His Thought.* Translated by Tomas Spiers and Anders Hallengren. West Chester, Pa.: Swedenborg Foundation.

Lamsa, George M. 1933. *The Holy Bible from the Ancient Eastern Text.* New York: Harper & Row. Reprint.

Lawlor, Robert. 1982. *Sacred Geometry.* London: Thames & Hudson.

Lewis, C. S. [1960] 1988. *The Four Loves.* New York: Harcourt, Brace & Co.

Lewis, Charlton T., and Charles Short. 1879. *A Latin Dictionary.* Oxford: Oxford University Press.

Liddell, Henry George, and Robert Scott. 1968. *A Greek-English Lexicon.* Edited by Henry Stuart Jones and others. Rev. ed. Oxford: Oxford at the Clarendon Press.

Lubac, Henri de. 1998. *Medieval Exegesis: The Four Senses of Scripture.* Translated by Mark Sebanc. Grand Rapids, Mich.: Eerdmans.

Luther, Martin. 1543. *Von den Juden und ihren Lügen.* Wittenberg.

Matt, Daniel C., ed. and trans. 2004. *The Zohar.* Stanford, Calif.: Stanford University Press. (Two volumes of a projected twelve.)

Matton, Sylvain. 1988. "Une Lecture alchimique de la Bible: Les *Paradoxes chymiques* de F. Thybourel." *Chrysopoeia* 2:401–422.

McCormick, John J. 1940. *Scholastic Philosophy.* Chicago: Loyola University Press.

Metzger, Bruce M., and Michael D. Coogan, eds. 1993. *The Oxford Companion to the Bible.* New York, Oxford: Oxford University Press.

The New Catholic Encyclopedia. 2003. 2nd ed. Detroit: Thomson/Gale; Washington, D.C.: Catholic University of America.

Origen. 1966. *Origen on First Principles, Being Koetschau's Text of the* De Principiis *Translated into English, Together with an Introduction and Notes by G. W. Butterworth.* Translated and annotated by G. W. Butterworth. New York: Harper & Row.

Orr, James, and others, eds. 1960. *International Standard Bible Encyclopedia.* 5 vols. Grand Rapids, Mich.: William B. Eerdmans.

Pasnau, Robert. 2007. "Mind and Extension (Descartes, Hobbes, More)." In *Forming the Mind: Essays on the Internal Senses and the Mind/Body Problem from Avicenna to the Medical Enlightenment,* edited by H. Lagerlund and O. Pluta. Dordrecht: Springer.

Pegis, Anton C., ed. 1948. *Introduction to St. Thomas Aquinas.* New York: Modern Library.

Philo of Alexandria. 1993. *The Works of Philo.* Translated by C. D. Yonge. Peabody, Mass.: Hendrickson.

The Philokalia: The Complete Text Compiled by St. Nikodimos of the Holy Mountain and St. Makarios of Corinth. 1979–1984. Translated and edited by G.E.H. Palmer, Philip Sherrard, and Kallistos Ware. Five vols. Boston: Faber and Faber.

Potts, John Faulkner. 1888–1902. *The Swedenborg Concordance. A Complete Work of Reference to the Theological Writings of Emanuel Swedenborg; Based on the Original Latin Writings of the Author.* 6 vols. London: Swedenborg Society.

Principe, Lawrence M., and William R. Newman. 2001. "Some Problems with the Historiography of Alchemy." In *Secrets of Nature: Astrology and Alchemy in Early Modern Europe,* edited by William R. Newman and Anthony Grafton. Cambridge, Mass.: MIT Press.

Rad, Gerhard von. 1972. *Genesis: A Commentary.* Rev. ed. Translated by John H. Marks. Philadelphia: Westminster Press.

Russell, Jeffrey Burton. 1981. *Satan: The Early Christian Tradition.* Ithaca, N.Y.: Cornell University Press.

Schmidt, Sebastian, trans. 1696. *Biblia Sacra sive Testamentum Vetus et Novum ex Linguis Originalibus in Linguam Latinam Translatum.* Strasbourg: J. F. Spoor.

Schmithals, Walter. 1997. *The Theology of the First Christians.* Translated by O. C. Dean, Jr. Louisville, Ky.: Westminster John Knox Press.

Schneider, Michael S. 1995. *A Beginner's Guide to Constructing the Universe: The Mathematical Archetypes of Nature, Art, and Science.* New York: Harper Perennial.

Scholem, Gershom. 1974. *Kabbalah*. Jerusalem: Keter Publishing House.

Shallo, Michael J. 1923. *Lessons in Scholastic Philosophy*. Philadelphia: Peter Reilly.

Smoley, Richard. 2005. "The Inner Journey of Emanuel Swedenborg." In *Emanuel Swedenborg: Essays for the New Century Edition on His Life, Work, and Impact*, edited by Jonathan S. Rose and others. West Chester, Pa.: Swedenborg Foundation.

Swedenborg, Emanuel. [1740–1741] 1955. *The Economy of the Animal Kingdom, Considered Anatomically, Physically, and Philosophically*. 2 vols. Translated by Augustus Clissold. Bryn Athyn, Pa.: Swedenborg Scientific Association. First edition of this translation: 1845–1846, London: W. Newbery, H. Bailliere, and Boston: Otis Clapp. A more accurate translation of the title of this work is *Dynamics of the Soul's Domain*.

———. [1744–1745] 1960. *The Animal Kingdom, Considered Anatomically, Physically, and Philosophically*. 2 vols. Translated by James John Garth Wilkinson. [Bryn Athyn, Pa.]: Swedenborg Scientific Association. First edition of this translation: 1843–1844, London: W. Newbery. A more accurate translation of the title of this work is *The Soul's Domain*.

———. 1976a. *The Economy of the Animal Kingdom, Considered Anatomically, Physically, and Philosophically, Transaction III*. Translated by Alfred Acton. Bryn Athyn, Pa.: Swedenborg Scientific Association. First edition: 1918, Philadelphia: Swedenborg Scientific Association.

———. 1976b. *The Five Senses*. Translated by Enoch S. Price. Bryn Athyn, Pa.: Swedenborg Scientific Association. First edition of this translation: 1914, Philadelphia: Swedenborg Scientific Association.

———. 1976c. *A Philosopher's Note Book*. Translated by Alfred Acton. Bryn Athyn, Pa.: Swedenborg Scientific Association. First edition: 1931, Philadelphia: Swedenborg Scientific Association.

———. 1976d. *Three Transactions on the Cerebrum*. 2 vols. Translated by Alfred Acton. Bryn Athyn, Pa.: Swedenborg Scientific Association. First edition: 1938, Philadelphia: Swedenborg Scientific Association.

———. 1978. *The Spiritual Diary of Emanuel Swedenborg*. Vol. 4, pages 91–494, and vol. 5. Translated by James F. Buss. New York: Swedenborg Foundation. First edition: 1889, London: J. Speirs.

———. [1749–1756] 1983–1999. *Arcana Caelestia, Principally a Revelation of the Inner or Spiritual Meaning of Genesis and Exodus*. 12 vols. Translated by John Elliott. London: Swedenborg Society.

———. 1984. *Psychological Transactions and Other Posthumous Tracts 1734–1744*. Translated by Alfred Acton. 2nd ed. Bryn Athyn, Pa.: Swedenborg Scientific Association.

———. 1994–1997. *Apocalypse Explained*. 6 vols. Translated by John C. Ager, revised by John Whitehead, and edited by William Ross Woofenden. West Chester, Pa.: Swedenborg Foundation.

———. 1998–2002. *Emanuel Swedenborg's Diary, Recounting Spiritual Experiences during the Years 1745 to 1765*. 3 vols. Translated by J. Durban Odhner. Bryn Athyn, Pa.: General Church of the New Jerusalem. The first three volumes, in English, of the six volumes of Swedenborg's Latin work *Experientiae Spirituales*, edited by J. Durban Odhner (Bryn Athyn, Pa.: Academy of the New Church, 1983–1997). Further volumes forthcoming.

———. 2001a. *Rational Psychology.* Translated by Norbert H. Rogers and Alfred Acton. Bryn Athyn, Pa.: Swedenborg Scientific Association. Revision of 1950 edition, Philadelphia: Swedenborg Scientific Association.

———. 2001b. *Swedenborg's Dream Diary.* Edited by Lars Bergquist and translated by Anders Hallengren. West Chester, Pa.: Swedenborg Foundation.

———. [1771] 2006. *True Christianity.* Translated by Jonathan S. Rose. West Chester, Pa.: Swedenborg Foundation.

Tafel, R. L. 1877. *Documents Concerning the Life and Character of Emanuel Swedenborg.* Vol. 2, parts 1 and 2. London: Swedenborg Society.

Theological Dictionary of the Old Testament. 1986. Edited by G. Johannes Botterweck and Helmer Ringgren and translated by John T. Willis. Vol. 5. Grand Rapids, Mich.: William B. Eerdmans.

Tremellius, Immanuel, Fr. Junius, and Theod. Beza, trans. 1669. *Biblia Sacra.* Amsterdam: Joh. Jac. Schipper.

Tulk, Charles Augustus. 1994. "The Internal Sense of the Bible According to the Early Church Fathers." *Arcana* 1(2):19–34.

Voltaire. 1924. *Philosophical Dictionary.* Selected and translated by H. I. Woolf. New York: Knopf.

———. [1764] 1962. *Philosophical Dictionary.* Translated by Peter Gay. New York: Harcourt, Brace, & World.

Waldung, Wolfgang. 1595. *Pulvis Scholasticus, Ostendens, Quibus Laborum Alpibus Se Teneant: In Quae Misceriarum et Aerumnarum Deserta Incidant; Quod Odii . . . Maria Transire Oporteat Scholarum Doctores Dictus.* Noriberg: Kauffmann.

Zimmer, Heinrich. 1951. *Philosophies of India.* Edited by Joseph Campbell. London: Routledge & Kegan Paul.

Index to Prefaces, Reader's Guide, Introduction, and Notes

A

Abraham (Abram), 607 note 87
L'abrégé des ouvrages d'Em. Swedenborg, 116–117 note 81
Active. *See* Forces, active and passive
Acton, Alfred, 68 note 10
Adam, 621 note 208, 629 note 292
Affection, 57
Africans, Swedenborg's opinion of, 52, 54, 647 note 478
Afterlife. *See also* Spiritual world
  Jewish views of, 628 note 281
Agrippa, Cornelius, 110 note 65
Alchemy, 638 note 373
Allegorical exegesis, 81 and note 23, 82, 83, 84
Altar, horns of, 650 note 520
"Anakim," 633 note 331
Ancient Word, 88
Angelic spirits. *See* Spirits
Angels, 40 and note 28, 46–47, 50, 79, 87, 109, 111 and note 66, 112, 595 note 3, 643–644 note 446. *See also* Heavenly communities
  their perception of the Bible, 95–96
Animals, souls of, 615 note 152
Anthony, St., of the Desert, 607 note 84
Anti-Semitism, 52–55
Aquinas, Thomas, 603 note 51, 642 note 421
Arcana Coelestia, 64, 69. *See also* Secrets of Heaven
Aristotle, 615 note 153, 639 note 395, 652 note 542
"Army," 608 note 92
Athanasius, 607 note 84, 634 note 346
Atheism, 616 note 157
Attributes, 6, 7 figure 1
Augustine, 614 note 151, 621 note 207, 634 note 346, 644 note 452, 647 note 472, 652 note 542
Autonomy, 612 note 133

B

Bae, Je Hyung, 3
Bae, Philip Kyung, 3
Balzac, Honoré de, 115, 117 note 81
Barruel, Augustin de, 117 note 81
Baudelaire, Charles, 115
Bayside Korean Church, 3
Bede, the Venerable, 634 note 346
Being, 635 note 353
Benz, Ernst, 66, 88
Benzelius, Erik, 53
Berkeley, George, 642 note 421
Bernard of Clairvaux, 634 note 346
Beyer, Gabriel, 36 note 25, 66 note 5, 86, 595 note 2
Bible. *See also* History, biblical
  alchemical readings of, 638 note 373
  allegorical or spiritual exegesis of, 634 note 346
  books containing an inner meaning, 86
  citations from (*see* Scripture references)
  exegesis of (*see* Exegesis)
  Hebrew Bible used by Swedenborg, 77 note 19
  historical accuracy in, 85–86, 100–101
  inner meaning of, 25, 64, 75, 79, 80, 84, 95–105, 596–597 note 8
  as inwardly meaning rebirth, 43
  literal meaning of, 75, 79, 80, 81 and note 23, 89, 95, 96, 100
  as the means for uniting heaven and earth, 95
  parallel phrasing in, 609 note 110
  punctuation in, 635 note 350
  as revealed by God, 75, 80, 84, 95
  styles (modes) of, 85–86, 87, 89
  Swedenborg's favorite Latin version of, 599 note 19
  Swedenborg's indexes and concordances to, 21
  Swedenborg's translations of
    gender-inclusive terms in, 604–605 note 61, 624 note 234
    issues in, 8–11
    literal, 599 note 19
  time and space in relation to inner meaning of, 50
  verse and chapter numbering in, 5
  word breaks in, 635 note 350

Bilfinger, George Bernard, 652 note 542
Black Africans, Swedenborg's opinion of, 52, 647 note 478
Blackness, 647 note 478
Blake, William, 115
Blood
  as the medium for the soul, 646 note 463
  qualities of, 646 note 466
"Bloods," 606 note 76
"Bodily," 6–7, 57–58, 599–600 note 23, 605 note 66
Body, interaction with the mind, 615 note 153
Boehme, Jacob, and Behmenists, 66 and note 5, 67 and note 7
Borges, Jorge Luis, 115
Brahms, Johannes, 71, 72
Brain, location of functions in, 635–636 note 356
Breath, also meaning spirit or wind, 609 note 106, 637 note 371, 652 note 532
"Brothers and sisters," 624 note 234

C
Calvin, John, 81
Camel, 611 note 126
Canaan, extent of, 611 note 124
Careri, Giovanni Francesco Gemelli, 652 note 542
Cartesian philosophy, 65, 76–77
Catholicism. *See* Roman Catholicism
Champollion, Jean-François, 68 note 10
Charity and faith, teachings on, 78, 89–95
Chastity, defined, 606 note 77
Cherubim, 620 note 193
Christ. *See* Jesus Christ
Christian groups, conjugal experimentation among, 644–645 note 452
"Christian world," 597 note 13
Church(es), 5–6, 25, 47–49
  ancient, 5, 48–49, 87–88, 91, 99–100
  Christian, 6, 48, 88–89, 100, 101
  "Church Militant," 607 note 83
  "Church Triumphant," 607 note 83
  decline of, 87, 88, 89, 97, 99, 101, 102
  defined, 598 note 16
  earliest, 5, 48–49, 50, 85, 87, 97, 99, 107, 605 note 70, 616 note 159
  heavenly, 48–49, 50
  Hebrew, 100–101
  Jewish, 5–6, 48, 53, 87, 88, 100–101

  new, 68 note 9, 89, 117
  spiritual, 48–49, 97, 103–105
  spiritual and heavenly, 101
Clement of Alexandria, 596 note 8, 644 note 452
Clemm, Heinrich Wilhelm, 116 note 79
Close of the age, 604 note 55
Clowes, John, 11, 117
Communion, 619–620 note 190
Conatus, 70, 74
Concordances of the Bible, 21
Conjugal experimentation among Christian groups, 644–645 note 452
"Conscience," 608 note 98
Control and dominance, 55–56
Cookworthy, William, 117
Cooper, Lisa Hyatt, 45 note 35, 46 note 36
Correspondences, 45 figure 4, 47, 68–77, 86, 90, 91, 109, 110, 619 note 189
Creation, 97
  rebirth process correlating with, 44–45
Creation story, having an inner meaning, 598 note 15
Cross-references, Swedenborg's, 22, 35–36
Cubit, 634 note 345
Cudworth, Ralph, 67
Cush, 608 note 95, 610 note 118

D
D'Aillant de la Touche, Jean François, 116 note 81
Damnation, 104
"David" meaning Psalms, 601 note 29, 608 note 89
Decalogue, 633 note 329
Deism, 614 note 147
Demons, devils, and evil spirits, 41, 42–43. *See also* Spirits
Descartes, René, 615 note 153, 628 note 279, 628 note 280, 642 note 421, 646 note 463, 652 note 542
Devastation, 104, 114, 601–602 note 34, 602 note 35, 626 note 249
The Devil, 114, 612–613 note 140, 618 note 176
Devils. *See* Demons, devils, and evil spirits
Dippel, Johann Konrad, 67, 628 note 278
A Disclosure of Secrets of Heaven . . . See Secrets of Heaven
Disease, skin, 636 note 359
Divine love and wisdom, 43
Divine Love and Wisdom, 117 note 83

Divine Providence, 117 note 83
Doctrinal and theological discussions, in the front field of *Secrets of Heaven,* 27, 35
Dole, George F., 107
Dominance and control, 55–56
Dominant (ruling) love, 71 note 12, 92, 114
Dostoevsky, Feodor, 115
Dove, 647 note 476
Draft of "Sacred Scripture," 81 note 23
Dreams of a Spirit-Seer, 116 note 80
Dynamics of the Soul's Domain, 19–20, 110

E

Earth, 632 note 321, 637 note 368
Earthly, 6, 7 figure 1
Earthly heaven, 38 figure 3, 38–39
Eastern sea, 602 note 48
Elliott, John, 8 note 10, 11
Emerson, Ralph Waldo, 115
Empiricism, 608 note 91
End field, in the structure of *Secrets of Heaven,* 26, 29 figure 1, 30
The Enlightenment, 18 note 1, 20, 118
Enoch, 630 note 305
Ephraim, 625 note 241
Epiphanius, 644 note 452
Epistles of Paul, references to, 636 note 363
Ernesti, Johann August, 116
Ether, 645 note 453
Ethiopia, 608 note 95
Ethiopians, 52
Ethnicity and race, 51–55
Eucharist, 619–620 note 190
Euclid, 31
Eunuch, 625 note 245
Euphrates, 608 note 97
Evening, as the twilight before dawn, 602 note 40, 649 note 493
Evil, inherited, 42 and note 31, 43, 621 note 207
Evil spirits. *See* Spirits
Exegesis
　confident nature of Swedenborg's, 22
　of Genesis and Exodus in *Secrets of Heaven,* 18
　Secrets of Heaven distinguished from other works of, 18 note 1
　in structure of *Secrets of Heaven,* 26, 27–30
　Swedenborg's planned additional works of, 23–24, 24–25 note 14
Existence, continued, 641–642 note 421

Exodus as having to do with the spiritual church, 103–105
Extension, 628 note 280
"Eye of a needle," 611 note 126

F

Failure to thrive, 645 note 456
Fair copy, 22 and note 10
Faith alone, 90, 92, 640 note 396
The Fall, 614 note 149
Fat, 623 note 226
Fiber, 631 note 315
Final cause, 649 note 501
Fisher, spiritual, 605 note 63
The Flood, 641 note 408
Forces, active and passive, 639–640 note 395
Free will, 71, 94
Fricker, Johann Ludwig, 116 note 79
Front field, in the structure of *Secrets of Heaven,* 26–27, 28 figure 1
Furies, 652 note 541

G

Gehenna, 625 note 239, 636 note 358
Gender issues
　attitudes of Swedenborg towards women, 51–52, 55–56, 57
　gender-inclusive terms in Swedenborg's Bible translations, 604–605 note 61, 624 note 234
　human being, gender-neutral translation of, 9
General category, as sustaining particular items, 605 note 65
Genesis
　as having to do with the development of churches, 97–101
　as having to do with the Lord's inner development, 101–103
Gentiles, 616–617 note 164
Geometric reasoning in the middle field of *Secrets of Heaven,* 30–35
Giants, 620 note 195, 631 note 317
Glorification (transformation), 25, 42, 43
God. *See also* Jesus Christ
　attributing human emotions to, 617 note 166
　names of, 5, 42, 596 note 7, 620 note 199, 639 note 384
　nature of, 41–43
　Trinity within, 42

God's kingdom, defined, 620 note 194
Goethe, Johann Wolfgang von, 115
Good spirits. *See* Spirits
Goodness and truth, 104, 603 note 49
Gregory the Great, 634 note 346, 642 note 421
Ground, 632 note 321, 637 note 368
Guardian beings, 620 note 193

H
Hades, 114 note 76
Hahn, Philipp Matthäus, 116 note 79
Halldin, Johann Gustav, 117 note 84
Hart, John, 23 note 12
Hartknoch, Johann Friedrich, 116 note 80
Hartley, Thomas, 117
Heaven
  abstract qualities as visible in, 605 note 64, 612 note 139, 643 note 441
  divisions of, 6, 38 and figure 3
  impossibility of telling lies in, 622 note 210, 643 note 441
  kingdoms of, 6, 603 note 49
  light of, 601 note 33
  orientation in, 609–610 note 111
  as a single human form, 109, 596 note 5 (*see also* Universal human)
  speech in, 622 note 210
  the three heavens, 111 note 66, 613 note 146, 615 note 155
Heaven and Hell, 24, 75, 107, 113, 117
Heaven, hell, and their inhabitants, 106–109
Heavenly, 6, 7 figure 1, 46
Heavenly and spiritual, distinction between, 87, 92, 111 notes 66 and 67
Heavenly church, 48–49, 50
Heavenly communities, 109, 112
Heavenly heaven, 38 and figure 3
Heavenly person, 97
Heavenly sense of Scripture, 25
Hebrew Bible used by Swedenborg, 77 note 19
Hebrew language, 53
  vowels of, 643 note 438
Hell(s), 6, 38 and figure 3, 39, 40, 42, 625 note 239
  communities in, 113
Hells and devastation, 113–114
Helmont, Franciscus Mercurius van, 67
Heres, city of, 626 note 256
Heresy, 624 note 230

Hermetic philosophy, 66, 67
Hiddekel, 608 note 96
Hieroglyphic Key, 68–71, 74, 75, 76, 77, 79 note 20
Hindmarsh, Robert, 68 note 10
History, biblical, 77, 78, 85–89, 97–101
Holographic nature of human beings, 650 note 517
Holographic perspective on time and space, 50, 51 note 40
Holy Supper, 619–620 note 190
Homer *(poet),* 645 note 458
Hooght, Everard van der, 77
Horns of the altar, 650 note 520
"House," meaning the Temple in Jerusalem, 602 note 47
Humans, 621 note 208, 629 note 292
  as essentially the same as spirits, angelic spirits, and angels, 111 and note 66
  as small versions of the universal human, 109–111

I
Idiomatic *vs.* literal translation of Scripture references, 8–11
"Image," 606 note 75
Indexes
  of the Bible, 21
  of *Secrets of Heaven,* 22
Influx, 637 note 367
Inherited evil, 42 and note 31, 43
Innate ideas, concept of, 94
Inner meaning of the Bible, 596–597 note 8
Inner self, 597–598 note 14
Intellect, 45, 603 note 51
  and will, 92–93 (*see also* Will)
Intentionality, 45
Interchapter material, in *Secrets of Heaven,* 30 note 20
Internal historical sense of Scripture, 25

J
Jacob, 618–619 note 179
Jah, 601 note 30
James, William, 601 note 34
Jehovah, 5, 42, 600 note 28, 639 note 384
  "Jehovah Sabaoth," 611 note 122
Jehovih, 600 note 28
"Jeremiah" meaning Lamentations, 602 note 42

Jerome, 634 note 346
Jesus Christ
  glorification (transformation) of, 25, 42, 43
  nature of, 41–43
  Second Coming of, 6
  Swedenborg's visions of, 20
  in time and space, 49, 50
Jewish church. *See* Church: Jewish
Jews and Judaism, 52–55, 618 note 170
  as part of the "Christian world," 597 note 13
  Swedenborg's attitude toward, 619 note 182, 620 note 191, 621 note 203
  views of afterlife of, 628 note 281
"John" meaning the Book of Revelation, 605 note 67
John of the Cross, 601–602 note 34
Johnson, P. H., 3
Jonsson, Inge, 65, 66
Jot, 597 note 11
Journal of Dreams, 20, 602 note 34
Judas, 619 note 179
Jung-Stilling, Johann Heinrich, 114 note 76
Justification, 640 note 396

K

Kabbala, 66, 67, 110 and note 63, 596–597 note 8
Kant, Immanuel, 116
Keller, Helen, 115
Kemper, Johan, 53
Kidneys, 623 note 223
Kies, Johannes, 116 note 79
Kraus, Hans-Joachim, 82

L

Labyrinth, 614 note 147
Lamm, Martin, 65, 66, 83, 94
Land, 632 note 321, 637 note 368
Last Judgment, 6 and note 7, 24, 39 note 27, 604 note 55, 614 note 147, 651 note 529
  as occurring in 1757, 651 note 529
Last Judgment, 24, 41, 106 note 54
Latin sources for this translation, 3–4
Lavater, Johann Caspar, 115
The Law, 597 note 9
The Law and the Prophets, 604 note 58
Layers, 630 note 301
Leade, Jane, 67 note 7
Le Boys des Guays, Jean-François-Étienne, 117 note 81

Leeuwenhoek, Antoni van, 18 note 1
Leibniz, Gottfried Wilhelm, 66, 615 note 153, 652 note 542
Leon, Rabbi Moses de, 597 note 8
Leprosy, 636 note 359
Levels, corresponding, of God, humanity, and nature, 70–77
Lewis, John, 23 notes 12 and 13
Light of heaven, 601 note 33
"Likeness," 606 note 75
Literal *vs.* idiomatic translation of Scripture references, 8–11
Locke, John, 94
The Lord, 41–43. *See also* God: names of
  absolute sovereignty of, 84
  defined, 5, 42, 596 note 7
  the subject of the Bible as the life and inner development of, 97, 98, 100, 101–103
Love
  and faith, 90–92
  for the Lord and one's neighbor, 92, 114
  types of, 631 note 316
Lower earth. *See* Underground realm
Luther, Martin, 81, 84, 621 note 203
Lutheranism, 82, 114
Lying, as impossible in heaven, 622 note 210, 643 note 441

M

Macrocosm, individual as, 110–111, 650 note 517
Male privilege, 632 note 325
Malebranche, Nicolas de, 66, 652 note 542
"Man," 604–605 note 61
Manasseh, 625 note 241
Marchant, John, 116–117
Marriage, 55–56, 606 note 77
  heavenly, 606 note 79, 613 note 141, 625 note 245
  music as analogous to, 606 note 78
Marriage Love, 23 note 12, 108 note 58
Mary, mother of God, 41–42
Material world
  properties of objects in, 628 note 280
  worship of, 616 note 157
Maximus the Confessor, 614 note 149
Measurement, 634 note 345
  Hebrew, 632–633 note 326, 633 note 327
Memorable occurrences, 77, 78, 105–114, 595–596 note 4

Mercy seat, 621 note 204
Les merveilles du ciel et de l'enfer et des terres planétaires et astrales, 116 note 81
Metaphor, 642 note 423
Methodological agnosticism, 65 and note 2
Microcosm, individual as, 110–111, 650 note 517
Middle field, in the structure of *Secrets of Heaven,* 26, 27–35, 28–29 figure 1
"Mighty," 633 note 334
Mind, interaction with the body, 615 note 153
"Minha," 628 note 276
Moët, Jean Pierre, 117 note 81
More, Henry, 67
Morveau, Louis Joseph Bernard Philibert Guyton de, 116 note 81
"Moses" meaning Genesis, Exodus, Leviticus, Numbers, Deuteronomy, 608 note 89
Mourning, 643 note 440
Music, as analogous to marriage, 606 note 78

N
Name, 612 note 134
Natural philosophy, 67
Nature, 67, 70, 73, 76, 77
Neighbor, commandment to love, 91–92
Neoplatonism, 66, 67, 69, 75, 110 note 63
"Nephilim," 620 note 195, 631 note 317
Nerve, 631 note 315
New Church, 68 note 9, 89, 117
New Jerusalem, 24, 106 and note 55
Noah, 99, 629 note 285
Non-Jews, 616 note 164
Nordensköld, August, 77
Nourse, John, 23 note 12
Numbering conventions, 4–5, 22

O
Oetinger, Friedrich Christoph, 106, 116, 118
The Old Testament Explained, 8, 9, 21–22, 23
Origen, 81 and note 24, 82, 83, 596 note 8, 634 note 346
Original sin, 42 note 31, 621 note 207
"Orions," 603 note 53
Other Planets, 24, 35, 107
Outer self, 597–598 note 14

P
Paracelsus, 67, 110 note 65, 646 note 466
Paradise, 597 note 10

Particular items, as sustained by general category, 605 note 65
Passive. *See* Forces, active and passive
Pernety, Antoine-Joseph, 116 note 81
Philanthropic and Exegetic Society, 117
Philo of Alexandria (Philo Judaeus), 81 and note 23, 82, 83, 596 note 8
Philo-Semitism, 53
Philosophical and Metallurgical Works, 18 and note 3, 19
Phrath, 608 note 97
Pico della Mirandola, Giovanni, 110 note 65
Piety, financial rewards of, 640 note 397
Pigs, debristling of, 652 note 534
Pinhole camera, 51 note 40
Plants, growing on roofs, 619 note 188
Plato, 24, 637 note 372, 652 note 542
Pleasure, relationship to good, 637–638 note 372
Plurals, 599 note 20, 606 note 76, 608 note 93, 618 note 174
Polemics, 53–54
Polygamy, 647 note 473
Pordage, John, 67 note 7
Potts, John Faulkner, 4, 11
Pre-Flood people, 631 note 319
Preview sections, in the structure of *Secrets of Heaven,* 29 figure 1, 31–34, 32–33 figure 2
Principia, 18 note 3
Prometheus, 623 note 226
Propositions, in the structure of *Secrets of Heaven,* 29 figure 1, 31–34, 32–33 figure 2
"Proprium." *See* Selfhood
Protestant Reformation, 81, 89, 114
Protestants, 52 note 41, 54
Providence, 70–71, 74
Purgatory, 39

R
Race and ethnicity, 51–55
Rationalism, 65–66, 69, 71, 84, 118
  rationalist Bible criticism, 80
Raven, 647 note 472
Rebirth, 25, 43–47. *See also* Regeneration
Regeneration, 93, 94, 97 and note 42, 98 figure 2
  states of, 645 note 459
  struggles involved in, 607 note 85
Religions, diversity of, 47–48, 54
"Remnant," 599 note 22
Repetition in the middle field of *Secrets of Heaven,* 30–35

"Rephaim," 620 note 195
Representation, 598 note 17
Reuss, Jeremias Friedrich, 116 note 79
Revelation Unveiled, 25 note 14, 36 note 25, 52 note 41
Richard of St. Victor, 634 note 346
Roman Catholicism, 52 note 41, 54, 82, 84, 88–89, 92, 114
Roofs, plant growth on, 619 note 188
Rüdiger, Andreas, 67
Rydelius, Andreas, 652 note 542

S
"Sabaoth," 611 note 122
Sabbath, 626 note 249
Sacrifices, 597 note 9
La sagesse angélique sur l'amour divin et sur la sagesse divine, 116 note 81
Sanhedrin, 624 note 238
Satan, 612 note 140
Satyrs, 41
Schelling, Friedrich Wilhelm Joseph von, 115
Schi'ur Koma, 110
Schmidt, Sebastian, 8, 77 note 19, 599 note 19
"Scholarly dust," 630 note 306
Schönberg, Arnold, 115
Schuchard, Marsha Keith, 66
Scripture references
    Genesis 1:14, page 603 note 50
    Genesis 1:26, page 649 note 502
    Genesis 1–15, page 27
    Genesis 2, pages 607 note 82, 650 note 514
    Genesis 2:1, page 611 note 122
    Genesis 2:2, 3, pages 615–616 note 156
    Genesis 2:11–14, page 611 note 127
    Genesis 2:18–25, page 641 note 415
    Genesis 2:22, 23, page 613 note 143
    Genesis 2:22–25, page 650 note 514
    Genesis 2:23, page 612 note 132
    Genesis 2:24, page 607 note 81
    Genesis 2:25, page 9
    Genesis 3:4, 5, pages 615–616 note 156
    Genesis 3:13, page 616 note 162
    Genesis 3:14, page 616 note 163
    Genesis 3:15, page 607 note 81
    Genesis 3:16, pages 55, 632 note 325
    Genesis 3:19, page 621 note 200
    Genesis 4:10, page 606 note 76
    Genesis 4:20, page 627 note 263
    Genesis 5, page 635 note 355
    Genesis 5:22, page 630 note 304
    Genesis 5:29, page 631 note 310
    Genesis 6:4, page 633 note 334
    Genesis 6:14, page 636 note 357
    Genesis 6:16, page 639 note 387
    Genesis 6:18, page 639 note 387
    Genesis 6:19, page 641 note 410
    Genesis 6:21, 22, page 642 note 429
    Genesis 7:2, page 650 note 514
    Genesis 7:2, 3, page 641 note 410
    Genesis 7:10, page 643 note 442
    Genesis 8:14, 18–19, page 643 note 442
    Genesis 8:15, page 649 note 504
    Genesis 9:7, page 643 note 442
    Genesis 10, 11, page 607 note 87
    Genesis 10:7, page 610 note 118
    Genesis 10:30, page 643 note 442
    Genesis 15:18, page 611 note 124
    Genesis 16:8, page 616 note 162
    Genesis 16–40, page 27
    Genesis 17:5, page 607 note 87
    Genesis 18:32, page 629 note 290
    Genesis 20:16, page 643 note 442
    Genesis 21:17, page 616 note 162
    Genesis 22:1, page 617 note 167
    Genesis 22:18, 23, page 643 note 442
    Genesis 23–43, page 47
    Genesis 24:29, page 598 note 17
    Genesis 27:17, 45, page 643 note 442
    Genesis 27:36, page 618 note 179
    Genesis 29:13, page 643 note 442
    Genesis 29:32, page 649 note 498
    Genesis 37:1, page 643 note 442
    Genesis 38:7, 10, page 617 note 167
    Genesis 41:51, page 625 note 241
    Genesis 41–50, page 27
    Genesis 48:20, page 625 note 241
    Genesis 49:17, page 80
    Exodus 1:1–6, pages 103–104
    Exodus 1–40, page 27
    Exodus 3:14, page 651 note 523
    Exodus 3:14, 15, page 600 note 28
    Exodus 4:2, page 616 note 162
    Exodus 4:14, page 617 note 167
    Exodus 6:3, page 600 note 28
    Exodus 12, page 612 note 137
    Exodus 12:6, page 602 note 40
    Exodus 14:10–15, page 640 note 401
    Exodus 15:9, page 643 note 442
    Exodus 15:24–25, page 640 note 401

Scripture references *(continued)*
 Exodus 16:2–12, page 640 note 401
 Exodus 16:4, page 630 note 303
 Exodus 16:12, page 602 note 40
 Exodus 17:1–7, page 640 note 401
 Exodus 17:9–13, page 648 note 486
 Exodus 20:7, page 600 note 28
 Exodus 20:17, page 632 note 325
 Exodus 21:23–25, page 623 note 218
 Exodus 23:10, 11, page 626 note 249
 Exodus 24:4–8, page 597 note 9
 Exodus 25, 26, 28, 30, page 610 note 114
 Exodus 25:17–22, page 621 note 204
 Exodus 26, 27, page 610 note 115
 Exodus 29:12, page 650 note 520
 Exodus 29:39, 41, page 602 note 40
 Exodus 30:8, page 602 note 40
 Exodus 32:34, page 617 note 167
 Exodus 32:35, page 640 note 401
 Exodus 34:16, page 629 note 291
 Leviticus 3:15, page 623 note 227
 Leviticus 4:30, page 650 note 520
 Leviticus 8:10, 11, page 625 note 247
 Leviticus 11, 15, page 649 note 492
 Leviticus 14:34, 44, 55, page 636 note 359
 Leviticus 15:19–33, page 632 note 325
 Leviticus 16, page 621 note 204
 Leviticus 16:13–15, page 621 note 204
 Leviticus 16:14, 19, page 625 note 247
 Leviticus 23:5, page 602 note 40
 Leviticus 23:15, page 626 note 247
 Leviticus 24:19–20, page 623 note 218
 Leviticus 25:2–5, page 626 note 249
 Leviticus 25:8, 10, page 626 note 247
 Leviticus 26:3, page 630 note 303
 Leviticus 26:18, 24, page 617 note 167
 Numbers 5:11–31, page 632 note 325
 Numbers 6:26, page 624 note 229
 Numbers 9:3, 5, 11, page 602 note 40
 Numbers 11:1, page 617 note 167
 Numbers 13:33, page 631 note 317
 Numbers 19, page 649 note 492
 Numbers 24:5, page 610 note 113
 Numbers 28:4, 8, page 602 note 40
 Numbers 28:11, 12, 18–20, 26–28, page 626 note 247
 Numbers 32:13, page 617 note 167
 Numbers 33:52, page 606 note 75
 Numbers 36:6–9, page 629 note 291
 Deuteronomy 1:28, page 633 note 331

Deuteronomy 2:10, 11, 21, page 633 note 331
Deuteronomy 7:3, 4, page 629 note 291
Deuteronomy 9:2, page 633 note 331
Deuteronomy 9:4–6, page 53
Deuteronomy 11:6, page 638 note 380
Deuteronomy 13:3, page 617 note 167
Deuteronomy 19:21, page 623 note 218
Deuteronomy 27:15, page 648 note 481
Deuteronomy 28:26, page 650 note 510
Deuteronomy 29:27, page 617 note 167
Deuteronomy 30:7, page 617 note 167
Deuteronomy 32:7, page 600 note 26
Deuteronomy 32:28, 32–33, page 53
Joshua 7:6, page 617 note 168
Joshua 11:21, 22, page 633 note 331
Joshua 14:12, 15, page 633 note 331
1 Samuel 2:3, page 607 note 88
1 Samuel 4:4, page 621 note 206
1 Samuel 6:5, page 606 note 75
1 Samuel 15:27, page 642 note 425
2 Samuel 1:2, page 617 note 168
2 Samuel 6:2, page 621 note 206
2 Samuel 8:3–6, page 611 note 124
2 Samuel 15:32, page 617 note 168
2 Samuel 22:11, page 620 note 193
1 Kings 1:50, page 650 note 520
1 Kings 2:4, page 630 note 303
1 Kings 2:28, page 650 note 520
1 Kings 6, 7, page 610 note 114
2 Kings 11:18, page 606 note 75
2 Kings 16:10, page 606 note 75
2 Kings 19:15, page 621 note 206
2 Kings 22:17, page 648 note 481
2 Kings 23:10, page 625 note 239
1 Chronicles 1:9, page 610 note 118
1 Chronicles 5:1, page 625 note 241
1 Chronicles 9:33, page 627 note 264
1 Chronicles 15:19–22, page 627 note 264
1 Chronicles 25:1–31, page 627 note 264
1 Chronicles 25:7, page 627 note 264
1 Chronicles 28, 29, page 610 notes 114 and 115
2 Chronicles 3, 4, page 610 note 114
2 Chronicles 5:12, 13, page 627 note 264
Job 19:27, page 623 note 223
Psalms 2:2, page 618 note 170
Psalms 4:6, page 624 note 229
Psalms 9:16, page 648 note 481
Psalms 11:4, page 635 note 352
Psalms 15:1, 2, page 633 note 338

Psalms 16:7, page 623 note 223
Psalms 18:10, page 620 note 193
Psalms 18:50, page 618 note 170
Psalms 25:21, page 633 note 338
Psalms 26:3, page 630 note 303
Psalms 28:4, page 648 note 481
Psalms 29:10, page 641 note 408
Psalms 33:6, page 609 note 108
Psalms 37:37, page 633 note 338
Psalms 40:2, page 638 note 377
Psalms 44:1, page 600 note 26
Psalms 50:10, page 650 note 509
Psalms 50:11, page 650 note 509
Psalms 63:9, page 617 note 169
Psalms 72, page 611 note 120
Psalms 73:21, page 623 note 223
Psalms 77:5, page 600 note 26
Psalms 78:10, page 630 note 303
Psalms 78:34, page 617 note 167
Psalms 79:2, page 650 note 510
Psalms 80:1, page 621 note 206
Psalms 99:1, page 621 note 206
Psalms 104:2, page 602 note 46
Psalms 115:4, page 648 note 481
Psalms 118:27, page 650 note 520
Psalms 119:1, page 630 note 303
Psalms 129:6, page 619 note 188
Psalms 135:15, page 648 note 481
Psalms 139:15, page 617 note 169
Psalms 143:5, page 600 note 26
Psalms 146:4, page 621 note 200
Proverbs 3:33, page 617 note 167
Proverbs 23:16, page 623 note 223
Ecclesiastes 9:5, page 621 note 200
Ecclesiastes 9:10, page 621 note 200
Isaiah 2:8, page 648 note 481
Isaiah 4:3, page 599 note 22
Isaiah 5:8, page 629 note 288
Isaiah 6:9–13, pages 602 note 35, 638 note 377
Isaiah 6:12, page 629 note 288
Isaiah 7:14, pages 618 note 175, 623 note 221
Isaiah 7:22, pages 10, 629 note 288
Isaiah 9:2, 3, page 633 note 338
Isaiah 9:6, 7, page 609 note 101
Isaiah 9:8, page 627 note 267
Isaiah 10:3, page 651 note 528
Isaiah 10:20, page 627 note 267
Isaiah 10:20–22, page 599 note 22
Isaiah 11, page 618 note 170
Isaiah 11:10–12, page 633 note 338

Isaiah 13:6, page 602 note 35
Isaiah 14:2–23, page 618 note 176
Isaiah 14:12, pages 612 note 140, 618 note 176
Isaiah 14:32, page 633 note 338
Isaiah 16:4, page 602 note 35
Isaiah 17:7, page 609 note 103
Isaiah 17:8, page 648 note 481
Isaiah 19:2, page 624 note 232
Isaiah 19:23–25, page 624 note 234
Isaiah 22:1, page 625 note 242
Isaiah 22:11, page 609 note 103
Isaiah 23:7, page 600 note 26
Isaiah 23:12, page 618 note 175
Isaiah 23:15–17, page 649 note 500
Isaiah 24:1–23, pages 621 note 202, 638 note 377
Isaiah 24:13, page 629 note 288
Isaiah 24:16, page 642 note 425
Isaiah 25:7, page 633 note 338
Isaiah 26:14, page 621 note 200
Isaiah 27:6, page 627 note 267
Isaiah 30:17, pages 9–10
Isaiah 30:26, pages 625 note 247, 649 note 500
Isaiah 32:17, 18, page 609 note 101
Isaiah 33:8, 9, page 602 note 35
Isaiah 33:20, page 635 note 352
Isaiah 37:16, page 621 note 206
Isaiah 37:17, page 635 note 352
Isaiah 37:19, page 648 note 481
Isaiah 37:22, page 618 note 175
Isaiah 37:26, page 600 note 26
Isaiah 39:7, page 623 note 221
Isaiah 40:28, page 609 note 103
Isaiah 42:5, page 609 note 103
Isaiah 42:11, page 9
Isaiah 42:14, 15, page 602 note 35
Isaiah 42:22, page 602 note 46
Isaiah 43:1, 15, page 609 note 103
Isaiah 43:22, 23, page 629 note 296
Isaiah 44:2, 24, page 609 note 103
Isaiah 44:23, page 617 note 169
Isaiah 45:1, page 618 note 170
Isaiah 45:12, page 602 note 46
Isaiah 47:1, page 618 note 175
Isaiah 47:8–15, page 611 note 128
Isaiah 49:5, page 609 note 103
Isaiah 49:17–19, page 602 note 35
Isaiah 51:3, page 638 note 377
Isaiah 51:9, page 600 note 26
Isaiah 51:15, page 602 note 46

Scripture references *(continued)*
- Isaiah 51:17–23, pages 602 note 35, 621 note 202
- Isaiah 52:7, page 609 note 101
- Isaiah 53:12, page 621 note 200
- Isaiah 54:2, page 602 note 46
- Isaiah 54:5, page 609 note 103
- Isaiah 54:10, page 609 note 101
- Isaiah 55:4, page 10
- Isaiah 56:7, page 609 note 101
- Isaiah 58:2, page 633 note 338
- Isaiah 63:9, 11, page 600 note 26
- Isaiah 66:24, page 625 note 239
- Jeremiah 1:16, page 648 note 481
- Jeremiah 1:18, page 638 note 378
- Jeremiah 3:14–16, page 633 note 338
- Jeremiah 7:31–32, page 625 note 239
- Jeremiah 7:33, page 650 note 510
- Jeremiah 8:17, page 614 note 151
- Jeremiah 10:3, pages 10, 648 note 481
- Jeremiah 10:8–9, page 10
- Jeremiah 13:14, page 624 note 232
- Jeremiah 14:17, page 618 note 175
- Jeremiah 15:20, page 638 note 378
- Jeremiah 16:5, page 609 note 101
- Jeremiah 17:5, page 617 note 167
- Jeremiah 17:10, page 9
- Jeremiah 17:24, 25, page 609 note 101
- Jeremiah 23:3, page 633 note 338
- Jeremiah 25:5, page 632 note 322
- Jeremiah 25:6, 7, 14, page 648 note 481
- Jeremiah 25:11, 12, page 649 note 500
- Jeremiah 29:6, page 623 note 221
- Jeremiah 31:4, page 618 note 175
- Jeremiah 31:7, page 627 note 267
- Jeremiah 31:11, page 633 note 334
- Jeremiah 32:17, 21, page 648 note 482
- Jeremiah 32:30, page 648 note 481
- Jeremiah 44:8, page 648 note 481
- Jeremiah 44:13, page 617 note 167
- Jeremiah 46:26, page 600 note 26
- Jeremiah 48:10, page 617 note 167
- Jeremiah 49:28, page 627 note 261
- Jeremiah 50:20, page 599 note 22
- Lamentations 1:7, page 600 note 26
- Lamentations 1:15, page 618 note 175
- Lamentations 2:10, page 617 note 168
- Lamentations 2:13, page 618 note 175
- Lamentations 2:17, page 600 note 26
- Lamentations 2:21, page 617 note 167
- Lamentations 4:20, page 618 note 170
- Lamentations 5:21, page 600 note 26
- Ezekiel 1, page 620 note 193
- Ezekiel 1:5, page 641 note 419
- Ezekiel 1:5, 10, 26, 28, page 606 note 75
- Ezekiel 1:27, page 10
- Ezekiel 4:6, page 629 note 295
- Ezekiel 5:6–7, page 630 note 303
- Ezekiel 7:22, page 617 note 167
- Ezekiel 8:2, page 10
- Ezekiel 9:2, 3, 11, page 613 note 145
- Ezekiel 10:2, 6, 7, page 613 note 145
- Ezekiel 12:19, 20, pages 621 note 202, 638 note 377
- Ezekiel 14:16, 18, page 623 note 221
- Ezekiel 18:4, page 621 note 200
- Ezekiel 18:9, 17, page 630 note 303
- Ezekiel 20:12, page 609 note 101
- Ezekiel 23:14, page 606 note 75
- Ezekiel 26:19–21, page 621 note 202
- Ezekiel 26:20, page 617 note 169
- Ezekiel 27:30, page 617 note 168
- Ezekiel 31:14, 16, 18, page 617 note 169
- Ezekiel 32:18, 24, page 617 note 169
- Ezekiel 34:5, 8, page 650 note 510
- Ezekiel 36:3–12, pages 602 note 35, 621 note 202, 638 note 377
- Ezekiel 36:27, page 630 note 303
- Ezekiel 37:3, page 616 note 162
- Ezekiel 39:9–12, page 649 note 500
- Ezekiel 40–41, page 605 note 62
- Ezekiel 47:9–20, page 605 note 63
- Daniel 7:9–14, page 651 note 528
- Daniel 9:24–25, page 649 note 500
- Daniel 9:27, page 651 note 528
- Daniel 10:5, page 613 note 145
- Daniel 12:6, 7, page 613 note 145
- Hosea 1–3, page 613 note 141
- Hosea 6:1, 2, page 649 note 500
- Hosea 6:2, page 10
- Hosea 9:7, page 651 note 528
- Hosea 9:11, page 623 note 221
- Amos 3:14, page 650 note 520
- Amos 4:10, page 617 note 167
- Amos 5:3, page 599 note 22
- Amos 9:7, page 624 note 234
- Amos 9:11, page 600 note 26
- Jonah 1:3, page 610 note 119
- Jonah 1:17–2:10, page 649 note 500
- Micah 3:5, 6, page 602 note 39

INDEX TO PREFACES, GUIDE, INTRODUCTION, & NOTES 669

Micah 4:8, page 618 note 175
Micah 5:2, page 600 note 26
Micah 5:7, page 599 note 22
Micah 6:8, page 630 note 304
Micah 7:14, 20, page 600 note 26
Zephaniah 1:14–18, page 602 note 35
Zephaniah 2:14, page 10
Zephaniah 3:14, page 618 note 175
Haggai 2:9, page 609 note 101
Zechariah 8:3, page 10
Zechariah 9:9, page 618 note 175
Zechariah 12:1, page 602 note 46
Malachi 2:2, page 617 note 167
Malachi 3:3, page 623 note 221
Malachi 3:4, page 600 note 26
Malachi 4:6, page 617 note 167
Matthew 3:16, page 647 note 476
Matthew 4:19, page 605 note 63
Matthew 5:38, page 623 note 218
Matthew 6:30, page 621 note 202
Matthew 8:10, 26, page 621 note 202
Matthew 8:20, page 606 note 73
Matthew 9:6, page 606 note 73
Matthew 10:23, page 606 note 73
Matthew 10:39, page 612 note 133
Matthew 11:19, page 606 note 73
Matthew 12:8, 32, 40, page 606 note 73
Matthew 13:24–30, 36–43, page 626 note 259
Matthew 13:37, 41, page 606 note 73
Matthew 13:39, 40, page 604 note 55
Matthew 14:31, page 621 note 202
Matthew 16:8, page 621 note 202
Matthew 16:13, 27, 28, page 606 note 73
Matthew 17:9, 12, 22, page 606 note 73
Matthew 18:11, page 606 note 73
Matthew 19:12, page 625 note 245
Matthew 19:24, page 611 note 126
Matthew 19:28, page 606 note 73
Matthew 20:1–16, page 616 note 160
Matthew 20:18, 28, page 606 note 73
Matthew 20:32, page 616 note 162
Matthew 21:28–32, page 616 note 160
Matthew 23:27, page 597 note 14
Matthew 23:33, page 652 note 540
Matthew 24:3, page 651 note 528
Matthew 24:3–14, page 651 note 528
Matthew 24:15, 16, page 621 note 202
Matthew 24:32, page 616 note 160
Matthew 24:37, 39, 44, page 606 note 73
Matthew 25:13, 31, page 606 note 73

Matthew 25:31–46, page 651 note 528
Matthew 25:34–36, page 90
Matthew 26:2, 24, 45, 64, page 606 note 73
Matthew 26:26–28, page 597 note 9
Matthew 26:26–29, page 620 note 190
Matthew 26:50, page 616 note 162
Mark 1:10, page 647 note 476
Mark 1:17, page 605 note 63
Mark 2:10, 28, page 606 note 73
Mark 4:3–20, page 601 note 32
Mark 4:40, page 621 note 202
Mark 8:38, page 606 note 73
Mark 9:12, 31, page 606 note 73
Mark 9:33–35, page 628 note 282
Mark 9:43–45, page 625 note 239
Mark 10:25, page 611 note 126
Mark 10:33, 45, page 606 note 73
Mark 10:51, page 616 note 162
Mark 12:1–11, page 616 note 160
Mark 13:26, page 606 note 73
Mark 13:28, page 616 note 160
Mark 14:21, 41, 62, page 606 note 73
Mark 14:22–24, page 597 note 9
Mark 14:22–25, page 620 note 190
Mark 16:15, page 642 note 426
Mark 16:19, 20, page 600 note 25
Luke 3:22, page 647 note 476
Luke 5:24, page 606 note 73
Luke 6:5, 22, page 606 note 73
Luke 7:9, page 621 note 202
Luke 7:34, page 606 note 73
Luke 8:25, page 621 note 202
Luke 9:22, 26, 44, 56, 58, page 606 note 73
Luke 11:30, page 606 note 73
Luke 12:8, 10, 40, page 606 note 73
Luke 12:28, page 621 note 202
Luke 13:6–9, page 616 note 160
Luke 13:32, page 649 note 500
Luke 17:6, page 621 note 202
Luke 17:21, page 650 note 513
Luke 17:22, 24, 26, 30, page 606 note 73
Luke 17:34, page 602 note 39
Luke 18:8, page 621 note 202
Luke 18:8, 31, page 606 note 73
Luke 18:10–14, page 597 note 14
Luke 18:25, page 611 note 126
Luke 18:41, page 616 note 162
Luke 19:10, page 606 note 73
Luke 20:9–16, page 616 note 160
Luke 21:7, page 651 note 528

Scripture references *(continued)*
  Luke 21:27, 36, page 606 note 73
  Luke 21:29–30, page 616 note 160
  Luke 22:14–20, page 620 note 190
  Luke 22:19–20, page 597 note 9
  Luke 22:22, 48, 69, page 606 note 73
  Luke 22:24–26, page 628 note 282
  Luke 22:26, page 629 note 283
  Luke 23:43, page 597 note 10
  Luke 24:3, 34, page 600 note 25
  John 1:4, page 597 note 12
  John 1:32–34, page 647 note 476
  John 1:51, page 606 note 73
  John 2:19–21, page 649 note 500
  John 3:13, 14, page 606 note 73
  John 4:22, page 619 note 182
  John 5:6, page 616 note 162
  John 5:27, page 606 note 73
  John 6:27, 53, 62, page 606 note 73
  John 7:1, page 619 note 182
  John 8:28, page 606 note 73
  John 8:44, page 53
  John 9:4, page 602 note 39
  John 11:9, 10, page 602 note 39
  John 12:23, page 606 note 73
  John 13:31, page 606 note 73
  John 14:27, page 609 note 101
  John 18:4, 7, page 616 note 162
  John 18:36, page 620 note 191
  John 19:31, page 619 note 182
  John 20:2, 13, 15, 18, 20, 25, 28, page 600 note 25
  John 20:15, page 616 note 162
  John 21:7, 12, 15, 16, 17, 20, page 600 note 25
  John 21:15–17, page 616 note 162
  John 21:21, page 600 note 25
  Acts 1:6, page 600 note 25
  Acts 2:36, page 600 note 25
  Acts 7:59–60, page 600 note 25
  Acts 8:16, page 600 note 25
  Acts 9:15, page 616 note 164
  Acts 13:47, page 616 note 164
  Romans 2:28–29, pages 598 note 14, 636 note 363
  Romans 7:22–23, page 636 note 363
  Romans 10:17, pages 625 note 244, 636 note 363
  1 Corinthians 4:5, page 600 note 25
  1 Corinthians 9:1, 5, page 600 note 25
  1 Corinthians 11:3, page 641 note 417
  1 Corinthians 13:2, page 623 note 222
  2 Corinthians 3:6, page 8 note 10
  2 Corinthians 4:16, pages 598 note 14, 636 note 363
  2 Corinthians 5:17, pages 642 note 426, 651 note 525
  2 Corinthians 12:2, page 613 note 146
  Galatians 2:20, page 612 note 133
  Galatians 5:6, page 648 note 489
  Galatians 6:15, pages 642 note 426, 651 note 525
  Ephesians 1:22, 23, page 641 note 417
  Ephesians 4:22–24, page 602 note 36
  Ephesians 5:2, page 597 note 9
  Ephesians 5:23, page 641 note 417
  Colossians 1:18, page 641 note 417
  Colossians 3:9–10, page 602 note 36
  1 Thessalonians 1:3, page 648 note 489
  Hebrews 5:9–10, page 636 note 363
  Hebrews 6:10, page 648 note 489
  Hebrews 7:14, page 600 note 25
  Hebrews 7:27, page 597 note 9
  Hebrews 9, page 597 note 9
  Hebrews 9:26, page 597 note 9
  Hebrews 10:1, page 597 note 9
  1 Peter 3:20–21, page 634 note 346
  Revelation 1:12, 13, page 625 note 247
  Revelation 2:7, page 597 note 10
  Revelation 4:5, page 626 note 247
  Revelation 9:20, page 648 note 481
  Revelation 12:9, page 618 note 176
  Revelation 14:4, 5, page 618 note 175
  Revelation 17:1–5, page 645 note 455
  Revelation 20:11–15, page 651 note 528
  Revelation 20:23, page 614 note 147
  Revelation 21:2, page 613 note 141
  Revelation 21:9, page 613 note 141
Second Coming, 6, 89, 90
Secrets, 595 note 1
Secrets of Heaven, 63, 77, 106
  audience for, 51–52
  Bible citation anomalies in, 602 note 45
  consisting of three strands, 77, 78–114, 119–124
    the first strand: method, history, and doctrine, 78–95, 119–120
    the second strand: biblical exegesis, 95–105, 120–123
    the third strand: accounts of memorable occurrences, 105–114, 123–124
  content of, 1–2, 36
  describing the Lord's life and inner development, 97, 101–103

as divinely revealed, 64, 79, 83, 84, 96–97
editions and translations of, 3–4, 14–15
emendations and errata to, 3
as an exegesis of Genesis and Exodus, 64, 75, 77, 78, 95–105, 118, 120–123
experiential material in, 4, 595–596 note 4
historical context of, 1–2
history of religious development in, 78, 85–89, 97–101
indexing and cross-referencing of, 22, 35–36
"introductory parts" in, 77
manuscript versions of, 4, 14, 22–23
method of biblical exegesis in, 77, 78, 79–85
numbering conventions used in, 4–5, 22 and note 9
place in Swedenborg's life and work, 18–24
planned extent of, 23–24, 24–25 note 14, 608 note 90, 620 note 197, 627 note 266
problematic aspects of, 5–7, 51–58
providing accounts of Swedenborg's spiritual experiences, 64, 77, 78, 105–114, 118, 123–124
reception and influence of, 115–118
spiritual teachings in, 64, 77, 78, 89–95
structure of (*see* Structure of *Secrets of Heaven*)
title of, 1, 18 note 1, 63, 64
translating, issues in, 1, 3–11
typographic conventions used in, 4–5, 24–30
writing and publishing of, 21–23
Sefer ha-Zohar, 596–597 note 8
Selfhood, 46, 612 note 133
Self-love, 93
and love for the world, 92, 97, 114
Sensation, spirits' powers of, 37
Senses, physical, 97, 622 note 212
Sensual pleasures, 58
Seven, 625 note 246
Shaddai, 609 note 109
Sheba, 610 note 118
Sirens, 41, 645 note 458
Snakes, 614 note 151, 618 note 171
snake in Garden of Eden, 55
Sola scriptura, doctrine of, 81
Son of Humankind, 604 note 60, 606 note 73
Soul, 652 note 542
of animals, 615 note 152
Soul-Body Interaction, 605 note 63
The Soul's Domain, 20
Space and time, 49–51
in the spiritual world, 50, 112–113

Spirit, also meaning breath or wind, 609 note 106, 616 note 161, 637 note 371, 652 note 532
Spirits
evil, 94, 613 note 140
attack of, 607 note 84
evil spirits, demons, and devils, 41, 42–43
good, 40 and note 28, 41, 94
spirits, angelic spirits, and angels, 40 and note 28, 111 notes 66 and 67
Spiritual, 6, 7 figure 1, 45
Spiritual and heavenly, distinction between, 87, 92, 111 notes 66 and 67
Spiritual church, 48–49
Spiritual Experiences, 21, 106 note 52
Spiritual heaven, 38 and figure 3
Spiritual person, 97
Spiritual sense of Scripture, 25
Spiritual world, 36–41, 76, 77, 91
defined, 6
diagram of, 38 figure 3
Jews in, 53
overlapping physical world, 41, 47, 49
sensation in, 37
Swedenborg's experiences in, 26–27, 36, 37 note 26, 50
time and space in, 50, 112–113
Strindberg, August, 115
Structure of *Secrets of Heaven*, 24–36
chapter organization, 26–27
diagrams of, 28–29 figure 1, 32–33 figure 2
end field, 26, 29 figure 1, 30
flexibility in reading allowed by, 35–36
formatting devices for, 27–30
front field, 26–27, 28 figure 1
geometric reasoning and repetition, 30–35
indexing and cross-referencing, 4–5, 22, 35–36
"interchapter" material, 30 note 20
levels of inner meanings influencing, 25–26
middle field, 26, 27–35, 28–29 figure 1
preview sections and propositions, 29 figure 1, 31–34, 32–33 figure 2
summaries, 28 figure 1, 30
typographic conventions distinguishing, 26–30
Sukkot, 627 note 262
Summaries, in the structure of *Secrets of Heaven*, 28 figure 1, 30
Suph, 641 note 413
"Survivors," 599 note 22

Swedenborg, Emanuel, 63
    attitudes regarding race and gender, 51–56, 647 note 478
    breathing of, 609 note 107
    date of spiritual awakening of, 598–599 note 18
    empiricism of, 608 note 91
    experiences in spiritual world, 26–27, 36, 37 note 26, 50
    knowledge of philosophy, 67, 69
    interest in microscopes, 34–35 and note 23
    Lutheran background of, 82
    place of *Secrets of Heaven* in life and work of, 19–24
    scientific background of, 64, 65, 69, 73, 76, 84, 118
    sources of his work, 64–68
    spiritual crisis of, 65, 68, 84, 94, 110
    spiritual reorientation of, 19–21
    visionary experiences, 20, 64, 65, 75, 77, 78, 79, 85 note 28, 112
    visions of Jesus Christ, 20
Swedenborgs und anderer irrdische und himmlische Philosophie, 116
Symbolism, 598 note 17

T

Tabernacle, 610 note 114
Tafel, J.F.I., 116 note 80
Tar, 636 note 362
Tarshish *(country)*, 610 note 119
Tarshish *(precious stone)*, 610 note 117
Temple, 610 note 114
Ten Commandments, 633 note 329
Tetragrammaton, 5
Theological and doctrinal discussions, in the front field of *Secrets of Heaven*, 27, 35
Theological argumentation, polemical nature of, 53–54
Theorie der Geister-Kunde, 114 note 76
Tigris, 608 note 96
Time and space, 49–51
    in the spiritual world, 50, 112–113
Titans, 631–632 note 319
Traité curieux des charmes de l'amour conjugal dans ce monde et dans l'autre, 116 note 81
Transformation. See Glorification
Translating *Secrets of Heaven*, 1, 3–11
Transliteration of Hebrew and Greek words, 10–11
Trinity, 42

True Christianity, 24, 44 note 34, 52 note 41
Truth and goodness, 603 note 49
Typographic conventions, 4–5, 24–30
Typology, 634 note 346
Tyre, king of, 610 note 116

U

Underground realm, 38 figure 3, 39–40, 617–618 note 169
Understanding, 45 and figure 4
Universal human, 40, 108 and note 59, 109–113, 596 note 5, 622 note 209, 633 note 330, 635 note 354, 650 note 517

V

"Virgin," 607 note 80
Volition, 45 and figure 4
Voltaire, 644 note 452
von Meyer, Johann Friedrich, 114 note 76

W

Ware, Richard, 23 note 12
Western esotericism, 66, 68 and note 9
Western sea, 602 note 48
White Horse, 24, 106–107
Whitehead, Alfred North, 24
"Wife," in Hebrew, 611–612 note 132
Wilkinson, James John Garth, 68 note 10
Will, 45 and figure 4, 70–71, 74, 92–93, 603 note 51. See also Free will
Wind, also meaning breath or spirit, 616 note 161, 637 note 371, 652 note 532
Wolff, Christian, 66, 652 note 542
Women, Swedenborg's attitude toward, 51–52, 55–56, 57
The Word. See also Bible
    narrative parts of, 607 note 86
    prophetic parts of, 607 note 86
    Swedenborg's use of the term, 595 note 2
World of spirits, 6, 38 figure 3, 39, 595 note 3
Worldliness, 58 note 45
Worship and Love of God, 20–21, 23
Wunsch, William F., 31 note 23

Y

Yahweh, 5, 600–601 note 28, 639 note 384
"Young woman," 607 note 80

Z

Zeus, 623 note 226

Index to *Secrets of Heaven,* Volume 1

This index to *Secrets of Heaven* 1–946 is a compilation by Alicia L. Dole based on the first volume of the Lisa Hyatt Cooper translation and the relevant entries of the six-volume *Swedenborg Concordance* by John Faulkner Potts (London: Swedenborg Society, 1888–1902).

Potts's concordance is keyed to Swedenborg's original Latin, and as a consequence the Latin provides the backbone of the present index as well. This Latin basis results in index entries that may prove unexpected. For example, in *Secrets of Heaven* 343 Swedenborg describes how all togetherness and unity derive from charity. The Latin word translated "unity" in this passage is *unio.* In the Cooper translation, however, *unio* is sometimes represented as "union," and by a necessarily arbitrary choice "union" is the heading that represents the Latin word in the index, though it is followed in parentheses by the alternate translation "unity." Thus the entry "all togetherness and unity coming from charity" appears under the heading "Union (unity)."

Even though such an indexing method necessarily entails some disadvantages for the reader, it far better represents Swedenborg's collocation of Latin concepts than an index based on the irrelevant vagaries of English use. Furthermore, the disadvantages of the system are largely mitigated by cross-references from synonyms to main headings. Thus a reader seeking a reference to the concept of unity deriving from charity can find it by first looking under the heading "Unity" and following the cross-reference "*See also* Union." In this index, then, the cross-references bear an unusual importance.

Although Potts's concordance has been utilized extensively here, this compilation differs significantly from that of Potts. In his introduction to his concordance, Potts states: "While this Concordance claims to be complete, the fact must not be overlooked that it is a selection. . . . Every word has had to pass under judgment. . . . This was inevitable, unless the Concordance were to fill forty volumes" (Potts 1888–1902, ix). This index is even more selective: though all entries pertaining to this volume in Potts's concordance were examined for possible inclusion, not all were chosen. Some passages that Potts cites as containing a given word are simply not sufficiently definitive to be of interest to the inquiring reader. On the other hand, many passages have been added to this index that do not occur in Potts's concordance.

Such determinations of inclusion and exclusion are obviously subjective and imperfect. It is hoped, however, that sufficient inclusion has been made that the index will assist readers in finding most of the significant passages in their areas of interest.

Reference numbers in this index correspond to Swedenborg's section numbers in *Secrets of Heaven;* subsection numbers are separated from section numbers by a colon.

A

Abel. *See also* Cain; Charity
    Abel meaning charity, 325, 326, 341, 342, 343, 345, 350, 351, 366, 436, 916:3
    Abel's offering meaning worship motivated by charity, 326, 354
    Cain's murder of Abel meaning detached faith putting an end to charity, 329, 366, 369, 436
    "Jehovah looked on Abel and on his offering" meaning charity and worship from charity was pleasing to the Lord, 354
Abraham, 665
    Abraham meaning a saving faith, 64, 264:2
    a spirit seeking Abraham, Isaac, and Jacob in the spiritual world, 940:2
Abram, 64, 66, 440, 796, 921:2
Abyss (chasm)
    abyss meaning hell, 756:2, 845:2
    abyss meaning our cravings and the resulting falsities, 18, 756:1
    abyss meaning trials, 756:1, 845
    abysses and sea depths said to be drained (devastated) before a person is regenerated, 18
    reasoning about the mysteries of faith resulting in a dark chasm, 206:2, 215
Academic disciplines, 521. *See also* Fact
Acknowledgment, 5, 14, 32:2, 206, 226, 304, 393. *See also* Belief; Faith; Knowledge
    acknowledging as different from knowing, 302, 303, 654, 896
    acknowledgment and faith existing where charity exists, 654
    acknowledgment as the second step of rebirth, 896
    acknowledgment of our own nature as necessary for admission into heaven, 189
    acknowledgment requiring the rational mind's assent, 896:2

faith
    as knowing, acknowledging, and believing, 896
    as more than acknowledgment of doctrine, 36, 654
    our life as built of the things that we acknowledge, 303
    people cannot profane what they do not acknowledge, 302, 303, 408, 410
    religious truth depending on acknowledgment to take root, 880
Acre, 576:1
Act. *See* Action; Work
Action (deed). *See also* Making; Work
    action and will as a single entity in ancient times, 363
    a charitable action needing charity and the Lord behind it, 161
    thoughts, words, and deeds lying open in heavenly people, 99
Adah, 427
    Adah and Zillah compared to Leah and Rachel, 409
    Adah meaning the mother of a new church's heavenly and spiritual attributes, 405, 412, 413, 436
    the church meant by Adah and Zillah, 333, 409
    the human and his wife meaning the new church previously symbolized by Adah and Zillah, 434, 435, 436
Adam, 4. *See also* Human being
    Adam in Paradise meaning the earliest church's belief in the Lord, 64
    Adam meaning "ground," 313, 479, 566:1, 566:5
    Adam meaning the earliest church, 64, 313, 478, 479
    the Hebrew word *adam* meaning "a human," 477:4, 478

inherited evil not coming from Adam, 313, 494:2
Adultery
  an adulterous spirit allowed to visit heaven, 539
  connection between cruelty and adultery, 824
  false principles of boys regarding adultery, 829:2
  the group "marriages" of those who condoned adultery, 826
  the hells of those who spent their lives in adultery and lechery, 824–829
  outwardly respectable women who were drawn to adultery, 831
  those who commit adultery and are deceptive, 827
Advent. *See* Coming
Affection. *See* Emotion
Age. *See also* Time
  an age as the longest interval in the Word, 900
  an age meaning ten years, 433
Aid. *See also* Service
  "an aid that seems to be his" meaning a sense of autonomy, 138, 140, 142, 146
Alone, being
  being alone meaning the desire to be led by oneself, 138, 139
  households in the earliest church living alone, 414:4, 471
  living alone meaning led by the Lord, 139
Altar, 919, 921, 923
  the altar as the main object to represent the Lord, 921
  altars as a main feature of worship in the ancient church, 920:1, 920:4
  altars built as memorials before people knew about sacrifices, 921:2
  thorn and thistle on the altars meaning profanation, 273
Alternation. *See also* Cycle
  alternation of bodily and worldly desires with faith and charity, 933:3–4
  our alternating between no life and true life, 933:2
Ammonite, 576:2
Amorite, 289
Anakim, 581:2, 583. *See also* Nephilim
Ancestor. *See* Parent

Angel. *See also* Heaven; Spirit; Spirit, angelic
  angel choirs, 418:2
  angels acknowledging that only the Lord keeps them from hell, 868
  angels as in charge of us when we are regenerate, 50:3
  angels as unable to help us while we are unregenerate, 50:2, 270
  angels becoming images of the Lord when they perform useful activities, 454
  angels being with those newly arrived in the spiritual world, 314, 315, 454
  angels communicating by ideas rather than words, 607:2
  angels conveying their own happiness to others, 549
  angels' defense of us during trials, 270, 737:1, 751:1, 761
  angels fighting with evil spirits on our behalf, 227, 263, 270, 761
  angels forming the inner self of the universal human, 911:2
  angels giving us the power to turn toward the Lord, 233:2
  angels guiding us, 50:3, 300
  angels' happiness
    coming from usefulness, 454
    as so immense that the human mind cannot grasp it, 32:2
  angels having no knowledge of time, matter, or space, 488:3
  angels having no power except through the Lord, 50:3, 233:2, 300, 653, 904
  angels inspiring us with goodness and truth, 50:3, 904:1
  angels living in the third heaven, 459
  angels loving their neighbor more than themselves, 454, 548, 549
  angels perceiving that they live from the Lord, 155
  angels' perception of goodness and truth, 104, 125, 167, 228
  angels' perception of the Word, 64, 167, 855
  angels preventing evil spirits from harming us, 454
  angels seeing spiritual realities in the Word, separate from the words and names, 64
  angels' selfhood, 141, 252, 633
    living selfhood as a sensation that affects all angels, 155

Angel *(continued)*
  angels using the remnant to protect us against evil spirits, 660, 737, 751
  charity providing the visible form of angels, 553:2
  good spirits, angelic spirits, and angels, 322, 457, 459, 634, 911:2
  heaven set up so that each angel is the center of all, 549
  heavenly angels, 394
    belonging to the area of the heart in the universal human, 418:2
    having perception, 202, 597
    knowing only the faith of love, 32:2, 202, 880:3
    knowledge and intelligence of, 34:1
    present when we awake from death, 170, 172–185
    present with heavenly people, 87
    similar to the people of the earliest church, 201, 597:2, 875:4
    speech of, 173, 174, 180, 202, 880:3
  the heavenly person being in the company of angels, 99
  keen perceptions of spirits and angels, 301, 322
  the Lord binding us to him through angels, 637
  the Lord called "the angel of the covenant," 666:1
  our having at least two evil spirits and two angels with us, 697, 904
  the people of the earliest church speaking with angels, 125
  spiritual angels
    belonging to the area of the lungs in the universal human, 418:2
    present at our resuscitation from death, 178, 181
      doing everything to help us, 314
      giving us back our sight, 182
      teaching us about the next life, 314, 315
    receiving from the Lord a perception through conscience, 203
    similar to the regenerate people living after the Flood, 201, 393
    using intellectual concepts to confirm their faith, but never relying on those concepts, 203
  virtue and kindness shaping angels, 553:1

Angelic spirit. *See* Spirit, angelic
Anger. *See also* Hatred
  anger against the Lord in the realm of evil spirits, 357
  anger as our reaction to everything that thwarts our self-love, 357
  anger meaning charity withdrew, 355, 357, 359
  Cain's burning anger and fallen face meaning a worse state for those who separated faith, 327
  Jehovah described as, but never being, angry, 245, 357, 592
Animal (creature). *See also* Animal, wild; Beast; Created being; *specific animals*
  animals having faculties similar to humans', 196:2
  animals living by their proper code, 637:2
  animals meaning good things, 46
  animals meaning the contents of the intellect and will, 45
  animate creatures meaning faith brought alive by love, 30:2
  brute animals compared to humans, 443, 671
  clean animals meaning positive emotions, 714, 715
  humans before rebirth being like animals, 848:1
  living soul meaning every animal in general, 670
  those closest to the Lord in heaven called living creatures, 46:3 (*see also* Guardian being)
  unclean animals meaning types of craving and malice, 719
Animal, wild, 908. *See also* Animal; Beast
  the animalistic nature of the pre-Flood people, 239, 272, 274
  the earliest people living like animals before becoming spiritual people, 286
  the earliest people recognizing themselves as wild animals, 841
  every kind of wild animal meaning all spiritual goodness, 774
  every wild animal and every beast that was with him [Noah] in the ark meaning everything that was in the people of the ancient church, 841
  every wild animal that is with you, of all flesh, meaning everything that was alive in the people called Noah, 908:1

the guardian beings or angels seen by Ezekiel called four "wild animals," 908:2
the Hebrew word for wild animal meaning a living being, 774, 841
our belief that we can be saved even if we live like a savage beast, 916:3
our living like animals when our inner being cannot direct our outer being, 272
our outer selves giving us our identity as animals, 272
the prophets making a distinction between animals of the earth and animals of the field, 46:3
the significance of the order in which "beast" and "wild animal" appear, 47
wild animal, 46:2
   meaning a living being, 774, 908:1–2
   meaning a nonliving thing, or a savage creature, 908:3
   meaning a positive feeling, 246
   meaning a regenerate person, and so a living quality in such a person, 908:2
   meaning both what is living in us and what is lifeless, 841
   meaning good things in the inner self, 916:1
   meaning sensual pleasure, 803:1
   meaning those who have no love for their neighbor, 870:3
the wild animal of the earth
   meaning a spiritual person's earthly plane, 58
   meaning cravings and appetites, 45
   meaning what the will is intent on, 44
the wild animal of the field meaning emotions (feelings), 194, 242, 246

Anointing, 886. *See also* Oil

Anxiety (distress), 318, 537. *See also* Distress; Pain; Trial
earthly tribulation as anxiety rising from attacks on earthly loves, 847:2
misery and distress from being controlled by evil spirits, 270
those who are spiritually dead feeling little distress, 270

The apostles, the Lord explaining the Word's inner meaning to, 1

Appearance. *See also* Image; Likeness
our possession of truth and goodness as an appearance, 633
passages in the Word that speak according to human appearances, 588, 589
used to support false premises, 589
the simple at heart learning from the appearances in the Word, 926

Appetite, 911:3. *See also* Craving; Pleasure

Arabia, 382:4, 414:2

Ararat, 854. *See also* Mountain

Ark, Noah's, 657, 719. *See also* Noah
"the ark came to rest" meaning rebirth, 851
the ark depicting the formation of the church called Noah, 605, 811
the ark meaning rebirth and the struggles leading up to it, 606
the ark meaning those in the church called Noah, 602, 605, 639, 655:1, 896:1
the ark's measurements meaning their remaining traces of goodness and truth (remnant), 602, 649
the ark's structure meaning protection of the will, 642
"enter the ark, you and all your household," meaning what exists in the will, 710
entering the ark meaning being prepared, 711
entering the ark meaning being saved, 667, 764, 767, 779
going out of the ark meaning freedom (liberty), 891, 905, 912, 918
"Noah entered the ark" meaning he was protected, 741, 748
staying in the ark meaning slavery, 891, 905
the unclean animals brought into the ark meaning the evil in the unregenerate people called Noah, 719
the water rising and lifting the ark meaning the faltering of the people called Noah, 789

The ark of Moses, having hidden meanings, 639:2

The ark of the covenant
the ark having hidden meaning, 639
the ark meaning the Lord and heavenly things, 308, 666:5, 878:7
the ark's repose meaning a time of peace, 85:2
the ark's travels meaning conflict and trial, 85:2
the furnishings associated with the ark meaning what is heavenly and spiritual, 296
Uzzah's putting his hand out onto the ark meaning human autonomy, 878:7

Arm. *See also* Hand
  an arm becoming visible in the world of spirits, 878:8
  arm meaning power, 574, 878
Army
  the army of the heavens meaning falsities, 666:5
  their army meaning love and faith, 82, 83
Aroma. *See* Fragrance
Arrival. *See* Coming
Artisan
  an artisan in bronze or iron meaning those who know about earthly good and truth, 421, 424
  an artisan meaning one who is wise, understanding, or knowledgeable, 424
  an artisan of any art meaning one who knows about truth and goodness, 424
  artisans who cast idols meaning people who teach falsity, 424
Assassin, in the spiritual world, 816
Assyria
  Assyria meaning a logical person, 870:3
  Assyria meaning rationalizations constructed from facts, 120, 130
  Assyria meaning the intellect, 655:2
  Assyria meaning the reasoning mind, 118, 119
  a cedar meaning Assyria as a spiritual church, 776:5
  the king of Assyria meaning delusions, falsities, and faulty reasoning, 705:2
  the river in Assyria meaning insane reasoning and the falsity it spawns, 130
Atonement, 645
  atonement as the Lord's function, 716:3
  the third and seventh days meaning atonement, 901:3
Attitude. *See* Opinion
Attribute (quality). *See also* Subject
  any feature attributed to a thing having its quality from that thing, 568:1
  human traits frequently used to describe Jehovah's attributes, 588–589, 592:1
Aura
  auras in heaven corresponding to earthly aromas, 925:2
  auras of love and faith clearly perceived in heaven, 925:2
Authority. *See* Power
Autonomy. *See* Selfhood

Aven, 273
Awareness. *See* Knowledge

B

Baby. *See* Infant
Babylon
  the captivity in Babylon, 395:2, 728:4, 755:3
  the mighty of Babylon meaning those in the trap of self-love, 583
Badger skins, 296
Balance
  balance in the spiritual world, 592:2
  the design of heaven consisting of balance, 689
  humans and all that exists being in perfect balance, 689
Bandit. *See* Outlaw
Baptism, 870:1
Bath *(unit of measurement)*, 576:1
Battle. *See* Conflict
Bear *(the animal)*, 45
Bearing. *See* Birth
Beast (animal), 774. *See also* Animal; Animal, wild
  the animal meaning the outer self, 477:4
  animals of the earth distinguished from animals of the field, 46:3
  the beast meaning both the wild animal of the earth and the bird in the heavens, 58
  a beast meaning what we produce in the sixth stage of regeneration, 12, 39:2, 48
  beasts (animals) meaning feelings (emotions), 45, 46, 142, 143, 194, 242, 246, 594, 714, 715, 719, 744, 803, 810
  beasts (animals) meaning the things of the will, 44, 52, 142, 594, 673, 674, 715, 909
  beasts as bad or good, 45, 715, 719
  beasts as having to do with regeneration, 47
  beasts meaning corrupt desires, 594, 803
  clean animals meaning the good effects of charity, 921:1, 922
  every kind of beast meaning earthly goodness, 774
  humans compared to animals, 714, 715
Beauty of angels coming from charity, 553
Beginning (origin)
  in the beginning, on the first of the month, meaning a starting point, 894
  beginning meaning the earliest times, 15
  beginning meaning the first period of rebirth, 16

the beginning of spiritual life, 186, 316, 894
the beginnings meaning the ancient church, 55:1, 477:2
laws coming from heavenly origins, 162
Being (existence). *See also* Entity; Essence; Existence
Being as not attributed to anything that ceases to be, 726
the belief that to lack selfhood is nonexistence, 206:2
charity as our existence, 840
Jehovah as being, 300, 630, 708, 726, 840, 926
the name Jehovah coming from beingness, 300
Being, inner (inner self, person of depth), 8, 9, 10. *See also* Being, outer
the ability to reason coming from the Lord through the inner self, 118, 657
angels as the universal human's inner self, 911:2
angels controlling the inner self, 270
being one flesh meaning the inner and outer beings coexisting in the outer being, 160
clinging to one's wife meaning to have an inner being within our outer being, 160
the earliest people
as people of depth, 54, 920:1
receiving instruction from the Lord through the inner self, 608
expanse meaning the inner self, 24, 30:3
goodness and truth coming from the Lord through the inner self, 27, 857:1
heaven meaning the inner self, 16, 24:3, 82, 89, 477:3, 911:2, 931:3
heavenly people
the inner being distinguished from the outer being in, 159
the outer self serving the inner self in, 91, 95
reformation beginning in the inner self of, 89
ruling the inner self first and the outer self secondarily, 52
humans no longer able to receive instruction through the inner self, 608, 609
the inner and outer being acting together, 161
the inner being as a person's soul, 3
the inner self containing the remnant, 8, 19, 561, 857
the inner self directing the outer self
by means of the rational mind, 268
after regeneration, 52
the inner self having nothing of our own, 268
the later generation of the earliest church unable to distinguish between the inner and outer beings, 159
leaving father and mother meaning leaving the inner being behind, 160
"let [the animals] swarm throughout the earth" meaning the way the inner self acts on the outer, 913
lights meaning love and faith shining through our inner self into our outer self, 31:3, 39
the Lord making a distinction between the inner and the outer being, 24:1
the Lord storing goodness and truth in our inner being, 268, 561, 563, 661:2, 711
the Lord working through our inner self, 857, 933:3
man meaning the inner being, 156, 158
our awareness that an inner being exists, 24:2, 24:3, 27
our awareness that truth and goodness come from the Lord through the inner self, 24:3, 27
our identity as humans coming from the Lord through our inner self, 272
our living like animals when our inner being is separated from our outer being, 272
the purpose of trials as subordinating the outer self to the inner, 857:2, 933:4
regeneration taking us from the outer self to the inner, 24:3, 47, 64
spiritual people
the outer self not willing to serve the inner self in, 91, 95
ruling the outer self first and the inner self secondarily, 52
Being, outer (outer self, shallow people), 272, 913. *See also* Being, inner
the ability to reason as belonging to the outer self, 268
creeping things as having to do with the outer self, 40
dry land meaning the outer being, 27
the earth meaning our outer self, 909, 913
goodness and truth being planted in the feelings and memory of the outer self, 268
the ground meaning the outer self, 90, 267, 268, 269, 275, 278

Being, outer *(continued)*
    our outer self battling our inner self before regeneration, 95
    our outer self coming to life, 94
    our outer self serving our inner self after regeneration, 95, 933:4
    the outer self corresponding with the inner self after regeneration, 911:2
    regeneration moving from the outer self to the inner, 24:3, 47, 64
    the sense of autonomy in the outer being, 156
    shallow people only knowing facts, 111
    spirits forming the universal human's outer self, 911:2
Belief (faith, trust). *See also* Acknowledgment; Faith; Opinion; Unbelief
    belief in the Lord leading us to rely on the Word for wisdom, 128
    the evil of trusting oneself and one's senses, 231–233
    faith being to live as the Lord teaches, 34, 44
    faith in the Lord as life, 30
    nonbelief compared to winter, 34:2
    our life as built through what we acknowledge and believe, 303
    simple belief in the Word, 196:3, 589, 735, 926
    snakes meaning those who believe only in their senses, 191, 194, 196, 235
    unbelief coming from reliance on sensory evidence, 128, 191, 194, 196, 229, 233:3, 235, 647
Belly, 828
    belly meaning the things that are closest to the earth, 247
Bird, 922:1. *See also* Flying thing; Winged creature
    birds in (of) the heavens
        meaning comprehension of truth, 40:3, 477:3, 778, 866
        meaning what we produce in the fifth stage of regeneration, 11, 39, 48
    birds meaning attachment to falsity, 803
    birds meaning false notions, 778, 866
    birds meaning matters of the intellect or reason, 40, 44, 52, 55:4, 142, 595, 674, 715, 723, 745, 776, 802, 803, 909
    birds meaning spiritual truth, 776, 777, 916, 921:1
    birds meaning the earthly plane of existence, 58

Birth. *See also* Child; Firstborn
    the births of Noah, 610, 611
    the births of the heavens and the earth meaning the ways in which a heavenly person is formed, 89
    the book of births, 469, 470
Birthright. *See* Firstborn
Blessing, 358
    fruit trees meaning blessings, 273
    the Lord blessing and saying things meaning he operates, 55:3
    the Lord's blessing meaning fruitfulness and multiplication, 43
Blindness, 212, 382:1, 489:1. *See also* Eye; Seeing
    blindness resulting from relying on sensory evidence, 128, 195:2, 196:1, 210, 241
Blood, 378, 716:2–4
    "the blood cries out" meaning guilt, 373, 376
    blood meaning hatred, 374
    blood meaning wickedness, 374:2
    the blood of the covenant meaning the Lord, 666:5
    the voice of blood meaning charity that has been extinguished, 330
    the voice of blood meaning violence inflicted on charity, 373, 374:1
Blood relative
    the relationships between virtues and truths in a regenerate person compared to those among blood relatives, 917
    ties between people in the next life compared to those among blood relatives, 685
Blue-violet, 424
Blushing (being ashamed), 217, 249, 264:1. *See also* Shame
    "they were naked and did not blush" meaning they were innocent, 163, 165 (*see also* Nakedness)
Bodily. *See also* Body; Flesh; The senses
    cultivating the ground from which they were taken meaning becoming body-centered, 305, 345
    flesh meaning a person in general and a body-centered (body-oriented) person in particular, 574, 627:1, 631, 661:3, 780, 800
    flesh under the heavens meaning our bodily plane, 661:3
    the heel meaning an orientation toward the body, 250

immersion in bodily and worldly concerns closing the path to heaven, 69
people who are focused on bodily (carnal) concerns
  denying that everything is the Lord's, 123
  destroying all comprehension of truth, 627, 628
  sense of autonomy as all-important to, 141
  when goodness and truth seem to have left our inner self we become, 268
  the proper hierarchy being heavenly, spiritual, earthly, and then bodily concerns, 911
  self-love carrying us toward bodily and earthly preoccupations, 309
  traveling on its belly meaning the sensory level turning away from heavenly values toward bodily and earthly ones, 242
  visitors to heaven having their bodily desires and delusions put to sleep, 542
Body (flesh). *See also* Bodily; Flesh; Spirit
  the belief of newly arrived spirits that they still live in the body, 178, 320
  the belief that life is located in the body, 443
  the body of the spirit, 446
  the cooperation of each part of the body, 550
  the death of the body, 70
  the earth's population compared to the human body, 637:1
  the human body compared to the earth, 909
  humans as spirits clothed in flesh, 69, 447
  love and faith working in our inner being in the same way warmth and light work in our outer body, 30:3
  self-love causing the senses of the earliest people to serve the body, 243
  things from the Lord having the equivalent of a physical body, 41
  wild animals meaning traits that rise from the body, 45
Bond (restraint). *See also* Connection
  charity forming the bond between the Lord and us, 379, 389
  evil spirits held by the bonds and restraints of their desires, 695
  external restraints compared to internal restraints, 81:3
  our bond with heaven, 530:1, 661:3

Bone (skeleton), 41, 149, 827. *See also* Rib; Skeleton
  bone meaning a sense of autonomy, 148, 149:1, 156, 157
Book of births, 469, 470
Border. *See* End
Bough, 119
Boulder. *See* Rock
Bowls, golden, 420:5
The brain
  the brain's structure, 501
  the intellect relating to the left side of the brain and the will relating to the right side, 641, 644
  the relationship between the soul and the brain, 444
Bramble, 273
Branch, 55:4
Bread. *See also* Food
  bread from the produce of the ground meaning charity, 343
  bread meaning everything of a spiritual or heavenly character, 276, 415:2
  bread meaning heavenly food, 623:1, 680
Breath. *See also* Spirit; Wind
  breath meaning the life of faith and love, 97
  the breath of life meaning the life in those who have been reborn, 661:3
  the breath of lives meaning the life force in heavenly people, 76
  breathing and breath meaning a life force, 97, 805:1
  breathing into the human's nostrils the breath of lives, meaning to put life into our faith and love, 94
  the earliest people perceiving others' love and faith from their breathing, 97
  flesh that has the breath of life in it meaning a newly created being, 772, 780
Breathing
  external breathing replacing internal breathing, 608, 805:3
  internal breathing of the earliest people similar to the angels', 607:2–3, 805:2–3
  the Lord constantly breathing his life even into evil people, 714
  silent breathing on awakening from death, 169
Breeze, 218, 221

Bride. *See also* Wife
  a bride meaning the church, 253
  the Lord's bride and wife meaning selfhood brought to life by the Lord, 155
Brier, 273
Bronze
  bronze meaning a somewhat profound heavenly quality, 643
  bronze meaning earthly goodness, 421, 424, 425, 426:2
  the bronze snake meaning the Lord's sensory level, 197, 425
Brook, 795:3
Brother. *See also* Abel; Cain; Esau; Jacob
  all in the early Christian church calling each other "sister" or "brother," 367:2
  brother meaning charity, 341, 342, 366, 367
Bruise
  bruise meaning charity being wiped out, 427, 431
  Lamech killing a man for his wound and a little child for his bruise meaning devastation, 406
Building, meaning reconstructing what has fallen down, 151, 153
Bulwark, 402:4
Burial (grave), 817, 901:2, 901:4
Burnt offering, 96, 870:2, 934:3. *See also* Offering; Sacrifice
  burnt offering meaning the Lord, 921
  burnt offerings as a main element in representative worship, 920, 921, 923
  burnt offerings meaning worship, 919, 921:3, 921:5, 922, 923, 925:1, 925:4
Butter
  honey and butter meaning spiritual and heavenly qualities, 195:3, 680:5
Buttocks, 818

C

Cain. *See also* Abel; Faith alone
  anger kindled in Cain meaning charity departing, 357
  Cain, or faith, as the first offspring of the earliest church, 338
  Cain and Abel compared to Jacob and Esau, 367
  Cain killing Abel meaning a detached faith extinguishing charity, 329, 366, 369, 436, 916:3
  "Cain knew his wife, and she conceived and delivered Enoch" meaning one schism's spontaneously producing another, 400
  Cain meaning the devastation of the earliest church, 407, 409
  Cain meaning the teaching that faith was separate from love (charity), 325, 326, 327, 329, 335, 337:3, 338, 340, 341, 347, 355, 356, 362, 363, 369, 384, 392, 394, 395, 398, 409, 436, 916:3
  the mark put on Cain, 330, 392, 394, 436, 609, 920:4
  the sacred ban on violating the detached faith meant by Cain, 392, 395:1, 432, 433, 436
Call. *See* Voice
Calm. *See* Tranquility
Canaan, 585, 620
  Canaan meaning heaven, 1, 115
  the rivers marking the boundaries of Canaan, 567
Captivities of the Jews, 395:2, 728:4, 755:3
Category (general kind, genus). *See also* Generality; Kind
  all things being divided into broad and specific categories, 775:1
  the contents of the intellect and of the will dividing into countless major categories, 644, 675
  in heaven all heavenly and spiritual goodness and truth carefully distinguished into their genera, 775:1
  innumerable general kinds of hatred and vengefulness, 693, 816
  innumerable general kinds of spiritual goodness and truth, 775:1
Cattle, 45, 715, 922:1
Caves, in hell, 814
Cedar, 643:4
  a cedar in Lebanon meaning the ability to reason, 119
  a cedar meaning a spiritual person or entity, 776:2, 886:2
  a cedar meaning Assyria as a spiritual church, 776:5
Center, 501
  each angel as a center of all the rest, 549
Change. *See* Alternation; Cycle
Chaos, preceding order, 842:3

Character (personality, psyche), 377, 482:2, 483:2, 542, 568:1, 665. *See also* Nature; Personality
  angels able to determine a person's character merely by looking, 803:2
  character determining how fully the remnant can operate, 635
  the character of the pre-Flood people, 562, 570, 573
  children acquiring their personality (character) from their parents, 471, 494:2
  the new psyche (character) given to the human race after the Flood, 310, 312, 393, 530:2, 608, 640, 736, 765
  our will determining our character, 379
  two types of mentality before and after the Flood also existing today, 736
Charity (kindness, love for others), 12, 148, 161, 259, 318, 343, 345, 353:2, 358, 361, 363, 384, 394, 415:1, 576:3, 854, 880:3, 886:1, 896:2, 921:1, 922, 932. *See also* Faith; Faith alone; Love; Neighbor
  Abel meaning charity, 325, 326, 341, 342, 343, 345, 350, 351, 366, 436, 916:3 (*see also* Abel)
  anger meaning charity has left, 355, 357, 359
  brother meaning charity, 341, 342, 366, 367
  bruise meaning charity being wiped out, 427, 431
  Cain killing Abel meaning a detached faith extinguishing charity, 329, 366, 369, 436, 916:3 (*see also* Cain)
  charitable goodness (neighborly good, neighborly kindness), 294, 341, 343, 848:2, 875:3, 884, 885:1, 886, 925:2
    coming before the truth of charity, 615
    coming through the conscience rather than the will, 875:4
  charity as heavenly, 353
  charity as love for one's neighbor, 325, 351, 393, 615, 654
  charity as mercy, 615
  charity as our existence, 840
  charity as the ancient church's distinguishing feature, 612, 615, 765, 834–836, 916
  charity as the bond between us and the Lord, 379, 389, 440, 904:2
  charity as the brother of faith, 366, 367
  charity as the church's second-born, 341, 342
  charity as the main concern of faith, 344, 365, 379, 393, 438, 654, 916:2
  charity being destroyed when faith is made more important, 329, 335, 362, 369, 370, 436, 916:3
  charity compared to flame, 365, 854
  charity constituting the church, 809
  charity existing alongside faith, 328
  charity in a regenerating person, 834, 840, 854, 862, 935:2
  charity needing to rule faith, 363, 365
  charity providing the visible form of angels, 553:2
  the church called Noah receiving charity through truth, 310:2, 640, 765
  cold meaning no faith or charity, 933, 934:1, 935:1
  "day" or "sun" meaning charity, 862
  earthly charity, 845, 847
  Enosh meaning charity introduced through faith, 336, 436 (*see also* Enosh)
  Esau meaning charity, 367:2
  evil as present when charity is lacking, 364
  the Flood meaning no charity remained in the earliest church, 798
  fruit as having to do with charity, 348, 627:2, 885:1
  hatred opposing charity, 374:1
  heat meaning faith and charity, 933, 934
  a human being meaning love and charity, 768:3
  Jehovah as present in love and charity, 709, 840
  "just" as having to do with the goodness involved in charity, 612, 615, 712, 922:3
  a little child meaning charity, 406, 427, 430
  the Lord giving us charity through faith, 337:3, 371, 393
  mountains as having to do with love and charity, 795, 854, 859
  our preparation to receive charity, 653:2, 654, 875:3
  our supposing acts of neighborly kindness to be our own doing, 9
  religious knowledge leading to charity, 459, 615
  Seth meaning a faith that will allow charity to take hold (to grow), 335, 436, 437, 438, 439
  a spiritual church acting from charity, 916:2
  usefulness as the good that comes of love and charity, 454
  the voice of blood meaning violence inflicted on charity, 330, 373, 374:1

Charity *(continued)*
  works (deeds) of charity as dead without life from the Lord, 880:2, 880:3
  worship inspired by charity as pleasing to the Lord, 326, 354, 440, 925:1
Chest
  the chest meaning love for others (charity), 148, 259
  the chest meaning things higher than the earth, 247
Child. *See also* Birth; Conception; Daughter; Firstborn; Infant; Offspring; Son
  child of light meaning a spiritual person, 51
  children acquiring their personality (character) from their parents, 471, 494:2
  children borne in pain meaning the truth produced by a church in a state of conflict, 261, 264
  the children of Israel meaning regenerate people, 842:5, 901:4
  killing a little child for his bruise meaning destroying charity, 427
  a little child meaning innocence or charity, 406, 427, 430
  our children inheriting our evil tendencies, 313, 494:2
Child of God. *See* Son of God
Children of humankind. *See also* Son of humankind
  children of humankind meaning those who believe in the Lord, 477:3
Choir. *See* Angel: angel choirs
The Christian church. *See* Church, Christian
Christianity (Christian), 2, 3. *See also* Church, Christian; Church, early Christian; Non-Christians
  Christians compared to non-Christians, after death, 932:2
  Christians in hell, 816, 826
  devastation of Christians, 410
  false beliefs of Christians, 916:3
  the way people live in the Christian world being despicable, 916:3
Church (religion). *See also* Faith; *the names of individuals that are used as the names of churches;* Teaching
  the ancient church (*see* Church, ancient)
  the Christian church (*see* Christianity; Church, Christian; Church, early Christian)
  the church after the Flood, 231
  the church always remaining with a few individuals, 407, 468, 530, 932:2
  the church as the Lord's kingdom on earth, 768:3
  church attenders in hell, 831:1
  the church called "a woman," "a wife," "a bride," "young woman," and "daughter," 253
  the church called "Daughter," "Virgin," and "Wife," 54
  the church compared to the heart and lungs, 468:2, 637:1, 931:1
  the church described as militant, 59
  the church developing out of its doctrine, 530, 769
  a church meaning a person who has been reborn, 246, 932
  the church representing the Lord's kingdom, 471
  churches producing heresies, 362
  churches tending to dwindle over time, 407, 468, 494:2, 530, 788
  the church's deterioration, 407, 408, 409, 468, 494:2, 497, 530
  the church's devastation, 408, 885, 931:2
  the church's end, 267
  the church's outward motions as lifeless, 870:2
  each individual as a church, 82, 768, 869, 872
  the earliest church (*see* Church, earliest)
  the face of the ground meaning the area where the church exists, 564, 566, 567, 593
  female meaning the church, 476
  ground meaning the church, 386, 566, 809, 869, 872
  the heavenly church (*see* Church, heavenly)
  the human race's existence depending on the church, 636, 637, 931
  the inner church (*see* Church, inner)
  the Jewish church (*see* Church, Jewish)
  the kingdom of God meaning the Lord's true church, 29:2
  Lamech meaning the ninth church, 465, 523, 526
  the Lord as the totality of the church, 768:3
  love as the all-in-all of the church, 768:3
  a new church (*see* Church, new)
  Noah meaning the ancient church (*see* Church, ancient; Noah)
  the offspring of a church having the same character as the church, 533

the outer church (*see* Church, outer)
qualities of the will, not intellectual traits, described as being the church, 809
religion based on love rather than faith, 709
rise and fall of a church, 408, 501
the role of conscience in the church, 393
"seed from the Lord" available to people inside and outside the church, 932
Seth meaning the second church, 462, 496, 497
the spiritual church (*see* Church, spiritual)
wife meaning the church, 54, 253, 255, 289, 768:3, 770, 886:3, 906, 915
woman meaning the church, 237, 250, 252, 253, 255, 261, 262, 402:5

Church, ancient. *See also* Flood: the people who followed the Flood; Noah; Shem, Ham, and Japheth
the ancient church as a spiritual church, 597, 607, 765
rather than heavenly, 805:3
the ancient church called "ancient" because it existed at the time of the Flood, 530:2
the ancient church having conscience rather than perception, 393, 573, 597, 607, 608, 765
the ancient years meaning the ancient church, 349:2
the beginnings meaning the ancient church, 55:1, 477:2
charity as the ancient church's distinguishing feature, 612, 615, 765, 834–836, 916
the evil of trusting oneself afflicting the ancient church, 231
"generation after generation" meaning the ancient churches, 477:3
the members of the ancient church having articles of faith that they could grasp through the senses, 608
Noah meaning the ancient church, 466, 468, 528, 529, 530, 534, 597:1, 773
other churches existing at the same time as the ancient church, 640
the people of the ancient church being reborn first as to the intellect, 670
regenerate people in the ancient church, 897
Shem, Ham, and Japheth forming the ancient church, 773, 788, 915
sons meaning the truth known to the ancient church, 489

the worship of the ancient church, 796, 920:1, 920:4, 921:1
a young shoot in the field meaning the ancient church, 93

Church, Christian. *See also* Christianity; Church, early Christian
the Christian church existing in Europe, 567
the Christian church of Swedenborg's day being in ruins, 407

Church, earliest, 219. *See also* Adam; Heavenly; Nephilim; The pre-Flood people
ancient times meaning the earliest church, 55, 477:2
the deterioration of the earliest church, 920:3
the earliest church acknowledging no faith besides love, 32:2, 337:1, 393
the earliest church beginning to believe only what they could grasp with the senses, 191, 235
the earliest church representing the heavenly kingdom, 483:2
the earliest church's general principles being heavenly, eternal truths, 597:3
the earliest people, 414:4
aware of the symbolism of place-names, 115
aware that they were no more than animals, 715
being condemned when they turned to loving themselves, 243, 279
being deep thinkers, 54, 442
the character of, 200, 201, 209
the communication of, 607:2
comparisons (similes) of, 54, 108, 195, 643, 715, 746, 776, 800, 909
confirming generalities through perception, 597:2
each household of the earliest people having its own identity, 471
the evil in them gushing out of their will, 209
the first chapters of Genesis dealing with the regeneration of, 286
genealogies created by, 339, 400
given perception of faith (truth) through love, 200, 310:1, 337:1, 597:3, 640 (*see also* Perception)
goodness leading to truth in, 200, 209
as heavenly, 85, 201–202, 241, 310, 337, 597
internal breathing giving them access to deep concepts, 607:3

Church, earliest *(continued)*
  the earliest people *(continued)*
    living divided into households, clans, and nations, 470, 471, 483:2
    living together in heaven, 483:2
    the Lord appearing as a human being to, 49:1
    marriage love being like heaven to, 162:2
    never thinking about faith on the basis of facts, 202
    not as concerned with facts as people of Swedenborg's day, 605
    receiving instruction through the inner self, 608
    receiving revelations regarding goodness and truth directly into their will, 895
    representing the Lord's kingdom, 471
    the senses serving the inner self in, 243
    speaking with the Lord and angels, 125
    their descendants having a different character, 241
    their faces being in harmony with their inner self, 358
    their mode of writing, 66:1, 403, 605, 742, 755:1, 801:1
    thinking of heavenly attributes represented by everything around them, 241
    using external objects to contemplate the Lord, 54
    weaving representative images into a narrative, 66:1, 403
    will and intellect forming one mind in, 310:1, 398, 640, 875:4, 927:2
    worshiping on mountains, 795:1
  the end of the earliest church, 200, 560
  Enosh, Kenan, Mahalalel, Jared, Enoch, and Methuselah meaning descendants of the earliest church, 463–464
  the evil of trusting oneself afflicting the earliest church, 231
  the first descendants of the earliest church having heavenly-spiritual good, 282
  human (human being) meaning the earliest church, 137, 277, 288, 313, 461, 477
  the human, Seth, and Enosh constituting the earliest church, 502, 505
  later generations of the earliest church, 54, 131, 133, 137, 142, 159, 161, 190, 206:2, 208, 230, 237, 464, 800, 920:3, 920:4
  the Lord's love for the earliest church, 414:4
  the passing away of the earliest church at the time of the Flood, 280, 800
  perception in the earliest church, 125, 159, 310:1, 337:1, 340, 371, 393, 483, 495, 503, 597, 895:2, 92c:1
  the propagation of the earliest church, 460
  the second and third generations of the earliest church having earthly good, 282
Church, early Christian, 477:2. *See also* Christianity; Church, Christian; Nation
  all in the early Christian church calling each other "sister" or "brother," 367:2
  the early Christian church ebbing away from true faith over time, 407
  the early Christian church possessing conscience rather than perception, 393
  Esau meaning the early Christian church, 367:2
  the Lord raising up the early Christian church at the time of his coming, 931:2
  the people Israel meaning the early Christian church, 477:2
  the sons of the desolate one meaning the truth known to the early Christian church, 489:2
  the waning of the earliest church, 495
Church, heavenly. *See also* Church, earliest
  the daughter of Zion meaning a heavenly type of church, 415:2
  God's likeness meaning the earliest church as a heavenly church, 461, 469
  the heavenly church able to communicate with heaven, 784
  human meaning a heavenly church, 477:1, 565
  Judah meaning a heavenly church, 768:2, 795:5
Church, inner, 768:2. *See also* Church, outer
  Adah and Zillah as the inner church and the outer church, 409
  heavenly and spiritual qualities making up the inner church, 422
  the inner church and the outer church forming one church, 409
  Israel meaning the inner church, 422
  Leah and Rachel as the outer church and the inner church of the Jews, 409, 422
Church, Jewish (Jewish religion), 231, 353:1, 407. *See also* Israel; Jacob; Jew
  the earliest church as the foundation of the Jewish church, 886:1
  every activity in the Jewish church representing the Lord, 31:3, 85:2, 921:1

fig tree meaning the Jewish church, 885:2
the Jewish church composed of an inner church and an outer church, 422
the Jewish church living divided into households, clans, and tribes, 471
Leah meaning the Jewish church, 422
the sons of the married one meaning the truth known to the Jewish church, 489:2
the Word's literal meaning dealing with the external facts of the Jewish religion, 1
Church, new, 28, 31:2, 40:3, 728:4. *See also* Adah; Enosh; Human being; Noah; Zillah
the Lord always bringing a new church to life when the previous one perishes, 931:2
morning meaning a new church, 408
a new church beginning among those outside the present church, 409, 410
a new church beginning when the present church has been thoroughly devastated, 408, 409, 410, 411
son meaning the beginnings of a new church, 526
Church, outer. *See also* Church, inner
Jacob meaning the outer church, 768:2
Leah meaning the outer church of the Jewish church, 409, 422
Church, representative, 352, 409, 730:1, 730:5, 796
burnt offerings as a main element in representative worship, 920, 921, 923
the Jewish church representing inner things, 101
the worship of the representative church, 349:1, 418:1, 716:2, 923
Church, spiritual, 870:3. *See also* Church, ancient; Spiritual
the ancient church as a spiritual church, 597, 607, 765, 805:3
a cedar meaning Assyria as a spiritual church, 776:5
Israel meaning a spiritual church, 710, 768:2
people in a spiritual church perceiving as true only what they learn, 895:2
a spiritual church acting from charity, 916:2
a wife like a grapevine meaning the spiritual church, 886:3
City
cities in hell, 940–942
"city" as having to do with spiritual things, 793

the city called Enoch, 399, 403
city meaning a doctrinal or heretical teaching, 402:1, 402:3
city meaning being heavenly or spiritual, 402:2
the city of Zion meaning the spiritual aspect of faith, 402:1
the Holy City meaning the Lord's kingdom, 402:1
Clan. *See* Family; House
Clothes, 424. *See also* Loincloth; Tunic
beautiful clothes in heaven, 165, 297
clothes meaning heavenly-spiritual good and earthly good, 297
clothes meaning objects of thought, 623:2
clothes meaning things that come from the deepest levels of being, 32:2
heavenly goodness as unclothed, 297
Jehovah clothing the human and his wife meaning teaching them, 292
Cloud
the clouds of the heavens (sky) meaning the literal meaning of the Word, 49:4
the day of cloud meaning falsity, 488:3
Cockatrice, 251
Coldness, 34. *See also* Heat; Winter
cold and heat meaning the condition of a regenerating person, 933, 935:1, 936
cold meaning no faith or charity, 933, 934:1, 935:1
coldness in hell, 817
Color, 184, 681, 731. *See also* Blue-violet
Coming (arrival)
every arrival of the Lord entailing a beginning for those who are regenerating and an end for those who are not, 728:1
the Lord's Coming delivering humankind from destruction, 581, 631, 637:2
the Lord's Coming introducing a new church, 31:2
the Lord's Coming occurring at the end of the Jewish church, 408
the middle of the years meaning the Lord's Coming, 482:2
morning meaning the Lord's Coming, 22
the number seven meaning the Lord's Coming, 728:1, 901
prophecies in the Word regarding the Lord's Coming, 25, 31:2, 250
there being a last judgment when the Lord came into the world, 900, 931:2

Coming *(continued)*
    the voice of one shouting, meaning a proclamation of the Lord's Coming, 220

Command (commandment, requirement). *See also* The Decalogue; Law
    the commandment concerning love to be placed above all others, 396:2
    every activity required of the Jewish church representing the Lord, 31:3, 85:2, 921:1
    "as God had commanded" meaning it happened in this way, 682, 732, 750
    "as God had commanded" meaning preparation to receive truth and goodness, 783
    for the Lord, to command being to prepare someone and to act, 783

Communication (contact, sharing). *See also* Speaking; Voice
    communication and perception in the spiritual world, 925:2
    communication of all feelings and thoughts in heaven, 549
    degrees of communication with heaven, 784
    the earliest people having communication with heaven, 784, 805:3
    our contact with heaven and hell, 697, 931:1
    our life depending on communication with heaven and the world of spirits, 50:1, 687, 784
    sharing of joy in the angelic state, 549
    sharing of thoughts in the spiritual world, 315, 443

Community (group)
    coming into a community of good spirits after death, 187
    compartments meaning heavenly communities, 644
    each of us associated with a group of hellish spirits, 697
    heavenly communities, 471, 644, 684–691
        all together forming a single human being, 684
        distinguished from each other by differences in love and faith, 684, 686
        each community an image of the whole of heaven and a heaven-in-miniature, 684
        each community forming a single personality, 684
        a heavenly community as harmony among many, 687, 690
        no angel or spirit having any life without being part of a heavenly community, 687
        no community exactly the same as another, 690
        no community having the same kind of perception as another, 483:1
        our being in constant association with a heavenly community, 687

Compact. *See* Pact

Company
    our being in the company of angels after death, 315
    our being in the constant company of spirits while on earth, 784:2

Comparisons (similes), of the earliest people, 54, 108, 195, 643, 715, 746, 776, 800, 909

Compartment
    the compartments in the ark meaning the will and the intellect, 640, 644
    compartments meaning heavenly communities, 644

Compassion. *See* Mercy

Compatibility. *See* Harmony

The completion of the heavens and the earth, meaning a person that has become spiritual, 82, 84

Concept. *See* Fact; Idea; Knowledge; Thought

Conception *(of a child)*, meaning thinking, 261

Conclusion (closure), 753, 804, 899. *See also* End

Condemnation (damnation), 243, 278, 279, 301, 561
    evil spirits accusing and condemning us during trials, 751:2, 761
    evil spirits' pleasure in condemning humans, 741
    people who are spiritually dead rushing toward damnation, 270

Conflict (battle, fighting, strife, struggle), 90, 261. *See also* Trial
    the conflict we experience as spiritual people, 55:4, 63, 81:3, 653
    evil spirits fighting for control over us, 263
    heavenly people experiencing no conflict, 81:3, 84, 87
    the Lord fighting on our behalf during spiritual trials, 63, 88, 653
    our awareness of the conflict between evil spirits and angels over control of us, 227

our being in constant battle while we are being reborn, 59:1
our senses causing strife as we regenerate, 12
strife caused by the outer self's unwillingness to serve the inner self, 91
Confusion, 842:3
Connection (link), 379, 389, 904:2. *See also* Bond
angels, spirits, and heavenly communities depending on a tight link to heaven and the world of spirits, 687
our life depending on a connection with the spiritual world, 50:1, 687, 697, 784
Conscience, 537. *See also* Perception
the belief that conscience is useful only for controlling common people, 206:2
conscience as a means of dividing the intellect from the will, 863, 875:3, 875:5, 918
conscience as a new will, 918, 927:3
conscience as an alertness to what is inside us, 219
conscience as an inner voice (call), 224, 371, 393, 607:1, 608, 895:2
conscience as formed from knowledge of goodness and truth, 310:2
conscience as formed from knowledge of Scripture, 371
conscience as what senses the conflict between angels and evil spirits present with us, 227, 751
conscience coming from teachings of faith, 765
conscience coming from what has been heard and learned, 895:2
conscience in the ancient church (*see* Church, ancient)
conscience replacing perception after the Flood, 371, 393, 573
conscience replacing perception when faith was separated from love, 371
the difference between perception and conscience, 597:1
faith as a function of conscience, 896:2
"Jehovah said to Cain" meaning conscience spoke, 359, 371
the Lord's instilling the goodness of charity and then conscience in the intellect, 875:3
our struggles felt as the gnawings of conscience, 857:2

the pseudo-conscience of those dividing faith from charity, 916:3
the role of conscience in the church, 393
the source of perception, inner dictates, and conscience, 227
spirits in hell who have no conscience, 831
spiritual angels
having conscience, 203, 597:1
receiving from the Lord a perception through conscience, 203
spiritual people
conscience as the basis for actions in, 875:3
conscience as the field in which trials do their work in, 762
conscience as the internal restraints in, 81:3
feeling free when they obey their conscience, 918
having conscience rather than perception, 104, 597:1
neighborly good in spiritual people coming from conscience, 875:4
the truth that spiritual people speak coming from conscience, 875:5
spiritual tests taking place only with those who have conscience, 762, 847:2
spiritually lifeless people lacking conscience, 104
those who have faith having charity and conscience, 896:2
the voice of Jehovah (Jehovah speaking) meaning conscience, 219, 359, 360, 371
Contact. *See* Communication
Contract. *See* Pact
Control. *See* Rule
Conviction. *See* Faith
Corpse, 175, 814, 916:3
Corruption, 568
"all flesh had made their way corrupt on the earth" meaning preoccupation with the bodily level destroyed all comprehension of truth, 627
corrupt meaning unmitigated falsity, 625
corruption stemming from delusions, 622
"the land was corrupt" meaning people's dreadful delusions, 621
the word "corruption"
as having to do with delusions, 622
as having to do with the intellect, 621
Covenant. *See* Pact

Crag, 795:4
Craving (appetite, desire, longing, self-interest, yearning), 18, 45, 207, 251:2, 306, 623:1, 643:4, 645, 808, 847. *See also* Appetite; Desire
  anger as a reaction to whatever blocks our selfish desires, 357
  beasts meaning corrupt desires, 594, 803
  corrupted people having desire instead of will, 568:1, 585, 652
  daughters meaning cravings, 555, 568, 569
  desire replacing a will for good, 568:2
  doing evil as associated with cravings, 622
  evil spirits rousing our cravings, 59, 641, 653, 660, 751:3
  false premises leading to cravings, 233:3
  fire meaning punishment of corrupt desire, 574:3
  the Lord diverting our delusions and cravings to goodness and truth, 24:3, 25, 868:2, 887
  Nephilim as those who merged the teachings of faith with their desires, 557, 582, 640
  only self-interest as truly our own, 105
  our cravings controlling us, 59:1, 892
  our cravings shutting down during trials, 857:2
  our inability to rid ourselves instantaneously of cravings, 59:1
  our intellect driven by hell if filled with corrupt desires, 845
  our lives being built through our cravings, 760
  our thinking ceasing if our cravings were removed, 33
  our will as made up of the yearnings we cultivate, 794:2
  the outer self containing cravings, 857
  people in hell restrained by their own desires, 695
  people who have hardened themselves in falsity on the basis of desire, 845:2
  the pre-Flood people's cravings
    annihilating them, 559, 601
    called a matter of will, although they had no true will, 801:1
    defiling the church's truths, 570, 571, 582, 593
    growing out of self-love, 808
    as insane, 307
    starting to control them, 555
  regenerate people being horrified by perverted desire and false thinking, 892:2
  teachings of faith merged with cravings, 794:2
  trials involving cravings as inseparable from trials involving the intellect, 757
  truth as unable to coexist with corrupt desires, 794:2
  two categories of selfish desire, 808
  yearning for evil as involvement in it, 139
Crawling. *See* Creeping
Created being, 780
  created beings meaning those to whom the gospel must be preached, 46:3
Creation
  "create" as having to do with a spiritual person, 476
  creation meaning regeneration, 16, 62, 88, 472, 593
  the creation of a heavenly person, 435
  the creation of a spiritual person, 435
  the creation of the world and the first human, 4
  Moses receiving accounts of creation from the descendants of the earliest church, 66:1
Creator, the Lord called, 88
Creature. *See* Animal; Created being
Creeping (crawling), 41
  a crawling thing crawling, meaning bodily and earthly yearnings, 803
  a creeping animal
    meaning all aspects of the will, 594
    meaning bodily and sensual pleasures, 594
  creeping animals of the water (fish), 39, 42:1
    meaning facts known by the outer self, 40
    meaning humans at the beginning of regeneration, 39
    meaning what the intellect grasps, 44
  creeping, crawling animals meaning what we acquire though our senses, 746
  a creeping thing
    meaning good things in the outer self, 916:1
    meaning sensual pleasure, 810
  a creeping thing creeping, meaning attributes in the outer self corresponding to the ideas and urges of the inner self, 911
  every creeping thing creeping on the earth meaning all goodness on the sensory and bodily levels, 774
  everything creeping on the ground meaning the sensory level and sensual pleasure, 746, 909

from human to beast to creeping animal meaning whatever was in the will of the earliest church's descendants would annihilate them, 594
something creeping on the ground meaning the lowest level of the intellect and will, 674
that which creeps meaning what the will is intent on, 44, 774
a thing creeping on the earth meaning truth in the outer self, 916

Crops. *See* Ground; Reaping; Seed

Cruelty, 814, 818, 819, 824

Crying (shouting), 375. *See also* Shouting
"his blood cries out" meaning guilt, 376
shouting from the head of the mountains meaning worshiping the Lord with love, 795:4

Culmination. *See* End

Cultivation, 89, 94, 284
cultivating the garden and guarding it meaning the freedom to enjoy heavenly qualities but not to claim possession of them, 122
cultivating the ground meaning becoming body-centered, 305, 345
cultivating the ground meaning developing a schism or heresy, 380, 381
one who cultivated the ground meaning people who lack charity, 341, 345

Curse, 272, 273
a curse from the ground meaning corrupt theology, 330
a curse meaning turning away from what is heavenly, 245, 269, 379, 927
"a curse on you from the ground" meaning Cain turned away, 378
the ground that Jehovah cursed meaning something entirely false and evil, 531
the Lord never cursing anyone, 245, 269, 592:1

Curtain, 414:2

Cush. *See* Ethiopia

Cycle (alternation, change), 37. *See also* Alternation
alternations existing in regenerate people, 935, 936
the coldness of bodily and worldly concerns alternating with the warmth of faith and charity, 933:3
daily and yearly cycles as metaphors for spiritual and heavenly cycles, 37

heavenly and spiritual values alternating with bodily and worldly values, 933:3
the pre-Flood people unable to alternate between heavenly and spiritual pursuits and bodily and worldly pursuits, 933:4

D

Damnation. *See* Condemnation

Dan, 259:1

Darkness (dimness, shadow, vagueness), 31:1, 181, 443
being in shadow before being reborn, 31:2
darkness meaning falsity, 38
darkness meaning our sense of self-sufficiency, 21
darkness meaning our state before regeneration, 7, 17
the darkness of physical life passing into daylight in the next life, 448:1
"I will bring shadow over your land" meaning to blot out love and faith, 31:1

Daughter. *See also* Female; Son
daughter meaning goodness, 486, 490, 518, 568:1
daughter meaning the church, 54, 253
daughters meaning cravings, 555, 568, 569
daughters meaning the goodness conceived in the church, 489, 491, 532
daughters meaning the goodness produced by the marriage of faith and love, 55:2
daughters meaning what is in the will, 568

David, 66:2, 255, 666:2, 666:4

Dawn, meaning the Lord, 920:1

Day, 24:1, 28, 488:3, 901:1, 931. *See also* Evening; Night; Time
the breeze of the day meaning a trace of perception remaining in the church, 221
daily cycles as metaphors for spiritual cycles, 37
the darkness of physical life passing into daylight in the next life, 448:1
day and night meaning concepts in the intellect of a regenerate person, 936
day meaning a state of faith, 221
day meaning any whole period of time, 893:2
day meaning charity, 862
day meaning goodness, 38
day meaning times and states in general, 23, 482:2, 487, 488, 493, 931:1
days of distress meaning the wretched afterlife of unbelievers, 34:2

Day *(continued)*
    "days of old" meaning the earliest church, 249, 349:2, 477:3
    "days of old" meaning the time before the Flood, 274
    the end of some days meaning the passage of time, 347
    forty days (*see* Forty)
    the greater light that rules by day meaning love, 30:2, 32, 709
    the phases of the church compared to day and night, 221, 267, 271
    seven days (*see* Seven: seven days)
    the seventh day (*see* Seventh: the seventh day)
    the six days of creation meaning stages in regeneration, 6–13, 62, 63, 221 (*see also* Six)
    what belongs to the Lord compared to the day, 21

Deaf, 196:1
    the deaf meaning those who submit to truth, 489:1

Death (lifelessness), 169, 173, 177. *See also* Resurrection
    anyone deprived of goodness and truth as dead, 680
    characteristics of lifeless people, 81, 104
    a dead body meaning our own propensities, 901:2
    "the dead" meaning people inflated with self-love, 290
    death meaning eternal damnation, 304
    dying from eating the fruit of the tree meaning faith would perish, 198
    hell as death, 290, 304
    "the human died" meaning perception ceased to exist, 492, 494
    our being dead
        on our own, 39:1
        when our outer self is disconnected from our inner self, 272
    our change from being lifeless to being spiritual, 73, 81
    the steps from bodily life to eternal life, 168–181, 314
    those who are spiritually dead not feeling distress, 270

Debate. *See* Sophistry

The Decalogue. *See also* Command
    the Decalogue meaning the remnant, 576:4
    the tablets of the Decalogue, 576:4

Deceit (fraud), 358, 623:2
    evil spirits whose hatred involves deceit, 821
    the hells of deceivers, 827, 830

Deed. *See* Action; Work

Defloration, 828

Deluge. *See* Flood

Delusion (conviction [based on delusion], hallucination, persuasion, self-deception), 68, 448:2, 542, 622, 643:3, 655:2, 695, 794:1, 806, 819, 831:3, 842:1, 868:2, 938, 939. *See also* Illusion; Nephilim; The pre-Flood people
    appealing to the eyes meaning delusion, 207
    convincing ourselves of false ideas, 570, 589:1
    a delusion being a complex of feelings and impulses, 803:1
    the delusions of the pre-Flood people (*see* The pre-Flood people)
    delusions rejecting truth and soaking up falsity, 798
    delusions replacing perception in the pre-Flood people, 586a:1
    evil spirits flooding us with delusions, 641, 660, 705:3, 790, 842:1
    our life as built of the things we persuade ourselves of, 303:1
    pitch meaning horrendous delusions, 643:4
    self-delusion using truth to justify self-love and materialism, 794:1
    sons meaning delusions, 568:2

Demon. *See also* Devil; Hell; Spirit, evil
    evil demons disturbing us to the point of despair, 840
    wicked demons being evil spirits who attack through our cravings, 751:3

Depth. *See* Being, inner

Desecration. *See* Profanation

Deserving (earning, merit). *See also* Reward
    the good we do to earn a place in heaven as motivated by self-interest, 876
    thoughts about being deserving tainting what we do, 874

Desire (longing), 273. *See also* Craving; Emotion; Will
    "desirable for lending insight" meaning sensual pleasure, 207, 209
    "he longs for you, but you rule him," meaning charity wanting but being unable to reside in faith because of faith's desire to rule, 361, 365

heavenly people acting on the Lord's pleasure rather than on their own desire, 85:3
a tree desirable in appearance meaning perception of truth, 102
Desolation (abandonment, ruination), 427, 623:1, 705
  desolate places meaning falsities, 153
  desolation referring to the spiritual aspects of faith in a church's final stage, 411
  "ruination" as having to do with spiritual things, 793
Despair, 383, 699
  despair during spiritual trials, 840
Destruction. *See also* Devastation
  "I will destroy them together with the earth" meaning the human race would meet its end along with the church, 637:1
  our destroying ourselves if not held back from evil, 929
Devastation (being wiped out, destruction, ruin, waste), 18, 19, 406, 409, 428, 488:3. *See also* Destruction; Flood
  the age-old wastelands meaning faith's heavenly qualities laid waste, 613
  the Christian church of Swedenborg's day being in ruins, 407
  the church being devastated
    when faith is gone, 407
    when the goodness and truth associated with faith are gone, 530:1
  the church being in the final stage of destruction at the time of the Lord's Coming, 728:1
  devastation as the process we undergo after death to dispel our evil and falsity, 698
  devastation (being wiped out) as having to do with the heavenly aspects of faith, 411, 431, 793
  the devastation of a church needing to be complete
    before a new church can arise, 408, 411
    so that faith and charity will not mingle with what is profane, 408
  the devastation of those in the underground realm, 699
  devastation taking place with people who do not know because they are untaught and with those who know but do not want to know, 410
  every arrival of the Lord entailing a beginning for those who are regenerating and an end for those who are being destroyed, 728:1
  Lamech meaning devastation or the absence of faith, 405, 406, 427, 428, 527 (*see also* Lamech)
  a nucleus of the church always existing, unrecognized by those whose faith has been destroyed, 407
  the ruination of the pre-Flood people, 239, 272, 273
  spiritual devastation removing the barriers to our acquiring truth and goodness, 18
  wastelands meaning evil, 153
Devil (diabolical), 817. *See also* Demon; Hell; Spirit, evil
  devil meaning all evil spirits and evil itself, 251
  the Devil's crew taking delight in tormenting each other, 695
  evil and falsity inviting the diabolical crowd, 696
  hell forming a single devil, 694
  love for the Lord chasing away the Devil, 364
  sin meaning the Devil, 364
  those who do not lead good lives becoming devils after death, 697
Devoutness. *See* Reverence
Dictate. *See* Voice
Dimension, 444–446. *See also* Height; Length; Measurement; Width
  earthly dimensions meaning greater or lesser perfection, nature, or amount, 650
  numbers and dimensions in the Word having heavenly and spiritual symbolism, 639, 648:1
Dimness. *See* Darkness
Dippel, Johann Konrad *(plausible identification; not mentioned by name)*, 443
Dirt, 247
  dirt meaning those who turn their eye in a bodily and earthly direction, 249
  dirt meaning what is damned and hellish, 249, 275, 278
  to form a human, dirt from the ground, meaning to form our outer self, 94
Disease. *See* Illness
Distance. *See* Space
Distinction, 21
  making a distinction meaning our awareness of the inner and outer being, 24

Distress, 34:2. *See also* Anxiety; Misery; Pain; Trial
  trials as distress over things that conflict with what we love, 847:2
The Divine-Human One. *See also* Human being; The Lord
  the Lord uniting his divine and human selfhoods in the context of his human nature, 256
  sun meaning the Lord's divinity, and light meaning his humanity, 32:2
Doctrine. *See* Teaching
Dog, 45
Doing. *See* Making
Domination. *See* Governance; Rule
Door, 364
  door meaning hearing the message, 652, 656
Doubt. *See also* Skepticism
  doubt resulting from using sensory evidence as the basis for belief, 233:3
  the earliest people beginning to doubt, 194
Dove. *See also* Turtledove
  a dove meaning the truth and goodness of faith, 870:1, 871, 875:1, 876, 878:1, 882, 890, 891
  a dove meaning the use of the intellect for religion, 870:3
  the dove returning to the ark meaning apparently religious goodness and truth, 876
  sending the dove out meaning the right conditions for receiving the goodness and truth of faith, 871, 882, 890
Downpour
  downpour (rain) meaning struggle (trials), 729, 759, 843, 844, 845
  a flooding downpour meaning the ruination that falsity causes, 739:2
Dragon, 257, 828
Dreams, the earliest people being taught through, 125, 597:2
Drowning. *See* Flood; Suffocation
Dry
  dry land meaning people in whom there is nothing spiritual left, 806
  dry land meaning the outer being, 27
Drying (drained)
  drained off (drying up) meaning falsity no longer appears, 895, 898
  "drying up" meaning apparently getting rid of falsity, 868
  the earth dried up meaning rebirth, 902
Dung, 824:2

E

Ear, 656. *See also* Hearing
The earliest people. *See* Church, earliest
Earth (land), 931. *See also* Ground
  the belief that the Last Judgment means the end of the earth, 931:2
  "earth" as having to do with regeneration, 17, 25, 82
  "the earth is filled" meaning the proliferation of truth and goodness, 55:3
  earth (land) distinguished from ground, 90, 268, 566, 620, 636, 662, 872, 895
  earth (land) meaning love, or will, 55:2, 585, 620, 632, 636
  earth (land) meaning something that contains, 28, 566:4, 620
  earth (land) meaning the area surrounding the ground, 566:2, 620, 636
  earth (land) meaning the outer self, 16, 27, 28, 82, 89, 90, 477:3, 909, 913
  earth (land) meaning the presence or absence of the church, 566, 567, 620, 662
  earth meaning a person, 29, 89, 566:4, 626
  earth meaning a person in the church, 636, 662
  God created heaven and earth meaning regeneration of the inner self and outer self, 16
  land meaning people in whom heavenly love and the church died away, 566, 620, 636
  spreading out the earth meaning regeneration, 25
  vacant, empty earth meaning a person before regeneration, 17
Earth (planet), 637
  throughout all the days of the earth meaning the planet will not last forever, 931
Earthly, 40:2. *See also* Goodness, earthly
  the earthly dimension involving the carrying out of works of charity through the body, 880:2
  the earthly level as a reservoir for spiritual qualities, 880:2
  the earthly level receiving life from the spiritual level, 880:2

the earthly, spiritual, and heavenly levels of
   the human being, 880:2
the heel meaning what is bottommost on the
   earthly level, 250, 259
spiritual people's earthly food, 12, 56, 58, 59:1
Earthly goodness. *See* Goodness, earthly
East, 101, 130
   east meaning the Lord, 98, 101, 920:4
   on the east of the Garden of Eden meaning a
      heavenly quality from which an intelli-
      gent understanding comes, 306
   east wind meaning the dispersal of falsity
      and evil, 842
   living to the east of Eden meaning living by
      the intellect's dictates, 398
Eating. *See also* Food
   eating bread in the sweat of the face mean-
      ing rejecting what is heavenly, 276
   eating from the tree of knowledge meaning
      relying on sensory evidence in matters of
      faith, 128, 192
   eating from the tree of lives meaning
      acknowledgment of love and faith, 304
   eating meaning knowing, 125, 304
   eating meaning living, 270, 274
   good for eating, meaning intense desire, 207
   the man's eating, meaning the rational
      mind's consent, 207, 265
Eber, 470, 737:1
Eden, 4, 46:2, 303:2. *See also* Garden; Paradise;
   River
   being thrown out of Eden meaning being
      deprived of understanding and wisdom,
      305–307
   Cain's residence to the east of Eden meaning
      removing faith from its former seat, 330,
      398
   Eden meaning love, 98, 100, 107, 305, 398
   Eden meaning self-love in worldly people, 130
   Eden meaning wisdom, or the will to do
      good, 305
   the Garden of Eden meaning a heavenly per-
      son, 79, 99, 122
   living to the east of Eden meaning living by
      the intellect's dictates, 398
   the river from Eden meaning wisdom born
      of love, 107
   trees of Eden meaning religious knowledge
      from the Word, 130

Education. *See* Instruction; Teaching
Egypt, 870:3. *See also* Pharaoh
   Egypt meaning factual information, 31:1,
      117:1, 119, 130
   Egypt meaning occult knowledge, 130
   Egypt meaning sophistry about divine sub-
      jects, 195:3, 273
   Egyptians meaning the wicked, 842:5
Eight. *See* Eighth; Number
Eighth
   Methuselah meaning the eighth church, 463,
      516, 523
Elohim, 300
Emotion (affection, feeling, passion), 41,
   149:2, 545, 549. *See also* Craving; Desire;
   Love; *specific emotions*
   beasts (animals) meaning feelings (emo-
      tions), 45, 46, 142, 143, 194, 242, 246,
      594, 714, 715, 719, 744, 803, 810
   emotions having an unlimited number of
      parts, 545
   good reproducing itself in our feelings, 913
   our whole being entering into our emotions,
      803
Emptiness
   emptiness meaning the absence of truth, 17
   emptiness meaning the stage before regener-
      ation, 7, 17
End (border, close, culmination). *See also*
   Conclusion
   border meaning organized knowledge and
      sensory evidence, 655:1
   the end of all flesh meaning the human race
      could not avoid destruction, 631
   the end of the age occurring in Swedenborg's
      time, 32
   predictions of the close (culmination) of the
      age, 34:2, 411, 931:2
Enemy, 249
Enjoyment. *See* Joy; Pleasure
Enoch
   the city called Enoch, 399, 403
   Enoch as the seventh church, 463, 513, 516
   "Enoch walked with God" meaning to
      develop the doctrine concerning faith,
      518, 519:1, 520, 614
   "Enoch was no more, because God took him,"
      meaning this church preserved doctrines
      for later use, 464, 520, 521, 609, 920:4

Enoch *(continued)*
 the heresy called Enoch, 331, 399, 401, 404
 the meaning of the name Enoch, 401, 519
 the people called Enoch making a theology from the earliest church's perceptions, 464, 519, 521, 522, 609, 736, 920:4
 two different churches called Enoch, 485
Enosh
 the church called Enosh, 324, 336, 496, 640
 Enosh as a spiritual person, 439
 Enosh as the third church, 463, 498, 500, 502, 505
 Enosh meaning a church that considered charity to be faith's principal concern, 438, 439
 Enosh meaning charity implanted through faith, 336, 436
 the meaning of the name Enosh, 336, 439, 477:4
 perception in the church called Enosh, 502, 505
Entity. *See also* Being
 belief in a Supreme Entity, 206:1
Ephah, 576:1
Ephraim, 264:1, 382:3, 870:3
Esau
 Esau and Jacob meaning the brotherhood of charity and faith, 367
 Esau meaning charity, 367:2
 Esau meaning the early Christian church, 367:2
Essence. *See also* Being
 essence diminishing from the center to the periphery, 501
 a name meaning the essence of a thing, 144, 145
Eternity (forever). *See also* Life: eternal life
 "days of old" meaning the earliest church, 349:2, 477:3
 living forever meaning being saved to all eternity, 298
 living forever meaning eternal damnation, 304
 there is nothing more important than our eternal life, 794:2
Ethiopia (Cush)
 Ethiopia meaning those with heavenly attributes, 349:2
 Ethiopians meaning religious knowledge, 117:1
 the land of Cush meaning our mental abilities, 116, 117

Eunuch, 394
Euphrates (Phrath). *See also* Eden; River
 the Euphrates (Phrath) meaning factual knowledge, 113, 120, 130
Europe, 567
Eve
 Eve meaning "life" in Hebrew, 291, 476
 Eve meaning the true church of the earliest times, 281
Evening, 28, 883
 evening meaning everything that is our own, 22
 evening meaning when there is no faith, 22
Evidence. *See* Fact; The senses
Evil (badness, wickedness), 209, 230, 488:3, 842:5. *See also* Hell; Spirit, evil; Wickedness
 the absence of faith leading to falsity and evil, 231
 all our purposes as evil when we are disconnected from the Lord, 389
 angels defending us from evil, 761
 angels giving us a horror of evil after regeneration, 50:3
 angels preventing us from rushing into evil, 50:2
 devil meaning evil itself, 251:2
 dispelling evil by means of goodness, 719, 731
 the evil afflicting all churches being trusting oneself rather than the Lord, 231
 evil allowed to those who yearn for it, 139
 evil as a matter of the will, 845:1
 evil as what condemns us, 845:1
 evil inherited from the parents, 313, 633, 719, 868
 the evil of the people in the land meaning evil present in the will, 585
 evil spirits adopting wickedness as their own, 233:2
 evil we have committed being rendered harmless but never removed, 719, 868, 929
 falsity and evil being their own punishment, 391, 696
 in hell, evil rebounding on the evildoer, 592:2, 696, 689, 868:2
 hereditary evil (*see* Heredity)
 human selfhood (sense of autonomy) as wickedness (evil) itself, 154, 164, 597:3, 633, 868

humans consisting of evil and falsity, 39, 55:3, 154, 233:2, 761, 868, 929
inherited evil (*see* Heredity)
the Lord fighting on our behalf against evil and falsity, 63
night meaning evil, 38
no life existing in evil or falsity, 30:2
nothing bad coming from the Lord, 592:1, 696
our adopting evil as our own through the belief that we live independently, 150, 592:1, 761
our evils being tempered by means of goodness during regeneration, 561, 719
our seeing evil as good before regeneration, 21
our throwing ourselves into hell if the Lord did not hold us back from evil and falsity, 789, 929
the snake meaning evil, 250, 251:1, 257
wickedness coming from relying on sensory evidence in matters of religion, 127, 233:3, 251:1
Evil spirit. *See* Spirit, evil
Examining religious mysteries through factual knowledge, 233:1, 448:2. *See also* Scrutiny
Excrement (feces), hells of, 827, 943
Existence, 42:1. *See also* Being
  to continue in existence is constantly to come into existence, 775:2
Expanse (spreading out)
  expanse meaning the inner self, 24, 30:3
  spreading out the earth meaning regeneration, 25
Expression. *See* Word
Extension (stretching out). *See also* Space
  the spirit having extension in space, 444, 445
  stretching out the heavens meaning regeneration, 25
Eye, 831:3. *See also* Blindness; Seeing
  angels rolling a membrane off the eye on revival from death, 183
  eyes meaning the intellect, 212
  opening of one's eyes meaning an inner voice, 212
  "their eyes were opened" meaning perceiving that they were behaving wrongly, 193
Eyesight. *See* Seeing

F
Fabrication, 565, 586a:1
  a fabrication meaning self-centered thinking, 586a:2
  a fabrication meaning what we persuade ourselves is true, 586a:1
  "what the heart fabricates" meaning the evil connected with self-love, 586a:1, 928
Face, 387, 398, 607:2, 641, 830
  the face being lifted meaning charity shone out, 358
  the face meaning the deepest levels of being, 32:2, 358
  the face of the abyss meaning our cravings and falsities, 18
  "the face of the ground had dried up" meaning falsity no longer appears, 898
  the face of the ground meaning the area where the church exists, 564, 566, 567, 593
  the face of the water meaning knowledge of truth and goodness, 19
  Jehovah's face meaning mercy, peace, and everything good, 222–223, 358, 387
  one's face falling meaning a change on the deeper levels, 355, 358, 359
Fact (knowledge, scientific concept, secular knowledge), 24:1, 27, 30:2, 102, 118, 119, 120, 121, 128, 202, 204, 215, 264:1, 340, 605. *See also* Knowledge; Reason; The senses
  acquiring knowledge as permitted, useful, and pleasurable, 129
  basing belief on factual knowledge
    as blotting out faith, 31:1
    the insanity of, 647
    leading to doubt and denial, 233:3, 301
    self-love (selfhood) involved in, 205, 208, 210
  the belief that our life exists on the level of facts and knowledge, 657
  branches meaning facts we know, 55:4
  creeping animals of the waters (fish) meaning facts, 40:1, 42:1
  the Euphrates meaning facts and sensory impressions, 120, 130
  evil as rising from fixation on facts and the senses, 251:1
  facts as the "food" of people focused on the physical world, 56

Fact *(continued)*
  factual knowledge
    in heavenly people, 75
    in the lowest level of the intellect, 657
    as too coarse to explore heavenly qualities, 233:1
    used only to confirm the truth in the Word, 128
  fish meaning facts, 40:1–2, 42
  knowledge as different from acknowledgment or belief, 896:1
  knowledge as the first step of rebirth, 896:1
  knowledge used to support false assumptions, 129, 206:2
  the Lord entering our understanding, reason, and knowledge, 99, 657
  the Lord making a distinction between religious knowledge and secular knowledge, 24:1
  the lowest compartment of the ark meaning facts, 657
  our being able to grasp truth on the factual level prior to regeneration, 671
  people today using facts unknown to the ancients to confirm their point of view, 196:1, 232
  people who depend on factual knowledge not believing in the spirit, 196:2, 446
  Pharaoh and the Egyptians meaning sensory evidence and factual information, 31:1, 120, 195:3
  sea creatures meaning general categories of facts, 42:1
  shallow people believing secular facts are wisdom and faith, 111
  "shrub of the field" and "plant of the field" meaning rational ideas and factual knowledge with a heavenly and spiritual origin, 91
  the snake meaning the senses and facts, 251:1, 251:2
  spiritual angels using scientific concepts to confirm their beliefs, 203
  spiritual people believing their intelligence to be a product of facts and rationality, 99
  trees of Eden meaning facts and religious knowledge from the Word, 130
  using facts to investigate religious mysteries, 42:2, 308
    as causing the fall of the earliest church and every church, 127
    heavenly people as not, 80
    the impossibility of, 233
  wisdom from the Lord bringing light to factual knowledge, 129

Faith (belief, conviction, religion), 31, 43, 53, 77, 198, 202, 328, 335, 336, 381, 409, 436. *See also* Belief; Charity; Church; Faith alone; Love; Teaching
  Cain meaning faith separated from love (*see* Faith alone)
  a dove meaning the truth and goodness of faith, 870:1, 871, 875:1, 876, 878:1, 382, 890, 891
  the earliest people perceiving faith only from love, 310:1, 325, 337, 393, 398, 597:3
  the faith acknowledged in heaven, 5
  faith as a function of conscience, 896:2
  faith as heavenly when it comes from love, 353
  faith as knowing, acknowledging, and believing, 896:2
  faith as more than knowledge and acknowledgment of doctrines, 36, 654, 896
  faith as obedience to the teachings of faith, 36, 344
  faith as the core of heavenly-spiritual people, 200
  faith as the form of love, 668
  faith compared to night, 709, 862
  faith compared to the moon, 862
  faith containing religious knowledge, 620
  faith (conviction) as an attribute of the intellect, 30:3, 48, 52, 53, 310, 709
  faith in the heart as a saving faith, 30:2
  faith in the intellect, 30:2
  faith leading to charity, 310:2, 330, 371
  faith separated from love in the people who lived after the Flood, 371, 393
  faith serving charity, 372
  faith wanting to rule charity, 365, 398
  faith without charity as mere knowledge, 379
  the first form of faith being memorized faith, based on facts, 30:2
  the function of faith as understanding truth and goodness, 419
  the goodness belonging to faith (religious good), 264:2, 420:4, 424, 530:1, 770
    being cut off from, 385, 387, 398
    charity as, 654
    coming from the Lord through our deepest levels, 876

the truth of faith depending on, 654, 874, 880:1
heavenly angels unable to tolerate a purely factual treatment of faith, 202
the interconnection of faith and love called a marriage, 55
the lack of faith in Swedenborg's day, 32:1
the life force of faith being absent if we believe that goodness and truth come from ourselves, 29:1, 39:1
living faith coming from the Lord, 290
living faith preparing us to be human, 95
the Lord as the essence and life of faith, 30:1, 256
love and faith as united, 34, 36, 60, 63
love and faith compared to heat and light, 30:3, 34:2, 365
love containing faith, 620
love for the Lord and our neighbor as the primary teaching of faith, 36
man meaning faith, 340, 367:1, 427, 429, 476
Noah meaning the faith that comes of charity, 598:1
nonbelief and belief without love compared to winter, 34:2
nonbelief coming from dependence on sensory evidence, 128, 231
our preparation to receive the living power of faith, 29:1
the peril of using facts to investigate religious mysteries, 42:2, 80, 126, 192, 198, 204, 206, 233, 298, 306, 308:2
the progress of faith (conviction) in those who are being reborn, 10–12, 30:2, 48
receiving life from the Lord through faith, 30:2, 39:2
seed meaning faith, 255, 264:2, 368, 437, 620, 726
spiritual people acknowledging truth and goodness from faith, 81:1
things from the Lord having life because they contain faith, 41
those who are heavenly knowing of no faith separate from love, 32:2, 81:1, 202, 393, 459
the tree that has fruit meaning religious good, 57
twelve meaning faith, 575, 577
Faith alone, the doctrine of, 34, 371, 398, 433, 436. *See also* Cain
  Cain meaning the teaching that faith was separate from love (charity), 325, 326, 327, 329, 335, 337:3, 338, 340, 341, 347, 355, 356, 362, 363, 369, 384, 392, 394, 395, 398, 409, 436, 916:3
  detached faith having our own selves at the core, 724
  faith separate from love as no kind of faith, 36, 341, 379, 381, 724
  faith without charity shattering the bond between us and the Lord, 379
  the Lord as not present in faith separated from love and charity, 724, 904:2
  the theory that faith alone saves, annihilating charity, 369
  those who prove from the Word that faith alone brings salvation, 794:2
Fallacy. *See* Falsity; Illusion
Falsification, of religious teachings, 337
Falsity (misconception), 896, 898. *See also* Delusion; Evil; Illusion
  birds meaning attachment to falsity, 803
  confirming false assumptions through facts, 589:1, 794
  the conviction that falsity is truth, suffocating spiritual and heavenly qualities, 806
  cravings giving rise to falsities, 18, 59, 857:1, 892
  darkness meaning falsity, 38
  each falsity as an effigy of hell, 803:2
  every falsity appearing to be a fact, 790
  evil spirits calling forth our misconceptions, 653
  evil spirits flooding us with falsities, 790:1
  false beliefs leading to false actions, 233:3
  falsities adopted in ignorance as relatively easy to dispel, 735, 803:2
  falsity interfering before regeneration, 865:1
  falsity separated from the contents of the will after the Flood, 895:1
  falsity staying with us after rebirth, 868, 887
  fighting falsities during times of trial, 653
  the Lord bending our falsities toward truth, 24:3, 25, 887
  our inability to receive truth while governed by falsity, 653:2, 875
  the pre-Flood people's attachment to falsity, 803
  the time before regeneration as marked by falsity, 22
  those who have hardened themselves in falsity, 129, 845:2

Falsity *(continued)*
  water meaning falsities, 739:1, 739:3, 789, 790, 794:1, 847:1, 857:1, 871, 877, 887
Family (clan), 313, 470, 685, 917. *See also* House
  "by their families" meaning pairs, 914, 917
Fantasy. *See* Delusion; Illusion
Farmer, 368
Fat (rich), 415
  fat from sacrifices as holy, 353
  fat meaning the heavenly aspects of charity, 353:2
  fat meaning the quality of heaven, 353
Father, 412, 413, 415, 417, 423, 496, 498, 518, 533. *See also* God; Mother
  leaving father and mother meaning leaving the inner being behind, 160
  the Lord as the only Father known in heaven, 15
  "Noah fathered three sons" meaning three kinds of theology would rise out of that church, 616–617
Favor (grace). *See also* Mercy
  the distinction between mercy and favor (grace), 598:3
  favor focusing on spiritual aims, 598:3
  the Lord's favor as having to do with salvation, 598:1
  spiritual people acknowledging the Lord's favor rather than his mercy, 598:2
Fear. *See also* Horror
  angels instilling in regenerate people a horror and fear of evil and falsity, 50:3
  evil people fearing everyone, 390, 391
  fear in hell and the world of spirits, 695, 815, 939, 941, 942
  fear restraining lifeless people, 81:3
  hiding themselves from Jehovah God's face meaning fearing an inner dictate, 218, 222
The Feast of Booths, 414:4
Feeling (sensing). *See also* Emotion; Sensation; The senses
  basing belief on seeing and feeling, 194
  the spirit as what actually senses things, 322:2, 447
Female (woman), 944. *See also* Bride; Daughter; Mother; Wife; Woman; Young woman
  female meaning goodness, 669, 725, 749
  female meaning the church, 476
  female meaning the qualities of love, 476
  female meaning the will in the spiritual being, 54, 476
  male and female meaning the marriage between faith and love, 475, 476
  old women growing young in heaven, 553
  the will ruling the intellect in women, 568:2
Field. *See also* Earth; Ground
  field meaning doctrine, 368
  field meaning the church or regenerate individual, 246, 368
  field meaning the outer self of a heavenly person, 90
  ground meaning the area surrounding a field, 377, 566:2, 620, 636
Fifteen, meaning something meager, 798, 813. *See also* Five
Fifth. *See also* Five
  birds meaning what we produce in the fifth stage of regeneration, 11, 48
  Mahalalel as the fifth church, 463, 506
Fifty, meaning the few remaining traces, 647. *See also* Five; One hundred fifty
Fig tree
  fig tree meaning earthly good, 216, 217, 885:2
  fig tree meaning the Jewish church, 885:2
Fighting. *See* Conflict
Figure of speech, 776:2. *See also* Comparisons
Filth (foulness)
  the foul Jerusalem, 940:2
  utter filth residing in us, 724
Fire, 308:2, 825. *See also* Flame
  fire and flame meaning evil and cravings, 739:3
  fire meaning love, 934
  fire meaning punishment of corrupt desire, 574:3
  fire meaning self-love and its craving, 934:3
  fire meaning the Lord, 934:3
  fire offerings meaning love, 925:1 (*see also* Burnt offering)
  the flaming fire meaning something heavenly and spiritual, 934:2
  flying fire snake meaning desire felt by self-love, 251:2
  heavenly love felt by ungodly individuals as a burning fire, 934:3
  spirits in hell descending into a fire, 814

First
- in the beginning, on the first of the month, meaning a starting point, 894
- faith as the first offspring of the earliest church, 338
- the first heaven, 544, 684
- the first human, 4, 313
- the first river, Pishon, meaning the intelligence that goes with a faith based on love, 110
- knowledge as the first step of rebirth, 896:1
- our first stage extending from infancy to just before regeneration, 7

Firstborn (birthright), 352, 897:2. *See also* Birth
- Esau and Jacob's birthright, 367
- firstborn of the flock meaning holiness, 350, 352

Fish, 11. *See also* Creeping
- fish as having to do with the intellect, 52
- fish meaning facts, 40:1–2, 42
- huge fish in hell, 819

Five, meaning a little, 649, 798. *See also* Fifteen; Fifth; Fifty; Number

Flame, 831:2. *See also* Fire
- charity compared to flame, 365, 854
- the flame of a sword turning itself meaning self-love, 306, 309
- the flaming fire meaning something heavenly and spiritual, 934:2

Flax, 25

Flesh, 627, 631, 661:1, 661:3. *See also* Bodily; Body
- all flesh meaning what lies in the will, 670
- flesh creeping on the earth meaning people became absorbed with sensory and bodily matters, 800
- flesh from one's flesh meaning the sense of autonomy of our outer being that has life, 156, 157
- flesh in place of the rib meaning the part of our identity that is alive, 147, 148, 149:2
- flesh meaning a person in general and a body-centered (body-oriented) person in particular, 574, 627:1, 631, 661:3, 780, 800
- flesh meaning attributes with a living quality, 148
- flesh meaning the body-centered part of the will, 670
- flesh that had the breath of lives in it meaning a newly created being, 780
- one flesh meaning the inner being and the outer being coexist, 160
- our flesh coming to life when the Lord stirs charity and faith in us, 780
- "they are flesh" meaning people became body-centered, 572, 574

Flock, 352. *See also* Sheep; Shepherd
- the flock meaning those who are taught the goodness involved in charity, 343
- the shepherd of the flock meaning the good actions that charity inspires, 415:1

Flood (deluge, drowning, inundation), 756:2, 842:5, 893:2. *See also* Ark, Noah's; Nephilim; Noah; The pre-Flood people; Rain; Suffocation
- the earliest church ending with the Flood, 271, 307
- false premises and warped reasoning drowning us, 705:3
- flood meaning a deluge of evil and falsity, 660, 787
- the Flood meaning the "drowning" of those cut off from their remnant, 662
- the Flood meaning the false ideas that swamped the pre-Flood people, 787
- the Flood meaning the pre-Flood race's extinction by the inundation of self-deception, 563, 660
- flood meaning the struggles leading up to regeneration, 606
- flood waters as evil and falsity imprisoning people before regeneration, 876
- floods of water meaning times of both trial and ruin, 705, 729, 739, 787, 842:5
- floods of water meaning times of desolation and trial, 790:1
- heaven's floodgates meaning a flood of falsities, 757
- influx from evil spirits compared to a flood, 660, 705:3, 787
- the people who followed the Flood described by qualities of the intellect, 209
    - given a new character to prevent the world's destruction, 200, 311
    - having spiritual rather than heavenly seed inside them, 310:2
    - truth leading to goodness in, 209
- trials as deluges of falsities stirred up by evil spirits, 790:1

Floodgates, of heaven, 576:3, 757, 760, 845
Flying thing, 745, 772, 776, 777. *See also* Bird; Winged creature
Fold, 415. *See also* Livestock
Fondness. *See* Emotion
Food, 57, 677, 680, 681. *See also* Bread; Eating
  angelic food as everything of a spiritual or heavenly character, 276:1
  food meaning facts, 56
  food meaning goodness and pleasure, 678
  food meaning spiritual and heavenly nourishment, 680:4
  food meaning things enjoyed by a worldly person, 56
  food meaning what harmonizes with a person's life, 56
  goodness and truth as our genuine food, 680:1
  heavenly food as things enjoyed by a heavenly person, 56
  the Lord giving us heavenly and spiritual food during times of trial, 59:1
  the Lord providing food appropriate to each individual, 677
  a plant, or grass, meaning a spiritual person's earthly food, 58
  a plant, or grass, meaning spiritual food, 57
  the pleasures of evil and falsity and bodily, worldly, and earthly pleasures as lethal foods, 680:1
  spiritual food as things enjoyed by a spiritual person, 56
Foot
  foot meaning the earthly level, 425
  foot meaning things fairly low on the earthly level, 259:1
Foreseeing, 598:1
  it being foreseen that the character of the human race would change, 393, 394, 521, 587:1, 609, 927:2–3
  Jehovah foreseeing everything from eternity, 587:1
Forever. *See* Eternity
Forty. *See also* Forty-two; Four
  forty days and nights foreshadowing the Lord's trials, 730:1
  forty days meaning how long the church called Noah lasted, 786
  the number forty
    meaning how long trials last, 730, 760, 786, 862
    meaning the duration of both trials and devastation, 730:2
Forty-two, having the same meaning as forty, 730:3
Foulness. *See* Filth
Foundation, 613
Four. *See* Forty; Forty-two; Fourth; Number
  the four states (stages) after trials, 833–837, 863, 880:1, 889
  guardian beings called "four wild animals" in Ezekiel, 908:2
  the river in the garden of Eden branching into four rivers, 78, 107, 116, 118, 121, 130, 567, 658
Fourth
Kenan meaning the fourth church, 463, 500
Fragrance (aroma, scent, smell), 886:2, 925. *See also* Frankincense; Incense; Perfume; Stenches
  earthly aromas corresponding to auras of love and faith in heaven, 925:2
  fragrance meaning perception, 96
  "Jehovah smelled a restful smell" meaning worship inspired by charity was pleasing to the Lord, 925:1, 925:3
  pleasant smells meaning the good embraced by charity and the truth espoused by a faith coming from charity, 925:2
Frankincense, 113
Freedom (liberty), 891
  all freedom coming from a love for goodness, 891, 892
  being led by the Lord as freedom, 892:2, 905
  going out of the ark meaning liberty (freedom), 891, 905, 912, 918
  Noah's state of freedom, 891
  our feeling free when controlled by cravings and falsity, 892
  spiritual people who act in accord with their conscience acting freely, 918
Fruit, 501. *See also* Reproduction
  the ban on touching the fruit of the tree of the garden (the tree of knowledge) meaning not to think about religious goodness and truth from oneself, 198, 202
  deeds inspired by charity yielding fruit, 348
  fruit as what the Lord gives the heavenly person, 57
  fruit meaning the good that results from love and charity, 885:1

fruit meaning the goodness and truth produced by perception, 199
fruit meaning wisdom, 57, 198
a fruit of faith meaning an action from charity, 161
the fruit of one's deeds meaning a life inspired by charity, 627:2
fruit of the ground meaning doing what faith requires without loving others, 346, 348
fruit that they were not to eat meaning religious goodness and truth that they were not to learn about from themselves, 198
fruit that they were to eat meaning the goodness and truth revealed by the earliest people, 198, 199
fruits of goodness called daughters, 55:2
fruits of truth called sons, 55:2
seed leading to new fruit as what the Lord gives the spiritual person, 57
tree that has fruit meaning religious good, 57
Fruitfulness. *See* Reproduction
Fugitive
being a wanderer and fugitive on the earth meaning not knowing what is true or good, 330, 380, 382:1
Furies, in hell, 814, 818, 944
Future, being the same as the present to the Lord and angels, 730:5

G

Garden, 225, 710. *See also* Eden; River
the "garden" in worldly people, 130
garden meaning anything good or true, 225
garden meaning intelligence (understanding), 98, 100, 305
the Garden of Eden (*see* Eden)
a human being compared to a garden, 108
Gate, 655:1
Gathering
"he was to gather it to him" meaning what is true, 679
Gehenna, 940:1
the city in hell called Gehenna's Judgment, 942
the hell below Gehenna, 815
the hell called Gehenna, 825, 826
sirens punished in Gehenna, 831
Genealogies, created by the earliest people, 339, 400

Generality (whole), 245, 545, 597, 865:1. *See also* Category
the earliest church receiving perception of general principles, 597:2–3
every general statement containing thousands of individual concepts, 865:1
every whole having an unlimited number of parts, 545:2
the general category to which a particular thing belongs allowing it to come into being and continue in existence, 42:1
general ideas preparing the mind for specifics, 848:3, 868:2
a general rule having its existence from specific cases, 917
our general viewpoint governing all our specific perceptions, 920:2
sea creatures meaning general categories of facts, 42:1
Generation, 612:1, 712
"generation after generation" meaning the ancient churches, 477:3
"generation after generation" meaning the religions that came after the Flood, 337:2
"generation" as plural when having to do with the intellect and as singular when having to do with the will, 712
"generations" as having to do with faith, 613
Genesis
the first three chapters of Genesis dealing with the earliest people, 137, 286
Genesis 1 dealing with the spiritual person and Genesis 2 dealing with the heavenly person, 51, 81, 872
the inner sense of the first chapter of Genesis dealing with regeneration, 4, 737:2, 860, 893:2
the name God used in Genesis 1, 300, 624
Gentile. *See also* Nation; Non-Christians
the fate of those who profane true faith as worse than that of gentiles, 593
a new church arising among gentiles, 410
Genus. *See* Category
Ghost, 443
Gihon. *See also* Eden; River
Gihon meaning knowledge about goodness and truth, or love and faith, 116
Glory, 455
strength and glory meaning the Word's inner meaning, 49:4

Goat, 294, 296, 715
God, 300. *See also* Jehovah; The Lord
   "Enoch walked with God" meaning to develop the doctrine concerning faith, 518, 519:1, 520, 614
   "Enoch was no more, because God took him," meaning this church preserved doctrines for later use, 464, 520, 521, 609, 920:4
   "as God had commanded" meaning it happened in this way, 682, 732, 750
   "as God had commanded" meaning preparation to receive truth and goodness, 783
   "God remembered" meaning the end of trial and the beginning of renewal, 840
   "God said" meaning that is how it was, 630
   God's kingdom (*see* Kingdom, the Lord's)
   human beings called gods by virtue of their power, 300
   the name God
     coming from his powerful ability, 300
     not as sacred as the name Jehovah, 624
     used in Genesis 1, 300
     used when no church exists, 619, 624
     used when the context is before rebirth, 840
   there being only one God, 300
   "you will be like God" meaning being able to lead themselves, 204
Gog, 737:2
Going out
   going and coming back meaning a stage of fluctuation, 856, 867
   going out from before Jehovah meaning being cut off from the good in a loving faith, 398
Gold, 117
   gold meaning an imitation of good, 424
   gold meaning goodness, 110, 115, 117:1
   gold meaning heavenly goodness, 425
   gold meaning the goodness belonging to wisdom or to love, 113
   gold meaning the most profound heavenly quality in us, 643:1
Goodness, 17, 21, 29:1, 55:3, 105, 200, 207, 209, 548:2, 668, 671, 678, 725, 735, 863, 868:2, 876, 880:1, 890, 895, 913, 916:1. *See also* Angel; Goodness, earthly; Goodness, heavenly; Goodness, heavenly-spiritual; Goodness, spiritual; Heaven; Truth
   all freedom coming from a love for goodness, 891, 892
   all good coming from love and so from the Lord, 112
   anyone deprived of goodness and truth as dead, 680
   the belief that everything connected with self-love is good, 20, 911:3
   the channel for goodness and truth from the Lord being blocked before regeneration, 857:1
   charitable goodness (*see* Charity: charitable goodness)
   daughter meaning goodness, 55:2, 486, 489, 490, 491, 518, 532, 568:1
   day meaning goodness, 38
   dispelling evil by means of goodness, 719, 731
   the earliest people given perception of goodness and truth, 125, 597:2, 895:2
   earthly goodness, spiritual goodness, and heavenly goodness, 775:2
   "extremely good" meaning a marriage of faith and love, 60
   female meaning goodness, 669, 725, 749
   gold meaning goodness, 110, 113, 115, 117:1, 425
   good actions in the different stages of regeneration, 9–12, 48, 52
   good not being good without something heavenly at its core, 225
   good spirit (*see* Spirit; Spirit, good)
   goodness and pleasure as the constituents of human life, 678
   goodness and truth, 198, 199
     coming from the Lord alone, 20, 24, 27, 29:1, 39
     coming from the Lord through the inner self, 27, 857:1
     destroyed among the pre-Flood people, 635, 731, 798
     as our genuine food, 680:1
   the goodness belonging to faith (*see* Faith: the goodness belonging to faith)
   goodness leading to truth in the earliest people, 200, 209
   the goodness that comes of love (*see* Love)
   knowledge of goodness and truth (*see* Knowledge: knowledge of goodness and truth)
   life being present in goodness, 668, 671, 678

the Lord as goodness itself, 21
the Lord diverting our delusions and cravings to goodness and truth, 24:3, 25, 868:2, 887
the Lord storing goodness and truth in our inner being, 268, 561, 563, 661:2, 711
man and wife meaning truth united to goodness, 430:2, 713, 718, 725
neighborly good (*see* Charity: charitable goodness)
our evils being tempered by means of goodness during regeneration, 561, 719
our inability to do good on our own, 44, 105, 233:2, 735, 848:2, 868:1, 874, 876, 882
our misconception that we do good on our own, 24:3, 29:1, 47, 39, 55:3, 874
people focused on externals having no idea of what is good, 20
perception as a feeling for whether a thing is true and good, 104, 495, 503, 521
perception of goodness and truth as the main influence in heaven, 483:1
preparation with truth and goodness, 677, 711, 719, 737:1, 781, 783
profanation of the Word destroying goodness and truth in us, 571
recognizing truth on the basis of goodness as a heavenly trait, 511
the remnant as a knowledge of truth and goodness, 19, 561, 711
those who do not lead good lives becoming devils after death, 697
usefulness as the good that comes of love and charity, 454
"very good" meaning the Lord making us likenesses of himself, 63
a will to do good, 305, 306, 568:2, 585, 632, 633, 634:2, 640, 671, 928
wives meaning goodness, 668, 718, 742, 770, 915
Goodness, earthly, 292, 294, 296, 297, 775:2. *See also* Earthly; Goodness
bronze meaning earthly goodness, 421, 424, 425, 426:2
earthly goodness remaining in the third stage of the earliest church, 193, 216, 224, 282
every kind of beast meaning earthly goodness, 774
fig tree meaning earthly good, 216, 217, 885:2
the middle of the tree of the garden meaning earthly good, 218, 225
the people called Noah retaining a trace of earthly goodness, 628, 635
Tubal-cain meaning earthly goodness and truth, 421, 436
Goodness, heavenly, 775. *See also* Goodness; Heavenly
gold meaning heavenly goodness, 425
heavenly goodness as unclothed, 297
Goodness, heavenly-spiritual, 282, 297. *See also* Goodness; Heavenly-spiritual
Goodness, spiritual, 292, 294, 296, 775. *See also* Goodness; Spiritual
every kind of wild animal meaning all spiritual goodness, 774
a grapevine meaning spiritual good, 217
an organ meaning spiritual good, 419
Gopher wood, 640, 643:1, 643:4
Governance, 450. *See also* Rule
the form of government in heaven, 548:1
higher levels in a human being governing lower ones, 911
the Lord's governance, 50, 141, 227, 581:1, 592, 597:3, 911, 918
self-governance (*see* Selfhood)
Grace. *See* Favor
Grape, 885:2
Grapevine
a grapevine meaning spiritual good, 217
a wife like a grapevine meaning the spiritual church, 886:3
Grass, 58. *See also* Plant
Grave. *See* Burial
Greed (miserliness), 548:3, 938–940
Grief. *See* Misery; Regret; Sorrow
Ground (soil), 593, 809. *See also* Field; Planting; Seed
Adam meaning "ground," 313, 479, 566:1, 566:5
cultivating the ground from which they were taken meaning becoming body-centered, 305, 345
the earliest people comparing the human body to the ground, 909
earth (land) meaning the area surrounding the ground, 566:2, 620, 636
"the face of the ground had dried up" meaning falsity no longer appears, 898

Ground *(continued)*
  falsity driven out to prepare the "soil" in us for religious truth, 875:2
  "ground" as having to do with the intellect, 809, 895:1
  the ground as the area surrounding a field, 377, 566:2, 620, 636
  "ground" in spiritual people being in their intellect, 875:3, 895:1
  "ground" in the earliest people being in their will, 895:1
  ground meaning a person who adopts a heresy, 386
  ground meaning a schism or heresy, 330, 373, 377, 380, 381
  ground meaning the area where the church exists, 566, 567, 593
  ground meaning the church, or the people in the church, 386, 566, 809, 869, 872, 898
  ground meaning the outer self, 90, 267, 268, 275, 278
  ground meaning theology, 566:3, 566:4
  ground used in reference to faith, 348, 620
  the land as the area surrounding the ground, 566:2, 636, 662
  one who cultivated the ground meaning people who lack charity, 341, 345
  regenerate people called ground because they have been planted with heavenly seed, 268
  the "soil" of our minds prepared to receive charity through matters of fact, reason, and understanding, 654
  an unregenerate person as soil in which no seed of goodness or truth has been planted, 17
Group. *See* Community
Guardian being
  guardian beings called "four wild animals" in Ezekiel, 908:2
  guardian beings guarding the way to the tree of lives, 285
  the guardian beings meaning the Lord's providence protecting us from profaning the mysteries of faith, 306, 308
Guarding. *See also* Preservation; Protection
  being a guardian meaning serving, 370, 372
  cultivating the garden and guarding it meaning the freedom to enjoy heavenly qualities but not to claim possession of them, 122

Guidance. *See* Leading
Guilt, "the blood cries out" meaning, 373, 376

H
Hair
  evil spirits having their hair scraped off, 939
Half-light, 865:1, 883
Hallucination. *See* Delusion; Illusion
Ham. *See* Shem, Ham, and Japheth
Hand, meaning power, 195:2, 878
Happiness (joy), 452, 540. *See also* Joy; Pleasure
  all happiness coming from the Lord, 32:2, 552
  the angelic state as conveying one's own happiness to others, 549
  angels finding happiness in usefulness, 454
  the earliest people finding their greatest happiness in marriage, 54
  heavenly happiness as inexpressible, 549
  life holding no joy unless it is active, 454
  love as heavenly angels' source of happiness, 32:2
Harmony
  a heavenly community as harmony among many, 687, 690
  unity as formed out of harmony among many parts, 457
Harnessing, 55:4
Harp, 420
  harp meaning knowledge of goodness and truth, 420:4
  harp meaning religious truth, 420:5, 424
  harp meaning spiritual qualities of faith, 417, 418
Harvest. *See* Ground; Reaping; Seed
Hatred, 251:1
  blood meaning hatred, 374
  the different kinds of hatred, 374:1
    as countless, 693, 816
    different hells for, 693, 816
    different kinds of snakes meaning, 251:1
  hatred against love for the Lord dominating the world of spirits, 59:2
  hatred as the source of all wickedness, 374:2, 374:3
  hatred of the Lord and one's neighbor constituting hell, 693
  hatred opposing charity, 374:1
  hatred putting a gulf between us and the Lord, 904:2

the hells of those who spent their lives in hatred, revenge, and cruelty, 814–823
our hatreds transformed into horrors in the spiritual world, 819
punishment in hell as necessary to extinguish the way of life acquired from acts of hatred, 815
self-love and materialism as forms of hatred, 33, 251:1, 694, 760, 911:3
those who hate as killing in their hearts, 374:1, 374:3
venom meaning hatred, 251:1
Havilah, 110, 115
Hazor, 382:4
Head, 172, 447
the head and face as having to do with our heavenly and spiritual qualities, 259:1
head meaning the highest things, 247
the snake's head meaning the tyranny of evil and self-love, 250, 257
Hearing (rumor)
door meaning hearing the message, 652, 656
faith being gained through hearing, 654
hearers meaning those who have faith, 367:2
the relationship between hearing and intellectual activity, 656
rumor meaning properties of the intellect, 623:2
the sensitive hearing of spirits, 322:1
Heart, 148, 170, 318. *See also* Pulse
the church compared to the heart, 468:2, 637:1
the earliest people assigning heavenly things to the heart's province, 418:2
hard-heartedness meaning no happiness in marriage love, 162:2
the heart meaning the will, 105
heavenly angels belonging to the province of the heart in the universal human, 418:2
the marriage of the heart and lungs, 418:2
Heat. *See also* Coldness; Summer; Warmth
being hot meaning having a wealth of charity, 934:1
cold and heat meaning the condition of a regenerating person, 933, 935:1, 936
heat coming from the Lord through our inner self, 933:3
heat meaning a challenge to the will, 739:2
heat meaning faith and charity, 933, 934

Heaven, 162:1, 300, 661:1, 661:3. *See also* Angel; Church, heavenly; Heavenly; Hell; Joy; Kingdom, the Lord's; The Lord; Spirit, good; Universal human; World of spirits
admission to heaven
acknowledgment of our own nature as necessary for, 189
as gradual for believers, 316, 317
as immediate for some, 317, 318, 319
as impossible for those carrying desires and delusions from the world, 542
often happening after a period of time in the world of spirits, 319
simplistic ideas of, 453
some innocence necessary for, 164
as up to the Lord alone, 537
all joy and happiness in heaven coming from the Lord alone, 552
the ancient heavens of heavens meaning the wisdom of the earliest church, 219
auras of love and faith clearly perceived in heaven, 925:2
beautiful clothes in heaven, 165, 297
the belief that
entry to heaven is through a door, 453
heaven is our being high up, 450
heaven is our being the greatest, 452
heaven is leisure and being waited on, 454, 455
heavenly joy is praising and celebrating the Lord, 456
heavenly joy is standing inside a glorious ring of light, 455
misfortune, poverty, and renunciation of pleasure are necessary for admission to heaven, 892:1
Canaan meaning heaven, 1, 115
communication of all feelings and thoughts in heaven, 549
communities in heaven (*see* Community: heavenly communities)
contact between humankind and heaven
angels providing, 50:1–2, 697
the church providing, 931:1
as necessary for our survival, 637:2, 661:3, 687
countless kinds of happiness in heaven, 457
the design of heaven consisting of balance, 689

Heaven *(continued)*
  each individual in heaven communicating joy to all others, 549
  the earliest people living together in heaven, 483:2
  the faith acknowledged in heaven, 5
  the first heaven, 544
    good spirits inhabiting, 684
  the greatest in heaven being the one who is least, 452
  harmony in heaven, 457, 545:1, 687
  heaven and heavenly joy, 449–459, 537–546, 547–553
  heaven as different for each person, 457, 690, 692
  heaven as mutual love, 537, 547, 916:2
  heaven called the "universal human," 550, 911:2
  heaven forming a single human being, 550, 684, 694, 911:2
  a heaven meaning a regenerate person, 29:2, 911:2
  heaven meaning the inner self, 16, 24:3, 82, 89, 477:3, 911:2, 931:3
  heavenly choirs, 418:2
  the heavenly marriage (*see* Marriage: the heavenly marriage)
  "the heavens and the earth were completed" meaning our having become spiritual, 82
  the heavens as not pure in the Lord's sight, 633
  the heavens meaning the truth that we understand and the good that we will, 661:3
  heaven's sense of self, 252
  humankind's direct communication with heaven, 609, 784, 920:3
  immersion in bodily and worldly concerns closing the path to heaven, 69
  Jerusalem meaning heaven, 1
  Jesus Christ acknowledged and revered as Lord throughout heaven, 14
  the Lord alone ruling heaven, 548:1
  the Lord as the only Father known in heaven, 15
  the Lord governing all of heaven as a single individual, 911:2
  the Lord organizing all of heaven according to differences in love and faith, 111
  love as the life of heaven, 32:2
  a new heaven meaning the inner self of regenerate people, 931:3
  our becoming an image of heaven after regeneration, 911:1–2
  our bond with heaven, 530:1, 661:3
  Paradise meaning heaven, 1, 63
  perception in heaven, 483:1, 483:2, 536, 925:2
  perception of goodness and truth as the main influence in heaven, 483:1
  a person as a miniature heaven, 644, 911:2
  the richness of the Word's inner meaning as perceived in heaven, 167
  the second heaven, 167, 459, 684
  spirits taught about heaven and its joy, 314, 537, 540, 541, 542, 543, 544
  stretching out the heavens meaning regeneration, 25
  the third heaven
    angels as inhabiting, 634:2, 684
    richness of perception of angels in, 167
  the three heavens, 459, 544, 684, 911:2
    as clearly distinguished from each other, 634:2, 684
    presenting the image of a single person, 911:2
  unprepared spirits trying to enter heaven, 538, 539, 546
  visitors to heaven having their bodily desires and delusions put to sleep, 542
  the whole of heaven and its individual inhabitants tracing their origin to the Lord, 551
Heavenly, 51, 89, 296, 414:1, 418:2, 643:1, 886:1. *See also* Church, earliest; Church, heavenly; Goodness, heavenly; Heaven; Heavenly-spiritual; Spiritual
  the ark meaning the Lord and heavenly things, 308, 666:5, 878:7
  the autonomy of a heavenly person, 141, 633, 780
  bread meaning heavenly food, 623:1, 680
  charity as heavenly, 353
  a curse meaning turning away from what is heavenly, 245, 269, 379, 927
  the earliest church representing the heavenly kingdom, 483:2
  the formation of a heavenly person, 89
  a fruit tree meaning a heavenly person, 776:2

the Garden of Eden meaning a heavenly person, 79, 99, 122
Genesis 2 dealing with the heavenly person, 81
God's work meaning a heavenly person, 84
heavenly angelic spirits compared to spiritual angelic spirits, 201, 459
heavenly angels (*see* Angel: heavenly angels)
"heavenly" as having to do with love for the Lord, 61, 847:2
heavenly church (*see* Church, heavenly)
heavenly communities (*see* Community: heavenly communities)
heavenly goodness (*see* Goodness, heavenly)
heavenly joy (*see* Joy: heavenly joy)
the heavenly level of a human being, 880:2
the heavenly marriage (*see* Marriage: the heavenly marriage)
heavenly perception, 805:3, 865:2
heavenly people, 47, 73, 75, 80, 110, 117:2, 126, 162, 197, 288, 865:2
　acknowledging that everything is the Lord's, 123, 141, 633
　acknowledging the Lord's mercy, 598:2
　the autonomy of, 141, 633, 780
　being in the company of angels, 99
　being led by the Lord, 139
　blessed with inner peace, 85:3, 91
　compared to spiritual people and lifeless people, 81
　concentrating on the Lord, 81, 85:3, 337
　enjoying only heavenly food, 56
　as free from conflict, 81, 84, 87, 93
　the inner life of, 99, 121
　the intelligence (understanding) of, 98, 121
　knowing of no faith separate from love, 32:2, 81:1, 202, 393, 459
　perception in, 80, 81:1, 81:3, 99
　proceeding from love, 52, 53, 81, 83, 337, 459
　recognizing truth on the basis of goodness, 511
　ruling from the inner self, 52, 89, 91, 95, 159, 243
　thoughts, words, and deeds lying open in, 99
　a heavenly person as a Sabbath, 84–88, 666:1
　the heavenly plane coming from the Lord, 775:2, 880:2

the heavenly quality (aspect) of faith, 117:2, 402:1–3, 411–413, 420:2, 612:3
the heavenly quality (aspect) of love, 353:2, 886:1, 925:3
heavenly seed, 29, 268, 310:1, 653:2, 726
heavenly spirits, 318, 459
heavenly things as having to do with the will, 61
"human" meaning a heavenly person, 288, 565
a likeness meaning a heavenly person, 51, 52, 85:2, 288, 469, 472, 473
the members of the earliest church having a heavenly character (*see* Church, earliest)
the morning meaning a heavenly person, 86
mountains as having to do with heavenly things, 793, 795
our becoming heavenly when love takes charge, 12
our senses unable to teach us about heavenly matters, 128
the proper hierarchy being heavenly, spiritual, earthly, and then bodily concerns, 911
a royal offspring meaning a heavenly person, 337:2
the seventh day meaning a heavenly person, 74, 84, 85, 86, 87, 395:1
the whole of heaven as a heavenly person, 162 (*see also* Universal human)
Heavenly-spiritual, 282, 353:2. See also Heavenly; Spiritual
　clothes meaning heavenly-spiritual good and earthly good, 297
　heavenly-spiritual people, 143, 161, 200, 282
Hebrew, 618
　Hebrew words distinguishable as heavenly or spiritual by sound, 793
Heel
　heel meaning what is bottommost on the earthly level, 250, 259:1
　the name Jacob coming from the word for heel, 259:1
Height, 273. See also Dimension
　height meaning holiness, 795:5
　the height of Noah's ark meaning the remnant's goodness, 650
　the idea of height causing the earliest people to think of heaven and the Lord, 920:1

Height *(continued)*
  the Lord said to dwell in the heights and called the Highest One, 920:1
  the origin of worship on high places, 796
Hell, 278, 279, 316, 692–700, 814–823, 824–831, 845:2, 938–946. *See also* Demon; Devil; Evil; Gehenna; Heaven; Punishment; Spirit, evil; Torture
  abyss meaning hell, 756:2, 845:2
  the appearances of the hells, 756:2, 819
  the damnation of all as the whole effort of hell, 694
  a different hell for each person, 457, 692
  a different hell for every variety of hatred, 693, 816
  the effort to dominate being part of hell's influence, 905
  the evil and falsity of bodily life turning into the hallucinations and punishments of hell, 868:2
  evil as what condemns us and drags us to hell, 845:1
  hell consisting of hatred for the Lord and our neighbor, 693
  hell forming a single devil, 694
  hell meaning the underground realm, 247
  the hells of deceivers and witches, 830–831
  the hells of the greedy, 938, 939, 940
  the hells of those who spent their lives in adultery and lechery, 824–829
  the hells of those who spent their lives in hatred, revenge, and cruelty, 814–823
  the Lord never sending anyone to hell, 696
  the Lord turning all punishment in hell to some good use, 696
  miser's hells, the foul Jerusalem, and the hells of those who pursued sensual pleasure, 938–946
  our throwing ourselves into hell if the Lord did not hold us back from evil and falsity, 789, 929
  our will causing us to rush toward hell, 35
  pain experienced in hell, 322:1, 829:1, 831:3
  people, spirits, and angels rushing toward hell on their own, 868:1
  Swedenborg's education in the spiritual world regarding hell, 5, 699
Helping. *See* Service
Heredity, 828
  hereditary evil causing the deterioration of churches, 494:2
  hereditary evil growing in each succeeding generation, 313
  inherited evil coming from sins committed by parents, 313, 494:2
  inherited evil made harmless through regeneration, 313
  inherited evil not coming from Adam, 313, 494:2
  inherited evil not loosened by goodness from the Lord, 719
  inherited evil remaining after regeneration, 868:1
  our inherited evil and the way we live our lives determining the nature of the Lord's mercy, 633
Heresy, 324, 332, 337, 442, 794:1. *See also* Irad; Lamech; Mehujael; Methushael; Schism; Teaching
  ground meaning a heresy (schism), 330, 373, 377, 380, 381
  heresies arising wherever a church exists, 362
  the heresy called Cain, 409
  the heresy called Enoch, 331, 399, 401, 404
  names meaning heresies and doctrines, 402, 404, 468:1
  one heresy spontaneously producing another heresy, 400, 401
Hiddekel. *See also* Eden; River
  the river Hiddekel meaning the ability to reason, 118
Hiding, 165, 193, 213, 224, 226, 414:1
  being hidden from your [Jehovah's] face meaning to be cut off from the good inherent in a loving faith, 385, 387
  hiding themselves from Jehovah's face meaning fearing an inner dictate, 218, 222
Hill, 795:2
History (narrative)
  the earliest people's manner of writing being to assemble symbols into a history (narrative), 66:1, 403, 605
  historical accuracy in the Word's literal meaning, 66:2, 482:1, 755:4, 755:5
  the Word's appearance as unpolished history in its literal meaning, 855
Hittite, 289
Holiness
  firstborn of the flock meaning holiness, 350, 352

height meaning holiness, 795:5
holiness and justice as the heavenly aspect of faith, 612:3
the Holy Supper, 276:1
the number three indicating holiness because of the Lord's resurrection on the third day, 720, 901:1, 901:4, 901:5
the seventh month meaning holiness, 852
the twenty-seventh day meaning holiness, 901:1

Homer *(unit of measurement)*, 576:1
Honesty (honor, respectability), 825, 831:1. *See also* Uprightness
those who are outwardly honest, 821:1
Honey, 195:3, 680:5
Honor. *See* Honesty; Uprightness
Horror, 50:3, 828. *See also* Fear
Horse, 187, 188, 828
horses meaning the rational level, 574:2
House (household), 162:1. *See also* Family
the earliest people living divided into households, clans, and nations, 470, 471, 483:2
house (household) meaning the will, 710
house meaning a church, or the mind of someone in the church, 710
the Jewish church living divided into households, clans, and tribes, 471
Human being (humankind, ourselves, person), 306, 594. *See also* The Divine-Human One; Heavenly: heavenly people; Human race; Humanity; Spiritual; Universal human
Adam as the human's name, meaning "ground," 566:1
the deeper plane in humans distinguishing us from animals, 714
Enosh meaning person (a human being), 336, 439, 477:4
the first human, 4, 313
forming a human, dirt from the ground, meaning to form our outer self, which was not previously human, 94
heavenly people acquiring their humanity from the Lord, 288
the Hebrew word *adam* meaning "a human," 478
the human and his wife
meaning the earliest church, 338, 339
meaning the new church previously symbolized by Adah and Zillah, 434, 435, 436
"human being" and "son of humankind" meaning the Lord, 49:2
a human being meaning love and charity, or the totality of the church, 768:3
"the human died" meaning perception ceased to exist, 492, 494
human (human being)
meaning a heavenly church, 477:1, 565
meaning a heavenly person, 288, 565
meaning an individual of the earliest church, 288
meaning goodness coming from love, 776:3
meaning love of goodness, 477:3
meaning the actual nature of something, 810
meaning the earliest church, 137, 277, 288, 313, 338, 461, 477
meaning the Lord or his qualities, 49:1, 288
the human, Seth, and Enosh constituting the earliest church, 502, 505
from human to animal to creeping thing to the bird of the heavens meaning the nature of the evil of the descendants of the earliest church, 810
from human to beast to creeping animal meaning whatever was in the will of the earliest church's descendants would annihilate them, 594
"the human was made into a living soul" meaning our outer self brought to life, 94
humanity meaning those who possess faith, 477:4
humankind
meaning the pre-Flood people, 565
meaning the spiritual being, 55:1
humans as animals, 714
humans as dead on their own, 39:1
humans as lower than animals, 637:2
humans as organs designed to receive life, 149:2
humans as spirits clothed with flesh, 69, 447
humans before regeneration consisting of cravings and distortions, 59:1
humans containing nothing but evil and falsity, 39:1
humans living opposite to the pattern ordained for them, 637:2
humans plunging headlong into destruction of themselves and everyone else if left on their own, 637:2
humans' survival depending on a connection with the Lord, 637:2, 687, 697

Human being *(continued)*
  the Lord appearing as a human being to the earliest people, 49:1
  the Lord as the only human, 49:1, 477:1, 565, 768:3
  the Lord creating us able to communicate with spirits and angels, 69
  our humanity depending on
    a life of love, 95
    love and faith from the Lord, 714
    loving belief in the Lord, 477:1
    the remnant, 530:2, 565
    the will to do good and the comprehension of truth, 306
  people who are spiritually dead as no longer human, 270
  "person" and "humankind" meaning those who are wise, or who acknowledge and believe, 303:2
  a person as a miniature heaven, 644, 911:2
  person meaning someone in the church, 477:4
  the pre-Flood people going from being human to being nonhuman, 240
  the prophets seeing the Lord as a human being, 49:3
Human race. *See also* The Divine-Human One; Human being; Humanity
  the human race meeting its end if the church died, 636, 637:1
  humans needing constant connection with the Lord to survive, 637:2
  the Lord foreseeing how the human race could be saved, 598:1
  the Lord's Coming preventing the human race's destruction, 581, 631, 637:2
Humanity, 477:1. *See also* The Divine-Human One; Human being; Human race
  anything coming from the Lord appearing human in the spiritual world, 41
Humankind. *See* Human being; Human race; Humanity
Hundred. *See* One hundred fifty; One hundred thirty; One hundred twenty; Three hundred; Three hundred sixty-five
Husband, 827, 829:2. *See also* Man; Marriage; Wife
  husband meaning the Lord, 289
  husband meaning the rational capacity, 261, 265
  true marriage involving one husband and one wife, 865:2

I

Idea (concept, mental image), 608. *See also* Fact; Image; Knowledge; Thought
  all ideas shared in the spiritual world, 315
  desires as clinging to ideas, 582
  each of our ideas as an image of us, 803:2
  the earliest people speaking in ideas, 607:2
  every concept containing something of both intellect and will, 590
  every idea coming from outside, 150
  every mental image of an angelic spirit as alive, 41
  ideas as the means of communication in the spiritual world, 582
  ideas coming through the outer self rather than through the inner self, 608
  keen perception in the spiritual world regarding ideas, 301
  profane images and holy images clinging together in our mind, 301, 582
  spirits being recognizable by their ideas, 803:2, 821:2
Identity. *See* Character; Selfhood
Idleness. *See* Leisure
Idol, 847:3, 878:8. *See also* Sculpture
  idols meaning falsities, 424
  representations lacking inner meaning as idolatrous, 349:1, 409, 639:2, 716:3, 921:4, 922:1
  wooden idols meaning appetites (cravings), 643:3, 643:4
Ignorance (lack of understanding). *See also* Simplicity
  darkness meaning ignorance regarding faith, 17
  the innocence of those who are ignorant about truth and goodness, 593
  those who live in ignorance as unable to profane holy things, 661:1
  the widespread lack of understanding regarding the blessings and happiness of heaven, 540, 547
Illness
  bodily illness taking the place of spiritual struggles, 762
  the outer self subsiding during illness, 268, 762, 857:2
Illumination. *See* Light

Illusion (fallacy). *See also* Delusion; Falsity
fallacies coming from believing the Word's literal meaning, 735
the Lord bending our illusions and cravings toward goodness and truth, 24:3, 25, 868:2, 887

Image (prefiguration, symbol), 50. *See also* Appearance; Idea; Likeness
the custom of the earliest people to express everything through representative images, 403
God's image meaning spiritual people, 12, 48, 51, 473
"God's image" referring to love, 53
"his image" referring to faith, 53
an image compared to a likeness, 51, 473, 481, 484
our becoming an image of heaven when we have regenerated, 911:1–2
our becoming God's image on the sixth day, 62
our becoming images of hell when the proper hierarchy of heavenly, spiritual, earthly, and bodily concerns is destroyed, 911:1, 911:3
the representative or prefigurative forms in the church symbolizing the Lord, 308:1

Imagination. *See* Delusion

Impulse. *See* Will

Incense, 925:3. *See also* Fragrance; Frankincense

Independence. *See* Self; Selfhood

Infant (baby, little child, toddler), 154, 164, 814:2. *See also* Child; Innocence
an angel appearing as a little child, 546
babies, toddlers, and children meaning three levels of love, 430:1
our first stage extending from infancy to just before regeneration, 7
a toddler in the street meaning newborn truth, 655:2
toddlers and children meaning innocence and charity, 430:2

Inflow. *See* Influence; Influx

Influence (coming in, entering, flowing in, inflow, influx). *See also* Influx
freedom as an aspect of the Lord's influence, 905
hell's influence involving domination, 905
influence from spirits and angels entering the human brain, 641
the influence of angelic spirits compared to that of evil spirits, 641
the influence of the angelic heavens on the world of spirits, 730:5
influx from evil spirits compared to a flood, 660, 705, 787
the inner being's influence on the outer being, 161
Jehovah's spirit meaning an inflow of truth and goodness, 573
the Lord entering heavenly people through love and spiritual people through faith, 99
the Lord flowing into the things we understand, then into our rational mind, and then into the facts stored in our memory, 99, 657
our life depending on inflow from the Lord, 657
truth and good coming from the Lord through the inner self, 27

Influx. *See also* Influence
influx as acquiring evil and falsity from the hells and goodness and truth from the Lord, 904:3
influx as our receiving life from the Lord through our heavenly level, 880:2
influx as the connection between the soul and the body, 657, 904:3

Inherited evil. *See* Heredity

Injury, those who enjoy causing, 822

Inner being. *See* Being, inner

Inner church. *See* Church, inner

Inner meaning. *See* Meaning, inner

Inner self. *See* Being, inner

Inner voice. *See* Conscience; Voice

Innocence, 163, 165, 430, 540, 544, 546. *See also* Child; Infant; Nakedness; Simplicity
charity and innocence, 430
innocence almost eliminating evil and falsity, 164
innocence impossible without love and charity, 430:1
the innocence of ignorance, 593
the innocent appearing like children in the spiritual world, 154, 165
lamb meaning innocence and love, 430:1
a little child meaning innocence, 430:1
the Lord infusing our selfhood (self-direction) with innocence, 136, 164, 252

Innocence *(continued)*
  no one let into heaven without some innocence, 164
  states of innocence in the three heavens, 544
  "they were naked and did not blush" meaning they were innocent, 163, 165
Insight. *See* Intelligence; Knowledge
Instruction (education, teaching), 206, 245, 895. *See also* Teaching
  Enoch meaning teach, 519:1
  humans no longer able to receive instruction through the inner self, 608, 609
  ideas from doctrine providing a framework for instruction, 608
  "make" and "clothe" meaning instruction, 292
Instrument, 420
  each musical instrument having its own symbolism, 420:1, 420:4
  a harp meaning spiritual truth, 419
  heavenly aspects of faith celebrated by wind instruments, 420:2
  an organ meaning spiritual good, 419
  spiritual choirs sounding like stringed instruments, 418:2
  stringed instruments meaning the spiritual qualities of faith, 418:1
Integrity. *See* Honesty; Uprightness
Intellect (understanding), 48, 398. *See also* Intelligence; Mind; Reason; Will
  the belief that the intellect makes a person human, 477:1
  birds and fish as having to do with the intellect, 40:1, 44, 52, 673, 674
  faith truly understood following faith consisting of memorized facts, 30:2
  intellect and will (*see also* Will: will and intellect)
    forming one mind in the earliest people, 927:2 (*see also* Church, earliest: the earliest people)
    kept separate in spiritual people, 895:1 (*see also* Spiritual)
    as our two basic faculties, 35
  the intellect of the people called Noah, 641, 645, 757, 927 (*see also* Church, ancient; Noah)
  intellect reigning in the male sex, 568:2
  intellectual information coming from spirits and angels, 641
  the life of the intellect as made of every falsity that we adopt, 794:2
  the Lord flowing into what we understand, then into what we grasp rationally, and then into the facts we know, 99, 657
  male meaning the intellect, 54, 476
  matters of understanding
    symbolized by the top compartments in the ark, 657
    symbolized by the top row of windows in the Temple at Jerusalem, 655:2, 658
  our mind being united when the will rules the intellect, 35
  "the smaller light" (faith) being placed in our intellect, 30:3
  spiritual angels using intellectual concepts to confirm their religious beliefs, 203
  spiritual people's intellect as the ground where truth is sown, 895:1
  spiritual things as having to do with our intellect, 61
  the three levels of the human intellect as factual knowledge, reason, and true understanding, 657
  trials involving the intellect, 653:1, 702, 734, 735, 749, 751:2, 753, 757
  window meaning the intellect (understanding), 602, 642, 651, 652, 653:2, 655, 658, 863
Intelligence (insight, understanding), 34:1, 110, 306. *See also* Intellect; Mind; Reason; Wisdom
  an artisan meaning one who is wise, understanding, or knowledgeable, 424
  being thrown out of Eden meaning being deprived of understanding and wisdom, 305–307
  "desirable for lending insight" meaning sensual pleasure, 207, 209
  on the east of the Garden of Eden meaning a heavenly quality from which an intelligent understanding comes, 306
  Ephraim meaning an intelligent understanding of truth, 264:1, 382:3, 870:3
  the four rivers from Eden meaning intelligence, 107
  garden meaning intelligence (understanding), 98, 100, 305
  the garden on the east in Eden meaning the intelligence of heavenly people, 77, 98

the intelligence of heavenly people, 98, 121
Israel meaning the ability to understand, 119
knowledge and intelligence of heavenly
    angels, 34:1
leaf meaning intelligence, 57
the rational capacity imitating an intelligent
    understanding, 265
spiritual people feeling their intelligence
    comes from themselves, 99
those left to their own devices as lacking
    understanding, 214
Interconnection. *See* Connection
Interval. *See* Time
Inundation. *See* Flood
Investigating. *See* Examining
Irad, 404
Iron
    iron meaning a somewhat deep spiritual
        quality, 643:1
    iron meaning earthly truth, 421, 425, 426
Ishmael, 340
Israel, 665, 730:4, 795:3. *See also* Church, Jewish; Jacob
    the children of Israel meaning regenerate
        people, 842:5, 901:4
    the cities of Judah and Israel meaning all
        doctrinal teachings as a whole, 402:3
    the elders of Israel meaning heavenly people,
        121
    "the house of Israel" and "the people Israel"
        meaning the early Christian church,
        477:2
    Israel meaning a spiritual being, 55:1
    Israel meaning a spiritual church, 710, 768:2
    Israel meaning the ability to understand, 119
    Israel meaning the inner church, 422
    the Lord called "the God of Israel," 300,
        308:1, 489:2
    the twelve tribes of Israel, 493, 577

J

Jabal
    Jabal meaning holy love and the resulting
        good actions, 412, 413, 416, 436
    Jabal meaning the heavenly aspects of a new
        church, 333
Jacob, 940:2. *See also* Church, Jewish; Israel
    Esau and Jacob meaning the brotherhood of
        charity and faith, 367
    the Holy One of Jacob meaning the Lord,
        489:2
    Jacob meaning the Jewish church, 259:1, 422
    Jacob meaning the outer church, 768:2
    Jacob wanting to supplant Esau, 367:2
    the name Jacob coming from the word for
        heel, 259:1
Japheth. *See* Shem, Ham, and Japheth
Jared
    Jared meaning the sixth church descended
        from the earliest church, 463, 510, 513
    the nature of the church called Jared, 514, 515
Javelin, 878:6
Jehovah, 99, 292, 340, 354, 396:1, 398, 531, 573,
    576:1, 795:3, 921:1, 925. *See also* God; The
    Lord
    actions being attributed to Jehovah, 926
    calling on the name of Jehovah meaning
        worship from charity, 440
    the day of Jehovah meaning devastation,
        488:3
    human traits frequently used to describe
        Jehovah's attributes, 588–589, 592:1
    "I have acquired the man Jehovah" meaning
        faith among those called Cain acknowledged as a thing in itself, 338, 340, 429
    invoking Jehovah's name as common to all
        worship of the Lord, 440, 441
    Jehovah as being, 300, 630, 708, 726, 840,
        926
    Jehovah as existence and life itself, 840
    Jehovah as present in our love and charity,
        709, 840
    Jehovah as the fountain of mercy, peace, and
        goodness, 245
    Jehovah foreseeing everything from eternity,
        587:1
    Jehovah God meaning the Lord, 269
        and also heaven, 298, 300
    Jehovah (Jehovah God) never angry at or
        cursing anyone, 245, 269, 357, 588:1, 592:1
    "Jehovah said" meaning a thing happens in
        this way, 708, 926
    Jehovah's face meaning mercy, 222–223, 224,
        358, 387
    Jehovah's inquiries as an opportunity for
        confession, 226
    Jehovah's spirit meaning truth and goodness
        flowing in, 573

Jehovah *(continued)*
  the name Jehovah
    coming from beingness, 300
    as sacred, 624
    used when the topic is charity, 709, 840
    used when the topic is the will or love, 709
    used where a church exists, 624
  the name Jehovah God first used in the Word when a heavenly person is discussed, 89, 300
  the voice of Jehovah (Jehovah speaking), 218, 219
    meaning conscience, 219, 359, 360, 371
    meaning perception, 370, 371
  walking with Jehovah meaning living a life of love, 519:1, 519:3
Jehovih. *See* The Lord Jehovih
Jerusalem. *See also* New Jerusalem
  the hell called the foul Jerusalem, 940
  Jerusalem meaning heaven, 1
  Jerusalem meaning the spiritual aspects of faith, 402:2
  "Jerusalem the Holy" meaning the Lord's kingdom, 402:1
Jesus Christ, revered as Lord in heaven, 14. *See also* The Lord
Jew, 276:2, 302, 303, 308, 353, 447, 716:3, 788:2, 824, 908:3, 940, 941. *See also* Church, Jewish; Israel; Jacob; Judah
The Jewish church. *See* Church, Jewish
The Jewish religion. *See* Church, Jewish
Jonah, 901:4
Jordan, 901:4
Joshua, 878:6, 878:7
  Joshua representing the Lord, 901:4
Jot, 2
Joy, 457. *See also* Happiness; Pleasure
  all joy and happiness in heaven coming from the Lord alone, 552
  all joy as resulting from love, 33
  the belief that heavenly joy
    is being at leisure, 454
    is not affected by one's life in the world, 547
    is our being the greatest, 452
    is praising and celebrating the Lord, 456
    is standing inside a glorious ring of light, 455
  heaven and heavenly joy, 449–459, 537–546, 547–553

  heavenly joy, 545
    bodily pleasure compared to, 540, 541, 545:2
    as the joy of shared love, 537, 547, 549
    levels of, 543
    our most profound joy as our, 543
    our not knowing what heavenly joy is, 449, 537, 538, 540, 541, 547
    spirits learning the nature of, 537, 540, 541, 543, 544
    Swedenborg permitted to experience, 545
    as unique to each individual, 690
    an unprepared spirit suffering from experiencing, 537
  joy coming from a life of love for the Lord, 33
  joy in serving others as the nature of love, 548:3
Jubal
  Jubal meaning the spiritual aspects of a new church, 333, 417
  Jubal meaning the spiritual gift of faith, 436
Judah
  Judah meaning a heavenly church, 768:2, 795:5
  the name Judah meaning "This time I will acclaim Jehovah," 340
Judgment. *See also* Last Judgment
  the city in hell called Gehenna's Judgment, 942
  exercising judgment meaning being wise, 158
  integrity and judgment meaning the spiritual aspect that develops out of the heavenly aspect of faith, 612:3
  judgment meaning the things advocated by truth, 612:1
Justice
  holiness and justice as the heavenly aspect of faith, 612:3
  "just" as having to do with the goodness involved in charity, 612, 615, 712, 922:3
  justice meaning goodness flowing from charity, 922:3
  justice meaning the things urged by good, 612:1

K

Kenan, 507
Kenan meaning the fourth church, 463, 500
Kidneys, 348, 353:1
  the fat of the kidneys of wheat, 353:3

Killing (murder), 374:1, 374:3, 389
  Cain's murder of Abel meaning charity destroyed by those who detached faith from it, 329, 366, 369, 436, 916:3
  evil and falsity as what kill a person, 389
  evil people constantly fearing murder, 390
Kind, 29:1, 42:1. *See also* Category
Kindness. *See* Charity
King. *See* Monarch
Kingdom, the Lord's (God's kingdom), 49:4
  the garden in Eden meaning the Lord's kingdom, 99
  the Holy City meaning the Lord's kingdom, 402:1
  the Lord's kingdom consisting in mutual love, 916:2
  the meaning in the Word of "God's kingdom," 29:2
  New Jerusalem meaning the Lord's kingdom in heaven and on earth, 648:1, 935:3, 940:1
  our having the Lord's kingdom inside us when we act from charity, 916:2
Knowledge (insight), 24:1, 27, 678. *See also* Acknowledgment; Fact; Intelligence; Reason
  depending on knowledge for belief, 229
  a distinction made between religious knowledge and secular knowledge, 24:1
  eating meaning knowing, 125, 304
  enlightenment coming from charity rather than religious knowledge, 854
  Ethiopians meaning religious knowledge, 117:1
  the face of the water meaning knowledge of truth and goodness, 19
  faith as more than knowledge and acknowledgment of doctrines, 36, 654, 896
  faith as the container of religious knowledge, 620
  the fruit of the tree from which they were to eat meaning religious knowledge, 199
  knowledge of goodness and truth, 78, 116, 380, 382, 420:4
    conscience as formed from, 310:2
    our awareness of, 24:1
    the pre-Flood people withheld from, 285
    the remnant as, 19, 561, 711
    stored with secular facts in our memory, 27
    those in the spiritual world receiving, 188, 189
  knowledge replacing perception, 125
  the knowledge that truth and good come from the Lord, 27
  the Lord giving us charity through knowledge of faith, 393
  love providing heavenly angels with all religious knowledge, 34:1
  "morning" as having to do with truth and religious knowledge, 22
  the regenerate person finding pleasure and nourishment in religious knowledge, 12
  religious insights as necessary for good actions, 44
  religious knowledge involving both truth and goodness, 419
  the remnant as religious knowledge stored away, 8, 19
  seas meaning a body of religious and secular knowledge, 28
  spiritual angels being led to charity by religious knowledge, 459
  "spiritual" as having to do with religious knowledge, 61
  waters meaning religious and secular knowledge, 28

L

Labor. *See* Work
Lakes (ponds), in hell, 819, 820, 941
Lamb, 922:1
  lamb meaning innocence and love, 430:1
  lamb meaning positive feelings, 143, 715
  lambs as good animals, symbolizing good things in us, 45
Lamech
  Adah and Zillah as the wives of Lamech, 409
  charity dying out in the church called Lamech, 384
  the church called Lamech passing away right before the Flood, 533
  the church destroyed by those called Lamech, 441
  Lamech as a church devastated, 526, 527, 532
  Lamech meaning devastation or the absence of faith, 405, 406, 427, 428, 527
  Lamech meaning the ninth church, 465, 523, 526
  Lamech's wives meaning a new church, 409, 427

Lamech *(continued)*
  no faith remaining in the church called
    Lamech, 332, 409
  no perception remaining in the church
    called Lamech, 467, 526, 527
  two different churches called Lamech, 485
Lameness, 210
Lamp
  lamps meaning heavenly attributes that yield
    spiritual attributes, 886:2
  lamps meaning holy love, 716:4
Lampstand, 552
  lampstand meaning the Lord, 716:4, 886:2
Land. *See* Earth; Ground
Lantern, 716:5
Last Judgment
  the belief that the end of the earth is the
    same as the Last Judgment, 931:2, 931:3
  the last judgment of the earliest church as
    when it perished, 931:2
  the last judgment of the Jewish church as
    when the Lord came into the world,
    931:2
  the numbers three and seven as holy because
    of their connection with the Last Judg-
    ment, 900
  there being a last judgment
    for each person, 900, 931:3
    for every church when it is devastated, 931:2
    when the Lord came into the world, 900,
      931:2
Law, 568:2. *See also* Command
  the Law and the Prophets meaning the
    teachings of faith and the Word, 36
  the law for marriage, 162:1, 266
  the laws of the Lord's kingdom as all
    founded on the law to love the Lord and
    one's neighbor, 548:1
  laws ordaining what is true and right having
    heavenly origins, 162:1, 266
Laziness. *See* Leisure
Leading (guidance), 24:3
  angels giving us guidance, 50:3, 300
  freedom as being led by the Lord, 892:2, 905
  heavenly people being led by the Lord, 139
  "my yoke is mild" meaning the Lord's gentle
    leading after regeneration, 905
  our desire to lead ourselves, 132, 138, 139, 205
  self-love having a desire to be led by oneself
    rather than the Lord, 205

  a shepherd meaning one who leads and
    teaches, 343
  "you will be like God" meaning being able
    to lead themselves, 204
Leaf. *See also* Plant
  leaf meaning intelligence, 57
  leaf meaning truth, 884, 885
  leaf said to serve as medicine, 57, 885:1
  leaves meaning the doctrinal precepts pre-
    served in the Jewish church, 885:2
  sewing leaves together meaning to make
    excuses, 216
Leah
  Leah meaning the Jewish church, 422
  Leah meaning the outer church of the Jew-
    ish church, 409, 422
Learning. *See* Knowledge
Leather tunic, 282, 292, 294, 295, 297
Leaving father and mother, meaning leaving
  the inner being behind, 160
Lebanon, 886:2
Lechery, 824–829
Left, 886:2
  intellectual information from angels coming
    into the left side of the brain, 641, 644
Leisure (laziness), 944
  heaven believed to be a life of leisure, 454
Length, 488:2. *See also* Dimension
  length meaning something holy, when
    ascribed to distance, 650
  length of time meaning what lasts to eter-
    nity, 650
Leopard, 430:1
Letter. *See* Meaning, literal
Level. *See also* Bodily; Earthly; Fact; Heavenly;
  Reason; The senses; Spiritual
  our seeing one confused whole rather than
    distinct levels of a human, 24:2
  three levels of the intellect, 655:2, 657, 658
Levi
  Levi meaning charity, 342
  Levi meaning love, 352
  the tribe of Levi as priests, 342, 352
Leviathan. *See* Sea creature
Liberty. *See* Freedom
Life (animate [quality]), 29:1, 30:2, 37, 41, 156,
  179, 657, 726. *See also* The other life
  an active life as essential to happiness, 454
  all life coming from the Lord, 32:2, 149:2,
    155, 657, 726

animals having life, 443
being given life meaning receiving the Lord's life, 726
the belief
  that life is in what we can sense and learn about, 657
  that life is located in the body, 443
  that living from the Lord is a fantasy, 206:2
  that the life of a spirit is vague, 443
  that we are alive on our own, 150
the body possessing no life, 447
breathing and breath meaning a life force, 97, 805:1
cravings and delusions as our life before regeneration, 59:1
the different appearance in the spiritual world of what is not alive from what is alive, 671
eternal life (living forever; *see also* Eternity)
  entry into, 182–189, 314–319
  as eternal happiness, 726
  life that is not eternal as not life, 726
  meaning eternal damnation, 304
  nothing being more important than our, 794:2
  spiritual conflict as necessary to attain, 59:2
  the steps by which we move from bodily life to, 168–189, 314
everything coming from the Lord having life, 41
everything containing life from the Lord as immensely fruitful, 43
everything seeming alive to the earliest people, 920:2
goodness and pleasure as the constituents of human life, 678
the Hebrew word for wild animal meaning a living being, 774, 841 (*see also* Animal, wild)
human selfhood as lifeless, 149:2, 150
humans as organs designed to receive life, 149:2
humans having a deeper plane of life than animals, 714
the inner being as what lives, 3
the land of the living meaning heaven, 290
life as a product of love, 32:2, 33
life as present in goodness but not in truth, 668
life as the purpose of rebirth, 848:1
life coming through faith in the Lord, 290

life consisting in sensation, 322:2
life flowing into us from the Lord, 657
life from the Lord giving us life after death, 714
the life in goodness coming from the Lord, 671
life in the outer self, 94, 95
the life of angels and spirits depending on their being part of a community, 687
the life of faith and love from the Lord differentiating us from animals, 714
the life of spirits, 320–323
lives meaning love and faith, 304
"the living" meaning believers, 290
a living soul meaning every animal in general, 670 (*see also* Animal)
a living soul meaning what comes from the Lord, 41
the Lord as life itself, 2, 20, 41, 290
the Lord as the only living being, 290
the Lord constantly breathing his life even into evil people, 714
the Lord's selfhood as life, 149:2
the meaning in the Word of "breath of lives," 76, 94, 661:3, 780
the nature of a love determining the nature of the resulting life, 33
no one lacking faith in the Lord can have life, 30:1
nothing that is ours having life, 39:1, 41
only a heavenly and spiritual life as real, 933:2
only one life force in existence, 290
our alternation during regeneration between no life and true life, 933:2
our doing evil in spite of living from the Lord, 233:2
our earlier way of life needing to be destroyed before we can be reborn, 848:1
our fate after death depending on our life in the world, 633, 687, 697
our having no life on our own, 150
our ignorance regarding spiritual or heavenly life, 17
our life built of the things we believe, 303:1
our life depending on a connection with the Lord through heaven and angels, 50:1, 687, 697
our living the same kind of life after death as before, 70, 316, 687

Life *(continued)*
  our receiving life
    from the Lord through faith, 30:2
    when we are reborn, 16, 39:2, 933:2
  our spirit as the living part of us, 447
  people who have love having faith and heavenly life, 34:2
  self-love and materialism producing an imitation of life, 33
  the tree of lives
    meaning love and the faith it leads to, 105
    taking from the tree of lives and eating, meaning learning about and acknowledging love and faith, 304
  truth acquiring its life from goodness, 678
  truth and goodness in unregenerate people as not living, 671
Lifting (raising), meaning the presence of charity, 358, 361, 363
Light, 31:2, 448:1. *See also* Half-light; Heat
  Ararat meaning a bit of light, 854
  the belief that heavenly joy consists in standing inside a glorious ring of light, 455
  brilliant light seen at resurrection, 186
  child of light meaning a spiritual person, 51
  everything of the Lord's belonging to the light, 21
  faith without love compared to light in winter, 34:2, 365
  faith's truths compared to rays of light, 854
  the great light meaning the Lord as the source of all love, 32:2
  the great lights meaning love and faith, 31:1, 32:1
  the greater light placed in our will and the smaller in our intellect, 30:3
  the greater light that rules by day meaning love, 30:2, 32, 709
  the Jewish church commanded to keep a light burning perpetually, 31:3
  lack of light in us before regeneration, 18, 19
  light called good because it is from the Lord, 21
  light meaning faith, 30–32, 34, 666:1
  light meaning our awareness that the Lord exists and that he is goodness and truth, 20
  light meaning the Lord's humanity, 32:2
  light meaning truth, 20, 22, 38, 519:2, 893:1, 896:1
  the light of heaven, 322:1

  lights meaning love and the faith that comes from love, 30:2, 31:1, 31:3
  love and faith compared to heat and light, 30:3, 34:2, 365
  a new light shining out when a church has been completely devastated, 408, 410
  the smaller light that rules by night meaning faith from love, 30:2, 32
  two lights meaning love and faith kindled in our inner self, 10, 39:1
Likeness. *See also* Appearance; Image
  the earliest people as likenesses of the Lord, 503
  God's likeness meaning the earliest church as a heavenly church, 461, 469
  a likeness as an exact copy, 51
  "likeness" as having to do with faith, 281
  a likeness meaning a heavenly person, 51, 52, 85:2, 288, 469, 472, 473
  "very good" meaning the Lord making us likenesses of himself, 63
Link. *See* Connection
Lion, 430:1
Lips of song, meaning a spiritual quality, 353:2
Literal meaning. *See* Meaning, literal
Livestock
  the father of livestock meaning good actions from holy love, 413, 415
Logic. *See* Reason; Sophistry
Loincloth. *See also* Clothes; Tunic
  making loincloths for themselves meaning to feel shame, 216, 224
Longing. *See* Craving; Desire; Emotion
The Lord, 31:3, 49:1, 54, 123, 141, 197, 425. *See also* Coming; The Divine-Human One; Faith; God; Goodness; Heaven; Heavenly; Influence; Influx; Jehovah; Jesus Christ; Resurrection, the Lord's
  all life coming from the Lord, 32:2, 149:2, 155, 657, 726
  all love coming from the Lord, 32:2 (*see also* Love)
  day (morning) meaning what is the Lord's, 21, 22
  a distinction between what is the Lord's and what is our own, 8
  east meaning the Lord, 98, 101, 920:4
  every aspect of the Word as having to do with the Lord, 1, 2, 771

everything that comes from the Lord having life, 41
genuine life as a life of love from the Lord, 33
goodness and truth coming from the Lord alone, 20, 24, 27, 29:1, 39
hatred putting a gulf between us and the Lord, 904:2
human traits often used to describe the Lord's attributes, 588–589, 592:1
Jehovah God meaning the Lord, 269, 300
joy and happiness in heaven coming from the Lord alone, 552 (*see also* Joy)
light called good because it is from the Lord, 21 (*see also* Light)
the Lord alone having true autonomy, 149:2 (*see also* Selfhood)
the Lord as closest during our trials though seeming absent, 840
the Lord as goodness and truth itself, 20, 24
the Lord as life itself, 2, 20, 41, 290 (*see also* Life)
the Lord as the essence and life of faith, 30:1, 256
the Lord as the fountain of mercy, peace, and goodness, 245
the Lord as the only human, 49:1, 477:1, 565, 768:3 (*see also* Human being)
the Lord at work during our trials, 63
the Lord called Redeemer, One-Who-Forms-from-the-Womb, Maker, and Creator, 16
the Lord constantly fighting on our behalf, 63
the Lord controlling and arranging absolutely everything, 592:1
the Lord entering into a compact with us when he regenerates us, 665 (*see also* Pact)
the Lord governing us through spirits and angels, 50:1, 50:3, 581:1
the Lord never angry or punishing, 245, 588:1, 592:1, 696
the Lord present with us to the extent that we love our neighbor and have faith, 904:2, 904:3
the Lord speaking to everyone, 904:1
the Lord working through our inner self, 857, 933:3 (*see also* Being, inner)
the Lord's human nature, 32:2, 256, 352, 414:4
the Lord's kingdom (*see* Kingdom, the Lord's)
the Lord's love for the earliest church, 414:4
the Lord's mercy as unknowable, 588:1 (*see also* Mercy)
the Lord's selfhood as life, 149:2
our awareness that the Lord exists, 20, 24
our survival depending on the Lord's constant protection of us, 59:2, 694
the remnant meaning the things in us that are the Lord's, 8 (*see also* Remnant)
the Word using different names for the Lord, 300
The Lord Jehovih, 300
Love, 10, 32:2, 33, 34, 43, 94, 97, 352, 353:2, 364, 415, 430:1, 709, 716:4, 768:3, 885:1, 886, 925:3. *See also* Charity; Faith; Heaven; Heavenly; Life; The Lord; Love, mutual; Neighbor; Self-love
acting with love, 12, 48
all freedom coming from a love for goodness, 891, 892
all love as the Lord's, 352
babies, toddlers, and children meaning levels of love, 430
the commandment concerning love to be placed above all others, 396:2
dwelling in a tent meaning holy love, 413, 414:1
the earliest people perceiving faith only from love, 200, 310:1, 337:1, 597:3, 640 (*see also* Church, earliest)
earth (land) meaning love, 585, 620, 636
Eden meaning love, 98, 100, 107, 305, 398
faith as the form of love, 668
fire meaning love, 934
genuine life as a life of love from the Lord, 33
genuine love as loving the Lord above all and loving our neighbor as ourselves, 33
"God's image" referring to love, 53
the greater light that rules by day meaning love, 30:2, 32, 709
heavenly angels knowing only the faith of love, 32:2, 202, 880:3
heavenly communities distinguished from each other by differences in love and faith, 684
a human being meaning love and charity, 768:3 (*see also* Human being)
innocence impossible without love and charity, 430:1
Jabal meaning holy love and the resulting good actions, 412, 413, 416, 436

Love *(continued)*
    joy resulting only from love, 33 *(see also* Joy)
    the laws of the Lord's kingdom as all founded on the law to love the Lord and one's neighbor, 548:1
    a life of love making us human, 95
    lights meaning love and the faith that comes from love, 30:2, 31:1, 31:3
    the Lord entering heavenly people through love and spiritual people through faith, 99
    the Lord present in love and charity, 709, 724
    the Lord present with us to the extent that we have love, 904:3
    love and charity consecrating faith, 724
    love and faith as united, 34, 36, 60, 63
    love and faith bringing us to life, 39:2
    love and faith compared to warmth and light, 30:3, 34:2, 365
    love as an attribute of the will, 30:3, 48, 53
    love as the heavenly aspect of the Lord's mercy, 597
    love as the life of heaven, 32:2
    love as the source of happiness in heaven, 32:2
    love coming before faith in a heavenly person, 53
    love coming from the Lord alone, 30:3, 32:2
    love coming second to faith in the spiritual person, 53, 81:1, 459, 484
    love containing faith, 620
    love for others *(see* Charity)
    marriage love being like heaven to the earliest people, 162:2
    the mind unified when love reigns, 310:1
    mountains as having to do with love and charity, 795, 854, 859
    the nature of love determining the nature of life, 33
    no life existing without love, 33
    no love belonging to us, 352
    the only wisdom coming from love, 112
    our conflict ceasing when love takes charge, 12
    our proper code of life being to love one another as we love ourselves, 637:2
    people who have love also having faith and heavenly life, 34:2
    selfish love, 714
    self-love and materialism being opposed to genuine love, 33
    speaking truth from the Word as not holy unless from love, 724
    the sun meaning love, 32:1, 253, 255, 337:2
    the sun meaning the Lord as the source of all love, 32:2
    the teaching that faith was separate from love (charity), 325, 326, 327, 329, 335, 337:3, 340, 347, 355, 356, 362, 363, 369, 392, 394, 395, 398, 409, 436, 916:3 *(see also* Cain; Faith alone)
    the tree of lives meaning love in heavenly people, 77
    trials as distress over things that conflict with what we love, 847:2
    usefulness as the good that comes of love and charity, 454
    walking with Jehovah meaning living a life of love, 519:1, 519:3
Love, mutual (sharing of love), 684, 685
    mutual love (sharing of love) in heaven, 537, 547, 551, 553:1, 694, 916:2
Lucifer, a snake or dragon called, 254, 257
Lungs, 148
    the lungs as having to do with things of a spiritual nature, 418:2
Lute, 420

M

Magic (occult, sorcery)
    Egypt meaning occult knowledge, 130
    magic as wisdom resulting from insane reasoning, 130
    sorceresses in hell, 831
Mahalalel
    Mahalalel as the fifth church, 463, 506
    those called Mahalalel preferring truth to usefulness, 511
Making, 88. *See also* Action; Creation; Work
    "making" as having to do with a heavenly or perfected person, 472, 593
    "making" meaning instruction, 292
Male. *See also* Father; Female; Husband; Man; Son
    intellect ruling in the male, 568:2
    male and female meaning the marriage between faith and love (intellect and will), 54, 475, 476

"male" coming first when the subject is spiritual things, 476
male meaning intellectual concerns or the truth that faith embraces, 770
male meaning something true, 669, 672, 725, 749, 770
male meaning the intellect in the spiritual being, 54, 476
marriage resulting from the male's being ruled by the intellect and the female by the will, 568:2
"two of each, a male and a female, were to enter the ark" meaning goodness connected with truth, 668

Man (husband), 406, 583. *See also* Human being; Husband; Male; Woman
husband and wife meaning marriage, 725
husband meaning the Lord and every heavenly quality, 289
laws about men's privileges and wives' submission in the Jewish church, 568:2
man and wife
  meaning falsity united to evil, 713, 721
  meaning intellectual properties of truth and will-oriented properties of good, 430:2
  meaning truth united to goodness, 430:2, 713, 718, 725
"man and wife" as having to do with the will, 725
man meaning a wise and understanding person, 158
man meaning faith, 340, 367:1, 427, 429, 476
man meaning intellectual concerns, or truth that faith embraces, 770
man meaning the ability to reason (rational capacity), 191, 207, 261, 265
man meaning the inner being, 156, 158
man meaning the intellect, 429, 476, 770
the man's eating, meaning the rational mind's consent, 207, 265
one man (husband) and one wife representing the heavenly marriage, 162:1, 865:2

Manna, 276:1, 276:2
Manners. *See* Mores
Mark
  "Jehovah put a mark on Cain" meaning the Lord singled faith out in a special way, 396:1, 398

the mark put on Cain meaning a sacred ban on violating faith detached from love, 330, 392, 394, 436, 609, 920:4
marking meaning to single out or distinguish, 396

Marriage. *See also* Adultery; Husband; Marriage love; Wife
all thoughts and feelings involving the marriage of intellect and will, 718
daughters meaning the goodness produced by the marriage of faith and love, 55:2
the earliest church marrying within the clan, 471
the earliest people finding their greatest happiness in marriage, 54
everything that exists depending on some kind of marriage, 672, 718, 747
faith combining with love as a marriage between spiritual and heavenly things, 60
the heavenly marriage, 394
  eunuch meaning those who enter into, 394
  as existing in our selfhood, 155, 252
  as existing only in those who are reborn, 665
  as heaven united to the Lord through its sense of self, 252
  one man (husband) and one wife representing, 162:1, 865:2
  repetitions in the Word as having to do with, 683
  as the source of marriage on earth, 54, 162:1
  as the truest compact, 665
heavenly people abhorring the idea of marriage with multiple partners, 865:2
husband and wife meaning marriage, 725
the Jewish church marrying within the clan, 471
the law for marriage having heavenly origins, 162:1, 266
male and female meaning the marriage between faith and love (intellect and will), 54, 475, 476
the marriage between thought and will, 590
marriage love (*see* Marriage love)
marriage meaning the interconnection of intellect and will (faith and love), 54, 55, 60
the marriage of heavenly and spiritual attributes in the Word, 683
the marriage of the heart and lungs, 418:2

Marriage *(continued)*
  marriage resulting from the male's being ruled by the intellect and the female by the will, 568:2
  a married land meaning intellect coupled with will, or faith with love, 55:2
  the passive and active natures in substances joining together in a marriage, 718
  polygamous marriage, 162:1, 865:2
  true marriage involving one husband and one wife, 865:2
  truth acting on its own as unable to enter into marriage with goodness, 725
  two meaning marriage, 720
Marriage love, 828. *See also* Husband; Marriage; Wife
  hard-heartedness meaning no happiness in marriage love, 162:2
  marriage love being like heaven to the earliest people, 162:2
Material. *See* Bodily
Materialism, 943. *See also* World
  love for the material world, 152, 230, 760
  those who worship the material world, 206:1, 775:2
Meaning. *See also* Meaning, inner
  our hearing the meaning more than the words when we pay close attention to the meaning of a speaker's words, 241
Meaning, highest. *See also* Meaning, inner
  the garden planted by Jehovah God on the east in Eden meaning the Lord himself, in the highest sense, 99
Meaning, inner (inner sense), author's table of contents, 1–5, 65, 605, 618. *See also* Meaning, highest; Meaning, literal; The Word
  historical events in the Word having an inner meaning, 66:2
  the inner meaning of the Word having been lost, 217
  the Lord giving Swedenborg the opportunity to learn the inner meaning of the Word, 67
  the many secrets (hidden information) contained in the Word's inner meaning, 1, 4, 37, 64, 167, 310, 937
  prophetic parts of the Word as unintelligible except in the inner meaning, 66:2
  the richness of the Word's inner meaning as perceived in heaven, 167
  strength and glory meaning the Word's inner meaning, 49:4
  the Word containing life in its inner meaning, 2, 3, 64
  the Word's inner meaning focusing on the Lord and his kingdom, 49:4
  the Word's inner meaning looking to the next life, 67
  the Word's inner sense always having some other import, 851
Meaning, literal (letter), 167. *See also* History; Meaning, inner; The Word
  angels knowing nothing of the Word's literal contents, 64, 65
  the clouds of the heavens (sky) meaning the literal meaning of the Word, 49:4
  none of the Word's secrets appearing in its literal meaning, 1, 4, 37, 64
  simple belief in the Word's literal meaning, 196:3, 589, 735, 926
  the Word in its letter being dead without its inner life, 3, 755:5
  the Word's literal meaning provided for those who cannot grasp anything beyond ordinary human experience, 926
  the Word's literal words acting as containers filled with innumerable heavenly secrets, 937
Measurement, 602, 648:1. *See also* Dimension; Height; Length; Width
  measurements as having to do with Jehovah's holy attributes, 576:1
Medicine, leaf meaning, 57, 885:1
Mehujael, 404
Memory, 27, 268, 913. *See also* Fact; Knowledge; Remembering
  memorized facts as the first form of faith to bring life, 30:2
Memphis. *See* Moph
Meninges, 501
Mercy (pity), 587:2. *See also* Favor
  charity as mercy, 615
  fire meaning the Lord's mercy, 934:3
  "God remembers" meaning he shows mercy, 840
  Jehovah as the fountain of mercy, peace, and goodness, 245

Jehovah's face meaning mercy, 222–223, 224, 358, 387
the Lord always looking at us with mercy, 223
the Lord having mercy on each of us according to our circumstances, 587:2
the Lord never abandoning evil people, because his mercy is so great, 714
the Lord showing mercy to everyone, 904:2
the Lord's mercy
  compared to a ruler's good favor, 451
  concerns the salvation of the whole human race, 598:1
  involving everything the Lord does for us, 587:2
  keeping angels from throwing themselves into hell, 868:1
  keeping us from throwing ourselves into hell, 35, 587:2
  love as the heavenly aspect of, 597
  our inherited evil and the way we live our lives determining the nature of, 633
  our turning away from, 588:3
  transcending human comprehension, 588:1
  wisdom and love as the heart of, 590
"mercy" as having to do with heavenly aims, 598:3
mercy called *misericordia*, 587:2
mercy compared to favor, 598:2, 598:3
mercy pertaining to heavenly people, 598:2
our idea of mercy formed from feelings we recognize, 588:1
punishment as an act of mercy, 587:2
regret and heartfelt grief meaning the Lord's mercy, 559, 587:1, 588
the Spirit of God meaning the Lord's mercy, 7, 19, 24:1
the tree of lives meaning the Lord's mercy, 105
water from the sanctuary meaning the Lord's living energy and mercy, 57
Merit. *See* Deserving; Reward
Messiah, 250, 276:2, 395:1, 408, 716:3, 940:2. *See also* Coming; Jesus Christ; The Lord
Metaphors. *See* Comparisons
Methuselah
  the church called Methuselah passing away right before the Flood, 533
  Methuselah meaning something that is dying, 527
  Methuselah meaning the eighth church, 463, 516, 523
  Methuselah's age, 515
Methushael
  Methushael meaning one of the heresies stemming from Cain, 404
  Methushael meaning something that is dying, 527
Middle
  in the middle of the garden meaning in the will that belongs to the inner self, 105
  the middle of the garden meaning the inmost core, 200, 218
  the middle of the tree of the garden meaning earthly good, 218, 225
  windows of the middle story meaning matters of reason, 655:2
Might. *See also* Power; Strength
  the mighty of Babylon meaning those who have fallen into the trap of self-love, 583
  the Nephilim called "mighty men" from their love for themselves, 580, 583
Milk
  wine and milk meaning spiritual and heavenly drink, 680:5
Mind. *See also* Idea; Intellect; Reason; Thought
  general ideas preparing the mind for specifics, 848:3, 868:2
  the mind split in two when we claim to believe but act otherwise, 35, 44
  the mind unified when love reigns, 310:1
  profane images and holy images clinging together in our mind, 301, 582
  the "soil" of our minds prepared to receive charity through matters of fact, reason, and understanding, 654
  truth unable to take root in a mind filled with falsity, 875:2
  will and intellect forming one mind, 111, 116
  in the earliest people, 310:1, 398, 640, 875:4, 927:2
  when the will is in charge, 35
Misconception. *See* Falsity; Illusion
Misery (unhappiness), 267, 270. *See also* Distress; Sorrow
  misery arising when the outer self turns away from the heavenly side, 279

Misfortune. *See also* Trial
  misfortune enabling worldly concerns to fade away, 8
  misfortunes replacing spiritual trials, 762
  the outer self "dying" during times of misfortune, 268

Mist, meaning the peaceful calm that follows trials, 90, 91

Moab, 576:2

Mode
  the earliest people's mode of writing, 66:1, 742, 801:1 (*see also* Church, earliest)
  the Word's four modes of writing, 66 (*see also* Writing)
  the Word's prophetic mode hiding religious mysteries, 66:2, 302

Monarch (royalty). *See also* Queen
  all monarchs representing the Lord's royal power, 665
  monarch meaning the Lord, 337:2
  a royal offspring meaning a heavenly person, 337:2

Month. *See also* Time
  in the beginning, on the first of the month, meaning a starting point, 894
  the longest and shortest intervals in the Word called days, weeks, months, years, or ages, 900
  the second month meaning all stages preceding rebirth, 900
  the seventh month meaning holiness, 852
  the seventh month meaning spiritual people after enduring tribulation, 851
  the tenth month meaning the remnant's truth, 858
  two months (the second month) meaning combat, 755:2

Moon, 31, 488:3
  moon meaning assumptions based on falsities, 666:5
  moon meaning faith, 32:1, 253, 337:2, 395:1, 709, 862

Moph, 273

Mores (manners), 788:2, 822

Morning. *See also* Dawn; Day; Evening
  "morning" as having to do with truth and religious knowledge, 22
  morning meaning a heavenly person, 86
  morning meaning a new church, 408
  morning meaning being created anew, 22
  morning meaning every coming of the Lord, 22
  morning meaning everything of the Lord's, 22
  morning meaning the later stages of regeneration, 22
  morning meaning when a new light shines out after a church has been devastated, 408
  morning meaning when there is faith, 22

Mortar, 824:1

Moses, 85:2, 162:2, 300, 308:1, 340, 639:2, 730:4, 878:5–6, 921:2, 934:3. *See also* The ark of Moses
  Moses receiving accounts of creation from descendants of the earliest people, 66:1
  Moses speaking to spirits and angels, 784:2

Mother, 548:3. *See also* Female
  Adah meaning the mother of a new church's heavenly and spiritual attributes, 405, 412, 413, 436
  mother meaning the church, 281, 287, 289, 290, 494:1
  Zillah meaning the mother of a new church's earthly aspects, 405, 421

Mountain, 795. *See also* Zion
  the earliest people worshiping the Lord on mountains, 795:1, 920:1
  Jehovah's mountain meaning the Lord in relation to the good coming from love, 795:3
  mountains as having to do with the Lord and his heavenly qualities, 793, 795
  mountains meaning self-love, 795:1
  mountains meaning the earliest church, 337:2, 795:1, 795:2
  mountains meaning the good effects of love and charity, 795:1–3, 854, 859
  the mountains of Ararat meaning a bit of light, 854
  the tops of the mountains appeared meaning religious truth began to be visible, 859

Mouth, 174, 348
  in its mouth meaning becoming visible, 884

Multiplying. *See also* Reproduction
  the evil of the people in the land multiplied meaning the will for good began to disappear, 585
  let them multiply meaning increases in truth, 913
  multiplying as having to do with faith, 43
  truth multiplying in our memory, 913

Mummy, 876
Murder. *See* Killing
Music, 418:1. *See also* Angel: angel choirs; *individual musical instruments;* Instrument; Singing
Mustard
  birds nesting in the mustard tree's branches meaning true ideas within the facts we know, 55:4
  a mustard plant meaning faith becoming more closely connected with love, 55:4
  a mustard seed meaning the small trace of goodness we have before regeneration, 55:3
Mutual love. *See* Love, mutual
Myrrh, 113
Mystery (hidden information, secret), 302. *See also* Meaning, inner
  biblical verses enfolding the mysteries of regeneration, 47
  the earliest mode of the Word woven of heavenly secrets, 742
  heavenly people not to depend on sensory evidence when they inquire into the mysteries of faith, 80, 126
  impossibility of examining religious mysteries through factual knowledge, 233:1
  not putting out their hand and taking from the tree of lives meaning not to be taught the mysteries of faith, 298
  reliance on sensory evidence or secular knowledge when investigating religious mysteries causing the fall of the earliest church and every church, 127
  religious mysteries not revealed until there is no ability to believe, 303:2
  those who want to use facts to initiate themselves into religious mysteries, 42:2
  well-educated people who reason about the mysteries of faith, 206
  the Word containing more hidden information than can be explained, 1, 4, 37, 64, 167, 310

N

Naamah, 421
Nakedness (nudity), 224. *See also* Innocence
  blushing at their nakedness meaning their integrity and innocence deserted them, 165
  the earliest people described as naked on account of their innocence, 295
  the innocent in heaven appearing like naked toddlers, 165
  nakedness meaning being left to one's own devices, 214
  nakedness meaning innocence, 165
  nakedness (nudity) as a matter of shame when innocence is lacking, 213
  nakedness (nudity) meaning being involved in evil, 295
  "they realized that they were naked" meaning they recognized their loss of innocence, 213
  "they were naked and did not blush" meaning they were innocent, 163, 165
Name, 404. *See also individual names*
  the ancients giving a name to every new phenomenon, 340
  angels picturing what names in the Word symbolize, 64
  the earliest people assigning names with symbolic meaning, 339
  a name meaning the essence of a thing, 144, 145
  names in ancient times indicating where people were from and what they were like, 144
  names meaning doctrines or churches, 337:1, 402, 404, 468:1, 483:1
  names not used in heaven, 145
  names referring not to individuals but to some larger entity (development), 468:1, 470
  naming something meaning recognizing its nature, 142, 144, 145, 479
Narrative. *See* History
Nation (tribe), 410. *See also* Gentile; Non-Christians
  the church transferred to non-Jewish nations, 409
  the day of the nations meaning wickedness, 488:3
  the earliest people living divided into households, clans, and nations, 470, 471, 483:2
  the Jewish church living divided into households, clans, and tribes, 471
  a nation comprising a number of clans, 470
  nations meaning evil, 139, 622
  nations meaning those who trust in their own abilities, 249

Nature. *See also* Character; Personality; Tendency; World
  acknowledgment of our own nature as necessary for admission into heaven, 189
  committing a sin imposing on us a nature coming from that sin, 313, 494:2
  the Lord's human nature, 32:2, 256, 352, 414:4
  naming something meaning recognizing its nature, 142, 144, 145, 479
Neighbor, 870:3. *See also* Charity
  angels loving their neighbor more than themselves, 454, 548, 549
  charity as love for one's neighbor, 325, 351, 393, 615, 654
  genuine love as loving the Lord above all and loving our neighbor as ourselves, 33
  hatred of the Lord and one's neighbor constituting hell, 693
  heaven made of loving one's neighbor more than oneself, 454
  hills meaning neighborly love, 795:2
  the laws of the Lord's kingdom as all founded on the law to love the Lord and one's neighbor, 548:1
  the Lord present in neighborly love, 904:2
  the Lord present with us to the extent that we love our neighbor, 904:2, 904:3
  loving ourselves and worldly goods involving hatred of one's neighbor and the Lord, 33
  neighborly good (*see* Charity: charitable goodness)
  the possible extent of neighborly love in this life and the next, 548:2, 548:3
  self-love opposed to love for the Lord and our neighbor, 33, 760
Nephilim, 567, 581, 583. *See also* The pre-Flood people
  the Anakim and the Rephaim as descendants of the Nephilim, 581:2
  Nephilim as those who merged falsity with their cravings, 927:2
  Nephilim as those who merged the teachings of faith with corrupt desires, 557, 582, 640
  the Nephilim called "mighty men" from their love for themselves, 580, 583
  the Nephilim meaning those who disregarded anything holy because of delusions of self-importance, 557, 580, 581:1
  the pre-Flood people as Nephilim, 581
Nest, 55:4, 776:4, 776:5

Nettle, 273
New church. *See* Church, new
New Jerusalem (new Jerusalem), 655:2
  the measurements of the New Jerusalem showing that numbers and dimensions are symbolic, 648
  the New Jerusalem meaning the Lord's kingdom in heaven and on earth, 648:1, 935:3, 940:1
The next life. *See* The other life
The next world. *See* The other life
Night, 38. *See also* Day; Evening
  day and night meaning concepts in the intellect of a regenerate person, 936
  faith compared to night, 709, 862
  forty days and nights meaning how long trials last, 730, 760, 786, 862
  night meaning a state lacking in faith, 221
  night meaning early faith not yet bound to charity, 862
  night meaning evil, 38
  night meaning no faith, or no charity, 931:3
  nights meaning times of anxiety, 786
  the phases of the church compared to day and night, 221, 267, 271
  the smaller light that rules by night meaning faith springing from love, 30:2, 32
  what is our own is compared to the night, 21
Nine. *See* Ninth; Number
Ninth
  Lamech meaning the ninth church, 465, 523, 526
Noah, 531, 535, 612:1, 740, 865:1. *See also* Ark, Noah's; Church, ancient; Flood; Shem, Ham, and Japheth
  the ark meaning the church called Noah, 602, 605, 639, 655:1, 896:1 (*see also* Ark, Noah's)
  the church (or the people) called Noah, 64, 535, 600, 602, 611, 664, 682, 719, 732, 788, 841, 902
  being saved, 767
  believing in rather than loving the Lord, 784:1
  believing in the teachings of the earliest church, 736
  as capable of rebirth, 628, 635
  coming from the descendants of the earliest church, 788
  conscience in, 765
  having a similar condition to the pre-Flood people, 788:1

having an entirely different psyche than the earliest church, 371, 597, 607, 608, 609, 640, 736, 765

having first adherents that wavered between truth and falsity, 788:2

having rational truth and earthly good, 628, 635

having to be reborn first as to their intellect, 641, 645, 652–653, 670

the Lord separating the will from the intellect in, 640–642

not able to be taught through the inner self, 609

preserving the doctrinal teachings of faith, 788:2

the process of rebirth in, 653:2, 765

receiving charity through truth, 640, 765

regenerated so that the heavenly seed would not die out, 726

the seed of goodness and truth growing in, 731

as spiritual rather than heavenly, 598:2, 765

their preparation in regard to the will, 709

their state before rebirth, 599, 628

the three stages of regeneration of, 871, 874, 880, 889, 890

the time after the trials of, 832, 838

the trials of, 605, 606, 702, 728:1, 730, 737:1, 751:1, 755:1, 763, 765, 840, 862, 874

the Flood meaning the trials of the people called Noah, 705:1

forty days meaning how long the church called Noah lasted, 786

"God spoke to Noah" meaning the Lord's presence with this church, 904:1

Noah and his sons meaning the people of the ancient church, 915

Noah and his wife meaning the church, 906

Noah and Shem, Ham, and Japheth together constituting the ancient church, 768, 788:1

"Noah built an altar to Jehovah" meaning the worship of the ancient church, 920:1, 921:1

"Noah entered the ark" meaning he was protected, 741, 748

"Noah fathered three sons" meaning three theologies would rise out of that church, 616–617

Noah going out of the ark meaning freedom, 905, 914

Noah meaning a church that arose in order for the human race to be saved, 559, 596, 598:1

Noah meaning a new church, 467, 596, 597, 598:1, 605, 838

Noah meaning a time of rest, 531, 851

Noah meaning doctrine from the earliest church, 530:1

Noah meaning faith coming of charity, 598:1

Noah meaning the ancient church, 466, 468, 528, 529, 530, 534, 597:1, 773

Noah meaning the earliest church's remnant before and after the Flood, 64, 407, 468:1, 468:2, 530:2

Noah meaning the progenitor of the ancient church, 773, 788, 915

Noah meaning the progenitor of the three churches that followed the Flood, 466, 529, 773

Noah meaning the qualities of the church, 764, 768:1

Noah meaning the tenth church, 466

"Noah opened the window of the ark" meaning religious truth appeared to them, 863

"Noah removed the roof of the ark and looked" meaning the light of truth once falsity had been removed, 893:1, 896

"Noah sent a dove out from him to see" meaning the right conditions for taking in faith's truth and goodness, 871, 874–878, 880, 882–884, 887, 888, 890, 891

Noah's sons, Shem, Ham, and Japheth, 765, 768:1, 769

Noah's time in the ark meaning captivity by evil and falsity, 905

"Noah's wife" meaning the actual church, and "his sons' three wives with them" meaning the actual churches that developed out of that church, 770

Nod, 398

Non-Christians, 845:1, 847:3, 916:3. *See also* Gentile; Nation

good actions done by non-Christians, 671, 932:2

non-Christians embracing true faith more easily than Christians in the next world, 932:2

Non-Jewish nation. *See* Gentile; Nation

North
  coming from the north meaning the sensory and earthly levels, 426:2
  north meaning falsity, 737:2
  people of the north meaning blindness resulting from sophistry about divine subjects, 195:3
Nostril, 94, 805. *See also* Fragrance
  nostrils meaning anything pleasing, 96
Nourishment. *See also* Food
  faith and love as spiritual and heavenly nourishment, 680:4
  green plants meaning nourishment for the earthly self, 58, 59
Nucleus. *See* Remnant
Nudity. *See* Nakedness
Number, 578. *See also specific numbers*
  angels and spirits having no idea what a number is, 716:1, 813
  the earliest people using numbers to symbolize aspects of the church, 487:2, 575
  the factors of a number indicating its meaning, 737:1
  no numbers in heaven, 901:1
  numbers having a purely symbolic meaning, 487:2, 493, 575, 576:1, 647, 648:2, 716:2, 716:5, 737:1, 813
  round numbers substituted for an exact figure, 730:3

O

Obedience, 627:2
  angelic spirits participating in the heavenly marriage more from obedience than from charity, 394
  faith as obedience to the teachings of faith, 36, 344
  the outer self's obedience to the inner self, 91, 95, 857:2, 911, 913, 933:4
  spiritual people feeling free when they obey their conscience, 918
Object, 920
Oblation, 349:2. *See also* Burnt offering; Offering
Obliteration
  all substance was obliterated meaning cravings, 807, 808, 809
  "Jehovah said, 'I will obliterate the human'" meaning humanity would annihilate itself, 592:1
  obliterating all substance meaning human self-sufficiency is obliterated, 727, 731
Occult. *See* Magic
Offering. *See also* Burnt offering; Sacrifice; Worship
  Abel's offering meaning worship motivated by charity, 326, 350, 354
  Cain's offering meaning worship motivated by a detached faith, 326, 355, 356
  fire offerings meaning love, 925:1
  "Jehovah looked on Abel and on his offering" meaning charity and worship from charity was pleasing to the Lord, 354
  offering meaning worship, 346, 349, 355
Offspring, 310:1, 338, 533, 828. *See also* Child; Generation
  a royal offspring meaning a heavenly person, 337:2
Oil
  anointing of priests and kings with olive oil, 886
  oil meaning the heavenly aspect of love and charity, 886:1
  oil meaning the holy quality of love, 716:2
Old, 553:1
  "days of old" meaning the earliest church, 349:2, 477:3
  "days of old" meaning the time before the Flood, 274
Old Testament, 2, 45
  every part of the Old Testament holding an inner message, 1
Olive
  anointing of priests and kings with olive oil, 886
  the olive leaf meaning religious truth, 884, 886:3
  olive tree meaning the goodness that charity inspires, 884, 886
  two olive trees meaning what is heavenly and what is spiritual, 886:2
Omnipotence. *See also* Power
  hands meaning omnipotence, 878:3
  Moses' staff and Joshua's javelin meaning the Lord's omnipotence, 878:6
One. *See* First; Number; One hundred fifty; One hundred thirty; One hundred twenty; Ten
One hundred. *See* One hundred fifty; One hundred thirty; One hundred twenty

One hundred fifty, meaning an ending point and a starting point, 813, 849
One hundred thirty
   one hundred thirty years meaning the interval before the new church came into being, 481
One hundred twenty
   "the days of humankind will be one hundred twenty years" meaning they ought to have traces of faith left, 575
   that the number 120 means remaining traces of faith as seen from its factors, ten and twelve, 575
Opening of one's eyes, meaning an inner voice, 212
Operation, the Lord's, 55:3
Opinion (belief). *See also* Principle
   opinions (beliefs) regarding the spirit, 196:2–3, 322, 443–448
   simplicity and ignorance excusing false beliefs, 347
   those who stick to false opinions, 806
Order. *See* Command
Order (code of life, pattern, structure), 842:2, 911:2
   the Lord restoring proper order through regeneration, 675, 911:1
   order destroyed when bodily and earthly demands control spiritual and heavenly ones, 911:1, 911:3
   our living opposite to our ordained pattern of life, 637:2
   our proper code of life being to love one another as we love ourselves, 637:2
Organ *(musical instrument)*, 417, 418
   an organ meaning spiritual good, 419
Organ *(organism)*. *See also individual organs*
   humans as organs designed to receive life, 149:2
Organization. *See* Order
Origin. *See* Beginning
The other life (the next life)
   everyone's thoughts perceived clearly in the other life, 315, 318
   everything we do and think during bodily life coming back in the other life, 561, 823
   the next life as a continuation of this one, 70
   people coming into the next life not realizing they are there, 320
   the short interval between the death of the body and revival in the next life, 70
   the Word's inner meaning as having to do with the other life, 67
The other world. *See* The other life
Outer. *See also* Being, outer; Church, outer
   overcoming outer attributes such as cravings and falsities, 857:1
Outer being. *See* Being, outer
Outlaws, in hell, 820, 941
Owl, 866

P

Pact (compact, covenant)
   the heavenly marriage as the truest compact, 665
   the Lord as the pact (covenant) itself, 666
   the Lord called "the angel of the covenant," 666:1
   the Lord entering into a compact with us when he regenerates us, 665
   the Lord's covenants with the children of Jacob being rituals with a representative meaning, 665
   a pact meaning rebirth, 665, 666
   a pact meaning union, 665
   the Sabbath referred to as an eternal pact, 666:1
Pain (distress), 261, 263, 531. *See also* Distress; Torture
   pain in hell, 322:1, 829:1, 831:3
Pair, 669, 671, 674, 747. *See also* Two
   "pairs" as having to do with intellectual matters, 717
   "by their families" meaning pairs, 914, 917
   two each meaning pairs, or elements that answer to each other, 717, 743, 747, 772, 779
Parable, 302
Paradise, 64, 540. *See also* Eden
   Paradise meaning heaven, 1, 63
Parent. *See also* Father; Heredity; Mother
   children acquiring their personality (character) from their parents, 471, 494:2
   the evil committed by parents, 494:2
   evil inherited from the parents, 313, 633, 719, 868
Part
   every whole having an unlimited number of parts, 545:2

Part *(continued)*
 the idea of "parts outside of parts," 446
 unity as formed out of harmony among many parts, 457
Passing away, 800
 "all that is on the earth will pass away" meaning the death of the people in the church, 662
Passion. *See* Emotion
Path, 842:5. *See also* Road; Street; Way
 path meaning truth or faith, 519:1, 612:3, 627, 795:5
 paths in the spiritual world, 189
Pattern. *See* Order
Peace, 92, 540, 925:3. *See also* Rest; Tranquility
 the Lord as the fountain of mercy, peace, and goodness, 245
 the Lord giving us peace during trials, 59:1
 peace after trials, 90, 92
 the state of the Lord's kingdom as a state of peace, 85:1, 925:3
Perception, 125, 126, 220, 224, 225, 503, 536. *See also* Conscience
 the ability to perceive, 482:2, 511, 608
  given by our selfhood when this is brought to life by the Lord, 155
  given by the Lord's life, 99
 the ability to perceive minute differences, 502, 507, 521, 545:1
 angels' perception of the Word, 64, 167, 855
 the church called Lamech having no remaining perception, 467
 the church called Noah having no perception, 530:2, 608
 conscience replacing perception after the Flood, 371, 393, 573
 the difference between perception and conscience, 597:1
 fragrance meaning perception, 96
 heavenly angels' perception, 202, 597:1
 heavenly people's perception, 80, 81:1, 81:3, 99
 Jehovah's speaking meaning perception, 370, 371
 learning from doctrine contrasted to recognizing by perception, 521
 no perception of goodness or truth in the pre-Flood people, 558, 573, 586a:1, 920:3
 perception as a feeling for whether a thing is true and good, 104, 495, 503, 521
 perception as unknown today, 104, 483:2, 536
 perception depending on love being given primary importance, 371
 perception in angels, 104, 155, 202, 203, 228, 443
 perception in heaven, 483:1, 483:2, 536, 925:2
 perception in the earliest church, 125, 159, 310:1, 337:1, 340, 371, 393, 483, 495, 503, 597, 895:2, 920:1
  as its distinguishing feature, 371, 597:1
  its members being in a continual state of perception, 125
  as its most important attribute, 483:1
 perception in the spiritual world, 391, 443, 549
 the source of perception, inner dictates, and conscience, 227
 spiritual angels having conscience rather than perception, 104, 203, 597:1
 spiritual people having conscience rather than perception, 104, 597:1
 spiritual perception, 203
 a trace of perception remaining in the third stage of the earliest church, 193, 218, 221
 tree meaning perception, 77, 102, 103, 125, 218
Perfection, 633, 935:2
 perfection as ongoing in the next life, 894
Perfume, 117. *See also* Fragrance
 perfumes meaning the heavenly characteristics of love, 925:3
Person. *See* Human being; Man; Personality; Woman
Personality. *See also* Character; Nature
 individuals' personalities disregarded in the Word's inner meaning, 665
 members of a heavenly community forming a single personality, 684
Persuasion. *See* Delusion; Illusion
Perversion, 798, 892:2
 evil spirits perverting all the good and true things that are the Lord's, 681
 the human will as completely perverted, 895:1
 the Lord's life in us perverted when the outer self is disconnected from the inner self, 272
Pestle, 824:1
Pharaoh
 Pharaoh called a great sea creature, 42, 130
 Pharaoh meaning sensory evidence and factual information, 31:1, 42:1

pharaoh meaning the Lord's royal power, 665
Phenomenon, 801:2
Philistine, 705:3
Philosophy, 233:2
  philosophers speaking of the spirit, 196:3
Phrath. *See* Euphrates
Physical. *See* Bodily
Pig, 939
Pillar, surrounding Swedenborg on a visit to hell, 699
Pishon, 115. *See also* Eden; River
  the first river, Pishon, meaning the intelligence that goes with a faith based on love, 110
Pitch, 643:4
Pity. *See* Mercy
Place. *See also* Space
  no moving from place to place in the spiritual world, 699
Plagues, meaning devastation, 730:4
Planet. *See* Earth
Plant (grass). *See also* Leaf; Planting
  eating the grass of the field meaning living like an animal, 274
  evil spirits leaving us "green plants" as our only nourishment during trials, 59:1
  green plant meaning a spiritual person's earthly food, 58, 59
  the Lord giving us "seed-bearing plants" during trials, 59:1
  the plant bearing its seed meaning something useful, 29:1
  plant (grass) meaning spiritual food, 56, 57
  plant meaning a spiritual person's earthly food, 58
  plant of the field meaning rational ideas and factual knowledge with a heavenly-spiritual origin, 91
  plants meaning good actions, 9
  plants meaning truth and goodness that we believe come from ourselves, 39:2
  the seed-bearing plant meaning a true idea with a useful goal, 57
  seed-bearing plants meaning spiritual food, 56
  the shrub and the plant sprouting from the ground and watered by the mist meaning the factual knowledge and reason of heavenly people, 75
  the tender plant meaning what first grows in us during regeneration, 29:1
Planting (sowing). *See also* Ground; Plant; Seed
  faith containing the religious knowledge that is planted, 620
  the Lord sowing the will of the earliest people with the seed of goodness, 895:1
  our "ground" as in our intellectual part, where truth is sown, 895:1
  seed sown in the will compared to seed sown in the intellect, 895:2
  that the Lord will always be planting seeds in us, 932:1
  what we hear from the Word as seeds sown in the memory, 880:1
Plaster, 739:2
Pleasure (appetite, gratification), 45, 831:1, 944, 945. *See also* Appetite; Craving; The senses
  creeping thing meaning sensual pleasure, 810
  "desirable for lending insight" meaning sensual pleasure, 207, 209
  the hell of those whose sole aim was sensory pleasure, 943
  our being carried away by the pleasure our vices bring us, 892:1
  our constructing our lives through pleasures, 760
  renunciation of pleasure, 892:1, 945
Pleasure (joy, revel, savor), 85:3, 353:2. *See also* Happiness; Joy
  heavenly joy and pleasure, 545:2
  the Lord giving us periods of joy during trials, 59:1
  marriage as the earliest people's greatest pleasure, 54
  the pleasure of vices, 892
  the pleasures of heavenly joy, 545:2
  river of pleasures meaning the spiritual quality belonging to faith from love, 353:2
  savors meaning religious knowledge, 42:2
Plunder, 576:3
Plural, 50:3, 253, 298, 300, 304, 374:3, 478, 712. *See also* Singular
Poison. *See* Venom
Pond. *See* Lakes
Population. *See* Human race
Possession, 79
  Arabia and the children of the east meaning the possession of heavenly riches (qualities), 382:4, 414:2

Possession *(continued)*
  cultivating the garden and guarding it meaning the freedom to enjoy heavenly qualities but not to claim possession of them, 122
  water meaning our spiritual possessions, 739:1
Poverty, 561
  the belief that misfortune, poverty, and renunciation of pleasure are necessary for admission to heaven, 892:1
Power. *See also* Might; Omnipotence; Selfhood; Strength
  angels aware that they have no power except from the Lord, 50:3
  desire for power, 451
  hand meaning power, 195:2, 878
  the name "God" coming from his power, 300
  our apparent ability to act under our own power, 233:2
  Uzzah's putting his hand out onto the ark meaning his own, independent power, 878:7
Praise. *See also* Worship
  the belief that heavenly joy lies in praising and celebrating the Lord, 456
  frankincense and myrrh called "Jehovah's praises," 113
  praising the Lord with music, 420
Preaching, 724, 795:4
Prefiguration. *See* Image
The pre-Flood people, 312, 554, 793, 801, 803, 920:3. *See also* Flood; Nephilim
  the cataclysm of the pre-Flood church, 635
  contact with hell opening for the pre-Flood people, 920:3
  the delusions of the pre-Flood people, 285, 562, 570, 581
    adopted because of their mental character, 562, 581:2, 661:1
    causing their destruction, 560, 563, 594, 601
    destroying their remnant, 560, 562, 563, 579, 594, 607:3, 635, 661:2
    destroying what was heavenly in them, 726
    eradicating everything true or good in them, 573, 635, 798
    shutting off access to the remnant, 563, 571, 660, 798
    staying with them after death, 311
  falsity in the pre-Flood people, 794:1
  goodness and truth destroyed among the pre-Flood people, 635, 731, 798
  the nature of the pre-Flood people's evil, 810
  no living faith surviving in the pre-Flood people, 661:3
  no rationality remaining in the pre-Flood people, 238
  the overpowering effect of the pre-Flood people on other spirits, 311, 562, 581
  the pre-Flood people as entirely possessed by evil spirits, 660
  the pre-Flood people immersing religious teachings in their desires (cravings), 555, 560, 570, 573, 586a, 661:1
  the pre-Flood people loving their autonomy, 237
  the pre-Flood people thrown out of the Garden of Eden, 303:2
  the pre-Flood people unable to be saved, 927:2, 933:4
  the pre-Flood people withheld from knowledge of goodness and truth for their protection, 285
  the pre-Flood people's attachment to falsity, 803
  the pre-Flood people's character as totally different from that of those living after the Flood, 310:2, 640, 736
  the pre-Flood people's cravings growing out of self-love, 808
  the separate hell of the pre-Flood people, 311
Premeditation, 830
Preparation, 868:2
  entering the ark meaning being prepared, 711
  falsity driven out to prepare the "soil" in us for religious truth, 875:2
  "as God had commanded" meaning preparation to receive truth and goodness, 783
  living faith preparing us to be human, 95
  our needing to be prepared with truth and good before being tested, 711, 737:1
  our preparation for eternal life, 697
  our preparation to receive the living power of faith, 29:1
  preparation with true thoughts and good impulses as necessary for rebirth, 711, 719
  the "soil" of our minds prepared to receive charity through matters of fact, reason, and understanding, 654

unprepared spirits trying to enter heaven, 538, 539, 546
Presence
  the future being the same as the present to the Lord, 730:5
  "God spoke to Noah" meaning the Lord's presence with this church, 904:1
  the Lord as present in neighborly love, 904:2
  the Lord as present with us to the extent that we have love, 904:3
Preservation (safeguarding), 609, 645. *See also* Guarding; Protection
  "Enoch was no more, because God took him," meaning this church preserved doctrines for later use, 464, 520, 521, 609, 920:4
  the Lord preserving states of goodness and truth in us, 561
  our survival depending on the Lord's preserving us every moment, 59:2, 694
  a remnant of the church always preserved, 468:2, 530:1
Pretense, 358
Priest, 342, 352, 382:1, 665, 886:1, 921:3
Principle (assumption, point of view), 130, 570. *See also* Opinion
  daily life of the earliest people confirming their general principles, 597:2
  false principles of those with a good secular education, 206
  false principles (points of view) confirmed by proofs, 581, 589, 794
  the Lord as the source of our principles, 129
  our thoughts coming from our principles, 128, 129
Privilege, 568:2
Proclamation, 220
Profanation, 306, 308, 576:2, 623:1, 720, 900
  in a church undergoing devastation, any faith or charity is mingled with something profane, 408
  the Nephilim profaning the holy attributes of faith, 582
  a new church arising when profanation is no longer possible, 408, 410
  only those who acknowledge faith able to profane it, 302, 303:1, 408, 410, 593, 661:1
  our being damned when we mingle holy and profane things together, 301
  profanation depriving us of any remaining traces of goodness and truth, 571
  profanation of truth through immersing it in cravings, 570, 571, 582, 586a:1, 794:2, 863 (*see also* Nephilim; The pre-Flood people)
  profanation perceived immediately in the next world, 582
  profane images and holy images clinging together in our mind, 301, 582
  religious mysteries hidden in representative acts and objects to prevent profanation, 302
  thorn and thistle on the altars meaning profanation, 273
Prophet
  the Law and the Prophets meaning the teachings of faith and the Word, 36
  the prophetic mode of the Word, 66:2, 302, 801
  prophets meaning those who teach, 382:1
Prostitute, 828
Protection. *See also* Guarding; Preservation
  angels using the remnant to protect us against evil spirits, 660, 737, 751
  the Lord protecting the remnant, 259:2
  the Lord's constant protection, 59:2, 694, 741
  "Noah entered the ark" meaning he was protected, 741, 748
Providence, 306, 308. *See also* Foreseeing
  the guardian beings meaning the Lord's providence keeping us from profaning the mysteries of faith, 306, 308
  the Lord's providence ensuring that the teachings of faith would be safeguarded, 609
Prudence. *See* Shrewdness
Psalms, the mode of David's, 66:2
Psyche. *See* Character; Personality
Pulse, 176
Punishment, 817. *See also* Devil; Hell; Spirit, evil; Torture
  evil and falsity turning into the punishments of hell, 592:2, 689, 696, 868:2
  evil spirits' delight in punishing one another, 391, 695
  falsity and evil carrying their own punishment, 391, 696
  the Lord converting the negative consequences of punishment into good, 592:2, 696
  the Lord never punishing anyone, 245, 592:2
  punishment as an act of mercy, 587:2
  punishment in hell, 815, 816, 829, 831:3

Q

Queen, 945. *See also* Monarch
Quiet. *See* Rest

R

Rabbi, 940:2
Race. *See* Nation
Rachel
    Rachel meaning a new church among non-Jewish nations, 422
    Rachel meaning the inner church of the Jewish church, 409, 422
Rain. *See also* Downpour; Flood
    rain meaning calm after battle, 90
    rain meaning the calm of a heavenly person, 91, 93
    rainfall meaning trial, 729, 844
Rainbow, 868:2
Ram, 294, 296, 715
Rat, 938, 940:1
Rationality. *See* Reason
Raven, 864, 865:1, 866, 870:3
Reality. *See* Being
Reaping (crops, harvest), 273, 937. *See also* Ground; Seed
    sowing and reaping meaning the regenerating person, or the church, 930, 932
Reason (logic, rationality), 75, 91, 202, 238, 655:2. *See also* Intellect; Mind; Sophistry
    the ability to reason
        becoming hellish when it consents to self-dependence, 238, 267
        belonging to the outer self, 268
        coming from the Lord through the inner self, 118, 657
        imitating an intelligent understanding, 265
        the inner self directing the outer self by means of, 268
    animals having something like reason, 196:2
    Assyria meaning the reasoning mind, 118, 119
    birds meaning logical reasoning, 40:1
    a cedar in Lebanon meaning the ability to reason, 119
    confirming the Word through rational argument, 128
    the heel meaning the bottommost things in the rational mind, 259:1
    the husband (man) meaning the rational capacity, 191, 207, 261, 265
    our sense of autonomy deceiving our rational capacity, 229
    the rational mind of spiritually dead people, 270
    reason as the middle level of the intellect, 657
    reason coming from understanding, which comes from wisdom, which comes from the Lord, 121
    reason reigning in males, 266, 568:2
    spiritual angels using rational concepts to confirm their religious beliefs, 203
    the third river out of Eden meaning the faculty of reason, 78, 118
    truth on the rational plane, 628, 635, 671
Reasoning. *See* Reason; Sophistry
Rebel, 451, 897:2
Rebirth. *See* Regeneration
Recognition. *See* Acknowledgment; Knowledge
The Red Sea. *See* The Suph Sea
Reed, 25
Reformation, 59:1
    the intellect having to be reformed before the will could be, 641, 645, 652
    our being reformed when charity forms the basis of thought and action, 654
    the purpose of trials being to reform us, 653:1
    a spiritual person's reformation beginning in the outer self, 89
Regeneration (rebirth), 4, 16, 17, 39:2, 46:1, 47, 63, 85:2, 246, 264:2, 671, 848, 860, 883, 898, 908:2. *See also* Ark, Noah's; Noah; Trial
    beasts as having to do with regeneration, 12, 39:2, 47, 48
    being regenerate as having faith, 896:2
    birds as having to do with regeneration, 11, 39:2, 48
    charity in a regenerating person, 834, 840, 854, 862, 935:2
    the children of Israel meaning regenerate people, 842:5, 901:4
    cold and heat meaning the condition of a regenerating person, 933, 935:1, 936
    creation meaning regeneration, 16, 62, 88, 472, 593
    darkness meaning our state before regeneration, 7, 17

"earth" as having to do with regeneration, 17, 25, 82
field meaning a regenerate individual, 246, 368
the first chapters of Genesis dealing with the regeneration of the earliest people, 286
freedom resulting from regeneration, 892:1
good actions in the different stages of regeneration, 9–12, 48, 52
ground meaning regenerate people, 268
a heaven meaning a regenerate person, 29:2, 911:2
Noah meaning a new rebirth, 531
our being made human through regeneration, 313, 848:1
our seemingly good qualities as dead until we regenerate and the Lord gives them life, 671
the pre-Flood people as incapable of rebirth, 601, 933:4
before regeneration, 18, 19, 671
    the channel for goodness and truth from the Lord being blocked, 857:1
    falsity interfering, 865:1
    our being in a state of slavery, 81:3, 892:1
    our consisting of cravings and distortions, 59:1
    our outer self battling our inner self, 95
    our seeing evil as good, 21
during regeneration, 24:3, 29:1, 55:1, 55:3, 59, 848:1, 887, 933
    evil needing to be dispelled, 719, 894
    our being in constant battle, 59:1
    our evils being tempered by means of goodness, 561, 719
    our receiving life from the Lord, 933:2, 933:3
    our senses causing strife, 12
after regeneration, 929, 935:2
    angels being in charge of us, 50:3
    everything evil and false remaining in us, 868, 887
    good spirits taking the place of evil spirits, 63, 87
    the inner self directing the outer self, 52, 268
    our becoming an image of heaven, 911:1–2
    the outer self corresponding with the inner self, 911:2
    the outer self obeying the inner self, 91, 95, 857:2, 911, 913, 933:4
regeneration as the Lord restoring us to proper order, 675, 911:1
regeneration continuing in the next life, 894
regeneration existing to give us life, 848:2, 933:2
regeneration occurring step by step, 62
the regeneration of a spiritual person, 875
regeneration progressing from the outer self to the inner, 24:3, 47, 64
the remnant stored away until we begin to regenerate, 8, 711, 737:1
the remnant used by angels to defend us against evil spirits during regeneration, 737:1
the six days of creation meaning stages in regeneration, 6–13, 62, 63, 221
sowing and reaping meaning the regenerating person, 930, 932
stages of regeneration, 6–13, 29:2, 62, 395:2
stages of regeneration following trials, 835, 871, 874, 880:1, 889
the steps of rebirth as knowledge, acknowledgment, and belief, 896:1
things necessary for rebirth
    preparation with true thoughts and good impulses, 677, 711, 719
    the remnant, 628, 635, 755:2
    spiritual devastation, 18
trial as the beginning of regeneration, 848:1
unregenerate people governed differently than regenerate people, 50:2, 50:3
the work of God's fingers meaning a regenerate person, 63
Regret (repentance, sorrow). *See also* Sorrow
"Jehovah was sorry" meaning mercy, 586b, 587:1, 588:1
the Lord's mercy described as regret, 559, 587:1, 588
regret as having to do with wisdom, 586b, 590
regrets meaning great mercy, 588:3
the third stage of regeneration as one of repentance, 9, 29:2
Reign. *See* Governance; Rule
Religion. *See* Church; Faith; *the individual churches;* Teaching
Religious good. *See* Faith: the goodness belonging to faith

Remembering. *See also* Memory
   "God remembered" meaning the end of struggle, 840
   "God remembers" meaning he shows mercy, 840
Remnant (remaining traces), 19, 468:3, 468:4, 561, 576:3, 649, 680:5, 857:1, 886:3
   the ark's measurements meaning the remnant (remaining traces), 602, 649, 650
   blocking off access to the remnant, 660, 661:1
   the Lord protecting the remnant, 259:2
   the Lord working through the remnant, 560
   Noah as the remnant of the earliest church **that survived the Flood**, 407
   a nucleus (remnant) of the church always remaining when the church is devastated, 407, 468:2, 530:1, 932:2
   our being like animals without the remnant, 530:2, 560, 565, 661:2
   our depriving ourselves of any remaining traces of goodness and truth, 571
   our life depending on the remnant, 468:2, 560
   people formed so that they could acquire remnants, 556
   the pre-Flood people destroying the remnant, 560, 562, 594, 660, 661:2, 798
   regeneration not possible without a remnant, 628
   the remnant as a knowledge of truth and goodness, 19, 561, 711
   the remnant being something that belongs to the Lord, 8, 576:4
   the remnant consisting of religious knowledge acquired from early childhood on, 8, 561, 661:2
   the remnant holding spiritual and heavenly life within it, 468:2, 560
   a remnant remaining in the people called Noah, 628, 635
   the remnant stored away, 268, 259:2, 563, 661:2
      in the inner self, 19, 268, 561
      until our outer nature has been devastated, 19
      until we begin to regenerate, 8, 711, 737:1
   the remnant used by angels to defend us against evil spirits, 737:1
   self-deception adhering to the remnant, 563

   the size of the remnant in us, 530:2
   ten meaning the remnant, 468:4, 575, 576, 737:1, 755:2, 798, 858
Repentance. *See* Regret
Repetition. *See also* Word
   repetitions in the Word, 100, 435, 590, 682, 707, 734, 765, 782, 793, 801
      as having to do with the heavenly marriage, 683
Rephaim, 290, 581:2. *See also* Nephilim
Repose. *See* Rest
Representation, 44c. *See also* Church, representative; Meaning, inner; Symbolism
   the custom of the earliest people to express **everything** through representative images, 403
   the earliest people weaving representative images into a narrative, 66:1, 403
   every activity in the Jewish church representing the Lord, 31:3, 85:2, 921:1
   inner realities represented by external objects, 54, 66:1
   the personality of individuals disregarded in favor of the qualities they represent, 665
   religious mysteries hidden in representative acts and objects to prevent profanation, 302
   the world of spirits as a representative world, 167
Reproduction (fruitfulness). *See also* Fruit
   everything with life from the Lord reproducing beyond measure, 43
   goodness reproducing in our feelings, 913
   goodness reproducing itself when the outer self obeys the inner self, 913
   "let them reproduce" meaning increases in goodness, 913
   the Lord's blessing meaning fruitfulness, 43
   reproducing as having to do with love, 43
   reproduction meaning the generation of goodness from the marriage of faith and love, 55:1
Requirement. *See* Command
Respectability. *See* Honesty; Uprightness
Rest (repose), 63, 87. *See also* Peace
   "Jehovah smelled a restful smell" meaning worship inspired by charity was pleasing to the Lord, 925:1, 925:3
   the Lord resting from all his work meaning the person is regenerated, 84

Noah meaning a time of rest, 531, 851
Sabbath meaning rest (repose), 84, 85, 851
spiritual people becoming the Lord's rest after having endured tribulation, 851
the spiritual person embodying a holy restfulness, 855
Restraint. *See* Bond
Resurrection (revival). *See also* Resurrection, the Lord's
brilliant light seen at resurrection, 186
heavenly angels present during resurrection, 170–185
only a day or two between death and resurrection, 70
our being taught during revival, 314, 315
revival from death and entry into eternal life, 70, 168–181, 182–185, 314–319
spiritual angels helping us after revival, 182, 314, 315
Resurrection, the Lord's, 14
the Lord's resurrection involving everything sacred and entailing the resurrection of all people, 901:1
the number three indicating holiness because of the Lord's resurrection on the third day, 720, 901:1, 901:4, 901:5
Reuben
the name Reuben coming from a word for seeing, 897:2
the name Reuben meaning Jehovah "has seen my unhappiness," 340
Reuben meaning faith, 342, 897:2
Revelation, 198, 199
needing proof to believe revelations, 194, 208
the people of the earliest church receiving revelations that gave them a perception of goodness and truth, 125, 597:2, 609, 895:2
the revelations of the earliest church replaced by articles of doctrine, 608, 609
voice meaning revelation, 219
Reverence (devoutness), apparent, 9, 724
Revival. *See* Resurrection
Reward. *See also* Deserving
the belief that we are rewarded for doing good on our own, 735
Rib. *See also* Bone
the rib from which the woman was built meaning a sense of autonomy, 138
a rib meaning a sense of self devoid of life, 147, 148, 151

Riches, 114, 382:4, 944, 945. *See also* Fat; Possession; Wealth
Arabia and the children of the east meaning the possession of heavenly riches, 382:4
the earliest people not striving after riches, 230
resources and treasures meaning spiritual riches, 368, 426:2
Tyre meaning those who have spiritual and heavenly riches, 425, 426:1
Right, 886:2. *See also* Uprightness
evil spirits flooding the right side of the human brain with cravings, 641
the right hand meaning omnipotence, 878:3
volitional matters belonging to the right hemisphere of the brain, 644
River. *See also* Eden; Euphrates; Garden; Gihon; Hiddekel; Pishon
the river in Assyria meaning insane reasoning and the falsity it spawns, 130
the river in the garden of Eden branching into four rivers, 78, 107, 116, 118, 121, 130, 567, 658
the river from Eden meaning wisdom born of love, 107
"the river of pleasures" and "the light" meaning the spiritual quality belonging to a faith from love, 353:2
the rivers marking the boundaries of Canaan, 567
rivers meaning all aspects of wisdom, 108
rivers meaning loathsome discharges from hell, 756:2
water and rivers meaning things that stimulate growth, 108
Road, meaning truth, 627:3, 795:5. *See also* Path; Street; Way
Robber. *See* Outlaw
Rock (boulder), 581:1, 795:3. *See also* Crag; Stone
Rod, 426:4
Roof
Noah removing the roof of the ark, 883, 890, 893:1, 896:1
roof meaning falsity, 893:1, 896:1
Root, 382:3, 875:1, 880:1
Rope, 414:2
Royalty. *See* Monarch
Ruby, 655:1
Ruin. *See* Devastation
Ruination. *See* Desolation

Rule (control, domination), 50:2, 831. *See also* Command; Governance
  evil spirits' efforts to dominate us, 50:2, 59:1, 660, 905
  the greater light that rules by day meaning love, 30:2, 32, 709
  "harness the earth and rule" meaning spiritual people subject to conflict, 55:4
  "he will rule over you" meaning the church will be ruled by rationality, 261
  the rule evil spirits have over us, 50:2, 227
  self-love wishing to dominate, 257, 760, 911:3
  the smaller light that rules by night meaning faith springing from love, 30:2, 32

S

Sabbath, 86, 883. *See also* Seventh: the seventh day
  the eve of the Sabbath meaning a spiritual person beginning to turn heavenly, 86, 480
  a heavenly person as a Sabbath, 84–88, 666:1
  the Lord as the Sabbath, 85:1, 666:1
  the Lord's kingdom as the Sabbath, 85:1
  Sabbath meaning rest (repose), 84, 85, 851
Sacrifice, 349:1, 353:1, 921. *See also* Burnt offering; Offering
  altars built as memorials before people knew about sacrifices, 921:2
  sacrifices as a means of worshiping the Lord, 921:5
  sacrifices meaning the Lord, 1
  sacrifices meaning worship from the faith that comes of love, 923
Salvation. *See also* Regeneration
  entering the ark meaning being saved, 667, 764, 767, 779
  living forever meaning being saved to all eternity, 298
  the Lord foreseeing how the human race could be saved, 598:1
  no hope of salvation for those who intermingle holy and profane things, 301, 302
  Noah meaning a church that arose in order for the human race to be saved, 559, 596, 598:1
  our belief that we can be saved even if we live like a savage beast, 916:3
  the pre-Flood people unable to be saved, 927:2, 933:4
  the salvation of the human race at the time of the Flood, 598:1, 608, 767
  the theory that faith alone saves, annihilating charity, 369
  those who prove from the Word that faith alone brings salvation, 794:2
Sanctuary, meaning the Lord, 57, 109
Satan, 251:2, 482:2. *See also* Devil
Saying, 55:3, 366, 383. *See also* Speaking
  "God said" meaning that is how it was, 630
  "Jehovah said" meaning a thing happens in this way, 708, 926
  "Jehovah said to Cain" meaning conscience spoke, 359, 371
Scent. *See* Fragrance
Schism, 400. *See also* Heresy; Teaching
  ground meaning a schism, 373, 377, 380, 381
Science. *See* Knowledge
Scripture. *See* The Word
Scrutiny (examining), 192, 204. *See also* Examining
Sculpture (idol), 643:4, 920:4. *See also* Idol
  a sculpture meaning the falsity we adopt as our own, 215, 586a:2
Sea. *See also* The Suph Sea
  seas meaning a body of religious and secular knowledge, 28
  seas meaning knowledge of truth and good stored in our memory, 27
Sea creature (sea monster). *See also* Whale
  big sea creatures meaning general categories of facts, 42:1
  the sea monster swallowing Jonah, 42:2
Seba, 117:2
Second, 896. *See also* Two
  charity as the church's second-born, 341, 342
  the second heaven, 167, 459, 684
  the second month meaning combat, 755:2
  the second month meaning stages that precede rebirth, 900
  Seth meaning the second church, 462, 496, 497
Secret. *See* Mystery
Sect, 337:1. *See also* Heresy
Secular knowledge. *See* Fact

Seed (sowing), 254, 437, 726. *See also* Ground; Planting; Reaping
　every charitable kindness being seed from the Lord, 932:2
　heavenly seed, 29, 268, 310:1, 653:2, 726
　the Lord as the sower of seeds, 29:2, 932
　the mustard seed meaning the good we have before developing a spiritual orientation, 55:3
　the plant bearing its seed meaning something useful, 29:1
　the seed leading to new fruit as what the Lord gives a spiritual person, 57
　seed meaning faith, 255, 264:2, 368, 437, 620, 726
　the seed of a woman meaning the Lord, 256
　the seed-bearing plant meaning a true idea with a useful goal, 57
　seeds always being planted in us by the Lord, 932:1
　seeds of goodness and truth planted in our outer self, 268
　the snake's seed meaning all unbelief, 250, 254
　sowing and reaping meaning the regenerating person, and the church, 930, 932
　spiritual seed, 310:2
　the woman's seed meaning faith in the Lord, 250, 255, 256
Seeing (eyesight, looking), 182. *See also* Eye; Light; Perception
　the eyesight of spirits, 322:1
　looking (seeing) meaning acknowledging and believing, 896:1, 897
　the name Reuben coming from a word for seeing, 340, 897:2
Self (independence, one's own, oneself), 32:2, 150, 204, 552. *See also* Selfhood; Self-love
　angels, when not reflecting, believing that they live on their own, 155
　anything we do on our own as evil, 55:3, 233:2
　the belief that we can acquire faith on our own, 546
　the belief that we live independently, 150
　the Lord allowing us to think we do good deeds and think true thoughts on our own, 47, 874, 904:3
　the Nephilim's delusions about their own importance, 557, 580, 581:1
　our being dead on our own, 39:2
　our deeds being lifeless when we believe that they come of our own doing, 9, 29:1, 39:1
　our inability to do good on our own, 44, 105, 233:2, 735, 848:2, 868:1, 874, 876, 882
　those who believe in simplicity that they can do good on their own, 735
　using our own powers to enter into religious mysteries, 42:2, 198
　wanting to be led by ourselves and the world, 138
Self, inner. *See* Being, inner
Self, outer. *See* Being, outer
Self-absorption. *See* Self; Selfhood; Self-love
Self-deception. *See* Delusion
Selfhood (autonomy, identity, independence, one's own power, sense of self), 8, 123, 138, 140, 142, 151, 155, 256, 268, 561, 714. *See also* Self; Self-love
　angels' selfhood, 141, 155, 252, 633
　the appearance of selfhood in the spiritual world, 149:2, 154, 164
　the autonomy of heavenly people, 141, 633, 780
　the belief that to lack selfhood is the same as nonexistence, 206:2
　bone meaning a sense of autonomy, 148, 149:1, 156, 157
　the church's heavenly sense of self, 253, 261, 262
　the desire for autonomy, 132, 146, 159
　the feeling of independent existence as necessary for union with the Lord, 252
　flesh meaning identity (autonomy) that has life, 147, 148, 156
　flesh meaning the things that are our own, 574:2
　the heavenly marriage existing in our selfhood, 155, 252
　heavenly, spiritual life linked with a sense of independence, 135, 160
　human selfhood, 41, 149:2, 207
　　believing not in the Lord or his Word but in ourselves, 210
　　as evil and falsity, 39:1, 154, 215, 389, 633, 731, 868:2

Selfhood *(continued)*
: human selfhood *(continued)*
  : as the evil and falsity coming from self-love and materialism, 210
  : as hellish, 141, 210, 252
  : as inherently dead, 41, 149:2, 150, 597:3
  : lacking understanding, wisdom, truth, and goodness, 214
  : as love for ourselves and the material world, 152
  : needing to die before we can be reborn, 730:1, 731
  : seeming to disappear when brought to life by the Lord, 731
  : as what deceives us, 152
  : as wickedness itself, 154, 164, 597:3
  : the later generations of the earliest church striving for autonomy, 131, 133, 137, 142, 161, 190, 237
  : the Lord alone having true autonomy, 149:2
  : the Lord born to unite his divine selfhood to a human one, 256
  : the Lord infusing our selfhood with innocence, 136, 164, 252
  : the Lord's selfhood as life, 149:2
  : the nature of autonomy in a body-oriented or worldly person, in a spiritual person, and in a heavenly person, 141
  : our being on our own when disconnected from the Lord, 389
  : our inability to do good under our own power, 44, 105, 233:2, 735, 848:2, 868:1, 874, 876, 882
  : our sense of autonomy shaken off during trials, 8, 730:1, 731
  : rib meaning a sense of self (autonomy), 138, 147, 148, 151
  : selfhood brought to life by the Lord, 149:2, 155
  : a sense of autonomy yielded to humankind, 132, 134
  : spiritual people believing in their own autonomy, 141
  : woman meaning a sense of self (autonomy) brought to life by the Lord, 151, 155
  : woman meaning selfhood (self-love), 152, 191, 194, 207

Self-interest. *See* Craving; Self; Selfhood; Self-love

Selfishness. *See* Self; Selfhood; Self-love

Self-love, 33, 273, 808. *See also* Nephilim; Self; Selfhood
: the belief that everything connected with self-love is good, 20, 911:3
: the earth meaning self-love, 636
: the pre-Flood people dominated by self-love, 583, 808
: self-love as a form of hatred, 33
: self-love as hatred for others and the Lord, 251:1
: self-love as the reigning evil of the third stage of the earliest church, 230
: self-love deceiving our rational capacity into believing only our senses, 191, 229
: self-love involving a desire to be led by oneself rather than the Lord, 205
: self-love involving the desire to dominate everything, 257, 760, 911:3
: self-love opposed to love for the Lord and our neighbor, 33, 760
: the snake meaning self-love, 250, 251, 257
: the woman meaning self-love, 191

Sensation (touch), 272, 321, 322:1. *See also* Emotion; Sense; The senses

Sense (sensation), 12, 229, 444. *See also* Bodily; Feeling; Meaning; Meaning, literal; Sensation; The senses; Shrewdness
: the evil of trusting oneself and one's senses, 231–233
: the impossibility of our senses teaching us about heavenly matters, 128
: the spirit as what senses things during bodily life, 322:2, 447
: spirits as human in respect to their senses, 320, 444
: there being no life without sensation, 322:2

Sense of self. *See* Selfhood

The senses (sense experience, sense impressions, sensory evidence, sensory level, sensory plane, sensory pleasure), 195:1, 196:2, 197, 198, 202, 657. *See also* Appetite; Bodily; Craving; Pleasure
: blindness caused by confidence in sensory evidence, 128, 195:2, 196:1, 210, 241
: everything that creeps on the ground meaning the sensory level, 746
: Pharaoh and the Egyptians meaning sensory evidence and factual information, 31:1, 120, 195:3

the pre-Flood people being immersed in what belonged to their senses and their body, 276:2
refusing to believe without confirmation by evidence from the senses, 208
relying on sensory evidence or secular knowledge to inquire into the mysteries of faith, 80, 126, 128
the sensory capacities serving the inner self in the earliest people, 243
the sensory experience becoming the primary force rather than a tool in later generations of the earliest church, 241, 243
the sensory plane turning toward earthly things and away from heavenly values, 247, 249, 263
the snake meaning sensory abilities (the senses), 191, 192, 194, 195:1, 196:1, 197, 229, 235, 242, 244, 249, 251
truth gained through the senses, 425, 777

Sensing. *See* Feeling

Serpent. *See* Snake

Service (helping). *See also* Obedience; Usefulness
angels helping us, 50:3
angels wanting nothing more than to be of service (be helpful) to us after resurrection, 314, 315, 316, 318

Seth, 435
the church called Seth compared to the earliest one, 462, 481, 484
Seth meaning a new faith through which charity would be implanted, 335, 436
Seth meaning the second church, 462, 496, 497
the three churches called the human, Seth, and Enosh together constituting the earliest church, 502
two different churches called Seth, 485

Seven, 395:1, 433, 728:3. *See also* Number; Seventeen; Seventh; Seventy; Week
"of every clean animal you are to take yourself seven each, seven each," 713
the number seven, 395:1, 482:1, 901
having to do with the Last Judgment, 900
having to do with the will, 717
meaning the Lord's Coming, 728:1
meaning things that are holy, 395:1, 482:1, 713, 716, 724, 728:2, 813, 881, 900

seven days
meaning the beginning of a new church and the end of the old, 728:5
meaning the beginning of the third stage of regeneration, 889
meaning the beginning of trials and the end of ruin, 728:1, 753
meaning the start of a divine visitation, 728:3

Seventeen, 755, 853

Seventh. *See also* Twenty-seventh
Enoch as the seventh church, 463, 513, 516
the seventh day (*see also* Sabbath)
as consecrated, 84
the Lord as, 716:1
meaning a heavenly person, 74, 84–88, 395:1
meaning atonement, 901:3
the seventh month meaning a spiritual person after trials, 851
the seventh month meaning holiness, 852

Seventy, 395:2, 728:2. *See also* Seventy-seven
the number seventy as holy, 433
seventy years of captivity meaning the end of devastation and the start of becoming a new person, 728:4

Seventy-seven
being avenged seventy-seven times meaning damnation, 432, 433

Sewing, 216

Shadow. *See* Darkness

Shame, 213, 829:1. *See also* Blushing
making loincloths for themselves meaning to feel shame, 216, 224 (*see also* Nakedness)

Sharing. *See* Communication

Sharing of love. *See* Love, mutual

Sheba, 117

Sheep, 45, 143, 294, 296. *See also* Flock; Shepherd

Shem, Ham, and Japheth, 788
the churches referred to as Shem, Ham, and Japheth together forming the ancient church, 773, 915
"Noah fathered three sons, Shem, Ham, and Japheth," meaning three kinds of theology, 600, 616, 617
Shem, Ham, and Japheth meaning qualities of the churches that developed out of the ancient church, 764, 768
Shem, Ham, and Japheth meaning the people of the church, 765, 768:1

Shem, Ham, and Japheth *(continued)*
  Shem, Ham, and Japheth meaning the three ancient churches, 534
  Shem, Ham, and Japheth meaning true concepts of faith, 765, 769
Shepherd, 342, 415:1, 416. *See also* Flock; Sheep
  the Lord called the shepherd, 294
  a shepherd meaning one who leads and teaches, 343
  a shepherd of a flock meaning one who does the good inspired by charity, 341, 343
Shoham, 110, 115
Shouting, 420:1. *See also* Crying
Shrewdness (good sense), 197, 266
Shrub, 75, 90, 91. *See also* Plant
Sickness. *See* Illness
Sidon, 264:1
Silence
  silent breathing, 169, 607:2
  silent speech of angels, 173, 174, 180
Silver, 643:3
  silver meaning our deepest possible spiritual quality, 643:1
  silver meaning spiritual truth, 425
  silver meaning truth, 113, 424
Simeon, 352
  the name Simeon meaning that Jehovah had heard Leah was not as well loved, 340
  Simeon meaning faith in action, 342
Simile. *See* Comparisons
Simplicity
  the simple at heart learning from the appearances in the Word, 926
  simple belief in the Word's literal meaning, 196:3, 589, 735
  simplicity and ignorance excusing false beliefs, 347
Sin, 361, 364, 865:2
  blood meaning every kind of sin, 374:1
  committing a sin, 313, 494:2, 698
  sin meaning the Devil, 364
Sinai, 795:5, 934:3
Singing (song), 418, 420. *See also* Angel: angel choirs
  lips of song meaning a spiritual quality, 353:2
  singing meaning something spiritual, 418:1, 418:2, 420:1
  the voice of song meaning spiritual or intellectual aspects of faith, 100
  a voice singing in the windows meaning misguided logic based on illusions, 655:2
Singular, 30:2, 34, 50:3, 218, 298, 478, 712. *See also* Plural
Siren, 831. *See also* Magic
Six, 84. *See also* Number; Six hundred; Sixth
  the number six
    being relatively profane, 900
    meaning hard work and combat, 85:2, 730:3, 737:1
    meaning in general every preceding stage, 900
    meaning the dispersing of falsity, 737:2
    meaning the holy quality of faith, 737:3
  six days meaning the consecutive stages of regeneration, 6–13, 62, 63, 221
  the six stages of regeneration, 6–13, 29:2, 48
Six hundred
  the number six hundred meaning a beginning, 893:2
  six hundred years meaning the first stage of trial, 733, 737:1, 755:2, 893:2
Sixth
  a beast meaning what we produce in the sixth stage of regeneration, 12, 39:2, 48
  Jared meaning the sixth church descended from the earliest church, 463, 510, 513
  our becoming God's image on the sixth day, 62
  our becoming spiritual people in the sixth stage of regeneration, 12, 48
  the sixth day meaning we have become spiritual and begin to be heavenly, 82–83, 484
  the sixth stage of regeneration, 12, 13
Skeleton, 824:2. *See also* Bone
Skepticism, 70, 194, 232. *See also* Doubt; Unbelief
Skull, 501
Slavery. *See also* Rule
  our being in a state of slavery prior to regeneration, 81:3, 892:1
  staying in the ark meaning slavery, 891, 905
Sleep. *See* Slumber
Slumber, meaning a state where we think we have autonomy, 147, 150
Smell. *See* Fragrance; Stenches
Snake (serpent), 242, 244, 247, 259:2
  the bronze snake meaning the Lord's sensory level, 197, 425

deaf snakes, 196:1
a flying fire snake meaning the desire felt by self-love, 251:2
flying snakes, 196:1, 251:2
snake meaning a person who uses false logic concerning the mysteries of faith, 195:1, 206:2
the snake meaning evil in general and self-love in particular, 250, 251:1, 257
the snake meaning sensory abilities (the senses), 191, 192, 194, 195:1, 196:1, 197, 229, 235, 242, 244, 249, 251
a snake meaning watchfulness, 197
a snake or dragon being called Lucifer, 254, 257
snake venom meaning false logic concerning the mysteries of faith, 195:1
the snake's head meaning the tyranny of evil and self-love, 250, 257
snakes in hell, 815, 819, 825, 830, 831:3
snakes meaning hatred, 251:1
the snake's seed meaning all unbelief, 250, 254
Soil. *See* Ground
Sole *(of the foot)*, 875:1
Son (child), 489:2. *See also* Birth; Daughter; Firstborn; Son of God; Son of humankind
children meaning the good deeds and true ideas of faith, 264:2
a foreigner's sons (children) meaning falsities, 489:1, 790:4
sons and daughters meaning truth and goodness, 486, 489:1, 491, 518, 568
sons and daughters meaning what is conceived and born in a church, 532, 533
sons (children) meaning truth, 55:2, 261, 264, 289, 489, 668, 742, 906
sons meaning what is in the intellect, 568:2
Son of God (child of God)
God's child meaning a person of heavenly character, 51
sons of God meaning the teachings of faith, 569, 570
Son of humankind. *See also* Children of humankind
son of humankind meaning everyone who has been reborn, 49:2
Son of Humankind meaning the Lord, 49:2, 49:3, 264:2
son of humankind meaning wisdom and understanding, 49:2

Song. *See* Singing
Sophistry (debate, false logic, reasoning), 195:3, 653:1. *See also* Mystery; Reason; Snake
debate regarding faith leading to doubt and denial, 215, 301
Egypt meaning sophistry about divine subjects, 195:3, 273
false logic (reasoning) concerning the mysteries of faith, 195, 241
intellectual approaches to investigating the spirit, 448:2
Philistines meaning those who reason about spiritual matters using false premises, 705:3
sophistry bolstering our false assumptions, 129
Sorcery. *See* Magic; Witch
Sorrow, 762. *See also* Regret
The soul, 794:2, 815. *See also* Spirit
influx as the connection between the soul and the body, 657, 904:3
the inner being as a person's soul, 3 (see also Being, inner)
a living soul, 44, 94
meaning every animal in general, 670
meaning things that contain life because they come from the Lord, 41
meaning what lies in the intellect, 670
meaning what we produce in the sixth stage of regeneration, 48
opinions concerning the soul, 443–448
our soul being revived from death, 180, 181, 182, 314, 315, 316
the relationship between the soul and the brain, 444
what the life of the soul is like, 320–323
Sound, 420:5. *See also* Hearing; Music
Hebrew words distinguishable as heavenly or spiritual by sound, 793
South
people in the south meaning those who have access to the light of truth and yet extinguish it, 402:4
Sowing. *See* Ground; Planting; Seed
Space (distance). *See also* Dimension; Place; Time
angels having no knowledge of time, matter, or space, 488:3
length meaning something holy, when ascribed to distance, 650
the spirit having extension in space, 444, 445

Speaking (communicating, conversation, talking). *See also* Communication; Saying; Voice
   the conversation of spirits, 322:2
   the earliest people speaking with angels, 125
   the earliest people's manner of speaking, 241, 607:2
   "God spoke to Noah" meaning the Lord's presence with this church, 904:1
   heavenly angels' speech, 202
      as silent, 174, 180
   Jehovah speaking, 359, 360, 370, 371
   the Lord continually talking with everyone, 904:1, 904:3
   our being created capable of communicating with spirits and angels, 69
   Swedenborg hearing and speaking with angels and spirits, 5, 67, 68, 70, 322:1
   verbal speech, 608

Spirit, 97, 215, 444, 643:2, 830. *See also* Body; Breath; The soul; Spirit, angelic; Spirit, evil; Spirit, good; World of spirits
   beliefs regarding the spirit, 196:2–3, 322, 443–448
      denial that the spirit exists, 196:2, 196:3, 206, 233:3, 320, 446
   communication with spirits, 69, 597:2, 784:2
   good spirits living in the first heaven, 459
   Jehovah's spirit meaning an inflow of truth and goodness, 573
   newly arrived spirit(s), 185, 318, 320, 454, 547
      not believing that they are spirits, 320, 444, 447, 938, 941:2
      wishing to enter heaven though unprepared, 537, 538, 539
   our being accompanied by at least two angels and two spirits, 50:1
   our being governed through angels and spirits, 50:1
   our being spirits clothed with flesh, 69, 447
   the spirit as the part of us that is alive, 447
   the Spirit of God meaning the Lord's mercy, 7, 19, 24:1
   spirits' faculties compared to the faculties of humans, 321, 322:1
   spirits forming the outer self of the universal human, 911:2
   Swedenborg constantly in the company of spirits and angels, 5, 59:2
   what the life of the soul or spirit is like, 320–323

Spirit, angelic, 41, 167, 394, 538, 546, 552, 592:2. *See also* Angel
   angelic spirits forming the intermediate self of the universal human, 911:2
   angelic spirits' influence on us, 641
   angelic spirits living in the second heaven, 167, 459, 684
   heavenly angelic spirits compared to spiritual angelic spirits, 201, 459

Spirit, evil, 63, 175, 751:3, 761, 815, 816, 842:2. *See also* Demon; Devil; Hell; Satan
   angels and evil spirits battling over control of us, 227, 263, 741, 751
   evil spirits adopting wickedness as their own, 233:2
   evil spirits as angry at the Lord, 357
   evil spirits connecting us to hell, 697, 756:2
   evil spirits' efforts to dominate us, 50:2, 59:1, 660, 905
   evil spirits flooding us with delusions, 641, 660, 705:3, 790, 842:1
   evil spirits longing to destroy both soul and body, 815
   evil spirits loving only selfhood, or autonomy, 150
   evil spirits opposing everything that is good and true, 59:1
   evil spirits stirring up our evils and falsities, 653:1, 705:3, 711, 741, 751, 787, 790, 904:1
   evil spirits who act on our intellect compared to those who act on our will, 653, 751:2
   the Lord constantly protecting us against evil spirits, 59:2, 741, 905
   the Lord seeming far away to those swept up by evil spirits, 904:1
   the nature of evil spirits, 814:1, 818, 830, 831
   our association with evil spirits, 233:2, 357, 592:1, 653, 697, 751, 904:1, 904:3
   punishing each other as the greatest joy of evil spirits, 391, 592, 695

Spirit, good, 941:1. *See also* Spirit
   good spirits taking the place of evil spirits when we have regenerated, 63, 87
   our entering a community of good spirits on revival from death, 187, 316

Spiritual, 46:2, 51, 54, 55:1, 56, 57, 81:2, 286, 653:2, 784:1. *See also* Heavenly; Heavenly-spiritual; Israel
   autonomy in spiritual people, 141
   conscience in spiritual people, 81:3, 104, 875:3, 875:4, 875:5

"create" as having to do with a spiritual person, 476
intellect separate from will in spiritual people, 875:4
love coming second to faith in the spiritual person, 53, 81:1, 459, 484
our becoming spiritual people in the sixth stage of regeneration, 12, 48
our being in conflict while we are becoming spiritual, 55:4, 59:1, 81:3
the rebirth of a spiritual person, 89, 653:2, 875
the sixth day meaning a spiritual person, 82, 484
spiritual angels (*see* Angel: spiritual angels)
"spiritual" as having to do with religious knowledge and the intellect, 61
spiritual church (*see* Church, spiritual)
spiritual goodness (*see* Goodness, spiritual)
spiritual people compared to lifeless people and heavenly people, 81
spiritual people ruling the inner self from the outer self, 52
a spiritual person as an image of the Lord, 12, 48, 50, 51, 53, 62, 473, 477:1
spiritual trials (*see* Trial)
the structure of the inner life in spiritual people as upside down, 99
water meaning something spiritual, 790:1
The spiritual world. *See* Heaven; Hell; The other life; World of spirits
Swedenborg's experiences in the spiritual world (*see* Swedenborg, Emanuel)
Spite. *See* Hatred
Spreading out. *See* Expanse
Spring *(of water)*, 756:1. *See also* Wellspring
Spring (springtime), 34:2, 553:1
Stage. *See* State
Star, 184, 940:2
Start. *See* Beginning
State (stage), 549, 561, 891
  day meaning a state, 23, 221, 482:2, 487:1, 488, 493
  each state of this life returning to us in the next life, 561, 823
  the four states (stages) after trials, 833–837, 863, 880:1, 889
  our state before regeneration, 7, 17, 892:1
  the six stages of regeneration, 6–13, 29:2, 48
  the state of the Lord's kingdom as a state of peace, 85:1, 925:3
  states of innocence in the three heavens, 544
  years meaning states, 482:2, 486, 487:1, 488:1, 493, 515, 893:2
Statue. *See* Sculpture
Statute, 37. *See also* Command; Law
Stenches (smells), in hell, 814:1, 824:2, 825
Stone. *See also* Rock; Ruby; Shoham
  precious stones meaning religious truth, 114
  stone meaning a spiritual quality of the lowest kind, 643:1
  stone meaning the lowest plane of the intellect, 643:2
  stone meaning truth (facts) learned through the senses, 425, 643:3
Storing away
  knowledge of truth and good being stored away in our memory, 27
  the remnant stored away, 8, 19, 259:2, 268, 561, 563, 661:2, 711, 737:1
Storm, 842:3, 842:4
Street, 655:2. *See also* Path; Road; Way
Strength, 11. *See also* Might
  the Lord strengthening us in truth and goodness through spiritual trials, 63
  strength and glory meaning the Word's inner meaning, 49:4
Stretching out. *See* Extension
Strife. *See* Conflict
Stringed instruments, 418
Structure. *See* Order
Struggle. *See* Conflict; Trial
Stumbling block, 309
Subduing
  the Lord subduing our evil and falsity, 868:2
  misfortune and illness subduing our life of pleasure and desire, 762
  trials subduing our external qualities and making them obedient to inner qualities, 857:2
Subject. *See also* Attribute
  the nature of the subject determining the nature of the things said about it, 103, 386, 568:1, 620, 721
Substance, 731, 801:2, 808
  spiritual substance, 272
Suffocation (drowning), 563
  the Flood meaning the "drowning" of those cut off from heaven, 662
  the nature of the pre-Flood people killing by suffocating, 562
  the pre-Flood people suffocating themselves by merging faith with their foul desires, 560

Sulfur, 643:1, 643:3
Summer, 37. *See also* Heat; Warmth; Winter
   regenerate people alternating between summer (charity) and winter (no charity), 930, 935–936
Sun
   the sun meaning love, 32:1, 253, 255, 337:2
   the sun meaning the Lord, 32:2
   the sun meaning the Lord's divinity, 32:2
   "suns" (windows) meaning ideas in the intellect coming from charity, 655:1
The Suph Sea (the Red Sea), 842
Sweat, 276:1
Swedenborg, Emanuel, 150
   the Lord allowing Swedenborg to learn the hidden inner meaning of the Word, 67
   Swedenborg not concerned that some will disbelieve his claims, 68
   Swedenborg's experience in the spiritual world, 5, 59:2, 699
     being continuous over several years, 227, 322:1, 681
     in being resuscitated from death, 168–181
     hearing and speaking with angels, 5, 67, 68, 70, 322:1
     speaking with people he knew during their physical life, 70, 448:1
Sword
   the flame of a sword turning itself meaning self-love, 306, 309
   sword meaning punishment inflicted on falsity, 574:3
Syllable. *See* Word
Symbol. *See* Image
Symbolism. *See also* Meaning, inner; Representation
   angels picturing what names in the Word symbolize, 64
   animals having a symbolic meaning in the ancient church, 922:1
   the earliest people assigning names with symbolic meaning, 339
   the earliest people aware of the symbolism of place-names, 115
   the earliest people's manner of writing being to assemble symbols into a history (narrative), 66:1, 403, 605
   numbers having a purely symbolic meaning, 487:2, 493, 575, 576:1, 647, 648:2, 716:2, 716:5, 737:1, 813

T

Tabernacle (booth, hut). *See also* Tent
   the tabernacle meaning a godly person, 414:3, 414:4
   the tabernacle meaning the Lord's human quality, 414:4
   tents, the tabernacle, and the Temple having the same symbolism, 414:3–4
The tablets of the Decalogue. *See* The Decalogue
Talking. *See* Speaking
Tambourine, 420:3, 420:4
Tar, 638, 639, 642, 645
Tare, 408, 731
Teaching (doctrine), 402:3, 518, 555, 557, 570, 788:2, 885:2. *See also* Church; Faith; Heresy; Instruction; Schism
   the church called Cain preserving the teachings of faith, 609, 920:4 (*see also* Cain; Faith alone)
   the church called Enoch developing doctrine from the perceptions of the earliest church, 464, 519, 521, 609, 920:4 (*see also* Enoch)
   churches developing from doctrine, 530
   city meaning a doctrinal or heretical teaching, 402:1, 402:3
   the creation of a distinct doctrine concerning faith, 325, 340, 337:3, 355 (*see also* Cain; Faith alone)
   doctrinal concepts making the church only if they look to charity, 809
   doctrinal teachings as the truth of the church, 570
   doctrine as knowledge received through the physical senses, 521
   faith involving more than the teachings of faith, 36, 654, 896
   falsification of religious teachings, 337
   field meaning doctrine, 368
   ideas from doctrine providing a framework for instruction, 608
   individuals' names symbolizing doctrines or churches, 337:1, 404, 468:1, 483:1, 530
   knowing by perception compared to learning from doctrine, 521
   Noah meaning doctrine from the earliest church, 530:1
   Noah's sons meaning doctrinal teachings, 769
   the revelations of the earliest church replaced by articles of doctrine, 608, 609

sons of God meaning the teachings of faith, 569, 570
the Word being the teachings of faith, 36
Temple, 113, 308, 425, 639:2, 643:2, 643:4, 648:2, 728:4
   a new temple meaning a new church, 40:2
   the new temple meaning the Lord's kingdom, 648:1
   the Temple meaning the church and heaven, 82
   a temple to the Lord meaning a godly (heavenly, reborn) person, 40:2, 414:3, 414:4
   tents, the tabernacle, and the Temple having the same symbolism, 414:3–4
   the windows in the Temple at Jerusalem, 655:2, 658
Ten. *See also* Number; Tenth
   the number ten as holy, 468:4
   ten meaning the remnant, 468:4, 575, 576, 737:1, 755:2, 798, 858
Tendency, 313. *See also* Nature
Tense. *See* Time
Tent, 412, 413, 414, 415, 416. *See also* Tabernacle
   dwelling in a tent meaning holy love, 413, 414:1
   tent meaning something heavenly, 414:1
   tent, tabernacle, or temple meaning the Lord's human quality, 414:4
Tenth. *See also* Ten
   Noah meaning the tenth church, 466
   the tenth month meaning the truth belonging to the remnant, 858
   tithes (portions equaling one tenth) meaning the remnant (remaining traces), 468:3–4, 680:5, 901:4
Territory, the church's, 567
Test. *See* Conflict; Trial
Theology. *See* Church; Faith; Teaching
Thing. *See* Phenomenon
Third, 9. *See also* Three
   Enosh as the third church, 463, 498, 500, 502, 505
   the third day having the same meaning as the seventh day, 93, 720, 901:3
   the third heaven, 167, 634:2, 684
   the third river out of Eden meaning the faculty of reason, 78, 118
   the third stage of regeneration as one of repentance, 9, 29:2

Thirty. *See also* One hundred thirty; Three
   the number thirty meaning the few remaining traces, 647
Thistle, 272, 273
Thorn, 272, 273
Thought, 33, 362, 444, 586a:1. *See also* Idea; Image; Mind
   the belief that the spirit is thought, 444, 445
   the belief that we think for ourselves, 904:3
   bird meaning thoughts, 745, 778
   conception and the bearing of children meaning all thinking, 261, 264:1
   the earliest people being engaged with deep thought, 442, 605
   faith seen as mere thought, 36
   in a heavenly person, all thoughts lying open to the Lord, 99
   the marriage between thought and will, 590
   our thoughts being apparent to angels, 228
   spirits thinking more clearly than during bodily life, 322:2
   thoughts as perceived clearly in the other life, 318, 443, 549, 823, 830
   thoughts returning vividly in the next life, 823
   the thought-speech of heavenly angels, 174, 180
Three. *See also* Number; Third; Thirty; Three hundred; Three hundred sixty-five
   "Noah fathered three sons" meaning three kinds of theology would rise out of that church, 616–617
   the number three indicating holiness because of the Lord's resurrection on the third day, 720, 901:1, 901:4, 901:5
   the number three meaning something holy or sacrosanct, 482:1, 900, 901
   the three heavens (*see* Heaven: the three heavens)
   three levels of the intellect, 655:2, 657, 658
Three hundred, meaning the few remaining traces, 647
Three hundred sixty-five
   all Enoch's days were three hundred sixty-five meaning they were few, 520
Throne, 255
Time (interval). *See also* Age; Cycle; Day; Month; Week; Year
   angels having no notion of time, 488:3
   day meaning times and states in general, 23, 482:2, 487, 488, 493, 931:1

Time *(continued)*
    the longest and shortest intervals in the Word called days, weeks, months, years, or ages, 900
    periods of time in the Word representing circumstances (states), 482:1, 493, 893:2
Tithe. *See* Tenth
Toddler. *See* Child; Infant
Toleration
    the Lord tolerating punishment of others rather than carrying it out, 592:2
Tooth, 819, 820
Torment. *See* Torture
Torture (abuse, pain, pang, torment), 697. *See also* Pain; Punishment
    evil spirits' delight in torturing each other, 391, 695
    the Lord never inflicting pain, 696
    our bringing on our own punishment and torture, 696
    torment endured by evil spirits, 322:1, 695, 696, 816, 824, 828, 830, 831:3
Touch. *See* Sensation; Sense; The senses
    the ban on touching the fruit, 198, 202
    spirits' sense of touch, 322:1
Trampling, 250, 258
Tranquility (calm, peace), 90. *See also* Peace
    angels' selfhood bringing them tranquility, 141
    heavenly people blessed with inner peace, 85:3, 91
    the Lord nourishing us with calm during trials, 59:1
    the outer self enjoying tranquility when struggles are over, 92
    rain (mist) meaning the calm of a heavenly person, 91, 93
Traveling. *See* Walking
Treasure, 368, 426:2. *See also* Riches
Tree, 130. *See also* Cedar; Fig tree; Mustard; Olive
    the fruit of the tree in the middle of the garden, 198, 204
    the fruit of the tree of the garden, 198, 199
    a fruit tree, 9, 29:1, 59:1, 273, 776:2
    the middle of the tree of the garden, 218, 225
    a tree meaning a person, 885:1, 920:1
    a tree meaning knowledge, 368
    a tree meaning perception, 77, 102, 103, 125, 218
    a tree meaning the good we have when faith is connected to love, 55:4
    the tree of knowledge, 77, 102, 126, 128, 192, 199, 200, 202
    the tree of lives, 77, 102, 105, 200, 285, 298, 304, 306
    the tree that has fruit, 56, 57
    the tree that produces seed, 56, 57
    trees of Jehovah, 776:4
    trees of the field, 795:4
Trial (adversity, crisis, struggle, temptation, test), 728:1, 755, 762, 847. *See also* Conflict
    angels defending us during time of trial, 270, 737:1, 751:1, 761
    downpour (rain) meaning struggle (trials), 729, 759, 843, 844, 845
    evil spirits bringing up falsities during trials, 653:1, 705:3, 751:1, 790:1
    floods meaning trial, 606, 705, 729, 739, 787, 790:1, 842:5 (*see also* Flood)
    forty days and nights meaning how long trials last, 730, 760, 786, 862
    the Lord as closer than we can believe during trials, 840
    the Lord establishing order in us after trials, 841
    the Lord never leading anyone into crisis, 245
    misfortune and illness as the kind of trial most experience today, 762, 847:2
    our belief in God faltering during trials, 840
    our needing to be prepared with truth and good before being tested, 711, 737:1
    our outer self dying in times of trial, 268
    our sense of autonomy shaken off during trials, 8, 730:1, 731
    the purpose of trials, 892:2
        to destroy our old life, which is made of our cravings, 760
        to enable the things of the outer self to be separated from those of the inner self, 8
        to give us a new capacity for receiving goodness and truth, 868:2
        to make our external qualities obedient to inner qualities, 857:2, 933:4
        to reform us, 653:1
        to strip away everything self-centered and bodily so that we can be reborn, 730:1
    rainfall meaning trial, 729, 844
    the remnant used by angels to defend us during trials, 737:1, 751:1
    in seven days meaning the beginning of trials, 728:1, 753, 755:2

spiritually dead people as unable to withstand trial, 270, 705:3
struggle as heavenly, spiritual, or earthly, 847:2–3
struggles as battles between the evil spirits and angels present with us, 741, 751:1, 761
trials as little known today, 751:1, 762
trials involving distress over things that conflict with what we love, 847:2
trials involving the intellect, 653:1, 702, 734, 735, 749, 751:2, 753, 757
trials involving the will, 702, 734, 751:3, 755:1, 756:1, 757, 760, 845:1
the trials of the new church called Noah, 605, 606, 702, 728:1, 730, 737:1, 751:1, 755:1, 763, 765, 832, 838, 840, 862, 874 (*see also* Noah)
vacillation (fluctuation) following trials, 847:1, 848:1, 848:3, 851, 867

Tribe. *See* Nation

Trouble. *See* Trial

Trumpet, 424

Trust. *See* Belief

Truth, 17, 29:1, 57, 110, 114, 393, 420:5, 424, 671, 765, 854, 859, 884, 885, 895:1. *See also* Faith; Falsity; Goodness; Knowledge
all truth coming from faith and so from the Lord, 112
all truth growing out of goodness, 668, 671, 724, 725, 863, 880:1
the axioms of the earliest church being eternal truths, 597:3
birds meaning comprehension of truth, 40:3, 477:3, 866
birds meaning spiritual truth, 776, 777, 916, 921:1
birds meaning true ideas, 55:4, 778
the church called Noah receiving charity through truth, 310:2, 640, 765
the difference between knowing the truth, acknowledging it, and believing it, 896:1
doctrinal teachings as the truth of the church, 570
iron meaning earthly truth, 421, 425, 426
knowing what is true as of primary importance, 794:2
the laws of the Lord's kingdom being eternal truths, 548:1
light meaning truth, 20, 22, 38, 519:2, 893:1, 896:1
the Lord bending our falsities toward truth, 24:3, 25, 887
male meaning something true, 669, 672, 725, 749, 770
no life in truth except through goodness, 668, 678
the olive leaf meaning religious truth, 884, 886:3
a path (way) meaning truth or faith, 519:1, 612:3, 622, 627, 795:5
preoccupation with the bodily level destroying comprehension of truth, 627:1, 628
religious truth depending on acknowledgment to take root, 880
silver meaning spiritual truth, 425
silver meaning truth, 113, 424
sons (children) meaning truth, 55:2, 261, 264, 289, 489, 668, 742, 906
those who prefer truth to being useful, 511
true ideas adopted for selfish reasons as lacking religious good, 874
truth acting on its own as unable to enter into marriage with goodness, 725
truth as the form of goodness, 668
truth as the spiritual aspect of the Lord's influx, 880:2
truth gained through the senses, 425, 777
the truth of faith depending on the goodness belonging to faith, 654, 874, 880:1
truth on the rational plane, 628, 635, 671
truth unable to coexist with corrupt desires, 794:2
truth unable to take root in a mind filled with falsity, 875:2
using earthly truth to confirm spiritual and heavenly truth, 129
vacillating between truth and falsity, 788:2, 789, 833, 847:1, 848, 857:1

Tubal-cain
Tubal-cain meaning earthly goodness and truth, 421, 436
Tubal-cain meaning the earthly aspects of the church represented by Adah and Zillah, 333, 423

Tunic. *See also* Clothes; Loincloth
a leather tunic meaning spiritual and earthly goodness, 282, 292, 294, 295, 297

Turning
our culpability for turning away from the Lord, 233:2

Turning *(continued)*
    our turning away from the Lord rather than his turning away from us, 223, 588:3
    those who separated faith from love turning away from the Lord, 330
    turning away from the Lord's face, 247, 278

Turtledove, 870:2–3. *See also* Dove

Twelve. *See also* Two
    the number twelve meaning all aspects of faith, 575, 577
    the number twelve meaning the holy things of faith, 648:2
    the twelve tribes of Israel, 493, 577

Twenty. *See also* One hundred twenty; Twenty-seventh; Two
    "the days of humankind will be one hundred twenty years" meaning they ought to have traces of faith left, 575
    that the number 120 means remaining traces of faith as seen from its factors, ten and twelve, 575

Twenty-seventh
    the twenty-seventh day meaning holiness, 901:1

Two. *See also* Number; Pair; Second; Twelve; Twenty; Twenty-seventh
    Noah taking two each, or pairs, as having to do with intellectual matters, 717
    two each meaning pairs, or elements that answer to each other, 717, 743, 747, 772, 779
    two each meaning things that are relatively profane, 720
    two lights meaning love and faith kindled in our inner self, 10, 39:1
    two meaning a few, 649
    two meaning hard work, combat, and dispersing something, 755:2, 900
    two meaning marriage, 720
    two months (the second month) meaning combat, 755:2
    "two of each, a male and a female, were to enter the ark" meaning goodness connected with truth, 668
    two olive trees meaning what is heavenly and what is spiritual, 886:2
    two terms frequently used in the Word for a single idea, 100, 590 *(see also* Repetition)

Tyranny. *See* Rule

Tyre, 425, 426:1

U

Unbelief, 250, 254

Underground realm, 247, 539, 699, 817. *See also* World of spirits

Understanding. *See* Intellect; Intelligence

Unhappiness. *See* Misery

Union (unity). *See also* Connection; Unity
    all togetherness and unity coming from charity, 343
    the union between heaven and the Lord depending on heaven's feeling of independent existence, 252

Unity. *See also* Union
    the common whole in heaven contributing to unity among the individual pieces, 684
    unity formed out of harmony among many, 457

Universal human, 318, 418:2
    the church in relation to the universal human, 931:1
    heaven called the "universal human," 550, 911:2

Uprightness (integrity), 165. *See also* Honesty
    the church called Noah retaining integrity rather than perception, 530:2
    upright meaning the truth involved with charity (goodness), 612, 615, 712

Urine, 820

Usefulness, 57, 511, 696. *See also* Service
    angelic life consisting in usefulness, 454
    being useful as acting from knowledge of goodness and truth, 503
    the Lord's kingdom as a realm of purpose and usefulness, 696
    seed-bearing plants as having to do with usefulness, 29:1, 57
    usefulness as the good that comes of love and charity, 454
    usefulness as the means by which the Lord gives us life, 503

V

Vacillation (wavering), 788, 847:1
    the ark going on the face of the water meaning how the people wavered between truth and falsity, 788, 789
    vacillation between good and evil, 847:1

vacillation between truth and falsity occurring after spiritual trials, 833, 848
"the waters going" meaning vacillation between truth and falsity, 857:1
Variety. *See also* Category
  variety in heaven, 536, 553:2, 690
  the Word holding incredible richness and variety, 167, 855, 937
Vengeance
  being avenged seventy-seven times meaning damnation, 432, 433
  the hells of those who are vengeful, 814, 815, 816
  innumerable general kinds of hatred and vengefulness, 693, 816
  sevenfold vengeance meaning there was a sacred ban, 392, 432
Venom (poison), 251:1, 817
  snake venom meaning false logic concerning the mysteries of faith, 195:1
  venom meaning hatred, 251:1
Violence, 623
  full of violence meaning the pre-Flood people's unclean desires, 621, 623:1
  the land is filled with violence meaning no will to do good, 632
  violence as having to do with the will, 621, 623:2
  violence meaning the damage people inflict on holy things through profanation, 623:1
  the voice of blood meaning violence inflicted on charity, 330, 373, 374:1
Viper, 259:2. *See also* Snake
Virgin. *See* Young woman
Virtue. *See* Goodness
Vision, 125, 212, 597:2. *See also* Seeing
Vocabulary. *See* Word
Voice (call, dictate, speech), 211, 212, 218, 222, 375, 573, 655:2. *See also* Communication; Conscience; Speaking
  the ancient church having an inner voice called conscience, 607:1, 608
  the inner call of perception or conscience, 224, 227, 371, 393, 895:2
  regenerate people hearing an inner call, 220
  speech by Jehovah meaning conscience spoke, 219, 359, 360, 371
  voice meaning everything that accuses, 374:1
  voice meaning revelation, 219
  the voice of blood meaning violence inflicted on charity, 330, 373, 374:1
  the voice of Jehovah, 219
    meaning an inner dictate, 218
  the voice of one shouting, meaning a proclamation of the Lord's Coming, 220
  voices in the spiritual world, 448:1
Void, 7, 17. *See also* Emptiness
Volition. *See* Will
Vowel, 793

W

Wail (weeping), 699, 814:2
Walking (traveling), 247
  walking as having to do with truth and faith, 519:1
  walking meaning living, 519:1
  walking with God meaning the doctrine concerning faith, 518, 519:1, 520, 614
  walking with Jehovah meaning living a life of love, 519:1, 519:3
Wall, 699, 739:2
Wandering, 391, 398
  being a wanderer meaning not knowing what is true or good, 330, 380, 382:1
  the wanderer and fugitive on the earth meaning falsity and evil from corrupt theology, 330
Warmth. *See also* Heat; Summer
  faith without love compared to sunlight without warmth, 34:2
  warmth in our outer flesh compared to love in our inner being, 30:3
Waste. *See* Devastation
Watchfulness, 197
Water, 382:2, 623:1. *See also* Flood; River; Sea
  water from the sanctuary meaning the living mercy of the Lord, 57
  water meaning difficulties, 790:3
  water meaning falsities, 739:1, 739:3, 789, 790, 794:1, 847:1, 857:1, 871, 877, 887
  water meaning our spiritual possessions, 739:1
  water meaning something spiritual, 790:1
  water meaning the intellectual elements of faith, 739:1, 795:3
  water meaning the spiritual aspects of faith, 680:3

Water *(continued)*
    water meaning the things we truly understand, grasp rationally, and know about, and also the opposites of these things, 790:1
    watering the garden meaning to give understanding, 107
    the waters gathered into one place (seas) meaning the knowledge in our outward memory, 27
    waters meaning religious and secular knowledge, 28
    the waters over the expanse meaning the knowledge in the inner self, 24:1
    the waters under the expanse meaning facts belonging to the outer self, 24:1

Wavering. *See* Vacillation

Way (path). *See also* Path; Road; Street
    a path (way) meaning truth or faith, 519:1, 612:3, 622, 627, 795:5
    ways meaning a life spent obeying what has been commanded, 627:2

Wealth, 230, 451, 685, 945. *See also* Riches

Web, 623:2

Week. *See also* Seven; Time
    "seventy weeks" and "seven weeks" meaning the Lord's Coming, 728:2
    stretches of time divided in seven and called weeks, 395:1, 728:4, 900
    a week meaning any whole period, 893:2

Weeping. *See* Wail

Wellspring, 353:2. *See also* Spring

Well-wishing, 361, 364, 452, 585

Whale, 42:1, 819. *See also* Sea creature

Whole. *See* Generality

Wickedness, 383. *See also* Evil
    blood meaning wickedness, 374:2
    hatred as the source of all wickedness, 374:2, 374:3
    wickedness as having to do with the will, 623:2

Width, 648:1. *See also* Dimension
    width meaning truth, 647
    width of the ark meaning the remnant's truth, 646, 650

Wife, 400, 770. *See also* Bride; Female; Husband; Marriage; Woman
    clinging to one's wife meaning to have an inner being within our outer being, 160
    the human and his wife meaning a new church, 434, 435, 436
    the human and his wife meaning the earliest church, 338, 339
    husband and wife meaning marriage, 725
    Lamech's wives meaning a new church, 409, 427
    the law for marriage of one man and one wife, 162:1
    man and wife
        meaning falsity united to evil, 713, 721
        meaning truth united to goodness, 430:2, 713, 721, 725
    Noah and his wife meaning the church, 906
    one man and one wife representing the heavenly marriage, 162:1, 865:2
    "she will be called wife" meaning our selfhood when the inner and outer beings are joined, 156
    true marriage involving one husband and one wife, 865:2
    a wife being under the influence of her husband's good sense, 266, 568:2
    a wife meaning an element of the will, or something good, 770, 915
    a wife meaning faith's truth, or faith, 915
    a wife meaning selfhood brought to life by the Lord, 155
    a wife meaning the church, 54, 253, 255, 289, 768:3, 770, 886:3, 906, 915
    wives meaning goodness, 668, 718, 742, 770, 915

Wild animal. *See* Animal, wild

Wilderness, 100
    outlaws in a wilderness in hell, 941
    wilderness meaning a church that has no faith, 220

Will (volition), 105, 116, 585, 640, 641, 643:2, 643:3, 644, 670, 710, 774. *See also* Intellect
    the ability to understand rising from the will (volition), 585, 590, 628, 732, 863
    beasts (animals) meaning the things of the will, 44, 52, 142, 594, 673, 674, 715, 909
    the church as having to do with the will, 809
    conscience as a means of dividing the intellect from the will, 863, 875:3, 875:5, 918
    conscience as a new will, 918, 927:3
    corrupted people having desire instead of will, 568:1, 585, 652
    daughters meaning what is in the will, 568
    the earliest people receiving revelations regarding goodness and truth directly into their will, 895
    earth (land) meaning will, 55:2, 585, 632

every essential quality coming from the will, 809
every perverse yearning contributing to the life of our will, 794:2
evil spirits acting on our will, 653:1, 751:3
evil (wickedness) as a matter of the will, 623:2, 845:1
female meaning the will, 54, 476
the "greater light" being placed in our will, 30:3
the heart meaning the will, 105
heavenly things as having to do with the will, 61
the human will as completely evil, 875:4, 928, 933:3
life flowing from the Lord into our will, 657
the Lord dividing our will from our intellect, 640, 641, 652, 863, 875:3, 875:4
love as an attribute of the will, 30:3, 48, 53
"man and wife" as having to do with the will, 725
marriage meaning the interconnection of intellect and will, 54, 55 (*see also* Marriage)
the new will we receive from the Lord, 652, 918, 928, 933:3
our calling self-interest our will, 105, 634:1
trials involving the will, 702, 734, 751:3, 755:1, 756:1, 757, 845:1
violence as having to do with the will, 621, 623:2
a wife meaning an element of the will, 770, 915
will and intellect, 594, 644, 652, 712, 732
  constituting the mind, 111, 116, 310:1
  distinguished from each other, 641, 644, 801:2
  everything in our intellect coupled with something in our will, 672, 718, 863
  making one mind and therefore one life, 35, 652
  our inability to distinguish between will and intellect, 634:1
  as our two basic faculties, 35
  the will regulating the intellect, 35, 398, 628
the will as a person's real identity, 379, 585, 808
the will as the main thing the Lord possesses, 105
the will driving everything, 35
will in the earliest people, 398, 628, 640, 875:4, 895:1, 927:2
will in the people called Noah, 635, 642
will in the pre-Flood people, 209, 594, 635, 801:1, 927:2
will ruling the intellect in females, 568:2
a will to do good, 305, 306, 568:2, 585, 632, 633, 634:2, 640, 671, 928
willing as what makes a person human, 585
Wind, 739:2. *See also* Spirit
  east wind meaning the dispersal of falsity and evil, 842
  wind as a metaphor for spirit or life, 97
  wind instruments, 420:2
Window
  "suns" (windows) meaning ideas in the intellect, 655:1
  window meaning the intellect (understanding), 602, 642, 651, 652, 653:2, 655, 658, 863
  the windows in the Temple at Jerusalem, 655:2, 658
  windows meaning falsity resulting from the misuse of reason, 655:2
  windows of the middle story meaning matters of reason, 655:2
Winged creature, 772, 776:1, 777. *See also* Bird; Flying thing
Winter, 880:1. *See also* Coldness; Summer
  faith without love compared to light in winter, 34:2, 365
  regenerate people alternating between summer (charity) and winter (no charity), 930, 935–936
  winter meaning a life devoid of love, 34:2
Wisdom, 49:2, 130, 219, 273, 305, 424. *See also* Intelligence; Knowledge; Mystery
  Eden meaning wisdom, 305
  fruit meaning wisdom, 57, 198
  gold meaning the goodness belonging to wisdom or to love, 113
  heavenly people receiving wisdom from the Lord, 121
  human being meaning wisdom and understanding, 49:2
  human selfhood lacking wisdom, 214
  human wisdom, 42:1, 775:1
  learning from the Word as the way to acquire wisdom, 128, 129
  the only wisdom coming from love, 112
  a person (humankind) meaning those who are wise, 303:2
  regret as having to do with wisdom, 586b, 590
  river meaning wisdom, 78, 107, 108

Wisdom *(continued)*
  shallow people believing secular facts are wisdom and faith, 111
  those wanting to learn wisdom from the world, 130
  those wanting to receive wisdom from themselves, 301
  wisdom and love as the heart of the Lord's mercy, 590
  wisdom as not ours but the Lord's, 109, 121, 124, 129
Witch (sorceress), 831. *See also* Magic
Wolf, 45, 430:1
Woman, 153, 553, 825, 831, 944, 945. *See also* Female; Wife; Young woman
  the human meaning both the man and the woman, 478
  the meaning in the Word of a woman being built out of a rib, 134, 138, 151, 152, 153, 155
  the woman meaning self-love (selfhood), 152, 191, 194, 207
  woman meaning the church, 237, 250, 252, 253, 255, 261, 262, 402:5
  the woman taking the fruit meaning being seduced by self-love, 207, 208, 229
  a woman (wife) meaning selfhood (sense of self) brought to life by the Lord, 151, 155, 156
  the woman's seed, 250, 255, 256
Wood
  gopher wood, 640, 643:1, 643:4
  wooden idols meaning appetites (cravings), 643:3, 643:4
  wood meaning a heavenly quality of the lowliest kind, 643:1
  wood meaning desire, 643:2, 643:3
  wood meaning goodness on the bodily level, 425
  wood meaning the contents of the will, 643:2, 643:3
  wood meaning the lowest plane of the will, 643:2, 643:4
Word (expression, verbal, vocabulary), 241. *See also* Repetition
  angels not knowing the meaning of even one word of the Word, 64
  the earliest people speaking without words, 607:2
  every expression in the Word coming from the Lord, 2, 771
  the precision of word choice in the Word, 621
  spiritual themes having one vocabulary and heavenly themes another, 793
  verbal speech, 608
  the Word giving a spiritual expression and a heavenly expression for one idea, 100
The Word, 44, 130, 245, 865:1. *See also* Meaning, highest; Meaning, inner; Meaning, literal; Old Testament; Word
  angels' perception of the Word, 64, 167, 855
  confirming the Word through knowledge and sensory evidence, 128, 129
  every aspect of the Word as having to do with the Lord, 1, 2, 771
  learning from the Word as the way to acquire wisdom, 128, 129
  the many secrets (hidden information) contained in the Word's inner meaning, 1, 4, 37, 64, 167, 310, 537
  the marriage of heavenly and spiritual attributes in the Word, 683
  profanation of the Word destroying goodness and truth in us, 571
  repetitions in the Word, 100, 435, 590, 682, 683, 707, 734, 765, 782, 793, 801
  the Word as spiritual, 426:1
    and heavenly, 680:1
  the Word being the teachings of faith, 36
  the Word holding incredible richness and variety, 167, 855, 937
  the Word speaking according to human appearances, 589:1, 865:2, 926
  the Word's contents pertaining to heaven, the church, and faith, 2, 155
  the Word's modes of writing, 66, 302, 742, 801:1
Work (deed), 531. *See also* Action; Making; Operation, the Lord's
  the earthly dimension involving the carrying out of works of charity through the body, 880:2
  God's work meaning a heavenly person, 84
  God's work meaning spiritual people after they have developed a heavenly nature, 88
  good works being the good that charity urges, 848:2
  the Lord resting from all his work meaning the person is regenerated, 84

work meaning the inability to perceive truth without effort, 531
the work of God's fingers meaning a regenerate person, 63
works (deeds) of charity as dead without life from the Lord, 880:2, 880:3
World, 130. *See also* Earth; Materialism
alternation of bodily and worldly desires with faith and charity, 933:3, 933:4
the belief that heavenly joy is not affected by one's life in the world, 547
the creation of the world and the first human, 4 (*see also* Creation)
facts as the "food" of people focused on the physical world, 56
the "garden" in worldly people, 130
immersion in bodily and worldly concerns closing the path to heaven, 69
the impossibility of loving worldly advantages and heavenly ones at the same time, 760
lethal foods as evil and worldly pleasures, 680:1
loving ourselves and worldly goods involving hatred of one's neighbor and the Lord, 33
misfortune enabling worldly concerns to fade away, 8
the nature of autonomy in a worldly and body-centered person, 123, 141
the other world (*see* The other life)
our fate after death depending on our life in the world, 633, 687, 697
the spiritual world (*see* Heaven; Hell; The other life; World of spirits)
wanting to be led by ourselves and the world, 138
wanting to learn wisdom from the world, 128, 130
the world's destruction, 200, 256, 311, 931:2
World of spirits, 878:8. *See also* Underground realm
admission to heaven often happening after a period of time in the world of spirits, 319
angels' thoughts made visible in the world of spirits, 730:5
fear in hell and the world of spirits, 695, 815, 939, 941, 942
the influence of the angelic heavens on the world of spirits, 730:5
the Lord freeing the world of spirits, 581:1

our life depending on communication with heaven and the world of spirits, 50:1, 687, 784
the world of spirits as a representative world, 167
the world of spirits dominated by hatred for the Lord, 59:2
Worship, 795:4, 921:3. *See also* Altar; Burnt offering; Offering; Sacrifice
farmers meaning worshipers, 368
invoking Jehovah's name as common to all worship of the Lord, 440, 441
mountains as having to do with worship of the Lord, 795:4
the origin of worship on high places, 796
those who worship the material world, 206:1, 775:2
worship based on a detached faith as not pleasing, 326, 355
worship based on charity as pleasing, 326, 354, 440, 925:1
the worship of the ancient church, 796, 920:1, 920:4, 921:1
the worship of the earliest church, 795:1, 796, 920:1, 920:2
Wound, 250, 259:1
Lamech killing a man for his wound and a little child for his bruise meaning devastation, 406
wound meaning faith had been abandoned, 427, 431
Writing. *See also* History; Mode
the Word's four modes of writing, 66
the writing of the ancient church, 920:4
the writing of the earliest people, 66:1, 403, 605, 742, 755:1, 801:1

Y

Year, 481, 575, 728:4. *See also* Time
an age meaning ten years, 433
the ancient years meaning the ancient church, 349:2
the longest and shortest intervals in the Word called days, weeks, months, years, or ages, 900
the middle of the years meaning the Lord's Coming, 482:2
six hundred years meaning the first stage of trial, 733, 737:1, 755:2, 893:2

Year *(continued)*
    the Word calling a whole period a year, 893:2
    yearly cycles as a metaphor for the cycles of spiritual and heavenly things, 37
    years meaning specific states, 486, 487:1, 488:1
    years meaning states, 482:2, 493, 893:2
    years meaning the times and states of the church, 515

Yoke
    "my yoke is mild" meaning the Lord's gentle leading after regeneration, 905

Young woman (virgin), 828. *See also* Female; Woman
    the church called Virgin (young woman), 54, 253

Youth, 187–188, 829:2
    our seeming to be in the prime of youth when we are first among angels, 187
    youthfulness of those who know how to share love in heaven, 553

Z

Zillah, 426:2, 427
    Adah and Zillah compared to Leah and Rachel, 409
    the church meant by Adah and Zillah, 333, 409
    the human and his wife meaning the new church previously symbolized by Adah and Zillah, 434, 435, 436
    Zillah meaning the mother of a new church's earthly aspects, 405, 421

Zion
    the city of Zion meaning the spiritual aspect of faith, 402:1
    the daughter of Zion meaning a heavenly type of church, 415:2
    the mountain of Zion
        meaning the heavenly aspect of faith, 402:1
        meaning the Lord, 795:3

Biographical Note

EMANUEL SWEDENBORG (1688–1772) was born Emanuel Swedberg (or Svedberg) in Stockholm, Sweden, on January 29, 1688 (Julian calendar). He was the third of the nine children of Jesper Swedberg (1653–1735) and Sara Behm (1666–1696). At the age of eight he lost his mother. After the death of his only older brother ten days later, he became the oldest living son. In 1697 his father married Sara Bergia (1666–1720), who developed great affection for Emanuel and left him a significant inheritance. His father, a Lutheran clergyman, later became a celebrated and controversial bishop, whose diocese included the Swedish churches in Pennsylvania and in London, England.

After studying at the University of Uppsala (1699–1709), Emanuel journeyed to England, Holland, France, and Germany (1710–1715) to study and work with leading scientists in western Europe. Upon his return he apprenticed as an engineer under the brilliant Swedish inventor Christopher Polhem (1661–1751). He gained favor with Sweden's King Charles XII (1682–1718), who gave him a salaried position as an overseer of Sweden's mining industry (1716–1747). Although he was engaged, he never married.

After the death of Charles XII, Emanuel was ennobled by Queen Ulrika Eleonora (1688–1741), and his last name was changed to Swedenborg (or Svedenborg). This change in status gave him a seat in the Swedish House of Nobles, where he remained an active participant in the Swedish government throughout his life.

A member of the Swedish Royal Academy of Sciences, he devoted himself to studies that culminated in a number of publications, most notably a comprehensive three-volume work on natural philosophy and metallurgy (1734) that brought him recognition across Europe as a scientist. After 1734 he redirected his research and publishing to a study of anatomy in search of the interface between the soul and body, making several significant discoveries in physiology.

From 1743 to 1745 he entered a transitional phase that resulted in a shift of his main focus from science to theology. Throughout the rest of his life he maintained that this shift was brought about by Jesus Christ, who appeared to him, called him to a new mission, and opened his perception to a permanent dual consciousness of this life and the life after death.

He devoted the last decades of his life to studying Scripture and publishing eighteen theological titles that draw on the Bible, reasoning, and his own spiritual experiences. These works present a Christian theology with unique perspectives on the nature of God, the spiritual world, the Bible, the human mind, and the path to salvation.

Swedenborg died in London on March 29, 1772, at the age of eighty-four.